2013
CHURCH AND CLERGY
TAX GUIDE

PLUS: INFORMATION ON
THE AMERICAN TAXPAYER RELIEF ACT OF 2012

2012	2013
TAX RETURN PREPARATION	YEAR-ROUND USE

The Most Comprehensive and Authoritative
Tax Guide Available for Both Churches and Clergy

UPDATED ANNUALLY!

RICHARD R. HAMMAR, J.D., LL.M., CPA

CHRISTIANITY TODAY
a global media ministry

YourChurchResources.com

1229 746X   71⁵⁰

2013
HURCH AND CLERGY
TAX GUIDE

2012 TAX RETURN PREPARATION | **2013** YEAR-ROUND USE

For any other use, including tuition-based classroom use, advance permission must be obtained from the copyright holder. For information, contact:
Your Church Resources Permissions
Christianity Today
465 Gundersen Drive
Carol Stream, IL 60188
Phone: (877) 247-4787
E-mail: cltodaycustserv@christianitytoday.com

Visit our website: YourChurchResources.com
Unless otherwise noted, Scripture quotations are taken from the HOLY BIBLE, NEW INTERNATIONAL VERSION ®.
Copyright © 1973, 1978, 1984 by International Bible Society. Used by permission of Zondervan Publishing House. All rights reserved.

Credits
Author: Richard R. Hammar, J.D., LL.M., CPA
Editor: Dawn M. Brandon
Executive Editor: Marian Liautaud
Art Director: Phil Marcelo
Cover Designer: Phil Marcelo
Cover image © Phil Marcelo

1-61407-900-5
978-1-61407-900-2

15 14 13   1 2 3 4
Printed in the United States of America.

We gratefully acknowledge the assistance of the Orlando-based CPA firm of Batts, Morrison, Wales & Lee, P.A., in the preparation of the illustrated tax return in Chapter 13. Batts, Morrison, Wales & Lee, P.A. is dedicated exclusively to serving nonprofit organizations and their affiliates. The firm's website is nonprofitcpa.com.

THE AMERICAN TAXPAYER RELIEF ACT OF 2012

Tax law changes that will affect clergy and churches

CONTENTS

In the early hours of 2013 Congress enacted the American Taxpayer Relief Act of 2012 (ATRA or the "Act") in order to avoid the so-called "fiscal cliff." We've extracted provisions from the 157-page Act that are of most relevance to churches and church employees and included them in this special supplement. We inserted this supplement just before going to press with the complete *2013 Church & Clergy Tax Guide* to ensure that readers would have the most up-to-date tax information in one book.

The American Taxpayer Relief Act of 2012 has two major features—an increase in the tax rates paid by the wealthiest Americans, and an extension of several tax benefits scheduled to expire at the end of 2011 or 2012.

Some expiring tax benefits were not extended. Most notably, Congress chose not to extend the so-called payroll tax "holiday" that reduced the Social Security taxes for both employees and the self-employed for the past two years. This results in a tax increase for three out of every four Americans in 2013.

1. EXPIRATION OF THE REDUCTION IN SOCIAL SECURITY TAXES

Prior to 2011 employees paid a 6.2 percent Social Security tax on all wages earned up to the annual "wage base" and self-employed individuals paid a 12.4 percent Social Security self-employment tax on all of their self-employment income up to the same threshold.

Congress enacted legislation in 2010 providing for a payroll tax and self-employment tax "holiday" during 2011 of two percentage points off the employee share of Social Security tax, and the Social Security component of self-employment taxes. This meant that the employee share of Social Security taxes dropped from 6.2 percent to 4.2 percent of wages, and the Social Security component of self-employment taxes dropped from 12.4 percent to 10.4 percent of self-employment earnings. This reduction in taxes was enacted to stimulate the economy by increasing the take-home pay of millions of workers.

Congress enacted legislation in 2012 temporarily extending the payroll tax cut for employees and self-employed persons through 2012.

The American Taxpayer Relief Act of 2012 does not extend the reduction in Social Security taxes after 2012. This has the following consequences:

- Employees and self-employed workers will have a tax increase of 2 percent of their earned income under $113,700.
- This tax increase will impact an estimated 77 percent of all workers.
- To illustrate, for a church employee earning $40,000 in 2013, the additional tax will be $800.
- Churches, like any employer, must take into account the elimination of the reduction in Social Security taxes when withholding Social Security taxes from nonminister employees.
- Ministers are self-employed for Social Security, and pay the self-employment tax rather than Social Security and Medicare taxes. Their self-employment taxes will increase 2 percent beginning in 2013. To illustrate, a minister earning $50,000 in 2013 in the exercise of ministry will pay an additional $1,000 in self-employment taxes.
- The housing allowance exclusion applies only to income taxes, and not self-employment taxes. As a result, the 2 percent hike in self-employment taxes will apply not only to a minister's salary, but also to any church-designated housing allowance and the annual rental value of a church-provided parsonage.
- Ministers should take into account the hike in self-employment taxes when computing their quarterly estimated tax payments for 2013 and future years.

✿ **KEY POINT.** The Affordable Care Act (the new healthcare law) contains an additional hike in Social Security and self-employment taxes for higher-income taxpayers. It increases the Medicare tax paid by both employees and self-employed persons by an additional 0.9 percent on wages in excess of a threshold amount beginning in 2013. However, unlike the general 1.45 percent Medicare tax on employee wages, or the 2.9 percent Medicare tax on self-employed workers, this additional tax is on the combined wages of the employee and the employee's spouse, in the case of a joint return. The threshold amount is $250,000 in the case of a joint return or surviving spouse, $125,000 in the case of a married individual filing a separate return, and $200,000 in any other case.

2. IMPACT ON CHARITABLE CONTRIBUTIONS

Some analysts are predicting that charitable contributions will decline as a result of the American Taxpayer Relief Act, for three reasons:

First, charitable contributions are discretionary outlays and many high-income taxpayers may cut back on their contributions to offset the impact of higher taxes. According to the latest IRS statistics, higher-income taxpayers pay a larger percentage of their household income to charity than lower-income taxpayers. Will higher taxes cause the rich to cut back on their contributions? It's too soon to tell, but the possibility exists.

Second, the reinstatement of the "Pease limitation" (addressed below), which caps charitable contributions for the wealthy at 20 percent of the amount of their contributions, may cause higher-income taxpayers to cut back on their giving. Note that the Pease limit impacts taxpayers at a lower level ($300,000 for joint filers) than the higher-income tax rates ($450,000 for joint filers), which may disincentivize charitable giving for a larger group of taxpayers.

Third, many taxpayers make some or all of their contributions by payroll deductions at work. Many of these taxpayers were stunned to see smaller paychecks in the early weeks of 2013 following the expiration of the 2 percent reduction in Social Security taxes that prevailed for the previous 2 years. Some undoubtedly will seek to offset the financial impact of higher Social Security withholdings by reducing or canceling contributions made by payroll deduction.

✿ **KEY POINT.** Several studies on the impact of charitable contribution limits on charitable giving have produced conflicting results. Some studies suggest that charitable giving is adversely affected by less favorable deduction rules, while other studies indicate that the effect is minimal.

3. PERMANENTLY EXTEND THE 10 PERCENT BRACKET

Under prior law, the 10 percent individual income tax bracket expired at the end of 2012. Upon expiration, the lowest tax rate would increase to 15 percent. The Act extends the 10 percent individual income tax bracket for taxable years beginning after December 31, 2012.

4. PERMANENTLY EXTEND THE 25 PERCENT, 28 PERCENT, AND 33 PERCENT INCOME TAX RATES FOR CERTAIN TAXPAYERS

Under prior law, the 25 percent, 28 percent, 33 percent, and 35 percent individual income tax brackets expired at the end of 2012. Upon expiration, the rates were to increase to 28 percent, 31 percent, 36 percent, and 39.6 percent respectively. The Act permanently extends the 25 percent, 28 percent, 33 percent rates on income at or below $400,000 (individual filers), $425,000 (heads of households) and $450,000 (married filing jointly) for taxable years beginning after December 31, 2012, but lets the 35 percent rate for income above these amounts expire, which reinstates a tax rate of 39.6 percent for taxable income above these amounts.

TABLE O-1

FEDERAL INCOME TAX RATES FOR 2013

RATE	SINGLE FILERS	JOINT RETURNS
10%	$0 - $8,925	$0 - $17,850
15%	$8,925 - $36,250	$17,850 - $72,500
25%	$36,250 - $87,850	$72,500 - $146,400
28%	$87,850 - $183,250	$146,400 - $223,050
33%	$183,250 - $398,350	$223,050 - $398,350
35%	$398,350 - $400,000	$398,350 - $450,000
39.6%	$400,000 and up	$450,000 and up

Note that the table reflects marginal tax rates (the tax rates that apply only to the corresponding income described in the table). For example, a married couple with taxable income of $100,000 will not pay the 25 percent rate on this entire amount. Rather, the first $17,850 of taxable income will be taxed at 10 percent, and income from $17,850 to $72,500 will be taxed at 15 percent. Only income from $72,500 to $100,000 will be taxed at 25 percent, meaning that the couple's effective tax rate will be 16.9 percent. This rate will be even lower when deductions, credits, and exclusions are considered.

✵ **KEY POINT.** The $400,000, $425,000, and $450,000 amounts are adjusted annually for inflation beginning in 2014.

✵ **KEY POINT.** The continuation of the lower tax rates for income up to $400,000 (individual filers), $425,000 (heads of households) and $450,000 (married filing jointly) is misleading, since many higher-income taxpayers will have little if any tax relief due to the application of the alternative minimum tax.

✵ **KEY POINT.** Many analysts have noted that the permanent extension of the Bush-era tax cuts for middle and lower-income Americans will make it more difficult to achieve significant reductions in the $16.5 trillion federal deficit, which many do not believe will be possible without greater contributions from middle and lower-income taxpayers.

5. PERMANENTLY REPEAL THE PERSONAL EXEMPTION PHASEOUT FOR CERTAIN TAXPAYERS

In order to determine taxable income, an individual reduces adjusted gross income by any personal exemptions, deductions, and either the applicable standard deduction or itemized deductions. Personal exemptions generally are allowed for the taxpayer, his or her spouse, and any dependents. For 2012, the amount deductible for each personal exemption is $3,800. This amount is adjusted annually for inflation.

Prior to EGTRRA, the exemption was phased out as a result of the Personal Exemption Phaseout ("PEP") for taxpayers with adjusted gross income (AGI) above a certain level.

EGTRRA repealed the PEP over five years, beginning in 2006. The phaseout was reduced by one-third in taxable years beginning in 2006 and 2007, and by two-thirds in taxable years beginning in 2008 and 2009. The repeal was fully effective for taxable years beginning in 2010. In explaining the reason for repealing the phaseout, a congressional conference committee noted that "the personal exemption phase-out is an unnecessarily complex way to impose income taxes and the hidden way in which the phase-out raises marginal tax rates undermines respect for the tax laws."

The Tax Relief, Unemployment Insurance Reauthorization and Job Creation Act of 2010 (TRUIRJCA) extended the PEP repeal through 2012.

The American Taxpayer Relief Act of 2012 extends the PEP repeal on income at or below $250,000 (individual filers), $275,000 (heads of households) and $300,000 (married filing jointly) for taxable years beginning after December 31, 2012.

✵ **KEY POINT.** The $250,000, $275,000, and $300,000 amounts are adjusted annually for inflation beginning in 2014.

6. PERMANENTLY REPEAL THE ITEMIZED DEDUCTION LIMITATION FOR CERTAIN TAXPAYERS

In his acceptance speech during the 1988 Republican National Convention, presidential candidate George H.W. Bush famously pledged, "Read my lips: no new taxes." Two years later, as president, he reluctantly broke his promise and signed the Omnibus Budget Reconciliation Act of 1990. This Act raised taxes in a number of ways, including the so-called "Pease" limit on itemized deductions (named after Ohio congressman Don Pease who first proposed it). This limit required certain itemized deductions, including charitable contributions, to be reduced by 3 percent of a taxpayer's adjusted gross income over $100,000 (adjusted annually for inflation), but not by more than 80 percent.

In 2001, Congress enacted a law (EGTRRA) that phased out the Pease limit by one-third in 2006 and 2007, by two-thirds in 2008 and 2009, and by 100 percent in 2010. EGTRRA contained a "sunset" provision calling for this and many other provisions to expire at the end of 2010. This would have reinstated the Pease limit beginning in 2011. However, Congress enacted legislation in 2010 extending the elimination of the Pease limit through 2012.

The American Taxpayer Relief Act of 2012 permanently extends the repeal of the Pease limit on income at or below $250,000 (individual filers), $275,000 (heads of households) and $300,000 (married filing jointly) for taxable years beginning after December 31, 2012.

✻ **KEY POINT.** The $250,000, $275,000, and $300,000 amounts are adjusted annually for inflation beginning in 2014.

EXAMPLE. A married couple with adjusted gross income of $400,000 in 2013 makes charitable contributions to their church of $50,000. Based on these facts alone, the couple's Pease limitation would be $3,000 (3 percent of the amount by which their AGI exceeds the $300,000 threshold amount for married couples filing a joint return). As a result, the couple's charitable contribution deduction would be $47,000 ($50,000 less $3,000).

EXAMPLE. A single person with adjusted gross income of $500,000 in 2013 makes charitable contributions to his church of $75,000. Based on these facts alone, the donor's Pease limitation would be $7,500 (3 percent of the amount by which his AGI exceeds the $250,000 threshold amount for single persons). As a result, the donor's charitable contribution deduction would be reduced from $75,000 to $67,500.

7. PERMANENTLY EXTEND THE 2001 MODIFICATIONS TO THE CHILD TAX CREDIT

Generally, taxpayers with income below certain threshold amounts may claim the child tax credit to reduce federal income tax for each qualifying child under the age of 17. In 2001, EGTRRA increased the credit from $500 to $1,000 and expanded refundability. The amount that may be claimed as a refund was 15 percent of earnings above $10,000.

The American Taxpayer Relief Act of 2012 permanently extends these provisions for taxable years beginning after December 31, 2012.

8. TEMPORARILY EXTEND THE 2009 MODIFICATIONS TO THE CHILD TAX CREDIT

The American Recovery and Reinvestment Act of 2009 (ARRA) provided that earnings above $3,000 would count towards refundability. The bill extends the ARRA child tax credit expansion for five additional years, through 2017.

9. PERMANENTLY EXTEND MARRIAGE PENALTY RELIEF

In the past, when two persons were married, they often paid more taxes than if they had remained single. This discrepancy is known as the "marriage penalty." This penalty arose in several contexts, including the following: (1) A married couple's combined income often put them in a higher tax bracket than if they had remained single; (2) the standard deduction for a married couple was less than the standard deductions for two single persons; and (3) the earned income tax credit penalized married couples since their combined income placed them in or above the phaseout ranges for the credit. EGTRRA reduced the marriage penalty in the following ways:

1—income tax rates

It increased the 15 percent income tax rate for a married couple filing a joint return to twice the size of the corresponding rate for a single person filing a single return. The increase was phased-in over four years, beginning in 2005.

2—the standard deduction

The standard deduction for married persons filing jointly was increased to twice the standard deduction for single persons.

3—the earned income tax credit

Prior to EGTRRA the earned income credit penalized some individuals because they received a smaller earned income credit if they were married than if they were not married. This was due to the fact that the combined income of married couples made it more likely that they would enter or exceed the phaseout limits that reduce the amount of the credit due to higher earned income. In order to minimize this penalty, EGTRRA increased the phaseout amount for married taxpayers who file a joint return. For married taxpayers who file a joint return, EGTRRA increased the beginning and ending of the earned income credit phaseout by $3,000. These beginning and ending points have been adjusted annually for inflation after 2002. For 2012, the threshold phaseout amounts for single taxpayers, and married couples filing jointly, with one child are $17,090 and $22,300, respectively. The completed phaseout amounts are $36,920 and $44,130, respectively.

The American Taxpayer Relief Act of 2012 extends the marriage penalty relief for the standard deduction, the 15 percent bracket, and the earned income tax credit (EITC) for taxable years beginning after December 31, 2012.

10. PERMANENTLY EXTEND EXPANDED COVERDELL ACCOUNTS

Coverdell Education Savings Accounts are tax-exempt savings accounts used to pay the higher education expenses of a designated beneficiary. EGTRRA increased the annual contribution amount from $500 to $2,000 and expanded the definition of education expenses to include elementary and secondary school expenses. The Act extends the changes to Coverdell accounts for taxable years beginning after December 31, 2012.

11. PERMANENTLY EXTEND THE EXPANDED EXCLUSION FOR EMPLOYER-PROVIDED EDUCATIONAL ASSISTANCE

An employee may exclude from gross income up to $5,250 for income and employment tax purposes per year of employer-provided education assistance. Prior to 2001, this incentive was temporary and only applied to undergraduate courses. EGTRRA expanded this provision to cover both undergraduate and graduate education, and extended the expanded exclusion through 2010. In 2010, Congress extended the expanded exclusion through 2012.

The American Taxpayer Relief Act of 2012 permanently extends the changes to this provision for taxable years beginning after December 31, 2012.

12. PERMANENTLY EXTEND THE EXPANDED STUDENT LOAN INTEREST DEDUCTION

Certain individuals who have paid interest on qualified education loans may claim an above-the-line deduction for such interest expenses up to $2,500. Prior to 2001, this benefit was only allowed for 60 months and phased-out for taxpayers with income between $40,000 and $55,000 ($60,000 and $75,000 for joint filers). EGTRRA eliminated the 60-month rule and increased the income phaseout to $55,000 to $70,000 ($110,000 and $140,000 for joint filers).

The American Taxpayer Relief Act of 2012 extends the changes to this provision for taxable years beginning after December 31, 2012.

13. PERMANENTLY EXTEND THE EXPANDED DEPENDENT CARE CREDIT

The dependent care credit allows a taxpayer a credit for an applicable percentage of child care expenses for children under 13 and disabled dependents. EGTRRA increased the amount of eligible expenses from $2,400 for one child and $4,800 for two or more children to $3,000 and $6,000, respectively. EGTRRA also increased the applicable percentage from 30 percent to 35 percent.

The American Taxpayer Relief Act of 2012 permanently extends the changes to the dependent care credit made by EGTRRA for taxable years beginning after December 31, 2012.

14. PERMANENTLY EXTEND THE INCREASED ADOPTION TAX CREDIT AND THE ADOPTION ASSISTANCE PROGRAMS EXCLUSION

Taxpayers that adopt children can receive a tax credit for qualified adoption expenses. A taxpayer may also exclude from income adoption expenses paid by an employer. EGTRRA increased the credit from $5,000 ($6,000 for a special needs child) to $10,000, and provided a $10,000 income exclusion for employer-assistance programs. The Patient Protection and Affordable Care Act of 2010 extended these benefits to 2011 and made the credit refundable.

The American Taxpayer Relief Act of 2012 extends for taxable years beginning after December 31, 2012, the increased adoption credit amount and the exclusion for employer-assistance programs as enacted in EGTRRA.

15. PERMANENT ESTATE, GIFT, AND GENERATION SKIPPING TRANSFER TAX RELIEF

EGTRRA phased-out the estate and generation-skipping transfer taxes so that they were fully repealed in 2010, and lowered the gift tax rate to 35 percent and increased the gift tax exemption to $1 million for 2010.

In 2010, TRUIRJCA set the exemption at $5 million per person with a top tax rate of 35 percent for the estate, gift, and generation skipping transfer taxes for two years, through 2012. The exemption amount was indexed beginning in 2012.

The American Taxpayer Relief Act of 2012 makes permanent the indexed TRUIRJCA exclusion amount and indexes that amount for inflation going forward, but sets the top tax rate to 40 percent for estates of decedents dying after December 31, 2012.

16. PORTABILITY OF UNUSED EXEMPTION

TRUIRJCA allowed the executor of a deceased spouse's estate to transfer any unused exemption to the surviving spouse for estates of decedents dying after December 31, 2010, and before December 31, 2012. The American Taxpayer Relief Act of 2012 makes permanent this provision and is effective for estates for decedents dying after December 31, 2012.

17. REUNIFICATION

Prior to EGTRRA, the estate and gift taxes were unified, creating a single graduated rate schedule for both. That single lifetime exemption could be used for gifts and bequests. EGTRRA decoupled these systems. TRUIRJCA reunified the estate and gift taxes. The American Taxpayer Relief Act of 2012 permanently extends unification and is effective for gifts made after December 31, 2012.

18. PERMANENTLY EXTEND THE CAPITAL GAINS AND DIVIDEND RATES

Under prior law, the capital gains and dividend rates for taxpayers below the 25 percent tax bracket was equal to 0 percent. For those in the 25 percent bracket and above, the capital gains and dividend rates were 15 percent. These rates expired at the end of 2012. Upon expiration, the rates for capital gains become 10 percent and 20 percent, respectively, and dividends are subject to the ordinary income rates.

The American Taxpayer Relief Act of 2012 extends the lower capital gains and dividends rates on income at or below $400,000 (individual filers), $425,000 (heads of households), and $450,000 (married filing jointly) for taxable years beginning after December 31, 2012. For income in excess of $400,000 (individual filers), $425,000 (heads of households), and $450,000 (married filing jointly), the rate for both capital gains and dividends will be 20 percent.

❖ **KEY POINT.** The $400,000, $425,000, and $450,000 amounts are adjusted annually for inflation beginning in 2014.

❖ **KEY POINT.** The effective tax rate for many high-income taxpayers will be 23.8 percent because of the 20 percent capital gains and dividends tax rate plus the new 3.8 tax on investment income that was a feature of the Affordable Care Act (the healthcare reform legislation).

19. TEMPORARILY EXTEND THE AMERICAN OPPORTUNITY TAX CREDIT

The American Opportunity Tax Credit is available for up to $2,500 of the cost of tuition and related expenses paid during the taxable year. Under this tax credit, taxpayers receive a tax credit based on 100 percent of the first $2,000 of tuition and related expenses (including course materials) paid during the taxable year and 25 percent of the next $2,000 of tuition and related expenses paid during the taxable year. Forty percent of the credit is refundable. This tax credit is subject to a phaseout for taxpayers with adjusted gross income in excess of $80,000 ($160,000 for married couples filing jointly).

The American Taxpayer Relief Act of 2012 extends the American Opportunity Tax Credit for five additional years, through 2017.

20. TEMPORARILY EXTEND THIRD-CHILD EITC

Under prior law, working families with two or more children qualified for an earned income tax credit equal to 40 percent of the family's first $12,570 of earned income. In 2009 Congress increased the earned income tax credit to 45 percent for families with three or more children and increased the beginning point of the phaseout range for all married couples filing a joint return (regardless of the number of children) to lessen the marriage penalty.

The American Taxpayer Relief Act of 2012 extends for five additional years, through 2017, the 2009 expansions that increased the EITC for families with three or more children and increased the phaseout range for all married couples filing a joint return.

21. PERMANENTLY EXTEND REFUND AND TAX CREDIT DISREGARD FOR MEANS-TESTED PROGRAMS

Prior law ensured that the refundable components of the EITC and the Child Tax Credit did not make households ineligible for means-tested benefit programs and included provisions stating that these tax credits did not count as income in determining eligibility (and benefit levels) in means-tested benefit programs, and also did not count as assets for specified periods of time. Without them, the receipt of a tax credit would put a substantial number of families over the income limits for these programs in the month that the tax refund is received. A provision enacted as part of TRUIRJCA disregarded all refundable tax credits and refunds as income for means-tested programs through 2012.

The American Taxpayer Relief Act of 2012 permanently extends this provision for any amount received after December 31, 2012.

22. PERMANENT AMT PATCH

Under prior law a taxpayer received an exemption of $33,750 (individuals) and $45,000 (married filing jointly) under the alternative minimum tax (AMT). Prior law also did not allow nonrefundable personal credits against the AMT.

The American Taxpayer Relief Act of 2012 increases the exemption amounts for 2012 to $50,600 (individuals) and $78,750 (married filing jointly) and for future years indexes the exemption and phaseout amounts for inflation. It also allows the nonrefundable personal credits against the AMT. These changes are effective for taxable year beginning after December 31, 2011.

❖ **KEY POINT.** Some analysts speculate that the reason Congress previously enacted a series of two-year "patches" to the AMT, rather than a one-time permanent fix, was to present a far more positive budgetary outlook based on the tenuous assumption that the AMT would not be patched in the future.

23. DEDUCTION FOR CERTAIN EXPENSES OF ELEMENTARY AND SECONDARY SCHOOL TEACHERS

The Act extends for two years the $250 above-the-line tax deduction for teachers and other school professionals for expenses paid or incurred for books, supplies (other than non-athletic supplies for courses of instruction in health or physical education), computer equipment (including related software and service), other equipment, and supplementary materials used by the educator in the classroom.

24. MORTGAGE DEBT RELIEF

Under current law, taxpayers who have mortgage debt canceled or forgiven after 2012 may be required to pay taxes on that amount as taxable income. Under the Act, up to $2 million of forgiven debt is eligible to be excluded from income ($1 million if married filing separately) through tax year 2013. This provision was created in the Mortgage Debt Relief Act of 2007 to prevent the taxation of so-called "shadow income" from foreclosures and cancelled debts through 2010. It was extended through 2012 by the Emergency Economic Stabilization Act of 2008.

25. PARITY FOR EXCLUSION FROM INCOME FOR EMPLOYER-PROVIDED MASS TRANSIT AND PARKING BENEFITS

This provision would extend through 2013 the increase in the monthly exclusion for employer-provided transit and vanpool benefits from $125 to $240, so that it would be the same as the exclusion for employer-provided parking benefits.

26. DEDUCTION FOR STATE AND LOCAL GENERAL SALES TAXES

Congress enacted legislation in 2004 providing that, at the election of the taxpayer, an itemized deduction may be taken for state and local general sales taxes in lieu of the itemized deduction for state and local income taxes. Taxpayers have two options with respect to the determination of the sales tax deduction amount. They can deduct the total amount of general state and local sales taxes paid by accumulating receipts showing general sales taxes paid, or they can use tables created by the IRS. The tables are based on average consumption by taxpayers on a state-by-state basis, taking into account filing status, number of dependents, adjusted gross income, and rates of state and local general sales taxation.

Taxpayers who use the tables may, in addition, deduct eligible general sales taxes paid with respect to the purchase of motor vehicles, boats, and other items specified by the IRS. Sales taxes for items that may be added to the tables would not be reflected in the tables themselves.

This provision was added to address the unequal treatment of taxpayers in the nine states that assess no income tax. Taxpayers in these states cannot take advantage of the itemized deduction for state income taxes. Allowing them to deduct sales taxes will help offset this disadvantage.

This deduction was scheduled to expire after 2005, but Congress extended it through 2009, and again through 2011.

The American Taxpayer Relief Act of 2012 extends for two years (through 2013) the election to take an itemized deduction for state and local general sales taxes in lieu of the itemized deduction permitted for state and local income taxes.

27. ABOVE-THE-LINE DEDUCTION FOR QUALIFIED TUITION RELATED EXPENSES

EGTRRA created an above-the-line tax deduction for qualified higher education expenses. The maximum deduction was $4,000 for taxpayers with AGI of $65,000 or less ($130,000 for joint returns) or $2,000 for taxpayers with AGI of $80,000 or less ($160,000 for joint returns).

The American Taxpayer Relief Act of 2012 extends the deduction to the end of 2013.

28. TAX-FREE DISTRIBUTIONS FROM INDIVIDUAL RETIREMENT PLAN FOR CHARITABLE PURPOSES

Congress enacted legislation in 2006 allowing tax-free qualified charitable distributions of up to $100,000 from an IRA to a church or other charity. Note the following rules and conditions:

- A qualified charitable distribution is any distribution from an IRA directly by the IRA trustee to a charitable organization, including a church, that are made on or after the date the IRA owner attains age 70½.
- A distribution will be treated as a qualified charitable distribution only to the extent that it would be includible in taxable income without regard to this provision.

- This provision applies only if a charitable contribution deduction for the entire distribution would be allowable under present law, determined without regard to the generally applicable percentage limitations. For example, if the deductible amount is reduced because the donor receives a benefit in exchange for the contribution of some or all of his or her IRA account, or if a deduction is not allowable because the donor did not have sufficient substantiation, the exclusion is not available with respect to any part of the IRA distribution.

This provision, which was scheduled to expire at the end of 2011, is extended for two more years (through 2013) by the American Taxpayer Relief Act of 2012.

The Act also contains a transition rule under which an individual can make a rollover during January of 2013 and have it count as a 2012 rollover. Also, individuals who took a distribution in December of 2012 will be able to contribute that amount to a charity and count as an eligible charitable rollover to the extent it otherwise meets the requirements for an eligible charitable rollover.

29. ENHANCED CHARITABLE DEDUCTION FOR CONTRIBUTIONS OF FOOD INVENTORY

The Act extends for two years (through 2013) the provision allowing businesses to claim an enhanced deduction for the contribution of food inventory.

CONTENTS

CONTENTS

CONTENTS

Preface

LONG AGO AN EMINENT JUDGE OBSERVED:

In my own case the words of such an act as the income tax . . . merely dance before my eyes in a meaningless procession: cross-reference to cross-reference, exception upon exception—couched in abstract terms that offer no handle to seize hold of—leaving in my mind only a confused sense of some vitally important, but successfully concealed purport, which it is my duty to extract, but which is within my power, if at all, only after the most inordinate expenditure of time. I know that these monsters are the result of fabulous industry and ingenuity, plugging up this hole and casting out that net, against all possible evasion . . . that they were no doubt written with a passion of rationality; but that one cannot help wondering whether to the reader they have any significance save that the words are strung together with syntactical correctness. I. Dillard, The Spirit of Liberty: Papers and Addresses of Learned Hand 213 (1960).

Former Treasury Secretary Paul O'Neill once lamented that "our tax code is so complicated, we've made it nearly impossible for even the Internal Revenue Service to understand."

Sound familiar? Few persons have more ably described the frustrations created by the federal income tax. Our tax law is so complex that it is incomprehensible to most taxpayers. A small and declining number of taxpayers are able to complete a Form 1040. And, as if this were not enough, the tax law is always changing.

Ministers' taxes are especially frustrating, since a number of unique rules apply to the reporting of ministers' federal income and Social Security taxes. The reporting of ministers' income taxes also involves a number of complex and sometimes controversial issues. To illustrate, a debate has raged for years over the question of whether ministers should report their federal income taxes as employees or as self-employed persons. With so many unique and complex rules, it's no wonder there is confusion among tax practitioners, the courts, and even within the IRS regarding the application of tax law to ministers.

This book has two objectives. The first is to help *ministers* (1) understand the many unique features of our tax laws that apply to them;

(2) correctly report their federal income taxes; (3) understand the basis for exempting themselves from Social Security (and why it does not apply to most ministers); (4) correctly report Social Security taxes (if not exempt); and (5) reduce income tax and Social Security liability as much as possible.

A second objective is to help *church treasurers, board members, bookkeepers, attorneys, CPAs, and tax practitioners* understand (1) the definition of "income" in the church environment; (2) how to handle and report employee business expenses; (3) the substantiation rules that apply to charitable contributions; (4) how to handle designated contributions; and (5) the federal tax reporting requirements that apply to churches and church employees.

Most tax guides lose most if not all of their relevance after April 15. This book is different—it was designed to have direct and immediate relevance to ministers, churches, and their advisers *throughout the year*. For example, entire chapters are devoted to charitable contributions, clergy retirement plans, Social Security, and church reporting requirements. Other chapters contain vital information of continuing relevance, such as the mechanics of the housing allowance and a business-expense reimbursement policy. A generous supply of illustrations and legal forms makes this a resource that you will refer to again and again throughout the year.

Since tax laws change from year to year, this book is republished annually to provide readers with information that is as accurate and up to date as possible. This edition addresses all of the important tax developments that occurred up until the time of publication in 2012.

Of course, I welcome your suggestions for future editions. Please send your ideas to Church Law & Tax Resources, Christianity Today, 465 Gundersen Drive, Carol Stream, IL 60188. My objective is to make this resource the most helpful, accurate, and comprehensible guide available.

Richard R. Hammar, J.D., LL.M., CPA

SUMMARY OF IMPORTANT TAX CHANGES

The hardest thing in the world to understand is the income tax.

Albert Einstein

Congress has enacted the following major tax laws since 2001, each of which contains provisions that will affect tax reporting by both churches and ministers for 2012 and future years.

- Tax Relief, Unemployment Insurance Reauthorization, and Job Creation Act of 2010
- Small Business Jobs Act of 2010
- Education Jobs and Medicaid Assistance Act of 2010
- Homebuyer Assistance and Improvement Act of 2010
- Hiring Incentives to Restore Employment (HIRE) Act of 2010
- Timing of Haiti earthquake relief donations (2010)
- Affordable Care Act (2010)
- American Recovery and Reinvestment Act of 2009 (ARRA)
- Emergency Economic Stabilization Act of 2008
- Housing Assistance Tax Act of 2008
- Heroes Earnings Assistance and Relief Tax Act of 2008
- Mortgage Forgiveness Debt Relief Act of 2007
- Pension Protection Act of 2006
- Tax Increase Prevention and Reconciliation Act of 2005
- American Jobs Creation Act of 2004
- Jobs and Growth Tax Relief Reconciliation Act of 2003
- Economic Growth and Tax Relief Reconciliation Act of 2001

The main provisions in these laws that took effect in 2012 or later are summarized in this introduction and throughout this text.

TAX LAW CHANGES MADE BY CONGRESS

✿ **KEY POINT.** Many of the tax benefits summarized below expire at the end of either 2011 or 2012, unless extended by Congress. As of the date of publication of this text, Congress has not acted. As a result, the availability of those benefits expiring at the end of 2011 in preparing tax returns for 2012 and beyond, and of those benefits expiring at the end of 2012 in preparing tax returns for 2013 and beyond, is dependent on congressional action.

President George W. Bush promised tax relief during the presidential campaign of 2000, and Congress delivered by enacting the Economic Growth and Tax Relief Reconciliation Act (EGTRRA)

in May 2001. The Act's most publicized feature was a $1.35 trillion package of tax cuts. However, the Act also contained more than 440 other tax law changes.

An unprecedented feature of EGTRRA was a sunset provision that revoked all of the hundreds of tax law changes at the end of 2010 unless Congress voted to extend them. Without congressional action, the tax law in effect in 2001, prior to the enactment of EGTRRA, would be reinstated beginning in 2011.

Congress enacted the Tax Relief, Unemployment Insurance Reauthorization, and Job Creation Act (the "Tax Relief Act") late in 2010, which extended many of the tax breaks under EGTRRA and other laws through either 2010, 2011, or 2012, meaning that some will be available when preparing your 2012 tax return. But unless Congress acts, none of these tax breaks will be available after 2012. And some benefits, as noted below, expired at the end of 2011 and will not be available in preparing 2012 income tax returns unless extended by Congress.

TAX RELIEF, UNEMPLOYMENT INSURANCE REAUTHORIZATION, AND JOB CREATION ACT OF 2010

1. Extension of expiring provisions

Here is a summary of the expiring provisions of most relevance to clergy and church staff. While many expire at the end of 2012 and are available in preparing 2012 tax returns, others expired at the end of 2011 and are no longer available. It is likely that Congress will extend some of these benefits, making them available in preparing tax returns for 2012 and possibly beyond.

- **Income tax rates.** Prior to EGTRRA, there were five income tax rates, depending on a taxpayer's income (15 percent, 28 percent, 31 percent, 36 percent, and 39.6 percent). EGTRRA created a new 10 percent income tax bracket for a portion of taxable income that was previously taxed at 15 percent, and the 15 percent income tax bracket was modified to begin at the end of the new low-rate income tax bracket. The pre-EGTRRA income tax rates of 28 percent, 31 percent, 36 percent, and 39.6 percent were phased down over six years to 25 percent, 28 percent, 33 percent, and 35 percent. The Tax Relief Act extended for two years (through 2012) the lower income tax rates for all taxpayers.
- **Capital gains and dividends.** Under prior law, the capital gains and dividend rates for taxpayers below the 25 percent

income tax bracket was equal to zero percent. For those in the 25 percent tax bracket and above, the capital gains and dividend rates were 15 percent. These rates were to expire at the end of 2010, and higher rates (10 percent and 20 percent) were to apply. The Tax Relief Act extends the lower capital gains and dividends rates for all taxpayers for an additional two years, through 2012.

- **Child Tax Credit.** Generally, taxpayers with income below certain threshold amounts may claim the Child Tax Credit to reduce federal income tax for each qualifying child under the age of 17. In 2001 Congress increased the credit from $500 to $1,000 and made it refundable up to 15 percent of earnings above $10,000. In 2009 Congress amended the law to allow earnings above $3,000 to count toward refundability for 2009 and 2010. The Tax Relief Act extends these changes (which were scheduled to expire at the end of 2010) for an additional two years, through 2012.

- **Marriage penalty relief.** For many years, married couples filing a joint tax return paid more taxes than if they were unmarried filing individual returns. In 2001 Congress ended this so-called "marriage penalty" by (1) increasing the basic standard deduction for a married couple filing a joint return to twice the basic standard deduction for an unmarried individual filing a single return and (2) increasing the 15 percent income tax rate bracket for a married couple filing a joint return to twice the size of the corresponding rate bracket for an unmarried individual filing a single return. These provisions were to have expired at the end of 2010, but both were extended by the Tax Relief Act for two years (through 2012).

- **Child and Dependent Care Credit.** The Child and Dependent Care Credit allows taxpayers a credit for a percentage of childcare expenses for children under 13 and for disabled dependents. In 2001 Congress increased the amount of eligible expenses from $2,400 for one child and $4,800 for two or more children to $3,000 and $6,000, respectively, and increased the applicable percentage from 30 percent to 35 percent. The Tax Relief Act extends these changes (which were scheduled to expire at the end of 2010) for two years, through 2012.

- **Earned Income Tax Credit.** Under prior law, working families with two or more children qualified for an Earned Income Tax Credit equal to 40 percent of the family's first earned income, up to a specified amount. In 2009 Congress increased the Earned Income Tax Credit to 45 percent of a family's earned income, up to a specified amount, for families with three or more children and increased the beginning point of the phaseout range for all married couples filing a joint return (regardless of the number of children). The Tax Relief Act extends for an additional two years, through 2012, the increased credit for families with three or more children and the higher phaseout ranges for all married couples filing a joint return.

- **Coverdell Education Savings Accounts.** Coverdell Education Savings Accounts are tax-exempt savings accounts used to pay the higher-education expenses of a designated beneficiary. In 2001 Congress increased the annual contribution amount from $500 to $2,000 and expanded the definition of education expenses to include elementary and secondary school expenses. These changes, which were to have expired at the end of 2010, were extended by the Tax Relief Act through 2012.

- **Employer-provided educational assistance.** An employee may exclude from taxable income up to $5,250 per year of employer-provided education assistance. Prior to 2001, this incentive was temporary and only applied to undergraduate courses. Congress enacted legislation in 2001 that expanded this provision to graduate education and extended it to the end of 2010. The Tax Relief Act extends the changes to this provision for an additional two years, through 2012.

- **American Opportunity Tax Credit.** The American Opportunity Tax Credit is available for up to $2,500 of the cost of tuition and related expenses paid during the taxable year. Under this tax credit, taxpayers receive a tax credit based on 100 percent of the first $2,000 of tuition and related expenses (including course materials) paid during the taxable year and 25 percent of the next $2,000 of tuition and related expenses paid during the taxable year. Forty percent of the credit is refundable (i.e., payable to individuals with no income tax liability). This tax credit is subject to a phaseout for taxpayers with adjusted gross income in excess of $80,000 ($160,000 for married couples filing jointly). The Tax Relief Act extends this credit, which was scheduled to expire at the end of 2010, for an additional two years, through 2012.

- **Alternative Minimum Tax (AMT).** The Act allowed an individual to offset the entire regular tax liability and alternative minimum tax liability by nonrefundable personal credits for 2010 and 2011. The individual AMT exemption amount for 2011 was (1) $74,450 in the case of married individuals filing a joint return and surviving spouses, (2) $48,450 in the case of other unmarried individuals, and (3) $37,225 in the case of married individuals filing separate returns. Without these changes, the AMT exemption amounts would have plummeted in 2010 and beyond, exposing tens of millions of Americans to the AMT.

- **Energy-efficient new homes credit.** The Tax Relief Act extends through 2011 the credit for manufacturers of energy-efficient residential homes.

- **Energy-efficient appliances.** The Act extends through 2011 the credit for United States–based manufacture of energy-efficient clothes washers, dishwashers, and refrigerators.

- **Energy-efficient existing homes.** The Act extends through 2011 the credit for energy-efficient improvements to existing homes. Standards for eligible improvements are updated to reflect advances in energy efficiency.

- **Above-the-line deduction for certain expenses of elementary and secondary school teachers.** The Act extends through 2011 the $250 above-the-line tax deduction for teachers and other school professionals for expenses paid or incurred for books, supplies (other than non-athletic supplies for courses of instruction in health or physical education), computer equipment (including related software and service), other equipment, and supplementary materials used by the educator in the classroom.

- **Deduction of state and local general sales taxes.** Congress enacted legislation in 2004 that provided an itemized deduction for state and local general sales taxes in lieu of the itemized deduction for state and local income taxes. Taxpayers could deduct the total amount of general state and local sales taxes they paid by accumulating receipts showing general sales taxes paid, or they could use tables created by the IRS. This provision was adopted to address the unequal treatment of taxpayers in the nine states that have no income tax. Taxpayers in these states cannot take advantage of the itemized deduction for state income taxes. Allowing them to deduct sales taxes helps offset this disadvantage. This deduction, which was scheduled to expire at the end of 2009, was extended by the Tax Relief Act through 2011.

- **Above-the-line deduction for qualified tuition and related expenses.** Under prior law, an above-the-line deduction of up to $4,000 was available for qualified education expenses incurred by a taxpayer or a taxpayer's spouse or dependent. Qualified education expenses included tuition and certain related expenses required for enrollment or attendance at an eligible educational institution (any college, university, vocational school, or other postsecondary educational institution eligible to participate in a student aid program administered by the Department of Education). Student activity fees and expenses for course-related books, supplies, and equipment were included in qualified education expenses only if the fees and expenses had to be paid to the institution as a condition of enrollment or attendance. This deduction, which was scheduled to expire at the end of 2009, was extended through 2011 by the Tax Relief Act.

- **Extension of tax-free distributions from Individual Retirement Accounts (IRAs) for charitable purposes.** The Act extends through 2011 a provision that permits tax-free distributions to charity from an IRA of up to $100,000 per taxpayer, per taxable year. Distributions are eligible for the exclusion only if made on or after the date the IRA owner attains age 70½ and only to the extent the distribution would be includible in gross income (without regard to this provision).

- **Parity for mass-transit benefits.** The Act extends through 2011 the increase in the monthly exclusion for employer-provided transit and vanpool benefits to that of the exclusion for employer-provided parking benefits.

- **Refundable tax credits disregarded for means-tested programs.** Prior law ensured that the refundable components of

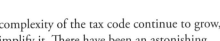

"The sheer girth and complexity of the tax code continue to grow, in spite of efforts to simplify it. There have been an astonishing 4,400 legislative changes to the Code from 2000 to September of this year."

—IRS Commissioner Douglas Shulman in a keynote address before the AICPA Fall 2010 meeting

the Earned Income Tax Credit and Child Tax Credit did not make households ineligible for means-tested benefit programs and did not count as income in determining eligibility (and benefit levels) in such programs. Without these provisions, the receipt of a tax credit could put a substantial number of families over the income limits for these programs in the month that the tax refund was received. The Tax Relief Act disregards all refundable tax credits and refunds as income for means-tested programs. The proposal is effective for amounts received after December 31, 2009, and does not apply to amounts received after December 31, 2012.

- **Extension of enhanced charitable deduction for contributions of food inventory.** The Act extends through 2011 a provision allowing businesses to claim an enhanced deduction for the contribution of food inventory.

- **Personal Exemption Phaseout.** Personal exemptions allow a certain amount per person to be exempt from tax ($3,800 for 2012). Due to the Personal Exemption Phaseout (PEP), the exemptions are phased out for taxpayers with income above a certain level. The PEP was repealed in 2010. This repeal was extended by the Tax Relief Act through 2012.

- **Itemized deduction limitation.** Generally, taxpayers itemize deductions if their total deductions are more than the standard deduction amount. Since 1991 the amount of itemized deductions is reduced for taxpayers with income above a certain amount. This limitation is generally known as the "Pease limitation." It was repealed for 2010. The Tax Relief Act extends the repeal of the Pease limitation for an additional two years, though 2012.

The Tax Relief Act of 2010 contained two other significant provisions that were not extensions of expiring provisions:

- **Payroll tax "holiday."** Under prior law, employees paid a 6.2 percent Social Security tax on all wages earned up to the annual "wage base" ($110,100 for 2012) and self-employed individuals paid a 12.4 percent Social Security self-employment tax on all their self-employment income up to the same threshold. The Tax Relief Act provided a payroll tax and self-employment tax "holiday" during 2011 of two percentage points off the employee share of Social Security tax, and the Social Security component of self-employment taxes. This meant that the employee share of Social Security taxes dropped from 6.2 to 4.2 percent of wages, and the Social Security component of self-employment taxes dropped from 12.4 to 10.4 percent of self-employment earnings. This reduction in taxes was enacted to stimulate the economy by increasing the take-home pay for millions of workers. Congress enacted legislation in 2012 temporarily extending the 2 percent payroll tax cut for employees and self-employed persons through 2012.

- **Estate tax relief.** In 2001, Congress phased out the estate tax which was fully repealed in 2010. The Tax Relief Act revives the estate tax, but establishes an exemption of $5 million per person and $10 million per couple and a top tax rate of 35 percent for two years, through 2012. The exemption amount is indexed beginning in 2012 and was $5,120,000 for 2012. Under prior law, couples had to do complicated estate planning to claim their entire exemption. The Tax Relief Act allows the executor of a deceased spouse's estate to transfer any unused exemption to the surviving spouse without such planning. If Congress does not act, the exemption amount will drop to $1 million in 2013, and the top estate tax rate will increase from 35 percent to 55 percent.

Some expired tax provisions were not extended by the Tax Relief Act. These include:

- **Additional standard deduction for state and local real property taxes.** Congress enacted legislation in 2008 that provided a limited tax deduction for state and local property taxes to nonitemizers by increasing their standard deduction by the lesser of (1) the amount allowable to the taxpayer as a deduction for state and local taxes or (2) $500 ($1,000 in the case of a married individual filing jointly). The increased standard deduction was determined by taking into account real estate taxes for which a deduction was allowable to the taxpayer.
- **Making work pay credit.** In the past, eligible individuals could claim a refundable income tax credit for two years (2009 and 2010). The credit was the lesser of (1) 6.2 percent of an individual's earned income or (2) $400 ($800 in the case of a joint return). Taxpayers could elect to receive this benefit through a reduction in the amount of income tax withheld from their paychecks or through claiming the credit on their tax returns. The credit expired at the end of 2010 and was not renewed. The withholding tables for 2011 are no longer adjusted for this credit.
- **Deduction of state and local tax on the purchase of qualified motor vehicles.** In the past, taxpayers could claim an above-the-line deduction for qualified motor vehicle taxes. Qualified motor vehicle taxes included any state or local sales or excise tax imposed on the purchase of a qualified motor vehicle. A qualified motor vehicle was a passenger automobile, light truck, or motorcycle which has a gross vehicle weight

of not more than 8,500 pounds that was acquired for use by the taxpayer after February 17, 2009, and before January 1, 2010, the original use of which begins with the taxpayer. The deduction was limited to the tax on up to $49,500 of the purchase price of a qualified motor vehicle. Congress has not extended this deduction.
- **Waiver of minimum required distribution rules for IRAs and defined contribution plans.** In general, persons participating in IRAs and defined benefit plans must begin receiving "required minimum distributions" by a certain age in order to avoid penalties. Congress suspended this rule for 2009 but has not done so for any subsequent year.

AFFORDABLE CARE ACT (2010)

The United States Supreme Court, in a 5-4 decision written by chief justice John Roberts, ruled that the individual mandate is not a valid exercise of Congress's power to regulate commerce. The Court stressed that Congress is an "enumerated powers" institution that can only do those things that are expressly authorized by the Constitution. It acknowledged that the Constitution grants Congress the power to "regulate Commerce." But it noted that the power to *regulate* commerce presupposes the existence of commercial activity to be regulated:

> *The individual mandate, however, does not regulate existing commercial activity. It instead compels individuals to become active in commerce by purchasing a product, on the ground that their failure to do so affects interstate commerce. Construing the Commerce Clause to permit Congress to regulate individuals precisely because they are doing nothing would open a new and potentially vast domain to congressional authority. Every day individuals do not do an infinite number of things. In some cases they decide not to do something; in others they simply fail to do it. Allowing Congress to justify federal regulation by pointing to the effect of inaction on commerce would bring countless decisions an individual could potentially make within the scope of federal regulation, and—under the Government's theory—empower Congress to make those decisions for him. . . .*
>
> *The individual mandate forces individuals into commerce precisely because they elected to refrain from commercial activity. Such a law cannot be sustained under a clause authorizing Congress to "regulate Commerce."*

To the surprise of many Court watchers, the Court went on to rule that Congress had the authority to create the individual mandate under its constitutional authority to collect taxes. The Court observed:

> *The Affordable Care Act's requirement that certain individuals pay a financial penalty for not obtaining health insurance may*

reasonably be characterized as a tax. Because the Constitution permits such a tax, it is not our role to forbid it, or to pass upon its wisdom or fairness. . . .

The Federal Government does not have the power to order people to buy health insurance. [The individual mandate] would therefore be unconstitutional if read as a command. The Federal Government does have the power to impose a tax on those without health insurance. [The mandate] is therefore constitutional, because it can reasonably be read as a tax.

The second provision of the Affordable Care Act challenged by the plaintiffs was the "Medicaid expansion" (summarized above). The Court acknowledged that the Act dramatically increases state obligations under Medicaid by requiring states to expand their Medicaid programs by 2014 to cover all individuals under the age of 65 with incomes below 133 percent of the federal poverty line. It agreed that Congress has the authority "to offer funds under the Affordable Care Act to expand the availability of health care, and requiring that states accepting such funds comply with the conditions on their use." But "what Congress is not free to do is to penalize states that choose not to participate in that new program by taking away their existing Medicaid funding." As a result, the portion of the Act giving the secretary of Health and Human Services the authority to do so was unconstitutional. The Court observed:

Congress has no authority to order the states to regulate according to its instructions. Congress may offer the states grants and require the states to comply with accompanying conditions, but the states must have a genuine choice whether to accept the offer. The states are given no such choice in this case: They must either accept a basic change in the nature of Medicaid, or risk losing all Medicaid funding. The remedy for that constitutional violation is to preclude the Federal Government from imposing such a sanction. That remedy does not require striking down other portions of the Affordable Care Act.

The Court concluded: "The Framers created a Federal Government of limited powers, and assigned to this Court the duty of enforcing those limits. The Court does so today. But the Court does not express any opinion on the wisdom of the Affordable Care Act. Under the Constitution, that judgment is reserved to the people."

The significance of the Supreme Court's ruling on churches and church employees is addressed in Chapter 5 of this guide.

EMERGENCY ECONOMIC STABILIZATION ACT OF 2008

In 2008 Congress enacted the Emergency Economic Stabilization Act to address the economic turmoil generated by the weaknesses in the credit and financial markets. The tax changes of most interest to churches and church staff are summarized below.

2. Extension of exclusion of income from discharge of qualified principal residence indebtedness

Normally, debt forgiveness results in taxable income. But under the Mortgage Forgiveness Debt Relief Act of 2007, taxpayers can exclude debt forgiven on their principal residence if the balance of their loan was less than $2 million ($1 million for a married person filing a separate return). Homeowners whose mortgage debt was partly or entirely forgiven may be able to claim the special tax relief by filling out Form 982 and attaching it to their federal income tax return.

The Mortgage Forgiveness Debt Relief Act applied only to debt forgiven in 2007, 2008, or 2009. Debt reduced through mortgage restructuring, as well as mortgage debt forgiven in connection with a foreclosure, may qualify for this relief. In most cases, eligible homeowners only need to fill out a few lines on Form 982 (specifically, lines 1e, 2, and 10b).

The debt must have been used to buy, build, or substantially improve the taxpayer's principal residence and must have been secured by that residence. Debt used to refinance qualifying debt is also eligible for the exclusion, but only up to the amount of the old mortgage principal just before the refinancing.

Debt forgiven on second homes, rental property, business property, credit cards, or car loans does not qualify for the new tax-relief provision. In some cases, however, other kinds of tax relief, based on insolvency, for example, may be available. See Form 982 for details.

Borrowers whose debt is reduced or eliminated receive a year-end statement (Form 1099-C) from their lender. By law, this form must show the amount of debt forgiven and the fair market value of any property given up through foreclosure.

The Emergency Economic Stabilization Act of 2008 extends the exclusion of forgiven home mortgage debt from the end of 2009 through 2012.

PENSION PROTECTION ACT OF 2006

Congress enacted the massive 900-page Pension Protection Act in 2006. While the main focus of the Act is pension reform, it also includes a number of unrelated provisions that will be of direct relevance to every church. Most notably, the Act imposes new requirements on the substantiation of charitable contributions.

These requirements take effect immediately and affect countless contributions made to churches. In summary, the Act affects nearly everyone, since it applies to the millions of Americans enrolled in pension or retirement plans as well as persons who make charitable contributions to their church or favorite charity.

Following is a summary of the main provisions that took effect in 2012 or later.

Elimination of EGTRRA "sunset" provision

The Economic Growth and Tax Relief Reconciliation Act of 2001 (EGTRRA) contained a number of favorable provisions pertaining to retirement plans. However, these provisions were scheduled to expire at the end of 2010 as a result of a "sunset" provision. The Pension Protection Act of 2006 repealed this sunset provision. Summarized below are the key provisions affected by this change.

3. Increases in the IRA contribution limits, including the ability to make "catch-up" contributions

EGTRRA increased the maximum annual dollar contribution limit for IRA contributions from $2,000 to $3,000 for 2002 through 2004 to $4,000 for 2005 through 2007 and to $5,000 for 2008. After 2008 the limit is adjusted annually for inflation in $500 increments. It has remained unadjusted at $5,000 for 2008 through 2012. It is $5,500 for 2013.

In addition, individuals who have attained age 50 may make additional "catch-up" IRA contributions. The maximum contribution limit (before application of the phaseout limits that apply to taxpayers with adjusted gross income above a specified amount) for an individual who has attained age 50 before the end of the taxable year is increased by $500 for 2002 through 2005 and $1,000 for 2006 and thereafter.

Both the increased annual contribution limits and the special catch-up contribution option were scheduled to expire at the end of 2010. The Pension Protection Act made both of these provisions permanent.

4. Increase in allowable contributions to a 403(b) plan

EGTRRA substantially increased the amount that could be contributed to an employee's 403(b) account. It amended the tax code to allow employees to contribute up to the lesser of (1) the limit on annual additions or (2) the limit on elective deferrals. The limit on annual additions is the lesser of 100 percent of includible compensation, or $40,000. The $40,000 amount is indexed for inflation and, in 2012, was $50,000. It is $51,000 for 2013.

The limit on elective deferrals specifies the maximum amount that an employee can contribute to his or her 403(b) account through salary reduction. EGTRRA increased this amount from $10,000 to $11,000 in 2002. In 2003 and thereafter the limit was increased in $1,000 annual increments until it reached $15,000 in 2006, with indexing in $500 increments thereafter. For 2012 this amount was $17,000. It is $17,500 for 2013.

These two limits allow employees to contribute far more to their 403(b) account than was possible prior to the enactment of

EGTRRA. They were scheduled to expire at the end of 2010 but were made permanent by the Pension Protection Act of 2006.

5. Catch-up contributions to 403(b) plan

EGTRRA substantially increased the limit on elective deferrals under a 403(b) annuity for individuals who have attained age 50 by the end of the year by allowing them to make additional, or catch-up, contributions to their account so long as no other elective deferrals may otherwise be made because of the application of any limitation of the tax code (e.g., the annual limit on elective deferrals) or of the plan itself. The additional amount of elective contributions that may be made by an eligible individual is the lesser of (1) the applicable dollar amount, or (2) the participant's compensation for the year reduced by any other elective deferrals of the participant for the year. EGTRRA defined the applicable dollar amount under a 403(b) annuity as $1,000 in 2002 and increased it by $1,000 each year until it reached $5,000 in 2006. It is adjusted for inflation in future years. (It increased to $5,500 for 2010 and remains at $5,500 through 2012.) Catch-up contributions are not subject to any other contribution limits and are not taken into account in applying other contribution limits. In addition, such contributions are not subject to applicable nondiscrimination rules. The generous catch-up contribution limits introduced by EGTRRA were to expire at the end of 2010. However, they were made permanent by the Pension Protection Act of 2006.

✿ **KEY POINT.** EGTRRA reduced the income tax rates for all taxpayers. These rate reductions, like EGTRRA's retirement provisions, were scheduled to expire after 2010 as a result of a sunset provision unless extended in whole or in part by Congress. The Pension Protection Act of 2006 did not make the income tax rate cuts permanent.

TAX INCREASE PREVENTION AND RECONCILIATION ACT OF 2005

Congress enacted the Tax Increase Prevention and Reconciliation Act (TIPRA) in 2005. The Act contains a number of provisions of interest to church leaders. For example, it extended the lower tax rates on capital gains and dividends that were scheduled to increase after 2008; prevented several tax provisions from expiring in the near future; and protected millions of Americans from being subject to the alternative minimum tax (AMT). The key provisions of the legislation are summarized below.

6. Reduced tax rates for capital gains

For taxable years beginning before 2009, the maximum rate of tax on the adjusted net capital gain of an individual was 15 percent. Any adjusted net capital gain which otherwise would be taxed at a 10 or 15 percent ordinary income rate was taxed at a 5 percent rate (zero for taxable years beginning after 2007). For taxable years beginning after 2008, the maximum rate of tax on the adjusted

INTRODUCTION

TABLE 1

INCOME TAX RATES FOR 2012
(Single Persons)

| TAXABLE INCOME | | | PLUS THIS | OF TAXABLE INCOME |
OVER	NOT OVER	PAY	PERCENT	OVER
$0	$8,700	$0.00	10%	$0
$8,700	$35,350	$870.00	15%	$8,700
$35,350	$85,650	$4,867.50	25%	$35,350
$85,650	$178,650	$17,422.50	28%	$85,650
$178,650	$388,350	$43,482.50	33%	$178,650
$388,350	No limit	$112,683.50	35%	$388,350

TABLE 2

INCOME TAX RATES FOR 2012
(Married Persons Filing Jointly)

| TAXABLE INCOME | | | PLUS THIS | OF TAXABLE INCOME |
OVER	NOT OVER	PAY	PERCENT	OVER
$0	$17,400	$0	10%	$0
$17,400	$70,700	$1,740	15%	$17,400
$70,700	$142,700	$9,735	25%	$70,700
$142,700	$217,450	$27,735	28%	$142,700
$217,450	$388,350	$48,665	33%	$217,450
$388,350	No limit	$105,062	35%	$388,350

TABLE 3

UNIFIED CREDIT EXEMPTION
Highest Estate and Gift Tax Rules

CALENDAR YEAR	ESTATE AND GENERATION-SKIPPING TRANSFER (GST) DEATHTIME TRANSFER TAX EXEMPTION	HIGHEST ESTATE AND GIFT TAX RATE
2002	$1 million	50%
2003	$1 million	49%
2004	$1.5 million	48%
2005	$1.5 million	47%
2006	$2 million	46%
2007	$2 million	45%
2008	$2 million	45%
2009	$3.5 million	45%
2010	Repeal of estate and GST	35% (gift tax only)
2011	$5 million	35%
2012	$5.12 million	35%

net capital gain of an individual was scheduled to increase to 20 percent. Any adjusted net capital gain which otherwise would be taxed at a 10 or 15 percent rate was to be taxed at a 10 percent rate. In addition, any gain from the sale or exchange of property held more than five years that would otherwise have been taxed at the 10 percent rate was to be taxed at an 8 percent rate.

Any gain from the sale or exchange of property held more than five years and the holding period for which began after 2000, that would otherwise have been taxed at a 20 percent rate, was to be taxed at an 18 percent rate.

The Tax Relief Act of 2010 extends the lower capital gains tax rates of 0 and 15 percent through 2012. The lower capital gains rates that apply to capital gains expire at the end of 2012 unless extended by Congress.

7. Reduced tax rates for dividends

Ordinary (taxable) dividends are the most common type of distribution from a corporation or a mutual fund. They are paid out of earnings and profits and are ordinary income to you. This means they are not capital gains. You can assume that any dividend you receive on common or preferred stock is an ordinary dividend unless the paying corporation or mutual fund tells you otherwise. Ordinary dividends will be shown in box 1a of the Form 1099-DIV you receive.

Qualified dividends are the ordinary dividends subject to the same 0 percent or 15 percent maximum tax rate that applies to net capital gain. They should be shown in box 1b of the Form 1099-DIV you receive. Qualified dividends are subject to the 15 percent rate if the regular tax rate that would apply is 25 percent or higher. If the regular tax rate that would apply is lower than 25 percent, qualified dividends are subject to the 0 percent rate.

To qualify for the 0 percent or 15 percent maximum rate, the dividends must have been paid by a U.S. corporation or a qualified foreign corporation, and you must have held the stock for more than 60 days during the 121-day period that begins 60 days before the ex-dividend date. The ex-dividend date is the first date following the declaration of a dividend on which the buyer of a stock is not entitled to receive the next dividend payment. When counting the number of days you held the stock, include the day you disposed of the stock, but not the day you acquired it.

The lower capital gains rates that apply to dividends expire at the end of 2012 unless extended by Congress.

MISCELLANEOUS CHANGES

8. Reduction in income tax rates
Income taxes are computed by applying the appropriate income tax rates to taxable income. The tax rates for 2012, for both single persons and married persons filing jointly, are summarized in Tables 1 and 2.

9. Phaseout and repeal of estate and generation-skipping transfer taxes
In 2001 Congress phased out the estate tax, which was fully repealed in 2010. Congress enacted the Tax Relief, Unemployment Insurance Reauthorization, and Job Creation Act in 2010 that revived the estate tax but established an exemption of $5 million per person and $10 million per couple and a top tax rate of 35 percent for two years, through 2012. The exemption amount is indexed beginning in 2012 and was $5,120,000 for that year. The current estate tax rate structure is summarized in Table 3.

✱ **New in 2013.** The federal gift tax applies to the transfer by gift of any property. The general rule is that any gift is a taxable gift. However, many exceptions to this rule exist, including gifts to charity, gifts to a spouse, and gifts that are not more than the annual exclusion for the calendar year. A separate annual exclusion applies to each person to whom a taxpayer makes a gift. For 2012 the annual exclusion was $13,000. The amount for 2013 is $14,000. This means taxpayers can give up to $13,000 to any number of people in 2013 and none of the gifts will be subject to the federal gift tax.

10. Backup withholding
If a self-employed worker performs services for your church (and earns at least $600 for the year) but fails to provide you with a Social Security number, the church is required by law to withhold a specified percentage of the compensation paid as "backup withholding." The backup withholding is reported to the IRS on Form 945. A self-employed person can avoid backup withholding by providing the church with a correct Social Security number. The church will need the correct number to complete the worker's Form 1099-MISC. Churches can be penalized if the Social Security number they report on a Form 1099-MISC is incorrect unless they have exercised due diligence. A church will be deemed to have exercised due diligence if it has self-employed persons provide their Social Security numbers on IRS Form W-9. It is a good idea for churches to present self-employed workers (e.g., guest speakers, contract laborers) with a Form W-9 and then to "backup withhold" unless the worker completes and returns the form.

The backup withholding rate (which is tied to the income tax rates) was 28 percent in 2012. It increases to 31 percent beginning in 2013 unless Congress acts to extend the lower income tax rates.

OTHER TAX LAW DEVELOPMENTS OF INTEREST TO MINISTERS AND LAY CHURCH EMPLOYEES

11. Housing allowances for clergy with two homes addressed by federal appeals court
In 2010 the United States Tax Court ruled that a minister could apply a housing allowance to expenses incurred in owning two homes. The court acknowledged that section 107 of the tax code, which contains the housing allowance exclusion, refers to a minister's "home" in the singular; but it concluded that this did not limit the application of a housing allowance to only one home.

In early 2012, a federal appeals court reversed the Tax Court's opinion and limited the application of a minister's housing allowance to expenses incurred in only one home (the principal residence).

The appeals court conceded that the tax code states that singular terms also include their plural forms, but it noted that this rule did not apply if "the context indicates otherwise." Therefore, the "singular includes the plural provision" should only apply if the context of the housing allowance reasonably supports such an application. The court concluded that it did not, for two reasons:

First, the word *home* is defined by the dictionary as "the house and grounds with their appurtenances habitually occupied by a family; one's principal place of residence; domicile." The court concluded that the word *home*, according to this definition, "has decidedly singular connotations."

Second, the court concluded that the history of the parsonage and housing allowance exclusions provided additional context for the term *home*. It noted that congressional committee reports describing the parsonage and housing allowance exclusions consistently use singular expressions ("a dwelling house," "a home," and "the home"), demonstrating that Congress intended for the parsonage and housing allowance exclusions to apply to only one home.

In further support for its conclusion, the court stressed that income exclusions should be "narrowly construed," therefore, "we do not believe that this court should construe any ambiguity in [the tax code] to favor a more expansive reading of the parsonage allowance income exclusion."

INTRODUCTION

Many ministers own two homes. In many cases, this is due to the fact that the minister has accepted a call in another community and purchases a home in that community but has not yet sold the prior home. In some cases, the minister has not moved but decides to purchase a new home in the same community and is in the process of selling the former home. The Tax Court's decision in the *Driscoll* case suggested that these ministers, at least in some cases, might be able to apply a housing allowance to the expenses of owning both homes. That option has been eliminated by the federal appeals court's recent ruling.

What is the impact of this ruling on ministers and churches? Consider two points:

First, ministers who relied on the *Driscoll* case by claiming housing allowance exclusions on their 2010 or 2011 tax returns based on expenses incurred in owning two homes should contact a tax professional to assist in preparing and submitting to the IRS an amended tax return (Form 1040X) for these years. The amended return should restate the nontaxable amount of the housing allowance to reflect housing expenses only on the pastor's principal residence.

Second, many churches have their pastors fill out a housing expense form each year that lists anticipated housing expenses for the following year. The church board uses this form to declare pastors' housing allowances. It would be prudent to amend this form to clarify that it should only list expenses incurred in owning a principal residence, and not a second home. *Driscoll v. Commissioner, 2012-1 U.S.T.C. ¶50,187 (11th Cir. 2012).*

12. Housing allowance challenged in federal court

The Freedom from Religion Foundation (FFRF) and several other plaintiffs filed a lawsuit in a federal district court in California challenging the constitutionality of the parsonage exclusion and housing allowance. The lawsuit alleged that the parsonage exclusion and housing allowance were available only to clergy and therefore amounted to an unconstitutional establishment of religion.

This legal challenge was dealt a fatal blow as a result of a recent United States Supreme Court case. The high court ruled (5-4) that a group of Arizona taxpayers lacked standing to challenge the constitutionality of a state law that gave tax credits for contributions to school tuition organizations (STOs) that provided scholarships to students attending private schools, including religious schools. It noted that the courts have consistently ruled that standing cannot be based on a plaintiff's status as a federal taxpayer because the "injury" is too remote or speculative.

The Court acknowledged a limited exception to taxpayer standing in cases challenging legislation on the basis of the First Amendment's nonestablishment of religion clause. Taxpayers have standing in such cases to challenge direct transfers of tax revenue to religious organizations, since "the taxpayer's allegation in such cases would be that his tax money is being extracted and spent in violation of specific constitutional protections against such abuses of legislative power." But the Court concluded that there is a difference between direct transfers of tax revenues to religious organizations, and credits and deductions, and it limited taxpayer standing to the former context.

This ruling left no doubt that the plaintiffs challenging the housing allowance lacked standing, since a tax exclusion rather than a direct transfer of tax revenue to religion was involved. As a result, the plaintiffs voluntarily dismissed their challenge on June 17, 2011.

But the Freedom from Religion Foundation revived its constitutional challenge to the housing allowance in a lawsuit filed in September 2011 in the federal district court for the western district of Wisconsin. FFRF has attempted to avoid the taxpayer standing issue in the Wisconsin litigation, making it more difficult to predict the outcome.

13. Revoking an exemption from Social Security

Will Congress give ministers another opportunity to revoke an exemption from Social Security? It does not seem likely, at least for now. No bills were introduced in Congress in 2012 that would have authorized ministers to revoke an exemption from Social Security.

14. Ministerial exception affirmed by Supreme Court

In a ringing endorsement of religious liberty, the United States Supreme Court unanimously affirmed the so-called "ministerial exception" barring civil court review of employment disputes between churches and ministers. The case involved a claim by a "called" teacher at a church-related school in Michigan that the school committed unlawful disability discrimination in terminating her employment. The Court's ruling has potential significance in two tax contexts.

Significance of being ordained, commissioned, or licensed. The Court noted that the plaintiff's status as a commissioned minister in the Lutheran church did not, by itself, "automatically ensure coverage" under the ministerial exception. But it concluded that "the fact that an employee has been ordained or commissioned as a minister is surely relevant, as is the fact that significant religious training and a recognized religious mission underlie the description of the employee's position."

While one's status as an ordained, commissioned, or licensed minister is not determinative or even essential, it is relevant in deciding if a person is a minister for purposes of the ministerial exception.

This aspect of the Court's opinion could serve as justification for liberalizing the current definition of *minister* in the context of federal tax law. Several provisions in the federal tax code apply to ministers, including, most notably, the housing allowance. The tax code and regulations refer to "ordained, commissioned, or licensed" ministers in describing persons who qualify as ministers for tax purposes. The

Tax Court amplified upon this definition in a 1989 ruling, *Knight v. Commissioner*, 92 T.C. 199 (1989). This definition has been endorsed by the IRS in its audit guidelines for ministers.

Under this test, the following five factors must be considered in deciding whether a person is a minister for federal tax reporting:

(1) Does the individual administer the sacraments?
(2) Does the individual conduct worship services?
(3) Does the individual perform services in the "control, conduct, or maintenance of a religious organization" under the authority of a church or religious denomination?
(4) Is the individual "ordained, commissioned, or licensed"?
(5) Is the individual considered to be a spiritual leader by his or her religious body?

Only the fourth factor is required in all cases (the individual must be ordained, commissioned, or licensed). The remaining four factors need not all be present for a person to be considered a minister for tax reporting.

By defining the term *minister* to apply only to "ordained, commissioned, or licensed ministers," the tax code, regulations, Tax Court, and IRS adopted a definition more restrictive than the analysis applied by the Supreme Court in the *Hosanna-Tabor* case, and this may serve as a basis for liberalizing the Tax Court definition to include persons who perform ministerial functions but who are not formally recognized as ordained, commissioned, or licensed ministers.

Time spent performing religious duties. Another important aspect of the Court's ruling in the *Hosanna-Tabor* case was its conclusion that a finding of ministerial status cannot be based solely on the amount of time a person spends on religious functions. In rejecting the appeals court's conclusion that the ministerial exception did not apply because of the limited time the teacher devoted to religious tasks, the Court observed: "The issue before us, however, is not one that can be resolved by a stopwatch. The amount of time an employee spends on particular activities is relevant in assessing that employee's status, but that factor cannot be considered in isolation, without regard to the nature of the religious functions performed."

The Court acknowledged that the teacher's religious duties "consumed only 45 minutes of each workday, and that the rest of her day was devoted to teaching secular subjects." However, the Court noted that it was unsure whether any church employees devoted all their time to religious tasks: "The heads of congregations themselves often have a mix of duties, including secular ones such as helping to manage the congregation's finances, supervising purely secular personnel, and overseeing the upkeep of facilities."

This aspect of the Court's rulings will be helpful in several contexts, including the following:

Ministerial status for tax purposes. The IRS and the Tax Court have, in some cases, contended that a person is not a minister for tax purposes because of the limited time the person devotes to religious functions. The Supreme Court concluded in the *Hosanna-Tabor* case that the plaintiff was a minister despite the fact that her religious duties occupied less than 45 minutes per day. The Court noted that ministerial status cannot be resolved by a stopwatch.

The Court also noted that many ministers devote less than all their time to religious tasks: "The heads of congregations themselves often have a mix of duties, including secular ones such as helping to manage the congregation's finances, supervising purely secular personnel, and overseeing the upkeep of facilities."

This will be a helpful precedent to persons whose ministerial status is challenged by the IRS on the basis of the limited time spent on religious duties.

Property tax exemption. Many churches own tracts of vacant land for recreation or future expansion. Are such properties exempt from taxation? Many courts have said no based on the requirement of many state property tax exemption laws that exempt property be used exclusively for exempt purposes. How can this requirement be satisfied when a tract of church-owned vacant land is used sporadically or not at all for religious purposes?

Some courts have taken the opposite view and have ruled that church-owned vacant land may be exempt from tax even though used infrequently for religious purposes. To illustrate, the Kentucky Supreme Court ruled that a 10-acre tract of largely vacant property that a church had acquired for future expansion was exempt from property taxation due to its occasional use for church purposes. *Freeman v. St. Andrew Orthodox Church, Inc.*, 294 S.W.3d 425 (Ky. 2009). The tax assessor determined that the property was subject to taxation based on its infrequent use for religious purposes. In rejecting the assessor's denial of exemption, the court made the following significant comment:

> We recognize that churches are unique. For the most part, they are never "occupied" in the conventional sense. A vast majority of properties owned by institutions of religion such as churches, mosques, tabernacles, temples, and the like, are used for places of worship at specified times and may remain vacant for substantial periods during the week. We further recognize that adjacent facilities, such as activity buildings, gymnasiums, even shelters, may be owned by religious institutions, but perhaps utilized irregularly on an as needed basis. School buildings owned by religious institutions may, in fact, sit idle for a great deal of time. This would not preclude these buildings from being occupied. . . . It is precisely for these reasons that we find that the trial court's findings were supported substantially by the evidence in this case as to the property not being rented out as residences.

This case is significant because of the court's recognition that many buildings owned by religious, educational, and charitable institutions are vacant for significant periods of time but are nevertheless entitled to exemption because of their occasional exempt use. A university classroom building comes to mind. Such buildings are often vacant for several months during the year. The same is true for many churches, whose property is used for religious purposes for no more than a few hours each week. In many states, the exemption of church property from taxation is limited to property that is "used exclusively for religious worship." Yet the exempt status of churches that conduct a single, one-hour worship service weekly has never been questioned on the ground of infrequent use.

This conclusion is reinforced by the Supreme Court's ruling in the *Hosanna-Tabor* case because of the Court's conclusion that the plaintiff was a minister despite the fact that her religious duties "consumed only 45 minutes of each workday, and that the rest of her day was devoted to teaching secular subjects." The Court noted that "the heads of congregations themselves often have a mix of duties, including secular ones such as helping to manage the congregation's finances, supervising purely secular personnel, and overseeing the upkeep of facilities." This language will be helpful to churches in demonstrating that church-owned vacant land is exempt from taxation despite infrequent use. *Hosanna-Tabor Evangelical Lutheran Church and School v. E.E.O.C., 132 S.Ct. 694 (2012).*

15. Pastor responsible for all payroll taxes an employing church fails to withhold or pay to the government

A federal district court in North Carolina ruled that a pastor was responsible for 100 percent of payroll taxes that her employing church failed to withhold or pay over to the government. The pastor filed for bankruptcy protection from her creditors. The IRS filed a claim for $88,000 with the bankruptcy court based on its assertion that the pastor was liable for $88,000 in unpaid payroll tax obligations of her church since she was a "responsible person" liable for unpaid payroll tax obligations. The pastor asked the court to reject the IRS claim on the grounds that she was not a "responsible person" and that any recognition of the IRS claim was barred by the First Amendment's guaranty of religious freedom. The bankruptcy court rejected the pastor's defenses, and the case was appealed to a federal district court.

The court began its opinion by noting that "federal law requires employers to withhold federal income taxes and Social Security taxes from employee wages and remit those taxes to the United States. The employer holds these taxes in trust for the United States." And, although the employer "remains liable for the unpaid payroll taxes, its officers and agents may incur personal liability for the unpaid payroll taxes." Section 6672 of the tax code states: "Any person required to collect, truthfully account for, and pay over any tax imposed by this title who willfully fails to collect such tax, or truthfully account for and pay over such tax, or willfully attempts in any manner to evade or defeat any such tax or the payment thereof, shall . . .

be liable to a penalty equal to the total amount of tax evaded, or not collected, or not accounted for and paid over."

In order for an individual to be held personally liable under this section, "(1) the party assessed must be a person required to collect, truthfully account for, and pay over the tax, referred to as a 'responsible person'; and (2) the responsible person must have willfully failed to insure that the withholding taxes were paid."

Responsible person. The court noted that the question of who within an organization is a "responsible person" required to collect and pay the payroll taxes to the United States is a "pragmatic, substance-over form inquiry into whether an officer or employee so participated in decisions concerning payment of creditors and disbursement of funds that he effectively had the authority—and hence a duty—to ensure payment of the corporation's payroll taxes." In other words, the "crucial inquiry is whether the person had the effective power to pay the taxes—that is, whether he had the actual authority or ability, in view of his status within the corporation, to pay the taxes owed."

When making the determination of who is a "responsible person," courts have considered several factors that are indicative of this authority, including whether the employee "(1) served as an officer of the company or as a member of its board of directors; (2) controlled the company's payroll; (3) determined which creditors to pay and when to pay them; (4) participated in the day-to-day management of the corporation; (5) possessed the power to write checks; and (6) had the ability to hire and fire employees. No single factor is controlling or dispositive in the responsible person inquiry."

The bankruptcy court concluded, and the district court agreed, that the pastor was a responsible person. In support of this conclusion, both courts referenced the bylaws of the pastor's church, which specify that the pastor shall act "as CEO over all spiritual and business matters." Additionally, the bylaws provide that the pastor shall be the "Chief Executive Officer of the said organization and shall be a continuing member of all boards and committees." The pastor "shall be an ex-officio member of all standing committees, and shall have the general powers and duties of supervision and management usually vested in the office of president of a corporation."

Freedom of religion. The pastor argued that the courts were barred by the First Amendment guaranty of religious freedom from making a determination regarding "responsible person" status on the basis of a church's bylaws. The court acknowledged that "the civil courts are obliged to play a limited role at times in resolving church disputes, the limited role being premised on First Amendment principles that preclude a court from deciding issues of religious doctrine and practice, or from interfering with internal church government. First Amendment values are jeopardized when church litigation turns on the resolution by civil courts of controversies over religious doctrine and practice." However, the court concluded that the pastor "has not shown how mere citation of the bylaws in the bankruptcy court's order is a challenge to the ecclesiastical decisions or religious customs of the church in violation of the [First Amendment]. In its most favorable light, the pastor asks the court to make the logical leap to hold that the mere citation of the church bylaws as part of the responsible person analysis under section 6672 is prohibited by the First Amendment. The case law, while limited in this specific context, does not appear to support this argument."

The court also stressed that the bankruptcy court's analysis of the church bylaws

> was limited to a few paragraphs. . . . The bankruptcy court noted that the bylaws provide that the pastor shall be the CEO and a member of all boards and committees and . . . shall execute in the name of the church all deeds, bonds, mortgages, contracts and other documents, and have the powers and duties of supervision and management usually vested in the office of president of a corporation. . . .

> The bankruptcy court interpreted the bylaws as authorizing the pastor to have decision making authority and supervision over business matters. The pastor argues that this interpretation now forces her to concern herself with secular affairs. Putting aside the fact that the plain language of the bylaws suggests that the pastor does concern herself with such affairs, the bankruptcy court did not base its decision on the bylaws alone. Contrarily, close examination of the bankruptcy court's order reveals that it placed great emphasis on what the pastor actually did as the church's pastor, including co-signing a $178,000.00 construction loan, disbursing and withholding payments to vendors and staff, signing a corporate resolution authorizing a bank account which authorized her to sign checks on behalf of the church, and hiring and firing employees.

> While the pastor argues that the bankruptcy court impermissibly interpreted the bylaws in such a way as to infringe upon her First Amendment rights, the court finds no support in the case law that the bankruptcy court's findings or analysis did anything of the kind.

Section 6672 contains no exemption for church officers or employees. As a result, any church officer or employee having the authority to pay withheld taxes to the government is potentially liable for 100 percent of the taxes owed if the church for any reason fails to withhold or pay them. The court enumerated several functions of the pastor that made her a "responsible person" liable for the unpaid payroll taxes. In addition, the court ruled that the First Amendment guaranty of religious freedom is not violated if a court examines a church's bylaws to determine if a pastor, or other church employee, is a "responsible person." *Vaughn v. Internal Revenue Service, 2012-2 U.S.T.C. ¶50,487, (E.D.N.C. 2012).*

16. Conviction of priest for embezzlement of church funds affirmed by appeals court

A Florida appeals court affirmed the conviction of a parish priest for embezzlement of church funds. The Catholic priest was charged with grand theft of funds from his church based on his use of church funds for his personal benefit rather than for the benefit of the church. The evidence at trial included the following:

- Testimony of the church bookkeeper, who stated that the priest asked to see the cash collected in the offerings and would keep some cash and return a reduced sum to the bookkeeper to be deposited into the church's operating accounts.
- Testimony of another church employee that the priest would keep cash from the weekly offering and would instruct her to deposit only a part of the weekly offering. She testified that the priest retained $4,600 in cash from just one week's offerings.
- Testimony that to avoid detection, the priest instructed the bookkeeper to create fake deposit slips to send to the diocese to hide the fact that cash was given directly to him. The priest was present when the cash from the offerings was counted.
- Testimony of a church employee that she gave the priest a shoebox with about $11,000 in cash, and the priest returned the box with only $2,000 in cash remaining. After this employee attended a bookkeepers' training class sponsored by the diocese, she informed the priest that she could no longer participate in counting the offertory. When the priest cursed at her, she resigned the same day.
- The church paid the priest's travel expenses for frequent trips out of state to places such as Las Vegas, Ireland, and the Bahamas.
- An internal audit by an outside auditor revealing that expenses listed as reimbursements for credit card payments were, by and large, "not church-related expenses." The auditor found checks written directly to the priest for $30,640 without any accompanying receipts or documentation to justify payment to the priest. The priest also wrote checks to the bookkeeper from his previous parish. A diocesan official questioned the priest about these payments and told him that the former secretary was not entitled to payments from the church's accounts. Despite this admonition, the priest wrote checks totaling $43,000 to his former secretary. The priest also wrote checks to a Catholic high school to cover the tuition expenses for his former secretary's son.

A diocesan official testified that priests draw both a salary and a car allowance. The funds to pay salaries and automobile allowances are derived from the general fund raised at each church. Although the diocese has no particular control over church accounts, the official stated that a priest's personal expenses would not be paid out of the parish's operating account, since the priest receives a salary package.

The diocesan official also testified that the priest is allowed to make distributions from parish accounts without permission of the bishop as long as the distribution does not exceed $50,000 and the distribution is "for the good of the parish." However, priests were instructed to keep records of distributions, and these accounts devoted to charitable works were required to be reported to the diocese quarterly.

The chief financial officer for the diocese testified that the diocese promulgated explicit written procedures regarding how offerings were to be counted and deposited. The diocese, according to the CFO, monitored the finances of each parish to ensure that each priest was properly administering his duties. However, he conceded that some parishes would hold funds in unreported accounts to keep reported account balances low to avoid incurring larger fund-raising goals during the diocese's annual fund-raising appeal.

A forensic examiner testified for the prosecution that during the priest's tenure as pastor, there was a cash shortfall of roughly $372,343, and almost $487,000 in parish funds were misappropriated by the priest.

The defense presented the following exculpatory evidence:

- A forensic examiner employed by the defense testified that the priest deposited $134,000 in cash in other church accounts.
- Another priest testified that parishes keep "slush funds" in separate accounts either to help needy parishioners or to reduce the amount of money they would be expected to remit to the diocese as part of the annual fund-raising appeal.
- Other witnesses stated that parish priests have substantial discretion in spending church funds. A former diocesan official testified that a parish priest would have the discretion to pay for a past employee's child to attend a Catholic high school and to pay for vacations out of the parish's operating account.
- The defense also presented the testimony of a former parishioner who decided to make a $100,000 gift to the priest out of appreciation for the priest's past services. The parishioner wrote checks to both the priest and the parish to avoid the priest's liability for federal gift taxes, but the parishioner intended that the checks written to the parish were for the priest's use "as he so chose."
- The priest offered justifications for the expenditures. For example, he testified that he paid his former secretary out of church funds in order to prevent her from suing the diocese. He also testified that he paid many church employees in cash and that he believed he had unfettered discretion to spend parish funds.

A jury convicted the priest of the lesser offense of grand theft of property valued between $20,000 and $100,000. The priest appealed, claiming that the state's evidence was insufficient for a conviction. He insisted that the discretion accorded to priests foreclosed any inference that he took the property of another. The appeals court rejected the priest's arguments and affirmed his conviction. It observed:

In this case, the state presented evidence from officials of the diocese that a parish priest is supposed to use parish money

only for parish purposes. [Diocesan officials] testified that the priest's expenditures for [his former secretary and her son] and for vacations would not be valid parish purposes. Further, the forensic examiner testified that thousands of dollars in cash from the offertory were unaccounted for and that a significant amount of parish money was spent on items that [diocesan officials] testified were not parish related. Significantly, [these officials] testified that money collected from the offertory is collected from the parish members for parish purposes. There was also testimony from staff at the parish that fake deposit slips were used to cover up the fact that cash was taken from the offertory.

The state has introduced evidence inconsistent with the priest's claim of innocence. The case rises and falls on the intent of the priest when he used parish money and removed cash from the weekly offertory and whether it was for his personal benefit, not related to parish purposes. Ultimately, intent is a question of fact to be decided by the jury. We find that there was sufficient competent evidence of grand theft for the jury to find the priest guilty.

The court also rejected the priest's contention that the prosecution of this case led to an "excessive entanglement with religion" in violation of the First Amendment. It observed: "Purely secular disputes involving religious institutions and third parties do not create excessive entanglement of church and state when they involve neutral principles of law."

Many churches have established discretionary funds that their pastor can use at his or her discretion, often with little if any oversight or accountability. This case illustrates that such arrangements can lead to the expenditure of church funds for personal purposes having little, if anything, to do with the furtherance of church purposes, and this in turn may lead to criminal liability. *Guinan v. State, 65 So.3d 589 (Fla. App. 2011).*

17. Conviction upheld for pastor and spouse guilty of tax crimes for failure to disclose church compensation

A federal appeals court affirmed the conviction of a pastor and his wife on several tax crimes based on various forms of church compensation they failed to disclose on their tax returns. The pastor ("defendant") had served as senior pastor of a church since 1981. His wife played an active role in church life during her husband's ministry and began to draw a salary from the church as a copastor in about 2000. Over the course of their time with the church, the couple were cochairs of the church's board of directors and served on a number of committees within the church, including those responsible for financial decisions. The pastor had final authority over employee salaries and church finances.

When the defendant first became pastor at the church, his salary was about $10,000. By 2001 his salary had increased to $148,000. It reached $300,000 by 2007. Between 2001 and 2007, the church provided him with substantial benefits, in addition to his salary, that he underreported on his tax returns. He received housing allowances of between $130,000 and $160,000 per year, travel allowances of $19,000 to $48,000 per year, payments for his children's tuition and his federal income tax liability, and unlimited use of a luxury car leased by the church in addition to an annual vehicle allowance. He also received annual bonuses of $35,000 to $50,000 as well as separate Christmas bonuses. He had use of a church credit card and received reimbursements for purported business-related expenses that remained unsubstantiated. Taken together, his total church compensation between 2001 and 2007 totaled nearly $3.9 million. During that time, his wife received compensation from the church in the form of salary, bonuses, allowances, and reimbursements totaling nearly $1 million. The defendant and his wife earned additional income from speaking at other churches.

The IRS reconstructed the couple's income for the years 2002–2007 and determined that they had understated their taxable income by $2,486,771 between 2002 and 2007, resulting in a tax deficiency of $664,352 for those years. The federal government eventually obtained a 19-count indictment against the couple. Their trial resulted in conviction on charges of conspiracy to defraud the United States, tax evasion and aiding and abetting the same, and for the defendant, filing false tax returns. Following a four-week trial that involved the admission of over 90,000 pages of documentary evidence and the testimony of more than 70 witnesses, the defendants were both convicted on several counts. The defendant was sentenced to 105 months' imprisonment and restitution in the amount of $1.3 million, and his wife to 80 months' imprisonment and restitution in the amount of $1.2 million. The couple appealed their convictions and sentences.

Willfulness. The couple argued that their crimes required willfulness, which the government failed to prove. The court disagreed:

> Willfulness with respect to tax crimes has been defined in essence as a knowledge requirement, or the "intentional violation of a known legal duty." When applied, the doctrine of willful blindness permits the government to prove knowledge by establishing that the defendant "deliberately shielded himself from clear evidence of critical facts that are strongly suggested by the circumstances." Willful blindness may satisfy knowledge in a criminal tax prosecution, where "the evidence supports an inference that a defendant was subjectively aware of a high probability of the existence of a tax liability, and purposefully avoided learning the facts pointing to such liability." United States v. Poole, 640 F.3d 114, 122 (4th Cir. 2011).

> These conditions were satisfied here. The defendant denied knowledge of his legal obligations and testified that he and his wife did not know that their tax returns contained a deficiency. But the government presented evidence to suggest that defendants were aware of a "high probability" that they were understating their income to the IRS. For example, defendants'

tax returns for 2001 to 2007 claimed personal deductions of nearly $1.6 million despite reporting about $1.8 million of taxable income. During those years, defendants deposited into their bank accounts and spent over $3 million more than they reported as income on their tax returns.

> In addition, the government introduced evidence indicating that the defendants purposely avoided learning the fact of their liability. Between 2002 and 2007, several auditors and church administrators advised them that they were underreporting their income, but defendants never raised these concerns with their personal CPA, who could easily have explained the law. They also failed to clarify their alleged confusion regarding the tax treatment of honoraria and "love offerings," instead simply excluding these payments from income. Their CPA testified that they never informed him of the substantial compensation from the church that they specifically structured so as not to appear on their W-2s. . . . In light of the defendants' denial of knowledge and the evidence supporting an inference of deliberate ignorance on the part of defendants, the court's provision of a willful blindness instruction was not an abuse of discretion.

"Love gifts" and reimbursements. The trial court instructed the jury that

> any amount transferred by or for an employer to or for the benefit of an employee is income. Such payments are not gifts under the Internal Revenue Code and may not be excluded from gross income regardless of how the payments by the employer to the employee are characterized.

> Additionally, payments by an employer to an employee, or on the employee's behalf as reimbursements for business-related expenditures, must be included in the gross income of the employee unless the expenses are ordinary and necessary business expenses, the business nature of the expenses has been substantiated, and any unsubstantiated payments have been returned to the employer.

The court rejected the defendant's claim that this jury instruction unfairly shifted the burden of proof to themselves. It observed:

> It is apparent that the relationship between an employer and employee is one that is commonly established for some kind of mutual benefit, a dynamic that is altogether different from the "detached and disinterested generosity" that normally prompts the tender of a gift. Commissioner v. Duberstein, 363 U.S. 278, 285 (1960). The instruction at issue correctly explained the relevant tax law, which is clear that payments from an employer to an employee are not gifts, but are presumed to be included in gross income. A taxpayer must report as gross income "all income from whatever source derived" unless "excluded by law." To be sure, section 102(a) of the Code excludes from gross income "the value

of property acquired by gift." But the Code is explicit that payments from an employer to an employee do not constitute gifts under §102(a), which "shall not exclude from gross income any amount transferred by or for an employer to, or for the benefit of, an employee." I.R.C. section 102(c).

Absent a clarifying instruction, the jury may have mistaken the testimony from several witnesses that the church's payments to the couple were "gifts" as a legal conclusion that these payments were nontaxable. To prevent juror confusion, the district court alerted the jury that as a matter of law, payments from an employer to an employee do not qualify as nontaxable gifts, irrespective of the employer's intent. But the jury was left to determine that the defendants did in fact receive payments from their employer—an uncontroversial point which the defendants essentially conceded.

With regard to employer reimbursements, the court noted that

the government retained its burden of proof on every element of the charges, including the burden to establish that the defendants failed to report income to the IRS. Before the burden shifted to the defendants to demonstrate the deductibility of unreported income, the government established that the defendants received several millions of dollars from their employer that they omitted from gross income. This offer of proof created a presumption that the income was taxable as a matter of law. In turn, the defendants failed to establish that these payments satisfied the reimbursement criteria [for an accountable arrangement] pursuant to section 72 of the tax code.

Limiting testimony. The trial court limited the defendants' ability to elicit testimony from additional witnesses about their belief that payments from the church to the defendants constituted gifts. These witnesses would have testified concerning the belief within the church community that many of the church's payments to the defendants were nontaxable gifts. This evidence, even if mistaken on the law, was relevant to show the defendants' own ignorance of their legal duties, thereby refuting the essential element of willfulness.

The appeals court concluded that it was well within the trial court's discretion to limit testimony in order to prevent juror confusion regarding the taxability of income from the church.

Sentence enhancement based on use of "sophisticated means." The trial court "enhanced" the defendants' prison sentences, pursuant to the federal sentencing guidelines, for their use of "sophisticated means." The appeals court rejected the defendants' claim that this enhancement was improper:

The enhancement applies to "especially complex or especially intricate offense conduct pertaining to the execution or concealment of an offense." . . . So it was here. The defendants' scheme

spanned many years and involved multiple organizations. . . . The court adopted the presentence report, which identified a variety of sophisticated techniques used by defendants to conceal their tax evasion. They structured their compensation so as to prevent the inclusion of income on their W-2 forms, drawing payments from the church operating account, rather than the payroll account. They disguised wages as allowances and reimbursements for which they instructed church employees not to issue 1099 forms to disclose additional income to the IRS. They directed church employees to manipulate church financial records to conceal their income and misrepresented their financial situation to the IRS in the church's application for section 501(c)(3) tax-exempt status. . . . Taken together, the assorted methods of executing the offense involved especially intricate offense conduct that rose to the level of sophisticated means.

Sentence enhancement based on abuse of a position of trust. The defendants' sentences also were enhanced, pursuant to the federal sentencing guidelines, for abusing a position of trust. The appeals court agreed with this enhancement:

The abuse of trust enhancement enables the sentencing court to punish those who wield their power to criminally take advantage of those who depend upon them most. As leaders of the church, the defendants were entrusted with the spiritual wellbeing and financial stewardship of their religious community. They exploited the trust of their unsuspecting congregation to conceal criminal acts from the government, as well as the church, and to maintain an extravagant lifestyle lived at the church's expense. We thus affirm the district court's application of the abuse of trust enhancement. United States v. Jinwright, 2012-2 U.S.T.C. ¶50,417 (4th Cir. 2012).

18. Inflation adjustments for 2012

Some tax benefits were adjusted for inflation for 2012. But many remained unchanged due to the low rate of inflation. Key changes affecting 2012 returns include the following:

- The value of each personal and dependency exemption, available to most taxpayers, is $3,800.
- The standard deduction for 2012 is $11,900 for married couples filing a joint return and $5,950 for singles and married individuals filing separately. Nearly two out of three taxpayers take the standard deduction rather than itemizing deductions such as mortgage interest, charitable contributions, and state and local taxes.
- Tax-bracket thresholds increase for each filing status. For a married couple filing a joint return, for example, the taxable-income threshold separating the 15 percent bracket from the 25 percent bracket is $70,700 (up from $69,000 for 2011).
- You may be able to claim the earned income credit for 2012 if (1) you do not have a qualifying child and you earned less than $13,980 ($19,190 if married); (2) a qualifying child lived with you and you earned less than $36,920 ($42,130 if

married filing jointly); (3) two qualifying children lived with you and you earned less than $41,952 ($47,162 if married filing jointly); or (4) three or more qualifying children lived with you and you earned less than $45,060 ($50,270 if married filing jointly). The maximum earned income credit for 2012 is (1) $475 with no qualifying child; (2) $3,169 with one qualifying child; (3) $5,236 with two qualifying children; and (4) $5,891 with three or more qualifying children.

- For contributions to a traditional IRA, the deduction phaseout range for an individual covered by a retirement plan at work begins at income of $92,000 for joint filers and $58,000 for a single person or head of household.

- Participants in most employer-sponsored 403(b) plans could contribute up to $17,000 in 2012. Individuals age 50 or over could make an additional, catch-up contribution of up to $5,500. The annual contribution limit increases to $17,500 for 2013, but the catch-up limit remains unchanged at $5,500.

19. Working after retirement

Many churches employ retired persons who are receiving Social Security benefits. Persons younger than full retirement age may have their Social Security retirement benefits cut if they earn more than a specified amount. Full retirement age (the age at which you are entitled to full retirement benefits) for persons born in 1943–1954 is 66 years. In the year you reach full retirement age, your monthly Social Security retirement benefits are reduced by $1 for every $3 you earn above a specified amount ($3,340 per month for 2013). No reduction in Social Security benefits occurs for income earned in the month full retirement age is attained (and all future months). Persons who begin receiving Social Security retirement benefits prior to the year in which they reach full retirement age will have their benefits reduced by $1 for every $2 of earned income in excess of a specified amount. For 2013 this annual amount is $15,120.

20. Housing allowances and the earned income credit

An unanswered question is whether a housing allowance (or annual rental value of a parsonage) should be treated as earned income when computing the earned income credit. If so, then earned income will be higher, making it more likely that a minister will not qualify for the earned income credit. In the 2001 tax law (EGTRRA), Congress clarified that the term "earned income" includes only "amounts includible in gross income for the taxable year." However, Congress added that earned income also includes "net earnings from self-employment." The problem is that ministers are always considered self-employed for purposes of Social Security with respect to their ministerial services, and so their entire church compensation constitutes "net earnings from self-employment" unless they filed a timely exemption application (Form 4361) that was approved by the IRS. Logically, then, housing allowances should be treated as earned income for those ministers who have not exempted themselves from self-employment taxes by filing Form 4361. On the other hand, ministers who have exempted themselves from self-employment taxes should not treat their housing allowance as earned income in computing the earned income credit.

As illogical as this result may seem, it is exactly what the IRS instructions to Form 1040 require, and for now the IRS national office is taking the position that there is nothing it can do to change the law as enacted by Congress. So for now, whether a minister's housing allowance (or annual rental value of a parsonage) is included within the definition of earned income for purposes of the earned income credit depends on whether the minister is exempt or not exempt from paying self-employment taxes. This issue is discussed fully in Chapter 7.

21. Standard mileage rates for 2012

The standard business mileage rate was 55.5 cents per mile for business miles driven during 2012. The standard mileage rates were 23 cents per mile driven for medical or moving expenses and 14 cents per mile driven in the service of charitable organizations.

* **New in 2013.** For 2013 the mileage rates are 56.5 cents (business), 24 cents (medical and moving), and 14 cents (charitable).

22. Earnings subject to the self-employment tax

The self-employment tax rate (15.3 percent) does not change in 2012. The 15.3 percent tax rate consists of two components: (1) a Medicare hospital insurance tax of 2.9 percent and (2) an old-age, survivor, and disability (Social Security) tax of 12.4 percent. There is no maximum amount of self-employment earnings subject to the Medicare tax. The tax is imposed on all net earnings, regardless of amount.

For 2012 the maximum earnings subject to the Social Security portion of self-employment taxes (the 12.4 percent amount) is $113,700. Stated differently, persons who receive compensation in excess of $113,700 in 2013 pay the combined 15.3 percent tax rate for net self-employment earnings up to $113,700 and only the Medicare tax rate of 2.9 percent on earnings above $113,700. These rules directly impact ministers, who are considered self-employed for Social Security purposes with respect to their ministerial services. Ministers should take these rules into account in computing their quarterly estimated tax payments.

Congress enacted legislation reducing the Social Security portion of FICA and self-employment taxes by two percentage points in 2011 and 2012. This meant that a minister's share of the Social Security component of self-employment taxes decreased from 12.4 to 10.4 percent of self-employment earnings. It is unlikely that Congress will extend the lower rates for 2013 or future years. Check the Social Security Administration website for current information.

23. Simplified definition of "highly compensated employee"

A number of tax-favored rules do not apply if there is discrimination in favor of highly compensated employees. These include (1) simplified employee pensions (SEPs); (2) 403(b) tax-sheltered annuities (churches and qualified church-controlled organizations are exempt from this nondiscrimination rule); (3) qualified employee discounts; (4) cafeteria plans; (5) flexible spending arrangements; (6) qualified tuition reductions; (7) employer-provided educational assistance; and (8) dependent care assistance.

For 2012 a highly compensated employee was one who (1) was a 5 percent owner of the employer at any time during the current or prior year (this definition will not apply to churches) or (2) had compensation for the previous year in excess of $115,000 and, if an employer elects, was in the top 20 percent of employees by compensation. The $115,000 amount is adjusted for inflation. It remains at $115,000 for 2013.

24. Luxury car limit adjustments for inflation

Ministers and lay church employees who use the actual-expense method of computing their car expenses can claim a deduction for depreciation. The amount of depreciation you can claim in any given year is limited. These limits are known as the luxury car limits. The 2012 limits are summarized in Table 4. The 2013 limits were not available at the time of publication of this guide.

25. Phaseout of personal exemption for high-income taxpayers

Personal exemptions allow a certain amount per person to be exempt from tax ($3,800 for 2012). Due to the Personal Exemption Phaseout (PEP), the exemptions are phased out for taxpayers with income above a certain level. The PEP was repealed in 2010. This repeal was extended by the Tax Relief and Jobs Creation Act through 2012.

26. New per diem rates for substantiating the amount of travel expenses incurred in 2012 and 2013

The IRS allows taxpayers to substantiate the *amount* of their business expenses by using per diem (daily) rates. Taxpayers still must

---

TABLE 4

LUXURY CAR DEPRECIATION LIMITS

TAX YEAR	MAXIMUM DEPRECIATION DEDUCTION FOR CARS FIRST PLACED IN SERVICE IN 2012
First	$3,160*
Second	$5,100
Third	$3,050
Each succeeding year	$1,875

* This amount is increased by $8,000 to $11,160 if bonus depreciation is claimed. Several conditions must be met to qualify for bonus depreciation, including the fact that the car must have been purchased and first used for business purposes in the year of acquisition.

---

have records substantiating the date, place, and business purpose of each expense. Separate rates are set for meals and lodging, and separate rates for high-cost localities and all other communities. See the most recent edition of IRS Publication 1542 for applicable rates.

In some cases, using the per diem rates will simplify the substantiation of meals and lodging expenses incurred while engaged in business travel. However, a number of restrictions apply, and these are explained in Chapter 7 of this tax guide.

27. IRS not addressing ministerial status in letter rulings

The IRS announced in January that it will no longer issue private letter rulings addressing the question of "whether an individual is a minister of the gospel for federal tax purposes." This means taxpayers will not be able to obtain clarification from the IRS in a letter ruling on their status as a minister for any one or more of the following matters: (1) eligibility for a parsonage exclusion or housing allowance; (2) eligibility for exemption from self-employment taxes; (3) self-employed status for Social Security; or (4) exemption of wages from income tax withholding. *Revenue Procedure 2012-3.*

28. IRS not addressing housing allowances for retired ministers

The IRS has announced that it will no longer issue private letter rulings addressing the question of "whether amounts distributed to a retired minister from a pension or annuity plan should be excludible from the minister's gross income as a parsonage allowance." *Revenue Procedure 2012-3.*

29. IRS not addressing treating forgiveness of debt as a charitable contribution

The IRS has announced that it will no longer issue private letter rulings addressing the question of "whether a taxpayer who advances funds to a charitable organization and receives therefore a promissory note may deduct as contributions, in one taxable year or in each of several years, amounts forgiven by the taxpayer in each of several years by endorsement on the note." To illustrate, a church member transfers $5,000 to her church and receives in return a promissory note from the church promising to pay back the note in annual installments over the next five years. Each year, on the due date of the annual installment, the note holder "forgives" the payment. Can the note holder treat the forgiven installment as a charitable contribution deduction? This is the question the IRS no longer will address in private letter rulings. *Revenue Procedure 2012-3.*

30. IRS declining to address gifts in letter rulings

The IRS has announced that it will no longer issue private letter rulings addressing the question of "whether a transfer is a gift within the meaning of section 102" of the tax code. To illustrate, a pastor retires after many years of service to the same church. The church presents him with a check in the amount of $10,000. Is this check taxable compensation or a tax-free gift? This is a question the IRS no longer will address in private letter rulings. *Revenue Procedure 2012-3.*

31. Identity theft addressed by IRS

The IRS and the Justice Department have announced the results of a massive national sweep cracking down on suspected identity theft perpetrators as part of a stepped-up effort against refund fraud and identity theft.

Working with the Justice Department's Tax Division and local U.S. Attorneys' offices, the nationwide effort targeted 105 people in 23 states. The coast-to-coast effort included indictments, arrests and the execution of search warrants involving the potential theft of thousands of identities and taxpayer refunds.

"This unprecedented effort against identity theft sends a strong, unmistakable message to anyone considering participating in a refund fraud scheme this tax season," said IRS Commissioner Doug Shulman. "We are aggressively pursuing cases across the nation with the Justice Department, and people will be going to jail. This is part of a much wider effort underway at the IRS to help protect taxpayers."

The national effort is part of a comprehensive identity theft strategy the IRS has embarked on that is focused on preventing, detecting, and resolving identity theft cases as soon as possible. In addition to the law-enforcement crackdown, the IRS has stepped up its internal reviews to spot false tax returns before tax refunds are issued and is working to help victims of the identity theft refund schemes.

➡ **TIP.** To help taxpayers, the IRS created a new, special section at irs.gov dedicated to identity theft matters. It features YouTube videos, tips for taxpayers, and a special guide to assistance. The information includes how to contact the IRS Identity Protection Specialized Unit and tips to protect against phishing schemes that can lead to identity theft.

Identity theft occurs when someone uses another's personal information without his or her permission to commit fraud or other crimes using the victim's name, Social Security number, or other identifying information. When it comes to federal taxes, taxpayers may not be aware they have become victims of identity theft until they receive a letter from the IRS stating that more than one tax return was filed with their information or that IRS records show wages from an employer the taxpayer has not worked for in the past.

The IRS urges taxpayers who believe they are at risk of identity theft due to lost or stolen personal information to contact the IRS immediately so the agency can take action to secure their tax account. The taxpayer should contact the IRS Identity Protection Specialized Unit at 1-800-908-4490. The taxpayer will be asked to complete the IRS Identity Theft Affidavit, Form 14039, and follow the instructions on the back of the form based on his or her situation.

32. Millions of tax returns flagged for suspected identity theft

IRS deputy commissioner Steven Miller disclosed at a recent conference that the IRS has flagged 2.6 million tax returns for possible identity theft. According to Miller, the IRS has seen a significant increase in refund fraud schemes, many of which target church members with bogus claims of free money. A common scam promises refunds to people who have little or no income and normally don't have a tax filing requirement. Under the scheme, promoters claim they can obtain for their victims a college education tax credit or nonexistent stimulus payment even if the victim was not enrolled in or paying for college.

The IRS has already detected and stopped thousands of these fraudulent claims. Nevertheless, the scheme can still be quite costly for victims. Promoters may charge exorbitant up-front fees to file these claims and are often long gone when victims discover they've been scammed.

The IRS is reminding people to be careful because all taxpayers, including those who use paid tax preparers, are legally responsible for the accuracy of their returns and must repay any refunds received in error.

To avoid becoming ensnared in this scheme, the IRS says taxpayers should beware of any of the following:

- Fictitious claims for refunds or rebates based on false statements of entitlement to tax credits.
- Unfamiliar for-profit tax services selling refund and credit schemes to church members.
- Internet solicitations that direct individuals to toll-free numbers and then solicit Social Security numbers.
- Homemade flyers and brochures implying credits or refunds are available without proof of eligibility.
- Offers of free money with no documentation required.
- Promises of refunds for "Low Income–No Documents Tax Returns."
- Claims for the expired Economic Recovery Credit Program or for economic stimulus payments.
- Unsolicited offers to prepare a return and split the refund.
- Unfamiliar return preparation firms soliciting business from cities outside of the normal business or commuting area.

EXAMPLE. An Ohio woman was sentenced to 75 months in prison and ordered to pay more than $3 million in restitution after she pleaded guilty to mortgage fraud, tax fraud, credit card fraud, and aggravated identity theft. This individual had filed approximately 140 false returns using stolen personal information.

EXAMPLE. A Georgia woman was sentenced to 72 months in prison and three years of supervised release and was ordered to pay approximately $290,000 in restitution for filing hundreds of false tax returns using identities stolen from deceased persons.

33. IRS statistics

The IRS issued several statistical summaries in 2012 analyzing data for 2009 and 2010. Here is a roundup of some of the key findings:

- For tax year 2010, the number of individual tax returns filed increased by 2.4 million, or 1.7 percent.
- Adjusted gross income (AGI) rose $462.7 billion, or 6.1 percent, from 2009 to 2010, compared to a 7.7 percent decrease from 2008 to 2009.
- Total tax liability increased 9 percent to $1.1 trillion.
- Some components of AGI showed decreases between 2009 and 2010. The most notable was taxable interest, which decreased 16.9 percent. Other components of AGI showed large gains for 2010, including IRA distributions, net gain less loss, and unemployment compensation, which increased 62.2 percent, 57.4 percent, and 43.9 percent, respectively.
- For 2010, individuals filed 142.8 million tax returns. Of those returns, 84.7 million (or 59 percent) were taxable, which means that at the return level, the taxpayer reported total income tax greater than zero. Adjusted gross income (AGI) reported on taxable returns was almost $8.1 trillion, while total income tax was $951.7 billion.
- For tax year 2010, individual taxpayers who itemized deductions reported $170.2 billion in deductions for charitable contributions.
- Schedule A itemized deductions were claimed on 32.6 percent of individual tax returns for 2010.
- For 2010, nearly 100 billion individual tax returns were e-filed.
- According to IRS Publication 4822, Taxpayer Filing Attribute Report, almost 60 percent of taxpayers pay a tax return preparer to prepare their tax return and 32 percent use tax preparation software.
- The average individual refund amount for tax year 2011 was $2,913.
- The Earned Income Tax Credit was claimed on 26.8 million tax returns for 2011.

TAX CHANGES OF INTEREST TO CHURCHES

34. Voluntary Classification Settlement Program launched

The Voluntary Classification Settlement Program (VCSP) is a voluntary IRS program that provides an opportunity for employers to reclassify their workers as employees for employment tax purposes for future tax periods, with partial relief from federal employment taxes. To participate in this program, the employer must meet certain eligibility requirements, apply to participate in the VCSP by filing Form 8952, Application for Voluntary Classification Settlement Program, and enter into a closing agreement with the IRS.

The VCSP is available for employers who want to voluntarily change the prospective classification of their workers. The program applies to taxpayers who are currently treating their workers (or a class or group of workers) as independent contractors or other non-employees and want to prospectively treat the workers as employees.

The employer must have consistently treated the workers as non-employees and must have filed all required Forms 1099 for the workers to be reclassified under the VCSP for the previous three years to participate in the VCSP. Additionally, the employer cannot currently be under audit by the IRS and cannot currently be under audit concerning the classification of the workers by the Department of Labor or by a state government agency.

If the IRS or the Department of Labor has previously audited a taxpayer concerning the classification of the workers, the taxpayer will be eligible only if the taxpayer has complied with the results of that audit.

Exempt organizations may participate in the VCSP if they meet all of the eligibility requirements.

An employer participating in the VCSP will agree to prospectively treat the class or classes of workers as employees for future tax periods. In exchange, the employer

- will pay 10 percent of the employment tax liability that may have been due on compensation paid to the workers for the most recent tax year;
- will not be liable for any interest and penalties on the amount; and
- will not be subject to an employment tax audit with respect to the worker classification of the workers being reclassified under the VCSP for prior years.

In addition, as part of the VCSP program, the employer will agree to extend the period of limitations on assessment of employment taxes for three years for the first, second, and third calendar years beginning after the date on which it has agreed under the VCSP closing agreement to begin treating the workers as employees.

To participate in the VCSP, an employer must apply using Form 8952, Application for Voluntary Classification Settlement Program. The application should be filed at least 60 days from the date the employer wants to begin treating its workers as employees.

35. Authority of bankruptcy trustees to recover charitable contributions made by bankrupt debtors

A bankruptcy court in Colorado addressed the authority of bankruptcy trustees to recover charitable contributions made by bankrupt debtors within a year of filing a bankruptcy petition. A married couple (the "debtors") filed for Chapter 7 bankruptcy relief on December 31, 2009. In 2008 the debtors' gross earned income was $6,800 and they received $22,036 in Social Security benefits. Throughout 2008 the debtors made 25 donations to their church totaling $3,478. In 2009 the debtors' gross earned income was $7,487 and they received $23,164 in Social Security benefits. Throughout 2009 the debtors made seven donations totaling $1,280 to their church.

The bankruptcy trustee attempted to avoid these charitable contributions and have the church return them to the court on the basis of a provision in the Bankruptcy Code that empowers a trustee to recover any transfer of funds or assets by a debtor for less than "reasonably equivalent value" within a year of filing a bankruptcy petition. The church cited section 548 of the Bankruptcy Code, which was amended by the Religious Liberty and Charitable Donation Protection Act of 1997 (RLCDPA) to provide a defense against a bankruptcy trustee's power to recover transfers by debtors within a year of filing a bankruptcy petition. Amended section 548 provides: "A transfer of a charitable contribution to a qualified religious or charitable entity or organization shall not be considered to be a [voidable] transfer in any case in which—(A) the amount of that contribution does not exceed 15 percent of the gross annual income of the debtor for the year in which the transfer of the contribution is made."

The court addressed two questions: (1) are Social Security payments included in gross annual income for purposes of the section 548 exception; and (2) if transfers exceed 15 percent, is the entire transferred amount voidable or just the transferred amount that exceeds 15 percent?

Social Security payments. The court noted that the plain language of section 548 was ambiguous as to whether gross annual income should include Social Security benefits. It also noted that the Bankruptcy Code does not define the term *gross annual income*, and no court has defined the term within the meaning of section 548. However, the court noted that the Bankruptcy Code does exclude Social Security benefits when calculating current monthly income, and the Internal Revenue Code only includes Social Security benefits in gross annual income if the taxpayer's modified adjusted gross income for the taxable year plus one-half of Social Security benefits received during the taxable year exceeds a "base amount" ($32,000). The court concluded that Social Security benefits are not included in computing gross annual income under section 548, and as a result, only 15 percent of the debtors' other income was shielded from the bankruptcy trustee.

Voidable amount. If a debtor contributes more than 15 percent of gross annual income to a church, is the entire contribution recoverable by the bankruptcy trustee, or only the portion that exceeds 15 percent of gross annual income? The court concluded that only the excess above 15 percent is recoverable. It observed:

> *The RLCDPA was created to reverse the trend among the courts allowing avoidance actions to recover funds contributed by debtors to churches. The House Report states, "the safe harbor*

protects annual aggregate contributions up to 15 percent of the debtor's gross annual income." The term "up to" indicates an intent by Congress to bifurcate the avoidance amount beyond the 15 percent threshold. . . . It is doubtful that Congress would protect a debtor's right to donate 15 percent of their gross annual income to a charitable organization, but allow a trustee to avoid all donations if one cent over the 15 percent threshold is donated. From the church's perspective, voiding entire transfers above 15 percent of a debtor's gross annual income would place an undue burden upon churches. If the entire donation amount is voided churches would be obligated to investigate a donor's financial background in order to use funds within two years of receipt.

This case is significant because it represents the only court to address the question of whether Social Security payments are included in computing gross annual income for purposes of applying the section 548 exclusion. The court concluded that gross annual income excludes Social Security benefits, meaning that Social Security beneficiaries' contributions to their church are more likely to be recoverable by bankruptcy trustees. But the court also ruled that if a bankruptcy debtor contributes more than 15 percent of gross annual income to his or her church, the bankruptcy trustee can recover only the contributions in excess of 15 percent of gross annual income. *In re McGough, 2011 WL 2671253 (D. Colo. 2011).*

36. The contemporaneous requirement in contribution receipts

Donors must substantiate individual cash contributions of $250 or more "by a contemporaneous written acknowledgment of the contribution by the donee organization." Donors cannot substantiate individual cash contributions of $250 or more with canceled checks. They must receive a written acknowledgment from the church or charity.

The IRS explains the contemporaneous requirement as follows: "For the written acknowledgment to be considered contemporaneous with the contribution, a donor must receive the acknowledgment by the earlier of the date on which the donor actually files his or her individual federal income tax return for the year of the contribution, or the due date (including extensions) of the return."

The Tax Court addressed the contemporaneous requirement in a recent case. A taxpayer made several contributions to a church (Church A) during 2007. The contributions to Church A were reported in a letter from the church dated January 19, 2010, indicating that the taxpayer contributed a total of $7,500, and several copies of checks, all for amounts of $250 or more. In addition, the taxpayer made several contributions to a second church (Church B). These contributions are reflected in a "tithing statement" from the church dated January 19, 2010, stating that the taxpayer contributed a total of $2,255, and several copies of checks, some of which are for amounts less than $250. The IRS disallowed any charitable contribution deduction for these contributions, and the taxpayer appealed to the Tax Court.

The court began its ruling by observing: "In general, a taxpayer is entitled to deduct charitable contributions made during the taxable year to or for the use of certain types of organizations. A taxpayer is required to substantiate charitable contributions; records must be maintained. A contribution of cash in an amount less than $250 may be substantiated with a canceled check, a receipt, or other reliable evidence showing the name of the donee, the date of the contribution, and the amount of the contribution."

The court noted that contributions of cash or property of $250 or more require the donor to obtain "contemporaneous written acknowledgment of the donation" from the charity. At a minimum, the contemporaneous written acknowledgment "must contain a description of any property contributed, a statement as to whether any goods or services were provided in consideration, and a description and good faith estimate of the value of any goods or services provided in consideration." Further, a written acknowledgment is contemporaneous "if it is obtained by the taxpayer on or before the earlier of (1) the date on which the taxpayer files a return for the taxable year in which the contribution was made, or (2) the due date (including extensions) for filing the return."

The court concluded that the taxpayer was not entitled to deduct the $7,500 she contributed to Church A: "The taxpayer introduced a letter from the church dated January 19, 2010, and copies of several checks, each for more than $250 and made out to the church's pastor and his wife. The letter does not state whether she received goods or services in exchange for contribution and was not received by the earlier of her return's filing date or its due date of April 15, 2008. Thus, there is no contemporaneous written acknowledgment from the donee that would permit petitioner to deduct the contributions."

The court also concluded that the taxpayer could not deduct most of the contributions she made to Church B: "To substantiate the contributions, the taxpayer introduced checks made out to Church B and a 2007 tithing statement from Church B dated January 19, 2010. Because the taxpayer did not receive the tithing statement by the earlier of her return's filing date or its due date of April 15, 2008, it is not a contemporaneous written acknowledgment. Thus, she does not have proper substantiation for the contributions of $250 or more."

However, the court concluded that the tithing statement and canceled checks substantiated the taxpayer's contributions of less than $250. As a result, she was entitled to deduct individual contributions of less than $250, which amounted to $355.

The court also upheld the imposition of a negligence penalty by the IRS. It noted that a taxpayer may be liable for a penalty of 20 percent of the portion of an underpayment of tax that is due to negligence or disregard of rules or regulations or attributable to a substantial understatement of income tax. *Negligence* is defined by the tax code as any failure to make a reasonable attempt to comply with the provisions of the Code, including a failure to keep adequate books and records or to substantiate items properly. Negligence "has also been defined as the failure to exercise due care or the failure to do what a reasonable person would do under the circumstances."

The court noted that the taxpayer's records were insufficient to substantiate several of her claimed deductions, and she failed to keep adequate books and records. Furthermore, she was a tax return preparer with more than 15 years' experience and yet improperly deducted the cost of numerous items. The court noted that the negligence penalty is not imposed with respect to any portion of the underpayment as to which the taxpayer shows that he or she acted with reasonable cause and in good faith. However, the taxpayer "offered no evidence that she acted with reasonable cause and in good faith. Accordingly, we hold that petitioner is liable for an accuracy-related penalty due to negligence or disregard of rules or regulations." *Linzy v. Commissioner, T.C. Memo. 2011-264.*

➥ **TIP.** To avoid jeopardizing the tax deductibility of charitable contributions, churches should advise donors at the end of 2012 not to file their 2012 income tax returns until they have received a written acknowledgment of their contributions from the church. This communication should be in writing. To illustrate, the following statement could be placed in the church bulletin or newsletter for the last few weeks of 2012 or included in a letter to members: "***Important notice:*** *To ensure the deductibility of your church contributions, please do not file your 2012 income tax return until you have received a written acknowledgment of your contributions from the church. You may lose a deduction for some contributions if you file your tax return before receiving a written acknowledgment of your contributions from the church.*"

37. Tax Court disallowance of $23 million charitable contribution

A successful real estate broker and appraiser donated several properties to his charitable remainder unitrust and claimed a charitable contribution deduction in the amount of $23 million. The IRS audited the tax return on which the deduction was claimed and denied any deduction on the ground that the donor failed to comply with the substantiation requirements that apply to donations of noncash property valued by the donor in excess of $5,000.

The donor did not obtain an appraisal of any of the donated properties prior to their donation, and he filled out his federal income tax return himself, including Form 8283 (Noncash Charitable Contributions), which is used to substantiate donations of property valued at more than $5,000 and which includes a summary of the "qualified appraisal" the donor previously obtained for the donated property.

The donor conceded that he did not read the instructions before completing Form 8283 because "it seemed so clear that he didn't think he needed to." In section B, the appraisal summary, he used his own appraisals of the donated properties. He didn't report his basis in any of the donated properties but stated that he had bought all the properties "in the 1970s and 1980s."

Soon after the IRS started an audit of the donor's tax return, it became obvious that a key issue was going to be the lack of a qualified appraisal for any of the donated properties performed by a qualified appraiser. The donor quickly retained two professional appraisers to provide an appraisal of the properties. These appraisals resulted in amounts close to, and in some cases less than, the donor's own appraisals.

The IRS disallowed any charitable contribution deduction on the ground that the substantiation requirements for donations of noncash property were not met. The donor appealed to the United States Tax Court.

The tax code and regulations. For most contributions of noncash property valued by the donor at more than $5,000, the tax code and regulations impose the following substantiation requirements:

(1) The donor must obtain a *qualified appraisal* of the donated property that (a) is made not earlier than 60 days before the date of contribution of the appraised property nor later than the due date of the return on which a deduction is first claimed; (b) is prepared, signed, and dated by a qualified appraiser; (c) includes a statement that the appraisal was prepared for income tax purposes; and (d) includes the appraised fair market value of the property on the date (or expected date) of the contribution. The regulations contain a detailed definition of a qualified appraiser.

The court noted that "the most important requirement is that the appraisal be done by a qualified appraiser . . . which the regulations say cannot be the donor or taxpayer claiming the deduction or the donee of the property." The donor in this case "did the appraisals, was the donor and the taxpayer claiming the deductions. He was also, in his capacity as the trustee of the trust, the donee. There is no way we can possibly find that he was a qualified appraiser for the gifts."

(2) The donor must attach a completed *qualified appraisal summary* (Part B of IRS Form 8283) to the tax return on which the charitable contribution deduction is claimed. The appraisal summary must be signed and dated by both the qualified appraiser who prepared the qualified appraisal and a representative of the donee charity. It also must include several items of information, including a description of the donated property; the date the donor acquired the donated property and the manner of acquisition; the cost or basis of the donated property; a statement as to whether the contribution was made by means of a bargain sale and the amount of any consideration received from the donee for the contribution; the name, address, and taxpayer identification number of the

qualified appraiser; and the appraised fair market value of the property on the date of contribution.

The court concluded that the donor's Form 8283 did not constitute a valid qualified appraisal summary because it failed to comply with several of these requirements: "[The donor] failed to include information about several of these categories on his Form 8283 and the attached statements. For instance, he didn't include his bases in the properties, there is no bargain-sale statement, and there are no statements from a qualified appraiser." In addition, the donor did not seek independent appraisals until after the IRS audit started (well after his returns were due)."

The court concluded that "there is no dispute that the donor didn't follow the regulations. His appraisals weren't qualified because he did them himself, his attached statements weren't appraisal summaries, and his untimely independent appraisals came too late to be either qualified appraisals or remedial appraisal summaries. This means the IRS has to win unless . . . we find that the donor has raised a genuine dispute that he substantially complied with the regulations."

Substantial compliance. The donor insisted that even if he failed to strictly comply with the regulation, he should still get a deduction because he substantially complied. The court acknowledged that it had previously ruled that a taxpayer who donated property to a charity had substantially complied with the law even though a separate appraisal had not been obtained and the qualifications of the appraiser were omitted from the appraisal summary attached to the donor's tax return. The court noted that the donor had obtained an appraisal of the property prior to the time he decided to donate it to charity and that this appraisal contained substantially all the information required by law. When the donor later decided to donate the property to charity, he simply enclosed a copy of this appraisal with the tax return on which a charitable contribution was claimed. The court concluded that the qualified appraisal rules are "directory, not mandatory," and therefore they could be met by substantial, rather than strict, compliance. The fact that the donor did not obtain a new appraisal did not preclude a charitable contribution deduction. *Bond v. Commissioner, 100 T.C. 32 (1993).*

However, the court noted that since the *Bond* case, "few taxpayers have succeeded in showing substantial compliance," and their "fatal mistakes" have included:

- Failing to get an appraisal. *Todd v. Commissioner, 118 T.C. 334 (2002); Hewitt v. Commissioner, 166 F.3d 332 (4th Cir. 1998); Jorgenson v. Commissioner, T.C. Memo. 2000-38.*
- Failing to fill out section B of Form 8283 (the appraisal summary). *See Hewitt (above); Smith v. Commissioner, T.C. Memo. 2007-368, aff'd, 364 Fed. Appx. 317 (9th Cir. 2009).*
- Having someone without expertise in appraisals complete the appraisal. *Smith (above) (CPA wasn't licensed appraiser); D'Arcangelo v. Commissioner, T.C. Memo. 1994-572*

(high-school principal not qualified to appraise art supplies and was employee of donee and therefore ineligible to be qualified appraiser).

- Having an appraisal prepared at the wrong time (i.e., either more than 60 days before the gift or after the return was filed). *See Jorgenson (above) (appraisal prepared after tax return filed); D'Arcangelo (above) (appraisal at least six years before gift); Friedman v. Commissioner, T.C. Memo. 2010-45 (appraisals performed years after due dates of returns).*

- Including insufficient information or inappropriate information in an appraisal or appraisal summary. *See Smith (above) (appraisal of partnership shares "terse" and appraisal actually of assets held by partnership, not the shares themselves).*

The court concluded:

> *The cases make clear that substantial compliance requires a qualified appraisal. . . . Since it is an essential requirement of [the tax code] that the taxpayer obtain a qualified appraisal, we can't excuse failure to do so as substantial compliance. . . . There is no dispute that the donor was not a qualified appraiser under the regulations, since he was both the donor and trustee for the donee. The attachment to the Form 8283, therefore, cannot be a qualified appraisal. Its fatal flaws include its preparation by an ineligible appraiser and its lack of enough detailed information to put the IRS on notice of the nature of the donation.*

The court concluded its opinion with these words:

> *Accordingly, we hold that the donor is not entitled to any charitable deduction. . . . We recognize that this result is harsh—a complete denial of charitable deductions to a donor that did not overvalue, and may well have undervalued, his contributions—all reported on forms that even to the Court's eyes seemed likely to mislead someone who didn't read the instructions. But the problems of misvalued property are so great that Congress was quite specific about what the charitably inclined have to do to defend their deductions, and we cannot in a single sympathetic case undermine those rules.*

This case provides church leaders with a useful review of the substantiation requirements that apply to gifts of noncash property. Note the following points in particular.

First, contributions of noncash property for which a donor claims a charitable contribution deduction of more than $5,000 must comply with special substantiation requirements. The donor must obtain a qualified appraisal of the donated property from a qualified appraiser and attach an appraisal summary to the tax return on which the deduction is claimed (this is done on IRS Form 8283, Section B). As the donor in this case learned, a failure to comply with this requirement may lead to the loss of a charitable contribution deduction.

❖ **KEY POINT.** Donors who claim a deduction of more than $500,000 for a contribution of property must attach a copy of the qualified appraisal of the property to their tax return. This does not apply to contributions of cash, inventory, publicly traded stock, or intellectual property. In figuring whether a deduction is over $500,000, combine the claimed deductions for all similar items donated to any charitable organization during the year.

Second, these substantiation requirements ordinarily will not be excused based on "substantial compliance."

Third, the regulations recognize two limited exceptions: (1) If it is impossible for a donor to obtain the donee charity's signature on the appraisal summary, the donor's deduction will not be disallowed provided he or she attaches a statement to the appraisal summary explaining why it was not possible to obtain the donee's signature. (2) If a donor fails to attach the appraisal summary to the tax return, the IRS may request that the donor submit the appraisal summary within 90 days of the request. If such a request is made and the donor complies, a deduction will not be disallowed provided that the donor's failure to attach the appraisal summary was a good faith omission and a qualified appraisal was completed within the specified period.

➥ **TIP.** Do not assume that donors are familiar with the substantiation rules that apply to gifts of noncash property. Church treasurers should obtain copies of Form 8283 each year to give to persons who donate noncash property to the church during the year. You can download copies of Form 8283 from the IRS website (irs.gov). Or you can order them by calling the IRS forms hotline at 1-800-TAX-FORM. In either case, be sure to get the form and the instructions (two separate documents).

➥ **TIP.** Ask donors of noncash property to be sure they obtain a qualified appraisal if you believe they may claim a charitable contribution deduction of more than $5,000.

❖ **KEY POINT.** Stock is a special case. No qualified appraisal is required for donations of publicly traded stock, and a qualified appraisal is required for privately held stock only if the claimed value exceeds $10,000.

For a full explanation of the substantiation requirements that apply to all forms of charitable contributions, see Chapter 8.

38. Designated scholarship gifts

A member of Congress asked the IRS for an opinion regarding a question submitted by a constituent. The question was whether contributions to a church's scholarship fund are tax-deductible if the donor suggests that the church use the contributions to pay for the college tuition costs of the pastor's daughter. The IRS responded as follows:

> *An individual can take a deduction for a charitable contribution or gift to or for the use of a charitable organization, including a*

church. . . . However, if a donor earmarks the contribution to a particular individual, the donor must treat it as being a gift to the designated individual and not as a tax-deductible contribution. Various courts have ruled that contributions to a church fund for missionaries are not deductible if there is a commitment or understanding that the church will use the contributions only for a particular individual. The law allows a deduction only if the church has full control of the donated funds and discretion as to their use.

39. Deducting charitable contributions: eight essentials

In 2012 the IRS released a list of "eight essential tips" on deducting charitable contributions. Here is the list:

(1) If your goal is a legitimate tax deduction, then you must be giving to a qualified organization. Also, you cannot deduct contributions made to specific individuals, political organizations or candidates. See IRS Publication 526, Charitable Contributions, for rules on what constitutes a qualified organization.

(2) To deduct a charitable contribution, you must file Form 1040 and itemize deductions on Schedule A. If your total deduction for all noncash contributions for the year is more than $500, you must complete and attach IRS Form 8283, Noncash Charitable Contributions, to your return.

(3) If you receive a benefit because of your contribution such as merchandise, tickets to a ball game or other goods and services, then you can deduct only the amount that exceeds the fair market value of the benefit received.

(4) Donations of stock or other non-cash property are usually valued at the fair market value of the property. Clothing and household items must generally be in good used condition or better to be deductible. Special rules apply to vehicle donations.

(5) Fair market value is generally the price at which property would change hands between a willing buyer and a willing seller, neither having to buy or sell, and both having reasonable knowledge of all the relevant facts.

(6) Regardless of the amount, to deduct a contribution of cash, check, or other monetary gift, you must maintain a bank record, payroll deduction records or a written communication from the organization containing the name of the organization and the date and amount of the contribution. For text message donations, a telephone bill meets the record-keeping requirement if it shows the name of the receiving organization, the date of the contribution and the amount given.

(7) To claim a deduction for contributions of cash or property equaling $250 or more, you must have a bank record, payroll

deduction records or a written acknowledgment from the qualified organization showing the amount of the cash, a description of any property contributed, and whether the organization provided any goods or services in exchange for the gift. One document may satisfy both the written communication requirement for monetary gifts and the written acknowledgment requirement for all contributions of $250 or more.

(8) Taxpayers donating an item or a group of similar items valued at more than $5,000 must also complete Section B of Form 8283, which generally requires an appraisal by a qualified appraiser.

For more information on charitable contributions, refer to Form 8283 and its instructions, as well as Publication 526, Charitable Contributions. For information on determining the value of donations, refer to Publication 561, Determining the Value of Donated Property. All are available at IRS.gov or by calling 800-TAX-FORM (800-829-3676). IRS Tax Tip 2012-57.

40. Tax Court decision regarding expenses incurred in performing charitable services

A taxpayer performed volunteer activities as a cheerleading coach for a youth football and cheerleading league. She claimed that she made various unreimbursed charitable contributions regarding her cheerleading activities, including paying for a charter bus rental and the use of her and her ex-husband's automobiles for travel to and from team practices and games. The IRS disallowed a charitable contribution deduction for any of these expenses, and the taxpayer appealed to the Tax Court.

Bus rental. The court noted that for a contribution of $250 or more, a taxpayer must substantiate the contribution with a written acknowledgment from the charity. A taxpayer who incurs unreimbursed expenses "incident to the rendition of services" is treated as having obtained a written acknowledgment if the taxpayer (1) "has adequate records . . . to substantiate the amount of the expenditures and (2) acquires a contemporaneous statement from the [charity] containing: (A) a description of the services provided by the taxpayer; (B) a statement of whether the [charity] provides any goods or services in consideration, in whole or in part, for the unreimbursed expenditures; and (C) [a description and good faith estimate of the value of any goods or services provided by the charity]."

The court noted that the taxpayer claimed she was entitled to a deduction for a $660 contribution she made in order to fund the cheerleading group's bus rental. In support of her position, she provided a charter confirmation form and a money order receipt. However, "because her contribution was for an amount greater than $250, she is required to substantiate it by producing a written acknowledgment from the charity. She has failed to present any form of written acknowledgment from the charity relating to her contribution. As a result, her contribution of the $660 charter bus rental fee is not deductible as a charitable contribution."

Auto mileage. The taxpayer claimed she was entitled to a deduction for automobile mileage expenses associated with her and her ex-husband's travel to and from team practices and games. In support, she produced a MapQuest directions printout. The printout detailed the number of miles she and her ex-husband traveled over the course of a season while driving to and from team practices and games. The printout provides detailed information, including (1) the distance for each trip taken; (2) the number of trips taken per week; and (3) the number of weeks during which the trips took place. The court ruled that the taxpayer was entitled to a charitable contribution deduction in the amount of the charitable mileage rate of 14 cents per mile multiplied by the 1,857 miles she and her ex-husband traveled to and from team practices and games during the year. *Bradley v. Commissioner, T.C. Summary Opinion 2011-120 (2011).*

41. Recommended Form 1099-R improvement to enhance compliance

Generally, distributions from pensions, annuities, profit-sharing and retirement plans, IRAs, and insurance contracts are reported to recipients on Form 1099-R. Many churches and church pension plans have difficulty completing this form, and this difficulty is compounded in the case of ministers who receive a housing allowance.

The Treasury Inspector General for Tax Administration (TIGTA) conducted a review to determine whether the IRS has effective controls and processes in place to ensure that taxpayers and retirement income providers are correctly computing and reporting the taxable portion of retirement income on Form 1099-R. TIGTA estimated that as much as $4.2 billion of the "tax gap" (the difference in taxes paid and taxes owed) can be attributed to underreported retirement income.

TIGTA found that given the magnitude of underreporting, even small improvements in the IRS's examination of tax returns with retirement income could increase taxpayer compliance and generate substantial revenue to the federal government to reduce the tax gap.

"Our report found that correctly reporting taxable amounts of retirement distributions on Form 1099-R can be confusing for taxpayers," said J. Russell George, Treasury Inspector General for Tax Administration. "By implementing TIGTA's recommendation to clarify the form, the IRS can reduce taxpayer confusion and improve compliance," he added.

TIGTA recommended that the IRS revise Form 1099-R to clarify the meaning of the "taxable amount not determined" box in order to reduce taxpayer confusion and include the dates needed to identify retirement savings program distributions and transfers not rolled over within 60 days as required.

The IRS substantially agreed with TIGTA's recommendations and plans to revise the instructions to Form 1099-R to clarify taxpayer responsibilities and the amounts to report. The IRS plans to consider the feasibility and the benefits of including the dates of

distributions and their respective contributions to identify distributions not rolled over within 60 days.

42. National denomination ruled not liable for losses suffered by retirement plan beneficiaries

A federal court in Minnesota ruled that a national denomination was not liable for losses suffered by beneficiaries of a denominational retirement plan because it did not exercise sufficient control over the fund to be liable for the actions of the fund's managing board. Four retired ministers (the "plaintiffs") sued their denomination (the "national church") to recover losses they incurred in a denominational pension fund. The pension fund is a defined contribution retirement plan under section 403(b) of the tax code. The plan is a "church plan" that is exempt from ERISA absent an election to the contrary. Under the plan, defined contributions are made on behalf of participating members into their individual accounts. Plan participants have options for directing their plan accumulations. Before retirement, the accounts are considered "active," and plan participants can direct their accumulations into funds invested in the equity or fixed income markets.

In December 2008, the plan sent a letter to the plaintiffs stating that their retirement accounts were subject to market risk and that they should expect their distributions to be decreased in 2010. In September 2009, the plan informed participants that, due to the market downturn, it was underfunded by 26 percent and that, effective January 1, 2010, monthly payments would decrease by 9 percent and would likely decrease by an additional 9 percent in both 2011 and 2012.

Plaintiffs sued the national church and the board of pensions that managed the retirement plan (the "defendants"), asserting that, under state law, the defendants were required to invest and manage retirement funds as a prudent investor and that the defendants breached their fiduciary duties by failing to prudently invest and manage the retirement fund and failing to preserve the trust corpus, which caused the fund to become significantly underfunded and reduce plaintiffs' monthly payments.

Fiduciary duties. The court concluded that the national church was not a fiduciary with respect to the retirement plan, so the plaintiffs' breach of fiduciary claim against the national church had to be dismissed. The court noted that the plan's managing board, and not the national church, was the plan fiduciary in charge of administering and managing the plan. It pointed to language in the national church's governing documents making the plan's managing board, rather than the national church, responsible for the plan's investment and administration.

The plaintiffs argued that the national church was a fiduciary with respect to its duty to elect members of the plan's governing board and that this imposed on it a limited duty to monitor the board's activities. It observed that "a person with discretionary authority to appoint, maintain and remove plan fiduciaries is himself deemed a fiduciary with respect to the exercise of that authority. Implicit in the fiduciary duties attaching to persons empowered to appoint and remove plan fiduciaries is the duty to monitor appointees. The scope of the duty to monitor appointees is relatively narrow." The court stressed that "the duty to monitor is limited and does not include a duty to review all business decisions of plan administrators" because "that standard would defeat the purpose of having trustees appointed to run a benefits plan in the first place." The court concluded that the plaintiffs' lawsuit did not allege that the national church violated any duty to monitor, and therefore it failed to adequately allege that the national church violated a fiduciary duty owed to the plaintiffs.

"Church plan" status. The court rejected the plaintiffs' assertion that the plan's status as a church plan somehow made the national church liable for the actions of the plan's managing board. It acknowledged that a church plan must be "established and maintained . . . by a church" and that a plan maintained by a third party, such as a pension board, is "established and maintained . . . by a church" if the third party "is controlled by or associated with a church or a convention or association of churches." Church-plan status is awarded not only to plans controlled by a church but also to plans associated with a church. An organization is "associated with" a church "if it shares common religious bonds and convictions with that church."

The court concluded that "the plan's status as a church plan did not require that the [national church] exercise control over the board or plan, let alone control over the board's actions at issue in this lawsuit, to the extent that [national church] is liable for the board's actions. Here, the [plaintiffs] do not allege that [the national church] controls the board with regard to the decisions at issue in this litigation."

Alter ego liability. As an alternative means of holding the national church liable, the plaintiffs alleged that the plan and its governing board were an "alter ego" of the national church and that "injustice and fundamental unfairness would result if the national church was not held accountable" for the board's misconduct.

The court noted that "there is a presumption of separateness between a parent and subsidiary corporation and that "a court may pierce the corporate veil to hold a party liable for the acts of a corporate entity if the entity is used for a fraudulent purpose or the party is the alter ego of the entity. When using the alter ego theory to pierce the corporate veil, courts look to the reality and not form, with how the corporation operated and the individual defendant's relationship to that operation."

Under Minnesota law, piercing the corporate veil "requires (1) analyzing the reality of how the corporation functioned and the defendant's relationship to that operation and (2) finding injustice or fundamental unfairness."

The court listed the following factors that are significant in applying the first prong: "whether there is insufficient capitalization for purposes of corporate undertaking, a failure to observe corporate formalities, nonpayment of dividends, insolvency of debtor corporation at time of transaction in question, siphoning of funds by dominant shareholder, nonfunctioning of other officers and directors, absence of corporate records, and existence of the corporation as merely a facade for individual dealings."

The plaintiffs did not allege any improper transfer of assets between the national church and the plan or its board. Nor did they allege any other type of misuse of the corporate form or plan to harm the plaintiffs. The plaintiffs alleged that the plan is undercapitalized, but "there is no allegation that the national church played any role in that situation. Beyond the conclusory allegation of undercapitalization, there are no factual allegations to support the first prong of piercing the corporate veil."

The court acknowledged that the national church and the retirement plan "share a close relationship." However, it concluded:

> *The national church's Constitution shows the separation of the corporate structures governing the national church and the board. For example, the Constitution provides that "separate incorporation shall be maintained" for the board. It enumerates the board's responsibilities in operating and managing benefit plans, which include autonomy and independence. The documents referenced [by the plaintiff] demonstrate that the national church and the board are separate corporate entities, and the plaintiffs provide no factual allegation that these corporate formalities have been disregarded.*

The court also concluded that the plaintiffs failed to establish the second prong. It noted that the plaintiffs' lawsuit alleged that the plan's board was "an alter ego or instrumentality of the [national church], and injustice and fundamental unfairness would result if the [the national church] is not held accountable for the liabilities resulting from shortfalls in the retirement plan due to undercapitalization or the board of pensions' lack of resources to cover its liabilities." But the court stressed that this "barebones allegation that injustice or fundamental unfairness will result" if the national church is not liable was insufficient. It noted that there was no allegation in the plaintiffs' lawsuit that the national church played any role in any underfunding or that the plan was underfunded when the national church created it. As a result, the plaintiffs "failed to allege facts to support their legal conclusion of injustice or unfairness."

The court concluded that "although corporations are related, there can be no piercing of the veil without a showing of improper conduct" by the parent corporation.

Breach of contract. The plaintiffs' final argument was that the retirement plan and its governing board were guilty of a breach of contract. The court agreed that the retirement plan constituted a contract with the plaintiffs and other beneficiaries, and it concluded that the plaintiffs' allegations of a breach of the contract were sufficient to avoid a dismissal of this theory of liability: "The [plaintiffs] claim that the board breached the terms of the plan because, although the plan promised that plaintiffs' annuity benefits were guaranteed for life and that all increases to those benefits would be permanent, the board implemented an across-the-board 9 percent decrease in the participants' monthly annuity benefits."

The board insisted that its actions were a response to the adverse economic conditions caused by the recession and were necessary to preserve and maintain the plan. The court concluded that it "did not have the information necessary to conclude whether, in fact, a cut in payments was required to preserve the fund, the amount of any required cut, or whether the fund's underfunding was, itself, a breach of fiduciary duty. The question of whether the board's actions were required by—or a breach of—its fiduciary duty is one that cannot be resolved at the motion to dismiss stage."

Many beneficiaries of denominational retirement plans have suffered substantial losses during the "great recession." But as this case illustrates, those losses are not necessarily attributable to the denomination itself if the retirement plan is a separate corporation with a separate board and the denomination exercises little, if any, supervision or control over the management decisions of the plan. Further, retirement funds and their governing boards are not necessarily liable for beneficiaries' losses if the individual accounts are self-directed and no promises are made that are later broken. The risk of liability for retirement funds can be reduced in several ways, including allowing beneficiaries to direct their own investments, providing educational and training resources to beneficiaries, and repeatedly stressing that all investments involve risk. *2011 WL 2970962 (D. Minn. 2011).*

43. Church employer identification numbers

A church asked the IRS if it was required to have an employer identification number (EIN). The IRS responded with a letter that provided, in part:

> *An organization seeking exemption under section 501(c)(3) of the Code is required to apply for recognition of exemption on Form 1023. However, churches, their integrated auxiliaries, and conventions or associations of churches seeking section 501(c)(3) status are excepted from this application requirement. Churches that meet the requirements of section 501(c)(3) are automatically considered tax exempt and are not required to apply for and obtain recognition of tax-exempt status from the IRS.*
>
> *Although there is no requirement to do so, many churches seek recognition of tax-exempt status from the IRS because such recognition assures church leaders, members, and contributors that the church is recognized as exempt and qualifies for related*

tax benefits. For example, contributors to a church that has been recognized as tax-exempt would know that their contributions generally are tax-deductible.

Unlike churches, religious organizations that wish to be tax exempt generally must apply to the IRS for tax-exempt status unless their gross receipts do not normally exceed $5,000 annually.

All section 501(c)(3) organizations, including churches and religious organizations, must abide by certain rules:

- *Their net earnings may not inure to any private individual or shareholder,*
- *They must not provide a substantial benefit to private interests,*
- *They must not devote a substantial part of their activities to attempting to influence legislation,*
- *They must not participate in, or intervene in, any political campaign on behalf of (or in opposition to) any candidate for public office, and*
- *The organization's purposes and activities may not be illegal or violate fundamental public policy.*

Churches and religious organizations are generally exempt from income tax and receive other favorable treatment under the tax law; however, certain income of a church or religious organization may be subject to tax, such as income from an unrelated business.

An EIN is also known as a Federal Tax Identification Number, and is used to identify a business or non-individual entity. Every organization, including a church, should have an EIN, even if it will not have employees. An EIN is a unique number that identifies the organization much like a social security number identifies an individual. There are many instances in which an EIN is necessary even if the organization is not applying for tax-exempt status. For example, a church needs an EIN when it opens a bank account, in order to be listed as a subordinate in a group ruling, or if it files returns with the IRS (e.g., Forms W-2, 1099, 990-T).

44. The neighborhood land rule

Many churches rent some or all of their property. For example, a church purchases several homes adjacent to its property to facilitate future expansion. The church has no immediate plans to expand its facilities, so it rents the homes. One of the issues that arises in such cases is the application of the federal unrelated business income tax, which is a tax on the net income generated by a church or other public charity from an unrelated trade or business.

In general, rental income received by a church is exempt from the unrelated business income tax, but an exception applies in the case of rental income derived from debt-financed property. Section 514 of the tax code states that income from dividends, interest, annuities, royalties, rents, and capital gains and losses must be included in the definition of unrelated business taxable income to the extent it derives from debt-financed property. The amount of income included is proportional to the debt on the property. Debt-financed property is any property held to produce income and that is subject to an "acquisition indebtedness," such as a mortgage, at any time during the tax year.

The tax code specifies that if an exempt organization acquires real property mainly to use for exempt purposes within 10 years, it will not be treated as debt-financed property if it is in the neighborhood of other property that the organization uses for exempt purposes and if the intent to use the property for exempt purposes within 10 years is not abandoned. This exception to the definition of debt-financed property is referred to as the "neighborhood land rule."

The neighborhood land rule does not apply to property 10 years after its acquisition. Further, the rule applies after the first five years only if the organization satisfies the IRS that use of the land for exempt purposes is reasonably certain before the 10-year period expires. The organization need not show binding contracts to satisfy this requirement; but it must have a definite plan detailing a specific improvement and a completion date, and it must show some affirmative action toward the fulfillment of the plan. This information should be forwarded to the following address for a ruling at least 90 days before the end of the fifth year after acquisition of the land:

> Internal Revenue Service
> Commissioner, TE/GE
> Attention: T:EO:RA
> P.O. Box 120, Ben Franklin Station
> Washington, DC 20044

The income tax regulations authorize the IRS to grant a reasonable extension of time for requesting the ruling if the organization can show good cause. If the neighborhood land rule does not apply because the acquired land is not in the neighborhood of other land used for an organization's exempt purposes or because the organization fails to establish after the first five years of the 10-year period that the property will be used for exempt purposes, but the land is used eventually by the organization for its exempt purposes within the 10-year period, the property is not treated as debt-financed property for any period before the conversion.

The neighborhood land rule applies to churches, but with two important differences:

- the period during which the church must demonstrate the intent to use the acquired property for exempt purposes is increased from 10 to 15 years, and
- the land need not be in the same "neighborhood" as the church.

As a result, if a church acquires land for exempt purposes within 15 years after the time of acquisition, the property is not treated as

APPLYING THE NEIGHBORHOOD LAND RULE TO CHURCHES

Section 514 of the tax code contains a special "neighborhood land rule" that exempts rents from debt-financed church property from the unrelated business income tax so long as a church

- has a definite plan to use the land for exempt purposes within 15 years, including a "specific improvement and a completion date, and some affirmative action toward the fulfillment of such a plan";
- informs the IRS of its plan at least 90 days before the end of the fifth year after acquiring the land and requests a ruling;
- does not abandon its intent during the 15 years following acquisition; and
- demolishes any structures on the property as part of its plans to use the property for exempt purposes.

debt-financed property so long as the church does not abandon its intent to use the land in this manner within the 15-year period.

This exception for churches does not apply to any property after the 15-year period expires. Further, this rule will apply after the first five years of the 15-year period only if the church establishes to the satisfaction of the IRS that use of the acquired land in furtherance of its exempt purposes is reasonably certain before the 15-year period expires. Relevant information should be sent to the IRS at the above-referenced address.

If a church (for the period after the first five years of the 15-year period) cannot establish to the satisfaction of the IRS that use of acquired property for its exempt purpose is reasonably certain within the 15-year period, but the land is, in fact, converted to an exempt use within the 15-year period, the land is not treated as debt-financed property for any period before the conversion.

The same rule for demolition or removal of structures (discussed below) applies to a church.

In a recent case, a church purchased land through the use of debt financing in the neighborhood of its existing facility in order to build a larger facility. The land consisted of several acres of undeveloped land with the exception of two small buildings. The church borrowed funds to buy the land. It rented a portion of the property for cattle grazing and also received royalty payments from a lease of mineral rights to an oil company.

INTRODUCTION

The church asked the IRS for a ruling that the neighborhood land rule applied, and therefore the rental and royalty income the church received from its debt-financed property was not subject to the unrelated business income tax.

The IRS began its ruling by noting: "You purchased land on which to build a new, larger church campus. You acquired the land subject to acquisition indebtedness. You did not immediately use substantially all of the property for an exempt purpose related to your exempt function. Thus, the land is considered to be debt-financed property."

In general, the IRS continued, "any income derived from rents or royalties from debt-financed property . . . would be treated as unrelated business taxable income." However, the IRS noted that there are exceptions to the general rule. For example, "when land is acquired for exempt use within 10 years (extended to 15 years for churches), it is not treated as unrelated business taxable income. This exception is commonly referred to as the neighborhood land rule."

Under the neighborhood land rule, "an organization may acquire land adjacent to or within one mile of the organization's present location and convert the land to exempt purpose use within 10 years of acquisition. Any structure on the land when acquired by the organization must be demolished or removed. For churches [the tax code] provides special rules. The land must be converted to exempt use within 15 years of acquisition and the neighborhood test of proximity to an existing location is not applied."

To use the neighborhood land rule, "an organization must apply after the first five years and establish to the satisfaction of the [IRS] that it is reasonably certain that the land will be used [for exempt purposes] within the required time period."

The IRS noted that the church had submitted its ruling request in a timely manner, at least 90 days prior to five years after the date of acquisition of the land at issue. It further noted that

> *within the required period, you have taken steps to convert the land to your exempt use. You have demolished structures that existed on the land at the time of acquisition. You have constructed a new church campus of buildings and put it into use for your congregation. You have put your former location up for sale. While the property allows room for future growth, your church campus is substantially complete and converted to exempt use within 15 years of the land acquisition. Thus, your property will not be treated as debt-financed land . . . because you qualify for the exception under the neighborhood land special rule for churches.*

Since the church's property is not treated as debt-financed land for 15 years from the date of acquisition, "any rents or royalties received during that time period will not be treated as unrelated business taxable income," and it is "not subject to imposition of tax on unrelated business income for such rents or royalties for the stated period."

THE DEMOLITION RULE

The neighborhood land rule applies to any structure on the land when acquired only so long as the intended future use of the land in furtherance of the organization's exempt purpose requires that the structure be demolished or removed in order to use the land in this manner. As a result, during the first five years after acquisition (and for later years if there is a favorable ruling), improved property is not debt-financed so long as the organization does not abandon its intent to demolish the existing structures and use the land in furtherance of its exempt purpose. If an actual demolition of these structures occurs, the use made of the land need not be the one originally intended as long as its use furthers the organization's exempt purpose.

The neighborhood land rule does not apply to structures erected on land after its acquisition. When the neighborhood land rule does not initially apply, but the land is used eventually for exempt purposes, a refund or credit of any overpaid taxes will be allowed for a prior tax year. A claim must be filed within one year after the close of the tax year in which the property is actually used for exempt purposes.

The IRS concluded: "Based on the information you have submitted, it is reasonably certain that the debt-financed land will be used for an exempt church purpose within 15 years of its acquisition. Therefore, the property is exempt from the debt-financed property unrelated business taxable income provisions of [the tax code] as a result of the neighborhood land rule exception . . . for 15 years beginning on the date the land was acquired."

Relevance to church leaders. Before renting property or negotiating for mineral royalties, church leaders should be familiar with

- the debt-financed property exception to the exemption of rental income from the unrelated business income tax;
- the eligibility requirements for application of the neighborhood and rule; and
- the demolition rule.

The services of a tax attorney will be invaluable in ensuring full compliance with the law. *IRS Letter Ruling 201206018.*

45. Transfer of sales proceeds from dissolved church to pastor as compensation for unpaid wages

A Pennsylvania court addressed the issue of whether a church acted properly when it dissolved due to declining attendance, sold its assets, and transferred most of the sales proceeds to the pastor as compensation for wages it was previously unable to pay.

The church was established in 1902. In 1999 the church hired a new pastor for a starting weekly salary of $150, out of which $90 was treated as a nontaxable housing allowance. The pastor subsequently received periodic salary increases and, eventually, his entire salary was treated as a housing allowance. He was also paid separately for his maintenance work. As of 2008, his annual salary was $17,930. In 2007, 13 members of the church's congregation unanimously approved the revision to the church's constitution to provide that "in the event of the dissolution of this corporation, all of its debts shall be fully satisfied, including any compensation and benefits due to its Pastor."

At an annual congregational meeting in 2008, eight voting members of the church, including the pastor and his wife and two children, voted to dissolve the church and sell the church's property. They also adopted a motion by the pastor's son to compensate the pastor for his past service after the sale of the church's property. A committee formed to determine the amount of compensation for the pastor proposed to pay him up to $635,000. Between 1999 and 2008, the church's annual income ranged from $26,474 to less than $35,000.

Later that year the pastor and his wife and son signed an agreement to sell the church's property to another church for $750,000. A week later, six remaining voting members (including the pastor and his wife and two children) unanimously voted to dissolve the church and approved the compensation package for the pastor. After receiving a net amount of $690,000 from the sale of the property in 2009, and pursuant to the procedure for dissolving a nonprofit corporation described in the state nonprofit corporation law, the church asked a court to approve its proposed distribution of the proceeds from the sale of its assets. The church informed the court that it "owed its pastor and other employees compensation for periods of time when they were uncompensated due to the church's financial struggles."

The state opposed the proposed distribution of the church's assets on the grounds that the church failed to seek the court's approval prior to the sale of its assets and that by voting to approve the compensation package, the pastor and other members of the church board violated a fiduciary duty imposed by the nonprofit corporation law and engaged in "self-dealing to inure benefits to private individuals."

The court concluded that the pastor's claim for compensation for his past service would be unenforceable under contract law. It noted that contracts, to be enforceable, must by supported by "consideration," meaning that both parties must receive something of value in exchange for their commitments. The court noted that the church's commitment to pay the pastor $635,000 in back wages was unenforceable, since "past services" are never valid consideration for current obligations and commitments. As a result, the court concluded that payment of additional sums to the pastor in excess of his specified salary would constitute a gift, which would be inconsistent with the charitable purposes of the church.

The church appealed, claiming that the proposed payment to the pastor is consistent with its charitable purposes. It asserted that its members desired to compensate the pastor appropriately and that the church's constitution also expresses a desire to compensate him adequately. The church also cited the provision of its revised constitution requiring payment of all debts, including any compensation and benefits owed to the pastor, upon dissolution.

A state appeals court dismissed the church's appeal on a technical ground. It noted that the trial court's ruling was in the context of the church's petition to dissolve its corporate status, and as such, it was not appealable until the broader issue of dissolution was adjudicated. Once the trial court reaches a decision on the church's petition to dissolve its corporate status, then the entire case, including the court's prior ruling addressing the distribution of the sales proceeds, would be appealable as a final order of the court.

This case addresses a question that often arises when a small, struggling church dissolves, sells its assets, and transfers the proceeds to its pastor or in some cases other employees or directors. In many such cases, the justification for distributing the proceeds from the sale of church assets to the pastor is that he or she was not "adequately compensated" in the past, and this is a way make amends. But as the trial court in this case noted, such dispositions of the proceeds from the sale of church assets has a number of potential legal and tax consequences, including the following:

(1) Disposition of the proceeds of the sale of church assets in the course of a dissolution of a church often is governed by state nonprofit corporation law. The Pennsylvania Nonprofit Corporation Act applied in this case, and it gave the civil courts authority to review the disposition of church assets in the course of a dissolution. The lesson is clear: church leaders should never distribute the proceeds of a sale of church assets to individuals without the assistance of legal counsel to ensure compliance with state nonprofit corporation law.

(2) A church board that authorizes the distribution of proceeds from the sale of church assets to a pastor or any other individual may be in violation of their fiduciary duties to the church, which could expose them to personal liability.

(3) A church's distribution of proceeds from the sale of church assets to a pastor or any other individual jeopardizes the church's tax-exempt status, since it may amount to prohibited "inurement" of a church's resources to the personal benefit of a private individual. The IRS defines *inurement* as follows:

Churches and religious organizations, like all exempt organizations under IRC section 501(c)(3), are prohibited from engaging in activities that result in inurement of the church's or organization's income or assets to insiders (i.e., persons having a personal and private interest in the activities of the organization). Insiders could include the minister, church board members, officers, and in certain circumstances, employees. Examples of prohibited inurement include the payment of dividends, the payment of unreasonable compensation to insiders, and transferring property to insiders for less than fair market value. The prohibition against inurement to insiders is absolute; therefore, any amount of inurement is, potentially, grounds for loss of tax-exempt status. In addition, the insider involved may be subject to excise tax. See the following section on Excess benefit transactions. Note that prohibited inurement does not include reasonable payments for services rendered, payments that further tax-exempt purposes, or payments made for the fair market value of real or personal property. IRS Publication 1828.

(4) The trial court concluded that the $635,000 paid to the minister was not a legitimate debt of the church that could lawfully be discharged in the dissolution proceeding, since the minister provided no "consideration" (value) to the church in return for its commitment to pay this amount. To the contrary, the only "consideration" was that the minister's past services did not amount to consideration. As a result, the court characterized the church's proposed payment of $635,000 to the minister as a gift.

(5) The payment of an "excess benefit" to an officer or director (or relative) of a church or any other tax-exempt entity may result in substantial penalties called "intermediate sanctions." These penalties can be as much as 225 percent times the amount of the excess benefit. This tax is paid by the recipient of the excess benefit, which would be the minister in this case.

(6) An excise tax equal to 10 percent of an excess benefit may be imposed on an exempt organization's managers who authorized the payment of an excess benefit to an officer or director (or relative). This tax may not exceed $20,000 with respect to any single transaction and is only imposed if the manager knowingly participated in the transaction and the manager's participation was willful and not due to reasonable cause.

(7) To be exempt from federal income tax, a church must be organized exclusively for exempt purposes. This requirement is referred to by the IRS as the "organizational test" of tax-exempt status. The income tax regulations specify (a) that an organization is not organized exclusively for exempt purposes unless its assets are dedicated to an exempt purpose and (b) that an organization's assets will be presumed to be dedicated to an exempt purpose if, upon dissolution, the assets would, by reason of a provision in the organization's articles of incorporation, be distributed to another exempt organization.

In summary, the distribution of church assets to a minister or other private individual raises an array of legal and tax issues of considerable importance. Such transactions should never be contemplated without the assistance of legal counsel. *In re First Church, 2011 WL 2302540 (Pa. Common. 2011).*

46. Preserving property tax exemptions

In 2007 a church (the "plaintiff") acquired property through a warranty deed from another church. The title company incorrectly listed the church's mailing address on the deed. At the time of the conveyance, the property was exempt from taxation on the basis of its religious use. The use of the property did not change when ownership changed; the property was used for religious services by both the old and the new owners.

Late in 2007, a local tax assessor sent the plaintiff a "Notification of Status Change" for the 2008–09 tax year. This notice was sent to the incorrect address listed on the deed. The notice stated: "An application is enclosed with this notice for you to file . . . for a tax exemption on the above referenced location." The reason listed on the notice for the status change was a "change of ownership." The 2009–10 tax statement for the property also was sent to the plaintiff at the incorrect address listed on the deed. Neither statement was received by the plaintiff, and both were returned unopened to the assessor's office by the post office. No payments were made when the property taxes became due.

The plaintiff did not receive this notice, which was returned unopened to the assessor by the post office with the notation "NMR," no mail receptacle, on the envelope. The assessor placed the unopened notice in the plaintiff's file. The assessor did not search its records or other sources to locate a different address for the plaintiff.

In 2010 the plaintiff first discovered that its property was being taxed. It immediately filed an application for tax exemption for tax years 2008–09 and 2009–10. The assessor denied the exemption for both tax years because the exemption applications were not timely filed. However, the assessor granted the plaintiff's property tax exemption for tax year 2010–11 and for future years. The plaintiff appealed to the Oregon Tax Court the denial of its property tax exemption for 2008–09 and 2009–10.

The court's ruling. The state tax court began its opinion by quoting the property tax exemption statute: "Before any . . . property may be exempted from taxation . . . for any tax year, the institution or organization claiming the exemption shall file with the county assessor, on or before April 1 of the assessment year, a statement . . . listing all property claimed to be exempt and showing the purpose for which such property is used." An exemption application may be filed as late as December 31 of the assessment year for which an exemption is desired upon payment of a late filing fee. The court concluded: "When the plaintiff acquired the property in 2007 this constituted a change in ownership that required plaintiff to file a new application. The latest plaintiff could have filed an application for exemption was December 31, 2008, for the 2008–09 tax year, and December 31, 2009, for the 2009–10 tax year. Plaintiff did not file an application for exemption for tax years 2008–09 and 2009–10 until December 3, 2010. Accordingly, plaintiff failed to timely file exemption applications for those years."

Improper address. The court acknowledged that the plaintiff did not receive notice of the exemption status change or the tax statements because the assessor sent the notices to the wrong address. The plaintiff claimed that the assessor was obligated to determine the church's correct address through a search of its internal records or of other available sources, particularly once he was put on notice that the plaintiff's address of record was incorrect. Additionally, the plaintiff claimed that the assessor could have searched other sources, such as the Internet, and learned that no mail was accepted at the address on the deed.

In rejecting the plaintiff's request that a property tax exemption be granted for prior years based on the assessor's failure to send notices to the correct address, the court observed:

> *While it is definitely a good idea for the county to examine its returned mail, arguing about whether the county might have found the [plaintiff] earlier overlooks the point that the county ought not to have had to look for the [plaintiff] at all. . . . It is not the county's obligation to search for the taxpayer. Instead, it is the taxpayer's responsibility to search the county and make sure its records are correct.*

> *The legislature has placed the burden on taxpayers to notify county assessors of their true and correct address. [The assessor] did not have a duty to locate any other address for the plaintiff either by searching its internal records or by searching some other source.*

"Where, as here, a taxpayer fails to provide the tax collector or assessor with correct address information and, as a result, the taxes are not paid, that error comes at a cost. That cost is the imposition of interest and, eventually, foreclosure." *Hawkins v. Lane County Assessor, 2009 WL 5103232 (Md. App. 2009).*

Returned mail. The plaintiff also noted that the returned notice was marked with the notation "NMR," meaning "no mail receptacle," which indicated not only that the plaintiff's address was incorrect but that there was no address at all. Furthermore, the plaintiff noted that it was the title company that incorrectly listed plaintiff's address on the deed. The court rejected these defenses:

> *The court has held taxpayers responsible for interest and penalties that were incurred on a late property tax payment when the title company incorrectly listed the address where all property tax statements should be sent. Additionally, taxpayers were held responsible for taxes and interest when their appeal was dismissed as untimely, despite the fact that tax notices were sent to an address with no mail receptacle. Thus, the facts that the title company incorrectly listed the plaintiff's address where property tax statements should be sent and that the address provided on the recorded deed did not have a mail receptacle do not relieve the plaintiff of the duty to keep the tax collector informed of the correct address.*

This case contains two important lessons for church leaders. First, many churches have purchased a building and grounds from another church or charity. It is a common assumption that since the property continues to be used for exempt purposes, its exemption from property taxation continues uninterrupted. In most jurisdictions, this assumption is incorrect, since any transfer of ownership, even from one church to another, requires the property's exempt status to be applied for again.

Second, this case illustrates that in most jurisdictions it is the responsibility of the property owner to ensure that the local tax assessor's records contain a correct mailing address. Church leaders should not assume that church property will be entitled to exemption from tax if no exemption application is filed, even if the failure to apply for an exemption was due to the fact that the local assessor sent tax statements and related information to the wrong address. And this is so even if, as in this case, the error was attributable to the title company rather than to the church.

The bottom line is that church leaders should pay special attention to property tax exemption requirements when purchasing a building or land, even from another church or charity. Here are some important tips:

- Do not assume that a property tax exemption automatically "goes with the land" to a new owner.
- When purchasing property, be sure your church's mailing address is correctly listed on the deed, since this is the address typically used by the assessor's office.
- If you do not hear from the assessor's office within a reasonable time after acquiring property, this may indicate a problem with the property's tax exemption that should be addressed promptly.
- Find out what requirements must be met in order for newly acquired church property to become exempt from property taxes. Go to the assessor's office and obtain the necessary forms.
- Confirm that the assessor's office has the correct address for the church. And, just as importantly, be sure the assessor's office has the correct name of the church. It is common for churches to change their name from time to time, and this can result in confusion when important notices are received at

the church's correct address but to an addressee whose name is unfamiliar to the person opening mail in the church office.

- Periodically contact the assessor's office to confirm the exempt status of church property as well as the church's name and address.
- The services of an attorney can be helpful in obtaining and maintaining a church's exemption from property taxes.

Byzantine Catholic Bishop v. County Assessor, 2011 WL 4444186 (Ore. Tax 2012).

47. Ohio Supreme Court ruling that an entire 80-acre tract owned by a church qualified for exemption from property taxation

After many years of expansion, a church decided to open a second church. It acquired 79 acres, on which it constructed a large church building with classrooms. The property includes two softball diamonds, a soccer field, and a jogging path that follows the circumference of the property. The church views itself as conducting a sports ministry in connection with the recreational portions of the property and conducts 14 events, including church-sponsored soccer teams and flag football games. Most of the participants in those events are community members who are not congregants of the church. The city also has sports leagues that use the property. During the summer months, the church stages a day camp for children age 6 through eighth grade, with several hundred participants. The jogging path is used by the general public without restriction. An estimated 3,000 people utilize the property each year, most of whom were not congregants of the church.

The church paid all costs to develop and maintain the property but does not charge the public to use the recreational facilities. The property does not generate income for the church. The mayor of the city testified that the city itself benefited because the church developed and made the property available for public use, thereby providing public recreational facilities that the city would otherwise have to pay for itself.

The church filed an application that sought to exempt the property from taxation. The application asked for an exemption of 58 acres as land associated with a house of public worship and sought exemption for another 21 acres as land used exclusively for a charitable use. A city tax commission ruled that the 21 acres, which were used exclusively for recreational purposes, did not qualify for exemption as land devoted to a charitable use. The commission concluded that the recreational property was used by the public, not the church, and therefore it was not eligible for exemption. The church appealed.

The Ohio Supreme Court ruled that the disputed 21 acres were exempt from taxation under a state law that exempted "property belonging to institutions that is used exclusively for charitable purposes." It rejected the commission's argument that "merely holding the property open to the public and allowing various third parties

to use it" is not a charitable use and "does not qualify [the property] for exemption." It also rejected the argument that church-owned property cannot qualify for a charitable exemption, noting that "any institution, irrespective of its charitable or noncharitable character, may take advantage of a tax exemption if it is making exclusive charitable use of the property."

This case is a useful precedent for any church that owns land used for recreational purposes. While not binding in any state other than Ohio, the case can be cited as persuasive authority for the proposition that land owned by a church and used for recreational purposes qualifies for exemption from taxation. *The Chapel v. Testa, 950 N.E.2d 142 (Ohio 2011).*

48. IRS to release guidance on church audits

Ruth Madrigal from the Treasury Department's Office of Tax Policy disclosed at a recent conference that the IRS soon will be releasing additional guidance on church audit procedures and protections.

49. Tax Court denial of charitable contribution deduction for services performed for a church without charge

A taxpayer owned and operated as a sole proprietorship a lawn care business. The taxpayer's church purchased a tract of 10 to 15 acres on which to build a house of worship. The taxpayer cleared the land for the church so it could begin construction. For each year in issue, he deducted as a charitable contribution the amount he would have billed the church for his services. The IRS audited the taxpayer's tax return and disallowed any charitable contribution deduction for the services he performed for his church without charge. The Tax Court affirmed the IRS position. It concluded:

> *[The tax code] allows a deduction for charitable contributions. A taxpayer may not, however, claim a deduction for services rendered to a charitable organization. The amounts of the taxpayer's charitable contributions in issue are for services he performed for his church. He testified that he cleared 10 to 15 acres of church-owned land so that a house of worship could be built. He also testified that for each of the years in issue he provided the church financial director a bill for his services. In return taxpayer stated that he was given a "receipt" or "paper" from the church confirming he had made a contribution to the church in the amount stated on the bill. He is not allowed charitable contribution deductions for the services he provided to the church.* Leak v. Commissioner., U.S. Tax Court, T.C. Summary Opinion 2012-39 (2012).

50. Small-employer health insurance tax credit

One of the main objectives of President Obama's health care reform law (the Affordable Care Act) was universal health coverage. The Act contains several provisions to achieve this goal. One of them is a new tax credit that will help small businesses and small tax-exempt organizations afford the cost of providing health insurance for their employees. The credit is up to 25 percent of the cost of health insurance premiums paid by a qualifying employer for its employees.

The new credit is specifically targeted for those employers with low- and moderate-income workers and is designed to encourage small employers to offer health insurance coverage for the first time or maintain coverage they already have. In general, the credit is available to small employers that pay at least half the cost of single coverage for their employees.

Many churches qualify for this credit. It is explained fully in Chapter 5, section D.7, of this text.

51. Social Security changes for 2013
See Table 5 for a summary of 2013 Social Security changes.

52. Retaining Forms W-2
It is a good practice for employees to keep copies of all Forms W-2 issued to them by their employer until they confirm that the earnings reported on their W-2s correspond to the earnings credited to them on the Social Security benefit statement that is automatically issued each year to all Americans aged 25 and over.

One of the main purposes of the Social Security benefit statement is to encourage taxpayers to check the accuracy of Social Security records and to make corrections. If earnings reflected on an employee's Social Security benefit statement are underreported, the easiest way to correct the record is for the employee to present a copy of his or her W-2 for the year in question to the nearest Social Security office. While proof of earnings is possible without a Form W-2, it is much more difficult and time consuming.

53. Changes in 2012 Form W-2 and Form W-3
The 2012 Form W-2 and Form W-3 are similar to the 2011 forms, but note the following:

- **Employee Social Security tax withholding.** The 4.2 percent rate of Social Security tax withholding (for employees only) is extended for wage payments made in 2012.
- **Form W-3, Kind of Employer.** To improve document matching compliance, box b of Form W-3 was expanded in 2011 to include a new section, Kind of Employer, which contains five new checkboxes. Filers are required to check one of these new checkboxes. Be sure to check the "None apply" checkbox if none of the other checkboxes apply. The specific instructions for the checkboxes in box b, Kind of Employer, of the 2012 Form W-3 include examples for various types of section 501(c) organizations.
- **Reporting the cost of coverage of group health insurance.** You must report the cost of employer-sponsored health coverage in box 12 using code DD. However, transitional relief applies to certain employers and certain types of plans.

54. Increase in wages subject to FICA tax
The FICA tax rate (7.65 percent for both employers and employees, or a combined tax of 15.3 percent) does not change in 2013. The

---

TABLE 5

2013 SOCIAL SECURITY AMOUNTS

	2013
Tax rate—employees	7.65%*
Tax rate—self-employed	15.3%
Maximum taxable earnings (Social Security tax only)	$113,700
Maximum taxable earnings (Medicare tax)	No limit
Retirement earnings tax-exempt amount (for workers under full retirement age)[†]	$15,120

*Churches and their nonminister employees are subject to Social Security and Medicare taxes (except for churches that exempted themselves from these taxes by filing a timely Form 8274 with the IRS, in which case their nonminister employees are treated as self-employed for Social Security purposes). The combined Social Security and Medicare tax rate is 15.3 percent of each employee's wages. This rate is paid equally by the employer and employee, with each paying a tax of 7.65 percent of the employee's wages. This 7.65 percent rate is comprised of two components: (1) a Medicare hospital insurance (HI) tax of 1.45 percent and (2) an old-age, survivor, and disability (Social Security) tax of 6.2 percent. For 2011 and 2012, Congress provided a temporary payroll tax holiday of two percentage points off the employee share of Social Security tax. This meant that the employee's share of Social Security taxes dropped from 6.2 to 4.2 percent of wages for 2011 and 2012. It is unlikely that Congress will extend the lower rates for 2013 or future years. Check the Social Security Administration website for current information.

[†] Your Social Security retirement benefits are reduced if your earnings exceed a certain level, called a "retirement earnings test exempt amount," and if you are under your "normal retirement age" (NRA). NRA, also referred to as "full retirement age," varies from age 65 to age 67 by year of birth. For persons born in 1943–1954, the NRA is 66 years. For people attaining NRA after 2012, the annual exempt amount in 2013 is $15,120, meaning that you can earn up to this amount with no reduction in Social Security retirement benefits. For every $2 earned above this amount, Social Security retirement benefits are reduced by $1. A modified annual earnings test applies in the year a worker attains full retirement age. Social Security benefits are reduced by $1 for every $3 of earnings above a specified amount for each month prior to full retirement age. (This amount is $3,340 for 2013.) Beginning with the month an individual attains full retirement age, no reduction in Social Security retirement benefits occurs, no matter how much the person earns.

7.65 percent tax rate is comprised of two components: (1) a Medicare hospital insurance (HI) tax of 1.45 percent and (2) a Social Security (old-age, survivor, and disability) tax of 6.2 percent. No maximum amount exists for wages subject to the Medicare hospital insurance (the 1.45 percent HI tax rate). The tax is imposed on all wages, regardless of amount. For 2013 the maximum wages subject to the Social Security portion of FICA taxes (the 6.2 percent amount) increases to $113,700. Stated differently, employees who receive wages in excess of $113,700 in 2013 pay the full 7.65 percent tax rate for wages up to $113,700 and the HI tax rate of 1.45 percent on all earnings above $113,700. Employers pay an identical amount.

Congress enacted legislation reducing the Social Security portion of FICA and self-employment taxes by two percentage points in 2011 and 2012. This meant that a nonminister employee's share of the Social Security component of FICA taxes decreased from 6.2 to 4.2 percent of wages. It is unlikely that Congress will extend the lower rates for 2013 or future years. Check the Social Security Administration website for current information.

55. IRS postponement of enforcing new nondiscrimination rules for insured group health plans

Section 10101(d) of the Patient Protection and Affordable Care Act (the Affordable Care Act) adds section 2716 to the Public Health Service Act (PHS Act). Section 2716 provides that an insured group health plan must satisfy the nondiscrimination requirements of section 105(h)(2) of the tax code (i.e., the plan does not discriminate in favor of highly compensated individuals as to eligibility to participate, and the benefits provided under the plan do not discriminate in favor of participants who are highly compensated individuals).

Section 2716 specifies that the term "highly compensated individual" in this context has the meaning given by section 105(h)(5) (an individual who is one of the five highest paid officers, or among the highest paid 25 percent of all employees (other than employees who have not completed three years of service, or not attained age 25, or are part-time or seasonal employees).

An insured group health plan that fails to comply with these rules may be subject to (1) an excise tax of $100 for each day in the noncompliance period with respect to each individual to whom such failure relates, limited in the case of failures due to reasonable cause and not applicable in limited circumstances, such as where a failure is due to reasonable cause and not to willful neglect and is corrected within a specified time period), or (2) a civil action to enjoin a noncompliant act or practice or for other appropriate equitable relief.

The Treasury Department and the IRS, as well as the Departments of Labor and Health and Human Services (collectively, the Departments), have determined that compliance with section 2716 should not be required (and thus, any sanctions for failure to comply do not apply) until after regulations or other administrative guidance of general applicability have been issued. In order to provide insured group health plan sponsors time to implement any changes required as a result of the regulations or other guidance, the Departments anticipate that the guidance will not apply until plan years beginning

a specified period after issuance. Before the beginning of those plan years, an insured group health plan sponsor will not be required to file IRS Form 8928 with respect to excise taxes resulting from the incorporation of section 2716 into the tax code.

IRS Notice 2011-1 concludes: "Thus, if a self-insured plan fails to comply with §105(h), highly compensated individuals lose a tax benefit; if an insured group health plan fails to comply with section 2716, the plan or plan sponsor may be subject to an excise tax, civil money penalty, or a civil action to compel it to provide nondiscriminatory benefits."

56. The IRS's "Dirty Dozen" tax scams

Each year the IRS publishes a list of the "Dirty Dozen," 12 of the most blatant tax scams affecting American taxpayers. The list for 2012 included attempts by donors to maintain control over donated assets and various schemes involving the donation of noncash assets. Often, donations of noncash property are highly overvalued or the charity receiving the donation promises that the donor can purchase the items back at a later date at a price the donor sets. The Pension Protection Act of 2006 imposed increased penalties for inaccurate appraisals and new definitions of qualified appraisals and qualified appraisers for taxpayers claiming charitable contributions.

57. Charitable contribution deduction disallowed for lack of substantiation

A married couple (the "taxpayers") timely filed their 2007 income tax return. On their attached Schedule A, the taxpayers claimed a deduction of $25,171 for charitable contributions made by cash or check. Most of the contributions were made by check to their church. Except for five checks totaling $317, the checks the taxpayers wrote to their church were for amounts larger than $250. In 2009 the IRS sent a notice to the taxpayers disallowing their charitable contribution deduction for 2007. In response, the taxpayers produced records of their contributions, including copies of canceled checks and a letter from the church that acknowledged contributions from them during 2007 totaling $22,517 (the "first acknowledgment"). The IRS did not accept the first acknowledgment and informed the taxpayers that it lacked a statement regarding whether any goods or services were provided in consideration for the contributions.

The taxpayers obtained a second letter from the church (the "second acknowledgment") that contained the same information found in the first acknowledgment as well as a statement that no goods or services were provided to them in exchange for their contributions.

The IRS concluded that the taxpayers were not entitled to a deduction for any of their contributions of $250 or more because of their failure to comply with the substantiation requirements. It noted that the church's first letter to the taxpayers failed to comply with the written acknowledgment requirement because it did not include a statement regarding whether any goods or services were provided in consideration for their contribution. And the second letter, which included the statement, was not contemporaneous. The couple conceded that they had not strictly complied with the tax code's substantiation requirements. But they insisted that they had substantially complied with the requirements and therefore were entitled to deduct their contributions.

The Tax Court agreed with the IRS and denied any deduction for contributions of $250 or more. The taxpayers claimed that the omission of a statement regarding goods or services in the church's first letter was sufficient to indicate that no goods or services were provided in consideration for their contributions. The court disagreed, noting that "the express terms of the statute require an affirmative statement." The court also agreed with the IRS that the church's second letter, which included the required statement that no goods or services were provided to the donors in consideration of their contribution, did not meet the tax code's "contemporaneous" requirement because it was issued after the earlier of the date on which the taxpayer files a return for the taxable year in which the contribution was made or the due date (including extensions) for filing such return.

The court rejected the taxpayers' argument that they should be allowed to deduct their donations to their church because they had "substantially complied" with the tax code's substantiation requirements. It acknowledged that it had found substantial compliance in prior cases that involved compliance with the "essential purpose" of the substantiation requirements despite a lack of strict compliance. But in the present case, the taxpayers had not complied with the "essential purpose" of the law, which includes both the contemporaneous requirement and the requirement that the charity's written acknowledgement indicate whether any goods or services were provided in consideration of the contribution. *Durden v. Commissioner, TC Memo. 2012-140 (2012).*

EXPLANATION OF TERMS

A few legal terms are used occasionally in this book. They are listed below, along with definitions to assist you in understanding the text.

Internal Revenue Code (the "tax code," "Code," or "IRC")
The federal tax law enacted by Congress. It covers several subjects, including federal income taxes, Social Security taxes, and withholding and estimated tax procedures. It is important to recognize that Congress, not the IRS, enacts federal tax laws. The IRS is an administrative agency established by Congress to assist in the administration of the tax laws enacted by Congress.

Regulations ("Treasury regulations" or "Treas. Reg.")
Regulations are interpretations of the Internal Revenue Code issued by the Treasury Department. They provide taxpayers with guidance as to the meaning and application of the Code. They are inferior to and may never contradict the Code itself.

Internal Revenue Service (IRS)
An administrative agency that is part of the Treasury Department. It was created by Congress and exists to administer and enforce federal tax laws. It is subordinate to Congress and has no authority to make law.

Revenue rulings ("Rev. Rul.") and Revenue procedures ("Rev. Proc.")
Official pronouncements of the national office of the IRS. Like regulations, they are designed to provide guidance on tax issues. Usually they pertain to a specific issue. They are inferior in authority to both the Code and regulations.

IRS Private Letter Rulings ("IRS Letter Rulings")
IRS responses to individual tax questions submitted by taxpayers. These letters can be relied upon only by the taxpayers to whom they are specifically directed. They cannot be cited or used as precedent by other taxpayers in similar circumstances.

AGI
Adjusted gross income.

Court decisions
A number of federal court decisions are referred to in the text. The initials "S. Ct." or "U.S." refer to a United States Supreme Court decision. The initials "F.2d" or "F.3d" refer to a federal appeals court decision. The initials "F. Supp." refer to a federal district court decision. The initials "T.C." or "T.C.M." refer to a decision of the United States Tax Court. However, note that the initials "T.C." refer to a ruling by all 19 judges comprising the full United States Tax Court, while the initials "T.C.M." refer to a "memorandum" decision by only one Tax Court judge. Tax Court decisions rendered by all 19 judges ("T.C.") have much more presidential value than memorandum decisions. United States Supreme Court rulings are binding in all state and federal courts. Federal appeals court rulings are binding in all federal courts in the respective federal circuit (there are 11 geographical circuits). Federal district court and tax court decisions ordinarily are not binding on any other court. Any federal court has the authority to interpret contested provisions of the tax code.

1 THE INCOME TAX RETURN

Tax collectors also came to be baptized. "Teacher," they asked, "what should we do?"
"Don't collect any more than you are required to," he told them.

Luke 3:12–13

CHAPTER HIGHLIGHTS

■ *Ministers not exempt from taxes.* Ministers are not exempt from paying federal income taxes.

■ *Filing a tax return.* Ministers are required to file a federal income tax return if they have earnings of $400 or more (if they are not exempt from Social Security).

■ *Form 1040.* Most ministers must use Form 1040 (rather than Form 1040A or 1040EZ).

■ *Penalties.* Ministers are subject to substantial penalties for not filing a tax return (if required) and for reporting inaccurate information on a tax return.

■ *Audit risk.* The risk of being audited is small. But it is much higher for self-employed persons and even higher for self-employed persons who receive only one or two Forms 1099-MISC (as is true for many ministers who report their federal income taxes under self-employed status).

■ *Exemption from income tax withholding.* Ministers are exempt from federal tax withholding, whether they report their income taxes as employees or as self-employed. However, if a minister reports income taxes as an employee, he or she may request voluntary withholding of income taxes and self-employment taxes.

■ *Estimated taxes.* Since ministers are exempt from federal tax withholding, they must prepay their income taxes and self-employment taxes by using the estimated tax reporting procedure. The only exception would be ministers who report their income taxes as employees and who elect voluntary withholding of both income taxes and self-employment taxes. Estimated taxes must be paid in quarterly installments. Use IRS Form 1040-ES.

A. FILING YOUR RETURN

1. CLERGY NOT EXEMPT FROM FEDERAL INCOME TAXES

❂ **KEY POINT.** Ministers are not exempt from paying federal taxes.

The United States Supreme Court has ruled that the First Amendment guaranty of religious freedom is not violated by subjecting ministers to the federal income tax. *Murdock v. Pennsylvania, 319 U.S. 105 (1943).*

The courts have rejected every attempt by ministers (some with mail-order credentials) to claim exemption from income taxes. Examples of arguments that have been rejected by the courts include the following:

- A minister claimed that his income was not taxable, since he was "a minister of the gospel of Jesus Christ living by the grace and mercy of God, and not by receipt of worldly income."
- A minister attempted to avoid income taxes by characterizing his compensation as "remuneration received for assigned services as an agent of the church, and not income or wages."
- A minister claimed that the religious tenets of his church forbade members to pay income taxes, therefore it would violate the first amendment guaranty of religious freedom for him to be required to pay taxes.
- A minister stopped filing tax returns when his study of the Bible led him to the conclusion that he was a "one-man church."
- A minister defended his refusal to pay income taxes by claiming that he was not a citizen of the United States but rather of "that place where one day I intend to permanently reside, which is Heaven," and that he had been "supernaturally provided for by the Lord Jesus Christ through the unsolicited free-will love offerings of others" and received no taxable wages.

All of these claims, and many like them, are treated as frivolous by the IRS and the courts. Often such ministers are required to pay substantial penalties in addition to back taxes and interest.

EXAMPLE. A federal court rejected a couple's claim that they were entitled to an exemption from federal income tax because they "labor for the ministry." The court concluded, "Income received by ministers whether from the church itself or from other private employers or sources is not exempt from income tax. The income received by taxpayers must be included in gross income required to be reported for income tax purposes according to the Internal Revenue Code." The court acknowledged that ministers' income (from the exercise of ministry) is exempt from federal income tax withholding but noted that "while certain income of ministers may be exempt from withholding of income tax, the income received by ministers, even from religious activities . . . is not exempt from payment of income tax." Further, "the fact that a church itself may be exempt from payment of income taxes does not mean that the income received by ministers is exempt." *Pomeroy v. Commissioner, 2003-2 USTC 50,568 (D. Nev. 2003).*

Tax protestors

Some tax protestors use religion in a futile attempt to excuse the nonpayment of taxes. Some argue that payment of income taxes violates their constitutional right to freely exercise their religion, and many have attempted to escape taxes through the creation of "mail-order churches." Unfortunately, such cases, along with celebrated televangelist scandals and excesses, have encouraged a governmental cynicism toward churches and ministers.

Here are some tax positions the IRS and courts consider frivolous:

- The Sixteenth Amendment (which permits a federal income tax) is invalid because it contradicts the Constitution.
- A taxpayer can make a "claim of right" to exclude the cost of his labor from income.
- Only income from a foreign source is taxable.
- Citizens of states, such as New York, are citizens of a foreign country and therefore not subject to tax.
- A taxpayer can escape income tax by putting assets in an offshore bank account.
- A taxpayer can eliminate tax by establishing a corporation sole (discussed below).
- A taxpayer can place all of his assets in a trust to escape income tax while still retaining control over those assets.
- Nothing in the tax code imposes a requirement to file a return.
- Filing a tax return is voluntary.
- Because taxes are voluntary, employers don't have to withhold income or employment taxes from employees.
- A taxpayer can refuse to pay taxes if the taxpayer disagrees with the government's use of the taxes it collects.
- A taxpayer can avoid taxation by filing a return that reports zero income and zero tax liability.
- A taxpayer can avoid taxation by filing a return with an attachment that disclaims tax liability.
- A taxpayer can deduct the amount of Social Security taxes he or she paid and get a refund of those taxes.
- A taxpayer may sell (or purchase) the right to use dependents in order to increase the amount of the earned income credit.

- Income taxes violate the Constitution's ban on involuntary servitude and self-incrimination.
- The United States Tax Court is unconstitutional.
- Income received in the form of paper currency (Federal Reserve notes) is not legal tender, since it is not redeemable in gold or silver, and is not taxable as income until paid in gold or silver.
- Claiming deductions or tax credits to avoid supporting war, defense, or abortion.
- Claiming excessive withholding allowances on Form W-4. Tax protestors are active in promoting their views on websites and in seminars, and they often appear convincing to the uninformed.

✹ **KEY POINT.** Congress has increased the penalty for claiming frivolous positions on a tax return from $500 to $5,000.

Congress has enacted legislation designed to discourage the use of tax protestor arguments. Besides the normal penalties for failure to pay taxes (including potential criminal penalties for willfully evading taxes or refusing to file a return), tax protestors face an array of additional penalties, including a $5,000 penalty for claiming a "frivolous" position on a tax return and a $25,000 penalty for maintaining a frivolous tax position (or a position designed solely for delay) before the Tax Court. *IRC 6702, 6673.*

Corporations sole

Some persons are promoting the use of "corporations sole" by churches and church members as a lawful way to avoid all government laws and regulations, including income taxes and payroll taxes. Church leaders are informed that by structuring their church as a corporation sole, they will become an "ecclesiastical" entity beyond the jurisdiction of the government. Individuals are told that by becoming a corporation sole, they can avoid paying income taxes. The promoters, who often use e-mail and the Internet, make it all sound believable with numerous references to legal dictionaries, judges, and ancient cases. As this section will demonstrate, such claims are false. Any material you receive promoting the corporation sole scam should be discarded.

What is a corporation sole?

A corporation sole is a type of corporation that allows the incorporation of a religious office, such as the office of bishop. One court described such corporations sole as follows:

A corporation sole enables a bona fide religious leader, such as a bishop or other authorized church or other religious official, to incorporate under state law, in his capacity as a religious official. One purpose of the corporation sole is to ensure the continuation of ownership of property dedicated to the benefit of a religious organization which may be held in the name of its chief officer. A corporation sole may own property and enter into contracts as a natural person, but only for the purposes of the religious entity and not for the individual office holder's personal benefit. Title to property that vests in the office holder as a corporation sole passes not to the office holder's heirs, but to the successors to the office by operation of law. A legitimate corporation sole is designed to ensure continuity of ownership of property dedicated to the benefit of a legitimate religious organization.

Corporations sole are recognized in only the following 11 states: Alabama, Alaska, Arizona, California, Colorado, Hawaii, Montana, Nevada, Oregon, Washington, and Wyoming. If your church is not in one of these states, it cannot form a corporation sole, and you should ignore any information you receive to the contrary.

A typical example of a corporation sole statute is section 10002 of the California Corporations Code (enacted in 1878), which provides: "A corporation sole may be formed under this part by the bishop, chief priest, presiding elder, or other presiding officer of any religious denomination, society, or church, for the purpose of administering and managing the affairs, property, and temporalities thereof." Section 10008 specifies that "every corporation sole has perpetual existence and also has continuity of existence, notwithstanding vacancies in the incumbency thereof."

These sections in the California Corporations Code illustrate the purpose of the corporation sole—to provide for the incorporation of an ecclesiastical office so that it is not affected by changes in the persons who occupy that office. The corporation sole is designed for use by an individual ecclesiastical officer and not by churches or other religious organizations.

Are corporations sole exempt from government laws?

Absolutely not. Consider the following two points. First, a church cannot incorporate as a corporation sole. Only the presiding officer of a religious organization can do so. A church officer's decision to incorporate as a corporation sole has no effect on the relationship of the church with the government.

Second, not one word in any corporation sole statute suggests that a corporation sole is an "ecclesiastical corporation" no longer subject to the laws or jurisdiction of the government. In fact, most corporation sole statutes clarify that such corporations *are* subject to all governmental laws and regulations. A good example is the California Corporations Code, which specifies that "the articles of incorporation may state any desired provision for the regulation of the affairs of the corporation *in a manner not in conflict with law*" (emphasis added).

Similarly, the Oregon corporations sole statute specifies that such corporations differ from other corporations "only in that they shall have no board of directors, need not have officers and shall be managed by a single director who shall be the individual constituting the corporation and its incorporator or the successor of the incorporator." This is hardly a license to avoid compliance with tax or reporting obligations. Nothing in the corporation sole statutes of any state would remotely suggest such a conclusion.

In summary, a church officer who incorporates as a corporation sole will not exempt his or her church from having to withhold taxes from employees' wages, issue Forms W-2 and Forms 1099-MISC, file quarterly Forms 941 with the IRS, or comply with any other law or regulation. Further, an officer who incorporates as a corporation sole will not insulate his or her church from legal liability.

Can individuals avoid taxes by forming a corporation sole?

No. In fact, the IRS has issued a warning to persons who promote or succumb to such scams. *See Revenue Ruling 2004-27.* The IRS noted that participants in these scams are provided with a state identification number that can be used to open financial accounts. They claim that their income is exempt from federal and state taxation because this income belongs to the corporation sole, a tax-exempt organization. Participants may further claim that, because their assets are held by the corporation sole, they are not subject to collection actions for the payment of federal or state income taxes or for the payment of other obligations, such as child support.

The IRS has noted that promoters, including return preparers, are recommending that taxpayers take frivolous positions based on this argument. Some promoters are marketing a package, kit, or other materials that claim to show taxpayers how they can avoid paying income taxes based on this and other meritless arguments. The IRS concluded:

A taxpayer cannot avoid income tax or other financial responsibilities by purporting to be a religious leader and forming a corporation sole for tax avoidance purposes. The claims that such a corporation sole is described in section 501(c)(3) and that assignment of income and transfer of assets to such an entity will exempt an individual from income tax are meritless. Courts repeatedly have rejected similar arguments as frivolous, imposed penalties for making such arguments, and upheld criminal tax evasion convictions against those making or promoting the use of such arguments.

EXAMPLE. The Tax Court has observed that while corporations sole cannot be used by individuals to evade taxes, they are a legitimate legal entity when used for their intended purpose. It defined a corporation sole as "a corporate form authorized under certain state laws to enable bona fide religious leaders to hold property and conduct business for the benefit of the religious entity" and noted that the corporation sole "originated in the common law of England, where it was used to ensure that property dedicated to the church would remain so, rather than passing to the heirs of the bishop or other church leader. The corporation sole operates to ensure that property held in the name of the church's titular head passes, by operation of law, to his successors in office." The court concluded that a pastor's establishment of a bona fide church as a corporation sole was not evidence of a scheme to evade taxes: "Because we have concluded that the church was a legitimate church, we reject [the IRS's] contention that [the pastor's] choice to organize it as a corporation sole suggests that he fraudulently intended to evade taxes." The court stressed that churches, whether formed as corporations

TABLE 1-1

ADJUSTED FILING REQUIREMENTS FOR 2012
(for persons under 65 years of age)

FILING STATUS	STANDARD DEDUCTION	PERSONAL EXEMPTIONS	FILE IF GROSS INCOME EXCEEDS
Single	$5,950	$3,800	$9,750
Married filing jointly	$11,900	$7,600	$19,500
Married filing separately	$5,950	$3,800	$3,800
Head of household	$8,700	$3,800	$12,500
Surviving spouse	$11,900	$3,800	$15,700

TABLE 1-2

ADJUSTED FILING REQUIREMENTS FOR 2012
(for persons 65 or older)

FILING STATUS	FILE IF GROSS INCOME EXCEEDS
Joint return, one spouse age 65 or older	$20,650
Joint return, both spouses age 65 or older	$21,800
Single, age 65 or older	$11,200
Head of household, age 65 or older	$13,650
Married filing separately, age 65 or blind	$3,800
Surviving spouse, age 65 or older	$16,850

sole or not, are exempt from federal income taxes, so organizing a legitimate church as a corporation sole could not be characterized as tax evasion. *101 T.C.M. 1550 (2011).*

Members of religious or apostolic associations

Ministers who are members of religious or apostolic associations having a common treasury do not have to report any income received in connection with duties required by the association if they have taken a vow of poverty and no portion of the net income of the association is distributable to them. *See Revenue Procedure 72-5, IRC 501(d).* If a member of an association has a share in its net income, then he or she must include such share (whether distributed or not) in gross income as a dividend received. The association must file an annual information return (Form 1065) along with a Schedule K-1 that identifies the members of the association and their portions of net income and expenses. However, such associations are not required to publicly disclose Schedule K-1.

2. WHO MUST FILE A RETURN

Not everyone is required to file an individual federal income tax return (Form 1040). For 2012 a federal income tax return (with appropriate schedules) must be filed only if your gross income exceeds your applicable standard deduction plus personal exemptions (an exception is made for married taxpayers filing separately). Tables 1-1 and 1-2 illustrate the filing requirements for most persons.

✱ **New in 2012.** For 2012 the standard deduction amount (listed in Table 1-1) increases by $1,450 for single persons if either age 65 or older or blind ($2,900 if both) and $1,150 for married

persons filing jointly if either spouse is age 65 or older or blind ($2,300 if a spouse is both age 65 or older and blind, and $4,600 if both are age 65 or older and blind). This adjustment in the standard deduction amount will affect the filing requirements of some taxpayers, as illustrated in Table 1-2.

EXAMPLE. Pastor L is 67 years of age. His spouse is 66. Pastor L filed an application for exemption from Social Security coverage that was approved by the IRS in 1980. Pastor L and his spouse file a joint return for 2012. Their standard deduction for 2012 is $14,200 ($11,900 basic standard deduction plus an additional $1,150 for each spouse because each is at least 65 years of age). Since Pastor L and his spouse are each entitled to a personal exemption of $3,800, they need not file a return for 2012 unless their income exceeds $21,800.

✱ **New in 2012.** The amount of income needed to file a federal tax return increased in 2012 for most taxpayers.

The standard filing requirements are subject to an important exception—any taxpayer who has net earnings from self-employment of $400 or more must file an income tax return even if his or her gross income is less than the minimum amounts discussed above. This exception can apply to ministers in either of two ways:

Ministers who report their income taxes as employees

Ministers are treated as self-employed for Social Security purposes with respect to services performed in the exercise of their ministry, even if they report their federal income taxes as employees. As a result, ministers who report their income taxes as employees must file a tax return for 2012 if they had net ministerial (or other self employment) compensation of $400 or more.

However, ministers who report their income taxes as employees and who have applied for and received IRS recognition of exemption from self-employment (Social Security) taxes are subject to the higher filing requirements discussed above unless they have net self-employment earnings of $400 or more from some other source. Such sources can include secular self-employment activities, guest speaking appearances in other churches, or fees received directly from church members for performing personal services such as funerals, weddings, and baptisms. See Chapter 9 for details regarding the exemption from self-employment taxes.

Ministers who report their income taxes as self-employed persons

Ministers who report their federal income taxes as self-employed persons and who receive net earnings of at least $400 from the performance of ministerial (or secular) duties must file a federal tax return regardless of whether they are exempt from Social Security coverage.

✿ **KEY POINT.** Ministers are required to file a federal income tax return if they have net self-employment earnings of $400 or more from any source.

EXAMPLE. Pastor T has never exempted himself from Social Security coverage. He is single, works part time as an associate pastor of a church, and received $7,500 in compensation from the church in 2012. He has no other income. Pastor T must file an income tax return. While single persons ordinarily are not required to file a return (for 2012) if they earn less than $9,500, they must file if they have net earnings from self-employment of $400 or more. Since Pastor T is self-employed for Social Security purposes with respect to services performed in the exercise of his ministry, he must file a return if he has net earnings of $400 or more.

3. WHICH FORM TO USE

✿ **KEY POINT.** Most clergy must use Form 1040 (rather than Form 1040A or Form 1040EZ).

You must use Form 1040 if you meet any one of several conditions, including any one or more of the following:

- Your taxable income is $100,000 or more.
- You itemize your deductions.
- You had income that cannot be reported on Form 1040EZ or Form 1040A.
- You claim any adjustments to gross income other than the adjustments listed on Form 1040A.
- Your Form W-2, box 12, shows uncollected employee tax (Social Security and Medicare tax) on group term life insurance.
- You claim any credits other than those listed on Form 1040A.
- You have to file other forms with your return to report certain exclusions, taxes, or transactions.
- You pay self-employment taxes (reported on Schedule SE).

✿ **KEY POINT.** Nonminister employees of a church that elected to exempt itself from the employer's share of FICA taxes by filing a timely Form 8274 with the IRS must use Form 1040 if they receive wages of $108.28 or more.

Most clergy must use Form 1040, since they will have income from self-employment (remember that ministers always are treated as self-employed for Social Security purposes with respect to their ministerial services). It is possible, however, for a minister to qualify for the simpler Form 1040A if he or she (1) has applied for and received IRS recognition of exemption from self-employment taxes, (2) reports income taxes as an employee, (3) has no self-employment earnings from any source (ministerial or secular), (4) has less than $100,000 in taxable income, and (5) does not itemize deductions.

EXAMPLE. Pastor A is senior minister of a church. He has exempted himself from self-employment (Social Security) taxes, earned $45,000 in 2012 from the church (his only source of income), and does not plan to itemize deductions. Pastor A may be eligible to use the simpler Form 1040A. However, he must use Form 1040 if he satisfies any one or more of several conditions listed above.

4. ELECTRONIC FILING

An increasing number of taxpayers are choosing to use e-file, which lets them electronically file an accurate tax return or get an extension of time to file without sending any paper to the IRS. The 2012 filing season set a series of records, highlighted by 100 million tax returns being filed electronically, representing 70 percent of all individual tax returns.

The IRS expects further increases in e-filers in future years because of the following benefits:

(1) Taxpayers receive faster refunds (average e-file refund is issued in 14 days).
(2) IRS computers quickly and automatically check for errors or other missing information, making e-filed returns more accurate and reducing the chance of getting an error letter from the IRS.
(3) Computer e-filers receive an acknowledgment that the IRS has received their returns.
(4) Taxpayers can create their own Personal Identification Number (PIN) and file a completely paperless return using their tax preparation software or tax professional, meaning there is nothing to mail to the IRS.
(5) E-filers with a balance due can schedule a safe and convenient electronic funds withdrawal from their bank account or pay with a credit card.
(6) Taxpayers in most states and the District of Columbia can e-file their federal and state tax returns in one transmission

to the IRS. You can electronically file a federal tax return in three ways: through a tax professional, using a personal computer, or using Free File.

✻ New in 2012. A recently passed law requires certain paid tax-return preparers to electronically file federal income tax returns that they prepare and file for individuals, trusts, and estates. Those are Forms 1040, 1040A, 1040EZ, and 1041.

E-filing with a tax professional

Most tax professionals file returns electronically for their clients. You can prepare your own return and have a professional transmit it electronically, or you can have a professional both prepare it and transmit it. Look for the "Authorized IRS e-file Provider" sign. Tax professionals may charge a fee to e-file your return. Your tax professional will ask you to sign Form 8453 (Declaration for Electronic Filing). Both spouses must sign if a joint return is being filed. Your tax professional will file the form with the IRS and will give you the required preparer-signed copy of your return, including a copy of the completed Form 8453. This material is for your records. Do not mail this copy to the IRS. Your tax professional can file your return electronically any time during the filing season; however, sending the payment for a balance due by April 15 is still your responsibility. You may pay a balance due to the IRS by check, direct debit, or credit card. All balance-due payments, regardless of method of payment, must be authorized or sent to the IRS by April 15 to avoid late-payment penalties or interest charges.

E-filing using a personal computer

If you have a computer, Internet connection, and tax preparation software, you can e-file your return electronically from your home. Here's how it works: You prepare your tax return on a personal computer, using commercially available software, and transmit the information via the Internet to an electronic return transmitter that converts the file you send to a format that meets IRS specifications and transmits it to the IRS. The IRS checks the return and notifies the transmitter (who then informs you) whether the return has been accepted or rejected. Most returns are accepted the first time they are transmitted. If you choose not to use a Self-Select PIN as your signature, or if you have certain paper forms to submit, you will need to mail in a paper signature document. You will send the completed Form 8453 to the appropriate IRS service center when the electronic return is accepted. Signing this document indicates that you have verified and agree with the return information. If your return is not accepted, the electronic return transmitter will provide you with customer support to correct your return and resubmit it.

➠ TIP. In several states you can simultaneously e-file your federal and state tax returns.

Free File

Another option for filing your tax return is Free File. This program stemmed from negotiations between the government and the commercial tax software industry on ways to provide free tax software and free e-filing services to taxpayers with modest incomes. The private sector agreed to provide the free services to at least 60 percent of the nation's taxpayers as part of the initial contract. In return the IRS agreed to not create its own tax preparation software. Members of the tax software industry (Free File Alliance) provide these free tax preparation and electronic filing services, not the IRS. Once you choose a particular company, you will be sent directly to the company's commercial website. A list of companies is provided on the IRS website.

The Free File program is limited to taxpayers with an adjusted gross income (AGI) of $57,000 or less. Taxpayers who used Free File in past filing seasons might not qualify for the free services for the 2012 filing season. Each participating software company sets its own eligibility requirements. After choosing a company, click on the company's title, which sends you directly to the company's website. You may then begin the preparation of your tax return. The company's software prepares and e-files your income tax returns using proprietary processes and systems. Electronically filed returns are transmitted by the company to the IRS using the established e-file system, which uses secure telephone lines. An acknowledgment file, notifying you that the return has been either accepted or rejected, is sent via e-mail from the company.

If you do not qualify for the selected company's free offer, you may want to check other Free File company offers by accessing the IRS Free File web page. If you do not qualify for the company's free offer but continue with the preparation and e-filing process with this company, please be aware that you will be charged a fee for preparing and e-filing your federal tax return.

❖ KEY POINT. Charges may apply to the preparation of state tax returns.

5. PAYING INCOME TAXES WITH A CREDIT CARD

Taxpayers can make credit- and debit-card payments whether they file electronically or file a paper return. Payments can be submitted via tax software when filing electronically. Credit- and debit-card payments can also be made over the telephone or online.

The IRS does not set or collect any fee for card payments. However, the IRS authorizes private companies processing the payments to charge a convenience fee. The taxes paid and convenience fee are listed separately on your statement.

Some tax-software developers offer integrated e-file and e-pay combinations for those who choose to use a credit or debit card to pay a balance due. The software accepts both the electronic tax return and the card information. The tax return and tax payment data are forwarded to the IRS, and the card data is forwarded to the payment processor.

For the current filing season, the IRS has contracted with three companies to accept credit- and debit-card payments from both electronic and paper filers. Each company offers both phone and Internet payment services, and each charges a convenience fee for the service. Fees are based on the amount of the tax payment and may vary between companies. The three companies are

- Official Payments Corporation, 1-888-UPAY-TAX (1-888-872-9829), 1-877-754-4413 (Customer Service);
- Link2Gov Corporation, 1-888-PAY-1040 (1-888-729-1040), 1-888-658-5465 (Customer Service); and
- RBS WorldPay, Inc., 1-888-9-PAY-TAX (1-888-972-9829), 1-888-877-0450 (Customer Service).

Anyone may use these services to charge taxes to credit cards including American Express, Discover, MasterCard, or VISA.

Taxpayers also can pay taxes electronically by authorizing an e-pay option, such as an electronic funds withdrawal from a checking or savings account.

Individuals can use any of these options to (1) pay taxes owed on an income tax return; (2) pay projected tax due when requesting an automatic extension of time to file; (3) pay quarterly estimated taxes; or (4) make a credit-card payment for past-due tax.

Employers, including churches, can use these options to make a credit-card payment for taxes owed on employment tax returns (Form 941). The payment can be made for the balance on the current return that is due. See the IRS website (irs.gov) for details.

6. RECORDKEEPING

You must keep records so that you can prepare a complete and accurate income tax return. The law does not require any special form of records. However, you should keep all receipts, canceled checks, and other evidence to prove amounts you claim as deductions, exclusions, or credits. Records should be retained for as long as they are important for any income tax law. In general you should keep records that support an item of income or a deduction appearing on a return until the statute of limitations (the period during which the IRS can audit your return) runs out. Usually this is three years after the date a return was filed (or three years after the due date of the return, if later). However, in some cases it is wise to keep records for a longer period of time, since a six-year limitations period applies in some situations, and in others (e.g., no return was filed or a return was fraudulent) there is no time limitation on the authority of the IRS to begin an audit. The time limitation rules are summarized later in this chapter (section A.15).

Specific recordkeeping requirements with respect to the following exclusions and deductions are discussed later in this tax guide:

- Housing allowances (Chapter 6)
- Business expenses (Chapter 7)
- Charitable contributions (Chapter 8)

Records of transactions affecting the basis (cost) of some assets should be retained until after the expiration of the limitations period for the tax year in which the asset is sold.

✿ **KEY POINT.** Churches have recordkeeping requirements too. These requirements are addressed in Chapter 11.

7. HOW TO FIGURE YOUR TAX

Here are some basics you need to know when figuring your tax.

Gross income

If you file Form 1040 (rather than Form 1040A), you must find your gross income, AGI, and taxable income before you can figure your tax. Gross income is your income after deducting all exclusions allowed by law. It is the starting point for determining your tax liability, and its various components are reported directly on Form 1040 (lines 7–22).

Since gross income is net of any exclusions, *no exclusions are reported on Form 1040*. Exclusions are discussed fully in Chapters 5 and 6 of this tax guide.

EXAMPLE. Pastor M rents his home, and his church provided him with a rental allowance of $10,000 for 2012. Assuming that Pastor M had actual rental expenses of at least $10,000 in 2012, his gross income would not reflect the $10,000 allowance, since it is an exclusion from gross income. This means that Pastor M's Form W-2 (box 1) would report his church compensation less the $10,000. Pastor M should report his church compensation less the $10,000 as wages on line 7 of Form 1040. This is the approach taken by the IRS in Publication 517. Note, however, that the housing allowance is an exclusion for federal income tax purposes only. It must be included in Pastor M's self-employment earnings (Schedule SE of Form 1040) in computing his self-employment tax liability (assuming he has not exempted himself from Social Security coverage).

Adjusted gross income (AGI)

AGI is gross income minus various adjustments that are reported on Form 1040, lines 23–37.

Taxable income

If you do not itemize deductions, your taxable income is your AGI less the standard deduction ($5,950 for single persons and

$11,900 for married persons filing jointly) and less the deduction for your exemptions. If you itemize your deductions, your taxable income is your AGI less your itemized deductions and less your deduction for your exemptions. If you must itemize your deductions (this rule applies to various categories of taxpayers, including a married person filing a separate return if his or her spouse itemizes deductions), then you should refer to the instructions accompanying Form 1040 for the more complicated rules that apply in such a case. The rules described above are discussed in greater detail in the chapters that follow. Tax liability is determined by taking your income tax liability (ordinarily computed from a table) less any credits (Form 1040, lines 47–54), plus any other taxes (Form 1040, lines 56–60, including self-employment taxes), minus payments already made (Form 1040, lines 62–71) through withholding or estimated tax payments.

8. WHEN TO FILE

The deadline for filing your 2012 federal tax return is April 15, 2013. Your return is filed on time if it is properly addressed and postmarked no later than the due date. The return must have sufficient postage.

➡ **TIP.** Many post offices will remain open until midnight on April 15, 2013, to accommodate late filers.

9. EXTENSIONS OF TIME TO FILE

Taxpayers can obtain an automatic six-month extension (from April 15 to October 15, 2013) of time to file their 2012 Form 1040. To get the automatic extension, you must file a Form 4868 by April 15, 2013, with the IRS service center for your area. Your Form 1040 can be filed at any time during the six-month extension period.

An extension only relieves you from the obligation to file your return; it is not an extension of the obligation to pay your taxes. Therefore, you must make an estimate of your tax for 2012 and pay the estimated tax with your Form 4868. When you file your Form 1040, list the estimated payment made with your Form 4868 as a prior payment of taxes on line 68. If your actual tax liability for 2012 is more than the amount you estimated and enclosed with your Form 4868, you may have to pay an underpayment penalty.

✿ **KEY POINT.** Taxpayers can get an automatic six-month extension of time to file their tax returns by filing Form 4868, Automatic Extension of Time to File. The extension gives taxpayers until October 15, 2013, to file their tax returns. In previous years only a four-month extension was automatic, and taxpayers who needed more time had to make a second request.

➡ **TIP.** The IRS has urged taxpayers who need more time to complete their tax returns to e-file their extensions. Taxpayers can e-file the extension from a home computer or through a tax professional who uses e-file. Taxpayers can e-file their extensions at no cost. Several companies offer free e-filing of extensions through the Free File Alliance; these companies are listed on the IRS website (irs.gov).

The IRS expects to receive 10 million extensions during 2013.

✿ **KEY POINT.** The IRS may postpone for up to one year certain tax deadlines for taxpayers who are affected by a presidentially declared disaster. The tax deadlines the IRS may postpone include those for filing income, estate, certain excise, and employment tax returns; paying taxes associated with those returns; and making contributions to an IRA. If the IRS postpones the due date for filing a return and for paying a tax, it may abate the interest on underpaid tax that would otherwise accrue for the period of the postponement. This extension to file and pay does not apply to information returns or to employment tax deposits.

10. REFUNDS

✿ **KEY POINT.** The IRS has announced that more people than ever are using Where's My Refund, the popular Internet-based service that helps taxpayers check on their federal income tax refunds. Taxpayers can securely access their personal refund information through the IRS website, irs.gov. All you need to do is enter your Social Security number, filing status, and the amount of your expected refund. *IRS News Release IR-1006-52.*

If you overpay income or Social Security taxes, you can get a refund of the amount you overpaid. Or you may choose to apply all or a part of the overpayment to your next year's estimated tax (if applicable). If you are due a refund, no interest will be paid if the refund is made within 45 days of the due date of the return. If the refund is not made within this 45-day period, interest will be paid for the period from the due date of the return or from the date you filed, whichever is later.

In general, a taxpayer must file a refund claim within three years of the filing of the return or within two years of the payment of the tax, whichever period occurs later. A refund claim that is not filed within these time periods is rejected as untimely.

The tax code permits the statute of limitations on refund claims to be "tolled," or suspended, during any period of a taxpayer's life in which he or she is unable to manage financial affairs by reason of a medically determinable physical or mental impairment that can be expected to result in death or to last for a continuous period of not less than 12 months. Tolling does not apply during periods in which the taxpayer's spouse or another person is authorized to act on the taxpayer's behalf in financial matters.

▲ **CAUTION.** *The IRS has issued a consumer alert about an Internet scam in which consumers receive e-mail informing them of a tax refund. The e-mail, which claims to be from the IRS, directs the consumer to a link that requests personal information, such as Social Security number and credit card information. This scheme is an attempt to trick e-mail recipients into disclosing personal and financial data. The information fraudulently obtained is then used to run up charges on credit cards, apply for new loans and credit cards, and obtain other services or benefits in the victim's name. The IRS never asks for personal identifying or financial information in unsolicited e-mail. If you receive an unsolicited e-mail purporting to be from the IRS, take the following steps: (1) Do not open any attachments to the e-mail, in case they contain malicious code that will infect your computer. (2) Contact your local IRS office to report a possible e-mail scam. Contact information is available on the IRS website (irs.gov).* **IRS News Release IR-2009-71.**

11. IF YOU OWE ADDITIONAL TAXES

If your tax liability exceeds the amount of taxes that have been withheld or the amount of your estimated tax payments (or other payments), you should enclose a check for the additional tax with your return. In addition, you may be liable for an underpayment penalty (discussed in Chapter 1, section D.2) and interest.

12. AMENDED RETURNS

If, after filing your return, you find that you did not report some income, you claimed deductions or credits you should not have claimed, or you did not claim deductions or credits you could have claimed, you should correct your return. Use Form 1040X to correct the Form 1040 or Form 1040A that you previously filed.

The amended return should be filed within three years of the date you filed your original return (including extensions) or within two years from the time you paid your tax, whichever is later. A return filed early is considered filed on the due date.

➡ **TIP.** The deadline for filing Form 1040X is extended for certain people who are physically or mentally unable to manage their financial affairs. For details, see IRS Publication 556.

13. AUDIT RISK

✪ **KEY POINT.** The risk of being audited is small, but it is much higher for self-employed persons (especially if they only receive one or two Forms 1099-MISC).

The IRS examined 1.11 percent of all 2010 individual income tax returns in fiscal year 2011. The examination or audit rates are listed in Table 1-3.

Most examinations are conducted by correspondence, and many taxpayers do not realize that they were being audited. When analyzing examination coverage rates, one must recognize differences in the types of contacts that are counted in audit statistics. Examinations range from issuance of an IRS notice asking for clarification of a single tax return item that appears to be incorrect (correspondence examination) to a full, face-to-face interview and review of the taxpayer's records. Face-to-face examinations are generally more comprehensive and time consuming for the IRS and for taxpayers, and they typically result in higher dollar adjustments to the tax amounts. Thus, caution should be used when combining statistics from the various examination function programs into overall examination rates. To illustrate, during fiscal year 2010, 70 percent of all examinations were conducted via correspondence.

Some taxpayers have a much higher risk of being audited because of a number of considerations, including unusually large itemized deductions and the existence of moving or education expenses. Itemized deductions that exceed ranges established by the IRS also increase your audit risk.

14. PENALTIES

✪ **KEY POINT.** Taxpayers are subject to substantial penalties for not filing a tax return (if one is required) and for reporting inaccurate information on a tax return. Some taxpayers view the risk of being audited as so low that they deliberately underreport income, overstate expenses, or adopt questionable interpretations of the tax laws. You should bear in mind the following penalties before adopting aggressive tax positions.

Accuracy-related penalties

Penalties are imposed for various inaccuracies in tax returns, as noted below.

Negligence or disregard

If an underpayment of tax is due to negligence or a disregard of tax law, a negligence penalty is imposed. This is computed by multiplying 20 percent by the amount of the underpayment of taxes that is due to negligence or disregard. *IRC 6662(b)(1).*

"Negligence" includes (1) failure to make a reasonable attempt to comply with the tax law; (2) failure to exercise reasonable care in the preparation of a tax return; or (3) failure to keep adequate records or to substantiate items properly. The term "disregard" includes any careless, reckless, or intentional disregard of federal tax law. Reliance on the advice of a tax adviser does not relieve a minister of liability for either the negligence or disregard penalties.

=== **TABLE 1-3** ===

EXAMINATION AND AUDIT RATES

ADJUSTED GROSS INCOME	PERCENTAGE OF RETURNS EXAMINED IN FISCAL YEAR 2009	PERCENTAGE OF RETURNS EXAMINED IN FISCAL YEAR 2010	PERCENTAGE OF RETURNS EXAMINED IN FISCAL YEAR 2011
All returns	1.00	1.10	1.11
0	4.04	3.19	3.42
$1–under $25,000	0.97	1.18	1.22
$25,000–under $50,000	0.70	0.73	0.73
$50,000–under $75,000	0.68	0.78	0.83
$75,000–under $100,000	0.57	0.64	0.82
$100,000–under $200,000	0.67	0.71	1.00
$200,000–under $500,000	1.86	1.92	2.66

Taxpayers can avoid the negligence penalty only "with respect to any portion of an underpayment if it is shown that there was a reasonable cause for such portion and that the taxpayer acted in good faith with respect to such portion." *IRC 6664(c)*. You can avoid the penalty for disregard of rules or regulations if you adequately disclose on your return a position that has at least a reasonable basis (discussed below).

Substantial understatement

Taxpayers who substantially understate their income tax are subject to a substantial understatement penalty. *IRC 6662(b)(2)*. This penalty is computed by multiplying 20 percent by the portion of an underpayment of income taxes that is due to a substantial understatement. A substantial understatement of income taxes exists if an understatement exceeds the greater of (1) 10 percent of the actual income taxes that should have been paid or (2) $5,000. However, the amount of an understatement is reduced by either of the following:

- any portion of an understatement that is due to taxpayer reliance on substantial authority—including the tax code, income tax regulations, most IRS rulings and published materials, court cases, and the "blue book" (a general explanation of tax legislation prepared by the Congressional Joint Committee on Taxation).
- any portion of an understatement for which the taxpayer includes an adequate disclosure of his or her reasonable position in a statement attached to the tax return. A congressional committee observed that a "reasonable position" is "a relatively high standard" that means more than "not patently improper" or "not frivolous." Disclosures should be made on IRS Form 8275. Form 8275-R is used to disclose a position that is contrary to the income tax regulations (Form 8275 should not be used in such cases).

EXAMPLE. Pastor S failed to properly report several items, including a salary he paid his wife for performing duties at the church, without satisfactory explanation. He also failed to prove that many of his business expense deductions (claimed on Schedule C) were for business purposes and failed to keep adequate books and records to support the amounts claimed on his tax returns. Pastor S explained that he was too busy to keep records. The Tax Court upheld an IRS assessment of a negligence penalty. The court defined negligence as "the lack of due care, or the failure to do what a prudent person would do under the circumstances." *Shelley v. Commissioner, T.C. Memo. 1994 432 (1994).*

EXAMPLE. Same facts as the previous example. The Tax Court also ruled that Pastor S would be liable for the penalty for substantially understating his tax liability if the understatement exceeded the greater of 10 percent of his actual income taxes or $5,000. The court noted that this penalty is not available if "there was substantial authority for the taxpayer's treatment of the items in issue or if the relevant facts relating to the tax treatment were adequately disclosed on the returns." However, the court concluded that "the record does not demonstrate that either exception applies."

EXAMPLE. The Tax Court upheld an IRS assessment of a negligence penalty against a pastor who attempted to deduct commuting expenses as a business expense. The court concluded that "the record in this case is replete with examples of [the pastor's] negligence. [He] claimed deductions for numerous items which in many cases are either nondeductible or lack substantiation. Accordingly, we find that [the pastor is] subject to the addition to tax for negligence for all the years at issue." *Clark v. Commissioner, 67 T.C.M. 2458 (1994).*

EXAMPLE. The Tax Court disallowed a $25,000 charitable contribution deduction for gifts of two items of property, since the donors failed to obtain qualified appraisals and attach qualified appraisal summaries (IRS Form 8283) to their tax return as required by law. The Tax Court further ruled that the IRS could assess an accuracy-related penalty against the taxpayers. Section 6662 of the tax code permits the IRS to assess a penalty of 20 percent on the amount of underpayment of tax attributable to a "substantial understatement" of tax. A substantial understatement of tax is defined as an understatement of tax that exceeds the greater of 10 percent of the tax required to be shown on the tax return or $5,000. The understatement is reduced to the extent that the taxpayer has (1) adequately disclosed his or her position or (2) has substantial authority for the tax treatment of the item. The court concluded that neither the taxpayers nor their accountant "provided an explanation why timely qualified appraisals were not conducted for the noncash charitable contributions and why the appraisal summaries on Form 8283 were not fully completed. We, therefore, sustain [the] imposition of the accuracy-related penalty with regard to the underpayment associated with the . . . noncash charitable contributions." *Jorgenson v. Commissioner, 79 T.C.M. 1444 (2000).*

EXAMPLE. A pastor reported $28,000 as income from his church. The IRS audited the pastor's tax return and concluded that he understated his taxable income by $24,000 and overstated several business expense deductions. The pastor insisted that the $24,000 of unreported income came from voluntary gifts or offerings from members of the congregation, which were not taxable. The Tax Court rejected this argument, noting that "we have no evidence as to the dominant reason for the transfers. Instead, all we have is his characterization of the transfers as gifts, which in itself has little or no evidentiary value. On the other hand, the evidence that we do have strongly suggests that the transfers were not [nontaxable] gifts. The transfers arose out of the pastor's relationship with the members of his congregation presumably because they believed he was a good minister and they wanted to reward him. Furthermore, the pastor testified that without the gifts his activity as a minister was essentially a money-losing activity. In short, as the pastor recognized, the so-called gifts were a part of the compensation he received for being a minister. As such, the transfers are not excludable from income."

In addition, the court concluded that the pastor had overstated his business expense deductions by $19,000, mostly due to his failure to substantiate these deductions. The court imposed a negligence penalty against the pastor based on his understatement of income and overstatement of expenses. It concluded: "Negligence is a lack of due care or the failure to do what a reasonable and ordinarily prudent person would do under the circumstances. The question then is whether [the pastor's] conduct meets the reasonably prudent person standard. We do not believe that the pastor's conduct meets this standard. The law surrounding the disputed items is not complex. With respect to the claimed deductions, the pastor was required to maintain

records, which he failed to do. Furthermore, there is no indication that he sought the advice of a qualified tax advisor concerning any of the disputed items." *Swaringer v. Commissioner, T.C. Summary Opinion 2001-37 (2001).*

EXAMPLE. The Tax Court upheld the assessment of a negligence penalty against a woman who had inadequate receipts from her church to substantiate her cash contributions. The donor's cash contributions amounted to $22,000, most of which consisted of individual contributions of $250 or more. The court concluded that the church receipts failed to substantiate any contribution of $250 or more because they failed to state whether the church had provided any goods or services in exchange for the contributions, as required by the tax code. The court also upheld the assessment by the IRS of a penalty equal to 20 percent of the underpayment in tax "attributable to, among other things, negligence or disregard of rules or regulations."

The penalty for negligence does not apply to an underpayment of tax to the extent the taxpayer can show both reasonable cause and good faith. Negligence "includes any failure by the taxpayer . . . to substantiate items properly." In upholding the penalty, the court observed: "[The donor], a long-time self-professed frequent contributor to charitable organizations, should have been aware that the acknowledgments failed to satisfy the special substantiation requirement of [the tax code] and she should have asked the charities to satisfy that requirement before deducting her contribution to those organizations in excess of $250. Not only is the requirement to obtain a proper acknowledgment set forth in the tax code and in the regulations, it is also contained in both the instructions for preparing Schedule A and IRS Publication 526 (Charitable Contributions)." *Kendrix v. Commissioner, T.C. Memo. 2006-9.*

Substantial valuation misstatement

Taxpayers who understate their income taxes in any year by $5,000 or more because they misstated the value of property on their tax return are subject to a penalty. *IRC 6662(b)(3).* The penalty only applies if the misstated value is at least 150 percent of the property's actual value. The penalty is computed by multiplying 20 percent by the amount of the underpayment of income taxes, The penalty rate increases to 40 percent for "gross" valuation misstatements (overstated value is at least 200 percent of the property's actual value). *IRC 6662(e).* There is no disclosure exception for this penalty.

❖ **KEY POINT.** The Pension Protection Act of 2006 lowered the thresholds for imposing accuracy-related penalties on a taxpayer. A substantial valuation misstatement exists when the claimed value of any property is 150 percent or more of the amount determined to be the correct value. A gross valuation misstatement occurs when the claimed value of any property is 200 percent or more of the amount determined to be the correct value. Also, the "reasonable cause" exception to the accuracy-related penalty does not apply in the case of gross valuation misstatements of charitable deduction property. *IRC 6664(c)*.

A common example of valuation overstatements involves overvaluations of properties donated to charity. Such overvaluations result in inflated charitable contribution deductions and a corresponding understatement of income taxes. However, the tax code clarifies that taxpayers who comply with the substantiation requirements that apply to contributions of noncash property valued by the donor in excess of $5,000 are not subject to this penalty even if there is an overvaluation. These requirements include a qualified appraisal of the donated property and the inclusion of a qualified appraisal summary (IRS Form 8283) with the donor's tax return on which the contribution is claimed. See Chapter 8 for complete details.

Property overvaluations that are not enough to trigger this penalty may still be subject to the negligence or substantial understatement penalties discussed previously.

✤ **KEY POINT.** The tax code specifies that no accuracy-related penalty (including negligence and substantial understatement) shall be imposed with respect to any underpayment of taxes if the taxpayer had reasonable cause for the underpayment and acted in good faith.

Fraud

The fraud penalty, which is imposed at a rate of 75 percent, applies to the portion of any underpayment of income taxes that is due to fraud. *See IRC 6663*. If the IRS establishes by "clear and convincing evidence" that any portion of an underpayment of income taxes is due to fraud, then the entire underpayment is treated as fraudulent except for any portion that the taxpayer can prove (by a preponderance of the evidence) is not based on fraud.

The IRS must establish fraud by a high standard (clear and convincing evidence). Once it does so, the taxpayer can rebut the presumption of fraud by a lesser standard of proof (a preponderance of the evidence). No accuracy-related penalty (defined above) can apply to any portion of an understatement of income taxes on which the fraud penalty is imposed. However, an accuracy-related penalty can be assessed against any portion of an underpayment that is not due to fraud.

EXAMPLE. The Tax Court ruled that a pastor who failed to report as taxable income deposits he made into a church bank account over which he exercised complete control was not guilty of fraud. The court noted that the tax code imposes a penalty "equal to 75 percent of the portion of the underpayment which is attributable to fraud." Taxpayers commit fraud when they "evade taxes known to be owing by conduct intended to conceal, mislead, or otherwise prevent the collection of taxes." The IRS bears the burden of proving fraud and must establish it by clear and convincing evidence. To satisfy this burden of proof, the IRS must show that (1) an underpayment in tax exists and (2) the taxpayer

intended to conceal, mislead, or otherwise prevent the collection of taxes. If the IRS establishes that any portion of an underpayment is attributable to fraud, the entire underpayment is treated as attributable to fraud. The IRS insisted that there was sufficient circumstantial evidence in the record to conclude that petitioners fraudulently intended to evade taxes. It pointed to a number of facts, including the establishment of the petitioners' church as a "corporation sole," but the court concluded that the IRS failed to meet the high standard of proving fraud by clear and convincing evidence. *101 T.C.M. 1550 (2011)*.

Sanctions and costs

The Tax Court can impose a penalty of up to $25,000 if a taxpayer (1) initiates an action primarily for delay, (2) takes a position that is frivolous, or (3) unreasonably fails to pursue available administrative remedies within the IRS. *IRC 6673*. This penalty is designed to reduce the large numbers of lawsuits brought by taxpayers who claim frivolous positions. The Tax Court also can require a taxpayer's attorney to pay the costs of litigating a frivolous lawsuit (including court costs and attorneys' fees incurred by the government).

Failure-to-file penalty

If you do not file your return by the due date, you may have to pay a failure-to-file penalty. The failure-to-file penalty currently is 5 percent of your unpaid taxes for each month or part of a month after the due date that the tax is not paid—but ordinarily not more than 25 percent of your tax (if fraudulent, 15 percent per month, with a maximum of 75 percent of your tax). The penalty is waived if you can show reasonable cause for not filing your return on time. *IRC 6651*.

Frivolous income tax return

Taxpayers can be assessed a penalty of $5,000 for filing a "frivolous" return that does not include enough information to figure the correct tax, or a return that contains information that shows on its face that the tax shown on the return is substantially incorrect, if the return was filed due to a frivolous position or out of a desire to delay or interfere with the administration of the federal tax laws. This penalty is in addition to any other penalty allowed by law. *IRC 6702*.

Criminal penalties

In addition to the civil penalties discussed above, a taxpayer can be subject to criminal penalties for a willful attempt to evade taxes. Criminal liability requires an affirmative act (typically filing a false return). Omissions are generally insufficient. Tax evasion is a felony punishable by a fine of not more than $100,000 ($500,000 for a corporation) or a prison sentence of up to five years or both. *IRC 7201*.

✤ **KEY POINT.** The United States Supreme Court has ruled that taxpayers cannot be guilty of a criminal violation of the tax law for taking positions based on ignorance or a misunderstanding of the law, or a sincere belief that they are not violating the law. A taxpayer who failed to pay taxes or file returns for several years was prosecuted on several counts of willfully violating the law. He maintained that he could not be convicted of willfully violating the law, since he had a good faith belief that he was not a taxpayer and that wages are not taxable. The taxpayer's beliefs arose from his own study of the Constitution and federal tax law and from information he received while attending several seminars sponsored by a tax protestor group. In a surprise ruling, the Supreme Court agreed with the taxpayer that he could not be convicted of willfully violating the law if he sincerely believed that wages are not taxable, even if this belief was not "objectively reasonable." *Cheek v. United States, 111 S. Ct. 604 (1991).*

EXAMPLE. Pastor O claimed on his 2012 income tax return a deduction for a contribution he made in 2010 but forgot to claim, as well as an unallowable deduction for the education expenses incurred by his dependent children in attending a private school. He sincerely believed he was legally entitled to claim both deductions on his 2012 return. Pastor O's taxes were underpaid by $4,000 because of these deductions. Such conduct amounts to negligent disregard of the tax laws and subjects Pastor O to a penalty of 20 percent of the amount of the underpayment (a total penalty of $800, excluding interest). Pastor O also will have to pay the full $4,000 of underpaid taxes.

EXAMPLE. Pastor W believes that ministers should not pay taxes. He bases his belief on his interpretation of the Bible. In 2012 Pastor W had church income of $40,000. Assume that Pastor W should have paid federal taxes of $5,000. In addition to having to pay the $5,000 tax deficiency, Pastor W will be subject to a delinquency penalty for fraudulently failing to file a tax return. The penalty is 15 percent of the net amount of tax due for each month that the return is not filed (up to a maximum of five months or 75 percent—a total of $3,750 in this case). The IRS has the burden of proving that the taxpayer fraudulently failed to file a return. Pastor W also may be liable for criminal penalties on the basis of a willful attempt to evade taxes. However, the likelihood of a criminal conviction under these circumstances is reduced by the Supreme Court's decision in the *Cheek* case (discussed earlier).

EXAMPLE. Pastor J's church failed to designate a portion of his 2012 compensation as a housing allowance. In January 2013 Pastor J had his church board retroactively designate a 2012 housing allowance although he knew that retroactive housing allowances are not allowed. He claimed a housing allowance exclusion on his 2012 tax return, which results in a $4,000 understatement of his tax liability. Pastor J may be subject to any of the following penalties: (1) the negligence penalty, which would be 20 percent of the underpayment of $4,000 (for a total penalty of $800); (2) a substantial understatement penalty, which would be 20 percent of the underpayment of $4,000 (for a total penalty of $800); or (3) if the IRS can establish that Pastor J acted fraudulently, it could assess the fraud penalty, which would be 75 percent of the underpayment of $4,000 (for a total

penalty of $3,000). These penalties are in addition to Pastor J's obligation to pay the $4,000 tax deficiency (plus interest). Pastor J's actions also may violate the Sarbanes-Oxley Act (see section H of this chapter).

EXAMPLE. Pastor G purchased a home many years ago, and last year he paid off the mortgage loan. In order to boost his housing allowance exclusion this year, he takes out a home equity loan (secured by a mortgage on his home) that he uses to pay for a new car and his daughter's college expenses. Pastor G is aware that some courts have ruled that a housing allowance cannot be used to pay for home equity loan repayments unless the loan is for home improvements. However, he believes that he is entitled to apply his housing allowance to his home equity loan payments because the loan is secured by a mortgage on his home and "I will lose my home if I don't repay it." Pastor G's position results in an understatement of his income taxes of $6,000. Under these facts Pastor G may be subject to any one of the following penalties (in addition to having to pay the tax deficiency of $6,000): (1) the negligence penalty, which would be 20 percent of the underpayment of $6,000 (for a total penalty of $1,200); or (2) a substantial understatement penalty, which would be 20 percent of the underpayment of $6,000 (for a total penalty of $1,200).

EXAMPLE. Same facts as the preceding example, except that Pastor G makes an adequate disclosure of his position by including a properly completed IRS Form 8275 with his Form 1040. Such a disclosure may avoid the penalty for substantial understatement of tax—at the cost of disclosing to the IRS the questionable position that is being asserted. To avoid the penalty, Pastor G's disclosed position must be reasonable.

EXAMPLE. A federal appeals court affirmed the enhanced prison sentence of a pastor who failed to report on his income tax return more than $500,000 in compensation and benefits received from his church. A church hired a new pastor, under whose leadership the church membership grew from 500 to 2,000 people. Weekly church income grew from $7,000 to $40,000. The church provided the pastor with compensation of $110,000. However, the pastor chose to supplement his salary by taking money directly from the Sunday collection without reporting it on his tax returns. He also failed to report on his tax return several fringe benefits, such as a church-provided car that he used for both personal and church business, making personal credit-card and life-insurance payments with church funds, and using the church credit card for personal expenditures.

From these benefits and the weekly draws on the collection plate, the government calculated that the pastor had additional gross income in the amount of $520,602 in the years 1996–2001, resulting in a large tax deficit. The government indicted the pastor on five counts of willfully making and subscribing a false income tax return, and one count of failure to file an income tax return. The

FAILURE OF MINISTERS TO FILE INCOME TAX RETURNS

Question. We just learned that our youth pastor has not filed a tax return since graduating from seminary seven years ago. What should we do?

Answer. Unfortunately, this is a common problem for ministers, and the reason is simple—churches are not required to withhold either income taxes or Social Security taxes from the wages of ministers who are performing ministerial services. This is due to the fact that (1) ministers are classified as self-employed by the tax code for Social Security purposes (so they pay the self-employment tax in lieu of having Social Security and Medicare taxes withheld from their wages by their employing church), and (2) the tax code exempts the wages of ministers from income tax withholding.

Unless they elect voluntary tax withholding, ministers are required to prepay their federal income taxes and self-employment taxes using the estimated tax procedure. This requires the minister to estimate income taxes and self-employment taxes for the year and to pay one-fourth of this amount on each of the following four dates: April 15, June 15, September 15, and the following January 15.

The problem is that few seminaries inform ministerial students of their obligation to prepay their taxes using the estimated tax procedure. Many new ministers assume that their church will operate like a secular employer and withhold these taxes. When they realize that nothing is being withheld, they may rationalize their failure to pay taxes or file tax returns (e.g., "ministers must be exempt from taxes" or "I probably am not earning enough to trigger withholding"). This leads to nonpayment of taxes and, in many cases, to a failure to file a tax return.

In time some of these ministers realize that they owe back taxes, but they are unsure how to proceed. Some fear imprisonment. What should be done? Consider the following nine points.

(1) If a tax return is not filed by the due date (including extensions), a taxpayer may be subject to the failure-to-file penalty unless reasonable cause exists.

(2) Taxpayers who did not pay their tax liability in full by the due date of the return (excluding extensions) may also be subject to the failure-to-pay penalty unless reasonable cause exists.

(3) Interest is charged on taxes not paid by the due date. Interest is also charged on penalties.

(4) Ministers who have not filed one or more tax returns should consult with a CPA or tax attorney to determine whether taxes were owed and, if so, to discuss options.

(5) Taxpayers who owe taxes but are financially unable to pay them may qualify for assistance in making payments through either an installment agreement or an offer in compromise. Discuss these options with your tax adviser.

(6) There is no penalty for failure to file if you are due a refund. But if you want to file a return or otherwise claim a refund, you risk losing a refund altogether. A return claiming a refund would have to be filed within three years of its due date for a refund to be allowed.

(7) After the expiration of the three-year window, the refund statute prevents the issuance of a refund check and the application of any credits, including overpayments of estimated or withholding taxes, to other tax years that are underpaid.

(8) The statute of limitations for the IRS to assess and collect any outstanding balances does not start until a return has been filed. In other words, there is no statute of limitations for assessing and collecting the tax if no return has been filed.

(9) Church leaders should discuss tax filing requirements with every new minister, especially those who are recent seminary graduates. How do they plan to pay their income taxes and self-employment taxes? Through voluntary withholding? The estimated tax procedure? If the latter, provide them with a current copy of IRS Form 1040-ES (including the instructions). This is the form used to compute estimated taxes. It also includes payment vouchers that are used with each quarterly tax payment.

pastor was found guilty of some of the charges and was sentenced to prison under section 7206(1) of the tax code, which specifies that "any person who willfully makes and subscribes any return, statement, or other document, which contains or is verified by a written declaration that it is made under the penalties of perjury, and which he does not believe to be true and correct as to every material matter . . . shall be guilty of a felony and, upon conviction

thereof, shall be fined not more than $100,000 or imprisoned not more than three years, or both, together with the costs of prosecution." The sentence prescribed by section 7206(1) can be "enhanced" due to several factors, including abuse of a position of trust and obtaining more than $10,000 in income from illegal sources without reporting it. A federal appeals court ruled that the enhancement of the pastor's sentence in this case was justified.

This case demonstrates that a church employee's failure to report compensation and taxable fringe benefits as taxable income on his or her income tax return may result in criminal liability for making a false income tax return. And the criminal penalty may be enhanced due to an abuse of a position of trust or obtaining more than $10,000 in income from illegal sources without reporting it. *United States v. Ellis, 440 F.3d 434 (7th Cir. 2006).*

EXAMPLE. A federal appeals court ruled that a pastor was properly convicted and sentenced to prison for filing a fraudulent tax return as a result of his failure to report several items of taxable income. At the pastor's trial, the prosecution documented $110,000 of unreported taxable income for various personal expenses for the pastor and members of his family by the church. These items included insurance policies, monthly payments on a loan the pastor had taken out to purchase a car for his daughter, and payments for a time-share property. The prosecution noted that the pastor's annual salary was $115,000 but that he had acquired numerous "luxury items" that seemed excessive in light of his salary, including two time shares, a 2.73 carat diamond ring, a projection television, a camcorder, a DVD player, and custom-made clothes. According to the prosecution, the excessiveness of his lifestyle relative to his reported income was indicative of fraud. A federal appeals court affirmed the conviction. *2009 WL 723206 (11th Cir. 2009).*

EXAMPLE. A federal appeals court affirmed the conviction of a pastor and his wife (the "defendants") on several tax crimes based on various forms of church compensation they failed to disclose on their tax returns.

The defendants' total church compensation between 2001 and 2007 totaled nearly $3.9 million. During that time, the wife received compensation from the church in the form of salary, bonuses, allowances, and reimbursements, totaling nearly $1 million. The IRS reconstructed the couple's income for the years 2002–2007 and determined that they understated their taxable income by $2,486,771 between 2002 and 2007, resulting in a tax deficiency of $664,352 for those years.

The federal government eventually obtained a 19-count indictment against the couple. Their trial resulted in conviction on charges of conspiracy to defraud the United States, tax evasion and aiding and abetting the same, and for the defendant, filing false tax returns. Following a four-week trial that involved the admission of over 90,000 pages of documentary evidence and the testimony of more than 70 witnesses, the defendants were both convicted on several counts. The pastor was sentenced to 105 months' imprisonment and restitution in the amount of $1.3 million, and his wife to 80 months' imprisonment and restitution in the amount of $1.2 million.

The couple appealed their convictions and sentences. The court concluded that the couple had willfully failed to report taxable income and attempted to conceal the true extent of their compensation from church staff, the congregation, and the IRS. The defendants' sentences were enhanced, pursuant to the federal sentencing guidelines, for abusing a position of trust. The appeals court agreed with this enhancement: "The abuse of trust enhancement enables the sentencing court to punish those who wield their power to criminally take advantage of those who depend upon them most. As leaders of the church, the defendants were entrusted with the spiritual well-being and financial stewardship of their religious community. They exploited the trust of their unsuspecting congregation to conceal criminal acts from the government, as well as the church, and to maintain an extravagant lifestyle lived at the church's expense. We thus affirm the district court's application of the abuse of trust enhancement." *United States v. Jinwright, 2012-2 U.S.T.C. ¶50,417 (4th Cir. 2012).*

15. LIMITATION PERIODS

For how many years can the IRS question or audit your income tax returns? Consider the following three possibilities:

- **Three years.** In general, the IRS may audit your returns to assess any additional taxes within three years after the date a return is filed (or within three years after the due date of the return, if later).

EXAMPLE. Pastor W filed his 2009 tax return on April 10, 2010. The IRS ordinarily may audit Pastor W's 2009 return only if it does so by April 15, 2013.

- **Six years.** The three-year period during which the IRS may audit your returns is expanded to six years if you omit from gross income an amount greater than 25 percent of the amount reported on your return.
- **No limit.** The IRS can audit returns without any time limitation in any of the following situations: (1) a false or fraudulent return is filed with the intent to evade tax; (2) a taxpayer engages in a willful attempt in any manner to defeat or evade tax; or (3) a taxpayer fails to file a tax return. *IRC 6501(c).*

✿ **KEY POINT.** Whenever a taxpayer is requested by the IRS to extend the statute of limitations on an assessment of tax, the IRS must notify the taxpayer of the taxpayer's right to refuse to extend the statute of limitations or to limit the extension to particular issues.

Section 6502(a)(1) of the tax code specifies that "where the assessment of any tax imposed by this title has been made within the period of limitation properly applicable thereto, such tax may be collected . . . within 10 years after the assessment of the tax."

CHURCH & CLERGY TAX GUIDE 2013

16. CHOOSING WHETHER TO PREPARE YOUR OWN TAX RETURNS OR TO USE A PAID PREPARER

Ministers can prepare their own tax returns. While ministers' taxes present several unique rules, these rules are not complex. Unfortunately, many people confuse uniqueness with complexity. With a little effort most ministers should be able to comprehend these rules sufficiently to prepare their own tax returns. The information provided in this tax guide, together with IRS Publication 17 (*Your Federal Income Tax*), should be all the information needed in most cases.

Of course, some ministers will prefer, for a variety of reasons, to have someone else prepare their tax returns. If that is your choice, be sure you select someone with experience in the preparation of ministers' tax returns (preferably a tax attorney or a CPA). You may wish to share a copy of this book with the person you select.

Important considerations

Before deciding to have someone else prepare your tax return, consider the following:

- More than half of all income tax returns prepared by paid preparers contain errors, according to an IRS study. What were the most common mistakes? Failing to claim the standard deduction; entering dollars and cents in the area for dollars; failing to claim (or incorrectly stating) the amount of a refund; failing to total the multiple entries on Schedule C; filing a Schedule SE even though net self-employment earnings are less than $400; using the wrong filing status (joint, head of household, etc.); and failing to check the age/blind box.
- Paid preparers are subject to a penalty of $1,000 per return (or 50 percent of the income they earned for preparing the return, if greater) for any understatement in taxes that is due to an "unreasonable position," which is defined by law to mean a lack of a reasonable basis. *IRC 6694.* As a result, competent paid preparers generally avoid overly aggressive positions when completing ministers' tax returns.
- The IRS has established a Return Preparer Program that can trigger audits of *all returns prepared by certain return preparers who intentionally or negligently disregard federal tax law (code, regulations, and rulings).* Ministers and church staff should be cautious when dealing with nonprofessional or "mail-order" return preparers, especially those who promise significant tax savings or are not attorneys or CPAs. *See Internal Revenue Manual §4.11.51.*

Tips on selecting a tax preparer

Let's assume you've decided to have your tax return prepared by a professional. The next step is to find someone who is experienced and competent in the preparation of ministers' tax returns. Here are some tips to help you find such a person:

- If possible, stick with a CPA or tax attorney. These professionals have completed a rigorous educational program, passed a difficult qualifying examination, and are subject to a comprehensive body of professional ethics.
- Try to use someone local.
- Find other ministers in your community who have their tax returns prepared by a professional, and ask questions. Who do they use? Are they pleased? What is the cost? How many ministers' tax returns does the person prepare?
- Call CPAs listed in your telephone directory: ask if they prepare ministers' tax returns and, if so, ask how many they prepare.
- When you find one or more possible candidates, consider asking a few simple questions that should be answered easily by anyone with any experience in handling ministers' tax returns. Here are a few examples: (1) Are ministers employees or self-employed for Social Security purposes? *Ministers always are self-employed for Social Security purposes with respect to their ministerial income.* (2) Can I claim my housing allowance exclusion in computing my self-employment taxes? *Absolutely not—ever.* (3) If I report my church wages as an employee, are my wages subject to FICA taxes? *The answer is never.* (4) If I report my church wages as an employee, are my wages subject to income tax withholding? *No, unless a minister elects voluntary withholding.* (5) What is the minister's housing allowance? *The portion of a minister's salary designated in advance by an employing church for housing expenses. This amount is not taxable in computing a minister's income taxes to the extent it is used to pay housing expenses and does not exceed the home's fair rental value.*

Persons who are familiar with ministers' taxes should be able to answer all of these questions knowledgeably.

B. FILING STATUS

1. SINGLE

You must file as single if on the last day of last year you were unmarried or separated from your spouse either by divorce or separate maintenance decree and you do not qualify for another filing status. State law governs whether you are married, divorced, or legally separated.

2. MARRIED

If you were married as of the last day of last year, you and your spouse may be able to file a joint return, or you may choose to file separate returns. You are considered married even if you are living separate and apart, provided that you and your spouse were not legally separated under a decree of divorce or separate maintenance. (As noted below, you may be able to report your taxes as a head of household under these circumstances if you meet certain requirements.) If your spouse died during the year, you are considered married for the whole year. If you and your spouse both have income, you should figure your tax both on a joint return and on separate returns to see which way gives you the lower tax. In most cases you will pay more taxes if you file separately. If you do file separately and one spouse itemizes deductions, the other spouse ordinarily should itemize deductions too, since he or she cannot take the standard deduction.

3. QUALIFYING WIDOWS AND WIDOWERS

The last year for which you may file a joint return with your deceased spouse is the year of your spouse's death. However, for the two years following the year of death, you may be able to figure your tax using the joint rates. These rates are lower than the rates for single or head of household status. To use the joint rates, you must file as a qualifying widow or widower and meet all of the following conditions: (1) you were entitled to file a joint return with your spouse for the year your spouse died; (2) you did not remarry before the end of the current year; (3) you have a child who qualifies as your dependent for the year; and (4) you paid more than half the cost of keeping up your home, which is the principal home of that child for the entire year.

> **EXAMPLE.** Pastor B died in 2010. His surviving spouse has not remarried and has continued during 2011 and 2012 to keep up a home for herself and her two dependent children. For 2010 Pastor B's surviving spouse was entitled to file a joint return for herself and her deceased husband. For 2011 and 2012 she may use the joint rates because she is a widow with dependent children.

4. HEAD OF HOUSEHOLD

➡ **TIP.** If you qualify to file as head of household, your tax rate usually will be lower than the rates for single or married filing separately. You will also receive a higher standard deduction than if you file as single or married filing separately.

You may be able to file as head of household if you meet all the following requirements:

- You are unmarried or "considered unmarried" on the last day of the year.
- You paid more than half the cost of keeping up a home for the year.
- A "qualifying person" lived with you in the home for more than half the year (except for temporary absences, such as school). However, if the qualifying person is your dependent parent, he or she does not have to live with you.

The terms *qualifying person* and *keeping up a home* are defined in IRS Publication 501.

c. PERSONAL EXEMPTIONS AND DEPENDENTS

✱ **New in 2012.** For 2012 you will not lose part of your deduction for personal exemptions, regardless of the amount of your adjusted gross income.

Taxpayers may deduct an amount for each available personal or dependent exemption in computing taxable income. For 2012 each exemption is worth $3,800. You may claim a personal exemption for yourself and one for your spouse, and an exemption for each of your dependents.

1. DEPENDENTS

A dependent is either a qualifying child or a qualifying relative.

Qualifying child
In general, a qualifying child must meet all of the following conditions.

- The child must be your child (including an adopted child, stepchild, or eligible foster child), brother, sister, stepbrother, stepsister, or a descendant of any of them.
- The child must have lived with you for more than half of 2012. An exception applies, in certain cases, for children of divorced or separated parents.
- At the end of 2012, the child must be under age 19, or under age 24 and a student, or any age and permanently and totally disabled.
- The child must not have provided over half of his or her own support in 2012.
- The child is not filing a joint return for the year (unless that joint return is filed only as a claim for refund).
- If the child meets the rules to be a qualifying child of more than one person, you must be the person entitled to claim the child as a qualifying child.

Qualifying relative
In general, a qualifying relative must meet all of the following conditions:

- The person must be either your relative or any other person (other than your spouse) who lived in your home all year as a member of your household. If the person is not your relative, your relationship must not violate local law.

- The person cannot be your qualifying child (see above) or the qualifying child of another person in 2012.
- The person must have gross income of less than $3,800. If the person is permanently and totally disabled, certain income from a sheltered workshop may be excluded for this purpose.
- You must have provided over half of the person's support in 2012. Exceptions apply, in certain cases, for children of divorced or separated parents and for a person supported by two or more taxpayers.

Other rules concerning dependents

The following rules also apply in determining if a person is your dependent.

- If you are a dependent of another person in 2012, you cannot claim any dependents on your return.
- If the dependent is married, he or she cannot file a joint return unless the return is filed only as a claim for refund and no tax liability would exist for either spouse if they had filed separate returns.
- A dependent generally must be a U.S. citizen, U.S. national, or a resident of the United States, Canada, or Mexico.
- New "tie-breaker rules" apply if a child meets the conditions to be a qualifying child of two or more people and more than one person claims the child as a qualifying child.

For more information on dependents, see IRS Publication 501.

✿ **KEY POINT.** Persons who claim personal exemptions for dependents as well as the dependent care credit must include on their tax return the name and Social Security number of each dependent. The IRS can deny a dependency exemption and dependent care credit to any taxpayer who fails to provide the correct Social Security number of a dependent on his or her tax return. If a person whom you expect to claim as a dependent does not have a Social Security number, either you or that person should apply for one as soon as possible. You can apply for a number by filing IRS Form SS-5 with the Social Security Administration. You can obtain a Form SS-5 from any IRS or Social Security office.

EXAMPLE. The Tax Court denied dependency deductions to a family with 10 children because none of the children had a Social Security number. The parents wrote "NA" in the section of Form 1040 where Social Security numbers (SSNs) of dependents are to be listed. The court relied on tax code section 151(e), which states: "No exemption shall be allowed under this section with respect to any individual unless the [taxpayer identification number] of such individual is included on the return claiming the exemption." *Kocher v. Commissioner, T.C. Memo. 2000-238 (2000).*

2. PHASEOUT OF PERSONAL EXEMPTION FOR HIGH-INCOME TAXPAYERS

✿ **KEY POINT.** Personal exemptions allow a certain amount per person to be exempt from tax (currently $3,800). Due to the Personal Exemption Phaseout (PEP), the exemptions are phased out for taxpayers with income above a certain level. The PEP was repealed in 2010. This repeal was extended by the Tax Relief Act through 2012.

In order to determine taxable income, an individual reduces adjusted gross income by any personal exemptions, deductions, and either the applicable standard deduction or itemized deductions. Personal exemptions generally are allowed for the taxpayer, his or her spouse, and any dependents.

Prior to the Economic Growth and Tax Relief Reconciliation Act of 2001 (EGTRRA) the deduction for personal exemptions was phased out for higher-income taxpayers with adjusted gross income over certain thresholds. The total amount of exemptions that could be claimed by a taxpayer was reduced by 2 percent for each $2,500 (or portion thereof) by which the taxpayer's adjusted gross income exceeds the applicable threshold.

EGTRRA repealed the personal exemption phaseout over five years, beginning in 2006. The phaseout was reduced by one-third for 2006 and 2007 and by two-thirds for 2008 and 2009. The repeal was fully effective for 2010. The repeal was extended by the Tax Relief and Jobs Creation Act through 2012.

In explaining the reason for repealing the phaseout, a congressional conference committee noted that "the personal exemption phaseout is an unnecessarily complex way to impose income taxes and the hidden way in which the phaseout raises marginal tax rates undermines respect for the tax laws."

D. TAX WITHHOLDING AND ESTIMATED TAX

The federal income tax is a "pay as you go" tax. You must pay your tax as you earn or receive income during the year. You can pay as you go in two ways: tax withholding and quarterly estimated tax payments. These two procedures will be summarized in this section.

1. WITHHOLDING

✿ **KEY POINT.** Ministers are exempt from income tax withholding whether they report their income taxes as employees or as self-employed. They pay their estimated taxes for the year in quarterly installments.

❋ **KEY POINT.** Ministers who report their income taxes as employees can elect voluntary withholding.

Most employers are required to withhold federal income taxes from employees' wages as they are paid.

Exceptions

Some exceptions to the withholding requirement do exist, including the following:

Wages paid to ministers for services performed in the exercise of ministry

The tax code exempts wages paid for "services performed by a duly ordained, commissioned, or licensed minister of a church in the exercise of his ministry" from income tax withholding. *IRC 3401(a)(9)*. This means a church is not required to withhold income taxes from wages paid to ministers who report and pay their income taxes as employees. This exemption only applies to "services performed in the exercise of ministry." This significant term is defined fully in Chapter 3.

❋ **KEY POINT.** The exemption of ministers' wages from income tax withholding does not apply to nonminister church employees. To illustrate, one federal court ruled that the services of a church secretary, organist, custodian, and choir director were not covered by the exemption, and so the church was required to withhold taxes from the wages of these workers (all of whom were treated as employees by the church). *Eighth Street Baptist Church, Inc. v. United States, 295 F. Supp. 1400 (D. Kan. 1969).* A church's withholding obligations with respect to nonminister employees (and employees who elect voluntary withholding) are covered in Chapter 11.

Self-employed workers

Persons who are self-employed for income tax purposes report and prepay their income taxes and Social Security taxes by means of the estimated tax procedure (discussed below). Self-employed persons are not subject to tax withholding.

IRS Tax Guide for Churches and Religious Organizations

The IRS *Tax Guide for Churches and Religious Organizations* (Publication 1828) contains the following paragraph on the application of tax withholding to ministers:

Unlike other exempt organizations or businesses, a church is not required to withhold income tax from the compensation that it pays to its duly ordained, commissioned, or licensed ministers for performing services in the exercise of their ministry. An employee minister may, however, enter into a voluntary withholding

agreement with the church by completing IRS Form W-4, Employee's Withholding Allowance Certificate.

IRS audit guidelines for ministers

The IRS has issued audit guidelines for use by its agents in auditing ministers. The guidelines specify:

Although a minister is considered an employee under the common law rules, payments for services as a minister are considered income from self employment. . . . A minister, unless exempt, pays social security and Medicare taxes under the Self-employment Contributions Act (SECA) and is not subject to Federal Insurance Compensation Act (FICA) taxes or income tax withholding.

Payment for services as a minister, unless statutorily exempt, is subject to income tax, therefore the minister should make estimated tax payments to avoid potential penalties for not paying enough tax as the minister earns the income. If the employer and employee agree, an election can be made to have income taxes withheld. Even though a minister may receive a Form 1099-MISC for the performance of services, he or she may be a common law employee and should in fact be receiving a Form W-2.

Voluntary withholding

Ministers who report their income taxes as employees can enter into a voluntary withholding arrangement with their church. Under such an arrangement, the church withholds federal income taxes from the minister's wages just as it would for any nonminister employee. Some ministers find voluntary withholding attractive, since it avoids the additional work and discipline associated with the estimated tax procedure.

How is a voluntary withholding arrangement initiated?

A minister who elects to enter into a voluntary withholding arrangement with his or her church need only file a completed IRS Form W-4 (Employee's Withholding Allowance Certificate) with the church. The filing of this form is deemed to be a request for voluntary withholding.

Can a voluntary withholding arrangement be revoked?

Voluntary withholding arrangements may be terminated at any time by either the church or minister, or by mutual consent of both. Alternatively, a minister can stipulate that the voluntary withholding arrangement terminates on a specified date. Of course, a voluntary withholding arrangement will affect the church's quarterly Form 941 (see Chapter 11).

What about a minister's self-employment taxes?

Remember that ministers are always deemed to be self-employed for Social Security purposes with respect to services performed in the exercise of ministry. Therefore, a church whose minister elects voluntary withholding is only obligated to withhold the minister's federal income tax liability. The minister is still required to use the estimated tax procedure to report and prepay the self-employment tax (the Social Security tax on self-employed persons).

Consider the following alternative. Ministers who report their income taxes as employees (and who are not exempt from Social Security) should consider filing an amended Form W-4 (Withholding Allowance Certificate) with their church, indicating on line 6 an additional amount of cash to be withheld from each pay period that will be sufficient to pay the estimated self-employment tax liability by the end of the year. IRS Publication 517 states: "If you perform your services as a common-law employee of the church and your salary is not subject to income tax withholding, you can enter into a voluntary withholding agreement with the church to cover any income and self-employment tax that may be due."

A church whose minister has elected voluntary withholding (and who is not exempt from Social Security taxes) simply withholds an additional amount from each paycheck to cover the minister's estimated self-employment tax liability for the year and then reports this additional amount as additional income tax withheld on its quarterly Forms 941. The excess withheld income tax is reported on line 62 of Form 1040 and is applied to all taxes the minister reports on Form 1040, including both income taxes and self-employment taxes.

Since any tax paid by voluntary withholding is deemed to be timely paid, a minister who pays self-employment taxes using this procedure will not be liable for any underpayment penalty (assuming that a sufficient amount of taxes are withheld).

➡ **TIP.** Ministers who report their income taxes as employees should consider the convenience of voluntary withholding with respect to both income taxes and self-employment taxes.

A self-employed minister is free to enter into an unofficial withholding arrangement whereby the church withholds a portion of his or her compensation each week and deposits it in a church account, then distributes the balance to the minister in advance of each quarterly estimated tax payment. No Forms W-4 should be used, and the withholdings are not reported on Form 941. A church's withholding obligations under federal law are explained (and illustrated) fully in Chapter 11.

2. ESTIMATED TAX

✿ **KEY POINT.** Ministers' compensation is exempt from federal income tax withholding whether they report their income taxes as employees or as self-employed.

✿ **KEY POINT.** Ministers must prepay their income taxes and self-employment taxes using the estimated tax procedure (unless they elect voluntary withholding).

Application to ministers

Compensation paid to ministers for services performed in the exercise of their ministry is exempt from income tax withholding (see above). As a result, ministers are required to prepay their taxes using the estimated tax procedure unless they request voluntary withholding.

Since ministers are self-employed for Social Security with regard to services performed in the exercise of ministry, they must use the estimated tax procedure to report and prepay their self-employment taxes (assuming they are not exempt) unless they have entered into a voluntary withholding arrangement with their employing church.

▲ **CAUTION.** *The exemption of ministers from income tax withholding, coupled with an unfamiliarity with the estimated tax requirements, has caused many younger and inexperienced ministers to refrain from reporting or paying their taxes. It is essential that ministers be familiar with the rules discussed below.*

Form 1040-ES

Estimated taxes are computed and reported on IRS Form 1040-ES.

Who should make estimated tax payments

In 2013 you must make estimated tax payments if you expect to owe at least $1,000 in tax for 2013 (after subtracting your withholding and refundable credits) and you expect your withholding and refundable credits to be less than the smaller of (1) 90 percent of the tax shown on your 2013 tax return, or (2) 100 percent of the tax shown on your 2012 tax return (110 percent of that amount if the adjusted gross income shown on that return is more than $150,000, or if married filing separately, more than $75,000). If you did not file a 2012 tax return or if that return did not cover 12 months, item (2) above does not apply.

If you are required to pay estimated taxes but fail to do so, you will be subject to an underpayment penalty. Since the penalty is figured separately for each quarterly period, you may owe a penalty for an earlier payment period even if you later paid enough to make up the underpayment. If you did not pay enough tax by the due date of each of the payment periods, you may owe a penalty even if you are due a refund when you file your income tax return.

✿ **KEY POINT.** Stated differently, if your estimated taxes for the current year will be $1,000 or more (after subtracting any tax withholdings and credits), you will owe a penalty for not paying quarterly estimated taxes to the IRS. However, the penalty is avoided if the estimated taxes you pay this year are at least (1) 90 percent of your tax liability for the current year, or (2) 100 percent of your tax liability for the previous year (110 percent for certain high-income taxpayers) if your tax return covered the entire year.

EXAMPLE. Pastor T's 2012 income tax return (which was for the entire calendar year) showed a tax of $7,000. Pastor T expects that her 2013 tax liability will be $7,500. She also anticipates that no taxes will be withheld from her 2013 income as a minister (her only source of income). Pastor T is exempt from Social Security taxes on her ministerial earnings (she submitted a timely Form 4361 exemption application to the IRS in a prior year). Under these facts, Pastor T's estimated tax will be $7,500 (tax liability of $7,500 with no withholding). Since Pastor T's estimated tax for 2013 will be at least $1,000 and none of it will be subject to withholding, she must make estimated tax payments for 2013.

EXAMPLE. Same facts as the preceding example, except that Pastor T has entered into a voluntary withholding agreement with her church and estimates that $6,500 will be withheld from her compensation in 2013. Must she make estimated tax payments? Yes, since the total amount of income taxes to be withheld from her compensation in 2013 is less than the lesser of (1) 90 percent of her estimated total tax liability for 2013 (90 percent x $7,500 = $6,750), or (2) 100 percent of the tax shown on her 2012 return ($7,000). If she fails to pay estimated taxes, she will be subject to a penalty (as explained later in this section).

EXAMPLE. Pastor G did not make estimated tax payments for 2012 because he thought he had enough tax withheld from his wages (through voluntary withholding) to cover his total tax liability. Early in January 2013 Pastor G made an estimate of his total 2012 tax and realized that his withholdings were $2,000 less than the amount needed to avoid a penalty for underpayment of estimated tax. On January 10, 2013, he made an estimated tax payment of $3,000, which was the difference between his withholding and his estimate of total tax. His final tax return showed his total tax to be $500 less than his estimate, so he was due a refund. Pastor G does not owe a penalty for the quarterly estimated tax payment due January 31, 2013. However, he may owe a penalty through January 10, 2013 (the day he made the $3,000 payment), for underpayments for the previous quarterly periods.

Estimated tax procedure for 2013

The four-step procedure for reporting and prepaying estimated taxes for 2013 is summarized below:

Step 1: Obtain a copy of IRS Form 1040-ES.

Obtain a copy of IRS Form 1040-ES prior to April 15, 2013. Note that Form 1040-ES consists of a worksheet, instructions, and four dated payment vouchers. You can obtain a copy from any IRS office, the IRS website (irs.gov), many public libraries, or by calling the toll-free IRS forms hotline at 1-800-TAX-FORM (1-800-829-3676).

Step 2: Compute estimated taxes for 2013.

Compute your estimated tax for 2013 on the Form 1040-ES worksheet. This is done by estimating adjusted gross income (AGI) and then subtracting estimated adjustments, deductions, exemptions,

and credits. Use the data set forth on your previous year's tax return as a helpful starting point. To determine your estimated taxes for 2013, estimated taxable income is multiplied by the applicable tax rate contained in the Tax Rate Schedule reproduced on Form 1040-ES. Remember to include your estimated Social Security tax on the worksheet if you are not exempt and to include your housing allowance exclusion in computing your estimated earnings subject to the self-employment tax (the housing allowance is excluded from income only in computing your income tax liability, not your self-employment tax).

✱ **New in 2013.** The tax cuts enacted by Congress in recent years will result in lower taxes, and thus lower estimated tax payments, for many taxpayers. However, some of the tax deductions and credits expired at the end of 2011 or 2012, making them unavailable in 2013 unless Congress acts to extend them. Be sure your estimated tax calculations for 2013 take into account the applicable tax rates, deductions, credits, and exclusions.

Step 3: Pay estimated taxes in quarterly installments.

If estimated taxes (federal income taxes and self-employment taxes) are more than $1,000 for 2013 and the total amount of taxes to be withheld from your compensation is less than the lesser of (1) 90 percent of the total taxes (income and Social Security) to be shown on your actual 2013 tax return, or (2) 100 percent of the total taxes (income and Social Security) shown on your 2012 return (110 percent for certain high-income taxpayers), you must pay one-fourth of your total estimated taxes in four quarterly installments, as follows:

FOR THE PERIOD	DUE DATE
January 1 – March 31	April 15
April 1 – May 31	June 15
June 1 – August 31	September 15
September 1 – December 31	January 15 (following year)

➡ **TIP.** You do not have to make the payment due January 15 if you file your tax return by January 31 and pay the entire balance due with your return.

Payments that are mailed must be postmarked no later than the due date. If the due date for making an estimated tax payment falls on a Saturday, Sunday, or legal holiday, the payment will be on time if you make it on the next day that is not a Saturday, Sunday, or legal holiday.

Payment vouchers. You must send each payment to the IRS, accompanied by one of the four payment vouchers contained in Form 1040-ES. If you paid estimated taxes last year, you should receive a copy of your 2013 Form 1040-ES in the mail with payment vouchers preprinted with your name, address, and Social Security number.

If you did not pay estimated taxes last year, you will have to get a copy of Form 1040-ES from the IRS. After you make your first payment (April 15, 2013), you should receive a Form 1040-ES package in your name with the preprinted information. There is a separate payment voucher for each of the four quarterly payment periods. Each one has the due date printed on it. Be sure to use the correct payment voucher.

➤ **TIP.** Estimated tax payments can be made electronically using electric funds withdrawal or a credit or debit card. See the instructions to Form 1040-ES for details.

Starting a job midyear. A minister may become liable for estimated tax payments midway through a year. For example, a minister may change churches midway through the year, leaving a church that voluntarily withheld taxes and going to a church that does not withhold taxes. In such a case the minister should submit a payment voucher by the next filing deadline, accompanied by a check for a prorated portion of the entire estimated tax liability for the year.

EXAMPLE. Pastor K graduates from seminary in May 2013 and assumes the position of associate pastor of a church on July 20, 2013. Pastor K had no income for the year until he began working for the church. Pastor K estimates his total tax liability for 2013 to be $5,000. He should obtain a Form 1040-ES and submit the third payment voucher on or before September 15, 2013, along with a check for half of the total tax (i.e., $2,500). He should send the remaining half with his January 15, 2014, payment voucher.

Changing your quarterly payments. After making your first or second estimated tax payment, changes in your income, deductions, credits, or exemptions may make it necessary for you to refigure your estimated tax and adjust your remaining quarterly payments accordingly.

EXAMPLE. Pastor H's church board fails to designate a housing allowance for 2013 until May 1, 2013. Pastor H's April 15 estimated tax payment was based on his annual earnings less an anticipated housing allowance. The delayed designation of a housing allowance will almost certainly affect Pastor H's estimated taxes for 2013, and so his remaining quarterly payments should be recalculated to avoid an underpayment penalty.

Step 4: Compute actual taxes at the end of the year.

At the end of 2013, compute your actual tax liability on Form 1040. Only then will you know your actual income, deductions, exclusions, and credits. Estimated tax payments rarely reflect actual tax liability. Most taxpayers' estimated tax payments are either more or less than actual taxes as computed on Form 1040.

The consequences of overpayment and underpayment of estimated taxes are summarized below.

Overpayment (estimated tax payments exceed actual tax liability). If you overpaid your estimated taxes (i.e., your estimated tax payments plus any withholding were more than your actual taxes computed on Form 1040), you can elect to have the overpayment credited against your first 2013 quarterly estimated tax payment or spread out in any way you choose among any or all of your next four quarterly installments. Alternatively, you can request a refund of the overpayment.

Underpayment (estimated tax payments were less than actual tax liability). If you underpaid your estimated taxes (i.e., your estimated tax payments plus any withholding were less than your actual taxes computed on Form 1040), you may have to pay a penalty. In general, you will not be subject to an underpayment penalty for 2013 if any of the following situations applies:

- You had no tax liability for 2011, you were a U.S. citizen or resident alien for the entire year, and your 2011 tax return was (or would have been, had you been required to file) for a full 12 months.
- The total tax shown on your 2012 return, minus the amount of tax you paid through withholding, is less than $1,000. To determine whether the total tax is less than $1,000, complete Part 1, lines 1 through 7, of Form 2210.

You will not have an underpayment for any quarter in 2013 in which your estimated tax payment is paid by the due date for that quarter and equals or exceeds the lesser of 22.5 percent of the tax shown on your 2013 return or 25 percent of the tax shown on your 2012 return (if your 2012 return covered all 12 months of the year). If you are subject to the 110 percent rule for high-income taxpayers, discussed earlier, substitute 27.5 percent for 25 percent.

❀ **KEY POINT.** The penalty is figured separately for each quarterly payment period, so you may owe the penalty for an early period even if you later pay enough to make up the underpayment. Contrary to popular belief, payment of your entire 2013 estimated tax liability by January 15, 2014, or by April 15, 2014, will not relieve you of the underpayment penalty if you did not pay any estimated taxes during the previous quarters. Waiting until the end of the year to pay the full amount of estimated taxes will result in an underpayment penalty for the three preceding quarters. *Veis v. United States, 88-2 USTC ¶ 9616 (D. Mont. 1988).* If, however, you file your 2013 Form 1040 and pay the actual taxes due by January 31, 2014, you will have no penalty for the payment due on January 15, 2014, if you failed to make your fourth quarterly payment by that date.

EXAMPLE. Pastor J does not elect voluntary withholding of any taxes and does not use the estimated tax procedure. Instead, he simply computes his taxes for the year and sends in a check with his Form 1040. Pastor J will be assessed a penalty for failure to pay each of the four quarterly payments he missed.

EXAMPLE. Pastor K estimates that his taxes for 2013 will be $8,000. He pays his first quarterly installment of $2,000 on April 15, 2013, but only pays $1,000 for his second quarterly installment on June 15, 2013, and another $1,000 for his third quarterly installment on September 15, 2013. He attempts to "make up the difference" by paying a fourth quarterly installment of $4,000 on January 15, 2014. While Pastor K has paid his entire estimated tax of $8,000, he will be assessed an underpayment penalty for failure to pay his full second and third installments on time.

Form 2210

You can use Form 2210 to see if you owe a penalty and to figure the amount of the penalty. If you owe a penalty and do not attach Form 2210 to your Form 1040, the IRS will compute your penalty and send you a bill. You do not have to fill out a Form 2210 or pay any penalty if (1) your total tax less income tax withheld is less than $1,000, or (2) you had no tax liability last year and you were a United States citizen or resident for the entire year.

The IRS can waive the underpayment penalty if it determines that (1) in 2012 or 2013 you retired after reaching age 62 or became disabled, and your underpayment was due to reasonable cause; or (2) the underpayment was due to casualty, disaster, or other unusual circumstance, and it would be inequitable to impose the penalty.

➥ **TIP.** For more information, see IRS Publication 505 (*Tax Withholding and Estimated Tax*).

Special rule for high-income taxpayers

High-income taxpayers cannot avoid the underpayment penalty by paying estimated taxes for the current year of at least 100 percent of last year's tax. A high-income taxpayer is one with AGI for the previous year of at least $150,000 ($75,000 for married persons filing separately). For such persons the 100 percent rule is replaced with a 110 percent rule, meaning they will be subject to an underpayment penalty unless they have paid estimated taxes for the current year of at least the lesser of (1) 90 percent of the current year's actual tax liability, or (2) 110 percent of last year's actual tax liability.

E. IF YOUR RETURN IS EXAMINED

Tax returns are examined to verify the correctness of your reported taxes. An IRS computer program selects most returns that are examined. Under this program (called the discriminant function system, or DIF), selected entries on your return are evaluated and the return

is given a score. Returns are then screened by IRS personnel. Those returns having the highest probability for error are selected for examination.

The IRS describes its procedure for selecting tax returns for examination as follows:

> *We accept most taxpayers' returns as filed. If we inquire about your return or select it for examination, it does not suggest that you are dishonest. The inquiry or examination may or may not result in more tax. We may close your case without change; or, you may receive a refund. The process of selecting a return for examination usually begins in one of two ways. First, we use computer programs to identify returns that may have incorrect amounts. These programs may be based on information returns, such as Forms 1099 and W-2, on studies of past examinations, or on certain issues identified by compliance projects. Second, we use information from outside sources that indicates that a return may have incorrect amounts. These sources may include newspapers, public records, and individuals. If we determine that the information is accurate and reliable, we may use it to select a return for examination.* IRS Publication 1 (Your Rights as a Taxpayer).

✿ **KEY POINT.** The IRS is prohibited from using "financial status" or "economic reality" examination techniques to determine the existence of unreported income of any taxpayer unless the IRS has independent and reasonable proof that there is a likelihood of unreported income.

Other returns are selected because of discrepancies among forms (e.g., stated compensation differs from amounts reported on Forms W-2 or 1099-MISC).

An examination of your return does not suggest a suspicion of dishonesty. It may not even result in more tax. Many audits are closed without any change in your reported tax, and in others taxpayers receive refunds.

The examination (or audit) may be conducted by correspondence, or it may take place in your home or place of business, an IRS office, or the office of your attorney or accountant. The place and method of examination is determined by the IRS, but your wishes will be considered. You may act on your own behalf, or you may have someone represent you or accompany you. An attorney, CPA, enrolled agent (someone other than an attorney or CPA who is enrolled to practice before the IRS), or the person who prepared your return and signed it as the preparer may represent or accompany you. You must furnish your representative (if any) with a power of attorney (Form 2848).

If your return is selected for examination, you will be contacted by the IRS and asked to assemble records supporting the items on your return that are being investigated. When the examination is completed, you will be advised of any proposed change in your taxes and the reasons for any such change. If you agree with the findings of the examiner, you will be asked to sign an agreement form. By signing the form, you indicate that you agree with the changes. If you owe any additional tax, you may pay it when you sign the agreement.

If you do not agree with changes proposed by the examiner, the examiner will explain your appeal rights. This includes your right to request an immediate meeting with a supervisor to explain your position if your examination takes place in an IRS office. If an agreement is reached, your case will be closed. If an agreement is not reached at this meeting or if your examination occurs outside of an IRS office, you will be sent (1) a letter notifying you of your right to appeal within 30 days; (2) a copy of the examination report explaining the proposed adjustments; (3) an agreement or waiver form; and (4) a copy of IRS Publication 5 (which explains your appeal rights in detail).

If, after receiving the examiner's report, you decide to agree with it, simply sign the agreement or waiver form and return it to the examiner. If you decide not to agree with the examination report, you may appeal your case within the IRS or take it immediately to the federal courts. For a complete explanation, obtain a copy of IRS Publication 556.

F. OFFERS IN COMPROMISE

What options are available to ministers who cannot afford to pay their taxes? This is an important question. Many ministers have been audited by the IRS and assessed several thousands of dollars of taxes and penalties but have no prospect for paying their bill. In some cases they incorrectly claimed a housing allowance exclusion in computing both their income taxes and self-employment taxes (it is an exclusion only in computing income taxes). In other cases ministers who have reported their income taxes as self-employed are reclassified as employees by the IRS, which often results in hundreds, if not thousands, of dollars in additional taxes. Some ministers have incorrectly assumed that they are exempt from Social Security, though they have never received IRS confirmation of their exempt status.

Obviously, these ministers can face many thousands of dollars in taxes and penalties. For these and other reasons, ministers sometimes are burdened with enormous tax liabilities without any reasonable prospect of payment. In many cases these tax liabilities are due to the complex and confusing tax rules that apply to ministers. What can be done in such cases? This section and section G address two possibilities: offers in compromise and installment agreements.

An offer in compromise (OIC) is an agreement between a taxpayer and the IRS that settles the taxpayer's tax liabilities for less than the

10-YEAR COLLECTION STATUTE

Generally the collection statute is 10 years from the date that your liability was assessed. Circumstances may extend the 10-year collection statute, such as when a taxpayer files for bankruptcy or files an offer in compromise. For assistance in calculating the remaining time on your collection statute, call this toll-free number: 1-800-829-1040.

full amount owed. Absent special circumstances, an offer will not be accepted if the IRS believes that the liability can be paid in full as a lump sum or through a payment agreement.

In most cases the IRS will not accept an OIC unless the amount offered by the taxpayer is equal to or greater than the reasonable collection potential (RCP). The RCP is how the IRS measures the taxpayer's ability to pay. It includes the value that can be realized from the taxpayer's assets, such as real property, automobiles, bank accounts, and other property. The RCP also includes anticipated future income, less certain amounts allowed for basic living expenses.

The IRS cautions taxpayers to be wary of promoters' claims "that tax debts can be settled through the offer in compromise program for 'pennies on the dollar.'"

1. THREE TYPES OF OIC

The IRS may accept an offer in compromise based on three grounds:

- **Doubt as to collectibility.** Doubt exists that the taxpayer could ever pay the full amount of tax liability owed within the remainder of the statutory period for collection. Use IRS Form 656 to submit the offer.

EXAMPLE. A church employee owes $20,000 for unpaid tax liabilities and agrees that the tax she owes is correct. The employee's monthly income does not meet her necessary living expenses. She does not own any real property and does not have the ability to fully pay the liability now or through monthly installment payments.

- **Doubt as to liability.** A legitimate doubt exists that the assessed tax liability is correct. Possible reasons to submit a doubt as to liability offer include: (1) the IRS made a mistake interpreting the law; (2) the IRS failed to consider the taxpayer's evidence; or (3) the taxpayer has new evidence. Use IRS Form 656-L to submit the offer.

EXAMPLE. Jon served as a church treasurer from 2001 to 2011. In 2013 the church accrued unpaid payroll taxes, and Jon was assessed a trust fund recovery penalty (under section 6672 of the tax code) as a responsible party of the church. Since Jon had resigned prior to the payroll taxes accruing and was not contacted prior to the assessment, there is legitimate doubt that the assessed tax liability is correct.

- **Exceptional circumstances (effective tax administration).** There is no doubt that the tax is correct, and there is potential to collect the full amount of the tax owed, but an exceptional circumstance exists that would allow the IRS to consider an OIC. To be eligible for compromise on this basis, a taxpayer must demonstrate that the collection of the tax would create an economic hardship or would be unfair and inequitable. Use IRS Form 656 to submit the offer.

2. OIC PAYMENT OPTIONS

Taxpayers may choose to pay the offer amount in a lump sum or in installment payments. The tax law provides rules for lump-sum offers and periodic-payment offers. A lump-sum offer is defined as an offer payable in five or fewer installments. If a taxpayer submits a lump-sum offer, the taxpayer must include with Form 656 a nonrefundable payment equal to 20 percent of the offer amount. This payment is required in addition to the $150 application fee. The 20 percent amount is called "nonrefundable" because it cannot be returned to the taxpayer even if the offer is rejected or returned to the taxpayer without acceptance. The 20 percent amount will be applied to the taxpayer's tax liability. The taxpayer has a right to specify the particular tax liability to which the IRS will apply the 20 percent amount.

The offer is considered a periodic-payment offer under the tax law if it is payable in six or more installments. When submitting a periodic-payment offer, the taxpayer must include the first proposed installment payment along with Form 656. This payment is required in addition to the $150 application fee. This amount is nonrefundable, just like the 20 percent payment required for a lump-sum offer. Also, while the IRS is evaluating a periodic-payment offer, the taxpayer must continue to make the installment payments provided for under the terms of the offer. These amounts are also nonrefundable. These amounts are applied to the tax liabilities, and the taxpayer has a right to specify the particular tax liabilities to which the periodic payments will be applied.

3. PAYMENTS AND APPLICATION FEES

In general, a taxpayer must submit a $150 application fee with Form 656. There are two exceptions to this requirement. First, no application fee is required if the OIC is based on doubt as to

liability. Second, the fee is not required if the taxpayer is an individual who qualifies for the low-income exception. This exception applies if the taxpayer's total monthly income falls at or below 250 percent of the poverty guidelines published by the Department of Health and Human Services. Section 4 of Form 656 contains the Low Income Certification guidelines to assist taxpayers in determining whether they qualify for the low-income exception. A taxpayer who claims the low-income exception must complete section 4 of Form 656.

If the IRS accepts the taxpayer's offer, the IRS expects that the taxpayer will have no further delinquencies and will fully comply with the tax laws. If the taxpayer does not abide by all the terms and conditions of the OIC, the IRS may determine that the OIC is in default. To avoid a default, the taxpayer must timely file all tax returns and timely pay all taxes for five years or until the offered amount is paid in full, whichever period is longer. When an OIC is declared to be in default, the agreement is no longer in effect and the IRS may then collect the amounts originally owed, plus interest and penalties.

If the IRS rejects an OIC, the taxpayer will be notified by mail. The letter will explain the reason the IRS rejected the offer and will provide detailed instructions on how the taxpayer may appeal the decision to the IRS Office of Appeals. The appeal must be made within 30 days from the date of the letter. In some cases, an OIC is returned to the taxpayer, rather than rejected, because the taxpayer has not submitted necessary information, has filed for bankruptcy, has failed to include a required application fee or nonrefundable payment with the offer, or has failed to file tax returns or pay current tax liabilities while the offer is under consideration. A return is different from a rejection because there is no right to appeal the IRS's decision to return the offer.

Here are some steps the IRS has taken to make the OIC program more effective:

- In evaluating a taxpayer's ability to pay, the IRS considers the taxpayer's own expenses rather than using national averages.
- Instead of the old, stringent application guidelines that often led to immediate rejections, the IRS works with taxpayers to fine-tune their compromise offers—a step that is designed to result in the acceptance of more offers.
- Taxpayers are asked to provide fewer financial documents to qualify for smaller compromise offers.
- New deferred payment procedures provide more opportunities for compromise offers to be submitted by taxpayers who may have been excluded under the old guidelines.
- A short-term deferred payment option allows taxpayers up to two years to pay the compromise offer.
- Specially trained IRS experts are devoted to handling compromise offers. These offer specialists bring more consistency to the OIC program and centralize offer processing.

- Independent reviews are conducted for each rejected compromise offer. These reviews assess whether rejection is in the best interest of the taxpayer and the government.

EXAMPLE. The United States Tax Court ruled that the IRS can ignore a pastor's tithes as a "living expense" in evaluating an offer in compromise. The court noted that the IRS *Internal Revenue Manual* concedes that if a minister is required "as a condition of employment" to tithe to a church, then this is a necessary living expense that can be considered in evaluating an offer in compromise submitted by the minister. The "only thing to consider is whether the amount being contributed equals the amount actually required and does not include a voluntary portion." In this case, the court concluded there was no evidence that the person was employed as a pastor, and it rejected his argument that tithing was a "condition of employment" even with respect to earnings from a secular employer, since he was required by church doctrine to tithe on such earnings.

The court also rejected the pastor's claim that the IRS's disregard of tithing expenses in evaluating offers in compromise violates the First Amendment guaranty of religious freedom, since the effect of this policy was to reduce the funds taxpayers have to support their religion and divert those funds to the U.S. Treasury. The court concluded, "It may well be true that paying their taxes will leave the pastor and his wife with less funds to support their religion. But this is a burden, common to all taxpayers, on their pocketbooks, rather than a recognizable burden on the free exercise of their religious beliefs." *Pixley v. Commissioner, 123 T.C. 15 (2004).*

G. INSTALLMENT AGREEMENTS

You can request a monthly installment plan if you cannot pay the full amount you owe. To be valid, your request must be approved by the IRS. However, if you owe $10,000 or less in tax and you meet certain other criteria, the IRS must accept your request. Before you request an installment agreement, you should consider other, less costly alternatives, such as a bank loan. You will continue to be charged interest and penalties on the amount you owe until it is paid in full.

Unless your income is below a certain level, the fee for an approved installment agreement has increased to $105 ($52 if you make your payments by electronic funds withdrawal). If your income is below a certain level, you may qualify to pay a reduced fee of $43.

For more information about installment agreements, see Form 9465, Installment Agreement Request.

Installment agreements may be set up in various ways:

- direct debit from your bank account,
- payroll deduction from your employer,
- regular installment agreement, or
- credit card.

➡ **TIP.** The IRS recommends that before requesting an installment agreement, you should consider other less costly alternatives, such as a bank loan or credit card payment.

H. THE SARBANES-OXLEY ACT

The Sarbanes-Oxley Act was enacted by Congress in 2002 following several financial scandals involving high-profile companies. While the main purpose of the Act is to increase corporate accountability for companies that issue and sell stock to the general public, some of the Act's provisions apply to churches. These include the following.

1. DESTRUCTION AND FALSIFICATION OF RECORDS

The Act amends federal criminal law to include the following new crime: "Whoever knowingly alters, destroys, mutilates, conceals, covers up, falsifies, or makes a false entry in any record, document, or tangible object with the intent to impede, obstruct, or influence the investigation or proper administration of any matter within the jurisdiction of any department or agency of the United States . . . or in relation to or contemplation of any such matter or case, shall be fined under this title, imprisoned not more than 20 years, or both."

2. WHISTLEBLOWER PROTECTION

The Act amends federal criminal law to include this crime: "Whoever knowingly, with the intent to retaliate, takes any action harmful to any person, including interference with the lawful employment or livelihood of any person, for providing to a law enforcement officer any truthful information relating to the commission or possible commission of any federal offense, shall be fined under this title or imprisoned not more than 10 years, or both."

Most of the provisions of the Act are in the form of amendments to federal securities laws (the Securities Act of 1933 and the Securities and Exchange Act of 1934). Since religious organizations are exempt from these laws (except for fraudulent acts), they are not covered by the Act's provisions. However, the two sections quoted above are amendments to federal criminal law. Since federal criminal law contains no blanket exemption for religious organizations, such organizations are subject to these provisions.

❖ **KEY POINT.** Persons who falsify records or documents may be liable on other grounds as well. For example, the intentional falsification of tax forms may result in liability for civil or criminal fraud.

EXAMPLE. A church has 50 members and one full-time employee (its pastor). It also has a part-time office secretary and an independent contractor who performs custodial services. The church does not have a CPA firm audit its financial statements. The pastor discovers in June 2013 that the church board failed to designate a housing allowance for him for that year. He creates a housing allowance that he dates December 31, 2012, and which purports to designate a housing allowance for all of 2013. The church is not a public company (i.e., it does not issue and sell stock to the general public) and therefore is not subject to most of the provisions of the Sarbanes-Oxley Act. However, the Act makes it a crime to knowingly falsify any document with the intent to influence "the investigation or proper administration of any matter within the jurisdiction of any department or agency of the United States . . . or in relation to or contemplation of any such matter or case," and this provision contains no exemption for churches or pastors. It is possible that the pastor's falsification of the 2012 housing allowance violates this provision, exposing him to a fine or imprisonment of up to 20 years.

The Act does not define the "proper administration of any matter within the jurisdiction of any department or agency of the United States . . . or in relation to or contemplation of any such matter," but several courts have construed this same language in other contexts and noted that it "must be given a broad, non-technical meaning" and pertains generally to "all matters within the authority of a government agency" and is not limited to submissions of written documents to governmental agencies. These factors raise the possibility that the pastor's actions violate Sarbanes-Oxley. But even if they do not, the pastor's actions may expose him to civil or criminal penalties under the tax code.

EXAMPLE. A church bookkeeper falsifies an application for property tax exemption for a building owned by the church in order to avoid the church having to pay property taxes. The Sarbanes-Oxley Act makes it a crime to knowingly falsify any document with the intent to influence "the investigation or proper administration of any matter within the jurisdiction of any department or agency of the United States . . . or in relation to or contemplation of any such matter or case," and this

provision contains no exemption for churches or church employees. In this case, however, the falsified record pertained to a local law and not a federal law, so the Act does not apply. However, the bookkeeper's actions may expose her to civil or criminal penalties under other state or federal laws.

EXAMPLE. A church staff member realizes that the church failed to complete a Form I-9 (immigration form) for each new worker for the past several years. In order to avoid any penalties for noncompliance, the staff member completes a Form I-9 for each employee hired over the past three years and backdates each form to the date of hire. The church is not a public company and therefore is not subject to most of the provisions of the Sarbanes-Oxley Act. However, the Act makes it a crime to knowingly falsify any document with the intent to influence "the investigation or proper administration of any matter within the jurisdiction of any department or agency of the United States . . . or in relation to or contemplation of any such matter or case," and this provision contains no exemption for churches or pastors. It is possible that the staff member's falsification of the I-9 forms violates this provision in the Sarbanes-Oxley Act, exposing him to a fine or imprisonment of up to 20 years.

The Act does not define the "proper administration of any matter within the jurisdiction of any department or agency of the United States . . . or in relation to or contemplation of any such matter," but several courts have construed this same language in other contexts and noted that it "must be given a broad, non-technical meaning" and pertains generally to "all matters within the authority of a government agency" and is not limited to submissions of written documents to governmental agencies. These factors raise the possibility that the staff member's actions violate Sarbanes-Oxley. But even if they do not, the actions may expose the staff member to civil or criminal penalties under other federal or state laws.

EXAMPLE. A church employee learns that the church is not paying over withheld income taxes and FICA taxes to the government. The employee notifies the local IRS office. When the pastor learns that the employee notified the IRS, he fires him. Has the pastor violated the Sarbanes-Oxley Act's whistleblower provision? Possibly. The Act amends federal criminal law to include the following crime: "Whoever knowingly, with the intent to retaliate, takes any action harmful to any person, including interference with the lawful employment or livelihood of any person, for providing to a law enforcement officer any truthful information relating to the commission or possible commission of any federal offense, shall be fined under this title or imprisoned not more than 10 years, or both." The pastor's decision not to pay over withheld taxes to the government may be a federal offense, since section 7202 of the tax code imposes criminal penalties upon "any person required to collect, account

SUPREME COURT AFFIRMS TAXPAYER RIGHT TO MINIMIZE TAXES

For the first time in 73 years, the United States Supreme Court affirmed the right of taxpayers to minimize taxes. In a unanimous ruling, the court quoted from a 1935 decision: "The legal right of a taxpayer to decrease the amount of what otherwise would be his taxes, or altogether avoid them, by means which the law permits, cannot be doubted." *Gregory v. Helvering, 293 U.S. 465 (1935).*

But the court cautioned: "The rule is a two-way street: While a taxpayer is free to organize his affairs as he chooses, nevertheless, once having done so, he must accept the tax consequences of his choice, whether contemplated or not . . . and may not enjoy the benefit of some other route he might have chosen to follow but did not. . . . The question here, of course, is not whether alternative routes may have offered better or worse tax consequences [but] whether what was done . . . was the thing which the [tax code] intended." *Boulware v. U.S. 2008 WL 552880 (U.S. 2008).*

for, and pay over any tax imposed by this title who willfully fails to collect or truthfully account for and pay over such tax." As a result, the pastor's dismissal of the employee for reporting the possible violation of this section may trigger liability under Sarbanes-Oxley.

Note that this section requires that the employee provide to a "law enforcement officer" information relating to the commission of a federal offense. Is an IRS agent a law enforcement officer? Federal law defines this term as "an officer or employee of the federal government, or a person authorized to act for or on behalf of the federal government or serving the federal government as an adviser or consultant—(A) authorized under law to engage in or supervise the prevention, detection, investigation, or prosecution of an offense." Construed broadly, this could include an IRS agent. In summary, it is possible that the pastor's dismissal of the church employee violated the whistleblower provision under Sarbanes-Oxley. If so, this would be a felony exposing the pastor to a fine of not more than $10,000 or imprisonment of not more than five years, or both, together with the costs of prosecution. Finally, note that apart from the pastor's potential liability for violating Sarbanes-Oxley under these circumstances, the dismissed employee may be able to sue the pastor and church under state law for wrongful termination or some other theory of liability.

I. RIGHT TO MINIMIZE TAXES

While *evasion* of taxes will subject a taxpayer to civil and possibly criminal penalties, every taxpayer has the legal right to *avoid* or *minimize* taxes. As Judge Learned Hand remarked: "Over and over again the courts have said that there is nothing sinister in so arranging one's affairs as to keep taxes as low as possible. Everybody does so, rich or poor; and all do right, for nobody owes any public duty to pay more tax than the law demands; taxes are enforced exactions, not voluntary contributions." *Newman v. Commissioner, 159 F.2d 848 (2d Cir. 1947).*

Another federal appeals court judge has observed that "it is a well settled principle that a taxpayer has the legal right to decrease the amount of what otherwise would be his taxes, or to avoid them altogether, by means which the law permits." *Jones v. Grinnell, 179 F.2d 873 (10th Cir. 1950).*

➡ **TIP.** Note that while taxpayers have a legal right to minimize or avoid taxes, they are subject to civil and possibly criminal penalties for tax evasion.

J. NOTIFYING THE IRS OF A CHANGE OF ADDRESS

The IRS has explained how to notify it of a change in address. Many taxpayers are surprised to learn that IRS notices are legally effective even if never received, so long as they are mailed to a taxpayer's last known address. The Tax Court has ruled that the address listed on a taxpayer's most recent federal tax return is his or her "last known address" unless the taxpayer has given the IRS "clear and concise notification" of a different address.

To effectively notify the IRS of a change in address, a taxpayer must send a change-of-address notification to the IRS Service Center serving the taxpayer's old address or to the Chief, Taxpayer Service Division, in the local IRS district office. The IRS has developed a form (Form 8822) that is designed specifically to notify it of a change of address. Taxpayers are encouraged to use this form in notifying the IRS of any change in their address, since it will satisfy the "clear and concise notification" requirement and will identify the specific IRS office to which the notification should be sent.

The IRS has stated that informing the U.S. Postal Service of a change of address will not constitute clear and concise notification to the IRS. Predictably, the IRS Form 8822 is seldom used by taxpayers to notify the IRS of a change of address.

✹ **KEY POINT.** Each year millions of dollars in refund checks are returned to the IRS as "undeliverable" by the U.S. Postal Service. Taxpayers who are due a refund and have not yet received their check are urged to call the IRS at 1-800-829-1040 or visit the IRS website at irs.gov (refund checks can be traced on-line using your Social Security number). Taxpayers can eliminate the possibility of lost, stolen, or undeliverable refunds by electing direct deposit. Also, they can avoid delays in receiving their refunds by sending their new address to the IRS on Form 8822. The Postal Service returned most of the refund checks to the IRS because it could not deliver them. Thousands of checks were returned because the names or addresses on the checks were incorrect.

✹ **KEY POINT.** Taxpayers who submit a Form 8822 to the IRS following a change in address not only ensure prompt delivery of refund checks; they also avoid the problems that arise when the IRS sends a notice of additional tax or penalties to a taxpayer at his or her "last known address" that is no longer the taxpayer's residence.

2 MINISTERS AND CHURCH STAFF: EMPLOYEES OR SELF-EMPLOYED?

Say to the Levites: "When you present the best part, it will be reckoned to you as the product of the threshing floor or the winepress. You and your households may eat the rest of it anywhere, for it is your wages for your work at the Tent of Meeting."

Numbers 18:30–31

CHAPTER HIGHLIGHTS

■ ***Reporting income taxes as an employee.*** Most ministers should report their federal income taxes as employees, because they will be considered employees under the tests currently used by the IRS and the courts. Most ministers will be better off reporting as employees, since (1) the value of various fringe benefits will be nontaxable, including the cost of employer-paid health insurance premiums, (2) the risk of an IRS audit is substantially lower, and (3) reporting as an employee avoids the additional taxes and penalties that often apply to self-employed ministers who are audited by the IRS and reclassified as employees.

■ ***Ministers' dual tax status.*** While most ministers are employees for federal income tax reporting purposes, they all are self-employed for Social Security purposes (with respect to services they perform in the exercise of their ministry). This means ministers are not subject to Social Security and Medicare taxes, even though they report their income taxes as employees and receive a W-2 from their church. Rather, they pay the self-employment tax.

■ ***Nonminister church workers.*** The IRS and the courts will apply the same tests used in determining the correct reporting status of ministers to determine the reporting status of nonminister church workers for income tax reporting purposes.

■ ***Tests for determining employee status.*** At least five recognized tests exist for determining whether a minister or lay worker is an employee or self-employed for federal income tax reporting purposes. These include (1) the "common-law employee" test set forth in the income tax regulations; (2) the "20-factor" test announced by the IRS in 1987; (3) the "7-factor" test announced by the United States Tax Court in 1994 in two cases addressing the correct reporting status of ministers; (4) a "12-factor" test developed by the United States Supreme Court and used by a federal appeals court in a case addressing the correct reporting status of a minister; and (5) the tax regulations' treatment of corporate officers.

INTRODUCTION

Whether a minister or other church staff member is an employee or self-employed is an important question. Unfortunately, it also can be a complex and confusing one. This chapter addresses this question on the basis of the most recent precedent. The focus of this chapter will be on the correct reporting status of ministers and nonminister staff members for *federal income tax* reporting purposes. The correct reporting status of these individuals for Social Security purposes is also addressed in this chapter but is addressed more fully in Chapter 9.

✿**KEY POINT.** The importance of the distinction between employee and self-employed status for purposes of computing business expense deductions is addressed fully in Chapter 7.

A. MINISTERS

1. OVERVIEW

✿**KEY POINT.** Most ministers should report their federal income taxes as employees, since (1) the value of various fringe benefits will be nontaxable; (2) audit risk is much lower; (3) reporting as an employee avoids the additional taxes and penalties often assessed against ministers who are reclassified as employees by the IRS; (4) the IRS considers most ministers to be employees; and (5) most ministers are employees under the tests applied by the IRS and the courts.

✿**KEY POINT.** While most ministers are employees for federal income tax reporting purposes, all ministers are self-employed for Social Security purposes with respect to services performed in the exercise of ministry (they have a "dual tax status"). The question of whether ministers should report their federal income taxes as employees or as self-employed persons has generated a good deal of controversy. It is a significant question for many reasons, including the following:

Reporting compensation

Employees report their compensation directly on Form 1040 (line 7—wages) and deduct unreimbursed (and nonaccountable reimbursed) business expenses on Schedule A only if they itemize deductions and only to the extent that such expenses exceed 2 percent of adjusted gross income (only 50 percent of business meals and entertainment expenses are counted). Self-employed persons report compensation and business expenses on Schedule C. Business expenses are, in effect, deductible whether the minister itemizes deductions or not and are not subject to the two percent floor.

Adjusted gross income (AGI)

AGI ordinarily will be higher if a minister reports as an employee, since unreimbursed (and nonaccountable reimbursed) business expenses are deductions from AGI. Self-employed persons deduct business expenses in computing AGI. AGI is a figure that is important for many reasons. For example, the percentage limitations applicable to charitable contributions and medical expense deductions are tied to AGI.

Form W-2 or Form 1099-MISC?

Ministers working for a church or church agency should receive a Form W-2 each year if they are employees, and a Form 1099-MISC if they are self-employed (and receive at least $600 in compensation).

❈ **KEY POINT.** The Tax Court has ruled that ministers who report their income taxes as self-employed will be reclassified as employees if their church issues them a Form W-2 instead of a Form 1099-MISC.

Tax-deferred annuities

Favorable tax-deferred annuities (also known as 403(b) annuities) offered by nonprofit organizations (including churches) may only be available to employees. This issue is addressed in Chapter 10.

❈ **KEY POINT.** Self-employed ministers can participate in qualified retirement plans including 403(b) tax-sheltered annuities. They are exempt from the general ban on self-employed persons participating in 403(b) plans.

❈ **KEY POINT.** In the case of contributions made to a church plan on behalf of a minister who is self-employed, the contributions are nontaxable to the extent that they would be if the minister were an employee of a church and the contributions were made to the plan.

Tax treatment of various fringe benefits

Certain fringe benefits provided by a church on behalf of a minister are excludable from the minister's income only if he or she is an employee. Examples include medical insurance premiums paid by a church on behalf of its minister; group term life insurance (up to $50,000) provided by a church on behalf of a minister; amounts payable to employees on account of sickness, accident, or disability pursuant to an employer-financed plan; employer-sponsored "cafeteria plans," which permit employees to choose between receiving cash payments or a variety of fringe benefits.

Audit risk

Self-employed persons face a higher risk of having their tax returns audited. Why? IRS data reveals that the voluntary reporting percentage (i.e., persons who voluntarily report the correct amount of income) is far greater for employees covered by mandatory income tax withholding. As a result, the IRS scrutinizes the tax returns of self-employed persons (who are not subject to tax withholding) more closely than those of employees.

❈ **KEY POINT.** The IRS estimates that 70 percent of workers who should be treated as employees but who report their income taxes as self-employed file no income tax returns.

Consequences of being reclassified as an employee

Taxpayers who report their federal income taxes as self-employed often incur penalties and additional taxes if they are audited by the IRS and reclassified as employees. This is because many persons who report as self-employed deduct their unreimbursed (and nonaccountable reimbursed) business expenses as a deduction on Schedule C. If they are reclassified by the IRS as employees, their business expense deduction will be allowable only as an itemized deduction on Schedule A, and then only to the extent that the expenses exceed two percent of AGI. Taxpayers who are not able to itemize end up with no deduction for their business expenses.

> **EXAMPLE.** Pastor C reports his income taxes as self-employed. His business expenses are not reimbursed by his church. In the past Pastor C has deducted his business expenses on Schedule C. In 2013 he is audited by the IRS and reclassified as an employee. One result of this reclassification is that Pastor C's unreimbursed business expenses are deductible only as an itemized expense on Schedule A. If he is not able to use Schedule A (70 percent of all taxpayers cannot), then he gets no deduction. If he is able to use Schedule A, his business expense deduction is reduced by two percent of his AGI.

The primary disadvantage of employee status is that most business expenses are deductible only as itemized deductions on Schedule A (i.e., the minister must be able to itemize deductions in order to deduct them), and they are deductible only to the extent that they exceed two percent of AGI. As we will see in Chapter 7, this disadvantage can be overcome simply by having your employing church adopt an "accountable reimbursement policy," under which the church reimburses you for those business expenses you periodically substantiate.

Table 2-1 summarizes the main differences between employee and self-employed status.

2. SELECTING THE CORRECT STATUS— FIVE TESTS

The IRS and the courts have applied a variety of tests to determine whether a particular worker is an employee or self-employed for income tax reporting purposes. These include the following:

(1) the common-law employee test,
(2) the 20-factor test adopted by the IRS,
(3) a 7-factor test applied by the Tax Court in two cases involving the correct reporting status of ministers,

(4) a 12-factor test applied by a federal appeals court in concluding that a minister was self-employed rather than an employee for federal income tax reporting purposes, and
(5) the tax regulations' treatment of corporate officers.

Each of these tests is summarized below.

Test 1—the common-law employee test
The income tax regulations contain the following common-law employee test for determining whether a worker is an employee or self-employed. This test is used frequently by the IRS and the courts.

TABLE 2-1

EMPLOYEE OR SELF-EMPLOYED
What difference does it make?

ISSUE	IF AN EMPLOYEE	IF SELF-EMPLOYED	HOW TO DECIDE IF A WORKER IS AN EMPLOYEE OR SELF-EMPLOYED
SOCIAL SECURITY	• Employer and employee each pay FICA tax of 7.65% of employee wages (total tax of 15.3%). • Ministers (except for certain chaplains) are never employees with regard to their ministerial duties. (They do not pay FICA taxes). • Nonminister church workers who are employees for income taxes are employees for Social Security (unless church filed a timely waiver from FICA taxes—in which case they are treated as self-employed for Social Security).	• Pay 15.3% self-employment tax. • Use Schedule SE (Form 1040). • Ministers always are self-employed with regard to their ministerial duties. • Nonminister church workers who are self-employed for income taxes are self-employed for Social Security.	Use income tax tests.
INCOME TAXES	• Wages are reported by employer on Form W-2. • Wages are reported by worker on line 7 (Form 1040). • Unreimbursed and nonaccountable reimbursed expenses are deducted on Schedule A (subject to 2% floor). • Audit risk is low. • Some fringe benefits (such as employer-paid medical insurance premiums and cafeteria plans) are tax-free.	• Income is reported by employer on Form 1099-MISC. • Wages are reported by worker on Schedule C and line 12 (Form 1040). • Unreimbursed and nonaccountable reimbursed expenses are deducted on Schedule C. • Audit risk is higher. • Some fringe benefits (such as employer-paid medical insurance premiums and cafeteria plans) are taxable. • Church issues 1099 (if annual compensation is $600 or more).	IRS applies a 3-factor "common law employee" test or an older 20-factor test. The Tax Court has adopted various tests—all focus on the degree of control exercised by the employer over the details of how the worker performs his or her job.
RETIREMENT	Some retirement plans are available only to employees (including tax-sheltered annuities or 403(b) plans—for nonminister church staff).	Some retirement plans are available only to self-employed persons (Keogh plans).	Use income tax tests.
LEGAL LIABILITY	Employer is liable for misconduct of employees in course of their employment (respondeat superior).	Employer generally is not liable for misconduct of self-employed workers.	Some courts follow income tax factors; others apply broader or narrower tests.

MINISTERS AND CHURCH STAFF: EMPLOYEES OR SELF-EMPLOYED?

Generally the relationship of employer and employee exists when the person for whom services are performed has the right to control and direct the individual who performs the services, not only as to the result to be accomplished by the work but also as to the details and means by which that result is accomplished. That is, an employee is subject to the will and control of the employer not only as to what shall be done but how it shall be done. In this connection, it is not necessary that the employer actually direct or control the manner in which the services are performed; it is sufficient if he has the right to do so.

The right to discharge is also an important factor indicating that the person possessing that right is an employer. Other factors characteristic of an employer, but not necessarily present in every case, are the furnishing of tools and the furnishing of a place to work to the individual who performs the services. In general, if an individual is subject to the control or direction of another merely as to the result to be accomplished by the work and not as to the means and methods for accomplishing the result, he is not an employee. Generally, physicians, lawyers, dentists, veterinarians, contractors, subcontractors, public stenographers, auctioneers, and others who follow an independent trade, business, or profession, in which they offer their services to the public, are not employees. Treas. Reg. 31.3401(c)-1(b). See also IRS Publication 517.

In Publication 15a the IRS notes that "in any employee-independent contractor determination, all information that provides evidence of the degree of control and the degree of independence must be considered." It then addresses three factors to be considered in applying the common-law employee test: behavioral control, financial control, and the relationship of the parties:

Behavioral control. *Facts that show whether the business has a right to direct and control how the worker does the task for which the worker is hired include the type and degree of:*

Instructions that the business gives to the worker. An employee is generally subject to the business' instructions about when, where, and how to work. All of the following are examples of types of instructions about how to do work. All of the following are examples of types of instructions about how do work:

- When and where to do the work.
- What tools or equipment to use.
- What workers to hire or to assist with the work.
- Where to purchase supplies and services.
- What work must be performed by a specified individual.
- What order or sequence to follow.

The amount of instruction needed varies among different jobs. Even if no instructions are given, sufficient behavioral control may exist if the employer has the right to control how the work results are achieved. A business may lack the knowledge to instruct some highly specialized professionals; in other cases, the task may require little or no instruction. The key consideration is whether the business has retained the right to control the details of a worker's performance or instead has given up that right.

Training that the business gives to the worker. An employee may be trained to perform services in a particular manner. Independent contractors ordinarily use their own methods.

Financial control. *Facts that show whether the business has a right to control the business aspects of the worker's job include:*

The extent to which the worker has unreimbursed business expenses. Independent contractors are more likely to have unreimbursed expenses than are employees. Fixed ongoing costs that are incurred regardless of whether work is currently being performed are especially important. However, employees may also incur unreimbursed expenses in connection with the services that they perform for their employer.

The extent of the worker's investment. An independent contractor often has a significant investment in the facilities or tools he or she uses in performing services for someone else. However, a significant investment is not necessary for independent contractor status.

The extent to which the worker makes his or her services available to the relevant market. An independent contractor is generally free to seek out business opportunities. Independent contractors often advertise, maintain a visible business location, and are available to work in the relevant market.

How the business pays the worker. An employee is generally guaranteed a regular wage amount for an hourly, weekly, or other period of time. This usually indicates that worker is an employee, even when the wage or salary is supplemented by a commission. An independent contractor is often paid a flat fee or on a time and materials basis for the job. However, it is common in some professions, such as law, to pay independent contractors hourly.

The extent to which the worker can realize a profit loss. An independent contractor can make a profit or loss.

Type of relationship. *Facts that show the parties' type of relationship include:*

- **Written contracts describing the relationship the parties intended to create.**
- **Whether or not the business provides the worker with employee-type benefits, such as insurance, a pension plan, vacation pay, or sick pay.**
- **The permanency of the relationship.** *If you engage a worker with the expectation that the relationship will*

continue indefinitely, rather than for a specific project or period, this is generally considered evidence that your intent was to create an employer-employee relationship.

- **The extent to which services performed by the worker are a key aspect of the regular business of the company.** If a worker provides services that are a key aspect of your regular business activity, it is more likely that you will have the right to direct and control his or her activities. For example, if a law firm hires an attorney, it is likely that it will present the attorney's work as its own and would have the right to control or direct that work. This would indicate an employer-employee relationship.

Test 2—the IRS 20-factor test

KEY POINT. The three-factor common-law employee test described above was formulated several years after the 20-factor test. However, the IRS has not repealed the 20-factor test, so both tests remain legitimate means for determining the reporting status of workers.

The IRS has developed a list of 20 factors to be used "as an aid in determining whether an individual is an employee under the common law rules." *Revenue Ruling 87-41.* There is considerable overlap between these 20 factors and the several factors enumerated by the IRS in describing the more recent common-law employee test (see above). In most cases, a worker's status will be the same under both tests.

The 20 factors were "developed based on an examination of cases and rulings considering whether an individual is an employee." The IRS cautioned that "[t]he degree of importance of each factor varies depending on the occupation and the factual context in which the services are performed" and that "if the relationship of employer and employee exists, the designation or description of the relationship by the parties as anything other than that of employer and employee is immaterial."

The 20 factors are listed in Table 2-2. Ministers who report their income taxes as self-employed should carefully consider these factors to determine if they have a substantial basis for reporting as self-employed. The same is true of any lay church workers who are treated as self-employed for income tax reporting purposes.

Another factor, not mentioned in the IRS 20-factor test, is the parties' own characterization of their relationship. For example, if a church and its minister enter into a written contract that specifically characterizes the minister as self-employed, this would be an additional factor to consider.

Illustration 2-1 presents a clause that may be used by a church wishing to characterize its minister as self-employed rather than as an employee. The clause could be inserted in the contract of employment or simply adopted as a resolution by the church board and included

═══════ **ILLUSTRATION 2-1** ═══════

CLAUSE CHARACTERIZING A MINISTER AS SELF-EMPLOYED

Note: Do not use this form without the advice of a tax professional.

The church board and Pastor L agree and intend that Pastor L's status for federal income tax reporting purposes shall be that of a self-employed person rather than that of an employee in view of the board's determination, based on its review and consideration of all the facts and circumstances, that Pastor L does not satisfy the common-law employee test. In particular, it is the board's conclusion that it does not have the authority to control the methods or means by which Pastor L conducts his services on behalf of the church.

in the board's official minutes. Keep in mind that such a clause by itself, as the IRS observed in Revenue Ruling 87-41, will have little, if any, relevance and will never result in a minister being characterized as self-employed if he or she fails the common-law employee test or a majority of the 20 factors. It is merely one factor that will be considered, but one that could be given considerable weight in a close case.

KEY POINT. A church will offset the effect of such a clause by issuing its minister a Form W-2 instead of Form 1099-MISC at the end of each year.

Test 3—the Tax Court's 7-factor test

In 1994 the United States Tax Court issued two rulings addressing the correct tax reporting status of ministers. In one case the court found that a Methodist minister was an employee for federal income tax reporting purposes. *Weber v. Commissioner, 103 T.C. 378 (1994), aff'd, 60 F.3d 1104 (4th Cir. 1995).* In the second case the court concluded that a Pentecostal Holiness pastor was self-employed for income tax reporting purposes. *Shelley v. Commissioner, T.C. Memo. 1994-432 (1994).* These cases are summarized later in this section. While the court reached different conclusions in these two cases, it applied the same test for determining the correct tax status of ministers. The test, along with an explanation of each factor, is set forth in Table 2-3.

The court made two additional points that should be considered in applying this test: (1) "No one factor dictates the outcome. Rather, we must look at all the facts and circumstances of each case." (2) "The threshold level of control necessary to find employee status is generally lower when applied to professional services than when applied to nonprofessional services."

KEY POINT. The Tax Court did not refer to the IRS 20-factor test (discussed above). Ministers who report their income taxes as self-employed probably will have a better chance of prevailing under the 7-factor test than under the more restrictive 20-factor test.

====== **TABLE 2-2** ======

DETERMINING A WORKER'S STATUS USING THE IRS 20-FACTOR TEST

Note: In order to determine if a pastor or lay church worker is an employee or self-employed for federal income tax reporting purposes, follow these simple steps: (1) read the description of each factor in the table below; (2) check the appropriate column ("EE" refers to employee and "SE" refers to self-employed); and (3) total the check marks for each column. The column with more marks indicates the worker's correct status.

FACTOR	EE	SE
1. Instructions. Is the worker required to comply with instructions about when, where, and how to work? If so, check EE; if not, check SE.		
2. Training. Is the worker trained by an experienced employee or by other means? If so, check EE; if not, check SE.		
3. Integration. Are the worker's services integrated into the employer's business operations? If so, check EE; if not, check SE.		
4. Services rendered personally. Must services be rendered personally by the worker? If so, check EE. If the worker may hire a substitute to perform the work without the church's knowledge or consent, check SE.		
5. Hiring, supervising, and paying assistants. Does the church hire, supervise, and pay assistants to assist the worker? If so, check EE. If the worker hires, supervises, and pays his or her own assistants, check SE.		
6. Continuing relationship. Is there a continuing working relationship between the church and worker? If so, check EE; if not, check SE.		
7. Setting hours of work. Does the employer establish set hours of work? If so, check EE. Is the worker a "master of his own time"? If so, check SE.		
8. Full time required. Must the worker devote full time to the church's business? If so, check EE. If the worker is hired "by the job" and may offer his or her services to other employers, check SE.		
9. Doing work on employer's premises. If the worker must perform his or her duties on the church's premises, check EE. If not, check SE.		
10. Order or sequence of work. If the worker must perform services in an order or sequence set by the church, check EE. If not, check SE.		
11. Oral or written reports. If the worker is required to submit regular oral or written reports to the employer, check EE. If not, check SE.		
12. Payment by hour, week, month. If the worker is paid by the hour, week, or month, check EE. If paid by the job on a lump-sum basis (even if paid in installments), check SE.		
13. Payment of business expenses. Does the church pay the worker's business expenses? If so, check EE; if not, check SE.		
14. Furnishing of tools and materials. If the church furnishes tools and materials for the worker's use, check EE. If the worker provides his or her own tools and materials, check SE.		
15. Significant investment. Does the church furnish all necessary facilities (equipment and premises)? If so, check EE; if not, check SE.		
16. Realization of profit or loss. May the worker realize a profit or suffer a loss as a result of his or her services? If so, check SE; if not, check EE.		
17. Working for more than one organization at a time. Does the worker perform services for a number of organizations besides your church? If so, check SE. If not, check EE.		
18. Making services available to the general public. Does the worker make his or her services available to the general public (by having his or her own office and assistants, holding a business license, advertising in newspapers and telephone directories)? If so, check SE; if not, check EE.		
19. Right to discharge. Can the church dismiss the worker at any time? If so, check EE; if not, check SE. Self-employed persons usually cannot be fired if they produce results that fulfill their contract specifications.		
20. Right to resign. Can the worker end the relationship with the church at any time without incurring liability? If so, check EE; if not, check SE. A self-employed person usually agrees to complete a specific job and is responsible for its satisfactory completion or is legally obligated to make good for failure to complete the job.		

TABLE 2-3	TABLE 2-4

THE TAX COURT'S 7-FACTOR TEST

FACTOR	EXPLANATION
1. Degree of control exercised by the employer over the details of the work	The more control exercised by an employer over the details of the work, the more likely the worker is an employee.
2. Which party invests in the facilities used in the work	Workers employed by an employer who provides the facilities used in the work are more likely to be employees.
3. Opportunity of the individual for profit or loss	Employees generally do not realize profits or losses as a result of their work (they are paid a salary); self-employed workers often do realize profits or losses.
4. Whether the employer has the right to discharge the worker	If the employer can discharge a worker, this indicates that the worker is an employee.
5. Whether the work is part of the employer's regular business	Workers who are furthering the employer's regular or customary business are more likely to be employees.
6. Permanency of the relationship	The more permanent the relationship, the more likely the worker is an employee.
7. Relationship the parties believe they are creating	Ordinarily the parties assume that a worker is an employee who is issued a W-2 and who receives several fringe benefits.

THE SUPREME COURT'S 12-FACTOR TEST

FACTOR	EXPLANATION
1. The hiring party's right to control the manner and means by which the product is accomplished	Such control indicates a worker is an employee.
2. The skill required	The more skill required the more likely a worker is self-employed.
3. Source of the instrumentalities and tools	Workers who provide their own tools or instruments are more likely self-employed.
4. Location of the work	If the work occurs on the employer's premises, this indicates the worker is an employee.
5. Duration of the relationship between the parties	The longer the relationship, the more likely a worker is an employee.
6. Whether the hiring party has the right to assign additional projects to the hired party	Such a right indicates a worker is an employee.
7. Extent of the hired party's discretion over when and how long to work	The more discretion, the more likely the worker is self-employed.
8. Method of payment	Employees typically are paid by the hour or week; self-employed workers typically are paid by the job.
9. The hired party's role in hiring and paying assistants	Self-employed workers hire and pay their own assistants; employees do not.
10. Whether the work is part of the regular business of the hiring party	An employee's work is part of the regular business of the employer.
11. Whether the hiring party is in business	Employees are more likely to work for organizations that provide services or products to the public.
12. Provision of employee benefits	Employees are more likely to receive fringe benefits.

Test 4—the Supreme Court's 12-factor test

In 1992 the Supreme Court listed 12 factors to be considered in deciding whether a worker is an employee or self-employed. *Nationwide Mutual Insurance Company v. Darden, 503 U.S. 318(1992)*. The court observed that each factor must be considered and that none is decisive. The 12 factors, along with an explanation of whether they support employee or self-employed status, are summarized in Table 2-4.

Test 5—the corporate-officer test

The income tax regulations specify:

The term "employee" includes every individual performing services if the relationship between him and the person for whom he performs such services is the legal relationship of employer and employee. . . . Generally, an officer of a corporation is an employee of the corporation. However, an officer of a corporation who as such does not perform any services or performs only minor services and who neither receives nor is entitled to receive, directly or indirectly, any remuneration is not considered to be an employee of the corporation. *A director of a corporation in his capacity as such is not an employee of the corporation.* Treas. Reg. 31.3401(c)-1.

Similarly, IRS Publication 15a states: "For employment tax purposes, no distinction is made between classes of employees. Superintendents, managers, and other supervisory personnel are all employees. An **officer of a corporation** is generally an employee; however, an officer who performs no services or only minor services, and neither receives nor is entitled to receive any pay, is not considered an employee. A **director of a corporation** is not an employee with respect to services performed as a director."

3. COURT DECISIONS AND IRS RULINGS

Five court decisions and four IRS rulings have addressed the question of whether a minister is an employee or self-employed for federal income tax reporting purposes. These cases and rulings are discussed below, and they are summarized in the Appendix at the end of this chapter.

Alford v. United States, 116 F.3d 334 (8th Cir. 1997)

A federal appeals court ruled that an Assemblies of God minister was self-employed rather than an employee for federal income tax reporting purposes. The court used a 12-factor test in reaching this result that was announced by the United States Supreme Court in 1992 (summarized in Table 2-4).

The facts of the case can be quickly summarized. Pastor James Alford is an ordained Assemblies of God minister who served as pastor of an Assemblies of God church in Hampton, Arkansas, for several years. He reported his income taxes as a self-employed person while serving as pastor of the church. The IRS audited Pastor Alford's 1986, 1987, and 1988 tax returns and determined that he should have reported his income taxes as an employee rather than as self-employed. As a result, all of Pastor Alford's business expenses were shifted from Schedule C to Schedule A and were deductible only to the extent they exceeded 2 percent of his AGI.

Pastor Alford paid the additional taxes assessed by the IRS and then filed a lawsuit in a federal district court in Arkansas, seeking a refund. The district court rejected Pastor Alford's request for a refund. It agreed with the IRS that he was an employee and that the IRS had correctly assessed the additional taxes. The district court concluded, however, that Pastor Alford was not an employee of the local Arkansas church that he served. But it found that "an extremely close relationship exists" among the national and regional Assemblies of God agencies and the local church that Pastor Alford served and that "the control exercised by each of them should be considered together." The district court concluded that Pastor Alford was an employee because of the "significant control by [his church] through its supervision by the District Council and the National Church, over the manner in which [he] performed his work."

Pastor Alford appealed the district court's ruling to the eighth circuit court of appeals (its decisions are binding in the states of Arkansas, Iowa, Minnesota, Missouri, Nebraska, North Dakota, and South Dakota). The court reversed the district court's decision and

concluded that Pastor Alford was self-employed rather than an employee for income tax reporting purposes. As a result, it ordered the IRS to refund to Pastor Alford the additional taxes he paid because of the erroneous decision by the IRS that he was an employee.

Was Pastor Alford an employee of his local church?

The court began its opinion by selecting the test to apply in deciding whether Pastor Alford was an employee or self-employed. It adopted a test set forth in a Supreme Court decision in 1992:

> [Besides considering] the hiring party's right to control the manner and means by which the product is accomplished, [a court must also look at] the skill required; the source of the instrumentalities and tools; the location of the work; the duration of the relationship between the parties; whether the hiring party has the right to assign additional projects to the hired party; the extent of the hired party's discretion over when and how long to work; the method of payment; the hired party's role in hiring and paying assistants; whether the work is part of the regular business of the hiring party; whether the hiring party is in business; [and] the provision of employee benefits. Nationwide Mutual Insurance Company v. Darden, 503 U.S. 318 (1992).

The Supreme Court clarified that "all of the incidents of the relationship must be assessed and weighed with no one factor being decisive."

The appeals court concluded, on the basis of this test, that Pastor Alford was not an employee of the local church he served:

> We begin our analysis with Alford's relationship with the Hampton Church. Alford was pastor at the church for a total of about ten years. The local church hired Alford and paid him a salary of $24,400 in 1986, $23,425 in 1987, and $22,100 in 1988. The salary was negotiated by Alford and the church and, although it was not calculated as a percentage of the revenues of the Hampton Church, it was dependent in part upon local church revenue. The church paid Alford a $4000 housing allowance and he did not pay rent when he lived in the parsonage. The church paid Alford an additional $250 each quarter so that he could pay his Social Security taxes; paid for his health insurance; paid into a retirement fund set up by the national church; and provided Alford a credit card for gasoline, on which he charged up to $520 a year. He received an annual $750 Christmas gift from the congregation, in addition to his salary. The church provided a desk, chair, and copy machine for the pastor's use, but Alford used his own desk and chairs, and in addition provided and used for the benefit of the church his own car, typewriter, computer, and library. Alford signed a contract with the church and paid his own self-employment taxes.

> For the most part, Alford set his own schedule (except of course for regularly scheduled church services). He was free to perform weddings, funerals, and revivals for a fee, and was not required

to pay over any of the fees to the church. He was not expected to pay for a substitute pastor if one was necessary. Alford arranged for evangelists or special speakers at the Hampton Church, and contributed to special collections taken for them.

✸ **KEY POINT.** The IRS conceded that Pastor Alford was not an employee of the local church. But it insisted that if the authority of the regional and national churches to "control" him were considered, then the combined authority of the local, regional, and national churches was sufficient to make him an employee. As a result, the IRS itself contributed to the result in this case. When the court concluded that the combined control exercised over Pastor Alford by the local, regional, and national church bodies was insufficient to make him an employee, the only alternative was to treat him as self-employed.

Was Pastor Alford an employee of the combination of his local, regional, and national churches?

The IRS conceded that Pastor Alford was not an employee of his local church. But it insisted that he was an employee of the combination of the local, regional, and national churches. The trial court agreed on the grounds that "an extremely close relationship exists" among the local, regional, and national church entities, and "thus, the control exercised by each of them should be considered together." The trial court concluded that Pastor Alford was an employee because of the "significant control by the Hampton Church, through its supervision by the District Council and the National Church, over the manner in which [he] performed his work."

The appeals court rejected the conclusion of both the IRS and the trial court that the authority of the local, regional, and national church bodies over Pastor Alford should be combined. The court concluded:

Perhaps more telling in this case are the aspects of Alford's work for the Hampton Church that the General and District Councils had no right to control during the years in question. They did not locate the job at the Hampton Church for Alford nor could they have "placed" him as pastor there. They did not and could not have negotiated his salary and benefits. They could neither have guaranteed him a job (with the Hampton Church or any other local church) nor could they have guaranteed his salary. The regional and national churches could not have fired him from the job as pastor of the Hampton Church (although if he had lost his credentials the Hampton Church would have lost its affiliate status if it had kept him on as pastor). They could not have required him to retire. They did not observe or grade his performance at the Hampton Church to determine if his credentials should be renewed, nor did they regularly evaluate him. Clearly the national and regional entities had little if any control over—or right to control—the "manner and means" Alford employed in accomplishing his duties as pastor at the Hampton Church during 1986, 1987, and 1988.

The court concluded that "the General and District Councils' right to control Alford, in combination with the common law agency factors present in Alford's relationship with the Hampton Church that weigh in favor of employee status, do not suffice to render Alford an employee within the meaning of the relevant provisions of the tax code."

The *Alford* case ensures that the correct reporting status of ministers for income tax purposes will remain ambiguous.

Table 2-5 summarizes the court's analysis in this case.

Binding precedent. The court's decision will be binding only in the eighth federal circuit, which covers the following states: Arkansas, Iowa, Minnesota, Missouri, Nebraska, North Dakota, and South Dakota. The decision will be persuasive, but not binding, elsewhere.

Application to multistaff churches. Perhaps the most significant fact in the *Alford* case was that Pastor Alford was the only employee of a small church. Under such circumstances, a minister often will have a greater degree of autonomy and be subject to less control by

---

TABLE 2-5

THE ALFORD CASE

FACTS SUGGESTING EMPLOYEE STATUS	FACTS SUGGESTING SELF-EMPLOYED STATUS
Pastor Alford's salary, though not based on percentage of church income, was dependent on church revenue.	Pastor Alford provided his own furniture.
Church paid several fringe benefits, including (1) a portion of Alford's self-employment tax, (2) a housing allowance, and (3) health insurance.	He used his own car, computer, and library in the performance of his duties.
Church provided a credit card to purchase gasoline.	He set his own schedule.
Church provided an annual Christmas gift of $750.	He was free to perform weddings, funerals, and revivals for a fee and was not required to pay over any of the fees to the church.
Church provided a desk, chair, and copy machine.	He was not expected to pay for a substitute pastor if one was necessary.
	He arranged for evangelists or special speakers and contributed to special collections taken for them.

the church. It is doubtful that ministers in larger churches employing several full-time staff members will be able to support self-employed status on the basis of the *Alford* decision.

Weber v. Commissioner, 103 T.C. 378 (1994), affirmed, 60 F.3d 1104 (4th Cir. 1995)

The Tax Court concluded that a Methodist minister was an employee and not self-employed for federal income tax reporting purposes. The court began its opinion by asserting that Pastor Weber, "a United Methodist Minister, is an employee for federal income tax purposes." What factors led the court to reach this conclusion, and how will the ruling affect other ministers? These are critical questions.

The court noted that Pastor Weber had the burden of proving that he was self-employed for federal income tax purposes and not an employee. The court conceded that the tax code contains no definition of the term "employee." Whether an employer-employee relationship exists in a particular situation "is a factual question" to be decided on a case-by-case basis. How is this determination made? The court referred to common-law rules that are applied in making such a decision. These common-law rules are set forth in the income tax regulations and also in court decisions. The court quoted the income tax regulations' definition of an employer-employee relationship (noted above as "Test 1—the common-law employee test").

The court then referred to seven factors the courts consider in deciding whether a particular worker is an employee or self-employed. The court emphasized that "no one factor dictates the outcome . . . rather we must look at all the facts and circumstances of each case."

⚙ **KEY POINT.** The Tax Court announced a 7-factor test in 1994 for determining whether a minister is an employee or self-employed for federal income tax reporting purposes.

Table 2-3 summarizes the 7-factor test. The importance of this test cannot be overemphasized. The Tax Court ignored the IRS 20-factor test (discussed above) and substituted a 7-factor test. The court discussed each of the factors as follows:

Factor 1—degree of control exercised by the employer over the details of the work

The court emphasized that the right-to-control test is "the crucial test to determine the nature of a working relationship." The more control exercised by an employer over the details of a worker's job, the more likely the worker is an employee rather than self-employed. The court noted that the degree of actual control over a worker is important but not exclusive, since "we must examine not only the control exercised by an alleged employer, but also the degree to which an alleged employer may intervene to impose control." The court observed that "in order for an employer to retain the requisite control over the details of an employee's work, the employer need not stand over the employee and direct every move made by that employee." Further, and this is a point the court stressed repeatedly, "the degree of control necessary

to find employee status varies according to the nature of the services provided." In particular, "the threshold level of control necessary to find employee status is generally lower when applied to professional services than when applied to nonprofessional services." Therefore, less evidence of control (whether exercised or potential) is required to support a finding that a minister (or other professional) is an employee for income tax reporting purposes. The court quoted from a federal appeals court ruling: "From the very nature of the services rendered by . . . professionals, it would be wholly unrealistic to suggest that an employer should undertake the task of controlling the manner in which the professional conducts his activities."

The court then itemized several factors that demonstrated sufficient control over Pastor Weber to establish employee status. These are listed below:

- A Methodist bishop testified at trial that the church is "very proactive" and none of its members work without supervision.
- As a minister of the United Methodist Church, Pastor Weber was required to perform the numerous duties set forth in the Discipline. He agreed to perform those duties.
- Pastor Weber had to explain the position of the Discipline on any topic he chose to present in his sermons.
- Pastor Weber admitted that he followed the United Methodist theology in his sermons.
- Pastor Weber does not have the authority to unilaterally discontinue the regular services of a local church.
- Under the itinerant system of the United Methodist Church, Pastor Weber was appointed by the bishop to the positions he held. A bishop of the North Carolina Annual Conference determined where Pastor Weber would preach. Pastor Weber had no right to refuse the appointment.
- Pastor Weber could not establish his own church.
- Pastor Weber was bound by the rules stated in the Discipline regarding mandatory retirement at age 70 and involuntary retirement.
- Pastor Weber was required to obtain the approval of the relevant bishop before he transferred from one Annual Conference to another.
- The Annual Conference limits the amount of leave ministers can take during a year.
- Methodist ministers are required by the Discipline to be amenable to the Annual Conference in the performance of their duties in the positions to which they are appointed. The court noted that "the requirement that [Pastor Weber] be amenable to the Annual Conference is another indication of the control the Annual Conference had over [him]."
- A bishop testified at trial that ineffectiveness or unfitness ultimately may result in the termination of a minister's membership in the Annual Conference. A minister may be subject to termination from membership in the Annual Conference for the use of materials that do not conform to the United Methodist faith. Furthermore, one of the district

superintendent's responsibilities is to establish a clearly under-stood process of supervision for ministers.

The court concluded its discussion of the first factor in its 7-factor test by noting: "Normally the control factor is the most persuasive factor in determining whether an employment relationship exists. We are mindful, however, that where professional individuals are involved this control 'must necessarily be more tenuous and general than the control over nonprofessional employees.' Nevertheless, it is clear that [Pastor Weber] is subject to significant control."

Factor 2—which party invests in the facilities used in the work

The court then turned to the second factor in its 7-factor test. This factor asks which party (employer or worker) invests in the facilities used in the work. If the employer invests in or provides the facilities used by the worker to perform the work, this suggests an employer-employee relationship. The court observed: "[Pastor Weber] was not required to invest in the work facilities. The local churches provided him with a home. The local churches provided the church in which [he] gave his sermons, and which contained office space for per-forming his duties. The local churches bought religious materials for his ministry."

The court dismissed the relevance of Pastor Weber's assertion that he prepared the weekly church bulletin at home, used his own com-puter for church work, and purchased some of his own vestments and a personal library. The court noted that "his choice to work at home does not negate the fact that the local churches provided him with an office. [He] purchased computer equipment to make his work easier and to perform better. It does not prove that he was required to provide office equipment." With regard to Pastor Weber's assertion that he purchased his own vestments, the court observed that "vestments were not required by the local churches, nor were they necessary for him to perform his duties. [His] choice was merely his own preference." Finally, the court pointed out that many professionals acquire their own libraries "whether they are employees or independent contractors."

Factor 3—opportunity of the individual for profit or loss

The third factor is whether a worker has an opportunity to realize a profit or suffer a loss as a result of his or her services. Workers who are in a position to realize a profit or suffer a loss as a result of their services generally are self-employed, while employees ordinarily are not in such a position. The court concluded that this factor sup-ported employee status in this case. It observed:

> [Pastor Weber] was paid a salary, and provided with a parson-age, a utility expense allowance, and a travel expense allowance from each local church. Furthermore, if [he] was not assigned to a local church, the Annual Conference would pay him a minimum guaranteed salary, or if he were in special need, the Annual Conference could give him [special support]. Aside from minimal

> amounts earned for weddings and funerals and amounts spent on utilities and travel, [Pastor Weber] was not in a position to increase his profit, nor was he at risk for loss.

Factor 4—whether the employer has the right to discharge the worker

The authority of an employer to discharge a worker generally indicates that the worker is an employee rather than self-employed. The court concluded that Pastor Weber was subject to dismissal, and accord-ingly this factor supported employee status. The court observed: "The Annual Conference had the right to try, reprove, suspend, deprive of ministerial office and credentials, expel or acquit, or locate [Pastor Weber] for unacceptability or inefficiency. The clergy members of the executive session of the Annual Conference had the authority to disci-pline and fire [Pastor Weber]. These are other strong factors indicating that [Pastor Weber] was an employee rather than [self-employed]."

Factor 5—whether the work is part of the employer's regular business

The fifth factor addresses the nature of the worker's services. Is the worker furthering the employer's regular or customary business? If so, this indicates an employer-employee relationship. Again the court concluded that this factor supported a finding that Pastor Weber was an employee: "[Pastor Weber's] work is an integral part of the United Methodist Church. A minister has the responsibility to lead a local church in conformance with the beliefs of the United Methodist Church, to give an account of his or her pastoral minis-tries to the Annual Conference according to prescribed forms, and to act as the administrative officer for that church."

A bishop confirmed the integral part played by ministers in the mission of the Methodist Church. When asked "and with respect to the pastor of the local church, would you also agree that to further the local church's integral role in the mission of the United Meth-odist Church, the pastor must perform his or her responsibilities and duties in conformance with this mission in mind," the bishop responded, "Yes, sir."

Factor 6—permanency of the relationship

The sixth factor focuses on the permanency of the relationship between the employer and a worker. The more permanent the relationship, the more likely the worker is an employee. The court concluded that this factor suggested that Pastor Weber was an employee. The relationship between Methodist ministers and the United Methodist Church is "intended to be permanent as opposed to transitory." Pastor Weber

> has been an ordained United Methodist minister since 1978. [He] has conceded . . . that he is likely to remain a minister for his entire professional religious career, and that he is likely to remain affiliated with the North Carolina Annual Conference. The Annual Conference will pay a salary to a minister even when there are no positions with a local church available. The fact that

WHY MOST MINISTERS ARE BETTER OFF REPORTING THEIR FEDERAL INCOME TAXES AS EMPLOYEES

Most ministers will be better off reporting their federal income taxes as employees, since

- the value of various fringe benefits will be excludable, including the often significant cost of employer-paid health insurance premiums for the minister and his or her dependents;
- the risk of an IRS audit is substantially lower; and
- they avoid the additional taxes and penalties that often apply to self-employed ministers who are audited by the IRS and reclassified as employees.

ministers are also provided with retirement benefits indicates that the parties anticipate a long-term relationship. An independent contractor would not normally receive such benefits from a customer or client.

Further, Pastor Weber "does not make his services available to the general public, as would an independent contractor." He "works at the local church by the year and not for individuals 'by the job.'" The court also noted that Pastor Weber "was required to work at the church to which he was assigned, and was required to attend meetings."

Factor 7—relationship the parties believe they are creating

The final factor asks what kind of relationship the parties themselves thought they were creating. Did they intend for the worker to be an employee or self-employed? The court again ruled that this factor supported its conclusion that Pastor Weber was an employee rather than self-employed: "Because there was no withholding of income taxes and no Form W-2, we assume that [Pastor Weber] and his supervisors believed that ministers such as [Pastor Weber] were independent contractors. We give this factor little weight."

The court noted that the parties' characterization of their relationship was completely negated by the volume of fringe benefits made available to Pastor Weber. The court concluded that these fringe benefits demonstrated, far more strongly than the parties' outward intentions, that Pastor Weber was an employee rather than self-employed, since the level of benefits was virtually unknown to self-employed workers. The court observed:

[Pastor Weber] received many benefits that we find are typical of those provided to employees rather than independent contractors,

some of which follow. Each local church made contributions on [his] behalf . . . to a pension plan. [Pastor Weber] continued to receive his salary while on vacation. If needed, [he] would have been entitled to disability leave and paternity leave. If he could not be assigned to a local church, he would receive a guaranteed salary from the Annual Conference. If he were needy, he might be able to get [special relief] from the Annual Conference. A portion of the cost of [his] life insurance was paid by the local churches. The local churches paid a portion of the death benefit plan premiums, and [he] paid a portion. The local churches paid 75 percent of [his] 1988 health insurance premiums.

The court noted simply that "these enumerated benefits also indicate that [Pastor Weber] is an employee rather than self-employed."

Conclusion

The court concluded its lengthy analysis of the facts of this case by observing: "After considering all the facts and circumstances present in this case, we conclude that the factors that indicate [that Pastor Weber] was an employee outweigh those factors that indicate that he was self-employed. Accordingly, we hold that [his] ordinary and necessary trade or business expenses paid in 1988 were not properly listed on Schedule C, but are allowable as miscellaneous itemized deductions on Schedule A, subject to the 2 percent floor."

Identification of Pastor Weber's employer

Amazingly, having concluded its lengthy discourse on the reasons why Pastor Weber was an employee rather than self-employed, the court refused to identify his employer. The court simply noted that "the parties have stipulated that the only issue in dispute is whether [Pastor Weber] was an employee or was self-employed. We need not decide which part of the United Methodist Church is the employer." Unfortunately, the court left unanswered a fundamental question. Was Pastor Weber's employer the annual conference, the local church, or some other entity within the Methodist Church? While the 7-factor test may clearly support employee status for Pastor Weber, it is not so clear in identifying his employer. Some of the factors suggest that the annual conference is the employer, while others point to the local church. Pastor Weber contended that no one agency within the Methodist Church exercised sufficient control over him to be his employer, and therefore an employer-employee relationship could not exist. The court responded to this argument as follows:

[Pastor Weber] contends that an employee-employer relationship cannot exist because there is no entity which exercised sufficient control over [him] so that he may be classified as an employee. He claims that the control over a minister is deliberately spread in a way that ensures that the minister has the maximum freedom to be the man or woman of God, which the United Methodist Church believes the ministry is all about. We do not question this polity for religious purposes. However, we disagree with [Pastor Weber's] contention when we analyze this case by application of the relevant court decisions and regulations. We acknowledge

*that an important religious purpose is served by the organiza-
tional structure. Nonetheless, we find that there is sufficient
control over [Pastor Weber] as well as several other factors
which establish that he was an employee.*

The identification of Pastor Weber's employer is not an academic
question. It will determine a number of important issues, including payroll tax reporting issues and the availability of various fringe
benefits. One can only wonder if the court's refusal to address this
issue was based on the difficulty of answering it and the inconsistency of any answer with the court's decision. Perhaps this also
explains why the court took so long to announce its decision.

Tax Court's decision not applicable to all ministers

While the Tax Court's decision was considered a test case by several
Methodist ministers, it is not a test case for ministers in other denominations. While the court's 7-factor test can now be used to evaluate
the correct reporting status of other ministers, the court did not decide
that all ministers are employees for income tax reporting purposes.
Quite to the contrary, the Tax Court ended the *Weber* case with the
following comment: "We recognize that there may be differences with
respect to ministers in other churches or denominations, and the particular facts and circumstances must be considered in each case."

❖ **KEY POINT.** The Tax Court ended the *Weber* case by noting that
"there may be differences with respect to ministers in other churches
or denominations, and the particular facts and circumstances must
be considered in each case." In other words, the Tax Court was not
addressing the correct reporting status of all ministers.

Relevance of religious considerations

Some ministers point to theological considerations in support of their
self-employed status. For example, some say they are theologically
opposed to the notion that they are "controlled" by their church. The
Tax Court was not sympathetic to this view. It observed:

*[Pastor Weber's] basic position appears to be that because he is
a minister in a unique religious order he cannot be an employee.
While we have great respect for [his] religious dedication, religion is not the question before us.*

*[Pastor Weber] is seeking a business benefit. He wants to file a
Schedule C . . . and to claim business expenses on it. It is he who
has cast this case in business terms.*

The court also noted: "[Pastor Weber] contends that no one had
the right to control either the method or the means by which he
conducted his ministry. We do not agree."

Tax Court's decision upheld on appeal

In 1995 a federal appeals court upheld the Tax Court's decision in
the *Weber* case. It adopted the Tax Court's decision as its own. *Weber
v. Commissioner*, 60 F.3d 1104 (4th Cir. 1995).

❖ **KEY POINT.** The *Weber* case was a regular opinion of the Tax
Court, meaning that it was a decision by all of the court's judges.
On the other hand, the *Shelley* case (addressed below) was a memorandum decision of the court, meaning it was a ruling by only one
judge. Regular opinions, such as the *Weber* case, have much greater
precedential value than memorandum opinions, since they are
decisions by the full court. This conclusion is reinforced by the fact
that the *Weber* case was affirmed by a federal appeals court.

❖ **KEY POINT.** The Tax Court's decision in the *Weber* case was
upheld by a federal appeals court in 1995 by a 2-1 vote. This ele-
vates the significance of this ruling and makes it more likely that
the IRS will assert that ministers are employees for federal income
tax reporting purposes.

Radde v. Commissioner, T.C. Memo. 1997-490 (1997)

In 1997 the Tax Court ruled that a Methodist minister was an employee rather than self-employed for income tax reporting purposes.
The court applied the same 7-factor test it used in the *Weber* case
and concluded that there was no basis for distinguishing between
the two cases. The minister in question had served as both a senior
pastor and a denominational official for the years under audit.

Shelley v. Commissioner, T.C. Memo. 1994-432 (1994)

Moments after issuing its decision in the *Weber* case, the Tax Court
released a second opinion finding that a Pentecostal Holiness minister was self-employed rather than an employee for federal income
tax reporting purposes. This second decision confirms that the Tax
Court did not intend by its *Weber* decision to find all ministers to
be employees. It also assures that the correct reporting status of
individual ministers will be a continuing source of confusion and
controversy.

The Tax Court applied the same 7-factor test it applied in the *Weber*
case, but it concluded that Pastor Shelley was self-employed rather
than an employee for federal income tax reporting purposes. Here is
how the court analyzed each of the factors:

Factor 1—degree of control exercised by the employer over the details of the work

The court concluded that this factor supported a finding that Pastor
Shelley was self-employed for income tax reporting purposes, since
his employing church exercised insufficient control over the details
of his work. Here are some of the factors the court mentioned in
reaching its conclusion:

- Pastor Shelley was hired by the church because of his specialized skills and his particular style of ministry.
- He was free to use his own methods and style in the day-to-
  day conduct of his activities.
- He was chairman of the church board.

- He had the power to appoint and remove members of the church board. He also appointed members of the board to the various church committees.
- He was not supervised by anyone and was not evaluated regularly.
- He could hire, supervise, and fire assistants as he saw fit.
- He could delegate his duties to the church's associate pastor.
- He had the power to adjust his own salary and did so on occasion.
- He performed services for the church both on and off the church's premises.
- He was not restricted to performing services solely for his own congregation.
- He determined his own work hours.
- He was not subject to a mandatory retirement age.
- He was encouraged but not required to participate in continuing education.
- He was free to go on mission trips when he felt called to do so, and he was not required to request permission for a leave of absence.
- He was not assigned to the church by the state conference of the Pentecostal Holiness Church (the denomination that ordained him and with which his church was affiliated).
- He was free to establish his own church within the denomination and could serve temporarily as pastor of a church not affiliated with the Pentecostal Holiness Church.
- His state conference will not evaluate a pastor until approached with a problem, by a church, that the church board and congregation have been unable to resolve. Once involved, the conference's primary responsibility is to provide spiritual guidance and counseling to the pastor and to the church. The denomination's manual states that if serious conflicts that cannot be resolved develop between a pastor and the quadrennial conference (a regional denominational body), the quadrennial conference has the right to place the pastor on probation or to revoke his ordination certificate.

However, these measures would not be used unless the pastor was unable to accomplish the basic goals for which he was hired, "to lead in worship, to lead in the nurture of believers, and to win the lost to Christ," in a manner consistent with church doctrines. At no point would a quadrennial conference official step in and specifically tell the pastor how to run his church.

The court acknowledged that the denominational manual specified that ministers are "amenable to the quadrennial conference and the conference board." However, this did not alter its conclusion that insufficient control was exercised over Pastor Shelley by either his church or denomination to render him an employee for income tax reporting purposes. The court concluded:

After considering all the facts and circumstances affecting the issue of control, we are persuaded that [Pastor Shelley]

was "subject to the control or direction of another merely as to the result to be accomplished by the work and not as to the means and methods for accomplishing the result." Treas. Reg. 31.3401(c) 1(b). [His] primary responsibility was to help the church thrive. The record does not reflect that the church or the [state conference] retained any significant rights to control [his] efforts to accomplish this goal.

Factor 2—which party invests in the facilities used in the work

The court noted simply that while Pastor Shelley was not required to invest in the basic work facilities he used as a pastor, he did pay for the collection of his own substantial library (which he used in his ministry), and he regularly paid a portion of the expenses associated with continuing education courses and other church-related travel.

Factor 3—the opportunity of the individual for profit or loss

Members of the court did not consider this factor relevant under the circumstances of this case, since they "do not believe that the normal business risks of profit and loss are particularly applicable" to a minister. However, the court observed that "to the extent that this factor has any bearing, we note that [Pastor Shelley] had no guarantee from the [state conference] or the church that his salary would be maintained if the church was not successful or if he left the church and could not find another ministry within the [denomination]. In this sense, [he] did have some risk of loss."

Factor 4—whether the employer has the right to discharge the worker

The IRS insisted that the fact that procedures are available to remove a Pentecostal Holiness minister from a church or to revoke a minister's ordination certificate mandates a finding that Pastor Shelley was an employee. The Tax Court disagreed:

[Pastor Shelley] could not be fired at will by either the church board, the [state conference], or any other body within the [denomination]. Discharge of a pastor typically requires the involvement of the church board, the congregation, and the [state conference] board. According to the Manual, it is possible for the church board to vote to request that the congregation hold a vote of confidence with respect to a pastor. However, this possibility must be considered in conjunction with the fact that the pastor has the power to appoint and remove members of the church board. As stated above, the testimony offered at trial made clear that the [state conference] board will not evaluate a pastor or a minister until approached by a church with a problem that the church board and congregation have been unable to resolve. The procedures delineated in the Manual and by witnesses for dealing with dissension within the church are oriented more toward conflict resolution than termination, and differ from what we would expect to find in a typical employer-employee relationship. In the context of this case, we do not believe that the remote possibility that [Pastor Shelley] could be

forced to leave the church or could have his ordination certificate withdrawn indicates that [he] was an employee rather than an independent contractor.

Factor 5—whether the work is part of the employer's regular business

The court conceded that Pastor Shelley's work "was part of both the church's and the [denomination's] regular business." It noted that this "may tend to suggest that [he] was an employee; however, [it is] not significant enough to outweigh the conclusion we draw from the record that [Pastor Shelley] was an independent contractor [self-employed]."

Factor 6—permanency of the relationship

The court conceded that Pastor Shelley's relationship with the church and the denomination was reasonably permanent. It noted that this "may tend to suggest that [he] was an employee; however, [it is] not significant enough to outweigh the conclusion we draw from the record that [Pastor Shelley] was an independent contractor [self-employed]."

Factor 7—relationship the parties believe they are creating

The court noted that no written agreement existed between Pastor Shelley and his church or state conference disclosing the type of relationship the parties believed they were creating. However, the court noted that Pastor Shelley "did not have any income tax withheld from his salary and did not receive any Forms W-2 from the church, the [state conference], or any other body in the [denomination]. We assume, therefore, that petitioner and the other parties involved believed that petitioner was an independent contractor." The court rejected the assertion of the IRS that the church provided fringe benefits to Pastor Shelley that ordinarily are provided only to employees. As examples the IRS cited a biweekly salary, a health insurance plan provided by the state conference, disability leave, and vacation pay. The court observed:

While these benefits are more likely to be found in an employer-employee relationship, their presence does not eliminate the possibility that the taxpayer is an independent contractor, particularly in situations where the taxpayer maintains a relationship with a particular institution over a long period of time. . . . [Pastor Shelley] received some benefits typical of an employer-employee relationship. Nevertheless, considering [his] long-term relationship with the [denomination] we find it significant that there is no evidence that [he] received life insurance coverage or any retirement benefits through the [denomination, state conference] or the church.

Conclusion

The Tax Court concluded: "Based on the application of the enumerated factors to the facts and circumstances present in this case, we conclude that, during the years in issue, [Pastor Shelley] was an independent contractor and must report his business income and

expenses on Schedules C." The court added: "We are aware that *Weber v. Commissioner, 103 T.C. 378 (1994)*, involving a United Methodist minister, shares certain similarities with the instant case but holds that the taxpayer was an employee. We find that the [Pentecostal Holiness Church] did not have the same type of relationship with [Pastor Shelley] that the United Methodist Church does with its ministers. Accordingly, we conclude that the facts and circumstances present in this case warrant our reaching a different conclusion than that reached in *Weber.*"

IRS appeal

The IRS appealed the *Shelley* decision to the federal court of appeals for the eleventh circuit. The case was settled out of court while the appeal was pending.

Greene v. Commissioner, T.C. Memo. 1996-531 (1996)

In 1997 the Tax Court ruled that an Assemblies of God foreign missionary who resided in Bangladesh was self-employed rather than an employee for federal income tax reporting purposes. The court listed eight factors to be considered in deciding whether a worker is an employee or self-employed for federal income tax reporting purposes:

(1) the degree of control exercised by the [employer] over the details of the work; (2) which party invests in the facilities used in the work; (3) the taxpayer's opportunity for profit or loss; (4) the permanency of the relationship; (5) the [employer's] right of discharge; (6) whether the work performed is an integral part of the [employer's] business; (7) what relationship the parties believe they are creating; and (8) the provision of benefits typical of those provided to employees. No one factor is determinative; rather, all the incidents of the relationship must be weighed and assessed.

❖**KEY POINT.** The court restated the final factor in the 7-factor test (Table 2-3) as two separate factors. As a result, the 8-factor test is identical to the 7-factor test. The court concluded that the missionary was self-employed on the basis of these factors. Its conclusions are summarized below:

Factor 1—degree of control

The court noted that an employer's right to control the manner in which a person's work is performed "is ordinarily the single most important factor" in determining whether that person is an employee. The more control, the more likely the worker is an employee. The court mentioned three additional factors to be considered in applying this test: (1) a sufficient degree of control for employee status does not require the employer to "stand over the taxpayer and direct every move made by that person"; (2) "[t]he degree of control necessary to find employee status varies according to the nature of the services provided"; and (3) "[w]e must consider not only what actual control is exercised, but also what right of control exists as a practical matter."

Facts indicating control. The IRS insisted that the following facts demonstrated a sufficient degree of control for the missionary to be considered an employee:

- Missionaries qualify as professionals who require little supervision, therefore the absence of actual control should not be confused with an absence of the right to control.
- The Assemblies of God Division of Foreign Missions (DFM) maintained control over the missionary through its missions manual that dictated the manner in which he was to conduct his deputational and foreign ministry. Deputational ministry refers to the practice of Assemblies of God of missionaries raising their own financial support by visiting local churches.
- The national Assemblies of God organization (the "National Church") exercised control, or had the right to exercise control, over the missionary's ministerial credentials to such a degree that he was an employee. For example, the National Church (1) maintains specific requirements for ministerial licensing and ordination; (2) has the authority to discipline ministers based on their behavior and conduct; and (3) has the authority to withdraw ministerial credentials.

Facts indicating a lack of control. The court pointed to the following facts in concluding that insufficient control was exercised over the missionary to treat him as an employee:

- Neither the National Church nor DFM provided any type of professional training for the missionary.
- The DFM did not assign the missionary to minister in a particular country. The missionary selected Bangladesh, despite some reservations expressed by the DFM.
- The DFM did not direct the missionary to work on a particular project in Bangladesh. Rather, the missionary independently chose to become involved in student ministry. He decided to expand his foreign ministry to include a drug rehabilitation program. He was able to make this decision without seeking permission from the DFM. In fact, it appears that the DFM was not even aware of the missionary's plans to initiate a drug-rehabilitation clinic in Bangladesh.
- The missionary determined his own workdays and hours.
- The missionary used vacation and sick leave without notifying or seeking permission from the DFM.
- The missionary decided to return from his foreign ministry after only three years in the foreign field. He made this decision considering the needs of his school-aged children and the schedules of the other missionaries in his area. It appears that the DFM played little or no role in his field departure date.
- The missionary decided when his personal allowance (a monthly distribution for living expenses) would begin, and he had the power to designate the amount of his personal allowance up to the limit imposed by the DFM.
- The missionary was required to attend only one meeting every five years.

- Apart from filing periodic expense and activity reports, the missionary and the DFM did not communicate regularly. Specifically, the DFM did not contact him at all during his year of deputational ministry (when he visited churches in the United States, raising support). Likewise, the DFM communicated with the missionary infrequently while he served in the foreign field.
- The missionary was not directly supervised or evaluated by anyone.
- The court acknowledged that the DFM missions manual contains extensive information with respect to foreign ministry. However, it concluded that "the missions manual was intended by the DFM to be an informational reference for missionaries, not a set of rules controlling their day-to-day conduct."
- The court concluded that the IRS's emphasis on the National Church's control of the missionary's ministerial credentials was misplaced for two reasons. First, although the missionary was an ordained Assemblies of God minister, he worked as a missionary. The court observed that "the National Church's requirements for ministerial licensing and ordination, as well as its authority to discipline [the missionary] and withdraw his ministerial credentials, have little or no bearing as to the details and means by which [he] performed his duties as a missionary." Second, the court concluded that the control test is not satisfied "where the manner in which a service is performed is controlled by the threat of the loss of professional credentials. Carried to its logical extreme, this argument would serve to classify all ordained ministers as employees of the National Church, regardless of the type of service performed."

The Tax Court noted that the missionary's circumstances in this case "are very different" from those of a pastor of a local church:

[The taxpayer in this case] was employed as a foreign missionary, not a pastor. We think that the National Church's authority over the manner in which a pastor performs his or her duties is not highly probative in analyzing the National Church's control over the daily activities of a foreign missionary. This is because pastoring a local church and engaging in foreign mission work are two different jobs involving different qualifications, duties, and bodies of authority. Pastors are subject to the controls of a local church whereas missionaries are subject to the authority of the DFM. As previously discussed, the DFM exerted very little control over petitioner.

The court concluded:

In summary, the DFM lacked the control and lacked the right to control the manner and means by which [the taxpayer] performed his duties as a foreign missionary. Rather, the DFM facilitates foreign ministry by processing a missionary's collections and pledges and providing useful information to missionaries through the missions manual and a proposed foreign living budget. In other words, we view the DFM as a service provider relieving endorsed missionaries from the administrative burdens of collecting and processing their pledges and obtaining information regarding their country of service.

Factor 2—investment in facilities and equipment

The second factor in the Tax Court's 8-factor test is which party invests in the facilities used in the work. If the employer invests in the facilities, it is more likely that the worker is an employee. The court observed:

[The taxpayer's] sole compensation as a missionary was in the form of a "personal allowance" secured from funds that he raised during his deputational ministry. In this regard, we observe that if a donor fails to remit a pledged amount, the DFM makes no effort to contact the donor, much less obtain the donation. Additionally, the National Church does not guarantee missionaries minimum compensation or support. [The taxpayer] used his personal car and telephone to raise funds during his deputational ministry. [He] occasionally hired assistants at his own discretion and accepted responsibility for paying those assistants.

The IRS pointed out that the missionary was reimbursed for his expenses when he withheld costs from the offerings remitted to the DFM. The court did not find this relevant: "Even if [he] were regarded as receiving reimbursement for his expenses, this matter is more than outweighed by other evidence probative of his being an independent contractor, e.g., petitioner's efforts in securing the funding for his foreign ministry and his investment in his automobile and telephone." The court concluded that the second factor supported self-employed status.

Factor 3—opportunity for profit or loss

The third factor in the Tax Court's 8-factor test is the taxpayer's opportunity for profit or loss. The court noted that the National Church does not guarantee missionaries minimum compensation. Rather, compensation received by missionaries is in the form of a personal allowance, the amount of which depends on the total amount of funding that missionaries are able to secure during their deputational ministry. Additionally, upon resignation, missionaries forfeit any account balance they may have with the DFM and must reallocate their funds to another ministry. The court concluded that the third factor supported self-employed status.

Factor 4—permanency of the relationship

The fourth factor in the Tax Court's 8-factor test is the permanency of the relationship. The more permanent the relationship, the more likely the individual is an employee. The taxpayer conceded that missionary service is a lifetime career. Therefore, the court concluded that the fourth factor supported employee status.

Factor 5—the DFM's right of discharge

The fifth factor in the Tax Court's 8-factor test is whether the employer has the right to discharge the worker. If such a right exists, it is more likely that the worker is an employee. The court noted that the DFM did not have the power to prevent the taxpayer from serving as an Assemblies of God missionary in Bangladesh: "The DFM's most extreme form of discipline is the withdrawal of a missionary's endorsement. For a missionary, the practical consequence of losing the DFM's endorsement is one of administrative inconvenience, namely, that the missionary must collect and process pledges without the assistance of the DFM. In any event, unendorsed Assemblies of God missionaries can and do serve in the foreign field."

The IRS insisted that because the missionary is an Assemblies of God minister, the National Church has the right to revoke his ministerial credentials, and therefore the National Church can effectively discharge him. The court disagreed:

Indeed, the credentials committee [of the National Church] has the authority to withdraw the approval and recommend the recall of ministerial credentials. Although [the taxpayer] is an Assemblies of God minister subject to the disciplinary proceedings in the constitution and bylaws, he presently serves in the capacity of a foreign missionary. Thus, we think the more appropriate analysis considers the DFM's right to discharge [him] in his capacity as a missionary, rather than the National Church's right to recall [his] ministerial credentials.

The court concluded that the fifth factor supported self-employed status.

Factor 6—integral part of business

The sixth factor in the Tax Court's 8-factor test is whether the work performed is an integral part of the employer's business. The court noted that the DFM's primary mission is world evangelism and that the taxpayer's work as an Assemblies of God missionary was directly related to the accomplishment of that mission. Therefore, the court concluded that the sixth factor supported employee status.

Factor 7—relationship the parties believe they have created

The seventh factor in the Tax Court's 8-factor test is the relationship the parties believe they have created. That is, did the DFM and its missionaries believe their relationship was that of employer and employee, or did they believe their relationship was that of an employer and self-employed workers? The court concluded that the parties believed that missionaries were self-employed, based on the following factors: (1) the financial comptroller of the DFM testified that the DFM considered its missionaries to be self-employed; (2) the National Church issued the taxpayer a Form 1099-MISC each year reflecting nonemployee compensation for services rendered; (3) federal income tax was not withheld from the missionary's compensation (the court apparently was unaware of the fact that the compensation of ministers and missionaries is exempt from federal income tax withholding whether they report their income taxes as employees or as self-employed); and (4) the taxpayer thought he was self-employed, as evidenced by the fact that he reported his foreign ministry income and expenses on Schedule C. The court concluded that the seventh factor supported self-employed status.

Factor 8—employee-type benefits

The last factor in the Tax Court's 8-factor test is whether the employer provides employee-type benefits to the worker. The court noted that the DFM provided its missionaries with the following fringe benefits: (1) access to the National Church's retirement plan, and (2) access to the National Church's health insurance plan. On the other hand, the DFM has no policy regarding sick leave and does not maintain records reflecting either vacation or sick leave taken by missionaries. The court concluded that "although the matter is not free from doubt, we think that these facts support a finding that [the taxpayer] was an employee, not [self-employed]."

The court concluded its analysis of the eight factors by observing:

> *Some aspects of the relationship between [the missionary] and the National Church indicate that [he] was an employee, whereas other aspects of the relationship indicate that he was [self-employed]. After weighing the above factors, giving particular weight to the lack of control and the lack of the right to control that the National Church and the DFM had over endorsed missionaries, we conclude that [the taxpayer] was [self-employed], and not an employee.*

IRS Letter Ruling 9825002 (1998)

The IRS ruled that a minister who served as a denominational official was an employee for federal income tax reporting purposes. The minister was ordained in 1969 and has served as minister to several congregations. In the early 1990s he was appointed as a presiding elder of his church. As a presiding elder the minister supervises 27 churches; conducts quarterly conferences and preaches at churches within his district and advises congregations as needed; oversees the collection of assessments from each church; presides over district conferences and Sunday-school conventions; licenses ministry candidates; and confirms stewards, Sunday-school superintendents, and Christian-education directors. Denominational rules establish salary guidelines for each salaried worker. A presiding elder is guaranteed a minimum salary annually as well as additional allowances from each church. Fringe benefits provided to a presiding elder as part of his compensation package include an annual housing allowance, pension benefits, payment of the minister's self-employment tax, and insurance (health, disability, and malpractice). Denominational rules specify that a presiding elder may be expelled or suspended from all official standing in the church if charged with any one or more of various offenses.

The minister insisted that he was self-employed for income tax reporting purposes, but the IRS concluded that he was an employee. The IRS conceded that "for federal income tax purposes, an ordained minister may be an employee or an independent contractor." It concluded that the minister in this case was an employee on the basis of

the Tax Court's decision in the *Weber* case (finding that a Methodist minister was an employee). It noted that a minister's correct reporting status will be based largely on church structure and that the minister in this case was much closer to the facts in the *Weber* case than to those cases in which ministers were found to be self-employed.

IRS Letter Ruling 9414022 (1994)

In 1994 the IRS ruled that a youth pastor was an employee rather than self-employed for federal income tax reporting purposes. The youth pastor was responsible for the church's youth ministry and was qualified to carry out all the ordinances of the church when necessary, including baptisms and communion; he received instructions from the senior pastor; the senior pastor supervised him and retained the right to change the methods used in the performance of his duties; he was hired for an indefinite period of time and was required to follow a schedule established by the church; he performed his services at the church's location, and the church provided him with the materials, equipment, and supplies and reimbursed him for expenses incurred in performing his services; he received a salary for his services plus a housing allowance; he received paid vacation; the church did not carry worker's compensation for the youth pastor and did not deduct Social Security or federal income taxes from his pay; the church reported the youth pastor's income to the IRS on Form W-2; the youth pastor performed his services on a full-time basis, at least eight hours a day; the church retained the right to discharge the youth pastor at any time, while he retained the right to terminate his services at any time without either party incurring any liability; the youth pastor performed his services under the church's name and did not represent himself to the public as being in the business to perform such services for others; and he did not have a financial investment in the church and did not assume the risk of realizing a profit or suffering a loss.

The IRS, applying the 20-factor test for determining a taxpayer's correct reporting status, concluded that the youth pastor was an employee for income tax reporting purposes. The IRS concluded that "the church has the right to and does, in fact, exercise the degree of direction and control necessary in establishing an employer-employee relationship. Accordingly, we conclude that the [youth pastor] is an employee of the church." The IRS correctly pointed out that the youth pastor, like any minister, is self-employed for Social Security purposes with respect to services performed in the exercise of ministry.

IRS Letter Ruling 8333107 (1983)

In 1983 the IRS ruled that an associate pastor was an employee for income tax reporting purposes. The pastor was under the supervision of a senior pastor and had primary responsibilities for the music, arts, drama, and missions program of his church. His responsibilities included working with the music, arts, drama, and missions committees and assisting the lead pastor and congregation in all phases of the ministry. He served as the resource person, motivator, and administrator of various church activities.

The church required the associate pastor to perform services during regular working hours. His services were supervised and reviewed by the church, and he received instructions from the church. His day-to-day activities were reviewed almost weekly by the senior pastor. He was required to attend a workshop of a general informative nature, and his budget included funds for one week of formalized training per year. All of the associate pastor's duties had to be performed by him personally and could not be delegated by him to others. The church made contributions toward hospital or medical insurance for the associate pastor and provided him with an office in the church building. The associate pastor was paid an annual rate on a biweekly basis. He also was provided with lump-sum amounts for automobile and housing expenses. His services could be terminated for unsatisfactory performance. He had the right to terminate his services at any time.

Under these facts the IRS ruled that the associate pastor was an employee and not self-employed for federal income tax reporting purposes. It noted that "it is clear that [the church has] the right to direct and control the associate pastor to the degree necessary to create an employer-employee relationship."

4. IRS AUDIT GUIDELINES FOR MINISTERS

In 1995 the IRS released its first audit guidelines for ministers pursuant to its Market Segment Specialization Program (MSSP). The guidelines were intended to promote a higher degree of competence among agents who audit ministers. In 2009 the IRS released a newly revised version of the guidelines (the Minister Audit Technique Guide) that addresses a number of important issues and contains several examples.

✵ **KEY POINT.** The audit guidelines will instruct IRS agents in the examination of ministers' tax returns. They alert agents to the key questions to ask, and they provide background information along with the IRS position on a number of issues. It is therefore of utmost importance that ministers be familiar with these guidelines.

The IRS audit guidelines introduce the correct classification of ministers for federal tax purposes with the following observations:

> *A minister can be a common law employee for income tax purposes even though the payments for services as a minister is statutorily considered income from self employment for social security and medical taxes and the minister can even apply to be exempt from social security tax.*

> *The handling of business expenses for income tax purposes is determined by whether the minister is classified as an employee or an independent contractor. If an independent contractor then the business expenses are reported on the Schedule C. If an employee then the expenses are reportable subject to statutory limitations as an employee business expense itemized deduction. To be properly*

> *reported on Schedule C, a minister's expense must come from a trade or business of his own, other than that of being an employee.*

How, then, can a minister's correct reporting status be determined? The guidelines provide the following clarifications:

- *The tax code defines an employee as one who is such "under the usual common law rules applicable in determining the employer-employee relationship."*
- *This subject is complex and dependent on the facts and circumstances in each case, which is why it is highly litigated.*
- *IRS agents are instructed to conduct research on litigation that has occurred in their region to assist in making the correct classification. The guidelines note that litigation "has generally occurred where the minister claims independent contractor status and the Internal Revenue Service determines the minister was an employee."*
- *The Internal Revenue Service looks at factors that fall within three categories, namely behavioral control, financial control and the relationships of the parties. Behavioral control deals with facts that substantiate the right to direct or control the detail and means by which a worker performs the required services. Financial control deals with facts of the economic aspects of the relationship of the parties and if the worker has the opportunity for the realization of profit or loss. Some factors are: significant investment, unreimbursed expenses, making services available, and methods of payments. Relationship of the parties is important because it reflects the parties' intent concerning control.*
- *The courts consider various factors to determine an employment relationship between the parties. Relevant factors include: (1) the degree of control exercised by the principal over the details of the work; (2) which party invests in the facilities used in the work; (3) the opportunity of the individual for profit or loss; (4) whether or not the principal has the right to discharge the individual; (5) whether the work is part of the principal's regular business; (6) the permanency of the relationship; and (7) relationship the parties believe they are creating.*
- *No one factor dictates the outcome. Rather, we must look at all the facts and circumstances of each case.*

● **OBSERVATION.** The guidelines do not say that all ministers are employees for federal income tax reporting purposes. This flexible approach leaves open the possibility that some ministers will not be employees under the applicable tests. Note, however, that self-employed status will be the exception and that any minister reporting income taxes as self-employed must expect to have his or her status challenged if audited.

● **OBSERVATION.** The guidelines do not refer to the 20-factor test announced by the IRS in 1987 (*Revenue Ruling 87-41*) or to the 7-factor test utilized by the Tax Court in the *Weber* and *Shelley* cases (summarized above). Instead, they refer to the 3-factor analysis of the common-law employee test found in IRS Publication 15a and quoted above. This test focuses on behavior control, financial control, and the relationship of the parties.

The guidelines refer to the following authorities in support of these conclusions:

- In *Weber v. Commissioner*, 60 F.3rd 1104 (4th Cir. 1995), a federal appeals court addressed the issue of whether a minister was an employee or independent contractor. The court stated: "The right-to-control test is the crucial test to determine the nature of the working relationship. . . . The degree of control is one of great importance, though not exclusive. . . . Accordingly, we must examine not only the control exercised by the alleged employer, but also the degree to which an alleged employer may intervene to imposed control. . . . In order for an employer to retain the requisite control over the details of an employee's work, the employer need not stand over the employee and direct every move made by that employee. . . . Also, the degree of control necessary to find employee status varies according to the nature of the services provided."
- The threshold level of control necessary to find employee status is generally lower when applied to professional services than when applied to nonprofessional service. In *James v. Commissioner*, 25 T.C. 1296 (1956), the Tax Court stated that "despite this absence of direct control over the manner in which professional men shall conduct their professional activities, it cannot be doubted that many professional men are employees." In *Azad v. United States*, 388 F.2d 74 (8th Cir. 1968), a federal appeals court said that "from the very nature of the services rendered by . . . professionals, it would be wholly unrealistic to suggest that an employer should undertake the task of controlling the manner in which the professional conducts his activities." Generally a lower level of control applies to professional."
- The absence of the need to control the manner in which the minister conducts his or her duties should not be confused with the absence of the right to control. The right to control contemplated by the common law as an incident of employment requires only such supervision as the nature of the work requires. *McGuire v. United States, 349 F.2d 644 (9th Cir. 1965).*

⊙ **OBSERVATION.** It is surprising that the guidelines do not refer to either the *Weber* or *Shelley* cases (summarized above). Both cases involved the application of a 7-factor test for deciding whether a worker is an employee or self-employed for income tax reporting purposes.

5. HOW MINISTERS SHOULD DETERMINE THEIR CORRECT REPORTING STATUS

Ministers should review the tests described in this chapter in determining their correct reporting status for federal income tax reporting

purposes. Any of the tests can be used. The tests should be applied in light of the court decisions and IRS rulings summarized above.

6. ADDITIONAL CONSIDERATIONS

Note the following additional considerations.

IRS bias in favor of treating taxpayers as employees

The reason is simple—employees are subject to income tax withholding, and accordingly there is a greater likelihood that a person's taxes will be paid if he or she is an employee rather than self-employed. This consideration has no application to ministers, however, whose income is exempt by law from income tax withholding even if they are employees for income tax purposes. *IRC 3401(a)(9).*

Ministers who may be self-employed for income tax reporting purposes

A number of situations exist in which a minister is more likely to be self-employed for federal income tax reporting purposes. These include the following:

Itinerant evangelists

Unincorporated evangelists who conduct services in several churches during the course of a year ordinarily would be considered self-employed for purposes of both income taxes and Social Security taxes. They ordinarily would not be considered employees under either the Tax Court's 7-factor test or the IRS 20-factor test.

Guest speakers

Many ministers are called upon to conduct worship services in other churches on an occasional basis. To illustrate, Pastor D, who serves as senior minister at First Church, is invited to conduct a service at a church in another community. Ministers generally will be considered to be self-employed with respect to such occasional guest speaking commitments.

Supply pastors

Many ministers serve temporary assignments in local churches until a permanent minister can be selected. In some cases these ministers will be self-employed with respect to such an assignment. This will depend on an application of the Tax Court's 7-factor test (or the IRS 20-factor test). In general, the shorter the assignment, the more likely the minister will be considered self-employed.

Services provided directly to congregation members

IRS Publication 517 recognizes that it is possible for ministers who are employees of their churches for income tax reporting purposes to be self-employed for certain services (such as baptisms, marriages, and funerals) that are performed directly for individual members who, in turn, pay a fee or honorarium to the minister.

Church polity

In some cases a church's polity may suggest that ministers are self-employed rather than employees for income tax reporting purposes. For example, ministers who are not associated with a regional or national religious body that exercises control over their activities will find it easier in some cases to argue that they are self-employed for income tax reporting purposes. It is significant that the Tax Court ended the *Weber* case with the following comment: "We recognize that there may be differences with respect to ministers in other churches or denominations, and the particular facts and circumstances must be considered in each case."

Obtaining official determination of reporting status

Ministers can obtain an official determination of their reporting status by filing a Form SS-8 with the IRS. This can be a time-consuming and involved process, however, and the IRS demonstrates a decidedly pro-employee bias in its rulings. In other words, a minister wanting to report his or her income taxes as a self-employed person ordinarily will not be successful in obtaining IRS confirmation in response to an SS-8 application.

Ministers who elect self-employed status for theological reasons

Some ministers consider themselves to be under the control or authority of Jesus Christ rather than a local church or church board. Such persons feel they would be compromising their biblical authority by reporting as an employee, since it would amount to an acknowledgment of subordination to local church authority. Such a view, if corroborated by appropriate language in the church's charter or bylaws, might support self-employed status for income tax reporting purposes if in fact the church does not exercise meaningful control over the minister. Note, however, that an IRS auditor might want to determine whether the church board shares the minister's theology on this point. If church board members do not agree that they lack any meaningful control over the minister, it is highly unlikely that this argument will prevail. Also, note that the Tax Court dismissed the relevance of theological considerations in the *Weber* case (see above) by observing:

> [Pastor Weber's] basic position appears to be that because he is a minister in a unique religious order he cannot be an employee. While we have great respect for [his] religious dedication, religion is not the question before us. [Pastor Weber] is seeking a business benefit. He wants to file a Schedule C . . . and to claim business expenses on it. It is he who has cast this case in business terms. . . . [Pastor Weber] contends that no one had the right to control either the method or the means by which he conducted his ministry. We do not agree.

Losing the housing allowance exclusion

A common misconception is that ministers who report their income taxes as employees will lose the housing allowance exclusion. This is not so. The housing allowance is available to ministers whether they report their income taxes as employees or as self-employed. However, as noted above, certain fringe benefits provided by a church on behalf of a minister are excludable from the minister's income only if he or she is an employee for federal income tax reporting purposes. Examples include medical insurance premiums paid by a church on behalf of its minister; group term life insurance (up to $50,000) provided by a church on behalf of a minister; amounts payable to employees on account of sickness, accident, or disability pursuant to an employer-financed plan; and employer-sponsored "cafeteria plans," which permit employees to choose between receiving cash payments or a variety of fringe benefits.

Section 530 of the Revenue Act of 1978

In the late 1960s the IRS began vigorously challenging employer attempts to classify workers as self employed rather than as employees. In many cases employers were assessed large penalties for improperly classifying some workers as self-employed. Congress responded to these developments by enacting section 530 of the Revenue Act of 1978. Section 530 was designed to provide employers with relief from hostile IRS attempts to reclassify workers as employees. If employers meet certain requirements set forth in section 530, they are relieved of penalties that otherwise might apply because of their treatment of workers as self-employed.

The IRS has interpreted section 530 in ways that seriously undermine the protections it was designed to create. Congress responded to these IRS efforts by enacting legislation repudiating most of the schemes the IRS has used over the years to avoid section 530.

The important point to note is that section 530 only relieves *employers* of penalties for improperly classifying a worker as self-employed. It provides no relief to such workers in defending their self-employed status for purposes of their individual income tax returns. Section 530 is addressed more fully in Chapter 11 of this text. See also *IRS Publication 1976 (Do You Qualify for Relief under Section 530?).*

- ✦ **KEY POINT.** In 2009 the IRS issued revised audit guidelines for its agents to follow in auditing ministers. These guidelines state that section 530 of the Revenue Act of 1978 does not apply to ministers "since they are statutorily exempt from FICA and are subject to SECA."

- ✱ **New in 2012.** In 2012 the IRS launched the Voluntary Classification Settlement Program to assist employers in reclassifying self-employment workers to employees, with reduced penalties.

Voluntary Classification Settlement Program

The Voluntary Classification Settlement Program (VCSP) is a voluntary program that provides an opportunity for employers to reclassify their workers as employees for employment tax purposes for future tax periods with partial relief from federal employment taxes. To participate in this new voluntary program, the employer must meet certain eligibility requirements, apply to participate in the VCSP by filing Form 8952, Application for Voluntary Classification Settlement Program, and enter into a closing agreement with the IRS.

The VCSP is available for employers who want to voluntarily change the prospective classification of their workers. The program applies to taxpayers who are currently treating their workers (or a class or group of workers) as independent contractors or other nonemployees and want to prospectively treat the workers as employees.

The employer must have consistently treated the workers as non-employees and must have filed all required Forms 1099 for the workers to be reclassified under the VCSP for the previous three years to participate in the VCSP. Additionally, the employer cannot currently be under audit by the IRS and cannot be currently under audit concerning the classification of the workers by the Department of Labor or by a state government agency.

If the IRS or the Department of Labor has previously audited a taxpayer concerning the classification of the workers, the taxpayer will be eligible only if the taxpayer has complied with the results of that audit.

Exempt organizations may participate in the VCSP if they meet all of the eligibility requirements.

An employer participating in the VCSP will agree to prospectively treat the class or classes of workers as employees for future tax periods. In exchange, the employer

- will pay 10 percent of the employment tax liability that may have been due on compensation paid to the workers for the most recent tax year;
- will not be liable for any interest and penalties on the amount; and
- will not be subject to an employment tax audit with respect to the worker classification of the workers being reclassified under the VCSP for prior years.

In addition, as part of the VCSP program, the employer will agree to extend the period of limitations on assessment of employment taxes for three years for the first, second, and third calendar years beginning after the date on which it has agreed under the VCSP closing agreement to begin treating the workers as employees.

To participate in the VCSP, an employer must apply using Form 8952, Application for Voluntary Classification Settlement Program. The application should be filed at least 60 days from the date the employer wants to begin treating its workers as employees.

Officers and directors

The income tax regulations address the correct reporting status of officers and directors as follows:

> All classes or grades of employees are included within the relationship of employer and employee. Thus, superintendents, managers, and other supervisory personnel are employees. Generally, an officer of a corporation is an employee of the corporation. However, an officer of a corporation who as such does not perform any services or performs only minor services and who neither receives nor is entitled to receive, directly or indirectly, any remuneration is not considered to be an employee of the corporation. A director of a corporation in his capacity as such is not an employee of the corporation. Treas. Reg. 31.3401(c)(1)(f).

Legal responsibility of employers for acts of their employees

Most courts have reached the conclusion that ministers serving local churches are employees rather than self-employed for purposes of deciding whether the employing church is legally responsible for their conduct. For example, a federal appeals court concluded that a Methodist church was legally responsible for the copyright infringement of a minister of music, since "the only inference that reasonably can be drawn from the evidence is that in selecting and arranging the song . . . for use by the church choir [the minister] was engaged in the course and scope of his employment by the church." *Wihtol v. Crow, 309 F.2d 777 (8th Cir. 1962).*

Many other cases have concerned accidents involving motor vehicles driven by ministers in the course of church work. Such cases support the treatment of ministers as employees for income tax purposes, since the legal considerations employed in determining whether a minister is an employee for church liability purposes are substantially the same as those used in determining whether a minister is an employee for income tax purposes. Note, however, that some courts have not agreed with these rulings. To illustrate, the Kansas Supreme Court concluded that a Catholic priest was self-employed for purposes of determining the legal liability of his diocese for his misconduct even though the diocese "followed the majority of dioceses in issuing a W-2 form to each priest." *Brillhart v. Sheier, 758 P.2d 219 (Kan. 1988).*

Workers compensation

Ministers who report their federal income taxes as self-employed are not necessarily self-employed for workers compensation purposes. The term "employee" generally is defined more broadly under workers compensation laws than under federal tax law.

Penalties

As noted in Chapter 11, a church can be assessed penalties for reporting as self-employed a worker whom the IRS later determines to be an employee.

B. NONMINISTER STAFF

Many churches employ staff members other than ministers. In general, the same tests for determining whether a minister is an employee or self-employed for federal income tax reporting purposes will apply in evaluating the correct reporting status of nonminister staff. Some differences, however, should be noted:

1. SOCIAL SECURITY

Nonminister staff, unlike ministers, are not always treated as self-employed for Social Security. Nonminister staff who are employees for income tax reporting purposes under the tests discussed in this chapter generally must be treated as employees for Social Security. This means they will be subject to Social Security and Medicare taxes. One exception is that nonminister staff members employed by a church that exempted itself from payment of the employer's share of FICA taxes by filing a timely Form 8274 (discussed in Chapter 11) are treated as self-employed for Social Security.

✿ **KEY POINT.** The definition of "minister" for federal tax purposes is addressed fully in Chapter 3.

2. WITHHOLDING

Nonminister staff members who are employees for income tax reporting purposes are subject to income tax as well as Social Security and Medicare tax withholding.

✿ **KEY POINT.** Some churches have elected to exempt themselves from the employer's portion of FICA taxes for nonminister employees by filing a timely Form 8274 with the IRS. Such churches do not withhold FICA taxes from nonminister employees' wages. This exemption is addressed fully in Chapter 11, section B.

EXAMPLE. A church employed a worker to serve as church custodian under the following terms and conditions: (1) the position of church custodian is advertised for bids on a yearly basis; (2) the custodian is required to follow guidelines established by the church; (3) the custodian's duties include the cleaning of the church building and, when necessary, snow removal; (4) the custodian works at the church once each week; (5) the custodian is not required to perform services during regular working hours but rather performs his duties at his own discretion; (6) the church reviews the custodian's services only to the extent necessary to ensure that they are completed in accordance with church guidelines; (7) equipment and supplies are furnished to the custodian at no cost (the custodian purchases the necessary supplies and is reimbursed by the church treasurer); (8) the custodian is paid on a monthly basis; (9) the church assumes that the custodian will perform his services personally; (10) the custodian does not engage helpers to assist in the work; (11) the custodian is not eligible for bonuses, pensions, sick pay, or other fringe benefits; (12) the church does not make contributions toward hospital or medical insurance for the custodian; (13) no formal guidelines have been established for termination, but the custodian could be terminated for gross negligence; (14) the custodian can terminate his services at any time; (15) the custodian does not perform similar services for others.

It is the church's belief that the custodian is self-employed rather than an employee, and accordingly it has not withheld FICA taxes or income taxes from the custodian's compensation. The IRS disagreed, concluding that the custodian was an employee. The IRS observed: "Careful consideration has been given to the information submitted in this case. The facts show that the [custodian is] subject to certain restraints and conditions that are indicative of the church's control over [him]. The [custodian] performs personal services for the church on its premises and property. [He performs his] services according to guidelines established by the church. He renders his services personally and does not engage any helpers or assistants. The church provides him with the use of equipment and supplies in the performance of services at no cost. His services are supervised and reviewed. His services are necessary and incident to the church's operation. He is not engaged in an independent enterprise in which he assumes the usual business risks. He has a continuous relationship with the church as opposed to a single transaction. Both parties could terminate the agreement at any time." *IRS Letter Ruling 8505023.*

C. EXAMPLES

EXAMPLE. Pastor P is a retired minister who serves as an interim minister for churches in a given geographical region that are temporarily in need of ministerial services. Pastor P typically spends no more than three months with any particular congregation, is given great freedom with respect to the duties he performs and the manner or method of performance, and is issued a Form 1099-MISC form by each church. These facts suggest that Pastor P could report his income and business expenses as a self-employed person on Schedule C.

EXAMPLE. Pastor L is a minister of education at First Church. She has a specific job description, her services are under the direct supervision and control of her senior pastor, she is issued a Form W-2 each year, and she is required to follow prescribed methods in the performance of her duties. These facts strongly suggest that Pastor L is an employee for income tax reporting purposes.

EXAMPLE. Pastor G serves as pastor of a small congregation that has no other employees. He performs his duties free from any control or supervision by the church. Much of his work is performed off of church premises. He is issued a Form 1099-MISC each year, and his work agreement with the church characterizes him as self-employed. Under these facts, the federal appeals court's decision in the *Alford* case (discussed above) suggests that Pastor G may be a self-employed person for income tax reporting purposes. However, Pastor G should carefully evaluate the following three advantages of employee status before continuing to report as self-employed: (1) the value of various fringe benefits will be excludable, including the often significant cost of employer-paid health insurance premiums on the life of the minister and his or her dependents; (2) the risk of an IRS audit is substantially lower; and (3) as an employee he would avoid the additional taxes and penalties that often apply to self-employed ministers who are audited by the IRS and reclassified as employees.

EXAMPLE. Same facts as the previous example, except that Pastor G is senior minister of a church with two other ministers and ten lay employees. It is less likely that Pastor G will be able to use the *Alford* case to support his self-employed status, because ministers in larger churches tend to be subject to more control with respect to the manner in which they perform their duties.

EXAMPLE. Pastor M works in an administrative capacity for a church agency. Ordinarily, ministers who work in such a capacity will satisfy the definition of a common-law employee since they are subject to a greater degree of control and supervision with respect to the details and performance of their duties, and accordingly should report their income taxes as employees. The income tax regulations specify that "generally, an officer of a corporation is an employee of the corporation." *Treas. Reg. 31.3401(c)-1(f)*.

EXAMPLE. Pastor H serves as a church's youth minister. Ordinarily, ministers who work in such a capacity will satisfy the definition of a common-law employee, since they are subject to a greater degree of control and supervision with respect to the details and performance of their duties, and accordingly should report their income taxes as employees. *IRS Letter Ruling 9414022*.

EXAMPLE. Pastor C has been the senior minister at a church since 1997. He reports his income taxes as a self-employed person on Schedule C (Form 1040). The church issues Pastor C a Form W-2 at the end of each year and includes his compensation on its quarterly Form 941. Pastor C's predecessor was Pastor B, who reported his income taxes as an employee. The fact that the church issues Pastor C a Form W-2 rather than a 1099-MISC and includes his compensation on its quarterly employer's tax returns (Forms 941) would probably result in a determination that he is an employee for income tax reporting purposes in the event that his return is audited by the IRS.

EXAMPLE. Pastor W has reported his federal income taxes as a self-employed person for many years. In 2013 he decides to report his taxes as an employee. His employing church withholds FICA taxes from his pay throughout 2013 and, in addition, pays the employer's share of FICA taxes. Ministers are always deemed self-employed for Social Security purposes with respect to services performed in the exercise of their ministry (except for some chaplains), and accordingly they are never subject to FICA taxes with respect to such services. Pastor W's decision to report his income taxes as an employee did not change his self-employed status for Social Security purposes. The church is incorrectly treating Pastor W as an employee for FICA purposes. He should continue to pay the self-employment tax (the Social Security tax for self-employed persons).

EXAMPLE. Pastor T reports his income taxes as a self-employed person (using Schedule C). His church compensation for 2012 was $45,000. In addition, the church paid the annual premium ($4,500) on a health insurance policy for Pastor T and his family. Since Pastor T considers himself to be self-employed for federal income tax reporting purposes, he is not eligible for the exclusion of employer-paid health insurance premiums. Accordingly, the church must list the full $4,500 premium as income on Pastor T's Form 1099-MISC for 2012.

EXAMPLE. Pastor O reports her income taxes as a self-employed person. She had $4,000 of business expenses in 2012 that were not reimbursed by her church. She deducted all of them on Schedule C. She did not have enough expenses to itemize deductions on Schedule A. Pastor O is later audited by the IRS, and she is reclassified as an employee. She will not be able to deduct any of the $4,000 of business expenses, since they are deductible by an employee only as an itemized deduction on Schedule A. This result can be avoided if the church adopts an accountable reimbursement plan (see Chapter 7 for details).

EXAMPLE. In a case in which the IRS argued that "love offerings" given to a pastor by his church represented taxable compensation, the IRS conceded that the pastor was self-employed for income tax reporting purposes. *Swaringer v. Commissioner, T.C. Summary Opinion 2001-37 (2001)*.

EXAMPLE. A church submitted a Form SS-8 to the IRS requesting a determination regarding the correct reporting status of a church musician. The church had been reporting the musician as a self-employed worker and issued him a Form 1099-MISC each year. The church summarized the facts as follows: (1) the musician performed music on Sunday mornings for one hour; (2) he practiced for two hours each week; (3) he received instructions from the pastor via e-mail; (4) the musician provided his own instrument, while the church provided all of the other necessary supplies and materials he needed to fulfill his duties; (5) the musician received a weekly stipend for his services; (6) there was no written employment contract; (7) the musician's services were a necessary part of the church's activities; (8) the musician did not advertise his services to the general public, nor did he provide similar services for others; (9) the musician had a continuous relationship (for four years) with the church; (10) both parties had the right to terminate the relationship without incurring liability. On these facts, the IRS concluded that the musician was an employee rather than self-employed for income tax reporting purposes. The IRS concluded that the church "had the right to exercise direction and control over the worker to the degree necessary to establish that the worker was a common law employee and not an independent contractor operating a trade of business." It noted:

> *Evidence of control generally falls into three categories: behavioral controls, financial controls, and relationship of the parties, which are collectively referred to as the categories of evidence. In weighing the evidence, careful consideration has been given to the factors outlined below.*
>
> *Factors that illustrate whether there is a right to control how a worker performs a task include training and instructions. In this case, you retained the right to change the worker's method and to direct the worker to the extent necessary to protect your financial investment.*
>
> *Factors that illustrate whether there is a right to direct and control the financial aspects of the worker's activities include significant investment, unreimbursed expenses, the methods of payment, and the opportunity for profit or loss. In this case, the worker did not invest capital or assume business risks, and therefore, did not have the opportunity to realize a profit or incur a loss as a result of the services provided.*
>
> *Factors that illustrate how the parties perceive their relationship include the intent of the parties as expressed in written contracts; the provision, or lack of employee benefits; the right of the parties to terminate the relationship; the permanency of the relationship; and whether the services performed are part of the service recipient's regular business activities. In this case, the worker was not engaged in an independent enterprise, but rather the services performed by the worker were a necessary and integral part of your business. Both parties retained the right to terminate the work relationship at any time without incurring a liability.*

━━━ **APPENDIX** ━━━

ARE MINISTERS EMPLOYEES OR SELF-EMPLOYED FOR FEDERAL INCOME TAX REPORTING PURPOSES—A SUMMARY OF ALL RELEVANT CASES AND RULINGS

CASE	TEST	CONCLUSION
IRS Letter Ruling 9825002 (1998)	Applied 7-factor test adopted in the *Weber* case (see below).	Denominational official was an employee.
Alford v. United States, 116 F.3d 334 (8th Cir. 1997)	Considered (1) the hiring party's right to control the manner and means by which the product is accomplished; (2) the skill required; (3) the source of the instrumentalities and tools; (4) the location of the work (5) the duration of the relationship between the parties; (6) whether the hiring party has the right to assign additional projects to the hired party; (7) the extent of the hired party's discretion over when and how long to work; (8) the method of payment; (9) the hired party's role in hiring and paying assistants; (10) whether the work is part of the regular business of the hiring party; (11) whether the hiring party is in business; and (12) the provision of employee benefits.	Assemblies of God pastor who served as sole employee of a small church was self-employed.
Radde v. Commissioner, T.C. Memo. 1997-490 (1997)	Applied 7-factor test adopted in the *Weber* case (see below).	Methodist minister was an employee.
Greene v. Commissioner, T.C. Memo. 1996 531 (1996)	Applied an 8-factor test, which included all 7 factors in the *Weber* case (see below) plus an inquiry into whether fringe benefits provided by the employer are "typical" of those provided to employees.	Assemblies of God foreign missionary was self-employed.
Weber v. Commissioner, 103 T.C. 378 (1994), aff'd 60 F.3d 1104 (4th Cir. 1995)	Considered (1) the degree of control exercised by the employer over the details of the work; (2) which party invests in the facilities used in the work; (3) the opportunity of the individual for profit or loss; (4) whether the employer has the right to discharge the individual; (5) whether the work is part of the employer's regular business; (6) the permanency of the relationship; and (7) the relationship the parties believe they are creating.	Methodist minister was an employee.
Shelley v. Commissioner, T.C. Memo. 1994 432 (1994)	Applied 7-factor test adopted in the *Weber* case (see above).	Pentecostal Holiness minister was self-employed.
IRS Letter Ruling 9825002 (1998)	Applied 7-factor test adopted in the *Weber* case (see above).	Denominational official was an employee.
IRS Letter Ruling 9414022 (1994)	Applied 20-factor test of Revenue Ruling 87-41: (1) employees must comply with employer instructions; (2) employees are more likely to be trained; (3) employees' work is integral part of employer's business; (4) self-employed workers hire and pay substitutes; (5) self-employed workers hire and pay assistants; (6) employees have continuing relationship with employer; (7) employees work set hours; (8) employees are more likely to work full time; (9) employees do work on employer's premises; (10) employees do work in sequence set by employer; (11) employees submit oral or written reports; (12) employees are paid by hour or week, self-employed by the job; (13) employees are more likely to have business expenses reimbursed by employer; (14) self-employed provide their own tools and materials; (15) employees use equipment and facilities provided by employer; (16) self-employed may realize profit or loss; (17) self-employed work for more than one employer at same time; (18) self-employed advertise their services to the public; (19) employees can be dismissed; (20) employees can quit at any time.	Youth pastor was an employee.
IRS Letter Ruling 8333107 (1983)	Applied common-law employee test in the income tax regulations, which states that "generally the relationship of employer and employee exists when the person for whom services are performed has the right to control and direct the individual who performs the services, not only as to the result to be accomplished by the work but also as to the details and means by which that result is accomplished."	Associate pastor was an employee.

3 QUALIFYING AS A MINISTER FOR FEDERAL TAX PURPOSES

Even after this, Jeroboam did not change his evil ways, but once more appointed priests for the high places from all sorts of people. Anyone who wanted to become a priest he consecrated for the high places. This was the sin of the house of Jeroboam that led to its downfall and to its destruction from the face of the earth.

1 Kings 13:33–34

CHAPTER HIGHLIGHTS

■ *Four special tax rules.* A number of provisions in the federal tax code apply to ministers with respect to services they perform in the exercise of their ministry. These include:

(1) the housing allowance and parsonage exclusions;
(2) exemption from Social Security coverage (if several conditions are met);
(3) self-employed status for Social Security (if not exempt); and
(4) exemption from income tax withholding.

■ *Consistency.* Persons who qualify as ministers must be consistent with respect to the four special tax rules. For example, not only are they eligible for a housing allowance, but they also are self-employed for Social Security, are exempt from income tax withholding, and are eligible for exemption from self-employment taxes if they meet several conditions.

■ *Importance of ministerial services.* Persons who qualify as ministers for federal taxes will be eligible for the four special tax rules only with regard to *services they perform in the exercise of their ministry.* For example, a minister is not eligible for a housing allowance with respect to secular earnings. Also, a minister who has obtained exemption from Social Security coverage is not exempt with respect to income from secular employment. Services performed in the exercise of ministry include conducting religious worship, administering sacraments, and performing management functions for a church, a denomination, or an integral agency of a church or denomination (such as some religious colleges). Further, working for a secular organization can constitute the exercise of one's ministry if the work is done pursuant to a valid assignment by one's church or denomination (and the work furthers the purposes of the church or denomination).

■ *Who is a minister for federal tax purposes.* In deciding if a person is a minister for federal income tax reporting, the following five factors must be considered: (1) ordained, commissioned, or licensed status (required); (2) administration of sacraments; (3) conduct of religious worship; (4) management responsibilities in the local church or a parent denomination;

and (5) whether the person is considered a religious leader by the church or parent denomination. In general, the IRS and the courts require that a minister be ordained, commissioned, or licensed, and then they apply a "balancing test" with respect to the other four factors. The more of those factors a person satisfies, the more likely he or she will be deemed a minister for tax reporting.

■ *Possibility of the IRS not recognizing ministerial status of some ministers.* The IRS may not recognize the ministerial status of persons who receive ministerial credentials from a local church if (1) the church is affiliated with a parent denomination that does not recognize the local church's action; (2) the local church's charter or bylaws do not authorize it to confer ministerial credentials; (3) the church does not have an established history and practice of conferring ministerial credentials; and (4) the ministerial credentials result in no change in job description or duties.

■ *Conferral of ministerial status to obtain tax benefits.* Any attempt to confer ministerial credentials upon persons solely to qualify them for tax benefits, without changing their duties or responsibilities in any way, probably will not be recognized by the IRS or the courts.

INTRODUCTION

✿ **KEY POINT.** A number of provisions in the federal tax code apply to ministers with respect to services they perform in the exercise of their ministry. These include: (1) eligibility for the housing allowance and parsonage exclusions; (2) exemption from self-employment taxes (if several conditions are met); (3) self-employed status for Social Security (if not exempt); and (4) wages exempt from federal income tax withholding.

✿ **KEY POINT.** Persons who qualify as ministers for federal tax purposes must be consistent with regard to these four special tax rules—if one applies, then they all apply.

✿ **KEY POINT.** To be eligible for these four special tax rules, a person must satisfy two requirements: (1) qualify as a minister for federal tax purposes, and (2) receive compensation for services performed in the exercise of ministry (the rules only apply with respect to such compensation).

1. SPECIAL TAX RULES FOR MINISTERS

A number of provisions in the tax code apply specifically to ministers. However, the following four provisions are unique in that they use the same language in defining which persons are eligible for the special treatment:

(1) the exclusion (in computing income taxes) of housing allowances and the fair rental value of church-owned parsonages provided to ministers rent-free;

(2) the exemption of some ministers from self-employment taxes (e.g., Social Security taxes for the self-employed) if several conditions are met;

(3) treatment of ministers (who are not exempt) as self-employed for Social Security with respect to ministerial services; and

(4) exemption of ministers' wages from income tax withholding.

This example illustrates the significance of this subject:

EXAMPLE. A church has an ordained senior minister, a licensed associate minister, a nonordained youth minister, a nonordained music minister, a business administrator, four office secretaries, and two custodians. How many of these persons are eligible for a housing allowance? How many should be treated as self-employed for Social Security (and pay the self-employment tax rather than FICA taxes)? How many are eligible for exemption from Social Security coverage (assuming they meet all of the conditions)? How many are exempt from income tax withholding? These questions are confusing to many church leaders. This chapter is designed to provide guidance in resolving the same or similar issues in your church or organization on the basis of the most recent legal precedent.

2. DEFINITION OF "MINISTER"

The four special rules mentioned above are available only to ordained, commissioned, or licensed ministers of a church with respect to service performed in the exercise of ministry. The term "service performed in the exercise of ministry" is defined in the income tax regulations as follows:

[S]ervice performed by a minister in the exercise of his ministry includes the ministration of sacerdotal functions and the conduct of religious worship, and the control, conduct, and maintenance of religious organizations . . . under the authority of a religious

body constituting a church or church denomination. The following rules are applicable in determining whether services performed by a minister are performed in the exercise of ministry:

(i) Whether service performed by a minister constitutes the conduct or religious worship or the ministration of sacerdotal functions depends on the tenets and practices of the particular religious body constituting his church or church denomination.

(ii) Services performed by a minister in the control, conduct, and maintenance of a religious organization relates to directing, managing, or promoting the activities of such organization. Any religious organization is deemed to be under the authority of a religious body constituting a church or church denomination if it is organized and dedicated to carrying out the tenets and principles of a faith in accordance with either the requirements or sanctions governing the creation of institutions of the faith. . . .

(iii) If a minister is performing service in the conduct of religious worship or the ministration of sacerdotal functions, such service is in the exercise of his ministry whether or not it is performed for a religious organization.

(iv) If a minister is performing service for an organization which is operated as an integral agency of a religious organization under the authority of a religious body constituting a church or church denomination, all service performed by the minister in the conduct of religious worship, in the ministration of sacerdotal functions, or in the control, conduct, and maintenance of such organization is in the exercise of his ministry. (v) If a minister, pursuant to an assignment or designation by a religious body constituting his church, performs service for an organization which is neither a religious organization nor operated as an integral agency of a religious organization, all service performed by him, even though such service may not involve the conduct of religious worship or the ministration of sacerdotal functions, is in the exercise of his ministry.

If a minister is performing service for an organization which is neither a religious organization nor operated as an integral agency of a religious organization and the service is not performed pursuant to an assignment or designation by his ecclesiastical superiors, then only the service performed by him in the conduct of religious worship or the ministration of sacerdotal functions is in the exercise of his ministry. Treas. Reg. 1.1402(c)-5.

✤**KEY POINT.** The purpose of this chapter is not to explain the special tax rules that apply to ministers but rather to address who qualifies for them. Each rule is addressed fully in the following chapters in this text: (1) housing allowance (Chapter 6); (2) self-employed status for Social Security (Chapter 9); (3) exemption from self-employment (Social Security) taxes (Chapter 9); and (4) exemption from income tax withholding (Chapters 1 and 11).

A. MINISTERS EMPLOYED BY A CHURCH

✤ **KEY POINT.** For each of the past several years the IRS has announced that it will not issue private letter rulings addressing the question of whether an individual is a minister of the gospel for federal tax purposes. This means taxpayers will not be able to obtain clarification from the IRS in a letter ruling on their status as a minister for any one or more of the following matters: (1)eligibility for a parsonage exclusion or housing allowance; (2) eligibility for exemption from self-employment taxes; (3) self-employed status for Social Security; or (4) exemption of wages from income tax withholding. *Revenue Procedure 2012-3.*

The tax regulations quoted above make the four special tax rules discussed in this chapter available to

- ministers,
- with respect to compensation received for services performed in the exercise of ministry.

Each of these requirements is fully explained below on the basis of the most recent legal precedent.

1. QUALIFYING AS A MINISTER FOR TAX PURPOSES

Tax Court decisions

Unfortunately, Tax Court decisions have not always been helpful in deciding if a person is a minister for federal tax reporting. Consider the following cases:

Salkov v. Commissioner, 46 T.C. 190 (1966)

The court ruled that a Jewish cantor was eligible for a housing allowance, since he was the equivalent of a commissioned minister and was recognized as a religious leader by his congregation. The court observed that the cantor satisfied all three types of religious services described in the regulations (ministration of sacerdotal functions, conduct of religious worship, and the control, conduct, and maintenance of a religious organization), and accordingly he had to be regarded as a minister. The court reasoned that neither the Code nor the regulations "attempt to say what a minister is, but only what a minister does." The court left unclear the question of whether a minister must satisfy all three kinds of religious activities mentioned in the regulations to qualify as a minister for tax purposes. A

similar result was reached by the court a few years later in the case of *Silverman v. Commissioner*, 57 T.C. 727 (1972).

Lawrence v. Commissioner, 50 T.C. 494 (1968)

The Tax Court ruled that a nonordained but commissioned minister of education in a Southern Baptist church was not eligible for a housing allowance, since he was not a "minister of the gospel." The court emphasized that the minutes of the meeting at which the minister had been commissioned indicated that he had been commissioned a "minister of the gospel in religious education so that he may receive benefits of laws relative to the Social Security Act and Internal Revenue Service."

The court called such a commissioning "nothing more than a paperwork procedure designed to help him get a tax benefit . . . without giving him any new status." It noted that his duties were in no way changed by the commissioning. Such evidence convinced the court that the individual was not "recognized by his church as a minister of the gospel" and therefore could not be considered a minister for tax purposes.

The court rejected the individual's argument that he qualified as a minister because he "performed the duties of a minister of the gospel." The court observed that "even if it be thought that the status of a minister of the gospel in the Baptist religion could be established by proof of services performed, the evidence falls far short of showing the prescribed duties of a minister of education are equivalent to the services performed by a Baptist minister."

In particular, the court noted that "it is more important to note the religious rites and ceremonies which [the taxpayer] did not perform," including the only two ordinances of the Baptist faith— baptism and the Lord's Supper. The taxpayer admitted that he never administered either ordinance or assisted the regular pastor in their administration.

This decision seemed to require that a minister perform all three kinds of religious services described in the regulations, despite the fact that the regulations state that "if a minister is performing service in the conduct of religious worship *or* the ministration of sacerdotal functions, such service is in the exercise of his ministry whether or not it is performed for a religious organization" (emphasis added).

Kirk v. Commissioner, 51 T.C. 66 (1968)

A denomination maintained an office of Social Concerns that had 11 professional employees, 9 of whom were ordained ministers. The remaining 2 employees were not ordained, commissioned, or licensed ministers. All 11 employees performed essentially the same duties, which included the administration of programs with respect to a broad range of social issues and problems, including race relations, civil liberties, church and state relations, foreign policy, disarmament and nuclear weapons control, mental health, and problems associated with aging and overpopulation. All 11 employees were paid a housing allowance. One of the two nonminister employees was audited by the IRS, and his housing allowance exclusion was disallowed on the ground that he was not a minister. On appeal, the Tax Court agreed. It conceded that the employee performed the duties of a minister but concluded that he was not entitled to a housing allowance because he was not a minister. It observed:

> *Granting that petitioner performed services that are ordinarily the duties of a minister of the gospel, another requirement of the regulations is that petitioner be a minister of the gospel. Specifically the regulations require him to be "a duly ordained, commissioned, or licensed minister of a church or a member of a religious order." We have recognized that the purpose of this reference in the regulations is to exclude self-appointed ministers. . . . The regulation does not say only "ordained." It also says "commissioned or licensed." Commission means the act of committing to the charge of another or an entrusting; and license means an official document giving permission to engage in a specified activity. Petitioner is a member of a church which provides for the ordination of ministers. He does not claim to be ordained. Nor is he "licensed" in the sense that he has any official document or other indicia of permission, formally conferred upon him, to perform sacerdotal functions. We do not think he is "commissioned." No congregation or other body of believers was committed to his charge. The duty of spreading of the gospel, either by sermon or teaching, was not formally entrusted to his care. Petitioner here is merely a non-ordained church employee.*

Wingo v. Commissioner, 89 T.C. 922 (1987)

The Tax Court defined the term "minister" as follows: "In determining whether [one] is a minister, we must look at whether he performed the duties and functions of a minister within the three types of services set out in the regulations. In making that determination, we will also consider the additional factors as to whether he was ordained, or commissioned, or licensed, and whether [his church] considered him to be a religious leader." This language, along with other statements in the court's opinion, clearly indicates that to be a minister for tax purposes, one must satisfy all three types of religious services mentioned in the regulations. To illustrate, the court noted that "the regulations . . . describe *three types of services that a minister in the exercise of his ministry performs*," and that "*when a person performs all three types of services set forth in the regulations*, and is recognized as a minister or religious leader by his denomination, that person is a minister" (emphasis added).

The *Wingo* case was disturbing for two reasons. First, it was contrary to the specific wording of the regulations, which provide that "if a minister is performing service in the conduct of religious worship *or* the ministration of sacerdotal functions, such service is in the exercise of his ministry whether or not it is performed for a religious organization" (emphasis added). This language certainly recognizes that not all three types of services are essential. The IRS itself recognized this in a 1978 ruling in which it stated that licensed or commissioned clergy need not perform all the religious functions of ordained clergy in order to qualify for a housing allowance (or any of the other special tax provisions) but rather need only perform "substantially all" of such functions. The IRS also recognized that "when the individual's regular, full-time duties to the congregation are spiritual or religious in nature, such as leading the worship service, those duties are in the exercise of ministry." *Revenue Ruling 78-301.*

The *Wingo* case was also disturbing because it implied that only those clergy who work for churches or church-controlled organizations were eligible for the housing allowance and other special tax provisions, since only such clergy satisfied the third type of service mentioned in the regulations (the control, conduct, and maintenance of a religious organization "under the authority of a religious body constituting a church or church denomination"). This was clearly contrary to the regulations quoted above, which specifically recognize that "if a minister is performing service in the conduct of religious worship or the ministration of sacerdotal functions, *such service is in the exercise of his ministry whether or not it is performed for a religious organization*" (emphasis added).

Knight v. Commissioner, 92 T.C. 199 (1989)

The Tax Court's decisions, and in particular its 1987 decision in the *Wingo* case, demanded correction and clarification. The needed response occurred a few years later in the *Knight* decision. The *Knight* case presented the question of whether a "licentiate" minister in the Cumberland Presbyterian Church (CPC) was a minister for tax purposes.

Here are the facts: The taxpayer was presented as a candidate for ministry in the CPC in 1980 and became a licentiate in 1981. Becoming a licentiate in the CPC is a solemn occasion and a necessary step toward ordination. A licentiate (or licensed minister) is authorized to preach and perform certain other functions of the ministry. In 1984 the taxpayer was called by a local CPC church to serve as its minister, and he remained at the church during 1984 and 1985, during which time he preached, conducted worship services, visited the sick, performed funerals, and ministered to the needy. Because he was not ordained, he was not able to vote in the "session" (the local church's governing body), administer the sacraments (the Lord's Supper and baptism), or solemnize marriages. The taxpayer reported his income as a self-employed minister in 1984 and 1985 (using Schedule C) and never filed an application for exemption from Social Security taxes (Form 4361). The local church issued the taxpayer a Form 1099-MISC (rather than a W-2) and did not withhold taxes from his wages. The taxpayer was audited, and the IRS asserted that he owed self-employment taxes (i.e., Social Security taxes for self-employed persons) for 1984 and 1985. The taxpayer argued, somewhat inconsistently, that while he reported his income taxes as a self-employed person, he was an employee for Social Security and accordingly was not subject to the self-employment tax for 1984 or 1985.

WHO IS A MINISTER FOR FEDERAL TAX PURPOSES
The Tax Court's 5-Factor Test

Who is a minister for federal tax purposes? The Tax Court ruled in 1987 that a minister is one who

(1) administers sacraments;
(2) conducts religious worship;
(3) has management responsibility in a local church or religious denomination (control, conduct, or maintenance of a religious organization);
(4) is ordained, commissioned, or licensed; and
(5) is considered to be a religious leader by his or her church or denomination.

In 1989 the Tax Court ruled that only the fourth factor is required (ordained, commissioned, or licensed) and that a balancing test should be applied with respect to the remaining four factors. This more flexible test was adopted by the IRS in its audit guidelines for ministers.

The Tax Court noted that section 1402 of the tax code specifies that a "duly ordained, commissioned, or licensed minister of a church in the exercise of his ministry" is always self-employed for Social Security (unless a timely exemption application is filed that is subsequently approved by the IRS) and accordingly is subject to the self-employment tax. The question in this, therefore, was whether the taxpayer was a "duly ordained, commissioned, or licensed minister of a church in the exercise of his ministry."

The taxpayer, relying on the *Lawrence* case (discussed above), argued that he was not a minister for tax purposes, since he had not been formally ordained by the CPC, and could not participate in church government or administer the sacraments. The IRS maintained that he was a minister for tax purposes and that he should have paid self-employment taxes for 1984 and 1985.

The court reviewed its earlier decisions and interpreted them to mean that "the phrase 'ordained, commissioned, or licensed' is applicable to various classes of ministry within a particular religious body." The court acknowledged that the taxpayer could not administer the sacraments and that this same fact had led it to conclude in the *Lawrence* case that the taxpayer was *not* a minister for tax purposes. The court repudiated *Lawrence* to the extent that it precludes ministerial status to those clergy who are not authorized to administer sacraments. The court announced a new test for determining whether an individual is a minister: "Five factors [must

be] analyzed. Those factors are whether the individual (1) administers sacraments, (2) conducts worship services, (3) performs services in the 'control, conduct, or maintenance of a religious organization,' (4) is 'ordained, commissioned, or licensed,' and (5) is considered to be a spiritual leader by his religious body."

The Tax Court claimed to base its new test on the *Wingo* case as well as on the regulations quoted above. Surprisingly, the court claimed that the *Wingo* case never implied that "all of the ecclesiastical functions mentioned [in the regulations] must be performed" in order for one to be a minister for tax purposes. Such a statement is not supported by a careful reading of *Wingo* (as noted above).

The court concluded that the taxpayer (1) did not administer the CPC sacraments, (2) did conduct religious worship, (3) did not participate in the conduct, control, or maintenance of his church or denomination, (4) was duly licensed (though not ordained), and (5) was considered to be a religious leader by the CPC. Thus, three of the five factors were present, and accordingly the taxpayer satisfied the definition of a minister for tax purposes and was subject to the self-employment tax.

The court emphasized that its new test for ministerial status "is not an arithmetical test but a balancing test. Failure to meet one or more of these factors must be weighed by the court in each case." It did acknowledge that one of the five factors must be present in every case—the requirement that the individual be an ordained, commissioned, or licensed minister.

The court further observed that in weighing the significance of the limitations upon the taxpayer's ministry, "it appears that [his] incapacity to perform the Lord's Supper, baptism, marriage or to moderate the church session or otherwise participate in church government did not diminish the ministry that [the taxpayer] did perform. [He] preached, conducted worship, visited the sick, performed funerals, and ministered to the needy in the exercise of his ministry. [He] did perform one of the three significant ecclesiastical functions described [in the regulations]—the conduct of religious worship." Therefore, the taxpayer satisfied the definition of the term "minister," "notwithstanding that the CPC constitution provides for the ordination of a minister with higher authority and greater ministry."

Reeder v. Commissioner, T.C. Memo. 1993-287

A minister became a licensed Assemblies of God minister in 1971. During 1973 and 1974 he served as senior pastor of a local church. He left the church to pursue further seminary training, and he was ordained in 1980. On December 23, 1980, the minister filed an application for exemption from self-employment taxes (IRS Form 4361). The minister represented on the application for exemption that he was licensed in 1971 and ordained in 1980 and that 1973 and 1974 were the first years he had received ministerial earnings subject to Social Security tax. The minister's application for exemption was denied in 1981. The IRS noted that under federal law, an application for exemption must be filed no later than the due date of the federal tax return (Form 1040) for the second year in which a minister earns $400 or more in self-employment earnings, any portion of which comes from ministerial services. The IRS reasoned that the taxpayer became a minister when he was licensed in 1971, and accordingly the exemption application was due no later than April 15, 1973.

In 1983 the minister submitted a second Form 4361, but this time he stated that he was ordained in 1980 and did not refer to the date he was licensed. This second application was also denied. The IRS again reasoned that the taxpayer became a minister in 1971 when he was licensed and that the exemption application accordingly was due no later than April 15, 1973. The minister appealed this denial to the Tax Court. He argued that he was not an official minister until he was ordained in 1980, and therefore his application was filed on time. He acknowledged that he had been licensed in 1971 and had served as a pastor of a local church in 1973 and 1974. However, he insisted that his church was a dependent assembly under the direct supervision of his district and that only upon ordination was he able to participate in the governance of his church organization at a higher level than the local church.

The Tax Court agreed with the IRS that the taxpayer had become a minister for federal tax purposes when he was licensed in 1971, and accordingly both of his applications for exemption were filed too late. It noted that one of the requirements for exemption from self-employment taxes is that the applicant must be an "ordained, commissioned, or licensed minister." While this term is not defined in the tax code or regulations, the court did note that it had ruled in a previous case that whether an individual is an "ordained, commissioned, or licensed minister" depends on whether he or she performs the duties and functions of a minister.

The court referred to its previous 1987 ruling in *Wingo v. Commissioner*, 89 T.C. 922, 930 (1987), in which it addressed the question of whether a licensed local pastor of a church was a minister for federal tax purposes. In the *Wingo* case, the court pointed out that the income tax regulations describe three types of services a minister in the exercise of his ministry performs: "(1) the ministration of sacerdotal functions; (2) the conduct of religious worship; and (3) service in the control, conduct, and maintenance of religious organizations (including the religious boards, societies, and other integral agencies of such organizations), under the authority of a religious body constituting a church or church denomination." The court concluded in this case that the Assemblies of God minister became an "ordained, commissioned, or licensed minister" when he was licensed in 1971, since he satisfied all three of these conditions.

First, with respect to the ministration of sacerdotal functions, the court observed:

> As to the sacerdotal functions, [the minister's] own testimony is that while he was the pastor of the [local church] during 1973 and

1974, he could have performed a marriage or performed funeral services with permission or performed services with respect to the dedication of infants, and he did in fact perform the ministry functions of preaching and teaching, baptism, and communion. There is no requirement that to qualify as a "duly ordained, commissioned, or licensed minister" . . . an individual must be qualified to perform and actually perform every sacrament or rite of the religion.

Second, as to the conduct of religious worship, the court noted that "there is no dispute here that [the taxpayer] conducted the religious services of the church . . . during 1973 and 1974."

Third, as to the question of service in the control, conduct, and maintenance of the religious organization, the court observed:

> [The taxpayer] points out that during 1973 and 1974 he was the pastor of a local church which was a dependent church and subject to supervision under the constitution and bylaws of the [District]. [The taxpayer] argues that only upon ordination was he able to participate in the governance of his church organization at a higher level than the local church. In response to a similar argument, in Wingo v. Commissioner, we stated: "To perform services in the control, conduct, and maintenance of the church or organizations within the church, the minister need only have some participation in the conduct, control, and maintenance of the local church or the denomination."

The *Reeder* case is unfortunate, since the Tax Court applied the rigid *Wingo* case it repudiated in the *Knight* ruling. A few aspects of this decision are positive: First, the court clarified that "there is no requirement that to qualify as 'a duly ordained, commissioned, or licensed minister' . . . an individual must be qualified to perform and actually perform every sacrament or rite of the religion." Second, the court clarified that "[t]o perform services in the control, conduct, and maintenance of the church or organizations within the church, the minister need only have some participation in the conduct, control, and maintenance of the local church or the denomination." And finally, the court did not reverse or overrule the *Knight* decision. On the contrary, it did not even mention it. As a result, the *Knight* case can still be relied upon as a precedent.

Other legal precedents

Following are some additional legal precedents regarding qualification as a minister for tax purposes.

IRS Technical Advice Memorandum 8915001

In a 1989 Technical Advice Memorandum (released prior to the *Knight* decision), the IRS national office addressed the question of who is a minister for tax purposes. Specifically, the IRS was addressing the question of whether a minister had filed a timely application for exemption from Social Security taxes (Form 4361). The individual had been licensed in 1971 and ordained in 1980 and had submitted an application for exemption from Social Security taxes (Form 4361) in 1980. The parties conceded that if the individual became a minister for tax purposes at the time he was licensed, the exemption application was properly rejected, since it was too late; but if he became a minister for tax purposes upon his ordination in 1980, then the application was timely.

The IRS, applying the *Wingo* test, concluded that the individual became a minister for tax purposes in 1971 (when he was licensed), since at that time he performed all three kinds of ministerial services described in the regulations and mandated by the *Wingo* decision. The IRS observed that in determining whether an individual is a minister for tax purposes, "the courts have consistently examined *whether the individual has performed the three types of ministerial services set forth in . . . the regulations*" (emphasis added). In summary, the IRS reached the right result for the wrong reasons. There is no doubt that the individual satisfied the five-part test of ministerial status announced a few weeks later in the *Knight* decision. It is unfortunate that the IRS reached its conclusion by relying on the more restrictive test announced in the *Wingo* decision—a test repudiated in the *Knight* decision. The reliance by the IRS on the *Wingo* case in this ruling can be explained by the fact that it was released prior to the Tax Court's decision in the *Knight* case.

IRS Letter Ruling 9221025

The IRS addressed the question of whether commissioned ministers in a denomination that both commissions and ordains ministers are eligible for a housing allowance. A Protestant denomination (the "Church") with more than 5,900 congregations located throughout the United States recognizes two levels of ministry—commissioned and ordained. Generally, a candidate for commissioned minister completes four years of study at a college, operated by the Church, where the curriculum centers around courses in religion. Upon completion of the required education, the college faculty, on behalf of the Church, certifies that the candidate is fit for the position of commissioned minister. The certificate of fitness assures that the candidate is academically, theologically, and morally fit to have the status and authority of a commissioned minister. The certified candidate is then "called" by a congregation, and after accepting the call, the candidate is installed as a commissioned minister in a formal ceremony. Occasionally an individual may become a commissioned minister through a "colloquy," which requires the candidate to have achieved equivalent academic, religious, educational, and personal life qualifications. In addition, a colloquy candidate must pass oral and written examinations.

Commissioned ministers serve God and the Church by performing full-time public ministry functions, including: classroom teaching; evangelism; counseling individuals; leading Bible study groups; leading devotions; conducting worship services for youth; music ministry; giving the children's sermon at the regular Sunday worship service; addressing the congregation in a worship service on a subject in which the commissioned minister has expertise; coordinating lay church workers; administering or guiding a congregation's youth ministry; coordinating family ministry events; participating in ministries to those with special needs; and caring spiritually for the sick and imprisoned and their families. The Church regards teaching of the faith to the children and youth of the flock as a major duty of the pastoral office. Upon acceptance of a call and installation into a ministry position, a commissioned minister becomes a "member" of the Church.

The majority of commissioned ministers are called directly by local churches to serve in church-controlled parochial schools. The schools, for the most part, are not separate organizations from the churches. However, some of the schools are incorporated separately from a member congregation; but each such school is an integral agency of a member congregation. A commissioned minister also may be called by a congregation to be a deaconess or director of Christian education. In contrast, *ordained ministers* of the Church officiate in the public administration of the sacraments and lead in public worship. In certain situations a commissioned minister may lead in prayer, read the Scriptures in a church service, or perform a baptism. Under the doctrine of the Church, baptism is a sacrament.

The IRS national office concluded that commissioned ministers are eligible for a housing allowance. The IRS based its decision on a 1978 revenue ruling in which it stated that "if a church or denomination ordains some ministers of the gospel and licenses or commissions other ministers, the licensed or commissioned minister must perform substantially all the religious functions within the scope of the tenets and practices of his religious denomination to be treated as a minister of the gospel." *Revenue Ruling 78-301*. However, the IRS also relied squarely on the *Wingo* case. The IRS, applying the *Wingo* five-part test, concluded that the commissioned ministers were ministers for federal tax purposes, since they satisfied all five of the conditions set forth in that decision.

IRS Letter Ruling 199910055

The IRS ruled that three ordained deacons in a Methodist church who served as the ministers of education, music, and stewardship were ministers for federal tax purposes. After 20 years of study, the Methodist Church (the "Church") voted to establish the status of ordained deacon. Prior to this decision, elders were the only ordained members of the clergy. To qualify for ordination as either a deacon or an elder, an individual must meet the requirements set by the Church that are specified in its governing document. In addition, to be ordained, the individual must be recommended by the regional Conference and receive the affirmative vote of the ministerial members of the Conference. Through ordination the ordained individual is given the approval of the Church to serve as an ordained minister and the authority to carry out those acts reserved to members of the clergy. As a result, following ordination, an ordained elder or deacon has the authority to exercise the responsibilities and duties of an ordained minister.

According to the Church's governing document, an ordained deacon is permitted to give leadership in teaching and proclaiming the gospel, forming and nurturing disciples, performing marriages and funerals, and assisting the ordained elder in administering the sacraments. An ordained deacon has full right of voice and vote in the regional Conference where membership is held; may serve or hold office as a member of the clergy on the boards, commissions, or committees of the Conference; may be elected as a clergy delegate to the national Conference; must attend all sessions of the regional Conference; and, with the elder, is responsible for all matters of ordination, character, and Conference relations with members of the clergy. An ordained deacon is accountable to his or her regional Conference and bishop for the fulfillment of his or her call. An ordained elder is appointed to a position by a bishop. However, unlike an elder, an ordained deacon does not itinerate; nor does the Church guarantee an ordained deacon a position, salary, or place of employment. Ordained deacons are permitted to participate in the Church retirement plan for members of the clergy.

A Methodist church employed more than 50 persons, including three ordained deacons. The church asked the IRS whether these ordained deacons were ministers of the gospel performing services in the exercise of their ministry for purposes of eligibility for a housing allowance, self-employed status for Social Security, and exemption from income tax withholding. The ordained deacons served as a minister of education, a minister of music, and a minister of stewardship. As integral members of the church's pastoral team, the ordained deacons met with the church's elder to plan the worship services, assisted with the sacraments, and officiated at weddings and funerals. Each was required to preach at Sunday worship service. They participated with the elder in the weekly worship service. They also performed various other duties at the church, including confirmation preparation and membership reception.

The IRS ruled that the three ordained deacons were ministers of the gospel performing services in the exercise of their ministries. It observed:

> As ordained members of the clergy in the Church [they] conduct worship and assist with the sacraments. In addition, as ordained members of the clergy in full connection they perform services in the control, conduct and maintenance of the Church. Further, [the local church and national church] consider [them] to be religious leaders who can perform substantially all of the religious functions within the scope of the Church's tenets and practices. . . . Accordingly [they] are performing services as "ministers of the gospel." . . . Thus, [they] are eligible to have a portion of their salary designated as a parsonage allowance. Any parsonage allowance will be excluded from gross income, provided the allowance is designated and paid in accordance with [the tax code]. We further conclude that the services [they] perform are in the exercise of their ministry within the meaning of section 3121(b)(8) of the Code [which treats ministers as self-employed for Social Security].

The IRS cautioned that "nor does this ruling suggest that the Service has departed from its position in Revenue Ruling 59-270." In Revenue Ruling 59-270 (1959), the IRS ruled that a church's minister of music and minister of education, who performed some of the duties of a minister of the gospel, could not be treated as ministers for federal tax purposes, since neither was ordained, commissioned, or licensed as a minister of the gospel. In other words, ministers of music and education who hold no ministerial credentials should not assume, based on the IRS ruling, that they now qualify for a housing allowance.

Eade v. United States, (unpublished opinion, W.D. Va. 1991)

A federal court in Virginia ignored the *Knight* test and applied the *Wingo* ruling. The court ruled that a minister was entitled to exemption from self-employment taxes. In reaching its decision, the court concluded that the individual satisfied the definition of "minister," since he met all five of the factors required by the *Wingo* decision. It observed:

> The minister testified that he performed ministerial functions or the [church] beginning in March of 1985, that he conducted religious worship, and that the church was an independent Baptist church under the authority of a religious body comprised of deacons drawn from members of the church congregation. As to his qualifications for the ministry, the minister testified, without contradiction, that he received a B.A. in Bible Studies from a Tennessee Bible college, an M.A. in sacred literature from Liberty Baptist University, had earned credits toward a Ph.D. in church administration, and had been ordained a minister in the Baptist faith on January 26, 1985 after nomination by the ordination committee of the [church]. At that time the minister received a certificate of ordination. Thereafter, [the church], comprised of some 300–350 active members, issued a call for him to become their pastor, which call he accepted, assuming his pastoral duties in April of 1985. Applying the Wingo factors and the income tax regulations criteria, I find that the minister meets [all five requirements]. I find that he performs in accordance with his denomination's requirements for sacerdotal function, that he conducts religious worship and provides service that is under the control, conduct and maintenance of an organized and recognized religious body constituting an independent church belonging to that denomination widely known as Baptist. Further, I find that he is an ordained minister and that Colonial Baptist Church recognizes him as its religious leader by paying him a salary to minister to the needs of its congregants.

Ballinger v. Commissioner, 728 F.2d 1287 (10th Cir. 1984)

A federal appeals court ruled that a person who functioned as a minister could file an application for exemption from self-employment taxes despite the fact that he had not been ordained. The court observed:

> Not all churches or religions have a formally ordained ministry, whether because of the nature of their beliefs, the lack of a

denominational structure or a variety of other reasons. Courts are not in a position to determine the merits of various churches nor an individual's conversion from one church to another. Thus, we cannot hold that an individual who functions as a minister in a church which does not ordain, license or commission that individual in a traditional or legally formal manner is not entitled to the exemption. Nor can we hold that an individual who has a change of belief accompanied by a change to another faith is not entitled to the exemption. We interpret Congress' language providing an exemption for any individual who is "a duly ordained, commissioner or licensed minister of a church" to mean that the triggering event is the assumption of the duties and functions of a minister.

This language suggests that the court was limiting its conclusion to churches that do not formally ordain, commission, or license clergy. However, the case before the court involved a church that eventually did ordain the minister. As a result, this case would support the treatment of a person as a minister for federal tax purposes who performs the functions of a minister even though the person has not been formally ordained, commissioned, or licensed—whether or not he or she is associated with a church that credentials ministers. No other court has reached this rather questionable conclusion, so it should not be relied upon without the advice of a tax attorney or CPA.

Haimowitz v. Commissioner, T.C. Memo. 1997-40 (1997)

The Tax Court ruled that an administrator of a Jewish synagogue was not eligible for a housing allowance, since he was not ordained, commissioned, or licensed, and there was no evidence that a housing allowance had been properly designated for him. In ruling that the administrator was not a minister and therefore was not eligible for a housing allowance, the court made a number of important observations:

- While the tax code limits housing allowances to ministers of the gospel, neither the code nor the income tax regulations define this term.
- The income tax regulations do define "what a minister does." They list the following functions: the performance of sacerdotal functions; the conduct of religious worship; and the performance of services in control, conduct, and maintenance of religious organizations.
- In deciding whether an individual performs the functions of a minister, consideration must be given not only to the religious duties the individual performs but also to the religious duties that are not performed.
- The performance of some religious functions is not enough to make one a minister for federal tax purposes. The administrator in this case performed a number of religious functions, but these were largely administrative in nature. More importantly, he performed few of the duties of an ordained, commissioned, or licensed minister.

- The court stressed that no one can be a minister for federal tax purposes who is not, at a minimum, "ordained, commissioned, or licensed."
- The court referred to the fact that the administrator had no seminary training.

The court concluded that even if the administrator were a minister for federal tax purposes, he would still be ineligible for a housing allowance, since no evidence existed that a housing allowance had ever been properly designated for him.

IRS Tax Guide for Churches

The IRS issued a revised *Tax Guide for Churches and Religious Organizations* in 2008. This publication does not attempt to define the term "minister" for federal tax purposes. It simply states that "as used in this booklet, the term minister denotes members of clergy of all religions and denominations and includes priests, rabbis, imams, and similar members of the clergy." It is unfortunate that the IRS chose not to provide any assistance in defining this critical term in a book that is designed to help churches "voluntarily comply with tax rules." This is a major flaw in the IRS publication.

⚘ **KEY POINT.** Much of the confusion regarding the definition of the term "minister" could be eliminated by the following two recommendations: (1) Define the term "minister" to include anyone who satisfies two requirements: (a) the individual is ordained, commissioned, or licensed by a bona fide religious organization exempt from tax under section 501(c)(3) of the tax code—or the functional equivalent of an ordained, commissioned, or licensed minister in a non-Christian faith; and (b) the individual, by virtue of his or her status as an ordained, commissioned, or licensed minister, has the authority (whether exercised or not) to function as a minister in his or her religious community, including the authority to conduct worship, administer sacraments, or perform sacerdotal functions (preaching, teaching, marriages, funerals, counseling, baptisms, and communion). (2) Retain the present definition of the term "services performed in the exercise of ministry" as reflected in the income tax regulations, but acknowledge that a minister need not perform all of the functions of a pastoral minister in order to satisfy this definition.

⚘ **KEY POINT.** The definition of "minister" contained in a number of IRS and Tax Court rulings assumes that a minister is engaged in pastoral ministry. This is an unreasonably narrow definition, for it fails to recognize that many bona fide ministers are not engaged in pastoral ministry—they are employed by denominational agencies, seminaries and other religious schools, parachurch ministries, or as support staff in local congregations.

IRS audit guidelines for ministers

In 1995 the IRS released its first audit guidelines for ministers pursuant to its Market Segment Specialization Program (MSSP). The guidelines were intended to promote a higher degree of competence among agents who audit ministers. In 2009 the IRS released a newly revised version of the guidelines (the Minister Audit Technique Guide). The guidelines instruct IRS agents in the examination of ministers' tax returns.

The guidelines provide IRS agents with clarification on the meaning of the term "minister":

- The income tax regulations require that an individual be a "duly ordained, commissioned, or licensed minister of a church."
- The Tax Court, in *Salkov v. Commissioner*, 46 T.C. 190 (1966), ruled that the phrase "duly ordained, commissioned, or licensed minister of a church" must be interpreted "disjunctively." By this it meant that a person qualifies as a minister for tax purposes if he or she falls within any of these three categories. Ordained status, therefore, is not required.
- The guidelines add that "[t]he duties performed by the individual are also important to the initial determination whether he or she is a duly ordained, commissioned, or licensed minister. Because religious disciplines vary in their formal procedures for these designations, whether an individual is duly ordained, commissioned, or licensed depends on these facts and circumstances."

Legal rulings

The guidelines refer to the following legal rulings:

1. *Salkov v. Commissioner* (discussed above) and *Silverman v. Commissioner*, 57 T.C. 727 (1972). The guidelines note that the Tax Court, in holding that a cantor of the Jewish faith was a duly ordained, commissioned, or licensed minister, looked to "the systematic manner the cantor was called to his ministry and the ecclesiastical functions he carried out in concluding that he was a minister."

2. Revenue Ruling 78-301 (discussed above). The IRS followed the Tax Court decisions in *Salkov* and *Silverman* and held that a Jewish cantor who is not ordained but has a bona fide commission and is employed by a congregation on a full-time basis to perform substantially all the religious worship, sacerdotal, training, and educational functions of the Jewish denomination's religious tenets and practices is a minister of the gospel for federal tax purposes. The audit guidelines state that this ruling "revoked and modified prior revenue rulings to the extent that they required that an individual must be invested with the status and authority of an ordained minister fully qualified to exercise all of the ecclesiastical duties of a church denomination to be considered ministers."

3. *Knight v. Commissioner*, 92 T.C. 199 (1989) (discussed above). The guidelines, in commenting on the *Knight* case, note:

The Tax Court considered whether a licentiate of the Cumberland Presbyterian Church (a status that was less than

full ordination), who had not filed a timely exemption from self-employment tax, was a duly ordained, commissioned, or licensed minister in the exercise of required duties who was thus liable for self-employment tax. The petitioner argued that he was not formally ordained as a minister and could not administer church sacraments or participate in church government. Thus, he could not be a minister subject to IRC §1402(c). The court rejected this view, and looked at all the facts. In concluding that he was a licensed minister, it cited the facts that he was licensed by the church, he conducted worship services, and he was considered by the church to be a spiritual leader. The court also noted the petitioner preached, performed funerals, visited the sick, and ministered to the needy within the context of his duties for the church.

◑ **OBSERVATION.** The guidelines' reference to the *Knight* case is significant. The *Knight* case contains perhaps the best analysis of the terms "minister" and "exercise of ministry." The court applied a "balancing test," noting that a minister need not actually perform every category of ministerial service described in the income tax regulations. In prior rulings the IRS omitted any reference to this important decision. The guidelines take a different view. IRS agents will now consider this ruling. As a result, more bona fide ministers will, in fact, be considered ministers for tax purposes. This is an important clarification and one of the most important aspects of the guidelines.

4. *Lawrence v. Commissioner*, 50 T.C. 494 (1968) (discussed above). The guidelines, in commenting on the *Lawrence* case, note the Tax Court found that

a "minister of education" in a Baptist church was not a "duly ordained, commissioned, or licensed" minister for purposes of IRC §107. The petitioner held a Master's Degree in Religious Education from a Baptist Theological Seminary, but was not ordained. Although his church "commissioned" him after he assumed the position, the court interpreted the commissioning to be for tax purposes, as it did not result in any change in duties. Most significant, however, was the court's analysis of petitioner's duties or rather, the duties he did not perform. He did not officiate at Baptisms or the Lord's Supper, two Ordinances that closely resembled sacraments, nor did he preside over or preach at worship services. The court concluded that the evidence did not establish that the prescribed duties of a minister of education were equivalent to the duties of a Baptist minister.

◑ **OBSERVATION.** Unfortunately, the guidelines do not adequately distinguish between the terms "minister" and "service performed in the exercise of ministry." The failure to distinguish between these key terms has produced much confusion, and the guidelines provide little assistance. This will mean that agents auditing ministers' tax returns will continue to experience confusion. The guidelines' disregard of the *Wingo* case will help.

Conclusions

What conclusions can be drawn from these rulings? Consider the following:

1. The Tax Court has provided two definitions of the term "minister."

(a) The Knight *case (1989).* The definition announced by the Tax Court in the *Knight* case is now the preferred definition since it has been endorsed by the IRS in its audit guidelines for ministers. It is likely that this is the only test IRS agents will apply when auditing persons who claim to be ministers.

Under this test the following five factors must be considered in deciding whether a person is a minister for federal tax reporting: (1) Does the individual administer the "sacraments"? (2) Does the individual conduct worship services? (3) Does the individual perform services in the "control, conduct, or maintenance of a religious organization" under the authority of a church or religious denomination? (4) Is the individual "ordained, commissioned, or licensed"? (5) Is the individual considered to be a spiritual leader by his or her religious body? Only the fourth factor is required in all cases (the individual must be ordained, commissioned, or licensed). The remaining four factors need not all be present for a person to be considered a minister for tax reporting.

The Tax Court in the *Knight* case did not say how many of the remaining four factors must be met. It merely observed that "failure to meet one or more of these factors must be weighed . . . in each case." The court concluded that the taxpayer in question was a minister despite the fact that he only satisfied three of the five factors.

One may reasonably assume, however, that persons who claim to be ministers solely on the basis of the final three factors mentioned in the *Knight* case will not be deemed ministers by the IRS or the courts unless they can demonstrate that they are entitled to ministerial status on the basis of other considerations. After all, if a church is willing to ordain its bookkeeper and secretary, these persons could argue that they satisfy the final three factors in the *Knight* case (management responsibilities, ordination, and a "religious leader"). No doubt, the IRS and the courts will not accept such a conclusion. Considerations that suggest ministerial status, even if the first two *Knight* factors are not satisfied, would include (1) ordination to pastoral ministry and actual pastoral experience, and (2) formal theological training.

(b) The Wingo *case (1987).* The more restrictive definition announced by the Tax Court in the *Wingo* case has been applied by the IRS in two rulings and by two federal courts in addition to two Tax Court rulings. However, all of these rulings occurred prior to the issuance of the original IRS audit guidelines for ministers in 1995. The audit guidelines not only fail to mention the *Wingo* definition, but they specifically endorse the *Knight* definition discussed above.

To be a minister under the *Wingo* test, one must satisfy all five of the factors mentioned in the *Knight* decision. The *Wingo* definition is overly restrictive and would result in the denial of ministerial status to many persons who clearly are ministers. Examples include ministers of music, ministers of education, ministers to youths, and other associate ministers who often will not satisfy all five factors announced by the Tax Court in the *Wingo* decision. Even ordained ministers teaching at church-operated seminaries would be adversely affected by a literal application of the *Wingo* decision, to the extent that they do not satisfy all five of the factors for ministerial status.

✿ **KEY POINT.** The IRS does not mention the *Wingo* case in its audit guidelines for ministers, so it is unlikely the *Wingo* case will be applied by IRS agents when auditing ministers' tax returns. This indicates a preference by the IRS for the *Knight* definition of "minister."

✿ **KEY POINT.** The *Knight* definition is currently the preferred definition of the term "minister." This conclusion is based on the following two considerations: (1) The IRS audit guidelines for ministers refer to the *Knight* definition but do not even mention the *Wingo* case. (2) The most recent decision by the full Tax Court was the *Knight* case in 1989. While the *Reeder* case (which applied the *Wingo* definition) was decided in 1993, it was a Tax Court memorandum decision, meaning it was a ruling by only one of the court's many judges and has minimal precedential value. The IRS often ignores Tax Court memorandum decisions. By comparison, the *Knight* case was a decision by the full Tax Court and has a much greater precedential value.

✿ **KEY POINT.** The IRS has adopted the analysis in this chapter. In a 2003 ruling it observed: "A balancing test of factors is used to determine whether a person is considered a minister of the gospel. Under [the *Knight* and *Wingo* cases] there are five factors that collectively determine whether a person qualifies as a minister of the gospel. A minister of the gospel must do a majority of the following: administer sacerdotal functions; conduct worship services; perform services in the control, conduct and maintenance of a religious organization; be considered a spiritual leader by his or her religious body; and be ordained, licensed or commissioned. Under section 1402(c)(4) of the Code, at a minimum, the person is required to be duly ordained, licensed or commissioned." *IRS Letter Ruling 200318002.*

The following examples illustrate the application of these two definitions.

EXAMPLE. Pastor J is an ordained minister who serves as a minister of education at his church. He does not preach or conduct worship services, and he never administers the sacraments. He does have management responsibility in his local church and at regional and national meetings of his denomination. His duties include overseeing the educational program of his church, occasional counseling, and hospital visitation. Under the *Wingo* test, Pastor J would not be a minister for federal tax reporting, since he does not meet all five factors. Specifically, he does not conduct religious worship or administer sacerdotal functions. Under the IRS tax guide test, it is possible that Pastor J would be a minister for federal tax reporting so long as he has the ecclesiastical authority to conduct worship, administer sacraments, and perform sacerdotal functions—even though he does not perform any of these tasks. Under the IRS audit guidelines for ministers, it is likely that Pastor J would be a minister for federal tax reporting so long as he is a minister under the *Knight* definition. Under the Tax Court's decision in the *Knight* case, it is probable that Pastor J would be a minister for federal tax reporting. Pastor J must now decide whether to follow the *Knight* decision or the *Wingo* test. For the reasons stated above, the *Knight* definition of the term "minister" is now the preferred definition.

EXAMPLE. Pastor B is a minister of music at his church. He is not ordained, commissioned, or licensed. Pastor B is not a minister for federal tax purposes under either the *Wingo* or *Knight* cases, since he is not ordained, commissioned, or licensed.

EXAMPLE. Pastor C is a minister of music at her church. She is licensed, and her duties include leading religious worship and administering all of the music programs and activities of the church. However, Pastor C does not administer sacraments or engage in sacerdotal functions. Pastor C would not be a minister for federal tax purposes under the *Wingo* test, but she may be under the *Knight* test and the IRS audit guidelines. Further, if Pastor C's status as a licensed minister invests her with the ecclesiastical authority to conduct worship, administer sacraments, and perform sacerdotal functions, she may satisfy the IRS tax guide's test even though she does not actually perform some or all of these tasks.

EXAMPLE. Same facts as the previous example, except that Pastor C occasionally assists the senior pastor in administering communion. This limited performance of a sacerdotal function increases the likelihood that Pastor C will be considered a minister for federal tax purposes. The Tax Court noted in the *Reeder* case that "there is no requirement that to qualify as 'a duly ordained, commissioned, or licensed minister' . . . an individual must be qualified to perform and actually perform every sacrament or rite of the religion." However, the performance of only one sacerdotal function on an occasional basis will not necessarily make Pastor C a minister for federal tax purposes and probably would be of limited relevance. On the other hand, the Tax Court ruled in the *Haimowitz* case (discussed above) that the performance of some religious functions of an administrative nature will not make one a minister for tax purposes.

EXAMPLE. Pastor G, an ordained minister with 25 years of pastoral experience, is now employed as a full-time seminary professor. Pastor G does not preach or administer sacraments and accordingly would not be considered a minister under the *Wingo* case. This is an unreasonable result. Such a person clearly is a minister even though not presently serving in a traditional pastoral ministry. It is possible that Pastor G would be a minister under the *Knight* test and the IRS audit guidelines. Further, if Pastor G's status as an ordained minister invests him with the ecclesiastical authority to conduct worship, administer sacraments, and perform sacerdotal functions, he may satisfy the IRS tax guide's test even though he does not actually perform some or all of these tasks.

EXAMPLE. M is a teacher at a private religious school operated by a church. She is not a minister, and accordingly she is not eligible for a housing allowance exclusion. Assume further that M asks the church to commission her in order to render her eligible for a housing allowance. Even if the church complies with such a request, it is doubtful, based on the *Lawrence* decision, that she will become eligible for the housing allowance exclusion. Recall that the Tax Court in the *Lawrence* decision called Pastor Lawrence's commissioning "nothing more than a paperwork procedure designed to help him get a tax benefit . . . without giving him any new status." It emphasized that his duties were in no way changed by the commissioning. Such evidence convinced the court that the individual was not "recognized by his church as a minister of the gospel" and therefore could not be considered a minister for tax purposes. The following factors would further support this conclusion: (1) the local church's charter does not specifically authorize it to commission ministers; (2) the church has never before commissioned a minister; (3) the church is affiliated with a denomination that will not recognize the ministerial status of M.

EXAMPLE. The IRS ruled that full-time male and female teachers employed by parochial schools of a particular church denomination qualified as "duly ordained, commissioned, or licensed ministers of a church" for purposes of federal tax law. The teachers were graduates of a theological college conducted under the auspices of a church denomination for the express purpose of training full-time church workers. Upon graduation teachers are recommended as candidates for the teaching ministry in the congregations of the church and in its parochial schools. Although not ordained as pastors, the male teachers' duties as full-time teachers in the parochial schools include the teaching and preaching of the religious principles of the church to the children and youths of the various congregations and the conducting of the musical portion of their religious services. They also may be called upon to function in the place of a pastor during his absence or together with him as the needs for the ministrations of the pastor increase. The female teachers' duties include all of the above-prescribed functions except that they are never called upon to preach or to take the place of or assist a pastor in the conduct of religious services. Both the male and female teachers are called to their respective offices for life. Teachers may be removed from office only for the same reasons that apply to pastors. Under these facts, the IRS concluded that "the male teachers, although not duly ordained as pastors, are, in performing full-time services for the church by teaching, preaching, and, when needed, acting for or assisting an ordained pastor in the conduct of religious services, 'duly ordained, commissioned, or licensed ministers of a church' for purposes of [federal tax law], and that their services are performed in the exercise of their ministry. . . . The female teachers whose services appear to be restricted to the teaching of the religious principles of the church and to the direction of the musical portion of the church services do not qualify as 'duly ordained, commissioned, or licensed ministers of a church.'" *Revenue Ruling 57-107. See also IRS Letter Ruling 7939023. But compare IRS Letter Ruling 8614010.*

EXAMPLE. The IRS ruled that a "minister of administration" who was licensed by a denomination that also ordained ministers was not a minister for federal tax purposes, since he did not "perform substantially all the religious functions within the scope of the tenets and practices of his religious denomination." The IRS noted that the minister acknowledged that he had never conducted worship services, preached a sermon, conducted a funeral, performed a baptism, or administered communion and had no intention of performing any of these activities. The IRS concluded that because the minister had "not performed substantially all the religious functions within the scope of the tenets and practices of [his] religious denomination," he was not a minister of the gospel for federal tax purposes. *IRS Letter Ruling 8442130.*

✤**KEY POINT.** Any attempt to confer ministerial credentials upon persons solely to qualify them for tax benefits, without changing their duties or responsibilities in any way, probably will not be recognized by the IRS or the courts.

2. Whether persons who are ordained, commissioned, or licensed by their local church will be considered ministers is unclear.

In many religious faiths ministers are ordained, commissioned, or licensed by a local congregation rather than by a denominational agency. However, in some denominations ministers are ordained, commissioned, or licensed by the denomination rather than by local congregations. If a local church in such a denomination ordains, commissions, or licenses a minister, will such an individual be recognized as a minister by the IRS for federal tax purposes? This is an important question that has not been addressed directly by the IRS or the courts. The following factors probably would be considered by the IRS and the courts in making such a decision:

- *Recognition by the denomination.* Does the denomination recognize the ministerial status of ministers who are ordained, commissioned, or licensed by affiliated churches? For example, can such ministers participate in denominational benefit programs that are available to ministers, and can they vote at denominational meetings?

✤**KEY POINT.** Line 6 of the application used by ministers to exempt themselves from self-employment taxes (Form 4361) asks: "If you apply for the exemption as a licensed or commissioned minister, and your denomination also ordains ministers, please indicate how your ecclesiastical powers differ from those of an ordained minister of your denomination. Attach a copy of your denomination's bylaws relating to the powers of ordained, commissioned, or licensed ministers."

- *The church's charter and bylaws.* Does the church's corporate charter or other governing document authorize the church to ordain, commission, or license ministers? If such documents are silent regarding the authority of the local church to confer ministerial credentials, this would tend to support an IRS determination that the church's conferring of ministerial credentials (to quote the *Lawrence* case, discussed above) is "nothing more than a paperwork procedure designed to help [the individual] get a tax benefit . . . without giving him any new status."
- *Church practice.* Does the local church have a history or practice of ordaining, commissioning, or licensing ministers? If not, this would tend to support an IRS determination that the church's conferring of ministerial credentials (to quote the *Lawrence* case, discussed above) is "nothing more than a paperwork procedure designed to help [the individual] get a tax benefit . . . without giving him any new status."
- *Duties.* Have the duties of the minister changed since he or she was ordained, commissioned, or licensed by the church? If not, this would tend to support an IRS determination that the church's conferring of ministerial credentials (to quote the *Lawrence* case, discussed above) is "nothing more than a paperwork procedure designed to help him get a tax benefit . . . without giving him any new status."
- *Theological training.* Did the minister have any formal theological training prior to being ordained, commissioned, or licensed by the church? If not, this would tend to support an IRS determination that the church's conferring of ministerial credentials (to quote the *Lawrence* case, discussed above) is "nothing more than a paperwork procedure designed to help him get a tax benefit . . . without giving him any new status."
- *Pastoral experience.* Did the minister have any pastoral experience in a local church following his or her ordination, commissioning, or licensing (including conducting worship and administration of sacerdotal functions)? If not, this would tend to support an IRS determination that the church's conferring of ministerial credentials (to quote the *Lawrence* case, discussed above) is "nothing more than a paperwork procedure designed to help him get a tax benefit . . . without giving him any new status."
- *Commissioning.* In some cases a church that is affiliated with a denomination that ordains and licenses ministers will "commission" staff members in order to make them eligible

for a housing allowance. The Tax Court's decision in the Kirk case (discussed at the beginning of this chapter) is one of the few cases to specifically address the meaning of "commissioning." *Kirk v. Commissioner, 51 T.C. 66 (1968).* The court concluded, "Commission means the act of committing to the charge of another or an entrusting; and license means an official document giving permission to engage in a specified activity. Petitioner is a member of a church which provides for the ordination of ministers. He does not claim to be ordained. Nor is he licensed in the sense that he has any official document or other indicia of permission, formally conferred upon him, to perform sacerdotal functions. We do not think he is commissioned. No congregation or other body of believers was committed to his charge. The duty of spreading of the gospel, either by sermon or teaching, was not formally entrusted to his care. Petitioner here is merely a non-ordained church employee." It should be noted that this case dealt with an employee of a denominational agency who performed no sacerdotal functions and never conducted worship.

✷ **KEY POINT.** The IRS will never question the authority of a church to ordain, commission, or license anyone it wants. However, it may determine whether a person qualifies for ministerial status under federal tax law.

3. It is not necessarily true that a church worker will be better off, for tax purposes, by becoming a minister. For example, assume that a layperson serving as a youth minister is debating whether to have the church license or ordain him as a minister. Assume further that the person is earning $30,000 per year. By becoming a minister, the individual will have the benefit of a housing allowance exclusion in computing his federal income taxes. On the other hand, his Social Security tax rate increases from 7.65 percent (the employee's share of FICA taxes) to 15.3 percent (the self-employment tax), since one of the four special tax rules that apply to ministers is self-employed status for Social Security. In other words, whether he will be better off for tax purposes depends on whether the housing allowance exclusion offsets the additional $2,295 in Social Security taxes. As a result, church workers should not assume that they automatically will be better off for tax purposes if their church ordains, commissions, or licenses them. In many cases, they will not be.

Of course, many persons seek ministerial credentials not only for the housing allowance but also so they can exempt themselves from Social Security. As noted in Chapter 9, few ministers qualify for this special exemption. Further, even for those who do, the financial hardships often associated with such a decision make the avoidance of Social Security taxes a dubious benefit.

EXAMPLE. Pastor J is married and has one dependent child. He is not ordained, commissioned, or licensed. In 2012 he received a salary of $25,000 and, in addition, a housing allowance of $12,000. Since Pastor J is not ordained, commissioned, or licensed, he is not a minister for tax purposes. As a result, he is not eligible for a housing allowance exclusion and is an employee for FICA purposes. How much tax will J pay in 2012? Taking into account only three personal exemptions (at $3,800 each) and the standard deduction ($11,900) for the sake of simplicity, Pastor J's taxable income will be $13,700 ($37,000 - $23,300). J will pay $1,370 in federal income taxes (10 percent x $13,700). Taxable income is not reduced by a housing allowance, since Pastor J is not a minister for tax purposes. However, as a nonminister employee, Pastor J pays the employee's share of FICA taxes, which amounts to $2,830 ($37,000 x 7.65 percent), rather than the full self-employment tax. Pastor J's total tax bill for 2012 is $4,200 (income taxes plus employee's share of FICA taxes). Note that this example does not take into account the temporary "payroll tax holiday" in 2012 that reduces an employee's share of Social Security taxes from 6.2 to 4.2 percent.

EXAMPLE. Same facts as the previous example, except that Pastor J is a licensed minister. The IRS would consider Pastor J a minister for tax purposes. His taxable income for income tax purposes is reduced by the housing allowance ($12,000), assuming that the allowance does not exceed his housing expenses or the fair rental value of his home. This leaves no taxable income and no income tax liability. Pastor J has saved $1,430 in income taxes by being classified as a minister for tax purposes. However, as a minister Pastor J pays the self-employment tax, which will be $5,228 (salary plus housing allowance less 7.65 percent, multiplied by the self-employment tax rate of 15.3 percent). J's total tax bill for 2012 as a minister will be $5,228. In summary, Pastor J pays $1,028 more in taxes by being treated as a minister.

4. The status and function of a minister are easily confused. Part of the reason the IRS and the Tax Court struggle to define the term "minister" is that they confuse the status and functions of a minister. Both the IRS and the Tax Court refer to the income tax regulations' definition of "service performed in the exercise of ministry" in attempting to define the term "minister." But the tax code and regulations treat separately the concepts of minister and service performed in the exercise of ministry.

5. Persons seeking ministerial credentials solely to qualify for tax benefits should recognize the legal and theological implications of their position. Consider the following:

- As the Tax Court recognized in the *Lawrence* decision (discussed above), a commissioning of a minister solely to qualify him for tax benefits is "nothing more than a paperwork procedure designed to help him get a tax benefit . . . without giving him any new status." Such a minister, the court concluded, generally should not be treated as a minister for tax purposes, since he is not "recognized by his church as a minister of the gospel."

• 1 Kings 13:33–34 states, "Jeroboam did not change his evil ways, but once more appointed priests for the high places from all sorts of people. Anyone who wanted to become a priest he consecrated for the high places. This was the sin of the house of Jeroboam that led to its downfall and to its destruction from the face of the earth."

6. A minister may be ordained, commissioned, or licensed by another church or denomination. In a 1955 ruling, the IRS clarified that "there is no requirement that a minister must exercise his sacerdotal functions in a church of his faith. So long as he exercises that function, its exercise anywhere meets the test." *Special Ruling, September 1, 1955.*

2. SERVICE PERFORMED IN THE EXERCISE OF MINISTRY

✿ **KEY POINT.** Persons who qualify as ministers for federal tax purposes will qualify for the four special tax rules only with respect to *services they perform in the exercise of their ministry.*

An individual who satisfies the definition of a minister as described above is eligible for the four special tax provisions discussed in this chapter. However, it must be stressed that the special tax treatment will only apply with respect to service performed in the exercise of ministry.

In other words, ministers are not automatically eligible for a housing allowance exclusion or any of the other four special rules that apply to ministers. Each rule is available only with respect to compensation received by a minister for the performance of services in the exercise of ministry. To illustrate, if a minister has a part-time secular job, the housing allowance exclusion will *not* apply to such work, since it is not service performed in the exercise of ministry. Similarly, ministers who have exempted themselves from self-employment (Social Security) taxes are not exempt from paying FICA taxes on wages they earn from a secular job, since such a job is not the exercise of ministry.

Income tax regulations

As noted above, the income tax regulations define "service performed in the exercise of ministry" as follows:

> Service performed by a minister in the exercise of his ministry includes the ministration of sacerdotal functions and the conduct of religious worship, and the control, conduct, and maintenance of religious organizations . . . under the authority of a religious body constituting a church or church denomination. Treas. Reg. 1.1402(c)-5(b)(2).

> If a minister is performing service for an organization which is operated as an integral agency of a religious organization under the authority of a religious body constituting a church or church denomination, all service performed by the minister in the conduct of religious worship, in the ministration of sacerdotal functions, or in the control, conduct, and maintenance of such organization is in the exercise of his ministry. Treas. Reg. 1.1402(c)-5(b)(2)(iv).

> If a minister, pursuant to an assignment or designation by a religious body constituting his church, performs service for an organization which is neither a religious organization nor operated as an integral agency of a religious organization, all service performed by him, even though such service may not involve the conduct of religious worship or the ministration of sacerdotal functions, is in the exercise of his ministry. Treas. Reg. 1.1402(c)-5(b)(2)(v).

The regulations provide the following examples:

> Examples of specific services the performance of which will be considered duties of a minister . . . include the performance of sacerdotal functions, the conduct of religious worship, the administration and maintenance of religious organizations and their integral agencies, and the performance of teaching and administrative duties at theological seminaries. Also, the service performed by a qualified minister as an employee of the United States (other than as a chaplain in the Armed Forces, whose service is considered to be that of a commissioned officer in his capacity as such, and not as a minister in the exercise of his ministry), or a State, Territory, or possession of the United States, or a political subdivision of any of the foregoing, or the District of Columbia, is in the exercise of his ministry provided the service performed includes such services as are ordinarily the duties of a minister. Treas. Reg. § 1.107-1(a).

The above-quoted regulations identify eight examples of services performed by ministers in the exercise of their ministry:

(1) the ministration of sacerdotal functions;
(2) the conduct of religious worship;
(3) the control, conduct, and maintenance of religious organizations under the authority of a religious body constituting a church or church denomination;
(4) the administration and maintenance of religious organizations and their integral agencies;
(5) the performance of teaching and administrative duties at theological seminaries;
(6) the service performed by a qualified minister as an employee of the United States (other than as a chaplain in the Armed Forces) or a state, territory, or possession of the United States, or a political subdivision of any of the foregoing, or the District of Columbia, provided the service performed includes such services as are ordinarily the duties of a minister;
(7) all service performed by a minister in the conduct of religious worship, the ministration of sacerdotal functions, or

the control, conduct, and maintenance of an organization that is operated as an integral agency of a religious organization under the authority of a religious body constituting a church or church denomination;

(8) service performed by a minister, pursuant to an assignment or designation by his or her church, for an organization which is neither a religious organization nor operated as an integral agency of a religious organization.

The first four of these examples of services performed by ministers in the exercise of their ministry are illustrated below. The fifth and sixth examples are illustrated in the examples that appear later in this chapter. The final two examples are addressed separately in section C of this chapter.

Sacerdotal functions

The term "sacerdotal functions" generally includes baptisms, communion, marriages, funerals, and prayer for the sick. The Tax Court, in the *Reeder* decision (discussed above), made the following comment regarding the performance of sacerdotal functions:

> *As to the sacerdotal functions, [the minister's] own testimony is that while he was the pastor of the [local church] during 1973 and 1974, he could have performed a marriage or performed funeral services with permission or performed services with respect to the dedication of infants, and he did in fact perform the ministry functions of preaching and teaching, baptism, and communion. There is no requirement that to qualify as a "duly ordained, commissioned, or licensed minister" . . . an individual must be qualified to perform and actually perform every sacrament or rite of the religion.*

The income tax regulations (quoted above) clarify that "whether service performed by a minister constitutes the . . . ministration of sacerdotal functions depends on the tenets and practices of the particular religious body constituting his church or church denomination." The regulations also specify that "if a minister is performing service in . . . the ministration of sacerdotal functions, such service is in the exercise of his ministry whether or not it is performed for a religious organization."

The IRS has recognized that sacerdotal functions include, but are not limited to, baptism, holy communion, and the performance of marriage and funeral ceremonies. *IRS Letter Ruling 8915001.*

Religious worship

The income tax regulations (quoted above) clarify that "whether service performed by a minister constitutes the conduct of religious worship . . . depends on the tenets and practices of the particular religious body constituting his church or church denomination." The regulations also specify that "if a minister is performing service in the conduct of religious worship . . . such service is in the exercise of his ministry whether or not it is performed for a religious organization."

How much religious worship is necessary to satisfy this test? This is an interesting question. The IRS has ruled on a few occasions that the religious worship must be part of a minister's regular duties. In one case the IRS ruled that an ordained minister who served as administrator of a religious school was not engaged in services performed in the exercise of ministry despite the fact that his duties included conducting worship services three times each week for the students. The IRS noted that while the administrator performed religious services and sacerdotal functions on occasion, his "regular, full-time duties were administrative duties." *IRS Letter Ruling 8646018.*

Similarly, in 1968 the IRS ruled that an ordained minister employed by a charitable organization as its Director of Special Services was not engaged in the performance of services in the exercise of ministry despite the fact that he occasionally performed certain sacerdotal duties including the conduct of worship service. The IRS acknowledged that while the minister occasionally performed worship and some sacerdotal duties, his overall duties were not basically the conduct of religious worship or the ministration of sacerdotal functions as contemplated by the regulations. *Revenue Ruling 68-68.*

On the other hand, the Tax Court has ruled that a minister employed by a parachurch ministry was engaged in services performed in the exercise of ministry because he conducted staff devotions, despite the fact that his "regular, full-time duties were administrative duties." *Mosley v. Commissioner, T.C. Memo. 1994-457 (1994).* The court observed:

> *Daily worship services are conducted at [the parachurch ministry]. Apparently, they were conducted during the years in question. [The minister] conducts those services. They are conducted for employees engaged in [the organization's] marketing efforts. On occasion, the Lord's Supper is administered at those services. . . . [I]t seems clear that his activity in conducting worship services was known to, and approved by, the board of directors of the corporation. We think that his conduct of those services constitutes the conduct of religious services within the meaning of [the regulations]. . . . Clearly, [his] preaching and conduct of religious services constituted only a portion of [his] duties on behalf of [the organization].*

❖**KEY POINT.** See the discussion later in this chapter on the United States Supreme Court's 2012 decision in the *Hosanna-Tabor* case. This case directly addressed the question of how much time a teacher in a church-affiliated school had to be engaged in religious activities in order to qualify for ministerial status. Significantly, the Court concluded: "The issue before us, however, is not one that can be resolved by a stopwatch. The amount of time an employee spends on particular activities is relevant in assessing that employee's status, but that factor cannot be considered in isolation, without regard to the nature of the religious functions performed."

THE MINISTRY OF MUSIC

Many church music directors are not ordained, commissioned, or licensed, and so they are not considered "ministers" by the IRS for federal tax reporting purposes under the prevailing definition. This means: they are not eligible for a housing allowance; they are employees for Social Security purposes; their wages are not exempt from income tax withholding; and they are not eligible for exemption from self-employment taxes. Nowhere are the deficiencies of the current IRS definition of "minister" more apparent than in the context of church music directors.

In other contexts, many federal courts have described the central role of music directors to the mission of the church, even if they are not ordained, commissioned, or licensed. To illustrate, the civil courts uniformly recognize a rule called the "ministerial exception," which bars the courts from resolving employment-related disputes between churches and ministers. Several courts have concluded that church music directors qualify as ministers under this rule to the extent that their duties are central to fulfilling the church's mission. Consider the following stirring description of the pivotal role of music in the ministry of the church. It comes from a decision by a federal appeals court finding that the ministerial exception applied to a noncredentialed music director:

> At the heart of this case is the undeniable fact that music is a vital means of expressing and celebrating those beliefs which a religious community holds most sacred. Music is an integral part of many different religious traditions. It serves a unique function in worship by virtue of its capacity to uplift the spirit and manifest the relationship between the individual or congregation and the Almighty. Indeed, the church has presented ample undisputed evidence affirming the centrality of sacred music to the [Christian faith] and the importance of music ministry to the faith community. . . . Thus, inasmuch as [the music director's] duties involve the expression of the church's musical tradition, it is a fallacy to denominate them as merely secular. We refuse to demote music below other liturgical forms or to sever it from its spiritual moorings. . . . Nor can we [prefer] modes of religious expression that draw principally from the rational faculties, such as preaching or the teaching of theology, over those which summon the more lyrical elements of the human spirit. Indeed [as the Supreme Court once observed] "the inspirational appeal of religion in the guises of music, architecture, and painting is often stronger than in forthright sermon." The efforts of a music minister or teacher can thus influence the spiritual and pastoral mission of the church as much as one who would lead the congregation in prayer, preach from the pulpit, or teach theology in school. Employment Opportunity Commission v. The Roman Catholic Diocese of Raleigh, 213 F. 3d 795 (4th Cir. 2000).

So far, neither the IRS nor the Tax Court has been persuaded by this same logic to recognize music directors (who are not ordained, commissioned, or licensed) as ministers for purposes of federal tax law.

The control, conduct, and maintenance of religious organizations

The regulations include "the control, conduct, and maintenance of religious organizations . . . under the authority of a religious body constituting a church or church denomination" in the definition of service performed by a minister in the exercise of ministry. The regulation quoted above defines this as "directing, managing, or promoting the activities of such organization." This terminology is admittedly confusing.

The Tax Court, in the *Wingo* decision, in interpreting this language, noted that "the fact that [a minister] was not permitted to do all that [an ordained minister] could do does not mean that he performed no services in the control, conduct, and maintenance of his church or denomination. To perform services in the control, conduct, and maintenance of the church or organization within the church, the minister need only have some participation in the conduct, control, and maintenance of the local church or denomination."

The *Wingo* court also noted that a minister can be engaged in the control, conduct, or maintenance of either a local church or a denomination. To illustrate, the fact that a minister has the right to vote at national conventions of his or her denomination will constitute sufficient control, even if the minister possesses little, if any, control over a local church. This is often true of ordained youth pastors—they have the right to vote at national conventions (and thereby they are engaged in the control, conduct, and maintenance of their denomination) even though they possess little, if any, authority in their own congregation.

The Tax Court, in the *Reeder* decision (discussed above), made the following comment regarding the question of service in the control, conduct, and maintenance of the religious organization:

> [The taxpayer] points out that during 1973 and 1974 he was the pastor of a local church which was a dependent church and subject to supervision under the constitution and bylaws of the [District]. [The taxpayer] argues that only upon ordination was he

able to participate in the governance of his church organization at a higher level than the local church. In response to a similar argument, in Wingo v. Commissioner, *we stated: "To perform services in the control, conduct, and maintenance of the church or organizations within the church, the minister need only have some participation in the conduct, control, and maintenance of the local church or the denomination."*

The income tax regulations (quoted above) further clarify that

services performed by a minister in the control, conduct, and maintenance of a religious organization relates to directing, managing, or promoting the activities of such organization. Any religious organization is deemed to be under the authority of a religious body constituting a church or church denomination if it is organized and dedicated to carrying out the tenets and principles of a faith in accordance with either the requirements or sanctions governing the creation of institutions of the faith.

The IRS has recognized that services in the control, conduct, and maintenance of a religious organization can occur at either the local congregational level or in the context of a regional or national denomination. To illustrate, in one ruling the IRS noted that a minister satisfied this test because "[h]e was directly responsible for the local church as its administrative head or overseer, and he was chairman of the official board of the church. Thus, he was in charge of all the organizational concerns of his own congregation."

The IRS also noted that the minister was a member of a regional body of his denomination and in that role was part of the voting constituency of that body. As a voting member, "he had the opportunity to influence the conduct, control, and maintenance of the governing body of his church in [his denomination]. Also, [his] denomination recognized the taxpayer as a minister or religious leader, by licensing him as a minister." *IRS Letter Ruling 8915001.*

○ **OBSERVATION.** It is significant that the IRS audit guidelines for ministers do not require that all three categories of ministry described in the regulations be met in order for one to be a minister for tax purposes or be engaged in the performance of services in the exercise of ministry. This is a potentially significant admission by the IRS. Many bona fide ministers do not satisfy all three categories of ministry, and to suggest (as the IRS and Tax Court have in the past) that all three are required is inappropriate and naive.

Administration and maintenance of religious organizations and their integral agencies
This terminology is not defined in the tax code or regulations. The best indication of its meaning was provided by the IRS in a 1958 ruling:

This phrase was included in the regulations in view of the practice of some church denominations to select and approve

ordained ministers as the governing body, the administrators or overall managers, of a religious organization, or an integral agency of the church denomination, which they support or sponsor in order that the purposes and aims of such church denomination are carried into effect. Hence, ordained ministers appointed by a religious denomination to administer or manage a religious organization are engaged in carrying out the tenets and practices of their denominations and to an extent engaged in ecclesiastic duties. Ordained ministers employed by a religious organization in a capacity subordinate to the administrator or manager of such organization, are considered to be primarily engaged in secular duties, if the duties for which they are being remunerated are not ordinarily the duties of a minister of the gospel. Letter Ruling 5807234520A.

In another 1958 ruling the IRS observed: "The term 'maintenance' as used in the preceding sentences means the overall management and supervision necessary for effectuating the purposes and aims of an organization." *Revenue Ruling 5807024980A.*

In a 1960 ruling the IRS clarified that "the term 'maintenance' . . . does not relate to the upkeep of property, machinery, or equipment, but rather to the overall management and supervision necessary for effectuating the purposes and aims of an organization." *Letter Ruling 6008269790A.*

The IRS audit guidelines for ministers use the phrase "administration and maintenance of religious organizations" interchangeably with the phrase "control, conduct, and maintenance of religious organizations." As a result, "administration and maintenance" probably should be viewed as synonymous with "control, conduct, and maintenance."

IRS audit guidelines for ministers
The IRS audit guidelines for ministers instruct agents that the income tax regulations define the term "service performed by a minister in the exercise of the ministry" to include

- ministration of sacerdotal functions;
- conduct of religious worship; and
- control, conduct, and maintenance of religious organizations (including the religious boards, societies, and other integral agencies of such organizations) under the authority of a religious body constituting a church or denomination.

The guidelines note that the income tax regulations specify that whether service performed by a minister constitutes conduct of religious worship or ministration of sacerdotal functions depends on the tenets and practices of the particular religious body constituting the church or denomination.

The guidelines note that the income tax regulations associated with section 107 of the tax code (pertaining to the housing allowance) provide the following examples of services considered duties of a minister:

- performance of sacerdotal functions;
- conduct of religious worship;
- administration and maintenance of religious organizations and their integral agencies; and
- performance of teaching and administrative duties at theological seminaries.

◉ OBSERVATION. Once again, this list does not suggest or require that a person satisfy all of the categories to be a minister or be engaged in service performed in the exercise of ministry. To illustrate, a professor at a church-controlled seminary who seldom, if ever, conducts religious worship or performs sacerdotal functions would still be considered a minister engaged in ministry under the approach taken both in the regulations and the guidelines. This is an important clarification, since some previous IRS and Tax Court rulings have suggested that all categories of ministerial services must be performed.

The guidelines add that "the duties performed by the individual are also important to the initial determination whether he or she is a duly ordained, commissioned, or licensed minister. Because religious disciplines vary in their formal procedures for these designations, whether an individual is duly ordained, commissioned, or licensed depends on these facts and circumstances."

IRS Publication 517

IRS Publication 517, which addresses tax reporting for ministers, refers to "service performed in the exercise of ministry" as "ministerial services" and describes this term as follows:

Most services you perform as a minister, priest, rabbi, etc., are ministerial services. These services include:

- *performing sacerdotal functions,*
- *conducting religious worship, and*
- *controlling, conducting, and maintaining religious organization (including the religious boards, societies, and other integral agencies of such organizations) that are under the authority of a religious body that is a church or denomination.*

You are considered to control, conduct, and maintain a religious organization if you direct, manage, or promote the organization's activities. A religious organization is under the authority of a religious body that is a church or denomination if it is organized for and dedicated to carrying out the principles of a faith according to the requirements governing the creation of institutions of the faith.

Services for nonreligious organizations. *Your services for a nonreligious organization are ministerial services if the services are assigned or designated by your church. Assigned or designated services qualify even if they do not involve performing sacerdotal functions or conducting religious worship. If your services are*

not assigned or designated by your church, they are ministerial services only if they involve performing sacerdotal functions or conducting religious worship.

Services that are not part of your ministry. *Income from services you perform as an employee that are not ministerial services is generally subject to Social Security and Medicare tax withholding (not self-employment tax) under the rules that apply to employees in general. The following are not ministerial services.*

- *Services you perform for nonreligious organizations other than the services stated above.*
- *Services you perform as a duly ordained, commissioned, or licensed minister of a church as an employee of the United States, the District of Columbia, a foreign government, or any of their political subdivisions. This is true even if you are performing sacerdotal functions or conducting religious worship. (For example, if you perform services as a chaplain in the Armed Forces of the United States, the services are not ministerial services.)*
- *Services you perform in a government-owned and operated hospital. (These services are considered performed by a government employee, not by a minister as part of the ministry.) However, services that you perform at a church related hospital or health and welfare institution, or a private nonprofit hospital, are considered to be part of the ministry and are considered ministerial services.*

Books or articles. *Writing religious books or articles is considered to be in the exercise of your ministry and is considered ministerial services.*

The Hosanna-Tabor case

In a ringing endorsement of religious liberty, the United States Supreme Court, in a 2012 ruling, unanimously affirmed the so-called "ministerial exception" barring civil court review of employment disputes between churches and ministers. *Hosanna-Tabor Evangelical Lutheran Church and School v. E.E.O.C., 132 S.Ct. 694 (2012).*

The case involved a claim by a "called" teacher at a church-related school in Michigan that the school committed unlawful disability discrimination in terminating her employment. The Court's ruling has potential significance in defining the term *minister* for tax purposes. Consider the following two points:

1. Significance of being ordained, commissioned, or licensed

The Court noted that the plaintiff's status as a commissioned minister in the Lutheran church did not, by itself, "automatically ensure coverage" under the ministerial exception. But it concluded that "the fact that an employee has been ordained or commissioned as a minister is surely relevant, as is the fact that significant religious training and a recognized religious mission underlie the description of the employee's position."

While one's status as an ordained, commissioned, or licensed minister is not determinative or even essential, it is relevant in deciding whether a person is a minister for purposes of the ministerial exception.

This aspect of the Court's opinion could serve as justification for liberalizing the current definition of *minister* in the context of federal tax law. Several provisions in the federal tax code apply to ministers, including, most notably, the housing allowance. The tax code and regulations refer to "ordained, commissioned, or licensed" ministers in describing persons who qualify as ministers for tax purposes. The Tax Court amplified upon this definition in a 1989 ruling, *Knight v. Commissioner*, 92 T.C. 199 (1989). This definition has been endorsed by the IRS in its audit guidelines for ministers. Under this test, the following five factors must be considered in deciding whether a person is a minister for federal tax reporting:

- Does the individual administer the sacraments?
- Does the individual conduct worship services?
- Does the individual perform services in the "control, conduct, or maintenance of a religious organization" under the authority of a church or religious denomination?
- Is the individual ordained, commissioned, or licensed?
- Is the individual considered to be a spiritual leader by his or her religious body?

Only the fourth factor is required in all cases (the individual must be ordained, commissioned, or licensed). The remaining four factors need not all be present for a person to be considered a minister for tax reporting.

By defining the term *minister* to apply only to ordained, commissioned, or licensed ministers, the tax code, regulations, Tax Court, and IRS adopted a definition more restrictive than the analysis applied by the Supreme Court in the *Hosanna-Tabor* case. This may serve as a basis for liberalizing the Tax Court definition to include persons who perform ministerial functions but who are not formally recognized as ordained, commissioned, or licensed ministers.

2. Time spent performing religious duties

Another important aspect of the Court's ruling in the *Hosanna-Tabor* case was its conclusion that a finding of ministerial status cannot be based solely on the amount of time a person spends on religious functions. In rejecting the appeals court's conclusion that the ministerial exception did not apply because of the limited time the teacher devoted to religious tasks, the Court observed: "The issue before us, however, is not one that can be resolved by a stopwatch. The amount of time an employee spends on particular activities is relevant in assessing that employee's status, but that factor cannot be considered in isolation, without regard to the nature of the religious functions performed."

The Court acknowledged that the teacher's religious duties "consumed only 45 minutes of each workday, and that the rest of her day was devoted to teaching secular subjects." However, the Court noted that it was unsure whether any church employees devoted all their time to religious tasks: "The heads of congregations themselves often have a mix of duties, including secular ones such as helping to manage the congregation's finances, supervising purely secular personnel, and overseeing the upkeep of facilities."

This aspect of the Court's rulings will be helpful in several contexts, including the determination of ministerial status for tax purposes. The IRS and the Tax Court in some cases have contended that a person is not a minister for tax purposes because of the limited time the person devotes to religious functions. The Supreme Court concluded in the *Hosanna-Tabor* case that the plaintiff was a minister despite the fact that her religious duties occupied less than 45 minutes per day. The Court noted that ministerial status cannot be resolved by a stopwatch.

The Court also noted that many ministers devote less than all their time to religious tasks: "The heads of congregations themselves often have a mix of duties, including secular ones such as helping to manage the congregation's finances, supervising purely secular personnel, and overseeing the upkeep of facilities."

This will be a helpful precedent to persons whose ministerial status is challenged by the IRS on the basis of the limited time spent on religious duties.

Conclusions

The courts and the IRS have had little difficulty in deciding that a minister engaged in pastoral ministry in a local congregation is performing services in the exercise of ministry. As the IRS noted in Revenue Ruling 78-301, "when the individual's regular, fulltime duties to the congregation are spiritual or religious in nature, such as leading the worship service, those duties are in the exercise of ministry." Further, the income tax regulations (quoted above) clarify that "if a minister is performing service in the conduct of religious worship or the ministration of sacerdotal functions, such service is in the exercise of his ministry whether or not it is performed for a religious organization."

Consider the following examples:

EXAMPLE. Pastor R is an ordained youth minister. He regularly performs sacerdotal duties and conducts religious worship. He would be considered to be a minister under the *Knight* definition. As a minister he is eligible for the four special tax provisions discussed in this chapter (assuming that he otherwise qualifies) with respect to his services on behalf of the church.

EXAMPLE. R is the minister of music. She has not been ordained, commissioned, or licensed by her church or denomination, and she does not perform any sacerdotal duties. Her duties include directing the church choir, overseeing the music program at the church, and playing the organ during church services. She will not qualify for any of the four special provisions discussed above, since she is not ordained, commissioned, or licensed. (According to the *Knight* definition, one must be ordained, commissioned, or licensed in order to be a minister for federal tax purposes.) This means she is not eligible for a housing allowance exclusion or exemption from either Social Security taxes or income tax withholding. *Revenue Ruling 59-270.*

EXAMPLE. M retired from a secular job and began working as a church's "minister of visitation." His responsibilities include hospital visitation and visiting new and prospective members. He is not ordained, commissioned, or licensed, and he performs no sacerdotal functions or religious worship. He does not qualify for the four special tax provisions discussed in this chapter, since he is not an ordained, commissioned, or licensed minister, and he performs neither sacerdotal duties nor religious worship.

EXAMPLE. Pastor P is the senior minister of a church. The church is not affiliated with any sect or denomination. Pastor P has never been ordained or licensed. He is not eligible for any of the special tax provisions discussed in this chapter (including a housing allowance). Of course, his church is free to ordain or commission Pastor P, and this may entitle him to the special tax provisions. However, note that the Tax Court in the *Lawrence* decision warned that an individual would not qualify for such special tax provisions if he or she was ordained or commissioned solely for tax savings purposes. Further, the court noted in the *Salkov* case that an individual cannot become eligible for the special tax provisions by "ordaining" himself or herself.

EXAMPLE. B serves as business administrator of a church. The church "licenses" her as a "minister of administration" in order to make her eligible for a housing allowance. B performs no sacerdotal functions and does not conduct religious worship. She has no formal theological training, and her duties were in no way affected by her "license." The act of licensing B probably will not make her eligible for a housing allowance, according to the legal precedent cited above, since it is doubtful that she will satisfy a majority of the five criteria mentioned in the *Knight* case. Again, persons seeking special tax benefits through licensing or commissioning should pay special heed to the Tax Court's decision in *Lawrence* (discussed above).

EXAMPLE. The IRS ruled that a "licensed minister" in a denomination that both ordains and licenses its ministers was a minister for federal tax purposes, since he performed substantially all the functions of an ordained minister. The minister was licensed in 1971, and as a licensed minister he pastured a church, administered the ordinances of baptism and holy communion, preached sermons, and performed the services of marriage, burial, and

membership reception. He also was responsible for ministering to the needs of the people of the church, which included instructing candidates for membership and receiving them into the church, and counseling troubled or bereaved families. The minister was ordained in 1980 and filed an application for exemption from self-employment tax (Form 4361) in 1980. The IRS ruled that the minister qualified as a minister for tax purposes when he was licensed in 1971, and accordingly the Form 4361 was filed too late.

The IRS noted that the minister performed all three of the kinds of ministerial services described in the income tax regulations (sacerdotal functions, conduct of worship, and the "control, conduct, and maintenance" of a religious organization): "The taxpayer was heavily involved in all three of the types of services in his capacity as a licensed minister and pastor of a local church. . . . With respect to the first type of ministerial services, he was authorized to and in fact did administer sacerdotal functions. He administered the ordinances of baptism and holy communion, and presided at marriage and funeral ceremonies. Secondly, he conducted religious worship on a regular basis in his capacity as pastor of a local church. Thirdly, in his role as pastor of a local church he was involved in the control, conduct, and maintenance of religious organizations under the authority of a religious body. He was directly responsible for the local church as its administrative head or overseer, and he was chairman of the official board of the church. Thus, he was in charge of all the organizational concerns of his own congregation. . . . He was also a member of the District Council and in that role was part of the voting constituency of the District Council. As a voting member of the District Council, he had the opportunity to influence the conduct, control, and maintenance of the governing body of his church in [his] District. Also, [his] denomination recognized the taxpayer as a minister or religious leader, by licensing him as a minister." *IRS Letter Ruling 8915001.*

EXAMPLE. The Tax Court ruled that a minister was not exempt from Social Security, because his exemption application was filed too late. While enrolled in college, a student (John) was licensed as a "student local pastor" for the United Methodist Church ("the Church") and served in a local church in 1983 and 1984. His earnings exceeded $400 each year. John thereafter attended seminary, and during this time he was licensed and served as the local pastor of a church from 1985 to 1987. In 1987 he was ordained a deacon in the Church. In 1990 he was ordained an elder. The ordained ministry of the Church consists of deacons and elders.

In 1989 John filed an application for exemption from Social Security (self-employment) taxes by filing a Form 4361 with the IRS. He noted on the form that he had been ordained in 1987, when he was ordained a deacon. Therefore, the form was filed prior to the deadline. The Tax Court ruled that John's application for exemption had been filed too late, since the duties he performed as a licensed pastor in 1983 and 1984 were the performance of services as a minister. The court noted that as a licensed local pastor in 1983 and 1984, John was authorized to preside over the ministration of sacerdotal functions, such as baptism, communion, and marriage, and he conducted religious worship. Therefore, he "for those years acted in a manner consistent with the performance of service by a duly ordained, commissioned, or licensed minister within the meaning of [the tax code]."

The court conceded that as a licensed pastor John had no "voice or vote" on official matters of his denomination. But it noted that "to perform services in the control, conduct, and maintenance of the church or organizations within the church, the minister need only have some participation in the conduct, control, and maintenance of the local church or denomination." It concluded that during 1983 and 1984, as a licensed local pastor, John served "in the control, conduct, and maintenance" of his local church even though as a licensed local pastor he might not have done so with respect to his national denomination. Since John had net earnings of at least $400 derived for the performance of services as a minister in 1983 and 1984, his application for exemption from self-employment tax should have been filed prior to the due date of his 1984 federal income tax return (April 15, 1985). Because it was not, it was filed too late and was not effective. *Brannon v. Commissioner, T.C. Memo. 1999-370 (1999).*

B. MINISTERS NOT EMPLOYED BY A CHURCH

It is often difficult to determine if a minister is engaged in service performed in the exercise of ministry with respect to *services performed outside of the context of a local church.* The following examples, based on actual cases, will be instructive. They are arranged by job classification, as follows: (1) authors, (2) chaplains, (3) church administrators, (4) counselors, (5) employees of parachurch ministries, and (6) teachers and administrators.

1. AUTHORS

EXAMPLE. An ordained minister performed services for a religious organization under the authority of a religious body constituting a church. His services included the writing of religious books and articles (that is, books or articles which were religious in nature and were designed for the dissemination of religious ideas), through the sale of which he received royalty payments. The IRS ruled that "the writing of bona fide religious books or

articles by the minister is considered to be service performed in the exercise of his ministry." *Revenue Ruling 59-50.*

EXAMPLE. IRS Publication 517 states: "Writing religious books or articles is considered to be in the exercise of your ministry and is considered ministerial services. This rule also applies to members of religious orders and to Christian Science practitioners."

2. CHAPLAINS

EXAMPLE. The IRS ruled that ordained ministers serving as chaplains in government-owned and -operated hospitals are not engaged in service performed in the exercise of ministry for purposes of Social Security, and accordingly they are employees for FICA purposes (and, if exempt from self-employment taxes, the exemption does not apply). However, the chaplains are engaged in the exercise of ministry for purposes of the housing allowance and accordingly are eligible for this exclusion. The services performed by the chaplains included conduct of religious worship, ministration of sacerdotal functions, and spiritual counseling.

The IRS noted that service performed by a duly ordained, commissioned, or licensed minister of a church "as an employee of the United States, a State, Territory, or possession of the United States, the District of Columbia, a foreign government, or a political subdivision of any of the foregoing," is not considered to be "in the exercise of his ministry" even though such service may involve the ministration of sacerdotal functions or the conduct of religious worship. Such service is considered to be performed in his capacity as an employee of the government and not by a minister "in the exercise of his ministry." *Treas. Reg. § 1.1402(c)-5.* Accordingly, service of the type described above performed by a minister as a chaplain at a government-owned and -operated hospital is not considered to be "in the exercise of his ministry" for Social Security purposes, and compensation paid by such hospitals to their minister-employees is subject to income tax withholding.

On the other hand, the income tax regulations specify that "service performed by a qualified minister as an employee of the United States (other than as a chaplain in the Armed Forces, whose service is considered to be that of a commissioned officer in his capacity as such, and not as a minister in the exercise of his ministry), or a State, Territory, or possession of the United States, or a political subdivision of any of the foregoing, or the District of Columbia, is in the exercise of his ministry provided the service performed includes such services as are ordinarily the duties of a minister." *Treas. Reg. 1.107-1(a).* Accordingly, chaplains employed by government-owned and -operated hospitals are eligible for a housing allowance. *Revenue Ruling 71-258. See also IRS Letter Rulings 7727019, 7809092, 8004046, 8138184, 8519004, and 9743037.*

EXAMPLE. Ordained ministers employed as chaplains by state prisons are not engaged in the exercise of ministry for Social Security purposes. As a result, they are subject to FICA taxes. If they exempted themselves from self-employment taxes, the exemption does not apply. This result is based on the income tax regulations, which specify that service performed by a duly ordained, commissioned, or licensed minister of a church "as an employee of the United States, a State, Territory, or possession of the United States, the District of Columbia, a foreign government, or a political subdivision of any of the foregoing" is not considered to be "in the exercise of his ministry" even though such service may involve the ministration of sacerdotal functions or the conduct of religious worship. The regulations specify that "service performed by an employee of a state as a chaplain in a state prison is considered to be performed by a civil servant of the state and not by a minister in the exercise of his ministry." *Treas. Reg. § 1.1402(c)-5.* On the other hand, the regulations specify that, for purposes of determining the eligibility of a chaplain for a housing allowance, "service performed by a qualified minister as an employee of the United States . . . or a State, Territory, or possession of the United States, or a political subdivision of any of the foregoing, or the District of Columbia, is in the exercise of his ministry provided the service performed includes such services as are ordinarily the duties of a minister." *Treas. Reg. 1.107-1(a).*

EXAMPLE. Pastor C performs services as an employee of a nonprofit organization formed to provide a chaplaincy ministry of pastoral and theological care for and to hospitalized patients, including counseling and guidance of patients and their families, outpatients, staff, and medical personnel who may be connected with local hospitals and health organizations. The organization receives its operating funds from contributions by local churches. Pastor C is an ordained minister and was employed to perform services for the organization as the director of pastoral care at a public hospital. His daily duties include (1) spiritual and emotional counseling of patients and their families referred by the nursing staff and physicians (which occupies approximately 40 percent of his working hours); (2) performing religious rituals at the time of death for patients who pass away while in the hospital (15 percent of his working hours); (3) spiritual crisis counseling and notification of patients' ministers in emergency situations (15 percent); (4) pastoral counseling of the hospital staff and student nurses in time of stress (5 percent); (5) performing funeral services, wedding services, and bedside communion services (5 percent); and (6) speaking in the hospital chapel at various community and church group gatherings on the hospital chaplaincy program and performing devotional programs (5 percent). The IRS ruled that Pastor C is a minister and that his work constitutes service performed in the exercise of ministry, and accordingly he should be treated as a minister for federal tax purposes. It noted that "his services are principally spiritual counseling and the ministration of sacerdotal functions." *IRS Letter Ruling 8519004.*

EXAMPLE. Chaplain Boyd was an ordained minister employed full time by the City of Indianapolis ("City") as a police chaplain. The police department's chaplain program was established through its joint efforts with the Church Federation of Greater Indianapolis, Inc. ("Federation"). The Federation is an organization of Christian congregations and denominations in the Indianapolis metropolitan area. Chaplain Boyd claimed he was eligible for a housing allowance with respect to amounts so designated by the Federation. The IRS disagreed. It noted that the tax regulations require a housing allowance to be designated "pursuant to official action taken in advance of the payment of such amount by the employing church or other qualified organization." Since the Federation was not the chaplain's employing church (he was not a Federation employee and was not paid by it), the IRS asserted that he was eligible for a housing allowance only if the City was an "other qualified organization." The IRS concluded that this test was not met, and the chaplain appealed.

The Tax Court ruled that the City was an "other qualified organization" that could designate a housing allowance. It concluded: "As a police chaplain, Boyd was under the direct supervision of the Chief of Police. However, the Federation retained supervision over Boyd's ecclesiastical performance and maintained day-to-day contact with Boyd and other chaplains. Boyd's salary was originally paid by the Federation, but in the years at issue, his salary was paid by the City. The Federation was also involved in the operation of the police chaplain program. If a problem arose concerning a police chaplain, a police department official would usually contact the Federation to resolve the problem. When a vacancy occurred for a chaplain, the Federation assumed primary responsibility for finding a qualified person to fill the vacancy. The Federation annually designated a specific amount of Boyd's salary, in advance, as a housing allowance even though his salary was paid by the City. The City neither provided Boyd with a home nor designated any portion of his salary as a housing allowance."

The Tax Court concluded that the Federation was a qualified organization and that its designation of a portion of Boyd's salary as a housing allowance was valid. The Tax Court based its decision on the "constant and detailed involvement of the Federation" in the City's police chaplain program. The IRS later "acquiesced" in the court's ruling on the ground that the Federation's responsibilities toward the chaplain program were similar to those of an employer and that the Federation was closely involved with the police department in its employer-employee relationship with the ministers. *Boyd v. Commissioner, T.C. Memo. 1981-528 (1981).*

EXAMPLE. The IRS ruled that an ordained minister employed by a state department of corrections as a prison chaplain was not entitled to a housing allowance. The chaplain was an employee of the state and was compensated by the state. His denomination submitted a letter to the department of corrections endorsing his call to the chaplaincy ministry and stating that 45 percent of his salary constituted a housing allowance. The IRS noted that the tax regulations require a housing allowance to be designated "pursuant to official action taken in advance of the payment of such amount by the employing church or other qualified organization." Since the chaplain's denomination was not an employing church, he was eligible for a housing allowance only if the state department of corrections was an "other qualified organization." The IRS concluded that this test was not met: "In the present case, the [denomination] is not actively involved in the day-to-day conduct of the chaplain program of the state department of corrections. . . . The [denomination's] involvement with the program was limited to sending a letter to the state endorsing [the chaplain] and receiving annual reports from him. We do not believe that this level of involvement is sufficient . . . to qualify the [denomination] as an 'other qualified organization.' The [denomination] is not closely involved with the state in the conduct of its chaplain program and the responsibilities of the [denomination] are not similar to those of an employer." *IRS Letter Ruling 9052001.*

EXAMPLE. An ordained minister was employed by the federal government as a full-time chaplain in a Veterans Administration hospital. The IRS ruled that the chaplain was not eligible for a housing allowance. It noted that a housing allowance is "an amount paid to a minister to rent or otherwise provide a home if such amount is designated as rental allowance pursuant to official action taken in advance of such payment by the employing church or other qualified organization." It referred to title 5, section 5301, of the United States Code, which specifies that it is the policy of Congress that federal pay fixing for employees under the General Schedule be based on the principles that "(1) there be equal pay for substantially equal work within each local pay area; (2) within each local pay area, pay distinctions be maintained in keeping with work and performance distinctions; (3) federal pay rates be comparable with non-federal pay rates for the same levels of work within the same local pay area; and (4) any existing pay disparities between federal and nonfederal employees should be completely eliminated."

The IRS noted that the pay rates for General Schedule (GS) employees of the federal government are provided on the basis of the duties, responsibilities, and qualification requirements of the employees' positions and that "no portion of a GS pay rate for a chaplain or for any other GS employee is provided as a rental allowance or as anything other than basic pay for the work the employee performs." The federal pay comparability process "compares only basic pay and does not take into consideration extraneous benefits such as rental allowances for ministers, nor does it compare pay for individual occupations. It compares pay for levels of work. Thus, rather than comparing pay for federal chaplains with pay for non-federal clergymen, the comparability process compares pay for a GS grade with average basic pay for work of a similar level of difficulty and responsibility in several occupations in the private sector. The General Schedule pay rates

do not expressly provide for any rental allowance exclusion for ministers. Furthermore, the IRS has been advised by the U.S. Civil Service Commissioner that there are presently no statutory provisions relating to General Schedule employees authorizing anyone in a government agency to designate part of a minister's government compensation as a rental allowance as required by section 1.107-1(b) of the regulations. Accordingly, it is held that the taxpayer, a General Schedule employee, may not exclude any portion of his pay as a rental allowance under section 107 of the tax code." *Revenue Ruling 72-462.*

EXAMPLE. A chain of nonprofit nursing homes ("Challenge Homes") affiliated with the Assemblies of God Church ("Church") employed several ordained ministers as chaplains. Challenge Homes designated a portion of each chaplain's compensation as a housing allowance. The IRS later determined that none of the chaplains was eligible for a housing allowance, and the chaplains appealed to the Tax Court.

The court noted three ways the chaplains' services could constitute the exercise of ministry, making them eligible for a housing allowance: (1) The performance of worship and sacerdotal functions constitutes the exercise of ministry, as defined by the Church. But the court concluded that this test was not met, since there was "no evidence regarding what, if any, sacerdotal functions or religious worship services the chaplains actually conducted pursuant to their employment with Challenge Homes. Nor, and more importantly for this test, is there any evidence that the duties which the chaplains did perform for Challenge Homes constituted the conduct of religious worship or ministration of sacerdotal functions within the stated tenets and practices of the Assemblies of God Church." (2) The regulations specify that if a minister, pursuant to an assignment by his church, performs service for an organization which is not a religious organization, all service performed by him, even though such service may not involve the conduct of religious worship or the ministration of sacerdotal functions, is in the exercise of his ministry. This test was not met, since none of the chaplains had been assigned to a post by the Church. (3) The regulations specify that service performed by a minister in the exercise of ministry includes service "in the control, conduct, and maintenance of religious organizations under the authority of a religious body constituting a church or church denomination." The court concluded that this test was not met, since there was not sufficient evidence that Challenge Homes was under the authority of the Church.

The court acknowledged that many ties existed between the two entities but that these ties were not enough. It noted the following facts: (1) Challenge Homes advertised itself as a provider of nondenominational nursing home services whose primary source of revenue was from various agencies of government. (2) The charter of Challenge Homes states that no legal relationship exists between it and the Church. (3) The Church does not have right of approval or the right to remove directors of Challenge Homes, does not support Challenge Homes financially, and cannot legally require Challenge Homes to report on its operations. The court concluded that the chaplains "have not shown any objective manifestation of control by the Church over Challenge Homes. The record is devoid of any evidence that the Church ever made a suggestion to Challenge Homes about the operation or management of the nursing homes it ran." *Toavs v. Commissioner, 67 T.C. 897 (1977). See also Revenue Ruling 72-606.*

3. CHURCH ADMINISTRATORS

EXAMPLE. The Tax Court ruled that an administrator of a Jewish synagogue was not eligible for a housing allowance, since he was not ordained, commissioned, or licensed. The court noted that in deciding whether an individual performs the functions of a minister, consideration must be given not only to the religious duties the individual performs but also to the religious duties that are not performed. The performance of some religious functions is not enough to make one a minister for federal tax purposes. The administrator in this case performed a number of religious functions, but these were largely administrative in nature. More importantly, he performed few of the duties of an ordained, commissioned, or licensed minister. The court also noted that the administrator had no seminary training. *Haimowitz v. Commissioner, T.C. Memo. 1997-40 (1997).*

EXAMPLE. The IRS ruled that an ordained minister who was fully qualified to perform all of the sacerdotal functions of his church and who served as the "canon/administrator" of his local church was engaged in the exercise of ministry and accordingly was eligible for a housing allowance. His duties included supervising all aspects of the church's finances, fund-raising program, plant and equipment, kitchen operations, and housekeeping. The IRS noted that "examples of specific services the performance of which will be considered duties of a minister for purposes of [the housing allowance] include the performance of sacerdotal functions, the conduct of religious worship, the administration and maintenance of religious organizations and their integral agencies." The IRS concluded that "the regulations are specific concerning ministers who serve as administrators of religious organizations. Accordingly, we have concluded that you are performing services that are ordinarily the duties of a minister of the gospel and, as such, are eligible to receive a rental allowance exclusion." *IRS Letter Ruling 8142076.*

4. COUNSELORS

EXAMPLE. The IRS ruled that an ordained Presbyterian minister employed full time by a nonprofit pastoral counseling center was not eligible for a housing allowance. The minister spent 50 percent of his working hours providing "spiritual and pastoral

counsel to individuals about a variety of issues, including marital difficulties, depression, anxiety, sexual problems eating disorders and gender identity." His counseling approach was based on "applying Biblical principles of human nature and behavior" to the problems of patients. He spent 35 percent of his time preparing for and leading three small Bible study groups and two discussion groups of other ordained ministers; 10 percent of his time was spent preparing for and teaching Sunday-school classes in nearby congregations; and 5 percent of his time was spent on preaching, leading worship services, officiating at weddings, and administering the sacraments. Less than five percent of his time was taken up with administrative duties. The counseling center's board of directors designated a portion of the minister's compensation as a housing allowance. This practice was questioned by the IRS, and guidance was sought from the IRS national office.

The IRS national office concluded that the minister was not entitled to a housing allowance. It conceded that the taxpayer was a minister, but it concluded that he was not engaged in service performed in the exercise of his ministry and therefore was not eligible for a housing allowance with respect to his employment by the counseling center. It observed: "In the present case, the facts indicate that only five percent of the taxpayer's working hours are spent performing duties such as the conduct of religious worship or the performance of sacerdotal functions that are described in the income tax regulations as constituting service performed by a minister in the exercise of his ministry. Therefore, we conclude that the duties performed by the taxpayer for [the counseling center] are not service performed in the exercise of his ministry pursuant to . . . the income tax regulations." This ruling is unique in the sense that the IRS limited its analysis to the percentage of the minister's time that was spent performing worship or sacerdotal functions. Such an approach is questionable, since most pastoral ministers (like the pastoral counselor in this case) spend no more than five percent of their time conducting worship or administering the sacraments, and they spend a substantial amount of time engaged in counseling. Clearly, there is a need for the IRS to come up with a better justification for the result reached in this private letter ruling. *IRS Letter Ruling 9124059.*

EXAMPLE. An ordained minister was a full-time counselor for an organization that promoted recovery from addictive disorders, such as alcoholism and drug addiction, through spiritual ministration and counseling. Many of the organization's patients were referred by churches. The minister spent 75 percent of his time engaged in spiritual counseling; 20 percent in administration; and five percent in performing weddings and funerals, prayer services, and adult religious education classes. Under these circumstances the IRS concluded that the minister was not eligible for a housing allowance, since "the facts indicate that only five percent of the minister's working hours are spent performing duties such as the conduct of religious worship or the performance of sacerdotal functions that are described in [the income tax regulations] as constituting service performed by a minister in the exercise of his ministry." *IRS Letter Ruling 9231053.*

EXAMPLE. Pastor B is an ordained minister employed as a counselor by a nonprofit religious organization not associated with any particular church. His employment includes the following services: teaching Bible classes, performing spiritual counseling, conducting seminars and workshops, speaking at churches, acting as a liaison with area churches, preaching, attending ministerial alliance meetings, and conducting staff devotions. Pastor B requested a ruling from the IRS that his services were in the exercise of his ministry and accordingly that he was eligible for a housing allowance exclusion (and the other special tax provisions available to ministers). The IRS concluded that Pastor B was engaged in the performance of services in the exercise of his ministry and was eligible for a housing allowance and the other special tax provisions. It relied on the regulation (quoted above) which specifies that "if a minister is performing service in the conduct of religious worship or the ministration of sacerdotal functions, such service is in the exercise of his ministry whether or not it is performed for a religious organization." The IRS concluded that the services performed by Pastor B were "clearly ministerial in nature" and accordingly that the services he performed on behalf of his employer were in the exercise of his ministry.

This case suggests that a minister serving in a parachurch ministry may be engaged in service performed in the exercise of ministry if his or her job description is amended to reflect the following responsibilities: (1) weekly worship service; (2) weekly religious education classes; (3) religious counseling with employees or supporters as desired; (4) administration of sacraments or sacerdotal functions to employees or supporters as desired; (5) serving as liaison with area churches; (6) staff devotions; and (7) representation of the ministry at ministerial alliance meetings. *IRS Letter Ruling 8825025.*

5. PARACHURCH MINISTRIES

EXAMPLE. The Tax Court ruled that an ordained minister who worked for an evangelical ministry was eligible for a housing allowance. The ministry conducted crusades, produced religious television broadcasts, and published religious literature. The ministry provided the minister with a housing allowance. The IRS claimed that the minister was not eligible for a housing allowance. The income tax regulations specify that a housing allowance must be provided as compensation for ministerial services, and they define ministerial services to include the performance of sacerdotal functions; the conduct of religious worship; and "the control, conduct, and maintenance of religious organizations, under the authority of a religious body constituting a church." The IRS claimed that the minister was not eligible for a housing allowance, since his employer was

not a church, and therefore he was not a minister performing services under the authority of a church.

The Tax Court disagreed. It defined a church as follows: "To classify a religious organization as a church under the Internal Revenue Code, we should look to its religious purposes and, particularly, the means by which its religious purposes are accomplished. . . . At a minimum, a church includes a body of believers or communicants that assembles regularly in order to worship. When bringing people together for worship is only an incidental part of the activities of a religious organization, those limited activities are insufficient to label the entire organization a church." The court concluded that the evangelistic ministry in this case met this definition: "[It] has a far-ranging ministry that reaches its members through television and radio broadcasts, written publications, and crusades. It has loyal followers, some who attended worship services . . . and attended crusades held regularly in various cities. Many . . . were not associated with any other religious organization or denomination. In essence, [it] had the requisite body of believers, and, therefore, [the minister] performed services under the authority of a church. In addition, [he] was 'authorized to administer the sacraments, preach, and conduct services of worship' and was an ordained minister of the gospel." *Whittington v. Commissioner, T.C. Memo. 2000-296 (2000).*

EXAMPLE. An ordained Baptist minister established an exempt organization to produce videotapes to promote world missions. The minister was responsible for the "message" conveyed on the tapes. His other duties included preaching in local church missions conventions and marketing the tapes. He conducts daily worship services for employees of the organization to emphasize the importance of their work, and he performs sacerdotal duties (communion) on occasion. More than 30,000 churches have purchased or used the organization's videos. The organization designated a portion of the minister's compensation as a housing allowance. The IRS audited the minister and determined that he was not eligible for a housing allowance, since his services did not constitute the exercise of ministry. The minister appealed, and the Tax Court ruled that the minister's duties were in the exercise of his ministry and that he qualified for a housing allowance. The court noted that the regulations specify that a minister employed by a separate organization can be engaged in ministerial services (and eligible for a housing allowance) under any of three circumstances: (1) the minister is assigned to the position by a church or denomination; (2) the minister is engaged in the "control, conduct, and maintenance" of a religious organization under the control of a church or denomination; or (3) the minister conducts religious worship or performs sacerdotal functions. The court concluded that the minister did not qualify under the first two tests but that he did under the third test. It emphasized that the minister conducted daily worship services for the employees of the organization and occasionally administered communion. In addition, he preached at local church missions conventions on behalf of the organization. The court acknowledged that these activities comprised only a portion of the minister's duties, but it concluded that this did not matter since his duties as CEO of his parachurch ministry were his primary duties and constituted the performance of sacerdotal functions under the religious tenets of the Baptist faith.

The court relied in part on the testimony of a Baptist professor who testified that some ministers, such as the minister in this case, broaden their ministries beyond the local church to proclaim the gospel through other means (such as videotapes and other media). The professor testified that Baptist churches consider an ordained minister who "seeks to proclaim the Gospel in any fashion to any person or group of persons, or who provides church-related services to congregations," to be functioning as a minister in accordance with the overall purpose of his ordination. The court concluded that the minister in this case was fulfilling his ministry through his organization by producing missions tapes for local congregations. *Mosley v. Commissioner, T.C. Memo. 1994-457 (1994).*

EXAMPLE. An ordained minister was employed by a charitable organization as its Director of Special Services. The organization was neither a religious organization nor an integral agency of a religious organization. As Director of Special Services the minister's basic functions were the directorship of the organization's advisory council and the coordination of its cultural programs. In connection with his position, he occasionally performed certain sacerdotal duties, including the conduct of worship services. The IRS ruled that since the charitable organization was neither a religious organization nor an integral agency of one, the minister's duties did not qualify as those in the administration or maintenance of a religious organization or an integral agency. The IRS acknowledged that while the minister occasionally performed sacerdotal duties, his overall duties were not basically the conduct of religious worship or the ministration of sacerdotal functions as contemplated by the regulations. *Revenue Ruling 68-68. But see Mosley v. Commissioner, T.C. Memo. 1994-457 (1994).*

EXAMPLE. Rabbi L was hired by the United Jewish Appeal (UJA) to serve as its Director of the Rabbinic Advisory Council. The placement bureau of the Rabbinical Assembly, an organization of conservative rabbis, assisted the rabbi in securing this position. Prior to his employment with the UJA, Rabbi L served as a rabbi of various congregations and was provided housing by these congregations. The services Rabbi L performed with the UJA were in substantial part rabbinic in nature. He served as a consultant to the UJA and its staff regarding matters of Jewish law and practices. He functioned as staff chaplain, providing rabbinic counseling to staff and conducting services at meetings. He performed sacerdotal functions, conducting weddings and funerals for the staff and families. He directed religious services and observances at all UJA conferences and meetings and conducted study sessions on Jewish customs and practices for the executive staff of the UJA. He communicated with rabbis around the world

regarding the importance of the concept of charity and enlisted their support for programs sponsored by the UJA. In this respect he conducted seminars for various rabbinic groups and delivered Sabbath sermons to various congregations.

The Tax Court concluded that Rabbi L was engaged in service performed in the exercise of ministry and accordingly was eligible for a housing allowance. It observed: "The services petitioner performed with the UJA, though different than that of a rabbi of a specific congregation, were clearly rabbinic or 'ministerial' in nature. . . . [Rabbi L] performed many religious or sacerdotal functions similar to those performed by a rabbi with a defined congregation. [He] served as staff chaplain to the UJA and its staff, explaining matters of Jewish law and practices and conducting weddings and funerals for the staff and families upon their request. In addition, he directed religious services and observances at all conferences and meetings and conducted study sessions on Jewish customs and practices for the executive staff of the UJA. Thus, based on the entire record, we are convinced that the services petitioner performed for the UJA were in the exercise of his ministry within the meaning of the regulations." *Libman v. Commissioner, 44 T.C.M. 370 (1982).*

6. TEACHERS AND ADMINISTRATORS

➡ TIP. For additional examples involving teachers, see section C.1 of this chapter.

✿ KEY POINT. See the discussion earlier in this chapter on the United States Supreme Court's 2012 decision in the *Hosanna-Tabor* case. This case directly addressed the question of how much time a teacher in a church-affiliated school had to be engaged in religious activities in order to qualify for ministerial status. Significantly, the Court concluded: "The issue before us, however, is not one that can be resolved by a stopwatch. The amount of time an employee spends on particular activities is relevant in assessing that employee's status, but that factor cannot be considered in isolation, without regard to the nature of the religious functions performed."

EXAMPLE. Pastor N is an ordained minister who teaches theology at a church-operated seminary. He rarely conducts religious worship or administers sacerdotal functions. Is he a minister engaged in service performed in the exercise of ministry? The answer is yes. As noted above, the income tax regulations specify that "examples of specific services the performance of which will be considered duties of a minister . . . include . . . the performance of teaching and administrative duties at theological seminaries." *Treas. Reg. § 1.107-1(a).*

EXAMPLE. The IRS ruled that teachers and administrators employed by an interdenominational seminary that was not an integral agency of a particular church or denomination were not engaged in the exercise of ministry and accordingly were not eligible for a housing allowance. The IRS acknowledged that the income tax regulations define "service performed in the exercise of ministry" to include "the performance of teaching and administrative duties at theological seminaries." It further acknowledged that the regulations provide that "services rendered by an ordained minister in the conduct of religious worship or the ministration of sacerdotal functions are considered services in the exercise of a ministry whether or not it is performed for a religious organization or an integral agency thereof." However, the IRS concluded: "[T]he information submitted does not show which religious activities qualify in accordance with the tenets and practices of a particular religious body constituting a church or church denomination. Since the employer is an interdenominational seminary, it is difficult to envision how the duties of the faculty could in any significant amount be said to constitute the conduct of religious worship or the ministration of sacerdotal functions of a particular denomination." *IRS Letter Ruling 7833017.*

EXAMPLE. The IRS ruled that ordained ministers of the gospel who are employed as teachers and administrators by a seminary that is not an integral agency under the authority of a religious body constituting a church or church denomination are not engaged in the exercise of ministry and accordingly are not eligible for a housing allowance (unless they serve by virtue of an assignment from their church or denomination, as explained in the next section of this chapter). *Revenue Ruling 63-90.*

EXAMPLE. The IRS ruled that some full-time teachers employed by parochial schools of a particular church denomination qualified as "duly ordained, commissioned, or licensed ministers of a church" for purposes of federal tax law. The IRS concluded that "the male teachers, although not duly ordained as pastors, are, in performing full time services for the church by teaching, preaching, and, when needed, acting for or assisting an ordained pastor in the conduct of religious services, duly ordained, commissioned, or licensed ministers of a church for purposes of [federal tax law], and that their services are performed in the exercise of their ministry. . . . The female teachers whose services appear to be restricted to the teaching of the religious principles of the church and to the direction of the musical portion of the church services, do not qualify as duly ordained, commissioned, or licensed ministers of a church." *Revenue Ruling 57-107. See also IRS Letter Ruling 7939023. But compare IRS Letter Ruling 8614010.*

EXAMPLE. The IRS ruled that a minister who was employed as an administrator at a religious school was not a minister for federal tax purposes, since the school was not an integral agency of a church. A group of concerned parents joined together for the purpose of establishing a religious school. The articles of incorporation of the school specify that the school is independent and autonomous and not subject to ecclesiastical control from any convention, conference, association, council, group, church, or individual. The administrator's duties included conducting worship services three times each week for the students; ministering to the spiritual needs of parents and students through counseling; preaching in various churches as a representative of the school; attending ministerial meetings as the head of the school; establishing programs for the spiritual, mental, and physical development of students; disciplining the students; and acting as the business agent for the school. The IRS concluded that the school was not an integral agency of a church, and accordingly the administrator was not engaged in the performance of services in the exercise of ministry. The IRS acknowledged that the income tax regulations specify that if a minister is performing service in the conduct of religious worship or the ministration of sacerdotal functions, such service is in the exercise of his ministry whether or not it is performed for a religious organization. However, the IRS noted that while the administrator performed religious services and sacerdotal functions on occasion, his "regular, full-time duties were administrative duties." *IRS Letter Ruling 8646018. But see Mosley v. Commissioner, T.C. Memo. 1994-457 (1994).*

EXAMPLE. An ordained rabbi is employed full time as a religious instructor by a synagogue-controlled private school. In this capacity the rabbi teaches Judaic studies, leads daily worship services with the students in the school, trains students to conduct religious services, teaches students to read the Torah, assists with Bar Mitzvah training, and provides consultation to students, faculty, and administrators of the school with respect to Jewish religious practices. The rabbi also instructs students on the subjects of Jewish law, liturgy, holidays, customs, ethics, and values. The rabbi is a minister, and he is engaged in service performed in the exercise of ministry. Accordingly, he is eligible for a housing allowance. *IRS Letter Ruling 9126048.*

EXAMPLE. The IRS ruled that teachers and administrative staff employed by a church school are not eligible for a housing allowance. A church operates a private school for kindergarten through eighth grade. All of the teachers are certified by the state, and the school is accredited with the state's Department of Education. The school's teachers and administrative staff are not required to attend a Bible college, seminary, or other theological program. Membership in the church is not required to be employed in either teaching or administrative positions, but employees are required to attend a church. The school's board adopted a resolution granting teachers and administrative staff a housing allowance. The school later asked the IRS for a private letter ruling confirming that the teachers and administrative staff were eligible for a housing allowance.

The IRS ruled that the teachers and administrative staff were not eligible for a housing allowance. It observed, "A review of the duties and responsibilities of the teachers and administrative staff reflect the typical duties and responsibilities found in secular schools. These duties do not include duties performed by ministers of the gospel which generally are: performing the Lord's supper, baptism, marriage, moderating of church sessions, sitting on church boards of government, conducting worship services, performing funeral services and ministering to the sick and needy. Ministers of the church are either ordained or licensed. The school states that the teachers and administrative staff are commissioned as ministers of the gospel and that the commissioning took place after the date each employee began his or her duties at school. The commissioning process consists of a job interview and hiring process which culminates in the signing of an employment contract and the first day of work. The school represents that when the board approves the candidate for the teaching or administrative position, they instruct the administrator to commission the candidate by calling him or her to be a teacher or administrative staff member and that the commissioning takes place on each employee's date of hire." The IRS concluded that the teachers and administrative staff were not ministers of the gospel, since they were not ordained, commissioned, or licensed.

While it is true that the church commissioned them as ministers of the gospel, the IRS concluded that this was not sufficient to make them ministers for tax purposes. It explained its decision by referring to a 1968 Tax Court ruling: "In *Kirk v. Commissioner, 51 T.C. 66 (1968)* the Tax Court stated that the term 'commission' means 'the act of committing to the charge of another or an entrusting.' The court held that [a non-ordained church employee] was not commissioned because no congregation or other body of believers was committed to his charge. The duty of spreading the gospel, either by sermon or teaching, was not formally entrusted to his care. He was merely a nonordained church employee. Furthermore, all the services performed by him were of a secular nature." This case suggests that not all teachers and administrative staff employed by church schools are eligible for a housing allowance, especially if (1) they are not required to attend a Bible college, seminary, or other theological training program; (2) membership in the church is not required to be employed in either teaching or administrative positions; (3) all of the services they perform are "of a secular nature"; and (4) "none of the prescribed duties of the teachers and administrative staff are equivalent to the services performed by a church minister."

Of course, some teachers and administrative staff employed by church schools will qualify for a housing allowance. The income tax regulations themselves specify that "examples of specific services the performance of which will be considered duties of a minister . . . include . . . the performance of teaching and administrative duties at theological seminaries." *IRS Letter Ruling 200318002 (2003).*

EXAMPLE. The IRS ruled that a university was an integral agency of a religious denomination, and therefore its faculty, managers, executives, and administrators who were ordained, licensed, or commissioned ministers were eligible for a housing allowance.

The IRS based its ruling on the following factors: (1) The university is an official regional school of the denomination. (2) The denomination exercises indirect control over the university. While it does not appoint each member of the board, it does appoint 15 members that comprise a majority of the board. (3) The university's president is also a member of the board and must be approved by the board of directors of the denomination. (4) Even though the trustees and the employees of the university are not required to be members of the denomination, they must affirm their agreement with the denomination's Statement of Faith and offer to resign if they no longer agree with it. (5) The denomination approves all amendments to the university's articles of incorporation, bylaws, and mission statement. (6) The university teaches all subjects from a biblical perspective, and its graduate degree programs prepare men and women for positions as pastors, missionaries, and other religious posts. "Accordingly," the IRS concluded, "the denomination exercises indirect control over the university." (7) The university is required to provide annual reports, financial statements, and annual audits to the denomination. (8) During the three previous fiscal years, the university received contributions from the denomination totaling 12.8 percent of the total gifts it received during that period. (9) The university's articles of incorporation specify that if it were to cease operations, dissolve, or terminate its affiliation with the denomination, its property would become the property of the denomination. "Accordingly," the IRS concluded, "the university is an integral agency of the denomination."

The IRS further noted: "An, ordained, commissioned or licensed minister who is performing services in the control, conduct or maintenance of an integral agency of a religious organization is engaged in performing services in the exercise of his ministry. . . . Revenue Rulings 70-549 and 71-7 hold that ministers who serve on the faculty of a college that is an integral agency of a church but do not perform any ecclesiastical duties are engaged in performing services in the exercise of their ministry and hence are eligible to exclude a portion of their compensation as a rental allowance under section 107 of the Code. Revenue Ruling 62-171 holds that ordained ministers of the gospel who teach or have positions involving administrative and overall management duties in parochial schools, colleges or universities which are integral agencies of religious organizations are performing duties as ministers of the gospel for purposes of section 107 of the Code and hence are eligible to exclude a portion of their compensation as a rental allowance. In the present case, the university is an integral agency of the denomination. Accordingly, ordained, commissioned, or licensed ministers of the denomination who teach or serve in faculty, executive, management, or administrative positions are performing services in the exercise of their ministry for purposes of section 107 of the Code. The ministers are therefore entitled to exclude from their gross income amounts that are properly designated as rental allowances under section 107 of the Code and the applicable regulations." *IRS Private Letter Ruling 200803008 (2007).*

c. MINISTERS EMPLOYED BY INTEGRAL AGENCIES OR ON ASSIGNMENT

The income tax regulations contain two special definitions of the phrase "service performed in the exercise of ministry." These are explained on the following pages.

1. INTEGRAL AGENCIES OF A CHURCH OR DENOMINATION

If a minister is performing service for an organization which is operated as an integral agency of a religious organization under the authority of a religious body constituting a church or church denomination, all service performed by the minister in the conduct of religious worship, in the ministration of sacerdotal functions, or in the control, conduct, and maintenance of such organization is in the exercise of his ministry. What is an integral agency of a church or religious denomination? The IRS (in Revenue Ruling 72-606) has listed eight criteria to be considered in determining whether a particular institution is an integral agency of a religious organization:

(1) whether the religious organization incorporated the institution;

(2) whether the corporate name of the institution indicates a church relationship;

(3) whether the religious organization continuously controls, manages, and maintains the institution;

(4) whether the trustees or directors of the institution are approved by or must be approved by the religious organization or church;

(5) whether trustees or directors may be removed by the religious organization or church;

(6) whether annual reports of finances and general operations are required to be made to the religious organization or church;

(7) whether the religious organization or church contributes to the support of the institution; and

(8) whether, in the event of dissolution of the institution, its assets would be turned over to the religious organization or church.

EXAMPLE. Pastor T is an ordained minister employed in an administrative capacity by a nursing home. The institution is affiliated with but not controlled by a religious denomination. Although the old-age home had a corporate name that implied a church relationship and its articles of incorporation directed that upon dissolution all assets would be turned over to the sponsoring denomination, these facts were not sufficient to support a finding that the home was an integral agency of the denomination. Pastor T's administrative services in the control, conduct, and maintenance of the institution are not service performed in the exercise of ministry. Accordingly, he does not qualify for a housing allowance or any of the other special rules summarized above. *Revenue Ruling 72-606. See also IRS Letter Ruling 8329042.*

EXAMPLE. A college was ruled to be an integral agency of a church because of the following factors: (1) the board of directors of the college was indirectly controlled by the church because each board member had to be a member in good standing of the congregation; (2) every teacher was a member in good standing of the congregation; (3) the majority of students were members of the church; (4) all subjects taught at the college, whether in natural science, mathematics, social science, languages, etc., were taught with emphasis on religious principles and religious living; and (5) the college had a department which performed all the functions for ministerial training that a seminary offers. Accordingly, ordained ministers employed in teaching or administrative positions at the college were engaged in the exercise of ministry and were eligible for the special benefits (including a housing allowance) discussed above. *Revenue Ruling 70-549. See also IRS Technical Advice Memorandum 9033002, and IRS Letter Rulings 5907134570A, 7907160, 8011047, 8004087, 80929145, 8922077, 9144047, and 9608027.*

EXAMPLE. Pastor F is an ordained minister who serves as a professor of religion at Texas Christian University. He occasionally officiates at weddings, preaches sermons, and performs other sacerdotal functions, but these activities are not part of his employment at the university. The university has a close relationship with the Christian church (Disciples of Christ), but the church does not control or manage the university either directly or indirectly. In fact, the university only satisfies the last of the five factors listed in Revenue Ruling 70-549 (see preceding example). In addition, the university satisfies only two of the eight criteria cited in Revenue Ruling 72-606 (cited above). Accordingly, the university is not an integral agency of the church, and Pastor F is not eligible for any of the special provisions discussed above (including a housing allowance). Since he was not working for an integral agency of a church, he had to satisfy all three elements of the definition of "service performed by a minister in the exercise of his ministry" in order to qualify. He failed to satisfy all three elements with respect to his employment by the university. *Flowers v. Commissioner, 82-1 USTC para. 9114 (N.D. Tex. 1981).*

EXAMPLE. Pastor B, a duly ordained minister, is engaged by a public university to teach history. She performs no other service for the university, although from time to time she performs marriages and conducts funerals for relatives and friends. The university is neither a religious organization nor operated as an integral agency of a religious organization. Pastor B is not performing services for the university pursuant to an assignment or designation by her ecclesiastical superiors. The service performed by Pastor B for the university is not in the exercise of ministry. However, service performed by Pastor B in performing marriages and conducting funerals is in the exercise of ministry. Only as to the latter kinds of services will the four special tax provisions apply.

EXAMPLE. The IRS ruled that a minister who was employed as a guidance counselor and teacher by a church-affiliated school was eligible for a housing allowance. The IRS concluded that the school was an integral agency of six sponsoring churches, and therefore the services performed by the minister on behalf of the school were in the exercise of his ministry and qualified for a housing allowance.

The IRS based this conclusion on a 1972 ruling in which it listed eight criteria to consider in deciding whether a church-related institution is an integral agency of the church. *Revenue Ruling 72-606.* The IRS concluded that the school was an integral agency of the sponsoring churches: "Each of the six sponsoring congregations appoint [sic] two of their members to serve on the school board, and each is free to remove and/or replace its own representatives at will. The sponsoring congregations, through their respectively appointed board members, establish school policies, purchase equipment and supplies, maintain facilities, as well as approve and sign teacher contracts. The school board elects its own trustees and officers from among the board members appointed by the congregations. Each member of the school's staff is required to sign a 'Statement of Faith' embracing church doctrine. The treasurer of the school board presents monthly financial statements to the school board, and it is the responsibility of the members to report the financial operations of the school back to their respective congregations. The six sponsoring congregations provide annual cash contributions to the school. Additionally, four of the sponsoring congregations house branches of the school in their church facilities. In the event of dissolution of the school, its assets would become the sole property of the sponsoring congregations." As a result, the minister was eligible for a housing allowance. *IRS Letter Ruling 200002040.*

EXAMPLE. Pastor W works in an administrative capacity for the headquarters of his religious denomination. Such employment constitutes service performed in the exercise of ministry even if

Pastor W does not perform sacerdotal functions or conduct religious worship as part of his employment, since he is engaged in the control, conduct, and maintenance of a church organization. *Revenue Ruling 57-129.*

EXAMPLE. The IRS ruled that a faculty member at a church-affiliated college qualified for a housing allowance since the college was an integral agency of a religious denomination under the criteria enumerated in IRS Revenue Ruling 72-606 (see above). In particular, the IRS noted:

- The denomination instigated and approved the university's incorporation.
- The university is named in honor of the denomination's founder and is the official regional school of the denomination.
- The denomination exercises indirect control over the university. While it does not appoint each member of the university's board, it does appoint 15 members that comprise a majority of the board. Trustees may also be removed by a majority of the board. The university's president is also a member of the board and must be approved by the board of directors of the denomination. Even though the trustees and the employees of the university are not required to be members of the denomination, they must affirm their agreement with the denomination's statement of faith and offer to resign if they no longer agree with it. The denomination approves all amendments to the university's articles of incorporation, bylaws, and mission statement. Finally, the university teaches all subjects from a Biblical perspective and its graduate degree programs prepare men and women for positions as pastors, missionaries, and other religious posts. Accordingly, "the denomination exercises indirect control over the university."
- The university also meets the financial and reporting criteria set forth in Revenue Ruling 72-606. The university is required to provide annual reports, financial statements, and annual audits to the denomination. During the previous three fiscal years the university received contributions from the denomination totaling 12.8 percent of the total gifts it received during that period. Finally, the articles of incorporation provide that if the university were to cease operations, dissolve, or terminate its affiliation with the denomination without permission from the denomination, its property would become property of the denomination. Accordingly, we conclude that the University is an integral agency of the denomination.

The IRS concluded: "In the present case, the university is an integral agency of the denomination. Accordingly, ordained, commissioned, or licensed ministers who teach or serve in faculty, executive, management, or administrative positions are performing services in the exercise of their ministry for purposes of section 107 of the Code. The ministers are therefore entitled to exclude from their gross income amounts that are properly designated as rental allowances under section 107 of the Code and the applicable regulations." *IRS Private Letter Ruling 200925001 (2009).*

EXAMPLE. A church-affiliated family-services ministry was organized to provide homes for orphaned children as well as foster-care services. The IRS concluded that it was sufficiently related to its sponsoring church to be an "integral agency," and therefore ministers employed as "managers, executives, supervisors, and administrators" were eligible for a housing allowance. The IRS concluded, on the basis of the criteria listed in Revenue Ruling 72-606, that the ministry was an integral agency of the church. As a result, ministers employed by the ministry as "managers, executives, supervisors, or administrators" were eligible for a housing allowance on the basis of section 1.1402(c)-5 of the tax regulations, which specifies that an ordained, commissioned or licensed minister who is performing services in the control, conduct or maintenance of an integral agency of a religious organization is engaged in performing services in the exercise of his ministry. *IRS Letter Ruling 201023008 (2010).*

2. ASSIGNMENTS

As noted above, the income tax regulations specify that if a minister, pursuant to an assignment or designation by a religious body constituting his church, performs service for an organization which is neither a religious organization nor operated as an integral agency of religious organization, all service performed by him, even though such service may not involve the conduct of religious worship or the ministration of sacerdotal functions, is in the exercise of his ministry.

The regulations further provide that "if a minister is performing service for an organization which is neither a religious organization nor operated as an integral agency of a religious organization and the service is not performed pursuant to an assignment or designation by his ecclesiastical superiors, then only the service performed by him in the conduct of religious worship or the ministration of sacerdotal functions is in the exercise of his ministry."

The regulations contain the following two examples:

EXAMPLE. M, a duly ordained minister, is assigned by X, the religious body constituting his church, to perform advisory service to Y Company in connection with the publication of a book dealing with the history of M's church denomination. Y is neither a religious organization nor operated as an integral agency of a religious organization. M performs no other service for X or Y. M is performing service in the exercise of his ministry.

EXAMPLE. M, a duly ordained minister, is engaged by N University to teach history and mathematics. He performs no other service for N, although from time to time he performs marriages and conducts funerals for relatives and friends. N University is neither a religious organization nor operated as an integral agency of a religious organization. M is not performing the service for N pursuant to an assignment or designation by his ecclesiastical superiors. The service performed by M for N University is not in the exercise of his ministry. However, service performed by M in performing marriages and conducting funerals is in the exercise of his ministry.

Rulings

The IRS and the courts have addressed "assignments" of ministers in a few rulings that are summarized below.

Boyer v. Commissioner, 69 T.C. 521 (1977)

The *Boyer* case is the leading judicial interpretation of the assignment language in the regulations. In the autumn of 1969 Pastor Boyer, a Methodist minister, began teaching data processing at a community college having no affiliation with the United Methodist Church. At the end of his first year of teaching at this college, Pastor Boyer had the college send his ordaining body (Annual Conference) a letter requesting that he be assigned to the college as a professor. The Conference sent the college a letter appointing Pastor Boyer as professor but did not negotiate with the college as to Pastor Boyer's salary or duties and paid no portion of his compensation. The purpose of this appointment was to qualify Pastor Boyer for a housing allowance. The Tax Court, in rejecting Pastor Boyer's eligibility for a housing allowance, remarked:

[Pastor Boyer] began teaching at [the college] in 1969; [the college] requested his assignment . . . in May 1970, after he had completed an academic year at the institution. His assignment . . . was virtually pro forma—the ratification by the church of employment previously begun. In contrast, we believe that the "assignment" referred to in the regulations must be significant, in that the minister must have been assigned by the church for reasons directly related to the accomplishment of purposes of the church. Unless we read these regulations to require a genuine church-related purpose in the church's assignment of the minister, bootstrapping of the type attempted here by petitioner would enable any ordained minister, merely by obtaining a pro forma "assignment" after he secures secular employment, to qualify for the ministerial rental exclusion. The special benefits of section 107 would follow him through a purely secular career. We do not believe that Congress intended any such result. More is required than mere ordained status and the perfunctory ratification by religious authority of secular employment obtained by the minister for non-church related reasons.

The court further concluded that the regulations "contain an implicit requirement that the assignment by the church must be to further the purposes of the church" and that Pastor Boyer's assignment to the college "did not qualify as an assignment which transformed his secular duties at a state university school into service in the exercise of his ministry."

This case suggests that an assignment of a minister by his or her ordaining body, to satisfy the requirements of the regulations, must satisfy two requirements: (1) the assignment must precede and initiate the minister's new work assignment; and (2) the assignment must be directly related to the accomplishment of the purposes of the church or other ordaining body. Retroactive assignments, occurring after a minister has served for a period of time in a new position, do not fulfill these requirements. As the court noted, more is required than "pro forma" assignments involving little more than "perfunctory ratification by religious authority."

Tanenbaum v. Commissioner, 58 T.C. 1 (1972)

A rabbi was employed by the American Jewish Committee as its National Director of Interreligious Affairs. The Tax Court ruled that he was not eligible for a housing allowance, since his duties did not involve the conduct of religious worship or the performance of sacerdotal functions. The court made the following comments regarding assignment:

> In addition, the [rabbi] was not assigned to the American Jewish Committee by any religious body constituting his "church." In accepting his position with the American Jewish Committee, he functioned as an independent contractor, separate and apart from any association with a religious group.

> The [rabbi] argues that the [assignment] test cannot be met by him because the Jewish faith does not have a hierarchical order, and consequently, does not assign rabbis to occupy positions such as his. He contends that this test focuses primarily upon the type of activity involved and that his work with the American Jewish Committee is of a type covered by the regulation. We cannot agree. The [assignment] test unequivocally requires that the [minister] be working "pursuant to an assignment or designation by a religious body constituting his church" . . . and in the instant case the [rabbi] clearly was not.

This case demonstrates that an "assignment" is not effective unless a religious body has the authority to assign a minister to a position in furtherance of its mission and does so on its own initiative (rather than merely ratifying a position the minister unilaterally secures). Many Protestant churches and denominations have no legal or ecclesiastical authority to assign ministers to any position, and any attempt by them to do so would be ineffective. The organizational documents of a church or denominational agency should be reviewed carefully to determine whether it has the authority to assign ministers. Further, the practice of the church or denominational agency should be studied. Does it have an established practice of assigning ministers to their positions? If not, it is unlikely that any assignment would be recognized by the courts or by the IRS.

Libman v. Commissioner, 44 T.C.M. 370 (1982)

The Tax Court ruled that a rabbi employed by the United Jewish Appeal was eligible for a housing allowance because he performed ministerial duties and not because of any assignment. The court rejected the validity of a purported assignment of the rabbi by his "Rabbinical Assembly," since it lacked any authority to assign rabbis. The court observed that "since the Jewish faith does not have a hierarchical order and consequently does not assign rabbis to occupy positions such as this (although rabbinic organizations may assist in placement), under a strict reading of the regulation it is difficult for [the rabbi] or someone similarly situated to pass this test."

Once again, the implication is clear—religious bodies cannot assign clergy in order to qualify them for a housing allowance unless they have the ecclesiastical authority to do so and this authority is validated by actual practice.

Letter Ruling 8520043

The IRS concluded that a purported assignment of a minister by his church to teach at a college was not effective and did not qualify the minister for a housing allowance. The minister found and accepted his position as a teacher at the college before he was ordained. Shortly after accepting the teaching position, the minister was ordained. His ordaining body approved of his work at the college and gave him annual permission to continue. The IRS observed:

> The assignment envisaged in the regulations is more than a formality. In the case of Boyer v. Commissioner, 69 T.C. 521 (1977), a minister found employment as a teacher at a university on his own and later received an "assignment" from his church to that position. In concluding that the "assignment" was not of the type envisaged by the regulations, the court stated as follows:

> His assignment . . . was virtually pro forma—the ratification by the church of employment previously began. In contrast, we believe that the "assignment" referred to in the regulations must be significant, in that the minister must have been assigned by the church for reasons directly related to the accomplishment of purposes of the church. . . . More is required than mere ordained status and the perfunctory ratification by religious authority of secular employment obtained by the minister for non-church-related reasons.

> From the facts submitted it is apparent that [your church's] approval or ratification of your work at the college is not an assignment within the meaning of . . . the regulations.

This ruling represents another example of a purported assignment of a minister to a position that the minister previously secured on his own initiative. This does not meet the requirement of the regulations that the assignment must establish the minister's new position rather than ratify it after the minister on his or her own initiative has already secured it.

Letter Ruling 8826043

The IRS ruled that a pastoral counselor employed by a counseling center was not eligible for a housing allowance despite a purported assignment by his ordaining church. The church, in a letter to the minister, expressed its support of the minister's counseling practice; expressed its desire to support the minister in his counseling; and endorsed him as a counselor through the counseling practice in order to further the efforts and mission of the church. The IRS observed:

> *Applying the regulations as interpreted in* Boyer v. Commissioner *to the facts in this situation, we conclude that the services the minister performs through his counseling practice do not qualify as services in the performance of his ministry. [The regulations require] that services that are not performed for a religious organization be performed pursuant to an assignment or designation by the church. In your case, we find that the counseling services the minister performs are not pursuant to an assignment or designation by the church. Although the church states it commissions and endorses the minister in his counseling practice, this does not constitute an assignment or designation by the church. The church is supportive of the minister's counseling practice, but we find no evidence to suggest that the church specifically assigned the minister to perform such counseling services on its behalf. Also, it does not appear that the counseling services the minister performs are to directly further the purposes of the church. The minister performs his services free from the church's control, and he states his purpose is to meet human needs as effectively as possible, using the principles and teachings of his church. The intent of the counseling services is not to further any of the church's purposes (although the church may benefit from the minister's counseling). While the minister may provide his counseling services based on his church's religious beliefs, this does not meet the requirement that the minister be assigned to perform his services in order for them to qualify as services performed in the exercise of his ministry. [Emphases added.]*

In this ruling the IRS interpreted the assignment language of the regulations to require that (1) the assignment must result in services being performed by the minister "on behalf of" the assigning church; (2) the assignment must "directly further the purposes of the church"; (3) the assigned minister, in the performance of his or her duties, must intend to further the church's purposes; and (4) the assigned minister's services must remain subject to the assigning church's control.

Letter Ruling 8930038

The IRS reaffirmed its ruling in Letter Ruling 8826043 (summarized above) and rejected the minister's claim that a valid assignment can be inferred from the actions of his church. The IRS, in rejecting this view, observed:

> *Furthermore, the information provided states that counseling practice was originally associated with the church until the minister established the counseling practice as a sole proprietorship. As stated in a letter from the church to the minister, it was a shared goal of the church and the minister to make the counseling practice an independent counseling ministry in which the minister performs his services free from the church's control. The minister states that as a matter of religious doctrine, the church does not assign or designate its ministers to any particular work. However, while counseling may be viewed as an integral element by the church of its mission for the community, the services are performed for the general public as well as for church members and in this case is also conducted for purposes of financial independence.*

Conclusions

Based on the legal precedent reviewed above, a minister's eligibility for a housing allowance should not be based on an "assignment" unless the assignment satisfies the following conditions:

- The church or denominational agency that assigned the minister has the authority, by virtue of its organizational documents, to assign ministers to their positions.
- The church or denominational agency that assigned the minister has a history of assigning ministers to their positions.
- The church or denominational agency assigned the minister to a particular position solely on its initiative.
- The assignment establishes the employment relationship between the minister and his or her employer.
- The assignment results in services being performed by the minister on behalf of the assigning church or denominational agency.
- The assigned minister, in the performance of his or her duties, intends to further the purposes of the assigning church or denominational agency.
- The assignment directly furthers the purposes of the assigning church or denominational agency.
- The assigned minister's services are subject to the control of the church or denominational agency that assigned him or her.

EXAMPLE. Pastor C, a duly ordained minister, is assigned by his religious denomination to perform advisory service to a publishing company in connection with the publication of a book dealing with the history of the denomination. The publisher is neither a religious organization nor operated as an integral agency of a religious organization. Pastor C performs no other service for his denomination or the publisher. He is performing service in the exercise of ministry, and accordingly he is eligible for all of the four special tax provisions discussed in this chapter.

To summarize, this means that (1) he is eligible for a housing allowance exclusion; (2) he must pay self-employment taxes (the Social Security tax for self-employed individuals) rather than FICA taxes, assuming that he is not exempt; (3) if he is exempt from Social Security taxes (because his timely exemption application was approved by the IRS), then he pays no self-employment tax on compensation received from the publisher; and (4) his wages are not subject to federal income tax withholding, meaning that he must report and pay his income taxes (and self-employment taxes, if applicable) using the estimated tax procedure (Form 1040-ES).

D. MINISTERS' SPOUSES

Some churches have issued credentials to the spouses of ministers, often at the request of a minister in an attempt to achieve tax "benefits" for the spouse. For example, a church or denomination "licenses" a minister's spouse so the spouse will be eligible for a housing allowance with respect to distributions from the minister's retirement account following the minister's death. Note the following considerations.

First, the IRS has always maintained that churches and denominations can issue ministerial credentials to anyone they choose. As a result, no one will ever challenge or question the inherent right of a church to confer ministerial credentials. But whether the IRS or the courts will recognize a person as a minister for tax purposes is another matter. So, to the extent that the sole purpose for providing ministerial credentials to ministers' spouses is to enable them to receive housing allowances following the death of a minister spouse, this is an issue that ultimately would be determined by the IRS and the courts.

Second, the IRS ruled in 1972 that church pension boards cannot designate housing allowances for the surviving spouses of deceased ministers. *Revenue Ruling 72-249.* The IRS observed:

Prior to his retirement and death the husband was a minister of the gospel and pastor of a church. Shortly before he retired, in recognition of his years of past service, the church, through official action of its governing body, authorized the payment of a specific amount each month upon retirement, to be paid for so long as he lived with survivor benefits for his wife. The authorization designated a portion of the payment as a rental allowance. The wife was not a minister of the gospel and she did not perform any services for the church. . . . Until his death, and to the extent used to provide a home, the rental allowance paid to the retired minister was excludable from his gross income since it was paid as part of his compensation for past services and it was paid pursuant to official action of his church. However, the rental allowance exclusion does not apply to amounts paid to his widow since it does not represent compensation for services performed by her as a minister of the gospel. Accordingly, in the instant case, it is held that the rental allowance exclusion does not apply to amounts paid by the church to the minister's wife.

This ruling provides definitive guidance. Eligibility for a housing allowance requires that

- the recipient is a minister, and
- the allowance represents compensation for services performed in the exercise of ministry.

A minister's spouse who is granted ministerial credentials by a church or denomination may satisfy the first requirement but not necessarily the second. The second requirement is satisfied only if the housing allowance represents compensation for services performed in the exercise of ministry (as defined above) by the spouse *after* he or she was granted ministerial credentials.

EXAMPLE. A denominational pension plan asked the IRS for a ruling on the taxability of retirement benefits designated as a housing allowance to be received by a retired minister or a spouse beneficiary of a deceased minister. The IRS referred to Revenue Ruling 72-249 (see above) and concluded, "A housing allowance received by a retired minister from [a church pension board] may be excluded from his or her gross income to the extent allowed by section 107 of the tax code and the regulations thereunder. However, a housing allowance payable through [the pension board] to the spouse beneficiary of a deceased minister is includable in the gross income of that spouse beneficiary." *IRS Letter Ruling 8404101 (1984).*

EXAMPLE. A church grants a ministerial license to Susan, the 60-year-old wife of Pastor Ron. Susan wanted ministerial credentials so that retirement distributions she will receive from her husband's pension fund following his death could be designated as a nontaxable housing allowance. Susan has never received compensation for ministerial services. This arrangement will not work. The church or denominational pension plan cannot designate a portion of Pastor Ron's retirement income as a housing allowance following his death, since this does not represent compensation earned by Susan in the exercise of ministry following her receipt of ministerial credentials.

EXAMPLE. Same facts as the previous example. Susan insists that she assisted her husband throughout his ministry and performed essential ministerial functions. Does this mean the church pension fund can designate some or all of the payments made to her from her husband's account as a housing allowance following his death? No, it does not, since she was not a minister until she was 60 years of age, and thus all of the services she performed prior to that time do not count. Further, she received no compensation for any of these services and did not contribute to her own retirement fund, so there are no funds out of which a housing allowance can be declared for her.

EXAMPLE. Pastor Andy and his wife Emily are both ordained pastors. They serve as co-pastors of a church. Both are compensated for the performance of ministerial duties, and both contribute some of their compensation to a church pension fund. At her retirement, Emily can have the pension board designate some or all of the distributions from her account as a housing allowance (subject to applicable legal limits), since she meets both of the requirements for a housing allowance. She is a minister, and the housing allowance represents compensation for services she performed in the exercise of ministry following her receipt of ministerial credentials.

E. RELIGIOUS ORDERS

The tax code exempts from Social Security taxes and income tax withholding "services performed . . . by a member of a religious order in the exercise of duties required by such order." Neither the tax code nor the income tax regulations defines the term "religious order." To provide some certainty regarding the definition of a religious order, the IRS has identified seven characteristics that traditionally have been associated with religious orders. *IRS Revenue Procedure 91-20.* The IRS came up with this list by reviewing the court decisions that have addressed the issue. Here are the seven characteristics:

> *(1) The organization is described in section 501(c)(3) of the Code. (2) The members of the organization vow to live under a strict set of rules requiring moral and spiritual self-sacrifice and dedication to the goals of the organization at the expense of their material well-being. (3) The members of the organization, after successful completion of the organization's training program and probationary period, make a long-term commitment to the organization (normally, more than two years). (4) The organization is, directly or indirectly, under the control and supervision of a church or convention or association of churches, or is significantly funded by a church or convention or association of churches. (5) The members of the organization normally live together as part of a community and are held to a significantly stricter level of moral and religious discipline than that required of lay church members. (6) The members of the organization work or serve full-time on behalf of the religious, educational, or charitable goals of the organization, (7) The members of the organization participate regularly in activities such as public or private prayer, religious study, teaching, care of the aging, missionary work, or church reform or renewal.*

The IRS has stated that "generally, the presence of all the above characteristics is determinative that the organization is a religious order" and that "the absence of one or more of the other enumerated characteristics is not necessarily determinative in a particular case.

Generally, if application of the above characteristics to the facts of a particular case does not clearly indicate whether or not the organization is a religious order, the [IRS] will contact the appropriate authorities affiliated with the organization for their views concerning the characteristics of the organization and their views will be carefully considered." *Revenue Ruling 91-20. See also IRS Letter Ruling 9219012 (an organization was a religious order though it did not satisfy one of the seven criteria) and IRS Letter Rulings 9418012 and 9630011 (evangelical organizations were religious orders though they were not directly or indirectly under the control and supervision of a church or convention or association of churches or significantly funded by a church or convention or association of churches).*

It is interesting that one of the cases the IRS relied on involved a claim by a Baptist church that the services of its church secretary, organist, custodian, and choir director were exempt from tax withholding since the church was a religious order. In rejecting the church's claim, the court defined a "religious order" as "a religious body typically an aggregate of separate communities living under a distinctive rule, discipline or constitution; a monastic brotherhood or society." *Eighth Street Baptist Church, Inc. v. United States, 295 F. Supp. 1400 (D. Kan. 1969).*

Under the current IRS definition, few organizations will be able to justify an exemption from FICA or income tax withholding on the ground that they are religious orders. Organizations that currently are relying upon an exemption from FICA coverage or the income tax withholding rules on the basis of religious order status should carefully review the current IRS definition to assess its impact.

EXAMPLE. X is a nonprofit corporation organized and operated for the purpose of providing Christian education of the young, and care of the sick and elderly, in accordance with the historic beliefs of Y Church. Specifically, X provides Christian education in the form of small, self-supporting schools or missionary training centers. The underlying religious philosophy of that educational approach is that Christians should learn to live independently of the world's support and work cooperatively to support each other. Education at X is part academic and part vocational. Students, faculty, and staff learn and maintain their independence by building and maintaining their campus, growing their own food, and taking care of the sick and elderly in the surrounding community. The educational program also includes intensive religious instruction, worship, and service. Members of X agree to donate their services without compensation and acknowledge that any compensation paid for services they perform as directed by X belongs to X. X represents that members of X are under a vow of poverty. The IRS concluded that X was a religious order, since it "possesses the characteristics in Revenue Procedure 91-20 [quoted above] to a substantial degree." As a result, (1) X and its members were not subject to FICA tax on compensation (including goods, services, and cash allowances) received by a member for services performed in the exercise of duties required by X; (2) X was not liable for FICA tax withholding on compensation it provided to its members for services performed in the exercise of duties required by X; and (3) X was not liable for federal income tax withholding on compensation it paid to its members for services performed in the exercise of duties required by X. *IRS Letter Ruling 199938013.*

EXAMPLE. X is a nonprofit organization that exists for the purpose of propagating the gospel of Jesus Christ. It is exempt from federal income taxes under section 501(c)(3) of the tax code. X also has been recognized by the IRS as an ordaining institution and has a group exemption letter. X operates Y to carry out the goals of X. Y is under the control and supervision of a Church. The Church is the mother church of the numerous churches operating under X. Church and other churches operated under X provide the funding of Y. Prospective members of Y go through a six-year training program and a probationary period before they are admitted as members. The training program includes 15 hours of instruction per week, daily prayer and study, and daily participation in the ministry. Members are held to a strict level of moral and spiritual discipline, which requires daily prayer and communion with other members and prohibits the ownership of material possessions. They pledge to work full time on behalf of X for the rest of their lives, during which time their lives are not their own but are to be separated sacrificially and entirely in dedication to the goals of X. They are to live their lives in servitude and in obedience to all the commands of God. Members reside within 2 miles of the Church in parsonages owned by Church. There, the members conduct themselves as a community by participating daily with each other in the spiritual disciplines of prayer, study, and communion. Members give themselves continually to prayer, study, teaching, counseling, care of the weak, missionary work, and evangelism. The IRS concluded that "Y possesses all the characteristics in Revenue Procedure 91-20 [quoted above] to a substantial degree. Accordingly, based on our consideration of all the facts and circumstances, we conclude that Y is a religious order for federal tax purposes." *IRS Letter Ruling 199937013.*

Chapter 4 — INCOME

When a man works, his wages are not credited to him as a gift, but as an obligation.

Romans 4:4

CHAPTER HIGHLIGHTS

■ ***Income.*** Income includes much more than a salary. It may also include several other items, such as the following:

- bonuses,
- Christmas and special-occasion offerings,
- retirement gifts,
- the portion of a minister's Social Security tax paid by a church,
- personal use of a church-provided car,
- purchases of church property for less than fair market value,
- rental income,
- interest income,
- some forms of pension income,
- some reimbursements of a spouse's travel expenses,
- forgiven debts,
- severance pay,
- "love gifts,"
- embezzled funds,
- church-paid trips to the Holy Land, and
- nonaccountable reimbursements of a minister's business expenses.

■ ***Unreasonable compensation.*** Churches that pay "unreasonable compensation" to a minister jeopardize their tax-exempt status.

■ ***Intermediate sanctions.*** The IRS can impose an excise tax against a "disqualified person," and in some cases against church board members individually, if excessive compensation is paid to the disqualified person. Most senior pastors will meet the definition of a disqualified person. These taxes are substantial (up to 225 percent of the amount of compensation the IRS determines to be in excess of reasonable compensation). As a result, governing boards or other bodies that determine clergy compensation should be prepared to document any amount that may be viewed by the IRS as excessive. This includes salary, fringe benefits, and special-occasion gifts. If in doubt, the opinion of a tax attorney should be obtained.

■ ***Automatic excess benefits.*** The IRS deems any taxable fringe benefit provided to an officer or director of a tax-exempt charity (including a church), or a relative of such a person, to be an automatic excess benefit that may trigger intermediate sanctions, regardless of the amount of the benefit, unless the benefit was timely reported as taxable income by either the recipient or the employer.

■ ***Social Security income.*** Persons who are retired and who earn more than a specified amount of income may be taxed on some of their Social Security benefits.

■ ***Loans to ministers.*** Churches that make low-interest or no-interest loans to ministers may be violating state nonprofit corporation law. These kinds of loans also result in taxable income for the minister.

■ ***Discretionary funds.*** Many churches have established a fund that can be distributed by a minister in his or her sole discretion. Such discretionary funds can inadvertently result in taxable income for the minister if they are unrestricted.

■ ***Reimbursement of spouse's travel.*** Church reimbursements of a spouse's travel expenses incurred while accompanying an employee on a business trip represent taxable income for the employee unless the spouse's presence serves a legitimate business purpose and the spouse's expenses are reimbursed under an accountable arrangement.

■ ***Splitting income with a spouse.*** Many ministers have attempted to shift their church income to a spouse in order to achieve a tax benefit. These benefits include (1) reducing the impact on the minister of the annual earnings test that reduces the Social Security benefits of individuals between 62 and 65 years of age who earn more than specified amounts of annual income; and (2) lower tax rates. Income shifting often does not work because the arrangement lacks "economic reality." Ministers who have engaged in income shifting or who are considering doing so should carefully evaluate their circumstances in light of the information in this chapter.

INTRODUCTION

Your Form 1040 begins (lines 7–22) with the reporting of gross income. This chapter will summarize those items of gross income that are of greatest relevance to ministers.

The tax code excludes several items from gross income. These exclusions (including the housing allowance) will be considered in Chapters 5 and 6. Exclusions are not reported on your tax return. After computing your gross income, you are permitted to claim certain adjustments that reduce gross income. Gross income less the total of all available adjustments yields adjusted gross income (AGI). AGI is an important figure for several reasons. AGI and the various adjustments of greatest relevance to ministers are discussed in Chapter 7.

It is beyond question that ministers must report and pay federal income taxes on their taxable income. A number of ministers have attempted, unsuccessfully, to evade taxes through reliance on a variety of theories. Many of these theories are reviewed in Chapter 1, section A.1. The penalties for refusing to file income tax returns and for adopting frivolous positions on filed returns are reviewed in Chapter 1, section A.14.

A. GENERAL CONSIDERATIONS

Before addressing specific items of income, three preliminary issues must be addressed: (1) unreasonable compensation, (2) revenue based compensation arrangements, and (3) intermediate sanctions.

1. UNREASONABLE COMPENSATION

✿ **KEY POINT.** Churches that pay "unreasonable compensation" to a minister jeopardize their tax-exempt status.

One of the requirements for exemption from income taxation under section 501(c)(3) of the tax code is that no part of the net earnings of the church "inures to the benefit of any private shareholder or individual" other than reasonable compensation for services rendered. As a result, a church will jeopardize its tax-exempt status if it pays unreasonable compensation to an employee.

Loss of exempt status
Loss of a church's tax-exempt status would have several negative consequences:

- the church's net income becoming subject to federal (and possibly state) income taxation;
- donors no longer being able to deduct contributions to the church;
- ineligibility to establish 403(b) tax-sheltered annuities;
- possible loss of property and sales tax exemptions;
- loss of preferential mailing rates;

- possible loss of a housing allowance exclusion for ministers serving the church;
- possible inapplicability of a minister's exemption from self-employment (Social Security) taxes to compensation received from the church; and
- possible loss of ministers' compensation exemption from federal income tax withholding.

Clearly, church leaders should avoid any activity that jeopardizes a church's exemption from federal income taxation.

Unfortunately, the IRS and the courts have provided little guidance on the meaning of "reasonable" compensation. Summarized below are the key cases.

Church of Scientology v. Commissioner of Internal Revenue, 823 F.2d 1310 (9th Cir. 1987)
One federal appeals court concluded that combined annual income of $115,680 paid by a religious organization to its founder and his wife was not excessive. Unreasonable compensation sometimes is associated with payment of ministers' compensation based on a percentage of church income. For example, a small church with annual income of $20,000 agrees to pay its minister half of the church's annual compensation. This amount is certainly reasonable. However, assume that within a few years the church experiences substantial growth and its annual income increases to $500,000. If the church has not changed its method of paying its minister (i.e., the minister now receives annual compensation of $250,000), the IRS (and the courts) would almost certainly conclude that this amounts to unreasonable compensation.

Heritage Village Church and Missionary Fellowship, Inc., 92 B.R. 1000 (D.S.C. 1988)
The bankruptcy court in the "PTL" case also addressed the critical issue of what constitutes reasonable compensation for a minister. The bankruptcy court ruled that reasonable compensation for Jim Bakker would have been $133,100 in 1984, $146,410 in 1985, $161,051 in 1986, and $177,156 in 1987. These are the same figures computed by the IRS, and the court openly expressed its reliance upon the IRS calculations. The court found that Bakker's actual compensation for the four years in question amounted to more than $7.3 million and that much of this was in the form of bonuses and fringe benefits. To illustrate, Bakker's salary (as determined by the court) for the years in question was $228,500 in 1984, $291,500 in 1985, $265,000 in 1986, and $265,000 in 1987. However, the total amount of compensation and benefits attributable to Bakker for the same years was $1.2 million in 1984, $1.6 million in 1985, $1.9 million in 1986, and $2.7 million in 1987.

How did the court in the PTL case determine what was reasonable compensation for Jim Bakker? This is both an interesting and highly relevant question, since the IRS and the courts have provided little guidance in defining this significant term. In answering this question, the court noted that "the highest paid head of a government agency in the State of South Carolina with a salary approved by the legislature is the president of the University of South Carolina who, for the years in question, had a salary under $100,000." (The court undoubtedly overlooked the compensation paid to certain university football and basketball coaches—who also could be considered government employees.) The court also referred to the testimony of "expert witnesses" who had testified that normal salary of the highest compensated ministers "would run from $75,000 to $120,000" and that "bonuses were almost unheard of in the religious field, although fringe benefits would amount to about 30 percent of the salary." In responding to the view of one of Bakker's witnesses that the Bible mandates that a minister should get 10 percent of all donations and a "high priest" should receive 20 percent, the court commented that such a view "defies common sense and rational judgment."

➡ **TIP.** Ministers' compensation in excess of $150,000 should be reviewed by the church board or compensation committee to determine its reasonableness. This review should include comparisons with compensation paid by churches, other charities, and businesses of similar size (in terms of membership, staff size, or budget) in your area. For added assurance, you may wish to obtain a written opinion from a tax attorney as to the reasonableness of a compensation package in excess of $150,000. The $150,000 figure is near the "upper limit" of compensation paid to senior pastors of the largest churches, according to the *2012–2013 Compensation Handbook for Church Staff* (published by Christianity Today International). In calculating whether a minister's compensation exceeds $150,000, it is important to include all components of compensation (bonuses, fringe benefits, housing allowance or annual rental value of a parsonage, personal expenses paid by the church, personal use of church vehicles, etc.). As noted above, the negative consequences of a minister's compensation being classified by the IRS as unreasonable are so severe that precautionary measures are warranted.

The bankruptcy court's ruling in the PTL case is also relevant because it helps to clarify the meaning of ministerial compensation. Ministers sometimes find it difficult to determine what benefits are includable in their income for tax purposes. The PTL bankruptcy court concluded that following items were properly included in the income of Jim Bakker:

- salary,
- bonuses (note that the court found that bonuses were "almost unheard of in the religious field"),
- personal use of a PTL vehicle (e.g., the corporate jet),
- PTL contributions to Bakker's retirement fund,
- utilities paid by PTL on Bakker's parsonage "notwithstanding the fact that Jim Bakker also received a housing allowance during the entire period of not less than $2,000 per month,"
- Bakker's housing allowance of $2,000 per month (since he lived in a PTL-owned "parsonage" rent-free),

- numerous expenditures from the PTL general checking account for the use and benefit of Bakker for which insufficient documentation existed to justify their classification as a business expense,
- charges made on PTL credit cards on Bakker's behalf for which there was insufficient documentation to justify their classification as business expenses, and
- cash advances to Bakker that had been "written off" by PTL.

The IRS reached these same conclusions, but it added several additional items to Bakker's compensation, including personal use of PTL automobiles; the fair rental value of Bakker's "parsonage"; a "housekeeping and maintenance allowance" of $28,000 each year; the fair rental value of a PTL-owned condominium in Florida; and personal use by Bakker of the presidential suite in the Heritage Grand Hotel. Several important lessons can be learned from this case:

- Ministers should recognize that bonuses and many kinds of fringe benefits are includable in compensation. They are not tax-free gifts.
- Ministers who live in a church-owned parsonage without having to pay rent are free to exclude from income (for income tax purposes) the fair rental value of the parsonage. They also may exclude that part of their compensation that is designated by their employing church as a "parsonage allowance" to the extent that it is actually used to pay parsonage related expenses. Bakker's problem was that he not only lived in a parsonage without paying rent but also received a "housekeeping and maintenance allowance" (of about $28,000 each year) and a housing allowance (of $24,000 each year) despite the fact that PTL paid all of his housing expenses. Such payments, in the court's judgment, clearly were above any reasonable parsonage-related expenses.
- Church payments of ministers' expenses (whether by check or credit card) generally are includable in ministers' compensation unless the payments are made pursuant to an accountable reimbursement arrangement. As discussed fully in Chapter 7, under an accountable arrangement a church reimburses a minister only for those business expenses that are adequately substantiated. Reimbursements of business expenses without sufficient substantiation constitute nonaccountable reimbursements, and they are fully includable in a minister's income for tax reporting purposes. Further, any employer reimbursements of an employee's purely personal expenses constitute taxable income. PTL reimbursed many of Bakker's personal expenses, yet failed to report these reimbursements as taxable income.
- A minister who uses a church vehicle for personal reasons has received a material benefit that must be valued and included in his or her compensation. Again, this is not a tax-free gift.

❋ **KEY POINT.** Clergy income includes much more than a church salary.

Truth Tabernacle, Inc. v. Commissioner of Internal Revenue, T.C. Memo. 1989-451

The United States Tax Court addressed the issue of unreasonable compensation paid to ministers in an important decision. Truth Tabernacle was incorporated as an independent church in 1978. The church was a fundamentalist Christian congregation, and its doctrine included a belief in "the death, burial, and resurrection of the Lord Jesus Christ . . . the sovereignty of the Church of God . . . Jesus Christ as the head of the church . . . resurrection of the dead . . . and Jesus Christ coming back again to reign as King of Kings and Lord of Lords over all the earth." The church consisted of about 40 members and conducted worship services three times each week. Regular men's and women's Bible classes were held two or three times each month. Sunday-school classes were held every Sunday. Saturday night prayer services were conducted each week. The church's pastor (who was an ordained minister) performed sacerdotal functions, including dedications of children, baptisms, funerals, and marriages.

The IRS audited the church in 1986 (the audit covered the years 1983, 1984, and 1985). At the conclusion of the audit, the IRS revoked the church's tax-exempt status retroactively. The IRS alleged that (1) the church was not operated exclusively for religious purposes, and (2) the church paid unreasonable compensation to its minister. The Tax Court rejected the IRS position and ruled in favor of the church. In rejecting the IRS claim that the church had not acted exclusively for religious purposes, the court observed: "Petitioner was a small church operating on a modest budget provided by the weekly contributions of its members. Essentially all of its contributions during the audit years were used to pay the mortgage, utility and maintenance expenses on the church building. Its activities primarily consisted of various worship services conducted in the church building and the performance of sacerdotal rites. In our view the [church is operated exclusively for religious purposes]."

The court noted that in 1983 the church received contributions of $10,700 and incurred expenses of $12,200. In 1984 it had contributions of $13,700 and expenses of $13,500. In 1985 it had contributions of $16,200 and expenses of $16,200. The major expenses each year were the mortgage payments, utilities, and repairs on the church building. The mortgage alone amounted to $5,000 of the church's annual budget. In rejecting the IRS claim that the church paid unreasonable compensation to its minister, the court noted that the pastor was provided a car and an apartment free of charge (a custodian and a caretaker received rent-free apartments on the church's property in exchange for 20 hours of service each week) but otherwise received no salary. The court observed that

[in determining] whether compensation is reasonable or excessive . . . one factor to consider is whether comparable services would cost as much if obtained from an outside source in an arm's-length transaction. Applying that standard to the present case, and considering the meager benefits received by the

THE INDEPENDENT SECTOR'S REPORT TO THE UNITED STATES SENATE

In September of 2004 the chairman of the Senate Finance Committee, Senator Charles Grassley (R-IA), and the ranking member, Senator Max Baucus (D-MT), sent a letter to the Independent Sector (a national coalition of several hundred public charities) encouraging it to assemble an independent group of leaders from the charitable community to consider and recommend actions "to strengthen governance, ethical conduct, and accountability within public charities and private foundations."

The Independent Sector issued its report in June 2005. It contained over 100 recommendations for congressional and IRS action as well as recommended actions for charities themselves. These recommendations included several that pertain to compensation planning, including the following:

- The panel "generally discourages payment of compensation to board members of charitable organizations."
- Governing boards or compensation committees should review the charity's staff compensation program periodically, including salary ranges for particular positions.
- "Charitable organizations that pay for or reimburse travel expenses of board members, officers, employees, consultants, volunteers, or others traveling to conduct the business of the organization should establish and implement policies that provide clear guidance on their travel rules, including the types of expenses that can be reimbursed and the documentation required to receive reimbursement. Such policies should require that travel on behalf of the charitable organization is to be undertaken in a cost-effective manner. The travel policy should be provided to and adhered to by anyone traveling on behalf of the organization."
- "Charitable organizations should not pay for nor reimburse travel expenditures (not including de minimis expenses of those attending an activity such as a meal function of the organization) for spouses, dependents, or others who are accompanying individuals conducting business for the organization unless they, too, are conducting business for the organization."

[church's] minister and grounds keepers in return for services that they performed, we find that the benefits were within the bounds of reasonable compensation for those services. Accordingly, there was no inurement of [the church's] net earnings to any private individual.

It is difficult to comprehend why the IRS challenged the tax-exempt status of a church that so clearly qualified for exempt status. Clearly, if the exempt status of Truth Tabernacle could be challenged, then few churches are beyond challenge. The Tax Court's decision will be a useful tool in combating similar efforts in the future.

Variety Club Tent No. 6 Charities, Inc. v. Commissioner, T.C. Memo. 1997-575 (1997)

The Tax Court addressed the issue of inurement in an important case. The case involved a charity that was organized to benefit disabled and underprivileged children. It conducted bingo games to raise funds. The IRS revoked the charity's tax-exempt status on the ground that some of its earnings inured to the benefit of its treasurer and another officer. The IRS based its action on the following grounds: (1) the treasurer and another officer of the charity embezzled more than $130,000 of bingo earnings; (2) the charity paid the legal fees of the treasurer in defending himself against criminal charges associated with his embezzlement of bingo proceeds; and (3) the charity rented a building owned by its treasurer for the bingo games and paid him $26,000 in rent for eight months each year.

The charity appealed the IRS ruling. The Tax Court concluded that the embezzlement of a charity's funds by its treasurer did not constitute prohibited inurement. However, the court concluded that the payment of the legal fees of an officer for acts unrelated to his or her official duties may constitute inurement that will jeopardize the charity's exempt status. And even if a charity's charter or bylaws contains an indemnification provision, a failure to comply with its conditions may constitute inurement and jeopardize the charity's exempt status. Finally the court agreed that the charity's payment of $26,000 each year to its treasurer to rent his building for bingo sessions might amount to prohibited inurement—but only if the fee was unreasonable.

✸ **KEY POINT.** Another result of inurement is the potential disqualification of a church to receive tax-deductible charitable contributions. In one case, a religious ministry paid for a minister-employee's personal expenses, including scholarship pledges made in the minister's name and a season ticket for a local college football team. The Tax Court noted that the tax code allows a charitable contribution deduction for contributions made to a charity "no part of the net earnings of which inures to the benefit of any private shareholder or individual." The court noted that the minister received payments from his employer (football tickets and scholarship pledges) and that these payments inured to his benefit. In addition, the minister failed to establish that these payments were compensation. Accordingly, the minister was not allowed to deduct contributions he made to his employer. *Whittington v. Commissioner, T.C. Memo. 2000-296 (2000).*

EXAMPLE. A school paid for the founding family's automobiles, education, travel, expenses, insurance policies, and personal equipment. A federal court ruled that the expenditures were not ordinary and necessary expenses in the course of the school's operations. The court also held that the payment of such personal expenses for the founder's children by the school provided direct and substantial benefit to the founder of the school. The court held that these payments constituted prohibited inurement of the school's earnings to the founder. *John Marshall Law School v. United States, 228 Ct. Cl. 902 (1981).*

IRS Tax Guide for Churches

The IRS published a revised *Tax Guide for Churches and Religious Organizations* in 2008 (Publication 1828) that addresses inurement and private benefit as follows:

Inurement to insiders

Churches and religious organizations, like all exempt organizations . . . are prohibited from engaging in activities that result in inurement of the church's or organization's income or assets to insiders (i.e., persons having a personal and private interest in the activities of the organization). Insiders could include the minister, church board members, officers, and in certain circumstances, employees. Examples of prohibited inurement include the payment of dividends, the payment of unreasonable compensation to insiders, and transferring property to insiders for less than fair market value. The prohibition against inurement to insiders is absolute; therefore, any amount of inurement is, potentially, grounds for loss of tax-exempt status. In addition, the insider involved may be subject to excise taxes. See the discussion of excess benefit transactions below. Note that prohibited inurement does not include reasonable payments for services rendered, or payments that further tax-exempt purposes, or payments made for the fair market value of real or personal property.

Excess benefit transactions

In cases where an [exempt] organization provides an excess economic benefit to an insider, both the organization and the insider have engaged in an excess benefit transaction. The IRS may impose an excise tax on any insider who improperly benefits from an excess benefit transaction, as well as on organization managers who participate in such a transaction knowing that it is improper. An insider who benefits from an excess benefit transaction is also required to return the excess benefits to the organization.

Private benefit

An [exempt] organization's activities must be directed exclusively toward charitable, educational, religious, or other exempt purposes. Such an organization's activities may not serve the private interests of any individual or organization. Rather, beneficiaries of an organization's activities must be recognized objects of charity (such as the poor or the distressed) or the community at large (for example, through the conduct of religious services or the promotion of religion). Private benefit is different from inurement to insiders. Private benefit may occur even if the persons benefited are not insiders. Also, private benefit must be substantial in order to jeopardize exempt status.

2. CHURCHES PAYING MINISTERS A PERCENTAGE OF REVENUE

A number of churches pay their minister a percentage of church revenue. Are such compensation arrangements legally permissible? The Tax Court addressed this issue in a 1980 ruling, *People of God Community v. Commissioner*, 75 T.C. 127 (1980). The Tax Court, in the People of God Community case, revoked the exempt status of a religious organization on the grounds that it paid its three ministers a percentage of gross revenue. However, the circumstances of this case reveal that payments to the three ministers were unreasonable apart from the percentage arrangement. The ministers' salaries made up 86 percent of the organization's budget; in addition, the ministers received no-interest loans. Further, the amount of the salaries paid to the ministers was well in excess of the average salary of comparable ministers. Therefore, this case should not be interpreted as an absolute prohibition of all compensation arrangements for ministers based on a percentage of income. Churches are free to pay their ministers reasonable compensation for services rendered. Compensation packages based on a percentage of income are reasonable and appropriate so long as the amount of compensation paid to a minister under such an arrangement is reasonable in amount.

An absolute rule characterizing all percentage-of-income compensation arrangements as unreasonable would lead to absurd results. For example, many ministers serve small congregations and receive all of the church's income. In many cases, these arrangements result in compensation of less than $10,000 per year to a minister. There can be no doubt that such an arrangement is reasonable and permissible under these circumstances. Such arrangements are common, and neither the IRS nor any federal court has addressed the propriety of this specific issue.

On the other hand, there is no doubt that compensation arrangements based on a percentage of income would be impermissible and jeopardize a church's exempt status to the extent that they result in excessive or unreasonable compensation. To illustrate, assume that Pastor B begins a new church with a few people and agrees to be paid 50 percent of the annual church revenue. For a few years this arrangement results in modest income to the pastor. However, the church prospers, and after a number of years the pastor is paid in excess of $1 million per year. There is no doubt that this constitutes unreasonable compensation, and it jeopardizes the exempt status of the church—not because of the percentage arrangement but because of the amount of compensation.

✤ **KEY POINT.** The IRS has issued regulations addressing the use of revenue-based compensation arrangements by churches and other charities.

IRS regulations addressing intermediate sanctions

"Intermediate sanctions" refers to the excise taxes the IRS can assess against persons who receive "excess benefits" from a church or other charity. The tax regulations state that compensation arrangements based on a percentage of a tax-exempt organization's revenues do not necessarily constitute an excess benefit. Rather, "all relevant facts and circumstances" must be considered. The regulations note that relevant facts and circumstances include but are not limited to (1) the relationship between the size of the benefit provided and the quality and quantity of the services provided, and (2) the ability of the person receiving the compensation to control the activities generating the revenues on which the compensation is based. The regulations contain the following additional clarification: "A revenue-sharing transaction may constitute an excess benefit transaction regardless of whether the economic benefit provided to the disqualified person exceeds the fair market value of the consideration provided in return if, at any point, it permits a disqualified person to receive additional compensation without providing proportional benefits that contribute to the organization's accomplishment of its exempt purpose."

The application of the regulations to revenue-based pay is illustrated by the following examples.

> **EXAMPLE.** Pastor C serves as an officer and director of his church. The congregation has 300 members. His annual compensation is one-half of all church income. This year the church's income was $600,000, and Pastor C was paid $300,000. The board is concerned that this compensation arrangement may trigger intermediate sanctions against Pastor C and the board members personally. The regulations clarify that not all revenue-based compensation arrangements result in an excess benefit leading to intermediate sanctions. Rather, all of the relevant facts and circumstances must be considered. The regulations state that relevant facts and circumstances include but are not limited to (1) the relationship between the size of the benefit provided and the quality and quantity of the services provided, and (2) the ability of the person receiving the compensation to control the activities generating the revenues on which the compensation is based. Pastor C's compensation may be excessive under these criteria, since the IRS may conclude that the amount of Pastor C's compensation is not proportional to the quantity and quality of the services he provides.

This is a difficult and somewhat subjective inquiry, but note the following: (1) It is highly irregular for the chief executive officer of any organization (nonprofit or for-profit) to receive half of all the organization's revenue. While such arrangements may be justifiable when an organization's revenue is modest, they become increasingly irregular as an organization's revenue increases. Being paid half of a church's revenue may be reasonable for a small congregation with revenues of $60,000. But the same cannot be said of a church with revenue of $600,000. (2) It is likely the IRS will assert that C's compensation is excessive in light of the quality and quantity of services performed. It is true that Pastor C is providing professional and valuable services. However, these services must be placed in perspective. Few ministers serving a congregation of 300 members receive annual compensation of $300,000. As a result, Pastor C will have a difficult, if not impossible, task in convincing the IRS that his compensation is reasonably related to the value of his services. How can it be reasonable if few (if any) ministers serving congregations of similar size receive this level of compensation?

This conclusion is reinforced by the *2012–2013 Compensation Handbook for Church Staff* published annually by Christianity Today International. Any doubt with regard to reasonableness of ministers' compensation should be resolved on the side of caution because of the enormity of the sanctions that can be assessed against disqualified persons who are paid excessive compensation. In this example, if the IRS determines that reasonable compensation for Pastor C would have been $100,000, then he has an excess benefit of $200,000. He will face an excise tax of $50,000 (25 percent of the excess) and an additional tax of $400,000 if he does not correct the overpayment by returning it to the church in a timely manner. In addition, the church board members who authorized this arrangement may be assessed an excise tax of $20,000 (10 percent x $200,000), collectively, not individually. For more information about this tax, see the section "Tax on managers" in section A.3 of this chapter

EXAMPLE. Same facts as the previous example, except that the congregation has more than 1,000 members and its revenue this year is $1.5 million, resulting in compensation to Pastor C of $750,000. It is possible that Pastor C's compensation will be deemed excessive by the IRS and that Pastor C will be exposed to 25 percent and 200 percent excise taxes discussed in section A.3 of this chapter. In addition, the board is exposed to the 10 percent tax on managers.

EXAMPLE. A church with 200 members has annual revenue of $300,000. The board enters into a compensation arrangement with its pastor, Pastor E, under which Pastor E is paid an annual salary of $50,000 and receives a bonus of $25,000 if membership or revenue increases by 10 percent in any year. Assuming that Pastor E is a disqualified person, it is doubtful that this arrangement will result in an excess benefit leading to intermediate sanctions. The regulations clarify that not all revenue-based compensation arrangements result in an excess benefit leading to intermediate sanctions. Rather, all of the relevant facts and circumstances must be considered.

The regulations state that relevant facts and circumstances include but are not limited to (1) the relationship between the size of the benefit provided and the quality and quantity of the services provided, and (2) the ability of the person receiving the compensation to control the activities generating the revenues on which

the compensation is based. Pastor E's compensation will not be excessive under these criteria. First, the size of his compensation is reasonably related to the quality and quantity of services performed (i.e., full-time professional services). Second, Pastor E has only limited ability to control the activities generating church revenue (see the previous examples). Third, the regulations specify that "a revenue-sharing transaction may constitute an excess benefit transaction regardless of whether the economic benefit provided to the disqualified person exceeds the fair market value of the consideration provided in return if, at any point, it permits a disqualified person to receive additional compensation without providing proportional benefits that contribute to the organization's accomplishment of its exempt purpose."

However, an example in the regulations clarifies that if additional compensation is based entirely on a "proportional benefit" to the charity, then the added pay is not an excess benefit. The example states that a manager of a charity's investment portfolio, whose compensation consists of an annual salary plus a bonus equal to a percentage of any increase in the value of the charity's portfolio, is not receiving an excess benefit. While the manager's compensation (the bonus) is linked to the charity's revenue, the arrangement gives the manager "an incentive to provide the highest quality service in order to maximize benefits." Further, the manager "can increase his own compensation only if [the charity] also receives a proportional benefit. Under these facts and circumstances, the payment to [the manager] of the bonus described above does not constitute an excess benefit transaction." It could be argued that Pastor E's bonus is tied directly to a proportional benefit being received by the church (a 10 percent increase in membership or revenue) and therefore is not excessive.

3. INTERMEDIATE SANCTIONS

❂ **KEY POINT.** In a series of four rulings, the IRS assessed intermediate sanctions against a pastor as a result of excess benefits paid to him (and members of his family) by his church. Intermediate sanctions are substantial excise taxes the IRS can impose on certain persons who receive excess benefits from a tax-exempt organization. The IRS concluded that a pastor's personal use of church property (vehicles, cell phones, credit cards, etc.) and nonaccountable reimbursements (not supported by adequate documentation of business purpose) that a church pays its pastor are automatic excess benefits resulting in intermediate sanctions, regardless of the amount involved, unless they are reported as taxable income by the church on the pastor's Form W-2 or by the pastor on Form 1040 for the year in which the benefits are provided. This is a stunning interpretation of the tax code and regulations that will directly affect the compensation practices of many churches and expose some church staff members to intermediate sanctions. This section will explain intermediate sanctions, summarize the recent IRS rulings, and assess their relevance to pastors and church compensation practices.

Section 501(c)(3) of the tax code exempts churches and most other religious organizations and public charities from federal income taxation. Five conditions must be met to qualify for exemption. One is that none of the organization's assets inures to the private benefit of an individual other than as reasonable compensation for services rendered. Churches and other tax-exempt organizations that pay unreasonable compensation to an employee are violating one of the requirements for exemption and are placing their exempt status in jeopardy. However, the IRS has been reluctant to revoke the tax-exempt status of charities that pay unreasonable compensation, since this remedy is harsh and punishes the entire organization rather than the individuals who benefited from the transaction. For example, should Notre Dame University lose its tax-exempt status because of the compensation it pays to its head football coach?

For many years the IRS asked Congress to provide a remedy other than outright revocation of exemption that it could use to combat excessive compensation paid by exempt organizations. In 1996 Congress responded by enacting section 4958 of the tax code. Section 4958 empowers the IRS to assess intermediate sanctions in the form of substantial excise taxes against insiders (called "disqualified persons") who benefit from an "excess benefit transaction."

Section 4958 also allows the IRS to assess excise taxes against a charity's board members who approved an excess benefit transaction. These excise taxes are called "intermediate sanctions" because they represent a remedy the IRS can apply short of revocation of a charity's exempt status. While revocation of exempt status remains an option whenever a tax-exempt organization enters into an excess benefit transaction with a disqualified person, it is less likely that the IRS will pursue this remedy now that intermediate sanctions are available.

Definition of a "disqualified person"

Since intermediate sanctions apply only to disqualified persons (and in some cases managers), it is important for church leaders to be familiar with this term. The regulations provide helpful guidance. They define a disqualified person as *any person who at any time during the five-year period ending on the date of an excess benefit transaction was in a position to exercise substantial influence over the affairs of the tax-exempt organization, or any family member of such a person.*

Substantial influence

The income tax regulations specify the following persons would be in a position to exercise substantial influence over the affairs of a tax-exempt organization:

- **Voting members of governing body.** This includes any individual serving on the governing body of the organization who is entitled to vote on any matter over which the governing body has authority.

- **Presidents, chief executive officers, or chief operating officers.** This category includes any person who, regardless of title, has ultimate responsibility for implementing the decisions of the governing body or for supervising the management, administration, or operation of the organization. A person who serves as president, chief executive officer, or chief operating officer has this ultimate responsibility unless the person demonstrates otherwise.

- **Treasurers and chief financial officers.** This category includes any person who, regardless of title, has ultimate responsibility for managing the finances of the organization. A person who serves as treasurer or chief financial officer has this ultimate responsibility unless the person demonstrates otherwise. If this ultimate responsibility resides with two or more individuals who may exercise the responsibility in concert or individually, then each individual is in a position to exercise substantial influence over the affairs of the organization.

Family members

The term "disqualified person" includes family members of a disqualified person. The income tax regulations define "family members" as

- spouses,
- brothers or sisters (by whole or half blood),
- spouses of brothers or sisters (by whole or half blood),
- ancestors,
- children,
- grandchildren,
- great-grandchildren, and
- spouses of children, grandchildren, and great-grandchildren.

An exception

The income tax regulations specify that some persons are not in a position to exercise substantial influence over the affairs of a tax-exempt organization, including employees who receive compensation or other benefits from an exempt organization of less than the amount required of a "highly compensated employee" under section 414(q) of the tax code ($115,000 for 2013) and who do not meet the definitions of "family member" or "substantial influence" as defined in the preceding paragraphs.

✱ **New in 2013.** The annual wages used in the definition of a highly compensated employee remains at $115,000 for 2013.

EXAMPLE. Pastor T is senior pastor of a church and serves as president of the corporation and a member of the board (with the right to vote). Pastor T's church salary for the current year is $50,000. Since Pastor T serves as both president and a member of the board, he is not automatically exempted from the definition of a disqualified person even though he is not a "highly compensated employee." As a result, he will be subject to intermediate sanctions if the church pays him excessive compensation.

However, Pastor T's current level of compensation is not excessive. In summary, while he is a disqualified person, he is not subject to intermediate sanctions because his compensation is reasonable. However, he may be subject to penalties for automatic excess benefit transactions (addressed below).

EXAMPLE. Pastor C is an assistant pastor. He does not serve on the church board and is not an officer of the church. His church salary this year is $40,000. In addition, the church board is considering a gift of the parsonage to Pastor C in 2013. The parsonage has a current value of $175,000 (and is debt free). The board is concerned that the gift of the parsonage to Pastor C will expose him to intermediate sanctions. They do not need to be concerned. It is true that Pastor C will be a highly compensated employee if the parsonage is given to him, since he will have compensation of more than $115,000 (for 2013). But this in itself does not make him a disqualified person. The regulations require that he be in a position to exercise substantial influence over the affairs of the church. An assistant pastor who is neither an officer nor member of the board probably does not meet this test. Since Pastor C is not a disqualified person, he is not subject to intermediate sanctions. However, note that a church's exemption from federal income taxation may be jeopardized by excessive compensation paid to a staff member even if the recipient is not a disqualified person under section 4958.

EXAMPLE. Same facts as the previous example, except that Pastor C is a senior pastor who serves on the church board (with the right to vote). Under these circumstances, Pastor C will be deemed a disqualified person because of his status as a church board member. This will expose him to intermediate sanctions if he receives an excess benefit from the church. It is unlikely that the compensation paid to Pastor C would be deemed excessive, especially if he pastors a large church. See the *2012–2013 Compensation Handbook for Church Staff* published by Christianity Today International.

Excise taxes

Intermediate sanctions consist of the following three excise taxes:

1. Tax on disqualified persons

A disqualified person who benefits from an excess benefit transaction is subject to an excise tax equal to 25 percent of the amount of the excess benefit (the amount by which actual compensation exceeds the fair market value of services rendered). This tax is paid by the disqualified person directly, not by his or her employer.

2. Additional tax on disqualified persons

If the 25 percent excise tax is assessed against a disqualified person and he or she fails to correct the excess benefit within the taxable period (defined below), the IRS can assess an additional tax of 200 percent of the excess benefit. Section 4958 specifies that the disqualified person can correct the excess benefit transaction by

"undoing the excess benefit to the extent possible, and taking any additional measures necessary to place the organization in a financial position not worse than that in which it would be if the disqualified person were dealing under the highest fiduciary standards." The correction must occur by the earlier of the date the IRS mails a notice informing the disqualified person that he or she owes the 25 percent tax, or the date the 25 percent tax is actually assessed.

3. Tax on organization managers

An excise tax equal to 10 percent of the excess benefit may be imposed on the participation of an organization manager in an excess benefit transaction between a tax-exempt organization and a disqualified person. This tax, which may not exceed $20,000 with respect to any single transaction, is only imposed if the 25 percent tax is imposed on the disqualified person, the organization manager knowingly participated in the transaction, and the manager's participation was willful and not due to reasonable cause. There is also joint and several liability for this tax. A person may be liable for both the tax paid by the disqualified person and this organization manager tax in appropriate circumstances. This tax is explained more fully below.

Correcting an excess benefit transaction

Section 4958 specifies that a disqualified person who receives excess compensation is subject to an excise tax equal to 25 percent of the amount of compensation in excess of a reasonable amount. Further, if the excess benefit is not corrected, the disqualified person is liable for a tax of 200 percent of the excess benefit. The correction must occur within the taxable period.

The tax code defines "taxable period" as "the period beginning with the date on which the transaction occurs and ending on the earliest [sic] of (1) the date of mailing a notice of deficiency under section 6212 [of the tax code] with respect to the [25 percent excise tax] or (2) the date on which the [25 percent excise tax] is assessed."

How can a disqualified person correct an excess benefit transaction? The regulations answer this question as follows:

> *An excess benefit transaction is corrected by undoing the excess benefit to the extent possible, and taking any additional measures necessary to place the tax-exempt organization involved in the excess benefit transaction in a financial position not worse than that in which it would be if the disqualified person were dealing under the highest fiduciary standards.*

> *A disqualified person corrects an excess benefit only by making a payment in cash or cash equivalents (excluding payment by a promissory note) equal to the correction amount to the tax-exempt organization.*

EXAMPLE. A pastor is a member of his church's governing board. Last year the pastor was paid a monthly car allowance of

$400 and was not required to substantiate any business use of his car. Neither the church nor the pastor reported the allowances as taxable income. The pastor recently learned that these allowances may constitute automatic excess benefits, exposing him to substantial excise taxes. He is unable to send the church a check for $4,800, so he drafts a promissory note in which he promises to pay the church $4,800 within one year without interest. The IRS will not consider this promissory note to be a correction of the excess benefit.

A disqualified person may, with the agreement of the tax-exempt organization, make a correction by returning property previously transferred in the excess benefit transaction. In this case the disqualified person is treated as making a payment equal to the lesser of (1) the fair market value of the property determined on the date the property is returned to the organization; or (2) the fair market value of the property on the date the excess benefit transaction occurred.

The "correction amount," with respect to an excess benefit transaction, equals the sum of the excess benefit and interest on the excess benefit.

Abatement of the penalty

If a disqualified person corrects an excess benefit transaction during the taxable period, the 25 percent and 200 percent excise taxes are abated as follows:

- **The 25 percent excise tax.** This is abated only if the disqualified person can establish that (1) the excess benefit transaction was due to reasonable cause, and (2) was not due to willful neglect. For this purpose, "reasonable cause" means exercising "ordinary business care and prudence." "Not due to willful neglect" means that the receipt of the excess benefit was not due to the disqualified person's conscious, intentional, or voluntary failure to comply with section 4958 and that the noncompliance was not due to conscious indifference. Disqualified persons who cannot prove both of these requirements will be liable for the 25 percent excise tax even though they corrected the excess benefit transaction and paid federal income tax on the benefit as additional compensation.
- **The 200 percent excise tax.** This excise tax under section 4958 is automatically abated.

EXAMPLE. A church pays its pastor a salary that the board later determines to have resulted in an excess benefit of $100,000. The board persuades the pastor to correct the arrangement by returning the excess amount to the church. This is not enough to correct the excess benefit transaction, so the pastor is exposed to the 200 percent excise tax ($200,000). The regulations clarify that a correction involves more than a return of the excess benefit. The recipient of the excess benefit must repay the church or other tax-exempt organization "the sum of the excess benefit and interest on the excess benefit." In this example, this means that the pastor must pay the church an amount

sufficient to compensate it for the earnings it would have received on the excess amount had it not been paid to the pastor.

Definition of "excess benefit"

Section 4958(c)(1)(A) of the tax code defines an excess benefit transaction as follows:

The term "excess benefit transaction" means any transaction in which an economic benefit is provided by an applicable tax-exempt organization directly or indirectly to or for the use of any disqualified person if the value of the economic benefit provided exceeds the value of the consideration (including the performance of services) received for providing such benefit. For purposes of the preceding sentence, an economic benefit shall not be treated as consideration for the performance of services unless such organization clearly indicated its intent to so treat such benefit.

Stated simply, an excess benefit transaction is one in which the value of a benefit provided to an insider exceeds the value of the insider's services. The excess benefit can be an inflated salary, but it can also be any other kind of transaction that results in an excess benefit. Here are three examples:

- sale of an exempt organization's assets to an insider for less than market value,
- use of an exempt organization's property for personal purposes, and
- payment of an insider's personal expenses.

Section 4958 states that certain benefits are not considered in determining whether a disqualified person has received an excess benefit. Such benefits include "expense reimbursement payments pursuant to an accountable plan."

Reasonable compensation

An excess benefit occurs when an exempt organization pays a benefit to an insider in excess of the value of his or her services. In other words, an excess benefit is a benefit that is paid in excess of reasonable compensation for services rendered. The income tax regulations explain the concept of reasonable compensation as follows: "The value of services is the amount that would ordinarily be paid for like services by like enterprises (whether taxable or tax-exempt) under like circumstances (i.e., reasonable compensation)."

Compensation for purposes of determining reasonableness under section 4958 includes "all economic benefits provided by a tax-exempt organization in exchange for the performance of services." These include but are not limited to

- all forms of cash and non-cash compensation, including salary, fees, bonuses, severance payments, and deferred and non-cash compensation; and

- all other compensatory benefits, whether or not included in gross income for income tax purposes, including payments to plans providing medical, dental, or life insurance; severance pay; disability benefits; and both taxable and nontaxable fringe benefits (other than fringe benefits described in section 132), including expense allowances or reimbursements (other than expense reimbursements pursuant to an accountable plan) and the economic benefit of a below-market loan.

Nonaccountable expense reimbursements

Income tax regulations specify that certain benefits are disregarded under section 4958, meaning that they are not taken into account in determining whether an excess benefit transaction has occurred that would trigger intermediate sanctions. The benefits *not* taken into account include "expense reimbursement payments pursuant to accountable plans."

Under an accountable reimbursement plan, an employer reimburses expenses of an employee only after receiving adequate records substantiating the amount, date, location, and business purpose of each reimbursed expense (including receipts for each expense of $75 or more). These strict substantiation requirements apply to all local transportation expenses (including the business use of a car); out-of-town travel expenses (including travel, lodging, and meals); entertainment; business gifts; personal computers; and cell phones. Other business expenses can be substantiated under an accountable plan with slightly less detail.

An employer's reimbursement of employee expenses that does not satisfy the strict requirements of an accountable plan is considered "nonaccountable." Such reimbursements constitute taxable income for income tax reporting purposes. But they also may constitute an excess benefit transaction, triggering intermediate sanctions. This issue was addressed by the IRS in an article in the January 2004 edition of its *Continuing Professional Education* text. This article, for the first time, recognizes the concept of "automatic" excess benefit transactions that can result in intermediate sanctions regardless of whether they are excessive or unreasonable in amount. This major development is discussed later in this chapter.

The presumption of reasonableness

Income tax regulations clarify that compensation is presumed to be reasonable, and a transfer of property or the right to use property is presumed to be at fair market value, if the following three conditions are satisfied:

- the compensation arrangement or the terms of the property transfer are approved in advance by an authorized body of the tax-exempt organization composed entirely of individuals who do not have a conflict of interest (defined below) with respect to the compensation arrangement or property transfer;

- the authorized body obtained and relied upon appropriate "comparability data" prior to making its determination, as described below; and
- the authorized body adequately documented the basis for its determination at the time it was made, as described below.

If these three requirements are met, the IRS may rebut the presumption of reasonableness if it "develops sufficient contrary evidence to rebut the . . . comparability data relied upon by the authorized body." Some of these important terms are further defined by the regulations, as noted below.

Authorized body of the tax-exempt organization. An authorized body means "the governing body (i.e., the board of directors, board of trustees, or equivalent controlling body) of the organization, a committee of the governing body . . . or other parties authorized by the governing body of the organization to act on its behalf by following procedures specified by the governing body in approving compensation arrangements or property transfers."

An individual is not included in the authorized body when it is reviewing a transaction if that individual meets with other members only to answer questions and otherwise recuses himself or herself from the meeting and is not present during debate and voting on the compensation arrangement or property transfer.

A member of the authorized body does not have a conflict of interest with respect to a compensation arrangement or property transfer *only if* the member

- is not a disqualified person participating in or economically benefiting from the compensation arrangement or property transfer and is not a member of the family of any such disqualified person;
- is not in an employment relationship subject to the direction or control of any disqualified person participating in or economically benefiting from the compensation arrangement or property transfer;
- does not receive compensation or other payments subject to approval by any disqualified person participating in or economically benefiting from the compensation arrangement or property transfer;
- has no material financial interest affected by the compensation arrangement or property transfer; and
- does not approve a transaction providing economic benefits to any disqualified person participating in the compensation arrangement or property transfer who in turn has approved or will approve a transaction providing economic benefits to the member.

Comparability data. An authorized body has appropriate data as to comparability if, given the knowledge and expertise of its members, it has sufficient information to determine whether the compensation arrangement is reasonable or the property transfer is at fair market value.

In the case of compensation, relevant information includes but is not limited to

- compensation levels paid by similarly situated organizations, both taxable and tax-exempt, for functionally comparable positions;
- the availability of similar services in the geographic area of the applicable tax-exempt organization;
- current compensation surveys compiled by independent firms; and
- actual written offers from similar institutions competing for the services of the disqualified person.

In the case of property, relevant information includes but is not limited to current independent appraisals of the value of all property to be transferred and offers received as part of an open and competitive bidding process.

For organizations with annual gross receipts (including contributions) of less than $1 million reviewing compensation arrangements, the authorized body will be considered to have appropriate data as to comparability if it has data on compensation paid by three comparable organizations in the same or similar communities for similar services. An organization may calculate its annual gross receipts based on an average of its gross receipts during the three prior taxable years.

IRS regulations contain the following examples.

EXAMPLE. Z is a university that is an applicable tax-exempt organization for purposes of section 4958. Z is negotiating a new contract with Q, its president, because the old contract will expire at the end of the year. In setting Q's compensation for its president at $600x per annum, the executive committee of the Board of Trustees relies solely on a national survey of compensation for university presidents that indicates university presidents receive annual compensation in the range of $100x to $700x; this survey does not divide its data by any criteria, such as the number of students served by the institution, annual revenues, academic ranking, or geographic location. Although many members of the executive committee have significant business experience, none of the members has any particular expertise in higher education compensation matters. Given the failure of the survey to provide information specific to universities comparable to Z, and because no other information was presented, the executive committee's decision with respect to Q's compensation was not based upon appropriate data as to comparability.

EXAMPLE. Same facts as the previous example, except that the national compensation survey divides the data regarding

compensation for university presidents into categories based on various university-specific factors, including the size of the institution (in terms of the number of students it serves and the amount of its revenues) and geographic area. The survey data shows that university presidents at institutions comparable to and in the same geographic area as Z receive annual compensation in the range of $200x to $300x. The executive committee of the Board of Trustees of Z relies on the survey data and its evaluation of Q's many years of service as a tenured professor and high-ranking university official at Z in setting Q's compensation at $275x annually. The data relied upon by the executive committee constitutes appropriate data as to comparability.

EXAMPLE. X is a tax-exempt hospital that is an applicable tax-exempt organization for purposes of section 4958. Before renewing the contracts of X's chief executive officer and chief financial officer, X's governing board commissioned a customized compensation survey from an independent firm that specializes in consulting on issues related to executive placement and compensation. The survey covered executives with comparable responsibilities at a significant number of taxable and tax-exempt hospitals. The survey data are sorted by a number of variables, including the size of the hospitals and the nature of the service they provide, the level of experience and specific responsibilities of the executives, and the composition of the annual compensation packages. The board members were provided with the survey results, a detailed written analysis comparing the hospital's executives to those covered by the survey, and an opportunity to ask questions of a member of the firm that prepared the survey. The survey, as prepared and presented to X's board, constitutes appropriate data as to comparability.

EXAMPLE. Same facts as the previous example, except that one year later X is negotiating a new contract with its chief executive officer. The governing board of X obtains information indicating that the relevant market conditions have not changed materially, and it possesses no other information indicating that the results of the prior year's survey are no longer valid. Therefore, X may continue to rely on the independent compensation survey prepared for the prior year in setting annual compensation under the new contract.

EXAMPLE. W is a local repertory theater and an applicable tax-exempt organization for purposes of section 4958. W has had annual gross receipts ranging from $400,000 to $800,000 over its past three taxable years. In determining the next year's compensation for W's artistic director, the board of directors of W relies on data compiled from a telephone survey of three other unrelated performing-arts organizations of similar size in similar communities. A member of the board drafts a brief written summary of the annual compensation information obtained from this informal survey. The annual compensation information obtained in the telephone survey is appropriate data as to comparability.

Documentation. For a decision to be documented adequately, the written or electronic records of the authorized body must note

- the terms of the transaction that was approved and the date it was approved;
- the members of the authorized body who were present during debate on the transaction that was approved and those who voted on it;
- the comparability data obtained and relied upon by the authorized body and how the data was obtained; and
- any actions taken with respect to consideration of the transaction by anyone who is otherwise a member of the authorized body but who had a conflict of interest with respect to the transaction.

✿ **KEY POINT.** The regulations state that "the fact that a transaction between a tax-exempt organization and a disqualified person is not subject to the presumption of reasonableness neither creates any inference that the transaction is an excess benefit transaction, nor exempts or relieves any person from compliance with any federal or state law imposing any obligation, duty, responsibility, or other standard of conduct with respect to the operation or administration of any applicable tax-exempt organization."

EXAMPLE. A parachurch ministry's board includes the president. If the IRS later asserts that the president was paid excessive compensation, the president will not be able to rely on the presumption of reasonableness because of his presence on the board. However, if he recuses himself from the board meeting in which his compensation is discussed (and so is not present for the debate and voting on the compensation arrangement), he may not have a conflict of interest that would preclude the presumption of reasonableness.

EXAMPLE. Same facts as the previous example. The president does not serve on the board, but his wife does. The president recuses himself from the board meeting in which his compensation is determined, but his wife does not. The president will not be able to rely on the presumption of reasonableness, because one board member (the wife) is related to the president, and she did not recuse herself from the meeting that addressed her husband's compensation.

EXAMPLE. A church with 500 members and an annual budget of $1 million paid its senior pastor compensation of $200,000 in 2012. The pastor participated in the board meeting in which his compensation was determined. The church board is concerned that the pastor's compensation may be excessive. They begin doing salary comparisons of other churches and businesses in the area with a similar membership or budget. Such efforts will serve no purpose if the board is attempting to qualify the pastor for the rebuttable presumption of reasonableness. The pastor's

presence on the board and his participation in the meeting in which his compensation was determined disqualify him for the presumption of reasonableness. However, salary surveys will be relevant in determining whether the pastor's compensation is excessive.

EXAMPLE. Same facts as the previous example, except that the pastor recused himself from the board meeting in which his compensation was determined. The board's efforts to obtain salary comparisons may be helpful. If the board determines that similarly situated organizations, both taxable and tax-exempt, are paying persons in a functionally equivalent position a similar amount of compensation, this may establish a rebuttable presumption that the pastor's compensation is reasonable. This assumes that the pastor's recusing himself from the board meeting in which his compensation was determined avoided any conflict of interest.

EXAMPLE. Same facts as the previous example. Assume that the board learns that the average annual compensation paid to senior pastors by 20 similarly situated churches in the same area is $75,000. The board also determines that the average annual compensation paid by 10 local businesses with annual revenue of $1 million is $100,000. The results of the board's salary surveys clearly will not support the rebuttable presumption of reasonableness.

EXAMPLE. A church pays its senior pastor annual compensation of $75,000 this year. The pastor serves as a member of the church's governing board. The church board also provides the pastor with a new car (with a value of $25,000) in recognition of 30 years of service. The pastor recused himself from the board meetings in which his salary and the gift were approved. The gift of the car is fully taxable, so the pastor's total compensation for this year will be $100,000. The board obtains a copy of the *Compensation Handbook for Church Staff*, published biannually by Christianity Today, and determines that senior pastors in similarly situated churches are paid an average of $85,000 per year. This information may be used to support a rebuttable presumption of reasonableness, since the pastor's compensation (including the gift of the car) is not substantially above the average. This assumes that the pastor's recusing himself from the board meeting in which his compensation was determined avoided any conflict of interest.

➡ **TIP.** The intermediate sanctions law creates a presumption that a minister's compensation package is reasonable if approved by a church board that relied upon objective comparability information, including independent compensation surveys by nationally recognized independent firms. The most comprehensive compensation survey for church workers is the biannual *Compensation Handbook for Church Staff*, published by Christianity Today International.

Tax on managers

An excise tax equal to 10 percent of the excess benefit may be imposed on the participation of an organization manager in an excess benefit transaction between a tax-exempt organization and a disqualified person. This tax, which may not exceed $20,000 with respect to any single transaction, is only imposed if the 25 percent tax is imposed on the disqualified person, the organization manager knowingly participated in the transaction, and the manager's participation was willful and not due to reasonable cause. There is also joint and several liability for this tax. A person may be liable for both the tax paid by the disqualified person and this organization manager tax in appropriate circumstances.

An organization manager is not considered to have participated in an excess benefit transaction where the manager has opposed the transaction in a manner consistent with the fulfillment of the manager's responsibilities to the organization.

A person participates in a transaction knowingly if the person has actual knowledge of sufficient facts so that, based solely upon such facts, the transaction would be an excess benefit transaction. Knowing does not mean having reason to know. The organization manager will not be considered knowing if, after full disclosure of the factual situation to an appropriate professional, the organization manager relied on a professional's reasoned written opinion on matters within the professional's expertise or if the manager relied on the fact that the requirements for the rebuttable presumption have been satisfied.

Participation by an organization manager is willful if it is voluntary, conscious, and intentional. An organization manager's participation is due to reasonable cause if the manager has exercised responsibility on behalf of the organization with ordinary business care and prudence.

EXAMPLE. A church board gives a retiring pastor the church parsonage (having a value of $150,000). The board members later learn about intermediate sanctions and are concerned that they may each be liable for up to $20,000 as managers. The regulations clarify that the board members will not individually be liable for the 10 percent excise tax (up to $20,000). Rather, they will collectively be liable for an excise tax (as managers) of 10 percent of the amount of the excess benefit up to a maximum tax of $20,000. The total tax assessed for this single transaction will be allocated to the board members who participated in the decision. However, the liability is joint and several, meaning that if some board members are unable to contribute, the others pay more. Board members who dissent from the transaction and whose dissent is reflected in the board minutes may avoid the penalty.

Effect on tax-exempt status

The regulations caution that churches and other charities are still exposed to loss of their tax-exempt status if they pay excessive compensation. The fact that such compensation arrangements may trigger intermediate sanctions does not necessarily protect the organization's tax-exempt status.

The tax regulations specify that "in determining whether to continue to recognize the tax-exempt status of a tax-exempt organization . . . that engages in one or more excess benefit transactions that violate the prohibition on inurement . . . [the IRS] will consider all relevant facts and circumstances, including, but not limited to," the following:

(A) The size and scope of the organization's regular and ongoing activities that further exempt purposes before and after the excess benefit transaction or transactions occurred;

(B) The size and scope of the excess benefit transaction or transactions (collectively, if more than one) in relation to the size and scope of the organization's regular and ongoing activities that further exempt purposes;

(C) Whether the organization has been involved in repeated excess benefit transactions;

(D) Whether the organization has implemented safeguards that are reasonably calculated to prevent future violations; and

(E) Whether the excess benefit transaction has been corrected . . . or the organization has made good faith efforts to seek correction from the disqualified persons who benefited from the excess benefit transaction.

All factors will be considered in combination with each other. Depending on the particular situation, the IRS may assign greater or lesser weight to some factors than to others. The factors listed in paragraphs (D) and (E) will weigh more strongly in favor of continuing to recognize exemption where the organization discovers the excess benefit transaction or transactions and takes action before the IRS discovers the excess benefit transaction or transactions. . . . Correction after the excess benefit transaction or transactions are discovered by the IRS, by itself, is never a sufficient basis for continuing to recognize exemption.

EXAMPLE. The income tax regulations contain the following example: O is a large organization with substantial assets and revenues. O conducts activities that further exempt purposes. O employs C as its Chief Financial Officer. During Year 1, O pays $2,500 of C's personal expenses. O does not make these payments under an accountable plan. In addition, O does not report any of these payments on C's Form W-2 for Year 1. C does not report the $2,500 of payments as income on his individual federal income tax return for Year 1. O does not repeat this reporting omission in subsequent years and, instead, reports all payments of C's personal expenses not made under an accountable plan as income to C. O's payment in Year 1 of

CHURCH AUDIT PROCEDURES ACT

The Church Audit Procedures Act (addressed in Chapter 12 of this guide) applies to excess benefit transactions of churches. The tax regulations specify that "the procedures of section 7611 will be used in initiating and conducting any inquiry or examination into whether an excess benefit transaction has occurred between a church and a disqualified person. For purposes of this rule, the reasonable belief required to initiate a church tax inquiry is satisfied if there is a reasonable belief that a section 4958 tax is due from a disqualified person with respect to a transaction involving a church." *Treas. Reg. 53.4958-8(b).*

$2,500 of C's personal expenses constitutes an excess benefit transaction between an applicable tax-exempt organization and a disqualified person. Therefore, this transaction is subject to the appropriate excise taxes. In addition, this transaction violates the proscription against inurement in section 501(c)(3). The payment of $2,500 of C's personal expenses represented only a de minimis portion of O's assets and revenues; thus, the size and scope of the excess benefit transaction were not significant in relation to the size and scope of O's activities that further exempt purposes. The reporting omission that resulted in the excess benefit transaction in Year 1 is not repeated in subsequent years. Based on the application of the factors to these facts, O continues to be [an exempt organization] described in section 501(c)(3).

EXAMPLE. In one of the first court cases to address intermediate sanctions, the Tax Court concluded: "The intermediate sanction regime was enacted in order to provide a less drastic deterrent to the misuse of a charity than revocation of that charity's exempt status. . . . Although the imposition of [intermediate sanctions] as a result of an excess benefit transaction does not preclude revocation of the organization's tax-exempt status, the legislative history indicates that both a revocation and the imposition of intermediate sanctions will be an unusual case." *Caracci v. Commissioner, 118 T.C. 379 (2002).*

Application to churches

The regulations confirm that intermediate sanctions apply to churches, but they specify that the protections of the Church Audit Procedures Act apply. The Church Audit Procedures Act imposes detailed limitations on IRS examinations of churches. These limitations are explained fully in Chapter 12, section A.8, of this tax guide.

❖ **KEY POINT.** The IRS *Tax Guide for Churches and Religious Organizations* specifies that the protections of the Church Audit

Procedures Act "will be used in initiating and conducting any inquiry or examination into whether an excess benefit transaction has occurred between a church and an insider."

EXAMPLE. A Maryland court ruled that a church did not necessarily act improperly in paying off the home mortgage loans of the church's pastor and his son. A church congregation voted to sell the church property to another church for $900,000 in a duly called special business meeting. The congregation later convened another meeting to determine how to use the sales proceeds. A majority voted to use $400,000 to pay off mortgage loans on homes owned by the pastor and his son. Some of the church's members filed a lawsuit contesting the use of the sales proceeds to pay off mortgage loans on the two homes. The church insisted that its payment of the mortgage loans represented compensation for past services for which the pastor and his son had not been adequately paid, therefore constituting reasonable deferred compensation.

A state appeals court agreed. It observed, "A religious or charitable corporation may take past services into consideration . . . in compensating an employee, as may a court when that compensation is challenged." In support of its conclusion, the court noted that the tax code permits the IRS to assess substantial excise taxes (called "intermediate sanctions") against the officers of a tax-exempt organization who benefit from an excess benefit transaction, and pointed out that the tax regulations specify that "services performed in prior years may be taken into account" in determining reasonable compensation in the current year. However, the court concluded that the church members had established a "prima facie case" of unreasonable compensation "through the substantial sums paid for the benefit of the church's pastor and a member of his family." As a result, it sent the case back to the trial court to further address the question of what was fair and reasonable compensation for all of the services of the pastor and his son, including past services, in light of the purposes of the church. *First Baptist Church v. Beeson, 841 A.2d 347 (Md. App. 2004).*

Automatic Excess Benefit Transactions

An article entitled "Automatic Excess Benefit Transactions under IRC 4958" appeared in the IRS publication *Exempt Organizations Continuing Professional Education Technical Instruction Program for Fiscal Year 2004*. This article is significant, since it unexpectedly announced a new interpretation of section 4958. For the first time the IRS asserted that some transactions will be considered "automatic" excess benefit transactions resulting in intermediate sanctions regardless of the amount involved. Even if the amount involved in a transaction is insignificant, it still may result in intermediate sanctions. This is an important development, since it exposes virtually every pastor and lay church employee to intermediate sanctions that until now had been reserved for a few highly paid charitable CEOs. The term "excess" in effect has been removed from the concept of excess benefits.

The IRS article laid down the following principles:

(1) An economic benefit will be treated as compensation under section 4958 of the tax code (pertaining to intermediate sanctions) only if the exempt organization providing the benefit "clearly indicated its intent to treat the benefit as compensation for services when the benefit was paid."

(2) If the benefit is treated as compensation under section 4958, the IRS will consider the benefit along with any other compensation the disqualified person may have received to determine whether the total compensation was unreasonable (and therefore an excess benefit transaction resulting in intermediate sanctions).

(3) If the exempt organization did not "clearly indicate its intent to treat the benefit as compensation for services when the benefit was paid," then the benefit constitutes an automatic excess benefit resulting in intermediate sanctions, regardless of the amount of the benefit.

(4) An exempt organization is treated as "clearly indicating its intent to treat an economic benefit as compensation for services" only if it "provided written substantiation that is contemporaneous with the transfer of the particular benefit."

(5) If the written contemporaneous substantiation requirement is not satisfied, the IRS will treat the economic benefit as an automatic excess benefit transaction without regard to whether (a) the economic benefit is reasonable, (b) any other compensation the disqualified person may have received is reasonable, or (c) the aggregate of the economic benefit and any other compensation the disqualified person may have received is reasonable.

(6) One method of providing written contemporaneous substantiation is by the timely reporting of economic benefits, either by the exempt organization or by the disqualified person. The exempt organization reports the economic benefit as compensation on Form W-2 or Form 1099-MISC filed before the start of an IRS examination of either the exempt organization or the disqualified person for the year when the transaction occurred. The disqualified person reports the economic benefit as income on an original federal tax return (Form 1040) or on an amended federal tax return filed before the earlier of (a) the start of an IRS examination of either the exempt organization or the disqualified person for the year when the transaction occurred or (b) the first written documentation by the IRS of a potential excess benefit transaction involving either the exempt organization or the disqualified person.

(7) Other written contemporaneous evidence may be used to demonstrate that the organization, through the appropriate decision-making body or an officer authorized to approve compensation, approved a transfer as compensation in accordance with established procedures, which include but are not limited to (a) an approved written employment contract executed on or before the date of transfer; (b) appropriate documentation indicating that an authorized body approved the transfer as compensation for services on or before the date of the transfer; and (c) written evidence that existed on or before the due date of the appropriate federal tax return (Form W-2, Form 1099-MISC, or Form 1040), including extensions, of a reasonable belief by the exempt organization that under the tax code the benefit was excludable from the disqualified person's gross income.

(8) Reimbursements of expenses incurred by a disqualified person, paid by an exempt organization to the disqualified person, are disregarded under section 4958 if the expense reimbursements are made in compliance with an arrangement that qualifies as an accountable plan.

(9) Reimbursements of expenses incurred by a disqualified person, paid by an exempt organization to the disqualified person under an arrangement that is a nonaccountable plan, may be subject to intermediate sanctions under section 4958. If the exempt organization clearly indicates its intent to treat the reimbursements as compensation for services by satisfying the written contemporaneous substantiation requirements, the IRS will treat the reimbursements as compensation and add them to the disqualified person's other compensation to determine whether, in the aggregate, all or any portion of the disqualified person's compensation is unreasonable. However, if the organization does not satisfy the written contemporaneous substantiation requirements, the IRS will treat reimbursements paid under a nonaccountable plan as automatic excess benefit transactions without regard to whether (a) the reimbursements are reasonable, (b) any other compensation the disqualified persons may have received is reasonable, or (c) the aggregate of the reimbursements and any other compensation the disqualified person may have received is reasonable.

(10) A disqualified person (or an organization manager) who is liable for tax imposed by section 4958 is required to file Form 4720 (Return of Certain Excise Taxes on Charities and Other Persons). Form 4720 must be filed annually, reporting the excess benefit transactions that occurred which give rise to the tax liability under section 4958. If a disqualified person (or an organization manager) required to file Form 4720 did not file Form 4720 on or before the required due date, including extensions of time, a penalty of 5 percent of the amount of the correct tax under section 4958 would apply if the failure to file was not more than one month. For each additional month that the disqualified person (or the organization manager) did not file Form 4720, a penalty of 5 percent per month applies, but not exceeding 25 percent in total. If the disqualified person (or the organization manager) establishes that the

failure to file was due to reasonable cause and not due to willful neglect, the penalty would not apply.

(11) In examining economic benefits involving an exempt organization and its disqualified persons, the IRS will consider agreements, loans, and expense reimbursements or payments.

(12) The IRS will consider agreements providing any type of economic benefits to any disqualified persons, to any member of their family, and to any organizations in which the disqualified persons or any family members have an ownership interest. Agreements that may be reviewed include employment agreements, deferred compensation agreements, bonus agreements, retirement agreements, severance agreements, and agreements for the purchase or sale of any goods or services.

(13) The IRS will consider loan arrangements between the exempt organization and all disqualified persons and will review all loan documents. In particular, the IRS will determine whether payments were made in compliance with the loan documents.

(14) The IRS will consider all expense reimbursements made by the exempt organization to all disqualified persons and all expenses paid by the exempt organization to or on behalf of all disqualified persons.

The IRS article provides the following examples (dates have been updated).

EXAMPLE. A tax-exempt charity paid its president a salary of $50,000 per year. In 2012 it paid $35,000 for the president and the president's spouse to take a vacation cruise around the world. The charity intended for this benefit to be additional compensation to the president, at the rate of $7,000 per year, for services the president performed from 2007 through 2012. During 2012, as to the $35,000 payment, the charity withheld additional federal income taxes and employment taxes from the president's salary, reported the $35,000 payment as wages on its Form 941 for the appropriate calendar quarter, and paid the appropriate income taxes and employment taxes as to the $35,000. The charity reported $85,000 as compensation on the president's Form W-2 for 2012. The president reported $85,000 as compensation on Form 1040 for 2012. The IRS concluded that the charity's reporting of the $35,000 benefit satisfied the written contemporaneous substantiation requirements; therefore no automatic excess benefits occurred. Further, "whether the president is treated as having received compensation of $50,000 per year from 2007 through 2012 or as having received $85,000 of compensation in 2012, since neither amount was unreasonable, none of the $35,000 paid for the vacation cruise constituted an excess benefit transaction under section 4958." See principle (2) above.

EXAMPLE. Same facts as the previous example, except that the charity did not withhold additional federal income taxes or

employment taxes from the president's salary, did not report the $35,000 payment as wages on its Form 941 for the appropriate calendar quarter and did not pay the appropriate income taxes and employment taxes as to the $35,000. The charity reported only $50,000 as compensation on the president's Form W-2 for 2012. The president reported only $50,000 as compensation on Form 1040 for 2012.

In this example the charity did not "clearly indicate its intent to treat the benefit as compensation for services when the benefit was paid," and therefore the benefit constitutes an "automatic" excess benefit resulting in intermediate sanctions, regardless of the amount of the benefit. See principle (3) above. So, even though the total amount would not have constituted an excess benefit had the charity reported it as taxable income, the fact that it did not makes the transaction an "automatic" excess benefit. This will result in (1) an excise tax of $8,750 (25 percent of $35,000); (2) an excise tax of $70,000 (200 percent of $35,000); (3) a penalty for failing to file Form 4270 (assuming the president failed to do so).

If a disqualified person corrects an excess benefit transaction during the correction period, the 200 percent excise tax under section 4958 is automatically abated, and the 25 percent excise tax is abated if the disqualified person can establish that the excess benefit transaction was due to "reasonable cause" and was not due to "willful neglect." For this purpose, "reasonable cause" means exercising "ordinary business care and prudence." "Not due to willful neglect" means that the receipt of the excess benefit was not due to the disqualified person's conscious, intentional or voluntary failure to comply with section 4958, and that the noncompliance was not due to conscious indifference. If the president can establish that in 2012, when the charity paid $35,000 on the president's behalf, this excess benefit transaction was due to "reasonable cause" and was not due to "willful neglect," the IRS would abate the 25 percent excise tax. However, if the president cannot establish both of these requirements, the president would be liable for the 25 percent excise tax even though the president corrected the excess benefit transaction by paying $35,000 plus interest to the charity, and paid federal income tax on the $35,000 as additional compensation.

EXAMPLE. A charity paid its president a salary of $50,000 per year. It adopted an expense reimbursement program that qualifies as an "accountable plan." In 2012 the president traveled in connection with business and incurred travel expenses of $2,500. In 2012 the charity reimbursed the president $2,500 for these travel expenses. During 2012 the charity did not withhold and pay employment taxes on the $2,500 of expense reimbursements paid to the president. In addition, it did not report this $2,500 as wages on its Form 941 for the appropriate calendar quarter in 2012 and did not include this amount as wages on the president's Form W-2. The charity reported $50,000 as compensation on the president's Form W-2 for 2012. The president reported $50,000 as compensation on Form 1040 for 2012. The IRS concluded that "since the charity paid its president $2,500 under an accountable plan, the $2,500 is disregarded for purposes of section 4958." This means that the reimbursements do not constitute an "automatic" excess benefit.

EXAMPLE. Same facts as the previous example, except that in 2012 the president traveled on a personal matter and incurred travel expenses of $2,500. The charity reimbursed the president $2,500 for these travel expenses, but did not withhold and pay employment taxes or additional federal income taxes as to the $2,500 of expense reimbursements. In addition, the charity did not report this $2,500 as wages on its Form 941 for the appropriate calendar quarter in 2010 and did not include this amount as wages on the president's Form W-2 for 2012. The charity reported only $50,000 as compensation on the president's Form W-2 for 2012. The president reported $50,000 as compensation on Form 1040 for 2012.

The $2,500 reimbursement was nonaccountable, since the president failed to substantiate a business purpose. Neither the charity nor president "clearly indicated an intent to treat the benefit as compensation for services when the benefit was paid," since the charity did not report the $2,500 nonaccountable reimbursement as taxable income on Form 941 or Form W-2, and the president failed to report the amount as taxable income on Form 1040. As a result, the IRS will treat the reimbursement as an "automatic" excess benefit transaction without regard to whether (1) the reimbursement was reasonable; (2) any other compensation the disqualified persons may have received is reasonable; or (3) the aggregate of the reimbursements and any other compensation the disqualified person may have received is reasonable. So, even though the $2,500 reimbursement would not have constituted an excess benefit had the charity reported it as taxable income, the fact that it did not makes the transaction an "automatic" excess benefit. This will result in (1) an excise tax of $625 (25 percent of $2,500); (2) an excise tax of $5,000 (200 percent of $2,500); (3) a penalty for failing to file Form 4270 (assuming the president failed to do so).

If a disqualified person corrects an excess benefit transaction during the correction period, the 200 percent excise tax under section 4958 is automatically abated, and the 25 percent excise tax is abated if the disqualified person can establish that the excess benefit transaction was due to "reasonable cause" and was not due to "willful neglect." For this purpose, "reasonable cause" means exercising "ordinary business care and prudence." "Not due to willful neglect" means that the receipt of the excess benefit was not due to the disqualified person's conscious, intentional or voluntary failure to comply with section 4958, and that the noncompliance was not due to conscious indifference. If the president can establish that when the charity paid the $2,500 this excess benefit transaction

was due to "reasonable cause" and was not due to "willful neglect," the IRS would abate the 25 percent excise tax. However, if the president cannot establish both of these requirements, the president would be liable for the 25 percent excise tax even though the president corrected the excess benefit transaction by paying $2,500 plus interest to the charity, and paid federal income tax on the $2,500 as additional compensation.

Four IRS Rulings

In 2004 the IRS issued four private letter rulings that apply the principle of automatic excess benefit transactions to a variety of benefits that were provided by a church to its pastor and members of the pastor's family. These rulings are discussed separately below.

Ruling 1: IRS Letter Ruling 200435019

A church was founded by a pastor (Pastor B), who has been its only pastor and who also serves as the president and a director of the church. The church's bylaws specify that directors are appointed by Pastor B and serve until their death, disability, resignation, or removal by Pastor B. The other members of the church's board of directors are Pastor B's wife (who also serves as secretary-treasurer) and one of his sons (who is the vice president). Pastor B has two sons, C and D. The IRS addressed the consequences of the following transactions in this ruling:

(1) use of church credit cards by Pastor B's son D,
(2) church reimbursement of cell phone expenses incurred by Pastor B's son D, and
(3) the church-reimbursed, unsubstantiated travel expenses incurred by Pastor B's son D.

The IRS began its analysis by noting that intermediate sanctions under section 4958 only can be assessed against disqualified persons and that the regulations define a disqualified person as any person who at any time during the five-year period ending on the date of an excess benefit transaction was in a position to exercise substantial influence over the affairs of the tax-exempt organization, *or any family member of such a person.* Since Pastor B met the definition of a disqualified person, so did the members of his family, including his sons. As a result, the IRS could assess intermediate sanctions against his family members for any excess benefit paid by the church.

The IRS defined an excess benefit transaction (resulting in intermediate sanctions) as follows:

An excess benefit transaction is a transaction in which an economic benefit is provided by a tax-exempt organization, directly or indirectly, to or for the use of any disqualified person and the value of the economic benefit provided by the organization exceeds the value of the services received for providing such benefit.

Reimbursements of an employee's expenses by the exempt organization are disregarded for purposes of section 4958 if the reimbursements satisfy all of the requirements of [an accountable reimbursement plan]. . . .

Expenditures of organization funds by an employee that satisfy the [business deduction] requirements under sections 162 and 274, including the substantiation requirements of those provisions and the regulations thereunder, do not constitute excess benefits under section 4958.

Any reimbursement of expenses by the organizations to an employee, or direct expenditures of organization funds by the employee, are automatic excess benefits to the extent that they do not satisfy the requirements of [an accountable reimbursement plan] or sections 162 and 274 of the tax code and the regulations thereunder, unless they are substantiated as compensation. . . .

In this case, Pastor B and his son expended church funds, and used church assets, in a variety of ways described below. . . . The son does not contend that these expenditures and uses were intended as compensation to himself or his relatives. In any event, there is no evidence in the record that would satisfy the contemporaneous substantiation rules of the regulations.

It follows that unless the son can satisfy the accountable plan requirements or the requirements of sections 162 and (to the extent relevant) 274 and the regulations thereunder for ordinary and necessary business expenses, the expenditures and use of church funds described below must be treated as automatic excess benefits.

The IRS analysis of each transaction is summarized below.

(1) Use of church credit cards by Pastor B's son D. Pastor B's son D used a church credit card for gasoline purchases. The church insisted that its policy regarding personal use of any church credit cards is that credit cards are to be used only for church business and not for any personal use. In the event of any personal use, the person using the card would be obligated to reimburse the church 100 percent.

The IRS noted, "The church retained its credit card statements and a few receipts. It did not note any business purpose or relationship with respect to the entries on such statements. It did not maintain any records, account books, diaries, etc., to establish the business purpose or relationship of such expenditures." The IRS concluded:

[The tax code] provides that expenses must be ordinary and necessary to be a business deduction. The expenses must be contemporaneously documented with time, place, business purpose, and business relationship. The church maintained credit card statements and a few receipts. However, neither the church nor Pastor B's son documented the business purpose or

relationship of his expenditures. It does not appear that the son kept any account books, diary, or other records demonstrating that the charges he made on the church credit cards were for business purposes [emphasis added].

As a result, the IRS determined that the church's reimbursements of the son's credit card charges were nonaccountable, and since neither the church nor the son reported these reimbursements as taxable income, they constituted automatic excess benefits resulting in intermediate sanctions in the amount of 25 percent of the amount of the excess benefits plus an additional 200 percent of the amount of the excess benefits if the excess benefit transactions were not corrected within the taxable period (defined above).

While the son was personally liable for these intermediate sanctions, so was his father. The IRS observed:

We note that Pastor B was founder, president, and chief executive of the church. As a practical matter, he had total control of all the church's expenditures. He either approved of the excess benefit transactions by his son or he acquiesced in them. If Pastor B had withdrawn funds from the church and given them to his family members, there would have been no question that such gifts would be taxable excess benefits to him. By authorizing or allowing his son and other relatives, the natural objects of his bounty, to make unlimited expenditures of church funds for personal purposes, without any substantiation or evidence of a business purpose, he in effect improperly removed charitable assets from the church and gave them to his relatives. Accordingly, he not only is liable for the excess benefit transactions from which he personally benefited, but also is jointly and severally liable for all the excess benefits [paid to his son and other members of his family].

(2) Church reimbursement of cell phone expenses incurred by Pastor B's son D. The church provided Pastor B's son D with a cell phone and paid most, if not all, of the charges associated with this phone. The church insisted that its policy regarding personal use of cell phones was that personal telephone calls should not be charged to any church-paid phone and that any personal calls should be reimbursed 100 percent to the church.

The church provided the IRS with "voluminous records listing calls from the church's cellular phones." However, the documents "list only the telephone numbers, and do not indicate with whom the son spoke and the business reasons for their conversation. Aside from phone calls made to church phones that would most likely be church business, all other calls were not substantiated as required."

As a result, the IRS determined that the church's reimbursements of the son's cell phone charges were nonaccountable, and since neither the church nor the son reported these reimbursements as taxable income, they constituted automatic excess benefits resulting in intermediate sanctions in the amount of 25 percent of the amount of the excess benefits plus an additional 200 percent of the amount of the excess benefits if the excess benefit transactions were not corrected within the taxable period (defined above).

The IRS found Pastor B and his son "jointly and severally liable" for the intermediate sanctions, meaning that the IRS could collect the excise taxes from either of them.

(3) The church-reimbursed, unsubstantiated travel expenses incurred by Pastor B's son D.
The church reimbursed the travel expenses of Pastor B's son in connection with a seminar. The IRS concluded that the son had failed to substantiate that the trip was for business purposes. As a result, the church's reimbursement of the son's travel expenses was nonaccountable, and since neither the church nor the son reported the reimbursement as taxable income, it constituted an automatic excess benefit resulting in intermediate sanctions in the amount of 25 percent of the amount of the excess benefit plus an additional 200 percent of the amount of the excess benefit if the transaction was not corrected within the taxable period (defined above).

The IRS found Pastor B and his son "jointly and severally liable" for the intermediate sanctions, meaning that the IRS could collect the excise taxes from either of them.

Ruling 2: IRS Letter Ruling 200435020
This ruling involved the same church and pastor as Ruling 1 (summarized above). However, the transactions involved in this ruling were as follows:

(1) use of church credit cards by Pastor B,
(2) church reimbursement of cell-phone expenses incurred by Pastor B,
(3) personal use of church-owned vehicle,
(4) "second home" expenses paid by the church,
(5) home expenses of Pastor B's son paid by the church,
(6) home expenses on Pastor B's primary residence paid by the church, and
(7) payment of miscellaneous personal expenses on behalf of Pastor B.

The IRS applied the same definition of an excess benefit transaction (resulting in intermediate sanctions) that it used in Ruling 1. The IRS analysis of each transaction is summarized below.

(1) Use of church credit cards by Pastor B.
The church provided Pastor B with five credit cards, which he used to pay for meals, gasoline, department-store items, car repairs, groceries, hotel charges, and clothing. The church claimed that its policy regarding church credit cards was that they were to be used only for church business and not for any personal use. In the event of any personal use, the person using the card would be obligated to reimburse the church 100 percent.

The IRS noted, "The church retained its credit card statements and a few receipts. It did not note any business purpose or relationship with respect to entries on such statements. It did not maintain any records, account books, diary, etc. to establish the business purpose or relationship of such expenditures." The IRS concluded,

The tax code provides that expenses must be ordinary and necessary to be a business deduction. The expenses must be contemporaneously documented with time, place, business purpose, and business relationship. The church maintained its credit card statements and a few receipts. However, neither the church nor Pastor B documented the business purposes of these expenditures. It does not appear that Pastor B kept any account books, diaries, or other records demonstrating that the charges the family made on church credit cards were for business purposes.

As a result, the IRS determined that the church's reimbursements of Pastor B's credit card charges were nonaccountable, and since neither the church nor Pastor B reported these reimbursements as taxable income, they constituted automatic excess benefits resulting in intermediate sanctions in the amount of 25 percent of the amount of the excess benefits plus an additional 200 percent of the amount of the excess benefits if the excess benefit transactions were not corrected within the taxable period (defined above).

(2) Church reimbursement of cell-phone expenses incurred by Pastor B.
The church provided Pastor B with a cell phone and paid expenses associated with this phone. The IRS noted that cell phones are "listed property" under section 280F of the tax code, meaning that "strict substantiation requirements must be in place, otherwise the use of the cell phones is taxable to the employee." However, it concluded that the amount of expenses paid by the church were so low that they qualified as a nontaxable de minimis fringe benefit. A de minimis fringe benefit is one that is so minimal in value that it would be "unreasonable or administratively impractical" to account for it.

(3) Personal use of church-owned vehicle.
The church purchased a car that was parked in Pastor B's garage. Pastor B and his wife were the only persons who had access to the car. The church claimed that its policy regarding personal use of any vehicles it owned was that vehicles "are to be used only for business and not for any personal use. In the event of any personal use, any person utilizing the vehicle would be obligated to reimburse the church at the current IRS approved rate per mile." The church also declared, "There are no employee expense accounts or reimbursements other than described herein. All employees and ministers have their own vehicles for their personal use and consequently have little or no reason to drive a church-owned vehicle for personal use. All vehicles owned by the church are to be used for business exclusively."

The IRS concluded, "The car is kept at Pastor B's personal residence, and he and his wife are the only people with access to it. Pastor B argued that he drove this car occasionally, and only on business. However, use of a vehicle is treated as personal use unless a taxpayer substantiates business use." As a result, the IRS determined that Pastor B's exclusive access to the church-owned car constituted personal use of church property, and since no taxable income was reported during the year in question by either the church or Pastor B, the annual rental value of the car constituted an automatic excess benefit resulting in intermediate sanctions in the amount of 25 percent of the amount of the excess benefit plus an additional 200 percent of the amount of the excess benefit if the excess benefit transaction was not corrected within the taxable period (defined above).

(4) "Second home" expenses paid by the church. The church purchased a home that was used exclusively by Pastor B and his wife (in addition to their principal residence). The IRS noted that the church paid for several expenses associated with the home, including furnishings, utilities, security system, cable TV, and landscaping. The IRS determined that no business purpose had been proven for any of these expenses; therefore, church assets had been used for personal purposes without having been reported as taxable income by the church or Pastor B in the year the benefits were provided. Thus they constituted automatic excess benefits resulting in intermediate sanctions in the amount of 25 percent of the amount of the excess benefit plus an additional 200 percent of the amount of the excess benefit if the excess benefit transaction was not corrected within the taxable period (defined above).

✿ **KEY POINT.** The IRS provided some indication of how it will determine a home's fair rental value. This is an important point, since this value must be known in determining the nontaxable portion of a church-designated housing allowance for ministers who own their home. The IRS observed, "In the agent's report, she determined an annual amount of $X as rental value for the property. . . . She stated: 'Calling a property management company and asking about the house determined this rental value. I did not identify the address; rather I used the information about the house, how many acres, square footage and area, etc. The rental value was $X per month. This appears correct as the other houses owned and operated by Pastor B and the church were consistent with this value. The other rentals were not as spacious, nor did they have the amenities consistent with this property. In addition, the other rentals were in [an adjacent county] as opposed to [this county], which has a higher rental value. Those houses were being rented for approximately $Y/month.'"

(5) Home expenses of Pastor B's son paid by the church. The church purchased a home that was occupied by Pastor B's son for six months. The son did not pay rent, and he and his parents were the only persons having access to the home. After the son moved out of the home, his parents gave the church a check for the purpose of belatedly paying rent for their son's occupation of the home. The church paid monthly utility, landscaping, and cable TV expenses at the house. It also paid a monthly fee for a home security system.

The IRS determined that no business purpose had been proven for any of these expenses; therefore, church assets had been used for personal purposes without having been reported as taxable income by the church, Pastor B, or Pastor B's son in the year the benefits were provided. Thus they constituted automatic excess benefits resulting in intermediate sanctions in the amount of 25 percent of the amount of the excess benefit plus an additional 200 percent of the amount of the excess benefit if the excess benefit transaction was not corrected within the taxable period (defined above).

(6) Home expenses on Pastor B's primary residence paid by the church. The church paid for landscaping, cable TV, and a security alarm system for Pastor B's primary residence. The IRS determined that no business purpose had been proven for any of these expenses; therefore, church assets had been used for personal purposes without having been reported as taxable income by the church or Pastor B in the year the benefits were provided. Thus they constituted automatic excess benefits resulting in intermediate sanctions in the amount of 25 percent of the amount of the excess benefit plus an additional 200 percent of the amount of the excess benefit if the excess benefit transaction was not corrected within the taxable period (defined above).

✿ **KEY POINT.** These items were all legitimate housing expenses that were nontaxable for income tax reporting purposes because of the housing allowance; as a result, there was no need for the church or Pastor B to have reported them as taxable income.

(7) Payment of miscellaneous personal expenses on behalf of Pastor B. The church paid an investigator to conduct surveillance activities on Pastor B's daughter-in-law, and it paid attorney's fees for services rendered in connection with a personal dispute. The IRS determined that no business purpose had been proven for any of these expenses; therefore church assets had been used for personal purposes without being reported as taxable income by the church or Pastor B in the year the benefits were provided. Thus they constituted automatic excess benefits resulting in intermediate sanctions in the amount of 25 percent of the amount of the excess benefit plus an additional 200 percent of the amount of the excess benefit if the excess benefit transaction was not corrected within the taxable period (defined above).

The IRS concluded this ruling with the following observation:

> We note that Pastor B was founder, president, and chief executive of the church. As a practical matter, he had total control of all church expenditures. He either approved of the excess benefit transactions by his son or he acquiesced in them. If he had withdrawn funds from the church and given them to his family members, there would have been no question that such gifts would be taxable excess benefits to him. By authorizing or allowing his son and other relatives, the natural objects of his bounty, to make unlimited expenditures of church funds for personal purposes,

*without any substantiation or evidence of a business purpose, he
in effect improperly removed charitable assets from the church
and gave them to his relatives. Accordingly, he not only is liable
for the excess benefit transactions from which he personally
benefited, but also is jointly and severally liable for all the excess
benefits [provided to members of his family].*

Ruling 3: IRS Letter Ruling 200435021

This ruling involved the same church and pastor as Ruling 1 (summarized above). The transactions were identical to those described in Ruling 2, but in this ruling the IRS focused on Pastor B's wife. Since she was a family member of Pastor B, she was a disqualified person subject to intermediate sanctions. Further, Pastor B was jointly and severally liable for her penalties.

Ruling 4: IRS Letter Ruling 200435022

This ruling involved the same church and pastor as Ruling 1 (summarized above). However, the transactions involved in this ruling were as follows:

(1) use of church credit cards by Pastor B's son C,
(2) church reimbursement of cell-phone expenses incurred by Pastor B's son C, and
(3) the church's purchase of a computer from Pastor B's son C.

The IRS applied the same definition of an excess benefit transaction (resulting in intermediate sanctions) that it used in Ruling 1.

The IRS analysis of each transaction is summarized below.

(1) Use of church credit cards by Pastor B's son C. Pastor B's son C used a church credit card for gasoline purchases. The church insisted that its policy regarding personal use of any church credit cards is that credit cards are to be used only for church business and not for any personal use. In the event of any personal use, the person using the card would be obligated to reimburse the church 100 percent.

The IRS noted, "The church retained its credit card statements and a few receipts. It did not note any business purpose or relationship with respect to the entries on such statements. It did not maintain any records, account books, diaries, etc., to establish the business purpose or relationship of such expenditures." The IRS concluded:

*[The tax code] provides that expenses must be ordinary and
necessary to be a business deduction. The expenses must be
contemporaneously documented with time, place, business
purpose, and business relationship. The church maintained credit
card statements and a few receipts. However, neither the church
nor Pastor B's son documented the business purpose or relationship of his expenditures. It does not appear that the son kept any
account books, diary, or other records demonstrating that the
charges he made on the church credit cards were for business
purposes [emphasis added].*

As a result, the IRS determined that the church's reimbursements of the son's credit card charges were nonaccountable, and since neither the church nor the son reported these reimbursements as taxable income, they constituted automatic excess benefits resulting in intermediate sanctions in the amount of 25 percent of the amount of the excess benefits plus an additional 200 percent of the amount of the excess benefits if the excess benefit transactions were not corrected within the taxable period (defined above).

While the son was personally liable for these intermediate sanctions, so was his father. The IRS observed:

*We note that Pastor B was founder, president, and chief execu-
tive of the church. As a practical matter, he had total control of
all the church's expenditures. He either approved of the excess
benefit transactions by his son or he acquiesced in them. If
Pastor B had withdrawn funds from the church and given them
to his family members, there would have been no question that
such gifts would be taxable excess benefits to him. By authorizing or allowing his son and other relatives, the natural objects of
his bounty, to make unlimited expenditures of church funds for
personal purposes, without any substantiation or evidence of a
business purpose, he in effect improperly removed charitable
assets from the church and gave them to his relatives. Accordingly, he not only is liable for the excess benefit transactions from
which he personally benefited, but also is jointly and severally
liable for all the excess benefits [paid to his son and other members of his family].*

(2) Church reimbursement of cell phone-expenses incurred by Pastor B's son C. The church provided Pastor B's son C with a cell phone and paid most, if not all, of the charges associated with this phone. The church insisted that its policy regarding personal use of cell phones was that personal telephone calls should not be charged to any church-paid phone and that any personal calls should be reimbursed 100 percent to the church.

The church provided the IRS with "voluminous records listing calls from the church's cellular phones." However, the documents "list only the telephone numbers, and do not indicate with whom the son spoke and the business reasons for their conversation. Aside from phone calls made to church phones that would most likely be church business, all other calls were not substantiated as required."

As a result, the IRS determined that the church's reimbursements of the son's cell phone charges were nonaccountable, and since neither the church nor the son reported these reimbursements as taxable income, they constituted automatic excess benefits resulting in intermediate sanctions in the amount of 25 percent of the amount of the excess benefits plus an additional 200 percent of the amount of the excess benefits if the excess benefit transactions were not corrected within the taxable period (defined above). The IRS found

Pastor B and his son "jointly and severally liable" for the intermediate sanctions, meaning that the IRS could collect the excise taxes from either of them.

(3) The church's purchase of a computer from Pastor B's son C.
The church purchased a computer from Pastor B's son C. The IRS concluded that "there has been no evidence provided to substantiate that the church's purchase of a computer from C should be categorized as an arm's length transaction. Although counsel has argued that it was, and that the church benefited from the computer's capabilities, counsel has failed to provide any supporting documentation assessing the value and condition of the computer at the time it was sold. Accordingly, the sale of the computer constituted an excess benefit transaction attributable to C."

Church compensation practices

▲ **CAUTION.** *Churches often provide benefits to their employees besides a salary. These benefits may include personal use of church property, payment of personal expenses, and reimbursement of business or personal expenses under a nonaccountable arrangement. Often pastors and church treasurers are unaware that these benefits must be valued and reported as taxable income on the employee's Form W-2. This common practice may expose the pastor, and possibly church board members, to substantial excise taxes, since the IRS now views these benefits as automatic excess benefits resulting in intermediate sanctions unless the benefit was reported as taxable income by the church or pastor in the year it was provided. The lesson is clear. Sloppy church accounting practices can expose ministers, and in some cases church board members, to intermediate sanctions in the form of substantial excise taxes. Thus it is essential for pastors and church treasurers to be familiar with the concept of automatic excess benefits so these penalties can be avoided.*

Here are the key points that pastors, church treasurers, and church board members need to understand about intermediate sanctions:

(1) Section 501(c)(3) of the tax code prohibits tax-exempt organizations (including churches) from paying unreasonable compensation to any employee or other person. A violation of this requirement will jeopardize an exempt organization's tax-exempt status. The IRS can revoke an exempt organization's tax-exempt status if it pays an excess benefit to a disqualified person. However, in most cases the IRS will pursue intermediate sanctions rather than revocation of exempt status.

(2) Section 4958 of the tax code permits the IRS to assess intermediate sanctions in the form of excise taxes against insiders (called "disqualified persons") who receive an excess benefit from a tax-exempt organization. These taxes are 25 percent of the amount of an excess benefit and 200 percent of the amount of the benefit if the insider does not correct the excess benefit (i.e., return it) within the taxable period defined by law.

(3) A disqualified person includes an officer or board member of an exempt organization, or a relative of such a person.

(4) An excess benefit is any benefit paid by an exempt organization to an insider in excess of the reasonable value of services performed. It includes (a) excessive salaries, (b) "bargain sales" to an insider (sales of an exempt organization's property at less than market value), (c) use of an exempt organization's property at no cost, and (d) payment of an insider's personal and business expenses under a non-accountable plan (without a proper accounting of business purpose) unless the payment is reported as taxable income on the insider's Form W-2 or Form 1040.

(5) An excess benefit is treated as compensation when paid if the exempt organization reports the benefit as taxable income on a Form W-2 or Form 1099-MISC issued to the recipient or if the recipient reported the benefit as taxable income on his or her Form 1040. Other written evidence may be used to demonstrate that the organization approved a transfer as compensation in accordance with established procedures, which include but are not limited to (a) an approved written employment contract executed on or before the date of transfer; (b) appropriate documentation indicating that an authorized body approved the transfer as compensation for services on or before the date of the transfer; and (c) written evidence that existed on or before the due date of the appropriate federal tax return (Form W-2, Form 1099-MISC, or Form 1040), including extensions, of a reasonable belief by the exempt organization that under the tax code the benefit was excludable from the disqualified person's gross income.

(6) If an excess benefit is treated as compensation by the exempt organization in the year the benefit is paid, the IRS will consider the benefit along with any other compensation the disqualified person may have received to determine whether the total compensation was unreasonable (and therefore an excess benefit transaction resulting in intermediate sanctions).

(7) If an excess benefit is not reported as taxable compensation when paid, the IRS will assume that the entire amount of the benefit exceeds the value of any services provided by the recipient, and therefore the entire benefit constitutes an automatic excess benefit resulting in intermediate sanctions, regardless of the amount of the benefit.

(8) In four private rulings issued in 2004, the IRS assessed intermediate sanctions against a pastor because of the personal use of church property by himself and members of his family, and the reimbursement of expenses by the church under a nonaccountable plan without any substantiation of business purpose. Most importantly, the IRS concluded that these benefits were automatic excess benefit transactions resulting in intermediate sanctions, regardless of amount, since they were not reported as taxable income on the pastor's Form W-2 or Form 1040 for the year in which the benefits were paid.

(9) Churches that allow staff members to use a church-owned vehicle or other church property for personal purposes or that reimburse business or personal expenses of a staff member (or relative of a staff member) under a non-accountable arrangement may be engaged in an automatic excess benefit transaction that will subject the staff member to intermediate sanctions under section 4958 regardless of the amount of the benefits. This result can be avoided if the church or the pastor reports the benefits as taxable income during the year the benefits are received, and they may be partly or completely abated if the pastor corrects the excess benefit within the tax period defined by section 4958. This generally means returning the excess benefit to the church by the earlier of (a) the date the IRS mailed the taxpayer a notice of deficiency with respect to the 25 percent excise tax, or (b) the date on which the 25 percent excise tax is assessed. If a disqualified person corrects an excess benefit transaction during the taxable period, the 200 percent excise tax is automatically abated. If the disqualified person corrects the excess benefit transaction during the correction period, the 25 percent excise tax is abated only if the disqualified person can establish that (a) the excess benefit transaction was due to reasonable cause and (b) was not due to willful neglect.

The following examples will further illustrate these rules. Assume that each senior pastor in these examples meets the definition of a disqualified person.

EXAMPLE 1. A church uses an accountable reimbursement arrangement for the reimbursement of its senior pastor's business-related transportation, travel, entertainment, and cell-phone expenses. The church only reimburses those expenses for which the pastor produces documentary evidence of the date, amount, location, and business purpose of each expense within 30 days. By the end of the year, the church has reimbursed $4,000 for expenses. Since the church's reimbursement arrangement is accountable, neither the church nor the senior pastor is required to report the reimbursements as taxable income, and the reimbursements are not taken into account in deciding if church has provided an excess benefit to the pastor.

EXAMPLE 2. A church pays its senior pastor a salary of $45,000 this year. In addition, it reimburses expenses the pastor incurs for the use of his car, out-of-town travel, entertainment, and cell phone but does not require substantiation of the amount, date, location, or business purpose of reimbursed expenses. Instead, the pastor provides the church treasurer with a written statement each month that lists the expenses incurred for the previous month. The treasurer then issues a check to the pastor for this amount. This is an example of a nonaccountable reimbursement arrangement. Assume that the church reimburses $5,000 under this arrangement this year and that the amount is reported as taxable

income by the church on the pastor's Form W-2 for this year. Since the full amount was reported as taxable compensation by the church in the year the benefit was paid, it is not an automatic excess benefit resulting in intermediate sanctions. Rather, the IRS will consider the benefit along with any other compensation the pastor received to determine whether the total compensation was unreasonable (and therefore an excess benefit transaction resulting in intermediate sanctions). A salary of $45,000 plus $5,000 in reimbursements of nonaccountable expenses is not unreasonable, so the IRS will not assess intermediate sanctions.

EXAMPLE 3. Same facts as Example 2, except that the church did not report the $5,000 as taxable income on the pastor's Form W-2 in the year it was paid, and the pastor did not report it on his tax return (Form 1040) for that year. The church treasurer assumed that the pastor had "at least" $5,000 in business expenses, and so there was no need to report the nonaccountable reimbursements as taxable income. This is a dangerous assumption that converts the nonaccountable reimbursements into an automatic excess benefit and exposes the pastor to intermediate sanctions. An excess benefit is defined by section 4958 of the tax code as any compensation or benefit provided to a disqualified person in excess of the reasonable value of his or her services. It includes nonaccountable reimbursements of business and personal expenses—unless the reimbursements are reported as taxable compensation by the church or pastor in the year they are paid. Since the church did not "clearly indicate its intent to treat the benefit as compensation for services when the benefit was paid" (i.e., the benefit was not reported on the pastor's Form W-2 or Form 1040), the benefit constitutes an automatic excess benefit resulting in intermediate sanctions, regardless of the amount of the benefit. So even though the total amount would not have constituted an excess benefit had the church reported it as taxable income, the fact that it did not do so makes the transaction an automatic excess benefit. This will result in (1) an excise tax of $1,250 (25 percent of $5,000); (2) an excise tax of $10,000 (200 percent of $5,000); and (3) a penalty for failing to file Form 4270 (assuming the pastor failed to do so).

If a disqualified person corrects an excess benefit transaction during the correction period, the 200 percent excise tax is automatically abated, and the 25 percent excise tax is abated if the disqualified person can establish that the excess benefit transaction was due to reasonable cause and was not due to willful neglect. For this purpose, "reasonable cause" means exercising "ordinary business care and prudence." "Not due to willful neglect" means that the receipt of the excess benefit was not due to the disqualified person's conscious, intentional, or voluntary failure to comply with section 4958 and that the noncompliance was not due to conscious indifference. If the pastor can establish that the excess benefit transaction was due to reasonable cause and was not due to willful neglect, the IRS would abate the 25 percent excise tax. However, if the pastor cannot establish both of these requirements, he would be liable for the 25 percent excise tax even though he corrected the excess benefit transaction by paying $5,000 plus interest to the church and paid federal income tax on the $5,000 as additional compensation.

Note that managers (directors) who approve an excess benefit transaction are subject to an excise tax equal to 10 percent of the amount of the excess benefit—up to a maximum of $20,000 collectively.

EXAMPLE 4. Same facts as Example 3, except that the pastor is a church's youth pastor. Assuming that the youth pastor is not an officer of the church, a member of the governing board, or a relative of someone who is, he is not a disqualified person and therefore is not subject to intermediate sanctions. While the nonaccountable reimbursements constitute taxable compensation, and the failure by the church and pastor to report them as such exposes the pastor to back taxes plus penalties and interest, they are not an automatic excess benefit resulting in intermediate sanctions, since the youth pastor is not a disqualified person.

EXAMPLE 5. Same facts as Example 4, except that the youth pastor is the senior pastor's son. Assuming the senior pastor is president of the church corporation or a member of the governing board, he is a disqualified person, and so is his son. As a result, the nonaccountable reimbursements not reported as taxable compensation are an automatic excess benefit resulting in intermediate sanctions. The senior pastor and his son are jointly and severally liable for the intermediate sanctions, meaning that the IRS can collect them from either person. Church board members who approved the excess benefit transaction are subject to an excise tax equal to 10 percent of the amount of the excess benefit—up to a maximum of $20,000 collectively. See "Tax on managers" in section A.3 of this chapter for additional information

EXAMPLE 6. A church's senior pastor owns his home and is paid a salary and housing allowance each year by his church. The church owns a parsonage, and this year it allows the pastor's son and daughter-in-law to use it as their residence at no charge (neither the son nor daughter-in-law is a minister or church employee). The annual rental value of the parsonage is $12,000, but the church does not believe this constitutes taxable income and so does not report it on the pastor's Form W-2 or on any tax form issued to the son or daughter-in-law. The pastor does not report the $12,000 as taxable income on his tax return (Form 1040) for this year. The pastor, as president of the church corporation, is a disqualified person, and so is his son. The church's decision to allow the pastor's son to reside in the parsonage constitutes an excess benefit. Since the benefit was not reported as taxable income in the year it was provided, the rental value constitutes an automatic excess benefit resulting in intermediate sanctions. This is so even though the amount of the benefit by itself, or when added to the pastor's other church compensation, is reasonable

in amount. This will result in (1) an excise tax of $3,000 (25 percent of $12,000); (2) an excise tax of $24,000 (200 percent of $12,000); and (3) a penalty for failing to file Form 4270 (assuming the pastor failed to do so).

If a disqualified person corrects an excess benefit transaction during the correction period, the 200 percent excise tax is automatically abated, and the 25 percent excise tax is abated if the disqualified person can establish that the excess benefit transaction was due to reasonable cause and was not due to willful neglect. See Example 3 for more information. However, if the pastor cannot establish both of these requirements, he would be liable for the 25 percent excise tax even though he corrected the excess benefit transaction by paying $12,000 plus interest to the church and paid federal income tax on the $12,000 as additional compensation. Also, note that the senior pastor and his son are jointly and severally liable for the intermediate sanctions, meaning that the IRS can collect them from either person.

Church board members who approve an excess benefit transaction are subject to an excise tax equal to 10 percent of the amount of the excess benefit—up to a maximum of $20,000 collectively.

EXAMPLE 7. A church sends its pastor and his wife on an all-expense-paid trip to Hawaii in honor of their 25th wedding anniversary. The total cost of the trip is $8,000. The church treasurer assumes that this amount is a nontaxable fringe benefit and so does not report any of the $8,000 on the pastor's Form W-2. The pastor likewise assumes that the cost of the trip is a nontaxable benefit. The church's payment of these travel expenses constitutes an automatic excess benefit resulting in intermediate sanctions, since it was not reported as taxable income by either the church or pastor in the year the benefit was provided. This is so even though the amount of the benefit by itself, or when added to the pastor's other church compensation, is reasonable in amount. This will result in (1) an excise tax of $2,000 (25 percent of $8,000); (2) an excise tax of $16,000 (200 percent of $8,000); and (3) a penalty for failing to file Form 4270 (assuming the pastor failed to do so).

If a disqualified person corrects an excess benefit transaction during the correction period, the 200 percent excise tax is automatically abated, and the 25 percent excise tax is abated if the disqualified person can establish that the excess benefit transaction was due to reasonable cause and was not due to willful neglect. See Example 3 for more information. However, if the pastor cannot establish both of these requirements, he would be liable for the 25 percent excise tax even though he corrected the excess benefit transaction by paying $8,000 plus interest to the church and paid federal income tax on the $8,000 as additional compensation. Also, note that the senior pastor and his wife are jointly and severally liable for the intermediate sanctions, meaning that the IRS can collect them from either person.

Church board members who approve an excess benefit transaction are subject to an excise tax equal to 10 percent of the amount of the excess benefit—up to a maximum of $20,000 collectively. For more information on this tax, see "Tax on managers" in section A.3 of this chapter.

EXAMPLE 8. A church collected a "love offering" from the congregation during the Christmas season last year. The congregation was informed that donations would be tax-deductible, and donations were reported on the annual contribution summary provided to each member. Last year the pastor's love offering was $4,000. Both the pastor and church treasurer assumed that this amount was a nontaxable gift, so neither reported it as taxable income (on Form W-2 or Form 1040). The love offering constitutes an automatic excess benefit resulting in intermediate sanctions, since it was not reported as taxable compensation by either the church or pastor in the year the benefit was provided. This is so even though the amount of the benefit by itself, or when added to the pastor's other church compensation, is reasonable in amount. This will result in (1) an excise tax of $1,000 (25 percent of $4,000); (2) an excise tax of $8,000 (200 percent of $4,000); and (3) a penalty for failing to file Form 4270 (assuming the pastor failed to do so).

If a disqualified person corrects an excess benefit transaction during the correction period, the 200 percent excise tax is automatically abated, and the 25 percent excise tax is abated if the disqualified person can establish that the excess benefit transaction was due to reasonable cause and was not due to willful neglect. See Example 3 for more information. However, if the pastor cannot establish both of these requirements, he would be liable for the 25 percent excise tax even though he corrected the excess benefit transaction by paying $4,000 plus interest to the church and paid federal income tax on the $4,000 as additional compensation.

Church board members who approve an excess benefit transaction are subject to an excise tax equal to 10 percent of the amount of the excess benefit—up to a maximum of $20,000 collectively. For more information on this tax, see "Tax on managers" in section A.3 of this chapter.

EXAMPLE 9. A church pays its senior pastor a monthly car allowance of $400. The church does not require the pastor to substantiate that he uses the monthly allowances for business purposes and does not require him to return any excess reimbursements (the amount by which the allowances exceed actual business expenses) to the church. The church treasurer does not report these allowances as taxable income on the pastor's Form W-2, since he assumes that the pastor has "at least" $400 of expenses associated with the business use of his car each month. The pastor reports none of the allowances as taxable income on his tax return (Form 1040).

An excess benefit is defined by section 4958 of the tax code as any compensation or benefit provided to a disqualified person in excess of the reasonable value of his or her services. It includes nonaccountable reimbursements of business and personal expenses—unless the reimbursements are reported as taxable compensation by the church or pastor in the year they are paid. Since the church did not "clearly indicate its intent to treat the benefit as compensation for services when the benefit was paid" (i.e., the benefit was not reported on the pastor's Form W-2 or Form 1040), the benefit constitutes an automatic excess benefit resulting in intermediate sanctions, regardless of the amount of the benefit. So even though the total amount of the allowances ($4,800 per year) would not have constituted an excess benefit had the church reported them as taxable income, the fact that it did not do so makes the allowances an automatic excess benefit. This will result in (1) an excise tax of $1,200 (25 percent of $4,800); (2) an excise tax of $9,600 (200 percent of $4,800); and (3) a penalty for failing to file Form 4270 (assuming the pastor failed to do so).

If a disqualified person corrects an excess benefit transaction during the correction period, the 200 percent excise tax is automatically abated, and the 25 percent excise tax is abated if the disqualified person can establish that the excess benefit transaction was due to reasonable cause and was not due to willful neglect. See Example 3 for more information. However, if the pastor cannot establish both of these requirements, he would be liable for the 25 percent excise tax even though he corrected the excess benefit transaction by paying $4,800 plus interest to the church and paid federal income tax on the $4,800 as additional compensation.

Church board members who approve an excess benefit transaction are subject to an excise tax equal to 10 percent of the amount of the excess benefit—up to a maximum of $20,000 collectively. For more information on this tax, see "Tax on managers" in section A.3 of this chapter.

B. WAGES, SALARIES, AND EARNINGS

The most significant component of income for most ministers and church staff is compensation received for personal services. Church compensation paid to employees constitutes wages and is reported on Form 1040, line 7. Compensation paid to self-employed workers (independent contractors) constitutes self-employment earnings and is reported on Schedule C (Form 1040).

As we will see later (in Chapters 5–7), some items of income are not included on Form 1040, line 7, or on Schedule C. These include a housing allowance, a church's reimbursements of business expenses under an accountable reimbursement plan, and several kinds of fringe benefits.

Church compensation often consists of several items besides salary, which must be included on the Form W-2 or Form 1099-MISC issued to the worker at the end of the year.

✿ **KEY POINT.** The IRS has issued guidelines for its agents to follow when auditing ministers. The guidelines cover a range of issues, including sources of ministerial income. The guidelines list the following sources of taxable income (this list is not exhaustive): (1) compensation; (2) bonuses; (3) special gifts; (4) fees paid directly from parishioners for performing weddings, funerals, baptisms, and masses; (5) expense allowances for travel, transportation, or other business expenses received under a nonaccountable plan; and (6) amounts paid by a church in addition to salary to cover the minister's self-employment tax or income tax.

Addressed in the remainder of this section are several items of income that may be received by ministers and church staff.

▲ **CAUTION.** *Many church treasurers do not understand that the benefits described below constitute taxable income. If a benefit is taxable and is not reported as taxable compensation by the church or the recipient in the year it is provided, the IRS may be able to assess intermediate sanctions in the form of substantial excise taxes against the recipient, and possibly members of the church board, regardless of the amount of the benefit. See section A.3 of this chapter for more details.*

1. BONUSES

Bonuses paid to a minister or staff member for outstanding work or other achievement are income and must be included on Form W-2 (if an employee) or Form 1099-MISC (if self-employed). *Treas. Reg. 1.61-2(a)(1).* Note that the bankruptcy court in the PTL case (discussed above) remarked that "bonuses [are] almost unheard of in the religious field." *Heritage Village Church and Missionary Fellowship, Inc., 92 B.R. 1000 (D.S.C. 1988).*

2. CHRISTMAS AND OTHER SPECIAL-OCCASION GIFTS

▲ **CAUTION.** *Special-occasion gifts constitute taxable income except as otherwise noted. If not reported as taxable income by the church or the recipient in the year provided, the IRS may be able to assess intermediate sanctions in the form of substantial excise taxes against the recipient, and possibly members of the church board, regardless of the amount of the benefit. See section A.3 of this chapter for more details.*

✿ **KEY POINT.** The IRS has announced that it will no longer issue private letter rulings addressing the question of "whether a transfer is a gift within the meaning of section 102" of the tax code. *Revenue Procedure 2012-3.*

Ministers and lay church employees often receive special-occasion gifts during the course of the year. Examples include Christmas, birthday, and anniversary gifts.

Church leaders often do not understand how to report these payments for federal tax purposes. Only two options are available: (1) the payments represent taxable compensation for services rendered and should be reported as income on the Form W-2 or Form 1099-MISC issued to the recipient by the church, or (2) the payments represent a nontaxable gift and are not reported on the Form W-2 or Form 1099-MISC issued to the recipient.

Are special-occasion gifts made to ministers and lay church employees tax-free gifts? Or are they taxable compensation for services rendered? While in most cases such distributions will represent taxable compensation for services rendered, in some cases a reasonable basis may exist for treating them as nontaxable gifts. Here are the most relevant considerations:

The Duberstein case

The United States Supreme Court, in a case involving a retirement gift made to a church treasurer, conceded that it is often difficult to distinguish between tax-free gifts and taxable compensation. The court did attempt to provide some guidance, however, by noting that "a gift in the statutory sense . . . proceeds from a detached and disinterested generosity . . . out of affection, respect, admiration, charity or like impulses. . . . The most critical consideration . . . is the transferor's intention." *Commissioner v. Duberstein, 363 U.S. 278 (1960).*

The court added that "it doubtless is the exceptional payment by an employer to an employee that amounts to a gift" and that the church's characterization of the distribution as a gift is "not determinative—there must be an objective inquiry as to whether what is called a gift amounts to it in reality."

The Bogardus case

In another ruling the Supreme Court attempted to provide further guidance in distinguishing between a tax-free gift and taxable compensation:

> *What controls is the intention with which payment, however voluntary, has been made. Has it been made with the intention that services rendered in the past shall be requited more completely, though full acquittance has been given? If so, it bears a tax. Has it been made to show good will, esteem, or kindliness toward persons who happen to have served, but who are paid without thought to make requital for the service? If so, it is exempt.* Bogardus v. Commissioner, 302 U.S. 34, 45 (1936).

Section 102(c) of the tax code

Section 102(c) of the tax code specifies that the definition of the term "gift" shall not include "any amount transferred by or for an employer to, or for the benefit of, an employee." There are two exceptions to this rule:

First, the tax code permits employees to exclude from income certain "employee achievement awards." This exception is discussed later in this section.

Second, employees (including ministers) are still permitted to exclude from gross income (as a de minimis fringe benefit) the value of any gift received from an employer if the value is so insignificant that accounting for it would be unreasonable or administratively impracticable. *IRC 132(e)*. To illustrate, a traditional employer holiday gift of low fair market value (a turkey, fruitcake, etc.) will continue to be excludable from an employee's income.

❋ **KEY POINT.** Whether holiday or other special-occasion gifts can qualify as nontaxable de minimis fringe benefits is a question that is addressed fully in Chapter 5, section I.4.

❋ **KEY POINT.** A federal appeals court made the following observation regarding section 102(c) of the tax code in a case involving congregational gifts to a pastor that did not go to the church and that were not receipted by the church as charitable contributions: "Although the legislative history suggests that [this section] was enacted to address other fact situations, its plain meaning may not be ignored in this case. That meaning seems far from plain, however. The church members are not [the pastor's] 'employer,' and the question whether their payments to the [pastor] were made 'for' his employer seems little different than the traditional gift inquiry under Duberstein and Bogardus. We therefore decline the government's belated suggestion that we affirm on the alternative ground of section 102(c)." *Goodwin v. United States, 67 F.3d 149 (8th Cir. 1995)*.

EXAMPLE. A federal appeals court affirmed the conviction of a pastor and his wife on several tax crimes based on various forms of church compensation they failed to disclose on their tax returns, including "gifts" from their church. The court observed: "It is apparent that the relationship between an employer and employee is one that is commonly established for some kind of mutual benefit, a dynamic that is altogether different from the 'detached and disinterested generosity' that normally prompts the tender of a gift. *Commissioner v. Duberstein, 363 U.S. 278, 285 (1960)*. . . . Payments from an employer to an employee are not gifts, but are presumed to be included in gross income. A taxpayer must report as gross income 'all income from whatever source derived' unless 'excluded by law.' To be sure, section 102(a) of the Code excludes from gross income 'the value of property acquired by gift.' But the Code is explicit that payments from an employer to an employee do not constitute gifts under §102(a), which 'shall not exclude from gross income any amount transferred by or for an employer to, or for the benefit of, an employee.'" *I.R.C. section 102(c). United States v. Jinwright, 2012-2 U.S.T.C. ¶50,417 (4th Cir. 2012)*.

Income tax regulations

The income tax regulations specify that Christmas bonuses paid by an employer are taxable income for the recipient. *Treas. Reg. 1.61-2(a)(1)*.

The Banks case

The Tax Court ruled that special offerings made to a minister on her birthday, Mother's Day, the church's anniversary, and Christmas were taxable compensation for services rendered rather than nontaxable gifts. *Banks v. Commissioner, 62 T.C.M. 1611 (1991)*. The offerings were in addition to the pastor's salary and amounted to more than $40,000 annually. The minister considered them to be tax-free gifts and did not report any of them as income on her income tax returns. The IRS audited the minister and determined that the special offerings were personal income and not tax-free gifts. The Tax Court agreed. It based its decision entirely on the Supreme Court's definition of the term "gift" announced in its *Duberstein* decision (mentioned above).

The Tax Court concluded that there simply was no way the special-occasion offerings in this case could be characterized as a gift under the *Duberstein* test, for the following reasons:

- Ample testimony from church members indicated that they contributed to the special-occasion offerings in order to show their appreciation to the minister for the excellent job she had done. This testimony clearly demonstrated that the offerings were compensation for services rendered (and therefore taxable) rather than a tax-free gift proceeding from a "detached and disinterested generosity."
- The offerings were not spontaneous and voluntary but rather were part of a "highly structured program" for transferring money to the minister on a regular basis. Church members met to discuss the amounts of the four special-occasion offerings, and most members made donations or "pledges" of a suggested amount and were pressured into honoring their pledges. The existence of such a program suggested that the transfers were not the product of a "detached and disinterested generosity" but were designed to compensate the minister for her service as a minister.
- The church substantially increased the minister's salary following the discontinuance of the four special-occasion offerings so that the minister's total compensation remained basically the same.

The Goodwin case

A federal appeals court ruled that congregational offerings collected on four special days each year and presented to a pastor represented taxable compensation rather than tax-free gifts. *Goodwin v. United States, 67 F.3d 149 (8th Cir. 1995)*. About two weeks before each special occasion, the associate pastor made an announcement prior to the commencement of a church service that he would be collecting money for the special-occasion gift.

The pastor and his wife were not present in the sanctuary during this announcement. People wishing to donate placed money in an envelope and gave it to the associate pastor or one of the deacons. The money was never placed in the offering plates passed during the services. Any checks received were returned in order to maintain anonymity. The money was never counted and was not recorded in the church book or records. The congregation was advised that their contributions would not be receipted by the church and were not tax-deductible.

The IRS audited the pastor's tax returns for 1987–1989 and determined that the special-occasion gifts were in fact taxable compensation to the pastor. The congregational "gifts" to the pastor amounted to $12,750 in 1987, $14,500 in 1988, and $15,000 in 1989. The pastor's salary (not counting the special-occasion gifts) was $7,800 in 1987, $14,566 in 1988, and $16,835 in 1989.

Despite the church members' belief that they were giving to their pastor out of "love, respect, admiration and like impulses," the court concluded that the payments constituted taxable compensation to the pastor. The court based its decision on the *Duberstein* case (discussed above), from which it derived the following principles: (1) the donor's intent is "the most critical consideration," and (2) "there must an objective inquiry" into the donor's intent. The court concluded that the facts of the case demonstrated that the donors' intent was to more fully compensate their pastor, and accordingly the "gifts" represented taxable compensation. It based this conclusion on two factors:

- **Source of the "gifts."** The court concluded that the "gifts" were made by the congregation and not by individual donors, since (1) "the cash payments were gathered by congregation leaders in a routinized, highly structured program," and (2) "individual church members contributed anonymously, and the regularly-scheduled payments were made to [the pastor] on behalf of the entire congregation."
- **Size of the "gifts."** The court also noted that the gifts were a substantial portion of the pastor's overall compensation. It observed:

The congregation, collectively, knew that without these substantial, on-going cash payments, the church likely could not retain the services of a popular and successful minister at the relatively low salary it was paying. In other words, the congregation knew that its special occasion gifts enabled the church to pay a $15,000 salary for $30,000 worth of work. Regular, sizable payments made by persons to whom the taxpayer provides services are customarily regarded as a form of compensation and may therefore be treated as taxable compensation.

The IRS proposed that the court adopt the following test to determine whether transfers from church members to their minister represent nontaxable gifts: "The feelings of love, admiration and respect that professedly motivated the parishioners to participate in the special occasion offerings arose from and were directly attributable to the services that [the pastor] performed for them as pastor of the church. Since the transfers were tied to the performance of services by [the pastor] they were, as a matter of law, compensation."

The court rejected this test as too broad, noting that

it would include as taxable income every twenty dollar gift spontaneously given by a church member after an inspiring sermon, simply because the urge to give was tied to the minister's services. It would also include a departing church member's individual, unsolicited five hundred dollar gift to a long-tenured, highly respected priest, rabbi, or minister, a result that is totally at odds with the opinions of all nine [Supreme Court] Justices in Bogardus v. Commissioner: "Has [the payment] been made with the intention that services rendered in the past shall be requited more completely, though full acquittance has been given? If so, it bears a tax. Has it been made to show good will, esteem, or kindliness toward persons who happen to have served, but who are paid without thought to make requital for the service? If so, it is exempt" [emphasis added]. Bogardus v. Commissioner, 302 U.S. 34, 45 (1936).

❖ **KEY POINT.** The court acknowledged that a $20 gift spontaneously given by a church member to a pastor is a nontaxable gift rather than taxable compensation despite the fact that the "urge to give" was tied to the pastor's services. The court also acknowledged that modest retirement gifts made by church members to a retiring minister can represent tax-free gifts.

❖ **KEY POINT.** The court, in commenting on the *Duberstein* case, noted that "it is the rare donor who is completely 'detached and disinterested.'"

One additional aspect of the court's ruling is significant. The court noted that section 102(c) of the Code prohibits employers from treating as a tax-free gift "any amount transferred by or for an employer to, or for the benefit of, an employee." The court further noted that

although the legislative history suggests that [this section] was enacted to address other fact situations, its plain meaning may not be ignored in this case. That meaning seems far from plain, however. The church members are not [the pastor's] "employer," and the question whether their payments to the [pastor] were made "for" his employer seems little different than the traditional gift inquiry under Duberstein and Bogardus. We therefore decline the government's belated suggestion that we affirm on the alternative ground of section 102(c).

This is a potentially significant observation, since it raises some doubt as to the relevance and applicability of section 102(c) of the tax code to gifts made to ministers and lay church employees.

IRS Audit Guidelines for Ministers

In 1995 the IRS released its first audit guidelines for ministers pursuant to its Market Segment Specialization Program (MSSP). The guidelines were intended to promote a higher degree of competence among agents who audit ministers. In 2009 the IRS released a newly revised version of the guidelines (the Minister Audit Technique Guide). The guidelines instruct IRS agents in the examination of ministers' tax returns.

The guidelines inform IRS agents that "gifts given to a minister, other than retired ministers, may actually be compensation for services, hence includable in gross income" for tax purposes. The guidelines provide agents with the following assistance in deciding if a church's payment to a minister is a tax-free gift or taxable compensation for services rendered:

- The tax code provides that taxable income includes all income from whatever source derived unless specifically excluded. Section 102(a) of the tax code excludes the value of property acquired by gift. The guidelines state: "Whether an item is a gift is a factual question and the taxpayer bears the burden of proof. The most significant fact is the intention of the taxpayer."
- The issue of differentiating tax-free gifts and taxable compensation has been addressed in the following court rulings:

(1) In *Commissioner v. Duberstein*, 363 U.S. 278 (1960), the United States Supreme Court stated the governing principles in this area: The mere absence of a legal or moral obligation to make such a payment does not establish that it is a gift. And, importantly, if the payment proceeds primarily from "the constraining force of any moral or legal duty" or from "the incentive of anticipated benefit" of an economic nature, it is not a gift. And, conversely, "where the payment is in return for services rendered, it is irrelevant that the donor derives no economic benefit from it." A gift in the statutory sense, on the other hand, proceeds from a "detached and disinterested generosity," "out of affection, respect, admiration, charity or like impulses." And in this regard, the most critical consideration, is the transferor's "intention." "What controls is the intention with which payment, however voluntary, has been made."

(2) In *Bogardus v. Commissioner*, 302 U.S. 34, 43 (1937), the United States Supreme Court provided the following guidance in distinguishing between a tax-free gift and taxable compensation: "What controls is the intention with which payment, however voluntary, has been made. Has it been made with the intention that services rendered in the past shall be requited more completely, though full acquittance has been given? If so, it bears a tax. Has it been made to show good will, esteem, or kindliness toward persons who happen to have served, but who are paid without thought to make requital for the service? If so, it is exempt."

(3) In *Banks v. Commissioner*, T.C. Memo. 1991-641, the United States Tax Court addressed a "structured and organized" transfer of cash from members of a church to their pastor on four special days of each year. Prior to making the transfers, members of the church met to discuss the transfers. The amounts of the transfers were significant. The testimony of several members indicated that "the primary reason for the transfers at issue was not detached and disinterested generosity, but rather, the church members' desire to reward petitioner for her services as a pastor and their desire that she remain in that capacity." The court ruled the transfers were compensation for services hence included in taxable income.

(4) In *Lloyd L. Goodwin v. U.S.*, 67 F.3d 149 (8th Cir. 1995), a federal appeals court addressed the tax status of offerings collected from a church congregation on special occasion days. The collections were done by congregational leaders in a structured manner. The congregation knew that it probably could not retain the pastor's service at his relatively low salary without the additional payments. The court ruled that the funds were compensation for services, not gifts.

(5) The Tax Court had ruled in *Potito v. Commissioner*, T.C. Memo 1975-187, aff'd 534 F.2d 49 (5th Cir. 1976), that the value of a boat, motor, and boat trailer was included in taxable income as payment for services. The taxpayer, a minister, had not produced any evidence regarding the intention of the donors that the transfer of the property was out of "detached and disinterested generosity."

Conclusions

The legal precedents summarized above can be reduced to the following general principles.

Gifts from the general fund

Special-occasion gifts made to a minister or lay employee by the church out of the general fund should be reported as taxable compensation and included on the recipient's Form W-2 or 1099-MISC and on Form 1040.

Person-to-person gifts

Members are free to make personal gifts to ministers or lay employees, such as a card at Christmas accompanied by a check or cash. Such payments may be tax-free gifts to the recipient (though they are not deductible by the donor), especially when small in amount. See the *Goodwin* case (above).

Gifts funded through members' donations to the church

Many special-occasion gifts to ministers and lay church employees are funded through members' contributions to the church (i.e., the contributions are entered or recorded in the church's books as cash received, and the members are given charitable contribution credit). Such gifts should always be reported as taxable compensation and included on the recipient's Form W-2 or 1099-MISC and on Form 1040. Members who contribute to special-occasion offerings pre-approved by the church board ordinarily may deduct their contributions if they are able to itemize deductions on Schedule A (Form 1040).

Gifts funded through personal checks to the recipient collected by the church

Some churches collect an offering for distribution to a minister or lay church employee on a special occasion and instruct donors that (1) cash and checks will be accepted, but checks must be made payable directly to the pastor or lay employee; and (2) no contribution will be receipted by the church as a charitable contribution. In other words, the church is merely collecting the individual gifts and then distributing them to the recipient. This ordinarily is done for convenience. A reasonable basis exists for treating such gifts as nontaxable to the minister or lay employee, so long as (1) the offering satisfies the definition of a gift announced by the Supreme Court in the *Duberstein* case (summarized previously); and (2) the offering consists of cash and checks made payable directly to the recipient, donors are not given any charitable contribution credit for their contributions, and the offering is not recorded as income in the church's books of account.

Whether an offering will satisfy the *Duberstein* case will depend on several factors, including the intent of the donors who contribute to the offering (e.g., if they are simply wanting to provide additional compensation to their minister in recognition of services rendered, then the transfer ordinarily will be taxable compensation rather than a tax-free gift); whether a church adjusts its pastor's compensation on the basis of the special-occasion offerings collected on his or her behalf; and whether the contributions were spontaneous and voluntary as opposed to fixed amounts established under a "highly structured program" for transferring money to the minister on a regular basis.

Employee achievement awards

If you receive tangible personal property (other than cash, a gift certificate, or an equivalent item) as an award for length of service or safety achievement, you generally can exclude its value from your income. However, the amount you can exclude is limited to your employer's cost and cannot be more than $1,600 ($400 for awards that are not qualified plan awards) for all such awards you receive during the year. Your employer must make the award as part of a meaningful presentation, under conditions and circumstances that do not create a significant likelihood of it's being disguised pay. However, the exclusion does not apply to the following awards:

- A length-of-service award if you received it for less than five years of service or if you received another length-of-service award during the year or the previous four years.
- A safety achievement award if you are a manager, administrator, clerical employee, or other professional employee

or if more than 10 percent of eligible employees previously received safety achievement awards during the year.

The term "qualified plan award" means "an employee achievement award awarded as part of an established written plan or program of the taxpayer which does not discriminate in favor of highly compensated employees [for 2013, those earning annual compensation of $115,000 or more] as to eligibility or benefits." *IRC 274(j).*

Examples

❖ **KEY POINT.** Churches, being tax-exempt organizations, may not make any distribution of their funds other than as reasonable compensation for services rendered or as payments in direct furtherance of their exempt purposes. They cannot make "gifts" to ministers or lay employees. Therefore, to avoid jeopardizing a church's tax-exempt status, it ordinarily is advisable (with the exceptions noted above) for special-occasion distributions from a church to its employees be characterized as compensation for services rendered and reported on the minister's Form W-2 or 1099-MISC. *IRC 501(c)(3).*

EXAMPLE. A church board votes to award a "Christmas bonus" in the amount of $1,000 to Pastor C. The bonus is to be paid out of the church's general fund. Under these facts, Pastor C has clearly received taxable compensation of $1,000, and the Form W-2 issued by the church to Pastor C should reflect this fact.

EXAMPLE. A church collects an offering for its pastor once each year at Christmas. This practice has occurred for more than 25 years. A member of the church board announces the offering during a worship service, and members are advised that their contributions will be receipted by the church. The Christmas gift made to the pastor under these circumstances is taxable compensation and should be added to the pastor's Form W-2 or 1099-MISC.

EXAMPLE. Same facts as the previous example, except that a member of the board, in announcing the offering, informs church members that their contributions will not be receipted and will not be deductible. Members are informed that they will be making their gifts directly to the pastor and, accordingly, are instructed to make checks payable directly to the pastor and not to the church. The church collects the offering and transfers it to the pastor without receipting any contributions.

This example can be analyzed in two ways. The conservative approach, based on the *Goodwin* case (discussed above), would treat the Christmas gift to the pastor as taxable income. This was the view the IRS contended for in the *Goodwin* case, and presumably it reflects the IRS view on this issue.

A more aggressive approach would be to treat the gift to the pastor as a tax-free gift rather than as taxable compensation.

This view is based on the following considerations: (1) The members were not receipted for their contributions. (2) Members were informed that they were giving directly to the pastor. (3) Members did not deduct their contributions. (4) The church was acting merely as an intermediary. The gifts, in reality, were made by individual members directly to their pastor. (5) The church's minimal involvement in the arrangement (collecting and turning over the offering) did not amount to sufficient church involvement to prevent the offering from being characterized as an aggregate of individual gifts from members directly to their pastor. (6) Only one special-occasion offering was collected each year. (7) Members were not pressured or coerced into making contributions. Participating in the offering was voluntary. (8) The pastor was adequately compensated through salary and fringe benefits. (9) Most members contribute to such an offering out of sincere affection, respect, and admiration and not out of a desire to compensate the pastor more fully for services rendered. Pastors and churches should not select the "aggressive approach" without the advice of a tax professional.

EXAMPLE. A church collects an all-cash offering in commemoration of its pastor's 25th year of service. Donors are told to contribute cash or checks payable directly to the pastor and are informed that the offering will be given directly to the pastor without being processed through the church's accounts and that no charitable contribution credit will be received. See the previous example for the correct analysis.

3. RETIREMENT GIFTS

▲ **CAUTION.** *This benefit constitutes taxable income except as otherwise noted. If it is not reported as taxable income by the church or the recipient in the year it is provided, the IRS may be able to assess intermediate sanctions in the form of substantial excise taxes against the recipient, regardless of the amount of the benefit. See section A.3 of this chapter for more details.*

▲ **CAUTION.** *Section 409A of the tax code imposes several complex requirements on nonqualified deferred compensation plans, including documentation, elections, funding, distributions, withholding, and reporting. If a plan does not meet these requirements, participants in the plan are required to include in income immediately compensation otherwise deferred under the plan and pay taxes on such income, including an additional 20 percent tax and a tax generally based upon the underpayment interest that would have accrued had the amount been includible in income when first deferred. Nonqualified deferred compensation subject to the section 409A requirements is generally defined as compensation that workers earn in one year but that is not paid until a future year. Some exceptions apply. For example, section 409A does not apply to qualified plans (such as a section 401(k) plan) or to a section 403(b) plan. Any agreement to pay compensation to a current or former employee may be subject to the 409A requirements. Such payments should not be approved without the advice of a tax professional to ensure that the potential application of*

section 409A is fully addressed. Section 409A is addressed in Chapter 10, section A.2, of this guide.

❖ **KEY POINT.** The IRS has announced that it will no longer issue private letter rulings addressing the question of "whether a transfer is a gift within the meaning of section 102" of the tax code. To illustrate, a pastor retires after many years of service to the same church. The church presents him with a check in the amount of $10,000. Is this check taxable compensation, or a tax-free gift? This is a question the IRS no longer will address in private letter rulings. *Revenue Procedure 2012-3.*

It is common for churches to present a retiring minister or lay employee with a retirement gift. Sometimes these gifts are very generous. Should the church report such gifts as taxable compensation and include them on the recipient's Form W-2? Or can the church treat them as nontaxable gifts?

Federal tax law requires all forms of compensation to be reported as taxable income unless specifically excluded by law. Gifts are one such exclusion. The question, then, is whether retirement gifts are taxable compensation for services rendered or tax-free gifts. The answer to this question is not always clear. All of the relevant precedent is summarized below, followed by a series of conclusions.

Four cases from the 1950s

In a series of cases in the early 1950s, four federal appeals courts concluded that certain retirement gifts to ministers were tax-free gifts rather than taxable compensation. These four rulings are summarized below:

Schall v. Commissioner, 174 F.2d 893 (5th Cir. 1949)

A federal appeals court ruled that a church's retirement gift to its pastor represented a tax-free gift rather than taxable compensation. The pastor was forced to retire on the advice of his physician as a result of a long illness. He made no request of the congregation that any amount be paid to him after his resignation, and he had no knowledge that the church would agree to do so. He did not agree to render any services in exchange for the gift and in fact did not do so. The court concluded:

> *We are of opinion the Tax Court clearly erred in holding that the payments to [the pastor] were taxable income. Where, as here, all the facts and circumstances surrounding the adoption of the [gift] clearly prove an intent to make a gift, the mere use of the terms "salary" and "honorarium" do not convert the gift into a payment for services. Moreover, "a gift is none the less a gift because inspired by gratitude for past faithful service of the recipient. . . ." Manifestly, these payments to [the pastor] were non-taxable gifts, within the orbit of the rule defining same, as enunciated by this court in [another case]: "That only is a gift which is purely such, not intended as a return of value or made because of any intent to repay another what is his due, but bestowed only because of*

personal affection or regard or pity, or from general motives of philanthropy or charity."

Mutch v. Commissioner, 209 F.2d 390 (3rd Cir. 1954)

A federal appeals court ruled that monthly retirement gifts made by a church to its retired pastor were tax-free gifts rather than taxable compensation. The court noted that the church's action in providing for the monthly honoraria "was motivated solely and sincerely by the congregation's love and affection for [the pastor]." The court described the church's action as a "free gift of a friendly, well-to-do group who as long as they were able and because they were, wished their old minister to live in a manner comparable to that which he had enjoyed while actively associated with them." The court also observed: "[The pastor] had been adequately compensated as far as money could for his services in the past. He was not being tied into any promise of services in the future. The installment gift, while it could be stopped or changed at any time by the trustees, had no conditions attached to its acceptance. The court concluded that no other ruling 'justifies the taxing of this bona fide gift given [the pastor] with love and affection by his old congregation.'"

Kavanagh v. Hershman, 210 F.2d 654 (6th Cir. 1954)

A federal appeals court, in a one-paragraph opinion, ruled that a distribution of funds to a minister was a tax-free gift rather than taxable compensation. The court based its decision on the *Mutch* decision (summarized above).

Abernathy v. Commissioner, 211 F.2d 651 (D.C. Cir. 1954)

The *Abernathy* case was a one-paragraph decision issued by a federal appeals court in 1954. The ruling addressed the question of whether a $2,400 retirement gift paid by a church to its pastor "as a token of its gratitude and appreciation" and "in appreciation of his long and faithful service" represented taxable income or a tax-free gift. The federal court concluded that the transfer was a tax-free gift. It cited (without explanation) the *Schall*, *Mutch*, and *Kavanagh* decisions (summarized above) along with *Bogardus v. Commissioner*, 302 U.S. 34 (1936) (discussed below).

⚙ **KEY POINT.** The *Abernathy* case was referred to, with approval, by a federal court in 1994 in a ruling addressing the tax status of congregational gifts to a minister. *Goodwin v. United States, 94-2 U.S.T.C. ¶ 50,597 (S.D. Iowa 1994), affirmed, 67 F.3d 149 (8th Cir. 1995).*

IRS Revenue Ruling 55-422

In 1955 the IRS issued Revenue Ruling 55-422, in which it endorsed the four cases summarized above because of the following facts in each case: (1) "the payments were not made in accordance with any enforceable agreement, established plan, or past practice"; (2) the minister "did not undertake to perform any further services for the congregation and was not expected to do so" following his retirement; (3) "there was a far closer personal relationship between the [minister] and the congregation than is found in lay

employment relationships"; and (4) "the available evidence indicated that the amount paid was determined in light of the financial position of the congregation and the needs of the recipient, who had been adequately compensated for his past services."

Commissioner v. Duberstein, 363 U.S. 278 (1960)

In this case the United States Supreme Court addressed the question of whether a $20,000 retirement gift made by a church to a retiring lay officer was taxable compensation or a tax-free gift. The church board had authorized the gift in a resolution characterizing the gift as a "gratuity" and specifying that it had been made "in appreciation for services rendered." The trial court concluded that the distribution was a tax-free gift, but a federal appeals court disagreed. The appeals court conceded that the courts had uniformly treated retirement gifts to ministers as tax-free gifts, since "in such cases the parishioners are apt to be largely moved by gratitude for spiritual direction, kindness and affection and do not think in quantitative terms of whatever financial gains the pastor may have contributed to the [church]." *Stanton v. United States, 268 F.2d 727 (2nd Cir. 1959).* The case was appealed to the United States Supreme Court, which freely admitted the difficulty of distinguishing between tax-free gifts and taxable compensation. The Supreme Court did attempt to provide some guidance, however, by noting that "a gift in the statutory sense . . . proceeds from a detached and disinterested generosity . . . out of affection, respect, admiration, charity, or like impulses. . . . The most critical consideration . . . is the transferor's intention."

The court also observed that "it doubtless is the exceptional payment by an employer to an employee that amounts to a gift" and that the church's characterization of the distribution as a gift is "not determinative—there must be an objective inquiry as to whether what is called a gift amounts to it in reality."

Bogardus v. Commissioner, 302 U.S. 34 (1936)

Also relevant in resolving the issue of whether a particular distribution constitutes a tax-free gift or taxable compensation for services rendered is the following language from another Supreme Court decision:

> *What controls is the intention with which payment, however voluntary, has been made. Has it been made with the intention that services rendered in the past shall be requited more completely, though full acquittance has been given? If so, it bears a tax. Has it been made to show good will, esteem, or kindliness toward persons who happen to have served, but who are paid without thought to make requital for the service? If so, it is exempt.*

Perkins v. Commissioner, 34 T.C. 117 (1960)

In 1960 the Tax Court ruled that pension payments made by the United Methodist Church to retired ministers constituted taxable compensation rather than tax-free gifts. The court concluded that the pension payments could not be characterized as tax-free gifts, since they did not satisfy all of the conditions specified by the IRS in

Revenue Ruling 55-422 (discussed above). Specifically, the "pension payments were made in accordance with the established plan and past practice of the Methodist Church, there was no close relationship between the recipient [ministers] and the bulk of the contributing congregations, and the amounts paid were not determined in the light of the needs of the individual [ministers]."

Joyce v. Commissioner, 25 T.C.M. 914 (1966)

In 1966 the Tax Court ruled that retirement payments made by the General Conference of Seventh-Day Adventists to the widow of a former minister represented taxable income and not tax-free gifts. Upon retirement, ministers received monthly payments from the "sustentation fund" of the General Conference. Benefits were based upon the length of service of the minister. Benefits to the widow of a deceased minister were limited to three-quarters of the payment received by the deceased spouse. The General Conference issued the widow Forms 1099-MISC reporting the payments as taxable income. However, in reporting her taxes, the widow treated the payments as nontaxable gifts. The court noted that "the Ultimate criterion" in resolving such cases is "the basic or dominant reason that explains the action of the transferor." How is this "basis or dominant reason" to be determined? The court listed the following considerations:

- To constitute a gift the benefits paid must proceed from a "detached and disinterested generosity" or "out of affection, respect, admiration, and charity or like impulses."
- "The absence of a legal or moral obligation to make such payments . . . or the fact that payments are voluntary . . . do not [necessarily] establish that a gift was intended. However, payments which do proceed from a legal or moral obligation are not gifts."
- "Additional factors, which militate against a determination that gifts were intended, have been findings: (1) that a plan or past practice of payment was in existence; (2) that the needs of the widow were neither the prerequisite for, nor the measure of payment; and (3) that the transferor considered the payment as compensation, including the withholding of income tax."

The court acknowledged that "in determining that certain payments constituted gifts, courts have seized upon the following: that payments were made directly to the widow rather than to the estate; that the widow performed no services for the transferor; that full compensation had been paid for the services of the deceased husband; and that the transferor derived no benefit from the payment."

The court stressed that "[t]he determination of the transferor's dominant motive does not rest upon any single factor but is rather a conclusion reached after due consideration of all the relevant factors." It concluded that the payments made to the widow in this case represented taxable income on the basis of the following considerations:

- Benefits payable to a minister, and to a surviving spouse, are fixed according to a computation based upon the length of service by the employee to the church. In other words, they are paid according to a formal plan. The court concluded that "[t]he existence of a plan or practice is most persuasive against the theory that a payment is a gift, and, we think it is decisive where a benefit to the [employer] is expected." The court noted that the church benefited from the payments to widows by providing "an additional inducement for workers to enter the church's employ."
- The church made payments to the widow "without any inquiry into her financial condition."
- The amount of payments was "based on a computation which ignores financial condition, in that benefits are computed solely on the basis of length of service and the degree of major responsibility borne by the employee." The court stressed that "[t]his lack of consideration of [the widow's] financial status is a highly relevant factor in determining that the motive of the transferor was not to make a gift to [her]."
- The court noted that the church itself treated the payments as taxable income to the widow and so reported them on Forms 1099-MISC. The court observed that "[t]his factor, though not decisive, is, again, highly relevant to the determination that no gift was intended."
- The court noted that the church "recognized a moral obligation to make such payments to those employees, and their widows, who have loyally rendered service to the church. This fact alone has been held sufficient to prevent payments from constituting gifts."

The court acknowledged that the payments were made directly to the widow and that she did not perform any services for the church. It rejected the widow's argument that this factor required the payments to be treated as gifts to her, since she had otherwise failed to overcome all of the other factors supporting the court's decision that the payments were taxable.

✿ **KEY POINT.** A federal appeals court mentioned "a departing church member's individual, unsolicited five hundred dollar gift to a long-tenured, highly respected priest, rabbi, or minister," as an example of a retirement gift that clearly would be nontaxable to the recipient based on the "opinions of all nine Justices" in the Bogardus case ("Has it been made to show good will, esteem, or kindliness toward persons who happen to have served, but who are paid without thought to make requital for the service? If so, it is exempt"). *Goodwin v. United States, 67 F.3d 149 (8th Cir. 1995).*

Brimm v. Commissioner, 27 T.C.M. 1148 (1968)

In 1968 the Tax Court ruled that a severance gift made by a church-affiliated school to a professor was a nontaxable gift rather than taxable compensation. The professor (the "taxpayer") was employed by a church-related, two-year graduate school supported by the Southern Baptist Convention. It became apparent that, because of the small student body and the high cost of operations, the school would have to be closed.

Prior to the school's dissolution, its board of trustees adopted a resolution authorizing "a gift equivalent to one year's salary to each faculty member and staff member upon termination of his or her services with the school." Pursuant to this policy, the taxpayer received a "gift" of $8,600 in two annual installments bearing the notation "severance gift." The taxpayer did not report the two installments as taxable income on his tax returns since he regarded them to be a tax-free gift rather than taxable compensation for services rendered.

The IRS audited the taxpayer's tax returns and determined that the severance gifts constituted taxable income. On appeal, the Tax Court concluded that the severance payments were in fact nontaxable gifts: "It is clear from the evidence that the board of trustees of the school took their action in declaring and making a severance gift to the taxpayer, as well as to other members of the small staff, because they were grateful and appreciative of the past faithful and dedicated service rendered to the school." The court noted that the presence of affection, respect, admiration, and a deep sense of appreciation in the minds of trustees was demonstrated by the testimony of a member of the board who testified that the severance gifts were not intended to represent additional compensation, that were authorized solely as a means of showing appreciation to the faculty, and that there was no expectation of additional services being performed in return for the severance gifts. The court concluded:

> There is no doubt that the school's trustees were motivated by gratitude for the taxpayer's past faithful services, but, as the Supreme Court said in [the Bogardus case] "a gift is none the less a gift because inspired by gratitude for past faithful service of the recipient." Indeed, long and faithful service may create the atmosphere of goodwill and kindliness toward the recipient which tends to support a finding that a gift rather than additional compensation was intended. . . . We hold that the school intended to make, and did make, a gift which was made gratuitously and in exchange for nothing.

IRS Audit Guidelines for Ministers

In 1995 the IRS released its first audit guidelines for ministers pursuant to its Market Segment Specialization Program (MSSP). The guidelines were intended to promote a higher degree of competence among agents who audit ministers. In 2009 the IRS released a newly revised version of the guidelines (the Ministers Audit Technique Guide). The guidelines instruct IRS agents in the examination of ministers' tax returns.

Perhaps the biggest surprise in the revised audit guidelines is the following statement: "There are numerous court cases that ruled the organized authorization of funds to be paid to a retired minister

at or near the time of retirement were gifts and not compensation for past services. Revenue Ruling 55-422 discusses the fact pattern of those cases which would render the payments as gifts and not compensation."

Revenue Ruling 55-422 is summarized above. In this 1955 ruling, the IRS endorsed four federal appeals court cases holding that retirement distributions from a church to a pastor were tax-free gifts due to the following "fact patterns" in each case:

- "the payments were not made in accordance with any enforceable agreement, established plan, or past practice";
- the minister "did not undertake to perform any further services for the congregation and was not expected to do so" following his retirement;
- "there was a far closer personal relationship between the [minister] and the congregation than is found in lay employment relationships"; and
- "the available evidence indicated that the amount paid was determined in light of the financial position of the congregation and the needs of the recipient, who had been adequately compensated for his past services."

Conclusions

Consider the following conclusions in deciding whether to treat a retirement gift as taxable compensation or as a tax-free gift.

The current status of the four 1950s cases

The *Schall*, *Mutch*, *Kavanagh*, and *Abernathy* cases, summarized above, and Revenue Ruling 55-422, suggest that retirement gifts to ministers can, under limited circumstances, be treated as tax-free gifts rather than as taxable compensation so long as the "fact patterns" mentioned in these four cases (summarized above) are satisfied. The IRS has never officially revoked or even modified Revenue Ruling 55-422, and none of the four federal appeals court rulings has been qualified or overturned. However, three considerations have made such a conclusion questionable, prior to the release of the IRS modified audit guidelines for ministers in 2009:

1. The position of the IRS national office. The IRS national office sent the author of this text a letter stating that "Revenue Ruling 55-422 ceased to represent the Service's position on or before the date the Supreme Court decided *Commissioner v. Duberstein* [in 1960]." The *Duberstein* case is summarized above. The IRS also informed the author that (1) "for years after 1986, section 102(c) ensures that [retirement] payments are not excludable" by ministers who are employees for income tax reporting purposes, and (2) retirement gifts to self-employed ministers are now evaluated under the *Duberstein* and *Stanton* cases (summarized above).

The IRS's repudiation of Revenue Ruling 55-422, and the four federal appeals court rulings summarized above, is belied by the following considerations:

First, in Revenue Procedure 89-14, the IRS provided the following information concerning revenue rulings:

A revenue ruling is an official interpretation by the IRS of the internal revenue laws and related statutes, treaties, and regulations. . . . Revenue rulings are issued only by the IRS national office and are published for the information and guidance of taxpayers, IRS officials, and others concerned. . . .

Taxpayers generally may rely upon revenue rulings and revenue procedures in determining the tax treatment of their own transactions and need not request specific rulings applying the principles of a published revenue ruling or revenue procedure to the facts of their particular cases. However, taxpayers, IRS personnel, and others concerned are also cautioned to determine whether a revenue ruling or revenue procedure on which they seek to rely has been revoked, modified, declared obsolete, distinguished, clarified or otherwise affected by subsequent legislation, treaties, regulations, revenue rulings, revenue procedures or court decisions.

The IRS has never revoked, modified, declared obsolete, or distinguished Revenue Ruling 54-422.

Second, Revenue Ruling 55-422 was quoted with approval as recently as 1995 by the United States Tax Court. *Osborne v. Commissioner, 69 T.C.M. 1895 (1995)*. This is several years after the *Duberstein* case (1960) and effective date of section 102(c) of the tax code (1987), both of which events were previously cited by the IRS as its rationale for no longer following Revenue Ruling 55-422.

Third, other federal courts have affirmed the tax-free status of gifts made to ministers. To illustrate, in *Brimm v. Commissioner, 27 T.C.M. 1148 (1968)*, the United States Tax Court ruled that a severance gift made by a church-affiliated school to a professor was a nontaxable gift rather than taxable compensation. The professor (the "taxpayer") was employed by a church-related, two-year graduate school supported by the Southern Baptist Convention. It became apparent that, because of the small student body and the high cost of operations, the school would have to be closed. Prior to the school's dissolution, its board of trustees adopted a resolution authorizing "a gift equivalent to one year's salary to each faculty member and staff member upon termination of his or her services with the school." Pursuant to this policy, the taxpayer received a "gift" of $8,600 in two annual installments bearing the notation "severance gift." The taxpayer did not report the two installments as taxable income on his tax returns because he regarded them to be a tax-free gift rather than taxable compensation for services rendered.

The IRS audited the taxpayer's tax returns and determined that the severance gifts constituted taxable income. On appeal, the Tax Court concluded that the severance payments were, in fact, nontaxable gifts: "It is clear from the evidence that the board of trustees

of the school took their action in declaring and making a severance gift to the taxpayer, as well as to other members of the small staff, because they were grateful and appreciative of the past faithful and dedicated service rendered to the school." The court noted that the presence of affection, respect, admiration, and a deep sense of appreciation in the minds of trustees was demonstrated by the testimony of a member of the board who testified that the severance gifts were not intended to represent additional compensation, that were authorized solely as a means of showing appreciation to the faculty, and that there was no expectation of additional services being performed in return for the severance gifts. The court concluded:

There is no doubt that the school's trustees were motivated by gratitude for the taxpayer's past faithful services, but, as the Supreme Court said in [the Bogardus case] "a gift is none the less a gift because inspired by gratitude for past faithful service of the recipient." Indeed, long and faithful service may create the atmosphere of goodwill and kindliness toward the recipient which tends to support a finding that a gift rather than additional compensation was intended. . . . We hold that the school intended to make, and did make, a gift which was made gratuitously and in exchange for nothing.

Fourth, the IRS audit guidelines for ministers (2009), summarized above, contain the following statement: "There are numerous court cases that ruled the organized authorization of funds to be paid to a retired minister at or near the time of retirement were gifts and not compensation for past services. Revenue Ruling 55-422 discusses the fact pattern of those cases which would render the payments as gifts and not compensation." This appears to be an explicit recognition that Revenue Ruling 55-422 continues to accurately reflect the law.

2. Tax-exempt status. Neither Revenue Ruling 55-422 nor any of the four court decisions from the 1950s explains how a church can distribute any of its assets as a tax-free gift without jeopardizing its tax-exempt status. To be exempt from federal income taxation, a church must satisfy a number of requirements. One of these requirements is that none of its assets or income be distributed to any individual except as reasonable compensation for services rendered or for a charitable or religious purpose. *IRC 501(c)(3)*. Treating a retirement gift as a tax-free gift would appear to violate this requirement if the gift is paid out of church funds. The effect of this would be to call into question the tax-exempt status of the church itself. Significantly, the courts have consistently ruled that any amount of income distributed to an individual (other than as reasonable compensation or in furtherance of charitable or religious purposes) will jeopardize a church's tax-exempt status. This problem is avoided by characterizing the retirement gift as taxable compensation, assuming that the gift is reasonable in amount.

3. Section 102(c) of the tax code. Section 102(c) of the tax code specifies that the definition of the term "gift" shall not include "any amount transferred by or for an employer to, or for the benefit of, an employee." The tax code does permit employees to exclude from income certain employee achievement awards (addressed in the previous section) and *de minimis* fringe benefits whose value is so insignificant that accounting for them would be unreasonable or administratively impracticable. *IRC 132(e).*

✤ **KEY POINT.** A federal appeals court in 1995 made the following observation regarding section 102(c) of the tax code: "Although the legislative history suggests that [this section] was enacted to address other fact situations, its plain meaning may not be ignored in this case. That meaning seems far from plain, however. The church members are not [the pastor's] 'employer,' and the question whether their payments to the [pastor] were made 'for' his employer seems little different than the traditional gift inquiry under *Duberstein* and *Bogardus.* We therefore decline the government's belated suggestion that we affirm on the alternative ground of section 102(c)." *Goodwin v. United States, 67 F.3d 149 (8th Cir. 1995).*

✤ **KEY POINT.** Taxpayers generally are not liable for penalties if they rely on a published court decision in support of a tax position. Since the four 1950s cases summarized above have never been overruled, they probably would prevent a minister from being assessed penalties as a result of treating a retirement gift as nontaxable. However, it is virtually certain that the IRS would insist that the entire value of the retirement gift represents taxable income, requiring the minister to pay the additional taxes due on this unreported income. However, if the minister's position is supported by any one or more of the 1950s cases, it is doubtful that the IRS could impose penalties.

Conclusion. For unknown reasons, the IRS, in its recently issued audit guidelines for ministers, has seemingly changed course in its treatment of gifts to clergy as a result of the following statement: "There are numerous court cases that ruled the organized authorization of funds to be paid to a retired minister at or near the time of retirement were gifts and not compensation for past services. Revenue Ruling 55-422 discusses the fact pattern of those cases which would render the payments as gifts and not compensation."

▲ **CAUTION.** *Church leaders should not treat retirement gifts to clergy as nontaxable distributions on the basis of the precedent cited above without first obtaining the assistance of a tax attorney.*

Retirement gifts from the general fund

Retirement gifts made to a minister or lay employee by the church out of the general fund should be reported as taxable compensation and included on the recipient's Form W-2 or 1099-MISC and on Form 1040.

Person-to-person retirement gifts

Members are free to make retirement gifts directly to ministers and lay employees without going through the church. Such payments may be tax-free gifts to the recipient, especially if they are of nominal value (though they are not deductible by the donor). See the *Goodwin* case in the previous section of this chapter.

Retirement gifts funded through members' designated contributions to the church

Many retirement gifts to ministers and lay employees are funded through members' contributions to the church that are specifically designated for the retirement gift authorized by the board or church membership. For example, it is common for churches to collect a special offering to commemorate the retirement of a pastor or lay employee. Such gifts should always be reported as taxable compensation and included on the recipient's Form W-2 or 1099-MISC and on Form 1040. Members who contribute to such offerings may deduct their contributions if they are able to itemize deductions on Schedule A (Form 1040).

Retirement gifts funded through personal checks to the recipient collected by the church

Some churches collect a retirement offering for distribution to a minister or lay church employee and instruct donors that (1) cash and checks will be accepted, but checks must be made payable directly to the retiring pastor or lay employee; and (2) no contribution will be receipted by the church as a charitable contribution. In other words, the church is merely collecting the individual gifts and then distributing them to the recipient. This ordinarily is done for convenience. A reasonable basis exists for treating such gifts as nontaxable to the minister or lay employee, so long as (1) the offering satisfies the definition of a gift announced by the Supreme Court in the Duberstein case (summarized above); and (2) the offering consists of cash and checks made payable directly to the recipient, donors are not given any charitable contribution credit for their contributions, and the offering is not recorded as income in the church's books of account.

Whether an offering will satisfy the *Duberstein* case will depend on several factors, including the intent of the donors who contribute to the offering (e.g., if they are simply wanting to provide additional compensation to their minister in recognition of services rendered, the transfer ordinarily will be taxable compensation rather than a tax-free gift); whether a church adjusts its pastor's compensation on the basis of the special-occasion offerings collected on his or her behalf; and whether the contributions were spontaneous and voluntary as opposed to fixed amounts established under a "highly structured program" for transferring money to the minister on a regular basis.

4. PROPERTY PURCHASED FROM AN EMPLOYER

If a church allows an employee to buy property at less than fair market value, the employee ordinarily must report as taxable income the excess of the property's fair market value over the bargain sale price. *Treas. Reg. 1.61-2(d)(2).*

EXAMPLE. A church sells its parsonage to its pastor for a bargain price of $50,000 in cash. The parsonage has a fair market value of $150,000. The pastor realizes income of $100,000 from this transaction, and this income must be reflected on his Form W-2 or 1099-MISC and on his federal income tax return (Form 1040). Before making a bargain sale of church property to an employee, a church must also consider whether the employee's total compensation is unreasonable in amount. If it is, this may constitute prohibited inurement of a church asset to the personal benefit of a private individual in violation of one of the conditions for tax-exempt status listed in section 501(c)(3) of the tax code. It also may expose the retired minister to substantial excise taxes known as "intermediate sanctions" (discussed earlier in this chapter).

❖ **KEY POINT.** The IRS can impose intermediate sanctions (an excise tax) against an officer or director of a church or other charity, and in some cases against board members, if an officer or director is paid an excessive amount of compensation. The law clarifies that compensation may include property sold to an officer or director at an unreasonably low price. A rebuttable presumption arises that a sale is for a reasonable price if it is approved by an independent board on the basis of comparability data and if the basis for the board's decision is documented.

5. SICK PAY

Amounts received by an employee for personal injuries or sickness are includable in income if paid directly by an employer or if they represent insurance proceeds from a policy paid for by an employer (and the insurance premiums paid by the employer were not included in the employee's income). *IRC 104.* However, if an employee paid the premiums on an accident or health insurance policy, the benefits received under the policy ordinarily are not taxable (see Chapter 5, section E).

6. SOCIAL SECURITY TAX PAID BY A CHURCH

▲ **CAUTION.** *This benefit constitutes taxable income unless otherwise noted. If not reported as taxable income by the church or the recipient in the year provided, the IRS may be able to assess intermediate sanctions in the form of substantial excise taxes against the recipient, and possibly members of the church board, regardless of the amount of the benefit. See section A.3 of this chapter for more details.*

Social Security benefits are financed through two tax systems. Employers and employees each pay the Social Security and Medicare tax, which for 2013 is 7.65 percent of an employee's taxable wages (a total tax of 15.3 percent). Self-employed persons pay the self-employment tax, which for 2013 is 15.3 percent of net self-employment earnings. Ministers always are considered to be self-employed for Social Security with respect to service performed

in the exercise of ministry. This means they never pay Social Security or Medicare taxes with respect to such services. Rather, they pay the self-employment tax (15.3 percent)—unless they have filed a timely application for exemption from self-employment taxes and have received written approval of their exemption from the IRS.

❖ **KEY POINT.** The employee's share of Social Security and Medicare taxes consists of a Social Security tax of 6.2 percent plus a Medicare tax of 1.45 percent, for a total tax of 7.65 percent. Self-employed persons, including ministers, pay a self-employment tax consisting of a Social Security tax of 12.4 percent and a Medicare tax of 2.9 percent for a total tax of 15.3 percent. Congress granted a payroll tax holiday for 2011 and 2012 for both employees and self-employed persons by reducing their share of Social Security taxes two percentage points—from 6.2 to 4.2 percent for employees and from 12.4 to 10.4 percent for the self-employed. Medicare taxes and the employer's share of Social Security and Medicare taxes were not affected. Unless Congress acts, this tax reduction will not be available in 2013.

Because a minister pays a much higher Social Security tax than is required of employees, many churches agree to pay their minister an additional sum to cover a portion (e.g., one-half) of the minister's self-employment tax liability. This is perfectly appropriate. However, note that any amount paid to a minister to help pay the higher self-employment tax must be reported as additional compensation on the minister's Form W-2 and on the minister's Form 1040. The amount paid by the church must be reported as compensation for Social Security as well. *Revenue Ruling 68-507*

➤ **TIP.** Churches electing to pay half of a minister's self-employment tax may have a difficult time making this calculation, since it will not be clear what "half" of a minister's self-employment tax liability for the year will be until the minister completes a Form 1040 following the end of the current year. This topic is addressed more fully in Chapter 9. Churches desiring to pay a specified portion of a minister's self-employment tax should consider paying a fixed amount rather than half of the total self-employment tax liability. This will avoid the complexities involved in calculating half of a minister's self-employment tax.

7. TAXABLE FRINGE BENEFITS

▲ **CAUTION.** *These benefits constitute taxable income. If not reported as taxable income by the church or the recipient in the year provided, the IRS may be able to assess intermediate sanctions in the form of substantial excise taxes against the recipient, and possibly members of the church board, regardless of the amount of the benefit. See section A.3 of this chapter for more details.*

A fringe benefit is any material benefit provided by an employer to an employee (or self-employed person) apart from his or her stated compensation. Some fringe benefits must be valued and included in an employee's gross income in computing income taxes and Social Security taxes, while others are specifically excluded from taxable income.

As a general rule, a fringe benefit must be valued and included in an employee's gross income unless it is specifically excluded by law. Excludable fringe benefits are discussed in Chapter 5. This subsection will illustrate some *taxable* fringe benefits. One of the more common fringe benefits is an employer-provided car. Because of the complexity of valuing this benefit, it is addressed separately in the following subsection.

Moving expenses paid by employing church

Employer reimbursements of an employee's qualified moving expenses are treated as a tax-free fringe benefit in either of the following two situations:

- The employer pays a third party (such as a moving company) directly on behalf of the employee. In such cases the employer's reimbursements are not reported on the employee's Form W-2.
- The employer reimburses the employee directly. These reimbursements are reported in box 12 of Form W-2 and are identified using code P.

All other moving expense reimbursements (so-called nonqualified expenses), whether paid directly to a third party or not, will be treated as a taxable fringe benefit and will be included in wages (Form W-2, box 1) and are subject to income tax withholding and Social Security and Medicare taxes.

Employer-provided meals

Generally, if meals are provided to you by your employer as a means of increasing your compensation and there is no business reason for providing them, their value is income for you. In some cases, however, the value of employer-provided meals is not included in your income. See Chapter 5, section I.6 for details.

Miscellaneous

Many of the other components of income discussed in this chapter could be considered fringe benefits (e.g., Christmas gifts from the church, Social Security taxes paid by the church on behalf of its minister, and low-interest loans). In addition, some fringe benefits that ordinarily are excluded from gross income must be valued and added to income if they do not satisfy various conditions discussed in Chapter 5.

8. PERSONAL USE OF A CHURCH-PROVIDED CAR

✹ **KEY POINT.** The personal use of a church-provided car is income for a church staff member and must be valued and reported using one of four valuation methods.

▲ **CAUTION.** *This benefit constitutes taxable income except as otherwise noted. If it is not reported as taxable income by the church or the recipient in the year it is provided, the IRS may be able to assess intermediate sanctions in the form of substantial excise taxes against the recipient, regardless of the amount of the benefit. See section A.3 of this chapter for more details.*

One of the more common taxable fringe benefits for ministers is personal use of a church-owned car. If a church provides a car to a minister (or lay employee), the personal use of the car is a taxable noncash fringe benefit. The church must determine the value of this fringe benefit so it can be reported as taxable income on the staff member's Form W-2.

The church may use either general valuation principles or one of three special valuation rules to value the personal use of the vehicle. The employee must use general valuation principles unless the church chooses to use one of the three special valuation rules. If a church uses a special valuation rule, the employee may use that same valuation rule or the general valuation principles.

General valuation principles

Under the general valuation principles, the amount to add to a worker's income equals (1) the amount a person would have to pay to lease a comparable vehicle on comparable terms in the same geographical area, multiplied by (2) the percentage of total vehicle miles for the period that were of a personal (rather than business) nature.

You ordinarily cannot use a cents-per-mile rate to determine the value of the availability of an employer-provided car unless the same or comparable vehicle could be leased on a cents-per-mile basis for the same period of time the vehicle was available to you (i.e., one year). In other words, if you have access to the car for an entire year and a comparable vehicle in your community would not be leased at a cents-per-mile rate for a similar period of time, then you cannot use a cents-per-mile rule to value the availability of the car to you. You must use the general rule that is applied in your community to determine the lease value of a car (such as a fixed rate per week, month, or year).

Special automobile lease valuation rule

Under this rule, you determine the value of an automobile provided to an employee by using its annual lease value. For an automobile provided only part of the year, use either its prorated annual lease value or its daily lease value.

If the automobile is used by the employee for business purposes, you generally reduce the lease value by the amount that is excluded from the employee's wages as a working condition benefit. In order to do this, the employee must account to the employer for the business use. This is done by substantiating the usage (mileage, for example), the time and place of the travel, and the business purpose of the travel. Written records made at the time of each business use are the best evidence. Any use of a company-provided vehicle that is not substantiated as business use is included in income. The working condition benefit is the amount that would be an allowable business expense deduction for the employee if the employee paid for the use of the vehicle. However, you may choose to include the entire lease value in the employee's wages.

Consistency requirements

If you use the lease value rule, the following requirements apply.

- You must begin using this rule on the first day you make the automobile available to any employee for personal use. However, the following exceptions apply: If you use the commuting rule (discussed below) when you first make the automobile available to any employee for personal use, you may change to the lease value rule on the first day for which you do not use the commuting rule. If you use the cents-per-mile rule (discussed below) when you first make the automobile available to any employee for personal use, you may change to the lease value rule on the first day on which the automobile no longer qualifies for the cents-per-mile rule.
- You must use this rule for all later years in which you make the automobile available to any employee, except that you may use the commuting rule for any year during which use of the automobile qualifies.
- You must continue to use this rule if you provide a replacement automobile to the employee and your primary reason for the replacement is to reduce federal taxes.

Annual lease value

Generally, you figure the annual lease value of an automobile as follows:

- Determine the fair market value (FMV) of the automobile on the first date it is available to any employee for personal use.
- Using Table 4-1, read down columns 1 and 3 until you come to the dollar range within which the FMV of the automobile falls. Then read across to columns 2 and 4 to find the annual lease value.
- Multiply the annual lease value by the percentage of personal miles out of total miles driven by the employee.

Fair market value (FMV)

The FMV of an automobile is the amount a person would pay to buy it from a third party in an arm's-length transaction in the area in which the automobile is bought or leased. That amount includes all purchase expenses, such as sales tax and title fees. You do not have to include the value of a telephone or any specialized equipment added to or carried in the automobile if the equipment is necessary for your business. However, include the value of specialized equipment if the employee to whom the automobile is available uses the specialized equipment in a trade or business other than yours.

You may be able to use a safe-harbor value as the FMV. For an automobile you bought at arm's length, the safe-harbor value is your cost, including sales tax, title, and other purchase expenses.

Items included in annual lease value table

Each annual lease value in the table includes the value of maintenance and insurance for the automobile. Do not reduce the annual lease value by the value of any of these services that you did not provide. For example, do not reduce the annual lease value by the value of a maintenance service contract or insurance you did not provide. You can take into account the services actually provided for the automobile by using the general valuation rule discussed earlier.

Items not included

The annual lease value does not include the value of fuel you provide to an employee for personal use, regardless of whether you provide it, reimburse its cost, or have it charged to you. You must include the value of the fuel separately in the employee's wages.

You may value fuel you provided at FMV or at 5.5 cents per mile for all miles driven by the employee. If you reimburse an employee for the cost of fuel or have it charged to you, you generally value the fuel at the amount you reimburse or the amount charged to you if it was bought at arm's length. If you provide any service other than maintenance and insurance for an automobile, you must add the FMV of that service to the annual lease value of the automobile to figure the value of the benefit.

Four-year lease term

The annual lease values in the table are based on a four-year lease term. These values generally will stay the same for the period that begins with the first date you use this rule for the automobile and ends on December 31 of the fourth full calendar year following that date. Figure the annual lease value for each later four-year period by determining the FMV of the automobile on January 1 of the first year of the later four-year period and selecting the amount in column 2 or 4 of the table that corresponds to the appropriate dollar range in column 1 or 3.

If you provide an automobile to an employee for a continuous period of 30 or more days but less than an entire calendar year, you may prorate the annual lease value. Figure the prorated annual lease value by multiplying the annual lease value by a fraction, using the number of days of availability as the numerator and 365 as the denominator.

If you provide an automobile continuously for at least 30 days, but the period covers two calendar years, you may use the prorated annual lease value or the daily lease value.

If you provide an automobile to an employee for a continuous period of less than 30 days, use the daily lease value to figure its value.

TABLE 4-1

ANNUAL VEHICLE LEASE VALUE

MARKET VALUE OF VEHICLE	ANNUAL LEASE VALUE	MARKET VALUE OF VEHICLE	ANNUAL LEASE VALUE
$0 to 999	$600	$22,000 to 22,999	$6,100
$1,000 to 1,999	$850	$23,000 to 23,999	$6,350
$2,000 to 2,999	$1,100	$24,000 to 24,999	$6,600
$3,000 to 3,999	$1,350	$25,000 to 25,999	$6,850
$4,000 to 4,999	$1,600	$26,000 to 27,999	$7,250
$5,000 to 5,999	$1,850	$28,000 to 29,999	$7,750
$6,000 to 6,999	$2,100	$30,000 to 31,999	$8,250
$7,000 to 7,999	$2,350	$32,000 to 33,999	$8,750
$8,000 to 8,999	$2,600	$34,000 to 35,999	$9,250
$9,000 to 9,999	$2,850	$36,000 to 37,999	$9,750
$10,000 to 10,999	$3,100	$38,000 to 39,999	$10,250
$11,000 to 11,999	$3,350	$40,000 to 41,999	$10,750
$12,000 to 12,999	$3,600	$42,000 to 43,999	$11,250
$13,000 to 13,999	$3,850	$44,000 to 45,999	$11,750
$14,000 to 14,999	$4,100	$46,000 to 47,999	$12,250
$15,000 to 15,999	$4,350	$48,000 to 49,999	$12,750
$16,000 to 16,999	$4,600	$50,000 to 51,999	$13,250
$17,000 to 17,999	$4,850	$52,000 to 53,999	$13,750
$18,000 to 18,999	$5,100	$54,000 to 55,999	$14,250
$19,000 to 19,999	$5,350	$56,000 to 57,999	$14,750
$20,000 to 20,999	$5,600	$58,000 to 59,999	$15,250
$21,000 to 21,999	$5,850		

Figure the daily lease value by multiplying the annual lease value by a fraction, using four times the number of days of availability as the numerator and 365 as the denominator. However, you may apply a prorated annual lease value for a period of continuous availability of less than 30 days by treating the automobile as if it had been available for 30 days. Use a prorated annual lease value if it would result in a lower valuation than applying the daily lease value to the shorter period of availability.

Cents-per-mile rule

Under this rule an employer determines the value of a vehicle provided to an employee for personal use by multiplying the standard mileage rate by the total miles the employee drives the vehicle for personal purposes. This amount must be included in the employee's wages (or reimbursed by the employee). An employer can use the cents-per-mile rule if either of the following requirements is met.

- The employer reasonably expects the vehicle to be used regularly for business purposes throughout the year.
- The mileage test is met.

▲ **CAUTION.** *The cents-per-mile rule cannot be used if a vehicle's value when first made available to an employee for personal use is more than an amount determined by the IRS as the maximum automobile value for the year. The maximum automobile value for 2012 was $15,900.*

A vehicle is regularly used for business purposes if at least one of the following conditions is met.

- At least 50 percent of the vehicle's miles are for business purposes.
- The church sponsors a commuting pool that generally uses the vehicle each workday to drive at least three employees to and from work.

- The vehicle is regularly used for business purposes on the basis of all of the facts and circumstances. Infrequent business use of the vehicle, such as for occasional trips to the airport, is not regular use of the vehicle for business.

A vehicle meets the mileage test for a calendar year if both of the following requirements are met.

- The vehicle is actually driven at least 10,000 miles during the year. If the church owns or leases the vehicle only part of the year, reduce the 10,000-mile requirement proportionately.
- The vehicle is used during the year primarily by employees. Consider the vehicle used primarily by employees if they use it consistently for commuting. Do not treat the use of the vehicle by another individual whose use would be taxed to the employee as use by the employee. For example, if only one employee uses a vehicle during the calendar year and that employee drives the vehicle at least 10,000 miles in that year, the vehicle meets the mileage test even if all miles driven by the employee are personal.

If a church or other employer uses the cents-per-mile rule, the following requirements apply:

- The cents-per-mile rule must be implemented on the first day the vehicle is made available to any employee for personal use. However, if the commuting rule (see below) is applied when a vehicle is first made available to any employee for personal use, an employer can change to the cents-per-mile rule on the first day for which it does not use the commuting rule.
- An employer must use the cents-per-mile rule for all later years in which it makes the vehicle available to any employee and the vehicle qualifies, except that it can use the commuting rule for any year during which use of the vehicle qualifies. However, if the vehicle does not qualify for the cents-per-mile rule during a later year, an employer can use for that year and thereafter any other rule for which the vehicle then qualifies.
- An employer must continue to use the cents-per-mile rule if it provides a replacement vehicle to the employee and the primary reason for the replacement is to reduce federal taxes.

EXAMPLE. In 2012 a church purchased a car and permitted Pastor T to use it for both business and personal use throughout the year. The car cost $23,500. The cents-per-mile method of valuing the personal use of the car cannot be used by either the church or Pastor T, since the fair market value of the car when first provided to Pastor T was in excess of $15,900.

EXAMPLE. Same facts as the preceding example, except that the fair market value of the car when first provided to Pastor T (in 2012) was $12,500. The cents-per-mile method of valuing the personal use of the car by Pastor T can be used. Assume that

Pastor T drove the vehicle a total of 20,000 miles in 2012, of which 12,000 were for personal purposes (1,000 per month). The church calculates the value of this personal use by multiplying the number of personal miles driven in 2012 (12,000) by the standard mileage rate (55.5 cents) for a total of $6,660. This amount would be added to the minister's Form W-2 and Form 1040. This method should not be used if Pastor T cannot substantiate the number of personal miles the car was driven during the year.

EXAMPLE. Same facts as the previous example, except that the church required Pastor T to purchase his own gas. If the church uses the cents-per-mile special valuation rule, it can value the personal use of Pastor T's use of the car by multiplying all miles driven for personal purposes during the year by the standard mileage rate less 5.5 cents per mile. This reduces the valuation of the personal miles to $6,000.

Special commuting valuation rule

If an employer provides an employee with a vehicle and requires the employee to commute to and from work in the vehicle, then the value of the commuting miles (which are always deemed personal rather than business) can be computed at a rate of $3 per round-trip commute or $1.50 per one-way commute. The employer includes the value of all commuting on the employee's Form W-2. For this rule to apply, the following conditions must be satisfied:

- The vehicle is owned or leased by the church and is provided to an employee for use in connection with church business.
- For noncompensatory business reasons (e.g., security) the church requires the employee to commute to and from work in the vehicle.
- Under a written policy statement adopted by the church board, no employee of the church can use the vehicle for personal purposes, except for commuting or de minimis (minimal) personal use (such as a stop for lunch between two business trips).
- The church reasonably believes that, except for commuting and de minimis use, no church employee uses the vehicle for any personal purpose.
- The employee who is required by the church to commute to and from work in the vehicle is not a "control employee" (defined below).
- The church must be able to supply sufficient evidence to prove to the IRS that the preceding five conditions have been met.

The regulations define a control employee (for purposes of the commuting valuation rule) as an employee who qualifies as any one or more of the following in 2012:

- a board appointed, confirmed, or elected officer with annual compensation of $100,000 or more;
- a director (regardless of compensation); or
- any employee with annual compensation of $205,000 or more.

✱ New in 2013. For 2013 the $100,000 and $205,000 amounts remain unchanged. Obviously, senior ministers ordinarily will not be able to take advantage of this special commuting rule since they usually are directors of their church, and in some cases they are appointed or confirmed by the church board and receive compensation of $100,000 or more during 2013. In some cases, however, ministers may be eligible for the special commuting rule.

❋ KEY POINT. Income tax regulations give employers the option of defining a control employee by using the definition of a "highly compensated employee." If a church would like to use this substitute definition, it should specifically adopt it by a resolution of the church board. The board should adopt a resolution stating simply that "for 2013 and future years, unless otherwise provided, the definition of a highly compensated employee is substituted for the definition of a control employee for purposes of the special commuting valuation rule." For 2012 a highly compensated church employee is an employee who had compensation for the previous year in excess of $115,000 and, if an employer elects, was in the top 20 percent of employees by compensation. For 2013 the amount remains at $115,000.

Special conditions applicable to special valuation rules

An employer may not use any of the three special valuation rules unless one or more of the following four conditions is satisfied:

- The employer treats the value of the benefit as wages (for tax reporting).
- The employee includes the value of the benefit in income.
- The employee is not a control employee (defined above).
- The employer demonstrates a good faith effort to treat the benefit correctly for tax reporting purposes. *Treas. Reg. 1.61-21(c)(3)(ii).*

If none of these conditions is satisfied, the employer and employee must use the general valuation rule to value the personal use of an employer-provided car.

Unsafe conditions commuting rule

Under this rule the value of commuting transportation an employer provides to a qualified employee solely because of unsafe conditions is $1.50 for a one-way commute (that is, from home to work or from work to home). This amount must be included in the employee's wages or be reimbursed by the employee. You can use the unsafe conditions commuting rule if all of the following requirements are met:

- The employee would ordinarily walk or use public transportation for commuting.
- The employer has a written policy under which it does not provide transportation for personal purposes other than commuting because of unsafe conditions.

- The employee does not use the transportation for personal purposes other than commuting because of unsafe conditions.

These requirements must be met on a trip-by-trip basis.

A qualified employee (for 2012) is one who

- performs services during the year,
- is paid on an hourly basis,
- is not claimed as exempt from the minimum wage and maximum hour provisions of the Fair Labor Standards Act,
- is within a classification for which overtime pay is required, and
- received pay of not more than $115,000 in 2011.

Unsafe conditions exist if, under the facts and circumstances, a reasonable person would consider it unsafe for the employee to walk or use public transportation at the time of day the employee must commute. One factor indicating whether it is unsafe is the history of crime in the geographic area surrounding the employee's workplace or home at the time of day the employee commutes.

Reporting taxable income

The value of an employer-provided vehicle that is included in your income will be reported by your employer on your Form W-2 (or Form 1099-MISC if you are self-employed). On Form W-2 the amount of the benefit should be included in box 1 (wages, tips, and other compensation) and boxes 3 and 5 for nonminister employees. If an employer reports 100 percent of the annual lease value of a vehicle as taxable income for the employee, this amount also must be reported in box 14 of Form W-2 or in a separate statement to the employee so the employee can compute the value of any business use of the vehicle.

Employee reimbursements

The income tax regulations specify that if the employer and employee use one of the special valuation rules, the amount of reportable income is decreased by "any amount reimbursed by the employee to the employer." The regulations further specify that "the employer and employee may use the special rules to determine the amount of the reimbursement due the employer by the employee. Thus, if an employee reimburses an employer for the value of a benefit as determined under a special valuation rule, no amount is includable in the employee's gross income with respect to the benefit." *Treas. Reg. 1.61-21(c)(2)(ii)(B).*

Tax withholding

Must a church withhold taxes on the personal use of an employer provided vehicle? In answering this question, it is important to remember that ministers are exempt from income tax withholding with respect to compensation they receive from the performance of ministerial services unless they elect voluntary withholding, and they are never subject to Social Security or Medicare tax withholding on their ministry income. Of course, nonminister employees generally are subject to withholding of income taxes as well as Social Security and Medicare taxes.

An employer may elect not to withhold income tax on the value of an employee's personal use of an employer-owned vehicle. An employer does not have to make this election for all employees. However, an employer must withhold Social Security and Medicare taxes on such benefits for nonminister employees.

An employer electing not to withhold income taxes on the personal use of an employer-provided vehicle must notify the employee (in writing) of this election by the later of (1) January 31 of the year of the election, or (2) within 30 days after the date the employer first provides the employee with the vehicle. The election not to withhold taxes does not affect the employer's responsibility to report the value of the benefit as taxable income on the employee's Form W-2.

9. BELOW-MARKET INTEREST LOANS

▲ **CAUTION.** *Churches that make low-interest or no-interest loans to ministers or lay employees may be violating state nonprofit corporation law and generating taxable income.*

▲ **CAUTION.** *This benefit constitutes taxable income except as otherwise noted. If it is not reported as taxable income by the church or the recipient in the year it is provided, the IRS may be able to assess intermediate sanctions in the form of substantial excise taxes against the recipient, and possibly members of the church board, regardless of the amount of the benefit. See section A.3 of this chapter for more details.*

Section 7872 of the tax code treats certain loans in which the interest rate charged is less than the "applicable federal rate" (AFR) as the equivalent to loans bearing interest at the applicable federal rate, coupled with a payment by the lender to the borrower sufficient to fund all or part of the payment of interest by the borrower. Such loans are referred to as "below-market loans."

❖ **KEY POINT.** An advance of money to an employee to defray anticipated expenditures is not treated as a loan for purposes of section 7872 if the amount of money advanced "is reasonably calculated not to exceed the anticipated expenditures and if the advance of money is made on a day within a reasonable period of time of the day that the anticipated expenditure will be incurred." *Treas. Reg. §1.7872-2.*

Section 7872 deals with the treatment of loans with below-market interest rates. It specifically applies to what it terms "compensation-related loans," which include below-market loans directly or indirectly between an employer and an employee. In general, section 7872 operates to impute interest on below-market loans. In the case of employer-employee loans, the employer is treated as transferring the foregone interest to the employee as additional compensation, and the employee is treated as paying interest back to the employer.

Different rules apply depending on whether a loan is a demand loan or a term loan. A demand loan is a below-market loan if it does not provide for an interest rate at least equal to the applicable federal rate. A term loan is a below-market loan if the present value of all amounts due on the loan is less than the amount of the loan (i.e., the yield to maturity is lower than the applicable federal rate). With respect to demand loans, the imputed interest payments and deemed transfer of additional compensation are treated as being made annually. With respect to term loans, the lender is treated at the time of the loans as transferring the difference between the loan amount and the present value of all the future payments under the loan as additional compensation. The term loan is then treated as having original issue discount equal to the amount of the deemed transfer of additional compensation and, thus, subject to the original issue discount provisions of section 1272 of the tax code.

There is a de minimis exception from the application of the section 7872 imputation rules if loans between the parties in aggregate do not exceed $10,000. The de minimis exception does not apply if one of the principal purposes of the loan is tax avoidance.

❖ **KEY POINT.** Any below-market interest rate loan of $10,000 or more triggers taxable income in the amount of the interest that would have accrued at the applicable federal rate of interest. The long-term AFR applies to loans in excess of nine years; the mid-term rate applies to loans of more than three years but not more than nine years; the short-term rate applies to loans of three years or less.

Exceptions
Consider the following exceptions to the rules on below-market loans.

Loans of $10,000 or less
The rules for below-market loans do not apply to any day on which the total outstanding amount of loans between the borrower and lender is $10,000 or less. This exception applies only to (1) gift loans between individuals if the gift loan is not directly used to buy or carry income-producing assets, and (2) pay-related loans if the avoidance of federal tax is not a principal purpose of the interest arrangement. This exception does not apply to a term loan that previously has been subject to the below-market loan rules. Those rules will continue to apply even if the outstanding balance is reduced to $10,000 or less.

Loans with no tax effect
Also exempted from the below-market loan rules are loans for which the interest arrangement can be shown to have no significant effect on the federal tax liability of the lender or the borrower. Some of the facts the IRS considers in making such a decision include (1) the amount of the loan, (2) the cost of complying with the below-market loan rules, if they were to apply, and (3) any reasons other than taxes for structuring the transaction as a below-market loan.

This exception may apply in some cases to ministers. Consider the following examples.

EXAMPLE. Pastor G lived in the church parsonage for many years. In 2012 he purchased his own home. To assist in making the down payment on a new home, the church board loaned Pastor G $7,500 in 2012. The loan is a demand loan, at no interest. Neither the church nor Pastor G reported any foregone interest ($7,500 x the applicable interest rate) for 2012. Was this correct? Yes, since the amount of the loan was for less than $10,000. This assumes that tax avoidance was not the principal purpose of the arrangement.

EXAMPLE. Same facts as the previous example, except that the amount of the loan was $20,000. The IRS audits Pastor G's 2012 tax return and insists that he should have reported the foregone interest on the loan for that year at the applicable federal interest rate. Assuming that this rate was 5 percent, Pastor G would have to report an additional $1,000 of taxable income for 2012 ($20,000 x 5 percent). However, Pastor G argues that the no-interest loan had no significant effect on his federal tax liability. He points out that even if the church had charged him 5 percent interest, this amount could have been excluded from his taxable income as a housing allowance, since it was an expense of home ownership.

EXAMPLE. Same facts as the first example, except that the amount of the church loan was $100,000. Pastor G argues that the no-interest loan had no significant effect on his federal tax liability. It is unlikely that this argument will succeed, given the amount of the loan. As a result, it is likely that Pastor G will have to pay taxes on an additional $5,000 of income for 2012 ($100,000 x 5 percent).

Loans made by charitable organizations

The income tax regulations exempt loans made by a charitable organization if the primary purpose of the loan is to accomplish religious, charitable, or educational purposes. This exception ordinarily will not apply to below-market interest loans made by churches to ministers or lay employees, since the purpose of such loans is to assist or compensate the recipient rather than to fulfill specific exempt purposes. *Treas. Reg. 1.7872-5T(b)(11).*

Employee relocation loans

The regulations further specify that

> in the case of a compensation-related loan to an employee, where such loan is secured by a mortgage on the new principal residence . . . of the employee, acquired in connection with the transfer of that employee to a new principal place of work . . . the loan will be exempt from [tax] if the following conditions are satisfied: (a) The loan is a demand loan or is a term loan the benefits of the interest arrangements of which are not transferable by the employee and are conditioned on the future performance of substantial services by the employee; (b) the employee certifies to the employer that the employee reasonably expects to be entitled to and will itemize deductions for each year the loan is outstanding; and (c) the loan agreement requires that the loan proceeds be used only to purchase the new principal residence of the employee. Treasury Regulation 1.7872-5T(c)(1).

EXAMPLE. A church hires Pastor C as its music minister. Pastor C will be moving from another state and would like to purchase a home in her new community. The church board would like to assist her in making the down payment on a new home and loans her $25,000 at no interest, payable on demand. The church can help Pastor C qualify for the employee-relocation exception to the below-market loan rules by having Pastor C sign a promissory note in the amount of $25,000 that is secured by a mortgage on the new home and by having Pastor C sign a loan agreement containing the following provisions: (1) the benefits of the interest arrangement are not transferable by Pastor C; (2) the benefits of the interest arrangement are conditioned on the future performance of substantial services by Pastor C; (3) Pastor C certifies that she reasonably expects to be entitled to and will itemize deductions for each year the loan is outstanding; and (4) the loan proceeds will be used only to purchase the new principal residence.

Other concerns

Low-interest or no-interest loans can create the following additional concerns:

Inurement. One of the requirements for tax-exempt status under section 501(c)(3) of the Internal Revenue Code is that none of a church's assets can inure to the benefit of a private individual other than as reasonable compensation for services rendered. The IRS and the courts have ruled in a number of cases that low- or no-interest loans constitute prohibited inurement, which results in the loss of a charity's tax-exempt status. See section A.1 of this chapter.

Excess benefit transaction. According to section 4958 of the tax code, any benefit provided by a tax-exempt organization to an employee that exceeds the reasonable value of the employee's services constitutes an excess benefit transaction that exposes the employee to substantial excise taxes (called "intermediate sanctions") of up to 225 percent of the amount the IRS determines to be excessive compensation. This penalty only applies to "disqualified persons," who are officers or directors of the charity or a relative of such a person. In addition, members of the organization's board who approved the excess benefit are subject to an additional excise tax of 10 percent of the amount of the excess (up to a maximum penalty of $20,000 collectively). For more information about this tax, see "Tax on managers" in section A.3 of this chapter.

Nonprofit corporation law. Most state nonprofit laws provide that board members who authorize a loan to an officer or director are personally liable for the repayment of that loan. To illustrate, if a state nonprofit corporation law contains such a provision, church board members who approve a $100,000 loan will remain personally liable for its repayment until it is paid in full.

In summary, below-market interest loans raise a number of complex and significant legal and tax issues that need to be addressed. Church leaders should seek legal counsel before pursuing such a transaction.

Debt forgiveness. Any agreement or understanding that would involve the church "forgiving" the loan obligation could result in the entire balance of the loan being realized as taxable income. It also might trigger the complex regulations that apply to nonqualified deferred compensation arrangements, since this arrangement might be deemed nonqualified deferred compensation under the expansive definition contained in the regulations under section 409A of the tax code.

✵ **KEY POINT.** In 2004 the Senate Finance Committee sent a letter to the Independent Sector (a national coalition of several hundred public charities) encouraging it to recommend actions "to strengthen governance, ethical conduct, and accountability within public charities and private foundations." The Independent Sector issued its report in June of 2005. It contained over 100 recommendations for congressional and IRS action as well as recommended actions for charities themselves. These recommendations included amending the tax code to prohibit loans to board members of public charities. Congress has not responded to this recommendation.

10. "IN KIND" TRANSFERS OF PROPERTY

Churches occasionally give a minister or lay employee property without charge. Examples include automobiles, homes, and equipment. Such transfers result in taxable compensation to the recipient that must be valued and reported on his or her Form W-2 and Form 1040. Generally, the amount to be included in income is the fair market value of the property less any amount paid by the recipient for the property. For example, a federal court has ruled that a minister had to include in his gross income for federal income tax purposes the value of a boat and trailer received in payment for services as a minister. *Potito v. Commissioner, 534 F.2d 49 (5th Cir. 1976).*

11. ASSIGNMENTS OF INCOME

Ministers, like other taxpayers, occasionally attempt to "assign" income to a charity and thereby avoid income taxes on the assigned income. For example, Pastor G conducts services for two weeks at a church whose pastor is on vacation. The church wants to pay Pastor G income of $1,000 for these services, but Pastor G declines and requests that the money be applied to the church's building fund. Does Pastor G have to pay tax on the $1,000? In many cases the

answer will be yes. The United States Supreme Court addressed this issue in a landmark ruling in 1940. *Helvering v. Horst, 311 U.S. 112 (1940).* The *Horst* case addressed the question of whether a father could avoid taxation on bond interest coupons that he transferred to his son prior to the maturity date. The Supreme Court ruled that the father had to pay tax on the interest income even though he assigned all of his interest in the income to his son. It observed: "The power to dispose of income is the equivalent of ownership of it. The exercise of that power to procure the payment of income to another is the enjoyment and hence the realization of the income by him who exercises it."

The Supreme Court reached the same conclusion in two other landmark cases. *Helvering v. Eubank, 311 U.S. 122 (1940); Lucas v. Earl, 281 U.S. 111 (1930).*

EXAMPLE. A taxpayer earned an honorarium of $2,500 for speaking at a convention. He requested that the honorarium be distributed to a college. This request was honored, and the taxpayer assumed that he did not have to report the $2,500 as taxable income, since he never received it. The IRS ruled that the taxpayer should have reported the $2,500 as taxable income. It noted that "the amount of the honorarium transferred to the educational institution at the taxpayer's request . . . is includible in the taxpayer's gross income [for tax purposes]. However, the taxpayer is entitled to a charitable contribution deduction." The IRS further noted that "the Supreme Court of the United States has held that a taxpayer who assigns or transfers compensation for personal services to another individual or entity fails to be relieved of federal income tax liability, regardless of the motivation behind the transfer" (citing the *Horst* case discussed above). *Revenue Ruling 79-121.*

EXAMPLE. A church member signed a real estate contract agreeing to sell a rental property he owned. At the real estate closing, the member insisted that 8 percent of the sales price be paid to his church for a building project. The Tax Court ruled that the member had to report the full amount of the sale price as taxable gain and that the attempt to assign 8 percent of the gain to the church did not reduce the member's taxable gain. It observed that "the payment of part of the sales proceeds to the church was an anticipatory assignment of income which does not protect [the member] from taxation on the full amount of the gain realized on the sale." The court stressed that the member could claim a charitable contribution deduction for the amount he paid to the church, but he had to report the full amount of the sales price as taxable gain. *Ankeny v. Commissioner, 53 T.C.M. 827 (1987).*

EXAMPLE. No taxable income is incurred when a taxpayer performs purely gratuitous and volunteer services with no expectation of compensation. To illustrate, the IRS ruled that a professional entertainer who gratuitously rendered professional services as a featured performer at a fund-raising event for a charity did not receive taxable income, since he "was not entitled to, and received no payment for these services." *Revenue Ruling 68-503.*

EXAMPLE. A donor owned several shares of stock in Company A. Company B offered to purchase all shares of Company A at a huge premium over book value. The donor contributed several shares to his church and claimed a charitable contribution deduction for the inflated amount. The IRS conceded that a gift of stock had been made to the church. It insisted, however, that the donor should have reported the gain in the value of his stock that was transferred to the church. Not so, said the donor. After all, he never realized or enjoyed the gain but rather transferred the shares to the church to enjoy. The IRS asserted that the donor had a legal right to redeem his shares at the inflated amount at the time he transferred the shares to the church. As a result, he had "assigned income" to the church and could not avoid being taxed on it. The Tax Court agreed. It observed: "It is a well-established principle of the tax law that the person who earns or otherwise creates the right to receive income is taxed. When the right to income has matured at the time of a transfer of property, the transferor will be taxed despite the technical transfer of that property. . . . An examination of the cases that discuss the anticipatory assignment of income doctrine reveals settled principles. A transfer of property that is a fixed right to income does not shift the incidence of taxation to the transferee. . . . [T]he ultimate question is whether the transferor, considering the reality and substance of all the circumstances, had a fixed right to income in the property at the time of transfer." The court concluded that the donor had a "fixed right to income" at the time he donated the 30,000 shares to his church. *Ferguson v. Commissioner, 108 T.C. 244 (1997).*

EXAMPLE. A taxpayer earned $100,000 that he had deposited in the bank account of a third party. The Tax Court ruled that the taxpayer should have reported the $100,000 as taxable income, since his transfer of the income to the third party was "a classic assignment of income." Further, "because such assignments are ineffective for federal income tax purposes [the taxpayer] remained the party taxable on the income generated by his services." The court explained, "One of the primary principles of the federal income tax is that income must be taxed to the one who earns it. . . . Attempts to subvert this principle by deflecting income away from its true earner to another entity by means of contractual arrangements, however cleverly drafted, are not recognized as dispositive for federal income tax purposes. . . . The assignment of income rule applies with particular force to personal service income." *Johnston v. Commissioner, T.C. Memo. 2000-315 (2000).*

12. REFUSAL TO ACCEPT FULL SALARY

This section addresses two related issues: (1) refusing to accept one's full salary, and (2) returning excess salary.

Refusal to accept full salary

Sometimes a minister or lay employee refuses to accept the full amount of his or her church-approved salary, often because the church is experiencing short-term financial problems. Should the church report the amount that is refused as taxable income to the minister or lay employee? The constructive receipt doctrine specifies:

> *Income although not actually reduced to a taxpayer's possession is constructively received by him in the taxable year during which it is credited to his account, set apart for him, or otherwise made available so that he may draw upon it at any time, or so that he could have drawn upon it during the taxable year if notice of intention to withdraw had been given. Treas. Reg. 1.451-2(a).*

A number of courts have ruled that this principle requires employees to include in their taxable income any portion of their stated salary that they refuse to accept. On the other hand, some courts have reached the opposite conclusion. Perhaps the most notable case is *Giannini v. Commissioner,* 129 F.2d 638 (9th Cir. 1942). This case involved a corporate president whose annual compensation was 5 percent of the company's profits. In the middle of one year, the president informed members of his company's board of directors that he would not accept any further compensation for the year and suggested that the company "do something worthwhile" with the money. The company never credited to the president any further compensation for the year, nor did it set any part of it aside for his use. The amount of salary refused by the president was nearly $1.5 million, and no part of this amount was reported by the president as taxable income in the year in question. The IRS audited the president and insisted that the $1.5 million should have been reported as taxable income. The taxpayer appealed, and a federal appeals court rejected the IRS position:

> *The taxpayer did not receive the money, and . . . did not direct its disposition. What he did was unqualifiedly refuse to accept any further compensation for his services with the suggestion that the money be used for some worthwhile purpose. So far as the taxpayer was concerned, the corporation could have kept the money. . . . In these circumstances we cannot say as a matter of law that the money was beneficially received by the taxpayer and therefore subject to the income tax provisions.*

The court acknowledged that the United States Supreme Court has observed: "One who is entitled to receive, at a future date, interest or compensation for services and who makes a gift of it by an anticipatory assignment, realizes taxable income quite as much as if he had collected the income and paid it over to the object of his bounty." *Helvering v. Schaffner, 312 U. S. 579 (1941).* However, the court distinguished this language by observing that "the dominance over the fund and taxpayer's direction show that he beneficially received the money by exercising his right to divert it to a use." This was not true of the corporate president in the present case, the court concluded.

In summary, a reasonable basis exists for not treating as taxable income the portion of an employee's stated salary that is refused, particularly where the employee does not assign the income to a specified use but is content to leave the unpaid salary with the employer.

Returning excess salary

Some churches have paid an employee more than the salary authorized by the church board. In most cases this is due to an innocent mistake. But what happens if the church later discovers the mistake and attempts to correct it? Can the employee give back the excess to the church? And what if the mistake is discovered in the following year? How does a return of the excess affect the employee's taxable income and the church's payroll reporting obligations? The IRS has listed the following tax consequences when employees return to their employer in "Year 2" excess salary received in "Year 1":

- The employer does not reduce the employee's wages for Social Security and federal income tax withholding purposes for Year 2.
- The employer does not reduce the employee's taxable income for Year 1 or reduce the amount of income taxes withheld in that year.
- The repayment in Year 2 of excess salary received in Year 1 has no effect on the Form W-2 for Year 2. The employer should furnish to the employee a separate receipt acknowledging the repayment for the employee's records.
- To the extent additional Social Security taxes were paid in Year 1 because of the erroneous salary payment, the repayment of the excess salary in Year 2 creates an overpayment of Social Security taxes in Year 1, and credit may be claimed by the employer with respect to its Social Security tax liability for that prior year.
- The employee may claim in Year 2 a miscellaneous itemized deduction on Schedule A in the amount of the excess salary that was repaid.
- To the extent that repayments in Year 2 of erroneous salary paid in Year 1 result in a reduced amount of Social Security wages for Year 1 and reduced amounts of employee Social Security taxes paid for that year, the employer is required to furnish corrected Forms W-2 for Year 1 showing the employee's corrected "Social Security wages," corrected "Social Security tax withheld," corrected "Medicare wages and tips," and corrected "Medicare tax withheld." No changes should be made in the entries for "Wages, tips, other compensation" (box 1 of Form W-2) or for "Federal income tax withheld" (box 2 of Form W-2). *SCA 1998-026.*

13. DISCRETIONARY FUNDS

It is a common practice for a congregation to set aside a sum of money in a discretionary fund and give a minister the sole authority to distribute the money in the fund. In some cases the minister has no instructions regarding permissible distributions. In other cases the congregation establishes some guidelines, but these often are oral and ambiguous. Consider the following examples.

EXAMPLE. A congregation at an annual business meeting authorizes the creation of a "pastor's fund" in the amount of $10,000 with the understanding that Pastor T, the congregation's senior minister, will have the authority to distribute the fund for any purpose. Pastor T is not required to account to the congregation or church board for any distribution, and he is not prohibited from making distributions to himself. During 2012 Pastor T distributed the entire fund to members of the congregation who were in need. He did not distribute any portion of the fund to himself or to any family member.

EXAMPLE. Same facts as the previous example, except that Pastor T distributed $5,000 to his adult daughter in 2012 to assist her with the purchase of a home.

EXAMPLE. A church board sets aside $5,000 in a discretionary fund and authorizes Pastor D, its senior minister, to distribute the funds for "benevolent purposes." Pastor D is required to account to the church board for all distributions and is prohibited from making any distributions to himself or to any family member.

Many ministers and church treasurers are unaware of the potential tax consequences of these arrangements. The tax consequences of some of the more common arrangements are summarized below.

Situation 1

The congregation (or governing board) establishes a discretionary fund and gives a minister full and unrestricted discretion to distribute it.

To the extent the minister has the authority to distribute any portion of the discretionary fund for any purpose, including a distribution to him or herself, without any oversight or control by the governing board, the following consequences occur.

Taxable income

The IRS could assert that the full value of the discretionary fund constitutes taxable income to the minister, even if the minister does not benefit from the fund. The mere fact that the minister *could* benefit from the fund may be enough for the fund to constitute taxable income. The basis for this result is the "constructive receipt" rule, which is explained in income tax regulation 1.451-2(a):

> *Income although not actually reduced to a taxpayer's possession is constructively received by him in the taxable year during which it is credited to his account, set apart for him, or otherwise made available so that he may draw upon it at any*

time, or so that he could have drawn upon it during the taxable year if notice of intention to withdraw had been given. However, income is not constructively received if the taxpayer's control of its receipt is subject to substantial limitations or restrictions.

For a discretionary fund to constitute taxable income to a minister, it is essential that the minister have the authority to "draw upon it at any time" for his or her personal use. This means the fund was established without any express prohibition against personal distributions.

EXAMPLE. The Tax Court ruled that a pastor was required to report as taxable income $182,000 in deposits to a church bank account over which he exercised complete dominion and control. This case supports the view that church contributions to discretionary funds over which a pastor has complete control represent taxable income to the pastor. *101 T.C.M. 1550 (2011).*

Donations to the fund

The IRS likely would assert that donations by members of the congregation to the fund would not be tax-deductible as charitable contributions, since the fund is not subject to the full control of the congregation or its governing board. For a charitable contribution to be tax-deductible, it must be subject to the full control of the church or other charity. The IRS stated the rule as follows in an important ruling: "The test in each case is whether the organization has full control of the donated funds, and discretion as to their use, so as to insure that they will be used to carry out its functions and purposes." If a church sets up a discretionary fund and authorizes a minister to make distributions from the fund for any purpose without any oversight or control by the church, this fundamental test is not met.

EXAMPLE. A Florida appeals court affirmed the conviction of a parish priest for embezzlement of church funds. A Catholic priest was charged with grand theft of funds from his church based on his use of church funds for his personal benefit rather than for the benefit of the church. A diocesan official testified that the priest was allowed to make distributions from parish accounts, without permission of the bishop, as long as the distribution does not exceed $50,000 and the distribution is "for the good of the parish." However, priests were instructed to keep records of distributions, and these accounts devoted to charitable works were required to be reported to the diocese quarterly. The priest claimed that he believed he had unfettered control over church funds and was free to spend them as he wished, and as a result, he had no criminal intent to warrant his conviction of a crime.

The court disagreed: "In this case, the state presented evidence from officials of the diocese that a parish priest is supposed to use parish money only for parish purposes. [Diocesan officials] testified that the priest's expenditures for [his former secretary

and her son] and for vacations would not be valid parish purposes. Further, the forensic examiner testified that thousands of dollars in cash from the offertory were unaccounted for and that a significant amount of parish money was spent on items that [diocesan officials] testified were not parish related. Significantly, [these officials] testified that money collected from the offertory is collected from the parish members for parish purposes. There was also testimony from staff at the parish that fake deposit slips were used to cover up the fact that cash was taken from the offertory.

"The state has introduced evidence inconsistent with the priest's claim of innocence. The case rises and falls on the intent of the priest when he used parish money and removed cash from the weekly offertory and whether it was for his personal benefit, not related to parish purposes. Ultimately, intent is a question of fact to be decided by the jury. We find that there was sufficient competent evidence of grand theft for the jury to find the priest guilty."

The court also rejected the priest's contention that the prosecution of this case led to an "excessive entanglement with religion" in violation of the First Amendment. It observed: "Purely secular disputes involving religious institutions and third parties do not create excessive entanglement of church and state when they involve neutral principles of law." *Guinan v. State, 65 So.3d 589 (Fla. App. 2011).*

Situation 2
The congregation establishes a discretionary fund and gives a minister the discretion to distribute it for any purpose, but the congregation's governing board retains administrative control over the fund.

Under this scenario the fund may still constitute taxable income to the minister, but the donations of congregational members to the fund probably would be tax-deductible as charitable contributions since the congregational board exercises control over the funds. Board "control" could be established if the board simply reviewed all distributions to ensure consistency with the congregation's exempt purposes.

Situation 3
The congregation establishes a discretionary fund and gives a minister the discretion to distribute it only for specified purposes (such as relief of the needy) that are consistent with the congregation's exempt purposes. The minister does not qualify for distributions and is prohibited from making distributions to himself or herself. The congregation's governing board retains administrative control over the fund.

If a discretionary fund is set up by a resolution of a congregation's governing board that prohibits any distribution of the fund for the minister's personal use, then the constructive receipt rule is avoided and no portion of the fund represents taxable income to the minister. In the words of the income tax regulations, "Income is not constructively received if the taxpayer's control of its receipt is subject to substantial limitations or restrictions." As a result, in order to avoid the reporting of the entire discretionary fund as taxable income to the minister, it is essential that the fund be established by means of a congregational or board resolution that prohibits any use of the fund by the minister for personal purposes.

To provide a reasonable basis for assuring donors that their contributions to the fund are deductible, the following steps should be taken: (1) the board resolution should specify that the fund may be distributed by the minister only for needs or projects that are consistent with the congregation's exempt purposes (as set forth in the congregation's charter); and (2) the congregational board must exercise control over the funds. As noted above, board "control" could be established if the board simply reviewed all distributions to ensure consistency with the congregation's exempt purposes.

➻ **TIP.** Ministers can reduce, if not eliminate, the risk of constructive receipt of taxable income, and donors can be given reasonable assurance of the deductibility of their contributions, if a discretionary fund satisfies the following conditions:

- the church gives a minister discretion to distribute the fund only for specified purposes (such as relief of the needy) that are consistent with the congregation's exempt purposes;
- the church prohibits (in writing) the minister from distributing any portion of the fund for himself or herself or any family member; and
- the congregation or its governing board retains administrative control over the fund to ensure that all distributions further the church's exempt purposes.

Definition of "charity"

Ministers who are authorized to distribute discretionary funds for benevolent purposes must recognize that the IRS interprets the term "charity" narrowly. More is required than a temporary financial setback or difficulty paying bills. Ministers should keep this in mind when making distributions from a discretionary fund. Also, the church board should scrutinize every distribution to ensure that this strict test is satisfied. The income tax regulations define "charitable" to include "relief of the poor and distressed or of the underprivileged." The regulations define "needy" as

being a person who lacks the necessities of life, involving physical, mental, or emotional well-being, as a result of poverty or temporary distress. Examples of needy persons include a person who is financially impoverished as a result of low income and lack of financial resources, a person who temporarily lacks food or shelter (and the means to provide for it), a person who is the victim of a natural disaster (such as fire or flood), a person who is the victim of a civil disaster (such as civil disturbance), a person who is temporarily not self sufficient as a result of a sudden and severe personal or family crisis (such as a person who is the

victim of a crime of violence or who has been physically abused). Treas. Reg. 1.170A-4A(b)(2)(ii)(D).

Form 1099-MISC for recipients

In general, a Form 1099-MISC is issued only to self-employed workers who are paid compensation. Since most recipients of a minister's discretionary fund do not perform any services for their distribution, no Form 1099-MISC is required. *IRS Letter Ruling 9314014.*

14. NONACCOUNTABLE BUSINESS EXPENSE REIMBURSEMENTS

▲ **CAUTION.** *In a series of four rulings, the IRS concluded that a pastor's personal use of church assets (vehicles, cell phones, etc.) and nonaccountable reimbursements (not supported by adequate documentation of business purpose) that a church paid the pastor were automatic excess benefits resulting in intermediate sanctions, regardless of the amount involved, since they had not been reported as taxable income by the church on the pastor's Form W-2 or by the pastor on his Form 1040 for the year in which the benefits were provided. Intermediate sanctions are substantial excise taxes the IRS can impose on certain persons who receive "excess benefits" from a tax-exempt organization. These rulings are discussed fully in section A.3 of this chapter.*

A church's reimbursements of a minister's (or other staff member's) business expenses under a nonaccountable arrangement represent taxable income for the minister, whether the minister reports his or her income taxes as an employee or as self-employed. Therefore, it is important to recognize nonaccountable reimbursement arrangements. Reimbursed expenses are nonaccountable if the minister did not account to the employer for the expenses or return any excess reimbursements (employer reimbursements in excess of substantiated expenses) to the employer. Here are some examples of nonaccountable reimbursement arrangements:

- Your church pays a monthly car allowance to ministers or lay staff members without requiring any accounting or substantiation.
- Your church reimburses business expenses without requiring adequate written substantiation (with receipts for all expenses of $75 or more) of the amount, date, place, and business purpose of each expense.
- Your church only reimburses business expenses once each year. Business expenses must be accounted for within a "reasonable time" under an accountable arrangement. Generally, this means within 60 days.
- Your church provides ministers or lay staff with travel advances and requires no accounting for the use of these funds.

In each of these cases, the church's reimbursements are nonaccountable, meaning that they must be reported by the church as income to the recipient.

EXAMPLE. Pastor H receives a monthly car allowance of $300. Pastor H is not required to account for the use of any of these funds. This is an example of a nonaccountable reimbursement arrangement. The church is reimbursing business expenses (through a monthly car allowance) without requiring any accounting or substantiation. It must report all of the monthly allowances ($3,600) as income on Pastor H's Form W-2 (or Form 1099-MISC if self-employed). A failure to do so may convert the allowances into an automatic excess benefit transaction, exposing the pastor and possibly members of the church board to substantial excise taxes called "intermediate sanctions." Automatic excess benefit transactions are addressed in section A.3 of this chapter.

✿ **KEY POINT.** A church's reimbursements of an employee's business expenses are not included in the employee's income if the reimbursements are accountable. See Chapter 7 for details.

✿ **KEY POINT.** The IRS audit guidelines for ministers define a minister's income to include "expense allowances for travel, transportation, or other business expenses received under a nonaccountable plan."

15. EMPLOYER REIMBURSEMENTS OF A SPOUSE'S TRAVEL EXPENSES

As noted in Chapter 7, section C.2, a church must report reimbursements of the travel expenses of a spouse who accompanies a minister on a business trip as taxable income (ordinarily, to the minister) unless the spouse's presence on the trip serves a legitimate business purpose and the spouse's expenses are reimbursed under an accountable arrangement.

16. FORGIVENESS OF DEBT

▲ **CAUTION.** *This benefit constitutes taxable income except as otherwise noted. If it is not reported as taxable income by the church or the recipient in the year it is provided, the IRS may be able to assess intermediate sanctions in the form of substantial excise taxes against the recipient, and possibly members of the church board, regardless of the amount of the benefit. See section A.3 of this chapter for more details.*

Many churches have made loans to their minister. If the minister does not repay the loan and the church forgives the debt, taxable income is generated. Consider the following example:

EXAMPLE. A church hires Pastor B as a youth pastor. Pastor B was recently married and is in need of housing. He would like to buy a home but lacks the $15,000 needed for a down payment. The church board votes to loan Pastor B $15,000. Pastor B signs a no-interest $15,000 promissory note agreeing to pay the church back the $15,000 in 60 monthly installments of

$250. Pastor B pays all of the monthly installments or the first year, but in the second and third years he pays only half of the required installments. After three years Pastor B resigns his position to accept a pastoral position in another church. The balance due on his note is $9,000. Over the next several months, the church treasurer at Pastor B's former church writes him on three occasions and requests that the note be paid in full. Pastor B does not respond to any of these requests. The church board eventually decides to forgive the debt and makes no further contact with Pastor B.

What should a church treasurer do under these circumstances? The forgiveness of debt ordinarily represents taxable income to the debtor. *IRC 61(a)(12).* As a result, if a church makes a loan to an employee and the debt is later forgiven by the church, the church should report the forgiven debt as income for the employee. Here are the rules to follow, using the same facts as in the example:

- If the church has not yet issued a Form W-2 to Pastor B for his last year of employment, then it should report the forgiven debt on that form.
- If the church already has issued a Form W-2 to Pastor B for the last year of employment (within the past three years), two options remain:

(1) Issue a corrected Form W-2, reporting the full amount of the forgiven debt as additional compensation for the last year of employment. A corrected W-2 is prepared on Form W-2c. Be sure to note the year of the Form W-2 that is being corrected.
(2) Issue a Form 1099-MISC reporting the full amount of the forgiven debt in the current year. It is preferable to report the forgiven debt as income in the year the debt is actually forgiven rather than restating Pastor B's compensation for his last year of employment, since taxable income does not actually occur until the year in which the debt is forgiven (the current year).

- In addition to the forgiven debt ($9,000), Pastor B received income because no interest was charged by the church on the loan. In essence, this additional income consists of the amount of interest Pastor B would have paid the church had the applicable federal rate been charged by the church on the loan. A below-market term loan of less than $10,000 is not subject to these rules (assuming one of its principal purposes is not the avoidance of tax). Check with a CPA or tax attorney for assistance in making this calculation. Different rules apply for demand loans. See section A.9, above, for more information.

✿ **KEY POINT.** The instructions to Form 1099-MISC specify that "a canceled debt is not reportable on Form 1099-MISC. Canceled debts are required to be reported on Form 1099-C . . . by financial institutions, credit unions, federal government agencies [and] certain agencies connected with the federal government." As a result, a church is not legally required to report a canceled debt as income on a Form 1099-MISC issued to a former minister. On the other hand, the minister is legally required to report the forgiven debt as taxable income. Many churches prefer to issue a Form 1099-MISC to the minister, reporting the forgiven debt as income. Although not required, this ensures that the minister properly reports the canceled debt as income. The same objective often can be achieved by using a corrected Form W-2 (Form W-2c).

EXAMPLE. An employer paid the moving expenses of newly hired employees to relocate them to the employer's city. Employees were required to reimburse the employer for a portion of the moving expenses paid by the employer if they terminated their employment within one year after being hired. An employee voluntarily terminated her employment within one year of being hired, and the employer was unsuccessful in collecting $5,000 in moving expenses from the employee. The employer eventually wrote this amount off as uncollectible. The IRS ruled that the employer had to report the forgiven debt as taxable income for the former employee. It observed: "It is well settled that where an employee's debt to his employer is satisfied by canceling such debt, income is realized by the employee. Therefore, the employee must include in gross income the total amount of the debt that was canceled by [the employer]. The income realized upon cancellation of indebtedness arose as a result of an employment relationship. Accordingly, Form W-2 should be used to report the amount of indebtedness canceled. This form should be used even if the debt is canceled in a year subsequent to the year of employment." *IRS Letter Ruling 8315021.*

EXAMPLE. A minister failed to report the discharge of an educational loan as income on his tax return. The Tax Court ruled that the forgiven loan balance should have been reported as income. The court also upheld an IRS assessment of a negligence penalty against the minister. *Parker v. Commissioner, 65 T.C.M. 1740 (1993).*

Planned forgiveness of annual payments under a promissory note

A church wants to help its pastor purchase a new home, so it agrees to pay $50,000 of the purchase price. The pastor signs a promissory note agreeing to pay back the $50,000 in ten annual installments. The church board assures the pastor that the church will forgive each annual installment on the date it is due, so the pastor will not have to pay back anything. Is this transaction legitimate? What are the tax consequences?

The IRS released an internal memorandum (a "field service advisory") in 1999 that addresses the tax consequences of debt forgiveness. *FSA 9999-9999-170.* Here are the facts of the arrangement the IRS

IRS SUSPENDS RULINGS ON TREATING THE FORGIVENESS OF DEBT AS A CHARITABLE CONTRIBUTION

The IRS has announced that it will no longer issue private letter rulings addressing the question of "whether a taxpayer who advances funds to a charitable organization and receives therefore a promissory note may deduct as contributions, in one taxable year or in each of several years, amounts forgiven by the taxpayer in each of several years by endorsement on the note." To illustrate, a church member transfers $5,000 to her church and receives in return a promissory note from the church promising to pay back the note in annual installments over the next five years. Each year, on the due date of the annual installment, the note holder "forgives" the payment. Can the note holder treat the forgiven installment as a charitable contribution deduction? This is the question the IRS will no longer address in private letter rulings. *Revenue Procedure 2012-3.*

was addressing: A widow and mother of three adult children owned a partial interest in farmland. She suffered a stroke and was later determined by a court to be incompetent. A guardian was appointed to handle her financial affairs. The guardian sold the farmland to the children in exchange for non–interest bearing promissory notes signed by each child. The sales agreement called upon each child to pay the guardian $10,000 annually. However, the agreement contained a cancellation provision specifying that the payments owed by the children each year would be forgiven by the guardian. The children and guardian recognized that these annual cancellations of debt constituted gifts, but they had no tax impact, since they were not more than the annual gift tax exclusion of $10,000 for each child.

An IRS auditor determined that a completed gift had been made in the year the original sales agreement was signed, not each year that the annual payments under the promissory notes were forgiven. As a result, the full amount of the notes represented a gift to the children in the year of the sale. Since these amounts were far more than $10,000, the children's attempt to purchase their mother's farmland without exceeding the annual gift tax exclusion failed.

The IRS national office was asked to evaluate this arrangement. Specifically, it was asked whether a gift to the children occurred when the property was transferred in exchange for the non-interest bearing notes. It also was asked to clarify its position "concerning taxpayers' persistent use of the installment sale as an estate and gift tax avoidance technique." The IRS noted that the tax code imposes a "gift tax" on gifts and that "the value of the property transferred, determined as of the date of the transfer, is the amount of the gift." Further, the code specifies that if property is transferred for less than full value, "the amount by which the value of the property exceeds the value [received] shall be deemed a gift."

The IRS observed:

> *If an individual ostensibly makes a loan and, as part of a prearranged plan, intends to forgive or not collect on the note, the note will not be considered valuable consideration and the donor will have made a gift at the time of the loan to the full extent of the loan. However, if there is no prearranged plan and the intent to forgive the debt arises at a later time, then the donor will have made a gift only at the time of the forgiveness. . . . Transactions within a family group are subject to special scrutiny, and the presumption is that a transfer between family members is a gift.*

> *Whether the transfer of property is a sale or a gift depends upon whether, as part of a prearranged or preconceived plan, the donor intended to forgive the notes that were received at the time of the transfer.*

The IRS noted that the intent to forgive the notes was the determinative factor in this case and that "a finding of a preconceived intent to forgive the notes relates to whether valuable consideration was received and thus to whether the transaction was in reality a bona fide sale or a disguised gift."

The IRS pointed out that the children "did not execute separate notes" for each year, but rather "the indebtedness of each child . . . was represented by only one note." The children insisted that their arrangement represented a valid installment sale. The IRS disagreed:

> *It is difficult to conceive of this exchange as an installment sale where the intent of the [children] to make a gift to themselves . . . is so clearly evident at the time of the [sale agreement]. The [children] have not come forward with evidence to show that the notes represented an obligation portions of which could be forgiven annually. . . . The [IRS auditor] in this case has appropriately treated this entire transaction as a sham. . . . It is axiomatic that questions of taxation are to be determined with regard to substance rather than form. An examination of the objective facts of this case, therefore, can only lead to the conclusion that the children are entitled to a gift tax exclusion for [one year] only.*

The IRS national office conceded, in its internal memorandum, that "it is conceivable that a court would be inclined to treat this exchange as a bona fide transfer and strictly construe the relevant documents in accordance with their terms." In other words, the children might persuade a court that the transaction was legitimate and that they in fact made gifts each year in which the annual payments under the promissory notes were forgiven.

The IRS cautioned, however, that at a minimum the children had to prove "by some overt act" that the guardian had the "authority and discretion" to forgive the annual payments due under the promissory notes. It noted that an example of such an overt act "would be the cancellation by the [guardian] of a series of promissory notes on an annual basis." The IRS concluded that such evidence was not present in this case. It acknowledged that the sales agreement contained a cancellation provision calling for the cancellation of the annual installment payments each year under the notes. However, the IRS concluded that "the conspicuous absence of any evidence of forgiveness in any of the subsequent years" effectively negated the legal effect of the cancellation provision. It observed:

> *The facts of this case clearly indicate that an intent to make a disguised gift for illusory consideration was formed at the time of the original transaction, and at no time subsequent. . . . In the absence of a showing that there was no prearranged or preconceived plan to forgive any indebtedness, a transfer of real property for non-interest bearing notes must be treated as a gift at the time of the original transfer. Further, the substance of a transaction must prevail over its form where an examination of the facts and circumstances of a transaction suggests that it lacks economic substance.*

Lessons from the IRS memorandum

Church leaders can learn important lessons from the IRS memorandum. Consider the following:

No documentation

Many churches have advanced funds to a pastor to assist with the payment of a home. In some cases there is no clear understanding as to the nature of the arrangement and no documents are signed. It may not be until it is time for the church treasurer to issue the pastor a Form W-2 that the tax consequences of the transaction are addressed. If the amount advanced by the church is substantial, church leaders may attempt to characterize it as a loan to avoid reporting it as taxable compensation to the pastor. The IRS memorandum demonstrates that this may not be possible.

EXAMPLE. A church wanted to help its pastor buy a new home, so it gave him $50,000 cash in March 2012 to assist with the down payment. In January 2013 the church treasurer is preparing the pastor's Form W-2 for 2012 and wonders whether to report the $50,000 as additional compensation. She presents this question to the church board, which is opposed to treating the full amount as taxable in 2012. They come up with the idea of treating the $50,000 as a tax-free gift. As a result, the treasurer reports no part of the $50,000 as additional compensation on the pastor's W-2 for 2012 or any future year. This is incorrect. The $50,000 cannot be treated as a nontaxable gift to the pastor.

EXAMPLE. Same facts as the previous example, except that the pastor, treasurer, and board recognize that the $50,000 cannot be treated as a nontaxable gift. The board wants to minimize the tax impact to the pastor, so it comes up with the idea of treating the $50,000 as a non-interest bearing loan payable over 10 years. They also agree informally to forgive each annual installment of $5,000. However, no documents are signed. How much additional compensation should the treasurer add to the pastor's Form W-2 for 2012: (1) $5,000 (the amount of the first annual installment the church forgives); (2) $50,000 (the full amount of the loan); or (3) some other amount? The IRS memorandum addressed in this section suggests that the correct answer is (2). Why? The memorandum, which represents the thinking of the IRS national office, states that "if an individual ostensibly makes a loan and, as part of a prearranged plan, intends to forgive or not collect on the note, the note will not be considered valuable consideration and the donor will have made a gift at the time of the loan to the full extent of the loan." Since such a gift must be treated as taxable compensation, the entire $50,000 represents taxable income in 2012.

Adequate documentation

The IRS memorandum makes it clear that the existence of adequate documentation may lead to a different result. Consider the following examples:

EXAMPLE. A church wanted to help its pastor buy a new home. The board loaned $50,000 to the pastor in September 2012 to assist with the down payment. It prepared a non-interest-bearing 10-year promissory note in the amount of $50,000, which the pastor signed. The note is secured by a second mortgage on the pastor's new home. The board minutes reflect the board's intention that each annual payment ($5,000) will be forgiven when due. How much additional compensation should the treasurer add to the pastor's Form W-2 for 2012: (1) $5,000 (the amount of the first annual installment the church forgives); (2) $50,000 (the full amount of the loan); or (3) some other amount? The IRS memorandum suggests that the correct answer is (2). The memorandum, which represents the thinking of the IRS national office, states that "if an individual ostensibly makes a loan and, as part of a prearranged plan, intends to forgive or not collect on the note, the note will not be considered valuable consideration and the donor will have made a gift at the time of the loan to the full extent of the loan." The board minutes make it clear that there was a prearranged plan to forgive each year's installment, so the entire amount of the loan must be reported as income in the year of the transaction (2012).

EXAMPLE. Same facts as the previous example, except there was no explicit understanding or agreement that the board would forgive each annual installment. Rather, the board left the question open. As a result, the board minutes contain no indication of any prearranged plan to forgive each annual installment. How much additional compensation should the treasurer add to the pastor's Form W-2 for 2012: (1) $5,000 (the amount of the first annual

installment the church forgives); (2) $50,000 (the full amount of the loan); or (3) some other amount? The IRS memorandum suggests that the correct answer is (1). The memorandum states that "if there is no prearranged plan and the intent to forgive the debt arises at a later time, then the [church] will have made a gift only at the time of the forgiveness." This means that income is realized by the pastor each year to the extent that the board decides to forgive the annual installment due under the promissory note. Of course, if the board forgives each annual installment in the year it is due, it becomes increasingly possible that the IRS might view the entire arrangement as prearranged. If so, the analysis of the previous example might apply.

EXAMPLE. Same facts as the previous example, except that the church issues the pastor ten promissory notes for $5,000 each. The notes have "rolling" maturity dates, so that one note matures each year over the next 10 years. The IRS memorandum suggests that this arrangement will have an even greater likelihood of avoiding the inclusion of the entire $50,000 amount as income on the pastor's 2012 Form W-2. The IRS noted that to avoid treating the entire loan amount as a gift (or as income) in the year of the original transaction, the borrower must be able to prove "by some overt act" that the lender had the "authority and discretion" to forgive the annual payments due under the promissory note. It cited as an example of an "overt act" the cancellation by the lender of a series of promissory notes on an annual basis. Such acts, concluded the IRS, were evidence of "forgiveness in subsequent years."

❖ **KEY POINT.** This section only addresses the tax consequences of a church's forgiveness of a loan made to a pastor. It does not address the tax consequences of a church making a non-interest bearing loan to a pastor. That issue is addressed previously in this chapter.

17. SEVERANCE PAY

Many churches have entered into severance-pay arrangements with a pastor or other staff member. Such arrangements can occur when a pastor or staff member is dismissed, retires, or voluntarily resigns. Consider the following examples:

EXAMPLE. Pastor G is hired for a three-year term at an annual salary of $45,000. After two years the church membership votes to dismiss Pastor G. The church agrees to give Pastor G severance pay in the amount of $45,000 (the full amount of the third year's salary).

EXAMPLE. Pastor C is called by a church for an indefinite term. After 10 years Pastor C resigns to accept another position. The church board agrees to give Pastor C severance pay of $20,000.

EXAMPLE. Pastor T accepts a call as a pastor of a local church. After one year she is dismissed and is replaced by a male pastor.

Pastor T believes the church was guilty of sex discrimination. The church and Pastor T enter into a severance agreement in which Pastor T agrees to waive any claims she has against the church under state and federal law in exchange for its agreement to give her severance pay of $40,000 (representing one year's salary).

EXAMPLE. K has served as bookkeeper at her church for 20 years. She is 68 years old. The church board decides it is time for K to retire so that a younger person can take over her job. When the board learns that K has visited with an attorney, they offer her a severance pay of one year's full salary ($25,000).

Taxable income

Is severance pay paid by a church taxable income for the recipient? In most cases the answer is yes. The tax code imposes the income tax on "all income from whatever source derived," unless a specific exclusion applies.

One exclusion may apply in some cases. Section 104(a)(2) of the tax code specifies that gross income does not include the amount of any damages received (whether by suit or agreement and whether as lump sums or as periodic payments) "on account of personal physical injuries or physical sickness." However, there are two important exceptions to this exclusion. First, punitive damages are always taxable. Second, section 104(a) specifies that "emotional distress shall not be treated as physical injury or physical sickness" except for "damages not in excess of the amount paid for medical care . . . attributable to emotional distress." As a result, jury awards and settlements for employment discrimination and wrongful dismissal claims are fully taxable to the extent that they are based on emotional distress.

Church leaders must determine whether severance pay is taxable so it can be properly reported (on Forms W-2 and 941). Also, taxes must be withheld from severance pay that is paid to nonminister employees (and ministers who have elected voluntary withholding). Failure to properly report severance pay can result in penalties for both a church and the recipient.

✿ **KEY POINT.** The American Jobs Creation Act of 2004 specifies that the amount of monetary damages received on account of unlawful discrimination is reduced by the amount of the damages that are used to pay for attorneys' fees and court costs incurred in connection with the lawsuit. This rule applies to most forms of discrimination under state and federal law.

Nonqualified deferred compensation

Section 409A of the tax code imposes several complex requirements on nonqualified deferred compensation plans, including documentation, elections, funding, distributions, withholding, and reporting. If a plan does not meet these requirements, participants in the plan are required to include in income immediately compensation otherwise deferred under the plan and pay taxes on such income, including an additional 20 percent tax and a tax generally based

upon the underpayment interest that would have accrued had the amount been includible in income when first deferred. Nonqualified deferred compensation subject to the section 409A requirements is generally defined as compensation that workers earn in one year but that is not paid until a future year. Some exceptions apply. For example, section 409A does not apply to qualified plans (such as a section 401(k) plan) or to a section 403(b) plan. Any agreement to pay compensation to a current or former employee may be subject to the 409A requirements. Such payments should not be approved without the advice of a tax professional to ensure that the potential application of section 409A is fully addressed. Section 409A is addressed in Chapter 10, section A.2, of this guide.

Housing allowance

A related question is whether a church can designate any portion of severance pay as a housing allowance. This question has never been addressed by the IRS or any court. However, an argument can be made that a church can designate a portion of severance pay as a housing allowance if the severance pay is treated as taxable compensation rather than as damages in settlement of a personal injury claim. If the severance pay represents taxable income, as the IRS will almost certainly insist in most cases, it is because the amount paid represents compensation based on services rendered. Since a housing allowance must be designated out of compensation paid to a minister for services rendered in the exercise of ministry, a reasonable case can be made that a housing allowance can be designated with respect to taxable severance pay.

Of course, a housing allowance can only be designated for ministers. And designating severance pay as a housing allowance will be of little value if a minister transfers immediately to another church that designates a timely housing allowance. But a designation of a housing allowance will be useful in the case of a minister who is not immediately employed by another church or religious organization.

Also, note that housing allowances are not reduced by the portion of a minister's compensation that represents vacation pay, even though the minister ordinarily is not performing services in the exercise of ministry during vacation. The same principle supports the availability of a housing allowance designated out of a minister's severance pay.

The income tax regulations specify that "a rental allowance must be included in the minister's gross income in the taxable year in which it is received, to the extent that such allowance is not used by him during such taxable year to rent or otherwise provide a home." *Treas. Reg. 1.107-1(c).* This language suggests that the portion of a minister's severance pay that is designated as a housing allowance must be included in the minister's taxable income to the extent that it is not used in that same year. This rule may greatly diminish the tax benefit of designating some or all of a minister's severance pay as a housing allowance late in the year. Deferring severance pay (and a housing allowance) to the following year may not help, since this may trigger the limitations on nonqualified deferred compensation arrangements set forth in section 409A of the tax code and the regulations thereunder (see Chapter 10, section D, for details).

18. TRIPS TO THE HOLY LAND

▲ **CAUTION.** *This benefit constitutes taxable income except as otherwise noted. If it is not reported as taxable income by the church or the recipient in the year it is provided, the IRS may be able to assess intermediate sanctions in the form of substantial excise taxes against the recipient, regardless of the amount of the benefit. See section A.3 of this chapter for more details.*

Many churches have presented their minister with an all-expense paid trip to the Holy Land for the minister and the minister's spouse. Often such trips are provided to commemorate some special occasion, such as a birthday or anniversary. In many cases the value of such a trip is treated as a nontaxable gift to the minister. Is this correct? Unfortunately, the answer is no if either or both of the following statements are true:

- The trip is provided to honor the minister for his or her faithful services on behalf of the church.
- The trip is provided to enhance or enrich the minister's ministry. While a trip to the Holy Land can benefit one's ministry, such a trip is not a business expense under current law. The tax code provides that "no deduction shall be allowed . . . for expenses for travel as a form of education." *IRC 274(m)(2).* A committee report explaining this rule contains the following observations:

No deduction is allowed for costs of travel that would be deductible only on the ground that the travel itself constitutes a form of education (e.g., where a teacher of French travels to France to maintain general familiarity with the French language and culture, or where a social studies teacher travels to another state to learn about or photograph its people, customs, geography, etc.). . . .

The committee is concerned about deductions claimed for travel as a form of "education." The committee believes that any business purpose served by traveling for general educational purposes, in the absence of a specific need such as engaging in research which can only be performed at a particular facility, is at most indirect and insubstantial. By contrast, travel as a form of education may provide substantial personal benefits by permitting some individuals in particular professions to deduct the cost of a vacation, while most individuals must pay for vacation trips out of after-tax dollars, no matter how educationally stimulating the travel may be. Accordingly, the committee bill disallows deductions for travel that can be claimed only

on the ground that the travel itself is "educational," but permits deductions for travel that is a necessary adjunct to engaging in an activity that gives rise to a business deduction relating to education.

As a result, the church's payment of the cost of such a trip is treated as the payment of personal vacation expenses, and the full amount must be included as taxable income on the minister's Form W-2 (or 1099-MISC if self-employed). This includes transportation, meals, and lodging. It also includes all of the travel costs of the minister's spouse (and children) if these are paid by the church.

✿ **KEY POINT.** The IRS has ruled that the value of a free trip to a foreign country provided by a travel agency to a person who organizes a tour and solicits participants is taxable income. *Revenue Ruling 64-154.*

Consider the following two very limited exceptions to the general rule summarized above.

Short-term mission trips

If a church sends a minister to the Holy Land (or any other foreign country) for the primary purpose of engaging in religious activities, then the church's payment of the documented expenses incurred by the minister may be nontaxable as an accountable reimbursement of business expenses. This exception will be interpreted narrowly, and the IRS will scrutinize such cases for evidence of abuse. A two-week vacation cannot be turned into a business trip because of a couple of speaking engagements. On the other hand, if a church sends a minister on a short-term mission trip to a foreign country and the minister performs several religious services or engages in evangelistic activities or teaching at a seminary, then a reasonable basis exists for treating the trip as having a legitimate business purpose. In general, any element of personal pleasure (vacation, sightseeing, etc.) must represent less than 25 percent of the total trip time. See Chapter 7, section C.2, for more information on foreign travel.

Study at a foreign university

If a minister travels to a university in a foreign country for an educational course that is reasonably necessary for the enhancement of his or her duties, then a church's reimbursement of the costs of such a trip may constitute a nontaxable reimbursement of business expenses if adequate substantiation is provided.

19. PAYMENT OF PERSONAL EXPENSES

▲ **CAUTION.** *This benefit constitutes taxable income except as otherwise noted. If it is not reported as taxable income by the church or the recipient in the year it is provided, the IRS may be able to assess intermediate sanctions in the form of substantial excise taxes against the recipient, and possibly members of the church board, regardless of the amount of the benefit. See section A.3 of this chapter for more details.*

Churches sometimes pay the personal expenses of their minister or other church employees. Such payments ordinarily represent taxable income for the minister and other employees.

❖**KEY POINT.** The IRS can impose intermediate sanctions (an excise tax) against an officer or director of a church or other charity, and in some cases against board members individually, if an officer or director is paid an excessive amount of compensation. The law clarifies that the payment of personal expenses of an officer or director can be treated as compensation if it is clear that the employer intended the payments as compensation for services.

EXAMPLE. A religious ministry purchased season tickets for a college football team for a minister-employee. The ministry also made scholarship pledges to the college on behalf of the minister. The Tax Court ruled that these purchases constituted taxable income for the minister. It noted that "a third party's payment of a taxpayer's personal expenses is income to the taxpayer." *Whittington v. Commissioner, T.C. Memo. 2000-296 (2000).*

Pastors and other church staff members sometimes use church funds over which they have control to pay for personal expenses. All such expenditures should be reported as taxable income for the staff member who paid the personal expenses.

EXAMPLE. The Tax Court ruled that the owner of a small company who used company checks to pay for personal purchases should have reported the value of those checks as taxable income. Some churches have checkbooks requiring the signature of only one person. Persons with such authority may write checks for personal purposes without authorization and justify their acts on the ground that their purchases were indirectly for church purposes or, in some cases, to compensate for a "substandard salary." Whatever the reason, persons who write church checks for personal purposes not only will generate taxable income, but they may face criminal charges for embezzlement and tax fraud (assuming that the amount of the checks is not reported as taxable income). *Thompson v. Commissioner, T.C. Memo. 2004-2.*

20. FREQUENT-FLIER MILES

Ever since major airlines launched frequent-flier programs several years ago, uncertainty has existed concerning the tax treatment of frequent-flier miles—especially when those miles are earned by employees while engaged in business travel for their employer. Are employers required to report the value of these mileage awards as taxable income to employees? Or is this a tax-free fringe benefit?

Tax status of benefits
The IRS provided official guidance in 2002. It announced, "Consistent with prior practice, the IRS will not assert that any taxpayer has understated his federal tax liability by reason of the receipt or personal use of frequent flier miles or other in-kind promotional benefits attributable to the taxpayer's business or official travel. Any future guidance on the taxability of these benefits will be applied prospectively."

The IRS cautioned that "this relief does not apply to travel or other promotional benefits that are converted to cash, to compensation that is paid in the form of travel or other promotional benefits, or in other circumstances where these benefits are used for tax avoidance purposes." A "promotional benefit" is a program that allows travelers to accumulate frequent-flier miles through rental car companies or hotels. These promotional benefits may generally be exchanged for upgraded seating, free travel, discounted travel, travel-related services, or other services or benefits. The IRS did not address the tax status of such benefits. This means that the IRS could pursue a tax-enforcement program against these benefits, but most experts view this as unlikely. *IRS Announcement 2002-18.*

Using personal credit cards to purchase church supplies and equipment
Some church employees purchase church supplies and equipment using a personal credit card in order to earn frequent-flier miles awarded for purchases made using their card. For example, a church board has authorized the purchase of a new copy machine for the church at a cost of $10,000. The senior pastor purchases the copier using his personal credit card and then is reimbursed by the church. Is it appropriate for the pastor to purchase this church asset with his personal credit card in order to have the frequent flier miles accrue to his benefit?

One of the requirements for a church to maintain its exemption from federal income taxation is that none of its income or assets inures to the benefit of a private individual other than as reasonable compensation for services rendered. There is no materiality requirement. Any distribution of a church's income or assets for the private benefit of an individual may constitute prohibited inurement. The IRS has observed that "those in control may not, by reason of their position, acquire any of the charitable organization's funds [or assets]. If funds [or assets] are diverted from exempt purposes to private purposes, exemption is in jeopardy. . . . The test is whether, at every stage of the transaction, those controlling the organization guarded its interests."

It is certainly possible that the IRS would view the use of a pastor's personal credit card to purchase church assets in order to divert frequent-flier miles to his or her account as an example of prohibited inurement. Because of this risk, church leaders are advised to consult with a tax professional before pursuing such an arrangement.

21. SABBATICAL PAY

▲ **CAUTION.** *This benefit constitutes taxable income except as otherwise noted. If it is not reported as taxable income by the church or the recipient in the year it is provided, the IRS may be able to assess intermediate sanctions in the form of substantial excise taxes against the recipient, and* *possibly members of the church board, regardless of the amount of the benefit. See section A.3 of this chapter for more details.*

▲ **CAUTION.** *Section 409A of the tax code imposes several complex requirements on nonqualified deferred compensation plans, including documentation, elections, funding, distributions, withholding, and reporting. If a plan does not meet these requirements, participants in the plan are required to include in income immediately compensation otherwise deferred under the plan and pay taxes on such income, including an additional 20 percent tax and a tax generally based upon the underpayment interest that would have accrued had the amount been includible in income when first deferred. Nonqualified deferred compensation subject to the section 409A requirements is generally defined as compensation that workers earn in one year but that is not paid until a future year. Some exceptions apply. For example, section 409A does not apply to qualified plans (such as a section 401(k) plan) or to a section 403(b) plan. Any agreement to pay compensation to a current or former employee may be subject to the 409A requirements. Such payments should not be approved without the advice of a tax professional to ensure that the potential application of section 409A is fully addressed. Section 409A is addressed in Chapter 10, section A.2, of this guide.*

A sabbatical is an extended leave of absence during which a minister is free to pursue writing, education, or other activities. Churches that provide a minister with a sabbatical usually continue the minister's compensation in whole or in part during his or her absence. Sabbatical pay represents taxable income to the minister.

Can sabbatical pay be characterized as a nontaxable scholarship? Generally this is not possible, for two reasons. First, the income tax regulations specify that scholarships provided to employees by an employer as compensation for services cannot qualify as a nontaxable benefit. See Chapter 5, section C, for details. Second, few sabbaticals would meet the requirements for a nontaxable scholarship, as the following example illustrates.

> **EXAMPLE.** A professor was given a year off to pursue studies overseas. He was paid $27,000 during his sabbatical, and he treated this entire amount as a tax-free scholarship. The IRS ruled that the sabbatical income represented taxable income, and the Tax Court agreed. The court noted that scholarships are nontaxable only if certain conditions are met. The recipient must be "a candidate for a degree at an educational organization," and the scholarship must be used for qualified tuition. The court noted that the professor's sabbatical income was not a nontaxable scholarship since he was not a candidate for a degree and failed to prove that he used any portion of the income for qualified tuition expenses. This ruling will be useful to church leaders in evaluating the tax status of sabbatical income provided to pastors or other staff members. *Kant v. Commissioner, T.C. Memo. 1997-217.*

❖ **KEY POINT.** The question of whether expenses incurred by a church employee while on sabbatical leave can be treated as

legitimate business expenses that are deductible by the employee or reimbursable by the employing church under an accountable reimbursement arrangement is addressed in Chapter 7, section C.3 of this tax guide.

22. LOVE OFFERINGS

▲ **CAUTION.** *This benefit constitutes taxable income except as otherwise noted. If it is not reported as taxable income by the church or the recipient in the year it is provided, the IRS may be able to assess intermediate sanctions in the form of substantial excise taxes against the recipient, and possibly members of the church board, regardless of the amount of the benefit. See section A.3 of this chapter for more details.*

▲ **CAUTION.** *Section 409A of the tax code imposes several complex requirements on nonqualified deferred compensation plans, including documentation, elections, funding, distributions, withholding, and reporting. If a plan does not meet these requirements, participants in the plan are required to include in income immediately compensation otherwise deferred under the plan and pay taxes on such income, including an additional 20 percent tax and a tax generally based upon the underpayment interest that would have accrued had the amount been includible in income when first deferred. Nonqualified deferred compensation subject to the section 409A requirements is generally defined as compensation that workers earn in one year but that is not paid until a future year. Some exceptions apply. For example, section 409A does not apply to qualified plans (such as a section 401(k) plan) or to a section 403(b) plan. Any agreement to pay compensation to a current or former employee may be subject to the 409A requirements. Such payments should not be approved without the advice of a tax professional to ensure that the potential application of section 409A is fully addressed. Section 409A is addressed in Chapter 10, section A.2, of this guide.*

Churches sometimes collect "love offerings" from the congregation for a pastor, intern, or other staff member in recognition of services rendered. Such offerings must be reported as taxable income. If the recipient is an employee, the love offering should be added to his or her Form W-2. If the recipient is not an employee, the income should be reported on a Form 1099-MISC if $600 or more.

> **EXAMPLE.** A pastor reported $28,000 as income from his church. The IRS audited the pastor's tax return and concluded that he understated his taxable income by $24,000. The pastor insisted that the $24,000 of unreported income came from voluntary gifts or offerings from members of the congregation, which were not taxable. The IRS rejected this argument, and the pastor appealed to the Tax Court. The court agreed with the IRS that these "gifts" represented taxable income for the pastor. It conceded that gifts are not taxable but concluded that the distributions made by the church to the pastor were not gifts. It observed, "The evidence that we do have strongly suggests

that the transfers were not gifts. . . . The transfers arose out of the pastor's relationship with the members of his congregation presumably because they believed he was a good minister and they wanted to reward him. Furthermore, the pastor testified that without the gifts his activity as a minister was essentially a money losing activity. In short, as the pastor recognized, the so-called gifts were a part of the compensation he received for being a minister. As such, the transfers are not excludable from income." The court assessed a negligence penalty against the pastor because he failed to make a reasonable attempt to comply with the tax law. *Swaringer v. Commissioner, T.C. Summary Opinion 2001-37 (2001).*

EXAMPLE. A federal court rejected a couple's claim that they were entitled to an exemption from federal income tax because they "labor for the ministry." The court concluded, "Income received by ministers whether from the church itself or from other private employers or sources is not exempt from income tax. The income received by taxpayers must be included in gross income required to be reported for income tax purposes according to the Internal Revenue Code." The court acknowledged that ministers' income (from the exercise of ministry) is exempt from federal income tax withholding but noted that "while certain income of ministers may be exempt from withholding of income tax, the income received by ministers, even from religious activities . . . is not exempt from payment of income tax." Further, "the fact that a church itself may be exempt from payment of income taxes does not mean that the income received by ministers is exempt." *Pomeroy v. Commissioner, 2003-2 USTC 50,568 (D. Nev. 2003).*

EXAMPLE. A federal appeals court ruled that a pastor was properly convicted and sentenced to prison for filing a fraudulent tax return as a result of his failure to report several items of taxable income. The court rejected the pastor's claim that a $60,000 payment to him by the church represented a nontaxable love gift. *2009 WL 723206 (C.A.11 2009).*

EXAMPLE. A federal appeals court affirmed the conviction of a pastor and his wife on several tax crimes based on various forms of church compensation they failed to disclose on their tax returns, including "gifts" from their church. The court observed: "It is apparent that the relationship between an employer and employee is one that is commonly established for some kind of mutual benefit, a dynamic that is altogether different from the 'detached and disinterested generosity' that normally prompts the tender of a gift. *Commissioner v. Duberstein, 363 U.S. 278, 285 (1960).* . . . Payments from an employer to an employee are not gifts, but are presumed to be included in gross income. A taxpayer must report as gross income 'all income from whatever source derived' unless 'excluded by law.' To be sure, section 102(a) of the Code excludes from gross income 'the value of property acquired by gift.' But

the Code is explicit that payments from an employer to an employee do not constitute gifts under §102(a), which 'shall not exclude from gross income any amount transferred by or for an employer to, or for the benefit of, an employee.'" *I.R.C. section 102(c). United States v. Jinwright, 2012-2 U.S.T.C. ¶50,417 (4th Cir. 2012).*

23. EMBEZZLED FUNDS

Embezzled funds represent taxable income to the embezzler. Here are the main points to consider:

- The embezzler has a legal duty to report the full amount of the embezzled funds as taxable income on his or her tax return regardless of whether the employer reports the embezzled funds as taxable income on the employee's Form W-2 or Form 1099. If funds were embezzled in prior years, the employee will need to file amended tax returns for each of those years to report the illegal income, since embezzlement occurs in the year the funds are misappropriated.

  IRS Publication 525 states: "Illegal income, such as stolen or embezzled funds, must be included in your income on line 21 of Form 1040, or on Schedule C (Form 1040) or Schedule C-EZ (Form 1040) if from your self-employment activity."

- Federal law does not require employers to report embezzled funds on an employee's Form W-2 or on a Form 1099. This makes sense, since in most cases an employer will not know how much was stolen. How can an employer report an amount that is undetermined? Embezzlers are not of much help, since even when they confess to their acts, they typically admit to stealing far less than they actually took. This means that any attempt by an employer to report embezzled funds on an employee's Form W-2 or 1099 will almost always represent an understatement of what was taken.

- In rare cases, an employer may be able to determine the actual amount of embezzled funds as well as the perpetrator's identity. In such a case, the full amount may be added to the employee's Form W-2, or it can be reported on a Form 1099 as miscellaneous income. But remember, do not use this option unless you are certain that you know the amount that was stolen as well as the thief's identity.

- In most cases, employers do not know the actual amount of embezzled funds. The embezzler's "confession" is unreliable if not worthless. Reporting inaccurate estimates on a Form W-2 or 1099 will be misleading. Also, if you report allegedly embezzled funds on an employee's Form W-2 or 1099 without proof of guilt, this may expose the church to liability on the basis of several grounds. One of these is section 7434 of the tax code, which imposes a penalty of the greater of $5,000 or actual damages plus attorney's fees on employers that willfully file a fraudulent Form 1099.

- Employers that cannot determine the actual amount of funds an employee embezzled, or the employee's identity, will not be penalized by the IRS for failing to file a Form W-2 or 1099 that reports an estimate of the amount stolen.

Employers that are certain of the identity of the embezzler and the amount stolen may be subject to a penalty under section 6721 of the tax code for failure to report the amount on the employee's Form W-2 or 1099. This penalty is $50 or up to the greater of $100 or 10 percent of the unreported amount in the case of an intentional disregard of the filing requirement. For employers that are certain how much was stolen and who intentionally fail to report it, this penalty can be substantial. To illustrate, assume that church leaders know with certainty that a particular employee embezzled $100,000, but they choose to forgive the debt and not report the stolen funds as taxable income. Since this represents an intentional disregard of the filing requirement, the church is subject to a penalty of up to 10 percent of the unreported amount, or $10,000. But note that there is no penalty if the failure to report is due to reasonable cause, such as uncertainty as to how much was embezzled or the identity of the embezzler.

- If the full amount of the embezzlement is not known with certainty, church leaders have the option of filing a Form 3949-A (Information Referral) with the IRS. Form 3949-A is a form that allows employers to report suspected illegal activity, including embezzlement, to the IRS. The IRS will launch an investigation based on the information provided on the Form 3949-A. If the employee in fact has embezzled funds and not reported them as taxable income, the IRS may assess criminal sanctions for failure to report taxable income.

In many cases, filing Form 3949-A with the IRS is a church's best option when embezzlement is suspected.

- Most people who embezzle funds insist that they intended to pay the money back and were simply "borrowing" the funds temporarily. An intent to pay back embezzled funds is not a defense to the crime of embezzlement. Most church employees who embezzle funds plan to repay the church fully before anyone suspects what has happened. One can only imagine how many such schemes actually work without anyone knowing about it. The courts are not persuaded by the claims of embezzlers that they intended to fully repay the funds they misappropriated. The crime is complete when the embezzler misappropriates the church's funds to his or her own personal use. As one court has noted: "The act of embezzlement is complete the moment the official converts the money to his own use even though he then has the intent to restore it. Few embezzlements are committed except with the full belief upon the part of the guilty person that he can and will restore the property before the day of accounting occurs. There is where the danger lies and the statute prohibiting embezzlement is passed in order to

protect the public against such venturesome enterprises by people who have money in their control."

In short, it does not matter that someone intended to pay back embezzled funds. This intent in no way justifies or excuses the crime. The crime is complete when the funds are converted to one's own use—regardless any intent to pay them back.

- In some cases, employees who embezzle funds will, when confronted, agree to pay them back if the church agrees not to report the embezzlement to the police or the IRS. Does this convert the embezzled funds into a loan, thereby relieving the employee and the church of any obligation to report the funds as taxable income in the year the embezzlement occurred? Not necessarily, since any recharacterization of embezzled funds as a "loan" may trigger provisions in the church's bylaws pertaining to the lending of church funds. For example, many church bylaws require congregational authorization of any indebtedness, and this would include any attempt to reclassify embezzled funds as a loan. Of course, this would have the collateral consequence of apprising the congregation of what has happened, which is an outcome church leaders sometimes seek to avoid.

Also, note that recharacterizing embezzled funds as a loan would raise the concerns, addressed previously, pertaining to below-market loans, inurement, and excess benefit transactions. See section B.9 in this chapter.

- What if the embezzled funds are returned? The crime of embezzlement has occurred even if the embezzled funds in fact are paid back. Of course, it may be less likely that a prosecutor will prosecute a case under these circumstances. And even if the embezzler is prosecuted, this evidence may lessen the punishment. But the courts have consistently ruled that an actual return of embezzled funds does not purge the offense of its criminal nature or absolve the embezzler from punishment. As far as taxes are concerned, the embezzled funds represent taxable income, since the crime is complete. The employee may be able to claim the repayment as a miscellaneous itemized deduction on Schedule A (Form 1040), depending on the circumstances.

- Cases of embezzlement raise a number of complex legal and tax issues. Church leaders should seek legal counsel in responding to these issues.

24. CONTROL OVER CHURCH FUNDS

Contributions to church bank accounts over which a pastor exercises total control may represent taxable income to the pastor. This potential source of taxable income was addressed by the United States Tax Court. An ordained pastor (the "petitioner") established a church as a corporation sole under Utah law. He designated himself as "overseer" of the church. As overseer, he had full control over the corporation sole, including the authority to amend its articles of corporation sole and appoint his successor. He opened two bank accounts in the name of the church. The IRS audited the petitioners' tax returns for two years and concluded that all money deposited into the church's accounts (totaling $182,000) was income to the petitioners because they exercised full control over it and used it to pay personal expenses.

On appeal, the Tax Court observed:

> We generally have held that . . . a taxpayer's gross income includes deposits into all accounts over which the taxpayer has dominion and control, not just deposits into the taxpayer's personal bank accounts. A taxpayer has dominion and control over an account when the taxpayer has the freedom to use its funds at will.

> We have held that deposits made to a lawyer's "cash management" accounts were income to the taxpayer where she was the only signatory on the account, used it to pay personal expenses, and did not disclose its existence to her law firm's accountant. . . . Furthermore, we have held that deposits into the accounts of a purported trust for an investment project were income to a taxpayer where he had the power to make withdrawals, his Social Security number was the only one on the accounts, he was one of two signatories, his business address was on the accounts, and he made transfers into and out of the accounts. Finally, we have held that deposits made into the account of a purported church were includable in the taxpayers' gross income where the taxpayers were the owners of the bank accounts, exercised complete control over the funds in the accounts, and used those funds for personal expenditures. [We noted] that it was unnecessary to disregard the separate existence of the purported church in order to reach our conclusion that funds deposited in the church's accounts were income to the taxpayers. We stated: "It is not necessary to disregard the separate existence of the church or to challenge the tax status of the church as an entity in order to sustain [the IRS's] determinations in this case. Whether they were entitled to the funds or embezzled the funds from the church, petitioners exercised complete dominion and control over deposits into the various bank accounts that were the basis of respondent's determination. . . ."

> It is undisputed that petitioners were the only signatories on the church bank accounts and that the address listed on those accounts was that of petitioners. The petitioner testified that he used the money in the church bank accounts for mission trips, mission expenses, other ministry expenses, and church expenses. Petitioners contend that the large number of checks written to themselves or to cash, totaling more than $70,000, were all for use on their mission trips, and they contend that the dates of those withdrawals line up with the dates of their mission trips. Yet many of the withdrawal dates bear little relationship to the dates of their mission trips. . . . Petitioners have supplied no receipts, records, or other evidence to substantiate their testimony regarding the use of the cash they withdrew from the church bank accounts.

The court conceded that some of the funds the petitioners withdrew from the church account were used for their missionary expenses. However,

> the evidence also shows that petitioners sometimes used funds from the church bank accounts to pay their personal expenses, suggesting the likelihood that they also used some of the cash they withdrew from the church bank accounts for trips to pay their personal expenses. Petitioners produced no receipts or other documentation to show how the cash was used or how much money they spent on overseas mission trips. Because the burden of proof is on petitioners to produce such records and because petitioners have failed to produce any documentation, we conclude that petitioners have failed to meet their burden.

The court stressed that the petitioners

> had unfettered access to the funds in the church accounts, and there is no evidence that the church congregation had any say over how those funds were used. Indeed, the only member of the church congregation who testified at trial had no knowledge of the church's finances, suggesting that petitioners did not share any information about church finances with the congregation. The facts show that petitioners fully controlled the church accounts, used money in those accounts at will, including to pay personal expenses, and were not accountable to anyone in their congregation for their use of the church funds. Accordingly, we conclude that petitioners exercised dominion and control over the church bank accounts. Consequently, all deposits into those accounts, except those from nontaxable sources, are properly includable in petitioners' gross income.

The court rejected the petitioners' plea that their failure to supply records from the church to substantiate their testimony regarding the use of church funds should be excused because, pursuant to the Church Audit Procedures Act, the IRS cannot compel them to produce church records. The Act sets forth certain conditions the IRS must follow before it can obtain records of a church in connection with an examination of that church's tax liability. However, the court noted that the Act does not apply to "any inquiry or examination relating to the tax liability of any person other than a church." It observed: "Courts generally have held that where the IRS is examining the tax liability of an individual, such as a pastor, rather than the church itself [the Act] does not apply. We agree. Accordingly, petitioners' failure to produce church records that would substantiate their testimony about how they used the cash withdrawn from the church bank accounts is not excused by [the Act]."

Petitioners claimed that even if some of the expenses paid from the church account were personal, those amounts are not includible in their taxable income because they were for the purpose of providing a home for the petitioner, a minister of the gospel, and therefore are exempt from taxation as a housing allowance. The court disagreed:

> In order for a minister's housing allowance to be exempt from taxation . . . it must be designated as a housing allowance by an official action of the church in accordance with section 1.107-1(b), Income Tax Regs., which provides: "The term [housing] allowance means an amount paid to a minister to rent or otherwise provide a home . . . if such amount is designated as [housing] allowance pursuant to official action taken in advance of such payment by the employing church or other qualified organization. . . . The designation of an amount as [a housing] allowance may be evidenced in an employment contract, in minutes of or in a resolution by a church or other qualified organization or in its budget, or in any other appropriate instrument evidencing such official action. The designation referred to in this paragraph is a sufficient designation if it permits a payment or a part thereof to be identified as a payment of rental allowance as distinguished from salary or other remuneration."

The court concluded that the petitioner received no official salary from the church, and "nothing in the record suggests that it took any official action to designate a housing allowance for him. Accordingly, petitioners' argument that their personal housing expenses are exempt from taxation fails." *101 T.C.M. 1550 (2011).*

C. FEES FOR PERFORMING MARRIAGES, FUNERALS, AND BAPTISMS

Ministers often receive fees directly from church members for performing personal services such as marriages, funerals, or baptisms. Are these fees, which are paid directly from members to a minister, taxable income to the minister? The answer is yes. The income tax regulations specify that "marriage fees and other contributions received by a clergyman for services" are income for the minister. *Treas. Reg. 1.61-2(a)(1).* Note, however, that such fees ordinarily will be self-employment earnings for a minister if received directly from members, and not employee wages. As a result, they must be reported on a Schedule C (explained fully in Chapter 7).

D. SOCIAL SECURITY BENEFITS

✿ **KEY POINT.** Persons who are retired and who earn more than a specified amount of income may be taxed on some of their Social Security benefits. If you received Social Security benefits other than supplemental security income benefits (SSI) in 2012, part of the amount you received may be taxable.

If you received Social Security benefits during 2012, you will receive (before January 31, 2013) Form SSA-1099 showing the amount of benefits you received. In determining whether your Social Security benefits received in 2012 are taxable, consider the following rules:

(1) In general, if the only income you received during 2012 was your Social Security benefits, your benefits probably will not be taxable and you probably will not have to file a return.

(2) If you received other income in addition to Social Security benefits in 2012, your benefits generally will not be taxable unless your income is over a certain amount.

(3) To determine if any of your benefits are taxable, compare the "base amount" (see below) with the total of

- one-half of your benefits, plus
- all your other income, including tax-exempt interest.

  Your *base amount* is
- $25,000 if you are single, head of household, or qualifying widow(er), or married filing separately and lived apart for all of 2012.
- $32,000 if you are married filing jointly.

  Your Social Security benefits generally are not taxable if your total income plus one-half of your Social Security benefits is less than your base amount.

(4) If your total income plus one-half of your Social Security benefits is more than $25,000 if you are single, or more than $32,000 if you are married and file a joint return, then some of your Social Security benefits will be taxable. Generally, up to 50 percent of your benefits will be taxable. However, up to 85 percent of your benefits can be taxable if your income plus half of your Social Security benefits exceeds $34,000 ($44,000 if you are married and file jointly).

(5) If you are married and file a joint return for 2012, you and your spouse must combine your incomes and your benefits to determine whether any of your combined benefits are taxable. Even if your spouse did not receive benefits, you must add your spouse's income to yours to figure whether any of your benefits are taxable.

EXAMPLE. Pastor E and his spouse are over age 65 and file a joint return. They both received Social Security benefits during 2012. In January 2013 they received a Form SSA-1099 showing that net Social Security benefits of $6,600 were received by Pastor E and $3,400 by his spouse in 2012 (for a total of $10,000). Pastor E and his spouse had AGI of $25,000 in 2012, plus tax-exempt interest of $1,000. The benefits received by the Pastor E and his spouse are not taxable in 2012, since their income plus half of their Social Security benefits is less than $32,000.

EXAMPLE. Same facts as the previous example, except that Pastor E and his spouse had AGI of $35,000 in 2012. Under these facts, a portion of the Social Security benefits received by Pastor E and his spouse will be taxable, since their total income ($36,000) plus half of their Social Security benefits ($5,000) exceeds $32,000. Half of the excess (or $4,500) will be taxable.

For additional help, see IRS Publication 915.

E. OTHER INCOME

Section 61 of the tax code defines gross income as "all income from whatever source derived." This is an expansive definition that results in the inclusion of several items not specifically itemized on lines 7–22 of Form 1040. Accordingly, line 21 requests that "other income" be reported. Several kinds of income are reported on line 21. Some of the more common examples include

- a canceled debt, or a debt paid for you by another person (unless the person who canceled or paid your debt intended it to be a gift);
- the fair market value of a free tour you receive from a travel agency for organizing a group of tourists (in some cases this may be reported on Schedule C); and
- most prizes and awards.

✿**KEY POINT.** The amount by which a minister's church-designated housing or parsonage allowance exceeds actual housing expenses (and, for ministers who own their home, the annual rental value of the home) is an "excess allowance" that must be reported as taxable income. The excess should be reported on the minister's Form 1040 (line 7). It is not reported on line 21.

F. SPLITTING INCOME BETWEEN SPOUSES

Some ministers have attempted to "split" their church income with their spouse. This often is done to soften the impact of the Social Security annual earnings test (which reduces Social Security benefits to workers under "full retirement age" who earn more than an amount prescribed by law). Do such arrangements work? That was the question addressed by the Tax Court in the following important ruling.

1. SHELLEY V. COMMISSIONER, T.C. MEMO. 1994-432 (1994)

Pastor Shelley attempted to shift some of his church income to his wife so she could make an annual IRA contribution. He also claimed his wife's "income" as a business expense deduction on his tax return. He explained that his wife performed a variety of services, including visiting members of the congregation who were in the hospital or unable to leave their homes and assisting with weddings and funerals. Pastor Shelley acknowledged that his wife did not receive a paycheck but simply had access to the couple's joint checking account. Mrs. Shelley was not employed elsewhere during the years in question.

✿**KEY POINT.** Taxpayers have attempted to shift income to a spouse in two ways: (1) the taxpayer pays a "salary" out of his or her own income to a spouse; or (2) the taxpayer persuades the employer to pay a portion of his or her income to a spouse.

The IRS insisted that Pastor Shelley's "employment" of his wife was a "ruse" designed to generate compensation so that contributions to her IRA would be deductible. The IRS ruled that Mrs. Shelley's wages should be removed from the couple's joint tax return, and the deductions claimed for wages paid should not be allowed because Pastor Shelley failed to establish that an employment relationship existed between himself and his wife. Accordingly, the IRS concluded that Mrs. Shelley was not entitled to any IRA deductions and that the couple owed excise taxes for the excess contributions made to Mrs. Shelley's IRA.

The Tax Court noted that whether Mrs. Shelley was entitled to deduct IRA contributions "depends on whether she was employed and received wages during the years in issue." The court continued:

Section 162 [of the Code] allows the deduction of "a reasonable allowance for salaries or other compensation for personal services actually rendered." Compensation is deductible only if it is: (1) reasonable in amount, (2) for services actually rendered, and (3) paid or incurred. When there is a family relationship, the facts require close scrutiny to determine whether there was in fact a bona fide employer-employee relationship or whether the payments were made on account of the family relationship.

We find that [Pastor Shelley has] failed to substantiate that wages were actually paid to Mrs. Shelley or that a bona fide employer-employee relationship existed. [He] did not issue Mrs. Shelley a paycheck, nor did he document any of the services she performed. [He] was unable to offer any explanation for how Mrs. Shelley's salary was determined, and there was no employment contract between [him] and Mrs. Shelley. [He] did not withhold income taxes from the alleged wages paid to his wife as required by [law] nor did he file employment tax returns (Forms 941). While we do not doubt that Mrs. Shelley contributed to church activities, there is little indication that this was done in the context of an employer-employee relationship. [Pastor Shelley's] testimony strongly suggested that the deductibility of Mrs. Shelley's IRA contributions was one of the principal reasons he employed her. [He] testified that he stopped employing her when she began working at Florida A & M University (FAMU). He did not, however, hire anyone to replace her. Similarly, there is no indication that once employed at FAMU, Mrs. Shelley stopped performing the services for the church that she previously had performed. [Pastor Shelley has] failed to establish that the alleged wages were actually paid, that any employment contract existed, or that Mrs. Shelley was treated as an employee. Therefore, we sustain [the IRS position] on this issue.

The Tax Court concluded that the Shelleys improperly claimed an excess contribution to Mrs. Shelley's IRA and that they were subject to the 6 percent excise tax on such contributions. It did concede that the Shelleys' maximum allowable IRA contributions for the years under examination was $2,250 per year (the amount allowed for a married taxpayer whose spouse earns no income).

✿ **KEY POINT.** Many ministers have attempted to shift their church income to a spouse in order to achieve a tax benefit. These benefits include (1) rendering the spouse fully eligible for an IRA contribution; (2) reducing the impact on the minister of the annual earnings test that reduces the Social Security benefits of individuals between 62 years of age and full retirement age who earn more than a specified amount of annual income; and (3) lower tax rates. Income shifting often does not work, because there is no "economic reality" to the arrangement. Ministers who have engaged in income shifting, or who are considering doing so, should carefully evaluate their circumstances in light of this ruling.

✿ **KEY POINT.** Persons who have reached their full retirement age (66 years of age for persons born in 1943–1954) and who continue to work do not have their Social Security benefits reduced

by earning income over a specified amount. This eliminates one of the main motivations for splitting income with a spouse.

2. CONCLUSION

Ministers occasionally attempt to shift income to a spouse. One common reason is to divert income from the minister in order to avoid the annual Social Security earnings test. The courts have ruled consistently that the Social Security Administration may disregard "fictitious arrangements" among family members. As the Tax Court noted in the *Shelley* case, there must, in fact, be an employment relationship. In making this decision, the court referred to several factors, which are summarized below.

Factors indicating an employment relationship

The spouse performed meaningful services, including visiting members of the congregation who were in the hospital or unable to leave their homes and assisting with weddings and funerals.

Factors indicating that no employment relationship existed

- The spouse did not receive a paycheck but rather had access to a joint bank account in the names of herself and her husband.
- The spouse was not employed elsewhere.
- The spouse's "compensation" was designed to provide a tax benefit (an IRA contribution) and lacked any economic reality.
- The husband did not issue his wife a paycheck.
- The husband did not document any of the services his spouse performed.
- The husband could not explain how his wife's "salary" was determined.
- No employment contract existed between the husband and his wife.
- The husband did not withhold income taxes from the alleged wages paid to his wife.
- The husband did not file employment tax returns (Form 941).
- While the spouse clearly performed services on behalf of the church, no evidence existed that these services were performed in the context of an employer-employee relationship.
- The spouse's "salary" was discontinued when she obtained secular employment, though she continued to perform the same kinds of services on behalf of the church as she had done before.
- The husband did not hire anyone to replace his wife when she accepted secular employment.
- No evidence existed that the wife stopped performing the services for the church that she previously had performed.
- No evidence existed that wages were actually paid to the spouse, or that any employment contract existed, or that the spouse was treated as an employee.

This aspect of the court's decision will be relevant to those ministers who seek to divert a portion of their church income to a spouse in order to achieve one or more of the benefits summarized above.

The courts generally have been skeptical of attempts by taxpayers to shift income to a spouse. Here is an excerpt from a typical ruling:

> *Here the husband was in a position to control the business. His wife knew nothing about the duties of president of the company. The husband came into the office, he says to pay his own bills. But he also met with the company accountants. After he reached 70 years of age he admits he returned to work. . . . At that time he was exempted by regulation from any work deductions to his retirement benefits.* Both he and his wife admitted that his wife performed the same services both before and after she began to receive a salary. *She said she had drawn no salary prior to August 1977 so that her husband's Social Security contributions would be higher, enabling him to receive higher benefits. . . .* When the husband's salary was shifted to his wife that salary did not reflect an increase in her services to the company. It is a fair inference that the salary she received was intended as indirect compensation to her husband. . . . *Since the critical determination is whether the wife's wages reflected the services she rendered, and there is no evidence to explain or justify the dramatic increase in her salary from nothing to $22,400, the finding of the Social Security Administration is supported by substantial evidence. The determination of the Social Security Administration is affirmed. [Emphases added.]* Sutton v. Sullivan, 1990 WL 48027 (E.D.N.Y. 1990).

The message is clear—ministers should not attempt to obtain tax benefits by shifting income to a spouse unless the arrangement has economic reality. The guidelines provided by the Tax Court in the *Shelley* decision will be helpful in evaluating the likely success of such arrangements.

Chapter 5 — EXCLUSIONS FROM GROSS INCOME

After Jesus and his disciples arrived in Capernaum, the collectors of the two-drachma tax came to Peter and asked, "Doesn't your teacher pay the temple tax?" "Yes, he does," he replied. When Peter came into the house, Jesus was the first to speak. "What do you think, Simon?" he asked. "From whom do the kings of the earth collect duty and taxes—from their own sons or from others?" "From others," Peter answered. "Then the sons are exempt," Jesus said to him.

Matthew 17:24–27

CHAPTER HIGHLIGHTS

■ *Exclusions.* Some kinds of income are not taxable. These items are called exclusions. Most exclusions apply in computing both income taxes and self-employment taxes. They generally are claimed by not reporting them as income on a tax return.

■ *Parsonages and housing allowances.* The fair rental value of a church-provided parsonage and a minister's housing allowance are two examples of exclusions that apply in computing a minister's income taxes but not self-employment (Social Security) taxes. These exclusions are addressed fully in Chapter 6.

■ *Gifts.* Gifts are excludable from taxable income so long as they are not compensation for services performed.

■ *Life insurance and inheritances.* Life insurance proceeds and inheritances are excludable from taxable income.

■ *Scholarships.* Qualified scholarships are excludable from taxable income.

■ *Employer-paid medical insurance premiums.* Medical insurance premiums paid by an employer for employees (and their spouses and dependents) are excludable from taxable income. This exclusion is not available to self-employed individuals.

■ *Accident and health plans.* Amounts received by employees as reimbursements for medical care under an employer-financed accident and health plan are excludable from taxable income. This exclusion is not available to self-employed individuals.

■ *Employer-paid group life insurance.* Employees may exclude the cost of employer-provided group term life insurance so long as the amount of coverage does not exceed $50,000.

■ *Tuition reductions.* School employees may exclude from their taxable income a "qualified tuition reduction" provided by their employer. A qualified tuition reduction is a reduction in tuition charged to employees or their spouses or dependent children by an employer that is an educational institution.

■ *Lodging.* The value of lodging furnished to an employee on an employer's premises and for the employer's convenience may be excludable from taxable income if the employee is required to accept the lodging as a condition of employment. This exclusion is not available in the computation of self-employment taxes.

■ *Educational assistance.* Amounts paid by an employer for an employee's tuition, fees, and books may be excludable from the employee's taxable income. The exclusion may not exceed $5,250 per year.

■ *Employer-provided childcare.* The value of free childcare services provided by a church to its employees is excluded from employees' income so long as the benefit is based on a written plan that does not discriminate in favor of highly compensated employees. Other conditions apply.

■ *Nondiscrimination rules.* Many of the exclusions are not available to employees who are either "highly compensated employees" or "key employees" if the same benefit is not available on a nondiscriminatory basis to lower-paid employees.

■ *Employee status.* Some exclusions are available only to taxpayers who report their income taxes as employees and not as self-employed persons. Many, however, apply to both employees and self-employed persons.

INTRODUCTION

✸ **KEY POINT.** Some kinds of income are not taxable (they are called exclusions).

✸ **KEY POINT.** Most exclusions reduce both income taxes and self-employment taxes (though some apply only to one or the other).

❀ **KEY POINT.** The parsonage and housing allowance exclusions are the most important exclusions for ministers. Because of their importance, they are addressed separately in Chapter 6.

1. INCOME TAXES

Certain kinds of income are not included in gross income for federal income tax reporting purposes. These items are known as exclusions. The most important exclusions for ministers are the annual rental value of a church-provided parsonage and a housing allowance provided to ministers who own or rent their homes. Because of the importance of these exclusions, they are discussed separately and fully in Chapter 6. This chapter will summarize other common exclusions.

Exclusions are reductions from gross income. Since Form 1040 begins with an itemization of various categories of gross income, there is no place on the return to list, or "deduct," exclusions. They are "claimed" by simply not reporting them as taxable income.

2. SOCIAL SECURITY

Are items of income that are excludable in computing income taxes also excludable in computing Social Security taxes? Recall that ministers are always treated as self-employed for Social Security with respect to their ministerial services, so they pay the self-employment tax. The income tax regulations specify that "income which is excludable from gross income under any provision of subtitle A of the Internal Revenue Code is not taken into account in determining net earnings from self-employment," with certain exceptions. *Treas. Reg. 1.1402(a)-2(a).* The exceptions, which are included in income for self-employment tax purposes, include

- the housing allowance,
- the fair rental value of a church-provided parsonage,
- the foreign earned income exclusion, and
- meals and lodging provided for the convenience of an employer.

Apart from these exceptions, the general rule is that the exclusions discussed in this chapter are excludable in computing *both* income taxes and self-employment taxes.

A. GIFTS AND INHERITANCES

❀ **KEY POINT.** Gifts are excludable from taxable income if they are not compensation for services performed.

Money or property received as a gift or by inheritance is excluded from gross income (any income generated from money or property received as a gift or inheritance is taxable). Often it is difficult to determine whether a particular transfer of money or property is a nontaxable gift or taxable compensation for services rendered. The United States Supreme Court has provided some clarification by noting the following characteristics of a gift: "A gift in the statutory sense . . . proceeds from a detached and disinterested generosity . . . out of affection, respect, admiration, charity, or like impulses. . . . The most critical consideration is the transferor's intention." *Commissioner v. Duberstein, 363 U.S. 285 (1960).*

> **EXAMPLE.** Pastor C receives from a church member a Christmas card containing a check in the amount of $50 (payable directly to Pastor C). The check probably is a gift and so is excludable from income. *Goodwin v. United States, 67 F.3d 149 (8th Cir. 1995).*

> **EXAMPLE.** Pastor G receives an inheritance of $100,000 in 2013 from the estate of a deceased relative. The $100,000 is not included in Pastor G's taxable income in 2013. However, any interest earned on the inheritance will be taxable.

> **EXAMPLE.** Pastor K performs ministerial services for a neighboring church that temporarily is without a minister. In recognition of his services, the congregation presents him with an "honorarium" of $500. The honorarium represents compensation for services rendered and is not a gift. See Chapter 4, section B.22.

For a discussion of retirement and other special-occasion gifts to ministers and lay employees, see Chapter 4, sections B.2 and B.3, and Chapter 10, section D.

B. LIFE INSURANCE PROCEEDS

❀ **KEY POINT.** Life insurance proceeds and inheritances are excludable from taxable income.

Life insurance proceeds paid to you because of the death of an insured person ordinarily are not taxable income for you. However, if the proceeds are payable to you in installments, you must report as income the portion of each installment that represents earnings on the face amount of the policy. Generally, the taxable amount is that portion of each installment that exceeds the face amount of the policy divided by the number of annual installments you are to receive. For example, if the face amount of the policy is $100,000 and you are to receive 20 annual installments of $6,000, you would report as income $1,000 each year ($6,000 - ($100,000/20)).

c. SCHOLARSHIPS

✿KEY POINT. Qualified scholarships are excludable from taxable income.

1. OVERVIEW

A scholarship is nontaxable to the recipient only if it meets the following two requirements:

Candidate for a degree

The recipient is a candidate for a degree at an educational institution. The term "candidate for a degree" means a full- or part-time student who

- attends a primary or secondary school or is pursuing a degree at a college or university; or
- attends an accredited educational institution that is authorized to provide (1) a program that is acceptable for full credit toward a bachelor's or higher degree, or (2) a program of training to prepare students for gainful employment in a recognized occupation.

Qualified scholarship

A qualified scholarship is any amount received by a candidate for a degree as a scholarship that is used under the terms of the scholarship for

- tuition and fees paid to enroll in or to attend an educational institution; or
- fees, books, supplies, and equipment required for the courses at the educational institution. These items must be required of all students in the course.

Other clarifications

Note the following:

- An "educational institution" maintains a regular faculty and curriculum and has a regularly enrolled body of students in attendance at the place where it carries on its educational activities.
- A scholarship may still qualify as nontaxable even if the terms do not provide that it be used only for tuition and course-related expenses. It will qualify if the recipient uses the scholarship for tuition and course-related expenses. However, if the terms of the scholarship require its use for other purposes, such as room and board, or specify that the scholarship cannot be used for tuition or course-related expenses, the amount received is fully taxable. See Table 5-1.
- Churches that would like to make a nontaxable scholarship payment to a student should consider taking the following

precautions: (1) Prepare a written scholarship instrument that sets forth the terms and conditions of the scholarship, including a provision limiting the use of the proceeds to tuition, enrollment fees, books, and supplies. (2) Require an academic transcript to ensure that the student is enrolled at an educational institution. (3) Require receipt of an invoice or other record showing the amount of tuition (or other allowable expense) that is owed. (4) Consider paying the scholarship amount directly to the educational institution rather than to the student.
- Any portion of a "scholarship" received by a graduate student that represents compensation for required teaching or research responsibilities cannot be a qualified scholarship.

2. SCHOLARSHIPS FOR CHURCH EMPLOYEES

Section 1.117-4(c) of the income tax regulations specifies that the following payments shall not be considered to be amounts received as a scholarship:

(1) Any amount paid or allowed to, or on behalf of, an individual to enable him to pursue studies or research, if such amount represents either compensation for past, present, or future employment services or represents payment for services which are subject to the direction or supervision of the grantor.

(2) Any amount paid or allowed to, or on behalf of, an individual to enable him to pursue studies or research primarily for the benefit of the grantor.

═══ TABLE 5-1 ═══

TAX TREATMENT OF SCHOLARSHIP PAYMENTS

PAYMENT FOR	DEGREE CANDIDATE	NOT A DEGREE CANDIDATE
Tuition	Nontaxable	Taxable
Fees	Nontaxable	Taxable
Books	Nontaxable	Taxable
Supplies	Nontaxable	Taxable
Equipment	Nontaxable	Taxable
Room	Taxable	Taxable
Board	Taxable	Taxable
Travel	Taxable	Taxable
Teaching	Taxable	Taxable
Research services	Taxable	Taxable
Other services	Taxable	Taxable

However, amounts paid or allowed to, or on behalf of, an individual to enable him to pursue studies or research are considered to be amounts received as a scholarship or fellowship grant for the purpose of section 117 if the primary purpose of the studies or research is to further the education and training of the recipient in his individual capacity and the amount provided by the grantor for such purpose does not represent compensation or payment for the services described in subparagraph (1) of this paragraph. Neither the fact that the recipient is required to furnish reports of his progress to the grantor, nor the fact that the results of his studies or research may be of some incidental benefit to the grantor shall, of itself, be considered to destroy the essential character of such amount as a scholarship or fellowship grant.

According to this language, amounts paid by a church for the education of a pastor or other church employee cannot be treated as a nontaxable scholarship if paid "as compensation for services." This conclusion also applies to scholarships provided to the children of church employees.

The Supreme Court has upheld the validity of this regulation, stating that it comports with the "ordinary understanding of scholarships as relatively disinterested, no-strings educational grants, with no requirement of any substantial quid pro quo from the recipients." *Bingler v. Johnson, 394 U.S. 741 (1969).*

The United States Tax Court has observed that this regulation is "designed to distinguish relatively disinterested payments made primarily for the purpose of furthering the education of the recipient from payments made primarily to reward or induce the recipient's performance of services for the benefit of the payor." *Turem v. Commissioner, 54 T.C. 1494 (1970).*

❋ **KEY POINT.** The determination of whether particular payments to individuals are intended to be disinterested grants to further the recipient's education rather than compensation for either past or prospective employment services is ultimately a question of fact. A very important factor is whether the scholarship recipient maintained his or her employment with the employer while attending school.

EXAMPLE. The IRS addressed the question of whether amounts received by a taxpayer from his employer for tuition assistance for the education of his children were tax-free scholarships. The IRS concluded that they were not. It observed: "Section 1.117-4 of the regulation denies scholarship exclusion to amounts that are paid to an individual to enable him to pursue studies or research if such amounts represent compensation for past, present or future employment services. . . . When funds are made available as a part of the pattern of employment to the children of employees of a corporation for educational expenses, those amounts are includable as additional compensation in the employee's gross income. Funds will be considered to be received as a part of the pattern of employment

PAYING THE SCHOOL DEBTS OF EMPLOYEES

Some churches pay off some or all of the accrued school debts of staff members who have completed their education. Can such payments be characterized as a nontaxable scholarship? Section 117 of the tax code clearly limits the scholarship exclusion to "candidates for a degree." Once students graduate and accept employment with a church or other employer, it is doubtful that any payment the employer makes toward their school debts would be eligible for the scholarship exclusion under section 117, since they no longer are candidates for a degree. Neither the IRS nor any court has addressed this issue directly. Any further clarification will be provided when available.

when they are made available to the children of employees merely because of the parent's employment relationship, and without any substantial limitations on the right to receive the funds." If, however, the funds are only available to a limited number of the employees' children and are awarded on the basis of need or merit, they may be treated as tax-free scholarships. The IRS cautioned that "convincing evidence is required to establish that an educational grant from an employer to an employee or his dependents does not constitute compensation." *IRS Letter Ruling 8541002.*

EXAMPLE. A federal appeals court found that college education payments for a taxpayer's children made by an educational trust set up by his employer were taxable compensation. In determining that the payments were includable in the parent employee's taxable income, the court stated, "When such a benefit is created in an employment situation and in connection with the performance of services, we are unable to conclude that such a benefit [does not represent taxable compensation]." The court concluded: "The IRS argues that the amounts paid by the educational trust were generated by the employees in connection with their performance of services for their employer and were, therefore, compensatory in nature. We find this view to be amply supported by the record. The plan was adopted by the employer to relieve its most important employees from concern about the high costs of providing a college education for their children. It was hoped that the plan would thereby enable the key employees to render better service. Moreover, the eventual payment of benefits by the trust was directly related to the taxpayers' employment. This is illustrated quite graphically by the fact that only those expenses incurred by their children while the parent was employed by the employer were covered by the plan. . . . In substance, by commencing or continuing to be employed by their employer, the employees have allowed a portion of their earnings to be paid to their children." *Armantrout v. Commissioner, 570 F.2d 210 (7th Cir. 1978).*

EXAMPLE. A pastor takes a course at a local college in business administration. He is not a candidate for a degree. The church pays the tuition expense. The amount paid by the church is not a qualified scholarship, since the pastor is not a candidate for a degree, and the church's payment likely would be viewed by the IRS as compensation based on past or present services. However, the amount may be nontaxable as employer-provided educational assistance (see section I.7 of this chapter).

EXAMPLE. A church operates an unaccredited training program for persons wanting to engage in full-time ministry. Students attend the program for one year on a full-time basis. The program includes both classroom instruction and practical experience. Students who complete the program are given a certificate. Students are charged $8,000 to enroll in the program, representing both tuition ($4,000) and room and board ($4,000). Another church sends one of its members to the program and pays his entire enrollment fee. None of this amount can be treated as a nontaxable qualified scholarship, since the student is not a candidate for a degree at an accredited educational institution.

EXAMPLE. A church establishes a scholarship fund for seminary students. L is a church member who is pursuing a master's degree at an accredited seminary. The church board voted to award her a scholarship of $1,500 for 2013. So long as L uses the scholarship award for tuition or other course-related expenses, she need not report it as income on her federal tax return, and the church need not issue her a Form 1099-MISC. The better practice would be for the church to stipulate that the scholarship is to be used for tuition or other course-related expenses (e.g., fees, books, supplies). This will ensure that the scholarship does not inadvertently become taxable income because its specific use was not designated and the recipient used it for nonqualified expenses. See Chapter 8, section B.5, for a discussion of the deductibility of church members' payments to the scholarship fund.

EXAMPLE. A seminary maintains a four-year curriculum, leading to a degree that must be completed by all students who wish to graduate and be ordained into the ministry. The first, second, and fourth years are spent on campus, and the third year is spent in a church as an intern. The seminary selects the churches in which the students will serve during their third year. Interns are paid a monthly support allowance by their host church, as prescribed by the seminary. The IRS ruled that the amounts received from local churches by interns were not tax free scholarships but rather constituted taxable compensation for services rendered. *Revenue Ruling 57-522.*

EXAMPLE. A professor was given a year off to pursue studies overseas. He was paid $27,000 during his sabbatical, and he treated this entire amount as a tax-free scholarship. The IRS ruled that the sabbatical income represented taxable income, and the

PAYING FOR A PASTOR'S CONTINUING EDUCATION

Many churches pay some or all of the expenses incurred by their pastor in taking a course at a college or seminary. Do such payments represent taxable income to the pastor? Not if they qualify for one or more of the following rules:

1. Employer-provided educational assistance. Amounts paid by an employer (up to $5,250 annually) for an employee's education are not taxable to the employee if certain requirements are met. This exclusion is addressed later in this chapter.

2. Business expense reimbursements. If tuition and related fees associated with a course taken by a pastor at a college or seminary qualifies as a business expense, then the church can reimburse these expenses. If the church reimburses the expenses under an accountable arrangement, then the reimbursements are not taxable to the pastor. Whether education qualifies as a business expense is a question that is addressed in Chapter 7, section C.5.

3. Working condition fringe benefit. Certain job-related education provided by an employer to an employee may be nontaxable as a working condition benefit. To qualify, the education must meet the same requirements that would apply for determining whether the employee could deduct the expenses had the employee paid the expenses. The employer must require the employee to verify that the payment is actually used for qualifying educational expenses and to return any unused part of the payment.

Tax Court agreed. The court noted that scholarships are nontaxable only if certain conditions are met. The recipient must be "a candidate for a degree at an educational organization," and the scholarship must be used for qualified tuition. The court noted that the professor's sabbatical income was not a nontaxable scholarship, since he was not a candidate for a degree and failed to prove that he used any portion of the income for qualified tuition expenses. This ruling will be useful to church treasurers in evaluating the tax status of sabbatical income provided to pastors or other staff members. *Kant v. Commissioner, T.C. Memo. 1997-217.*

EXAMPLE. An employer paid an employee an $8,000 "commission" in addition to his regular salary. Throughout his employment, the employee was enrolled at a local university, earning an undergraduate degree. He had a verbal agreement with his employer that he would be reimbursed for certain educational expenses he incurred. He did not report the $8,000 as taxable income because he considered it to be a nontaxable scholarship. The Tax Court disagreed. It noted that the tax code excludes from taxable income "any amount received as a qualified scholarship by an individual who is a candidate for a degree" at certain educational institutions. However, a "qualified scholarship" does not include any amount received by a student which represents compensation for past, present, or future employment services. The court concluded that the $8,000 was "a form of compensation and not the result of disinterested generosity," and therefore it was not a nontaxable qualified scholarship. *Lewis v. Commissioner, T.C. Sum. Op. 2003-78 (2003).*

D. MEDICAL INSURANCE PREMIUMS

❋**KEY POINT.** Medical insurance premiums paid by an employer for employees (and their spouses and dependents) are excludable from taxable income (this exclusion is not available to self-employed individuals).

❋**KEY POINT.** Special rules apply to employer contributions to Medical Savings Accounts (discussed later in this chapter).

❋**KEY POINT.** Amounts contributed by an employer to an employee's Health Savings Account (HSA) are treated as employer provided coverage for medical expenses and are excludable from the employee's taxable income. *IRC 106(d).*

1. OVERVIEW

Churches often provide ministers and lay employees with accident or health insurance coverage and pay some or all of the premiums for such coverage. Income tax regulation 1.106-1 specifies that the gross income of an employee does not include

> *contributions which his employer makes to an accident or health plan for compensation (through insurance or otherwise) to the employee for personal injuries or sickness incurred by him, his spouse, or his dependents. . . . The employer may contribute to an accident or health plan by paying the premium (or a portion of the premium) on a policy of accident or health insurance covering one or more of his employees, or by contributing to a separate trust or fund.*

EXAMPLE. The IRS ruled that amounts furnished to a conference of churches by member churches to provide hospital and medical insurance coverage for ministerial employees were excludable from the ministers' gross income under section 106. *Revenue Ruling 70-179.*

Section 106 excludes from gross income both (1) accident and health insurance premiums paid by an employer and (2) payments made directly to employees by an employer to reimburse them for accident and health insurance premiums that they paid. However, the employer must require proof of prior payment of premiums as a condition of the reimbursement. *Revenue Ruling 85-44; Revenue Ruling 75-241; Revenue Ruling 67-360; Revenue Ruling 61-146; Adkins v. U.S., 882 F.2d 1078 (6th Cir. 1989).*

Amounts can be excluded as employer contributions only if employees do not have any right to receive them in cash or any other form. An important exception is a "health flexible spending arrangement" under section 125 of the tax code (discussed later in this chapter). Such an arrangement gives employees the right to receive cash or certain fringe benefits, including employer-paid premiums under an accident and health plan.

In summary, three rules are clear:

- Church employees' health insurance premiums paid directly to the insurer by the church are excludable from the employees' gross income for federal tax reporting purposes.
- Church employees' health insurance premiums paid directly to employees are excludable from the employees' gross income for federal tax reporting purposes if the church requires proof that the employees paid the premiums themselves. In other words, the church treats this arrangement like an accountable business expense reimbursement arrangement and only reimburses those expenses for which it receives adequate substantiation.
- If a church provides employees with cash in lieu of paying their health insurance premiums, the exclusion does not apply and the amount of cash distributed to employees is fully taxable. However, the cash provided to the employees can be tax-free if the church adopts a type of "cafeteria plan" called a "health flexible spending arrangement" (discussed later in this chapter).

The exclusion of employer-paid medical insurance premiums is a significant tax-free benefit for ministers and lay workers who report their income taxes as employees. In fact, it is one of the major reasons ministers and lay workers often are better off reporting their income taxes as employees rather than as self-employed (see Chapter 2). With the substantial increase in the cost of medical insurance over the past several years, this exclusion can reduce taxable income by thousands of dollars.

For church employees to enjoy the benefit of this exclusion, their employing church must adopt a written plan. Section 106 of the tax code does not explain what a "written plan" is, but several courts have defined the term in the related context of accident and health plans under section 105 of the tax code. Generally, these decisions indicate that such a plan meets the following conditions: (1) a commitment by an employer's board must be recorded in the board's minutes; (2) the employer "must be committed to certain rules and regulations governing payment"; (3) these rules "must be made known to employees as a definite policy and must be determinable before the employee's medical expenses are incurred"; (4) the plan must be called an "accident or health plan"; and (5) the plan must be operated on a consistent basis. This information will be helpful to employers in implementing a written plan to pay for employees' medical insurance.

▲ **CAUTION.** *Without a written plan, an employer's payment of employees' medical insurance premiums will constitute taxable income.*

Ministers and lay workers who report their federal income taxes as self-employed *are not eligible for this exclusion.* They must report any employer-paid medical insurance premiums as taxable income.

❈ **KEY POINT.** The Tax Court, in ruling that a Methodist minister had incorrectly reported his income taxes as self-employed, pointed out that by being reclassified as an employee, he would be eligible for the exclusion of employer-paid medical insurance premiums that he incorrectly had been claiming in the past. *Weber v. Commissioner 103 T.C. 378 (1994), aff'd 60 F.3d 1104 (4th Cir. 1995).*

❈ **KEY POINT.** Employer-provided coverage for qualified long-term care services is not treated as nontaxable employer provided medical insurance to the extent that such coverage is provided through a flexible spending arrangement. *IRC 106(c).*

EXAMPLE. The board of directors of a church adopts a written resolution agreeing to pay the medical insurance premiums of its minister and the minister's dependent family members (but not for any other church employee). For 2012 the premiums paid by the church were $4,000. If the minister reports income taxes as an employee, the $4,000 need not be reported on either Form W-2 or 1040. It does not matter that the same benefit is not made available to other church employees.

EXAMPLE. Same facts as the previous example, except that the church also agrees to pay the $1,000 annual deductible under the health insurance policy. Is the $1,000 deductible paid by the church excluded from its minister's taxable income? See section E (and examples) discussing amounts received under accident and health plans.

EXAMPLE. A church adopts a plan under which it agrees to pay up to $1,500 of each employee's medical insurance premiums. Employee T is covered by the medical insurance plan of a spouse (who is employed by a secular employer), so T requests a cash payment of $1,500 from the church. If the church agrees to do so, is this cash payment in lieu of medical insurance premiums excludable from T's taxable income? The answer is no. *See Revenue Ruling 75-241; Adkins v. U.S., 882 F.2d 1078 (6th Cir. 1989); Marshall v. Commissioner, 56 T.C.M. 1006 (1989).*

EXAMPLE. A church adopts a plan under which it agrees to pay up to $1,500 of each employee's medical insurance premiums. Employee G elects to receive $1,500 in cash in lieu of the church paying her medical insurance premiums for the year. However, G uses the $1,500 to pay her own medical insurance premiums and can document this. The IRS ruled in 1990 that G is not entitled to exclude the $1,500 from her federal taxes. The IRS concluded that workers receive taxable compensation if they can choose to have their employer pay their medical insurance premiums or receive an equivalent amount in cash. It does not matter that employees use the money to pay health insurance premiums, since they have the right to treat it as a cash benefit. This is all that is required to create taxable income under the "constructive receipt" rule (see Chapter 10, section A). *IRS Letter Ruling 9022060.*

EXAMPLE. D is a church employee. He pays his own health insurance premiums directly to an insurance company and is reimbursed by the church for the amount of the premiums. D does not have to report this amount as income for tax purposes so long as the church requires proof ("verification") that the insurance coverage exists and that the employee paid the premium. *IRS Letter Ruling 9022060.*

EXAMPLE. Same facts as the previous example, except that D reports his federal income taxes as a self-employed person and is issued a Form 1099-MISC by the church each year. As a self-employed person, D is not eligible for the exclusion of the cost of employer-paid medical insurance premiums. D would have to report as additional income the church's reimbursement of his medical insurance premiums (and the church should add the amount of the reimbursement to D's Form 1099-MISC).

2. NONDISCRIMINATION RULES

If an employer-adopted group medical plan only covers "highly compensated employees" (defined in section I of this chapter), the exclusion of employer-paid premiums may be disallowed unless the employer permits employees to continue their coverage after discontinuing their employment. *IRC 4980B.* This rule does not apply to "church plans" or "small employers." A church plan is defined as a plan maintained for its employees by a church or convention or association of churches exempt from federal income taxation under section 501(c)(3) of the tax code.

The IRS has ruled that an employee is entitled to exclude medical insurance premiums paid by his employer even though he is the only employee covered. *Revenue Ruling 58-90.*

3. SALARY REDUCTIONS

Many employers provide health insurance for their employees. This is a nontaxable fringe benefit under section 106 of the tax code. But what if an employer pays for this insurance by reducing the salaries of its employees? Must the employer report the salary reductions as taxable income, or are the reductions nontaxable?

The IRS addressed this question in a ruling. An employer provided health coverage for its employees through a group health insurance policy. The employer reduced its employees' salaries and applied the salary reduction amounts to the payment of the health insurance premiums. In other words, employees received lower salaries in exchange for employer-provided health coverage. The IRS concluded that the amount by which an employee's wages were reduced to cover the employer's payment of health insurance premiums was nontaxable. It based this conclusion on section 106 of the tax code, which states that "gross income of an employee does not include employer-provided coverage under an accident or health plan." The IRS noted that when the employer "applies the amount of employees' salary reduction to pay health insurance premiums, the premium payments are paid by the employer, not the employees, and are excludable from the employees' gross income under section 106 because they are paid by the employer."

But the IRS ruled that "reimbursements" made by the employer to its employees in the amount of their salary reductions (so their after-tax pay was the same as if there were no salary reductions) had to be reported as taxable income for the employees. The IRS observed that section 106 "allows an employee to exclude employer reimbursements for health insurance premiums, but *only* if those premiums are actually paid by the employee" (emphasis added). Here, however, "there is no employee-paid premium for the employer to reimburse, and therefore the reimbursement payments that the employer makes to employees are not excluded from gross income under section 106." *Revenue Ruling 2002-3.*

4. COBRA

The Consolidated Omnibus Budget Reconciliation Act of 1985 (COBRA) requires that certain employees covered under an employer's group health plan be permitted to elect continued health insurance coverage at their own expense after the termination of their employment. Employers must comply with this rule to avoid an excise tax penalty under section 4980B of the tax code. However, this penalty does not apply to "any church plan within the meaning of section 414(e)." This means that church plans are effectively exempted from the COBRA rules, since there is no penalty for violating them.

Section 414(e) of the tax code defines a "church plan" as "a plan established and maintained . . . for its employees (or their beneficiaries) by a church or by a convention or association of churches which is exempt from tax under section 501."

Many states have enacted laws providing for the continuation of medical insurance for terminating employees, and these laws should also be consulted.

5. AFFORDABLE CARE ACT (2010)

In 2010 Congress enacted the 2,500-page Patient Protection and Affordable Care Act (the "Affordable Care Act") in order to increase the number of Americans covered by health insurance and decrease the cost of health care. One of the key provisions in the Act is the "individual mandate," which requires most Americans to maintain "minimum essential" health insurance coverage as defined by the Secretary of Health and Human Services (HHS). The mandate does not apply to some individuals, such as prisoners and undocumented aliens. Many individuals will receive the required coverage through their employer or from a government program such as Medicaid or Medicare. But for individuals who are not exempt and do not receive health insurance through a third party, the means of satisfying the requirement is to purchase insurance from a private company.

The purpose of the individual mandate is to bring millions of uninsured, healthy young people into the insurance system in order to prevent the dramatic increase in premiums that otherwise would occur due to the Act's requirement that health insurers provide coverage for unhealthy persons with prior conditions.

Beginning in 2014, those who do not comply with the mandate must make a "shared responsibility payment" to the federal government. That payment is calculated as a percentage of household income, subject to a floor based on a specified dollar amount and a ceiling based on the average annual premium the individual would have to pay for qualifying private health insurance. In 2016, for example, the penalty will be 2.5 percent of an individual's household income, but no less than $695 and no more than the average yearly premium for insurance that covers 60 percent of the cost of 10 specified services (including prescription drugs and hospitalization). The Act provides that the penalty will be paid to the Internal Revenue Service with an individual's taxes and "shall be assessed and collected in the same manner" as tax penalties, such as the penalty for claiming too large an income tax refund. The Act, however, bars the IRS from using several of its normal enforcement tools, such as criminal prosecutions and levies. And some individuals who are subject to the mandate are nonetheless exempt from the penalty—for example, those with income below a certain threshold.

Another key provision of the Act is the Medicaid expansion. The current Medicaid program offers federal funding to states to assist pregnant women, children, needy families, the blind, the elderly, and the disabled in obtaining medical care. The Act expands the scope of the Medicaid program and increases the number of individuals the states must cover. For example, the Act requires state programs to provide Medicaid coverage by 2014 to adults with incomes up to 133 percent of the federal poverty level, though many states now cover adults with children only if their income is considerably lower and do not cover childless adults at all. The Act increases federal funding to cover the states' costs in expanding Medicaid coverage. But if a state does not comply with the Act's new coverage requirements, it may lose not only the federal funding for those requirements, but all of its federal Medicaid funds.

On the day the president signed the Act into law, Florida and 12 other states filed a complaint in the federal district court for the Northern District of Florida. Those plaintiffs were later joined by 13 additional states, several individuals, and the National Federation of Independent Business. The plaintiffs alleged, among other things, that the individual mandate provisions of the Act exceeded Congress's powers under the Constitution. The district court agreed, holding that Congress lacked constitutional power to enact the individual mandate. The district court determined that the individual mandate could not be severed from the remainder of the Act and, therefore, struck down the Act in its entirety.

A federal appeals court agreed that the individual mandate exceeds Congress's power under the Constitution. The court unanimously agreed that the individual mandate did not impose a tax and so could not be authorized by Congress's power under the Constitution to "lay and collect Taxes." The court also held that the individual mandate was not supported by Congress's power under the Constitution to "regulate Commerce . . . among the several States."

The United States Supreme Court agreed to determine the constitutionality of the Act and issued its ruling on June 28, 2012.

Individual mandate

The Supreme Court, in a 5-4 decision written by Chief Justice John Roberts, ruled that the individual mandate is not a valid exercise of Congress's power to regulate commerce. *National Federation of Independent Business v. Sebelius, 132 S.Ct. 2566 (2012).* The Court stressed that Congress is an "enumerated powers" institution that can only do those things that are expressly authorized by the Constitution. It acknowledged that the Constitution grants Congress the power to "regulate Commerce." But it noted that the power to regulate commerce presupposes the existence of commercial activity to be regulated:

The individual mandate, however, does not regulate existing commercial activity. It instead compels individuals to become active in commerce by purchasing a product, on the ground that their failure to do so affects interstate commerce. Construing the Commerce Clause to permit Congress to regulate individuals precisely because they are doing nothing would open a new and potentially vast domain to congressional authority. Every day individuals do not do an infinite number of things. In some cases they decide not to do something; in others they simply fail to do it. Allowing Congress to justify federal regulation by pointing to the effect of inaction on commerce would bring countless decisions an individual could potentially make within the scope of federal regulation, and—under the Government's theory—empower Congress to make those decisions for him. . . .

The individual mandate forces individuals into commerce precisely because they elected to refrain from commercial activity. Such a law cannot be sustained under a clause authorizing Congress to "regulate Commerce."

To the surprise of many Court watchers, the Court went on to rule that Congress had the authority to create the individual mandate under its constitutional authority to collect taxes. The Court observed:

The Affordable Care Act's requirement that certain individuals pay a financial penalty for not obtaining health insurance may reasonably be characterized as a tax. Because the Constitution permits such a tax, it is not our role to forbid it, or to pass upon its wisdom or fairness. . . .

The Federal Government does not have the power to order people to buy health insurance. [The individual mandate] would therefore be unconstitutional if read as a command. The Federal Government does have the power to impose a tax on those without health insurance. [The mandate] is therefore constitutional, because it can reasonably be read as a tax.

Medicaid expansion

The second provision of the Affordable Care Act challenged by the plaintiffs was the "Medicaid expansion" (summarized above). The Court acknowledged that the Act dramatically increases state obligations under Medicaid by requiring states to expand their Medicaid programs by 2014 to cover all individuals under the age of 65 with incomes below 133 percent of the federal poverty line. It agreed that Congress has the authority "to offer funds under the Affordable Care Act to expand the availability of health care, and requiring that states accepting such funds comply with the conditions on their use." But "what Congress is not free to do is to penalize states that choose not to participate in that new program by taking away their existing Medicaid funding." As a result, the portion of the Act giving the Secretary of HHS the authority to do so was unconstitutional. The Court observed:

Congress has no authority to order the states to regulate according to its instructions. Congress may offer the states grants and require the states to comply with accompanying conditions, but the states must have a genuine choice whether to accept the offer. The states are given no such choice in this case: They must either accept a basic change in the nature of Medicaid, or risk losing all Medicaid funding. The remedy for that constitutional violation is to preclude the Federal Government from imposing such a sanction. That remedy does not require striking down other portions of the Affordable Care Act.

The Court concluded: "The Framers created a Federal Government of limited powers, and assigned to this Court the duty of enforcing those limits. The Court does so today. But the Court does not express any opinion on the wisdom of the Affordable Care Act. Under the Constitution, that judgment is reserved to the people."

Impact on church employees

What is the significance of the Supreme Court's ruling upholding the constitutionality of the Affordable Care Act? Consider the following:

- All of the deadlines and requirements in the Act remain intact except for the Medicaid expansion (see above). The more important deadlines and requirements for churches are summarized below:
- Most Americans will be required to have health insurance that provides "minimum essential coverage" (as defined by the Secretary of HHS) by 2014 or face a monetary penalty of the greater of $95 or 1 percent of income in 2014, $325 or 2 percent of income in 2015, and $695 or 2.5 percent of income in 2016, up to a cap. Families will pay half the amount for children, up to a cap of $2,250 for the entire family. After 2016, dollar amounts will increase by the annual cost of living adjustment. The penalty applies to any period in which an individual does not maintain minimum essential coverage and is determined monthly.

   This provision is intended to bring actuarial integrity to a plan that aims to extend health care coverage to an additional 32 million Americans. There are limited exceptions for members of religious sects that are opposed on religious grounds to purchasing health insurance, individuals not lawfully present in the United States, incarcerated individuals, and members of "health care sharing ministries."

   Exemptions from the penalty will be made for those who cannot afford coverage, taxpayers with income below the filing threshold, those who have received a hardship waiver, and those who were not covered for a period of less than three months during the year.

✸ **KEY POINT.** The penalty is assessed through the tax code and accounted for as an additional amount of federal tax owed. However, the use by the IRS of liens and seizures of property otherwise authorized by the tax code for the collection of taxes does not apply to the collection of this penalty.

- Individuals are free to keep their existing insurance under a "grandfather" provision, subject to some conditions.

FROM THE DISSENTING OPINION
(agreeing with the Court's majority that the Constitution's commerce clause did not empower Congress to enact the Affordable Care Act)

"The striking case of *Wickard v. Filburn*, 317 U.S. 111 (1942), which held that the economic activity of growing wheat, even for one's own consumption, affected commerce sufficiently that it could be regulated, always has been regarded as the *ne plus ultra* of expansive Commerce Clause jurisprudence. To go beyond that, and to say the *failure* to grow wheat (which is *not* an economic activity, or any activity at all) nonetheless affects commerce and therefore can be federally regulated, is to make mere breathing in and out the basis for federal prescription and to extend federal power to virtually all human activity."

- Beginning in 2014, uninsured individuals can purchase insurance coverage through a state-operated "Exchange." An Exchange must offer four levels of benefits. Low-income persons may qualify for a tax credit to assist in paying their premiums.
- The Act prohibits health insurers from excluding coverage of preexisting conditions for children.
- The Act provides $5 billion in federal support for a new program to provide affordable coverage to uninsured Americans with preexisting conditions until new Exchanges are operational in 2014.
- The Act prohibits insurers from imposing lifetime limits on benefits.
- The Act stops insurers from rescinding insurance when claims are filed, except in cases of fraud or intentional misrepresentation of material fact.

✸ **KEY POINT.** See the table at the end of this section that summarizes the implementation dates for the key provisions in the Affordable Care Act.

Impact on churches

The health care reform legislation does not require employers to provide health insurance for their employees. Instead, the legislation places the responsibility to obtain coverage on individuals, subject to a penalty for noncompliance. However, an "applicable large employer" that does not offer coverage for all its full-time employees, offers minimum essential coverage that is unaffordable, or offers minimum essential coverage that consists of a plan under which the plan's share of the total allowed cost of benefits is less than 60 percent is required to pay a penalty if any full-time employee is certified

FROM THE DISSENTING OPINION

(disagreeing with the Court's majority that the
Affordable Care Act was a legitimate exercise
of the power of Congress to collect taxes)

"To say that the individual mandate merely imposes a tax is not to interpret the statute but to rewrite it. Judicial tax-writing is particularly troubling. Taxes have never been popular, and in part for that reason, the Constitution requires tax increases to originate in the House of Representatives. That is to say, they must originate in the legislative body most accountable to the people, where legislators must weigh the need for the tax against the terrible price they might pay at their next election, which is never more than two years off. The Federalist No. 58 'defended the decision to give the origination power to the House on the ground that the Chamber that is more accountable to the people should have the primary role in raising revenue.' We have no doubt that Congress knew precisely what it was doing when it rejected an earlier version of this legislation that imposed a tax instead of a requirement-with-penalty. Imposing a tax through judicial legislation inverts the constitutional scheme and places the power to tax in the branch of government least accountable to the citizenry."

to the employer as having purchased health insurance through a state Exchange with respect to which a tax credit or cost-sharing reduction is allowed or paid to the employee.

�֎ **KEY POINT.** The health care reform law contains no special exemptions for churches. Churches are subject to the same requirements and penalties as a for-profit employer. However, note that employers with fewer than 50 employees are not subject to the shared responsibility provisions of the new law.

An employer is an applicable large employer with respect to any calendar year if it employed an average of at least 50 full-time employees during the preceding calendar year. In counting the number of employees for purposes of determining whether an employer is an applicable large employer, a full-time employee (meaning, for any month, an employee working an average of at least 30 hours or more each week) is counted as one employee, and all other employees are counted on a prorated basis in accordance with regulations prescribed by the Secretary of HHS.

An applicable large employer that offers, for any month, its full-time employees and their dependents the opportunity to enroll in minimum essential coverage under an employer-sponsored plan is subject

to a penalty if any full-time employee is certified to the employer as having enrolled in health insurance coverage purchased through a state Exchange with respect to which a premium tax credit or cost-sharing reduction is allowed or paid to such employee or employees.

The penalty is an excise tax that is imposed for each employee who receives a premium tax credit or cost-sharing reduction for health insurance purchased through a state Exchange. For each full-time employee receiving a premium tax credit or cost-sharing subsidy through a state Exchange for any month, the employer is required to pay an amount equal to one-twelfth of $3,000. The penalty for each employer for any month is capped at an amount equal to the number of full-time employees during the month (regardless of how many employees are receiving a premium tax credit or cost-sharing reduction) in excess of 30, multiplied by one-twelfth of $2,000.

For calendar years after 2014, the $3,000 and $2,000 dollar amounts are increased by the percentage (if any) by which the average per capita premium for health insurance coverage in the United States for the preceding calendar year (as estimated by the Secretary of HHS no later than October 1 of the preceding calendar year) exceeds the average per capita premium for 2013 (as determined by the Secretary of HHS), rounded down to the nearest $10.

> **EXAMPLE.** A church has 12 employees. It is not subject to the employer shared responsibility provisions in the health care reform legislation that take effect in 2014, meaning that it will not be penalized for failing to provide minimum essential health coverage for its staff. Beginning in 2014, each employee is required to have minimum essential health coverage through an individual health insurance policy, an employer plan, or a church plan. Failure to obtain such coverage will expose the church's employees to a penalty. The church is not required to provide health insurance coverage for its employees beginning in 2014, but if it chooses not to do so, its employees will be required to provide for their own coverage through an individual insurance policy or an Exchange.

> **EXAMPLE.** A church has 60 employees. Beginning in 2014, if the church does not provide minimum essential health care coverage and has at least one full-time employee receiving a premium assistance tax credit (explained above), it is required to make a payment of $2,000 per full-time employee. The new law includes the number of full-time equivalent employees for purposes of determining whether an employer has at least 50 employees. But it exempts the first 30 full-time employees for the purposes of calculating the amount of the payment.

The small-employer health insurance tax credit
One of the main objectives of the Affordable Care Act is universal health care coverage. The Act contains several provisions to achieve this goal. One of them is a tax credit that will help small businesses and tax-exempt organizations afford the cost of providing health insurance for their employees. The credit is up

to 25 percent of the cost of health insurance premiums paid by a qualifying employer for its employees. This credit is addressed in the next section of this chapter.

Revenue raisers

The Affordable Care Act will impose massive new costs upon the federal government. Those costs will be offset, in part, through several revenue provisions, including the following:

- An excise tax of 40 percent on insurance companies and plan administrators for any health coverage plan that is above the threshold of $10,200 for single coverage and $27,500 for family coverage.
- The Affordable Care Act increases the additional tax on distributions from a Health Savings Account that is not used for qualified medical expenses from 10 percent to 20 percent of the disbursed amount. This change is effective for disbursements made during tax years starting after December 31, 2010.
- In order for a Health FSA to be a qualified benefit under a cafeteria plan, the maximum amount available for reimbursement of incurred medical expenses of an employee, the employee's dependents, and any other eligible beneficiaries with respect to the employee under the Health FSA for a plan year (or other 12-month coverage period) must not exceed $2,500. The $2,500 limitation is indexed to the Consumer Price Index for Urban Consumers (CPI-U) with any increase that is not a multiple of $50 rounded to the next lowest multiple of $50 for years beginning after December 31, 2012.
- The Act increases the adjusted gross income threshold for claiming the itemized deduction for medical expenses from 7.5 percent to 10 percent. Individuals age 65 and older would be able to claim the itemized deduction for medical expenses at 7.5 percent of adjusted gross income through 2016.
- The Act imposes an additional "hospital insurance" FICA tax on high-income taxpayers for compensation received and taxable years beginning after December 31, 2012.

Extension of dependent coverage

The Affordable Care Act contains two important provisions pertaining to health care coverage for children. Unfortunately, these provisions are not consistent and have led to confusion. Here is a summary of the provisions.

1. Group health plans and health insurance providers

The health care reform legislation requires plans that provide dependent medical coverage of children to continue to make the coverage available for an adult child until the child turns age 26 even if the young adult no longer lives with his or her parents, is not a dependent on a parent's tax return, or is no longer a student. The extended coverage must be provided not later than plan years beginning on or after September 23, 2010. This applies to all plans in the individual market, all new employer plans, and existing employer plans if the young adult is not eligible for employer coverage on his or her own.

YOUNG ADULTS UNINSURED

Young adults have the highest rate of uninsured of any age group. About 30 percent of young adults are uninsured, representing more than one in five of the uninsured. This rate is higher than any other age group and is three times higher than the uninsured rate among children.

In addition, young adults have the lowest rate of access to employer-based insurance. As young adults transition into the job market, they often have entry-level jobs, part-time jobs, jobs in small businesses, or other employment that typically comes without employer-sponsored health insurance. The uninsured rate among employed young adults is one-third higher than older employed adults.

There is a transition for certain existing group plans that generally do not have to provide dependent coverage until 2014 if the adult child has another offer of employer-based coverage aside from coverage through the parent. The new policy providing access for young adults applies to both married and unmarried children, although their own spouses and children do not qualify.

For plan or policy years beginning on or after September 23, 2010, plans and issuers must give children who qualify an opportunity to enroll that continues for at least 30 days, regardless of whether the plan or coverage offers an open enrollment period. This enrollment opportunity and a written notice must be provided not later than the first day of the first plan or policy year beginning on or after September 23, 2010. The new policy does not otherwise change the enrollment period or start of the plan or policy year.

Any qualified young adult must be offered all of the benefit packages available to similarly situated individuals who did not lose coverage because of cessation of dependent status. The qualified individual cannot be required to pay more for coverage than those similarly situated individuals. The new policy applies only to health insurance plans that offer dependent coverage in the first place. While most insurers and employer-sponsored plans offer dependent coverage, there is no requirement to do so.

2. Tax-free benefits for dependent children

Section 105(b) of the tax code excludes from an employee's taxable income any employer-provided reimbursements made directly or indirectly to the employee for the medical care of the employee or the employee's spouse or dependents. The Affordable Care Act amends section 105(b) to extend this exclusion to cover employer-provided

IRS REGULATIONS ADDRESS CAFETERIA PLANS

In 2007 the IRS issued proposed regulations addressing cafeteria plans. The key provisions include the following:

- The regulations clarify and amplify the general rule that section 125 is the exclusive means by which an employer can offer employees a choice between taxable and nontaxable benefits without the choice itself resulting in inclusion in taxable income by the employees. When employees may elect between taxable and nontaxable benefits, this election results in taxable income to employees unless a specific Internal Revenue Code section (such as section 125) intervenes to prevent income inclusion. As a result, except for an election made through a cafeteria plan that satisfies section 125 or another specific section of the tax code, any opportunity to elect among taxable and nontaxable benefits results in inclusion of the taxable benefit in taxable income, regardless of what benefit is elected and when the election is made.

- Participants in a cafeteria plan must be permitted to choose among at least one permitted taxable benefit (for example, cash, including salary reduction) and at least one qualified benefit. A plan offering only elections among nontaxable benefits is not a cafeteria plan. Also, a plan offering only elections among taxable benefits is not a cafeteria plan.

- A cafeteria plan must be in writing. The regulations require that the written plan specifically describe all benefits; set forth the rules for eligibility to participate and the procedure for making elections; provide that all elections are irrevocable; and state how employer contributions may be made under the plan (for example, salary reduction or nonelective employer contributions), the maximum amount of elective contributions, and the plan year. If the plan includes a flexible spending arrangement (FSA), the written plan must include provisions complying with the uniform coverage rule and the use-or-lose rule.

- The regulations require that the written cafeteria plan specify that only employees may participate in the cafeteria plan. Self-employed individuals are not treated as employees for purposes of section 125.

- Former employees (including laid-off employees and retired employees) may participate in a plan, but a plan may not be maintained predominantly for former employees.

- Examples of qualified benefits include group term life insurance; employer-provided accident and health plans, including health flexible spending arrangements; a dependent care assistance program; an adoption assistance program; and contributions to health savings accounts. A cafeteria plan may also offer long-term and short-term disability coverage as a qualified benefit.

- Qualified benefits must be current benefits. In general, a cafeteria plan may not offer benefits that defer compensation or operate to defer compensation.

- The regulations allow a written cafeteria plan to provide an optional grace period immediately following the end of each plan year, extending the period for incurring expenses for qualified benefits.

    A grace period may apply to one or more qualified benefits (for example, health FSA or dependent care assistance program), but in no event does it apply to paid time off or contributions to section 401(k) plans. Unused benefits or contributions for one qualified benefit may only be used to reimburse expenses incurred during the grace period for that same qualified benefit. The amount of unused benefits and contributions available during the grace period may be limited by the employer. A grace period may extend to the 15th day of the 3rd month after the end of the plan year (but may be for a shorter period). Benefits or contributions not used as of the end of the grace period are forfeited under the use-or-lose rule. The grace period applies to all employees who are participants (including through COBRA) as of the last day of the plan year. Grace period rules must apply uniformly to all participants.

- A cafeteria plan cannot offer any of the following benefits: scholarships, employer-provided meals and lodging, educational assistance, fringe benefits, or long-term care insurance. The regulations clarify that contributions to Archer Medical Savings Accounts; group term life insurance for an employee's spouse, child, or dependent; and elective deferrals to section 403(b) plans are also nonqualified benefits. A plan offering any nonqualified benefit is not a cafeteria plan.

- A cafeteria plan may not offer a health FSA that provides for the carryover of unused benefits.

- The regulations allow a cafeteria plan to offer after-tax employee contributions for qualified benefits or paid time off.

- Generally, a cafeteria plan must require employees to elect annually between taxable benefits and qualified benefits. Elections must be made before the earlier of the first day of the period of coverage or when benefits are first currently available. Annual elections generally must be irrevocable and may not be changed during the plan year. However, the regulations permit a cafeteria plan to provide for changes in elections based on certain changes in status.

(Continued on page 208)

IRS REGULATIONS ADDRESS CAFETERIA PLANS
(continued)

- If HSA contributions are made through salary reduction under a cafeteria plan, employees may prospectively elect, revoke, or change salary reduction elections for HSA contributions at any time during the plan year with respect to salary that has not become currently available at the time of the election.
- A cafeteria plan is permitted to include an automatic election for new employees or current employees. A new rule also permits a cafeteria plan to provide an optional election for new employees between cash and qualified benefits. New employees avoid gross income inclusion if they make an election within 30 days after the date of hire, even if benefits provided pursuant to the election relate back to the date of hire. However, salary reduction amounts used to pay for such an election must be from compensation not yet currently available on the date of the election. Also, this special election rule for new employees does not apply to any employee who terminates employment and is rehired within 30 days after terminating employment.
- New elections and revocations or changes in elections can be made electronically.
- Only an employee can make an election or revoke or change his or her election. An employee's spouse or dependent may not make an election under a cafeteria plan and may not revoke or change an employee's election.
- If an employee fails to use all contributions and benefits for a plan year before the end of the plan year (and the grace period, if applicable), those unused contributions and benefits are forfeited under the use-or-lose rule. Unused amounts are also known as experience gains. The regulations clarify that the employer sponsoring the cafeteria plan may retain forfeitures, use forfeitures to defray expenses of administering the plan, or allocate forfeitures among employees contributing through salary reduction on a reasonable and uniform basis.
- The regulations provide that after an employee incurs an expense for a qualified benefit during the coverage period, the expense must first be substantiated before the expense may be paid or reimbursed. All expenses must be substantiated.
- The regulations incorporate previously issued guidance on substantiating, paying, and reimbursing expenses for medical care incurred at a medical care provider when payment is made with a debit card.
- Discriminatory benefits provided to highly compensated individuals and key employees are included in these employees' gross income. The regulations provide additional guidance on the cafeteria plan nondiscrimination rules, including definitions of key terms, guidance on the eligibility test and the contributions and benefits tests, descriptions of employees allowed to be excluded from testing, and a safe harbor nondiscrimination test for premium-only plans. To illustrate, the regulations define "highly compensated individual" consistently with the section 414(q) definition of a highly compensated employee.

---

reimbursements for expenses incurred by an employee for the medical care of the employee's child who has not attained age 27 as of the end of the taxable year, including a child who is not an employee's dependent. As a result, the age, support, and other tests that ordinarily apply to dependents do not apply for purposes of section 105(b).

Section 106 of the tax code excludes from an employee's taxable income any amounts paid by an employer (through insurance or otherwise) to cover medical expenses incurred by the employee or a spouse or dependent. The IRS has stated that "there is no indication that Congress intended to provide a broader exclusion in section 105(b) than in section 106. Accordingly, IRS and Treasury intend to amend the regulations under section 106, retroactively to March 30, 2010, to provide that coverage for an employee's child under age 27 is excluded from gross income."

Abortion
With regard to abortion, the Affordable Care Act

- affirms that a state may prohibit abortion coverage in qualified health plans offered through an Exchange if the state enacts a law to provide for such prohibition.
- ensures that plans may elect whether to cover abortion.
- requires a segregation of funds for subsidy-eligible individuals in plans that cover abortions for which the expenditure of federal funds appropriated for the Department of Health and Human Services is not permitted. Subsidy-eligible individuals would pay one premium with two distinct payment transactions, with one going to an allocation account to be used exclusively for payment of such services.
- requires state insurance commissioners to ensure compliance with the requirement to segregate federal funds in accordance

with generally accepted accounting requirements and guidance from the Office of Management and Budget (OMB) and Government Accountability Office (GAO). Plans would be required to include in their benefit descriptions whether they cover abortion, as they will do for all other benefits. The allocation of the premium into its components would not be advertised or used in enrollment material. All applicants would see the same premium when they are choosing a plan.

- includes conscience language that prohibits qualified health plans from discriminating against any individual health care provider or health care facility because of its unwillingness to provide, pay for, provide coverage of, or refer for abortions.
- ensures that federal and state laws regarding abortion are not preempted.

Contraception and abortifacients

The Affordable Care Act requires that most health insurance plans cover women's preventive services without charging a copay or deductible beginning in August 2012. These preventive health services include coverage, without cost sharing, for "all Food and Drug Administration–approved contraceptive methods, sterilization procedures, and patient education and counseling for all women with reproductive capacity," as prescribed by a provider. Most group or individual health insurance coverage is required to provide this coverage.

The HHS website states: "Women will have access to all Food and Drug Administration–approved contraceptive methods, sterilization procedures, and patient education and counseling. These recommendations do not include abortifacient drugs. Most workers in employer-sponsored plans are currently covered for contraceptives. Family planning services are an essential preventive service for women and critical to appropriately spacing and ensuring intended pregnancies, which results in improved maternal health and better birth outcomes."

The requirement that churches and other religious employers provide contraception and certain "morning after" drugs such as Plan B and Ella that are not regarded as abortifacients by HHS because they prevent conception rather than "interfere with pregnancy" unleashed a tidal wave of opposition by the Catholic church and many Protestants. The United States Conference of Catholic Bishops drafted a letter expressing outrage at the rule and insisting on a change. The letter stated: "The drugs that Americans would be forced to subsidize under the new rule include Ella, which was approved by the FDA as an 'emergency contraceptive' but can act like the abortion drug RU-486. It can abort an established pregnancy weeks after conception. The pro-life majority of Americans—Catholics and others—would be outraged to learn that their premiums must be used for this purpose."

HHS regulations incorporate a narrow exemption for some religious employers, but many religious organizations consider it to be unacceptably narrow. The regulations define an exempt religious employer as one that

(1) has the inculcation of religious values as its purpose;
(2) primarily employs persons who share its religious tenets;
(3) primarily serves persons who share its religious tenets; and
(4) is a nonprofit organization under section 6033(a)(1) and section 6033(a)(3)(A)(i) or (iii) of the tax code. Sections 6033(a)(3)(A)(i) and (iii) refer to churches, their integrated auxiliaries, and conventions or associations of churches as well as to the exclusively religious activities of any religious order.

While this definition of an exempt religious employer would cover some churches, it would not cover many religious organizations, agencies, schools, and parachurch ministries. To illustrate, many church-affiliated universities, seminaries, and social-service agencies that provide social services for the underprivileged would not qualify.

✵ **KEY POINT.** In May 2012, several Catholic dioceses, universities, and institutions filed a lawsuit in federal court claiming that the imposition of the contraceptive mandate on several Catholic entities contrary to their religious convictions violates the First Amendment guaranty of religious freedom. This case is pending.

6. SMALL-EMPLOYER HEALTH INSURANCE CREDIT

One of the main objectives of President Obama's health care reform law (the Affordable Care Act) was universal health care coverage. The Act contains several provisions to achieve this goal. One of them is a new tax credit that will help small businesses and small tax-exempt organizations afford the cost of providing health insurance for their employees. The credit is up to 25 percent of the cost of health insurance premiums paid by a qualifying employer for its employees.

The new credit is specifically targeted for those employers with low- and moderate-income workers and is designed to encourage small employers to offer health insurance coverage for the first time or maintain coverage they already have. In general, the credit is available to small employers that pay at least half the cost of single coverage for their employees.

Eligible employers

In order for an employer to qualify for the credit, it must meet the following three requirements:

(1) it has fewer than 25 "full-time equivalent employees" (FTEs) for the tax year;
(2) the average annual wages of its employees for the year is less than $50,000 per FTE; and
(3) it pays premiums for health insurance coverage under a "qualifying arrangement."

AFFORDABLE CARE ACT EFFECTIVE DATES

(a summary of the effective dates of key provisions)

YEAR	PROVISION
2010	• Prohibits denial of coverage of children based on preexisting conditions. • In the past, insurance companies could search for an error or other technical mistake on a customer's application and use this error to deny payment for services when he or she got sick. The Affordable Care Act makes this illegal. • Insurance companies are prohibited from imposing lifetime dollar limits on essential benefits like hospital stays. • Insurance companies' use of dollar limits on the amount of insurance coverage a patient may receive will be restricted for new plans in the individual market and all group plans. In 2014 the use of annual dollar limits on essential benefits like hospital stays will be banned for new plans in the individual market and all group plans. • The Act provides consumers with a way to appeal coverage determinations or claims to their insurance company and establishes an external review process. • Up to four million small businesses are eligible for tax credits to help them provide insurance benefits to their workers. The first phase of this provision provides a credit worth up to 35 percent of the employer's contribution to the employees' health insurance. Small nonprofit organizations may receive up to a 25 percent credit. • All new plans must cover certain preventive services such as mammograms and colonoscopies without charging a deductible, copay, or coinsurance. • A new $15 billion fund will invest in proven prevention and public health programs, including smoking cessation and combating obesity. Funding begins in 2010. • The Act provides new coverage options to individuals who have been uninsured for at least six months because of a preexisting condition. States have the option of running this program in their state. If a state chooses not to do so, a plan will be established by the Department of Health and Human Services in that state. • Young adults are allowed to stay on their parents' plan until they turn 26 years of age. In the case of existing group health plans, this right does not apply if the young adult is offered insurance at work. • To preserve employer coverage for early retirees until more affordable coverage is available through the new Exchanges by 2014, the Act creates a $5 billion program to provide needed financial help for employment-based plans to continue to provide valuable coverage to people who retire between the ages of 55 and 65, as well as their spouses and dependents. • States will be able to receive federal matching funds for covering some additional low-income individuals and families under Medicaid for whom federal funds were not previously available. This will make it easier for states that choose to do so to cover more of their residents.
2011	• Seniors who reach the coverage gap ("donut hole") will receive a 50 percent discount when buying Medicare Part D–covered brand-name prescription drugs. Over the next 10 years, seniors will receive additional savings on brand-name and generic drugs until the coverage gap is closed in 2020. • To ensure that premium dollars are spent primarily on health care, the law generally requires that at least 85 percent of all premium dollars collected by insurance companies for large employer plans are spent on health care services and health care quality improvement. For plans sold to individuals and small employers, at least 80 percent of the premium must be spent on benefits and quality improvement.
2012	• Health care remains one of the few industries that relies on paper records. The Act institutes a series of changes to standardize billing and requires health plans to begin adopting and implementing rules for the secure, confidential, electronic exchange of health information. Using electronic health records will reduce paperwork and administrative burdens, cut costs, reduce medical errors, and most importantly, improve the quality of care.
2013	• To expand the number of Americans receiving preventive care, the law provides new funding to state Medicaid programs that choose to cover preventive services for patients at little or no cost. • As Medicaid programs and providers prepare to cover more patients in 2014, the Act requires states to pay primary care physicians no less than 100 percent of Medicare payment rates in 2013 and 2014 for primary care services. The increase is fully funded by the federal government.

(Continued on page 211)

AFFORDABLE CARE ACT EFFECTIVE DATES
(continued)

YEAR	PROVISION
2014	• The Act implements strong reforms that prohibit insurance companies from refusing to sell coverage or renew policies because of an individual's preexisting conditions. Also, in the individual and small-group market, the law eliminates the ability of insurance companies to charge higher rates due to gender or health status.
	• The Act prohibits new plans and existing group plans from imposing annual dollar limits on the amount of coverage an individual may receive.
	• Insurers will be prohibited from dropping or limiting coverage because an individual chooses to participate in a clinical trial. This applies to all clinical trials that treat cancer or other life-threatening diseases.
	• Tax credits to make it easier for the middle class to afford insurance will become available for people with income between 100 percent and 400 percent of the poverty line who are not eligible for other affordable coverage. The tax credit is advanceable, so it can lower your premium payments each month rather than making you wait until you file your tax return. It's also refundable, so even moderate-income families can receive the full benefit of the credit. These individuals may also qualify for reduced cost-sharing (copayments, coinsurance, and deductibles).
	• Starting in 2014, if your employer doesn't offer insurance, you will be able to buy it directly in an Affordable Insurance Exchange. An Exchange is a new transparent and competitive insurance marketplace where individuals and small businesses can buy affordable and qualified health benefit plans. Exchanges will offer you a choice of health plans that meet certain benefits and cost standards.
	• The Act implements the second phase of the small-business tax credit for qualified small businesses and small nonprofit organizations. In this phase, the credit is up to 50 percent of the employer's contribution to provide health insurance for employees. There is also up to a 35 percent credit for small nonprofit organizations.
	• Under the law, most individuals who can afford it will be required to obtain basic health insurance coverage or pay a fee to help offset the costs of caring for uninsured Americans. If affordable coverage is not available to an individual, he or she will be eligible for an exemption.
	• Workers meeting certain requirements, who cannot afford the coverage provided by their employer, may take whatever funds their employer might have contributed to their insurance and use these resources to help purchase a more affordable plan in the new health insurance Exchanges.
2015	• A new provision will tie physician payments to the quality of care they provide. Physicians will see their payments modified so that those who provide higher value

The credit is reduced for employers with more than 10 FTEs for the tax year. It is reduced to zero for employers with 25 or more FTEs. Further, the credit is reduced for employers that paid average annual wages of more than $25,000 for the year. It is reduced to zero for employers that pay average annual wages of $50,000 or more.

Figuring FTEs and average annual wages

The number of an employer's FTEs is determined by dividing the total hours of service for which the employer pays wages to employees during the year (but not more than 2,080 hours for any employee) by 2,080. The result, if not a whole number, is then rounded to the next lowest whole number (unless the result is less than one, in which case the employer rounds up to one FTE).

An employee's hours of service for a year include each hour for which an employee is paid or entitled to payment for the performance of duties for the employer during the employer's tax year and each hour of paid leave (except that no more than 160 hours of service are required to be counted for an employee on account of any single continuous period of paid leave). To calculate the total number of hours of service that must be taken into account for an employee for the year, the employer may use any of the following methods:

(1) determine actual hours of service from records of hours worked and hours for which payment is made or due, including hours for paid leave;

(2) use a days-worked equivalency whereby the employee is credited with eight hours of service for each day for which the employee would be required to be credited with at least one hour of service under method 1; or

(3) use a weeks-worked equivalency whereby the employee is credited with 40 hours of service for each week for which the employee would be required to be credited with at least one hour of service under method 1.

❋ **KEY POINT.** Employers do not have to use the same method for all employees. They may apply different methods for different classifications of employees if the classifications are reasonable and consistently applied. For example, it is permissible for an employer to use method 1 for all hourly employees and the method 3 for all salaried employees. Employers may change the method for calculating employees' hours of service for each taxable year.

Note that a church with 25 or more employees may qualify for the credit if some of its employees are part-time. This is because the limitation on the number of employees is based on FTEs. So a church with 25 or more employees could qualify for the credit if some of its employees work part-time.

The amount of average annual wages is determined by first dividing the total wages paid by the employer during the employer's tax year to employees who perform services for the employer during the tax year by the number of the employer's FTEs for the year. The result is then rounded down to the nearest $1,000 (if not otherwise a multiple of $1,000). Only wages that are paid for hours of service are taken into account. Wages for this purpose means wages subject to Social Security and Medicare tax withholding.

❋ **KEY POINT.** The $50,000 average annual wage limit is adjusted for inflation beginning in 2013.

Calculating the credit

Only premiums paid by the employer under an arrangement meeting certain requirements (a "qualifying arrangement") are counted in calculating the credit. Under a qualifying arrangement, the employer pays premiums for each employee enrolled in health care coverage offered by the employer in an amount equal to a uniform percentage (not less than 50 percent) of the premium cost of the coverage. However, a qualifying arrangement also includes an arrangement under which the employer pays at least 50 percent of the premium cost for single (employee-only) coverage for each employee enrolled in any health insurance coverage offered by the employer.

For tax years beginning in 2010 through 2013, only premiums paid to a health insurance provider for health care coverage are counted for purposes of the credit. A health insurance provider is either an insurance company or another entity licensed under state law to provide health insurance coverage.

The IRS has clarified that the term "health insurance provider" also includes "an arrangement under which an otherwise qualifying small church employer pays premiums for employees who receive medical care coverage under a church welfare benefit plan." This conclusion is based on the Church Plan Parity and Entanglement Prevention Act of 1999, which states that "for purposes of enforcing provisions of state insurance laws that apply to a church plan that is a welfare plan, the church plan shall be subject to state enforcement as if the church plan were an insurer licensed by the state." Based on this

provision, the IRS concluded that a church welfare benefit plan is subject to state insurance law enforcement as if it were licensed as an insurance company and, therefore, meets the definition of a health insurance provider for purposes of the credit. As a result, insurance premiums paid by churches to many denominational health plans will be counted for purposes of the credit.

Premiums for health care coverage that covers a wide variety of conditions, such as a major medical plan, are counted; and premiums for certain coverage that is more limited in scope, such as limited scope dental or vision coverage, are also counted. However, if an employer offers more than one type of coverage, such as a major medical plan and a separate, limited-scope dental or vision plan, the employer must separately satisfy the requirements for a qualifying arrangement with respect to each type of coverage the employer offers (meaning the employer cannot aggregate these different plans for purposes of meeting the qualifying arrangement requirement).

❋ **KEY POINT.** An arrangement under which an otherwise qualifying small-church employer pays premiums for employees who receive medical care coverage under a church welfare benefit plan may be a qualifying arrangement for purposes of the small-business health care tax credit.

❋ **KEY POINT.** Employer contributions to health reimbursement arrangements (HRAs), health flexible spending arrangements (FSAs), and health savings accounts (HSAs) are not taken into account for purposes of the small-business health care tax credit.

If an employer pays only a portion of the premiums for the coverage provided to employees under the arrangement, with employees paying the rest, the amount of premiums counted in calculating the credit is only the portion paid by the employer. For purposes of the credit, including the requirement to make a uniform contribution of not less than 50 percent of the premium, any premium paid pursuant to a salary reduction arrangement under a section 125 cafeteria plan is not treated as paid by the employer.

EXAMPLE. A church pays 80 percent of the premiums for employees' health insurance, with employees paying the other 20 percent pursuant to a salary reduction arrangement under a cafeteria plan. Only the 80 percent premium amount paid by the church counts in calculating the credit.

In addition, the amount of an employer's premium payments that counts for purposes of the credit is capped by the premium payments the employer would have made under the same arrangement if the average premium for the small-group market in the state in which the employer offers coverage were substituted for the actual premium. For example, if an employer pays 80 percent of the premiums for coverage provided to employees and the employees pay the other 20 percent, the premium amount that counts for purposes of the credit is the lesser of 80 percent of the total actual premiums paid or 80 percent of the premiums that would have been paid for the coverage if the average premium for the small-group market in the state were substituted for the actual premium. The average premium for the small-group market does not apply separately to each type of coverage the employer offers, but rather provides an overall cap for all health insurance coverage provided by a qualified employer.

Maximum credit amount

For tax years beginning in 2010 through 2013, the maximum credit for a tax-exempt qualified employer is 25 percent of the employer's premium expenses that count toward the credit. However, the amount of the credit cannot exceed the total amount of income and Medicare (i.e., hospital insurance) tax the employer is required to withhold from employees' wages for the year and the employer share of Medicare tax on employees' wages for the year.

If a minister is an employee for income tax reporting purposes, he or she is taken into account in determining an employer's FTEs for purposes of the health care tax credit. Also, premiums paid by the church for the health insurance coverage of a minister who is an employee can be taken into account in computing the credit, subject to limitations on the credit. If the minister is self-employed for income tax reporting purposes, he or she is not taken into account in determining an employer's FTEs or premiums paid.

Reducing the credit

The maximum credit goes to smaller employers—those with 10 or fewer full-time equivalent (FTE) employees—paying annual average wages of $25,000 or less. The credit is completely phased out for employers that have 25 or more FTEs or that pay average wages of $50,000 or more per year. Because the eligibility rules are based in part on the number of FTEs, not the number of employees, employers that use part-time workers may qualify even if they employ more than 25 individuals.

How is the credit reduced if the number of FTEs exceeds 10 or average annual wages exceed $25,000? If the number of FTEs exceeds 10, or if average annual wages exceed $25,000, the amount of the credit is reduced as follows:

- If the number of FTEs exceeds 10, the reduction is determined by multiplying the otherwise applicable credit amount by a fraction, the numerator of which is the number of FTEs in excess of 10 and the denominator of which is 15.
- If average annual wages exceed $25,000, the reduction is determined by multiplying the otherwise applicable credit amount by a fraction, the numerator of which is the amount by which average annual wages exceed $25,000 and the denominator of which is $25,000.

In both cases, the result of the calculation is subtracted from the otherwise applicable credit to determine the credit to which the employer is entitled. For an employer with both more than 10 FTEs and average annual wages exceeding $25,000, the reduction in the credit amount is equal to the sum of the amount of the two reductions. This sum may reduce the credit to zero for some employers with fewer than 25 FTEs and average annual wages of less than $50,000.

How to claim the credit

Small businesses can claim the credit for 2010 through 2013 and for any two years after that. For tax years 2010 to 2013, the maximum credit is 25 percent of premiums paid by eligible tax-exempt organizations. Beginning in 2014, the maximum tax credit will increase to 35 percent of premiums paid by eligible tax-exempt organizations.

Tax-exempt organizations will first use Form 8941 to figure their refundable credit, and then claim the credit on line 44f of Form 990-T. Though primarily filed by those organizations liable for the tax on unrelated business income, Form 990-T will also be used by any eligible tax-exempt organization to claim the credit, regardless of whether they are subject to this tax. Form 990-T has been revised to enable eligible tax-exempt organizations to claim the health care tax credit.

The deadline for filing Form 990-T is the 15th day of the fifth month following the end of a church's tax year (May 15 of the following year for most churches). To illustrate: to claim the credit for 2012, a church will need to file Form 990-T by May 15, 2013. For churches that operate on a fiscal-year basis, the deadline is the 15th day of the fifth month following the end of their fiscal year.

Note that qualifying tax-exempt employers (including churches) having no taxable income to be offset with a tax credit will claim a "refundable" tax credit, meaning that the amount of the credit that would otherwise have offset taxable income is refunded to them.

✤ **KEY POINT.** The credit is refundable so long as it does not exceed the employer's income tax withholding and Medicare tax liability.

✤ **KEY POINT.** Although the tax code requires section 501(c)(3) organizations to make their Form 990-T available for public inspection, this requirement does not apply to returns filed only to request a credit for the small-employer health insurance premiums. Also, there is no requirement that section 501(c)(3) organizations make Form 8941 available for public inspection. An organization filing a Form 990-T only to request a credit for the small-employer health insurance premium must write "Request for 45R Credit Only" across the top of the Form 990-T.

Years the credit is available

The credit is initially available for any taxable year beginning in 2010, 2011, 2012, or 2013. Qualifying health insurance for claiming the credit for this first phase of the credit is health insurance coverage purchased from an insurance company licensed under state law. As noted above, the IRS has clarified that qualifying health insurance includes "an arrangement under which an otherwise qualifying small church employer pays premiums for employees who receive medical care coverage under a church welfare benefit plan."

For taxable years beginning in years after 2013, the credit is only available to a qualified small employer that purchases health insurance coverage for its employees through a state "exchange" and is only available for a maximum coverage period of two consecutive taxable years, beginning with the first year in which the employer or any predecessor first offers one or more qualified plans to its employees through an exchange.

The maximum two-year coverage period does not take into account any taxable years beginning in years before 2014. As a result, a qualified small employer could potentially qualify for this credit for six taxable years, four years under the first phase and two years under the second phase.

Questions

This section addresses some common questions pertaining to the application of the small-employer health insurance tax credit to churches.

Question 1. Our church has a preschool with six employees. Are these employees taken into account in computing the small-employer health insurance tax credit?

Answer. Unfortunately, the tax code does not directly address this question, and the IRS has not provided any clarification. It is likely, though not certain, that the IRS would apply the "common-law rules" pertaining to the definition of an "employer" for employment tax purposes (i.e., withholding and payment of Social Security, Medicare, and income taxes) in computing the number of employees for purposes of the small-employer health insurance credit. These rules are found in several sources, including IRS Publication 15A:

> *Under common-law rules, anyone who performs services for you is your employee if you have the right to control what will be done and how it will be done. This is so even when you give the employee freedom of action. What matters is that you have the right to control the details of how the services are performed....*
>
> *If you have an employer-employee relationship, it makes no difference how it is labeled. The substance of the relationship, not the label, governs the worker's status. It does not matter whether the individual is employed full time or part time.... You generally have to withhold and pay income, social security, and Medicare taxes on wages that you pay to common-law employees.*

However, section 3401(d) of the tax code contains an important exception to the common-law rules by defining an employer as "the person for whom an individual performs or performed any service, of whatever nature, as the employee of such person, *except that if the person for whom the individual performs or performed the services does*

not have control of the payment of the wages for such services, the term employer means the person having control of the payment of such wages" (emphasis added).

According to this provision, a preschool employee that is performing services directly for the preschool rather than the church, and would therefore be an employee of the preschool under the common-law rules, is subject to the general rule of section 3401(d) that "if the person for whom the individual performs or performed the services does not have control of the payment of the wages for such services, the term *employer* means the person having control of the payment of such wages."

According to this precedent, it is likely that the employees of a church preschool would be considered church employees and included in computing the church's eligibility for the small-employer health insurance credit if (1) the preschool is not separately incorporated, (2) the preschool uses the church's employer identification number for reporting employment taxes, and (3) the church pays the wages of preschool employees.

On the other hand, if a church-affiliated preschool is separately incorporated, has its own employer identification number, and pays the wages of its employees, then it is unlikely that these employees would be included in determining the number of church employees for purposes of the small-employer health insurance tax credit.

In some cases, a preschool may be separately incorporated but use the church's employer identification number. Are the employees of such a preschool counted in computing the number of church employees for purposes of the credit? The answer is less clear in hybrid scenarios like this. Perhaps the main point would be the definition of an employer under section 3401(d) of the tax code as the entity "having control of the payment of wages." If the preschool employees' wages are paid by the church, then the church would be the employer, even if the preschool operates with some level of independence under the governing documents of itself and the church.

This analysis is necessarily tentative given the lack of clarification from the IRS. Any future developments will be reported in future editions of this guide. Church leaders should consult with a tax professional for assistance in determining the church's eligibility for the small-employer health insurance tax credit.

Question 2. Some ministers have elected voluntary withholding of income taxes and self-employment taxes. Will the wages of these ministers be counted in computing a church's average annual wages?

Answer. No. Section 45R of the tax code states that in computing the credit, the term "wages" has the meaning as in section 3121(a), which pertains to Social Security and Medicare taxes (FICA taxes) for employees. However, since 3121(a)(8) specifies that for Social Security and Medicare taxes a duly ordained, commissioned, or licensed minister of a church is self-employed with respect to services performed in the exercise of ministry, his or her compensation is not "wages" under section 3121 of the tax code and, therefore, is not taken into account in computing the church's average annual wages even if a minister has entered into a voluntary withholding arrangement with the church. As the IRS notes in Notice 2010-82: "Because compensation of a minister performing services in the exercise of his or her ministry is not subject to Social Security or Medicare tax under the Federal Insurance Contributions Act (FICA), a minister has no wages as defined under §3121(a) for purposes of computing an employer's average annual wages."

Question 3. What about ministers who have elected voluntary withholding of taxes? Will this affect the amount of the church's credit? If so, should churches reconsider whether they want to accommodate a pastor's request for voluntary withholding of income taxes and self-employment taxes?

Answer. Section 45R of the tax code, which contains the small-employer health insurance credit, limits the credit for tax-exempt employers (including churches) to "the amount of the payroll taxes of the employer during the calendar year in which the taxable year begins." Section 45R(f)(3) defines "payroll taxes" as the sum of the following three amounts:

(1) income taxes "required to be withheld from the employees of the tax-exempt eligible small employer,"

(2) Medicare taxes "required to be withheld from such employees," and

(3) the employer's share of Medicare taxes.

Ministers' wages are exempt from income tax withholding with respect to services performed in the exercise of their ministry, and they are not subject to Medicare taxes with respect to these services (instead, they pay self-employment taxes). So the "payroll tax limit" on the amount of the credit will not be affected by ministerial employees.

However, many pastors and churches have entered into voluntary withholding arrangements whereby the church withholds income taxes from a pastor's wages. In some cases, a pastor requests that additional income taxes be withheld to offset self-employment tax liability. These additional withheld taxes are deemed income taxes and not Social Security or Medicare taxes.

Of the three components of payroll taxes under section 45R(f)(3), the only one that would be affected by pastoral compensation would be withheld income taxes for pastors who have elected voluntary withholding. Are these voluntarily withheld income taxes counted in computing the payroll tax limit on the amount of the small-employer health insurance credit? The obvious answer is no, since these taxes are voluntarily withheld and not required to be held (to use the language of section 45R(f)(3)). However, this issue has not been addressed

or clarified by the tax code, regulations, IRS, or the courts, and so a definitive answer is not possible. Church leaders should consult with a tax professional in making a final decision. Note that if these voluntarily withheld taxes are included in computing the payroll tax limit, this will have the effect of increasing the credit for some churches.

Question 4. Does a church have to use Form 990-T if it is only claiming the credit?

Answer. The IRS has stated that "tax-exempt organizations will include the amount of the credit on Line 44f of revised Form 990-T (Exempt Organization Business Income Tax Return). Form 990-T has been revised to enable eligible tax-exempt organizations, even those that owe no tax on unrelated business income, to claim the small-business health care tax credit." An organization filing a Form 990-T only to request a credit for the small-employer health insurance premium must write "Request for 45R Credit Only" across the top of the Form 990-T.

Although the tax code requires section 501(c)(3) organizations to make their Form 990-T available for public inspection, this requirement does not apply to returns filed only to request a credit for the small-employer health insurance premiums. Also, there is no requirement that section 501(c)(3) organizations make Form 8941 available for public inspection.

Question 5. Are health insurance premiums paid by a church for its pastors included in computing the credit?

Answer. Yes. The following question and answer appears on the IRS website in the course of an explanation of the credit:

24. Can a tax-exempt organization described in section 501(c) include a minister in its calculation when determining eligibility for the small business health care tax credit?

A. The answer depends on whether, under the common-law test for determining worker status, the minister is considered an employee of the tax-exempt organization or self-employed. If the minister is an employee, he or she is taken into account in determining an employer's FTEs for purposes of the health care tax credit. Also, premiums paid by the employer for the health insurance coverage of a minister who is an employee can be taken into account in computing the credit, subject to limitations on the credit. If the minister is self-employed, he or she is not taken into account in determining an employer's FTEs or premiums paid.

Question 6. When calculating number of employees, are we to include all employees or only full-time employees?

Answer. To be eligible for the credit, an employer must have fewer than 25 "full-time equivalent employees" (FTEs) for the tax year and pay average annual wages of less than $50,000 per FTE.

The number of an employer's FTEs is determined by dividing (1) the total hours of service for which the employer pays wages to employees during the year (but not more than 2,080 hours for any employee) by (2) 2,080. The result, if not a whole number, is then rounded to the next lowest whole number (unless the result is less than one, in which case the employer rounds up to one FTE).

To calculate the total number of hours of service which must be taken into account for an employee for the year, the employer may use any of the following methods:

- *Method 1.* Determine actual hours of service from records of hours worked and hours for which payment is made or due, including hours for paid leave;
- *Method 2.* Use a days-worked equivalency, whereby the employee is credited with eight hours of service for each day for which the employee would be required to be credited with at least one hour of service under Method 1; or
- *Method 3.* Use a weeks-worked equivalency, whereby the employee is credited with 40 hours of service for each week for which the employee would be required to be credited with at least one hour of service under Method 1. Employers do not have to use the same method for all employees. They may apply different methods for different classifications of employees if the classifications are reasonable and consistently applied. For example, it is permissible for an employer to use Method 1 for all hourly employees and the Method 3 for all salaried employees. Employers may change the method for calculating employees' hours of service for each taxable year.

Question 7. Does this credit apply in a situation where the only paid staff member is the pastor, assuming the annual salary is less than $50,000?

Answer. Yes. The minister is counted in computing the number of employees, but his or her wages are not deemed to be compensation in computing the average annual wages limit of $50,000. So, in the case of a church with one pastor and no other paid staff, the church would have one employee and average annual wages of under $25,000 (ministers' compensation is excluded from the definition of "wages" in computing the credit), entitling it to the full credit of 25 percent times the health insurance premiums paid by the church for the pastor, assuming that the church pays at least half of the premium amount.

The credit is limited to the income taxes and Medicare taxes withheld by the church plus the church's share of Medicare taxes. But since ministers' wages are exempt from income tax withholding and ministers are not subject to FICA taxes with regard to compensation received for their ministerial services, a church will have no "payroll taxes" (income taxes and Medicare taxes withheld, plus the church's share of Medicare taxes). This probably means that a church with only one pastor and no other compensated employee will be ineligible for the credit, since it will have no payroll taxes and its credit cannot exceed the amount of payroll taxes paid. This is an open question that has not been answered by section 45R of the tax code or the IRS.

One possible solution would be for the pastor to elect voluntary withholding of income taxes. If the pastor increases income tax withholding to account for both income tax and self-employment tax liability, this could have the effect of increasing the payroll tax ceiling by enough to make the credit worthwhile. Note, however, that voluntary withholding is available only to ministers who report their income taxes as employees, which may be the incorrect status for some ministers who are the sole compensated worker at their church. Also, note that if the pastor is a church's sole compensated worker and the pastor reports income taxes as a self-employed worker, this may affect the church's eligibility for the credit, since the credit only applies to health insurance provided by an employer for its employees.

Churches with no employees other than a pastor should consult with a tax professional to resolve this issue. Any clarification will be presented in future editions of this guide.

E. AMOUNTS RECEIVED UNDER ACCIDENT AND HEALTH PLANS

✿ **KEY POINT.** Amounts received by employees as reimbursements for medical care under an employer-financed accident and health plan generally are excludable from taxable income (this exclusion is not available to self-employed individuals).

1. OVERVIEW

Churches commonly pay some or all of the medical expenses of their ministers or lay employees. This can include direct payment of expenses, reimbursing employees for expenses they have incurred, and paying a "deductible" amount on an employee's medical insurance. The tax consequences of such payments and reimbursements are not well understood.

Section 105(a) insurance benefits
Section 105(a) of the tax code specifies that amounts received by an employee through accident or health insurance for personal injuries or sickness shall be included in the employee's taxable income "to the extent such amounts (1) are attributable to contributions by the employer which were not includible in the gross income of the employee, or (2) are paid by the employer."

Section 105(b) "self-insured" benefits

Section 105(b) of the tax code provides an exception to the general rule requiring inclusion in income. It specifies that an employee's taxable income does not include amounts referred to in section 105(a) that are "paid, directly or indirectly, to the taxpayer to reimburse the taxpayer for expenses incurred by him for the medical care of the taxpayer, his spouse, and his dependents." This refers to employer-provided benefits that are not financed through insurance.

✿ **KEY POINT.** Section 105(b) permits employees to exclude from their taxable income amounts received under an employer-financed accident and health plan as payments for permanent injury or loss of bodily function, or as reimbursements of medical expenses. The payments can be made on behalf of a spouse or dependent of the employee. As part of the Affordable Care Act of 2010, Congress extended this benefit to cover employer-provided reimbursements for expenses incurred by an employee for the medical care of the employee's child who has not attained age 27 as of the end of the taxable year, including a child who is not an employee's dependent. As a result, the age, support, and other tests that ordinarily apply to dependents do not apply for purposes of section 105(b).

This exclusion assumes that the employer has established an accident or health plan. Unfortunately, the requirements for such a plan are not specified in the tax code. The regulations simply state that "an accident or health plan is an arrangement for the payment of amounts to employees in the event of personal injuries or sickness." The regulations further specify that "an accident or health plan may be either insured or uninsured, and it is not necessary that the plan be in writing or that the employee's rights to benefits under the plan be enforceable." Of course, a written plan is preferable, since it generally will eliminate any doubt regarding the existence or date of a plan. The regulations do require that notice of a plan be "reasonably available" to employees (if employees' rights under the plan are not enforceable).

Several courts have defined the term "accident or health plan." Generally, these decisions indicate that such a plan meets the following conditions: (1) a commitment by an employer's board must be recorded in the board's minutes; (2) the employer "must be committed to certain rules and regulations governing payment"; (3) these rules "must be made known to employees as a definite policy and must be determinable before the employee's medical expenses are incurred"; (4) the plan must be called an "accident or health plan"; and (5) the plan must be operated on a consistent basis.

EXAMPLE. A church provides health insurance coverage for its employees and their spouses and any child who has not attained age 27 as of the end of the taxable year. For 2013 the church provides health care coverage to Pastor Steve and his daughter, Emily. Emily will not attain age 27 in 2013. Emily is not eligible for health care coverage from her own employer. She is not a dependent of Pastor Steve, because she does not live with him and she provides more than half of her support. Because Emily will not attain age 27 during 2013, the health care coverage available to her under her father's plan is excludable from his taxable income under sections 105(b) and 106 of the tax code.

Nondiscrimination rules

Nondiscrimination rules regarding accident and health benefits are addressed below.

Self-insured plans

Employers may reimburse employee medical expenses under either a "self-insured" plan (e.g., reimbursements are paid out of the employer's own funds rather than through an insurance policy), or an insured plan. However, if reimbursements are made under a self-insured plan, nondiscrimination rules apply. Generally, these rules require that the plan not discriminate in favor of highly compensated individuals with regard to either amount of benefits or eligibility to participate. If a self-insured plan is discriminatory, then highly compensated individuals ordinarily must report some or all of the amount of the employer's reimbursements as taxable income.

If a reimbursement arrangement discriminates in favor of highly compensated individuals on the basis of the amount of benefits (e.g., highly compensated individuals receive a greater benefit than other participants in the plan), then such individuals must report the entire amount of the reimbursements as income.

More complicated rules determine how to compute the taxable portion of an employer's reimbursements if the plan discriminates on the basis of participation (rather than the amount of benefits). In general, a plan discriminates in favor of highly compensated individuals on the basis of eligibility to participate unless the plan benefits 70 percent or more of all employees. Some employees can be disregarded in applying this test, including those who have not completed 3 years of service, have not attained age 25, or are part-time or seasonal employees.

✿ **KEY POINT.** Who are highly compensated individuals? For churches, they include (1) one of the five highest paid officers, or (2) those employees among the highest paid 25 percent of all employees (some employees are not considered, including those who have not completed three years of service, have not attained age 25, are part-time or seasonal employees, and are not participants in the employer's plan).

The regulations specify that "benefits paid to participants who are not highly compensated individuals may be excluded from gross income . . . even if the plan is discriminatory." The fact that highly compensated employees must report some or all of their reimbursements as income does not affect the ability of non-highly compensated employees to fully exclude employer reimbursements.

Insured plans

Section 10101(d) of the Patient Protection and Affordable Care Act (the Affordable Care Act) adds section 2716 to the Public Health Service Act (PHS Act). Section 2716 provides that an insured group health plan must satisfy the nondiscrimination requirements of section 105(h)(2) of the tax code (i.e., the plan does not discriminate in favor of highly compensated individuals as to eligibility to participate, and the benefits provided under the plan do not discriminate in favor of participants who are highly compensated individuals).

Section 2716 specifies that the term "highly compensated individual" in this context has the meaning given by section 105(h)(5) (an individual who is one of the five highest paid officers, or among the highest paid 25 percent of all employees, other than employees who have not completed three years of service, or not attained age 25, or are part-time or seasonal employees).

An insured group health plan that fails to comply with these rules may be subject to (1) an excise tax of $100 for each day in the non-compliance period with respect to each individual to whom such failure relates, limited in the case of failures due to reasonable cause and not applicable in limited circumstances (such as where a failure is due to reasonable cause and not to willful neglect and is corrected within a specified time period), or (2) a civil action to enjoin a non-compliant act or practice or for other appropriate equitable relief.

The U.S. Department of the Treasury and the IRS, as well as the Departments of Labor and Health and Human Services (collectively, the Departments), have determined that compliance with section 2716 should not be required (and thus, any sanctions for failure to comply do not apply) until after regulations or other administrative guidance of general applicability has been issued. In order to provide insured group health plan sponsors time to implement any changes required as a result of the regulations or other guidance, the Departments anticipate that the guidance will not apply until plan years beginning a specified period after issuance. Before the beginning of those plan years, an insured group health plan sponsor will not be required to file IRS Form 8928 with respect to excise taxes resulting from the incorporation of section 2716 into the tax code.

IRS Notice 2011-1 states: "Thus, if a self-insured plan fails to comply with §105(h), highly compensated individuals lose a tax benefit; if an insured group health plan fails to comply with section 2716, the plan or plan sponsor may be subject to an excise tax, civil money penalty, or a civil action to compel it to provide nondiscriminatory benefits."

2. REIMBURSING EXPENSES BEFORE ADOPTING A PLAN

An internal IRS policy addresses the following question: "Are employer reimbursements under a self-insured accident and health plan for medical expenses incurred prior to the adoption of the plan excludable from gross income by the employee under section 105(b) of the Internal Revenue Code?" *IRP ¶ 80,600 (1999)*. The IRS policy concludes that "employer reimbursements under a self-insured accident and health plan for medical expenses incurred prior to the adoption of the plan are *not* excludable from gross income by the employee" (emphasis added).

The IRS noted that employers often adopt self-insured accident and health plans to cover medical expenses incurred prior to the date of the adoption of the plan but within the same taxable year. This is done in an attempt to allow employees to exclude these medical expense reimbursements from income.

> **EXAMPLE.** A church employee experiences a severe illness. The church board agrees to pay the $2,500 deductible on the employee's health insurance policy. The board assumes that this amount is nontaxable because it was motivated by charity. Several weeks later, however, the board learns that the payment is nontaxable only if the church had a formal accident and health plan in place. The board hastily drafts a few paragraphs describing its plan and inserts the text in the minutes of a board meeting.

The IRS noted:

> *The basic tenet of income taxation is that unless wages, benefits or other income fall within an explicit exclusion to the Internal Revenue Code's definition of gross income, they are included within that term. Exclusions and exemptions from income are matters of legislative grace and are construed narrowly. . . . [Tax code section] 105(b) states that gross income does not include amounts paid, directly or indirectly, to the employee to reimburse the employee for expenses incurred by him, his spouse or dependents for medical care. . . . However, section 105(b) does not apply unless the medical expense reimbursements are received under an accident or health plan.*

The IRS pointed out that the income tax regulations define "plan" as "an arrangement for the payment of amounts to employees in the event of personal injuries or sickness." The IRS conceded that a plan "need not be enforceable and need not be in writing." However, in order for a plan to exist, the employer "must be committed to certain rules and regulations governing payment. These rules must be made known to employees as a definite policy and must be determinable before the employee's medical expenses are incurred."

The IRS concluded that "payments for reimbursement of medical expenses incurred prior to the adoption of a plan are not paid or received under an accident or health plan for employees. Thus, these amounts are includible in the employee's gross income . . . and are not excludable under section 105(b) of the tax code."

The importance of the IRS policy is clear. Church leaders often distribute funds to ministers and lay employees to cover medical expenses without any serious consideration of the tax consequences. In most cases they simply assume that these payments are nontaxable. The IRS policy addressed in this section suggests that such an assumption may be erroneous and lead to needless tax complications. In many cases a church not only is required to report the payments or reimbursements as taxable income and add them to the employee's Form W-2, but the employee will need to report them on his or her tax return and pay taxes on them. All of this can be avoided, the IRS concluded, if the church simply adopts an adequate plan in advance of making the medical payments.

✱ **KEY POINT.** The IRS has issued another ruling confirming its position that amounts reimbursed under a self-insured medical expense reimbursement plan for medical expenses incurred by an employee prior to the adoption of an employer plan are not excludable from the employee's income under section 105(b) of the tax code. *Revenue Ruling 2002-58.*

✱ **KEY POINT.** The tax code and regulations do not define a "plan." The IRS policy simply states that an employer "must be committed to certain rules and regulations governing payment" and that these rules "must be made known to employees as a definite policy and must be determinable before the employee's medical expenses are incurred." While a plan need not be in writing, it certainly will be desirable for a church to set forth a plan in writing to eliminate any question regarding when it was adopted.

✱ **KEY POINT.** A plan may not operate retroactively. A church cannot reimburse an employee's medical expenses and later attempt to insulate these payments from tax by belatedly adopting a medical payment plan. These important rules are illustrated in the following examples.

EXAMPLE 1. Pastor M is the senior pastor of a church. He undergoes major surgery and incurs $10,000 of expenses that are not covered under any insurance policy. The church board decides to reimburse Pastor M for the full amount of $10,000. The church has no formal plan of reimbursing any employee's medical expenses. Several weeks after making the $10,000 reimbursement, the church treasurer learns that the reimbursement will represent taxable income to Pastor M unless it was made pursuant to an accident and health plan. The church board quickly adopts a written plan. The board's action is too late to avoid reporting the $10,000 reimbursement as taxable income to Pastor M under section 105 of the tax code.

EXAMPLE 2. Same facts as Example 1, except that the church board decides that their previous decision to reimburse the pastor's medical expenses constituted an accident and health plan. They rely on the fact that such a plan need not be in writing. It is likely that the board's argument will fail. According to the IRS internal policy, an employer "must be committed to certain rules and regulations governing payment," and these rules "must be made known to

employees as a definite policy and must be determinable before the employee's medical expenses are incurred." It is very unlikely that the IRS would consider the mere act of reimbursing the pastor's medical expenses to constitute a plan. If the church's argument were accepted, it would render the plan requirement meaningless, since any employer's payment or reimbursement of medical expenses would automatically constitute a plan.

EXAMPLE 3. Same facts as Example 1, except that the church treasurer learned of the plan requirement a few weeks before the reimbursement was made. Prior to making the reimbursement, the church board adopted a plan that stated: "Resolved, that the church will pay the unreimbursed medical expenses of the pastor." It is possible that this action will not constitute a valid plan. According to the IRS internal policy, an employer "must be committed to certain rules and regulations governing payment," and these rules "must be made known to employees as a definite policy and must be determinable before the employee's medical expenses are incurred." Does the one-sentence resolution by the church board satisfy this test? Unfortunately, the answer is not clear. The church could have eliminated any doubt by providing more detail in the resolution.

EXAMPLE 4. Same facts as Example 1. The church treasurer realizes by now that the $10,000 reimbursement cannot be excluded from the pastor's income as a payment under an accident and health plan under section 105 of the tax code. The church treasurer is wondering if the amount can be excluded from the pastor's income as a charitable or benevolent distribution from the church. This is a possibility, depending on the circumstances.

Churches certainly are free to make distributions to the poor and needy, since such distributions further a church's religious and charitable purposes. However, when churches make distributions to one of their own employees (such as the pastor in this example), it is less likely that the distribution will be viewed by the IRS or the courts as serving the church's religious and charitable purposes. This is so for the following two reasons: (1) Whenever an employee is the recipient of a church distribution, the immediate assumption is that the distribution represents additional taxable compensation for services rendered. (2) The income tax regulations define "charitable" quite narrowly. The term includes the "relief of the poor and distressed or of the underprivileged." The regulations define "needy" as "being a person who lacks the necessities of life, involving physical, mental, or emotional well-being, as a result of poverty or temporary distress. Examples of needy persons include a person who is financially impoverished as a result of low income and lack of financial resources, a person who temporarily lacks food or shelter (and the means to provide for it), a person who is the victim of a natural disaster (such as fire or flood), a person who is the victim of a civil disaster (such as civil disturbance), a person who is temporarily not self-sufficient as a result of a sudden and severe personal or family crisis (such as a person who is the victim of a crime of violence or who has been physically abused).”

It is unlikely, though not impossible, that the church's reimbursement of the pastor's medical bills would be deemed a charitable distribution under this definition.

EXAMPLE 5. Same facts as Example 1, except that the church board adopted a plan several months before reimbursing the pastor's medical bills that spelled out the church's commitment to paying the senior pastor's medical bills not covered under any available insurance coverage. The plan did not provide for the payment of any other employee's medical bills. Assuming that the board's action qualifies as an accident and health plan, it will not prevent the $10,000 reimbursement from being treated as taxable income to Pastor M. Why? Since the church's plan is self-insured (the pastor's medical expenses will be paid out of the church's general fund), the $10,000 is excludable from Pastor M's income only to the extent that the church's plan is not discriminatory. If Pastor M is one of the five highest paid officers, or is among the highest paid 25 percent of all employees, he may not exclude any of the $10,000 from his income for tax purposes if the same benefit is not available to non-highly compensated individuals.

EXAMPLE 6. A church purchases health insurance for Pastor G, who reports his income taxes as an employee. In order to reduce the cost of the insurance, the church elects a $1,000 deductible (e.g., the insurance pays for any expense only to the extent that it exceeds $1,000). The church established a "medical fund" for Pastor G in order to reimburse all of his medical expenses that are less than $1,000 (and not covered by insurance). The church does not provide health insurance or a medical fund for any other employee. The church's medical plan is self-insured and discriminatory (in favor of Pastor G, a highly compensated individual), and accordingly all of Pastor G's medical expenses reimbursed by the church represent taxable income and must be included on his Form W-2 and Form 1040 (as wages). However, the health insurance premiums paid by the church are not taxable to Pastor G.

EXAMPLE 7. Pastor E is injured in an automobile accident. The accident was caused by another driver. Pastor E accepts a settlement offer of $50,000 from the other driver's insurance carrier. The lump-sum distribution of $50,000 is not reportable as income by Pastor E. The reason for this rule is that the settlement merely compensated Pastor E for his injuries and did not provide him with any additional gain or benefits.

3. SEVERANCE PAY

Section 104 of the tax code excludes from taxable income "the amount of any damages received (whether by suit or agreement and whether as lump sums or as periodic payments) *on account of*

personal injuries or sickness" (emphasis added). As a result, severance pay that is intended to settle personal injury claims may be nontaxable. The tax treatment of severance pay arrangements is addressed in Chapter 4, section B.17. The term "personal injuries or sickness" excludes emotional distress.

F. CAFETERIA PLANS AND FLEX PLANS

1. CAFETERIA PLANS

A cafeteria plan, including a flexible spending arrangement, is a written plan that allows employees to choose between receiving cash or taxable benefits instead of certain "qualified benefits" (defined below) for which the law provides an exclusion from wages. If an employee chooses to receive a qualified benefit under the plan, the fact that the employee could have received cash or a taxable benefit instead will not make the qualified benefit taxable.

It is a basic rule of tax law that employees who are given the choice of receiving a tax-free fringe benefit or cash must report the value of the fringe benefit as taxable income (assuming they choose the fringe benefit) because they had the right to receive a taxable benefit (cash). For example, the cost of employer-provided health insurance ordinarily is a tax-free fringe benefit to employees. However, employees cannot exclude the cost of this benefit from their taxable income if they had the right (whether it was exercised or not) to receive cash instead of having their employer pay their health insurance premiums.

A cafeteria plan avoids this tax rule and permits employees to receive certain tax-free fringe benefits from their employer even though they had the right to receive cash instead. However, note that a cafeteria plan must present employees with a choice between cash and one or more specified nontaxable fringe benefits.

Employer contributions to a cafeteria plan are not taxable, even if they are funded through salary reductions. This makes such plans very attractive to employees. The term "cafeteria" refers to the choice employees have under such plans and not to an eating facility (as is commonly supposed).

✿ **KEY POINT.** The requirements for establishing and maintaining a cafeteria plan are complex. Churches interested in establishing such a plan should consult with a tax attorney or CPA.

Generally, a cafeteria plan does not include any plan that offers a benefit that defers pay.

Qualified benefits

Qualified benefits include the following:

- accident and health benefits (but not medical savings accounts or long-term care insurance),
- health savings accounts,
- adoption assistance,
- dependent care assistance, and
- group term life insurance coverage (including costs that cannot be excluded from wages).

The only taxable benefit a cafeteria plan may offer is cash. That is, employees can be given the option of choosing among any of the qualified benefits listed above or cash.

❈ **KEY POINT.** Employer contributions to the cafeteria plan are usually made pursuant to salary reduction agreements between the employer and the employee in which the employee agrees to contribute a portion of his or her salary on a pre-tax basis to pay for the qualified benefits. Salary reduction contributions are not actually or constructively received by the participant. Therefore, those contributions are not considered wages for federal income tax purposes. In addition, those sums generally are not subject to FICA. A salary reduction agreement is sufficient to satisfy the cash requirement of a cafeteria plan. Thus, a cafeteria plan need only offer a choice between one qualified benefit and salary reduction.

Benefits not allowed

A cafeteria plan cannot include the following benefits:

- Archer medical savings accounts,
- after 2013, a qualified health plan offered through an American Health Benefit Exchange,
- athletic facilities,
- de minimis (minimal) benefits,
- educational assistance,
- employee discounts,
- lodging on the business premises,
- meals,
- moving-expense reimbursements,
- no-additional-cost services,
- scholarships,
- transportation (commuting) benefits,
- tuition reduction, or
- working condition benefits.

Simple cafeteria plans

After December 31, 2010, eligible employers meeting contribution requirements and eligibility and participation requirements can establish a simple cafeteria plan. Simple cafeteria plans are treated as meeting the nondiscrimination requirements of a cafeteria plan and certain benefits under a cafeteria plan.

Eligible employer

You are an eligible employer if you employ an average of 100 or fewer employees during either of the two preceding years. If you establish a simple cafeteria plan in a year that you employ an average of 100 or fewer employees, you are considered an eligible employer for any subsequent year as long as you do not employ an average of 200 or more employees in a subsequent year.

Eligibility and participation requirements

These requirements are met if all employees who had at least 1,000 hours of service for the preceding plan year are eligible to participate and each employee eligible to participate in the plan may elect any benefit available under the plan. You may elect to exclude from the plan employees who (1) are under age 21 before the close of the plan year, (2) have less than one year of service with you as of any day during the plan year, (3) are covered under a collective bargaining agreement, or (4) are nonresident aliens working outside the United States whose income did not come from a U.S. source.

Contribution requirements

You must make a contribution to provide qualified benefits on behalf of each qualified employee in an amount equal to (1) a uniform percentage (not less than 2 percent) of the employee's compensation for the plan year or (2) an amount which is at least 6 percent of the employee's compensation for the plan year or twice the amount of the salary reduction contributions of each qualified employee, whichever is less.

If the contribution requirements are met using option 2 above, the rate of contribution to any salary reduction contribution of a highly compensated or key employee can not be greater than the rate of contribution to any other employee.

Written plan

A cafeteria plan must be set forth in a written agreement. The income tax regulations describe the required agreement in some detail, as follows:

> The written document embodying a cafeteria plan must contain at least the following information: (i) a specific description of each of the benefits available under the plan, including the periods during which the benefits are provided (i.e., the periods of coverage), (ii) the plan's eligibility rules governing participation, (iii) the procedures governing participants' elections under the plan, including the period during which elections may be made, the extent to which elections are irrevocable, and the periods with respect to which elections are effective, (iv) the manner in which employer contributions may be made under the plan, such as by salary reduction agreement between the participant and the employer or by nonelective employer contributions to the plan, (v) the maximum amount of employer contributions available to any participant under the plan, and (vi) the plan year on which the

cafeteria plan operates. Proposed Treas. Reg. 1.125-1 (question and answers, answer A-3).

Employees

Only employees may participate in a cafeteria plan. See Chapter 2 for a definition of "employee."

Discrimination in favor of highly compensated or key employees

If a cafeteria plan discriminates in favor of "highly compensated employees," then such employees lose the benefit of the exclusion and are taxed on the value of the benefits received. Further, the exclusion is denied to "key employees" if the qualified benefits provided to such employees exceed 25 percent of total nontaxable benefits provided to all employees under the plan. Special nondiscrimination rules apply to cafeteria plans that provide health benefits. *IRC 125(b)(2).* See section I of this chapter for definitions of "highly compensated employee" and "key employee."

Election requirements

For participants to avoid constructive receipt of taxable benefits, the plan must offer an election and participants must elect the amounts and types of benefits to be received prior to the beginning of the plan year. If salary reduction is permitted to pay for the benefits chosen, the salary reduction amount must be elected prior to the beginning of the plan year.

Generally, the plan may not permit participants to elect their benefit coverage, benefit reimbursement, or salary reduction for less than 12 months. However, this does not prohibit new employees from electing benefits for a part of the cafeteria-plan year.

Revocation of elections

After a participant has elected and begun to receive benefits under the plan, the plan may not allow the participant to revoke the benefit election during the period of coverage unless the revocation is due to one of the following events.

❃**KEY POINT.** The rules for revoking a coverage election also apply to group term life insurance, group health plans, dependent care assistance, and adoption assistance.

Health Insurance Portability and Accountability Act of 1996 (HIPAA) special enrollment rights

The Health Insurance Portability and Accountability Act of 1996 (HIPAA) requires group health plans to permit individuals to be enrolled for coverage following the loss of other health coverage or if a person becomes the spouse or dependent of an employee through birth, marriage, adoption, or placement for adoption. If a participant has a right to enroll in an employer's group health plan or to add coverage for a family member under HIPAA, the participant can revoke an existing election and make a new election under the cafeteria plan that conforms to the special enrollment right.

Changes in status

Under the change in status rules, a plan may permit participants to revoke an election and make a new election with respect to accident and health coverage, dependent care expenses, group term life insurance, or adoption assistance if a change in status occurs and the election change is "consistent" with the change in status. Change in status events are

- changes in legal marital status;
- changes in number of dependents;
- changes in employment status;
- cases where the dependent satisfies or ceases to satisfy the requirements for eligibility;
- changes in residence; and
- for purposes of adoption assistance, the commencement or termination of an adoption proceeding.

An election change is "consistent" if it is "on account of" and "corresponds with" a change in status event that affects eligibility for coverage. In the case of accident or health coverage (such as a health FSA), if a change in status results in an increase or decrease in the number of an employee's family members or dependents who may benefit from coverage under the plan, the eligibility requirement is satisfied. Election changes must be on a prospective basis only.

EXAMPLE. B is a church employer who has one child, C. The church maintains a calendar-year cafeteria plan that allows employees to elect coverage under a dependent care FSA. Prior to the beginning of 2013, B elects salary reduction contributions of $2,000 during the year to fund coverage under the dependent care FSA for up to $2,000 of reimbursements for the year. During the year, C reaches the age of 13, and B wants to cancel coverage under the dependent care FSA. When C turns 13, she ceases to satisfy the definition of a qualifying individual for the dependent care exclusion. As a result, C's attainment of age 13 is a change in status that affects B's employment-related expenses. Therefore, B may make a corresponding change under the cafeteria plan to cancel coverage under the dependent care FSA.

EXAMPLE. A church sponsors a calendar-year cafeteria plan under which employees may elect either employee-only or family health coverage. Before the beginning of the year, employee G elects family coverage under the cafeteria plan. G also elects coverage under the health FSA for up to $200 of reimbursements for the year to be funded by salary reduction contributions of $200 during the year. G is married to H, who is employed by another employer that does not maintain a cafeteria plan but does maintain an accident or health plan providing its employees with employee-only coverage. During 2013 H's employer adds family coverage as an option under its health plan; H elects family coverage under this plan, and G elects to revoke his election for health coverage and elect no health coverage under the church's cafeteria plan for the remainder of the year. The addition of family coverage by H's employer constitutes a "new coverage option." As a result, the church's cafeteria plan may permit G to revoke his health coverage election if H elects family health coverage under her accident or health plan. However, the church may not permit G to change his health FSA election.

2. FLEXIBLE SPENDING ARRANGEMENTS ("FLEX PLANS")

One popular type of cafeteria plan is the flexible spending arrangement (FSA). Many employees face the prospect of escalating medical costs and diminishing health benefits provided by their employer. FSAs were designed to address this predicament. Basically, a health FSA permits employees to pay for their medical expenses with pre-tax dollars (through a salary reduction). An FSA makes it easier for employees to pay for their medical expenses by eliminating federal taxes on the amount of the salary reductions.

A health FSA allows employees to be reimbursed for medical expenses. FSAs are usually funded through voluntary salary reduction agreements with your employer. No employment or federal income taxes are deducted from your contribution. The employer may also contribute.

✿ **KEY POINT.** For the health FSA to maintain tax-qualified status, employers must comply with certain requirements that apply to cafeteria plans. For example, there are restrictions for plans that cover highly compensated employees and key employees. The plans must also comply with rules applicable to other accident and health plans. Chapters 1 and 2 of IRS Publication 15-B explain these requirements.

Benefits of an FSA

You may enjoy several benefits from having an FSA:

- Contributions made by your employer can be excluded from your gross income.
- No employment or federal income taxes are deducted from the contributions.
- Withdrawals may be tax-free if you pay qualified medical expenses.
- You can withdraw funds from the account to pay qualified medical expenses even if you have not yet placed the funds in the account.

Qualifying for an FSA

Health FSAs are employer-established benefit plans. These may be offered in conjunction with other benefits as part of a cafeteria plan. Employers have complete flexibility to offer various combinations of benefits in designing their plan. You do not have to be covered under any other health care plan to participate.

Self-employed persons are not eligible for an FSA.

▲ **CAUTION.** *Certain limitations may apply if you are a highly compensated participant or a key employee.*

Contributions to an FSA

You contribute to your FSA by electing an amount to be voluntarily withheld from your pay by your employer. This is sometimes called a salary reduction agreement. The employer may also contribute to your FSA if specified in the plan. You do not pay federal income tax or employment taxes on the salary you contribute or the amounts your employer contributes to the FSA. However, contributions made by your employer to provide coverage for long-term care insurance must be included in income.

When to contribute

At the beginning of the plan year, you must designate how much you want to contribute. Your employer will deduct amounts periodically (generally, every payday) in accordance with your annual election. You can change or revoke your election only if there is a change in your employment or family status that is specified by the plan.

Amount of contribution

For tax years beginning after 2012, your contribution to your flexible spending arrangement made through a salary reduction is limited to $2,500. Beginning in tax years after 2013, the limit will be subject to a cost-of-living adjustment.

Changes made by the Affordable Care Act (2010)

The health reform legislation enacted by Congress in 2010 made the following change in health FSAs effective for tax years beginning after 2012. In order for a health FSA to be a qualified benefit under a cafeteria plan, the maximum amount available for reimbursement of incurred medical expenses of an employee, the employee's dependents, and any other eligible beneficiaries with respect to the employee, under the health FSA for a plan year (or other 12-month coverage period) must not exceed $2,500. The $2,500 limitation is indexed to the CPI-U (consumer price index—urban areas), with any increase that is not a multiple of $50 rounded to the next lowest multiple of $50 for years beginning after December 31, 2012.

▲ **CAUTION.** *A cafeteria plan that does not include this limitation on the maximum amount available for reimbursement under any FSA is not a cafeteria plan within the meaning of section 125 of the tax code. As a result, when an employee is given the option under a cafeteria plan maintained by an employer to reduce his or her current cash compensation and instead have the amount of the salary reduction be made available for use in reimbursing the employee for his or her medical expenses under a health FSA, the amount of the reduction in cash compensation pursuant to a salary reduction election must be limited to $2,500 for a plan year.*

The IRS has announced that plans may adopt the required amendments to reflect the $2,500 limit at any time through the end of calendar year 2014. IRS Notice 2012-40.

EXAMPLE. A church has 10 employees, and several years ago it implemented a health FSA plan to assist employees with their medical expenses. Beginning in 2013, in order for a health FSA to be a qualified benefit under a cafeteria plan, the maximum amount available for reimbursement of incurred medical expenses under the Health FSA for a plan year must not exceed $2,500. A cafeteria plan that does not include this limitation is not a cafeteria plan within the meaning of section 125 of the tax code.

EXAMPLE. A church does not provide health insurance for its employees but has established a health flexible saving account (health FSA). There is no limit on the amount of money that can be contributed to a Health FSA by an employee, but the plan must prescribe a maximum dollar amount. The church's FSA allows employees to contribute up to $5,000 annually. The entire balance in a health FSA must be used for qualifying medical expenses by the end of the year ("use it or lose it"). For 2012, Pastor Ted elected to have his salary reduced by $4,000 to fund his FSA. Pastor Ted is not required to pay income taxes or self-employment taxes on the $4,000 salary reduction. However, if he incurs less than $4,000 in medical expenses, any balance in the account at the end of the year is forfeited (subject to a grace period that runs until March 15 of the following year if certain conditions apply). Withdrawals from a health FSA are tax-free to an employee only if used for qualifying medical expenses (i.e., expenses that would qualify for the medical and dental expenses itemized deduction). However, even though nonprescription medicines (other than insulin) do not qualify for the medical and dental expenses deduction, they do qualify as expenses for FSA purposes.

EXAMPLE. Same facts as the previous example, except that the year is 2013. The most that Pastor Ted can contribute to his health FSA is $2,500. If the church fails to impose this cap on its FSA plan, the plan loses tax benefits that would otherwise apply. This means that the entire amount that Pastor Ted contributes to his FSA is taxable.

✿ **KEY POINT.** The Affordable Care Act (2010) conforms the definition of "qualified medical expenses" for FSAs, HSAs, and HRAs to the definition used for the medical expense itemized deduction. Over-the-counter medicine obtained with a prescription continues to qualify as a qualified medical expense, but nonprescription over-the-counter medications no longer qualify (except for insulin).

The IRS has announced:

- The $2,500 limit does not apply for plan years that begin before 2013.

- Plans may adopt the required amendments to reflect the $2,500 limit at any time through the end of calendar year 2014.
- In the case of a plan providing a grace period (which may be up to two months and 15 days), unused salary reduction contributions to the health FSA for plan years beginning in 2012 or later that are carried over into the grace period for that plan year will not count against the $2,500 limit for the subsequent plan year.
- Relief is provided for certain salary reduction contributions exceeding the $2,500 limit that are due to a reasonable mistake and not willful neglect and that are corrected by the employer.

✿ **KEY POINT.** The IRS has clarified that the $2,500 limit applies only to salary reduction contributions under a health FSA and does not apply to certain employer nonelective contributions (sometimes called flex credits); to any types of contributions or amounts available for reimbursement under other types of FSAs, health savings accounts, or health reimbursement arrangements; or to salary reduction contributions to cafeteria plans that are used to pay an employee's share of health coverage premiums (or the corresponding employee share under a self-insured employer-sponsored health plan). *IRS Notice 2012-40.*

Balance remaining at year-end

✿ **KEY POINT.** The IRS has amended the "use it or lose it" rule for FSAs.

The law specifies that any salary reductions not used to pay for medical expenses by December 31 are forfeited. This rule is often referred to as the "use it or lose it" rule. In 2005 the IRS amended this rule. In a published notice it stated:

A cafeteria plan document may, at the employer's option, be amended to provide for a grace period immediately following the end of each plan year. The grace period must apply to all participants in the cafeteria plan. Expenses for qualified benefits incurred during the grace period may be paid or reimbursed from benefits or contributions remaining unused at the end of the immediately preceding plan year. The grace period must not extend beyond the fifteenth day of the third calendar month after the end of the immediately preceding plan year to which it relates (i.e., "the 2 and 1/2 month rule"). If a cafeteria plan document is amended to include a grace period, a participant who has unused benefits or contributions relating to a particular qualified benefit from the immediately preceding plan year, and who incurs expenses for that same qualified benefit during the grace period, may be paid or reimbursed for those expenses from the unused benefits or contributions as if the expenses had been incurred in the immediately preceding plan year. The effect of the grace period is that the participant may have as long as 14 months and 15 days (the 12 months in the current cafeteria plan year plus the

---

grace period) to use the benefits or contributions for a plan year before those amounts are "forfeited" under the "use-it-or-lose-it" rule. IRS Notice 2005-42.

The IRS cautioned that during the grace period a cafeteria plan may not permit unused contributions to be cashed out or converted to any other taxable or nontaxable benefit. Unused benefits or contributions relating to a particular qualified benefit may only be used to pay or reimburse expenses incurred with respect to that particular qualified benefit. For example, unused amounts elected to pay or reimburse medical expenses in a health flexible spending arrangement (FSA) may not be used to pay or reimburse dependent care or other expenses incurred during the grace period.

The following examples illustrate this rule.

EXAMPLE. An employer with a flex-plan year ending on December 31, 2012, amended the plan document before the end of the plan year to permit a grace period that allows all employees to apply unused contributions remaining at the end of the plan year to medical expenses incurred during the grace period immediately following that plan year. The grace period adopted by the employer ends on the 15th day of the third calendar month after the end of the plan year (March 15, 2013, for the plan year ending December 31, 2012). Employee X timely elected salary reduction of $1,000 for a health FSA for the plan year ending December 31, 2012. As of December 31, 2012, X has $200 remaining unused in his health FSA. X timely elected salary reduction for a health FSA of $1,500 for the plan year ending December 31, 2013. During the race period from January 1 through March 15, 2013, X incurs $300 of unreimbursed medical expenses. The unused $200 from the plan year ending December 31, 2012, is applied to pay or reimburse $200 of X's $300 of medical expenses incurred during the grace period. Therefore, as of March 16, 2013, X has no unused benefits or contributions remaining for the plan year ending December 31, 2012. The remaining $100 of medical expenses incurred between January 1 and March 15, 2013, is paid or reimbursed from X's health FSA for the plan year ending December 31, 2013. As of March 16, 2013, X has $1,400 remaining in the health FSA for the plan year ending December 31, 2013.

EXAMPLE. Same facts as the previous example, except that X incurs $150 of medical expenses during the grace period (January 1 through March 15, 2013). As of March 16, 2013, X has $50 of unused benefits or contributions remaining for the plan year ending December 31, 2012. The unused $50 cannot be cashed out, converted to any other taxable or nontaxable benefit, or used in any other plan year (including the plan year ending December 31, 2013). The unused $50 is subject to the "use it or lose it" rule and is forfeited. As of March 16, 2013, X has the entire $1,500 elected in the health FSA for the plan year ending December 31, 2013.

Distributions from an FSA

Distributions from a health FSA must be paid only to reimburse you for qualified medical expenses you incurred during the period of coverage. You must be able to receive the maximum amount of reimbursement (the amount you have elected to contribute for the year) at any time during the coverage period, regardless of the amount you have actually contributed. The maximum amount you can receive tax-free is the total amount you elected to contribute to the health FSA for the year.

You must provide the health FSA with a written statement from an independent third party stating that the medical expense has been incurred and the amount of the expense. You must also provide a written statement that the expense has not been paid or reimbursed under any other health plan coverage. The FSA cannot make advance reimbursements of future or projected expenses.

❋**KEY POINT.** Debit cards, credit cards, and stored value cards given to you by your employer can be used to reimburse participants in a health FSA. If the use of these cards meets certain substantiation methods, you may not have to provide additional information to the health FSA.

Qualified medical expenses

Qualified medical expenses are those specified in the plan that would generally qualify for the medical and dental expenses deduction. These are explained in IRS Publication 502 (Medical and Dental Expenses). Examples include amounts paid for doctors' fees, prescription medicines, and necessary hospital services not paid for by insurance. You cannot receive distributions from your FSA for the following expenses:

- amounts paid for health insurance premiums,
- amounts paid for long-term care coverage or expenses, or
- amounts covered under another health plan.

❋**KEY POINT.** Nonprescription medicines (other than insulin) are not considered qualified medical expenses.

Employer participation

For the health FSA to maintain tax-qualified status, employers must comply with certain requirements that apply to cafeteria plans. For example, restrictions exist for plans that cover highly compensated employees and key employees. The plans must also comply with rules applicable to other accident and health plans (see above).

❋**KEY POINT.** The federal Department of Health and Human Services (HHS) has ruled that the HIPAA privacy rules apply to cafeteria plans and flex plans.

Employer reimbursements of medical expenses under an FSA can be made with an employer-issued credit, debit, or stored-value cards.

However, procedures must be in place to ensure that only allowable medical expenses are charged to the card.

✿ **KEY POINT.** You cannot deduct qualified medical expenses as an itemized deduction on Schedule A (Form 1040) that are equal to the distribution you receive from your FSA.

3. PRIVACY RULES

Does your church have a cafeteria plan or flex plan that allows employees to pay for medical expenses with pre-tax dollars through salary reductions? If so, you may be subject to privacy rules. Here is what church leaders should know:

- The Health Insurance Portability and Accountability Act of 1996 (HIPAA) required the federal Department of Health and Human Services (HHS) to publish rules for the electronic exchange, privacy, and security of health information. HHS published the final version of its "Privacy Rule" in 2002, and it took effect in 2003.
- The Privacy Rule applies to health plans and health care providers ("covered entities") that transmit health information in electronic form.
- Covered entities include employer-sponsored group health plans and church-sponsored health plans. An exception is available for a group health plan with less than 50 participants that is administered solely by the employer (and not a third-party administrator).
- In 2003 HHS ruled that cafeteria plans and flexible spending arrangements are covered entities for purposes of the Privacy Rule if they meet the definition of an "employee welfare benefit plan" under ERISA (a federal pension regulation law). This is a broad definition that will apply to most cafeteria plans and flexible spending arrangements established by churches. Again, an exception is made for plans with less than 50 participants that are administered solely by the employer.
- If your church meets the definition of a covered entity and operates a cafeteria plan or flex plan, you are required to comply with the various privacy protections spelled out in HIPAA's Privacy Rule. These protections are complex, so you should consult with an attorney for assistance. Basically, they limit the ways you can use your employees' personal medical information. Key provisions of these new standards include (1) employee access to medical records; (2) employer notification of employees of their privacy rights under the new law; (3) a prohibition of using employee medical information for any purpose other than health care; (4) requirement of written employee consent before an employer can release medical information to a life insurer, bank, marketing firm, or other outside business for purposes not related to the employee's health care; (5) requirement that written privacy policies and procedures be adopted by employers; and (6) special privacy

training for employees who will have access to medical information.
- Civil and criminal penalties exist for covered entities that misuse personal health information or violate the privacy requirements.

⟳ **RESOURCE.** More information about the application of HIPAA to churches is contained in Richard Hammar's special report, *Are Prayer Lists Illegal?* published by CHURCH LAW & TAX REPORT.

4. THE AFFORDABLE CARE ACT (2010)

The health care reform legislation (the Affordable Care Act) enacted by Congress in 2010 contains a number of provisions that affect cafeteria plans and flexible spending arrangements. Some provisions take effect immediately, while others take effect in a future year. See Section D.5 in this chapter for details.

G. OTHER HEALTH PLANS

There are a number of other tax-advantaged ways to provide medical benefits. These are summarized in Table 5-2. See IRS Publication 969 (Health Savings Accounts and Other Tax-Favored Health Plans) for additional information on several of these plans.

H. GROUP TERM LIFE INSURANCE

✿ **KEY POINT.** Employees may exclude the cost of employer-provided group term life insurance so long as the amount of coverage does not exceed $50,000.

This exclusion applies to life insurance coverage that meets all the following conditions:

- It provides a general death benefit that is not included in income.
- You provide it to a group of employees. See the "10-employee rule" later in this text.
- It provides an amount of insurance to each employee based on a formula that prevents individual selection. This formula must use factors such as the employee's age, years of service, pay, or position.

TABLE 5-2

COMPARISON OF TAX BENEFITS FOR HEALTH EXPENSES

(Based on a Report Prepared by the Joint Congressional Committee on Taxation)

PROVISION	TAX BENEFIT	CLASS ELIGIBLE	MAXIMUM DOLLAR LIMIT ON TAX BENEFIT	QUALIFIED EXPENSES
1. EMPLOYER CONTRIBUTIONS TO AN ACCIDENT OR HEALTH PLAN (IRC 106)	Exclusion from taxable income	Employees (including former employees)	No limit on amount excludable	Contributions to health plan for the taxpayer, spouse, and dependents
2. EMPLOYER RE-IMBURSEMENT OF MEDICAL EXPENSES (IRC 105)	Exclusion from taxable income	Employees (including former employees)	No limit on amount excludable	Medical-care expenses of the taxpayer, spouse, and dependents that would qualify for deduction as an itemized deduction on Schedule A, Form 1040, and certain nonprescription medications (e.g., antacid, allergy medicine, pain reliever, and cold medicine)
3. CAFETERIA PLANS (IRC 125)	Exclusion from taxable income (for salary reduction contributions)	Employees	No limit on amount excludable	Coverage under an accident or health plan (IRC 105,106)
4. HEALTH REIM-BURSEMENT ARRANGEMENTS (IRC 105, 106)	Employer-maintained arrangement providing exclusion from taxable income for amounts used to reimburse employees for medical expenses. Amounts remaining at the end of the year can be carried forward to reimburse medical expenses in later years. There is no tax-free accumulation of earnings	Employees (including former employees)	No limit on amount excludable. After 2012, contributions to a flexible spending arrangement made through a salary reduction are limited to $2,500. After 2013, the limit will be subject to an annual cost-of-living adjustment.	Medical-care expenses of the taxpayer, spouse, and dependents (that would qualify for deduction as an itemized deduction on Schedule A, Form 1040)
5. HEALTH FLEXIBLE SPENDING ARRANGEMENTS (FSAs) (IRC 105, 106, 125)	Employee salary-reduction arrangement providing exclusion from taxable income for amounts used to reimburse employees for medical expenses	Employees	No limit on amount excludable (limit of $2,500 annually after 2012)	Medical-care expenses of the taxpayer, spouse, and dependents (that would qualify for deduction as an itemized deduction on Schedule A, Form 1040), but not including insurance premium payments for other health coverage

(Continued on page 228)

TABLE 5-2

COMPARISON OF TAX BENEFITS FOR HEALTH EXPENSES
(continued)

PROVISION	TAX BENEFIT	CLASS ELIGIBLE	MAXIMUM DOLLAR LIMIT ON TAX BENEFIT	QUALIFIED EXPENSES
6. HEALTH SAVINGS ACCOUNTS	Employee contributions in cash or through a cafeteria plan are deductible; employer contributions are excludable. Amounts can be carried over from year to year. Distributions for qualified medical expenses are nontaxable	Persons with high deductible health plan (HDHP). For self-only plans, deductible amount at least $1,250 with out-of-pocket maximum not more than $6,250 (2013 amounts). For family plans, deductible amount at least $2,500 with out-of-pocket maximum not more than $12,500 (2013 amounts)	For 2013 the maximum annual HSA contribution for an eligible individual with self-only coverage is $3,250. For family coverage, the maximum annual HSA contribution is $6,450. Catch-up contribution for individuals who are 55 or older is $1,000	Medical-care expenses of the taxpayer, spouse, and dependents (that would qualify for deduction as an itemized deduction on Schedule A, Form 1040)
7. DEDUCTION FOR HEALTH INSURANCE EXPENSES OF SELF-EMPLOYED PERSONS (IRC 162(L))	Income tax deduction for cost of health insurance expenses of self-employed persons. Deduction does not apply to self-employment taxes	Self-employed persons	No specific dollar limit; deduction limited by amount of taxpayer's earned income from the trade or business	Insurance that constitutes medical care for the taxpayer, spouse, and dependents
8. ITEMIZED DEDUCTION FOR MEDICAL EXPENSES (IRC 213)	Itemized deduction for unreimbursed medical expenses to extent expenses exceed 7.5% of adjusted gross income (10% for alternative minimum tax purposes, and 10% after 2012)	Any individual who itemizes deductions and had unreimbursed medical expenses in excess of 7.5% of adjusted gross income (10% after 2012)	No maximum limit	Expenses for medical care (as defined under section 213) of the taxpayer, spouse, and dependents. Medicine or drugs must be prescribed

- You provide it under a policy you directly or indirectly carry. Even if you do not pay any of the policy's cost, you are considered to carry it if you arrange for payment of its cost by your employees and charge at least one employee less than, and at least one other employee more than, the cost of his or her insurance.

Group term life insurance does not include the following insurance:

- insurance that does not provide general death benefits, such as travel insurance or a policy providing only accidental death benefits.
- life insurance on the life of your employee's spouse or dependent. However, you may be able to exclude the cost of this insurance from the employee's wages as a de minimis benefit.

- insurance provided under a policy that provides a permanent benefit (an economic value that extends beyond one policy year, such as paid-up or cash surrender value), unless certain requirements are met.

Employee
For this exclusion, treat the following individuals as employees:

(1) a current common-law employee.
(2) an individual who was formerly your employee under (1) above.
(3) a leased employee who has provided services to you on a substantially full-time basis for at least a year if the services are performed under your primary direction and control.

The 10-Employee Rule

Generally, life insurance is not group term life insurance unless you provide it to at least 10 full-time employees at some time during the year. For this rule, count employees who choose not to receive the insurance unless, to receive it, they must contribute to the cost of benefits other than the group term life insurance. For example, count an employee who could receive insurance by paying part of the cost, even if that employee chooses not to receive it. However, do not count an employee who must pay part or all of the cost of permanent benefits to get insurance, unless that employee chooses to receive it. A permanent benefit is an economic value extending beyond one policy year (for example, a paid-up or cash-surrender value) that is provided under a life insurance policy.

Even if you do not meet the 10-employee rule, two exceptions allow you to treat insurance as group term life insurance. Under the first exception, you do not have to meet the 10-employee rule if all the following conditions are met:

(1) If evidence that the employee is insurable is required, it is limited to a medical questionnaire (completed by the employee) that does not require a physical.
(2) You provide the insurance to all your full-time employees or, if the insurer requires the evidence mentioned in (1), to all full-time employees who provide evidence the insurer accepts.
(3) You figure the coverage based on either a uniform percentage of pay or the insurer's coverage brackets that meet certain requirements.

The second exception generally will not apply to churches.

Do not consider employees who were denied insurance for any of the following reasons:

- They were 65 or older.
- They customarily work 20 hours or less a week or five months or less in a calendar year.
- They have not been employed for the waiting period given in the policy. This waiting period cannot be more than six months.

1. KEY EMPLOYEES

The exclusion of the cost of up to $50,000 of group term life insurance paid for by an employer is not available to "key employees" if the plan discriminates in their favor. For 2013 a key employee is an employee who is an officer of the employer having annual compensation greater than $165,000. *IRC 416(i).* This amount is adjusted annually for inflation in multiples of $5,000.

Section 79(d) of the tax code specifies that the nondiscrimination rules pertaining to key employees "shall not apply to a church plan

maintained for church employees." In this context a "church employee" does not include an employee of (1) "an educational organization which normally maintains a regular faculty and curriculum and normally has a regularly enrolled body of pupils or students in attendance at the place where its educational activities are regularly carried on," or (2) "an organization the principal purpose or functions of which are the providing of medical or hospital care or medical education or medical research, if the organization is a hospital."

2. GROUP TERM INSURANCE IN EXCESS OF $50,000

Exclusion from wages

You can generally exclude the cost of up to $50,000 of group term life insurance from the wages of an insured employee. You can exclude the same amount from the employee's wages when figuring Social Security and Medicare taxes. In addition, you do not have to withhold federal income tax on any group term life insurance you provide to an employee.

Coverage over the limit

You must include in your employee's wages the cost of group term life insurance beyond $50,000 worth of coverage, reduced by the amount the employee paid toward the insurance. Report it as wages in box 1 of a minister's Form W-2 and in boxes 1, 3, and 5 for nonminister employees. Also, show it in box 12 with code C. The amount is subject to Social Security and Medicare taxes, and you may, at your option, withhold federal income tax. Figure the monthly cost of the insurance to include in the employee's wages by multiplying the number of thousands of dollars of all insurance coverage over $50,000 (figured to the nearest $100) by the cost shown in the following table. For all coverage provided within the calendar year, use the employee's age on the last day of the employee's tax year. You must prorate the cost from the table if less than a full month of coverage is involved.

Compute the taxable income associated with excess coverage by referring to Table 5-3. Employers also must include the imputed cost of employer-provided group term life insurance on the life of a spouse or dependent if the coverage provided exceeds $2,000. *IRS Notice 89-110. Treas. Reg. 1.79(d)(2).* If part of the coverage for a spouse or dependents is taxable, use Table 5-3 to determine the imputed cost. The entire amount is taxable, not just the amount that exceeds $2,000.

EXAMPLE. A church pays the premiums on a $70,000 group term insurance policy on the life of Pastor B, with B's wife as beneficiary. Pastor B is 50 years old. The imputed cost of the excess coverage on Pastor B is $2.76 (23 cents x 12 months) per $1,000 of coverage. Since Pastor B had $20,000 of insurance in excess of the $50,000 exclusion amount, the church must include $55.20 in Pastor B's income ($2.76 x 20). The church

TABLE 5-3

COST PER $1,000 OF PROTECTION FOR A ONE-MONTH PERIOD

AGE	COST	AGE	COST
Under 25	5¢	50 through 54	23¢
25 through 29	6¢	55 through 59	43¢
30 through 34	8¢	60 through 64	66¢
35 through 39	9¢	65 through 69	$1.27
40 through 44	10¢	70 and above	$2.06
45 through 49	15¢		

should include this amount with wages in box 1 of Form W-2. This amount should also be reported in box 12 and labeled "C." Any includable amount is subject to income tax as well as Social Security and Medicare withholding for nonminister church employees.

EXAMPLE. Pastor Tim's church provides him with group term life insurance coverage of $200,000. Pastor Tim is 45 years old, is not a key employee, and pays $100 per year toward the cost of the insurance. The church must include $170 in his wages. The total cost of the insurance, $360 ($.15 x 200 x 12), is reduced by the cost of $50,000 of coverage, $90 ($.15 x 50 x 12), and by the $100 the pastor pays for the insurance. The church includes $170 in box 1 of the pastor's Form W-2. The church also enters $170 in box 12 with code C.

I. CERTAIN FRINGE BENEFITS

As noted in Chapter 4, a fringe benefit is any material benefit provided by an employer to an employee (or self-employed person) apart from his or her stated compensation. Certain fringe benefits are generally includable in an employee's gross income for both income tax and Social Security tax purposes. Such taxable fringe benefits are discussed in Chapter 4. Some fringe benefits are specifically excluded from income if certain requirements are satisfied. Several of these nontaxable fringe benefits are described in section 132 of the tax code.

Before summarizing these fringe benefits, it is necessary to define two important terms: "highly compensated employee" and "key employee." Many of the fringe benefits summarized below are excludable from taxable income only to the extent that the employee

is not highly compensated or a key employee. These terms, for 2013 and in the context of religious organizations, are summarized below:

- **Highly compensated employee (2013).** A highly compensated employee is an employee who (1) is a 5 percent owner of the employer at any time during the current or prior year (this definition will not apply to churches), or (2) has compensation for the previous year in excess of $115,000 and, if an employer elects, was in the top 20 percent of employees by compensation. The $115,000 amount is indexed for inflation and represents the 2013 amount (unchanged from 2012). *IRC 414(q)*.

  In applying the $115,000 test to ministers, do not include a housing allowance or the annual rental value of a parsonage. Section 414(q) of the tax code, which contains the definition of a highly compensated employee, defines the term "compensation" by referring to section 415(c)(3). The income tax regulations specify that for purposes of 415(c)(3), the term "compensation" means "the employee's wages . . . to the extent that the amounts are includible in gross income." *Treas. Reg. 1.415-2(d)(2).* Since a housing allowance is not "includible in gross income" (to the extent that it is used to pay for housing expenses and, for ministers who own their home, does not exceed the fair rental value of the home), it is not included in the definition of compensation and would not be considered in applying the $115,000 limit. The same would be true for the annual rental value of a parsonage provided to a minister.

- **Key employee (2013).** A key employee is an employee who is "an officer of the employer having annual compensation greater than $165,000." *IRC 416(i).* This amount is adjusted annually for inflation in multiples of $5,000.

1. NO-ADDITIONAL-COST SERVICE

If an employer offers an employee a service free of charge (or at a reduced price) that is the same service it offers to the public in the ordinary course of its business, and if the employer does not discriminate in favor of highly compensated employees in dispensing the service, the service is considered a no-additional-cost service and is excludable from the employee's income. In addition, the employer cannot incur substantial additional cost in providing the service to the employee. This exclusion ordinarily will not benefit ministers.

2. QUALIFIED EMPLOYEE DISCOUNTS

A qualified employee discount is a reduction in price that an employer offers employees on certain property or services it offers to the public in the ordinary course of its business. Such discounts cannot be excluded by highly compensated employees unless the same benefit is made available on substantially similar terms to lower-paid employees.

3. WORKING CONDITION FRINGE BENEFITS

Employees do not include in income the value of a working condition fringe benefit. A working condition fringe benefit is any property or service provided to you by your employer to the extent that you could have deducted the cost of the property or service as an employee business expense had you paid for it yourself. Note that this exclusion generally does not apply to self-employed ministers.

Perhaps the most common example of this exclusion for ministers is a church-provided car. If your church provides you with a car, the amount excludable as a working condition fringe benefit is the amount that would be allowable as an employee business expense deduction if you had to provide the car yourself. Your personal use of the car is a taxable noncash fringe benefit that your employer must value and include in your income for tax reporting purposes. See Chapter 4, section B.8. The employer may either include the actual value of your personal use of the car or include 100 percent of the value of the use of the car in your income (i.e., assume 100 percent personal use). If your employer elects the second alternative, you may be able to deduct the value of your business use of the car as a miscellaneous itemized deduction on Schedule A. (Use Form 2106 to compute the deduction.)

IRS regulations specify that an employer's reimbursement of a nonemployee spouse's travel expenses incurred while accompanying an employee on a business trip qualifies as a nontaxable "working condition fringe benefit" so long as the following conditions are met:

- the employer has not treated such amounts as compensation;
- the amounts would be deductible as a business expense without regard to the limitation on the deductibility of a spouse's travel expenses, meaning that the spouse's presence on the trip is for a legitimate business purpose; and
- the employee substantiates the expenses under an accountable arrangement.

The tax treatment of a spouse's travel expenses is addressed fully in Chapter 7.

Certain job-related education provided by a church to an employee may qualify for exclusion as a working condition fringe benefit. To qualify, the education must meet the same requirements that would apply for determining whether the employee could deduct the expenses had the employee paid the expenses. The education must meet at least one of the following tests:

- The education is required by the employer or by law for the employee to keep his or her present salary, status, or job. The required education must serve a bona fide business purpose of the employer.
- The education maintains or improves skills needed in the job.

However, even if the education meets one or both of the above tests, it is not qualifying education if it

- is needed to meet the minimum educational requirements of the employee's present trade or business or
- is part of a program of study that will qualify the employee for a new trade or business.

4. DE MINIMIS (MINIMAL) FRINGE BENEFITS

If your employer provides you with a fringe benefit so minimal in value that it would be unreasonable or administratively impractical to account for it, you will not have to include the value of such benefits in your income.

Excludable benefits
Examples of de minimis fringe benefits that are excludable from taxable income include

- occasional typing of personal letters (by yourself on church equipment, or on your behalf by another employee on church equipment);
- occasional personal use of the church duplicating machine;
- occasional office parties and picnics for employees and their guests;
- traditional holiday gifts of noncash property with low fair market value (such as turkeys and fruitcakes at Christmastime);
- coffee, doughnuts, and soft drinks furnished to employees;
- local telephone calls; and
- subscriptions to professional publications paid for by the employer on behalf of an employee.

Nonexcludable benefits
Examples of fringe benefits that are not excludable from taxable income as de minimis fringe benefits include the following (these items must be valued and reported as income to the employee):

- season tickets to sporting or theatrical events;
- the commuting use of a church-owned vehicle more than one day each month; and
- membership in a private country club or athletic facility. In determining whether a benefit is minimal, the frequency with which the benefit is provided must be considered. Therefore, if your employer provides you with a free lunch each day, such a benefit will not be de minimis; though the value of any one lunch would be.

EXAMPLE. In 2013 a church pays for two dinners for staff members (and their spouses) at local restaurants. This common church practice has never been challenged or questioned by the IRS, so it may be assumed that the church's payment of the cost of such customary functions constitutes a nontaxable working condition fringe benefit.

EXAMPLE. In 2013 a church pays for three dinners for members of its governing board (and their spouses) at local restaurants. This is a common church practice, and few if any churches (or any other organization) ever report the cost of such meals as taxable income to the board members. The availability of the working condition fringe benefit exclusion is not clear, since this exclusion generally applies only to employees and self-employed workers (most board members are volunteers serving without pay). It is possible that the working condition fringe benefit exclusion could apply to uncompensated board members under one of two theories: (1) board members are "uncompensated workers," or (2) board members become "self-employed" workers by virtue of the "in kind" compensation (occasional meals) provided to them by the church, and this qualifies them for treating the meals as a working condition fringe benefit.

✱ **New in 2013.** A transit pass (including tokens and fare cards) provided to an employee during 2013 at a discount not exceeding $125 per month can be excluded as a de minimis fringe benefit. Employees can also exclude from income the value of employer-provided parking of up to $240 per month for 2013.

Discounted meals

Some employers provide meals to employees at less than fair market value (i.e., the employer subsidizes the cost of meals). Under a special de minimis fringe rule, if your employer operates a cafeteria or other eating facility on or near the business premises for employees, you will not have to include in income the excess of the value of the meals over the fees charged to you. To qualify for this rule, (1) the revenue received by the employer must generally equal or exceed its operating cost; (2) the employer must own or lease the facility; (3) substantially all of the use of the facility must be by employees; (4) meals must be provided during or immediately before or after the workday; and (5) access to the facility must not be primarily for the benefit of officers, directors, or highly compensated employees.

Athletic facilities

Some churches operate athletic facilities (such as a gym or pool) on church property and make these facilities available to employees. You do not have to include in income the value of such a fringe benefit if substantially all of the use of the facility is by employees and their spouses and dependent children.

Holiday gifts to employees

Many churches provide employees and volunteers with gifts at Christmas. Common examples include hams, turkeys, fruit baskets,

small amounts of cash, or gift certificates. Church treasurers may assume that these gifts are so small that they need not be reported as taxable income. An IRS ruling suggests that this assumption is incorrect. *IRS Letter Ruling 200437030 (2004).*

▲ **CAUTION.** *A high-level IRS official has warned that the whole issue of de minimis fringe benefits is being scrutinized more closely and that employers should not assume that all relatively low-cost dinners and gifts provided to employees are tax-free. The official noted that gift certificates that can be exchanged for merchandise will not be considered de minimis if the cost of the merchandise is less than the value of the certificate and the employee receives the difference in cash. The official also cautioned against using any threshold amount (such as $25 or $75) to define "de minimis." The official noted that a de minimis gift is one that has a value that is so small that it would be unreasonable or administratively impractical to account for it. If the value of the gift is ascertainable, it is not a de minimis fringe benefit, regardless of the value.*

A charity annually provided employees with a ham, turkey, or gift basket as a holiday gift. Over the years, several employees complained about the gifts because of religious or dietary restrictions and requested a gift coupon of comparable value. In response, the charity began providing employees with a gift coupon having a face value of $35 instead of a ham, turkey, or gift basket. The coupons list food stores where the coupon is redeemable. The charity did not withhold or pay any employment taxes for any portion of the $35 gift coupons provided to employees.

The IRS ruled that these coupons represented taxable income that should have been added to the employees' Forms W-2. It rejected the charity's argument that the coupons were a de minimis fringe benefit (i.e., so low in value that they could be ignored for tax purposes).

The IRS conceded that taxable income does not include any fringe benefit that qualifies as a de minimis fringe benefit. Section 132(e)(1) of the tax code defines a de minimis fringe benefit as "any property or service the value of which is (after taking into account the frequency with which similar fringes are provided by the employer to the employer's employees) so small as to make accounting for it unreasonable or administratively impracticable."

The IRS concluded that cash can never be a de minimis fringe benefit, since it is not "unreasonable or administratively impracticable" to account for its value. The same conclusion applies to cash equivalents, such as gift coupons, even though the property acquired with the coupon would be a nontaxable de minimis fringe benefit had it been provided by the employer.

The IRS noted:

When an employee attends a staff meeting where two pots of coffee and a box of donuts are provided by the employer, the value of the benefit the employee receives is not certain or easily *ascertained. Further, the administrative costs associated with determining the value of the benefit and accounting for it may be more expensive than providing the benefit. In this case, there is no difficulty in determining the value or accounting for it; each employee that received a gift coupon received a cash equivalent fringe benefit worth $35.*

In support of its conclusion, the IRS cited the following considerations:

- The definition of de minimis fringe benefits in section 132 refers only to "property or services" and not to cash.
- The income tax regulations provide several examples of de minimis fringe benefits, and none involves cash. Rather, they include "occasional typing of personal letters by a company secretary; occasional personal use of an employer's copying machine; group meals, or picnics for employees and their guests; traditional birthday or holiday gifts of property (not cash) with a low fair market value; occasional theater or sporting event tickets; coffee, donuts, and soft drinks; local telephone calls; and flowers, fruit, books, or similar property provided to employees under special circumstances (e.g., on account of illness, outstanding performance, or family crisis)." Similarly, a congressional committee report provides illustrations of benefits that are excludable as de minimis fringe benefits, such as "traditional gifts on holidays of tangible personal property having a low fair market value (e.g., a turkey given for the year-end holidays)."
- "It is not administratively impracticable to account for even a small amount of cash provided to an employee because the value of the amount provided is readily apparent and certain. Accordingly . . . accounting for cash or cash equivalent fringe benefits such as gift certificates is never considered administratively impracticable under section 132."

The IRS concluded:

It is our view that the employer-provided gift coupon operates in essentially the same way as a cash equivalent fringe benefit such as a gift certificate. As with a gift certificate, it is simply not administratively impracticable to account for the employer provided gift coupons; they have a face value of $35. Accordingly, we conclude that an employer-provided holiday gift coupon with a face value of $35 that is redeemable at several local grocery stores is not excludable from gross income as a de minimis fringe benefit.

The IRS acknowledged that some courts have ruled that gift certificates of small amounts may be nontaxable fringe benefits, but it noted that all of these cases were decided many years ago, prior to the enactment of section 132, so they are no longer relevant.

✤ **KEY POINT.** The IRS based its ruling on the fact that gift coupons and certificates are cash equivalents. It should be noted that coupons and certificates are unlike cash in some fundamental ways. For example, they generally cannot be used everywhere; they often have expiration dates; in some cases they may be used only by the person to whom they are issued; and in some cases they may be used only once (with any unused balance being forfeited). The IRS did not address any of these dissimilarities.

✤ **KEY POINT.** The IRS rejected the charity's suggestion that any holiday gift with a value of less than $75 should be considered a nontaxable de minimis fringe benefit.

The following examples will illustrate the application of the IRS ruling to common church practices.

EXAMPLE. A church provides its nonpastoral employees with a turkey at Christmas. This is a nontaxable de minimis fringe benefit, so the value of the turkey need not be reported on the employees' Forms W-2. The income tax regulations provide several examples of de minimis fringe benefits, including "traditional birthday or holiday gifts of property (not cash) with a low fair market value."

EXAMPLE. A church provides its senior pastor with a $250 check as a Christmas gift. This is not a de minimis fringe benefit, and the entire value must be reported on the pastor's Form W-2.

EXAMPLE. A church provides employees with a $50 gift certificate redeemable at a local restaurant as a holiday gift. The certificate is a cash equivalent the value of which is readily ascertainable. It is not a nontaxable de minimis fringe benefit, despite the token amount, so it must be reported as taxable compensation.

EXAMPLE. A church provides employees with a $25 gift certificate redeemable at a local doughnut store. The certificate is a cash equivalent the value of which is readily ascertainable. It must be reported as additional income on employees' Forms W-2. It is not a nontaxable de minimis fringe benefit, despite the token amount, so it must be reported as taxable compensation.

EXAMPLE. A church provides employees with a Christmas card containing a $25 check. The value of the check must be reported as additional income on employees' Forms W-2. It is not a nontaxable de minimis fringe benefit, despite the token amount, so it must be reported as taxable compensation. The fact that the amount of a check is $25 is irrelevant. No cash gift provided to an employee, regardless of how small the amount, can be treated as a nontaxable de minimis fringe benefit.

EXAMPLE. A church treats its staff to a holiday dinner at a local restaurant. The value of each dinner averages $20. The value of the meals is a nontaxable de minimis fringe benefit. The income tax regulations provide several examples of de minimis fringe benefits, including "group meals or picnics for employees and their guests" and "traditional birthday or holiday gifts of property (not cash) with a low fair market value."

EXAMPLE. At the end of each year, a church provides volunteers who work in the church nursery or in children's ministries with a $25 gift certificate to a local restaurant in recognition of their selfless services. The IRS ruling addressed in this section suggests that the value of these certificates represents taxable income to the volunteers. However, since they are not employees, the church is not required to report the amount of the certificates on a Form W-2. No Form 1099-MISC is required either, assuming that the volunteers do not receive compensation of $600 or more during the year. It will be up to the volunteers to decide how to handle the certificates for tax purposes.

✿**KEY POINT.** Churches can avoid having the value of holiday gifts constitute taxable compensation by providing both employees and volunteers with noncash items of nominal amounts rather than cash or cash equivalents. Such items include turkeys, hams, gift baskets, and candy.

5. QUALIFIED TUITION REDUCTIONS

Many churches operate schools and offer tuition discounts to employees of both the school and church whose children attend the school. For example, a church operates a private school (kindergarten through grade 12). The annual tuition is $2,500. The school allows the children of its employees to attend at half tuition. The same rate applies to the children of church employees. For 2012, tuition reductions are provided to the children of five school employees and four church employees. Are there tax consequences to these tuition discounts? Do the tuition reductions represent taxable income to the parents, or are they nontaxable? If they are nontaxable, what conditions apply?

Qualification requirements

Section 117(d) of the tax code specifies that qualified tuition reductions are not taxable. To be qualified, however, certain conditions must be met. These include the following:

- The tuition reduction is provided to an employee of an "organization described in section 170(b)(1)(A)(ii)" of the tax code. This section refers to "an educational organization which normally maintains a regular faculty and curriculum and normally has a regularly enrolled body of pupils or students in attendance at the place where its educational activities are regularly carried on."
- The tuition reduction must be for education below the graduate level.
- The qualified tuition reduction must be provided to a current school employee, a former school employee who retired or became disabled, or a dependent child of a school employee.

- Highly compensated employees cannot exclude qualified tuition reductions from their gross income unless the same benefit "is available on substantially similar terms" to non-highly compensated employees. For 2012 the term "highly compensated employee" refers to any employee whose annual compensation for 2012 was $115,000 or more. The fact that a highly compensated employee must report the value of a tuition reduction in his or her income for tax reporting purposes does not affect the right of employees who are not highly compensated to exclude the value of tuition reductions from their income.

✱ **New in 2013.** The $115,000 limitation used in the definition of a highly compensated employee remains unchanged for 2013.

EXAMPLE. The IRS issued a "field service advisory" in which it concluded that tuition reductions provided by a school to graduate students who were employed by the school could not be excluded from tax as either a qualified tuition reduction or a working condition fringe benefit. The qualified tuition reduction exclusion did not apply, since this exclusion only applies to "education below the graduate level." The IRS also rejected the school's claim that the tuition reductions could avoid tax as a working condition fringe benefit. A working condition fringe benefit is any "property or service provided to an employee of the employer to the extent that, if the employee paid for such property or services, such payment would be allowable as a [business] deduction." *IRC 132.* However, section 132 states that the working fringe benefit exclusion is not available "to any fringe benefits of a type the tax treatment of which is expressly provided for in any other section" of the tax code. Since section 117(d) of the code addresses tuition reductions, graduate students who do not qualify for this exclusion cannot look to section 132 for relief. *Field Service Advice 200231016 (2002).*

Church employees

Many churches that operate private schools offer tuition discounts to employees of both the church and school and assume that the tax treatment is the same. But is it? Does the exclusion of qualified tuition reductions from a school employee's taxable income apply to church employees? As noted above, section 117(d) defines a qualified tuition reduction as "any reduction in tuition provided to an employee of an organization described in section 170(b)(1)(A)(ii) for the education (below the graduate level) at such organization." Section 170(b)(1)(A)(ii) refers to educational institutions that "normally maintain a regular faculty and curriculum and normally have a regularly enrolled body of pupils or students in attendance at the place where its educational activities are regularly carried on." In other words, tuition reductions granted to the employees of an educational institution are tax-exempt.

In the past it has not been clear whether the IRS or the courts would consider an employee who works directly for a church to be an employee of an educational institution, even if the church operates a private school. The eligibility of a church employee for a qualified tuition reduction was doubtful because of two considerations: (1) A church is a religious rather than an educational institution. (2) A qualified tuition reduction must be provided by an educational institution as described in section 170(b)(1)(A)(ii) of the tax code. This section is preceded by section 170(b)(1)(A)(i), which refers to churches as a separate category. This makes it difficult to argue that employees of a church described in section 170(b)(1)(A)(i) are eligible for an exclusion that is limited to employees of schools described in section 170(b)(1)(A)(ii).

IRS clarification

An IRS ruling directly addressed the eligibility of church employees for qualified tuition reductions and concluded that they are not eligible for the exclusion. *IRS Private Letter Ruling 200149030.* The IRS noted that nontaxable qualified tuition reductions must be provided by an educational organization described in section 170(b)(1)(A)(ii), which refers to schools.

The IRS conceded, however, that a school that is "operated as an activity or function of" a church may qualify as an educational organization for purposes of section 117(d), even though not separately organized or incorporated. It concluded:

> *An unincorporated school operated by a church or parish . . . or the school system of a synod or diocese, all may constitute "educational organizations" described in 170(b)(1)(A)(ii) for purposes of section 117(d). The employees generally of such an "educational organization" would be eligible to receive excludable "qualified tuition reductions" from their employer; the exclusion is not limited solely to individuals providing teaching services, but would extend to the employees generally within such function, including secretarial, managerial, administrative, and support function employees.*

> *However, in these circumstances, an excludable [qualified tuition reduction] could not be extended to church employees who were not employed within the context of the school function, or "educational organization," so defined. Thus, for example, a diocese operating a school system may not properly exclude from reportable wages as "qualified tuition reductions" . . . the value of tuition reduction benefits it might provide to employees of a hospital it also operates.*

Conclusions

Does your church operate a private school? If so, do you offer tuition discounts to both church and school employees? If you do, here are the main points to consider:

(1) **The fact that your school is a ministry of the church and is not separately incorporated does not prevent it from being treated as an educational institution under section**

117 of the tax code. This means that tuition reductions you offer to school employees may be nontaxable if they are qualified as defined above.

(2) **Qualified tuition reductions are nontaxable regardless of the school employee's position.** This benefit is not limited to teachers and administrators. As noted above, highly compensated employees are not eligible for this exclusion.

(3) **Most importantly, tuition reductions offered to church employees do not benefit from this exclusion and remain fully taxable.** To illustrate, if your church offers a 50 percent tuition reduction to school and church employees, and your annual tuition is $3,000, then you would have to report $1,500 of income to each church employee who is given a tuition discount because of a child attending the school. For school employees, the tuition reduction is a nontaxable benefit.

✲**KEY POINT.** Tuition reductions provided to church employees are taxable. But note that church employees are better off receiving a taxable tuition reduction than none at all. They get a valuable fringe benefit for the cost of taxes.

(4) **Some church employees may perform duties at a church-operated school.** Common examples are a senior pastor of a church who serves as president of a church school, or a youth pastor who teaches one or two courses each year at a church school. It is possible that these church employees may qualify for a nontaxable tuition reduction on account of the services they perform on behalf of the school. The IRS did not address this possible exception in its recent ruling. It could be argued that the pastor who teaches one course per semester at the school is a school employee for purposes of the qualified tuition reduction exclusion because he is performing services on behalf of the school for compensation.

To illustrate, the IRS ruled that a worker hired to teach English as a second language by a public school and who worked only three evenings per week was a school employee. *IRS Private Letter Ruling 9821053.* This ruling and others like it may support the availability of the qualified tuition reduction exclusion for pastors and other church employees who teach one or more classes each semester at a church-operated school. After all, this ruling leaves little doubt that the IRS considers part-time teachers who work only a few hours each week to be employees. The same logic may apply to the definition of a school employee for purposes of determining eligibility for the qualified tuition reduction exclusion. Churches that treat a minister or staff member who teaches a course at a church-operated school as a school employee should be consistent. Any teaching compensation should be reported as employee wages. If the school issues its own paychecks, it should do so for the minister or staff member. This is an aggressive tax position that should not be adopted without legal counsel.

What about pastors who serve as a church school's president? Should they be considered part-time school employees because their job description includes serving as the school's president? Does it matter whether they are paid for their services? Obviously, employees ordinarily must be paid something, although it does not necessarily have to be in the form of cash. But while pastors may not be compensated directly for their services as a school president, the argument could be made that if their job description includes these duties, a portion of their church salary should be considered school compensation. This, too, is an aggressive position that should not be adopted without legal counsel.

❋ **KEY POINT.** Efforts have been made in Congress, without success, to amend the tax code to clarify that church schools can provide nontaxable tuition discounts to employees of both the school and church.

❋ **KEY POINT.** Church employees who perform compensated or uncompensated services on behalf of a church-operated school should be sure that their job descriptions reflect their school services. This will increase the likelihood of their eligibility for the tuition reduction exclusion.

EXAMPLE. A pastor served as senior pastor of a Baptist church, and his wife served as principal of a private school operated by the same church. The couple received tuition discounts for their children who attended the school. The Tax Court noted that "by reason of their employment with the church and the school, petitioners, as well as all other full-time employees of the school, received tuition reductions for their children's education at the school." In fact, the court noted that the IRS had conceded that the couple's tuition discounts were not taxable. It is interesting that the court observed that the couple received tuition discounts "by reason of their employment with the church and the school." However, this language should not be pushed too far. After all, the wife was a school employee, and the tuition discounts were nontaxable by reason of her employment. Nevertheless, this case will of some value in supporting the nontaxability of tuition discounts received by the children of pastors and other church employees who are not employees of a school operated by their church. *Rasmussen v. Commissioner, 68 T.C.M. 30 (1994).*

EXAMPLE. A federal appeals court rejected the claim of one church that its school employees were really church employees and therefore exempt from the Fair Labor Standards Act (minimum wage and overtime pay). The church pointed out that the school was "inextricably intertwined" with the church, that the church and school shared a common building and a common payroll account, and that school employees were required to subscribe to the

church's statement of faith. The court rejected this reasoning without explanation. This case suggests that church employees should not assume that they can be treated as school employees in order to qualify for the exclusion of qualified tuition reductions. *Dole v. Shenandoah Baptist Church, 899 F.2d 1389 (4th Cir. 1990).*

Paying tuition through salary reductions

Many churches that operate schools have allowed school employees (with a child who attends the school) to pay for some of all of their child's tuition expenses through salary reduction. To illustrate, assume that a church operates a private religious school and provides employees with a tuition discount of 50 percent off of the regular annual tuition of $3,000 (for any child who attends the school). An employee earns annual income of $20,000 and sends a child to the school. The employee pays tuition of $1,500 (the regular tuition of $3,000 reduced by 50 percent). The church would like to reduce the employee's taxable compensation by $1,500 in order to pay for the remaining tuition. In other words, can the employee pay for the remaining tuition ($1,500) with pretax dollars through a salary reduction arrangement?

The answer is no. Salary reductions can reduce taxable income only if specifically authorized by law. For example, federal law specifically authorizes the payments of contributions to a 403(b) plan (tax-sheltered annuity) or to a cafeteria plan to be made through salary reductions. No authorization is given to pay for tuition expenses through salary reductions. Section 127 of the tax code permits employees, with certain limits, to exclude from taxable income the amounts paid by an employer for the employee's educational expenses. This benefit is available only to employees (not their children), and the education has to be at the college level.

Obviously, this exclusion is not available to the children of church employees. Section 117(a) of the tax code provides for the exclusion of qualified scholarships from a recipient's taxable income. This benefit is available to students who are pursuing a degree at a school that is accredited by a nationally recognized accreditation agency. This exclusion would not be relevant in this example, since the benefit is only available to the student and not to the student's parents.

EXAMPLE. A college provided certain of its employees the option of electing from a variety of fringe benefits, including payment of tuition expenses of employees' children attending private secondary schools. Employees desiring to take advantage of the tuition benefits would inform the college, which would then contact the high school, determine the tuition, and begin paying the high-school tuition as it became due. It made a corresponding reduction of the employee's salary, and the reduced amount was later reported on each employee's Form W-2. The college did not withhold federal income taxes on amounts by which the salaries of participating employees were reduced. The IRS claimed that these salary reductions did not reduce the employees' taxable compensation. It insisted that the employees' Forms W-2 should have reported the full amount of the salary reductions. A federal court agreed with the IRS position. The court based this conclusion on the following language in the tax regulations: "Any amount deducted by an employer from the remuneration of an employee is considered to be a part of the employee's remuneration and is considered to be paid to the employee as remuneration at the time that the deduction is made." Further, the court concluded that the college should have withheld taxes on the salary reductions. *Marquette University v. United States, 645 F. Supp. 1007(E.D. Wis. 1985).*

6. MEALS OR LODGING FURNISHED FOR THE CONVENIENCE OF THE EMPLOYER

Meals and lodging for employees

Section 119(a) of the tax code specifies that the value of **meals** furnished to an employee by an employer is not subject to income taxes or Social Security and Medicare taxes if the meals are furnished on the business premises of the employer and they are furnished for the convenience of the employer.

All meals furnished to employees on an employer's premises are for the convenience of the employer if the meals furnished to at least half of the employees are for the convenience of the employer. Generally, meals are for the convenience of the employer if the employer has a noncompensatory business reason for furnishing the meals (for example, there are few, if any, restaurants nearby, and the employer would have to provide employees with longer lunch breaks if they were not furnished meals at work).

In addition, you may exclude any occasional de minimis meal or meal money you provide to an employee if it has so little value (taking into account how frequently you provide meals to your employees) that accounting for it would be unreasonable or administratively impracticable. The exclusion applies, for example, to the following items:

- coffee, doughnuts, or soft drinks.
- occasional meals or meal money provided to enable an employee to work overtime.
- occasional parties or picnics for employees and their guests.

The de minimis exception does not apply to highly compensated employees who receive meals not available on the same terms to all other employees.

Section 119(a) of the tax code specifies that the value of **lodging** furnished to an employee by an employer is not subject to income taxes or Social Security and Medicare taxes if three tests are met:

- the lodging is furnished on the business premises of the employer;

- the lodging is furnished for the convenience of the employer; and
- the employee is required to accept such lodging as a condition of his employment.

The third requirement means that the employee is required to accept such lodging in order to enable him properly to perform the duties of his employment. Lodging will be regarded as furnished to an employee to enable him to perform his duties properly when, for example, the lodging is furnished because the employee is required to be available for duty at all times or because the employee could not perform the services required of him unless he is furnished such lodging.

To illustrate, if a church located in a high-crime area hires a security guard and requires that he reside in a home located on the church's premises, the value of such lodging need not be included in the gross income of the employee if the tests described above are satisfied.

✿**KEY POINT.** The tax code specifies that ministers may not claim an exclusion for meals or lodging furnished for the convenience of an employer in computing their self-employment tax liability. *IRC 1402(a)(8).*

EXAMPLE. A religious organization required that certain of its executive officers live in houses it owned and that they use the houses as the primary place for performing their duties. The executives were not charged for their use or occupancy of the homes. The lodging was furnished on the business premises of the employer, it was furnished for the convenience of the employer, and the employees were required to accept such lodging as a condition of their employment. Accordingly, the value of such lodging was not includable in the gross income of the employees for income tax purposes. *Revenue Ruling 77-80.*

EXAMPLE. A religious college provided meals and lodging to its faculty and staff members. The value of such meals and lodging was not excludable from the employees' gross income. They were not furnished for the convenience of the employer since they were "not functionally related to the educational or religious goals of the institution." In addition, the employees were not required to accept such arrangements as a condition of their employment. *Bob Jones University v. Commissioner, 670 F.2d 167 (Ct. Cl. 1982).*

EXAMPLE. A religious secondary school furnished lodging to its teachers. The value of such lodging was includable in the employees' gross income, since the lodging was not located on the business premises of the employer and was not the site of a significant portion of the employees' duties. *Goldsboro Christian School, Inc. v. Commissioner, 436 F. Supp. 1314 (D.D.C.1978), aff'd 103 S. Ct. 2017 (1983). See also IRS Letter Ruling 8213005.*

EXAMPLE. Ten "church centers" were engaged in religious activities including praying, preaching the gospel, ministering to the spiritual needs of members, and teaching the Bible. The centers employed full-time ordained ministers and lay workers who were required as a condition of their employment to live at the assigned church center. The primary service required of the ministers and lay workers was prayer. In addition, the ministers conducted Sunday services, held prayer meetings, counseled and helped church members, and carried out evangelistic work. The lay workers taught Bible school, administered the church's business affairs, organized and ran annual conventions, and maintained the facilities. Although the ministers and lay workers were not paid a salary, they were provided with meals and lodging.

The church centers asked the IRS for a ruling addressing the federal Social Security tax consequences of the meals and lodging provided to the full-time ordained ministers and full-time lay workers. With regard to the lay workers, the IRS concluded that the lodging was for the convenience of the employer and accordingly was not includable in gross income for either federal income tax or Social Security (FICA) purposes. Similarly, the IRS concluded that the meals furnished on the church premises for the lay employees were for the convenience of the employer and accordingly were not includable in gross income for federal tax purposes. However, with regard to the ordained ministers who were employed by the churches, the IRS noted that such persons are self-employed for Social Security with respect to service performed in the exercise of their ministries. Accordingly, they are not subject to FICA taxes but rather pay the self-employment tax with respect to such services.

The IRS further noted that section 1402(a)(8) of the tax code prevents the section 119 exclusion for meals and lodging from reducing a minister's net earnings. Thus, the value of meals and lodging provided by the churches to their ordained ministers "must be included in the ministers' net earnings from self-employment" for self-employment tax purposes. On the other hand, the ordained ministers were entitled to exclude from their taxable income for federal income tax purposes the value of the housing provided to them on a cost-free basis (the parsonage exclusion). *IRS Letter Ruling 9129037.*

EXAMPLE. A church provided a minister with a $300 monthly allowance for food and clothing. The minister claimed that the portion of these funds allocable to food was nontaxable based on the exclusion of meals provided for the convenience of an employer. The Tax Court disagreed, noting that "there is no indication that the amounts involved pertain to any meals provided by the church on the church premises." *Kalms v. Commissioner, 64 T.C.M. 153 (1992).*

Faculty lodging

If you are an employee of an educational institution and you are provided with lodging that does not meet the three conditions noted above, you still may not have to include the value of the lodging in income. However, the lodging must be qualified campus lodging, and you must pay an adequate rent.

"Qualified campus lodging" is lodging furnished to you, your spouse, or one of your dependents by or on behalf of the institution for use as a home. The lodging must be located on or near a campus of the educational institution.

The amount of rent you pay for the year for qualified campus lodging is considered adequate if it is at least equal to the lesser of (1) 5 percent of the appraised value of the lodging, or (2) the average of rentals paid by individuals (other than employees or students) for comparable lodging held for rent by the educational institution. If the amount you pay is less than the lesser of these amounts, you must include the difference in your income.

⚙ **KEY POINT.** The lodging must be appraised by an independent appraiser, and the appraisal must be reviewed on an annual basis.

> **EXAMPLE.** Carla, a college professor, rents a home from the college that is qualified campus lodging. The house is appraised at $100,000. The average rent paid for comparable university lodging by persons other than employees or students is $7,000 a year. Carla pays an annual rent of $5,500. She does not include in her income any rental value because the rent she pays equals at least 5 percent of the appraised value of the house (5 percent x $100,000 = $5,000). If Carla paid annual rent of only $4,000, she would have to include $1,000 in her income ($5,000 - $4,000).

⚙ **KEY POINT.** In some cases on-campus housing provided rent-free to a teacher or administrator who is a minister may qualify for the parsonage exclusion (addressed fully in Chapter 6). This assumes that the individual's duties on behalf of the school constitute the "exercise of ministry" (as defined in Chapter 3). The discussion of on-campus housing in this section assumes that the requirements for parsonage exclusion are not met.

7. EMPLOYER-PROVIDED EDUCATIONAL ASSISTANCE

Employer-paid educational expenses are excludable from the gross income and wages of an employee if provided under an educational assistance program. Section 127 provides an exclusion of $5,250 annually for employer-provided educational assistance. In order for the exclusion to apply, certain requirements must be satisfied. The educational assistance must be provided pursuant to a separate written plan of the employer, and the educational assistance program must not discriminate in favor of highly compensated employees.

Under the terms of the exclusion, employees are limited to an exclusion of up to $5,250 of the benefits they receive during a calendar year. This exclusion applies to both income tax and Social Security tax.

An educational assistance program in the context of church employers (1) is a separate written plan of an employer for the exclusive benefit of its employees to give them educational assistance; (2) cannot have eligibility requirements that discriminate in favor of officers or highly compensated employees or their dependents (as defined in section I of this chapter); (3) must not provide eligible employees with a choice between educational assistance and cash; and (4) must provide for reasonable notification of the availability and the terms of the program to eligible employees. *IRC 127.*

Employees

The term "employee" includes self-employed persons for purposes of this exclusion.

Educational assistance

Educational assistance provided by an employer includes payments for such expenses as tuition, fees, books, and equipment. It does not include payment for tools or supplies (other than books) that an employee may retain after the completion of a course, meals or lodging, or transportation. This exclusion applies to undergraduate and graduate education.

Examples

EXAMPLE. Pastor E is taking graduate-level counseling courses at a local seminary. His church pays his tuition, which amounted to $5,000 in 2012. The church's payment of Pastor E's tuition in 2012 may be nontaxable employer-provided educational assistance, since this benefit is not limited to undergraduate education.

EXAMPLE. An employer paid an employee an $8,000 "commission" in addition to his regular salary. Throughout his employment the employee was enrolled at a local university, earning an undergraduate degree. He had a verbal agreement with his employer that he would be reimbursed for certain educational expenses he incurred. The employee did not report the $8,000 as taxable income because he considered it to be nontaxable employer-paid educational assistance. The Tax Court disagreed. It noted that section 127 of the tax code excludes from taxable income "amounts paid by the employer for educational assistance to the employee," but only if the assistance is furnished pursuant to an "educational assistance program." An "educational assistance program" is a "separate written plan of an employer" which meets certain requirements. The court concluded that the $8,000 was not tax-free employer paid educational assistance, since "the amounts at issue were not provided pursuant to a written plan maintained by the employer as required by the statute." *Lewis v. Commissioner, T.C. Sum. Op. 2003-78 (2003).*

Working condition fringe benefit

Educational expenses that do not qualify for the section 127 exclusion or that are in excess of the annual $5,250 limit may be excludable from income as a working condition fringe benefit. In general, education qualifies as a working condition fringe benefit if the employee could have deducted the education expenses under section 162 if the employee paid for the education. In general, education expenses are deductible by an individual under section 162 if the education (1) maintains or improves a skill required in a trade or business currently engaged in by the taxpayer or (2) meets the express requirements of the taxpayer's employer, applicable law, or regulations imposed as a condition of continued employment. However, education expenses are generally not deductible if they relate to certain minimum educational requirements or to education or training that enables a taxpayer to begin working in a new trade or business.

8. EMPLOYER-PROVIDED DEPENDENT CARE

KEY POINT. Dependent care assistance provided by an employer to an employee may be a nontaxable fringe benefit. In addition, persons who incur childcare expenses to enable them to pursue gainful employment may be eligible for a childcare credit (explained in Chapter 7).

Payments made by employers to their employees for childcare may be excluded from income. *IRC 129.* The same applies to the value of childcare services made available to employees on the employer's premises. This benefit will apply to many churches that maintain childcare facilities and that offer childcare services at reduced or no cost to employees. For the exclusion to be available, the following requirements must be satisfied:

- The childcare payments, or the provision of childcare services directly on the employer's premises, must be authorized by a written plan of the employer for the exclusive benefit of its employees.
- The employer must notify each employee of the availability and terms of the plan.
- The employer, by January 31 of each year, must furnish to each employee a statement showing the amounts paid or expenses incurred by the employer in providing dependent care assistance to each employee during the previous year.
- The plan must not discriminate in favor of highly compensated employees (defined above).

If any of these rules is not met, only highly compensated employees are required to include the value of dependent care assistance in their gross income.

An employee may exclude the amount of childcare payments made by an employer, or the value of childcare services made available on the employer's premises, up to but not exceeding the lowest of the following three amounts: (1) the employee's earned income; (2) if an employee is married, the earned income of the employee's spouse; or (3) $5,000. In valuing childcare services provided on an employer's premises, take into account how often an employee's dependents utilize the facility and the value of the services provided.

This exclusion is not available with respect to payments made directly to an employee's dependents. Further, the amount of the exclusion will reduce the dollar limit on work-related expenses used in computing the childcare credit. Employers who reasonably believe that an employee will be able to exclude the entire value of employer-provided childcare assistance are not required to withhold taxes on any portion of the value of this benefit.

To calculate the correct amount of the exclusion, an employee must complete IRS Form 2441. The name, address, and taxpayer identification number of the childcare provider must be listed on the form. If the provider is a tax-exempt organization that does not have a federal taxpayer identification number, then only the name and address of the provider must be listed. This exclusion is available to both employees and self-employed persons.

❋ **KEY POINT.** The IRS can deny both a dependency exemption and dependent care credit to any taxpayer who fails to provide the correct Social Security number of a dependent on his or her tax return.

9. EMPLOYER-PAID MOVING EXPENSES

If you received a reimbursement for your allowable or qualified moving expenses (see Chapter 7, section H), how you report this amount and your expenses depends on whether the reimbursement was paid to you under an accountable plan or a nonaccountable plan.

Accountable plans

To be an accountable plan, your employer's reimbursement arrangement must require you to meet all three of the following requirements:

(1) Your expenses must have a business connection. That is, you must have paid or incurred deductible expenses while performing services as an employee of your employer. Two examples of this are the reasonable expenses of moving your possessions from your former home to your new home and traveling from your former home to your new home.

(2) You must adequately account to your employer for these expenses within a reasonable period of time. You adequately account for your moving expenses by giving your employer documentation of those expenses, such as a statement of expense, an account book, a diary, or a similar record in which you entered each expense at or near the time you had it. Documentation includes receipts, canceled checks, and bills.

(3) You must return any excess reimbursement or allowance within a reasonable period of time. What constitutes a "reasonable period of time" depends on the facts and circumstances of each situation. However, regardless of the facts and circumstances, actions that take place within the times

specified in the following list will be treated as taking place within a reasonable period of time:

- You receive an advance within 30 days of the time you have an expense.
- You adequately account for your expenses within 60 days after they were paid or incurred.
- You return any excess reimbursement within 120 days after the expense was paid or incurred.
- You are given a periodic statement (at least quarterly) that asks you to either return or adequately account for outstanding advances and you comply within 120 days of the statement.

If employee meets accountable plan rules

If for all reimbursements you meet the three rules for an accountable plan, your employer should not include any reimbursements of allowable expenses in your income in box 1 of your Form W-2. Instead, your employer should include the reimbursements in box 12 of your Form W-2 (using code P).

If employee does not meet accountable plan rules

You may be reimbursed by your employer, but for part of your expenses you may not meet all three rules. If your deductible expenses are reimbursed under an otherwise accountable plan but you do not return, within a reasonable period, any reimbursement of expenses for which you did not adequately account, then only the amount for which you did adequately account is considered paid under an accountable plan. The remaining expenses are treated as having been reimbursed under a nonaccountable plan.

Reimbursement of nondeductible expenses

You may be reimbursed by your employer for moving expenses, some of which are deductible expenses and some of which are not deductible. The reimbursements received for the nondeductible expenses are treated as paid under a nonaccountable plan.

Nonaccountable plans

A nonaccountable plan is a reimbursement arrangement that does not meet the three rules listed above. In addition, the following payments will be treated as paid under a nonaccountable plan: (1) excess reimbursements you fail to return to your employer, and (2) reimbursements of nondeductible expenses.

If an arrangement pays for your moving expenses by reducing your wages, salary, or other pay, the amount of the reduction will be treated as a payment made under a nonaccountable plan. This is because you are entitled to receive the full amount of your pay regardless of whether you had any moving expenses. If you are not sure if the moving expense reimbursement arrangement is an accountable or nonaccountable plan, ask your employer. Your employer will combine the amount of any reimbursement paid to you under a nonaccountable plan with your wages, salary, or other pay. Your employer will report the total in box 1 of your Form W-2.

�֎ **KEY POINT.** If an employer reimburses an employee's qualified moving expenses by paying the mover directly, these reimbursements are not reported on the employee's Form W-2.

J. REPORTING REQUIREMENTS (FORM 5500)

Employers no longer have to file an annual Form 5500 and Schedule F for so-called "pure fringe benefit plans." Employers who in the past filed Form 5500 and the Schedule F (Fringe Benefit Plan Annual Information Return) solely to meet the reporting requirements of section 6039D of the tax code ("fringe benefit plans")

should file neither Form 5500 nor Schedule F. In fact, the Schedule F has been eliminated, and Form 5500 has been modified so fringe benefit plan information cannot be reported.

Fringe benefit plans are often associated with ERISA group health plans and other welfare benefit plans. The exemption of pure fringe benefit plans from the Form 5500 filing requirement does not cover these associated welfare plans. But, in many cases, a Form 5500 was not required for the welfare plan because it was exempt from filing a Form 5500 report under Department of Labor regulations. For example, fully insured or unfunded welfare plans covering fewer than 100 participants at the beginning of the plan year are eligible for a filing exemption, as are church plans. Unless exempt, however, ERISA welfare plans must still file in accordance with the Form 5500 instructions on welfare plan filing requirements.

Form 5500 must be filed annually by every pension benefit plan. However, church plans are exempt from this requirement so long as they have not elected to be covered by ERISA. See Chapter 10 for more information about church retirement plans.

Chapter 6 PARSONAGES AND HOUSING ALLOWANCES

Joseph established it as a law concerning land in Egypt—still in force today—that a fifth of the produce belongs to Pharaoh. It was only the land of the priests that did not become Pharaoh's.

Genesis 47:26

CHAPTER HIGHLIGHTS

- **Parsonages.** Ministers who live in a church-owned parsonage that is provided rent-free as compensation for ministerial services do not include the annual fair rental value of the parsonage as income in computing their federal income taxes. The annual fair rental value is not deducted from the minister's income. Rather, it is not reported as additional income anywhere on Form 1040 (as it generally would be by nonclergy workers).

- **Parsonage allowances.** Ministers who live in a church-provided parsonage do not pay federal income taxes on the amount of their compensation that their employing church designates in advance as a parsonage allowance, to the extent that the allowance represents compensation for ministerial services and is used to pay parsonage-related expenses such as utilities, repairs, and furnishings.

- **Housing allowances.** Ministers who own their home do not pay federal income taxes on the amount of their compensation that their employing church designates in advance as a housing allowance, to the extent that the allowance represents compensation for ministerial services, is used to pay housing expenses, and does not exceed the fair rental value of the home (furnished, plus utilities). Housing-related expenses include mortgage payments, utilities, repairs, furnishings, insurance, property taxes, additions, and maintenance. Ministers who rent a home or apartment do not pay federal income taxes on the amount of their compensation that their employing church designates in advance as a housing allowance, to the extent that the allowance represents compensation for ministerial services and is used to pay rental expenses and does not exceed the fair rental value of the home (furnished, plus utilities).

- **Designating an allowance.** Parsonage and housing allowances should be (1) adopted by the church board or congregation, (2) in writing, and (3) in advance of the calendar year. However, churches that fail to designate an allowance in advance of a calendar year should do so as soon as possible in the new year (though the allowance will only operate prospectively). In designating housing allowances, churches should keep in mind that the nontaxable portion of a housing allowance cannot exceed the fair rental value of a minister's home (furnished, plus utilities). Therefore, nothing will be accomplished by designating allowances significantly above this limit.

- **Safety net housing allowances.** Churches should consider adopting a "safety net" allowance to protect against the loss of this significant tax benefit due to the inadvertent failure by the church to designate an allowance.

- **Equity allowances.** Churches should consider adopting an appropriate "equity allowance" for ministers who live in church-owned parsonages.

- **Amending the allowance.** Churches can amend an allowance during the year if the original allowance proves to be too low. But the amended allowance will only operate prospectively.

- **No retroactive application.** Under no circumstances can a minister exclude any portion of an allowance retroactively designated by a church.

- **Social Security.** A housing allowance and the annual rental value of a parsonage are exclusions only for federal income tax reporting. Ministers cannot exclude a housing allowance (or the annual fair rental value of a parsonage) when computing their self-employment (Social Security) taxes unless they are actually retired. The tax code specifies that the self-employment tax does not apply to "the rental value of any parsonage or any parsonage allowance provided after the [minister] retires." *IRC 1402(a)(8).*

- **Pension funds.** In some cases a church pension plan may designate a housing allowance for retired ministers.

- **Reporting.** Housing allowances are not required to be reported on a minister's Form W-2, but many churches do so by reporting the allowance (or the annual rental value of a parsonage) in box 14. The instructions to Form W-2 say this regarding box 14: "You may use this box for any information that you want to give to your employee. Label each item. Examples include . . . a member of the clergy's parsonage allowance and utilities." Box 14 is used by employers to communicate information to their employees and is ignored by the IRS. This is one way for a church to remind a minister of the amount of the church-designated housing allowance. IRS Publication 517 contains a comprehensive clergy tax filing illustration that includes a minister's housing allowance in box 14. So, while some churches use box 14 to report a minister's housing allowance, this is optional and not required. Further, a church does not need to issue two checks—one for salary and one for housing allowance.

■ *Setting the allowance.* There is no limit on the amount of a minister's compensation that can be designated by a church as a housing allowance (assuming that the minister's compensation is reasonable in amount). However, for ministers who own their home, a church ordinarily should not designate a housing allowance significantly above the fair rental value of the minister's home, since the nontaxable portion of a housing allowance cannot exceed this amount.

INTRODUCTION

The three most common housing arrangements for ministers are (1) living in a church-provided parsonage, (2) renting a home or apartment, or (3) owning a home. The tax code provides a significant benefit to each housing arrangement. The rules are summarized below:

- **Parsonages.** Ministers who live in a church-provided parsonage that is provided as compensation for ministerial services do not include the annual rental value of the parsonage as income in computing their federal income taxes.
- **Parsonage allowances.** Ministers who live in a church-provided parsonage do not pay federal income taxes on the amount of their compensation that their employing church designates in advance as a parsonage allowance, to the extent that the allowance represents compensation for ministerial services; is used to pay parsonage-related expenses such as utilities, repairs, and furnishings; and does not exceed the fair rental value of the parsonage (furnished, plus utilities).
- **Housing allowances (minister rents a home or apartment).** Ministers who rent a home or apartment do not pay federal income taxes on the amount of their compensation that their employing church designates in advance as a housing allowance, to the extent that the allowance represents compensation for ministerial services, is used to pay rental expenses, and does not exceed the fair rental value of the home (furnished, plus utilities).
- **Housing allowances (minister owns the home).** Ministers who own their home do not pay federal income taxes on the amount of their compensation that their employing church designates in advance as a housing allowance, to the extent that the allowance represents compensation for ministerial services, is used to pay housing expenses, and does not exceed the fair rental value of the home (furnished, plus utilities). Housing-related expenses include mortgage payments, utilities, repairs, furnishings, insurance, property taxes, additions, and maintenance.

These rules (summarized in Table 6-1) represent the most significant tax benefits enjoyed by ministers. Yet many ministers either fail to claim them or do not claim enough. In some cases this results from tax advisers who are unfamiliar with ministers' taxes.

✿**KEY POINT.** The Clergy Housing Allowance Clarification Act of 2002 amended the tax code to specify that the nontaxable portion of a housing allowance designated by a church for a minister who owns a home may not exceed either actual housing expenses or the fair rental value of the home (furnished, plus utilities). The fair rental value limit applies to 2002 and future years.

Because the rules for ministers living in church-owned parsonages differ from the rules that apply to ministers who own or rent their home, this chapter will be divided into two sections. Section A will summarize the requirements for obtaining the full benefit available

═══ **TABLE 6-1** ═══

TAX CONSEQUENCES OF VARIOUS CLERGY HOUSING ARRANGEMENTS

RULE	EXPLANATION
Parsonage	Annual fair rental value of a church-owned parsonage provided rent-free to a minister as compensation for ministerial services is excluded from income in computing federal income taxes.
Parsonage allowance	Ministers who live in a church-provided parsonage do not pay federal income taxes on the amount of their compensation that their employing church designates in advance as a parsonage allowance, to the extent the allowance represents compensation for ministerial services; is used to pay parsonage-related expenses such as utilities, repairs, and furnishings; and does not exceed the fair rental value of the parsonage (furnished, plus utilities).
Rental allowance	Ministers who rent a home or apartment do not pay federal income taxes on the amount of their compensation that their employing church designates in advance as a housing allowance, to the extent the allowance represents compensation for ministerial services; is used to pay rental expenses; and does not exceed the fair rental value of the home (furnished, plus utilities).
Housing allowance	Ministers who own their home do not pay federal income taxes on the amount of their compensation that their employing church designates in advance as a housing allowance, to the extent the allowance is used to pay housing expenses and does not exceed the fair rental value of the home.

to ministers who live in a church-owned parsonage. In section B the rules that apply to ministers who rent or own their homes will be considered.

A. PARSONAGES

❀ **KEY POINT.** Ministers who live in a church-owned parsonage that is provided as compensation for ministerial services do not include the fair rental value of the parsonage as income in computing their federal income taxes. The fair rental value is not deducted from the minister's income. Rather, it is not reported as additional income anywhere on Form 1040 (as it generally would be by nonclergy workers).

❀ **KEY POINT.** Ministers who live in a church-provided parsonage do not pay federal income taxes on the amount of compensation their employing church designates in advance as a parsonage allowance, to the extent that the allowance represents compensation for ministerial services and is used to pay parsonage-related expenses such as utilities, repairs, and furnishings.

1. OVERVIEW

Since 1921 ministers have been permitted to exclude from their gross income for income tax purposes the annual fair rental value of a church-owned parsonage provided to them rent-free as part of their compensation for services rendered to the church. Congress has never explained the justification for this rule. Presumably, it is based on the principle that the rental value of lodging furnished rent-free to an employee on an employer's business premises should be excluded from gross income if it is furnished "for the convenience of the employer" and the employee must accept such lodging in order to adequately perform his or her duties. *IRC 119.*

Section 107 of the tax code says simply that "in the case of a minister of the gospel, gross income does not include—(1) the rental value of a home furnished to him as part of his compensation; or (2) the rental allowance paid to him as part of his compensation, to the extent used by him to rent or provide a home and to the extent such allowance does not exceed the fair rental value of the home, including furnishings and appurtenances such as a garage, plus the cost of utilities."

Note the following four considerations.

Minister of the gospel

The rental value of a parsonage and a parsonage allowance are non-taxable fringe benefits for ministers. The definition of "minister" for federal tax purposes is addressed in Chapter 3.

Compensation for the exercise of ministry

The annual rental value of a parsonage and the portion of a minister's compensation designated in advance by his or her employing church as a parsonage allowance are excluded from income in computing federal income taxes only if they represent compensation for services performed in the exercise of ministry. The income tax regulations specify that the parsonage or parsonage allowance must be "provided as remuneration for services which are ordinarily the duties of a minister of the gospel." In other words, the parsonage and "parsonage allowance" exclusions are available only if

- the recipient is a minister of the gospel, and
- the benefit is made available to the minister as compensation for services which are ordinarily the duties of a minister of the gospel.

These eligibility requirements are addressed in Chapter 3.

An exclusion

A parsonage allowance and the annual rental value of a church-provided parsonage are exclusions from gross income rather than deductions in computing or reducing adjusted gross income. As a result, they are not reported on Form 1040. Many ministers find this confusing and think they are not receiving a tax benefit unless they can deduct something on their tax return. In fact, some ministers erroneously deduct the annual rental value of a parsonage. This practice clearly violates federal tax law.

Keep in mind that virtually any other worker who receives rent-free use of an employer-provided home must include the annual rental value of the home in his or her gross income for both income tax and Social Security tax purposes. Ministers, however, do not. This is a significant benefit. As noted below, the annual rental value of a parsonage (and any additional parsonage allowance designated by a church) must be included in self-employment earnings on Schedule SE (Form 1040) in computing a minister's Social Security tax liability.

> **EXAMPLE.** Frank lives in Chicago and works for a large company. His employer wants to transfer Frank to a Los Angeles office for two years and then return him to Chicago. The company allows Frank to live in a home it owns in Los Angeles for the two-year term. The annual rental value of the home provided to Frank rent-free is income to him in computing both income tax and Social Security tax. So if Frank's annual salary is $50,000 and the annual rental value of the Los Angeles home is $15,000, Frank's employer must report compensation of $65,000 on Frank's Form W-2.

> **EXAMPLE.** Same facts as the preceding example except that Frank is a minister who leaves a church in Chicago to accept a pastoral position in Los Angeles and that the Los Angeles church provides him with rent-free use of a church-owned parsonage. Frank's W-2 income (assuming that he is an employee) would be only $50,000 (not $65,000). The annual rental value of the

home is not reported as taxable income. This is a significant benefit compared to the previous example involving an employee who was not a minister, and it will result in a tax savings of several thousands of dollars. Some ministers erroneously deduct the rental value of their parsonage from their taxable income. For example, assume that Frank instructs his church treasurer to reduce his W-2 income by $15,000 so that only $35,000 is reported. This practice clearly violates federal law and should be avoided. The tax benefit is that Frank does not have to report the annual rental value of the home ($15,000) as income in addition to his $50,000 salary. Note that Frank would have to pay Social Security taxes on the rental value of the parsonage (assuming that he is not exempt from Social Security coverage).

Valuing the exclusion

Section 107 excludes the annual rental value of a parsonage provided rent-free to a minister as compensation for ministerial services as well as an allowance paid to a minister that is used to pay expenses incurred in maintaining the parsonage (e.g., utilities, repairs, furnishings). Ministers who live in a church-owned parsonage do not report the annual rental value of the parsonage as income, and the church is not required to declare an allowance in the amount of the annual rental value of the parsonage. The exclusion is automatic. However, if the minister incurs any expenses in living in the parsonage, he or she may exclude them only to the extent that they do not exceed a parsonage allowance declared in writing and in advance by the church board. See Illustration 6-1 for an example of a parsonage allowance designation.

EXAMPLE. Pastor W lives rent-free in a church-owned parsonage having an annual rental value of $6,000 in 2012. The church expects Pastor W to incur some expenses in living in the parsonage, so it provides him with an allowance of $200 each month. His salary (not including the monthly allowance) was $30,000 in 2012. On his 2012 federal income tax return, Pastor W would not report the annual rental value of the parsonage ($6,000) as income, even though the church never designated that amount as a parsonage allowance. However, he would have to report the total monthly allowances ($2,400) as income unless the church board declared a parsonage allowance in writing and in advance of at least $2,400. The rental value of the parsonage and parsonage allowance are taxable in computing self-employment taxes. *Eden v. Commissioner, 41 T.C. 605 (1961). See also Revenue Ruling 59-350.*

EXAMPLE. Pastor R lives rent-free in a church-owned parsonage having an annual rental value of $6,000 in 2012. The church pays the utilities charged to the parsonage, which amount to $3,000 for 2012. The IRS *Tax Guide for Churches and Religious Organizations* specifies that "a minister who is furnished a parsonage may exclude from income the fair rental value of the parsonage, including utilities." In effect, the church is designating this amount as a parsonage allowance each month by paying it. While the $3,000 does not represent taxable

---

PARSONAGE ALLOWANCE DESIGNATION FOR MINISTERS WHO LIVE IN A CHURCH-OWNED PARSONAGE

The following resolution was duly adopted by the board of directors of First Church at a regularly scheduled meeting held on December 15, 2012, a quorum being present:

Whereas, section 107 of the Internal Revenue Code permits a minister of the gospel to exclude from gross income the rental value of a parsonage furnished to him as part of his compensation, and a church-designated parsonage allowance paid to him as part of his compensation, to the extent the allowance represents compensation for ministerial services; is used to pay parsonage-related expenses such as utilities, repairs, and furnishings; and does not exceed the fair rental value of the parsonage (furnished, plus utilities); and

Whereas, Pastor John Smith is compensated by First Church exclusively for services as a minister of the gospel; and

Whereas First Church provides Pastor Smith with rent-free use of a church-owned parsonage as compensation for services that he renders to the church in the exercise of his ministry; and

Whereas, as additional compensation to Pastor Smith for services that he renders to the church in the exercise of his ministry, First Church also desires to pay Pastor Smith an amount to cover expenses he incurs in maintaining the parsonage; therefore, it is hereby

Resolved, that the annual compensation paid to Pastor Smith for calendar year 2013 shall be $50,000, of which $5,000 is hereby designated as a parsonage allowance pursuant to section 107 of the Internal Revenue Code; and it is further

Resolved, that the designation of $5,000 as a parsonage allowance shall apply to calendar year 2013 and all future years unless otherwise provided by this board; and it is further

Resolved, that as additional compensation to Pastor Smith for calendar year 2013 and for all future years unless otherwise provided by this board, Pastor Smith shall be permitted to live in the church-owned parsonage located at 123 Main Street, and that no rent or other fee shall be payable by Pastor Smith for such occupancy and use.

---

income to Pastor R for income tax reporting, it does for self-employment (Social Security) tax reporting; so Pastor R must add the $3,000 to self-employment earnings in computing the self-employment tax. The annual rental value of the parsonage ($6,000) is also subject to the self-employment tax.

EXAMPLE. IRS Publication 517 contains the following example: Pastor Roger Adams receives an annual salary of $39,000 as a full-time minister. The $39,000 includes $5,000 that is designated as a rental allowance to pay utilities. His church owns a parsonage that has a fair rental value of $12,000 per year. Pastor Adams is given the use of the parsonage. He is not exempt from SE tax. He must include $51,000 ($39,000 plus $12,000) when figuring net earnings from self-employment. The results would be the same if, instead of the use of the parsonage and receipt of the rental allowance for utilities, Pastor Adams had received an annual salary of $51,000 of which $17,000 ($5,000 plus $12,000) per year was designated as a rental allowance.

➤ **TIP.** Churches should declare a parsonage allowance in advance of each calendar year for any minister who lives in a parsonage to cover any miscellaneous expenses the minister may incur while living in the parsonage. The allowance should be declared in writing and be incorporated into the minutes of the board or other group that designates it. Churches failing to declare a parsonage allowance before January 1 need not wait until the following year to act. The declaration is effective from the date of its enactment. Therefore, a church failing to declare a parsonage allowance until March of 2013 (for 2013) can still provide its minister with an important tax benefit for the remainder of the year.

2. DESIGNATING A PARSONAGE ALLOWANCE

Ministers who live in a church-provided parsonage often incur expenses in maintaining the parsonage. Common examples include utilities, repairs, insurance, and furnishings. The portion of a minister's compensation that is designated in advance by the church as a parsonage allowance is not subject to federal income taxes, to the extent the allowance represents compensation for ministerial services; is used to pay parsonage-related expenses such as utilities, repairs, and furnishings; and does not exceed the fair rental value of the parsonage (furnished, plus utilities).

The income tax regulations specify that the designation of the allowance may be contained in "an employment contract, in minutes of or in a resolution by a church or other qualified organization or in its budget, or in any other appropriate instrument evidencing such official action." The regulations further provide that "the designation . . . is a sufficient designation if it permits a payment or a part thereof to be identified as a payment of rental allowance as distinguished from salary or other remuneration." *Treas. Reg. 1.107-1(b).*

In other words, the designation must simply distinguish a part of the minister's compensation as a parsonage allowance. This can be

done by giving a minister two separate checks—one designated as salary and the other as the parsonage allowance. This approach is not necessary, since a church that has designated a portion of a minister's compensation as a parsonage allowance has thereby made the required identification, and it is free to issue a minister one check per pay period that combines both salary and the parsonage allowance.

The church's designation should be in writing, although if a board orally agrees to a specific allowance and neglects to make a written record of its action, it could draft an appropriate record of its action at a later time, dated as of the earlier meeting. *Kizer v. Commissioner, T.C. Memo. 1992-584.*

Section 35 of *Robert's Rules of Order Newly Revised* (11th ed., 2011) recognizes a motion to "amend something previously adopted" as an incidental main motion by which a deliberative body an change an action previously taken or ordered. This would include amending the minutes of a church board to reflect a parsonage allowance that in fact was adopted at a prior meeting but that was not reflected in the minutes.

The Tax Court has ruled that an oral designation is sufficient, since "there is no requirement that the designation be in writing." *Libman v. Commissioner, 44 T.C.M. 370 (1982).* This practice should be avoided, however, since it will always create problems of proof.

A parsonage allowance should be designated by the same body (a board or the membership) that approves compensation. A parsonage allowance must be designated in advance, since it is nontaxable only to the extent it is used to pay parsonage-related expenses. Ideally, a parsonage allowance should be designated in advance of each new year. A sample resolution that accomplishes this is set forth as Illustration 6-6 at the end of this chapter. If a church fails to designate a parsonage allowance before the start of a new year, it is not lost for the entire new year. Rather, the church can designate a parsonage allowance at any time during the year, for the remainder of that year. To illustrate, if a church discovers on March 10, 2013, that it has not yet designated a parsonage allowance for its pastor for that year, it can do so on that date for the remainder of the year.

➤ **TIP.** Many ministers who live in a parsonage are unaware that they do not pay tax on that portion of their salary that is designated in advance by their church as a parsonage allowance (to the extent it is used to pay parsonage-related expenses). Such an allowance costs the church nothing, but it provides a minister with a significant tax benefit.

EXAMPLE. A minister reduced his taxable income by the amount of a parsonage allowance. The IRS audited the minister and determined that he was not eligible for a parsonage allowance, since no evidence existed that the church had ever designated one. The Tax Court agreed. It noted that the minister had the "burden of proving that the amount at issue was properly designated as a rental allowance by official church action before payment" and concluded that "the record is devoid of any such evidence." *Logie v. Commissioner, T.C. Memo. 1998-387.*

3. REASONABLE IN AMOUNT

An additional requirement, not mentioned in section 107, is that the annual rental value of a parsonage (or a parsonage allowance declared by a church) must be reasonable in amount. *IRC 501(c)(3).* Providing a minister with a parsonage (or parsonage allowance) that is excessive in amount may constitute unreasonable compensation." Such a finding could jeopardize the tax-exempt status of the church. It also could trigger intermediate sanctions against the minister and the church board members who approved the transaction. Intermediate sanctions are excise taxes the IRS can assess as a result of an "excess benefit transaction" favoring a director or officer. See Chapter 4, section A, for a discussion of unreasonable compensation and intermediate sanctions.

The IRS *Tax Guide for Churches and Religious Organizations* states that "a minister who is furnished a parsonage may exclude from income the fair rental value of the parsonage, including utilities. However, the amount excluded cannot be more than the reasonable pay for the minister's services."

EXAMPLE. A federal court noted that a prominent televangelist lived in a parsonage and also received a housekeeping and maintenance allowance and a housing allowance, despite the fact that his ministry paid all of his utilities and other housing expenses. Such payments clearly were above any reasonable parsonage-related expenses, in the court's judgment. This case illustrates that ministers who live in a parsonage and who pay none of the expenses of maintaining the parsonage are not eligible for a parsonage allowance exclusion. *Heritage Village Church and Missionary Fellowship, Inc., 92 B.R. 1000 (D.S.C. 1988).*

4. ELIGIBILITY FOR BOTH THE PARSONAGE EXCLUSION AND PARSONAGE ALLOWANCE

Can ministers who live in a church-owned parsonage also have a portion of their salary designated by their employing church as a parsonage allowance to the extent that they incur any out-of-pocket expenses in living in the parsonage? Section 107 of the tax code states that the gross income of a minister does not include the rental value of a church-provided residence or a rental or housing allowance paid to the minister. A reasonable basis exists for the view that ministers who live in a church-owned parsonage can exclude from gross income not only the annual rental value of the parsonage but also a parsonage allowance designated by the church, to the extent the allowance represents compensation for ministerial services; is used to pay parsonage-related expenses such as utilities, repairs, and

furnishings; and does not exceed the fair rental value of the parsonage (furnished, plus utilities).

IRS Publication 517

The current edition of IRS Publication 517 (Social Security and Other Information for Members of the Clergy and Religious Workers) clearly recognizes that ministers who live in a church-provided parsonage may have some of their compensation designated in advance by their employing church as a parsonage allowance: "You can exclude from gross income the fair rental value of a house or parsonage, including utilities, furnished to you as part of your earnings. However, the exclusion cannot be more than the reasonable pay for your services. *If you pay for the utilities, you can exclude any allowance designated for utility costs, up to your actual cost*" (emphasis added). IRS Publication 517 includes the following example.

EXAMPLE. Rev. Joanna Baker is a full-time minister. The church allows her to use a parsonage that has an annual fair rental value of $24,000. The church pays her an annual salary of $67,000, of which $7,500 is designated for utility costs. Her actual utility costs during the year were $7,000. For income tax purposes, Rev. Baker excludes $31,000 from gross income ($24,000 fair rental value of the parsonage plus $7,000 from the allowance for utility costs). She will report $60,000 ($59,500 salary plus $500 of unused utility allowance). Her income for SE tax purposes, however, is $91,000 ($67,000 salary + $24,000 fair rental value of the parsonage).

Revenue Ruling 59-350

In Revenue Ruling 59-350 the IRS ruled that a minister who lived in a church-owned parsonage could exclude from gross income that portion of his salary that was designated in advance by his employing church as a parsonage allowance. The IRS observed:

> [A] minister of the gospel who is furnished a parsonage rent-free may exclude a rental allowance to the extent used by him to pay for utilities so long as the employing church or church organization designates a part of his remuneration as a rental allowance....
>
> Therefore, a minister of the gospel is permitted to exclude from his gross income, under section 107(1) of the Code, the rental value of a home furnished him as part of his compensation and, in addition, may exclude from his gross income, under section 107(2) of the Code, the "designated" rental allowance, to the extent expended for utilities.
>
> Accordingly, [if] a minister of the gospel who is provided a home rent-free by a church or other qualified organization as part of his compensation ... pays for his utilities, [and] an amount of his compensation is designated as a "rental allowance" to cover the cost of his utilities, he may exclude from his gross income not only the rental value of the home but also the amount of the "rental allowance" to the extent used by him to pay for his utilities.

Revenue Ruling 63-156

In Revenue Ruling 63-156 the IRS stated:

A retired minister of the gospel is furnished rent-free use of a home pursuant to official action taken by the employing qualified organization in recognition of his past services which were the duties of a minister of the gospel in churches of his denomination. In addition, he is paid a rental allowance, within the meaning of section 107(2) of the Internal Revenue Code of 1954, for utilities, maintenance, repairs and other similar expenses directly related to providing a home.

The rental value of the home furnished to the retired minister as part of his compensation for past services is excludable from his gross income under section 107(1) of the Code. Also, the rental allowance paid to him as part of his compensation for past services is excludable under section 107(2) of the Code, to the extent used by him for expenses directly related to providing a home.

These precedents clearly support the view that ministers who live in church-owned parsonages can exclude from gross income not only the annual rental value of the parsonage but also a parsonage allowance designated by the church, to the extent it is used to pay for parsonage expenses.

5. SOCIAL SECURITY

Ministers cannot exclude a housing allowance (or the annual fair rental value of a parsonage) when computing their self-employment (Social Security) taxes unless they are retired. The tax code specifies that the self-employment tax does not apply to "the rental value of any parsonage or any parsonage allowance provided after the [minister] retires." *IRC 1402(a)(8).*

Therefore, in computing the Social Security tax on Schedule SE of Form 1040, nonretired ministers who live in a church-owned parsonage must *include* the annual rental value of the parsonage as income on line 2 (of either the short or long Schedule SE, whichever applies). A minister also must include as income any parsonage allowance paid by the church to cover miscellaneous expenses in maintaining the parsonage.

6. RENTAL VALUE OF A PARSONAGE

Ministers who have not exempted themselves from paying self-employment (Social Security) tax on their ministerial income must report any parsonage allowance and the annual rental value of a parsonage as income when reporting self-employment taxes on Schedule SE (Form 1040).

The rental value of a parsonage is a question to be determined in each case on the basis of its particular circumstances. Some have

suggested that a fair approximation of the monthly rental value of a home can be computed simply by taking 1 percent of the home's fair market value. For example, if a home has a fair market value of $100,000, its monthly rental value would be $1,000 ($100,000 x 1 percent) and its annual rental value would be $12,000. This method may yield accurate results in some cases, but it will yield inaccurate results in others. Generally, it yields excessive rental values. This approach has never been endorsed by the IRS or any court.

✿ **KEY POINT.** The IRS audit guidelines for ministers instruct agents that "determining the fair rental value [of a parsonage] is a question of all facts and circumstances based on the local market, but the church and minister have often already agreed on a figure and can provide documentary evidence."

✿ **KEY POINT.** The IRS provided some indication of how it will determine a home's fair rental value in a series of four letter rulings issued in 2004. The IRS observed, "In the agent's report, she determined an annual amount of $X as rental value for the property. . . . She stated: 'Calling a property management company and asking about the house determined this rental value, I did not identify the address; rather I used the information about the house, how many acres, square footage and area, etc.' The rental value was $X per month. This appears correct as the other houses owned and operated by Pastor B and the church were consistent with this value. The other rentals were not as spacious, nor did they have the amenities consistent with this property. In addition, the other rentals were in [an adjacent county] as opposed to [this county], which has a higher rental value. Those houses were being rented for approximately $Y/ month." *IRS Private Letter Rulings 200435019, 200435020, 200435021, 200435022.*

EXAMPLE. Pastor T lives in a church-owned parsonage. He is not exempt from Social Security coverage. In an effort to avoid any increase in Pastor T's Social Security tax liability, the church agrees to "rent" the parsonage to Pastor T for $1 each year. Pastor T then lists only $1 as the parsonage's rental value on his Schedule SE in computing his Social Security tax liability. This practice will not achieve its desired savings in Social Security taxes, since a minister must include the annual rental value of a church-provided parsonage as income on Schedule SE. The annual rental value of the parsonage is not $1. Rather, it is what houses of comparable size and quality in the same vicinity would rent for in an arm's-length transaction.

EXAMPLE. A minister was provided with a parsonage, and in addition, a portion of his annual compensation was designated a parsonage allowance to assist him in paying utilities, furnishings, and other miscellaneous expenses. The annual rental value of a parsonage is taxable in computing a minister's self-employment (Social Security) tax. The minister claimed that this amount includes any parsonage allowance designated by the church. As a result, he reduced his parsonage's annual rental value by the parsonage allowance designated by his church in computing his self-employment tax. The Tax Court ruled that this was improper, noting that the minister had "not proven that the stipulated annual rental value of the parsonage already includes amounts designated or received in cash relating to the utility and other household expenses of the parsonages." *Radde v. Commissioner, T.C. Memo. 1997-490 (1997).*

Some churches in high-cost areas purchase a parsonage in order to make housing available to their minister. However, the rental value of such parsonages often is very high, resulting in large increases in the minister's self-employment taxes. For example, assume that church purchased a parsonage several years ago that currently is worth several hundreds of thousands of dollars and that has an annual rental value of $25,000. A minister who lives in such a parsonage would need to add the full $25,000 annual rental value in computing his or her earnings subject to the self-employment tax. This will result in an increase in self-employment taxes of nearly $4,000 (without taking into account any available deductions).

While this is a significant tax increase, keep in mind the following considerations:

- The minister is still receiving a significant income tax benefit (the $25,000 is not taxable for income tax purposes).
- The minister is allowed to live in a home of substantial value.
- Lower-cost accommodations may be much farther away from the church.
- Ministers pay the full 15.3 percent self-employment rate only on earnings up to a specified amount ($113,700 for 2013), and they pay only the 2.9 percent Medicare component of self-employment taxes on all net earnings from self-employment in excess of this amount. So, to the extent that the annual rental value of the parsonage boosts the minister's earnings above $113,700 for 2013, only the excess is subject to the 2.9 percent Medicare tax.

EXAMPLE. Pastor H excluded a parsonage allowance from his reportable income though his employing church had never designated a portion of his compensation as a parsonage allowance. The Tax Court ruled that Pastor H was not entitled to exclude the allowance, since it had not been designated by his church prior to the time of its payment. *Hoelz v. Commissioner, 42 T.C.M. 1037 (1981).*

7. EQUITY ALLOWANCES

Ministers who live in church-owned parsonages experience a significant disadvantage—they do not acquire equity in a home. To illustrate, assume that Pastor E lives in church-owned parsonages throughout his 35-year career as a minister. When Pastor E retires, he must vacate the parsonage he is occupying, and he has no equity interest in any of the parsonages he has occupied that can be used to acquire a retirement home. If Pastor E had owned homes throughout his career, he would have accumulated equity in the amount of his combined principal mortgage payments plus any appreciation in the value of the homes he owned. At retirement, not only would Pastor E have a home in which he could remain, but he also would have accumulated a significant equity interest.

Some churches have helped ministers who live in parsonages avoid or at least reduce the adverse economic impact of this housing arrangement by providing them with an equity allowance over and above their stated compensation. This allowance is designed to partially or wholly compensate the minister for the lost opportunity of accumulating equity in a home.

Since the purpose of such an allowance is to assist the minister in obtaining suitable housing at retirement, it is important that the allowance not be available to the minister until retirement. One way churches can accomplish this is to deposit the annual equity allowance in a tax-favored retirement program not currently accessible to the minister. This is an excellent approach that can help to avoid a most unfortunate financial predicament for a minister who, often sacrificially, has devoted a lifetime to the church. However, since an equity allowance ordinarily does not compensate a minister for actual costs incurred in living in a parsonage, it is not excludable from income as a parsonage allowance.

⊷ TIP. Churches should consider adopting an appropriate equity allowance for ministers who live in church-owned parsonages.

▲ CAUTION. *Section 409A of the tax code imposes strict new requirements on most nonqualified deferred compensation plans (NQDPs). IRS regulations define an NQDP broadly to include any plan that provides for the deferral of compensation. This definition is broad enough to cover some forms of equity allowances, depending on how they are structured by a church. As a result, any church that is considering an equity allowance should contact a tax attorney to have the arrangement reviewed to ensure compliance with both section 409A and the final regulations. Such a review will protect against the substantial penalties the IRS can assess for noncompliance. It also will help clarify whether a deferred compensation arrangement is a viable option in light of the limitations imposed by section 409A and the final regulations. See Chapter 10, section A.2, in this guide for more information.*

8. IRS AUDIT GUIDELINES FOR MINISTERS

The IRS has issued audit guidelines for its agents to follow when auditing ministers. The guidelines provide agents with the following information regarding parsonages and parsonage allowances:

Internal Revenue Code section 107 provides an exclusion from gross income for a "parsonage allowance" . . . . The term "parsonage allowance" includes church provided parsonages, rental allowances with which the minister may rent a home and housing allowances with which the minister may purchase a home. A minister can receive a parsonage allowance for only one home. . . .

The value of the "allowed" parsonage allowance is not included in computing the minister's income subject to income tax and should not be included in W-2 wages. However, the parsonage allowance is subject to self-employment tax along with other earnings. If a church-owned parsonage is provided to the minister, instead of a housing allowance, the fair rental value of the housing must be determined. Determining the fair rental value is a question of all facts and circumstances based on the local market, but the church and minister have often already agreed on a figure and can provide documentary evidence.

The [parsonage allowance] exclusion only applies if the employing church designates the amount of the parsonage allowance in advance of the tax year. The designation may appear in the minister's employment contract, the church minutes, the church budget, or any other document indicating official action. An additional requirement . . . is that the fair rental value of the parsonage or parsonage allowance is not more than reasonable pay for the ministerial services performed.

The audit guidelines contain the following example:

EXAMPLE. A is an ordained minister. She receives an annual salary of $36,000 and use of a parsonage which has an annual rental value of $800 a month, including utilities. She has an accountable plan for other business expenses such as travel. A's gross income for arriving at taxable income for federal income tax purposes is $36,000, but for self-employment tax purposes it is $45,600 ($36,000 salary + $9,600 annual rental value of parsonage).

❋**KEY POINT.** The audit guidelines assist IRS agents in the examination of ministers' tax returns. They alert agents to the key questions to ask and provide background information along with the IRS position on a number of issues. It is of utmost importance that ministers be familiar with these guidelines.

❋**KEY POINT.** It is unfortunate that the guidelines state that the housing allowance "only applies if the employing church designates the amount of the allowance in advance of the tax year," since this statement is not true. The tax code does not impose such a requirement. It is true that a church's housing allowance designation may never be made retroactively and only operates prospectively. But this does not mean it has to be made in advance of a tax year. To illustrate, many churches fail to designate a housing allowance by the end of a calendar year

IRS TAX GUIDE FOR CHURCHES

The current edition of the IRS *Tax Guide for Churches and Religious Organizations* contains summaries of several rules that pertain to churches and ministers. The guide contains the following statements regarding parsonages and parsonage allowances:

- A minister's gross income does not include the rental value of a home (a parsonage) provided, or the rental allowance paid, as part of his or her compensation for services performed that are ordinarily the duties of a minister.
- A minister who is furnished a parsonage may exclude from income the fair rental value of the parsonage, including utilities. However, the amount excluded cannot be more than the reasonable pay for the minister's services.
- A minister who receives a parsonage or rental allowance excludes that amount from his income. The portion of expenses allocable to the excludable amount is not deductible. This limitation, however, does not apply to interest on a home mortgage or real estate taxes, nor to the calculation of net earnings from self-employment for SECA tax purposes.
- The fair rental value of a parsonage or housing allowance is excludable from income only for income tax purposes. These amounts are not excluded in determining the minister's net earnings from self-employment for Self-employment Contributions Act (SECA) tax purposes. Retired ministers who receive either a parsonage or housing allowance are not required to include such amounts for SECA tax purposes.

and discover the omission a few months into the new year. The church can still designate a housing allowance for the minister for the remainder of the new year. Unfortunately, unless the guidelines are amended, IRS agents may unnecessarily disallow any housing allowance exclusion under these facts. A strict interpretation of the audit guidelines would preclude ministers who are called to a church in midyear from receiving a housing allowance, since the allowance would not be designated "in advance of the tax year." This is clearly an incorrect result that undermines the "in advance of the tax year" language in the audit guidelines.

9. PARSONAGES PROVIDED TO RETIRED MINISTERS

The tax status of parsonages and parsonage allowances provided to retired ministers is addressed in Chapter 10, section E, of this text.

B. OWNING OR RENTING YOUR HOME

Ministers who own their home do not pay federal income taxes on the amount of their compensation that their employing church designates in advance as a housing allowance, to the extent that the allowance represents compensation for ministerial services, is used to pay housing expenses, and does not exceed the fair rental value of the home (furnished, plus utilities). Housing-related expenses include mortgage payments, utilities, repairs, furnishings, insurance, property taxes, additions, and maintenance.

Ministers who rent a home or apartment do not pay federal income taxes on the amount of their compensation that their employing church designates in advance as a housing allowance, to the extent that the allowance represents compensation for ministerial services and is used to pay rental expenses such as rent, furnishings, utilities, and insurance.

Many ministers rent their home. The apostle Paul did so for a brief time. Acts 28:30 states: "For two whole years Paul stayed there in his own rented house and welcomed all who came to see him."

1. OVERVIEW

The previous section addressed parsonages and parsonage allowances. Most ministers, however, do not live in a parsonage. Instead, they either own or rent a home. This section will address the tax rules that apply to these ministers. The tax code uses the term "rental allowance" for allowances paid to ministers who either rent or own their home. This terminology is confusing, so this text uses the term "housing allowance" for ministers who either rent or own their home.

❖ **KEY POINT.** The IRS audit guidelines for ministers state that the term "parsonage allowance" includes "church provided parsonages, rental allowances with which the minister may rent a home and housing allowances with which the minister may purchase a home."

Section 107 of the tax code specifies that "in the case of a minister of the gospel, gross income does not include—(1) the rental value of a home furnished to him as part of his compensation; or (2) the rental allowance paid to him as part of his compensation, to the extent used by him to rent or provide a home and to the extent such

allowance does not exceed the fair rental value of the home, including furnishings and appurtenances such as a garage, plus the cost of utilities."

Following are four important considerations to note:

- The housing allowance is available only to a minister of the gospel. This term is defined in Chapter 3.
- A housing allowance must represent compensation for services performed in the exercise of ministry. This term is defined in Chapter 3.
- The housing allowance is an exclusion from gross income rather than a deduction in computing or reducing adjusted gross income. As a result, it is not reported on Form 1040. In effect, the housing allowance is claimed by not reporting it as income. As will be explained later, if the actual housing allowance exclusion is less than the church-designated allowance, the minister will need to report the difference as additional income on his or her federal tax return. This assumes that the church reduced the minister's Form W-2 or 1099-MISC income by the amount of the allowance. Note further that the actual housing allowance exclusion must be reported as self-employment earnings on a nonretired minister's Schedule SE (Form 1040) in computing Social Security taxes, assuming the minister has not applied for and received an approved exemption from Social Security coverage.
- A housing allowance is nontaxable in computing a minister's federal income taxes only if the following requirements are met: (1) the allowance is designated in advance by official action of the church board or congregation; (2) the allowance is used by the minister to pay for housing-related expenses; and (3) in the case of ministers who own or rent their home, the allowance does not exceed the fair rental value of the minister's home (furnished, plus utilities). See Illustration 6-2 for an example of a church-designated housing allowance.

❖ **KEY POINT.** Parsonage and housing allowances should be (1) adopted by the church board or congregation, (2) recorded in written form (such as minutes), and (3) designated in advance of the calendar year. However, churches that fail to designate an allowance in advance of a calendar year should do so as soon as possible in the new year. The allowance will operate prospectively.

2. DESIGNATING THE HOUSING ALLOWANCE

❖ **KEY POINT.** The tax code limits the nontaxable portion of a church-designated housing allowance for ministers who own their home to the fair rental value of the home (furnished, plus utilities). Churches should keep this limit in mind when designating housing allowances. There is no benefit in designating allowances above this limit. To the contrary, designating a housing allowance substantially above this limit can create problems,

HOUSING ALLOWANCE DESIGNATION FOR MINISTERS WHO OWN THEIR HOME

The following resolution was duly adopted by the board of directors of First Church at a regularly scheduled meeting held on December 15, 2012, a quorum being present:

Whereas, ministers who own their home do not pay federal income taxes on the amount of their compensation that their employing church designates in advance as a housing allowance, to the extent that the allowance represents compensation for ministerial services, is used to pay housing expenses, and does not exceed the fair rental value of the home (furnished, plus utilities); and

Whereas, Pastor John Smith is compensated by First Church exclusively for services as a minister of the gospel; and

Whereas, First Church does not provide Pastor John Smith with a parsonage; therefore, it is hereby

Resolved, that the total compensation paid to Pastor John Smith for calendar year 2013 shall be $50,000, of which $15,000 is hereby designated as a housing allowance; and it is further

Resolved, that the designation of $15,000 as a housing allowance shall apply to calendar year 2013 and all future years unless otherwise provided by this board.

---

since ministers often wrongly assume that the entire allowance is nontaxable even though it exceeds their home's fair rental value (furnished, plus utilities). This error can lead to additional taxes in the event of an audit.

In general

The income tax regulations specify that the designation of the allowance may be contained in "an employment contract, in minutes of or in a resolution by a church or other qualified organization or in its budget, or in any other appropriate instrument evidencing such official action."

The regulations further provide that "the designation . . . is a sufficient designation if it permits a payment or a part thereof to be identified as a payment of rental allowance as distinguished from salary or other remuneration." *Treas. Reg. 1.107-1(b)*. In other words, the designation must simply distinguish a part of the minister's compensation as a housing allowance. This can be done by giving a minister two separate checks—one designated as salary and the other as the housing or rental allowance. But this approach

is not necessary, since a church that has designated a portion of a minister's compensation as a housing or rental allowance has thereby made the required identification, and it is free to issue a minister one check per pay period that combines both salary and the housing allowance.

The church's designation should be in writing, although if a board orally agrees to a specific allowance and neglects to make a written record of its action, it could draft an appropriate record of its action at a later time, dated as of the earlier meeting. *Kizer v. Commissioner, T.C. Memo. 1992-584.*

The Tax Court has ruled that an oral designation is sufficient, since "there is no requirement that the designation be in writing." *Libman v. Commissioner, 44 T.C.M. 370 (1982)*. This practice should be avoided, however, since it will always create problems of proof.

EXAMPLE. A traveling evangelist was denied any housing allowance exclusion despite his insistence that various churches in which he had conducted services had orally designated a portion of his compensation as a housing allowance. The Tax Court noted that there was no evidence of such designations and that the minister's testimony was "marred by numerous inconsistencies." *Holland v. Commissioner, 47 T.C.M. 494 (1983)*.

In summary, if your church board orally designated (in advance) a portion of your compensation as a housing or rental allowance, you should go ahead and claim the exclusion. The church board could "memorialize" its earlier action in a written resolution if your return is audited and your allowance questioned. Such a practice is not recommended.

In advance

Many churches fail to designate a housing allowance by the end of a calendar year for a variety of reasons and discover the omission a few weeks or months into the new year. Is it too late to do so for that year? According to the IRS regulations, the church can still designate a housing allowance for the minister for the remainder of the new year. The regulations state that a housing allowance "means an amount paid to a minister to rent or otherwise provide a home if such amount is designated as rental allowance pursuant to official action taken . . . *in advance of such payment* by the employing church or other qualified organization" (emphasis added). *Treas. Reg. 1.107-1(b)*. Similarly, IRS Publication 1828 states that "the minister's church or other qualified organization must designate the housing allowance pursuant to official action taken *in advance* of the payment."

As a result, a housing allowance only operates prospectively, never retroactively. This principle is a corollary of the requirement that a housing allowance is nontaxable only to the extent that it is used to pay for housing expenses. This requirement would be compromised if housing allowances could be designated retroactively, after housing expenses are incurred and paid. In such a case, some or all of the allowance would not be used to pay for housing expenses.

Unfortunately, the IRS audit guidelines for ministers incorrectly state that the housing allowance exclusion "only applies if the employing church designates the amount of the parsonage allowance *in advance of the tax year*" (emphasis added). It is unfortunate that the IRS audit guidelines for ministers contradict the IRS regulations and IRS Publication 1828. The regulations are more authoritative than the audit guidelines, but many IRS agents will follow the guidelines when auditing ministers, and this will result in the unnecessary denial of a housing allowance exclusion to ministers whose church failed to designate an allowance until after the start of the year.

▲ **CAUTION.** *Under no circumstances can a minister exclude any portion of a housing allowance retroactively designated by a church.*

▲ **CAUTION.** *In some cases retroactive designations of a housing allowance may violate the Sarbanes-Oxley Act (see section B.20 in this chapter).*

EXAMPLE. A pastor performed ministerial services for a congregation that provided him with a monthly rental allowance. The pastor excluded the amount of the housing allowance from his gross income each year in question. The pastor and his employing church later asked the IRS if they could amend the amount of the housing allowance to reflect the true cost of providing the home. The church claimed that the amount of the rental allowance was selected without understanding its legal consequences. The IRS rejected the church's request. It observed, "The church is attempting to increase the amount of the pastor's rental allowance through official action taken after payments were made. The tax code and regulation are clear in the treatment of rental allowances for ministers of the gospel. The church must designate the amount of its minister's rental allowance before the minister receives payment for his services. The church may not retroactively increase the amount of the taxpayer's rental allowance. The minister properly excluded from his gross income the amount of his compensation that was designated as rental allowance by his church in advance of payment." *IRS Technical Advice Memorandum 8120007 (1981).*

EXAMPLE. In preparing his income tax return for 2012, Pastor H discovers that his church failed to designate a housing allowance for 2012. He asks his church board to pass a resolution retroactively granting the allowance for 2012. Such a resolution is ineffective, and Pastor H will not be eligible for any housing allowance in 2012. *Hoelz v. Commissioner, 42 T.C.M. 1037 (1981); Ling v. Commissioner, 200 F. Supp. 282 (D.D.C. 1962).*

EXAMPLE. Pastor K was paid a salary by his church, but no portion of the salary was designated by the church as a housing

HOUSING EXPENSES TO INCLUDE WHEN COMPUTING YOUR HOUSING ALLOWANCE EXCLUSION

Ministers who own their homes should take the following expenses into account in computing their housing allowance exclusion:

- down payment on a home;
- payments (including prepayments) on a mortgage loan to purchase or improve your home (including both interest and principal);
- real estate taxes;
- property insurance;
- utilities (electricity, gas, water, trash pickup, local telephone charges; Internet access fees);
- furnishings and appliances (purchase and repair);
- structural repairs and remodeling;
- yard maintenance and improvements;
- maintenance items (household cleansers, light bulbs, pest control, etc.); and
- homeowners association dues.

allowance. The Tax Court ruled that Pastor K was not able to exclude any part of the expenses incurred in owning and maintaining his home as a housing allowance, since the church had not designated any portion of Pastor K's compensation as a housing allowance. *Eden v. Commissioner, 41 T.C. 605 (1964).*

EXAMPLE. A church board orally discussed a new minister's compensation package with him and agreed to pay him a salary of $30,000, out of which $6,250 was designated as a housing allowance. The board's housing allowance designation was not recorded in the church minutes or in any other writing. The IRS audited the minister and denied any housing allowance exclusion on the ground that no allowance had been properly designated.

The Tax Court disagreed and ruled that the minister was eligible for a housing allowance in the amount of $6,250. It observed: "It is clear that there was discussion about a parsonage allowance for [the minister], and that all of the members of the board of directors [of the church] who testified recollected that he was taking a cut in total compensation to come to their church. The recording secretary, the person whose obligation it was to keep the minutes of the various meetings, had a clear recollection of the discussion and thought that [the minister] was to receive the same amount as a parsonage allowance that he received at [his former church]." The court referred to a 1982 decision (*Libman v. Commissioner*)

in which it ruled that "there is no requirement that the parsonage allowance designation be in writing. Rather, we held, the designation requirement is satisfied upon satisfactory proof of official action." In the present case, the court concluded that there was sufficient evidence of a proper designation, in advance of the year in question, though never committed to writing. Accordingly, the minister was entitled to the housing allowance exclusion. *Kizer v. Commissioner, T.C. Memo. 1992-584.*

EXAMPLE. The IRS ruled that a pastor was not entitled to a housing allowance because there was no evidence that his employing church had designated an allowance for the year in question. In 1982 the church board adopted a motion stating simply that "the pastor's housing allowance for 1982 will be $10,000." The pastor claimed a housing allowance of $10,000 in the following year, although the church had not designated such an allowance. The pastor and church maintained that it was their understanding that the 1982 allowance was effective for future years until there was a salary change. As a result, the pastor claimed a $10,000 allowance in 1983. The church board, in 1984, adopted a resolution stating that "the pastor's salary and housing allowance for 1984 will be the same as 1983."

The IRS concluded, "You have not furnished any information or documents that show that the church designated a portion of your compensation as rental allowance for the year 1983 pursuant to official action taken in advance of your payments for 1983. In 1984, the church made a retroactive designation that $10,000 of your 1983 compensation was a rental allowance. However, this does not satisfy the requirement of [the tax regulations] that the designation must be made before the payments are made. Accordingly, we conclude that because the rental allowance for 1983 was not designated by official action before it was paid to you, you may not exclude $10,000 from your gross income." *IRS Private Letter Ruling 8511075.*

Who designates the allowance

Section 1.107-1(b) of the income tax regulations provides that the term "housing allowance" means an amount paid to a minister to rent or otherwise provide a home if such amount is designated as a housing allowance pursuant to official action taken in advance of the payment of such amounts by "the employing church or other qualified organization."

EXAMPLE. An ordained minister was employed as a chaplain by a municipal police department. The police department's chaplaincy program was established through its joint efforts with a local federation of churches. The minister claimed that amounts designated by the federation as a housing allowance were excludable from his gross income. The IRS maintained that because the minister was employed by the city and not by the federation, the city was the only "other qualified organization" eligible to designate a housing allowance. Since it failed to do so, the minister

was not eligible for a housing allowance. The Tax Court reversed the IRS determination and ruled that the minister was entitled to a housing allowance. It noted that as a police chaplain, the minister was under the direct supervision of the chief of police. However, the federation retained supervision over his ecclesiastical performance and maintained day-to-day contact with him and other chaplains. The federation was also involved in the operation of the police chaplaincy program. If a problem arose concerning a police chaplain, a police department official usually would contact the federation to resolve the problem. When a vacancy occurred for a chaplain, the federation assumed primary responsibility for finding a qualified person to fill the vacancy.

The federation annually designated a specific amount of the minister's salary in advance as a housing allowance even though his salary was paid by the city. The city neither provided him with a home nor designated any portion of his salary as a housing allowance.

The Tax Court concluded that the federation was an "other qualified organization" within the meaning of section 1.107-1(b) of the regulations and that its designation of a portion of his salary as a housing allowance was valid. The Tax Court based its decision on the "constant and detailed involvement of the federation" in the city's police chaplaincy program. The IRS later acquiesced in the court's ruling on the ground that the federation's responsibilities toward the chaplaincy program were similar to those of an employer and that the federation was closely involved with the police department in its employer-employee relationship with the ministers. *Boyd v. Commissioner, 42 T.C.M. 1136 (1981).*

3. FAILURE TO DESIGNATE A TIMELY HOUSING ALLOWANCE

Unfortunately, many churches fail to designate a housing allowance for their ministers. This practice denies ministers an important tax benefit. If your church fails to designate a housing allowance prior to January 1 for the new year, it should designate an allowance as soon as possible. The housing allowance will be effective from the date it is declared for the remainder of the year. See section B.2 of this chapter.

Matching allowances and expenses

Assume that Pastor B receives monthly compensation of $4,000 from First Church, that Pastor B owns or rents his home, that First Church fails to designate a housing allowance for Pastor B for 2013, and that the church board belatedly takes action on November 1, 2013, to designate Pastor B's entire remaining compensation for 2013 ($8,000) as a housing allowance. The question in such a case is how large a housing allowance exclusion Pastor B can claim. At the very least, he will be able to exclude housing expenses incurred in November and December. But what if his housing expenses amount to only $2,000 in November and December? Can Pastor B apply the rest of the housing allowance ($6,000) to housing expenses incurred in months prior to November? This important issue has never been addressed by the IRS or the courts.

Section 107 of the tax code provides that the housing allowance exclusion covers "the rental allowance paid to [a minister] as part of his compensation *to the extent used by him to rent or provide a home*" (emphasis added). This language suggests that the housing expenses must be paid out of the designated allowance, meaning that Pastor B (in the above example) would only be able to exclude housing expenses incurred in November and December.

A broader interpretation

Some interpret section 107 more broadly and claim that the critical event is the designation of a portion of Pastor B's salary as a housing allowance. Once an allowance is declared (even if later in the year), there is no reason why it should not be allocated to expenses incurred in prior months of the same year. Under this broader interpretation of section 107, the church's belated action would permit Pastor B to exclude his remaining salary of $4,000 from his gross income as a housing allowance exclusion (assuming his actual expenses in owning or maintaining his home are at least this amount for the year), resulting in a substantial savings in income taxes.

The main problem with this approach is that a housing allowance is nontaxable only to the extent it is used to pay for housing expenses. By November, Pastor B has already paid for most of his housing expenses for the first ten months of the year (mortgage payments, utilities, insurance, taxes, etc.), and so it impossible for him to use the $8,000 allowance designated in November for these expenses.

Ministers who adopt this broader interpretation must recognize that such a position has never been approved by the IRS or the courts, it may not be allowed, and it is an aggressive position that should not be pursued without professional advice. Clearly, the more reasonable interpretation of the regulation would be the first one described above.

> **EXAMPLE.** An administrator of a Jewish synagogue was not eligible for a housing allowance, since there was no evidence that a housing allowance had ever been properly designated for him. *Haimowitz v. Commissioner, T.C. Memo. 1997-40 (1997); McCurry v. Commissioner, 56 T.C.M. 253 (1988).*

4. THE CLERGY HOUSING ALLOWANCE CLARIFICATION ACT OF 2002

✸**KEY POINT.** Congress enacted the Clergy Housing Allowance Clarification Act in 2002. This Act amended the tax code to limit the nontaxable portion of a church-designated housing allowance for ministers who own their home to the fair rental value of the home (furnished, plus utilities). As a result, ministers who own a home do not include the portion of their salary designated in advance by their church as a "housing allowance" as income in computing their federal income taxes, to the extent it is used to pay for expenses incurred in owning the home, such as mortgage payments, utilities, repairs, property taxes, property insurance, and furnishings and does not exceed the fair rental value of the home.

Background

For many years, section 107 of the tax code stated that "in the case of a minister of the gospel, gross income does not include . . . the rental allowance paid to him as part of his compensation, to the extent used by him to rent or provide a home." This language required little explanation. The portion of a minister's church-designated housing allowance that was used to pay for housing-related expenses was nontaxable for federal income tax reporting purposes. Stated differently, ministers could exclude from taxable income the lesser of (1) the church-designated housing allowance, or (2) the actual amount of housing-related expenses paid during the year.

In 1971 the IRS imposed an additional limitation: the nontaxable portion of a church-designated housing allowance could not exceed the fair rental value of the minister's home (furnished, plus utilities). *Revenue Ruling 71-280.* As a result, a housing allowance was nontaxable only to the extent it was used to pay for housing expenses and did not exceed the fair rental value of the home (furnished, plus utilities).

The IRS offered various arguments to defend the annual rental value test, including the following: (1) the rental value test prevents ministers who own their homes from receiving a greater tax benefit than those who live in a church-provided parsonage; (2) the rental value test prevents ministers from acquiring expensive homes; and (3) the rental value test prevents ministers with other sources of income from acquiring more expensive homes by allocating a larger amount of their church compensation to a nontaxable housing allowance.

The Warren case

The United States Tax Court ruled in 2000 that a housing allowance is nontaxable for income tax reporting so long as it is used to pay for housing-related expenses. *Warren v. Commissioner, 114 T.C. 23 (2000).* The court threw out the annual "fair rental value" test the IRS adopted in 1971. The IRS appealed the *Warren* case to the ninth circuit federal court of appeals in California. On March 5, 2002, a three-judge panel of the court issued a surprising decision. Two of the panel's three judges issued an order asking the parties, and a law professor, to submit additional briefs to the court addressing the following issues:

- Does the court have the authority to consider the constitutionality of the housing allowance?
- If so, should the court exercise that authority?
- Is the housing allowance constitutional under the First Amendment's nonestablishment of religion clause?

In referring to the housing allowance, the court observed that "it appears that no similar exemption is afforded any member of any other profession, whether serving a for-profit or non-profit institution." This off-hand comment left little doubt that the court had made up its mind that the housing allowance was unconstitutional. This conclusion was reinforced by the court's reference to the following quotation from an earlier Supreme Court case: "When government directs a subsidy exclusively to religious organizations that is not required by the free exercise [of religion] clause and that either burdens non-beneficiaries markedly or cannot reasonably be seen as removing a significant state-imposed deterrent to the free exercise of religion . . . it provides unjustifiable awards of assistance to religious organizations and cannot but convey a message of endorsement to slighted members of the community." *Texas Monthly, Inc. v. Bullock, 489 U.S. 1 (1989)*.

One of the court's three judges passionately dissented from the court's order, noting that neither the IRS nor the minister had raised the issue of the constitutionality of the housing allowance, and therefore the court should not have done so on its own initiative. He observed:

> *The parties to this appeal have not questioned the constitutionality of the tax exclusion enacted by Congress and each party has advised the Court that they do not wish to do so. . . . Because the constitutional issue was not raised in the Tax Court, nor briefed or argued by the parties on appeal, and because it is unnecessarily and improvidently raised by my colleagues, I respectfully dissent from the order directing supplemental and court-appointed amicus briefing. This case can easily be decided without reaching the constitutionality of the statutory exclusion.*

Clergy Housing Allowance Clarification Act

In response to this threat to the housing allowance, the Clergy Housing Allowance Clarification Act of 2002 (H.R. 4156) was introduced in the House of Representatives. It was enacted on April 16, 2002, by a vote of 408 to 0. The Senate unanimously enacted the same bill on May 2. President George W. Bush signed it into law on May 20.

The Act had one purpose—to amend the tax code to reinstate the fair rental value limit on ministers' housing allowances so that the IRS would dismiss its appeal of the *Warren* case and thereby deprive the federal appeals court of the opportunity to address the constitutionality of the housing allowance on its own initiative. As amended, section 107 now reads: "In the case of a minister of the gospel, gross income does not include—(1) the rental value of a home furnished to him as part of his compensation; or (2) the rental allowance paid to him as part of his compensation, to the extent used by him to rent or provide a home and to the extent such allowance does not exceed the fair rental value of the home, including furnishings and appurtenances such as a garage, plus the cost of utilities."

The Act had the desired effect. The IRS agreed to dismiss the appeal of the *Warren* case, and the federal appeals court eventually issued an order formally dismissing the case.

> **EXAMPLE.** A retired pastor had $50,000 distributed from his retirement account in 2012 and had the entire amount designated as a housing allowance. The pastor used the distribution for a down payment on a new home and other housing related expenses. The fair rental value of the home (furnished, plus utilities) was $20,000. The nontaxable portion of the retired pastor's $50,000 housing allowance is limited to $20,000 (the fair rental value of his home). As a result, $30,000 of the housing allowance is taxable in computing income taxes.

5. FAIR RENTAL VALUE

The Clergy Housing Allowance Clarification Act of 2002 amended the tax code to limit the nontaxable portion of a housing allowance for ministers who own or rent their home to the annual fair rental value of the home furnished, plus utilities). Unfortunately, while the Act imposes a fair rental value limit, it does not explain what this means. The IRS has provided no help. Its audit guidelines for ministers instruct agents that "determining the fair rental value of a home is a question of all facts and circumstances based on the local market, but the church and minister have often already agreed on a figure and can provide documentary evidence."

In summary, ministers have been given no guidance by Congress, the IRS, or the courts regarding the meaning of "fair rental value." Here are three ways some ministers attempt to define this term:

- **Realtor's informal opinion.** Some ministers have a realtor drive by their home and provide an informal estimate as to the rental value of the home. Usually this will result in a range of possible values (e.g., "between $700 and $1,000 per month"). The realtor should be asked to provide his or her opinion in a signed letter that the minister can later use in the event of an audit. Given the refusal by the IRS to define the term "fair rental value," it is reasonable to assume that an IRS auditor would accept this method as reasonable.
- **Appraisal.** A minister could obtain a formal rental value from a local real estate appraiser. This approach will be expensive and, in most cases, will not be significantly different than a realtor's informal opinion. It is another option to consider.
- **The 1 percent rule.** Some have suggested that a fair approximation of the monthly rental value of a home can be computed simply by taking 1 percent of the home's fair market value. For example, if a home has a fair market value of $100,000, then its monthly rental value would be $1,000 ($100,000 x 1 percent), and its annual rental value would be $12,000. This method will yield accurate results in some cases but inaccurate results in others. Generally, this approach

yields excessive rental values. It has never been endorsed by the IRS or the courts.

❖ **KEY POINT.** The IRS provided some indication of how it will determine a home's fair rental value in a series of four letter rulings issued in 2004. The IRS observed, "In the agent's report, she determined an annual amount of $X as rental value for the property. . . . She stated: 'Calling a property management company and asking about the house determined this rental value, I did not identify the address; rather I used the information about the house, how many acres, square footage and area, etc.' The rental value was $X per month. This appears correct as the other houses owned and operated by Pastor B and the church were consistent with this value. The other rentals were not as spacious, nor did they have the amenities consistent with this property. In addition, the other rentals were in [an adjacent county] as opposed to [this county], which has a higher rental value. Those houses were being rented for approximately $Y/ month." *IRS Private Letter Rulings 200435019, 200435020, 200435021, 200435022.*

Home owned less than one year

One question that is not addressed by the tax code or by the IRS or the courts is whether the fair rental value limit should be prorated if a minister owns a home for less than one year. Consider an example. Pastor Tim accepts a pastoral position with a church in July 2013 and purchases a new home that he occupies for the last six months of the year. The church pays him a salary and a housing allowance. Assume that the annual fair rental value of the home is $15,000. However, since Pastor Tim only occupied the home for six months of the year, the rental value of the home for those months was $7,500.

When Pastor Tim computes the nontaxable amount of his church-designated housing allowance for 201, does the fair rental value limit refer to the *annual* fair rental value ($15,000) of his home or the *prorated* fair rental value for the portion of the year he occupied the home ($7,500)?

While the IRS has not addressed this question, it is likely that it would use a prorated rental value limit in calculating Pastor Tim's housing allowance exclusion. Here's why. For many years the tax code excluded the rental value of a parsonage from a minister's taxable income, but not a housing allowance designated by a church. This changed in 1954, when Congress amended the tax code (section 107) to make church-designated housing allowances nontaxable in computing income taxes to the extent they are used to pay housing expenses. A committee report explained this change as follows:

> Under present law, the rental value of a home furnished a minister of the gospel as a part of his salary is not included in his gross income. This is unfair to those ministers who are not furnished a parsonage, but who receive larger salaries (which are taxable) to compensate them for expenses they incur in supplying their own

home. Your committee has removed the discrimination in existing law by providing that the present exclusion is to apply to rental allowances paid to ministers to the extent used by them to rent or provide a home.

According to this language, the housing allowance exclusion was created to eliminate the tax code's former preference for ministers who reside in a parsonage. In the above example, this would mean that Pastor Tim's computation of his home's fair rental value should only be for the six months he lived there, since if he had lived in a church-provided parsonage, he would have occupied it for only six months. On the other hand, if Pastor Tim can use his home's fair rental value for the entire year as his limitation, this puts him in a *more favorable position* than he would have been in had he occupied the parsonage for six months.

Logically, then, the fair rental value should be prorated to reflect the portion of the year a minister actually occupies a home. This will result in more taxes (because of a lower rental value limit). Any official guidance will be reported in future editions of this tax guide.

Furniture

The tax code specifies that the nontaxable portion of a housing allowance (for ministers who own their home) cannot exceed "the fair rental value of the home, including furnishings and appurtenances such as a garage, plus the cost of utilities." Ministers and their tax advisors have interpreted this language in two ways:

(1) Some assume that "the rental value of the home, including furnishings" refers to the fair rental value of a *furnished* home. To illustrate, assume that a home has an annual fair rental value of $15,000 if unfurnished, but an annual fair rental value of $16,000 if it includes furnishings. The fair rental value limit refers to the $16,000 value.

(2) Some have argued that "the rental value of the home, including furnishings" means the fair rental value of a home *without* furnishings *plus* the fair rental value of rented furniture. To illustrate, assume that a home has an annual fair rental value of $15,000 if unfurnished and an annual fair rental value of $16,000 if it includes furnishings. However, the cost of renting furniture for the entire home is $5,000 per year. Therefore, "the rental value of the home, including furnishings," means the rental value of the unfurnished home ($15,000) plus the rental value of furnishing the home ($5,000), for a total rental value of $20,000. Obviously, this interpretation results in a much higher rental value, and this means that in many cases the housing allowance exclusion will be larger, resulting in lower taxes for the minister.

Neither the IRS nor any court has addressed this issue in a published ruling. Until definitive guidance is provided, the second option should be viewed as an aggressive tax position that likely would be rejected by the IRS in an audit, and it should not be used without the advice of a tax professional.

6. AMOUNT OF HOUSING ALLOWANCE

✿ **KEY POINT.** The tax code limits the nontaxable portion of a church-designated housing allowance for ministers who own or rent their home to the fair rental value of the home (furnished, plus utilities). As a result, ministers who own or rent a home do not include the portion of their salary designated in advance by their church as a housing allowance as income in computing their federal income taxes, to the extent it is used to pay for expenses incurred in owning or renting the home (i.e., mortgage payments, rental payments, utilities, repairs, property taxes, property insurance, and furnishings) and does not exceed the fair rental value of the home (furnished, plus utilities).

Method of determination

Some churches simply declare a percentage (e.g., 40 percent) of a minister's salary as a housing allowance. This practice should be avoided, since it bears no correlation to actual housing expenses. Others declare a monetary amount based on a minister's projected expenses for the year. In either case, the church should make a separate designation for each minister on staff (churches can designate housing allowances for all ministers on staff).

The allowance should be designated each year for each minister. General designations for several unspecified ministers are not adequate. In some cases it is appropriate for a church to designate a minister's entire church compensation as a housing allowance. For example, assume that Don is a minister of a small, mission church that is only able to pay him $5,000 per year. Assume further that Don works a part-time secular job to support himself. If Don has at least $5,000 of housing expenses, it would seem perfectly reasonable and appropriate for his church to designate his entire salary as a housing allowance. No court (or the IRS) has ever ruled that a housing allowance designated by a church cannot be fully claimed by a minister who has secular earnings. There is no requirement that ministers allocate their housing expenses to their church and secular earnings on a pro rata basis.

Some churches designate a housing allowance in the amount of a minister's actual housing expenses. This practice should be avoided, since it may not satisfy the requirement that housing allowances be designated in advance. Under this approach there is no way to know how much of a minister's compensation is a housing allowance until *after* expenses are incurred. This is not consistent with the income tax regulations.

Limitations

The IRS has stated that there are no limitations on how much of a minister's compensation can be designated by his or her employing church as a housing allowance. However, as noted above, this means little, since the nontaxable portion of a church-designated housing allowance for ministers who own or rent their home cannot exceed the lesser of (1) actual housing expenses, or (2) the fair rental value of the home (furnished, plus utilities).

In addition, the IRS has ruled that a housing allowance may not be excluded by a minister to the extent that it represents "unreasonable compensation" for the minister's services. *Revenue Ruling 78-448.* For example, a televangelist whose ministry designates hundreds of thousands of dollars of his compensation each year as a housing allowance would likely have the reasonableness of the allowance challenged by the IRS in the event of an audit. Providing a minister with a housing allowance (or parsonage) that is excessive in amount may constitute unreasonable compensation. Such a finding could jeopardize the tax-exempt status of the church or ministry. Further, the allowance may constitute an excess benefit transaction, triggering intermediate sanctions against the pastor (and the board members who approved it) in the form of substantial excise taxes. See Chapter 4, section A, for a discussion of unreasonable compensation and intermediate sanctions.

✿ **KEY POINT.** No limit has been placed on the amount of a minister's compensation that can be designated by a church as a housing allowance (assuming that the minister's compensation is reasonable in amount). However, a church ordinarily should not designate for a minister who owns or rents a home a housing allowance that is significantly above the minister's housing expenses or the fair rental value of the home (furnished, plus utilities), since the minister will not be able to exclude more than the lower of these amounts in computing federal income taxes.

EXAMPLE. The Tax Court ruled that the portion of a pastor's salary designated by his church as a housing allowance was not subject to income taxation despite the fact that it comprised most of his compensation. The pastor was employed by a small church that paid him an annual compensation of $13,500, of which $13,000 ($250 per week) was designated as a housing allowance. The IRS audited the pastor's tax return. It conceded that the church had designated the allowance, but disallowed it because the pastor had failed to prove that the allowance in fact was spent on housing expenses.

The Tax Court reversed the IRS determination and ruled that the pastor was entitled to exclude the housing allowance from his taxable income. It noted that the pastor had "credibly testified that the housing allowance provided by [the church] was insufficient to cover his mortgage expenses and utilities. In this respect [he] testified that his mortgage payment alone was approximately $1,000 per month before refinancing. Consequently, we find that the $13,000 per year parsonage allowance he received was used to provide a home. Accordingly, the $13,000 annual housing allowance . . . is not includable in petitioners' gross income."

In the past, some have questioned whether most or all of a pastor's compensation can be designated as a housing allowance. It is

DESIGNATING A MINISTER'S ENTIRE SALARY AS A HOUSING ALLOWANCE

Question. We have a part-time associate pastor who has asked the church to designate his entire salary as a housing allowance. Do we need to issue him a W-2 form at the end of the year reporting no income?

Answer. This is a surprisingly complex question. Here's why. Until 1974, section 6051 of the federal tax code required a Form W-2 to be issued to (1) each employee from whom income, Social Security, or Medicare tax is withheld or (2) each employee from whom income tax would have been withheld if the employee had claimed no more than one withholding allowance or had not claimed exemption from withholding on Form W-4. Churches were not required to issue a W-2 to pastors under this provision since their wages are exempt from tax withholding.

In 1974 Congress enacted a massive pension law (the Employee Retirement Income Security Act, or ERISA). This law added the following phrase to section 6051: "Every employer engaged in a trade or business who pays remuneration for services performed by an employee, including noncash payments, must file a Form W-2 for each employee." Unfortunately, the legislative history contains no explanation of why this language was added. In any event, it was broad enough to require churches to issue a Form W-2 to ministers even though they are not subject to tax withholding.

The 1974 amendment created some ambiguities, and the stated question highlights one of them. Read literally, the revised section 6051 requires a church to issue a Form W-2 to a minister even though all of the minister's income is designated as a housing allowance, no amount is shown in box 1 (wages), and no withholdings of income taxes or Social Security or Medicare taxes are reported. Why? Because the church is an employer "engaged in a trade or business who pays remuneration for services performed by an employee, including noncash payments." Of course, submitting to the IRS a Form W-2 that identifies a minister by name and Social Security number but has blank boxes for income and withholdings is not consistent with the purpose of the form, which is to report wages and withholdings to the IRS to ensure that the correct amount of taxes are paid. This purpose is not furthered by submitting blank forms. This, however, does not necessarily mean that a church is relieved of obligation to issue a Form W-2.

In 2000 the IRS addressed the question of whether election workers should be issued W-2 forms. Election workers are individuals who are generally employed to perform services for states and local governments at election booths in connection with national, state, or local elections. Government agencies typically pay election workers a set fee for each day of work. The IRS quoted section 6051 of the tax code and concluded that this section "does not require reporting of compensation that is not subject to withholding of FICA tax or income tax. . . . Section 6051 requires reporting of compensation subject to either FICA tax or income tax withholding. No reporting is required . . . for items of income that are not subject to withholding of FICA tax or income tax. If an election worker's compensation is subject to withholding of FICA tax, reporting is required by section 6051 regardless of the amount of compensation." *IRS Revenue Ruling 2000-6.*

This ruling suggests that a church may not be required to issue a W-2 to a part-time pastor whose entire income is designated as a housing allowance.

The IRS operates a centralized call site to answer questions about reporting information on W-2 forms. If you have any questions about completing a Form W-2, call the IRS at 1-866-455-7438, Monday through Friday, 8:30 A.M. to 4:30 P.M. Eastern time.

---

worth noting that neither the IRS nor the Tax Court questioned the housing allowance in this case on the ground that it comprised over 95 percent of the pastor's total church compensation. *Holmes v. Commissioner, T.C. Summary Opinion 2010-42 (2010).*

7. AMOUNT A MINISTER MAY CLAIM AS A HOUSING ALLOWANCE EXCLUSION

The housing allowance designated by a church is not necessarily exempt from tax in computing federal income taxes. Section 107 of the tax code specifies that a housing allowance is excluded from income tax only to the extent it is used for actual expenses incurred by the minister in owning or renting a home and does not exceed the fair rental value of the home (furnished, plus utilities).

For ministers who own their homes, actual expenses include:

- down payment on a home;
- payments (including prepayments) on a mortgage loan to purchase or improve your home (including both interest and principal);
- real estate taxes;
- property insurance;

- utilities (electricity, gas, water, trash pickup, local telephone charges; Internet access fees);
- furnishings and appliances (purchase and repair);
- structural repairs and remodeling;
- yard maintenance and improvements;
- appurtenances;
- maintenance items (household cleansers, light bulbs, pest control, etc.); and
- homeowners association dues.

✿**KEY POINT.** In 2007 the Tax Court characterized Internet expenses as utility expenses. This suggests that a housing allowance can be used to pay for Internet access expenses. *Soholt v. Commissioner, T.C. Summary Opinion 2007-49 (2007), is relying on Verma v. Commissioner, T.C. Memo. 2001-132.* In addition, the same analysis of telephone expenses (above) could be applied to Internet access fees.

If actual expenses exceed the church-designated allowance and the fair rental value of the home, the minister can only exclude the allowance. This illustrates why churches should always be liberal in designating housing allowances.

In Publication 517 the IRS states the rule as follows:

> *If you own your home and you receive as part of your salary a housing or rental allowance, you may exclude from gross income the smallest of:*
>
> - *The amount actually used to provide a home,*
> - *The amount officially designated as a rental allowance, or*
> - *The fair rental value of the home, including furnishings, utilities, garage, etc.*

EXAMPLE. Pastor C is paid a salary of $40,000 for year 2013. The church board designates $25,000 of this amount as a housing allowance. In February Pastor C purchases a new home and makes a down payment of $15,000. Assume that he has additional housing expenses of $7,000 for the year and that the fair rental value of the home (furnished, including utilities) is

TELEPHONE EXPENSES

Can ministers include the costs of both personal and business use of a home telephone in computing their housing allowance exclusion? Unfortunately, the tax code and regulations do not answer this question, and it has never been addressed by either the IRS or any court. So a definitive answer is not possible.

In a 1955 ruling, the IRS concluded that telephone expenses are a utility expense to which a housing allowance can be applied. *Letter Ruling 5509169250A.* While this ruling was a private letter ruling that cannot be cited as precedent in other cases, it remains the only instance in which the IRS has addressed the application of housing allowance to telephone expenses. This ruling makes sense. Section 107 of the tax code provides that the portion of a minister's church compensation that is designated as a housing allowance is not included in computing taxable income (for income tax reporting) to the extent that it is used to pay for housing-related expenses and, for ministers who own or rent their homes, does not exceed their home's annual fair rental value. There is no requirement that the housing expenses be business related. All that is required is that the expenses be incurred to rent or provide a home. To illustrate, ministers can use a housing allowance to pay for mortgage payments, property insurance, property taxes, electricity, natural gas, and water despite the fact that the vast majority of these expenses are incurred for purely personal reasons having nothing to do with the conduct of the minister's profession. They are excludable not because they are business related but because they are housing related. They are necessary and customary expenses for anyone who owns a home. Under this analysis, a housing allowance could be applied to the expenses incurred in maintaining a local land-line telephone so long as reasonably necessary to provide a home.

Clearly, the use of a land-line telephone for local calls (the base charge) is indispensable to a minister's home. Therefore, an argument could be made that such telephone expenses are includible in the housing allowance calculation (whether for business or personal use). Such expenses are like electricity expenses—they are reasonably necessary to provide a home, and as a result they are includible in their entirety in the housing allowance calculation despite the fact that a substantial portion of such expenses are not business related. This was the conclusion reached by the IRS in its 1955 ruling.

But it is far from clear that this same reasoning would apply to cell phones, which, unlike all of the other expenses mentioned previously, are mobile and not physically connected to the minister's home. As a result, applying a housing allowance to a cell phone should be viewed as an aggressive tax position, unsupported by any existing precedent, that should not be adopted without the advice of a tax professional. This is true even for those ministers who use a cell phone exclusively and do not have a land-line telephone in their home.

$10,000 for the portion of the year he occupied it. Pastor C's housing allowance is nontaxable only to the extent it does not exceed actual housing expenses or the rental value of his home. Stated differently, the amount of the housing allowance that is excluded in computing federal income taxes is the lowest of the following three amounts: (1) the church-designated housing allowance ($25,000); (2) actual housing expenses ($22,000); or (3) the rental value of the home ($10,000). Since the rental value is the lowest amount, this is the amount of Pastor C's housing allowance that is nontaxable.

EXAMPLE. Pastor L's roof collapsed during a snowstorm late in 2012. Knowing repairs would cost $5,000 and that he incurs about $10,000 of additional housing expenses per year, Pastor L has the church board designate $15,000 of his 2013 salary of $40,000 as a housing allowance. Assume that the fair rental value of the home (furnished, including utilities) is $10,000. Pastor L's nontaxable housing allowance would be the least of the following three amounts: (1) the church-designated housing allowance ($15,000); (2) actual housing expenses ($15,000); or (3) the rental value of the home ($10,000). Since the rental value is the lowest amount, this is the amount of Pastor L's housing allowance that is nontaxable.

EXAMPLE. A church board is considering the 2013 compensation package for Pastor B. It decides on total compensation of $30,000. Pastor B informs the board that he will have ordinary housing expenses of $10,000 but that he also will be incurring remodeling expenses of an additional $10,000. The board is uncomfortable designating two-thirds of Pastor B's total compensation as a housing allowance. If the fair rental value of the home is significantly lower than $20,000, there is no advantage in designating a housing allowance of this amount.

8. HOME EQUITY LOANS, SECOND MORTGAGE LOANS, AND REFINANCING

What happens to ministers who own their homes after they pay off their home mortgage loan? Are they still eligible for a housing allowance, and if so, for what expenses? Can they include the annual fair rental value of their home in computing their housing allowance exclusion?

Ministers who own their home may still claim a housing allowance exclusion (assuming they otherwise qualify), but since the exclusion may never exceed the actual expenses incurred in owning or maintaining a home, it will be reduced (often significantly) when the home mortgage loan is paid off. Ministers still will incur some expenses (e.g., utilities, repairs, improvements, furnishings, property taxes, and insurance) to which a housing allowance can be applied. But since the annual rental value of the home is not an actual expense, it cannot be included in computing the exclusion. *Swaggart v. Commissioner, 48 T.C.M. 759 (1984).*

In the past some ministers who had paid off their homes obtained a home equity loan (secured by a new home mortgage) and included the mortgage payments (principal and interest) in computing their housing allowance exclusion. The IRS has ruled that this practice is not permissible unless the home equity loan was obtained for direct housing-related expenses. The fact that the loan is secured by a mortgage on the home is not enough. *IRS Letter Ruling 9115051.* The Tax Court has agreed with this conclusion. *Rasmussen v. Commissioner, T.C. Memo. 1994-311.* The court observed:

> *Exemptions from gross income are to be construed narrowly . . . and [federal law does not] provide for the exclusion of payments on loans secured by a home if they are not used to "provide a home." The proceeds of the church loans were used to pay personal expenses of [the pastor and his wife] unrelated to their home. Thus, even assuming that the loans were secured by the [pastor's home, he has] not shown that the portion of the parsonage allowance used to repay the church loans was used for the maintenance or purchase of the home. On the record before us, we hold that [the pastor and his wife] have not proven that the portion of the parsonage allowance used to repay the church loans was used to provide a home as required by [federal law].*

✿**KEY POINT.** The Tax Court has concurred with an IRS private letter ruling that ministers cannot consider loan repayments as a housing expense in computing their housing allowance exclusion unless the loan is used for direct housing-related expenses. If the loan is for personal items such as a new car, a child's education, or medical expenses, it is not converted into a housing expense because it is secured by a mortgage on the minister's home.

A related and more difficult question is how to calculate a housing allowance when a minister adds to an existing home mortgage. For example, assume that a minister refinances a home mortgage and increases the indebtedness, or obtains a second mortgage loan on top of an existing home mortgage loan, or obtains a home equity loan. What are the tax consequences in these cases if the additional mortgage debt is obtained to finance expenses not directly related to the home (e.g., education, medical care, vacations, or a new car)? In each of these cases, the minister has a preexisting mortgage loan that was obtained solely to facilitate the purchase of the home. Unfortunately, neither the IRS nor any court has addressed this question. As noted above, both the IRS and the Tax Court have addressed what happens when a minister's home is paid off and the minister obtains a subsequent home mortgage loan to finance personal expenses such as medical care and education. Obviously, these rulings provide a reasonable basis for concluding that some form of allocation would be required when a minister adds to an existing mortgage debt for nonhousing expenses.

To illustrate, if a minister has an outstanding home mortgage loan in the amount of $50,000 and then obtains a second mortgage loan in the amount of $25,000 for various personal expenses, the mortgage interest payments allocable to the first loan could be considered in computing the minister's housing allowance exclusion, while the interest paid on the second mortgage loan would not. It would be easy to make such allocations in the case of a second mortgage loan or a home equity loan. The more difficult case involves refinancing. It is likely that the IRS and the courts would again apply some type of allocation rule. One possibility would be to make an allocation at the time of the refinancing. For example, if a minister with a $50,000 home mortgage debt refinances the indebtedness and increases it to $75,000, and if the additional $25,000 debt is used for personal expenses, then two-thirds of the interest payments could be allocated to the home and be included in computing the housing allowance exclusion, while one-third of the interest payments would be allocated to personal expenses and would not be included. Future rulings may provide further clarification.

9. HOUSING ALLOWANCES, DOWN PAYMENTS, AND MORTGAGE LOAN PREPAYMENTS

In the past it was much harder for taxpayers to avoid tax on the gain from the sale of a home. As a result, ministers often attempted to minimize or avoid taxes by having gain from the sale of a former home designated as a housing allowance and applied to the down payment on a new home. This practice is rarely used today because the tax code eliminates any tax on gain from a former home if the home was owned and occupied for at least two of the previous five years (gain may be partially excluded from tax even if the home was owned and occupied for less than two years). For married couples, up to $500,000 of gain is excluded (up to $250,000 for single persons).

Because of this liberal provision, the gain most ministers realize from the sale of a former home is not taxed. However, this is not always the case. For example, a minister may have owned and occupied a home for less than two of the previous five years, resulting in some of the gain from the sale of the home being taxable. In high-cost areas, some ministers my realize gain from the sale of a home that exceeds the $250,000/$500,000 exclusion limits. Can ministers minimize or avoid tax on the gain from the sale of a former home by having it designated as a housing allowance and applying it to the down payment on a new home? In the past, when the rules for excluding gain on the sale of a home were much more restrictive, a number of courts addressed this question. Those cases are still relevant today whenever ministers try to exclude gain from the sale of a former home by having it designated as a housing allowance. Consider the following precedent:

The Marine case (1967)

In 1967 the Tax Court addressed the question of whether a pastor can apply his housing allowance to housing expenses paid out of the gain from the sale of his former home. *Marine v. Commissioner, 47 T.C. 609 (1963).* A church's board of trustees adopted the following resolution: "For the [current] year and thereafter unless modified, all payments to Pastor Fred are to be considered rental allowance unless the payments exceed $20,000."

During the year, Pastor Fred received compensation of $13,500 from the church. In July he purchased a new home for $18,500. He made a cash deposit of $500 on the property at the time of signing the contract of sale. The balance was provided by a one-year mortgage loan of $18,000, which Pastor Fred received from a local bank. In August Pastor Fred sold his former home for $16,500. Of this amount, $15,000 was withheld from Pastor Fred at closing and paid over to his bank in partial satisfaction of the $18,000 mortgage loan. Pastor Fred paid an additional $3,000 in expenses associated with the ownership of his home (monthly mortgage payments, utilities, furnishings, insurance, and property taxes).

In preparing his federal income tax return for the year, Pastor Fred did not report any taxable income. He assumed that his entire salary of $13,500 was nontaxable, since the church had designated this entire amount as a housing allowance and he incurred housing expenses well in excess of this amount. The IRS audited Pastor Fred and determined that the housing allowance could be applied only to the $3,000 that he paid out of his own funds for housing expenses. The IRS refused to allow Pastor Fred to apply his housing allowance to the $15,000 proceeds from the sale of his former home that was used to pay down the mortgage loan on his new home. Pastor Fred appealed to the Tax Court.

The Tax Court agreed with the IRS that Pastor Fred could only apply his housing allowance to the $3,000 of out-of-pocket housing expenses he incurred in 1963. The court noted that the tax code originally only allowed ministers to exclude from taxable income the annual rental value of a parsonage. In 1954 the code was amended to allow ministers to exclude the portion of their income designated by their employing church as a housing allowance, to the extent it is used to pay for housing expenses. The reason for the 1954 amendment, noted the court, was to eliminate the prior law's discrimination against ministers who were not provided with a parsonage and who had to use their own income to provide a home. As a result, in enacting the 1954 code, "Congress not only continued to provide that the rental value of a house furnished to a minister would not be included in gross income, but also added a further provision that a rental allowance paid to a minister as part of his compensation was excludable from gross income to the extent used by him to rent or provide a home." The court concluded:

> *Plainly, the purpose of the new provision was to equalize the situation between those ministers who received a house rent free and those who were given an allowance that was actually used to provide a home. There certainly does not appear to be any intention to place ministers of the second category in a favored position. Yet, if Pastor Fred were to prevail here, his entire compensation for 1963 would escape taxation, a result that seems clearly contrary to the underlying purpose of the statute. And the words of the statute itself explicitly preclude that result, for it provides that the rental allowance is excludable from a minister's gross income only "to the extent used by him to rent or provide a*

home." The circumstance that Pastor Fred's entire compensation was artificially designated as a rental allowance pursuant to the statement signed by the board of trustees of the church cannot in fact convert into a rental allowance that which was plainly compensation for services, nor does it appear on this record that to the extent that the IRS refused to treat his compensation as an excludable rental allowance such compensation was actually "used by him to rent or provide a home." On the facts before us Pastor Fred did not use his entire 1963 compensation of $13,500 to rent or provide a home. True, he purchased a new residence in 1963 at a price which exceeded that amount. But the great bulk of that price was paid out of the proceeds of sale of his old residence.

The court's decision in the *Marine* case was based squarely on the principles of *discrimination* and *source* of income. Each principle is addressed below.

Discrimination

The court concluded that allowing ministers who own their homes to have their entire salary designated as a housing allowance would violate the purpose of the 1954 tax code amendment that sought to achieve equality between ministers who live in parsonages and those who own or rent their home. If ministers could have all or most of their church compensation designated as a housing allowance, they would be in a better position than ministers who live in church-owned parsonages.

The IRS applied this reasoning in a 1971 ruling that imposed the fair rental value limit on the nontaxable amount of ministers' housing allowances. *Revenue Ruling 71-280.* This ruling was repudiated by the Tax Court in a 2000 decision. *Warren v. Commissioner, 114 T.C. 23 (2000).* However, the IRS position was incorporated into the Clergy Housing Allowance Clarification Act of 2002 that was enacted by Congress and that reinstated the fair rental value limit as a matter of law.

Source

The court concluded that Pastor Fred's housing allowance could not be applied to proceeds from the sale of a home that he applied to the mortgage loan on his new home, since these proceeds were not compensation received for the performance of ministerial services. In other words, the source of funds used to pay for a minister's housing expenses must be compensation earned by the minister in the exercise of ministry. This is a correct statement. The income tax regulations specify that "in order to qualify for the exclusion, the home or rental allowance must be provided as remuneration for services which are ordinarily the duties of a minister of the gospel." Note that in the *Marine* case the $15,000 used to pay down the mortgage loan could be unequivocally traced to the proceeds from the sale of Pastor Fred's former home because the sales proceeds were withheld from him at closing and paid directly to his bank to be applied to his mortgage loan. There was no question that the mortgage loan prepayment was paid out of the sales proceeds and not out of Pastor Fred's church salary. Therefore, the housing allowance could not be applied to any of those proceeds.

But what if the sales proceeds had *not* been withheld from Pastor Fred at closing? What if they were paid to Pastor Fred directly, he deposited them in his bank account, and he later used some or all of them to make a large down payment on his new home or pay down the mortgage loan on a new home? In such a case there would be no way to trace the $15,000 to the proceeds from the sale of Pastor Fred's former home. The proceeds and Pastor Fred's church salary would be commingled, making it difficult, if not impossible, to determine the source of the funds used to pay down the mortgage loan. It would be just as reasonable to assume that the source of the mortgage loan prepayment was Pastor Fred's housing allowance as the proceeds from the sale of his home. There are two important qualifications to this view, however.

Other income. This view assumes a source of income in addition to the housing allowance. If a pastor's entire church compensation is designated as a housing allowance and the pastor has no other source of income (including a spouse's income), then it would be impossible to claim that the entire housing allowance should be nontaxable, even if the pastor had expenses of that much or more. After all, what income did the pastor use for living expenses? However, when a pastor has income in addition to a church salary, it makes a larger housing allowance more defensible.

Matching expenses to income. Housing allowances are nontaxable in computing federal income taxes only to the extent they are used to pay for housing expenses. The income tax regulations specify that "a rental allowance must be included in the minister's gross income in the taxable year in which it is received, to the extent that such allowance is not used by him during such taxable year to rent or otherwise provide a home." Does this requirement mean there must be a strict matching of housing allowances with actual housing expenses?

To illustrate, what if Pastor Fred had sold his former home in January and used $15,000 of the proceeds to make a down payment on a new home on January 31? By January 31 Pastor Fred has received only one-twelfth of his housing allowance for the year ($1,125). Can he only apply this amount to his down payment, or may he include the housing allowances he receives for the entire year ($13,500)? In other words, are housing allowances compared with housing expenses on an annual basis, or must allowances be matched with expenses on an ongoing basis throughout the year?

The following arguments and precedent clearly demonstrate that any matching is done annually. Consider the following points:

- The IRS has never required strict matching in any ruling involving a housing allowance.
- The IRS does require strict matching in its audit guidelines for ministers.
- The IRS does not require strict matching in Publication 517 (a publication addressing tax issues for ministers).

- No court has ever required strict matching in any case involving a housing allowance.
- Ministers will almost always violate a strict matching requirement with respect to some housing expenses. To illustrate, assume that Pastor J is paid on the second and fourth Fridays each month and that he makes his monthly mortgage and utilities payments on the first business day of each month. Under such an arrangement, Pastor J's monthly mortgage payment for January will occur before his first paycheck for the month. The important point to note is that Pastor J had received no income (or housing allowance) for the new year when he paid the mortgage and utilities bills. He cannot match the payment of these housing expenses to his housing allowance.

  Does this mean he cannot consider these expenses when computing the nontaxable portion of his housing allowance at the end of the year when he prepares his tax return? Neither the IRS nor any court has ever ruled that a housing allowance cannot be applied to housing expenses incurred in January (or any other month) prior to the receipt of a housing allowance of equal or greater value. The focus is on housing expenses incurred throughout the year and whether the housing allowance designated by the church for the year is sufficient to cover these expenses.

  Many other examples could be given. For example, what about a minister who incurs remodeling expenses or repairs of several thousand dollars in January that are far in excess of the housing allowance distributed in that month? Again, neither the IRS nor any court has ever suggested that these expenses must be matched to the housing allowance actually paid in January. Common sense, then, indicates that strict matching of housing allowances and housing expenses is not required. Doing so would be far too impractical and would lead to absurd results. Instead, the focus is on housing expenses incurred throughout the year and on a minister's church-designated housing allowance for the year.
- In 1984 the full Tax Court made these comments about the matching of housing expenses to housing allowances: "Section 1.107-1(c) [of the income tax regulations] provides that, for the allowance to be excludable, the use of the allowance to rent or provide a home must be in the taxable year in which the allowance is received. . . . The statute and the regulation appear to require an expenditure (or conceivably some equivalent action which may constitute a use) of an amount received as compensation in the same year." *Reed v. Commissioner, 82 T.C. 208 (1984).*
- Section 1.107-1(c) of the income tax regulations specifies that "a rental allowance must be included in the minister's gross income in the taxable year in which it is received, *to the extent that such allowance is not used by him during such taxable year to rent or otherwise provide a home*" (emphasis added). This language clearly applies an annual comparison of housing allowances to housing expenses. There is no need to match on a more frequent basis specific housing expenses with housing allowances actually received. So, for example, if a minister pays a monthly mortgage payment and utility bill in the first week of January, before receiving his first paycheck (including housing allowance) for the year, this does not prevent him from applying his housing allowances to these expenses when computing his taxes for the year. He need not match housing allowances actually received to the expenses paid on a daily, weekly, or monthly basis. It is done annually.

- IRS Publication 517 states that "if you own your home and you receive as part of your salary a housing or rental allowance, you may exclude from gross income the smallest of the amount actually used to provide a home, the amount officially designated as a rental allowance, or the fair rental value of the home, including furnishings, utilities, garage, etc." No suggestion is made here of matching housing expenses to housing allowance payments. Quite to the contrary, this language clearly indicates that the housing allowance is applied to housing expenses on an annualized basis. At the end of the year, ministers determine the nontaxable portion of their housing allowance by adding up all of the housing expenses they incurred during the year (subject to the annual fair rental value limitation).

- Section 461 of the tax code specifies that "the amount of any deduction or credit allowed by this subtitle shall be taken for the taxable year which is the proper taxable year under the method of accounting used in computing taxable income." The income tax regulations specify that "generally, under the cash receipts and disbursements method in the computation of taxable income, all items which constitute gross income (whether in the form of cash, property, or services) are to be included for the taxable year in which actually or constructively received. Expenditures are to be deducted for the taxable year in which actually made." *Treas. Reg. 1.461-1(c).*

EXAMPLE. A church designates $24,000 of Pastor T's 2013 compensation as a housing allowance. Pastor T resigns from the church on June 30, 2013. At the time of Pastor T's resignation, he had received half of his $24,000 housing allowance ($12,000) but had only incurred $10,000 in housing expenses. Can he apply the unused allowance ($2,000) to housing expenses incurred in the second half of the year, following his resignation? The preceding analysis suggests that he can. Also, note that the key consideration is that the $2,000 unused allowance represents compensation for ministerial services performed by Pastor T during the course of his employment in the first half of the year. Section 1.107-1(c) of the income tax regulations specifies that "a rental allowance must be included in the minister's gross income in the taxable year in which it is received, *to the extent that such allowance is not used by him during such taxable year to rent or otherwise provide a home*" (emphasis added). This language explicitly allows a housing allowance that constituted compensation for ministerial services to be excluded from a minister's taxable income if used to pay housing expenses during the same year.

Revenue Ruling 71-280 (1971)

Four years after the *Marine* decision, the IRS ruled that the non-taxable portion of a housing allowance for ministers who own their homes can never exceed the fair rental value of the home. *Revenue Ruling 71-280.* The IRS based its ruling squarely on the *Marine* case. It concluded:

> It is indicated in the Senate Report that Congress intended only to remove the discrimination in the existing law and did not intend to create a new discrimination in favor of another group by placing ministers who receive rental allowances in a better position than ministers who receive rent free homes. Consequently, a minister cannot exclude his entire compensation by the mere act of having it designated as a rental allowance. Marine v. Commissioner, 47 T.C. 609 (1967).

As a result, ministers who own their homes can only exclude housing expenses to the extent that they do not exceed *either* the church-designated allowance *or* the fair rental value of the home plus the cost of utilities. The fair rental value test was adopted by the IRS to eliminate any discrimination between ministers who live in parsonages and those who are purchasing a home. It was repudiated by the Tax Court in 2000. *Warren v. Commissioner, 114 T.C. 23 (2000).* However, it was later reinstated as an amendment to section 107 of the tax code by the Clergy Housing Allowance Clarification Act of 2002. See section B.4 of this chapter.

✤ **KEY POINT.** While no direct matching of housing allowances and housing expenses is required, this does not mean that housing allowances can be designated retroactively. A housing allowance must be designated in advance. This is simply another way of saying that a housing allowance is nontaxable only to the extent it is used to pay for housing expenses. This requirement cannot be met if a housing allowance is designated retroactively. In summary, while the matching of housing allowances and housing expenses is done on an annual basis, this assumes that the housing allowance was designated in advance. If a housing allowance is not designated until the middle of the year, it can be applied only to housing expenses incurred from that date through the end of the year.

EXAMPLE. M is a retired minister who rents a home. In December 2012 she informed her denominational pension board that she wanted a lump-sum distribution from her account of $100,000 in 2013, and she wanted the entire distribution to be designated as a housing allowance. M uses the distribution as a down payment on a new home in July 2013. She pays her living expenses with Social Security benefits and investment income. Assume that the rental value of the new home is $12,000 for the months it is occupied by M in 2013. What is the nontaxable portion of M's housing allowance? According to the *Marine* case, the nontaxable portion of the housing allowance would be limited to the rental value of the home for the months M occupied it

in 2013 ($12,000). This is the same result dictated by Revenue Ruling 71-280, IRS Publication 517, and section 107 of the tax code as amended by the Clergy Housing Allowance Clarification Act of 2002.

EXAMPLE. A church board is considering the 2013 compensation package for Pastor N. It decides on total compensation of $60,000. Pastor N asks the board to designate this entire amount as a housing allowance. He informs the board that he will have ordinary housing expenses of $15,000 but that he also will be purchasing a new home in 2013 and plans to make a large down payment (with the sale proceeds from his prior residence) of $45,000. Pastor N's spouse is employed as a college professor, and the couple plans on using her salary for living expenses in 2013. Pastor N later uses the entire $60,000 to pay for housing expenses in 2013. Assume that the rental value (including utilities) of the former and new homes, during the months Pastor N occupies them, is $12,000. What is the nontaxable portion of Pastor N's housing allowance? Section 107 of the tax code, as amended by the Clergy Housing Allowance Clarification Act of 2002, limits the nontaxable portion of a housing allowance for ministers who own their home to the fair rental value of their home (furnished, plus utilities). As a result, the housing allowance is nontaxable only if it is used to pay for housing expenses and does not exceed the annual rental value of the home. In this case, this means that the nontaxable housing allowance is limited to $12,000 (fair rental value).

10. AMENDING THE HOUSING ALLOWANCE

What if a church designates $10,000 of a minister's 2013 compensation as a housing allowance based on reasonable estimates of the minister's anticipated expenses, and the minister trades homes later in the year and incurs much greater housing expenses? Can the church amend its housing allowance designation?

While neither the IRS nor any court has addressed this question, it seems reasonable to conclude that the church can amend its housing allowance designation during the course of the year if changed circumstances render the allowance inadequate. Any change would only operate prospectively.

✤ **KEY POINT.** Churches can amend a housing allowance if the allowance proves to be too low. However, the amended allowance will only operate prospectively.

11. THE "DOUBLE DEDUCTION"

Ministers who own their homes and who itemize their deductions are eligible to deduct mortgage interest and property taxes on Schedule A, even though such items were excluded as part of the housing allowance exclusion. This is the so-called double deduction. *IRC 265.*

The IRS audit guidelines for ministers state that even though a minister's home mortgage interest and real estate taxes have been paid with money excluded from income as a housing allowance, he or she "may still claim itemized deductions for these items."

12. HOUSING EXPENSES PAID DIRECTLY BY A CHURCH

Some churches pay part or all of a minister's housing expenses directly. Can such payments be treated as a nontaxable housing allowance? It could be argued that by agreeing to pay for a minister's housing expenses, a church is, in effect, designating a housing allowance (in advance) in the amount of the expenses it paid. But the Tax Court has reached the opposite conclusion. A minister received a weekly "living allowance" from his church. He kept no records reflecting how these allowances were spent. In addition, his church paid his housing expenses (including mortgage payments, utilities, and furnishings). The court ruled that the weekly allowances were taxable and could not be classified as a nontaxable housing allowance. It observed:

> [The minister and his spouse] have not substantiated that any of their weekly allowances were used "to rent or provide a home." In fact, the record reveals that [the church] directly paid for such expenses. Moreover, the regulations require that prior to payment of a rental allowance, the employing church must designate the rental allowance in an employment contract or other appropriate instrument so as to clearly identify the portion of the minister's salary that is the rental allowance. As [the minister and his spouse] had no written agreement with the church concerning this matter, they have failed to comply with the regulations. Accordingly, for the years in issue, we hold that the weekly allowances received by petitioners must be included in their gross incomes. Pollard v. Commissioner, 48 T.C.M. 1303 (1984).

Based on this case, a church that pays a minister's housing expenses directly should designate in advance the amount it pays as a housing allowance, in addition to any other housing allowance it declares.

13. SAFETY NET ALLOWANCES

Many churches do not limit housing allowances to a particular calendar year. For example, if a church intends to designate $12,000 of its senior pastor's salary in 2013 as a housing allowance, its designation could state that the allowance is effective for calendar year 2013 *and all future years unless otherwise provided.* This clause may protect the pastor in the event that the board

neglects to designate an allowance prior to the beginning of a future year.

A church also would be wise to have a "safety net" designation to cover midyear changes in personnel, delayed designations, and other unexpected contingencies. To illustrate, such a designation could simply state that a specified percentage (e.g., 40 percent) of the compensation of all ministers on staff, regardless of when hired, is designated as a housing allowance for the current year and all future years unless otherwise specifically provided.

Such safety net designations should not be used as a substitute for annual housing allowance designations for each minister. They are simply a means of protecting ministers against inadvertent failures by the church board to designate a timely housing allowance.

❖ **KEY POINT.** Churches should consider adopting a "safety net" allowance to protect against the loss of this significant tax benefit due to the inadvertent failure by the church to designate a timely allowance.

14. OWNING TWO HOMES

In 2010 the United States Tax Court ruled that a minister could apply a housing allowance to expenses incurred in owning two homes. The court acknowledged that section 107 of the tax code, which contains the housing allowance exclusion, refers to a minister's "home" in the singular, but it concluded that this did not limit the application of a housing allowance to only one home.

In 2012 a federal appeals court reversed the Tax Court's opinion and limited the application of a minister's housing allowance to expenses incurred in only one home (the principal residence). The United States Supreme Court declined to review the case on appeal, leaving the appeals court's ruling intact.

The appeals court conceded that the tax code states that singular terms also include their plural forms, but it noted that this rule did not apply if "the context indicates otherwise." Therefore, the "singular includes the plural provision" should only apply if the context of the housing allowance reasonably supports such an application. The court concluded that it did not, for two reasons:

First, the word *home* is defined by the dictionary as "the house and grounds with their appurtenances habitually occupied by a family; one's principal place of residence; domicile." The court concluded that the word *home* according to this definition "has decidedly singular connotations."

Second, the court concluded that the history of the parsonage and housing allowance exclusions provided additional context for the term *home.* It noted that congressional committee reports describing the parsonage and housing allowance exclusions consistently use singular expressions ("a dwelling house," "a home," and "the home"), demonstrating that Congress intended for the parsonage and housing allowance exclusions to apply to only one home.

In further support for its conclusion, the court stressed that income exclusions should be "narrowly construed," and therefore "we do not believe that this court should construe any ambiguity in [the tax code] to favor a more expansive reading of the parsonage allowance income exclusion."

Many ministers own two homes. In many cases, this is due to the fact that the minister has accepted a call in another community, purchases a home in that community, but has not yet sold the prior home. In some cases the minister has not moved but decides to purchase a new home in the same community and is in the process of selling the former home. The Tax Court's decision in the *Driscoll* case suggested that these ministers, at least in some cases, might be able to apply a housing allowance to the expenses of owning both homes. That option has been eliminated by the federal appeals court's recent ruling.

What is the impact of this ruling on ministers and churches? Consider two points:

First, ministers who relied on the *Driscoll* case by claiming housing allowance exclusions on their 2010 or 2011 tax returns based on expenses incurred in owning two homes should contact a tax professional to assist in preparing and submitting to the IRS an amended tax return (Form 1040X) for these years. The amended return should restate the nontaxable amount of the housing allowance to reflect housing expenses only on the pastor's principal residence.

Second, many churches have their pastors fill out a housing expense form each year that lists anticipated housing expenses for the following year. The church board uses this form to declare pastors' housing allowances. It would be prudent to amend this form to clarify that it should only list expenses incurred in owning a principal residence, and not a second home. *Driscoll v. Commissioner, 2012-1 U.S.T.C. ¶50,187 (11th Cir. 2012).*

15. SEVERANCE PAY

Can a church designate some or all of a minister's severance pay as a housing allowance? This question is addressed in Chapter 4, Section B.17.

16. RETIRED MINISTERS

Retired ministers are eligible for a housing allowance exclusion if certain conditions are met. See Chapter 3, section D, and Chapter

10, section E, for details. However, the surviving spouse of a deceased minister is not eligible for the exclusion unless he or she also is a minister who otherwise qualifies. IRS Publication 517 states: "If you are a retired minister, you exclude from your gross income the rental value of a home (plus utilities) furnished to you by your church as a part of your pay for past services, or the part of your pension that was designated as a rental allowance. However, a minister's surviving spouse cannot exclude the rental value unless the rental value is for ministerial services he or she performs or performed."

Many ministers move into a retirement home following their retirement from ministry. Two costs are often associated with such living arrangements: (1) a lump-sum entrance fee, and (2) monthly or annual maintenance fees. The IRS has ruled that a lump-sum entrance fee paid by a retired minister to gain admission to a retirement community cannot be prorated over several years and claimed as a housing expense in those years. It can only be treated as a housing expense in the year it is actually paid. *IRS Letter Ruling 8348018 (1983); IRS Technical Advice Memorandum 8039007 (1980).*

What about monthly or annual maintenance fees? Can a retired minister's housing allowance (designated by a pension board) be applied to these fees? That depends. Section 107 of the tax code allows ministers to exclude from gross income the portion of their compensation designated in advance as a housing allowance, to the extent the allowance is used to "rent or provide a home." The regulations define this language as follows: "Circumstances under which a rental allowance will be deemed to have been used to rent or provide a home will include cases in which the allowance is expended (1) for rent of a home, (2) for purchase of a home, and (3) for expenses directly related to providing a home. Expenses for food and servants are not considered for this purpose to be directly related to providing a home."

As a result, a retired minister's housing allowance can be applied to any portion of a monthly maintenance fee charged by a retirement home that is "an expense directly related to providing a home." The regulations prohibit housing allowances from being applied to the costs of "food and servants"; therefore a housing allowance could not be applied to any portion of a maintenance fee that goes to food or housekeeping expenses.

17. TRAVELING EVANGELISTS

Traveling evangelists are entitled to a housing allowance exclusion if they maintain a permanent home and have local churches in which they conduct religious meetings declare in advance a portion of their compensation as a housing allowance. *See Revenue Ruling 64-326.* The requirement that each church designate a portion of an evangelist's compensation as a housing allowance is certainly an inconvenience, but it is well worth it. The Tax Court has rejected the contention of one evangelist that such a requirement impermissibly discriminates against evangelists. *Warnke v. Commissioner, 641 F. Supp. 1083 (D.C. Ky. 1986).*

Some evangelists have created nonprofit corporations. One of the justifications sometimes given for this procedure is to enable the evangelist to avoid the inconvenience of having each church designate a portion of his or her compensation as a housing or rental allowance—the idea being that the corporation can designate a portion of the evangelist's annual income as a housing allowance in a single action. See Chapter 3 for a discussion of which organizations can designate housing allowances.

Other evangelists have churches designate all of their compensation as a housing allowance during the first months of the year and then do not bother with allowances for the last several months of the year. A potential problem with this arrangement is that if evangelists have churches designate their entire compensation as a housing allowance, there will be no taxable income to report on a Form 1099-MISC, and an evangelist theoretically could avoid the reporting of any income.

To ensure accountability, it is recommended that churches issue evangelists and other guest speakers a Form 1099-MISC if paying them compensation (net of substantiated travel expenses) of $600 or more. Include a housing allowance designated by the church in computing the $600 amount, but also provide the evangelist or guest speaker with a written housing allowance designation on the church's stationery to confirm the housing allowance amount.

18. SOCIAL SECURITY

Ministers cannot exclude a housing allowance (or the annual fair rental value of a parsonage) when computing their self-employment (Social Security) taxes unless they are retired. The tax code specifies that the self-employment tax does not apply to "the rental value of any parsonage or any parsonage allowance provided after the [minister] retires." *IRC 1402(a)(8).*

The IRS *Tax Guide for Churches and Religious Organizations* states: "The fair rental value of a parsonage or housing allowance is excludable from income only for income tax purposes. These amounts are not excluded in determining the minister's net earnings from self-employment for Self-employment Contributions Act (SECA) tax purposes. Retired ministers who receive either a parsonage or housing allowance are not required to include such amounts for SECA tax purposes."

Therefore, in computing the Social Security tax on Schedule SE of Form 1040, nonretired ministers must include the actual housing allowance exclusion as income on line 2 of either the short or long Schedule SE (whichever applies). *IRC 1402(a)(8); Treas. Reg. 1.1402(a)-11(a); Flowers v. Commissioner, T.C. Memo. 1991-542.*

✿**KEY POINT.** A housing allowance and the annual rental value of a parsonage are exclusions only for federal income tax reporting. They must be included in a minister's self-employment earnings when computing the self-employment tax (the Social Security tax on self-employed persons) unless the minister is retired.

19. IMPACT ON BUSINESS EXPENSES

A decision of the United States Tax Court may limit the deductibility of some business and professional expenses for ministers who exclude a portion of their church compensation from gross income as a housing or rental allowance. *Dalan v. Commissioner, T.C. Memo. 1988-106.* See Chapter 7, section F, for a full discussion of the potential ramifications of this decision.

20. THE SARBANES-OXLEY ACT

In 2002 Congress enacted the Corporate and Auditing Accountability, Responsibility and Transparency Act, more commonly known as the "Sarbanes-Oxley Act." The Act was designed to restore investor confidence in the financial markets by holding companies issuing stock to much higher standards than previously done.

Most of the Act's provisions are amendments to the two main federal securities laws, the Securities Act of 1933 and the Securities Exchange Act of 1934. Churches are specifically exempted from these laws except for the antifraud provisions; so churches generally are not subject to most of the provisions of Sarbanes-Oxley.

A few provisions of the Act are not amendments to federal securities law but instead are amendments to federal criminal law. Since no blanket exemption for churches is granted under federal criminal law, it is clear that churches are subject to these provisions. One of these provisions amends federal criminal law to include the following new crime:

> *Whoever knowingly alters, destroys, mutilates, conceals, covers up, falsifies, or makes a false entry in any record, document, or tangible object with the intent to impede, obstruct, or influence the investigation or proper administration of any matter within the jurisdiction of any department or agency of the United States . . . or in relation to or contemplation of any such matter or case, shall be fined under this title, imprisoned not more than 20 years, or both.*

A number of requirements must be met in order to trigger liability for destruction or falsification of documents:

- an alteration, destruction, mutilation, or falsification of a record or document must take place;

- the alteration, destruction, mutilation, or falsification must be "knowing" (i.e., intentional); and
- the act must be done with the intent to impede, obstruct, or influence the investigation or proper administration of any matter within the jurisdiction of any department or agency of the United States "or in relation to or contemplation of any such matter."
- Just what is the "proper administration of any matter within the jurisdiction of any department or agency of the United States . . . or in relation to or contemplation of any such matter"? The Act does not define this language, but numerous federal court rulings have interpreted this same language in other contexts. These decisions clarify that this terminology "must be given a broad, nontechnical meaning"; pertains generally to "all matters within the authority of a government agency"; and is not limited to submissions of written documents to governmental agencies.

✿**KEY POINT.** Persons who falsify records or documents may be liable on other grounds as well. For example, the intentional falsification of tax forms may result in liability for civil or criminal fraud.

✿**KEY POINT.** Churches should periodically apprise board members and staff members of this provision in the Sarbanes-Oxley Act.

EXAMPLE. A church has 50 members and one full-time employee (its pastor). It also has a part-time office secretary and an independent contractor who performs custodial services. The pastor discovers in November 2013 that the church board failed to designate a housing allowance for him for that year. He prepares a document that he dates December 31, 2012, and that purports to designate a housing allowance for all of 2013.

The church is not a public company and therefore is not subject to most of the provisions of the Sarbanes-Oxley Act. However, the Act makes it a crime to knowingly falsify any document with the intent to influence "the investigation or proper administration of any matter within the jurisdiction of any department or agency of the United States . . . or in relation to or contemplation of any such matter or case," and this provision contains no exemption for churches or pastors. It is possible that the pastor's falsification of the 2013 housing allowance violates this provision in the Sarbanes-Oxley Act, exposing him to a fine or imprisonment of up to 20 years. The Act does not define the "proper administration of any matter within the jurisdiction of any department or agency of the United States . . . or in relation to or contemplation of any such matter," but several courts have construed this same language in other contexts and noted that it "must be given a broad, nontechnical meaning" and that it pertains generally to "all matters within the authority of a government agency" and is not limited to submissions of written documents to governmental agencies. These

factors raise the possibility that the pastor's actions violate Sarbanes-Oxley. But even if they do not, the pastor's actions may expose him to civil or criminal penalties under the tax code.

21. EXAMPLES

The following examples address the significant issues associated with the housing allowance exclusion.

Construction costs

EXAMPLE. Pastor B owns a home. In February 2013 he begins building a new home in the same community. Pastor B sells his home in June 2013 and moves into the new home on July 1. Can he include the construction costs from February to July in computing his housing allowance exclusion for 2013, in addition to the costs of maintaining his prior home?

The regulations interpreting section 107 of the tax code specify that "for purposes of section 107, the term 'home' means a dwelling place." The IRS and a federal appeals court have both ruled that a minister has only one "home"—his or her principal residence—and so no expenses incurred in constructing a new home can be counted in computing the housing allowance exclusion until it has become the minister's "dwelling place." *Driscoll v. Commissioner, 2012-1 U.S.T.C. ¶50,187 (11th Cir. 2012), addressed in section B.14 of this chapter; Revenue Ruling 72-588.*

A more difficult question is presented in a case in which a minister is building a home while living in a church-owned parsonage. Even here it would appear that the construction costs would not be excludable as a housing allowance until the minister actually moved into the home. Because of these uncertainties, it would be prudent for ministers who are contemplating building a new home to defer as much of the construction cost as is possible to the time when they will be occupying the home.

EXAMPLE. A minister spent a portion of his church-designated housing allowance to purchase and install new floors, new carpet, and new cabinets in his home. The IRS ruled that a housing allowance can be used to pay for "capital expenditures" for remodeling. *IRS Letter Ruling 8350005.*

"Double deduction" of mortgage interest and property taxes

EXAMPLE. Pastor Y owns a home and incurred housing expenses of $12,000 in 2012. These expenses include mortgage principal and interest, property taxes, utilities, insurance, property taxes, and repairs. The church designated (in advance) $12,000 of Pastor Y's 2012 compensation ($35,000) as a housing allowance. The church reports only $23,000 of taxable compensation on Pastor Y's Form

W-2 for 2012 ($35,000 - $12,000). Pastor Y is able to itemize expenses on Schedule A (Form 1040). He is able to claim itemized deductions on Schedule A for both his mortgage interest and his property taxes, even though his taxable income was already reduced by these items because of their inclusion in the housing allowance. This is often referred to as the "double deduction." In reality, it represents an exclusion and a deduction.

Down payments

EXAMPLE. Pastor G, an ordained minister, purchased a home in 2012 for $100,000. During 2012 he made a $15,000 down payment on the home and, in addition, paid $8,000 in principal and interest payments on his home loan, $3,000 for utilities, $1,000 for home furnishings, $750 for repairs, $500 for real property taxes, and $200 for homeowners insurance. Pastor G has receipts for all of these expenses. His church designated $15,000 of his salary of $35,000 as a housing allowance. The annual rental value of the home (including furnishings) is determined by a local real estate agent to be $17,000. Pastor G's housing allowance exclusion would be the lowest of the following three amounts: (1) actual expenses ($28,450); (2) the church-designated housing allowance ($15,000); or (3) the annual rental value of the home, including utilities ($17,000). The lowest of these three amounts is the housing allowance of $15,000, meaning that the entire allowance is excluded from income taxation.

This example illustrates the adverse tax impact of a church designating an allowance that is too low. In this case the church's low designation will have the effect of forcing Pastor G to unnecessarily include an additional $2,000 in gross income for 2012. Assuming that he is in the 15 percent tax bracket, this amounts to an additional tax liability of $300. The lesson is clear—churches should not designate an allowance for a home-owning minister that is less than estimated housing expenses or the rental value of the minister's home (furnished, including utilities).

Housing allowance designations

EXAMPLE. A church board adopts the following resolution: "The board authorizes a housing allowance for each member of the pastoral staff in the amount of their actual and substantiated housing expenses." This method of designating a housing allowance should be avoided, since the IRS and the courts may not consider this to be an advance designation of a portion of a minister's compensation as a housing allowance, as required by law. The church will not know the amount of the housing allowance until the end of the year. Therefore, it seems doubtful that this would satisfy the advance designation requirement. It is not enough to agree in principle to pay a minister a housing allowance, leaving to the future a determination of the amount of the allowance. A specific amount of a minister's compensation must be designated as a housing allowance.

EXAMPLE. A religious denomination seeks to relieve local churches of the burden of designating annual housing allowances for their ministers and accordingly makes a designation for all ministers ordained by the denomination. This general designation is not effective with respect to ministers of local churches, but it is effective with respect to minister-employees of the denomination. *Revenue Ruling 62-117; Revenue Ruling 75-22.*

EXAMPLE. The Tax Court ruled that a "federation" of churches that supervised a police chaplain (who was an ordained minister) could designate a portion of his salary as a housing allowance, despite the fact that his salary was paid by the police department. *Boyd v. Commissioner, 42 T.C.M. 1136 (1981).*

EXAMPLE. The IRS ruled that a regional denominational executive could not designate a portion of a state prison chaplain's salary as a housing allowance. The chaplain was an ordained minister with the Christian Church (Disciples of Christ). He excluded 45 percent of his wages as a housing allowance on the basis of a letter from a regional executive of the Christian Church, which "endorsed" his ministry and stated that 45 percent of his annual salary constituted a housing allowance.

The IRS noted that the income tax regulations specify that housing allowances must be declared "by the employing church or other qualified organization." The IRS concluded that the Christian Church was not actively involved in the day-to-day conduct of the state prison chaplain program. Its involvement was limited to sending a letter to the state endorsing the chaplain and receiving annual reports from him. It also concluded that "we do not believe that this level of involvement is sufficient . . . to qualify the Church as an 'other qualified organization'. . . . The Church is not closely involved with the state in the conduct of its chaplain program and the responsibilities of the Church are not similar to those of an employer." Accordingly, neither the Christian Church nor any of its executives could designate a housing allowance for the prison chaplain. The IRS disallowed the chaplain's exclusion of 45 percent of his salary as a housing allowance. *IRS Letter Ruling 9052001.*

Housing expenses that exceed housing allowance

EXAMPLE. Pastor D owns his home. His employing church designated $8,000 of his $35,000 compensation in 2012 as a housing allowance. Pastor D's housing expenses for 2012 were utilities of $3,500, mortgage payments of $6,200, property taxes of $2,000, insurance payments of $500, repairs of $1,000, and furnishings of $750. The annual rental value of the home (including furnishings) is $7,500. Pastor D's housing allowance exclusion would be the lowest of the following three amounts: (1) actual expenses ($13,950), (2) the church-designated housing allowance ($8,000), or (3) the annual rental value of the home (furnished, including utilities). The nontaxable amount of the housing allowance would be limited to $8,000, since it is the lowest of the three amounts.

Ministers who own their home debt-free

EXAMPLE. Pastor C is paid a salary of $35,000 for 2012 plus a housing allowance of $15,000. Pastor C has housing expenses of $15,000, consisting of mortgage payments on a conventional home loan of $10,000, utilities of $3,500, and property taxes and insurance of $1,500. The fair rental value of the home is $16,000 (furnished, plus utilities). Pastor C can claim the full church-designated housing allowance as an exclusion from taxable income for income tax reporting, since he has housing-related expenses of at least this amount (and his expenses do not exceed the fair rental value of the home).

EXAMPLE. Same facts as the previous example, except that Pastor C pays off his home mortgage loan. Pastor C is still eligible for a housing allowance, but it is excludable only to the extent of his actual housing-related expenses of $5,000. As a result, $10,000 of the housing allowance represents taxable income.

Purchasing a parsonage from the church

EXAMPLE. A church owned a home that it sold to its senior minister, Pastor D. The sales price was the home's fair market value at the time of the sale. Pastor D signed a promissory note and land contract agreeing to make monthly payments over a number of years until the sales price was paid in full. Title to the home remained in the name of the church until the note was paid in full. Under a "compensation agreement" adopted by the church, Pastor D was paid a salary (a portion of which was designated as a housing allowance by the church). The church also paid all of Pastor D's utility expenses. Principal and interest payments made by Pastor D to the church are properly included in computing his housing allowance exclusion, and he may also deduct the interest payments as an itemized deduction on Schedule A (if he is able to itemize deductions). *IRS Letter Ruling 8937025.*

Renting a home

EXAMPLE. Pastor R rents a home. His church designated a rental allowance of $7,500 for 2012. Pastor R's actual expenses incurred in renting the home (he has receipts for all of them) are $8,200. The annual rental value of the home (including furnishings and utilities) is $10,000. The housing allowance of a minister who rents a home is the least of the following amounts: (1) actual expenses incurred in renting the home, (2) the church-designated allowance, or (3) the fair rental value of the home (furnished, plus utilities). Pastor R's housing allowance exclusion for 2012 will be $7,500 (the least of these three amounts).

Second mortgages and home equity loans

EXAMPLE. Pastor C is paid a salary of $30,000 for 2013 plus a housing allowance of $10,000. Pastor C has housing expenses of

$10,000 in 2013, consisting of mortgage payments on a conventional home loan of $6,000, utilities of $2,500, and property taxes and insurance of $1,500. The fair rental value of the home is $11,000. Pastor C can claim the full church-designated housing allowance as an exclusion from taxable income when computing income taxes for 2013, since he had housing-related expenses of at least this amount (and his expenses do not exceed the fair rental value of the home).

EXAMPLE. Same facts as the previous example, except that Pastor C paid off his home mortgage loan at the end of 2009. Pastor C is eligible for a housing allowance in 2013, but it is nontaxable only to the extent of his actual housing-related expenses of $4,000. As a result, $6,000 of the $10,000 housing allowance represents taxable income.

EXAMPLE. Same facts as the previous example, except that Pastor C obtains a loan, secured by mortgage on his home, to pay for various personal expenses (a car, a vacation, a child's college education, and various medical bills). The loan payments amount to $6,000 in 2013. Pastor C cannot include any portion of the $6,000 in computing his housing allowance exclusion for the year, since these are not an expense of providing a home. Pastor C's housing allowance exclusion (the amount by which he can reduce his taxable income) is $4,000 (utilities, property taxes, and insurance). The excess housing allowance of $6,000 must be reported as taxable income.

EXAMPLE. Same facts as the previous example, except that Pastor C obtains a loan, secured by a mortgage on his home, to pay for remodeling expenses and furnishings. The full amount of these loan payments can be considered housing-related expenses in computing Pastor C's housing allowance for the year.

22. IRS AUDIT GUIDELINES FOR MINISTERS

The IRS has issued audit guidelines for its agents to follow when auditing ministers. The guidelines provide agents with the following information regarding housing allowances:

Internal Revenue Code section 107 provides an exclusion from gross income for a "parsonage allowance," housing specifically provided as part of the compensation for the services performed as a minister of the gospel. This includes the rental value of a home furnished to him or her as part of compensation or a housing allowance, to the extent that the payment is used to rent or provide a home and to the extent such allowance does not exceed the fair rental value (FRV) of the home, including furnishings and appurtenances such as a garage and the cost of utilities. The term "parsonage allowance" includes church provided parsonages, rental allowances with which the minister may rent a home and housing allowances with which the minister may purchase a home. A minister can receive a parsonage allowance for only one home.

A housing allowance must be included in the minister's gross income in the taxable year in which it is received to the extent that such allowance is not used by him during the taxable year to rent or otherwise provide a home or exceeds the FRV of the home including furnishings and appurtenances such as a garage and the cost of utilities. The value of the "allowed" parsonage allowance is not included in computing the minister's income subject to income tax and should not be included in W-2 wages. However, the parsonage allowance is subject to self-employment tax along with other earnings. (See special rules for retired ministers). . . .

The exclusion under section 107 only applies if the employing church designates the amount of the parsonage allowance in advance of the tax year. The designation may appear in the minister's employment contract, the church minutes, the church budget, or any other document indicating official action. . . .

The amount of the parsonage allowance excludible from gross income is the LEAST of:

- *The amount actually used to provide a home,*
- *The amount officially designated as a housing allowance, or*
- *The fair rental value (FRV) of the home, including furnishings and appurtenances such as a garage plus the cost of utilities.*

The IRS audit guidelines contain the following examples:

EXAMPLE 1. A is an ordained minister. She receives an annual salary of $36,000 and use of a parsonage which has a FRV of $800 a month, including utilities. She has an accountable plan for other business expenses such as travel. A's gross income for arriving at taxable income for Federal income tax purposes is $36,000, but for self-employment tax purposes it is $45,600 ($36,000 salary + $9,600 FRV of parsonage).

EXAMPLE 2. B, an ordained minister, is vice president of academic affairs at Holy Bible Seminary. His compensation package includes a salary of $80,000 per year and a $30,000 housing allowance. His housing costs for the year included mortgage payments of $15,000, utilities of $3,000, and $3,600 for home maintenance and new furniture. The fair rental value of the home, as furnished, is $18,000 per year. The three amounts for comparison are:

(a) Actual expenses of $21,600 ($15,000 mortgage payments + $3,000 utilities + $3,600 other costs)
(b) Designated housing allowance of $30,000
(c) FRV + utilities of $21,000 ($18,000 + $3,000 utilities)

B may exclude $21,000 from gross income but must include in income the other $9,000 of the housing allowance. The

entire $30,000 will be considered in arriving at net self-employment income.

EXAMPLE 3. C is an ordained minister and has been in his church's employ for the last 20 years. His salary is $40,000 and his designated parsonage allowance is $15,000. C's mortgage was paid off last year. During the tax year he spent $2,000 on utilities, and $3,000 on real estate taxes and insurance. The FRV of his home, as furnished, is $750 a month.

The three amounts for comparison are:

(a) Actual housing costs of $5,000 ($2,000 utilities + $3,000 taxes and insurance)
(b) Designated housing allowance of $15,000
(c) FRV + utilities of $11,000 ($9,000 FRV + $2,000 utilities)

C may only exclude his actual expenses of $5,000 for Federal income tax purposes. He may not exclude the FRV of his home even though he has paid for it in previous years. *Swaggart v. Commissioner, T.C. Memo. 1984-409.* The $15,000 will be included in the computation of net self-employment income.

EXAMPLE 4. Assume the same facts as in Example 3, except that C takes out a home equity loan and uses the proceeds to pay for his daughter's college tuition. The payments are $300 per month. Even though he has a loan secured by his home, the money was not used to "provide a home" and can't be used to compute the excludable portion of the parsonage allowance. The results are the same as for Example 3. The interest on the home equity loan may be deducted as an itemized deduction subject to the limitations, if any, of Internal Revenue Code section 163.

EXAMPLE 5. D is an ordained minister who received $40,000 in salary plus a designated housing allowance of $12,000. He spent $12,000 on mortgage payments, $2,400 on utilities, and $2,000 on new furniture. The FRV of his home as furnished is $16,000. D's exclusion is limited to $12,000 even though his actual cost ($16,400) and FRV and utilities ($18,400) are more. He may not deduct his housing costs in excess of the designated allowance.

EXAMPLE 6. E's designated housing allowance is $20,000. She and her husband live in one half of a duplex which they own. The other half is rented. Mortgage payments for the duplex are $1,500 per month. E's utilities run $1,800 per year, and her tenant pays his own from a separate meter. During the year E replaced carpeting throughout the structure at a cost of $6,500 and did minor repairs of $500. E must allocate her mortgage costs, carpeting, and repairs between her own unit and the rental unit in determining the amount of the excludable parsonage allowance. Amounts allocable to the rented portion for mortgage interest, taxes, etc., would be reported on Schedule E as usual. Her actual costs to provide a home were $14,300 ($9,000 mortgage payments, $1,800 utilities, and $3,500 for half the carpeting and repairs). The FRV for her unit is the same as the rent she charges for the other half, which is $750 a month, and she estimates that her furnishings add another $150 per month to the FRV. Her FRV plus utilities is $12,600 ($10,800 FRV + $1,800 utilities). E may exclude $12,600 for Federal income tax purposes.

Pursuant to Internal Revenue Code section 265(a)(6) and Rev. Rul. 87-32, even though a minister's home mortgage interest and real estate taxes have been paid with money excluded from income as a housing allowance, he or she may still claim itemized deductions for these items. The sale of the residence is treated the same as that of other taxpayers, even though it may have been completely purchased with funds excluded under Internal Revenue Code section 107.

Because expenses attributable to earned income which is exempt from tax are not ordinarily deductible, a minister's business expenses related to his or her earnings must be allocated and become partially nondeductible pursuant to IRC §265 This is discussed in detail in the section on Business Expenses.

Illustration 6-3 provides a worksheet for the computation of the amount that is excludable as a [housing] allowance.

✦ **KEY POINT.** The audit guidelines assist IRS agents in the examination of ministers' tax returns. They alert agents to the key questions to ask, and they provide background information along with the IRS position on a number of issues. It is therefore important for ministers to be familiar with these guidelines.

23. CONSTITUTIONALITY

The Freedom from Religion Foundation (FFRF) and several other plaintiffs filed a lawsuit in a federal district court in California challenging the constitutionality of the parsonage exclusion and housing allowance. The lawsuit alleged that the parsonage exclusion and housing allowance were available only to clergy and, therefore, amounted to an unconstitutional establishment of religion.

This legal challenge was dealt a fatal blow as a result of a 2011 United States Supreme Court case. *Arizona Christian School Tuition Organization v. Winn, 131 S.Ct. 1436 (2011).* The high court ruled (5-4) that a group of Arizona taxpayers lacked standing to challenge the constitutionality of a state law that gave tax credits for contributions to school tuition organizations (STOs) that provided scholarships to students attending private schools, including religious schools. It noted that the courts have consistently ruled that standing cannot be based on a plaintiff's status as a federal taxpayer because the "injury" is too remote or speculative.

ILLUSTRATION 6-3

EXCLUSION OF [HOUSING] ALLOWANCE UNDER INTERNAL REVENUE CODE §107
Home Owned or Rented/Housing Allowance Received

The exclusion is limited to the least of:

1. Amount designated as housing allowance
2. Amount actually used to provide a home which is composed of the following items:

   • Rent
   • House payments
   • Furnishing
   • Repairs
   • Insurance
   • Taxes
   • Utilities
   • Other Expenses

3. Fair rental value of home, including furniture, utilities, garage

Amount excludable from income tax liability is the least of 1, 2, or 3 above.

If Parsonage provided, you can deduct only the fair rental value.

The entire designated housing allowance is subject to self-employment tax unless you have been approved for exemption or are retired.

The Court acknowledged a limited exception to taxpayer standing in cases challenging legislation on the basis of the First Amendment's nonestablishment of religion clause. Taxpayers have standing in such cases to challenge direct transfers of tax revenue to religious organizations, since "the taxpayer's allegation in such cases would be that his tax money is being extracted and spent in violation of specific constitutional protections against such abuses of legislative power." But the Court concluded that there is a difference between direct transfers of tax revenues to religious organizations, and credits and deductions, and it limited taxpayer standing to the former context.

This ruling left no doubt that the plaintiffs challenging the housing allowance lacked standing, since a tax exclusion rather than a direct transfer of tax revenue to religion was involved. As a result, the plaintiffs voluntarily dismissed their challenge.

But the Freedom from Religion Foundation revived its constitutional challenge to the housing allowance in a lawsuit filed in

September 2011 in the federal district court for the western district of Wisconsin. It is attempting to demonstrate taxpayer standing by naming three of its executive officers as plaintiffs and asserting that the plaintiffs are ineligible for a housing allowance, since they are not ministers, and therefore they are directly affected by the tax code's housing allowance provision.

C. REPORTING HOUSING ALLOWANCES

Churches and ministers can report housing allowances for federal income tax purposes in various ways. Three methods are described below (for use in 2013), along with the advantages and disadvantages of each. Churches and ministers should select the method that works best for them.

METHOD 1: THE ACTUAL EXCLUSION METHOD

Few churches use this method. It consists of the following steps:

- **Minister provides estimate of next year's housing expenses.** The minister estimates 2013 housing expenses by December of 2012 on a form provided by the church (see Illustrations 6-4, 6-5, and 6-6).
- **Church designates a housing allowance.** The church board, in its December 2012 meeting, designates a portion of the minister's 2013 compensation as a housing allowance, based on the minister's estimated expenses (see Illustration 6-2).
- **Minister substantiates actual housing expenses.** In January 2014 the minister is required to substantiate actual housing or rental expenses by submitting documentary evidence to the church treasurer.
- **Church computes actual housing allowance exclusion.** By the end of January 2014, the church treasurer computes the minister's actual housing allowance exclusion for 2013 by selecting the lowest of the following three amounts:

  - the church-designated housing allowance for 2013,
  - actual housing or rental expenses paid for by the minister during the year 2013 and properly substantiated, or
  - the fair rental value of the minister's home (furnished, plus utilities).

- **Minister's Form W-2 compensation reduced by the actual exclusion.** The church treasurer reduces the amount of compensation reported on the minister's 2013 Form W-2 (or Form 1099-MISC) by the actual exclusion as determined above.

Advantages

- This method ensures that ministers will not claim the church-designated allowance as their exclusion (often a lower amount applies).
- It ensures that the church will not participate in the understatement of taxable income.
- The church exercises fiscal control over compensation packages.

Disadvantages

- It is difficult for some ministers to accumulate expenses and receipts by the due date of the church's Form W-2 (or 1099-MISC).
- This method imposes greater responsibilities on the church treasurer that are not mandated by the tax code or IRS regulations.
- The church treasurer must determine the portion of the housing allowance that is nontaxable. At a minimum, this will require a careful analysis of all of the pastor's substantiated housing expenses for the year. The treasurer will be responsible for deciding which expenses can be included in computing the housing allowance exclusion. These decisions can be complex and will be beyond the expertise of many church treasurers.
- By assuming responsibility for determining the correct amount of the housing allowance exclusion, the church may be liable for the payment of additional taxes and penalties if it incorrectly computes a minister's housing allowance exclusion.
- Income reported to the IRS on the quarterly Form 941 filed by the church during the year often will not be the same as the income reported on the Form W-2 issued to the minister, since the income reported on Form 941 is net of the church-designated housing allowance, while income reported on the Form W-2 reflects the minister's income less the actual nontaxable amount of the housing allowance. This can be addressed in an explanatory letter accompanying the Forms W-2 that are sent to the Social Security Administration (with the W-3 transmittal form).

METHOD 2: THE ESTIMATED EXCLUSION METHOD

This is a commonly used method consisting of the following steps:

- **Minister provides estimate of next year's housing expenses.** The minister estimates his or her 2013 housing or rental expenses by December 2012 on a form provided by the church (see Illustrations 6-4, 6-5, and 6-6). Note that some modifications in these forms will be necessary, since portions of them reflect Method 1 (above).
- **Church designates a housing allowance.** The church board, in its December 2012 meeting, designates a portion of the minister's 2013 compensation as a housing allowance, based on the minister's estimated expenses (see Illustration 6-2).

- **Minister's Form W-2 compensation reduced by church-designated housing allowance.** In January 2014 the church treasurer reduces the amount of compensation reported on the minister's 2013 Form W-2 (or 1099-MISC) by the church-designated housing allowance.
- **Minister reports any excess housing allowance as taxable income.** If the minister's actual exclusion is less than the church-designated allowance (according to the tests described under Method 1, above), it is the minister's responsibility to report the excess housing allowance as additional income on line 7 of his or her Form 1040 (if an employee) or on Schedule C (if self-employed).

Advantages

- This method imposes less administrative inconvenience on the church than Method 1.
- It is the method illustrated by the IRS in Publication 517.
- It avoids the lack of reconciliation between a church's Forms 941 and W-2, which is noted as a disadvantage to Method 1.

Disadvantages

- This method promotes the common practice of ministers claiming the church-designated housing allowance as their exclusion (even if a lower amount applies). This has the effect of understating taxable income, sometimes significantly.
- The church indirectly may contribute to the understatement of taxable income.

METHOD 3: THE NONACCOUNTABLE METHOD

This method is not commonly used. It consists of the following steps:

- **Minister requests housing allowance with no estimate of housing expenses.** The minister informs the church board during its December 2012 meeting of the appropriate housing allowance for the year 2013. No estimated expenses are

discussed, so Illustrations 6-4, 6-5, and 6-6 are not used. The board simply designates an allowance in the amount requested by the minister (see Illustration 6-2).
- **Church designates a housing allowance.** The church board, in its December 2012 meeting, designates a portion of the minister's 2013 compensation as a housing allowance based on the minister's request. It has no way of knowing whether the request reasonably reflects anticipated housing expenses.
- **Minister's Form W-2 compensation reduced by church-designated housing allowance.** In January 2014 the church treasurer reduces the amount of compensation reported on the minister's 2013 Form W-2 (or 1099-MISC) by the church-designated housing allowance.
- **Minister reports any excess housing allowance as taxable income.** If the minister's actual exclusion is less than the church-designated allowance (according to the tests described under Method 1, previous page), it is the minister's responsibility to report the excess housing allowance as additional income on line 7 of his or her Form 1040 (if an employee) or on Schedule C (if self-employed).

Advantages

There are no advantages in using this method other than the fact that it may be slightly easier for the minister (who is not required to estimate housing expenses for the following year).

Disadvantages

- The church exercises no internal control over the process of designating the allowance. It designates an amount without any assurance that it is reasonable in light of the minister's anticipated expenses for the new year.
- This method promotes the common practice of ministers simply claiming the church-designated housing allowance as their exclusion (though a lower amount may apply).
- The church indirectly may contribute to the understatement of taxable income.

ILLUSTRATION 6-4

HOUSING ALLOWANCE EXPENSE REPORT FORM FOR MINISTERS WHO *OWN* THEIR HOME

As a minister who owns a home, you do not pay federal income taxes on the amount of your compensation that the church designates in advance as a housing allowance, to the extent that the allowance represents compensation for ministerial services, is used to pay housing expenses, and does not exceed the fair rental value of your home (furnished, plus utilities). To assist the church in designating an appropriate housing allowance, please estimate on this form the housing expenses you expect to pay next year, and then return the form to the secretary of the church board prior to the board's December meeting.

HOUSING EXPENSE	ESTIMATED 2013 AMOUNT
Down payment on home	$
Mortgage payments on a loan to purchase or improve your home (include both principal and interest)	$
Real estate taxes	$
Property insurance	$
Utilities (electricity, gas, water, trash pickup, local telephone charges)	$
Furnishings and appliances (purchase and repair)	$
Structural repairs and remodeling	$
Yard maintenance and improvements	$
Maintenance items (household cleansers, light bulbs, pest control, etc.)	$
Homeowners association dues	$
Miscellaneous	$
TOTAL ESTIMATED EXPENSES FOR 2013	$

The above listed expenses represent a reasonable estimate of my housing expenses for next year. I understand and agree that

(1) The church board will not designate a portion of my compensation as a housing allowance until I complete and return this form. Retroactive designations of housing allowances are not legally effective.

(2) It is my responsibility to notify the church board in the event these estimates prove materially inaccurate during the year.

(3) The entire housing allowance designated by the church is not necessarily nontaxable. Rather, it is nontaxable for income tax purposes only to the extent that it does not exceed actual housing expenses or the annual rental value of my home (furnished, including utilities). Stated differently, the nontaxable amount is the *lowest* of three amounts: (a) actual housing expenses for the year, (b) the church-designated housing allowance, or (c) the annual rental value of my home (furnished, including utilities).

[Note: Include paragraph (4) only if the church uses the "actual exclusion" method for reporting housing allowances, as described above. If the church uses the "estimated exclusion" or "nonaccountable" methods, delete paragraph (4) and renumber paragraph (5) as paragraph (4).]

(4) I will have to account to the church treasurer for my actual 2013 housing expenses not later than January 20, 2014. This means I will have to present receipts substantiating my actual 2013 housing expenses. The church treasurer will then compute my actual housing allowance exclusion based on the information I have provided and the test described in the previous paragraph. The church treasurer will then reduce the income reported on my Form W-2 by the amount of the actual housing allowance exclusion. I understand that if I fail to account for my actual housing expenses by January 20, 2014, the church will include my entire housing allowance as income on my Form W-2 and that I will be responsible for claiming the exclusion on my income tax return.

(5) My housing allowance exclusion is an exclusion for federal income taxes only. I must add the nontaxable amount of my housing allowance as income in reporting my self-employment taxes on Schedule SE (unless I am exempt from self-employment taxes).

_____
Legible signature of minister

_____
Date

I attest that I received this form on _____
                                         Date

_____
Secretary of church board

=== **ILLUSTRATION 6-5** ===

HOUSING ALLOWANCE EXPENSE REPORT FORM FOR MINISTERS WHO *RENT* THEIR HOME

As a minister who rents a home or apartment, you do not pay federal income taxes on the amount of your compensation that the church designates in advance as a housing allowance, to the extent that the allowance represents compensation for ministerial services, is used to pay rental expenses, and does not exceed the fair rental value of the home (furnished, plus utilities). To assist the church in designating an appropriate amount, please estimate on this form the rental expenses you expect to pay next year, and then return the form to the secretary of the church board prior to the board's December meeting.

RENTAL EXPENSE	ESTIMATED 2013 AMOUNT
Rental payments	$
Property insurance	$
Utilities (electricity, gas, water, trash pickup, local telephone charges)	$
Furnishings and appliances (purchase and repair)	$
Structural repairs and remodeling	$
Yard maintenance and improvements	$
Maintenance items (household cleansers, light bulbs, pest control, etc.)	$
Miscellaneous	$
TOTAL ESTIMATED EXPENSES FOR 2013	$

The above listed expenses represent a reasonable estimate of my housing expenses for next year. I understand and agree that

(1) The church board will not designate a portion of my compensation as a housing allowance until I complete and return this form. Retroactive designations of housing allowances are not legally effective.
(2) It is my responsibility to notify the church board in the event these estimates prove materially inaccurate during the year.
(3) The entire housing allowance designated by the church is not necessarily nontaxable. Rather, it is nontaxable for income tax purposes only to the extent that it does not exceed my actual rental expenses for the year. Stated

differently, the nontaxable amount is the *lowest* of three amounts: (a) my actual rental expenses for the year, (b) the church-designated housing allowance, or (c) the fair rental value of the home (furnished, plus utilities).

[Note: Include paragraph (4) only if the church uses the "actual exclusion" method for reporting housing allowances, as described above. If the church uses the "estimated exclusion" or "nonaccountable" methods, delete paragraph (4) and renumber paragraph (5) as paragraph (4).]

(4) I will have to account to the church treasurer for my actual 2013 rental expenses not later than January 20, 2014. This means I will have to present receipts substantiating my actual 2013 rental expenses. The church treasurer will then compute my actual housing allowance exclusion based on the information I have provided and the test described in the previous paragraph. The church treasurer will then reduce the income reported on my Form W-2 by the amount of the actual housing allowance exclusion. I understand that if I fail to account for my actual rental expenses by January 20, 2014, the church will include my entire housing allowance as income on my Form W-2 and that I will be responsible for claiming the exclusion on my income tax return.
(5) My housing allowance exclusion is an exclusion for federal income taxes only. I must add the nontaxable amount of my housing allowance as income in reporting my self-employment taxes on Schedule SE (unless I am exempt from self-employment taxes).

_____
Legible signature of minister

_____
Date

I attest that I received this form on _____
                                        Date

_____
Secretary of church board

ILLUSTRATION 6-6

PARSONAGE ALLOWANCE EXPENSE FORM FOR MINISTERS WHO LIVE IN A CHURCH-OWNED PARSONAGE

As a minister who lives in a church-provided parsonage, you do not pay federal income taxes on the amount of your compensation that the church designates in advance as a parsonage allowance, to the extent that the allowance represents compensation for ministerial services, is used to pay parsonage expenses, and does not exceed the fair rental value of the parsonage (furnished, including utilities). To assist the church in designating an appropriate amount, please estimate on this form the parsonage expenses you expect to pay next year, and then return the form to the secretary of the church board prior to the board's December meeting.

PARSONAGE EXPENSE	ESTIMATED 2013 AMOUNT
Real estate taxes	$
Property insurance	$
Utilities (electricity, gas, water, trash pickup, local telephone charges)	$
Furnishings and appliances (purchase and repair)	$
Structural repairs and remodeling	$
Yard maintenance and improvements	$
Maintenance items (household cleansers, light bulbs, pest control, etc.)	$
Miscellaneous	$
TOTAL ESTIMATED EXPENSES FOR 2013	$

The above listed expenses represent a reasonable estimate of my parsonage expenses for next year. I understand and agree that

(1) The church board will not designate a portion of my compensation as a parsonage allowance until I complete and return this form. Retroactive designations of parsonage allowances are not legally effective.

(2) It is my responsibility to notify the church board in the event these estimates prove materially inaccurate during the year.

(3) The entire parsonage allowance designated by the church is not necessarily nontaxable. Rather, it is nontaxable for income tax purposes only to the extent that it does not exceed my actual parsonage expenses for the year. Stated dif-

ferently, the nontaxable amount is the *lowest* of the following amounts: (a) my actual parsonage expenses for the year, (b) the church-designated parsonage allowance, or (c) the fair rental value of the parsonage (furnished, plus utilities).

[Note: Include paragraph (4) only if the church uses the "actual exclusion" method for reporting housing allowances, as described above. If the church uses the "estimated exclusion" or "nonaccountable" methods, delete paragraph (4) and renumber paragraph (5) as paragraph (4).]

(4) I will have to account to the church treasurer for my actual 2013 parsonage expenses not later than January 20, 2014. This means I will have to present receipts substantiating my actual 2013 parsonage expenses. The church treasurer will then compute my actual parsonage allowance exclusion based on the information I have provided and the test described in the previous paragraph. The church treasurer will then reduce the income reported on my Form W-2 by the amount of the actual parsonage allowance exclusion. I understand that if I fail to account for my actual parsonage expenses by January 20, 2014, the church will include my entire parsonage allowance as income on my Form W-2 and that I will be responsible for claiming the exclusion on my income tax return.

(5) My parsonage allowance exclusion and the exclusion of the annual rental value of the parsonage are exclusions for federal income taxes only. I must add the nontaxable amount of my parsonage allowance and the annual rental value of the parsonage as income in reporting my self-employment taxes on Schedule SE (unless I am exempt from self-employment taxes).

_____

Legible signature of minister

_____

Date

I attest that I received this form on _____

Date

_____

Secretary of church board

Chapter 7 BUSINESS EXPENSES, ITEMIZED DEDUCTIONS, AND CREDITS

Have you never questioned those who travel? Have you paid no regard to their accounts?

Job 21:29

CHAPTER HIGHLIGHTS

- **Overview.** Church staff members can reduce their taxes by claiming various adjustments, deductions, and credits.

- **Adjustments.** An adjustment to gross income is a deduction that is available regardless of whether a taxpayer has enough expenses to itemize deductions on Schedule A. Common adjustments include the deduction of half the self-employment tax, IRA contributions, and moving expenses.

- **Deductibility of business expenses.** Most church staff members have business expenses. The deductibility of these expenses depends on whether a person is an employee or self-employed, whether the expenses are reimbursed by the church, and whether any reimbursed expenses are paid under an accountable or a nonaccountable reimbursement plan.

- **Unreimbursed business expenses.** Church staff members who are employees for income tax reporting purposes claim their unreimbursed business expenses on Schedule A to the extent such expenses exceed two percent of adjusted gross income (AGI). Unreimbursed expenses are those expenses paid out of an employee's own funds without any contribution from the church.

- **Employee business expenses reimbursed by a church under a nonaccountable arrangement.** Church staff members who are employees for income tax reporting purposes claim any business expenses reimbursed by their church under a *nonaccountable* reimbursement plan on Schedule—if they are able to itemize, and only to the extent such expenses exceed two percent of AGI. The full amount of the church's reimbursements must be included in the employee's income regardless of whether the expenses are deductible. A church has a *nonaccountable* plan if it reimburses staff members' business expenses without requiring adequate substantiation of the amount, date, place, and business purpose of the expenses, or if it does not require excess reimbursements to be returned to the church.

- **Employee business expenses reimbursed by a church under an accountable arrangement.** The limitations on the deductibility of employee business expenses (summarized

in the preceding two paragraphs) can be avoided if the church adopts an *accountable* reimbursement plan. An accountable plan is one that meets the following requirements: (1) only business expenses are reimbursed; (2) no reimbursement is allowed without an adequate accounting of expenses within a reasonable period of time (not more than 60 days after an expense is incurred); (3) any excess reimbursement or allowance must be returned to the employer within a reasonable period of time (not more than 120 days after an excess reimbursement is paid); and (4) an employer's reimbursements must come out of the employer's funds and not by reducing the employee's salary. Under an accountable plan, an employee reports to the church rather than to the IRS. The reimbursements are not reported as income to the employee, and the employee does not claim any deductions. This is the best way for churches to handle reimbursements of business expenses.

- **Self-employed staff members.** Church staff members who report their income taxes as self-employed deduct their business expenses directly on Schedule C. They are not subject to the 2 percent limitation that applies to employees, and they may deduct their expenses even if they are not able to itemize deductions on Schedule A.

- **Examples of business expenses.** Common business expenses for church staff members include transportation, travel, entertainment, books and subscriptions, education, cell phones, and vestments. In some cases a home computer and a home office qualify as business expenses.

- **Commuting.** Commuting to and from work is never a business expense—unless you meet the rigid requirements of a home office.

- **Automobile expenses.** Automobile expenses are the most significant business expense for many church staff members. These expenses can be deducted using either a standard mileage rate or the actual costs of operating the car for business miles. Most staff members choose the standard mileage rate because of its simplicity. It is available only if it is selected for the first year a car is used in your trade or business. The standard mileage rate for business miles driven during 2012 was 55.5 cents per mile. The standard business mileage rate for 2013 is 56.5 cents per mile.

- **Church-owned automobiles.** Church staff members should consider the advantages of using a church-owned car for their business travel. Such an arrangement can eliminate most recordkeeping and reporting requirements if several conditions are satisfied.

- **Per diem rates.** Church staff members can use new per diem rates to substantiate the amount of their lodging and meal expenses. If these rates are used, a minister need not retain receipts of actual meals and lodging expenses. Several conditions apply. These per diem rates can be used only in connection with an accountable reimbursement plan of the employer.

- **Home offices.** Most ministers have an office in their home. For the costs of such an office to be deductible as a business expense, several conditions must be satisfied. For example, the office must be used exclusively and regularly in the minister's trade or business. More stringent rules apply to ministers who are employees for income tax purposes.

- **Substantiation.** Business expenses must be substantiated by adequate evidence in order to support an income tax deduction or an expense reimbursement under an accountable reimbursement plan of an employer. Stricter substantiation rules apply to transportation, travel, and entertainment expenses.

- **The Deason rule.** This rule requires ministers to reduce their business expenses by the percentage of their total compensation that consists of a tax-exempt housing allowance. This reduction in business expenses does not apply to the computation of self-employment taxes (since the housing allowance is not deductible in computing these taxes).

- **Itemized deductions.** Church staff members who have itemized deductions in excess of their standard deduction ($11,900 for married couples filing jointly, $5,950 for single persons for 2012) may deduct these expenses on Schedule A. Itemized deductions include medical expenses (in excess of 7.5 percent of AGI), certain taxes and interest payments, charitable contributions, casualty and theft losses (uncompensated by insurance), and miscellaneous expenses.

INTRODUCTION

The preceding chapters have described several items that you must include in computing your gross income, and some of the exclusions that are not included in gross income. After your gross income is computed (and reported on Form 1040, line 22), you then compute your AGI by deducting various adjustments to gross income. Adjustments to gross income, and the more important itemized and business deductions, will be summarized in this chapter from both an employee and a self-employed perspective.

A. ADJUSTMENTS TO GROSS INCOME

❖ **KEY POINT.** Most church staff members can reduce their taxes by claiming various adjustments, deductions, and credits.

❖ **KEY POINT.** An adjustment to gross income is a deduction that is available to most church staff members regardless of whether they have enough expenses to itemize their deductions on Schedule A.

You may deduct certain adjustments from gross income in computing your adjusted gross income. The adjustments are reported and deducted on Form 1040, lines 23–37. For 2012 these adjustments consist of the following:

- IRA deduction, including a spouse's contribution (explained in Chapter 10);
- medical savings account deduction (explained in Chapter 5 and reported on line 36);
- health savings account deduction (explained in Chapter 5);
- moving expenses you pay that are not reimbursed by your employer;
- one-half of your self-employment tax;
- self-employed workers' health insurance deduction;
- a penalty incurred on an early withdrawal of funds from a time savings account; and
- alimony paid.

B. DEDUCTIONS: AN OVERVIEW

After you have figured your adjusted gross income, you are ready to either (1) subtract itemized deductions, or (2) subtract your applicable standard deduction. For the most part, itemized deductions are deductions for various kinds of personal expenses that are grouped together on Schedule A (Form 1040). They include deductions for medical expenses, taxes and interest you pay, charitable contributions, nonbusiness casualty and theft losses, and various miscellaneous deductions (including certain employee business expenses). Many of these deductions will be summarized below. Ordinarily you should itemize deductions only if they total more than your standard deduction. The standard deduction amounts for 2012 are set forth in Table 7-1.

As Table 7-1 illustrates, if a single taxpayer is blind or age 65 or older, the standard deduction is increased by an additional $1,450 (or by $2,900 if the taxpayer is both blind and at least age 65). If either married taxpayer (assuming they file a joint return) is blind or age 65 or older, the standard deduction is increased by an additional $1,150 ($2,300 if both).

c. BUSINESS AND PROFESSIONAL EXPENSES

✿ **KEY POINT.** Most church staff members have business expenses. The deductibility of these expenses depends on whether a staff member is an employee or self-employed, whether the expenses are reimbursed by the church, and whether any reimbursed expenses are paid under an accountable or a nonaccountable reimbursement arrangement.

Section 162 of the tax code authorizes taxpayers to deduct any ordinary and necessary expenses incurred in a trade or business. The exercise of ministry qualifies as a trade or business, so ministers are free to deduct most of the expenses they incur in the exercise of their ministry (subject to certain conditions and limitations described below).

The tax code specifically lists travel expenses (including meals and lodging), compensation paid for services, and rent paid for business property or equipment as examples of deductible business expenses. These certainly are not intended to be the only deductible business and professional expenses. Section 1.162-6 of the income tax regulations lists the following additional examples of business expenses:

- expenses paid or accrued in the operation and repair of an automobile used in making professional calls;
- dues to professional societies;
- subscriptions to professional journals;
- rent paid or accrued for office rooms;
- the cost of the fuel, light, water, telephone, etc., used in such offices;
- the hiring of office assistants; and amounts currently paid or accrued for books, furniture, and professional instruments and equipment, the useful life of which is short.

Other common examples of business expenses include entertainment, education, convention expenses, business gifts, insurance, and vestments (including cleaning).

EXAMPLE. Ministers who perform their duties with no expectation of receiving compensation are not engaged in a trade or business and cannot claim any deduction for business expenses.

However, they may be able to claim a charitable contribution deduction for expenses incurred in performing charitable activities. *Revenue Ruling 69-645; Thornton v. Commissioner, 57 T.C.M. 1119 (1989); Brydia v. Commissioner, 450 F.2d 954 (3rd Cir. 1971).*

Self-employed staff members report their unreimbursed business expenses and any church reimbursements of nonaccountable expenses on Schedule C (Form 1040). Reporting business and professional expenses on Schedule C has several advantages, including the following:

- **Business expenses are fully deductible.** Since self-employed workers list only their net self-employment earnings (i.e., after deducting all business and professional expenses) as a component of gross income on line 12 of Form 1040, they are able to deduct 100 percent of their business and professional expenses (but only 50 percent of business meals and entertainment expenses). They are not subject to the two percent AGI floor that applies to the deduction of *employee* business and professional expenses that are either unreimbursed or reimbursed under a nonaccountable reimbursement plan (these expenses are deductible only to the extent they exceed 2 percent of an employee's adjusted gross income).
- **Business expenses are deductible even if a person has insufficient deductions to itemize on Schedule A.** Business and professional expenses are deductible regardless of whether a self-employed worker itemizes deductions on Schedule A. Employees can claim unreimbursed business expenses

═══ **TABLE 7-1** ═══

STANDARD DEDUCTION AMOUNTS FOR 2012

FILING STATUS	STANDARD DEDUCTION
Married filing joint return	$11,900
Married filing separately	$5,950
Head of household	$8,700
Single	$5,950
Joint return, one spouse age 65 or older or blind	$13,050
Joint return, both spouses age 65 or older or blind	$14,200
Married filing separately, age 65 or older or blind	$7,100
Surviving spouse, age 65 or older or blind	$13,050
Head of household, age 65 or older or blind	$10,150
Single, age 65 or older or blind	$7,400

(including travel and transportation expenses), and business expenses reimbursed by their church under a nonaccountable arrangement, only as miscellaneous itemized deductions on Schedule A (line 21), as explained below. As a result, employees who cannot itemize deductions will not be able to deduct any of these expenses.

- **Adjusted gross income will be lower.** Self-employed workers who deduct reimbursed or unreimbursed business and professional expenses on Schedule C have a lower AGI than if these expenses were reported as miscellaneous itemized deductions on Schedule A. This will increase the amount of those itemized deductions that are available only to the extent they exceed a specified percentage of AGI (e.g., medical expenses and most miscellaneous expenses).
- **Self-employment tax may be reduced.** Reporting business and professional expenses on Schedule C may reduce a self-employed worker's self-employment (Social Security) tax liability, since this tax is based on net earnings from self-employment, and self-employed workers are not subject to the 2 percent limitation that applies to the deduction of employee business expenses.

❀ **KEY POINT.** Many church staff members who are treated as self-employed for federal income tax reporting purposes would be considered employees by the IRS, making these "advantages" of self-employed status illusory. See Chapter 2 for a full consideration of whether church staff members are employees or self-employed for income tax reporting purposes.

The performance of services as an employee also constitutes a trade or business. However, federal tax law permits the deduction of unreimbursed employee business expenses (i.e., your employing church does not reimburse you for such expenses) and nonaccountable reimbursed business expenses only as a miscellaneous itemized deduction on Schedule A. *This means that only employees who itemize their deductions will be able to deduct their unreimbursed and nonaccountable reimbursed business expenses.* Also, most miscellaneous expenses are deductible only to the extent they exceed two percent of AGI (only 50 percent of business meals and entertainment are counted).

These rules may result in more taxes for employees. However, the increased tax burden can be reduced, if not eliminated, if a church adopts an accountable reimbursement policy (as explained later in this chapter). Failure to do so will needlessly result in the payment of additional taxes. All of these rules, and the more common examples of business expenses, will be explained more fully below.

❀ **KEY POINT.** Church staff members who report their income taxes as employees compute most of their employee business expenses on Form 2106 and then carry over the net amount to Schedule A. Employees may be able to use a simplified Form 2106 to compute their business expense deduction. The simplified Form 2106-EZ is available to employees only if their

employer does not reimburse business expenses and if they do not claim any depreciation for a car used in their work.

❀ **KEY POINT.** Church staff members who are employees for income tax reporting purposes claim their unreimbursed business expenses on Schedule A—if they are able to itemize, and only to the extent such expenses exceed two percent of AGI.

❀ **KEY POINT.** Church staff members who are employees for income tax reporting purposes cannot claim any deduction for unreimbursed employee business expenses for which an employer reimbursement was available.

❀ **KEY POINT.** Church staff members who are employees for income tax reporting purposes claim any business expenses reimbursed by their church under a nonaccountable reimbursement plan on Schedule A—if they are able to itemize, and only to the extent such expenses exceed two percent of AGI.

❀ **KEY POINT.** The limitations on the deductibility of employee business expenses (summarized in the preceding paragraphs) can be avoided if the church adopts an accountable reimbursement plan, as explained later in this chapter.

1. TRANSPORTATION EXPENSES

❀ **KEY POINT.** Automobile expenses are a major business expense for most church staff members. These expenses can be deducted using either a standard mileage rate or the actual costs of operating the car for business miles. Most church staff members choose the standard mileage rate because of its convenience. However, it is available only if it is selected for the first year a car is used in your trade or business.

▲ **CAUTION.** *A church's reimbursement of employees' unsubstantiated business expenses are nonaccountable. If these reimbursements are not reported as taxable income to the employee in the year the reimbursements are paid, two consequences result: (1) the employee is subject to back taxes plus penalties and interest on the unreported income; and (2) if the benefits are provided to an officer or director of the church (a "disqualified person"), or a relative of such a person, they will expose the recipient and possibly other members of the church's governing board to intermediate sanctions in the form of substantial excise taxes, since the IRS views these benefits as automatic excess benefits unless reported as taxable income by the church or recipient in the year provided. This topic is covered fully in Chapter 4, section A.3. The lesson is clear: sloppy church accounting practices can be costly.*

Transportation expenses are expenses you incur for business transportation while not traveling away from home (as explained in the next section on travel expenses). These expenses include the cost of transportation by air, rail, bus, taxi, etc., and the cost of driving and maintaining your car. Transportation expenses include the ordinary and necessary costs of all of the following:

- Getting from one workplace to another in the course of your business or profession when you are traveling within the city or general area that is your tax home (as explained in the next section on travel expenses).
- Visiting clients or customers.
- Going to a business meeting away from your regular workplace.
- Getting from your home to a temporary workplace when you have one or more regular places of work. These temporary workplaces can be either within the area of your tax home or outside that area.

The first three examples commonly apply to church employees.

Transportation expenses do not include expenses you have while traveling away from home overnight. Those expenses are travel expenses as explained fully in the next section of this chapter. However, if you use your car while traveling away from home overnight, use the rules in this chapter to figure your car expense deduction.

This terminology is confusing. Note that transportation and travel expenses are distinct concepts for tax purposes. Generally, transportation expenses are all of the expenses associated with local transportation for business purposes (excluding commuting), while travel expenses are all of the expenses associated with travel (including meals and lodging) while away from home overnight for business purposes.

Temporary work location

If you have one or more regular work locations away from your home and you commute to a temporary work location in the same trade or business, you can deduct the expenses of the daily round-trip transportation between your home and the temporary location, regardless of distance.

If your employment at a work location is realistically expected to last (and does in fact last) for one year or less, the employment is temporary unless facts and circumstances indicate otherwise.

If your employment at a work location is realistically expected to last for more than one year, or if there is no realistic expectation that the employment will last for one year or less, the employment is not temporary, regardless of whether it actually lasts for more than one year.

If employment at a work location initially is realistically expected to last for one year or less, but at some later date the employment is realistically expected to last more than one year, that employment will be treated as temporary (unless facts and circumstances

indicate otherwise) until your expectation changes. It will not be treated as temporary after the date you determine it will last more than one year.

If the temporary work location is beyond the general area of your regular place of work and you stay overnight, you are traveling away from home. You may have deductible travel expenses as discussed in the next section.

No regular place of work

If you have no regular place of work but ordinarily work in the metropolitan area where you live, you can deduct daily transportation costs between home and a temporary work site outside that metropolitan area. Generally, a metropolitan area includes the area within the city limits and the suburbs that are considered part of that metropolitan area. You cannot deduct daily transportation costs between your home and temporary work sites within your metropolitan area. These are nondeductible commuting expenses.

Two places of work

If you work at two places in one day, whether or not for the same employer, you can deduct the expense of getting from one workplace to the other. However, if for some personal reason you do not go directly from one location to the other, you cannot deduct more than the amount it would have cost you to go directly from the first location to the second. Transportation expenses you have in going between home and a part-time job on a day off from your main job are commuting expenses. You cannot deduct them.

Commuting expenses

You cannot deduct the costs of taking a bus, trolley, subway, or taxi, or of driving a car between your home and your main or regular place of work. These costs are personal commuting expenses. You cannot deduct commuting expenses, no matter how far your home is from your regular place of work. You cannot deduct commuting expenses even if you work during the commuting trip.

> **EXAMPLE.** You sometimes use your cell phone to make business calls while commuting to and from work. Sometimes another church employee rides with you to and from work, and you have a business discussion in the car. These activities do not change the trip from personal to business. You cannot deduct your commuting expenses.

> **EXAMPLE.** The Tax Court upheld an IRS assessment of a negligence penalty against a pastor who attempted to deduct commuting expenses as a business expense. The court concluded that "the record in this case is replete with examples of [the pastor's] negligence. [He] claimed deductions for numerous items which in many cases are either nondeductible or lack substantiation. Accordingly, we find that [the pastor is] subject to the addition to tax for negligence for all the years at issue." *Clark v. Commissioner, 67 T.C.M. 2458 (1994).*

Parking fees

Fees you pay to park your car at your place of business are nondeductible commuting expenses. You can, however, deduct business-related parking fees when visiting a customer or client.

Office in the home

If you have an office in your home that qualifies as a principal place of business, you can deduct your daily transportation costs between your home and another work location in the same trade or business. See section C.9 in this chapter for assistance in deciding whether your home office qualifies as a principal place of business.

Examples of deductible transportation

The following examples show when you can deduct transportation expenses based on the location of your work and your home.

EXAMPLE. Pastor D lives in Town A and pastors a church in Town A. The church provides him with an office on the church's premises. Pastor D owns a home that is located ten miles from the church. He drives to work each day. The transportation expenses he incurs in driving to and from work are nondeductible commuting expenses. This means Pastor D cannot deduct them on his tax return, and his church cannot reimburse them under an accountable expense reimbursement arrangement. However, Pastor D can deduct the costs of going from one business location to another.

EXAMPLE. Same facts as the previous example, except that Pastor D takes a bus or subway to work each day. The transportation expenses he incurs in riding to and from work are nondeductible commuting expenses. This means Pastor D cannot deduct them on his tax return, and his church cannot reimburse them under an accountable expense reimbursement arrangement.

EXAMPLE. Same facts as the first example, except that Pastor D has an office in his home that qualifies for a home office deduction on his federal tax return. While it is rare for pastors to qualify for a home office deduction (see section C.9 of this chapter), if Pastor D qualifies for this deduction, he can deduct the cost of round-trip transportation between his home office and the church where he is employed.

EXAMPLE. Pastor G lives in Town B and pastors a church in Town B. The church provides him with an office on the church's premises. Pastor G owns a home that is located 10 miles from the church. Several days each month, he drives from his home to a local hospital to visit members of his congregation. According to Revenue Ruling 99-7 (see above), "if a taxpayer has one or more regular work locations away from the taxpayer's residence, the taxpayer may deduct daily transportation expenses incurred in going between the taxpayer's residence and a temporary work location in the same trade or business, regardless of the distance." Clearly, visiting the hospital is "in the same trade or business" of a pastor. The question is whether the hospital qualifies as a "temporary work location." If it does, the expenses the pastor incurs in traveling from home to the hospital are a business transportation expense that can be reimbursed by the church under an accountable arrangement (or, if unreimbursed, deducted by the pastor on Schedule A if he itemizes deductions).

As noted above, a temporary work location is one where you expect to work no more than one year or less. Neither the IRS nor any court has addressed the question of at what point a hospital that is regularly visited by a pastor ceases to be a "temporary work location." All that can be said is that at some point a local hospital that a pastor regularly visits over a period of time equal to or exceeding one year may cease to be a temporary work location. However, if Pastor G goes on to the church after stopping at the hospital, the miles he drives from a hospital to the church would constitute a transportation expense. The same is true at the end of the day—miles he drives from church to the hospital are a transportation expense, even if the hospital is on the way to the pastor's home.

EXAMPLE. Pastor J lives in Town A and pastors a church in Town A. He also has agreed to serve as an interim pastor for a church in Town B. He drives to Town B on Sunday afternoons to conduct a service and returns home the same day. He expects this assignment to last no more than six months. In general, if a taxpayer has a regular work location away from his residence, the taxpayer may deduct daily transportation expenses incurred in going between the taxpayer's residence and a temporary work location in the same trade or business, regardless of the distance. This is based on IRS Revenue Ruling 99-7, summarized above, in which the IRS ruled that "a taxpayer may deduct daily transportation expenses incurred in going between the taxpayer's residence and a temporary work location outside the metropolitan area where the taxpayer lives and normally works."

If you work at two places in one day, whether or not for the same employer, you can deduct the expense of getting from one workplace to the other. However, if for some personal reason you do not go directly from one location to the other, you cannot deduct more than the amount it would have cost you to go directly from the first location to the second.

EXAMPLE. Pastor H owns a home 15 miles from the church. In order to utilize the time it takes to drive to and from work each day, Pastor H has a telephone installed in his car. He uses the telephone for mostly church-related calls. The fact that Pastor H makes business calls while commuting will not change the character of such trips from commuting to business. His commuting expenses remain nondeductible. The same rule applies if Pastor H commutes to and from the church with an associate minister of the church and the two discuss church-related business during their commuting time. These rules do not violate a minister's constitutional guaranty of religious freedom. *Hamblen v. Commissioner, 78 T.C. 53 (1981).*

✿ **KEY POINT.** If a temporary work location is beyond the general area of your regular place of work and you stay overnight, you are traveling away from home. You may have deductible travel expenses as discussed later in this chapter.

You can compute your transportation expenses in one of two ways: (1) using the standard mileage rate; or (2) figuring actual expenses. Both of these options are explained below.

Method 1—standard mileage rate

✳ **New in 2012.** The standard mileage rate for business miles driven during 2012 was 55.5 cents per mile. The standard mileage rate for computing deductible medical or moving expenses for 2012 was 23 cents per mile. The mileage rate for providing services for charitable organizations is set by statute, not the IRS, and is 14 cents per mile until Congress increases it.

✳ **New in 2013.** The standard business mileage rate for 2013 is 56.5 cents per mile. The standard mileage rate for computing deductible medical or moving expenses for 2013 is 24 cents per mile.

✿ **KEY POINT.** The various options for handling car expenses are summarized in Table 7-2.

Overview

The simpler and more common method of computing your transportation expenses is to multiply the standard business mileage rate for each business mile you can substantiate. The standard mileage rate applies to all business miles. You may use the standard mileage rate instead of figuring your actual operating and fixed expenses, including depreciation, fuel, and repairs, in computing your deductible costs in operating a car. You can use the standard mileage rate regardless of whether you are reimbursed by your church for your business expenses.

You generally can use the standard mileage rate whether or not you are reimbursed and whether or not any reimbursement is more or less than the standard mileage rate.

Choosing the standard mileage rate. If you want to use the standard mileage rate for a car you own, you must choose to use it in the first year the car is available for use in your work. Then, in later years, you can choose to use either the standard mileage rate or actual expenses.

If you want to use the standard mileage rate for a car you lease, you must use it for the entire lease period. You must make the choice to use the standard mileage rate by the due date (including extensions) of your return. You cannot revoke the choice. However, in later years, you can switch from the standard mileage rate to the actual expenses method. If you change to the actual expenses method in a later year, but before your car is fully depreciated, you have to

estimate the remaining useful life of the car and use straight line depreciation.

EXAMPLE. Larry is a church employee who occasionally uses his own car for business purposes. He purchased the car in 2010, but he did not claim any unreimbursed employee expenses on his 2010 tax return. Because Larry did not use the standard mileage rate the first year the car was available for business use, he cannot use the standard mileage rate in 2012 to claim unreimbursed employee business expenses.

Standard mileage rate not allowed. You cannot use the standard mileage rate if you

- claimed a depreciation deduction for the car using any method other than straight line (for example, MACRS, as discussed later);
- claimed a section 179 deduction (discussed later) on the car;
- claimed the special depreciation allowance on the car; or
- claimed actual car expenses for a car you leased.

Personal property taxes. If you itemize your deductions on Schedule A (Form 1040), you can deduct on line 7 state and local personal property taxes on motor vehicles. You can take this deduction even if you use the standard mileage rate or if you do not use the car for business.

Parking fees and tolls. In addition to using the standard mileage rate, you can deduct any business-related parking fees and tolls. (Parking fees you pay to park your car at your place of work are nondeductible commuting expenses.)

EXAMPLE. Pastor A purchased a car in 2012 for business use. He drove the car 1,000 miles each month for business purposes during the year and elected to use the standard mileage rate to calculate his transportation expenses. Without considering any other rule or limitation, Pastor A is entitled to a deduction of $6,660 for the year (12,000 miles x 55.5 cents).

EXAMPLE. Pastor W purchased a car in 2012 for business use. He drove the car 15,000 miles for business purposes during the year and elected to use the actual expense method for computing his transportation expenses. Because of the complexity of this method, Pastor W would like to use the standard mileage rate for computing his transportation expenses in 2013. He may not do so, since he did not elect this method in the year he placed the car in service in his business.

Reimbursing business miles using the standard mileage rate

Many churches have adopted an accountable reimbursement arrangement that reimburses the business miles of employees using a mileage rate. Some churches use the IRS-approved rate, while others use a rate that is either higher or lower than the IRS rate.

TABLE 7-2

BUSINESS USE OF A CAR: A COMPARISON OF THE MAJOR TAX OPTIONS

CAR OWNER	METHOD	CHARACTERISTICS	TAX CONSEQUENCES
Minister	Actual expenses	• Minister computes actual expenses of operating car for business use. • Actual expenses include gas, oil, tires, repairs, tune-ups, batteries, washes, insurance, depreciation, interest on car loans, taxes, licenses, garage rent, parking fees, and tolls. • Annual depreciation deduction is limited by "luxury car" rules.	• Ministers can deduct expenses allocable to the business use of their car, and not reimbursed under an accountable plan, as an itemized deduction on Schedule A (for employees) or a Schedule C deduction (for self-employed). • Deduction is allowable only if records substantiate the amount, date, place, and business purpose of each expense. • Deduction is allowable only if records substantiate the business use of the car. • In many cases a larger deduction will be available than with the standard mileage rate—but the trade-off is that the recordkeeping requirements are much more complex.
Minister	Standard mileage rate	• Multiply current standard mileage rate by miles driven for business during the year. • Must be used in first year a car is used for business purposes. • Cannot be used for leased vehicles.	• Ministers can deduct expenses allocable to the business use of their car, and not reimbursed under an accountable plan, as an itemized deduction on Schedule A (for employees) or a Schedule C deduction (for self-employed). • Ministers must maintain records documenting the business nature of their business miles. • Ministers can still deduct parking fees and tolls. • Most ministers use this method because of its simplicity.
Church	Church-owned vehicle; no personal use permitted	• Church owns vehicle. • Vehicle kept on church's premises. • Written church policy prohibits personal use (including commuting). • Minister using car does not live on church's premises. • Church reasonably believes the vehicle is not used for any personal use.	There is no income to report (since no personal use is allowed).
Church	Church owned vehicle; no personal use allowed except for commuting (for security or other non-compensatory reasons)	• Church owns vehicle. • For noncompensatory reasons (such as vehicle security), the church requires the minister to commute. • Written church policy prohibits personal use (except commuting). • Minister using car is not a "control employee" (defined in Chapter 4, section B.8). • Church reasonably believes the vehicle is not used for any personal use.	• There is no income to report (since no personal use is allowed)—except for $3 per round trip commute or $1.50 per one-way commute. • No recordkeeping is required (since no personal use is allowed) except number of commutes.
Church	Church owned vehicle; no restrictions on personal use	None	• Personal use must be valued and reported as income on the minister's Form W-2 or 1099-MISC. • Use the general valuation method (discussed earlier) unless the church has elected one of the three special valuation rules.

Listed below are the rules that apply to a church's use of the standard mileage rate.

(1) Employees substantiate business miles with adequate records at least every 60 days and are reimbursed at the IRS approved rate. This is an accountable arrangement, and the church is not required to report the reimbursements as income on employees' Forms W-2. This assumes that employees (a) submit records, such as logs or diaries, substantiating the date, place, and business purpose of all miles driven for business purposes; (b) substantiate business miles within 60 days; and (c) are reimbursed by the church at the IRS-approved rate multiplied by the number of substantiated business miles.

> **EXAMPLE.** A church reimburses business miles driven by employees at the IRS-approved rate. In 2012 the church bookkeeper drives 300 substantiated miles each month on church business. The church treasurer reimburses the bookkeeper at the IRS-approved standard mileage rate for all business miles driven each month. The reimbursements are not reported as taxable income to the bookkeeper.

✿ **KEY POINT.** An employer may grant an additional allowance (in excess of the standard mileage rate) for parking fees and tolls. The IRS has ruled that "if an employer grants an allowance not exceeding [the standard mileage rate] to an employee for ordinary and necessary transportation expenses . . . [it also] may grant an additional allowance for the parking fees and tolls attributable to the traveling and transportation expenses as separate items." *Revenue Ruling 87-93.*

✿ **KEY POINT.** Section D of this chapter addresses the substantiation of business expenses.

(2) Employees substantiate business miles with adequate records at least every 60 days and are reimbursed at an amount HIGHER than the IRS-approved rate. This arrangement is accountable, but only up to the IRS-approved rate.

> **EXAMPLE.** A church maintains an accountable reimbursement arrangement, but reimburses employees' business miles at a rate of 75 cents per mile. Karen, a church employee, properly substantiates all of her business expenses for 2012, including 6,000 miles that she drove her car for church-related business. The church does not require Karen to return the amount by which her reimbursements exceed the IRS-approved rate. The fact that the church reimburses Karen's car expenses at a rate in excess of the IRS-approved rate will not render the entire reimbursement arrangement nonaccountable. Rather, only the amount by which the church's reimbursement rate exceeds the IRS rate is treated as nonaccountable. As a result, the church should add $1,170 (6,000 x 19.5 cents) to Karen's W-2, and Karen should report this amount as income on her Form 1040. The excess cannot be claimed as a deduction since it exceeds the IRS-approved rate.

Further, as noted below, the excess reimbursements will be subject to tax withholding, assuming that Karen is not a minister (or a minister who has elected voluntary withholding).

(3) Employees substantiate business miles with adequate records at least every 60 days and are reimbursed at an amount LOWER than the IRS-approved rate. This arrangement is accountable. The church should not report any reimbursements on an employee's Form W-2. Employees can claim a business expense deduction of the amount by which the IRS-approved standard mileage rate exceeds the church's reimbursement rate multiplied by their substantiated business miles.

> **EXAMPLE.** A church reimburses substantiated employee business miles at a rate of 30 cents per mile in 2012. Since this reimbursement rate is less than the IRS-approved rate (55.5 cents), church staff can claim a business expense deduction of 25.5 cents per mile multiplied by their substantiated business miles for the year. This deduction is subject to the limitations that apply to the deductibility of unreimbursed business expenses.

(4) Employees do not substantiate business miles with adequate records or within every 60 days. This is not an accountable arrangement, so the church's reimbursements must be added to each employee's Form W-2 as income. Employees can claim a business expense deduction for the business use of their car if they itemize deductions on Schedule A (Form 1040) and have sufficient records to substantiate miles driven for business purposes. The deduction is the standard mileage rate multiplied by the number of substantiated business miles. Employee business expenses are deductible only to the extent that they exceed 2 percent of the employee's adjusted gross income.

> **EXAMPLE.** A church requires its pastor to substantiate once each year (in December) all of the business miles he drove his car that year. He is then reimbursed for these miles at the IRS-approved standard mileage rate. This is not an accountable arrangement since the pastor is not required to substantiate business miles within a "reasonable time." The income tax regulations specify that 60 days is presumed to be a reasonable time. As a result, the church must report all of the reimbursements as income on the pastor's Form W-2.

> **EXAMPLE.** Each month Pastor R orally informs the church treasurer how many business miles she drove her car for the previous month. The treasurer reimburses Pastor R for these miles at the IRS-approved rate. This is not an accountable arrangement, since Pastor R does not adequately document the amount, date, place, and business purpose of her business miles. As a result, the church must report these reimbursements as income on Pastor R's Form W-2. The income tax regulations specifically prohibit "accounting" to an employer by means of a taxpayer's own oral or written statements. Therefore, a minister will not adequately account to his or her church by orally informing the church treasurer of the amount of business expenses incurred during a

particular month, or by signing a statement that merely recites what the minister's business expenses were.

▲ **CAUTION.** *Churches may expose employees and members of the church's governing board to substantial penalties if they fail to report taxable fringe benefits as taxable income. Examples of taxable fringe benefits that often are not reported as taxable income include use of a business mileage rate to reimburse car expenses that exceeds the IRS-approved standard business mileage rate, and reimbursement of employees' business miles without requiring adequate substantiation. If such reimbursements are not reported as taxable income to the employee in the year the reimbursements are paid, there are two possible consequences: (1) The employee is subject to back taxes plus penalties and interest on the unreported income. (2) If the benefits are provided to an officer or director of the church (a "disqualified person") or a relative of such a person, they will expose the recipient and possibly other members of the church's governing board to substantial excise taxes (called "intermediate sanctions"), since the IRS views these benefits as "automatic" excess benefits unless reported as taxable income by the church or recipient in the year provided. The lesson is clear: sloppy church accounting practices can be costly. See Chapter 4 for details.*

Withholding taxes

Ministers' wages are not subject to income tax withholding unless voluntary withholding is elected. But nonminister employee wages are subject to withholding (of income taxes and the employee's share of Social Security and Medicare taxes). The IRS maintains that employers must withhold payroll taxes from any mileage rate reimbursement that exceeds the IRS-approved rate. The IRS has provided the following clarification with regard to the timing of withholding:

> *In the case of a mileage allowance paid as a reimbursement, the excess . . . is subject to withholding and payment of employment taxes in the payroll period in which the payor reimburses the expenses for the business miles substantiated. In the case of a mileage allowance paid as an advance, the excess . . . is subject to withholding and payment of employment taxes no later than the first payroll period following the payroll period in which the business miles with respect to which the advance was paid are substantiated. If some or all of the business miles with respect to which the advance was paid are not substantiated within a reasonable period of time and the employee does not return the portion of the allowance that relates to those miles within a reasonable period of time, the portion of the allowance that relates to those miles is subject to withholding and payment of employment taxes no later than the first payroll period following the end of the reasonable period.*

Method 2—actual cost method

❊ **KEY POINT.** You can use the actual cost method to compute transportation expenses associated with the business use of your car. However, as this section demonstrates, doing so is too complicated for most taxpayers.

You may be able to compute the business use of your vehicle using the actual cost method instead of the standard mileage rate. Few ministers or lay church employees do so, however, because this method is complex and time-consuming. Using the standard mileage rate is much easier. While using the actual cost method takes discipline and perseverance, some studies suggest that you will have a higher deduction using this method than the standard mileage rate method, especially if your car is relatively new. The question is whether you consider the potential savings in taxes worth the extra inconvenience.

Actual transportation costs include the cost of local business travel by air, rail, bus, or taxi, and the cost of driving and maintaining your car, but not the cost of meals or lodging. You may not deduct the costs of commuting (e.g., by bus, subway, taxi, train, or car) between your home and your main or regular place of work. These costs are nondeductible personal expenses.

> **EXAMPLE.** Pastor F drives her car to and from work on most days but occasionally takes a bus. The cost of traveling to and from work (whether by bus or in her own car) is a commuting expense that is not deductible by Pastor F whether she reports her income taxes as an employee or as a self-employed person.

The most important element of transportation expense is your car. If you are required to use your car in your work, you can deduct the expenses associated with business use of the car. Deductible items include the cost of depreciation, licenses, gas, oil, tolls, lease payments, insurance, garage rent, parking fees, registration fees, repairs, and tires. If you have fully depreciated a car that you still use for business, you can continue to claim your other actual car expenses.

Business and personal use

If you use your car both for business and personal purposes, you must divide your expenses between business and personal use. For example, if you drive your car 20,000 miles during the year (12,000 miles for business and 8,000 miles for personal use), you can claim only 60 percent ($12,000/20,000) of the cost of operating the car as a business expense.

Employer-provided vehicle

If you use a vehicle provided by your employer for business purposes, you can deduct your actual unreimbursed car expenses. You cannot use the standard mileage rate.

Interest on car loans

If you are an employee, you cannot deduct any interest paid on a car loan. This interest is treated as personal interest and is not deductible.

Taxes paid on your car

If you are an employee, you can deduct personal property taxes paid on your car if you itemize deductions. Enter the amount paid on line 8 of Schedule A (Form 1040).

Generally, sales taxes on your car are part of your car's basis and are recovered through depreciation, discussed later.

Fines and collateral
You cannot deduct fines you pay or collateral you forfeit for traffic violations.

Depreciation and section 179 deductions
Generally, the cost of a car, plus sales tax and improvements, is a capital expense. Because the benefits last longer than one year, you generally cannot deduct a capital expense. However, you can recover this cost through the section 179 deduction (the deduction allowed by section 179 of the Internal Revenue Code), special depreciation allowance, and depreciation deductions. Depreciation allows you to recover the cost over more than one year by deducting part of it each year. The section 179 deduction, special depreciation allowance, and depreciation deductions are discussed later.

Generally, there are limits on these deductions. Special rules apply if you use your car 50 percent or less in your work or business.

You can claim a section 179 deduction and use a depreciation method other than straight line only if you do not use the standard mileage rate to figure your business-related car expenses in the year you first place a car in service.

If you claim either a section 179 deduction or use a depreciation method other than straight line in the year you first place a car in service, you cannot use the standard mileage rate on that car in any future year.

Computing depreciation and the section 179 deduction for the business use of a car is a complex task that is explained fully in IRS Publication 463 (available on the IRS website, irs.gov). A few minutes perusing this information will demonstrate why the overwhelming majority of church employees use the much simpler standard mileage rate rather than actual expenses to compute a business expense deduction.

EXAMPLE. A church hired a pastor whose home was 70 miles from the church. The pastor chose to remain in his home and commute to and from work at the church every Sunday and Wednesday. The pastor claimed a business expense deduction for depreciation on the car he used in commuting to and from work. To substantiate this deduction, he produced a letter signed by the six officers of the church stating that he was their pastor and containing a schedule of business miles traveled. The pastor claimed that he used his car to travel 12,643 business miles during the year under examination, which he claimed represented 70 percent of the total miles traveled during the year.

The IRS disallowed the claimed depreciation deduction, and the Tax Court agreed. It noted that the evidence showed that 11,523

of the 12,643 miles traveled were commuting miles from the pastor's home to the church and that "it is well settled that the cost of commuting between one's residence and regular place of employment is a nondeductible personal expense." The remaining 1,120 miles were used for business purposes, since they represented travel to transport church members to various functions at other churches. Therefore, these miles qualified as business miles, and a depreciation deduction was allowable for the total amount of depreciation for the year multiplied by the "business use percentage" (the percentage of total miles that the car was used for business purposes, or 1,120 divided by 12,643). *Clark v. Commissioner, 67 T.C.M. 2458 (1994).*

EXAMPLE. The Tax Court refused to allow a minister to use the actual expense method to compute a deduction for the business use of his car, since he could not prove the percentage of his total miles that the car was used for business purposes. The pastor often traveled by car in connection with his ministry, and he reported travel expenses on his tax returns using the actual expense method. The IRS audited the minister and recalculated his expenses using the standard mileage rate. The IRS reasoned that the pastor must use the standard rate method to determine car expenses, since he failed to prove the total miles driven each year.

The IRS conceded that the pastor drove 13,170 business miles in the year under examination and at least 12,274 business miles in the following year. These miles were not computed using a mileage log but by "reconstructing" the number of business miles by referring to actual receipts. However, during the years in question, the pastor kept no documentation that showed the personal use of his car or the total miles driven. The IRS claimed that without adequate substantiation of the total number of miles driven, it was unable to determine a business use percentage of the miles, and accordingly the pastor could not use the actual expense method for either year.

In using the actual expense method, a taxpayer multiplies expenses incurred in owning and operating a car by the business use percentage—the percentage of total miles the car is used for business purposes. If a taxpayer can prove business miles but not personal miles or total miles, then the business use percentage cannot be calculated, and the actual expense method cannot be used. Rather, the taxpayer must use the standard mileage rate (multiplying business miles by the applicable standard mileage rate). *Parker v. Commissioner, 65 T.C.M. 1740 (1994). See also Shelley v. Commissioner, T.C. Memo. 1994-432 (1994).*

Leasing a car
If you lease a car that you use in your ministry, you can use the standard mileage rate or actual expenses to figure your deductible car expenses. You can deduct the part of each lease payment that is for the use of the car in your business. You cannot deduct any part of a lease payment that is for personal use of the car, such as commuting.

You must spread any advance payments over the entire lease period. You cannot deduct any payments you make to buy a car, even if the payments are called lease payments.

If you lease a car that you use in your business for a lease term of 30 days or more, you may have to include an inclusion amount in your income for each tax year you lease the car. To do this, you do not add an amount to income. Instead, you reduce your deduction for your lease payment.

This reduction has an effect similar to the limit on the depreciation deduction you would have on the car if you owned it. The inclusion amount is a percentage of part of the fair market value of the leased car multiplied by the percentage of business and investment use of the car for the tax year. It is prorated for the number of days of the lease term in the tax year. The inclusion amount applies to each tax year that you lease the car if the fair market value of the car when the lease began was more than the amounts shown in Table 7-3.

Fair market value is the price at which the property would change hands between a buyer and a seller, neither having to buy or sell, and both having reasonable knowledge of all the necessary facts. Sales of similar property around the same date may be helpful in figuring the fair market value of the property. Figure the fair market value on the first day of the lease term. If the capitalized cost of a car is specified in the lease agreement; use that amount as the fair market value.

Inclusion amounts are listed in tables reproduced in IRS Publication 463. For each tax year during which you lease the car for business, determine your inclusion amount by locating the applicable appendix in Publication 463. To find the inclusion amount, do the following: (1) Find the line that includes the fair market value of the car on the first day of the lease term. (2) Go across the line to the column for the tax year in which the car is used under the lease to find the dollar amount. For the last tax year of the lease, use the dollar amount for the preceding year. (3) Prorate the dollar amount for the number of days of the lease term included in the tax year. (4) Multiply the prorated amount

by the percentage of business use for the tax year. This is your inclusion amount.

Employer-provided cars

❖ **KEY POINT.** Ministers should consider the advantages of using a church-owned car for their business travel. This will eliminate most recordkeeping and reporting requirements. Some conditions apply.

Many churches provide their minister with a church-owned car that the minister is free to use for both personal and business purposes. The minister's personal use of such a car must be valued and reported by both the church and minister as taxable income. The methods that can be used for computing the value of the personal use of the car are discussed in Chapter 4, section B.8.

However, note that if the church board adopts a resolution restricting use of the car to church-related activities, then the minister reports no income or deductions (use of the car is a nontaxable, noncash working condition fringe benefit); and better yet, no accountings, reimbursements, allowances, or recordkeeping is required. This assumes that the car is, in fact, used exclusively for church-related purposes. For churches and ministers to realize these tax benefits, the following conditions must be satisfied:

- The vehicle is owned or leased by the church and is provided to a minister (or other church employee) for use in connection with church business.
- When the vehicle is not being used for church business, it is kept on the church's premises (unless it is temporarily located elsewhere, such as a repair shop).
- No employee using the vehicle lives on the church's premises.
- Under a written policy statement adopted by the church board, no employee of the church can use the vehicle for personal purposes, except for de minimis (minimal) personal use (such as a stop for lunch between two business trips).
- The church reasonably believes that, except for de minimis use, no church employee uses the vehicle for any personal purpose.
- The church must be able to supply sufficient evidence to prove to the IRS that the preceding five conditions have been met. (The church must complete Part V, Section C of IRS Form 4562 for each employee provided with a church-owned vehicle, specifying that it satisfies the above requirements.) *Treas. Reg. 1.274-6T(a)(2).*

Commuting is always considered to be personal use of a car, and accordingly the procedure discussed in the preceding paragraph would not be available if a church allowed its minister to commute to work in a church-owned vehicle. Fortunately, the regulations permit certain church employees who use a church-owned vehicle

---

TABLE 7-3

DOES THE INCLUSION AMOUNT APPLY?

YEAR LEASE BEGAN	FAIR MARKET VALUE
2012	$18,500
2011	$18,500
2010	$18,500
2009	$18,500

exclusively for business purposes *except for commuting* to receive all of the benefits associated with business use of a church-owned vehicle if certain conditions are satisfied. These rules are explained fully in Chapter 4, section B.8.

2. TRAVEL EXPENSES

▲ **CAUTION.** *A church cannot reimburse employees' expenses under an accountable reimbursement arrangement that do not qualify as business expenses. Such reimbursements, as well as a church's reimbursement of employees' unsubstantiated business expenses, are nonaccountable. If these reimbursements are not reported as taxable income to the employee in the year the reimbursements are paid, one or both of the following consequences may result: (1) the employee is subject to back taxes plus penalties and interest on the unreported income; and (2) if the benefits are provided to an officer or director of the church (a "disqualified person"), or a relative of such a person, they will expose the recipient and possibly other members of the church's governing board to intermediate sanctions in the form if substantial excise taxes, since the IRS views these benefits as automatic excess benefits unless reported as taxable income by the church or recipient in the year provided. This topic is covered fully in Chapter 4, section A.3. The lesson is clear: sloppy church accounting practices can be costly.*

Overview

Travel expenses are your *ordinary and necessary* expenses while traveling *temporarily away from home* for your work or business. You can deduct these expenses if you prove them, as explained below. However, you may not deduct expenses that are lavish or extravagant or that are for personal or vacation purposes. Travel expenses do not include expenses for transportation while not traveling away from home or expenses for entertainment. These expenses are discussed elsewhere in this chapter. Deductible travel expenses include

- air, rail, and bus fares;
- operating and maintaining your car;
- taxi fares or other costs of transportation between the airport or station and your hotel, or from one work site to another;
- meals and lodging while you are away from home on business;
- cleaning and laundry expenses;
- telephone expenses; and
- tips.

Away from home

Your expenses must be for travel or temporary living (including meals and lodging) while you are away from home. You are considered to be traveling away from home if

- your duties require you to be away from the general area of your tax home (defined below) substantially longer than an ordinary day's work and

- you need to sleep or rest to meet the demands of your work while away from home.

This does not mean napping in your car. You do not have to be away from your home from dusk to dawn, as long as your relief from duty is long enough to get necessary sleep or rest. To satisfy these requirements, a trip ordinarily must be overnight.

EXAMPLE. Pastor W travels to another city to conduct a funeral service for a former member of his congregation. He leaves at 7:00 A.M. and returns home that evening at 6:00 P.M. Expenses incurred by Pastor W in making the trip are not travel expenses, since he was not away from home overnight or for a sufficiently long period of time that required sleep or rest. Pastor W's car expenses constitute transportation expenses but not the cost of meals. The deductibility of these expenses is explained fully in section C.1 of this chapter.

EXAMPLE. Same facts as the preceding example, except that Pastor W left home at 7:00 A.M. and did not return home until 11:00 A.M. the next day. Since this trip was overnight, the car, meals, and lodging expenses incurred by Pastor W are travel expenses. They are deductible according to the rules discussed at the beginning of this chapter.

Instead of deducting the actual cost of your meals and lodging while you are traveling away from home for business, you may be able to deduct a per diem allowance provided by your employer. Per diem allowances are explained in section E of this chapter.

Your tax home

It is important to determine where your tax home is, since you may deduct travel expenses only to the extent that they are incurred while you are traveling away from your home. Generally, your tax home is your regular place of employment or work, regardless of where you maintain your family home. It includes the entire city or general area in which your work is located.

✿ **KEY POINT.** Special rules apply in determining the tax home of persons who have no main place of work or who have multiple places of work. These rules rarely apply to church employees. They are explained in IRS Publication 463.

Determining temporary or indefinite

You will be considered away from home, and your travel expenses (including meals and lodging) will constitute travel expenses, if you are away from home on a *temporary* rather than on an *indefinite* basis. As a result, you must determine whether your assignment is temporary or indefinite when you start work. If you expect a job to last for *one year or less*, it is *temporary* unless facts and circumstances indicate otherwise. Employment that is initially temporary may become indefinite due to changed circumstances. A series of assignments to the same location, all for short periods but that together cover a long period, may be considered an indefinite assignment.

On the other hand, if your assignment or job is *indefinite*, the location of the assignment or job becomes your new tax home, and you cannot deduct your travel expenses while there. An assignment or job in a single location is considered indefinite if it is realistically expected to last for *more than one year*, regardless of whether it actually lasts for more than one year. If your assignment is indefinite, you must include in your income any amounts you receive from your employer for living expenses, even if they are called travel allowances and you account to your employer for them.

❖ **KEY POINT.** Expenses incurred in traveling away from home overnight for business purposes are deductible business expenses. These expenses include the costs of transportation, lodging, and meals. Since they are business expenses, they can be reimbursed under an employer's accountable reimbursement arrangement, and the reimbursements will not represent taxable income for the employee. However, if the travel is reasonably expected to last for more than one year, whether or not it actually does, it is considered indefinite, meaning that taxpayer's home changes to the work location, and none of the travel expenses can be treated as a business expense, since they are not incurred while "away from home." The IRS has created two exceptions to this rule.

EXAMPLE. The United States Tax Court ruled that an itinerant evangelist was not able to deduct his travel expenses, since he was never "away from home." A full-time evangelist did not have a church or a fixed base of operation for the conduct of his ministry. He and his spouse travel throughout the United States in a recreational vehicle and conduct religious services at churches for either a few days or a few weeks. The couple does not own or rent a residence. The couple's federal tax return was audited, and the IRS denied any deduction for the couple's travel expenses. The Tax Court agreed, noting that the tax code allows deductions for traveling expenses only if the expenses are incurred while "away from home." The court concluded: "Where the taxpayer has neither a principal place of business nor a permanent residence, he has no tax home from which he can be away. His home is wherever he happens to be." *Boyd v. Commissioner, T.C. Summary Opinion 2006-36.*

What travel expenses are deductible

Once you have determined that you are traveling away from your tax home, you can determine what travel expenses are deductible. Table 7-4 summarizes the more common travel expenses you may be able to deduct.

➥ **TIP.** When you travel away from home on business, you should keep records of all the expenses you have and any advances you receive from your employer. You can use a log, diary, notebook,

or any other written record to keep track of your expenses. The types of expenses you need to record, along with supporting documentation, are described later in this chapter (section D).

Separating costs

If you have one expense that includes the costs of meals, entertainment, and other services (such as lodging or transportation), you must allocate that expense between the cost of meals and entertainment and the cost of other services. You must have a reasonable basis for making this allocation. For example, you must allocate your expenses if a hotel includes one or more meals in its room charge.

Travel expenses for another individual

If a spouse, dependent, or other individual goes with you (or your employee) on a business trip or to a business convention, you generally cannot deduct his or her travel expenses. See "Travel expenses of a spouse," below.

Travel in the United States

Entirely for business

If your trip was entirely for business, you may deduct your ordinary and necessary travel expenses.

Primarily for business

If your trip was primarily for business and, while away at your business destination, you extend your stay for a vacation, make a nonbusiness side trip, or have other nonbusiness activities, you may deduct the travel expenses to and from your business destination as well as any business expenses incurred while at your business destination.

EXAMPLE. You work in Atlanta and make a business trip to New Orleans. On your way home, you stop in Mobile to visit relatives. You spend $1,300 for the nine days you are away from home for travel, meals, lodging, and other travel expenses. If you had not stopped in Mobile, you would have been gone only six days, and your total cost would have been $900. You may deduct $900 for your trip.

Primarily for pleasure

If your trip was primarily for vacation, the entire cost of the trip is a nondeductible personal expense except for any expenses incurred while at your destination that are directly and properly allocable to your business. A trip can be a vacation even though a promoter advertises that a trip to a resort or on a cruise ship is primarily for business. The scheduling of incidental business activities during a trip, such as watching instructional videos or attending seminars, will not convert a vacation into a business trip.

EXAMPLE. Pastor T lives in Minnesota. In January she is invited by a pastor friend in Florida to visit for a week. While in

TABLE 7-4

TRAVEL EXPENSES YOU CAN DEDUCT

(when you travel away from home for business purposes)

IF YOU HAVE EXPENSES FOR . . .	THEN YOU CAN DEDUCT THE COST OF . . .
Transportation	Travel by airplane, bus, or car between your home and your business destination. If you were provided with a ticket or you are riding free as a result of a frequent traveler or similar program, your cost is zero. If you travel by ship, see "Luxury water travel" and "Cruise ships" for additional rules and limits.
Taxi, commuter bus, and airport limousine	Fares for these and other types of transportation that take you between • the airport or station and your hotel, and • the hotel and the work location of your customers or clients, your business meeting place, or your temporary work location.
Baggage and shipping	Sending baggage and sample or display material between your regular and temporary work locations.
Car	Operating and maintaining your car when traveling away from home on business. You can deduct actual expenses or the standard mileage rate, as well as business-related tolls and parking. If you rent a car while away from home on business, you can deduct only the business-use portion of the expenses.
Lodging and meals	Your lodging and meals if your business trip is overnight or long enough that you need to stop for sleep or rest to properly perform your duties. Meals include amounts spent for food, beverages, taxes, and related tips.
Cleaning	Dry cleaning and laundry.
Telephone	Business calls while on your business trip. This includes business communication by fax machine or other communication devices.
Tips	Tips you pay for any expenses listed in this chart.
Other	Other similar ordinary and necessary expenses related to your business travel. These expenses might include transportation to or from a business meal, computer rental fees, and operating and maintaining a house trailer.

Florida the pastor friend invites Pastor T to conduct a worship service on a Sunday morning. Pastor T does so. Pastor T's travel is not deductible as either a business expense or charitable contribution. IRS Publication 463 states: "If your trip was primarily for personal reasons, such as a vacation, the entire cost of the trip is a nondeductible personal expense."

EXAMPLE. Assume that Pastor T is invited by a church in another state to come for a weekend and conduct three worship services. Pastor T's trip is for business purposes. If her travel expenses are unreimbursed, she can deduct them as a business expense. Alternatively, the host church can reimburse Pastor T's travel expenses as a legitimate business expense. If adequate substantiation is provided, then the reimbursement is accountable and need not be reported as taxable income to Pastor T. IRS Publication 463 states that "you can deduct all your travel expenses if your trip was entirely business related."

EXAMPLE. Same facts as the previous example, except that Pastor T decides to extend her trip by five days. IRS Publication 463

states: "If your trip was primarily for business and, while at your business destination, you extended your stay for a vacation, made a nonbusiness side trip, or had other nonbusiness activities, you can deduct your business-related travel expenses. These expenses include the travel costs of getting to and from your business destination, and you can deduct any business-related expenses at your business destination."

Sabbatical leave

Some churches grant their pastor a sabbatical from a few weeks to a year or more. In most cases the sabbatical is for no specific purpose other than rest and rejuvenation, while in others it is to enable the pastor to pursue research or other activities directly related to ministry. Any compensation the pastor receives from the church during the sabbatical represents taxable income and must be so reported by the church. But what about travel expenses (i.e., transportation, lodging, meals) incurred by the pastor while on sabbatical? Can these expenses be reimbursed by the church under an accountable reimbursement policy or deducted by the pastor as a business expense on his or her tax return?

In answering this question, keep the following points in mind:

(1) Travel expenses qualify as business expenses only if they are ordinary and necessary in the conduct of the pastor's business and the travel takes the pastor away from home for less than one year. It is doubtful that travel expenses incurred by a pastor while on sabbatical leave would qualify as an ordinary and necessary business expense if the purpose of the travel is rest, rejuvenation, sermon preparation, or strategic planning. The point is this—why must the pastor travel out of town to achieve these goals? Can they not be readily achieved without travel? Only ordinary *and necessary* travel expenses count as business expenses.

(2) If the pastor remains at home during the sabbatical leave, no travel expenses are incurred.

(3) Travel expenses of the pastor's family members would not be a reimbursable or deductible business expense.

(4) If the purpose of the sabbatical is research or some other activity that is directly tied to the performance of the pastor's duties and requires the pastor to be at a specific location away from home, then travel expenses may be legitimate business expenses. This requires more than a nebulous desire to do sermon preparation or strategic planning. The question is whether the travel to the specific location is necessary to the development of the pastor's professional skills. For example, is there a library at the destination that is indispensable to an article or book that the pastor is writing? If the same work could be done at home, then the travel cannot be deemed necessary and therefore would not be a legitimate business expense.

(5) The tax code does not permit "travel as a form of education" to qualify as a business expense. See generally *Keller v. Commissioner*, T.C. Memo. 1996-300 (1996).

Travel outside the United States

If any part of your business travel is outside the United States, some of your deduction for the cost of getting to and from your destination may be limited. How much of your travel expenses you can deduct depends in part on how much of your trip outside the United States was business related.

The tax code and regulations directly address foreign business trips. Following is a summary of the rules.

Foreign travel *entirely* for business

If your trip to a foreign country is entirely for business, then all of your travel expenses are deductible (or reimbursable under an accountable arrangement). Travel expenses include such items as transportation, meals, and lodging.

Some foreign trips are treated as if they were entirely for business, even though they were not. As a result, all travel expenses are deductible (and reimbursable under an accountable arrangement).

Here are the four "safe harbors" recognized by the tax code and regulations:

(1) No substantial control. A foreign trip is considered entirely for business if you did not have substantial control over arranging the trip. You do not have substantial control merely because you had control over the timing of the trip. You do not have substantial control over your trip if you: (a) are an employee who was reimbursed or paid a travel expense allowance; (b) are not related to your employer (church employees generally are not "related" to their employer); and (c) are not a managing executive. A managing executive is an employee who has the authority and responsibility, without being subject to the veto of another, to decide on the need for the business travel.

➡ TIP. The IRS maintains that self-employed persons generally have substantial control over arranging business trips, meaning that it is less likely that they will qualify for this safe harbor.

(2) Outside the United States no more than one week. A business trip is considered entirely for business if it involves travel outside the United States of not more than one week—even if the trip includes nonbusiness activities. One week means seven consecutive days. In counting days, do not count the day of departure, but do count the day of return to the United States.

EXAMPLE. You traveled to Brussels primarily for business. You left Denver on Tuesday and flew to New York. On Wednesday you flew from New York to Brussels, arriving the next morning. On Thursday and Friday you were engaged in business, and from Saturday until Tuesday you were sightseeing. You flew back to New York, arriving Wednesday afternoon. On Thursday you flew back to Denver. Although you were away from your home in Denver for more than a week, you were not outside the United States for more than a week. This is because the day you depart does not count as a day outside the United States. You can deduct your cost of the round-trip flight between Denver and Brussels. You can also deduct the cost of your stay in Brussels for Thursday and Friday while you conducted business. However, you cannot deduct the cost of your stay in Brussels from Saturday through Tuesday because those days were spent on nonbusiness activities.

(3) Less than 25 percent of time spent on personal activities. A trip is considered entirely for business if you were outside the United States for more than a week, but you spent less than 25 percent of the total time you were outside the United States on nonbusiness activities. For this purpose, count both the day your trip began and the day it ended.

EXAMPLE. You flew from Dallas to Nairobi, Kenya, where you spent 14 days on a mission trip and five days on personal matters. You then flew back to Dallas. You spent one day flying in each direction. Because only 5/21 (less than 25 percent) of your total time abroad was for nonbusiness activities, you can deduct as travel expenses what it would have cost you to make the trip if you had not engaged in any nonbusiness activity. The amount you can deduct is the cost of the round-trip plane fare and 16 days of meals (subject to the 50 percent limit), lodging, and other related expenses.

(4) Vacation not a major consideration. Your trip is considered entirely for business if you can establish that a personal vacation was not a major consideration, even if you have substantial control over arranging the trip.

→ **TIP.** You do not have to allocate your travel expenses if you meet one of the four safe harbor exceptions summarized above. In such cases, you can deduct the total cost of getting to and from your destination.

→ **TIP.** If you do not meet any of the above exceptions, you may still be able to deduct some of your expenses.

Foreign travel *primarily* for business

If you travel outside the United States primarily for business but spend some of your time on nonbusiness activities, you generally cannot deduct all of your travel expenses unless you qualify for one of the four exceptions summarized above. You can only deduct the business portion of your cost of getting to and from your destination. You must allocate the costs between your business and nonbusiness activities to determine your deductible amount. How do you make this allocation? In general, if your trip outside the United States was primarily for business, you must allocate your travel time on a day-to-day basis between business days and nonbusiness days. The days you depart from and return to the United States are both counted as days outside the United States. To figure the deductible amount of your round-trip travel expenses, multiply your expenses by the following fraction: the numerator (top number) is the total number of business days outside the United States; the denominator (bottom number) is the total number of travel days outside the United States.

Your business days include transportation days, days your presence was required, days you spent on business, and certain weekends and holidays. Count as a business day any day your presence is required at a particular place for a specific business purpose. Count it as a business day even if you spend most of the day on nonbusiness activities. Also, count as a business day any day you are prevented from working because of circumstances beyond your control. Count weekends,

THE PANEL ON THE NONPROFIT SECTOR RECOMMENDATIONS

In the midst of the financial scandals involving several prominent companies in 2002 and 2003, the media began focusing on allegations of questionable conduct by trustees and executives of public charities. In some cases the alleged abuses were clear violations of the law. In others the issue was whether certain practices met the high ethical standards expected of the charitable sector. These disclosures caught the attention of Congress. In September 2004 the chairman of the Senate Finance Committee, Senator Charles Grassley (R-IA), and the ranking member, Senator Max Baucus (D-MT), sent a letter to the Independent Sector (a national coalition of several hundred public charities) encouraging it to assemble an independent group of leaders from the charitable community to consider and recommend actions "to strengthen governance, ethical conduct, and accountability within public charities and private foundations." The Senate Finance Committee leadership requested a final report in 2005.

The Independent Sector responded by creating a Panel on the Nonprofit Sector, consisting of 24 leaders of public charities. The panel embarked upon a wide-ranging examination of how to strengthen the governance, accountability, and ethical standards of public charities. It convened several public hearings, obtained valuable input from advisory groups and work groups, and consulted with dozens

of professionals. The panel's final report was submitted to the Senate Finance Committee in 2005. It consists of nearly 100 recommendations for changes to be adopted by Congress, the IRS, or charities themselves. These recommendations included the following:

> *Charitable organizations that pay for or reimburse travel expenses of board members, officers, employees, consultants, volunteers, or others traveling to conduct the business of the organization should establish and implement policies that provide clear guidance on their travel rules, including the types of expenses that can be reimbursed and the documentation required to receive reimbursement. Such policies should require that travel on behalf of the charitable organization is to be undertaken in a cost-effective manner. The travel policy should be provided to and adhered to by anyone traveling on behalf of the organization. . . .*

> *Charitable organizations should not pay for nor reimburse travel expenditures (not including de minimis expenses of those attending an activity such as a meal function of the organization) for spouses, dependents, or others who are accompanying individuals conducting business for the organization unless they, too, are conducting business for the organization.*

holidays, and other necessary "standby days" as business days if they fall between business days. But if they follow your business meetings or activity, and you remain at your business destination for nonbusiness or personal reasons, do not count them as business days.

If you stopped for a vacation or other nonbusiness activity either on the way from the United States to your business destination or on the way back to the United States from your business destination, you must allocate part of your travel expenses to the nonbusiness activity. The part you must allocate is the amount it would have cost you to travel between the point where travel outside the United States begins and your nonbusiness destination and a return to the point where travel outside the United States ends.

You determine the nonbusiness portion of that expense by multiplying it by a fraction. The numerator of the fraction is the number of nonbusiness days during your travel outside the United States, and the denominator is the total number of days you spend outside the United States.

Travel primarily for vacation

If you travel outside the United States primarily for vacation, the entire cost of the trip is a nondeductible personal expense. This is true even if you spend some time attending brief professional seminars or a continuing education program. You can, however, deduct your registration fees and any other expenses incurred that were directly related to your business.

Luxury water travel

If you travel by ocean liner, cruise ship, or other form of luxury water transportation for the purpose of carrying on your trade or business, there is a limit on the amount you can deduct. You cannot deduct more than twice the federal per diem rate allowable at the time of your travel. For purposes of this limit, the federal per diem is the highest amount allowed as a daily allowance for living expenses to employees of the executive branch of the federal government while they are away from home but in the United States. The daily limit on luxury water travel does not apply to expenses you have to attend a convention, seminar, or meeting on board a cruise ship (see below). See IRS Publication 463 for the current per diem rates.

Conventions

You may deduct travel expenses for yourself, but ordinarily not those of your family, in attending a convention if you can show that your attendance benefits your own work or business. If the convention is for investment, political, social, or other purposes unrelated to your profession or business, you cannot deduct the expenses.

Ordinarily, no deduction will be allowed for expenses in attending a convention, seminar, or similar meeting that does not offer significant business-related activities, such as participation in meetings, workshops, lectures, or exhibits held during the day. Nonbusiness expenses, such as social or sightseeing expenses, are personal expenses and are not deductible. Your appointment or election as a delegate does not, in itself, determine whether you can treat travel expenses as a business expense.

EXAMPLE. Pastor O is the lead pastor of a church. He and his spouse attend an annual church convention in another state. The trip lasts six days. Pastor O attends business sessions and visits an exhibit area during the day. His spouse spends most of her time visiting with friends and relatives and occasionally attends business sessions and visits exhibits. She also assists her husband in entertaining friends. Pastor O can deduct the travel expenses he incurs in attending the convention, but not those of his spouse. This assumes that the deduction rules addressed in this chapter are satisfied. If their hotel room costs $115 per night, but a single room would have cost $90, then Pastor O can deduct $90 per night as lodging expense. He may deduct the total cost of driving a car, however. If he and his spouse used public transportation, he may deduct only his fare.

Convention agenda

The convention agenda or program generally shows the purpose of the convention. You can show your attendance at the convention benefits your trade or business by comparing the agenda with the official duties and responsibilities of your position. The agenda does not have to deal specifically with your official duties and responsibilities; it will be enough if the agenda is so related to your position that it shows your attendance was for business purposes.

You may not deduct expenses paid by others. If your expenses are paid by reimbursement or allowance, certain limitations may apply (see sections D and E of this chapter).

You may deduct only 50 percent of your business-related meal expenses incurred while traveling away from home. This rule may be avoided by an accountable reimbursement policy, as noted later, in section E of this chapter. You must show that the meal expense is directly related to the active conduct of your trade or business. Further, no deduction will be allowed for lavish or extravagant expenses.

❖ **KEY POINT.** The deductible portion of business meals and entertainment is limited to 50 percent of such expenses. This rule makes the adoption of an accountable business expense reimbursement arrangement desirable, since employers can fully reimburse all of a worker's business meal and entertainment expenses under such an arrangement.

Conventions held outside North America

You cannot deduct expenses for attending a convention, seminar, or similar meeting held outside North America unless the meeting is directly related to your trade or business. Also, it must be as reasonable to hold the meeting outside North America as in it. If the meeting meets these requirements, you also must satisfy the rules for deducting expenses for business trips in general, discussed above.

The following factors must be considered in deciding if it was reasonable to hold the meeting outside North America: (1) the purpose of the meeting and the activities taking place at the meeting; (2) the purposes and activities of the sponsoring organizations or groups; (3) the homes of the active members of the sponsoring organizations and the places at which other meetings of the sponsoring organizations or groups have been or will be held; and (4) other relevant factors you may present.

Examples

The following examples illustrate many of the rules summarized above. They are based on examples contained in the regulations.

EXAMPLE. Pastor E traveled from his home in Tulsa to New York City on Thursday. He flew from New York City to London on Friday. He conducted religious services at churches on Saturday and Sunday, and on Monday through Wednesday went sightseeing. He flew home on Wednesday, arriving home on Thursday. Although he was away from home for more than a week, he was not outside the United States for more than a week. This is because the day he departed does not count as a day outside the United States. He can deduct his cost of the round-trip flight. He can also deduct the cost of his stay in London for Friday and Saturday while he was engaged in business. However, he cannot deduct the cost of his stay in London on Monday through Wednesday because those days were spent on nonbusiness activities.

EXAMPLE. Pastor N goes on a ten-day tour of Israel. He has no business functions or activities, other than the enrichment of his ministry. This trip is primarily for vacation, and Pastor N's travel expenses are not tax-deductible. Any reimbursement of his expenses by the church must be reported on his Form W-2 or 1099-MISC as taxable compensation.

EXAMPLE. Pastor J travels from Seattle to Taiwan, where he spends 14 days on a preaching and teaching mission and 5 days on personal matters. He then flies back to Seattle. He spent 1 day flying in each direction. Because only 5/21 (5 out of 21 days, less than 25 percent) of his total time abroad was for nonbusiness activities, he can deduct as travel expenses what it would have cost him to make the trip if he had not engaged in any personal activity. The amount he can deduct is the cost of the round-trip plane fare and 16 days of meals (subject to the 50 percent limit), lodging, and other related expenses. Alternatively, the church can reimburse Pastor J's travel expenses. If the church has an accountable reimbursement arrangement, its reimbursement of these expenses is not reported as taxable compensation on Pastor J's Form W-2 or 1099-MISC.

Cruise ships

You can deduct up to $2,000 per year of your expenses of attending conventions, seminars, or similar meetings held on cruise ships.

All ships that sail are considered cruise ships. You can deduct these expenses only if all of the following requirements are met:

(1) The convention, seminar, or meeting is directly related to your profession or business.
(2) The cruise ship is a vessel registered in the United States.
(3) All of the cruise ship's ports of call are in the United States or in possessions of the United States.
(4) You attach to your return a written statement, signed by you, that includes information about

    (a) the total days of the trip (not including the days of transportation to and from the cruise ship port),
    (b) the number of hours each day that you devoted to scheduled business activities, and
    (c) a program of the scheduled business activities of the meeting.

(5) You attach to your return a written statement signed by an officer of the organization or group sponsoring the meeting that includes

    (a) a schedule of the business activities of each day of the meeting and
    (b) the number of hours you attended the scheduled business activities.

Annual foreign earned income exclusion

✳ **New in 2012.** For 2012 the maximum foreign earned income exclusion was $95,100 per qualifying person. If married and both individuals work abroad and both meet either the bona fide residence test or the physical presence test, each one can choose the foreign earned income exclusion. Together they can exclude as much as $190,200 for 2012.

If you meet certain requirements, you may qualify for the foreign earned income and foreign housing exclusions and the foreign housing deduction. If you are a U.S. citizen or a resident alien of the United States and you live abroad, you are taxed on your worldwide income. However, you may qualify to exclude from income up to $95,100 (for 2012) of your foreign earnings. In addition, you can exclude or deduct certain foreign housing amounts, but the amount of qualified housing expenses eligible for the housing exclusion and housing deduction is limited. The limitation is generally 30 percent of the maximum foreign earned income exclusion. For 2012 the housing amount limitation is $28,530 for the tax year. However, the limit will vary depending on the location of the qualifying individual's foreign tax home and the number of qualifying days in the tax year.

The foreign earned income exclusion is limited to the actual foreign earned income minus the foreign housing exclusion. Therefore, to exclude a foreign housing amount, the qualifying individual must first figure the foreign housing exclusion before determining the amount for the foreign earned income exclusion.

You may also be entitled to exclude from income the value of meals and lodging provided to you by your employer.

To claim the foreign earned income exclusion, the foreign housing exclusion, or the foreign housing deduction, you must satisfy all three of the following requirements.

(1) Your tax home (explained above) must be in a foreign country.

(2) You must have foreign earned income.

(3) You must meet one of the following tests:

- A U.S. citizen who is a bona fide resident of a foreign country or countries for an uninterrupted period that includes an entire tax year.
- A U.S. resident alien who is a citizen or national of a country with which the United States has an income tax treaty in effect and who is a bona fide resident of a foreign country or countries for an uninterrupted period that includes an entire tax year.
- A U.S. citizen or a U.S. resident alien who is physically present in a foreign country or countries for at least 330 full days during any period of 12 consecutive months.

The maximum annual exclusion is prorated on a daily basis if there is any part of the year that you do not qualify under either test.

If you qualify under any of these tests, you may also claim an additional exclusion based on what you spend for foreign housing. See the instructions for Form 2555 for details.

The foreign earned income exclusion and the foreign housing cost amount exclusion are figured on Form 2555, which must be attached to Form 1040. However, if you claim only the foreign earned income exclusion, you may be able to use Form 2555-EZ instead.

The minimum time requirements for bona fide residence and physical presence can be waived if you must leave a foreign country because of war, civil unrest, or similar adverse conditions in that country.

Foreign earned income is defined as wages, salaries, professional fees, and other amounts received as compensation for personal services performed in a foreign country. The place where you perform the services is what defines your income as foreign, not where or how you are paid. Foreign earned income does not include such items as interest, dividends, pensions, or annuities.

Net self-employment income is generally subject to self-employment tax even if it is nontaxable in computing income taxes due to the foreign earned income exclusion. However, if it was earned in a

country that has a Social Security agreement with the United States, which is called a "totalization agreement," it may be exempt from U.S. Social Security taxes, including the self-employment taxes.

Charitable travel

Treasury regulation 1.170A-1(g) specifies that "out-of-pocket transportation expenses necessarily incurred in performing donated services are deductible. Reasonable expenditures for meals and lodging necessarily incurred while away from home in the course of performing donated services also are deductible." Therefore, unreimbursed travel expenses incurred while away from home (whether within the United States or abroad) in the course of donated services to a tax-exempt religious or charitable organization are deductible as a charitable contribution.

The topic of charitable travel is addressed in Chapter 8, in the Introduction and in section D.1.

Tour guides

Some ministers lead tours to the Holy Land (or other destinations) and receive free travel by a tour company if they recruit a specified number of tourists to go along. Is the value of the free travel provided to a minister under such arrangement taxable income? The IRS says that it is:

> *If you received a free tour from a travel agency for organizing a group of tourists, you must include its value in your income. Report the fair market value of the tour on Form 1040, line 21, if you are not in the trade or business of organizing tours. You cannot deduct your expenses in serving as the voluntary leader of the group at the group's request. If you organize tours as a trade or business, report the tour's value on Schedule C or Schedule C-EZ (Form 1040).* IRS Publication 17. See also Revenue Ruling 64-154; GCM 35232 (1973); Revenue Ruling 74-473.

Often a minister will recruit enough tour group members to receive multiple free trips (which are used by members of the minister's family). The market value of these additional free trips also must be reported as taxable income by the minister.

Travel expenses of a spouse

✿ **KEY POINT.** IRS regulations permit churches to treat reimbursements of the travel expenses of a minister's spouse (incurred while accompanying the minister on business travel) as a nontaxable fringe benefit. Some conditions apply.

▲ **CAUTION.** *Churches often provide benefits to their senior pastor besides salary. These benefits may include the reimbursement of a spouse's travel expenses while accompanying the pastor on a trip. Often pastors and church treasurers are unaware that this benefit must be valued and reported as taxable income on the pastor's Form W-2 unless the spouse's presence on the trip serves a business purpose and the expenses are reimbursed under an ac-*

countable arrangement. This omission may expose the pastor, and possibly church board members, to substantial excise taxes, since the IRS views this benefit as an automatic excess benefit resulting in intermediate sanctions unless the benefit was reported as taxable income by the church or pastor in the year it was provided. It is essential for pastors and church treasurers to be familiar with the concept of automatic excess benefits so these penalties can be avoided. This topic is covered fully in Chapter 4, section A.3.

Most ministers attend conferences and conventions in the course of their ministry. Common examples include seminars and denominational meetings. In some cases ministers attend such events at their own expense, but often their travel expenses (including transportation, lodging, and meals) are reimbursed by their church. These expenses are legitimate business expenses so long as the primary purpose of the travel is church business. This means the expenses may be deductible by the minister or reimbursed by the church under an accountable arrangement. But what if the minister's spouse goes along? Can the church reimburse the spouse's travel expenses too? Are the tax consequences the same as for the minister, or do different rules apply? And what if the minister's children come too? These are important questions.

Hundreds of IRS rulings and court decisions prior to 1994 addressed spousal travel expenses, with the vast majority of them concluding that an employer's reimbursements of a spouse's travel expense were includable in taxable income and were *not deductible or reimbursable as business expenses.*

In 1994 section 274(m)(3) was added to the tax code. This section disallows any deduction for amounts "paid or incurred" with respect to a spouse, dependent, or other individual accompanying the taxpayer on business travel, unless the following three conditions are satisfied:

* the spouse, dependent, or other individual is an employee of the taxpayer;
* the travel of the spouse, dependent, or other individual is for a bona fide business purpose; and
* such expenses would otherwise be deductible by the spouse, dependent, or other individual.

Section 274(m)(3) eliminates any possibility of a deduction for a spouse's (or child's) travel expenses in most cases, since a minister's spouse (or child) rarely is an employee of the church.

Section 274(m)(3) also led many to conclude that a church's reimbursements of family members' travel expenses had to be treated as taxable income. Here's why. Section 132 of the tax code specifies that expenses paid by an employer on behalf of an employee represent a nontaxable working condition fringe benefit so long as the employee could have deducted the expense if he or she paid it directly. Since section 274(m)(3) prevents a deduction for the travel expenses of a minister's spouse in most cases, the implication

was that any reimbursement of such expenses by a church had to be reported as taxable income. In short, not only were the travel expenses incurred by a spouse or child not deductible, but a church's reimbursement of these expenses had to be reported as taxable income.

EXAMPLE. Pastor C and his spouse attend a church convention. The spouse is not an employee of the church, and she has no official duties at the convention. The church reimburses the travel expenses of both Pastor C and his wife (including transportation, lodging, and meals). According to section 274(m)(3) of the tax code, the travel expenses of Pastor C's spouse are not deductible (by either her or Pastor C), since she is not an employee and her presence at the convention did not serve a legitimate business purpose. Further, since her business expenses were not deductible, the church's reimbursements of her expenses represented taxable income.

IRS regulations

IRS regulations clarify that section 274(m)(3) does not prevent an employer's reimbursement of the travel expenses of an employee's spouse or family member from qualifying as a nontaxable working condition fringe benefit so long as these conditions are met:

* the employer has not treated such amounts as compensation;
* the amounts would be deductible as a business expense without regard to the limitation on the deductibility of a spouse's travel expenses, meaning that the spouse's presence on the trip is for a legitimate business purpose; and
* the employee substantiates the expenses under an accountable arrangement (described above). *Treas. Reg. 1.132-5(t).*

▲ **CAUTION.** *If any one of these conditions is not met, then a church's reimbursement of a nonemployee spouse's travel expenses will represent taxable income to the minister. The same applies to children who accompany a minister on a business trip.*

✿ **KEY POINT.** The regulations clarify that ministers need not report as taxable income a church's reimbursement of their spouse's travel expenses, even though the spouse is not an employee and therefore cannot deduct such expenses. However, note that this result assumes that the church has not reported the reimbursement of the spouse's expenses as income, the spouse's presence on the trip is for a legitimate business purpose, and the spouse's expenses are reimbursed under an accountable arrangement. If any of these conditions is not met, then the church's reimbursement of the spouse's travel expenses represents taxable income for the minister.

If a spouse is not a church employee and the spouse's presence on a trip does not serve a legitimate business purpose, then that portion of the church's reimbursement of the travel expenses of the minister and spouse attributable to the spouse's travel represents taxable income to the minister.

PROMOTING ACCOUNTABILITY THROUGH A SPOUSE'S PRESENCE

Some churches require that their minister be accompanied by his or her spouse while on business trips for accountability purposes. That is, the spouse's presence greatly reduces the risk of inappropriate conduct by the minister or false accusations that could be devastating to the minister's reputation and to the church as well. Many churches have been devastated by the sexual misconduct of their minister, and church leaders are justified in taking this risk seriously and in implementing procedures to prevent it. If the church board adopts a policy mandating a spouse's presence on the minister's business trips and explains the "business rationale" for such a policy, an argument could be made that the spouse's presence on the minister's business trips serves a legitimate business purpose regardless of whether the spouse is engaged in any other business activities on the trip.

However, this is a highly aggressive position that should not be adopted without the advice of a competent tax professional. Further, it should not be adopted if (1) it is not consistently followed (e.g., the church permits the spouse to accompany the minister on only selected business trips, or the church does not require spouses to accompany other staff members on business trips) or (2) one or more other church employees customarily accompany the minister on business trips, and these individuals could share the same accommodations and otherwise provide the same accountability as the minister's spouse.

This is not simply a matter of splitting the combined expenses in half. Rather, the amount to add to the minister's taxable income is the actual amount of additional travel expenses attributable to the spouse's travel. For example, if the minister and spouse drive their car to a church convention, the travel expenses allocable to the spouse would include any additional hotel room charge based on double occupancy as well as the spouse's meals. If the couple flies to their destination, the spouse's airfare would be included.

Examples
The application of section 274(m)(3) and the IRS regulations are illustrated by the following examples.

EXAMPLE. Pastor B is the senior minister of a church and is a member of the church's governing board by virtue of his position. He attends a church convention in another city. He is accompanied by his spouse, who was selected by the church as an official delegate. The spouse is not an employee of the church.

The spouse attends business meetings with her husband and votes on matters addressed at the convention. Pastor B's travel expenses were $800 (transportation, lodging, and meals), and travel expenses attributable to his spouse were an additional $400. The church reimburses fully those travel expenses of both Pastor B and his spouse that are adequately substantiated under an accountable arrangement.

Since the spouse is not an employee of the church, her travel expenses ($400) are not deductible as a business expense. However, since her presence on the trip serves a legitimate business purpose and her travel expenses were reimbursed under an accountable arrangement, the church's reimbursement of her travel expenses does not represent taxable income to either her or Pastor B.

EXAMPLE. Same facts as the previous example, except that the church issues a cash advance of $1,500 to Pastor B for all of the travel expenses he and his spouse incur while attending the church convention. No substantiation of actual business expenses is required. The IRS regulations do not apply to this situation, since the church is not reimbursing the spouse's travel expenses under an accountable arrangement. Accordingly, the full amount of the church's travel reimbursement represents taxable income and must be included on Pastor B's Form W-2 (or 1099-MISC). Pastor B will be able to deduct his travel expenses ($800) as an itemized deduction on Schedule A (or on Schedule C if self-employed), but the travel expenses incurred by his spouse ($400) are not deductible.

EXAMPLE. Same facts as the first example, except that Pastor B and his spouse must pay their own expenses in attending the church convention. Pastor B will be able to deduct his travel expenses ($800) as an itemized deduction on Schedule A (or on Schedule C if self-employed), but the travel expenses incurred by his spouse ($400) are not deductible, since she is not an employee of the church.

EXAMPLE. Same facts as the first example, except that Pastor B's spouse is a church employee. Since the spouse is an employee of the church and her presence on the trip serves a legitimate business purpose, her travel expenses ($400) are deductible as a business expense. Since the church reimbursed her expenses under an accountable arrangement, the reimbursement is not taxable income (it is not reported on her Form W-2), and there is no deduction to claim. As a church employee engaged in legitimate business travel, the treatment of the spouse is identical to that of Pastor B.

EXAMPLE. Same facts as the first example, except that Pastor B's spouse does not attend the convention as an official delegate of the church. She has no official duties at the convention and does not attend or participate in business sessions. She spends most of her time with friends and relatives who are at the convention. Since the spouse's presence on the trip does not serve a legitimate business purpose, the IRS regulations do not apply. As a result, her travel expenses reimbursed by the church ($400) represent taxable income to Pastor B. If the $400 is not reported as taxable income on the pastor's Form W-2 or Form 1040 for the year in which the reimbursement occurred, this omission will expose the pastor not only to the risk of back taxes and interest but also (if he is a "disqualified person," meaning an officer or director, or relative of an officer or director) to substantial excise taxes since the IRS views this as an automatic excess benefit transaction unless the benefit was reported as taxable income by the church or pastor in the year it was provided. Church board members who authorized the transaction are exposed to excise taxes of up to 10 percent of the amount of the excess benefit. This topic is covered fully in Chapter 4, section A.3.

EXAMPLE. Same facts as the preceding example, except that Pastor B's church board adopted the following resolution in 2013: "Whereas the scriptural qualifications for ministers include: above reproach, respectable, a good reputation (1 Timothy 3:2–7); and blameless, upright, and holy (Titus 1:7–8); and whereas the church has a significant interest in its minister adhering to these standards, since the church can be devastated if its minister violates them or is wrongfully accused of violating them; now therefore the official board resolves that its minister may not participate in any out-of-town business travel without the presence of his wife; and further resolves that the presence of the minister's wife on business trips serves the legitimate and essential business purpose of promoting and preserving the integrity of the minister's ministry and thereby protects the mission of the church; and further resolves that the substantiated travel expenses incurred by the minister's spouse in accompanying the minister on business trips as mandated by this policy shall be reimbursed by the church."

It is possible that the spouse's travel expenses incurred as a result of such a policy would be viewed as serving a legitimate business purpose and that the church's reimbursement of such expenses would represent a nontaxable working condition fringe benefit under the IRS regulations (so long as the spouse's expenses are reimbursed under an accountable arrangement). As noted above, this is an aggressive position that should not be adopted without the advice of a tax attorney or CPA. Further, the strength of this position will be greatly reduced, if not eliminated, if (1) it is not consistently followed (e.g., the church permits the spouse to accompany the minister on only selected business trips, or the church does not require spouses to accompany other staff members on business trips) or (2) one or more other church employees customarily accompany the minister on business trips, and these individuals could share the same accommodations and otherwise provide the same accountability as the minister's spouse.

EXAMPLE. Pastor C is an officer with a denominational agency. One of Pastor C's functions is to attend church conferences and conventions and to speak at local churches. Pastor C's spouse goes along on many of these trips. The denominational agency expects the spouse to accompany Pastor C on many of these trips, although the spouse performs no business function or purpose. The agency reimburses the travel expenses of both Pastor C and Pastor C's spouse under an accountable arrangement (only those expenses that are adequately substantiated are reimbursed). The spouse is not an employee of the agency. Since the spouse is not an employee of the agency, the spouse's travel expenses are not a business expense and cannot be deducted. However, it is possible that the agency's reimbursements of the spouse's expenses would not be included in Pastor C's income—if the spouse's presence on Pastor C's trips serves a legitimate business purpose.

While the likelihood that the spouse satisfies this condition is remote under these facts, it is possible. A few courts have suggested that a spouse's presence on a business trip can serve a business purpose if (1) the employee spouse is an executive officer; (2) the employer has a "long-standing practice of defraying the travel expenses" of the employee's spouse; (3) one of the business objectives of the employee's travel is to "promote the public image" of the employing institution, and this task reasonably required the presence of the employee's spouse on at least some occasions; (4) the spouse's presence is necessary to assist the employee in "developing and renewing personal contacts"; and (5) it is customary for the spouse to accompany the employee on some activities, and the spouse's absence would materially diminish the image that the employee was seeking to project of the employer. *See, e.g., United States v. Disney, 413 F.2d 783 (9th Cir. 1969); Bank of Stockton v. Commissioner, 36 T.C.M. 114 (1977).*

There is little doubt that the IRS would challenge the business purpose of the spouse under these facts. Reliance on the proposed regulations to avoid recognizing the agency's reimbursement of the spouse's expenses as taxable income to the minister would be a highly aggressive position under these facts that should not be pursued without the advice of a tax attorney. Note, however, that this position may be strengthened by the adoption of an official policy (as explained above) requiring the spouse to accompany the minister on business trips in order to promote accountability and protect against unethical and unscriptural behavior that could have a negative impact on the finances and reputation of the denominational agency.

Finally, note that treating the spouse's travel expenses as business expenses may expose Pastor C and members of the denomination's governing board to intermediate sanctions if the IRS determines that the spouse's presence on the trips served no legitimate business purpose. In such a case the denomination's reimbursement of the spouse's expenses constitutes the reimbursement of personal expenses. And since these reimbursements were not reported as taxable income during the year they were paid (because the denomination assumed they were accountable reimbursements of business expenses), the reimbursements constitute an automatic excess benefit exposing Pastor C and members of the denomination's governing board to intermediate sanctions. This topic is covered fully in Chapter 4, section A.3.

EXAMPLE. Same facts as the previous example, except that the spouse is a featured speaker at one or more special events held during the convention. Such responsibilities make it far more likely that the denomination's reimbursement of the spouse's travel expenses will be a nontaxable working condition fringe benefit, since the "business purpose" test is more likely satisfied. This assumes that the spouse's travel expenses are reimbursed under an accountable arrangement. If the denomination reimburses the spouse's expenses without adequate substantiation, or more than 60 days after incurring the travel expenses, then the reimbursements will represent taxable income for Pastor C and must be added to his Form W-2.

EXAMPLE. Pastor D is an associate minister of a church. He travels to another city to interview for a pastoral position at Second Church. Pastor D's spouse goes along on the trip but performs no specific business function. Pastor D and his spouse incur the following travel expenses in their trip to Second Church: airfare for Pastor D ($500); airfare for Pastor D's spouse ($500); hotel ($100 double occupancy—a single room would be $75); meals for Pastor D ($50); meals for Pastor D's spouse ($50). Second Church reimburses all of the travel expenses of both Pastor D and his spouse ($1,200) that they substantiate with receipts and other records.

The reimbursement of Pastor D's expenses ($625) by Second Church does not represent taxable income to Pastor D, since it is an accountable reimbursement of legitimate business expenses incurred on behalf of the church.

There is a reasonable basis for concluding that the church's reimbursement of the travel expenses allocable to Pastor D's spouse ($575) represents a nontaxable working condition fringe benefit under the IRS regulations, since (1) the spouse's presence on the trip served a legitimate business purpose, and (2) the spouse's expenses were reimbursed under an accountable arrangement. Accordingly, the church's reimbursement of the spouse's travel expenses ($575) would not be reported as income on Pastor D's Form W-2 or 1099-MISC. The basis for concluding that the spouse's presence on the trip serves a legitimate business purpose is the fact that many churches consider the spouse's presence during the interview process essential. The pastor and his or her spouse represent a model of marital fidelity to many congregations, and the spouse typically serves a variety of volunteer roles within the church. It would be unthinkable for most churches to hire a pastoral candidate without meeting and interviewing the candidate's spouse. This is an aggressive position, and there is no assurance that it would be accepted

by the IRS or the courts. Ministers should consult with a tax adviser before adopting this approach.

EXAMPLE. Same facts as the previous example, except that the couple brings their two minor children along on the trip at an additional cost of $1,100. Again, an argument can be made that the presence of the children on the trip serves a legitimate business function. The New Testament lists the following qualifications (among others) for a pastor: "He must manage his own family well and see that his children obey him with proper respect" (1 Timothy 3:4); "An elder must be blameless, the husband of but one wife, a man whose children believe and are not open to the charge of being wild and disobedient" (Titus 1:6). According to these verses, an argument can be made that a church would be legitimately interested in meeting the pastor's entire family before making an employment decision. Obviously this will not be true for all churches and would be less true for pastors with very young children. This is a highly aggressive position, and it is doubtful there is a reasonable basis for it. This means that ministers who take this position may be subject to penalties in addition to payment of back taxes and interest. Ministers should consult with a tax adviser before adopting this approach.

Charitable contributions

As noted in Chapter 8, unreimbursed expenses incurred while performing donated labor for a church may constitute a deductible charitable contribution. The income tax regulations specify:

> Unreimbursed expenditures made incident to the rendition of services to an organization contributions to which are deductible may constitute a deductible contribution. For example, the cost of a uniform without general utility which is required to be worn in performing donated services is deductible. Similarly, out-of-pocket transportation expenses necessarily incurred in performing donated services are deductible. Reasonable expenditures for meals and lodging necessarily incurred while away from home in the course of performing donated services are also deductible. Treas. Reg. 1.170A-1(g).

Another way for travel expenses of a spouse to be nontaxable under the IRS regulations would be if the spouse performed meaningful church-related business activities. Under these circumstances, the spouse's unreimbursed travel expenses could be claimed as a charitable contribution deduction. Consider the following examples:

EXAMPLE. A denomination's bylaws permit churches to send lay delegates to annual denominational meetings. These lay delegates, along with ordained ministers, comprise the eligible voters. Pastor G is an ordained minister who attends an annual meeting in another city. Pastor G's church selected his spouse to accompany him as an official delegate. Pastor G's spouse attends all business meetings and exercises her voting privileges. The travel expenses of Pastor G's spouse are not reimbursed by the church.

Pastor G's spouse can deduct her travel expenses as a charitable contribution. This conclusion is supported by the following language in IRS Publication 526 (Charitable Contributions): "If you are a chosen representative attending a convention of a qualified organization, you can deduct unreimbursed expenses for travel and transportation, including a reasonable amount for meals and lodging, while away from home overnight in connection with the convention." Alternatively, the church's reimbursement of the spouse's expenses may represent a nontaxable working condition fringe benefit under the IRS regulations.

EXAMPLE. Same facts as the previous example, except that the church does not select Pastor G's spouse to attend the meeting as a church delegate. The spouse's unreimbursed expenses are not deductible as a charitable contribution. IRS Publication 526 states: "You cannot deduct your expenses in attending a church convention if you go only as a member of your church rather than as a chosen representative. You can deduct unreimbursed expenses that are directly connected with giving services for your church during the convention."

EXAMPLE. Same facts as the previous example, except that after arriving at the location of the meeting, Pastor G's spouse visits a religious music publisher to consider music for the church. Her unreimbursed expenses in making this side trip can be claimed as a charitable contribution. However, this does not convert her expenses incurred in traveling to the meeting site to a deductible business expense. This conclusion is supported by the following language in IRS Publication 526: "You can deduct unreimbursed expenses that are directly connected with giving services for your church during the convention."

EXAMPLE. Pastor H is invited to speak at a church in a different city. His spouse accompanies him on the trip, but she performs no specific duties on behalf of the church. Her unreimbursed travel expenses are not deductible as a charitable contribution.

EXAMPLE. Same facts as the previous example, except that Pastor H's spouse is asked to speak to a Sunday-school class and sing a solo during the worship service at which her husband speaks. Her travel expenses are not reimbursed by either church.

While not certain, it is possible that the spouse's activities during the trip represent sufficient charitable activity for her unreimbursed travel expenses to be deductible as a charitable contribution. If the church reimburses these expenses, then the expenses would not be deductible as a charitable contribution, but as noted above, the reimbursements may be nontaxable if they meet the requirements of a working condition fringe benefit.

For more information on claiming a charitable contribution deduction for expenses incurred during charitable travel (and substantiation requirements), see Chapter 8, Introduction and section D.1.

3. ENTERTAINMENT EXPENSES

▲ **CAUTION.** *A church cannot reimburse employees' expenses under an accountable reimbursement arrangement that do not qualify as business expenses. Such reimbursements, as well as a church's reimbursement of employees' unsubstantiated business expenses, are nonaccountable. If these reimbursements are not reported as taxable income to the employee in the year the reimbursements are paid, two consequences result: (1) the employee is subject to back taxes plus penalties and interest on the unreported income; and (2) if the benefits are provided to an officer or director of the church (a "disqualified person"), or a relative of such a person, they will expose the recipient and possibly other members of the church's governing board to intermediate sanctions in the form of substantial excise taxes, since the IRS views these benefits as automatic excess benefits unless reported as taxable income by the church or recipient in the year provided. This topic is covered fully in Chapter 4, section A.3. The lesson is clear: sloppy church accounting practices can be costly.*

You may be able to deduct entertainment expenses you incur for your trade or business (i.e., your ministry). You may take the deduction only if you can demonstrate that the amounts spent are either (1) *directly related* to the active conduct of your ministry, *or* (2) *associated* with the active conduct of your ministry and the entertainment occurred directly before or after a substantial business discussion. These two tests are summarized below:

(1) **"Directly related" test.** In order to show that entertainment was directly related to the active conduct of your business, you ordinarily must be able to demonstrate either that the entertainment occurred in a clear business setting and is for your business or work or that you meet the following three requirements: (1) the main purpose of the entertainment was the transaction of business; (2) you did engage in business during the entertainment period; and (3) you had more than a general expectation of deriving income or some other specific business benefit at some indefinite future time.

Entertainment expenses generally are not considered directly related if you are not present or in situations where substantial distractions generally prevent you from actively conducting business. The following are examples of situations with substantial distractions:

- a meeting or discussion at a theater or sporting event;
- a meeting or discussion during what is essentially a social gathering, such as a party; or

- a meeting with a group that includes persons who are not business associates, at places such as restaurants, country clubs, athletic clubs, or vacation resorts.

(2) **Associated entertainment.** In order to show that entertainment was associated with the active conduct of your ministry, you must be able to demonstrate that the entertainment was associated with the active conduct of your trade or business and occurred directly before or after a substantial business discussion. Generally, an expense is associated with the active conduct of your trade or business if you can show that you had a clear business purpose for incurring the expense. The purpose may be to get new business or to encourage the continuation of an existing business relationship. Whether a business discussion is substantial depends on the facts of each case. A business discussion will not be considered substantial unless you can show that you actively engaged in the discussion, meeting, negotiation, or other business transaction to get income or some other specific business benefit. The meeting does not have to be for any specified length of time, but you must show that the business discussion was substantial in relation to the meal or entertainment. It is not necessary that you devote more time to business than to entertainment. You do not have to discuss business during the meal or entertainment.

Entertainment includes any activity generally considered to provide entertainment, amusement, or recreation. This covers entertaining guests at restaurants; social or athletic facilities; sporting events; or on hunting, fishing, vacation, or similar trips. Expenses are not deductible when a group of business acquaintances take turns picking up each other's entertainment checks without regard to whether any business purposes are served. Ministers incur entertainment expenses in a variety of situations. Common examples include entertaining denominational officials, guest speakers, church groups (youth, choir, the church board, etc.), or meeting with members at a restaurant for counseling purposes.

You may deduct only 50 percent of your business-related entertainment expenses, including meals. This 50 percent limitation is incorporated directly into the tax returns (line 9 of Form 2106, and line 24 of Schedule C). Note, however, that the 50 percent limitation *does not apply to expenses you incur that are reimbursed by your employer under an accountable reimbursement plan* (described in section E of this chapter). IRS Publication 463 (Travel, Entertainment, and Gift Expenses) states: "If you are an employee, you are not subject to the 50 percent limit on expenses for which your employer reimburses you under an accountable plan."

Publication 463 states that self-employed persons also can avoid the 50 percent limitation through use of an accountable reimbursement arrangement.

Church staff members who report their income taxes as employees may deduct their unreimbursed and nonaccountable reimbursed entertainment expenses only as a miscellaneous itemized deduction on Schedule A (you must be able to itemize deductions to claim them), and then only to the extent that all miscellaneous expenses exceed 2 percent of AGI. Further, only 50 percent of business meals and entertainment expenses would be deductible. These restrictive rules, which are explained fully in section E of this chapter, make the adoption of an accountable reimbursement policy essential. Self-employed workers may deduct their unreimbursed and nonaccountable reimbursed entertainment expenses directly on Schedule C regardless of whether they can itemize their deductions on Schedule A, and without regard to the 2 percent AGI floor. However, they will be subject to the 50 percent limitation on business meals and entertainment—unless their expenses are reimbursed under an accountable arrangement.

Entertainment expenses incurred in your home are especially scrutinized by the IRS. You must be able to demonstrate that your expenses were not purely social but rather had a primary business purpose. Entertainment expenses of spouses may also be deductible if their presence serves a legitimate business purpose or if it would be impracticable under the circumstances to entertain the business associate without including his or her spouse.

✿**KEY POINT.** The rules for deducting entertainment expenses are summarized in Table 7-5.

You must meet certain requirements for proving the amount spent and the business nature of the expense (described below). The IRS frequently challenges entertainment expenses, so you should be prepared to fully substantiate such expenses as described below.

EXAMPLE. Pastor S invites the church's board of trustees to his home for dinner and a board meeting. The expenses incurred by Pastor S and his guests for food and beverages ordinarily will constitute entertainment expenses.

EXAMPLE. Pastor S invites a friend and fellow minister to his home for dinner. The friend resides in another state and is visiting Pastor S for the day. Ordinarily such a visit will be a social visit, and the expenses associated with it will not be deductible.

EXAMPLE. Pastor K is the senior minister of a church. He takes an applicant for a staff position out to dinner, where they discuss the applicant's background and suitability for the position. The applicant's spouse comes along because it would be impractical to discuss the position solely with the applicant. Further, Pastor K's spouse accompanies her husband because the applicant's spouse is present. Pastor K pays everyone's meal expense. The cost of the meals of all four persons is a deductible entertainment expense.

If Pastor K is not reimbursed by the church for the expense, he may deduct it on Schedule A as a miscellaneous expense if

TABLE 7-5

WHEN ARE ENTERTAINMENT EXPENSES DEDUCTIBLE?

GENERAL RULE
- You can deduct ordinary and necessary expenses to entertain a client, customer, or employee if the expenses meet the "directly related" test or the "associated" test.

DEFINITIONS
- Entertainment includes any activity generally considered to provide entertainment, amusement, or recreation, and it includes meals provided to a customer or client.
- An ordinary expense is one that is common and accepted in your field of business, trade, or profession.
- A necessary expense is one that is helpful and appropriate, although not necessarily indispensable, for your business.

TWO TESTS (MUST MEET ONE)
1. **Directly related test**
   - Entertainment took place in a clear business setting, OR
   - Main purpose of entertainment was the active conduct of business, AND (a) you did engage in business with the person during the entertainment period, AND (b) you had more than a general expectation of getting income or some other specific business benefit.
2. **Associated test**
   - Entertainment is associated with your trade or business, AND
   - Entertainment directly precedes or follows a substantial business discussion.

OTHER RULES
- You cannot deduct the cost of your meal as an entertainment expense if you are claiming the meal as a travel expense.
- You can deduct expenses only to the extent that they are not lavish or extravagant under the circumstances.
- You generally can deduct only 50 percent of your unreimbursed entertainment expenses.

he reports his income taxes as an employee (and he is able to itemize), or on Schedule C if he is self-employed. If the church reimburses the expense but requires no substantiation of the amount or date of the expense or the business purpose of the entertainment and business relationship of those entertained, then the expense is reimbursed under a nonaccountable plan. The result is that Pastor K may deduct the expense on Schedule

A as a miscellaneous expense if he reports his income taxes as an employee (and he is able to itemize), or on Schedule C if he is self-employed. Further, the full amount of the reimbursement must be reported as income on his Form W-2 or 1099-MISC and on Form 1040. If Pastor K is reimbursed for the expense under an accountable reimbursement plan, he reports neither the reimbursement nor the expense on his tax return.

EXAMPLE. Pastor S claimed a deduction for expenses incurred in entertaining guests who came to visit. He claimed that many of the guests were associated with the church where he previously had been the pastor. The IRS denied any deduction for these expenses, and the Tax Court agreed. It observed: "Entertainment expenses, like travel expenses, must be substantiated strictly. . . . While we understand that [Pastor S] may have wanted to maintain good relations with his former parishioners, he has not established any business purpose for the entertainment expenses, nor has he established the business relationship between himself and the guests. When asked whether the out-of-town guests were business guests, [his] testimony indicated that he regarded the guests as personal. We find that [he] has failed to meet his burden of proof and sustain [the IRS's] disallowance of these claimed deductions." *Shelley v. Commissioner, T.C. Memo. 1994-432 (1994).*

EXAMPLE. The Tax Court addressed the deductibility of a pastor's entertainment expenses. The expenses were incurred as a result of the following three activities:

(1) Men's prayer breakfasts were held at a church parsonage almost every Friday. The pastor's wife prepared and served breakfast to the participants and recorded the number of men attending each breakfast on a calendar kept in the parsonage kitchen. Neither the congregation nor its board specifically directed the pastor to offer the prayer breakfasts, but the pastor insisted that the breakfasts were part of his work as the pastor of the congregation.
(2) The pastor and his wife also provided meals and lodging in the parsonage for a visiting choir group or for families who needed a meal or a place to stay while looking for a job, or while stranded in town because their car broke down. Some meals also were provided to church members and others who assisted in the construction of an addition to the church building during the summer. The pastor's wife recorded on the kitchen calendar on the appropriate date the number of people to whom she served individual meals and designated the meal as "breakfast," "lunch," "dinner," or "supper"; she also recorded the number of people staying overnight at the parsonage and the duration of their stay.
(3) The pastor and his wife provided meals and lodging in the parsonage for a young man who donated his time to help build an addition to the church building.

The IRS denied any entertainment deduction for these expenses, and the pastor appealed to the Tax Court. The court concluded that the expenses incurred in connection with the prayer breakfasts were deductible entertainment expenses. It observed, "We are persuaded that the prayer breakfast program was directly related to [the pastor's] employment as clergyman. [His] purpose was to conduct religious study and promote fellowship. Such a purpose is clearly within the functions of a pastor of a congregation. The fact that the church did not specifically require [him] to hold these breakfasts is a factor, but is not determinative. We are satisfied that [he] was given broad latitude in fulfilling his responsibilities as clergyman, and that this program was conducted within that broad authorization." However, the court concluded that the pastor could not deduct the other entertainment expenses, since he failed to demonstrate that they were directly related to his income-producing employment. *Onstott v. Commissioner, 41 T.C.M. 827 (1981).*

✢ **KEY POINT.** The deductible portion of business meals and entertainment is only 50 percent of such expenses. This makes the adoption of an accountable business expense reimbursement arrangement desirable, since employers can fully reimburse all of a worker's business meal and entertainment expenses under such an arrangement.

Lunch expenses

Ministers and church staff members commonly go out to lunch together on workdays. In many churches it is a weekly ritual. Since church matters are discussed, many church treasurers assume that the cost of the lunch can be reimbursed by the church under an accountable arrangement. As a result, the cost of such lunches is not added to the employees' taxable compensation for tax reporting purposes. But is this the correct way to handle lunch expenses? If your church has an accountable reimbursement arrangement, can you reimburse lunch expenses? If so, under what circumstances? Always? Whenever church matters are discussed? A recent Tax Court decision addresses this important question. While the case involved a medical technician, it is equally relevant to church staff. *Dugan v. Commissioner, T.C. Memo. 1998-373.*

Sample case

A medical technician and a physician shared office space. The two often met at lunchtime to discuss the treatment of their patients and the details of office administration and operations. The two met at other times as well, but they found that lunchtime was often the best opportunity to meet. They alternated paying for their meals together. On her federal income tax return, the technician deducted her share of these meal expenses (subject to the 50 percent reduction that applies to unreimbursed meal expenses). The IRS disallowed any deduction for the meals on the ground that they were not a legitimate business expense. The technician appealed to the Tax Court.

Were the technician's lunch expenses deductible? After all, she discussed both treatment procedures and office operations during these lunches. Unfortunately, the court agreed with the IRS that the expenses were not deductible. It began its opinion by noting that "daily meals are an inherently personal expense, and a taxpayer bears a heavy burden in proving they are deductible" as a business expense.

The court referred to a previous ruling involving attorneys. Members of a law firm met every workday at a restaurant to discuss work-related matters. Lunchtime was selected for meetings because the lawyers were litigators, and court was not in session over the noon hour. A federal appeals court conceded the business purpose for these lunch meetings and that lawyers "did not dawdle over their lunch" but concluded that the meals represented nondeductible personal expenses, not business expenses. It observed:

> [I]t is undeniable that eating together fosters camaraderie and makes business dealings friendlier and easier. It thus reduces the costs of transacting business, for these costs include the frictions and the failures of communication that are produced by suspicion and mutual misunderstanding, by differences in tastes and manners, and by lack of rapport. A meeting with a client or customer in an office is therefore not a perfect substitute for a lunch with him in a restaurant. But it is different when all the participants in the meal are coworkers, as essentially was the case here. . . . They know each other well already; they don't need the social lubrication that a meal with an outsider provides—at least don't need it daily. If a large firm had a monthly lunch to allow partners to get to know associates, the expense of the meal might well be necessary, and would be allowed by the Internal Revenue Service. But [the law firm in this case] never had more than eight lawyers and did not need a daily lunch to cement relationships among them.

> We may assume it was necessary for the [attorneys] to meet daily to coordinate the work of the firm, and also . . . that lunch was the most convenient time. But it does not follow that the expense of the lunch was a necessary business expense. The members of the firm had to eat somewhere. . . . Although it saved time to combine lunch with work, the meal itself was not an organic part of the meeting. *Moss v. Commissioner, 758 F.2d 211 (7th Cir. 1985).*

EXAMPLE. The Tax Court ruled that lunch expenses incurred by a group of government attorneys who met for lunch one day each month were not business related, despite the fact that business was discussed. The court did concede that "an occasional luncheon meeting with the staff to discuss the operation of the firm would be regarded as an ordinary and necessary expense," as would "a luncheon to mark an anniversary, retirement or other occasion for an employee," since such expenses "aid in building morale and loyalty and serve as an inducement for others to work more efficiently." *Wells v. Commissioner, 36 T.C.M. 1690 (1977).*

Like the attorneys' lunches, the lunches shared by the medical technician and the physician were not

integral to the technician's business objectives and have not been clearly linked to her production of income. They met at lunchtime because that was the most convenient and feasible time to meet. Their business relationship was well established and did not require "social lubrication," at least not as often as [she and the physician] dined together. Indeed, the frequency of their lunches together and the reciprocal nature of their meal arrangement belie the existence of any business purpose for the meals. . . . If taxpayers were permitted to deduct meal expenses in such circumstances then . . . only the unimaginative would dine at their own expense.

Conclusions

Entertainment expenses. Local lunch expenses incurred by church employees qualify as a business expense and can be reimbursed by a church under an accountable expenses reimbursement arrangement only if they qualify as entertainment expenses. The requirements for substantiating entertainment expenses are strict. You must demonstrate that the expenses are either (1) directly related to the active conduct of your ministry, or (2) associated with the active conduct of your ministry, and the entertainment occurred directly before or after a substantial business discussion.

In order to show that entertainment was *directly related* to the active conduct of your business, you ordinarily must be able to demonstrate that (1) you had more than a general expectation of deriving income or some other specific business benefit at some indefinite future time; (2) you did engage in business during the entertainment period; and (3) the main purpose of the entertainment was the transaction of business.

In order to show that entertainment was *associated* with the active conduct of your ministry, you must be able to demonstrate that you had a clear business purpose in incurring the expense and that the meal or entertainment directly preceded or followed a substantial business discussion.

Frequent staff lunches. Frequent lunches with the same members of the church staff are much less likely to qualify as a business expense, even if church business is discussed. For example, if the same three church staff members go out to lunch every Friday, it is very unlikely that any of these lunches will qualify as a business expense. After all, these persons work in the same office and presumably have considerable interaction during the week. A shared lunch under these circumstances does not constitute an ordinary and necessary business expense.

❖ **KEY POINT.** It is worth noting that the attorneys in the *Wells* case (summarized in the example above) met for lunch one day each month. This was considered too frequent to be business-related.

Occasional lunches with non-staff members. Such lunches are more likely to qualify as entertainment expenses, and as a result, the costs of these lunches can be reimbursed by the church under an accountable expense reimbursement arrangement. To illustrate, a lunch arranged by a pastor with a local architect to discuss new building plans would qualify as a business expense.

Occasional employee lunches. The Tax Court, in a previous decision (the *Wells* case, summarized in the example above) addressing the deductibility of lunch expenses incurred by attorneys one day each month, conceded that "an occasional luncheon meeting with the staff to discuss the operation of the firm would be regarded as an ordinary and necessary expense," as would "a luncheon to mark an anniversary, retirement or other occasion for an employee," since such expenses "aid in building morale and loyalty and serve as an inducement for others to work more efficiently."

Lunch expenses while traveling. This section only addresses the reimbursement of local lunch expenses. Lunch expenses incurred while church employees are away from town on business travel are business related and can be reimbursed under an accountable arrangement.

Other requirements of an accountable arrangement. In order for your church to reimburse expenses under an accountable expense reimbursement arrangement, you must have adopted a reimbursement arrangement that meets certain requirements. See section E of this chapter. If any of these three requirements is not satisfied, the church's reimbursement of a lunch expense is nonaccountable, and the full amount of the reimbursement must be allocated to the employees' Forms W-2.

Intermediate sanctions. If lunch expenses do not constitute a business expense, it is important for church leaders to recognize that the church's reimbursement of these expenses is nonaccountable and must be reported as taxable compensation. If these reimbursements are not reported as taxable income to the employee in the year the reimbursements are paid, two consequences result: (1) the employee is subject to back taxes plus penalties and interest on the unreported income; and (2) if the benefits are provided to an officer or director of the church (a "disqualified person"), or a relative of such a person, they will expose the recipient and possibly other members of the church's governing board to intermediate sanctions in the form of substantial excise taxes, since the IRS now views this as automatic excess benefit unless it was reported as taxable income by the church or recipient in the year it was provided. This topic is covered fully in Chapter 4, section A.3. The lesson is clear. Sloppy church accounting practices can be costly to church staff.

Unreimbursed expenses. This section addresses the tax consequences of a church's reimbursement of employee lunch expenses. In some cases, church employees pay for their own lunch expenses. Such unreimbursed expenses may be deducted as an employee business expense, but only if reimbursement from the church was not available. Further, church employees may deduct only 50 percent of business-related entertainment expenses, including meals. This 50 percent limitation is incorporated directly into the tax returns (line 9 of Form 2106, and line 24 of Schedule C). Note, however, that the 50 percent limitation does not apply to expenses that are reimbursed by an employer under an accountable reimbursement plan. IRS Publication 463 states: "As an employee, you are not subject to the 50 percent limit if your employer reimburses you under an accountable plan and does not treat your reimbursement as wages." Publication 463 states that the self-employed persons also can avoid the 50 percent limitation through use of an accountable reimbursement arrangement.

Examples

The examples below illustrate the issues addressed in this section.

EXAMPLE. A church has three pastors who, for many years, have gone out to lunch every Friday. Church business is almost always discussed at these lunches. The cost of the lunches is always charged to a church credit card, and the church treasurer has never reported the church's reimbursements as taxable income to the pastors by including it on their Forms W-2.

This is incorrect. According to the rulings summarized in this section, these lunches do not qualify as business expenses, and as a result, they should not be charged to the church credit card. If the pastors continue to charge the lunches to the church credit card, the treasurer will need to allocate the reimbursed expenses to the pastors and report the reimbursements as taxable income on their Forms W-2 at the end of the year, since the reimbursements are nonaccountable. The treasurer need not withhold additional income taxes, because the pastors' wages are exempt from income tax withholding (unless they have elected voluntary withholding).

If nonaccountable reimbursements of the expenses of any church officer or board member are not reported as taxable income on Form W-2 or Form 1040 in the year they are provided, they constitute an automatic excess benefit resulting in intermediate sanctions in the form of substantial excise taxes that can be assessed against the recipient and possibly members of the church's governing board who authorized the transaction. This topic is addressed in Chapter 4, section A.3. Nonaccountable reimbursements of the expenses of church employees who are not officers or directors are not automatic excess benefits and will not result in intermediate sanctions. But they still must be reported as taxable compensation. Failure to do so will expose the employees to back taxes plus penalties and interest.

EXAMPLE. Same facts as the previous example, except that non-minister church employees, rather than pastors, are involved. The answer is the same, except that the church will need to withhold income taxes and FICA taxes from the value of the lunches.

EXAMPLE. A pastor occasionally meets church members for lunch and charges the cost of these lunches to the church credit card. The purpose of these lunches is for the pastor to become better acquainted with members and to provide spiritual guidance as needed. These expenses qualify as an entertainment expense. As a result, the expenses reimbursed by the church are accountable so long as the requirements for an accountable reimbursement (summarized in this section) are satisfied.

EXAMPLE. Same facts as the previous example, except that the pastor informs the church treasurer each month of the approximate amount he spent during the previous month on such lunches, and he receives a reimbursement check. This arrangement is nonaccountable, since the substantiation requirements for an accountable arrangement are not met. As a result, the treasurer will need to add the value of all lunch expense reimbursements to the pastor's Form W-2 at the end of the year. If nonaccountable reimbursements are not reported as taxable income on the employee's Form W-2 or Form 1040 in the year they are provided, they constitute an automatic excess benefit resulting in intermediate sanctions in the form of substantial excise taxes that can be assessed against the recipient of the benefit and members of the church's governing board. This topic is covered fully in Chapter 4, section A.3.

EXAMPLE. A pastor takes the church staff out to lunch twice each year as a means of expressing appreciation for their hard work. The cost of these lunches is charged to the church credit card. These expenses represent a legitimate business expense, and as a result, they can be reimbursed by the church under an accountable arrangement so long as they are adequately substantiated. The church treasurer would not report any of the reimbursements as taxable income. The Tax Court has noted that "an occasional luncheon meeting with the staff to discuss the operation of the firm would be regarded as an ordinary and necessary expense," as would "a luncheon to mark an anniversary, retirement or other occasion for an employee," since such expenses "aid in building morale and loyalty and serve as an inducement for others to work more efficiently." *Wells v. Commissioner, 36 T.C.M. 1690 (1977).*

EXAMPLE. A church's two pastors go out to lunch once each month. Church business is always discussed, and the cost of the lunches is charged to the church credit card. A federal appeals court has observed that monthly lunches by law firm members "might well be necessary, and would be allowed by the Internal Revenue Service." *Moss v. Commissioner, 758 F.2d 211 (7th Cir. 1985).* On the other hand, the Tax Court has ruled that monthly lunch expenses incurred by government attorneys were not business-related, despite the fact that business was discussed. *Wells v. Commissioner, 36 T.C.M. 1690 (1977).* In summary, while legal support does exist for treating monthly lunch expenses as business-related, support also exists for the opposite conclusion. This suggests that the business nature of monthly lunch expenses may be challenged by the IRS but that no penalties would be assessed.

4. BUSINESS GIFTS

You may deduct the cost of business gifts. However, you cannot deduct more than $25 for business gifts you give, directly or indirectly, to any one individual during your tax year. Such gifts would include gifts made by a minister to church staff or board members.

EXAMPLE. The Tax Court ruled that $2,300 in expenses incurred by a minister in one year to pay for plants, flowers, and other gifts to members and staff were a nondeductible personal expense rather than a deductible business expense. The court observed: "[The minister] testified that the gifts stemmed from a desire to foster goodwill among his parishioners and staff; however, [he has] not provided sufficient evidence to prove that these expenses were not personal. We find that [the minister] failed to prove that the gifts were not personal expenses; therefore, [he is] not entitled to deductions for these amounts." *Shelley v. Commissioner, T.C. Memo. 1994-432 (1994).*

5. EDUCATIONAL EXPENSES

General educational expenses

You may deduct expenses you have for education, such as tuition, books, supplies, correspondence courses, and certain travel and transportation expenses, even though the education may lead to a degree, if the education (1) is required by your employer, or by law or regulation, to keep your salary, status, or job or (2) maintains or improves skills required in your present work.

However, you may not deduct expenses incurred for education, even if one or both of the above-mentioned requirements are met, if the education (1) is required in order to meet the minimum educational requirements to qualify you in your trade or business or (2) is part of a program of study that will lead to qualifying you in a new trade or business, even if you did not intend to enter that trade or business.

You can deduct the costs of qualifying, work-related education as a business expense even if the education could lead to a degree.

Deductible expenses

The following education expenses can be deducted:

- Tuition, books, supplies, lab fees, and similar items.
- Certain transportation and travel costs.
- Other education expenses, such as costs of research and typing when writing a paper as part of an educational program.

Nondeductible expenses

You cannot deduct personal or capital expenses. For example, you cannot deduct the dollar value of vacation time or annual leave you take to attend classes. This amount is a personal expense.

Unclaimed reimbursement

If you do not claim reimbursement that you are entitled to receive from your employer, you cannot deduct the expenses that apply to the reimbursement.

EXAMPLE. Your employer agrees to pay your education expenses if you file a voucher showing your expenses. You do not file a voucher, and you do not get reimbursed. Because you did not file a voucher, you cannot deduct the expenses on your tax return.

Transportation expenses

If your education qualifies, you can deduct local transportation costs of going directly from work to school. If you are regularly employed and go to school on a temporary basis, you can also deduct the costs of returning from school to home. You go to school on a temporary basis if your attendance at school is realistically expected to last one year or less and does, indeed, last one year or less; or you initially believed that your attendance at school would last one year or less, but at a later date your attendance is reasonably expected to last more than one year (your attendance is temporary up to the date you determine it will last more than one year.) If you are in either situation, your attendance is not temporary if facts and circumstances indicate otherwise.

If you are regularly employed and go directly from home to school on a temporary basis, you can deduct the round-trip costs of transportation between your home and school. This is true regardless of the location of the school, the distance traveled, or whether you attend school on nonworkdays. Transportation expenses include the actual costs of bus, subway, cab, or other fares, as well as the costs of using your car. Transportation expenses do not include amounts spent for travel, meals, or lodging while you are away from home overnight.

If you use your car, you may deduct your actual expenses, or you may use the standard mileage rate to figure the amount you can deduct (see transportation expenses, above). You may not deduct the cost of local transportation between your home and school on a nonworking day (this expense is a personal commuting expense).

If you travel away from home mainly to obtain qualifying education, you may deduct your expenses for travel, meals, and lodging while away from home. However, you may not deduct expenses for personal activities such as sightseeing or entertaining. Educational expenses do not include travel as a form of education.

Examples

EXAMPLE. A youth pastor takes a course at a nearby college three nights each week for three months. The course improves the youth pastor's job skills. Since he is attending school on a temporary basis, he can deduct his daily round-trip transportation expenses in going between home and school. This is true regardless of the distance traveled.

EXAMPLE. Assume the same facts as the previous example except that the youth pastor attends classes twice a week for 15 months. Since his attendance in school is not considered temporary, he cannot deduct his transportation expenses in going between home and school. However, if he goes directly from work to school, he can deduct the one-way transportation expenses of going from work to school. If he goes from work to home to school and returns home, his transportation expenses cannot be more than if he had gone directly from work to school.

EXAMPLE. Pastor D takes a counseling course at a local university. Expenses associated with the course are deductible educational expenses if the course maintains or improves job skills and is not a part of a program of study that will qualify Pastor D for a new trade or business.

EXAMPLE. Pastor D takes accounting courses at a local university in order to qualify for the CPA examination. Such courses are clearly part of a program of study that will qualify Pastor D for a new trade or business and accordingly are not deductible as education expenses, even if Pastor D insists that she is pursuing her studies solely to improve her job skills as a minister.

EXAMPLE. A minister who is not a college graduate can claim as education expenses the costs of obtaining a college degree if the degree will not qualify him for a new trade or business. *Glasgow v. Commissioner, 31 T.C.M. 310 (1972).*

EXAMPLE. Pastor B, a minister of music, enrolled in several music courses at a local college. Expenses associated with such courses were not deductible education expenses, since the courses qualified the minister for a new trade or business of being a public school or junior college instructor. *Burt v. Commissioner, 40 T.C.M. 1164 (1980).*

EXAMPLE. J is a 25-year-old seminary student. She is not employed while attending school and has never previously served as a minister of a church. Her educational expenses are not deductible, since they (1) are not related to a current job, (2) are required in order to meet the minimum educational requirements to qualify her in her "trade or business," and (3) are part of a program of study that will lead to qualifying her in a new trade or business.

EXAMPLE. A minister who serves a local church without compensation cannot deduct the cost of his educational expenses, since an uncompensated minister is not engaged in trade or business. *IRS Letter Ruling 9431024.*

EXAMPLE. The Tax Court ruled that a minister could not deduct the cost of courses he took at a local university to complete his undergraduate degree, even though he took the courses to enhance his ministerial skills. The minister enrolled in various courses at a local university (including Introduction to Counseling, Internship in Ministry Practice, Death and Dying as a Life Cycle, Modern Social Problems, The Family, Community, Ethics in Human Services, Symphonic Choir, Basic Writing, and Writing Strategies). These courses were not required for him to continue as a local pastor. He later earned a bachelor's degree in human services. On his tax return he claimed a deduction of $9,698 for "continuing education." The amount claimed represented tuition, books, and course-related fees incurred for the courses taken at the university.

The IRS disallowed the deduction, and the minister appealed. The Tax Court agreed that the educational expenses were not deductible. It acknowledged that education expenses are deductible as business expenses if the education "maintains or improves skills required by the taxpayer in his employment or meets the express requirements of an employer imposed as a condition for the taxpayer's continued employment." However, education expenses are not deductible if they are "made by an individual for education which is part of a program of study being pursued by him which will lead to qualifying him in a new trade or business." This is so even if the courses meet the express requirements of the employer.

Whether the education qualifies a taxpayer for a new trade or business depends upon the "tasks and activities which he was qualified to perform before the education and those which he is qualified to perform afterwards." The court noted that it had "repeatedly disallowed education expenses where the education qualified the taxpayer to perform significantly different tasks and activities. Further, the taxpayer's subjective purpose in pursuing the education is irrelevant, and the question of deductibility is not satisfied by a showing that the taxpayer did not in fact carry on or did not intend to carry on a new trade or business." The court agreed that the courses the minister took qualified him for a new trade or business and that the expenses of a college education are almost always nondeductible personal expenses.

The court concluded, "We conclude that the courses, which ultimately led to his bachelor's degree, qualified him in a new trade or business. The courses provided him with a background in a variety of social issues that could have prepared him for employment with several public agencies and private nonprofit organizations outside of the ministry. Whether or not he remains in the ministry is irrelevant; what is important under the regulations is that the degree 'will lead' him to qualify for a new trade or business." The court noted that it is "all but impossible" for taxpayers to establish that a bachelor's degree program does not qualify them for a new trade or business. *Warren v. Commissioner, T.C. Memo. 2003-175 (2003).*

Employer-provided educational assistance

Some educational expenses paid by your employer may be excluded from your income. See the discussion of employer-provided educational assistance programs in Chapter 5, section I.7.

6. SUBSCRIPTIONS AND BOOKS

The income tax regulations specify that "a professional . . . may claim as deductions the cost of . . . subscriptions to professional journals [and] amounts currently paid for books . . . the useful life of which is short." *Treas. Reg. 1.162-6.*

The cost of a subscription will be deductible as a business expense if it is related to the conduct of a minister's trade or business. Professional clergy journals (such as *Church Law & Tax Report*) and specialized clergy periodicals clearly satisfy this test. News magazines may also qualify if a minister can demonstrate that the information contained in such periodicals is related to his or her ministry (e.g., sources of illustrations for sermons). The cost of a general circulation daily newspaper is not deductible.

The unreimbursed cost of books that are related to one's ministry is a business expense. The same is true for the cost of books reimbursed by the church under a nonaccountable arrangement. Deduct the cost of any book that you acquired for use in your ministry and that has a useful life (not the same as its physical life) of less than one year. For example, the cost of a book that you purchase and read, but have no intention of using again, can be deducted in full in the year of purchase.

The unreimbursed cost of commentaries or theological dictionaries and encyclopedias that are acquired for extended reference use also may be deducted fully in the year of purchase using the section 179 deduction (see section C.1 in this chapter). Most ministers prefer to deduct the entire cost of reference books in the year of purchase using the section 179 deduction. Alternatively, ministers can allocate the purchase price of reference books to their useful life by means of annual depreciation deductions. The depreciation deduction is computed using the Modified Accelerated Cost Recovery System (MACRS) method. See IRS Publication 946 for details.

Property must be used more than 50 percent for business purposes to be eligible for a section 179 deduction or to use the MACRS method of computing depreciation. You must indicate on IRS Form 4562 that you have elected to claim the section 179 deduction in the year of acquisition. Form 4562 is submitted with your Form 1040.

Religious books generally are used exclusively in a minister's work, so no allocation is required between business and personal use.

Ministers who are self-employed for income tax purposes claim the deduction for book and subscription expenses directly on Schedule

C. Ministers who report their income taxes as employees may deduct these expenses only as an itemized deduction on Schedule A. This means that they cannot claim any deduction if they do not have sufficient deductions to itemize on Schedule A. This rule is avoided if business expenses are reimbursed by one's employer under an accountable arrangement (see section E of this chapter).

❈ **KEY POINT.** Often a church will pay for the cost of a minister's periodicals and books. The question of whether the minister or the church retains ownership of books paid for by the church following the minister's resignation is addressed fully in section E of this chapter.

EXAMPLE. Pastor S claimed deductions for the costs of publications used in his ministry. He claimed that he was reimbursed by the church for amounts he spent on business publications in excess of $1,600. He presented canceled checks and a summary of some of the publication expenses for each of the years in issue. The IRS disallowed the deductions in full, arguing that the evidence failed to establish that the publications were related to his business. The Tax Court disagreed, concluding that "based on [Pastor S's] testimony and notations made on the checks, we conclude that [he] has established that the expenses were related to his ministry and that he has substantiated the claimed deduction in each of the years in issue." *Shelley v. Commissioner, T.C. Memo. 1994-432 (1994).*

EXAMPLE. An ordained minister wrote several manuscripts on religion and other subjects but only submitted one for publication (it was not accepted). The minister claimed a depreciation deduction of $8,000 for depreciation on his professional library of 6,400 books (with an alleged purchase price of $160,000), plus an additional $1,320 for depreciation on various office equipment, such as desks, bookcases, filing cabinets, furniture, and computers. He insisted that he was engaged in the trade or business of writing, so he was entitled to deduct the depreciation on his library and home office equipment.

The IRS denied any deduction for the minister's library, and the Tax Court agreed. It observed that for the minister to be able to deduct writing expenses, "he must prove that profit was the primary or dominant purpose for engaging in the activity." The court referred to the income tax regulation's list of factors to consider in deciding whether a taxpayer is engaged in an activity with a profit objective: "(1) the manner in which the taxpayer carried on the activity; (2) the expertise of the taxpayer or his advisers; (3) the time and effort expended by the taxpayer in carrying on the activity; (4) the expectation that the assets used in the activity may appreciate in value; (5) the success of the taxpayer in carrying on other similar or dissimilar activities; (6) the taxpayer's history of income or loss with respect to the activity; (7) the amount of occasional profits that are earned; (8) the financial status of the taxpayer; and (9) whether elements of personal pleasure or recreation are involved. No single factor is controlling, and we do not reach our decision by merely counting the factors that support each party's position." *Treas. Reg. 1.183-2(b).*

The court concluded that the minister's writing activity was not motivated by profit according to these considerations, and as a result he could not deduct depreciation expenses associated with this activity: "[He] did not carry on this activity in a business-like manner, as he did not maintain any books and records. Moreover [he] submitted only one manuscript for publication and earned no income from his writing activity. In addition, he did not demonstrate that he changed his operation to improve profitability, had a business plan, or investigated the basic factors that affect profitability." *Nauman v. Commissioner, T.C. Memo. 1998-217.*

7. PERSONAL COMPUTERS

▲ **CAUTION.** *A church cannot reimburse employees' expenses under an accountable reimbursement arrangement that do not qualify as business expenses. Such reimbursements, as well as a church's reimbursement of employees' unsubstantiated business expenses, are nonaccountable. If these reimbursements are not reported as taxable income to the employee in the year the reimbursements are paid, two consequences result: (1) the employee is subject to back taxes plus penalties and interest on the unreported income; and (2) if the benefits are provided to an officer or director of the church (a "disqualified person"), or a relative of such a person, they will expose the recipient and possibly other members of the church's governing board to intermediate sanctions in the form of substantial excise taxes, since the IRS views these benefits as automatic excess benefits unless reported as taxable income by the church or recipient in the year provided. This topic is covered fully in Chapter 4, section A.3. The lesson is clear: sloppy church accounting practices can be costly to church staff.*

❈ **KEY POINT.** The IRS has issued audit guidelines for its agents to follow when auditing corporate executives. The guidelines are instructive in evaluating the compensation packages provided to senior pastors and other church employees. The guidelines specify: "Special record-keeping rules apply to computers except for those used exclusively at the business establishment and owned or leased by the person operating the business. Detailed records are required to establish business use of computers that can be taken home or are kept at home by the executives. There are no recordkeeping exceptions like 'no personal use' available for computers. . . . This requires documentation of business usage in order for the purchase and operational cost to be an allowable deduction and not included as income to the executive."

Many church employees are provided with a church-owned computer that they use in the performance of their duties. Others own a computer that they use for both personal and business purposes. The tax rules associated with both scenarios are summarized below.

Church-owned computer

There are no tax issues associated with the use of an employer-provided computer exclusively for business purposes, since no taxable income is generated as a result of such an arrangement. However, many employees uses an employer-provided computer for personal reasons, and this personal use constitutes a taxable fringe benefit that must be valued and reported on their Form W-2. If the personal use is minimal or infrequent, it may qualify as a nontaxable de minimis fringe benefit (see Chapter 5, section I.4). If the personal use is significant, then it must be valued and reported as taxable income. The IRS has not clarified how this is done other than to say it depends on the facts and circumstances; but many employers follow one of the following two rules:

- The employer provides employees who use an employer-owned computer for occasional personal use (including Internet access) with a taxable "stipend" that is a good faith estimate of the value of the personal use.
- The income tax regulations specify that "if an employer exercises sufficient control and imposes significant restrictions on the personal use of a company copying machine so that at least 85 percent of the use of the machine is for business purposes, any personal use of the copying machine by particular employees is considered to be a [nontaxable] de minimis fringe." *Treas. Reg. 1.132-6.* Some employers apply this rule to employer-provided computers that are located on their business premises. That is, so long as the computer is used at least 85 percent of the time for business purposes, any personal use by an employee is deemed to be a nontaxable de minimis fringe benefit. This rule would not apply to copy machines or computers that are not located on the employer's premises. That is, if a church provides an employee with a portable computer that is often taken home by the employee, there is no presumption that personal use is a de minimis fringe benefit.

Note that neither of these options has ever been officially recognized by the IRS or the courts.

Personally owned computer

Church employees who purchase a computer that is used for business as well as personal use may be entitled to deduct the cost of the computer in the year of purchase or to claim an annual depreciation deduction over the useful life of the computer. However, note that personal computers are "listed property" and, as a result, are subject to strict substantiation requirements regarding business use. Here are the rules that apply:

Depreciation
You can claim a depreciation deduction for a computer that you use in your work as an employee if its use is

- for the convenience of your employer and
- required as a condition of your employment.

For the convenience of your employer. Your use of the computer in your home must be for the convenience of your employer. This means you must be able to clearly demonstrate that you cannot perform your job without the home computer. The fact that the computer enables you to perform your work more easily and efficiently is not enough. Further, you must prove that the computers available at your place of employment are insufficient to enable you to properly perform your job. Obviously, this is a difficult test to satisfy.

Required as a condition of your employment. Your use of the computer in your home must be required as a condition of your employment. This means you must not be able to properly perform your duties without the computer. It is not necessary that your employer explicitly requires you to use the computer. On the other hand, it is not enough that your employer merely states that your use of the home computer is a condition of your employment. If you are an employee and these tests are not met, you cannot deduct any of the cost of your home computer. *IRC 280F, Revenue Ruling 86-129.*

If you are an employee and you meet both tests described above, or if you are self-employed, then you can claim a section 179 deduction if you use your home computer more than 50 percent of the time during the year in your work. This means you can deduct the entire cost (up to $560,000 for 2012) in the year of purchase. However, this assumes that you can substantiate your "business use percentage" (the percentage of total use that consists of business use). Your section 179 deduction is limited to the percentage of business use of the computer.

You compute your section 179 deduction on Form 4562. Section 4562 requires the following information regarding personal computers: (1) date first placed in service as a business asset; (2) business use percentage for the year; (3) cost; and (4) evidence to support the business use claimed. Your evidence supporting the business use of the computer must be in writing.

▲ **CAUTION.** *If you do not claim a section 179 deduction on Form 4562, you will not be eligible for the deduction. You will have to depreciate the computer over its useful life (five years) and claim a depreciation deduction each year.*

If you cannot prove your business use percentage, or if your business use percentage is less than 50 percent of total use, then you may not expense the cost in the year of purchase by claiming a section 179 deduction. Instead, you must depreciate the computer using the straight-line method over the five-year recovery period (i.e., the annual depreciation expense is the cost of the computer divided by five years). Using your computer to keep track of your personal investments does not count in determining whether you satisfy the "50 percent business use" test. On the other hand, if you meet the 50 percent business use test without considering use of the computer for investments, you may include your use of the computer for investments in computing your deduction.

❖ **KEY POINT.** Section 280F(d)(4)(B) of the tax code exempts from the definition of listed property "any computer or peripheral equipment used exclusively at a regular business establishment and owned or leased by the person operating such establishment. [Any] portion of a dwelling unit shall be treated as a regular business establishment if (and only if) the requirements of [a home office deduction are met]."

EXAMPLE. The Tax Court ruled that a minister was not entitled to a tax deduction for the purchase of a computer that he used in his ministry. It noted that the tax code imposes strict substantiation requirements on the business use of any property designated as "listed property" and that personal computers are included in this definition. The court concluded: "The taxpayer's testimony described the purchase of video equipment and tapes for preparing, editing, and duplicating video tapes for [his] ministry. He claimed that he bought such equipment in 2001 but also testified that he could not remember honestly. This testimony is insufficient to satisfy the strict substantiation requirement of applicable to computers as listed property." *Vigil v. Commissioner, T.C. Summary Opinion 2008-6 (2008).*

EXAMPLE. Pastor R purchases a personal computer (for $2,000 in 2013) that he uses 60 percent for business, 20 percent for investments, and 20 percent for personal activities. Since he uses it more than 50 percent for business purposes, he can take the Modified Accelerated Cost Recovery System (MACRS) depreciation deductions over the five-year recovery period, or he can expense the cost of the computer in the year of purchase by claiming a section 179 deduction. Since costs incurred in investment activities ordinarily are deductible, Pastor R computes his annual depreciation deduction by multiplying the annual MACRS percentage (from tables in IRS publication 946) by his unadjusted basis in the computer (original cost less any section 179 deduction) times the combined business and investment usage (80 percent).

EXAMPLE. Same facts as the preceding example, except that Pastor R uses the computer 40 percent for business, 30 percent for investments, and 30 percent for personal activities. Since his business usage is less than 50 percent, he is not eligible for the section 179 deduction and must figure a depreciation deduction under the MACRS using the straight-line method over the "alternative depreciation system" (ADS) recovery period. *Treas. Reg. 1.280F-6T(d)(5).*

EXAMPLE. The Tax Court ruled that an employee could not claim any deduction for the business use of her personal computer, since she failed to maintain any records demonstrating the percentage of total use that was for business purposes. *Kelly v. Commissioner, T.C. Memo. 1997-185.*

EXAMPLE. A taxpayer purchased a personal computer and deducted the entire cost as a business expense in the year of purchase.

The IRS audited the taxpayer and disallowed the deduction. It pointed out that the taxpayer failed to make any section 179 election in the year the computer was purchased, so he could not deduct the full cost of the computer in that year. The Tax Court agreed. It noted that section 179 of the tax code permits a taxpayer to deduct the entire cost of many kinds of business equipment in the year of purchase—but only if a section 179 election is made on the taxpayer's tax return. This is done on Form 4562, the depreciation schedule that accompanies Form 1040. If this election is not made, then a taxpayer has no choice but to claim annual depreciation deductions over the useful life of the computer or other business equipment. *Fors v. Commissioner, T.C. Memo. 1998-158 (1998).*

EXAMPLE. A taxpayer claimed a business expense deduction for his personal computer equipment. The IRS denied the deduction, and the taxpayer appealed. The Tax Court noted that any computer or peripheral equipment is "listed property" that is subject to stricter substantiation rules. Among other things, the taxpayer must demonstrate that business use exceeds 50 percent. The court concluded: "Based on his testimony and the evidence introduced at trial, petitioner failed to establish the percentage of business use for the computer and peripheral equipment. Rather, at trial petitioner merely asserted 'these are office expenses' and then proceeded to name each item purchased and the amount purportedly incurred for it. Furthermore, even if petitioner had established the business-use percentage for such items, he failed to satisfy all of the stringent substantiation requirements." *Whalley v. Commissioner, 72 T.C.M. 1422 (1996).*

EXAMPLE. A school adopted a rule requiring teachers to switch from written report cards and evaluations to a computerized format. The school had eight computers that were available for faculty and student use. One teacher purchased a $3,233 personal computer and deducted the entire cost on her tax return as a section 179 deduction. The teacher claimed that due to the insufficient number of computers available at her school for faculty to use in preparing their reports, and the confidentiality and security problems which existed at the school, it was necessary for her to purchase a computer to properly perform the duties of her employment. She also claimed that without her own computer she would be unable to timely prepare her reports and evaluations, and for these reasons she argued that the computer was required as a condition of employment.

The Tax Court denied the deduction. It noted that the computer was "listed property," and as such the teacher could not claim a section 179 deduction for the full cost unless her use of the computer was for the convenience of the employer and was required as a condition of her employment. The court noted that the purchase of the computer was not required as a condition of her employment: "Although a computer was needed [by the teacher] to file her reports and evaluations, the school had computers which could be used for this purpose. Furthermore, we note that

there were several teachers who did not own personal computers and, nonetheless, they were able to file timely reports and evaluations. . . . In short, it is amply clear on this record that a personal computer was not required for the proper performance by school teachers of their employment duties. Although it may have been more convenient for [the teacher] to use her own personal computer, we must, as the statute requires, focus on the convenience of the employer and not the convenience of the employee. Moreover, the record shows that . . . the school continually purchased additional computers available for faculty and student use. Consequently, it is evident that the 'convenience of employer' requirement is not satisfied since [the teacher's] purchase of a personal computer did not spare her employer the cost of providing her with suitable equipment with which to engage in her job responsibilities." *Bryant v. Commissioner, 66 T.C.M. 1594 (1993).*

➠ **TIP.** Some churches provide a personal computer to their pastors or other staff members. If the computer is used for personal as well as business purposes, the personal use should be valued and reported as taxable income. See section C.7 in this chapter for further information.

8. CLOTHING AND LAUNDRY

You may be able to deduct the cost of clothing (including cleaning expenses) that you use in your ministry if the clothing (1) is of a type specifically required as a condition of employment, (2) is not adaptable to general or continued usage to the extent that it could take the place of ordinary clothing, and (3) is not so worn.

As with any professional or business expense, such an expense is deductible on Schedule C by a self-employed minister and may be deductible on Schedule A by a minister-employee (to the extent that he or she itemizes deductions, and then only to the extent that most miscellaneous expenses exceed 2 percent of adjusted gross income)—see section E of this chapter for further details. Ministers can avoid these restrictions by having their church adopt an accountable reimbursement policy (explained fully in section E).

EXAMPLE. Pastor P serves as senior pastor of a church. Ministers in his denomination wear ordinary clothing (not vestments) in the performance of their ministerial duties. Pastor P believes he should be able to claim the cost of his suits as a business expense, since he must wear suits in the performance of his duties. His position is in error and would not be upheld by the IRS or the courts, since he does not satisfy the second and third conditions discussed above and may not be considered to have met the first.

EXAMPLE. A church pays a monthly clothing allowance to its minister. The Tax Court concluded that these amounts represented taxable income and were not deductible. The court observed that the tax law "provides a comprehensive definition of gross income" and that this term "includes income realized in any form, whether in money, property, or services." Accordingly, "income may be realized in the form of clothing as well as in cash." In rejecting any deduction for the cost of the taxpayer's clothing, the court noted that "the cost of acquisition and maintenance of uniforms is deductible generally if (1) the clothing is of a type specifically required as a condition of employment, (2) it is not adaptable to general usage as ordinary clothing, and (3) it is not so worn. There is no indication in this record that the amount of the clothing allowance is for uniforms or special clothing." *Kalms v. Commissioner, T.C. Memo 1992-394.*

EXAMPLE. Pastor S claimed laundry and dry cleaning deductions of more than $300 per year. To support the deductions, he presented canceled checks on which he had made notations. The IRS disallowed these deductions in full. The Tax Court mostly agreed: "Expenses of maintaining a professional wardrobe generally are nondeductible personal expenditures. Expenses for clothing are deductible only if the clothing is required for the taxpayer's employment, is not suitable for general and personal wear, and is not so worn. Thus [Pastor S] is permitted to deduct the cost of cleaning his robes and similar items. Only one check for $8 . . . bears a notation indicating that payment was for cleaning of [Pastor S's] robe and stole. Neither [Pastor S's] testimony nor the notations on the other checks in evidence, are sufficient to establish that the remaining cleaning expenses claimed were not personal. Consequently, [Pastor S is] entitled to deduct only $8 for laundry expenses." *Shelley v. Commissioner, T.C. Memo. 1994-432 (1994).*

EXAMPLE. A pastor claimed a deduction of $4,900 for robes and dry cleaning. He insisted that he was required to wear business suits that he would not otherwise have worn because of the nature of his employment. The Tax Court disallowed this deduction. It concluded, "[E]ven if this were correct, the cost of clothing is only deductible if the clothing is of a type specifically required as a condition of employment and is not adaptable as ordinary clothing. This rule also applies to the maintenance of such clothing. There is no indication in the record that the amounts disallowed were for clothing that could not be worn in an ordinary way." *Swaringer v. Commissioner, T.C. Summary Opinion 2001-37 (2001).*

9. OFFICE IN THE HOME

KEY POINT. Most ministers have an office in their home. For the costs of such an office to be deductible as a business expense, several conditions must be satisfied. For example, the office must be used exclusively and regularly in the minister's trade or business. More stringent rules apply to ministers who are employees for income tax purposes.

KEY POINT. Taxpayers can claim a home office deduction if they use their home office for largely administrative tasks—even if their income-generating activities occur at another location. But the home office must be used regularly and exclusively for business purposes.

Many ministers maintain an office in their home. For some ministers, their "home office" is simply a desk or table in a corner of a bedroom. For others, it is a separate room that is used either regularly or exclusively for business purposes. Can any of the expenses associated with such offices be deducted as a business expense?

General rule—housing allowance precludes a home office deduction

In 1964 the Tax Court ruled that section 265 of the tax code (which denies a deduction for any expense allocable to tax-exempt income) prevented a minister from deducting his unreimbursed transportation expenses to the extent they were allocable to his tax-exempt housing allowance. To illustrate, assume that a minister receives compensation of $50,000, of which $10,000 is an excludable housing allowance, and incurs unreimbursed business expenses of $1,500. Since one-fifth of the minister's compensation is tax-exempt, he should not be permitted to deduct one-fifth of his business expenses, since they are allocable to tax-exempt income and their deduction would amount to a double deduction. As a result, the minister can deduct only $1,200 of his unreimbursed business expenses. *Deason v. Commissioner, 41 T.C. 465 (1964).*

This principle is commonly thought to apply to the home office expenses of a minister, meaning that ministers who claim a housing allowance or parsonage exclusion are not entitled to the home office deduction. This is the view taken by the IRS in its audit guidelines for ministers.

KEY POINT. The IRS audit guidelines for ministers instruct IRS agents to take the position that ministers who exclude all of their housing expenses as a housing allowance exclusion have deducted all of the expenses associated with an office in the home and should not be able to claim any additional deduction of such expenses as an itemized (home office) deduction on Schedule A.

A limited exception

Some ministers are not able to claim all of their home expenses in computing their housing allowance exclusion. To illustrate, some churches designate an allowance that is less than actual expenses. Other churches fail to designate an allowance at all. In these cases, a partial home office deduction (in some cases a full deduction) may be permissible under the *Deason* ruling. Since neither the IRS nor any court has addressed or endorsed this position, it should not be adopted without the advice of a tax professional.

Four requirements for a home office deduction

Even if the limited exception applies, it is still unlikely that a home office deduction will be available because the requirements are so difficult to meet. For ministers to be eligible for a home office deduction, the following four requirements must be met:

Exclusive use

The home office must be exclusively used in the minister's "trade or business." This means the home office must not be used by other family members (for example, to watch television or do homework). The use of a part of your home for *both* personal and business purposes does not meet the exclusive use test. If, for example, you use a room in your home for personal purposes as well as a place where you prepare sermons and occasionally counsel church members, you may not deduct any expenses for the business use of that part of your home.

Regular basis

The home office must be used on a regular basis in the minister's "trade or business." This means the home office must be used on a continuous basis by the minister for professional purposes (e.g., preparing sermons, conducting counseling, doing research, contacting members, writing correspondence, preparing for board meetings). Occasional or incidental use of the office for such purposes is not enough, even if the office is used for no other purposes.

Convenience of the employer

If the minister is an employee, the home office must be for the convenience of the employer. This means the home office must do more than make the employee's job more easy or efficient—it must be essential to the performance of the job. This ordinarily is not the case when an office is available in the church.

The courts and the IRS have ruled that if an employer provides employees access to an office on its premises for the performance of their duties and an employee elects to conduct these duties at home as a matter of personal preference, the employee's use of the home office is not for the convenience of the employer, and no deduction is allowed.

Principal place of business

The home office must be the minister's principal place of business. You may have a principal place of business for each trade or business. For example, as a minister, your principal place of business ordinarily will be your church. Investment activities on your own behalf do not constitute a trade or business.

Taxpayers may be eligible for a home office deduction if they use their home office for largely administrative tasks—even if their income-generating activities occur at another location. The tax code specifies that a home office qualifies as a principal place of business if (1) the office is used by the taxpayer exclusively and regularly to conduct administrative or management activities related to a trade or business, and (2) there is no other fixed location where the taxpayer conducts substantial administrative and management activities of the trade or business.

Many activities are administrative or managerial in nature. The following activities performed by you or others will not disqualify your home office from being your principal place of business.

- You have others conduct your administrative or management activities at locations other than your home.
- You conduct administrative or management activities at places that are not fixed locations of your business, such as in a car or a hotel room.
- You occasionally conduct minimal administrative or management activities at a fixed location outside your home.
- You conduct substantial nonadministrative or nonmanagement business activities at a fixed location outside your home. (For example, you meet with or provide services to church members at a fixed location outside your home.)
- You have suitable space to conduct administrative or management activities outside your home but choose to use your home office for those activities instead.

Taxpayers who meet these requirements are eligible for a home office deduction even if they conduct some administrative and management activities at a fixed location of their business outside their home—so long as those activities are not substantial. For example, a taxpayer occasionally does minimal paperwork at another fixed location of the business. Further, taxpayers can claim a home office deduction even though they conduct substantial *nonadministrative* or *nonmanagement business activities* at a fixed location of their business outside their home. For example, a taxpayer meets with or provides services to customers or clients at a fixed location that is away from home.

Conclusions

Ministers who satisfy the requirements summarized above may be able to claim a full or partial deduction of their home office expenses—assuming that the limited exception applies. Perhaps even more importantly, they may be able to deduct their transportation costs from their home to their church, since they are traveling from one business location to another and, as a result, are not commuting. In many cases, these transportation costs will exceed the value of a home office deduction. However, ministers must recognize that few will be able to satisfy all of the requirements. After all, how many ministers have a home office that is used exclusively and regularly for business purposes and do not have an office in the church?

✿ **KEY POINT.** Those few ministers who satisfy the requirements for a home office will be permitted to deduct their home office expenses. Perhaps even more importantly, they may be able to deduct their transportation costs from their home to their church. This is a significant benefit, since these costs generally will far exceed the value of a home office deduction. However, ministers must recognize that few will be able to satisfy all four requirements for a home office deduction.

Computing the deduction

To figure the percentage of your home used for business, compare the square feet of space used for business to the total square feet in your home. Or, if the rooms in your home are approximately the same size, you may compare the number of rooms used for business to the total number of rooms in your home. You figure the business part of your expenses by applying the percentage to the total of each expense.

The deduction of home office expenses is limited to the gross income from that business use minus the sum of (1) the business percentage of the mortgage interest, real estate taxes, and casualty losses; and (2) the business expenses other than those related to the business use of a home. As a result, the deduction is limited to a modified net income from the business use of the home. Deductions in excess of the limit may be carried over to later years.

Deductible expenses include all the business portion of all operating expenses (utilities, repairs, mortgage payments, insurance, property taxes, etc.) plus depreciation.

As an employee, you must itemize deductions on Schedule A (Form 1040) to claim a deduction for the business use of your home and any other employee business expenses. If you have employee expenses for which you were not reimbursed, report them on Schedule A, line 21. If your employer paid part of your home office expenses, you may have to complete Form 2106. See IRS Publication 587 for details. Self-employed ministers compute their home office deduction on Form 8829 and report the deduction on Schedule C (line 30).

IRS audit guidelines for ministers

The IRS has published audit guidelines for its agents to follow when auditing ministers. The guidelines provide IRS agents with the following information regarding the business use of a home:

> In order for a home to qualify as a principal place of business . . . the functions performed and the time spent at each location where the trade or business is conducted are the primary considerations and must be compared to determine the relative importance of each.

> The church often provides an office on the premises for the minister, so the necessity of an office in the home should be questioned closely. Furthermore, since the total cost to provide the home is used in computing the exempt housing allowance, home office deductions for taxes, insurance, mortgage interest, etc. would be duplications. (Note that itemized deductions are allowable for mortgage interest and taxes.)

❖ KEY POINT. The guidelines instruct agents to "question closely" the necessity of a home office. This is a business expense that invites scrutiny. It should not be claimed unless there is a reasonable basis for it.

❖ KEY POINT. The guidelines take the view that a minister who excludes all of his or her housing expenses as a housing allowance exclusion has in effect already "deducted" all of the expenses associated with an office in the home and, accordingly, should not be able to claim any additional deduction of such expenses as an itemized (home office) deduction on Schedule A.

Examples

In each of the following examples, assume that the limited exception (see above) applies.

EXAMPLE. Pastor V reports his income taxes as an employee. He has an office at his church but also maintains an office in his home, where he occasionally does research and other work-related activities. He also uses his home office to monitor investments and assist his children with their homework. Pastor V is not eligible for a home office deduction for two reasons. First, his home office is not used exclusively for business purposes. Second, his home office is not for the convenience of his employer, since an office is available at the church where Pastor V can perform all of his work-related duties.

EXAMPLE. Pastor H is the pastor of a small congregation. He reports his income taxes as an employee. The church does not maintain an office for Pastor H, so he performs all of his work-related administrative tasks at a home office that he uses regularly and exclusively in performing his duties. While Pastor H performs all of his nonadministrative duties (preaching, sacraments) at the church, all of his administrative tasks (sermon preparation, business planning) are performed at his home office. Pastor H qualifies for a home office deduction.

EXAMPLE. A church provides Pastor K with a small office where she can perform many of her pastoral duties, including sermon preparation and counseling. The church does not require her to work at home. Pastor K prefers to use the office she has set up in her home and does not use the one provided by the church. She uses this home office exclusively and regularly for the administrative duties of her job. She must meet the convenience of the employer test, even if her home qualifies as her principal place of business for deducting expenses for its use. Her employer provides her with an office and does not require her to work at home, so she does not meet the convenience of the employer test and cannot claim a deduction for the business use of her home.

EXAMPLE. Pastor H had an office at the church (his principal place of work) and an office in his home, where he prepared sermons and performed other ministerial duties. The Tax Court ruled that he could not deduct the costs of daily round trips by car between his home and church. The transportation was commuting. *Hamblen v. Commissioner, 78 T.C. 53 (1981).*

PERSONAL USE OF AN EMPLOYER'S INTERNET CONNECTION

Many church employees have an Internet connection on their office computer. Employees who use the Internet connection for personal purposes are receiving a taxable fringe benefit unless the limited de minimis exception applies (see Chapter 5, section I.4). Under this exception, benefits that are so immaterial in value that it would be unreasonable and or administratively impractical to account for them are nontaxable. This exception would apply, for example, to an employee who uses an employer-provided Internet connection for a few minutes each month. It would not apply to employees who use an employer-provided Internet connection several times each month for significant amounts of time.

Internet usage is considered to be a utility expense by the Tax Court and, as a result, is not subject to the strict substantiation rules that apply to listed property. To illustrate, the Tax Court has noted that "Internet expenses are utility expenses. Strict substantiation therefore does not apply, and the Court may . . . estimate petitioners' deductible expense, provided that the Court has a reasonable basis for making an estimate."

Nevertheless, to avoid the problems associated with a failure to report taxable fringe benefits as taxable income, especially in the case of employees who are officers or directors (or their relatives), and to avoid the burden of accounting for personal use, a growing number of employers are adopting one of the following two approaches: (1) Characterize a small portion of employees' compensation as an Internet stipend to cover a reasonable estimate of the value of personal use. This amount is reported as taxable compensation to the employees. (2) Classify the estimated value of the personal Internet usage as an "in kind" taxable benefit.

EXAMPLE. A minister claimed a deduction for a home office based on the fact that approximately 18 percent of his home was used for a home office. Accordingly, the minister claimed a deduction for 18 percent of the maintenance and repair expenses incurred with respect to his home. The Tax Court denied any home office deduction. It noted that to deduct home office expenses, a taxpayer must prove that a specific portion of his residence was used exclusively for business. However, in this case, the court concluded that the minister's "testimony makes clear that the office was used both as an office and as a guest room. Thus, his office fails the exclusive use test. Accordingly, we find that the minister cannot claim deductions attributable to a home office." *Shelley v. Commissioner, T.C. Memo. 1994-432 (1994).*

EXAMPLE. A minister claimed that he used 20 percent of his home as a home office associated with his counseling ministry. The minister did all of his counseling in another office and used the office in his home (consisting of two rooms) to store his books and office equipment and to prepare for counseling sessions. He did not meet with or counsel clients at his home office but rather used his other office for that purpose. He claimed that he maintained his counseling books and accounting materials at the home office because the presence of these items in the other office would have "intimidated the clients." The Tax Court concluded that the minister could not claim a business expense deduction for any portion of the expenses associated with his home office. *Hairston v. Commissioner, T.C. Memo. Dec. 51,025(M) (1995).*

10. MOVING EXPENSES

The moving expense deduction is addressed in section H of this chapter.

11. TELEPHONE EXPENSES

If you use your home telephone for business purposes, you may not deduct any of the basic local service charge (including taxes) for the first telephone line into your home.

EXAMPLE. A minister used his home phone to speak with members of his congregation or to deal with other church-related matters. He did not have a separate telephone line for business calls. He claimed a business deduction of 75 percent of his total telephone expenses (including both local and long distance charges) on his federal tax returns for three years. The IRS audited the minister and disallowed all of the deductions, but the Tax Court ruled in the minister's favor. The court observed: "No deduction is allowed for a taxpayer's telephone expenses if the primary purpose of the telephone is personal rather than business. . . . The minister presented canceled checks paid to the telephone company and testified that approximately 75 percent of all local and long distance calls received at home were related to his business. He did not maintain a separate business telephone line. Due to the nature of his business and the hours devoted to his duties, we believe his approximation of the business use of his home phone. We hold that he has met his burden of proof as to the claimed telephone expenses and is entitled to the deductions claimed."

Note that this case was decided before the tax law was changed to deny any deduction for basic local telephone service for the first telephone line into a home. However, even under the new rule, the minister's deduction for 75 percent of his long distance calls would have been upheld. *Shelley v. Commissioner, T.C. Memo. 1994-432 1994).*

EXAMPLE. A minister engaged in a counseling ministry from a downtown office and also maintained an office in his home. The minister claimed a business expense deduction for telephone expenses incurred at his downtown office and his home office. The IRS disallowed the portion of the telephone expenses attributable to the minister's home office. The Tax Court disagreed with this conclusion, noting that the minister clearly "incurred some telephone expenses at home in the course of conducting his trade or business as a counselor" and that the deductibility of telephone expenses is not governed by the home office rules (the minister did not qualify for a home office deduction). The court further noted that the tax code disallows a deduction for "basic local telephone service with respect to the first telephone line" to any residence of the taxpayer, regardless of any business use of the telephone. The court added that "this section, however, does not apply in this case since [the minister has] not claimed local telephone service expenses." *Hairston v. Commissioner, T.C. Memo. Dec.51,025(M) (1995).*

EXAMPLE. The Tax Court denied a $2,000 deduction for a pastor's home telephone expenses. It concluded, "As we understand, the deduction claimed was for telephone expenses incurred on [the pastor's] home telephone. He has no records substantiating these expenditures as expenses incurred in his trade or business. He apparently did not keep the monthly telephone statements. He could have, but did not, obtain copies of statements from the telephone company. In addition, the cost of basic local telephone service with respect to the first telephone line is a personal expense and is not deductible. We sustain [the IRS's] disallowance of the deduction." *Swaringer v. Commissioner, T.C. Summary Opinion 2001-37 (2001).*

Cell phones

▲ **CAUTION.** *A church cannot reimburse employees' expenses under an accountable reimbursement arrangement that do not qualify as business expenses. Such reimbursements, as well as a church's reimbursement of employees' unsubstantiated business expenses, are nonaccountable. If these reimbursements are not reported as taxable income to the employee in the year the reimbursements are paid, two consequences result: (1) the employee is subject to back taxes plus penalties and interest on the unreported income; and (2) if the benefits are provided to an officer or director of the church (a "disqualified person"), or a relative of such a person, they will expose the recipient and possibly other members of the church's governing board to intermediate sanctions in the form of substantial excise taxes, since the IRS views these benefits as automatic excess benefits unless reported as taxable income by the church or recipient in the year provided. This topic is covered fully in Chapter 4, section A.3. The lesson is clear: sloppy church accounting practices can be costly.*

✱ **New in 2010.** Congress enacted the Small Business Jobs Act of 2010, which eliminated cell phones from the definition of "listed property."

PUBLICATION 15-B ADDRESSES CELL PHONES

IRS Publication 15-B contains the following explanation of the tax treatment of cell phones:

The value of an employer-provided cell phone, provided primarily for noncompensatory business reasons, is excludable from an employee's income as a working condition fringe benefit. Personal use of an employer-provided cell phone, provided primarily for noncompensatory business reasons, is excludable from an employee's income as a de minimis fringe benefit. You provide a cell phone primarily for noncompensatory business purposes if there are substantial business reasons for providing the cell phone. Examples of substantial business reasons include the employer's

- need to contact the employee at all times for work-related emergencies,
- requirement that the employee be available to speak with clients at times when the employee is away from the office, and
- need to speak with clients located in other time zones at times outside the employee's normal workday.

You cannot exclude from an employee's wages the value of a cell phone provided to promote good will of an employee, to attract a prospective employee, or as a means of providing additional compensation to an employee.

Many churches provide cell phones to some employees. In the past, this created special tax concerns due to the fact that cell phones were designated as "listed property" by section 280F of the tax code. "Listed property" includes various items that are acquired for business use but that lend themselves to personal use as well. This includes automobiles, computers, and entertainment or recreation-related items. The tax code and regulations impose stricter substantiation rules on these kinds of property to ensure that any personal use is identified and reported as taxable income. Section 1.274-5T of the income tax regulations specifies that no deduction shall be allowed for the use of listed property unless the taxpayer substantiates the following:

(1) **Amount.** The amount of each separate expenditure for an item of listed property, such as the purchase cost, and "the amount of each business use . . . based on the appropriate measure (i.e., time for listed property) . . . and the total use of the listed property for the taxable period."

(2) **Time.** The date of the expenditure or use with respect to an item of listed property.

(3) **Business purpose.** The business purpose of each expense or use associated with any listed property. This means that the business purpose of every cell phone call must be established with adequate records.

In 1989 cell phones were added to this category because the cost of acquiring and using them was so steep that Congress was concerned that taxpayers would claim inflated business expense deductions and reimbursements without reporting the inevitable personal use as taxable income. But over the years, as the cost of acquiring and using cell phones declined, the rationale for treating them as listed property diminished.

In 2010 Congress responded by amending the tax code to remove cell phones from the definition of listed property. As a result, the heightened substantiation requirements and special depreciation rules that apply to listed property do not apply to cell phones. This provision is effective for taxable years ending after December 31, 2009.

✱ **New in 2011.** The IRS provided important guidance on the tax rules that apply to personal use by employees of employer-provided cell phones and employer reimbursements of employees for their business use of their own cell phones.

In 2011 the IRS provided guidance to employers on two important issues: (1) personal use by employees of employer-provided cell phones and (2) reimbursement by an employer of an employee's business use of his or her own cell phone. *IRS Notice 2011-72.* The IRS guidance is summarized below.

Personal use of employer-provided cell phones
IRS Notice 2011-72 states:

Many employers provide their employees with cell phones primarily for noncompensatory business reasons. The value of the business use of an employer-provided cell phone is excludable from an employee's income as a working condition fringe to the extent that, if the employee paid for the use of the cell phone themselves, such payment would be allowable as a deduction under section 162 for the employee.

An employer will be considered to have provided an employee with a cell phone primarily for noncompensatory business purposes if there are substantial reasons relating to the employer's business, other than providing compensation to the employee, for providing the employee with a cell phone. For example, the employer's need to contact the employee at all times for work-related emergencies, the employer's requirement that the employee be available to speak with clients at times when the employee is away from the office, and the employee's need to speak with clients located in other time zones at times outside of the employee's normal work day are

possible substantial noncompensatory business reasons. A cell phone provided to promote the morale or good will of an employee, to attract a prospective employee or as a means of furnishing additional compensation to an employee is not provided primarily for noncompensatory business purposes.

This notice provides that, when an employer provides an employee with a cell phone primarily for noncompensatory business reasons, the IRS will treat the employee's use of the cell phone for reasons related to the employer's trade or business as a working condition fringe benefit, the value of which is excludable from the employee's income and, solely for purposes of determining whether the working condition fringe benefit provision in section 132(d) applies, the substantiation requirements that the employee would have to meet in order for a deduction under §162 to be allowable are deemed to be satisfied.

In addition, the IRS will treat the value of any personal use of a cell phone provided by the employer primarily for noncompensatory business purposes as excludable from the employee's income as a de minimis fringe benefit. The rules of this notice apply to any use of an employer-provided cell phone occurring after December 31, 2009. The application of the working condition and de minimis fringe benefit exclusions under this notice apply solely to employer-provided cell phones and should not be interpreted as applying to other fringe benefits.

What does this language mean as a practical matter? The IRS is taking the position that "when an employer provides an employee with a cell phone primarily for noncompensatory business reasons, the business and personal use of the cell phone is generally nontaxable to the employee. The IRS will not require recordkeeping of business use in order to receive this tax-free treatment." *IRS News Release IR-2011-93.*

The IRS has noted that "noncompensatory business reasons" include "the employer's need to contact the employee at all times for work-related emergencies."

Employer reimbursement of business use of employees' cell phones
IRS Notice 2011-72 only addresses the tax treatment of employees' personal use of employer-owned and -provided cell phones. It does not address employer reimbursements of employees' use of their personal cell phones for business purposes. In interim "audit guidance" provided to its agents, the IRS made the following observations:

Notice 2011-72 does not address the treatment of reimbursements received by employees from employers for the business use of an employee's personal cell phone. In cases where employers, for substantial noncompensatory business reasons, require employees to maintain and use their personal cell phones for business purposes and reimburse the employees for the business use of their personal cell phones, examiners should analyze reimbursements of

"Under the guidance issued today, where employers provide cell phones to their employees or where employers reimburse employees for business use of their personal cell phones, tax-free treatment is available without burdensome recordkeeping requirements. The guidance does not apply to the provision of cell phones or reimbursement for cell-phone use that is not primarily business related, as such arrangements are generally taxable." *IRS News Release IR-2011-93.*

employees' cell phone expenses in a manner that is similar to the approach described in Notice 2011-72. Specifically, in cases where employers have substantial business reasons, other than providing compensation to the employees, for requiring the employees' use of personal cell phones in connection with the employer's trade or business and reimbursing them for their use, examiners should not necessarily assert that the employer's reimbursement of expenses incurred by employees after December 31, 2009, results in additional income or wages to the employee.

However, the employee must maintain the type of cell phone coverage that is reasonably related to the needs of the employer's business, and the reimbursement must be reasonably calculated so as not to exceed expenses the employee actually incurred in maintaining the cell phone. Additionally, the reimbursement for business use of the employee's personal cell phone must not be a substitute for a portion of the employee's regular wages. Arrangements that replace a portion of an employee's previous wages with a reimbursement for business use of the employee's personal cell phone and arrangements that allow for the reimbursement of unusual or excessive expenses should be examined more closely.

The IRS has noted that

Examples of reimbursement arrangements that may be in excess of the expenses reasonably related to the needs of the employer's business and should be examined more closely include: (1) reimbursement for international or satellite cell phone coverage to a service technician whose business clients and other business contacts are all in the local geographic area where the technician works; or (2) a pattern of reimbursements that deviates significantly from a normal course of cell phone use in the employer's business (i.e., an employee received reimbursements for cell phone use of $100/quarter in quarters 1 through 3, but receives a reimbursement of $500 in quarter 4).

12. CLUB DUES

✿**KEY POINT.** Dues paid to clubs organized for business, pleasure, recreation, or social purposes cannot be claimed as a

business expense—other than dues paid to professional organizations, such as bar associations and medical associations, and civic or public service organizations, such as Kiwanis, Lions, and Rotary.

Many ministers belong to local clubs, including fitness and golf clubs. Some churches agree to pay the annual dues or fees to these clubs as a fringe benefit. In some cases, the minister (or church) treats the club dues as a business expense because membership in the club will either contribute to the minister's health or expose the minister and church to the community.

Section 274(a)(3) of the tax code specifies that "no deduction shall be allowed for amounts paid or incurred for membership in any club organized for business, pleasure, recreation, or other social purpose." As a result, dues paid to health and fitness clubs, golf clubs, airline and hotel clubs, and dinner clubs are no longer deductible as a business expense. However, dues paid to professional organizations, such as bar associations and medical associations, and civic or public service organizations, such as Kiwanis, Lions, Rotary, chambers of commerce, and trade associations, are not covered by this prohibition and may qualify as business expenses.

Two points should be emphasized:

- **Reimbursements.** Since most club dues cannot be treated as a business expense, a church cannot pay for or reimburse such dues under an accountable expense reimbursement arrangement. If a church pays for a minister's club dues, the full amount must be added to the minister's Form W-2 or 1099-MISC as additional taxable compensation. It is not a business expense that is reimbursable under an accountable arrangement.
- **Deductions.** Ministers cannot claim a business expense deduction for unreimbursed club dues that they pay themselves.

Club dues paid by an employer on behalf of an employee that cannot be treated as a business expense because of the prohibition of tax code section 274(a)(3) (quoted above) may be partly or fully nontaxable to the employee if they are a working condition fringe benefit. The income tax regulations state that "the amount, if any, of an employee's working condition fringe benefit relating to an employer-provided membership in the club is determined without regard to the application of section 274(a)(3) to the employee. To be excludible as a working condition fringe benefit, however, the amount must otherwise qualify for deduction by the employee under section 162." *Treas. Reg. 1.132-5(s).*

In other words, if a church pays for a pastor's club dues in a club organized for pleasure, recreation, or other social purposes and does not report the amount of these dues as taxable compensation to the pastor, the pastor can treat the dues as a nontaxable working condition fringe benefit to the extent that they could be treated as a business expenses if it were not for section 274(a)(3). The regulations give the following example:

EXAMPLE. Assume that Company X provides Employee B with a country club membership for which it paid $20,000. B substantiates, within the meaning of paragraph (c) of this section, that the club was used 40 percent for business purposes. The business use of the club (40 percent) may be considered a working condition fringe benefit, notwithstanding that the employer's deduction for the dues allocable to the business use is disallowed by section 274(a)(3), if X does not treat the club membership as compensation under section 274(e)(2). Thus, B may exclude from gross income $8,000 (40 percent of the club dues, which reflects B's business use). X must report $12,000 as wages subject to withholding and payment of employment taxes (60 percent of the value of the club dues, which reflects B's personal use). B must include $12,000 in gross income. X may deduct as compensation the amount it paid for the club dues which reflects B's personal use provided the amount satisfies the other requirements for a salary or compensation deduction under section 162.

EXAMPLE. A taxpayer claimed "physical fitness dues" of $720 on his tax return as an employee business expense. He insisted that a healthy body is important to the performance of his work and that "my tool is my body." The court noted that no tax deductions are allowed for "personal, living, or family expenses." It concluded that "a gym membership fee is an inherently personal expense." *Battle v. Commissioner, T.C. Summary Opinion 2007-27.*

13. FINANCIAL SUPPORT PAID BY MINISTERS TO LOCAL CHURCHES OR DENOMINATIONAL AGENCIES

Most ministers support their church with regular contributions. Some also make regular contributions to a denominational agency. Must this financial support be treated as a charitable contribution? Or is it possible to treat it as professional dues? This question was addressed directly in an unpublished "small" Tax Court decision in 1992. That case is explored below.

Forbes v. Commissioner, T.C. Sum. Op. 1992-167 (unpublished)

A local church adopted a "tithing policy" requiring every employee to pay a tithe of 10 percent of total compensation back to the church. The church strictly enforces the tithing policy. Tithing records are maintained on a computer and are periodically examined for all employees. Employees found to be delinquent in their tithes are required to become current. The church has dismissed several employees for failing to comply with the tithing requirement.

The church views its tithing policy as both moral and managerial. From a moral standpoint, the church believes that "a church

member whose wages are paid from the tithes of the parishioners, but refuses to participate in the support of the ministry, is dishonest and hypocritical." From a management standpoint, the church believes that an employee who disagrees with its basic tenets and is unwilling to comply with its policies is not fulfilling his or her employment commitment.

One of the church's ministers received $24,600 in wages from the church in one year, which consisted of salary, housing allowance, and miscellaneous amounts received for services performed at weddings, funerals, and other occasions. She paid a tithe of $2,460 back to the church, as required by the tithing policy. In computing her self-employment (Social Security) taxes for the year, she deducted this tithe as a "business expense."

The IRS audited the minister's tax return and claimed that she could only claim her tithe as a charitable contribution deduction and not as a business expense. As a result, the IRS concluded that it was improper for the minister to deduct the tithe in computing her Social Security taxes. While taxpayers can deduct business expenses in computing self-employment taxes, they cannot deduct charitable contributions. The minister appealed the IRS ruling to the Tax Court, claiming that her tithe was a business expense that she was entitled to deduct in computing her self-employment taxes.

The Tax Court concluded that the minister's tithes to the church represented a business or professional expense rather than a charitable contribution under the facts of this case. As a result, the minister properly deducted her tithes in computing her Social Security taxes. The court observed:

Under consideration of the record in this case, we agree with [the minister]. Tithing is required by [the church] as a matter of employment policy, and [the minister] must annually tithe 10 percent of the income she receives as a result of her position as a minister. Since [the church's] tithing policy is rigorously enforced, [the minister's] employment is, in a very real sense, dependent upon her willingness to give. The fact that she is tithing to a charitable organization to which she belongs and to which she might tithe 10 percent anyway is of little consequence given the facts in this case. Accordingly . . . we hold that [the minister] is entitled to compute her net earnings from self-employment by reducing her gross income from self employment by the $2,460 she paid to [the church] during the year in issue as a tithe.

Federal tax law permits taxpayers to deduct business and professional expenses, which are defined as "all the ordinary and necessary expenses paid or incurred during the taxable year in carrying on any trade or business." The court concluded that the minister's tithes satisfied this definition and accordingly could be deducted as a business expense. It is significant that *the IRS conceded* that the minister's tithes could be deducted as a business or professional expense except for a provision in federal law preventing taxpayers from claiming a business expense deduction for an item *that could be claimed as a charitable contribution.* The IRS claimed that this provision prevented the minister from deducting her tithes as a business expense—since she could have claimed them as a charitable contribution. Not so, said the court. It concluded that "payments made as an integral part of a taxpayer's trade or business" are deductible as business or professional expenses even if "the recipient of the payment is a charitable organization." That is, the critical question to ask is whether a payment satisfies the definition of a business expense. Is it an ordinary and necessary expense paid or incurred in carrying on a trade or business? If so, it is deductible as a business expense even though it may be possible to characterize it as a charitable contribution.

Further, the court suggested that it would be unrealistic to treat the minister's tithe to the church as a voluntary charitable contribution, since in no sense was it a voluntary transfer of funds to the church. Rather, it was a mandatory payment, and as such it could not be characterized as a charitable contribution.

❖ **KEY POINT.** The United States Supreme Court has observed that a gift or charitable contribution "proceeds from a detached and disinterested generosity . . . out of affection, respect, admiration, charity, or like impulses." Surely it would be inappropriate to classify mandatory financial support paid to a church by a minister or lay employee as a gift or contribution under this test, since in no sense does such support "proceed from a detached and disinterested generosity."

❖ **KEY POINT.** Another problem with characterizing financial support paid by clergy to their church or denomination is compliance with the written-acknowledgment requirement that applies to charitable contributions of $250 or more. For example, the acknowledgment (issued by the donee) must recite whether any "goods or services" were received by the donor in exchange for the contribution and, if so, the value of the goods or services. Ministers often receive a variety of goods and services from their church or denomination as a result of their financial support, and the valuation of these goods and services can be difficult. See Chapter 8, section D, for more information on these requirements.

Conclusions
Note the following additional considerations about this controversial decision:

This case suggests that in some cases mandatory contributions made by ministers and lay employees to a church can be treated as business expenses.
What is the practical effect of this result? Most importantly, it suggests that ministers may be able to deduct such contributions as a business expense in computing their self-employment (Social Security) tax on Schedule SE (of Form 1040). Remember, ministers are

considered self-employed for Social Security purposes with respect to their ministerial income. Consider the following examples:

EXAMPLE. Pastor D receives compensation of $40,000 for the year 2013 from his church (of which $10,000 is designated as a housing allowance). He makes contributions of $4,000 to his church and has other business expenses of $3,000. If the $4,000 in contributions to the church is mandatory, the Tax Court's ruling suggests that it can be deducted as a business expense in computing both income taxes and self-employment taxes. Pastor D would pay self-employment taxes on $33,000 (total compensation, including housing allowance, less the mandatory contributions and business expenses). Without taking into account any other facts or deductions (for the sake of simplicity), this would result in a tax of $4,950 ($33,000 x 15 percent).

EXAMPLE. Same facts as the previous example, except that Pastor D's contributions to the church do not meet the Tax Court's definition of "mandatory." Pastor D would pay self-employment taxes on $37,000 (total compensation, including housing allowance, less business expenses but not less contributions). Without taking into account any other facts or deductions (for the sake of simplicity), this would result in a tax of $5,550 ($37,000 x 15 percent). By not treating his contributions as a business expense, Pastor D will pay $600 in additional self-employment taxes.

Mandatory contributions may be reimbursable.
Many churches reimburse their minister's business expenses. If mandatory contributions to the church are considered to be business expenses, can a church reimburse them? This is a difficult question that the Tax Court's ruling did not address. Logically, if mandatory contributions are considered to be business expenses, they can be reimbursed under either an accountable or nonaccountable business expense reimbursement arrangement. However, neither the IRS nor any court has directly addressed this issue. This does not mean that the reimbursement of mandatory contributions would be wrong or illegal. It simply means that there is no direct precedent to support such a position, so it represents an aggressive position.

❖ **KEY POINT.** Though mandatory contributions may be reimbursable, churches, ministers, and lay church employees should consider this scripture: "The king replied to Araunah, 'No, I insist on paying you for it. I will not sacrifice to the Lord my God burnt offerings that cost me nothing.' So David bought the threshing floor and the oxen and paid fifty shekels of silver for them" (2 Samuel 24:24).

▲ **CAUTION.** *Treating a minister's financial support to a church or denominational agency as a business expense that can be reimbursed under an accountable arrangement may constitute an automatic excess benefit, exposing the minister to intermediate sanctions if the IRS determines that a* *taxable benefit was not reported as taxable income. See Chapter 4, section A.3, for details.*

Churches that elect to reimburse these expenses should understand that the reimbursements cannot be funded under an accountable arrangement by reducing the minister's compensation (a salary reduction plan).

To be treated as a business expense, contributions must be mandatory.

For contributions to a church to be treated by ministers and lay employees as a business expense rather than a charitable contribution, they must be "mandatory" under the Tax Court's rigid definition. Note the following elements that were mentioned by the court:

- The church adopted a formal "tithing policy" that required every employee to pay a tithe (10 percent) of gross income to the church.
- The church maintained tithing records on every employee.
- The church periodically reviewed the tithing records of all employees and required delinquent employees to become current.
- The church dismissed several employees for failing to comply with the tithing requirement.
- The church clearly articulated both a theological and managerial basis for its tithing policy.

EXAMPLE. Pastor K would like to reduce the amount of Social Security taxes he pays. He decides to deduct the contributions he makes to his church as a business expense in computing his self-employment taxes. He claims that if he does not set an example to his congregation by making contributions to the church, he may be asked to resign. The church has never adopted a formal tithing policy and has never dismissed (or even suggested dismissing) a minister for inadequate contributions. These contributions are not mandatory and are not deductible (for income tax or Social Security tax purposes) as a business expense.

The IRS conceded that mandatory contributions could be treated as business expenses.

As noted above, it is important to recognize that *the IRS conceded* that the minister's tithes could be deducted as a business or professional expense except for a provision in federal law preventing taxpayers from claiming a business expense deduction for an item *that could be claimed as a charitable contribution.* Since the Tax Court concluded that this provision did not apply, the contributions were deductible as a business expense.

Mandatory denominational support can be considered a business expense.

Some denominations require ministers to make contributions for their support. If these contributions are mandatory, they can be treated as business expenses and deducted in computing

self-employment taxes according to the Tax Court's decision. Once again, it is important to emphasize that the contributions must be mandatory. For example, the denomination's governing documents specify that ministers can lose their ordained status for failure to pay the required support.

❀ **KEY POINT.** Some ministers will prefer to report their mandatory contributions as a charitable contribution rather than as a business or professional expense. Some ministers will do so for theological reasons. Others will do so to reduce their audit risk, since the IRS may not accept the reasoning of the Tax Court in other cases.

Decisions in a "small" Tax Court case are not precedential.

The Tax Court's decision was a "small" Tax Court case, meaning it involved less than $50,000 and the taxpayer elected to pursue an expedited and simplified procedure authorized by section 7463 of the tax code. While small Tax Court cases are more quickly resolved, there is a trade-off: section 7463 specifies that "a decision entered in any case in which the proceedings are conducted under this section shall not be reviewed by any other court and shall not be treated as precedent for any other case." In other words, the decision of the Tax Court was final, and it cannot be cited as precedent in other cases. Obviously, this greatly limits the impact of the case. The IRS is free to completely ignore the decision in other cases.

▲ **CAUTION.** *Ministers who claim financial support they pay to their employing church or a denominational agency as a business expense rather than as a charitable contribution should recognize the following points: (1) They cannot cite the Forbes case (discussed above) as precedent for their position, since it was a small Tax Court case. (2) Even if the Forbes case could be cited as precedent, it would be of little or no benefit to most ministers because of the court's rigid definition of "mandatory" contributions. (3) No other court has ever said that financial contributions made by ministers to their employing church can be treated as a business expense. (4) Such a position almost certainly would be challenged by the IRS if the minister were audited. It is possible that the IRS would assess penalties in addition to back taxes and interest. (5) Treating a minister's financial support to a church or denominational agency as a business expense that can be reimbursed under an accountable arrangement may constitute an automatic excess benefit exposing the minister to intermediate sanctions if the IRS determines that a taxable benefit was not reported as taxable income. See Chapter 4, section A.3, for details.*

IRS audit guidelines for ministers

The IRS has published audit guidelines for its agents to follow when auditing ministers. The (revised) guidelines (2009) communicate the following information to agents regarding the tax treatment of ministers' financial support to a church or denominational agency:

Ministers often pay a small annual renewal fee to maintain their credentials, which constitutes a deductible expense. However, ministers' contributions to the church are not deductible as business expenses. They may argue that they are expected to donate generously to the church as part of their employment. This is not sufficient to convert charitable contributions to business expenses. The distinction is that charitable contributions are given to a qualifying organization (such as a church) for the furtherance of its charitable activities. Dues, on the other hand, are usually paid with the expectation that a financial benefit will result to the individual, as in a realtor's multilist dues or an electrician's union dues. A minister's salary and benefits are not likely to directly depend on the donations made to the church. They may still be deducted as contributions on Schedule A but may not be used as a business expense to reduce self-employment tax.

● **OBSERVATION.** The guidelines acknowledge that "small annual renewal fees" that are required to maintain a minister's credentials are deductible. This is an important clarification, since the IRS has challenged this proposition in several audits of ministers. There is no doubt that mandatory contributions to a credentialing body to maintain one's professional credentials represent a business expense, whether the taxpayer is a minister, attorney, physician, or any other professional.

● **OBSERVATION.** The guidelines inform agents that ministers' contributions to an employing church are not deductible as business expenses. They can be claimed only as charitable contributions. The guidelines reject the conclusion reached by the Tax Court in the *Forbes* case (discussed above). Ministers who treat contributions to their employing church as a business expense are taking an aggressive position that is now more likely to be scrutinized and challenged.

EXAMPLE. The United States Tax Court ruled that the IRS can ignore a pastor's tithes as a "living expense" in evaluating an offer in compromise. The court noted that the IRS *Internal Revenue Manual* concedes that if a minister is required "as a condition of employment" to tithe to a church, then this is a necessary living expense that can be considered in evaluating an offer in compromise submitted by the minister. The "only thing to consider is whether the amount being contributed equals the amount actually required and does not include a voluntary portion."

In this case the court concluded that there was no evidence that the pastor was employed as a pastor, and it rejected his argument that tithing was a condition of employment, even with respect to earnings from a secular employer, since he was required by church doctrine to tithe on such earnings. The court's decision, and the *Internal Revenue Manual* provision it cited, both acknowledge that a minister's contributions to a church can be a condition of employment. This is indirect support for treating these same contributions as a business expense. *Pixley v. Commissioner, 123 T.C. 15 (2004).*

D. RECORDKEEPING

1. KEEPING ADEQUATE RECORDS

You need to keep adequate records of business expenses for two reasons:

- to substantiate a deduction that you claim on your tax return for a business expense you incurred; and
- to substantiate reimbursements of business expenses under an accountable business expense reimbursement arrangement adopted by your employer. If you fail to keep the records prescribed by law, then you cannot claim a deduction for your business expenses, and you cannot obtain a reimbursement from your employer under an accountable reimbursement arrangement for business expenses you incur.

Three categories of business expenses

The kinds of records you need to substantiate a business expense depends on the type of business expense. The tax code divides business expenses into three categories for purposes of substantiation:

(1) local business transportation, overnight travel, entertainment, and gift expenses;
(2) expenses associated with "listed property"; and
(3) other business expenses.

Local business transportation, overnight travel, entertainment, and gift expenses

Section 274(d) of the tax code states that no deduction for local business transportation, overnight business travel (including meals and lodging), business entertainment, or gift expenses will be allowed unless a taxpayer can substantiate the information summarized in Table 7-6. You must be able to substantiate each item by adequate records or by sufficient evidence corroborating your own statement.

Expenses associated with "listed property"

The tax code defines "listed property" to include automobiles and computers (and peripheral equipment) that are used for business purposes. In order to substantiate a business expense for the use of any of these items of listed property, a taxpayer must prove (1) the amount of the expense; (2) the business use percentage (the percentage of total use of the listed property for the year that consisted of business use); (3) the date of the expense; and (4) business purpose.

If you are an employee, you can claim a depreciation deduction for the use of your listed property (whether owned or rented) in performing services as an employee only if your use is a business use. The use of your property in performing services as an employee is a business use only if the use is for your employer's convenience and is required as a condition of your employment. If these requirements are not met, you cannot deduct depreciation (including the section 179 deduction) or rent expenses for your use of the property as an employee. Whether the use of listed property is for your employer's convenience must be determined from all the facts. The use is for your employer's convenience if it is for a substantial business reason of the employer. The use of listed property during your regular working hours to carry on your employer's business generally is for the employer's convenience. Whether the use of listed property is a condition of your employment depends on all the facts and circumstances. The use of property must be required for you to perform your duties properly. Your employer does not have to require explicitly that you use the property. However, a mere statement by the employer that the use of the property is a condition of your employment is not sufficient.

If you cannot prove that you use listed property more than 50 percent for business purposes, you cannot take a section 179 deduction (you cannot deduct the full cost in the year of purchase) but rather must depreciate the property using the straight-line method over the property's "recovery period."

Other business expenses

For all other business expenses, you should be able to substantiate that such expenses were not only paid or incurred but also that they constitute ordinary and necessary business expenses. The income tax regulations provide the following information regarding the substantiation of this category of business expenses:

> *The tax code contemplates that taxpayers keep such records as will be sufficient to enable the [IRS] to correctly determine income tax liability. Accordingly, it is to the advantage of taxpayers who may be called upon to substantiate expense account information to maintain as adequate and detailed records of travel, transportation, entertainment, and similar business expenses as practical since the burden of proof is upon the taxpayer to show that such expenses were not only paid or incurred but also that they constitute ordinary and necessary business expenses. One method for substantiating expenses incurred by an employee in connection with his employment is through the preparation of a daily diary or record of expenditures, maintained in sufficient detail to enable him to readily identify the amount and nature of any expenditure, and the preservation of supporting documents, especially in connection with large or exceptional expenditures. Nevertheless, it is recognized that by reason of the nature of certain expenses or the circumstances under which they are incurred, it is often difficult for an employee to maintain detailed records or to preserve supporting documents for all his expenses. Detailed records of small expenditures incurred in traveling or for transportation, as for example, tips, will not be required.*
>
> *Where records are incomplete or documentary proof is unavailable, it may be possible to establish the amount of the*

> *expenditures by approximations based upon reliable secondary sources of information and collateral evidence. For example, in connection with an item of traveling expense a taxpayer might establish that he was in a travel status a certain number of days but that it was impracticable for him to establish the details of all his various items of travel expense. In such a case rail fares or plane fares can usually be ascertained with exactness and automobile costs approximated on the basis of mileage covered. A reasonable approximation of meals and lodging might be based upon receipted hotel bills or upon average daily rates for such accommodations and meals prevailing in the particular community for comparable accommodations. Since detailed records of incidental items are not required, deductions for these items may be based upon a reasonable approximation. In cases where a taxpayer is called upon to substantiate expense account information, the burden is on the taxpayer to establish that the amounts claimed as a deduction are reasonably accurate and constitute ordinary and necessary business expenses paid or incurred by him in connection with his trade or business. In connection with the determination of factual matters of this type, due consideration will be given to the reasonableness of the stated expenditures for the claimed purposes in relation to the taxpayer's circumstances (such as his income and the nature of his occupation), to the reliability and accuracy of records in connection with other items more readily lending themselves to detailed recordkeeping, and to all of the facts and circumstances in the particular case.* Treas. Reg. 1.162-17.

Estimating business expenses

Employees who incur transportation, travel, entertainment, or gift expenses, or expenses associated with the purchase or use of listed property, in connection with their employment must substantiate each element of an expense or use as noted above. Estimating the amount of such expenses is strictly prohibited, even though it is clear that a taxpayer incurred some expenses. This limitation supersedes the "*Cohan* rule," which allows taxpayers to estimate the amount of business expenses other than transportation, travel, entertainment or gift expenses, or expenses connected with listed property. *Cohan v. Commissioner, 39 F.2d 540 (2d Cir. 1930).*

Adequate records

To maintain adequate records, you should keep the proof you need in an account book, diary, statement of expense, or similar record. You should also keep documentary evidence that, together with your record, will support each element of an expense.

Documentary evidence

You generally must have documentary evidence, such as receipts, canceled checks, or bills, to support your expenses. Documentary evidence is not needed if any of the following conditions apply: (1) You have meals or lodging expenses while traveling away from home for which you account to your employer under an accountable plan, and you use a per diem allowance method that includes meals or lodging.

TABLE 7-6

HOW TO PROVE CERTAIN BUSINESS EXPENSES

IF YOU HAVE EXPENSES FOR:	THEN YOU MUST KEEP RECORDS THAT SHOW DETAILS OF THE FOLLOWING ELEMENTS:			
	AMOUNT	TIME	PLACE OR DESCRIPTION	BUSINESS PURPOSE AND BUSINESS RELATIONSHIP
TRAVEL	Cost of each separate expense for travel, lodging, and meals (Incidental expenses may be totaled in reasonable categories such as taxis, daily meals, etc.)	Dates you left and returned for each trip and number of days spent on business	Destination or area of your travel; name of city or other destination	• **Purpose:** Business purpose for the expense or the business benefit gained or expected to be gained • **Relationship:** Not applicable
ENTERTAINMENT	Cost of each separate expense (Incidental expenses such as taxis, telephones, etc., may be totaled on a daily basis.)	Date of entertainment	Name and address or location of place of entertainment; type of entertainment if not otherwise apparent	• **Purpose:** Business purpose for the expense or the business benefit gained or expected to be gained (For entertainment, the nature of the business discussion or activity. If the entertainment was directly before or after a business discussion: the date, place, nature, and duration of the business discussion, and the identities of the persons who took part in both the business discussion and the entertainment activity.) • **Relationship:** Occupations or other information (such as names, titles, or other designations) about the recipients that shows their business relationship to you (For entertainment you must also prove that you or your employee was present if the entertainment was a business meal.)
GIFTS	Cost of the gift	Date of the gift	Description of the gift	
TRANSPORTA-TION (VEHICLE)	Cost of each separate expense (For vehicle expenses, the cost of the vehicle and any improvements, the date you started using it for business, the mileage for each business use, and the total miles for the year.)	Date of the expense (for vehicle expenses, the date of the use of the vehicle)	Your business destination (name of city or other destination)	• **Purpose:** Business purpose for the expense • **Relationship:** Not applicable

(2) Your expense, other than lodging, is less than $75. (3) You have a transportation expense for which a receipt is not readily available.

Documentary evidence ordinarily will be considered adequate if it shows the amount, date, place, and essential character of the expense. A canceled check, together with a bill from the payee, ordinarily establishes the cost. However, a canceled check by itself does not prove a business expense without other evidence to show that it was for a business purpose.

EXAMPLE. A hotel receipt is enough to support expenses for business travel if it has all of the following information: (1) name and location of the hotel; (2) dates you stayed there; and (3) separate amounts for charges such as lodging, meals, and telephone calls.

EXAMPLE. A restaurant receipt is enough to prove an expense for a business meal if it has all of the following information: (1) the name and location of the restaurant; (2) the number of people served; and (3) the date and amount of the expense. If a charge is made for items other than food and beverages, the receipt must show that this is the case.

You do not have to record information in your account book or other record that duplicates information shown on a receipt as long as your records and receipts complement each other in an orderly manner.

You do not have to record amounts your employer pays directly for any ticket or other travel item. However, if you charge these items to your employer, through a credit card or otherwise, you must keep a record of the amounts you spend.

You should record the elements of an expense or of a business use at or near the time of the expense or use and support it with sufficient documentary evidence. A timely kept record has more value than a statement prepared later, when generally there is a lack of accurate recall. You do not need to write down the elements of every expense on the day of the expense. If you maintain a log on a weekly basis that accounts for use during the week, the log is considered a timely kept record. If you give your employer an expense account statement, it can also be considered a timely kept record. This is true if you copy it from your account book, diary, statement of expense, or similar record.

Proving business purpose

You must generally provide a written statement of the business purpose of an expense. However, the degree of proof varies according to the circumstances in each case. If the business purpose of an expense is clear from the surrounding circumstances, you do not need to give a written explanation.

> **EXAMPLE.** A minister who frequently visits church members in a local hospital does not have to give a written explanation of the business purpose for traveling to that destination. He can satisfy the requirements by recording the length of the route once, the date of each trip at or near the time of the trips, and the total miles he drove the car during the tax year.

Confidential information

You do not need to put confidential information relating to an element of a deductible expense (such as the place, business purpose, or business relationship) in your account book, diary, or other record. However, you do have to record the information elsewhere at or near the time of the expense and have it available to fully prove that element of the expense.

2. INCOMPLETE RECORDS

If you do not have complete records to prove an element of an expense, then you must prove the element with: (1) your own written or oral statement containing specific information about the element, and (2) other supporting evidence that is sufficient to establish the element. If the element is the cost, time, place, or

date of an expense, the supporting evidence must be either direct evidence or documentary evidence. Direct evidence can be written statements or the oral testimony of your guests or other witnesses, setting forth detailed information about the element. Documentary evidence can be receipts, paid bills, or similar evidence. If the element is either the business relationship of your guests or the business purpose of the amount spent, the supporting evidence can be circumstantial rather than direct.

Sampling

The income tax regulations specify: "[A] taxpayer may maintain an adequate record for portions of a taxable year and use that record to substantiate the business use of listed property for all or a portion of the taxable year if the taxpayer can demonstrate by other evidence that the periods for which an adequate record is maintained are representative of the use for the taxable year or a portion thereof." *Treas. Reg. 1.274-5T(c)(3)(ii)(A).*

> **EXAMPLE.** You keep adequate records during the first week of each month that show that 75 percent of the use of your car is for business. Invoices and bills show that your business use continues at the same rate in the later weeks of each month. Your weekly records are representative of the use of the car each month and are sufficient evidence to support the percentage of business use for the year.

Destroyed records

If you cannot produce a receipt for reasons beyond your control, you can prove a deduction by reconstructing your records or expenses. Reasons beyond your control include fire, flood, and other casualty.

3. SEPARATING AND COMBINING EXPENSES

Each separate payment is generally considered a separate expense that must be recorded separately in your records. You can make one daily entry in your record for reasonable categories of expenses. Examples are taxi fares, telephone calls, or other incidental travel costs. Meals should be in a separate category. You can include tips for meal-related services with the costs of the meals. Expenses of a similar nature occurring during the course of a single event are considered a single expense.

4. HOW LONG TO KEEP RECORDS AND RECEIPTS

You must keep records as long as they may be needed for the administration of any provision of the tax code. Generally, this means you must keep records that support your deduction for three years from the date you file the income tax return on which the deduction is claimed. A return filed early is considered filed on the due date.

ILLUSTRATION 7-1

DAILY BUSINESS MILEAGE AND EXPENSE LOG

DATE	DESTINATION	BUSINESS PURPOSE	START	STOP	MILES THIS TRIP	TYPE OF EXPENSE	AMOUNT
4/19	Local (St. Louis)	Visiting church members	8,097	8,188	91	Gas	$18.25
4/20	Indianapolis	Church conference	8,211	8,486	275	Parking	$2.00
4/21	Louisville	Seminary board	8,486	8,599	113	Gas	$16.50
						Repair flat tire	$8.00
4/22	Return to St. Louis		8,599	8,875	276	Gas	$17.25
4/23	Local	Hospital calls	8,914	9,005	91		
		WEEKLY TOTAL	8,097	9,005	908		$62.00
		TOTAL YEAR TO DATE			6,236		$993.00

Employees who give their records and documentation to their employers and are reimbursed for their expenses generally do not have to keep copies of this information. However, you may have to prove your expenses if any of the following conditions apply: (1) you claim deductions for expenses that are more than reimbursements; (2) your expenses are reimbursed under a nonaccountable plan; or (3) your employer does not use adequate accounting procedures to verify expense accounts.

5. EXAMPLES OF RECORDS

Examples of records that show the information you need to keep for different types of expenses are included as Illustrations 7-1 and 7-2.

E. REIMBURSEMENT OF BUSINESS EXPENSES

Most church employees incur out-of-pocket business expenses during the course of the year for transportation, travel, entertainment, education, books, and similar items. These expenses can be handled and reported in any one of three ways: (1) unreimbursed, (2) nonaccountable reimbursements, or (3) accountable reimbursements. These methods are summarized below.

1. UNREIMBURSED EXPENSES

Many churches do not reimburse their employees' business and professional expenses. Such employees have *unreimbursed* business

expenses. Some churches reimburse employees' business expenses only up to a specified amount. Such employees have unreimbursed expenses to the extent that they incur expenses in excess of what the church is willing to reimburse.

Church employees can deduct their business expenses only as a miscellaneous itemized deduction on Schedule A (of Form 1040), and then only to the extent such expenses exceed 2 percent of AGI. These rules have resulted in the nondeductibility of unreimbursed business expenses for many ministers and lay employees, since it is estimated that only about 30 percent of all taxpayers have sufficient expenses to be able to itemize deductions on Schedule A.

✿ **KEY POINT.** Employees cannot claim any deduction for unreimbursed employee business expenses for which an employer reimbursement was available.

Church staff who are self-employed for federal income tax reporting purposes can deduct their unreimbursed business expenses directly on Schedule C, regardless of whether they are able to itemize their expenses on Schedule A.

2. NONACCOUNTABLE REIMBURSED EXPENSES

▲ **CAUTION.** *If a church's reimbursement of an employee's expenses under a nonaccountable plan are not reported as taxable income in the year the reimbursements are paid, two consequences result: (1) the employee is subject to back taxes plus penalties and interest on the unreported income; and (2) if the reimbursed expenses were incurred by an officer or director of the church (a "disqualified person"), or a relative of such a person, they will expose the recipient and possibly other members of the church's governing board to intermediate sanctions in the form of substantial excise taxes, since the IRS views these benefits*

ILLUSTRATION 7-2

WEEKLY TRAVELING EXPENSE AND ENTERTAINMENT RECORD
(This is not an official internal revenue form)

EXPENSES	SUN		MON		TUE		WED		THU		FRI		SAT		TOTAL	
1. TRAVEL EXPENSES																
Airport																
Excess baggage																
Bus, train																
Cab, limousine																
Excess baggage																
Tips																
Porter																
2. MEALS AND LODGING																
Breakfast					6	75	6	00	5	25	7	00			25	00
Lunch			9	75	10	00	9	25	8	25	8	50			45	75
Dinner			22	00	18	25	17	50							57	75
Hotel, motel			50	00	50	00	50	00	45	00					195	00
(Detail in Schedule B)																
3. ENTERTAINMENT																
(Detail in Schedule C)									50	00					50	00
4. OTHER EXPENSES																
Postage																
Telephone, telegraph			1	50							1	00			2	50
Stationery, printing																
Stenographer																
Sample room					15	00	15	00							30	00
Advertising																
Assistant(s), model(s)					20	00	20	00							40	00
Trade shows																
5. CAR EXPENSES (List all car expenses—the division between business and personal expenses may be made at the end of the year.)																
(Detail mileage in Schedule A)																
Gas, oil, lube, wash																
Repairs, parts																
Tires, supplies																
Parking fees, tolls			4	00					3	00	3	00			10	00
6. OTHER (Identify)																
TOTAL			87	25	120	00	117	75	111	50	19	50			456	00

Note: Attach receipted bills for (1) ALL lodging and (2) any other expenses of $75.00 or more.

SCHEDULE A—CAR								
Mileage: End		57,600		57,620		57,650		57,660	57,840		
Start		57,445		57,600		57,620		57,650	57,660		
Total		155		20		30		10	180		395
Business Mileage		155		20		30		10	170		385

SCHEDULE B—LODGING								
Hotel, motel	NAME		Bay Hotel	Bay Hotel	Bay Hotel	Modern			
	CITY		Albany	Albany	Albany	Troy			

SCHEDULE C—ENTERTAINMENT						
DATE	ITEM	PLACE	AMOUNT		BUSINESS PURPOSE	BUSINESS RELATIONSHIP
August 9	Lunch	John's Steak House	15	00	Discuss purchases	Smith Construction
	Dinner	Troy	35	00		

as automatic excess benefits unless reported as taxable income by the church or recipient in the year provided. This topic is covered fully in Chapter 4, section A.3. The lesson is clear: sloppy church accounting practices can be costly.

Many churches reimburse some or all of their employees' business expenses. Reimbursements may be either nonaccountable or accountable. A reimbursement arrangement is nonaccountable if it fails to meet any one or more of the four requirements for an accountable reimbursement plan described in the following section.

A common example of a nonaccountable reimbursement arrangement is a monthly car allowance. Many churches pay their minister a monthly allowance to cover business use of an automobile without requiring any substantiation of actual expenses or a return of the amount by which the allowance exceeds actual expenses. Such a reimbursement arrangement is called a nonaccountable reimbursement arrangement, since the minister is not required to account for (substantiate) the actual amount, date, place, and business purpose of each reimbursed expense.

What are the tax consequences of a nonaccountable plan? That depends on whether a worker is an employee or self-employed for federal income tax reporting purposes.

Employees

For employees, the full amount of the church's reimbursements must be reported as income on Forms W-2 and 1040. An employee can deduct actual expenses only as a miscellaneous itemized deduction on Schedule A to the extent these expenses exceed 2 percent of AGI. These rules can be harsh, since the church's reimbursements are fully reported as income for the employee, who in many cases is unable to claim any deduction because of insufficient itemized expenses to use Schedule A.

Self-employed

For church staff who are self-employed for federal income tax reporting purposes, the full amount of the church's reimbursements must be reported by the church as income on Form 1099-MISC (and by the worker on Schedule C). The worker is then able to deduct expenses on Schedule C regardless of whether he or she is able to itemize expenses on Schedule A. This is seen by some to be an advantage of reporting income taxes as self-employed. However, because the IRS considers most workers (including ministers) to be employees for income tax reporting purposes, those who report their income taxes as self-employed should not assume that they are unaffected by the limitations on the deductibility of employee business expenses. In fact, this is one of the primary reasons the IRS targets self-employed workers. If it succeeds in reclassifying self-employed workers as employees, then their business expenses are shifted from Schedule C to Schedule A. For employees who do not have enough deductions to itemize on Schedule A, this means they receive no deduction for any of their business expenses.

✿ **KEY POINT.** The IRS has ruled that a minister may be able to deduct business expenses in computing self-employment taxes on Schedule SE even though the expenses were not deductible in computing income taxes because the minister could not use Schedule A. *Revenue Ruling 80-110.*

✿ **KEY POINT.** Church staff members who report their income taxes as employees cannot deduct any of their unreimbursed business expenses if they have insufficient itemized deductions to use Schedule A. If their church reimburses some or all of their expenses under a nonaccountable arrangement, all of the reimbursements must be reported as taxable income, without any offsetting deduction. For this reason, churches should avoid nonaccountable reimbursement arrangements.

Church staff who are self-employed for income tax reporting purposes are not affected by the limitations on the deductibility of employee business expenses, since they can deduct all of their business expenses (only 50 percent of business meals and entertainment) directly on Schedule C.

Examples of nonaccountable arrangements

Here are some common examples of nonaccountable reimbursement arrangements that should be avoided. If you currently have any of these arrangements, it is recommended that you consider switching to an accountable arrangement.

- Your church pays a monthly vehicle allowance to ministers or lay staff members without requiring any accounting or substantiation.
- Your church reimburses business expenses without requiring adequate written substantiation (with receipts for all expenses of $75 or more) of the amount, date, place, and business purpose of each expense.
- Your church only reimburses business expenses once each year. Business expenses must be accounted for within a "reasonable time" under an accountable arrangement. Generally, this means within 60 days.
- Your church provides ministers or lay staff with travel advances and requires no accounting for the use of these funds.
- Your church does not require employees to return excess reimbursements (reimbursements in excess of substantiated expenses) within 120 days.

EXAMPLE. Pastor B serves as a senior minister of a church and reports his federal income taxes as an employee. The church expects Pastor B to pay business expenses out of his own salary, so it reimburses none of Pastor B's business expenses. In other words, all of Pastor B's business expenses are unreimbursed. For 2012 Pastor B had total church compensation of $35,000 and unreimbursed business expenses of $3,000. He did not have enough itemized deductions to use Schedule A.

As an employee, the only way for Pastor B to deduct his unreimbursed business expenses is as an itemized deduction on Schedule A (to the extent that such expenses exceed 2 percent of his AGI). Since Pastor B does not have enough deductions to itemize on Schedule A, he cannot deduct any portion of his unreimbursed business expenses. According to IRS statistics, nearly two-thirds of all taxpayers cannot use Schedule A. This means that two out of three taxpayers who report their income taxes as employees (or who would be classified as employees by the IRS in an audit) will be unable to deduct their unreimbursed business expenses or expenses reimbursed under a nonaccountable arrangement. This result can be avoided if a church simply adopts an accountable business expense reimbursement arrangement.

EXAMPLE. Pastor H receives a monthly car allowance of $300. Pastor H is not required to account for the use of any of these funds. This is an example of a nonaccountable reimbursement arrangement. The church is reimbursing business expenses (through a monthly car allowance) without requiring any accounting or substantiation.

If Pastor H reports her income taxes as an employee (or as self-employed but is reclassified as an employee by the IRS in an audit) and has insufficient itemized deductions to use Schedule A, the following reporting requirements apply: (1) the church must report all of the monthly allowances ($3,600) on Pastor H's Form W-2; (2) Pastor H must report all of the monthly allowances ($3,600) as income on her Form 1040; and (3) Pastor H cannot deduct any of her car expenses, since these are deductible only as itemized deductions on Schedule A.

This result is even worse than the previous example, since in this case all of the monthly car allowances are includable on Pastor H's Form W-2, but she is unable to claim any offsetting deduction for her car expenses. This result can be avoided if a church adopts an accountable reimbursement arrangement. Also, note that a failure to report the $3,600 as taxable income will expose Pastor H, and possibly other members of the church board, to substantial excise taxes (called intermediate sanctions) if she is an officer or director. See Chapter 4, section A.3, for details.

3. ACCOUNTABLE REIMBURSED EXPENSES

✿ **KEY POINT.** A church's reimbursements of employee business expenses under an accountable plan are not reported as compensation on the employee's Form W-2 or 1040, and they are not taken into account in computing automatic excess benefits, as explained in Chapter 4, section A.3.

The adverse tax consequences associated with both unreimbursed and nonaccountable reimbursed expenses can be eliminated if a church adopts an accountable expense reimbursement arrangement.

This is one of the most important components of the compensation packages of ministers and lay church employees.

If a church adopts an accountable reimbursement arrangement, none of the church's reimbursements needs to appear on an employee's Form W-2 (or 1040), and there are no expenses for the employee to deduct. The employee, in effect, accounts to his or her employer rather than to the IRS. This is the ideal way for churches to handle the business expenses of ministers and any other church worker.

To be an accountable plan, your employer's reimbursement or allowance arrangement must comply with all four of the following four rules:

- **Business connection.** Your expenses must have a business connection—that is, you must have paid or incurred deductible expenses while performing services as an employee of your employer.
- **Adequate accounting.** You must adequately account to your employer for these expenses within a reasonable period of time (not more than 60 days after an expense is incurred).
- **Returning excess reimbursements.** You must return any excess reimbursement or allowance within a reasonable period of time (not more than 120 days after an excess reimbursement is paid). An excess reimbursement or allowance is any amount you are paid that is more than the business-related expenses you adequately accounted for to your employer.
- **Reimbursements not made out of salary reductions.** The income tax regulations caution that in order for an employer's reimbursement arrangement to be accountable, it must meet a reimbursement requirement in addition to the three requirements summarized above. The reimbursement requirement means that an employer's reimbursements of an employee's business expenses come out of the employer's funds and not by reducing the employee's salary.

Each of these requirements is explained in the following sections.

✿ **KEY POINT.** The income tax regulations that list the four requirements for an accountable plan refer to "employees." However, the regulations clarify that workers who are self-employed may have their business expenses reimbursed by an "employer" under an accountable arrangement.

✿ **KEY POINT.** The IRS has issued audit guidelines for its agents to follow when auditing ministers. The guidelines state: "If [a reimbursement] arrangement meets all the requirements for an accountable plan, the amounts paid under the arrangement are excluded from the minister's gross income and are not required to be reported on his or her Form W-2. If, however, the arrangement does not meet one or more of the requirements, all payments under the arrangement are included in the minister's gross income and are reported as wages on the Form W-2, even though no withholding at the source is required."

✿ **KEY POINT.** Taxpayers must have sufficient documentary evidence to substantiate the amount, date, place, and business purpose of most business expenses, but they will not need a receipt for any expense of less than $75.

Business connection

A reimbursement arrangement meets the business connection requirement if it reimburses employee expenses that could be claimed by the employee as a business expense deduction and that are paid or incurred by the employee in connection with the performance of services as an employee. The business connection requirement will not be satisfied if the employer "arranges to pay an amount to an employee regardless of whether the employee incurs or is reasonably expected to incur business expenses." See Tables 7-8 and 7-9.

Churches occasionally reimburse ministers for nonbusiness expenses. Such reimbursements, though they require an accounting, ordinarily must be included in the minister's wages for income tax reporting purposes, and they are not deductible by the minister. Such "personal, living, or family expenses" are not deductible, and the entire amount of a church's reimbursement must be included on the minister's Form W-2 and Form 1040.

Adequate accounting

You must adequately account to your employer for any business expense it reimburses. Following are the rules.

Adequate accounting—the general rule

Section 1.162-17 of the income tax regulations, which applies to all business and professional expenses *other than* listed property or transportation, travel, entertainment, and gift expenses, provides:

> The employee [or self-employed person] need not report on his tax return (either itemized or in total amount) expenses . . . paid or incurred by him solely for the benefit of his employer for which he is required to account and does account to his employer and which are charged directly or indirectly to the employer (for example, through credit cards) or for which the employee is paid through advances, reimbursements, or otherwise, provided the total amount of such advances, reimbursements, and charges is equal to such expenses. In such a case the taxpayer need only state in his return that the total of amounts charged directly or indirectly to his employer through credit cards or otherwise and received from the employer as advances or reimbursements did not exceed the ordinary and necessary business expenses paid or incurred by the employee. . . . To "account" to his employer . . . means to submit an expense account or other required written statement to the employer showing the business nature and the amount of all

> the employee's expenses (including those charged directly or indirectly to the employer through credit cards or otherwise) broken down into such broad categories as transportation, meals and lodging while away from home overnight, entertainment expenses, and other business expenses.

Adequate accounting—transportation, travel, entertainment, and gift expenses

The substantiation requirements for transportation, travel, entertainment, and gift expenses are set forth in section 1.274-5T(f) of the income tax regulations:

> For purposes of computing tax liability, an employee [or self-employed person] need not report on his tax return business expenses for travel, transportation, entertainment, gifts, or with respect to listed property, paid or incurred by him solely for the benefit of his employer for which he is required to, and does, make an adequate accounting to his employer . . . and which are charged directly or indirectly to the employer (for example, through credit cards) or for which the employee is paid through advances, reimbursements, or otherwise, provided that the total amount of such advances, reimbursements, and charges is equal to such expenses. . . . [A]n adequate accounting means the submission to the employer of an account book, diary, log, statement of expense, trip sheet, or similar record maintained by the employee in which the information as to each element of an expenditure or use [amount, time and place, business purpose, and business relationship] is recorded at or near the time of the expenditure or use, together with supporting documentary evidence, in a manner which conforms to all the "adequate records" requirements [described in section D of this chapter]. An adequate accounting requires that the employee account for all amounts received from his employer during the taxable year as advances, reimbursements, or allowances (including those charged directly or indirectly to the employer through credit cards or otherwise) for travel, entertainment, gifts, and the use of listed property.

Section 1.274-5T(f) goes on to provide that "an employee who makes an adequate accounting to his employer . . . will not again be required to substantiate such expense account information," except in the following cases: (1) an employee whose business expenses exceed the total of amounts charged to his employer and amounts received through advances, reimbursements, or otherwise and who claims a deduction on his return for such excess; or (2) employees in cases where it is determined that the accounting procedures used by the employer for the reporting and substantiation of expenses by such employees are not adequate, or where it cannot be determined that such procedures are adequate.

✿ **KEY POINT.** Note that an "adequate accounting" must be based on "adequate records." The adequate records requirement, including receipts for expenses of $75 or more, is explained in section D of this chapter.

Adequate accounting—listed property

The tax code defines "listed property" to include automobiles and computers (and peripheral equipment) that are used for business purposes. In order to substantiate a business expense for the use of any of these items of listed property, a taxpayer must prove (1) the amount of the expense; (2) the business use percentage (the percentage of total use of the listed property for the year that consisted of business use); (3) the date of the expense; and (4) the business purpose.

✿ **KEY POINT.** Accounting procedures will be considered inadequate to the extent that the employer does not require an adequate accounting from its employees or does not maintain such substantiation. The regulation cautions that "to the extent an employer fails to maintain adequate accounting procedures it will thereby obligate its employees to substantiate separately their expense account information."

✿ **KEY POINT.** Most churches implement an accountable reimbursement plan by having the church board pass an appropriate resolution containing the requirements summarized above. A reimbursement policy should be in writing, and it should clearly specify what expenses the church will reimburse. It also should describe the documentation and reporting that will be required. The church should retain the records and receipts presented by a minister in documenting the business nature and amount of business expenses he or she incurs (discussed more fully later).

✿ **KEY POINT.** A sample accountable reimbursement policy is reproduced as Illustration 7-3.

Credit cards

The IRS has issued audit guidelines for its agents to follow when auditing corporate executives. The guidelines are instructive in evaluating the compensation packages provided to senior pastors and other church employees. The guidelines specify:

> *Many employers provide corporate credit cards to executives and other employees. The difference between the rank and file credit card accounts and those maintained for executives is generally the method of reimbursement. Top level executives are permitted to use the card at will. A monthly statement may be mailed directly to the employer and the account may be paid in full without the submission of a business expense report. Lower level executives are generally required to submit an expense report and are reimbursed for business related expenses. Personal expenses paid on behalf of executives are taxable fringe benefits that should be included in wages. The determination of whether the corporation has an accountable plan should be made at the beginning of the examination. If executives are not required to substantiate that the expenses charged to the corporate credit card were for business expenses, the reimbursement is considered to have been made under a nonaccountable plan and the entire reimbursement is taxable to the executive, and wages for employment tax purposes.*

When employees should account for their business expenses

The income tax regulations specify that under an accountable reimbursement arrangement, an employee's accounting or substantiation of business expenses and the return of any excess reimbursements must occur within a reasonable time. The regulations state that "the determination of a reasonable period of time will depend on the facts and circumstances." However, the regulations provide the following two "safe harbors" that will satisfy the reasonable time requirement:

Fixed date method. Under the fixed date method, business expenses will be deemed substantiated within a reasonable amount of time if done within 60 days after the expenses are paid or incurred, and excess reimbursements will be deemed to have been returned to the employer within a reasonable amount of time if done within 120 days after the expenses are paid or incurred.

Periodic statement method. Under the periodic statement method, an employer gives employees a periodic statement (not less often than quarterly) setting forth the amount by which the employer's reimbursements exceed the amount of business expenses substantiated by the employee and requesting the employee to either substantiate the difference or return it within 120 days of the statement. Expenses that are substantiated or returned during the 120-day period satisfy the reasonable time requirement.

✿ **KEY POINT.** The regulations specify that if an employer has a plan or practice to provide amounts to employees in excess of expenses that are properly substantiated to avoid reporting and withholding on such amounts, the employer may not use either of the safe harbors for any years during which such plan or practice exists.

Tax withholding

Churches must recognize that business expense reimbursements or allowances paid to employees must be included on the employees' Forms W-2 and are subject to income tax and FICA withholding when paid—*unless* the reimbursements are paid under an accountable reimbursement plan. The withholding requirements will not apply to ministers, who are exempt from tax withholding (unless they have elected voluntary withholding). Nonminister church employees will be covered by these same rules.

How churches pay for expense reimbursements

A church can fund an accountable reimbursement plan in a variety of ways. First, it can agree to reimburse all substantiated business expenses without limitation. Second, it can agree to reimburse substantiated expenses up to a fixed limit (e.g., $4,000 per year). Any business expenses incurred by the minister in excess of this amount would be unreimbursed. Third, in the past, some churches reimbursed a minister's substantiated business expenses out of his or her own compensation. This approach was popular, since it did not "cost" the church anything. Under this approach, churches simply agreed to pay a minister's monthly business expenses out of the first weekly paycheck of the following month. Whatever was left after the substantiated expenses were reimbursed was classified as salary and reported on the minister's Form W-2. This practice has been repudiated by the IRS. Salary reduction arrangements are fully addressed later in this chapter.

Employee records and receipts

Regulation 1.274-5T(f) (quoted above) specifies that a reimbursement arrangement will not satisfy the requirements of an accountable arrangement "to the extent that the employer . . . does not require an adequate accounting from its employees or does not maintain such substantiation. To the extent an employer fails to maintain adequate accounting procedures he will thereby obligate his employees to separately substantiate their expense account information."

Making a nonaccountable arrangement accountable

An employee cannot make a nonaccountable arrangement accountable. The regulations specify that "if a payor provides a nonaccountable plan, an employee who receives payments under the plan cannot compel the payor to treat the payments as paid under an accountable plan by voluntarily substantiating the expenses and returning any excess to the payor."

Independent contractors

The income tax regulations permit independent contractors (i.e., self-employed persons) to be reimbursed for their business expenses; such reimbursements need not be reported as income to the extent that the self-employed individual properly accounts to his or her client or customer for each expense that is reimbursed.

Generally, the substantiation and accounting requirements described above for employees apply to self- employed as well. Since self-employed ministers are permitted to deduct their business expenses (whether unreimbursed or reimbursed under a nonaccountable plan) directly on Schedule C regardless of whether they can itemize deductions on Schedule A, there is less need for a reimbursement policy. However, an accountable reimbursement plan for self-employed persons would have the following advantages: (1) it would reduce the likelihood of additional taxes if the self-employed individual is audited by the IRS and reclassified as an employee; and (2) it will reduce audit risk by permitting the individual to report to his or her church rather than to the IRS.

Ownership of property purchased by a church under an accountable expense reimbursement arrangement

A question that often arises is, who owns property purchased by a pastor or lay employee if the purchase price is reimbursed by the church under an accountable arrangement? Let's illustrate the practical significance of this subject with a few examples.

EXAMPLE 1. A church adopted an accountable expense reimbursement arrangement several years ago. It reimburses those

expenses incurred by any of its employees who are adequately substantiated. To substantiate an expense, an employee must submit proof of its amount, date, location, and business purpose. Receipts are required for any expense of $75 or more. Substantiation of each expense must be completed within a month of the date the expense was incurred. Such an arrangement qualifies as an accountable expense reimbursement arrangement. Assume that Pastor D purchased a personal computer for $2,000 in 2012 that he uses entirely for work-related duties (sermon preparation, research, and communicating with church members and other ministers). In 2013, one year after purchasing the computer, Pastor D accepts a position at Second Church. A few days before moving, the church treasurer asks Pastor D about the computer. Will he be leaving it or taking it with him? Pastor D is unsure who should keep it, and so is the church treasurer.

EXAMPLE 2. Pastor B has served as pastor of First Church for 20 years. Over that time he has purchased several books and commentaries for a professional library that he maintains in his church office. Many of the books were purchased in the past few years. The church has reimbursed Pastor B for the purchase of all of these books. The reimbursements have amounted to $3,000. Pastor B accepts a position at Second Church. As his last day at First Church approaches, he begins to wonder about his library. Should he leave it for his successor at First Church? After all, the church paid for it. Or should he pack it up and take it with him? He asks the church treasurer for her opinion, but she is unsure. They agree to let the pastor take the library with him. This decision is based on the fact that a pastor's library is a matter of personal preference, so Pastor B's library may be of little, if any, use to his successor. Further, they assume that the next pastor probably will bring his own library with him from his previous church.

An accountant who attends First Church learns that Pastor B will be taking the library with him. The accountant questions the legality of this arrangement. The church board addresses this issue but does not know how to resolve it. They want to let Pastor B take the library with him, but they do not know how to explain such a decision to the accountant.

EXAMPLE 3. Pastor T is the youth pastor and resident "computer expert" at his church. During the three years he is employed by the church, he purchases several CDs and software programs to assist in the performance of his duties. The church reimbursed him for all of these purchases, which amounted to nearly $1,500. Pastor T accepts a position at another church. A question arises as to the ownership of the CDs and computer programs.

Unfortunately, the tax code and regulations do not address the question of who owns property purchased by an employee if the purchase price is reimbursed by the employer under an accountable reimbursement arrangement. And no guidance has been provided by the IRS or the courts. So what should ministers and church treasurers do? Here are some options:

The general rule. In general, when an employer reimburses an employee for the cost of property purchased by the employee for business use, it is the employer rather than the employee that is the legal owner of the property. After all, property purchased by an employee cannot be reimbursed under an accountable arrangement unless the employee substantiates the cost and business purpose of the property. In other words, it must be clear that the property will be used solely for the business purposes of the employer. Under these circumstances, there is little doubt as a matter of law that the employer is the legal owner of the property. The employer paid for it, and the accountable nature of the reimbursement arrangement ensures that it will be used by the employee within the course of his or her employment on behalf of the employer.

✸ **KEY POINT.** In many states a "resulting trust" arises by operation of law in favor of the person who purchases property in the name of another. The law presumes that it ordinarily is not the intention of a person paying for property to make a gift to the one receiving title.

A possible exception. In many cases the value of property diminishes rapidly, and in a sense is "used up" within a period of months or a few years. As a result, the question of ownership of the property when the employee leaves his or her job has little relevance, since the value is minimal.

EXAMPLE 4. A pastor purchases a small dictation machine for $49 in 2007. The church treasurer reimburses her for the cost of the machine under the church's accountable reimbursement arrangement. When she leaves the church in 2013, the value of the machine is negligible. The "value" of the machine has been "used up" over its useful life. The church has realized the full value for the purchase, and it would be pointless to insist that the machine remain with the church.

EXAMPLE 5. Pastor G purchased a "state of the art" computer in 1995 at a cost of $2,500. The church reimbursed the full purchase price, since the pastor used the computer exclusively for church-related work. The computer is an IBM 20-megahertz 286 model, with 1 RAM of memory and a hard disk storage space of 200 megabytes. It has no modem and no CD drive. Pastor G accepts a position at Second Church in 2013. He is still using the same computer, and a question arises as to the ownership of the machine. While the computer may have been "state of the art" in 1995, it is essentially worthless in 2013. Like the dictation equipment described in the previous example, the church has received full value for its purchase of the computer, and it would be pointless to insist that the computer remain with the church.

Inurement. Churches should be concerned about the issue of inurement when they allow a minister or other employee to retain ownership and possession of property purchased by the church for church use. Churches are exempt from federal income taxes so long as they comply with a number of conditions set forth in section 501(c)(3) of the tax code. One of those conditions is that "no part of the net earnings [of the church or charity] inures to the benefit of any private shareholder or individual." What does this language mean? The IRS has provided the following clarification:

An organization's trustees, officers, members, founders, or contributors may not, by reason of their position, acquire any of its funds. They may, of course, receive reasonable compensation for goods or services or other expenditures in furtherance of exempt purposes. If funds are diverted from exempt purposes to private purposes, however, exemption is in jeopardy. The Code specifically forbids the inurement of earnings to the benefit of private shareholders or individuals. . . . The prohibition of inurement, in its simplest terms, means that a private shareholder or individual cannot pocket the organization's funds except as reasonable payment for goods or services. IRS Exempt Organizations Handbook section 381.1.

It is possible that prohibited inurement occurs when a church allows a minister or other employee to retain ownership and possession of property purchased with church funds for church use. However, in many cases the value of the property will be so minimal that inurement probably is not a problem. To avoid any question, especially if the property has some appreciable residual value, the church could "sell" the property to the employee, or it could determine the property's market value and add that amount to the employee's final Form W-2 or 1099-MISC as additional compensation. In either case, the inurement problem would be avoided.

In deciding whether inurement has occurred, the relevant considerations will be as follows:

- the purchase price paid or reimbursed by the church,
- the "useful life" of the property,
- the date of purchase, and
- the residual value of the property at the time the pastor or lay employee is leaving his or her employment with the church. IRS regulations specify the useful life of several different kinds of property in order to allow taxpayers to compute depreciation deductions. These guidelines can be a helpful resource in deciding whether inurement has occurred.

Let's apply the inurement principle to the above five examples.

EXAMPLE 1. Inurement is a possibility according to the above criteria, since (1) the purchase price paid by the church was substantial; (2) a one-year-old computer still has a remaining "useful life" (according to IRS regulations, the useful life of computer equipment is five years); (3) the computer was purchased one year ago; and (4) the residual value of a one-year-old computer is still significant. To avoid jeopardizing the church's tax-exempt status as a result of prohibited inurement, the church has three options. First, it can ask Pastor D to return the computer. Second, it can let Pastor D keep the computer but add the current value of the computer to Pastor D's Form W-2. The computer's current value can be obtained by calling local computer dealers, especially those dealing in used equipment. Third, the church can sell the computer to Pastor D for its current value.

EXAMPLE 2. Inurement is a possibility according to the above criteria, since (1) the purchase price paid by the church was substantial; (2) some of the books still have a remaining "useful life" (according to IRS regulations, the useful life of books is seven years); (3) while some of the books were purchased more than seven years ago, many were purchased within the past seven years; and (4) the residual value of books purchased within the past seven years is still significant. To avoid jeopardizing the church's tax-exempt status as a result of prohibited inurement, the church has three options. First, it can ask Pastor B to return books purchased within the past seven years. Books purchased prior to that time are beyond their "useful life," according to IRS regulations, so their value is presumed to be insignificant. Second, it can let Pastor B keep the entire library but add the current value of books purchased within the past seven years to his Form W-2. The current value of these books can be obtained by calling a used book dealer. Third, the church can sell the books to Pastor B for their current value.

EXAMPLE 3. Inurement is a possibility according to the above criteria, since (1) the purchase price paid by the church was substantial; (2) the CDs and software programs still have a remaining "useful life" according to IRS regulations, the useful life of computer software is 36 months); (3) the CDs and software were purchased in the recent past (within the 36-month useful life specified by the IRS regulations); and (4) the residual value of the CDs and software is still significant. To avoid jeopardizing the church's tax-exempt status as a result of prohibited inurement, the church has three options. First, it can ask Pastor T to return the CDs and software. Second, it can let Pastor T keep the CDs and software but add the current value of these items to his Form W-2. The current value of CDs and software can be obtained from a local computer dealer, especially one that deals with used products. Third, the church can sell the CDs and software to Pastor T for their current value.

EXAMPLE 4. Inurement is not a possibility according to the above criteria, since (1) the purchase price paid by the church was minimal; and (2) the current residual value of a dictation machine that cost $49 four years ago is negligible. IRS regulations specify that the useful life of such equipment is seven years, and so the machine still has a remaining useful life. However, the age and minimal cost of the machine outweigh the significance of any remaining useful life.

ADVANTAGES OF AN ACCOUNTABLE REIMBURSEMENT PLAN

The implementation of an accountable reimbursement plan by a church is an important component of compensation planning. Consider the following benefits of such a plan:

- Employees report their business expenses to the church rather than to the IRS.
- Staff members who report their income taxes as employees (or who report as self-employed and who are reclassified as employees by the IRS in an audit) avoid the limitations on the deductibility of employee business expenses. These include (1) the elimination of any deduction if the employee cannot itemize deductions on Schedule A (two-thirds of all taxpayers cannot), and (2) the deductibility of business expenses on Schedule A as an itemized expense only to the extent these expenses exceed 2 percent of the employee's adjusted gross income.
- The *Deason* allocation rule (discussed earlier and in section F) is avoided. Under this rule, ministers must reduce their business expense deduction by the percentage of their total compensation that consists of a tax-exempt housing allowance.
- The 50 percent limitation that applies to the deductibility of business meals and entertainment expenses is avoided. Unless these expenses are reimbursed by an employer under an accountable arrangement, only 50 percent of them are deductible by either employees or the self-employed. See IRS Publication 463.
- Ministers who report their income taxes as self-employed minimize the tax impact of being reclassified as an employee by the IRS in an audit. One of the reasons the IRS targets self-employed workers is that by reclassifying them as employees, the IRS forces the business expense deduction to be moved from Schedule C (where it is deductible even if the taxpayer cannot itemize deductions on Schedule A) to Schedule A (where it is deductible only if the taxpayer can itemize deductions). Since only one-third of taxpayers can use Schedule A, the IRS often collects more taxes by reclassifying self-employed workers as employees. But if a self-employed worker's business expenses are reimbursed under an accountable arrangement, the IRS has much less incentive to reclassify the person as an employee.

EXAMPLE 5. Inurement is not a possibility according to the above criteria, even though the original cost was substantial, since (1) the computer has outlived its "useful life" (according to IRS regulations, the useful life of computer equipment is seven years); (2) the computer was purchased 15 years ago and is essentially obsolete; and (3) the residual value of a 15-year-old computer is negligible.

❖ **KEY POINT.** This section has focused on the ownership of property purchased by a pastor or lay employee when the purchase price is later reimbursed by the church under an accountable business expense reimbursement arrangement. The same analysis will apply, of course, if the church reimburses the purchase price under a nonaccountable arrangement. This section addresses accountable arrangements, since the vast majority of churches that reimburse business expenses claim to be doing so under an accountable arrangement.

Returning excess reimbursements

Under an accountable plan, you are required to return any excess reimbursement or other expense allowance for your business expenses to your employer. "Excess reimbursement" means any amount for which you did not adequately account within a reasonable period of time. For example, if you received a travel advance and you did not spend all the money on business-related expenses, or you do not have proof of all your expenses, you have an excess reimbursement. You must return an excess reimbursement to your employer within a reasonable period of time. While the meaning of a reasonable period of time depends on the facts of each case, the IRS will always accept 120 days as a reasonable period of time.

The income tax regulations specify that if an employer establishes an accountable arrangement but an employee fails to return, within a reasonable period of time, any reimbursements in excess of substantiated expenses, "only the amounts paid under the arrangement that are not in excess of the substantiated expenses are treated as paid under an accountable plan."

Using salary reductions to reimburse employee business expenses (the "reimbursement requirement")

The income tax regulations caution that in order for an employer's reimbursement arrangement to be accountable, it must meet a "reimbursement requirement" in addition to the three requirements summarized above (business connection, substantiation, and return of excess reimbursements). The reimbursement requirement is defined by the regulations as follows: "If [an employer] arranges to pay an amount to an employee regardless of whether the employee incurs (or is reasonably expected to incur) business expenses . . . the arrangement does not satisfy [the reimbursement requirement] and all amounts paid under the arrangement are treated as paid under a nonaccountable plan." *Treas. Reg. 1.62-2(d)(3).*

The IRS interprets this regulation to prohibit accountable reimbursement plans from reimbursing employee business expenses through salary reductions. Employers who agree to pay an employee a specified annual income and also agree to reimburse the employee's business expenses out of salary reductions have "arranged to pay an amount to an employee regardless of whether the employee incurs business expenses."

In explaining this regulation, the IRS observed:

> Some practitioners have asked whether a portion of an employee's salary may be recharacterized as being paid under a reimbursement arrangement. The final regulations clarify that if [an employer] arranges to pay an amount to an employee regardless of whether the employee incurs . . . deductible business expenses . . . the arrangement does not meet the business connection requirement of [the regulations] and all amounts paid under the arrangement are treated as paid under a nonaccountable plan. . . . Thus no part of an employee's salary may be recharacterized as being paid under a reimbursement arrangement or other expense allowance arrangement.

Let's illustrate this rule with an example.

EXAMPLE. A church pays its senior pastor, Pastor G, an annual salary of $52,000 ($1,000 each week). The church also agreed that it would reimburse Pastor G's substantiated business expenses through salary reductions. At the beginning of each month, Pastor G substantiates his business expenses for the previous month, and he is issued a paycheck for the first week of the next month consisting of both salary and expense reimbursement. Pastor G substantiated $400 of business expenses for January 2013 during the first week of February. The church issued Pastor G his customary check of $1,000 for the first week of February, but only $600 of this check represents taxable salary, while the remaining $400 represents reimbursement of Pastor G's business expenses. The church only accumulates the $600 to Pastor G's Form W-2 or 1099-MISC that it will issue at the end of the year.

Such arrangements are used by many churches. However, they are nonaccountable according to the regulation quoted above, since Pastor G would receive his full salary of $52,000 if he chose not to incur any business expenses. As a result, the church would report the full salary of $52,000 as income on Pastor G's Form W-2 or 1099-MISC.

The above-quoted regulation (imposing the reimbursement requirement) effectively put an end to a common church practice that allowed many ministers to enjoy the advantages of an accountable plan without any additional cost to the church. Unfortunately, regulation 1.62-2(d)(3), by imposing the reimbursement requirement, makes such arrangements nonaccountable. Such arrangements are not illegal. They simply cannot be considered accountable. Even if such arrangements meet the three requirements for an accountable reimbursement arrangement (described above), they do not meet the regulation's reimbursement requirement. This is so for the following two reasons:

- The employer is not "reimbursing" the employee's expenses. A reimbursement assumes that the employer is paying for the employee's business expenses out of its own funds. When an employer pays an employee for his or her business expenses through a salary reduction, it is the employee and not the employer who is paying for the expenses. Such an arrangement is not an employer reimbursement.
- The church has agreed "to pay an amount to an employee regardless of whether the employee incurs (or is reasonably expected to incur) business expenses," in violation of the reimbursement requirement prescribed by the regulations.

Employers are free to pay for an employee's business expenses through salary reductions, but they must recognize that such an arrangement is nonaccountable. The effect of this is that the salary reductions must be accumulated to the employee's taxable income, and the employer is obligated to withhold applicable taxes on the salary reductions. In summary, there are no tax advantages associated with such arrangements.

EXAMPLE. A church agreed to pay its youth minister, Pastor P, an annual salary for 2013 of $36,000 ($692 per week). In February of 2013, Pastor P accounts to the church treasurer for $300 of business and professional expenses that he incurred in the performance of his ministry in January 2013. Pastor P receives two checks for the first week in February—a check in the amount of $300, reimbursing him for the business and professional expenses he accounted for, and a paycheck in the amount of $392 (the balance of his weekly pay of $692). His weekly compensation remains $692, but $300 of this amount constitutes a business expense reimbursement. The same procedure is followed for every other month during the year.

Because of the income tax regulation discussed in this section, this arrangement constitutes a nonaccountable plan. As a result: (1) Pastor P's Form W-2 (or 1099-MISC) for 2013 must include the full salary of $36,000; (2) Pastor P must report $36,000 as income on his Form 1040; and (3) if Pastor P reports his income taxes as an employee (or as self-employed but is reclassified as an employee by the IRS in an audit), he can deduct his business expenses only as miscellaneous itemized deductions on Schedule A, to the extent they exceed 2 percent of AGI. The key point is this—accountable reimbursement arrangements cannot fund business expense reimbursements out of an employee's salary.

Salary "restructuring"

Can the regulation prohibiting the funding of business expenses under an accountable arrangement through salary reductions be avoided by proper drafting of an employee's compensation package?

Let's illustrate this important question with an example. Assume that Pastor K and his church are discussing compensation for the next year and that the church board proposes to pay Pastor K $50,000. However, since it will require Pastor K to pay his own business expenses, the church board decides to pay Pastor K a salary of $46,000 and establish a separate church account for $4,000, out of which substantiated business expenses will be reimbursed. At the end of the year, any balance remaining in the reimbursement account would belong to the church, not Pastor K. It would not be distributed to Pastor K as a "bonus" or as additional compensation.

Since Pastor K has no right to any of the reimbursement account funds ($4,000) unless he adequately substantiates his business expenses, this arrangement should be permissible under the regulation. The church has not "agreed to pay an amount to an employee regardless of whether the employee incurs deductible business expenses." Unfortunately, the IRS disagreed with this conclusion in a 1993 private letter ruling. *IRS Letter Ruling 9325023.*

In the 1993 ruling the IRS addressed the question of whether the following arrangement could be considered to be accountable:

> Company X proposes to modify the district manager's compensation arrangement to allow each district manager to elect on an annual basis and prior to the beginning of each calendar year to reduce the amount of gross commission payable to him for the upcoming calendar year. Under the arrangement, the district manager may elect to reduce his gross commissions by a percentage ranging from 0 to 40 percent. In exchange for the reduction in commissions, Company X will pay the district manager's business expenses for the calendar year up to a maximum amount equal to the amount by which the district manager elected to reduce his commissions. Company X will pay only for expenses that satisfy the business connection and substantiation requirements of . . . the income tax regulations. If the expenses a district manager incurs in a calendar year are less than the amount by which the gross commissions were reduced, the excess amounts will be forfeited and may not be carried over and used for expenses incurred in the next calendar year.

The IRS began its ruling by noting that "a gratuitous assignment of income does not shift the burden of taxation and the donor is taxable when the income is received by the donee." The IRS continued:

> If a district manager of Company X elects to forgo future compensation under the reimbursement arrangement in consideration of Company X's agreement to reimburse his business expenses up to an equivalent amount, the district manager is making an anticipatory assignment of future income to Company X for consideration (the reimbursements). Thus, when Company X reimburses a district manager, the district manager is treated as currently receiving the forgone compensation for which the reimbursement is a substitute. Accordingly, we conclude that when

Company X reimburses a district manager for employee business expenses, the reimbursements will be includible in the district manager's gross income in the taxable year when paid just as if the district manager had received the forgone compensation. We also conclude, as explained below, that the reimbursements are subject to employment taxes because they are not paid under an arrangement that is an accountable plan.

The IRS then quoted the following example that appears in the income tax regulations:

Employer S pays its engineers $200 a day. On those days that an engineer travels away from home on business for Employer S, Employer S designates $50 of the $200 as paid to reimburse the engineer's travel expenses. Because Employer S would pay an engineer $200 a day regardless of whether the engineer was traveling away from home, the arrangement does not satisfy the reimbursement requirement of [the regulations]. Thus, no part of the $50 Employer S designated as a reimbursement is treated as paid under an accountable plan. Rather, all payments under the arrangement are treated as paid under a nonaccountable plan. Employer S must report the entire $200 as wages or other compensation on the employees' Forms W-2 and must withhold and pay employment taxes on the entire $200 when paid.

The IRS noted that "the conclusion to be reached from this example is that an employer may not recharacterize a portion of an employee's salary as being paid under a reimbursement arrangement or other expense allowance arrangement." Further, the example illustrates that

in order to have an accountable plan . . . the code and regulations contemplate that the reimbursement or other expense allowance arrangement provided by an employer should be amounts paid to an employee in addition to salary. This conclusion is supported by the preamble to the final regulations published in the Federal Register on December 17, 1990, which provides that no part of an employee's salary may be recharacterized as being paid under a reimbursement arrangement or other expense allowance arrangement. [Emphasis added.]

The IRS concluded that the reimbursement arrangement proposed by Company X would

result in a portion of the district manager's salary being recharacterized as paid under a reimbursement or other expense allowance arrangement. Therefore, we conclude that the arrangement proposed by Company X would fail the reimbursement requirement of section 1.62-2(d)(3) of the regulations. Thus, the business connection requirement of section 1.62-2(d) would not be satisfied. Therefore, all amounts paid under the arrangement would be treated as paid under a nonaccountable plan. In accordance with section 1.62-2(c)(5) all amounts paid under the arrangement are includible in the district managers' gross incomes, must be

reported as wages or other compensation on the district managers' Forms W-2, and are subject to the withholding and payment of employment taxes (FICA, FUTA, and income tax).

IRS audit guidelines for ministers

The IRS has issued guidelines for its agents to follow when auditing ministers. The guidelines inform agents that if a church has a salary reduction arrangement which "reimburses" a minister for employee business expenses by reducing his or her salary, the arrangement will be treated as a nonaccountable plan. This is the result

regardless of whether a specific portion of the minister's compensation is designated for employee expenses or whether the portion of the compensation to be treated as the expense allowance varies from pay period to pay period depending on the minister's expenses. As long as the minister is entitled to receive the full amount of annual compensation, regardless of whether or not any employee business expenses are incurred during the taxable year, the arrangement does not meet the reimbursement requirement.

The guidelines instruct IRS agents to be alert to salary reduction arrangements that are used to fund reimbursements under an "accountable" arrangement. According to the IRS, accountable plans cannot reimburse employee business expenses out of salary reductions. The important point is this—the guidelines are educating IRS agents as to this issue, so it is now far more likely that salary restructuring and salary reduction arrangements will be discovered and questioned in an audit.

EXAMPLE. The IRS released a private letter ruling in 1999 in which it concluded that appropriate "salary restructuring" arrangements could avoid the prohibition on the use of salary reduction arrangements to pay for business expense reimbursements under an accountable arrangement, so long as (1) the restructuring arrangement was done in advance of the year; (2) employees are reimbursed for employee business expenses that would be deductible as business expenses on their personal tax returns; (3) employees who do not request reimbursement under the plan receive no additional compensation; and (4) employees requesting reimbursement must account for reimbursed expenses within 45 days after the expense is incurred.

The IRS concluded that the company's plan satisfied all the requirements for an accountable plan, and therefore: (1) reimbursements made to a consultant under the plan may be excluded from the consultant's income as payments made under an accountable plan; and (2) reimbursements made to a consultant under the plan are not wages subject to employment taxes and are not reportable on the consultant's Form W-2. *IRS Letter Ruling 199916011.* However, in a 2000 ruling the IRS withdrew its more liberal 1999 ruling, which no longer can be relied on. *IRS Letter Ruling 200035012.*

Conclusions

Ministers, lay staff members, church treasurers, and church board members should be aware of the following points:

- **Reimbursing employee business expenses out of church funds.** In order to eliminate any of the questions concerning the use of salary restructuring arrangements, a church should adopt an accountable reimbursement policy that reimburses business expenses out of church funds. Churches that are concerned with unlimited reimbursement arrangements can set a maximum amount that will be reimbursed per employee.

- **Salary reduction agreements.** Some churches prefer to "reimburse" employee business expenses out of the employee's own compensation through a salary reduction arrangement. The objective is to eliminate any additional cost to the church for an employee's business expenses. The tax code prohibits employers from paying for accountable reimbursements out of salary reductions. Such arrangements are not illegal. They simply cannot be considered accountable. Churches that use such an arrangement must recognize that all reimbursements paid through salary reduction are nonaccountable and must be reported on the minister's Form W-2.

- **Salary restructuring arrangements.** What about salary restructuring arrangements? Does the ban on using salary reduction arrangements to fund accountable expense reimbursements apply to these arrangements as well? The IRS answered yes to this question in a 1993 private letter ruling. It reversed itself in a 1999 ruling but in 2000 announced that the whole issue of salary restructuring arrangements was under review and that the 1999 ruling was being withdrawn. Therefore, church leaders should assume that the 1993 IRS ruling represents the IRS position with regard to salary reduction and salary restructuring arrangements.

- **The "two resolutions" option.** Some churches are using a "two resolutions" approach to avoid the ban on using salary restructuring arrangements to pay for a church's reimbursements of a minister's business expenses. Here is how it works. At the end of the year, when the church board or compensation committee is considering a compensation package for its minister for the following year, it adopts a resolution that authorizes a salary and housing allowance of specified amounts, along with other fringe benefits (excluding any reference to business expenses). These various components of compensation are added and result in "total compensation" to be paid to the minister in the following year. The board or compensation committee then adopts a second resolution that sets aside a specified dollar amount in a business expense reimbursement account that can be used to pay for business expenses incurred by the minister that are accounted for within a reasonable time under an accountable reimbursement arrangement. Whether the IRS and the courts would view this as a covert salary restructuring arrangement requiring all funds specified in the second resolution to be included

in the minister's taxable income remains to be seen. At best, it is an aggressive approach that should not be adopted without the advice of a tax professional.

Consider the following three examples.

EXAMPLE. In December 2012 a church board addresses the compensation package for its minister for 2013. It decides to set aside $50,000 for the minister's total compensation package consisting of the following components: salary of $35,000, a housing allowance of $10,000, and various fringe benefits amounting to an additional $5,000. During the same meeting the board discusses the minister's business expenses and agrees to create a business expense reimbursement account in the amount of $5,000 that it will use to pay for business expenses that the minister incurs and that are reimbursed by the church under an accountable reimbursement arrangement.

This arrangement may not be a salary reduction or salary restructuring arrangement, since the board elected to create the expense reimbursement account independently from its consideration of the minister's compensation. Further, the arrangement arguably meets all of the requirements for an accountable reimbursement arrangement. It meets the reimbursement requirement (summarized above) because (1) the church will only distribute funds from the $5,000 business expense account as reimbursements of substantiated expenses, and (2) reimbursements are entirely separate from salary. As a result, business expenses the minister incurs in 2013 may be reimbursed by the church out of the expense reimbursement account if the requirements for an accountable reimbursement arrangement are met, and such reimbursements will not represent taxable income to the minister.

Whether the IRS and the courts would accept this reasoning remains to be seen. At best, it is an aggressive approach that should not be adopted without the advice of a tax professional.

EXAMPLE. Same facts as the previous example, except that the church board decides to set aside $55,000 for the minister's compensation for 2013, and it breaks this down as follows: (1) a resolution authorizing total compensation of $50,000, consisting of salary of $35,000, a housing allowance of $10,000, and various fringe benefits amounting to an additional $5,000; and (2) a second resolution authorizing the creation of a business expense reimbursement account in the amount of $5,000 that will be used to pay for business expenses that the minister incurs and that are reimbursed by the church under an accountable reimbursement arrangement. An argument can be made that this arrangement should be treated like the arrangement in the previous example, since it is essentially the same arrangement. This view has not been addressed by the IRS or any court, so it remains untested and aggressive. Ministers and church treasurers should not rely on this approach without the advice of a tax professional.

EXAMPLE. In December 2012 a church board addresses the compensation package for its minister for 2013. It decides to set aside $55,000 for the minister's total compensation package and adopts a resolution authorizing total compensation of $55,000, consisting of salary of $35,000, a housing allowance of $10,000, various fringe benefits amounting to an additional $5,000, and the reimbursement of business expenses up to $5,000. This arrangement clearly would be regarded as a salary restructuring arrangement by the IRS, meaning that any of the minister's business expenses reimbursed by the church would not be accountable, and so the reimbursements would have to be reported as taxable income by the church.

There is very little difference, other than semantics, in these three examples. However, the precise language used by the church board may determine the tax consequences of the arrangement.

Additional examples

The following examples illustrate the most important principles addressed in section E.3.

EXAMPLE 1. A church pays its pastor compensation of $50,000 this year. In addition, it reimburses business expenses incurred by the pastor during the year up to $5,000 if the pastor provides adequate substantiation of each expense within 30 days. This is an accountable reimbursement arrangement. Amounts reimbursed by the church are not reported on the pastor's Form W-2 or by the pastor on Form 1040 (line 7).

EXAMPLE 2. Same facts as the Example 1, except that the church also reimburses some personal expenses of the pastor, such as the personal use of a car. The regulations specify that if an employer reimburses both business and personal expenses of an employee, the employer "is treated as maintaining two arrangements. The portion of the arrangement that provides payments for the deductible employee business expenses is treated as one arrangement that satisfies [the reimbursement requirement]. The portion of the arrangement that provides payments for the nondeductible employee expenses is treated as a second arrangement that does not satisfy [the reimbursement requirement] and all amounts paid under this second arrangement will be treated as paid under a nonaccountable plan." As a result, the church does not accumulate business expense reimbursements on the pastor's Form W-2, and the pastor does not report these reimbursements as taxable income on Form 1040 (line 7). However, the reimbursements of personal expenses are deemed nonaccountable. The church must report these reimbursements on the pastor's Form W-2, and the pastor must include them as taxable income on Form 1040 (line 7).

EXAMPLE 3. Same facts as Example 1, except that the church accepts the pastor's signed statement as to the amount of business expenses he incurs each month without any additional substantiation. This arrangement does not meet the substantiation requirement, so it is not accountable. Amounts reimbursed by the church are reported on the pastor's Form W-2, and the pastor must include them as taxable income on Form 1040 (line 7). He may be able to claim a business expense deduction on his tax return for business expenses he is able to substantiate.

EXAMPLE 4. A church provides a pastor with a monthly $400 car allowance. The church board is certain that the pastor incurs business expenses of at least this much each month and so does not require any additional substantiation. This arrangement does not meet the substantiation requirement, so it is not accountable. Amounts reimbursed by the church are reported on the pastor's Form W-2, and the pastor must include them as taxable income on Form 1040 (line 7). He may be able to claim a business expense deduction on his tax return for expenses incurred in the use of his car for business that he is able to substantiate.

EXAMPLE 5. A church issues its senior pastor a cash advance of $1,500 to cover all expenses incurred by the pastor in attending a church convention. The pastor is not required to substantiate any of her expenses. The entire amount represents a nonaccountable reimbursement, since the pastor is not required to substantiate expenses or return any excess reimbursement (in excess of substantiated expenses). The full amount of the cash advance must be reported by the church on the pastor's Form W-2, and the pastor must report it as taxable income on Form 1040 (line 7). She may be able to claim a business expense deduction on her tax return for business expenses incurred during the trip that she is able to substantiate.

EXAMPLE 6. Same facts as Example 5, except that the pastor substantiates $1,200 of business expenses but is allowed to keep the excess reimbursement ($300). The regulations specify that this arrangement is accountable up to the amount the pastor actually substantiates ($1,200), but it is considered nonaccountable with regard to the excess. As a result, the church must report the $300 excess on the pastor's Form W-2, and the pastor must include this amount as taxable income on Form 1040 (line 7).

EXAMPLE 7. In December 2012 a church board agreed to pay its senior pastor a salary of $60,000 for 2013 ($1,154 per week). In addition, the church agreed to "reimburse" the pastor's business expenses by reducing his salary. Each month, the pastor provided the church treasurer with the total amount of business expenses he incurred for the previous month. The pastor provided no substantiation other than his own statement. Some months the pastor orally informed the treasurer of the amount of expenses for the previous month, while in other months he provided the treasurer with a note showing the total expense amount. The treasurer then allocated the next weekly paycheck between salary and business expense "reimbursement."

To illustrate, in the first week of September, the pastor informed the treasurer that he had incurred business expenses of $400 in August. The church treasurer issued the pastor his customary check in the amount of $1,154 for the next week—but it was allocated between business expense reimbursement ($400) and salary (the balance of $754). Assume that the pastor incurs $5,000 of business expenses during 2013. The church treasurer issues the pastor a Form W-2 showing compensation of $55,000 (salary of $60,000 less the salary reductions that were allocated to substantiated business expenses).

This is incorrect. This arrangement does not meet the reimbursement requirement for two reasons: (1) The employer is not reimbursing the pastor's expenses. A reimbursement assumes that the employer is paying for the employee's business expenses out of its own funds. When an employer pays an employee for his or her business expenses through a salary reduction, it is the employee and not the employer who is paying for the expenses. Such an arrangement is not an employer reimbursement. (2) The arrangement also fails the reimbursement requirement because the church has agreed "to pay an amount to an employee regardless of whether the employee incurs (or is reasonably expected to incur) business expenses." The church treasurer should have treated this arrangement as nonaccountable. The full amount of the salary reductions should have been reported on the pastor's Form W-2, and the pastor should include this amount with taxable income on Form 1040 (line 7). He may be able to claim a business expense deduction on his tax return for expenses he is able to substantiate.

EXAMPLE 8. Same facts as Example 7, except that the church requires the pastor to adequately substantiate (amount, date, location, and business connection) each expense in order to be reimbursed for it through salary reduction. Even though this arrangement meets three of the requirements of an accountable plan (business connection, substantiation, and return of excess reimbursements), it is not accountable because it does not meet the reimbursement requirement for the same reasons mentioned in Example 7.

▲ **CAUTION.** *In Examples 7 and 8, the pastor and members of the church board may be subject to intermediate sanctions in the form of substantial excise taxes, since the nonaccountable reimbursements were not reported as taxable income in the year they were paid. See Chapter 4, section A.3 for a full explanation.*

4. OTHER RULES FOR SUBSTANTIATING EXPENSES

Sampling

You may maintain an adequate record for parts of a year and use that record to substantiate the amount of business expense for the entire year if you can demonstrate by other evidence that the periods for which an adequate record is kept are representative of your expenses throughout the entire year. The income tax regulations specify that "a taxpayer may maintain an adequate record for portions of a taxable year and use that record to substantiate the business use of listed property [such as a car] for all or a portion of the taxable year if the taxpayer can demonstrate by other evidence that the periods for which an adequate record is maintained are representative of the use for the taxable year or a portion thereof." *Treas. Reg. 1.274-5T(c)(3)(ii)(A).*

EXAMPLE. Pastor M uses his car for local business transportation to visit members and make hospital calls. He and his family also use the car for personal purposes. Pastor M maintains adequate records during the first week of each month that show that 75 percent of the use of the car is for business. Invoices and bills show that business use of the car continued at the same rate during the later weeks of each month. Such weekly records are representative of the use of the car each month and are sufficient evidence to support the percentage of business use for the year. *Treas. Reg. 1.274-5T(c)(3)(ii)(A).*

Standard mileage rate

Two special rules are in place for substantiating the amount of business expenses and should be considered, since they will be much easier to follow in many cases than accumulating receipts of actual expenses. These two special rules are (1) the standard mileage rate for computing the amount of the business use of a car, and (2) the per diem rates for determining the amount of travel expenses.

You can account to your employer for the amount of your car expenses by documenting the business nature of your monthly mileage (or any other accounting period) and then multiplying business miles by the standard mileage rate. Alternatively, you can account for all of your actual expenses in the manner described in section C of this chapter. In Revenue Ruling 87-93 the IRS announced: "If an employer grants an allowance not exceeding [the standard mileage rate] to an employee for ordinary and necessary transportation expenses not involving travel away from home, such an arrangement will be considered to be an accounting to the employer. . . . However, an employer may grant an additional allowance for the parking fees and tolls attributable to the traveling and transportation expenses as separate items."

Per diem rates

If your employer reimburses you for your expenses using a per diem or a car allowance, you can generally use the allowance as proof for the amount of your expenses. A per diem or car allowance satisfies the adequate accounting requirements for the amount of your expenses only if all the following conditions apply:

- Your employer reasonably limits payments of your expenses to those that are ordinary and necessary in the conduct of the trade or business.

ILLUSTRATION 7-3

ACCOUNTABLE REIMBURSEMENT POLICY

The following resolution was duly adopted by the board of directors of ______________________________ **(the "Church")** at a regularly scheduled meeting held on ______________________________ **(date)**, a quorum being present.

The Church hereby adopts an accountable expense reimbursement policy upon the following terms and conditions:

1. **Adequate accounting for reimbursed expenses.** Any employee (as defined below) now or hereafter employed by the Church shall be reimbursed for any ordinary and necessary business and professional expense incurred on behalf of the Church, if the following conditions are satisfied: (1) the expenses are reasonable in amount; (2) the employee documents the amount, date, place, and business purpose of each expense (including, in the case of entertainment expenses, the business relationship of the person or persons entertained) with the same kind of documentary evidence as would be required to support a deduction of the expense on the employee's federal tax return; and (3) the employee substantiates such expenses by providing the church treasurer with documentary evidence of such expenses (including receipts for any expense of $75 or more) no less frequently than monthly (in no event will an expense be reimbursed if substantiated more than 60 days after the expense is paid or incurred by an employee). Examples of reimbursable business expenses include local transportation, overnight travel (including lodging and meals), entertainment, books and subscriptions, education, vestments, and professional dues. Under no circumstances will the Church reimburse an employee for business or professional expenses incurred on behalf of the Church that are not properly substantiated according to this policy. Church and staff understand that this requirement is necessary to prevent the Church's reimbursement plan from being classified as a nonaccountable plan.

   The Church agrees to reimburse up to ______________________ (dollar amount, or "no limit") under this policy for each employee in 2013.
2. **Excess reimbursements.** Any Church reimbursement that exceeds the amount of business or professional expenses properly accounted for by an employee pursuant to this policy must be returned to the Church within 120 days after the associated expenses are paid or incurred by the employee, and shall not be retained by the employee.
3. **Tax reporting.** The Church shall not include in an employee's W-2 form the amount of any business or professional expense properly substantiated and reimbursed according to this policy, and the employee should not report the amount of any such reimbursement as income on Form 1040.
4. **Retention of records.** All receipts and other documentary evidence used by an employee to substantiate business and professional expenses reimbursed under this policy shall be retained by the Church.
5. **Employees.** For purposes of this policy, the term "employee" shall include the following persons: ______________________________
   ____

Attest: ____
Secretary of the Board

© 2013 *Christianity Today International*

- The allowance is similar in form to and not more than the federal rate (defined below).
- You prove the time (dates), place, and business purpose of your expenses to your employer within a reasonable period of time.

Use of the per diem rates is explained fully in IRS Publications 463 and 1542.

KEY POINT. Ministers whose churches have adopted an accountable reimbursement arrangement may use per diem rates to substantiate the amount of their lodging and meal expenses. If these rates are used, a minister need not retain receipts of actual meals and lodging expenses to substantiate the amount of such expenses. Several conditions apply.

5. SAMPLE REIMBURSEMENT POLICY

A sample accountable reimbursement policy is reproduced as Illustration 7-3. Please note that it may have to be modified to fit your situation. The reimbursement policy set forth in Illustration 7-3 can apply to either employees or self-employed workers. If you use it for a self-employed worker, the policy's reference to "employees" should be changed. As noted previously (see Chapter 2), the reimbursement of business expenses is one of many factors to consider in deciding whether a particular worker is an employee, rather than a self-employed person, under the IRS 20-factor test (it suggests the individual is an employee).

6. EXAMPLES ILLUSTRATING BUSINESS EXPENSE REIMBURSEMENTS

The rules addressed in this section are summarized in Table 7-7 and illustrated in following examples.

Accountable arrangements

EXAMPLE. Pastor G is the senior minister of a church. He is given a monthly allowance of $200 for business expenses. However, he is required to account for all business expenses incurred each month and is only given credit for those expenses that are sufficiently documented (as to amount, time and place, business purpose, and business relationship) by adequate records that would support a deduction on his income tax return. The proper reporting of this arrangement depends on whether Pastor G is required to return excess reimbursements to the church. If he is, and this requirement is stated in the church's written reimbursement policy, and the excess reimbursements must be returned within 120 days of the associated expense, then this is an accountable arrangement and the allowances are not reported on Pastor G's Form W-2 or 1040.

Car allowances

EXAMPLE. Pastor H is given a monthly car allowance of $300 by her church and is not required to substantiate the business purpose or amount of any of her business expenses. This is a classic example of a nonaccountable reimbursement arrangement— the church is reimbursing business expenses without requiring the necessary substantiation. If Pastor H reports her income taxes as an employee (or as self- employed, but is reclassified as an employee by the IRS in an audit), the following reporting requirements apply: (1) the church must report all of the monthly allowances ($3,600) on Pastor H's Form W-2; (2) Pastor H must report all of the monthly allowances ($3,600) as income on her Form 1040; and (3) Pastor H can deduct her actual expenses only as a miscellaneous itemized deduction on Schedule A (if she has sufficient itemized expenses to use Schedule A), and then only to the extent that such expenses exceed 2 percent of AGI.

Cash allowances

EXAMPLE. A church provides its minister, Pastor M, with a cash advance of $1,500 to attend a church convention. Pastor M's actual expenses in attending the convention were $1,200. He is not required to substantiate his expenses or return any excess reimbursement. This is a nonaccountable plan, meaning that the church must report the full $1,500 as income on Pastor M's Form W-2 (or 1099-MISC), and Pastor M must report the $1,500 as income on his Form 1040. Whether he can deduct any of his expenses depends on whether he is an employee or self-employed for income tax purposes (as explained above).

EXAMPLE. Same facts as the previous example, except that Pastor M is required to substantiate his expenses within 60 days after the convention and return excess reimbursements to the church. However, he is not required to return excess reimbursements within 120 days. Pastor M substantiates $1,200 of expenses but fails to return the excess $300 within 120 days. According to the income tax regulations, only the $300 excess reimbursement is treated as paid under a nonaccountable plan, so only $300 (not $1,500) is reported as income on Pastor M's Form W-2 (or 1099-MISC) and on his Form 1040.

Credit cards

EXAMPLE. Pastor G is the senior minister of his church. The church reimburses him for all of his business expenses by means of a credit card (in the church's name). Pastor G is not required to substantiate any expenses with adequate documentation but rather informs the treasurer at the end of each month of the expenses incurred during that month. If Pastor G received reimbursements of $4,000 in 2012, (1) the church would report the entire reimbursement amount ($4,000) as income on Pastor G's Form W-2, and Pastor G would report them as income on his Form 1040; (2) Pastor G can deduct the reimbursed expenses as a miscellaneous itemized deduction on Schedule A if he has sufficient expenses to itemize, but only to the extent the expenses exceed 2 percent of Pastor G's AGI. If the church's reimbursements are not reported as taxable income in the year they are paid, they expose Pastor G to back taxes (plus penalties and interest) and intermediate sanctions in the form of substantial excise taxes if Pastor G is an officer or director. Intermediate sanctions are addressed in Chapter 4, section A.

EXAMPLE. Pastor C has a church credit card that he uses for all church-related business expenses. Each month Pastor C submits a statement of all charges to the church treasurer, along with supporting receipts, documenting the amount, date, place, business relationship, and business nature of each expense. This is a proper reimbursement policy. As a result, Pastor C need not report any of the charges as income; he need not deduct any expenses; and the church need not report any of the reimbursements as compensation on Pastor C's Form W-2.

Failure to seek reimbursement of expenses

EXAMPLE. Reimbursement arrangements sometimes create an unexpected problem—employees cannot claim a deduction for business expenses for which they did not seek reimbursement. To illustrate, in one case a federal court refused to allow a taxpayer to claim a business expense deduction for several business expenses that could have been reimbursed under his employer's expense reimbursement arrangement. What is the rationale for this rule? A business expense, to be deductible, must be "ordinary and necessary." If an employee voluntarily chooses not to seek reimbursement for an expense from an employer, the presumption is that the expense was not necessary. *In re Williams, 95-2 USTC ¶50,349 (D. Ind. 1995).*

See also *Onstott v. Commissioner*, 41 T.C.M. 827 (1981) (in a case involving a minister's business expenses, the Tax Court noted that "if a taxpayer is entitled to reimbursement from his employer for an expenditure made in connection with his status as an employee, no trade or business expense deduction is allowed").

Mileage allowances

EXAMPLE. The IRS issued a ruling denying accountable status to an employer's reimbursements of employee business expenses. The employer reimbursed certain employees' business miles at a specified per diem (daily) rate or the standard mileage rate, whichever was greater. Odometer readings were not required on the employees' claim forms. The integrity of the claim was the responsibility of the employee. The IRS ruled that these employees were not reimbursed under an accountable arrangement. As a result, all of the employer's reimbursements of these expenses had to be reported as additional income on the employees' Forms W-2.

The IRS observed: "To meet the substantiation requirement . . . of the regulations for passenger automobiles, an arrangement must require the submission of information sufficient to [demonstrate the amount, date, and business purpose of each reimbursed expense]. The supervisor's auto arrangement does not require the submission of mileage records and, thus, does not meet the applicable substantiation requirements. In addition, the automobile arrangement provides for reimbursements at the rate of the greater of [a daily rate] or the applicable cents-per-mile rate without requiring the return of amounts in excess of actual or deemed substantiated expenses. Accordingly, the supervisor's auto arrangement does not meet the substantiation or return of excess requirements of . . . the regulations. Therefore, the supervisor's auto arrangement is a nonaccountable plan." *IRS Letter Ruling 9547001.*

Nonaccountable arrangements

EXAMPLE. Assume that Pastor B's church reimburses him for all of his business and professional expenses (by means of a credit card or cash reimbursements). However, Pastor B is not required to substantiate the business purpose or amount of any of these expenses. He simply informs the treasurer at the end of each month of the total expenses incurred during that month. Assume further that Pastor B cannot itemize deductions on Schedule A (he does not have sufficient deductions) and that he is an employee for income tax reporting purposes.

If Pastor B received reimbursements of $4,000 in 2012, (1) the church would report the entire reimbursement amount ($4,000) as income on Pastor B's Form W-2, and Pastor B would report them as income on his Form 1040; and (2) Pastor B can deduct the expenses as a miscellaneous itemized deduction on Schedule A if he has sufficient expenses to itemize, to the extent that these expenses exceed 2 percent of Pastor B's AGI. If a church's reimbursements of an employee's expenses under a nonaccountable plan are not reported as taxable income in the year the reimbursements are paid, they expose the employee to back taxes (plus penalties and interest) and intermediate sanctions in the form of substantial excise taxes if the employee is an officer or director (or a relative of one). Intermediate sanctions are addressed in Chapter 4, section A.3.

EXAMPLE. Same facts as the previous example, except that Pastor B is self-employed for income tax reporting purposes. The proper way to report this arrangement would be as follows: (1) the church reports all of the reimbursements ($4,000) as income on Pastor B's Form 1099-MISC; (2) Pastor B includes the total reimbursements ($4,000) as compensation on his Schedule C (Form 1040); and (3) Pastor B deducts his business expenses on Schedule C (regardless of whether he can itemize deductions on Schedule A, and not subject to the 2 percent AGI floor).

EXAMPLE. In 2012 Pastor W incurred $3,500 in church-related business expenses. He informed the church of this amount and received a full reimbursement. However, he did not document the business nature or amount of any of his expenses. The proper way to report this arrangement in 2012, assuming that Pastor W is an employee for income tax reporting purposes, is as follows: (1) the church reports all of the reimbursements ($3,500) as income on Pastor W's Form W-2; (2) Pastor W includes the total allowances ($3,500) as salary on his Form 1040; and (3) Pastor W deducts the expenses on Schedule A as a miscellaneous itemized deduction (if he is able to use Schedule A, and then only to the extent that such expenses exceed 2 percent of AGI).

If a church's reimbursements of an employee's expenses under a nonaccountable plan are not reported as taxable income in the year the reimbursements are paid, they expose the employee to back taxes, plus penalties and interest, and intermediate sanctions in the form of substantial excise taxes if the employee is an officer or director (or relative of an officer or director). Intermediate sanctions are addressed in Chapter 4, section A.3.

EXAMPLE. Pastor C brings all of his 2012 business expense receipts and records to the church treasurer at the end of the year and adequately substantiates $4,150 of expenses. The church treasurer issues Pastor C a check for this amount. This is not an accountable reimbursement, since expenses are not substantiated within 60 days. Therefore, the church must report the $4,150 as income on Pastor C's Form W-2. If Pastor C reports his income taxes as an employee (or as self-employed, but is reclassified as an employee by the IRS), he may deduct his expenses only as miscellaneous itemized deductions on Schedule A to the extent they exceed 2 percent of AGI. If a church's reimbursements of an employee's expenses under a nonaccountable plan are not reported as taxable income in the year the reimbursements are paid, they expose the employee to back taxes (plus penalties and interest) and intermediate sanctions in the form of substantial excise taxes if the employee is an officer or director. Intermediate sanctions are addressed in Chapter 4, section A.3.

Salary reduction arrangements

EXAMPLE. A church agreed to pay its youth minister, Pastor P, an annual salary for 2012 of $26,000, payable in weekly checks of $500. On February 1, 2012, Pastor P accounts to the church treasurer for $300 of business and professional expenses that he incurred in the performance of his ministry in January 2012. Pastor P receives two checks for the first week in February—a check in the amount of $300, reimbursing him for the business and professional expenses he accounted for, and a paycheck in the amount of $200. His weekly compensation remains $500, but $300 of this amount constitutes a business expense reimbursement. The same procedure is followed for every other month during the year.

Because of the income tax regulation discussed in this chapter, this arrangement will constitute a nonaccountable plan in 2012 and future years. As a result, (1) Pastor P's Form W-2 (or

---

TABLE 7-7

REPORTING TRAVEL, ENTERTAINMENT, GIFT, AND CAR EXPENSES AND REIMBURSEMENTS

IF THE TYPE OF REIMBURSEMENT ARRANGEMENT IS	THEN THE EMPLOYER REPORTS ON FORM W-2	AND THE EMPLOYEE REPORTS ON FORM 2106
AN ACCOUNTABLE PLAN WITH		
Actual expense reimbursements: adequate accounting made within 60 days of each expense AND excess reimbursements returned within 120 days	No amount	No amount
Actual expense reimbursements: adequate accounting within 60 days of each expense AND return of excess reimbursements both required BUT excess not returned	The excess amount as wages in box 1	No amount
Per diem or mileage allowance up to IRS-allowed rate: adequate accounting within 60 days of each expense AND excess reimbursements returned within 120 days	No amount	All expenses and reimbursements only if excess expenses are claimed; otherwise, form is not filed
Per diem or mileage allowance up to IRS-allowed rate: adequate accounting AND return of excess reimbursements both required BUT excess not returned	The excess amount as wages in box 1 (The amount up to the IRS-approved rate is reported only in box 12 [code L]. It is not reported in box 1.)	No amount
Per diem or mileage allowance EXCEEDS IRS-allowed rate: Adequate accounting up to IRS-approved rate only AND excess reimbursements not returned	The excess amount as wages in box 1 (The amount up to the IRS-approved rate is reported only in box 12 [code L]. It is not reported in box 1.)	All expenses (and reimbursements reported on Form W-2, box 12) only if expenses in excess of the federal rate are claimed; otherwise, form is not filed
A NONACCOUNTABLE PLAN WITH		
No requirement that the employee adequately account for business expenses within 60 days, or return excess reimbursements to the employer within 120 days (or both)	The entire amount as wages in box 1	All expenses
NO REIMBURSEMENT PLAN	The entire amount as wages in box 1	All expenses

1099-MISC) for 2012 must include the full salary of $26,000; (2) Pastor P must report $26,000 as income on his Form 1040; and (3) if Pastor P reports his income taxes as an employee (or as self-employed, but is reclassified as an employee by the IRS), he can deduct his business expenses only as miscellaneous itemized deductions on Schedule A, to the extent they exceed two percent of AGI. The key point is this: accountable reimbursement arrangements cannot fund business expense reimbursements out of an employee's salary.

Unreimbursed expenses

EXAMPLE. In 2012 Pastor D incurred $3,500 in church-related business expenses. His church expected him to pay such expenses out of his salary and accordingly did not reimburse him for these expenses or pay him an allowance. Assuming that the IRS would regard Pastor D as an employee for income tax reporting purposes, he can deduct his business expenses only as a miscellaneous expense on Schedule A—if he itemizes his expenses, and then only to the extent that they, together with most other miscellaneous expenses, exceed two percent of AGI. Because of the adverse tax impact of this method, many churches do not use it. A better method is the adoption of an accountable reimbursement plan that requires periodic accounting of reimbursed expenses by the minister, as described above. It costs the church nothing, yet it may result in significant tax savings to the minister.

EXAMPLE. A pastor claimed a deduction of $9,300 for car expenses. The IRS disallowed $8,000 of this amount. The pastor claimed that the deduction was based on the number of miles he drove in connection with the ministry. The court pointed out that to properly substantiate a deduction for the business use of a car, a taxpayer must have records to prove "the amount of the business use and total use of the automobile, the time of the use of the automobile, and the business purpose for the use. [Taxpayers] must maintain adequate records such as a log, diary, or trip sheet."

The pastor's records consisted of a document prepared by his secretary after the end of the year that contained headings as to the date of travel, the place of travel, the general purpose of the travel, and the mileage. But the court concluded that there were several "problems" with the information contained in this document: "It contains [the pastor's] transportation to and from his residence and his place of business which represents personal commuting and not deductible expenses. It also contains a trip to Los Angeles, California, that the pastor admits was erroneous. There are trips listed for which the stated mileage is obviously wrong. Furthermore, the reasons stated for the travel lack any specificity. In short, we do not find that the pastor's records satisfy the [substantiation] requirements." The court noted that the pastor's records stated that the reason for many of his trips was to attend a "conference" without

any description of the nature of the conference. *Swaringer v. Commissioner, T.C. Summary Opinion 2001-37 (2001).*

EXAMPLE. A taxpayer claimed a deduction for the business use of her car in the amount of $4,300, which she computed by multiplying the standard mileage rate by the number of miles she drove her car for business during the year. The Tax Court noted that the tax code imposes "stringent substantiation requirements for claimed deductions relating to the use of a [car]." The information that must be substantiated to claim a deduction for the business use of a car includes the following: "(1) [t]he amount of the expenditure; (2) the mileage for each business use of the automobile and the total mileage for all use of the automobile during the taxable period; (3) the date of the business use; and (4) the business purpose of the use of the automobile."

The taxpayer testified that she carried a calendar with her in her car and filled it out each day, recording any business activity she conducted. She further testified that she carried a "business miles log" on all of her business trips and made notes about these trips shortly after completing each trip.

The court conceded that the entries in the log and the notations on the calendar generally indicated the miles that were driven for business purposes. However, the court concluded that the taxpayer had failed to meet the substantiation requirements. It noted that she "had not substantiated all the required elements of her automobile use, her records are not reliable, and her testimony lacks credibility. . . . Although [her] records purport to provide the dates of business use of her automobile, miles driven for each business use, and evidence of business purpose, she has not provided the total mileage for all use of her automobile during the year. Thus, she has not substantiated all the elements required by the regulations. . . . When questioned about the pristine condition of the log and the fact that all entries in the log appear to have been made with the same pen, the taxpayer explained that she carried the log in a case with a pen. We also question the reliability of the information recorded in the taxpayer's records. Despite her testimony, we find it unlikely that the records were made contemporaneously with the activities recorded given the condition of the mileage log, the appearance of the entries in the log, and the mistakes in the log." *Aldea v. Commissioner, T.C. Memo. 2000-136 (2000).*

EXAMPLE. The Tax Court denied a taxpayer's $7,500 deduction for the business use of a car. The taxpayer had claimed a mileage expense deduction by multiplying the standard mileage rate by the miles he claimed he drove for business purposes. The court pointed out that use of the standard mileage rates "serves only to substantiate the amount of expenses and not the remaining elements of time and business purpose." It noted that the taxpayer relied on a computer-printout "mileage log" with daily listings of business trips identified only by abbreviations under a column titled "client."

The taxpayer insisted that all of the business miles listed on the mileage log were related to his employment. However, the court concluded that "nowhere does the record reveal the . . . business purpose of each trip recorded on the mileage log," and as a result, it ruled that the taxpayer was not entitled to any deduction for the business use of his car because of his failure to comply with the substantiation requirements.

The court also referred to "irregularities" in the taxpayer's mileage log. For example, "for those dates for which personal mileage is recorded, the mileage log invariably lists either 4, 5, or (more typically) 6 miles of personal travel for the day, for a total of 796 personal miles, compared with 25,096 total business miles recorded. Consulting our own experience, it seems improbable that the taxpayer's daily personal use of his vehicle would be so rigidly fixed and limited, especially in light of the much larger number of business miles he recorded." *Tamms v. Commissioner, T.C. Memo. 2001-201.*

F. THE DEASON RULE

In 1964 the Tax Court ruled that section 265 of the tax code (which denies a deduction for any expense allocable to tax-exempt income) prevented a minister from deducting his unreimbursed transportation expenses to the extent that they were allocable to his tax-exempt housing allowance. *Deason v. Commissioner, 41 T.C. 465 (1964).*

To illustrate, assume that a minister receives compensation of $30,000, of which $10,000 is a nontaxable housing allowance, and incurs unreimbursed business expenses of $1,500. Since one-third of the minister's compensation is tax-exempt, he should not be permitted to deduct one-third of his business expenses, since they are allocable to tax-exempt income and their deduction would amount to a double deduction. This was the conclusion reached by the Tax Court in the *Deason* case.

The IRS agreed with the *Deason* ruling but did not enforce it for several years. In fact, for years the *Internal Revenue Manual* instructed agents not to raise the *Deason* allocation rule when auditing ministers. Unfortunately, this position changed, probably because of a more recent Tax Court decision reaffirming the *Deason* ruling. *Dalan v. Commissioner, T.C. Memo. 1988-106.* In 1992 the Tax Court reaffirmed its rulings in both the *Deason* and *Dalan* decisions. *McFarland v. Commissioner, T.C. Memo. 1992-440.*

✿**KEY POINT.** The IRS has issued audit guidelines for its agents to follow when auditing ministers. The guidelines instruct agents

to apply the *Deason* allocation rule. The guidelines explain this rule as follows: "A minister may deduct ordinary and necessary business expenses. However, if a minister's compensation includes a housing allowance which is exempt from income tax, then that portion of the expenses allocable to this tax-exempt income is not deductible. Before this allocation is made, the total amount of business expenses must be determined."

✿**KEY POINT.** The audit guidelines will instruct IRS agents in the examination of ministers' tax returns. They alert agents to the key questions to ask, and they provide background information along with the IRS position on a number of issues. It is therefore important for ministers to be familiar with these guidelines.

EXAMPLE. A pastor was paid compensation of $78,000, consisting of a salary of $36,000 and a housing allowance of $42,000. He also received self-employment earnings of $21,000 for the performance of miscellaneous religious services (including weddings, funerals, and guest speaking). The pastor incurred business expenses of $25,000 that were not reimbursed by the church, including car expenses, books, office expenses, and business trips. The IRS audited the pastor's tax return and claimed that his deduction for business expenses had to be reduced by the percentage of his total church income that consisted of a housing allowance.

On appeal, the Tax Court noted that section 265 of the tax code provides that "no deduction shall be allowed for any amount otherwise allowable as a deduction which is allocable to one or more classes of income wholly exempt from taxes." The court noted that the pastor "received both nonexempt income and a tax-exempt parsonage allowance for his ministry work. The ministry expenses he attempts to deduct were incurred while he was earning both nonexempt income and a tax-exempt parsonage allowance. This is precisely the situation section 265 targets. . . . The parsonage allowance is a class of income wholly exempt from tax and section 265 expressly disallows a deduction to the extent that the expenses are directly or indirectly allocable to his nontaxable ministry income."

The court noted that since the pastor "failed to provide evidence that would allow the court to determine which of his ministry activities generated which expenses, the court will allocate the expenses on a pro rata basis. The court concludes that the pastor's Schedule C ministry activities generated 22 percent of his total ministry income, and therefore allocates 22 percent of his ministry expenses to Schedule C, and the balance to Schedule A. Because 54 percent of his ministry salary was his parsonage allowance ($42,000/$78,000), 54 percent of his Schedule A deductions are rendered nondeductible because of section 265. The pastor may deduct (subject to the 2 percent floor) the balance as itemized miscellaneous deductions on Schedule A." The court concluded that the reduced deduction for business expenses applied to both income taxes and self-employment taxes.

It has generally been assumed that the *Deason* rule does not apply to the computation of a minister's self-employment taxes, since the housing allowance is not tax-exempt in computing self-employment taxes. This understanding is contained in the IRS audit guidelines for ministers. However, the court ignored this logic and applied the *Deason* rule to the pastor's self-employment taxes. It observed, "In computing his net earnings from self-employment, a pastor must include all his earnings from his ministry, including his parsonage allowance, and may claim the deductions 'allowed by chapter 1 of the tax code which are attributable to such trade or business.' Because a portion of the pastor's deductions is allocable to his parsonage allowance, and is disallowed as a deduction by section 265, it may not be deducted in computing his net earnings from self-employment." Fortunately, this case is a "small case," meaning it cannot be cited as precedent. *Young v. Commissioner, T.C. Summary Opinion 2005-76.*

1. IRS AUDIT GUIDELINES FOR MINISTERS

The IRS audit guidelines for ministers explain the *Deason* rule as follows:

> *A minister may deduct ordinary and necessary business expenses. However, if a minister's compensation includes a parsonage or housing allowance which is exempt from income under IRC §107, the prorated portion of the expenses allocable to the tax exempt income is not deductible, per IRC §265, Deason v. Commissioner, 41 T.C. 465 (1964),* Dalan v. Commissioner, T.C. Memo. 1988-106, *and* McFarland v. Commissioner, T.C. Memo. 1992-440.
>
> *Before this allocation is made, the total amount of business expenses must be determined. Ministers are subject to the same substantiation requirements as other taxpayers.*

How do ministers reduce their business expenses to properly reflect this rule? The guidelines provide IRS agents with the following procedure:

> *Once total business expenses have been determined, the non-deductible portion can be computed using the following formula.*
>
> *Step 1*
> *Divide the allowable housing allowance or fair rental value (FRV) of parsonage by the total ministry income to get the nontaxable income percentage. Total ministry income includes salary, fees, expense allowances under nonaccountable plans plus the allowable housing allowance or FRV of the parsonage.*

> *Step 2*
> *Multiply the total business expenses times the nontaxable income percentage from step 1 to get the expenses allocable to nontaxable income which is not deductible.*

The audit guidelines illustrate the *Deason* rule with the following two examples.

EXAMPLE. F receives a salary of $36,000, an exempt housing allowance of $18,000 and an auto expense allowance of $6,000 for his services as an ordained minister. F incurs business expenses as follows: auto, $7,150; vestments, $350; dues, $120; publications and supplies, $300; totaling $7,920. His nondeductible expenses are computed as follows:

Step 1: $18,000 housing allowance/nontaxable income divided by $60,000 total ministry income ($36,000 salary, $18,000 housing, and $6,000 car allowance) equals 30 percent nontaxable income percentage.

Step 2: Total business expenses of $7,920 x 30 percent, the nontaxable income percentage equals $2,376 the nondeductible expenses.

Total expenses $7,920 less the nondeductible expenses of $2,376 equals the deductible expenses of $5,544.

F's deductible expenses are reported as Schedule A miscellaneous deductions since his church considers him an employee and issues a W-2. These expenses, along with any other miscellaneous deductions are subject to a further reduction of 2 percent of his adjusted gross income.

EXAMPLE. G received a salary of $12,000, a housing allowance of $9,000, and earned $3,000 for various speaking engagements, weddings, funerals, etc., all related to her ministry. She reports her salary as "wages" on page 1 of her Form 1040 and her fees on Schedule C. Because her actual housing costs ($6,000) were less than her housing allowance and the FRV of her home for the year, she must include $3,000 of her housing allowance as "other income" for income tax purposes. Her total business expenses are $4,500. The computation of deductible expenses is shown below:

Step 1: $6,000 (housing allowance actually exempt from income tax) divided by $24,000 total ministry income ($12,000 salary + $9,000 housing + $3,000 fees) equals 25 percent nontaxable income percentage.

Step 2: Total expenses $4,500 times 25 percent nontaxable income percentage equals $1,125 nondeductible expenses. Total expenses $4,500 less $1,125 equals $3,375 deductible expenses.

Note that this $3,375 would further be allocable between Schedule A miscellaneous deductions (related to salary) and Schedule C (related to other fees).

However, this allocation will not change G's self-employment tax, since all ministry income and ministry expenses are included in the computation, regardless of where they are reported on the return for income tax purposes. The allocation between Schedule A and Schedule C will also affect any AGI-dependent computations.

2. MINIMIZING OR AVOIDING THE DEASON RULE

Two important considerations can result in substantial tax savings for ministers:

- Since a housing allowance is not an exclusion or self-employment (Social Security) tax purposes, no reduction in business expenses is required in computing these taxes on Schedule SE. This understanding is affirmed in the IRS audit guidelines for ministers and in IRS Publication 517. It was questioned in a 2005 Tax Court decision, *Young v. Commissioner, T.C. Summary Opinion 2005-76* (see above).
- The adverse impact of the *Deason* ruling can be eliminated if a church simply adopts an accountable reimbursement arrangement (described in section E of this chapter). The reason is that section 265 of the tax code reduces any deduction for business expenses allocable to tax-exempt income. Under an accountable reimbursement arrangement, however, no deduction is claimed, since the employer's reimbursements are not reported as income.

The *Dalan* and *McFarland* cases dealt only with the *unreimbursed* business and professional expenses of self-employed ministers. However, it is likely that the same reduction rule will apply to business expenses reimbursed by a church under a nonaccountable plan and to all ministers, whether they are self-employed or employees for income tax reporting purposes, since section 265 of the tax code, upon which these cases are based, prohibits a deduction for any amount allocable to income that is exempt from tax. Whether a minister is an employee or self-employed, and whether business expenses are unreimbursed or reimbursed under a nonaccountable plan, the expenses are claimed as a deduction—on Schedule C for self-employed ministers, and on Schedule A for ministers who are employees.

3. PARSONAGES

What about ministers who live in church-owned parsonages? Are they affected by the *Deason* rule? The IRS *Tax Guide for Churches and Religious Organizations* states: "A minister who receives a parsonage or rental allowance excludes that amount from his income, and the portion of expenses allocable to the excludable amount is not deductible." This statement indicates that the IRS will apply the *Deason* rule to ministers who live in church-owned parsonages.

4. COMPUTING THE REDUCTION

Another ambiguity pertains to the proper manner of making the reduction in business and professional expenses called for by the *Deason* rule. IRS Publication 517 (Social Security and Other Information for Clergy and Other Religious Workers) presents a full-page example of a schedule that ministers can use to compute the reduction in their business expense deduction required by the *Deason* rule.

5. OTHER ITEMS OF NONTAXABLE INCOME

Ministers may have items of nontaxable income in addition to a housing allowance. Common examples include gifts, inheritances, life insurance proceeds, and interest on some government bonds. Must these items of nontaxable income be lumped together with a housing allowance in applying the *Deason* rule? In most cases the answer will be no. In the *Deason* case the Tax Court ruled that compensation earned by ministers in the exercise of their ministry cannot be used to pay business expenses incurred in earning this compensation. As a result, any business expense deduction must be reduced by the percentage of total compensation that is nontaxable as a result of the housing allowance. This principle does not apply to gifts, inheritances, life insurance proceeds, interest on government bonds, or most other forms of nontaxable income, since (unlike a housing allowance) they are not associated with services performed in the exercise of ministry. Therefore, business expenses incurred in the course of ministerial services need not be reduced by percentage of a minister's income that consists of such items.

6. CRITIQUE

A compelling argument can be made that the *Deason* case makes no sense when applied to ministers. The IRS (and the Tax Court) are saying that ministers must reduce their business expenses by the percentage of their total compensation that consists of a *tax-exempt* housing allowance. But a housing allowance is tax-exempt, under section 107 of the tax code, only "to the extent used to rent or provide a home." This being the case, it is impossible for one cent of a *tax-exempt* housing allowance to be used to pay for a minister's business expenses. Business expenses are neither directly nor indirectly allocable to a minister's tax-free housing allowance.

Many nonclergy taxpayers doubtless receive tax-exempt income and use that income to pay business expenses. There may be some logic in requiring such taxpayers to reduce their business expense deductions by the percentage of their total compensation that is tax-free. However, this logic does not apply in the case of a minister whose tax-exempt income is tax-exempt *only if used exclusively for housing-related expenses* rather than the payment of business expenses. Note, however, that both the IRS and the Tax Court have rejected this reasoning, and so it represents an aggressive position that should not be adopted without the advice of a tax professional.

G. ITEMIZED DEDUCTIONS

If your itemized deductions exceed your standard deduction (see section B of this chapter), you should report your itemized deductions on Schedule A (Form 1040). This section will summarize the itemized deductions.

Taxpayers may choose to claim either the standard deduction or itemized deductions (subject to certain limitations) for certain expenses incurred during the year. Prior to the enactment of the Economic Growth and Tax Relief Reconciliation Act of 2001 (EGTRRA), the total amount of allowable itemized deductions (with a few exceptions) was reduced by 3 percent of the amount of the taxpayer's adjusted gross income in excess of a specified amount ($132,950 in 2001). However, itemized deductions could not be reduced by more than 80 percent. The starting point for the phaseout ($132,950 in 2001) was adjusted annually for inflation.

EGTRRA repealed this limitation on itemized deductions over a five-year period beginning in 2006. The limit on itemized deductions was reduced by one-third in taxable years beginning in 2006 and 2007 and by two-thirds in taxable years beginning in 2008 and 2009. The overall limitation was repealed in 2010. The repeal was extended through 2012 by the Tax Relief and Job Creation Act of 2010. Unless extended further by Congress, the pre-2006 limitation on itemized deductions will apply after 2012.

The limitation on itemized deductions applied to all itemized deductions except medical expenses, investment interest, and casualty losses. *It did apply to charitable contribution deductions.*

1. MEDICAL EXPENSES

✶ **New in 2012.** The standard mileage rate allowed for operating a car for medical reasons was 23 cents per mile for 2012. The rate is 24 cents in 2013.

✶ **New in 2014.** The health care reform legislation enacted by Congress in 2010 increases the adjusted gross income threshold for claiming the itemized deduction for medical expenses from 7.5 percent to 10 percent beginning in 2013. Individuals age 65 and older would be able to claim the itemized deduction for medical expenses at 7.5 percent of adjusted gross income through 2016.

You may deduct certain medical and dental expenses (for yourself, your spouse, and your dependents) if you itemize your deductions on Schedule A, but only to the extent that your expenses exceed 7.5 percent of your AGI. You must reduce your medical expenses by the amounts of any reimbursements you receive for those expenses before applying the 7.5 percent test. Reimbursements include amounts you receive from insurance or other sources for your medical expenses (including Medicare). It does not matter if the reimbursement is paid to the patient, the doctor, or the hospital.

Deductible medical expenses
Deductible medical expenses include the following:

- fees for medical services;
- fees for hospital services;
- physical exams;
- meals and lodging provided by a hospital during medical treatment;
- medical and hospital insurance premiums that you pay;
- special equipment;
- special items (bandages, false teeth, artificial limbs, eyeglasses, hearing aids, crutches, etc.);
- transportation for necessary medical care;
- medicines and drugs requiring a prescription;
- the portion of a life-care fee or founder's fee paid either monthly or in a lump sum under an agreement with a retirement home that is allocable to medical care;
- wages of an attendant who provides medical care;
- the cost of home improvements if the main reason is for medical care;
- cost of lead-based paint removal from your home;
- special school or home for mentally or physically disabled persons;
- Medicare A premiums paid by ministers and others not covered under Social Security;
- Medicare B premiums; and
- Medicare D premiums.

Nondeductible medical expenses
The following items are *not* deductible as medical expenses:

- health savings account payments for medical expenses;
- flexible spending account reimbursements for medical expenses (if contributions were on a pre-tax basis);
- funeral services;

- health club dues;
- household help;
- life insurance;
- maternity clothes;
- payroll tax paid for Medicare insurance (Medicare A);
- nonprescription medicines and drugs;
- prescription drugs you ordered from another country (in most cases);
- vitamin supplements unless recommended by a physician as a treatment for a specific medical condition;
- teeth whitening;
- bottled water;
- weight-loss expenses not for the treatment of obesity or other disease;
- nursing care for a healthy baby;
- programs to stop smoking;
- toothpaste, cosmetics, and toiletries; and
- trips for general improvement of health.

Personal injuries

Amounts you receive for personal injuries you sustain in an accident present special problems. Do not reduce your medical expenses by any repayments you receive for loss of earnings or damages for personal injury. However, you must reduce your medical expenses by the portion of any personal injury award (whether by settlement or court judgment) that repays you for hospitalization and medical care.

If you receive a settlement or award after the year in which you were injured, the part of the settlement or award that compensates you for medical expenses you incurred and deducted in the year of the accident must be included in your income in the year you receive the settlement or award. If a portion of the settlement or award is allocable to future medical expenses, you must reduce any medical expenses you pay this year and in future years because of your injuries until the amount you receive in settlement has been completely used. You may include amounts you pay after that in your medical expenses.

2. TAXES

If you itemize your deductions on Schedule A, you may deduct certain taxes you pay during the year. These include (1) state and local income taxes, (2) real property taxes, (3) personal property taxes, and (4) for ministers (and others who are self-employed for Social Security), half of their self-employment taxes as an adjustment to gross income (line 27, Form 1040). The main types of deductible taxes are summarized below.

Income taxes

You may deduct state and local income taxes, including taxes on interest income that is exempt from federal income tax. You may not deduct state and local taxes on other exempt income. Deduct state and local income taxes withheld from your salary or paid by you on an estimated basis. However, estimated tax payments are not deductible if you later determine that no estimated taxes were necessary. If you receive a refund of state or local income taxes in a year after the year in which you paid them, you may have to include all or a part of the refund in your income in the year you receive it. If you did not itemize your deductions in the previous year, you do not have to include the refund.

Real estate taxes

Real estate taxes are any taxes on real property levied for the general public welfare. They generally do not include taxes charged for local benefits and improvements that increase the value of your property. If you bought or sold real estate during 2012, the real estate taxes ordinarily must be divided between the buyer and seller according to the number of days in the real property tax year (the period to which the tax relates) that each owned the property. The seller pays the taxes up to the date of the sale, and the buyer pays the taxes beginning with the date of sale. If your monthly mortgage payment includes an amount placed in escrow for real estate taxes, you may not deduct the total of these amounts included in your payments for the year. You may only deduct the amount of the tax that the lender actually paid to the taxing authority.

If you receive a refund in 2012 of real estate taxes you paid in 2012, you must reduce your deduction by the amount of the refund. If you receive a refund in 2012 of taxes you deducted in a prior year, you must include the refund in income in the year you receive it. However, you only need to include the amount of the deduction that reduced your tax in the earlier year. If you did not itemize deductions in the year you paid the tax, do not report the refund as income.

➡ **TIP.** Ministers who own their homes and pay real property taxes can include the full amount of such taxes in computing their housing allowance exclusion, and may also fully deduct the amount of the taxes as an itemized deduction on Schedule A (if they itemize their deductions). For a full discussion of the housing allowance, see Chapter 6.

Personal property taxes

To qualify as a deductible personal property tax, a state or local tax must meet three tests: (1) the tax must be based solely on the value of the personal property; (2) the tax must be charged on a yearly basis, even if it is collected more than once a year, or less than once a year; and (3) the tax must be charged on personal property.

Sales taxes

The American Jobs Creation Act of 2004 provided that, at the election of the taxpayer, an itemized deduction may be taken for state and local general sales taxes in lieu of the itemized deduction for state and local income taxes. Taxpayers have two options with respect to the determination of the sales tax deduction amount. They can deduct the total amount of general state and local sales taxes paid by accumulating receipts showing general sales taxes paid, or they can use tables created by the IRS (see IRS Publication 600).

The tables are based on average consumption by taxpayers on a state-by-state basis, taking into account filing status, number of dependents, adjusted gross income, and rates of state and local general sales taxation. Taxpayers who use the tables may, in addition, deduct eligible general sales taxes paid with respect to the purchase of motor vehicles, boats, and other items specified by the IRS. Sales taxes for items that may be added to the tables would not be reflected in the tables themselves.

This provision was added to address the unequal treatment of taxpayers in the nine states that assess no income tax. Taxpayers in these states cannot take advantage of the itemized deduction for state income taxes. Allowing them to deduct sales taxes will help offset this disadvantage.

❖ **KEY POINT.** This deduction was scheduled to expire after 2005, but Congress extended it through 2009, and the Tax Relief and Job Creation Act further extended it through 2011. Unless Congress extends it again, it will not be available in computing taxes for 2012.

➥ **TIP.** While the sales tax deduction mainly benefited taxpayers with a state or local sales tax but no income tax (taxpayers living in Alaska, Florida, Nevada, South Dakota, Texas, Washington, or Wyoming), it provided a larger deduction to any taxpayer who paid more in sales taxes than income taxes. For example, a person who purchased a new car might have had sales taxes in excess of state income taxes.

3. INTEREST

Interest is an amount paid for the use of borrowed money. To deduct interest on a debt, you must legally be liable for the debt. You may not deduct payments you make for someone else if you are not legally liable to make them. Both you and the lender must intend that the loan be repaid. In addition, there must be a debtor-creditor relationship between you and the lender.

If you own your home, your most significant interest deduction probably will be for mortgage interest you pay on your home. In most cases you will be able to deduct all of the interest you pay on any loans secured by your main home, including first and second mortgages, home equity loans, and refinanced mortgages. Whether your home mortgage interest payments are deductible depends on the date you took out the mortgage, the amount of the mortgage, and your use of the proceeds.

If all of your mortgages fit into one of the following categories, you can deduct *all* of your interest and report it on Schedule A (Form 1040).

(1) Mortgages you took out on or before October 13, 1987 ("grandfathered debt")
(2) Mortgages you took out after October 13, 1987, to buy, build, or improve your home ("home acquisition debt"), but only if throughout 2012 these mortgages, plus any grandfathered debt, totaled $1 million or less ($500,000 or less if married filing separately)
(3) Mortgages you took out after October 13, 1987, other than to buy, build, or improve your home ("home equity debt"), but only if throughout 2012 these mortgages totaled $100,000 or less ($50,000 or less if married filing separately) and totaled no more than the fair market value of your home reduced by (1) and (2)

If you had a main home *and* a second home, the dollar limits explained in the second and third categories described above apply to the total mortgage on both homes.

➥ **TIP.** Ministers who own their homes can deduct mortgage interest payments as an itemized deduction even though such payments were included in computing the housing allowance exclusion (the so-called double deduction). *IRC 265(a)(6).* However, ministers are subject to the limitations on mortgage loans discussed in this section.

It is not always easy to determine whether an item is deductible as interest. Consider the following items:

- **Late payment charges.** You may deduct a late payment charge if it was not for a specific service performed by your mortgage holder.
- **Points.** The term "points" is sometimes used to describe certain charges paid by a borrower. They are also called loan origination fees, maximum loan charges, or premium charges. If the payment of any of these charges is only for the use of money, it ordinarily is interest paid in advance and must be deducted in installments over the life of the mortgage (not deducted in full in the year of payment). However, points are deductible in the year paid if the following requirements are satisfied: (1) your loan is secured by your main home; (2) paying points is an established business practice in your area; (3) the points you paid were not more than the points generally charged in your area; (4) you use the cash method of accounting; (5) the points were not paid in the place of amounts that ordinarily are stated separately on the settlement statement, such as appraisal fees, attorney fees, and property taxes; (6) you use your loan to buy or build your main home; (7) the points were computed as a percentage of the principal amount of the mortgage; (8) the amount is

clearly shown on the settlement statement; and (9) the funds you provided at or before closing, plus any points the seller paid, were at least as much as the points charged.

- **Mortgage prepayment penalty.** A penalty that you are assessed for paying off a loan early is deductible as interest.
- **Service charges.** These amounts are not deductible as interest.
- **Credit investigation fees.** These amounts are not deductible as interest.
- **Credit card finance charges.** These amounts are deductible as interest. However, to the extent that they relate to personal items, they are not deductible.

Interest that you pay for personal reasons (i.e., interest on car loans, credit cards, and personal loans) no longer is deductible as an itemized deduction on Schedule A.

4. CHARITABLE CONTRIBUTIONS

The rules that govern the deductibility of contributions are of vital concern to ministers and churches. Because of the significance of these rules, they are considered separately in Chapter 8.

5. CASUALTY AND THEFT LOSSES

Most taxpayers have at some time suffered damage to their property as a result of hurricanes, earthquakes, tornadoes, fires, vandalism, car accidents, floods, or similar events. When property is damaged or destroyed by such events, it is called a casualty. If your property is stolen, you may also have a deductible theft loss. You must itemize your deductions on Schedule A to be able to claim a casualty or theft loss to nonbusiness property. To determine your deduction, you must reduce the amount of your casualty and theft losses by any insurance or reimbursement you receive. No deduction is allowed for a casualty or theft loss that is covered by insurance unless a timely insurance claim for reimbursement has been filed.

You can deduct personal casualty or theft losses only to the extent that: (1) the amount of each separate casualty or theft loss is more than $100, and (2) the total amount of all losses during the year (reduced by the $100 limit) is more than 10 percent of the amount on Form 1040, line 38.

The 10 percent of AGI limitation does not apply to a casualty loss that occurred in an area determined by the president of the United States to warrant federal disaster assistance. For information on disaster losses, see Publication 547.

To claim a casualty or theft loss, you must be able to show that the loss in fact occurred. In addition, the loss generally is defined as the lesser of (1) the decrease in fair market value of the property as a result of the casualty or theft or (2) your adjusted basis in the property before the casualty or theft.

Calculate nonbusiness casualty and theft losses on Form 4684 and report them on Schedule A as an itemized deduction.

H. MOVING EXPENSES

1. GENERAL RULES

In general, you may deduct a portion of your moving expenses incurred because of a change of job, or your acceptance of a new job, if you satisfy the following conditions:

Move related to start of work
Your move must be closely related, both in time and place, to the start of work at your new job location. In general, moving expenses incurred within one year from the date you first reported to work are considered closely related in time to the start of work at the new location. It is not necessary that you make arrangements to work before moving to a new location, as long as you actually do go to work. If you do not move within one year, you ordinarily may not deduct the expenses unless you can show that circumstances existed that prevented the move within that time. A move is generally not closely related in place to the start of work if the distance from your new home to the new job location is greater than the distance from your former home to the new job location.

Distance test
Your new job location must be at least 50 miles farther from your former home than your old job location was. For example, if your old job was 3 miles from your former home, your new job must be at least 53 miles from that home (measured according to the shortest of the more commonly traveled routes between those points).

Time test
If you report your income taxes as an employee, you must work full time for at least 39 weeks during the first 12 months after you arrive in the general area of your new job location. You do not have to work for one employer for the 39 weeks. However, you must work full time within the same general commuting area. If you report your income taxes as a self-employed person, you must work full time for at least 39 weeks during the first 12 months and for a total of at least 78 weeks during the first 24 months after you arrive in the area of your new job location.

If you are married and file a joint return and both you and your spouse work full time, either of you may satisfy the full-time work test. However, you may not combine your weeks of work.

You may deduct your moving expenses even if you have not met the time test by the due date of your 2012 return. You may do this if you expect to meet the 39-week test by the end of 2013 or the 78-week test by the end of 2013. If you do not meet the time test by then, you either must amend your 2012 return or report your moving expense deduction as other income on your Form 1040 for the tax year you cannot meet the test. These time tests do not apply in some situations that ordinarily are not relevant to ministers.

❋**KEY POINT.** The reporting of employee moving expenses and reimbursements is summarized in Table 7-8.

2. DEDUCTIBLE MOVING EXPENSES

Deductible moving expenses include the following:

- **Moving your household goods and personal effects.** You may deduct the cost of packing, crating and transporting your household goods and personal effects from your former home to your new one. You also may deduct the cost of storing and insuring household goods and personal effects within any consecutive 30-day period after the day your things are moved from your former home and before they are delivered to your new home.
- **Travel expenses.** You may deduct the cost of transportation and lodging (but not meals) for yourself and members of your household while traveling from your former home to your new home. You may deduct expenses of only one trip to your new home. However, all of the members of your household do not need to travel together.

3. NONDEDUCTIBLE MOVING EXPENSES

You may not deduct any of the following expenses as moving expenses:

- premove house-hunting expenses,
- temporary living expenses,
- the expenses of disposing of your former home and obtaining your new home,
- home improvements to help you sell your former home,
- loss on the sale of your former home,
- mortgage penalties,
- any part of the purchase price of your new home,
- meal expenses incurred while moving to your new home,
- storage charges (except those incurred in transit), or
- real estate taxes.

4. EMPLOYER REIMBURSEMENTS

If your allowable moving expenses (as defined above) are reimbursed by your employer under an accountable arrangement, then the reimbursements are not reportable as taxable income for you, and there are no deductions to report. Employer reimbursements that are not pursuant to an accountable arrangement must be included in your taxable income. As noted previously in this chapter, an accountable arrangement is one by which an employer reimburses only those expenses that are deductible and that are properly substantiated.

❋**KEY POINT.** You can use a standard mileage rate for transportation expenses incurred in moving. For 2012 the standard mileage rate for moving was 23 cents per mile. Do not use the standard mileage rate that is used for business travel. Use Form 3903 to compute the moving expense deduction for unreimbursed moving expenses (or expenses reimbursed under a nonaccountable arrangement).

❋**KEY POINT.** Qualified moving expenses an employer pays to a third party on behalf of the employee (e.g., to a moving company) are not reported on Form W-2. Qualified moving expense reimbursements an employer pays directly to an employee are reported in box 12 of Form W-2 and are identified using code P. All other moving expense reimbursements (nonqualified expenses) are included in wages (Form W-2, box 1) and are subject to income tax withholding and Social Security and Medicare taxes.

I. TAX CREDITS

A credit is a direct dollar-for-dollar reduction in your tax liability. It is much more valuable than deductions and exclusions, which merely reduce taxable income. Credits are reported on lines 47–54 of Form 1040, immediately after you compute your actual tax liability. For example, if your total tax liability amounted to $4,000 for 2012 and you have credits totaling $1,000, your tax liability is reduced to $3,000. The more common credits claimed by ministers are summarized in this section.

EXAMPLE. An ordained minister who qualified for the earned income credit was a part-time pastor of a church from which he received a salary of $2,400 and a housing and utility allowance of $600. During that year the minister received directly from individuals, fees totaling $500 for performing marriages, baptisms, and other personal services. The minister also received $2,000 of farming income. In an earlier year the minister had elected to be exempt from self-employment tax with respect to amounts received for services performed in the exercise of ministerial duties. This election was made by filing a Form 4361. As a result, the $2,400 of salary, the housing and utility allowance of $600, and the $500 of fees, all of which would otherwise be includible in net earnings from self-employment, were exempt from the self-employment tax. The $2,000 of income from farming was not exempt from self-employment tax. The gross income of $4,900 was also the minister's AGI for the year.

The IRS ruled that in computing the minister's earned income for purposes of the earned income credit, he should include the salary of $2,400 and the $600 housing and utility allowance. The $500 of fees received from individuals for performing marriages and other personal services was not received by the minister as an employee and thus is not earned income for purposes of the earned income credit. The $2,000 from farming is earned income because the election to be exempt from self-employment tax does not apply to services not performed in the exercise of the ministry. *Revenue Ruling 79-78.*

1. CHILD AND DEPENDENT CARE CREDIT

✿ **KEY POINT.** See Chapter 5, section I.8, for a discussion of the exclusion for employer-provided dependent care.

If you paid someone to care for a qualifying individual so you (and your spouse, if you are married) could work or look for work, you may be able to claim the credit for child and dependent care expenses. If you are married, both you and your spouse must have earned income unless one spouse was either a full-time student or was physically or mentally incapable of self-care. The expenses you paid must have been for the care of one or more of the following qualifying individuals:

- Your qualifying child who was under age 13 when care was provided and who lived with you for more than half the year. A noncustodial parent, however, cannot treat a child as

a qualifying person even if the parent may claim the child as an exemption.
- Your spouse who was mentally or physically not able to care for himself or herself and who has the same principal place of abode as you for more than one-half of the year.
- Your dependent who was physically or mentally not able to care for himself or herself, for whom you can claim an exemption, and who has the same principal place of abode as you for more than one-half of the year.

In addition to the conditions just described, to take the credit, you must meet all the following conditions:

- The care must be for one or more qualifying persons who are identified on your Form 1040 (usually this means the Social Security number of the qualifying person).
- You (and your spouse if filing jointly) must have earned income during the year.
- You must pay child and dependent care expenses so you (and your spouse if filing jointly) can work or look for work.
- Your filing status must be a status other than married filing separate.
- The payments for care cannot be paid to someone you can claim as your dependent or to your child who is under age 19, even if he or she is not your dependent.
- You must report the name, address, and taxpayer identification number (either the Social Security number or the employer identification number) of the care provider on your return. If the care provider is tax exempt, you need only report the name and address on your return. You can use Form W-10 (Dependent Care Provider's Identification and Certification) to request this information from the care provider. If you do not provide information regarding the

TABLE 7-8

REPORTING YOUR MOVING EXPENSES AND REIMBURSEMENTS

IF YOUR FORM W-2 SHOWS . . .	AND YOU HAVE . . .	THEN . . .
your reimbursements reported only in box 12 with code P	moving expenses greater than the amount in box 12	file Form 3903 showing all allowable expenses and reimbursements.
your reimbursement reported only in box 12 with code P	moving expenses equal to the amount in box 12	do not file Form 3903.
your reimbursement divided between box 12 and box 1	moving expense greater than the amount in box 12	file Form 3903 showing all allowable expenses but only the reimbursements reported in box 12.
your entire reimbursement reported as wages in box 1	moving expenses	file Form 3903 showing all allowable expenses but no reimbursements.
no reimbursement	moving expenses	file Form 3903 showing all allowable expenses.

care provider, you may still be eligible for the credit if it is shown that you exercised due diligence in attempting to provide the required information.

- If you exclude or deduct dependent care benefits provided by a dependent care benefits plan, the total amount you exclude or deduct must be less than the dollar limit for qualifying expenses (generally, $3,000 if one qualifying person was cared for or $6,000 if two or more qualifying persons were cared for). If two or more qualifying persons were cared for, the amount you exclude or deduct will always be less than the dollar limit, since the amount you can exclude or deduct is limited to $5,000.

If you qualify for the credit, complete Form 1040A, Schedule 2, or Form 2441 with Form 1040. If you received dependent care benefits from your employer (this amount should be shown on your Form W-2), you must complete Part III of Schedule 2 (Form 1040A) or Form 2441. You cannot use Form 1040EZ if you claim the Child and Dependent Care Credit.

The credit is a percentage, based on your adjusted gross income, of the amount of work-related child and dependent care expenses you paid to a care provider. There is a maximum dollar limit of dependent care expenses you can use for this credit. The amount of the maximum dollar limit depends on the taxable year and the number of qualifying children. These dollar limits must be reduced by the amount of any dependent care benefits provided by your employer that you exclude from your income. Refer to Publication 503 (Child and Dependent Care Expenses) for additional information.

If you pay someone to look after your dependent or spouse in your home, you may be a household employer. If you are a household employer, you may have to withhold and pay Social Security and Medicare taxes and pay a federal unemployment tax. For information, refer to Publication 926 (Household Employer's Tax Guide).

Special rules for ministers
Earned income includes wages, salaries, other taxable employee compensation, and net earnings from self-employment. IRS Publication 503 states: "Whether or not you have an approved Form 4361, amounts you received for performing ministerial duties as an employee are earned income. This includes wages, salaries, and other taxable employee compensation. However, amounts you received for ministerial duties, but not as an employee, do not count as earned income. Examples include fees for performing marriages and honoraria for delivering speeches. Any amount you received for work that is not related to your ministerial duties is earned income."

2. EARNED INCOME CREDIT

✸**KEY POINT.** The earned income credit (or advanced earned income credit payments you receive) has no effect on certain

welfare benefits, including temporary assistance for needy families, Medicaid and supplemental security income (SSI), food stamps, and low-income housing.

✱ **New in 2012.** The maximum earned income credit for 2012 is (1) $475 with no qualifying child, (2) $3,169 with one qualifying child, (3) $5,236 with two qualifying children, and (4) $5,891 with three or more qualifying children.

If you qualify for it, the earned income credit (EIC) reduces the tax you owe. Even if you do not owe tax, you can get a refund of the credit. Depending on your situation, the credit can be as high as $5,891. Also, you may be able to get part of the credit added to your pay instead of waiting until after the end of the year.

You cannot take the credit if your earned income (or AGI, if greater) is more than

- $13,980 ($19,190 if married filing jointly) if you do not have a qualifying child,
- $36,920 ($42,130 if married filing jointly) if you have one qualifying child,
- $41,952 ($47,162 if married filing jointly) if you have two qualifying children, or
- $445,060 ($50,270 if married filing jointly) if you have three or more qualifying children.

These limits are summarized in Table 7-9.

Housing allowances and the earned income credit
Should ministers treat a housing allowance (or annual rental value of a parsonage) as earned income when computing the earned income credit? If so, then earned income will be higher, making it more likely that a minister will not qualify for the earned income credit.

Section 32(c)(2)(A) of the tax code provides: "The term earned income means . . . wages, salaries, tips, and other employee compensation, but only if such amounts are includible in gross income for the taxable year, plus the amount of the taxpayer's net earnings from self-employment for the taxable year (within the meaning of section 1402(a))."

It is not clear if this language includes or excludes a minister's housing allowance or the annual rental value of a parsonage within the definition of earned income for purposes of the earned income credit. Consider the following points.

Ministers who report income taxes as employees
Section 32(c)(2)(A) includes within the definition of earned income both employee compensation and net earnings from self-employment. A pastor's salary obviously is included in earned income under this definition. But what about a housing allowance? Is it included because it constitutes net earnings from employment under code section 1402(a)? The answer is not clear. Pastors have

a dual tax status. While most are employees for federal income tax purposes, they are self-employed for Social Security with respect to services performed in the exercise of ministry. *IRC 3121(b)(8)(A).* This means that most ministers have "employee compensation" from their ministry, but this same compensation also constitutes "net earnings from self-employment" for purposes of the self-employment tax.

Read literally, section 32 would require ministers who report their church salary as employees to "double report" their salary in computing their income for purposes of the earned income credit, since their salary constitutes employee compensation and also is net earnings from self-employment within the meaning of section 1402(a). The instructions for line 64 (Form 1040) avoid this result for ministers who are not exempt from self-employment taxes.

Ministers who report their income taxes as self-employed

Section 32 only makes sense for those few ministers who report their church compensation as self-employment earnings in computing both income taxes and self-employment taxes. For these persons, there would be no double reporting of income in computing the earned income credit, and a housing allowance (or annual value of a parsonage) clearly would be included in the computation of earned income.

Ministers who are exempt from self-employment tax

About one-third of all ministers have exempted themselves from self-employment tax by filing a timely Form 4361 with the IRS. Such ministers do not report their church salary, housing allowance, or annual rental value of a parsonage as earnings from self-employment in computing their self-employment tax liability. As a result, while revised tax code section 32 would treat their church salary as earned income in computing the earned income credit, it would not treat a housing allowance or the annual rental value of a parsonage as earned income, since such amounts are not reported as net earnings from self-employment under section 1402(a). Is this what Congress intended? Ministers who have opted out of Social Security do not need to include their housing allowance (or annual rental value of a parsonage) in computing earned income for

purposes of the earned income credit, but those who have not opted out of Social Security must do so?

Chaplains

The income tax regulations specify that service performed by a duly ordained, commissioned, or licensed minister "as an employee of the United States, a State, Territory, or possession of the United States, the District of Columbia, a foreign government, or a political subdivision of any of the foregoing" is not considered to be "in the exercise of his ministry" even though such service may involve the ministration of sacerdotal functions or the conduct of religious worship. *Treas. Reg. § 1.1402(c)-5.* This means that government-employed chaplains are not self-employed for Social Security purposes and have no "section 1402(a)" earnings. Thus, they would not include a housing allowance or the annual rental value of a parsonage as earned income for purposes of the earned income credit. Here we see another absurd result. Why should chaplains enjoy this advantageous rule, but not other ministers?

Conclusions

In summary, the problem is that ministers are always self-employed for Social Security with respect to their ministerial services, and so their entire church compensation constitutes net earnings from self-employment unless they filed a timely exemption application (Form 4361) that was approved by the IRS. Logically, then, housing allowances should be treated as earned income for those ministers who have *not* exempted themselves from self-employment taxes by filing Form 4361. On the other hand, ministers who have exempted themselves from self-employment taxes should not treat their housing allowance as earned income in computing the earned income credit.

As illogical as this result may seem, it is exactly what the IRS instructions to Form 1040 require (as illustrated below), and this position is confirmed in IRS Publication 596 (see below). The IRS national office is taking the position that there is nothing it can do to change a law enacted by Congress. So for now, whether a minister's housing allowance (or annual rental value of a parsonage) is included within the definition of "earned income" for purposes of the earned income credit

TABLE 7-9

EARNED INCOME CREDIT LIMITS (2012)

	THREE OR MORE QUALIFYING CHILDREN	TWO QUALIFYING CHILDREN	ONE QUALIFYING CHILD	NO QUALIFYING CHILD
MAXIMUM CREDIT	$5,891	$5,236	$3,169	$475
PHASEOUT BEGINS	$17,090 ($22,300 if married filing jointly)	17,090 ($22,300 if married filing jointly)	17,090 ($22,300 if married filing jointly)	$7,770 ($12,980 if married filing jointly)
PHASEOUT ENDS	$45,060 ($50,270 if married filing jointly)	$41,952 ($47,162 if married filing jointly)	$36,920 ($42,130 if married filing jointly)	$13,980 ($19,190 if married filing jointly)

depends on whether the minister is exempt or not exempt from paying self-employment taxes. For further guidance with respect to this question, ministers should contact the IRS or their tax professional.

Computing the earned income credit for 2012

The earned income credit is based on the amount of your *earned income*, so you must compute your earned income in order to determine the amount of your credit. The instructions for line 64 (Form 1040) contain a six-step procedure and two worksheets (A and B) to assist you in determining whether you are eligible for the earned income credit and, if so, the amount of the credit. Following is a summary of the six-step procedure.

Steps 1–4

These steps will help you determine whether you are eligible for the credit.

Steps 5–6 for ministers who file Schedule SE (not exempt from self-employment taxes).

These ministers ordinarily report earnings on line 2 of Schedule SE that also were reported on Form 1040, line 7 (such as their church salary). If this is the case, then follow these instructions:

- Check the "Yes" box on line 1 of Step 5.
- Put "Clergy" on the dotted line next to line 64a of Form 1040. The reason for this requirement is to notify the IRS that the income reported on Form 1040, line 7, and on Schedule SE, line 2, may be substantially the same amount and should not be combined. Ministers have a dual tax status. For income tax purposes, many are employees. But for Social Security, they always are self-employed with regard to their ministerial services. As a result, it is common for ministers to report compensation in both places. While for most taxpayers this would indicate two sources of income, for ministers it does not.
- Determine how much of the amount on Form 1040, line 7, was also reported on Schedule SE, line 2, and then subtract this amount from the amount you reported on Form 1040, line 7, and enter the result in the first space of Step 5, line 2. Note that Step 5, line 2, refers to your Form 1040, line 7 wages, but it will not actually show line 7 wages, because the instructions for line 64 (Form 1040) state that ministers who are not exempt from self-employment taxes must reduce their line 7 income by "the amount on Form 1040, line 7, that was also reported on Schedule SE, line 2."

   If you are not exempt from self-employment tax, your wages will be reported on Worksheet B, line 1a, as net earnings from self-employment from Schedule SE, line 2. As a result, if you report the same amount in Step 5, line 2, you will be reporting your church income twice. The instructions avoid this result by directing ministers who are not exempt from self-employment tax to determine how much of the amount reported on Form 1040, line 7 (wages), was also reported on Schedule SE, line 2. This amount is subtracted

from the amount on Form 1040, line 7. The difference is entered in Step 5, line 2. This will include a minister's church salary but not the housing allowance or the fair rental value of a parsonage, since these items are not reported on line 7 (Form 1040).

- Be sure to answer "Yes" on line 3 of Step 5.

✿ **KEY POINT.** A housing allowance or the fair rental value of a parsonage will be reported as earnings on Schedule SE (Section A, line 3); therefore, it will be reported on Worksheet B, line 1a. This means that the housing allowance or fair rental value of a parsonage will be included in the definition of earned income for purposes of computing the earned income credit for ministers who have not exempted themselves from self-employment taxes.

➡ **TIP.** These rules are illustrated in IRS Publication 596 with Example 4.

Steps 5–6 for ministers who do not file Schedule SE (exempt from self-employment taxes)

Unfortunately, the IRS instructions for line 64 (Form 1040) only provide guidance to ministers who have *not* exempted themselves from self-employment taxes. While the instructions provide no specific guidance to ministers who *have* exempted themselves from self-employment taxes, they seem to suggest that these ministers do *not* include a housing allowance or the fair rental value of a parsonage in computing their earned income for purposes of the earned income credit, even though this is clearly not the intent of the law.

These ministers do not file Schedule SE, so they must check "No" in line 1 of Step 5 of the instructions for line 64 (Form 1040). They then report their Form 1040, line 7, income on line 2 of Step 5, which will be their church salary and any other compensation (including a spouse's compensation) less a housing allowance or the fair rental value of a parsonage. These ministers also use Worksheet A, since Worksheet B clearly does not apply. But nowhere on Worksheet A are these ministers required to include a housing allowance or the fair rental value of a parsonage in computing their earned income for purposes of the earned income credit. In other words, ministers who have exempted themselves from self-employment taxes and who apply the IRS instructions for line 64 (Form 1040) will have no way of knowing that they must include their housing allowance or the fair rental value of a parsonage as earned income in computing the earned income credit.

IRS Publication 596

This 68-page publication explains the earned income credit. The 2011 edition (the most recent available at the time of publication of this text) states: "The rental value of a home or a housing allowance provided to a minister as part of the minister's pay generally is not subject to income tax but is included in net earnings from self-employment. For that reason, it is included in earned income for the EIC (except in certain cases described in *Approved Form 4361 . . . below*).”

Publication 596 goes on to state:

> [I]f you have an approved Form 4361 [i.e., you are exempt from self-employment taxes with regard to ministerial income] amounts you received for performing ministerial duties as an employee count as earned income. This includes wages, salaries, tips, and other taxable employee compensation. A nontaxable housing allowance or the nontaxable rental value of a home is not earned income. Also, amounts you received for performing ministerial duties, but not as an employee, do not count as earned income. Examples include fees for performing marriages and honoraria for delivering speeches [emphasis added].

These excerpts from Publication 596 confirm that ministers who are employees for income tax reporting purposes and who have *not* exempted themselves from self-employment taxes by filing a timely Form 4361 with the IRS *include* their housing allowance or the fair rental value of a parsonage in computing earned income for purposes of the earned income credit. This result is illustrated in a comprehensive example (Example 4) in Chapter 7 of Publication 596.

But what about ministers who have exempted themselves from self-employment taxes by filing a timely Form 4361 with the IRS? Do they include a housing allowance or the rental value of a parsonage in computing their earned income for purposes of the earned income credit? As noted above, Publication 596 explicitly states, with regard to ministers who have filed Form 4361, that "a nontaxable housing allowance or the nontaxable rental value of a home is not earned income."

IRS Publication 517

IRS Publication 517 (Social Security and Other Information for Members of the Clergy and Religious Workers) contains the following information about the Earned Income Tax Credit:

> **Earned income.** *Earned income includes your:*
>
> 1. *Wages, salaries, tips, and other taxable employee compensation (even if these amounts are exempt from FICA or SECA), and*
> 2. *Net earnings from self-employment that are not exempt from SECA (you do not have an approved Form 4029 or 4361) with the following adjustments.*
>
>   a. *Subtract the amount you claimed (or should have claimed) on Form 1040, line 27, for one-half of your SE tax.*
>   b. *Add the amount you claimed on Form 1040, line 29, for the self-employed health insurance deduction.*
>   c. *Add any amount from Schedule SE, line 4b and line 5a.*
>
> *To figure your earned income credit, see the Form 1040 instructions for lines 64a and 64b.*

> **CAUTION.** *If you are a minister and have an approved Form 4361, your earned income will still include wages and salaries earned as an employee, but it will not include amounts you received for nonemployee ministerial duties, such as fees for performing marriages and baptisms, and honoraria for delivering speeches*

This language does nothing to clarify whether ministers include a housing allowance or rental value of a parsonage as earned income in computing the earned income credit.

Additional help

The computation of the earned income credit is complex. Here are some tips that will assist you in computing the credit:

- Refer to the instructions for Form 1040 (line 64) for assistance. Some taxpayers must use IRS Publication 596 to compute their earned income credit, but ministers generally are not required to do so.
- If you qualify for the earned income credit on the basis of the rules summarized above, you need to compute the amount of your credit. The IRS will do so if you like (see the instructions for Form 1040). Or you can compute the credit yourself. To figure the amount of your earned income credit, you must use the EIC Worksheet and EIC Table in the instruction booklet for Form 1040. In most cases the amount of your earned income credit depends on (1) whether you have no qualifying child, one qualifying child, or two or more qualifying children; and (2) the amount of your earned income and modified AGI.

➡ **TIP.** The IRS has a web-based tool to help taxpayers determine whether they are eligible for the Earned Income Tax Credit. The EITC Assistant will help take the guess work out of the EITC eligibility rules. By answering a few simple questions and providing some basic income information, the program will assist taxpayers in determining their correct filing status, determining whether their children meet the tests for a qualifying child, and estimating the amount of credit taxpayers may receive. A link to the EITC Assistant can be found on the IRS website, irs.gov.

Complexity

Unfortunately, determining eligibility for the EIC and computing the credit itself are so complicated that many taxpayers who qualify for the credit do not claim it. A good measure of the complexity of the credit is the fact that IRS Publication 596, which is supposed to explain the credit in simple terms, is 68 pages long!

As a result, Congress has ordered the IRS to establish a "public awareness program to inform the taxpaying public of the availability of the [earned income] credit. Such public awareness program shall be designed to assure that individuals who may be eligible are informed of the availability of such credit and filing procedures."

→ **TIP.** Denominational offices should advise ministers with dependent children of the availability of this important benefit.

Advance payments

In the past, some taxpayers who qualified for the Earned Income Tax Credit could choose to get "advance" EITC payments in their paycheck instead of waiting to get the credit in the following year when their tax return was filed.

Congress repealed the advance EITC effective for 2011 and future years.

3. CHILD TAX CREDIT

✱ **New in 2012.** Generally, taxpayers with income below certain threshold amounts may claim the Child Tax Credit to reduce federal income tax for each qualifying child under the age of 17. In 2001 Congress increased the credit from $500 to $1,000 and made it refundable up to 15 percent of earnings above $12,550. In 2009 Congress amended the law to allow earnings above $3,000 to count toward refundability for 2009 and 2010. The Tax Relief Act extends these changes (which were scheduled to expire at the end of 2010) for an additional two years, through 2012. Unless Congress acts, this credit will revert to its pre-2001 amount of $500, and the refundable part will be reduced.

An individual may claim a tax credit for each qualifying child under the age of 17. The amount of credit per child is $1,000 through 2012. A child who is not a citizen, national, or resident of the United States cannot be a qualifying child.

The credit is phased out for individuals with income over certain threshold amounts. Specifically, the otherwise allowable Child Tax Credit is reduced by $50 for each $1,000 (or fraction thereof) of modified adjusted gross income over $75,000 for single individuals or heads of households, $110,000 for married individuals filing joint returns, and $55,000 for married individuals filing separate returns. For purposes of this limitation, modified adjusted gross income includes certain otherwise excludable income.

To the extent the child credit exceeds the taxpayer's tax liability, the taxpayer is eligible for a refundable credit (the additional child tax credit) equal to 15 percent of earned income in excess of a threshold dollar amount (the "earned income" formula). The American Recovery and Reinvestment Act of 2009 modifies the earned income formula to apply to 15 percent of earned income in excess of $3,000 for taxable years beginning in 2009 and 2010. The Tax Relief and Job Creation Act of 2010 extends these changes through 2012. Unless extended by Congress, this credit reverts to $500 in 2013.

Earned income is defined as the sum of wages, salaries, and other taxable employee compensation plus net self-employment earnings. Unlike the EIC, which also includes the preceding items in its definition of earned income, the additional child tax credit is based only on earned income to the extent it is included in computing taxable income.

A committee report to the Tax Relief, Unemployment Insurance Reauthorization, and Job Creation Act of 2010 includes the following clarification in commenting on the Child Tax Credit:

> *Earned income is defined as the sum of wages, salaries, tips, and other taxable employee compensation plus net self-employment earnings. Unlike the EITC, which also includes the preceding items in its definition of earned income, the additional child tax credit is based only on earned income to the extent it is included in computing taxable income. For example, some ministers' parsonage allowances are considered self-employment income, and thus are considered earned income for purposes of computing the EITC, but the allowances are excluded from gross income for individual income tax purposes, and thus are not considered earned income for purposes of the additional child tax credit since the income is not included in taxable income.*

EXAMPLE. A couple had a valid, approved Form 4029 exempting themselves from Social Security and Medicare taxes on the basis of their membership in a recognized religious group conscientiously opposed to accepting benefits of any private or public insurance (including Social Security and Medicare) that makes payments in the event of death, disability, old age, or retirement. The couple had nine children and claimed a refundable "additional child tax credit" based on the husband's self-employment earnings from his carpentry business (the couple's only source of income). The IRS denied this credit on the ground that the husband's self-employment earnings were not "earned income" in calculating the additional child tax credit.

The court noted that section 24 of the tax code provides that the "additional child tax credit" is refundable and is equal to "15 percent of so much of the taxpayer's earned income (within the meaning of section 32) which is taken into account in computing taxable income for the taxable year as exceeds [$3,000]." The court concluded that the couple was not eligible for the additional child tax credit because they had no earned income. The term "earned income" in section 32 is defined to include net earnings from self-employment. However, section 32 goes on to exclude from the definition of earned income any services by an individual who has filed a Form 4029 exempting himself from self-employment taxes as a result of his membership in a recognized religious group that is opposed on religious grounds from receiving benefits from any public or private insurance program, including Social Security, that makes payments on the basis of old age or sickness. Since the couple had a valid and approved Form 4029, the husband's carpentry income was not "earned income," and therefore they were not eligible for the additional child tax credit. *Heilman v. Commissioner, T.C. Memo. 2011-210 (2011).*

4. EDUCATION CREDITS

Various tax benefits may be available to you if you are saving for or paying education costs for yourself or, in many cases, another student who is a member of your immediate family. Most benefits apply only to higher education. Listed below are eleven benefits for which you may be eligible:

- Lifetime Learning Credit;
- a tax deduction for student loan interest;
- tax-free treatment of a canceled student loan;
- tax-free student loan repayment assistance;
- a tax deduction for tuition and fees for education;
- qualified tuition programs (QTPs), which feature tax-free earnings;
- contributions to a Coverdell Education Savings Account (Coverdell ESA), which features tax-free earnings;
- early distributions from any type of individual retirement arrangement (IRA) for education costs without paying the 10 percent additional tax on early distributions;
- cash in savings bonds for education costs without having to pay tax on the interest;
- receiving tax-free educational benefits from your employer; and
- a business deduction for work-related education.

You generally cannot claim more than one of the benefits described in the lists above for the same qualifying education expense. Each of these tax benefits is explained fully in IRS Publication 970 (Tax Benefits for Education), available on the IRS website (irs.gov).

American Opportunity Tax Credit

The American Recovery and Reinvestment Act of 2009 modified the Hope Scholarship Credit for taxable years beginning in 2009 or 2010. The modified credit was referred to as the American Opportunity Credit. The allowable modified credit was up to $2,500 per eligible student per year for qualified tuition and related expenses paid for each of the first four years of the student's post-secondary education in a degree or certificate program. The modified credit rate was 100 percent on the first $2,000 of qualified tuition and related expenses, and 25 percent on the next $2,000 of qualified tuition and related expenses. For purposes of the modified credit, the definition of qualified tuition and related expenses was expanded to include course materials. The modified credit was extended by the Tax Relief and Job Creation Act of 2010 through 2012.

✱ **New in 2013.** Unless Congress acts, this credit expires at the end of 2012, and the less attractive Hope Scholarship Credit will be reinstated.

The modified credit is available with respect to an individual student for four years, provided the student has not completed the first four years of post-secondary education before the beginning of the fourth taxable year. As a result, the modified credit, in addition to other modifications, extends the application of the Hope Scholarship Credit to two more years of post-secondary education.

The modified credit is phased out for taxpayers with modified adjusted gross income between $80,000 and $90,000 ($160,000 and $180,000 for married taxpayers filing a joint return).

Forty percent of the allowable modified credit is refundable. However, no portion of the modified credit is refundable if the taxpayer claiming the credit is a child under age 18 or any child under age 24 who is a student providing less than one-half of his or her own support, who has at least one living parent and does not file a joint return.

Chapter 8 CHARITABLE CONTRIBUTIONS

Ascribe to the Lord the glory due his name; bring an offering and come into his courts.

Psalm 96:8

CHAPTER HIGHLIGHTS

■ **Introduction.** Most churches are funded almost entirely by charitable contributions. This makes an understanding of charitable contributions very important. Further, many unique and sometimes technical legal rules apply to charitable contributions that are not well understood by most donors or church leaders. Unfamiliarity with these rules can lead to unfortunate consequences, including the disallowance of charitable contribution deductions.

■ **Six requirements.** Charitable contributions generally must satisfy six requirements. A charitable contribution must be (1) a gift of cash or property, (2) claimed as a deduction in the year in which the contribution is made, (3) unconditional and without personal benefit to the donor, (4) made "to or for the use of" a qualified charity, (5) within the allowable legal limits, and (6) properly substantiated.

■ **Personal services.** The value of personal services is never deductible as a charitable contribution, but expenses incurred in performing services on behalf of a church or other charity may be.

■ **Rent-free building space.** The value of rent-free building space made available to a church cannot be claimed as a charitable contribution.

■ **Year of contribution.** Charitable contributions must be claimed in the year in which they are *delivered*. One exception is a check that is mailed to a charity—it is deductible in the year the check is mailed (and postmarked), even if it is received early in the next year.

■ **If a donor receives a benefit.** Charitable contributions generally are deductible only to the extent they exceed the value of any premium or benefit received by the donor in return for the contribution.

■ **Amount of deduction.** The amount of a contribution that can be deducted is limited. In some cases, contributions that exceed these limits can be carried over and claimed in future tax years.

■ **Recovery of charitable contributions by bankruptcy courts.** The bankruptcy code prevents bankruptcy trustees, in many cases, from recovering contributions made by donors to a church or other charity within a year of filing for bankruptcy.

■ **Designated contributions.** Designated contributions are those made to a church with the stipulation that they be used for a specified purpose. If the purpose is an approved project or program of the church, the designation will not affect the deductibility of the contribution. However, if a donor stipulates that a contribution be spent on a designated individual, no deduction ordinarily is allowed unless the church exercises full administrative control over the donated funds to ensure that they are being spent in furtherance of the church's exempt purposes. However, contributions to a church or missions agency that specify a particular missionary may be tax-deductible if the church or missions agency exercises full administrative and accounting control over the contributions and ensures that they are spent in furtherance of the church's mission.

■ **Direct contributions to an individual.** Direct contributions to missionaries or any other individual are not tax-deductible, even if they are used for religious or charitable purposes.

■ **Substantiation.** Charitable contributions must be properly substantiated. Special substantiation rules apply to (1) all cash contributions, (2) individual contributions of cash or property of $250 or more, (3) "quid pro quo" contributions in excess of $75, and (4) contributions of cars, boats, and planes. Additional requirements apply to contributions of noncash property valued by the donor at $500 or more. If the value is more than $5,000, the donor must obtain a qualified appraisal of the property and attach an appraisal summary (IRS Form 8283) to the tax return on which the contribution is claimed. In some cases a church that receives a donation of noncash property valued by the donor at more than $5,000 must submit an information return (IRS Form 8282) to the IRS if it disposes of the property within three years of the date of gift.

■ **Church treasurers.** Church treasurers need to be familiar with the many legal requirements that apply to charitable contributions so they can determine the deductibility of contributions and properly advise donors.

■ ***Appraisals.*** Churches are not appraisers, and they have no legal obligation to determine the value of donated property. They should provide donors with receipts or periodic summaries acknowledging receipt of cash or described property.

■ ***The Pension Protection Act of 2006.*** Congress enacted legislation in 2006 containing several provisions that will affect the deductibility and substantiation of charitable contributions. Those changes of most relevance to churches are addressed in this chapter.

INTRODUCTION

Section 170 of the tax code states that "there shall be allowed as a deduction any charitable contribution . . . payment of which is made within the taxable year." To be deductible, a contribution must meet six conditions. A charitable contribution must be

(1) a gift of cash or property,
(2) claimed as a deduction in the year in which the contribution is made,
(3) unconditional and without personal benefit to the donor,
(4) made "to or for the use of" a qualified charity,
(5) within the allowable legal limits, and
(6) properly substantiated.

These conditions are explained below.

1. GIFT OF CASH OR PROPERTY

Charitable contributions are limited to gifts of cash or property, but almost any kind of property will qualify, including cash, charges to a bank credit card, real estate, promissory notes, stocks and bonds, automobiles, art objects, books, building materials, collections, jewelry, easements, insurance policies, and inventory.

Donated services

No deduction is allowed for a contribution of services. Church members who donate labor to their church may not deduct the value of their labor.

❖**KEY POINT.** The value of personal services is never deductible as a charitable contribution, but expenses incurred in performing services on behalf of a church or other charity may be.

EXAMPLE. A church begins a remodeling project. S, a church member, donates 30 hours of labor towards the project. S is a carpenter who ordinarily receives $30 per hour for his services on the open market. S asks the church treasurer for a receipt showing

a contribution of $900 (30 hours times $30 per hour). The church may issue S a letter of appreciation acknowledging the hours of labor that were donated, but it should clarify that this amount is not deductible.

EXAMPLE. Same facts as the preceding example, except that S asks the church to pay him for his services, and then he donates the payment back to the church in the form of a contribution. This is a permissible arrangement, but it ordinarily will not result in any tax advantage to S, since his deduction is offset by the inclusion of the same amount in his income for income tax reporting purposes. If S cannot itemize deductions on Schedule A, he will actually be worse off for tax purposes by having the church pay him the $900 for his services, since he will have additional income without any offsetting deduction.

EXAMPLE. An attorney donates his time free of charge in representing a church. He is not entitled to a charitable contribution deduction for the value of his donated services. *Grant v. Commissioner, 84 T.C. 809 (1986).*

EXAMPLE. A commercial radio station broadcasts certain religious programs free of charge. It is not entitled to a charitable contribution deduction for the value of the free airtime. *Revenue Ruling 67-236.*

Unreimbursed expenses incurred in performing donated services

While the value of labor or services can never be deducted as a charitable contribution, any unreimbursed expenses incurred while performing donated labor for a church may constitute a deductible contribution. The income tax regulations specify:

> Unreimbursed expenditures made incident to the rendition of services to an organization contributions to which are deductible may constitute a deductible contribution. For example, the cost of a uniform without general utility which is required to be worn in performing donated services is deductible. Similarly, out-of-pocket transportation expenses necessarily incurred in performing donated services are deductible. Reasonable expenditures for meals and lodging necessarily incurred while away from home in the course of performing donated services are also deductible. Treas. Reg. 1.170A-1(g).

IRS Publication 526 (Charitable Contributions) states:

> You may be able to deduct some amounts you pay in giving services to a qualified organization. The amounts must be:

> • Unreimbursed,
> • Directly connected with the services,
> • Expenses you had only because of the services you gave, and
> • Not personal, living, or family expenses.

EXAMPLE. A taxpayer was entitled to deduct as a charitable contribution his out-of-pocket expenses incurred in carrying out evangelistic work for his church. *Smith v. Commissioner, 60 T.C. 988 (1965).*

EXAMPLE. A taxpayer's unreimbursed out-of-pocket expenses for vestments, books, and transportation while participating in a "diaconate program" of his church were deductible as charitable contributions. *Revenue Ruling 76-89.*

EXAMPLE. A donor claimed a charitable contribution deduction for the cost of an airplane ticket ($1,000) that she purchased in 2006 to travel to her native country and provide services to Catholic churches in that country. While she informed the pastor of her home church in Texas of the nature of her trip, she was not working in any official capacity for her church while engaged in rendering charitable services to Catholic churches in her native country.

The donor claimed the cost of her airfare as a deductible unreimbursed expense incurred in the performance of services to a qualified charitable organization. The Tax Court acknowledged that a taxpayer is permitted to deduct an unreimbursed expense made incident to the performance of services to qualified charitable organization and noted that such expenses include transportation expenses and reasonable expenses for meals and lodging while away from home. But the court, in denying any deduction for the donor's airfare, noted that she had "failed to show that any of the Catholic churches in the foreign country to which she rendered services was a qualified charitable organization."

The donor also claimed that she was performing missionary services on behalf of her local Catholic diocese while overseas. But the court noted: "Her local diocese did not have control over her services provided to the Catholic churches in the foreign country, and no legally enforceable trust or similar legal arrangement existed between her local church (as a member of that diocese) and the donor. She did not render services in the foreign country under the direction of, or to or for the use of her local church or the local diocese. The record shows only that her priest at her local church had some awareness of her work in her native country. Nor is there any evidence that she provided those services during the year in controversy to or for the use of the [US-based missions agency] of which she did not become a member until 2007." *Anonymous v. Commissioner. TC Memo. 2010-87 (2010).*

Use of a car in performing donated services

Volunteers often use their own vehicles when performing services on behalf of their church. These expenses may be either reimbursed by the church or unreimbursed.

Unreimbursed expenses

Volunteers who use their vehicles while performing services for a church may claim a charitable contribution deduction for the cost of using their vehicles if they receive no reimbursements from the church. This deduction may be computed in one of two ways:

First, a volunteer can use the charitable mileage rate of 14 cents per mile multiplied by all substantiated miles driven in the course of performing charitable services. Section 170(i) of the tax code specifies that "for purposes of computing the deduction under this section for use of a passenger automobile, the standard mileage rate shall be 14 cents per mile." This is the rate used to compute a charitable contribution deduction for unreimbursed charitable travel incurred while performing donated services for a charity.

Second, volunteers can deduct the actual cost of using their vehicles while performing charitable services. Actual costs include any out-of-pocket cost of operating or maintaining a vehicle. IRS Publication 526 (Charitable Contributions) states that "you can deduct unreimbursed out-of-pocket expenses, such as the cost of gas and oil that are directly related to the use of your car in giving services to a charitable organization. You cannot deduct general repair and maintenance expenses, depreciation, registration fees, or the costs of tires or insurance. . . . You can deduct parking fees and tolls, whether you use your actual expenses or the standard mileage rate."

Under either method of valuing a charitable contribution deduction for the use of a vehicle in performing charitable services, you must keep reliable written records of expenses incurred. If you claim expenses directly related to use of your car in giving services to a qualified organization, you must keep reliable written records of your expenses. Whether your records are considered reliable depends on all the facts and circumstances. Generally, they may be considered reliable if you made them regularly and at or near the time you had the expenses. Your records must show the name of the church or charity you were serving and the date each time you used your car for a charitable purpose. If you use the standard mileage rate of 14 cents a mile, your records must show the miles you drove your car for the charitable purpose. If you deduct your actual expenses, your records must show the costs of operating the car that are directly related to a charitable purpose.

The Tax Court has confirmed that the actual cost of using a vehicle for charitable purposes does not include depreciation:

> *The regulations do not specifically refer to depreciation, but the [IRS] contends that the statute and the regulations do not authorize a deduction for depreciation. We agree. Depreciation is a "decrease in value." It is not a payment, or expenditure, or an out-of-pocket expense. Hence, it cannot be considered as a contribution, payment of which is made within the taxable year. We accordingly conclude that the [IRS] properly disallowed as a charitable contribution that portion of the amount claimed on the automobile which represented depreciation.* Mitchell v. Commissioner, 42 T.C. 953 (1964).

Most volunteers use their vehicles for both charitable and personal purposes and may claim a contribution deduction only for costs associated with their charitable services. In other words, they must determine the percentage of the total miles their vehicle is used during the year for personal and charitable activities. They can then claim a deduction for their actual vehicle expenses multiplied by the percentage of their total miles that represent their charitable services (their "charitable use percentage"). Of course, the volunteer must be able to substantiate each charitable travel expense with adequate written records. The Tax Court has observed:

> Unreimbursed amounts expended by a taxpayer to enable him to provide his own services to a charitable organization are deductible only if the charitable work is the cause of the payments. When the expenditures are incurred in an activity which also benefits the taxpayer personally, a charitable deduction has not been allowed, even though the charity also benefits. Therefore, travel expenditures which include a substantial, direct, personal benefit, in the form of a vacation or other recreational outing, are not deductible. The burden of proving that such expenditures qualify as charitable contributions rests with petitioner. Tafralian v. Commissioner, T.C. Memo. 1991-33.

Reimbursed expenses

It is not clear that the charitable mileage rate can be used by charities to reimburse volunteers for expenses incurred in the course of charitable travel. Section 170(i) of the tax code states that "for purposes of computing the deduction under this section for use of a passenger automobile, the standard mileage rate shall be 14 cents per mile." Technically, this language only makes sense for unreimbursed expenses, since no deduction is allowed for reimbursed expenses (assuming the reimbursement is accountable). The mileage rate was created to assist individuals in valuing a charitable contribution deduction for the use of their vehicles in performing charitable services for which no reimbursement was provided. Further, IRS Publication 526 states, "You may be able to deduct some amounts you pay in giving services to a qualified organization. The amounts must be *unreimbursed*, directly connected with the services, expenses you had only because of the services you gave and not personal, living, or family expenses" (emphasis added).

Some charities do reimburse volunteers for expenses they incur in performing charitable work and reimburse miles at the charitable mileage rate for volunteers who are able to substantiate miles driven in performing charitable work. Neither the IRS nor the Tax Court has unequivocally approved such reimbursements, so they remain a questionable, though common, practice. At a minimum, reimbursements should satisfy the following requirements:

(1) If a mileage rate is used, it must be the charitable mileage rate (currently 14 cents per mile). The fact that this amount does not adequately reimburse the true cost of using a vehicle for charitable work is no justification for using a higher mileage rate. A mileage rate in excess of this amount will generate taxable income to the extent it exceeds the charitable mileage rate. This taxable income should be reported to the volunteer on a Form 1099-MISC if it equals or exceeds $600 in the same calendar year.

(2) The charitable mileage rate should only be used to reimburse substantiated charitable miles. That is, reimbursement should be limited to miles for which a donor has reliable written records substantiating a charitable purpose.

Some churches use the standard business mileage rate to reimburse volunteers for the use of a vehicle in performing charitable services. No unequivocal legal support exists for this position. In fact, the evidence strongly suggests that this practice is improper. To illustrate, several attempts have been made in Congress in recent years to increase the charitable mileage rate. Some have proposed that it be the same as the business mileage rate. Obviously, such legislation would be unnecessary if the business mileage rate could be used for charitable travel.

EXAMPLE. A church member used his car in performing lay religious activities. While he was denied a charitable contribution deduction for a portion of the depreciation and insurance expenses allocable to the car (they did not represent "payments"), he could deduct his out-of-pocket travel and transportation expenses. *Orr v. Commissioner, 343 F.2d 553 (5th Cir. 1965).*

EXAMPLE. A taxpayer could not deduct as a charitable contribution transportation expenses incurred in attending choir rehearsals at his church. The court concluded that attendance at choir rehearsals was a form of religious worship that benefited the taxpayer directly and that his participation in the choir only incidentally benefited the church. *Churukian v. Commissioner, 40 T.C.M. 475 (1980).*

EXAMPLE. A lay church member drove 2,000 miles during the year for charitable activities associated with her church. She had records to document the charitable nature of these miles. The IRS ruled that she could either (1) claim the charitable standard mileage rate of 14 cents per mile (2,000 miles x 14 cents = $280), or (2) deduct her actual out-of-pocket expenses in operating the car for charitable purposes. *Revenue Procedure 80-32.*

EXAMPLE. A taxpayer performed volunteer activities as a cheerleading coach for a youth football and cheerleading league. She claimed that she made various unreimbursed charitable contributions regarding her cheerleading activities, including car expenses she and her ex-husband incurred in traveling to and from team practices and games. In support, she produced MapQuest directions printouts providing the following information: (1) the distance for each trip; (2) the number of trips taken per week; and (3) the number of weeks during which the trips took place. The court ruled that the taxpayer was entitled to a charitable contribution deduction in the amount of the charitable mileage rate of 14 cents per mile multiplied by the 1,857 miles she and her ex-husband traveled to and from team practices and games during the year. *Bradley v. Commissioner, T.C. Summary Opinion 2011-120 (2011).*

EXAMPLE. A taxpayer owned and operated as a sole proprietorship a lawn-care business. The taxpayer's church purchased a tract of 10 to 15 acres on which to build a house of worship. The taxpayer cleared the land for the church so it could begin construction. He deducted as a charitable contribution the amount he would have billed the church for his services had he not donated his labor. The IRS audited the taxpayer's tax return and disallowed any charitable contribution deduction for the services he performed for his church without charge. The Tax Court affirmed the IRS position. It concluded: "The amounts of the taxpayer's charitable contributions at issue are for services he performed for his church. He testified that he cleared 10 to 15 acres of church-owned land so that a house of worship could be built. He also testified that for each of the years at issue he provided the church financial director a bill for his services. In return taxpayer stated that he was given a receipt from the church confirming he had made a contribution to the church in the amount stated on the bill. He is not allowed charitable contribution deductions for the services he provided to the church." *Leak v. Commissioner., U.S. Tax Court, T.C. Summary Opinion 2012-39 (May 1, 2012).*

Charitable travel (out of town)

Many lay church members participate in mission trips or other religious activities that take them away from home. Are persons who participate in such trips entitled to a charitable contribution deduction for their unreimbursed travel expenses?

Section 170(j) of the tax code states that "no deduction shall be allowed under this section for traveling expenses (including amounts expended for meals and lodging) while away from home, whether paid directly or by reimbursement, unless there is no significant element of personal pleasure, recreation, or vacation in such travel." The key phrase is "no significant element of personal pleasure, recreation, or vacation in such travel." Unfortunately, the tax code and regulations do not define this phrase. A conference committee report to section 170(j) provides the following clarification:

> *The disallowance rule applies whether the travel expenses are paid directly by the taxpayer, or indirectly through reimbursement by the charitable organization. For this purpose, any arrangement whereby a taxpayer makes a payment to a charitable organization and the organization pays for his or her travel expenses is treated as a reimbursement.*
>
> *In determining whether travel away from home involves a significant element of personal pleasure, recreation, or vacation,*

> *the fact that a taxpayer enjoys providing services to the charitable organization will not lead to denial of the deduction. For example, a troop leader for a tax-exempt youth group who takes children belonging to the group on a camping trip may qualify for a charitable deduction with respect to his or her own travel expenses if he or she is on duty in a genuine and substantial sense throughout the trip, even if he or she enjoys the trip or enjoys supervising children. By contrast, a taxpayer who only has nominal duties relating to the performance of services for the charity, or who for significant portions of the trip is not required to render services, is not allowed any charitable deduction for travel costs.*

The IRS has provided the following additional clarification in Notice 87-23:

> *[Section 170(j)] provides that no deduction is allowed for transportation and other travel expenses relating to the performance of services away from home for a charitable organization unless there is no significant element of personal pleasure, recreation, or vacation in the travel. For example, a taxpayer who sails from one Caribbean Island to another and spends eight hours a day counting whales and other forms of marine life as part of a project sponsored by a charitable organization generally will not be permitted a charitable deduction. By way of further example, a taxpayer who works on an archaeological excavation sponsored by a charitable organization for several hours each morning, with the rest of the day free for recreation and sightseeing, will not be allowed a deduction even if the taxpayer works very hard during those few hours. In contrast, a member of a local chapter of a charitable organization who travels to New York City and spends an entire day attending the organization's regional meeting will not be subject to this provision even if he or she attends the theatre in the evening. This provision applies whether the travel expenses are paid directly by the taxpayer or by some indirect means such as by contribution to the charitable organization that pays for the taxpayer's travel expenses.*

EXAMPLE. A donor claimed a charitable contribution deduction for the cost of an airplane ticket ($1,000) that she purchased in 2006 to travel to her native country and provide services to Catholic churches in that country. She claimed that she was performing missionary services on behalf of her local Catholic diocese while overseas. But the court noted: "Her local diocese did not have control over her services provided to the Catholic churches in the foreign country, and no legally enforceable trust or similar legal arrangement existed between her local church (as a member of that diocese) and the donor. She did not render services in the foreign country under the direction of, or to or for the use of her local church or the local diocese. The record shows only that her priest at her local church had some awareness of her work in her native country. Nor is there any evidence that she provided those services during the year in controversy to or for the use of the [US-based missions agency] of which she did not become a member until 2007." *Anonymous v. Commissioner. TC Memo. 2010-87 (2010).*

The current edition of IRS Publication 526 addresses this issue as follows:

Generally, you can claim a charitable contribution deduction for travel expenses necessarily incurred while you are away from home performing services for a charitable organization only if there is no significant element of personal pleasure, recreation, or vacation in the travel. This applies whether you pay the expenses directly or indirectly. You are paying the expenses indirectly if you make a payment to the charitable organization and the organization pays for your travel expenses.

The deduction for travel expenses will not be denied simply because you enjoy providing services to the charitable organization. Even if you enjoy the trip, you can take a charitable contribution deduction for your travel expenses if you are on duty in a genuine and substantial sense throughout the trip. However, if you have only nominal duties, or if for significant parts of the trip you do not have any duties, you cannot deduct your travel expenses.

Publication 526 provides the following examples (each is based on the precedent summarized above):

EXAMPLE. You are a troop leader for a tax-exempt youth group and take the group on a camping trip. You are responsible for overseeing the setup of the camp and for providing the adult supervision for other activities during the entire trip. You participate in the activities of the group and really enjoy your time with them. You oversee the breaking of camp, and you transport the group home. You can deduct your travel expenses.

EXAMPLE. You sail from one island to another and spend eight hours a day counting whales and other forms of marine life. The project is sponsored by a charitable organization. In most circumstances, you cannot deduct your expenses.

EXAMPLE. You work for several hours each morning on an archeological dig sponsored by a charitable organization. The rest of the day is free for recreation and sightseeing. You cannot take a charitable contribution deduction, even though you work very hard during those few hours.

EXAMPLE. You spend the entire day attending a charitable organization's regional meeting as a chosen representative. In the evening you go to the theater. You can claim your travel expenses as charitable contributions, but you cannot claim the cost of your evening at the theater.

Contributions of less than a donor's entire interest in property

Contributions of less than a donor's entire interest in property ordinarily are not deductible unless they fit within one of the following exceptions:

A contribution (not in trust) of an irrevocable remainder interest in a personal residence or farm

To illustrate, a donor who wants to give his home or farm to his church, but who wants to retain possession during his life, can retain a "life estate" in the property and donate a "remainder interest" to the church. The donor may deduct the value of the remainder interest that he has conveyed to the church, though this interest represents less than the donor's entire interest in the property. The valuation of a remainder interest is determined according to income tax regulation 1.170A-12.

A contribution (not in trust) of an undivided interest in property

Such an interest must consist of a part of every substantial interest or right the donor owns in the property and must last as long as the donor's interest in the property lasts. To illustrate, assume that a church member owns a 100-acre tract of land and that she donates half of this property to her church. While this represents a gift of only a portion of the donor's interest in the property, it is nevertheless deductible. *Treas. Reg. 1.170A-7.*

A contribution of an irrevocable remainder interest in property to a charitable remainder trust

A charitable remainder trust is a trust authorized by section 664 of the tax code, which provides for a specified distribution, at least annually, to one or more noncharitable income beneficiaries for life or for a term of years (ordinarily not more than 20), with an irrevocable remainder interest to a charity. Many churches and other religious organizations have found such trusts to be an excellent means of raising funds, since they provide the donor with a current charitable contribution deduction plus a stream of income payments, as well as assuring the charity that it will receive the trust property at some specified future date. Charitable remainder trusts can be either annuity trusts or unitrusts. The specified distribution to be paid at least annually must be a certain sum that is not less than 5 percent of the initial fair market value of all property placed in trust (in the case of a charitable remainder annuity trust) or a fixed percentage which is not less than 5 percent of the net fair market value of the trust assets, valued annually (in the case of a charitable remainder unitrust).

Rent-free use of a building

❖ **KEY POINT.** The value of rent-free building space made available to a church cannot be claimed as a charitable contribution.

A contribution of a partial interest in property that does not fit within one of the three categories described above ordinarily is not deductible as a charitable contribution. To illustrate, an individual who owns an office building and donates the rent-free use of a portion of the building to a charitable organization is not entitled to a charitable contribution deduction, since the contribution consists of a partial interest in property that does not fit within one of the exceptions described above.

This principle is illustrated in the income tax regulations with the following example: "T, an individual owning a 10-story office building, donates the rent-free use of the top floor of the building . . . to a charitable organization. Since T's contribution consists of a partial interest to which section 170(f)(3) applies, he is not entitled to a charitable contribution deduction for the contribution of such partial interest."

Obviously, the same principle would apply to rent-free use of equipment. *IRC 170(f)(3)(A).*

EXAMPLE. Mary owns a vacation home at the beach that she sometimes rents to others. For a fund-raising auction at her church, she donated the right to use the vacation home for one week. At the auction, the church received and accepted a bid from Lauren equal to the fair rental value of the home for one week. Mary cannot claim a deduction because of the partial interest rule. Lauren cannot claim a deduction either, because she received a benefit equal to the amount of her payment. *IRS Publication 526.*

EXAMPLE. A taxpayer used a spare bedroom in his home to perform services for a local charity and claimed a charitable contribution deduction of $100 per month. The IRS disallowed any deduction, and the Tax Court agreed. The court noted that the taxpayer "cannot deduct the $100 per month for the portion of the rent attributable to the second bedroom since the 'contribution' consists of less than his entire interest in the property." The tax code specifies that a charitable contribution must consist of the transfer of a donor's entire interest in the donated property, with three limited exceptions not relevant in this case. Since the donor in this case was not donating a partial interest in his property to charity, it could not be claimed as a charitable contribution. *Sizelove v. Commissioner, T.C. Summary Opinion 2008-15 (2008).*

Pledges

Pledges and subscriptions are commitments to contribute a fixed sum of money or designated property to a church or other charity in the future. Many churches base their annual budget, or the construction of a new facility, on the results of pledge campaigns.

Pledges raise two questions of interest to church leaders: (1) can pledges be deducted as charitable contributions, and if so, when; and (2) are pledges legally enforceable? Both questions are addressed below.

Can pledges be deducted as charitable contributions?

The income tax regulations specify that "any charitable contribution . . . actually paid during the taxable year is allowable as a deduction in computing taxable income irrespective of the method of accounting employed or of the date on which the contribution is pledged." *Treas. Reg. 1.170A-1.*

EXAMPLE. The IRS ruled that "the satisfaction of a pledge" is a tax-deductible charitable contribution. *Revenue Ruling 78-129.*

EXAMPLE. A federal appeals court ruled that pledges not paid during the year are not allowed as charitable contribution deductions for that year. *Mann v. Commissioner, 35 F.2d 873 (D.C. Cir. 1932).*

Are pledges legally enforceable?

Are such commitments enforceable by a church? Traditionally the courts refused to enforce pledges on the basis of contract law. Since donors who make a pledge normally receive nothing in exchange for the pledge, their commitment was considered "illusory" and unenforceable. In recent years, however, several courts have enforced pledge commitments. In most cases enforcement is based on the principle of detrimental reliance. That is, a church that relies to its detriment on a pledge in assuming debt or other legal obligation should be able to enforce the pledge. One court has noted:

> The consideration for a pledge to an eleemosynary [i.e., charitable] institution or organization is the accomplishment of the purposes for which such institution or organization was organized and created and in whose aid the pledge is made, and such consideration is sufficient. We therefore conclude that pledges made in writing to eleemosynary institutions and organizations are enforceable debts supported by consideration, unless the writing itself otherwise indicates or it is otherwise proved. Hirsch v. Hirsch, 289 N.E.2d 386 (Ohio 1972). See also Estate of Timko v. Oral Roberts Evangelistic Association, 215 N.W.2d 750 (Mich. 1974).

Another court observed that "the real basis for enforcing a charitable [pledge] is one of public policy—enforcement of a charitable pledge is a desirable social goal." The court continued: "Lightly to withhold judicial sanction from such obligations would be to destroy millions of assets of the most beneficent institutions in our land, and to render such institutions helpless to carry out the purposes of their organization." *Jewish Federation v. Barondess, 560 A.2d 1353 (N.J. Super. 1989).*

EXAMPLE. The Alabama Supreme Court ruled that a $250,000 pledge to a Jewish temple was legally enforceable. A temple member had paid only $4,000 of his pledge at the time of his death, and the temple asked a court to determine if the balance of the $250,000 pledge was enforceable. Heirs of the donor insisted that the pledge was unenforceable because the donor never signed a pledge card. The court disagreed: "Alabama law is clear that an unsigned pledge, when met with detrimental reliance, rises to the level of an enforceable pledge. The evidence in this case showed that the Temple detrimentally relied on [the donor's] pledge. The temple had used the pledge to encourage others to donate to the campaign. The temple even publicized the pledge in its newsletters and other advertisements. Moreover, the evidence indicated that, before his death, the donor had even made appearances at various meetings and fundraising activities to show his support for the campaign." *Ruttenberg v. Friedman, 2012 WL 1650388 (Ala. 2012).*

EXAMPLE. A Georgia court ruled that a person who promised to make a $25,000 contribution to a church could be compelled to honor his commitment. A church purchased property from an individual for $375,000. In the contract of sale the seller promised to donate $5,000 to the church each year for the next five years (for a total contribution of $25,000). When the promised donations were not made, the church sued the seller for breach of contract. The seller claimed that his promise to make the donations was unenforceable because of lack of "consideration" for his promise. A trial court ruled in favor of the seller, concluding that a commitment or promise is not enforceable unless the promissor receives something of value ("consideration") in return.

The court concluded that the seller received no value for his promise to make the donations, and therefore the promise was not enforceable. The church appealed, and a state appeals court agreed with the church. It observed: "Although [the seller] asserts the promise to pay the church $25,000 was without consideration . . . nothing in the [record] shows that to be the case. [The sales contract] recites that the promise to pay $25,000 was made as additional consideration for the church to buy [the seller's] property." *First Baptist Church v. King, 430 S.E.2d 635 (Ga. App. 1993).*

EXAMPLE. An Iowa court ruled that a pledge a donor made to his church was legally enforceable. The donor informed various relatives of his intent to pay for the church projects. He was later informed that the projects would cost between $115,000 and $150,000. Prior to the donor's death, and in reliance on his agreement to provide funds, work was begun on several projects. After the donor's death, some of his heirs challenged the enforceability of the pledge. A state appeals court concluded that it was enforceable, even without proof of "consideration" or "detrimental reliance" by the church. All that was needed was a definite promise to transfer funds or property. As the court noted, "where a subscription is unequivocal the pledgor should be made to keep his word." *In re Estate of Schmidt, 723 N.W.2d 454 (Iowa App. 2006).*

EXAMPLE. A New York court ruled that pledges made by members of a synagogue were legally enforceable. The court conceded that pledges, like any promise, generally are not legally enforceable unless the person making the pledge receives something of value (called "consideration") in return. But there are exceptions to this requirement, and one of them is "detrimental reliance." According to this exception, if a charity relies to its detriment upon the pledges of members, then those pledges are enforceable even though not supported by consideration in a traditional sense. The court applied this principle to pledges made to the synagogue: "The synagogue entered into contracts and incurred liability in reliance upon the pledge made by [its members]. Thus, [members] became legally bound to pay the full dues when billed. Since the synagogue relies upon persons' membership as of the time of budgeting, and the dues being billed, [members are] estopped from refusing to pay the dues." *Temple Beth Am v. Tanenbaum, 789 N.Y.S.2d 658 (Dist. Ct. 2004).*

✷ **KEY POINT.** The issue of whether ministers should treat the financial support they pay to their church or denomination as a charitable contribution or as a business expense is addressed in Chapter 7, section C.13.

Gifts of blank checks

A blank check is a check that is complete in all respects except for the designation of a payee. The person issuing the check specifies the date and an amount and signs the check but does not identify a payee. Occasionally a church will receive a blank check in the offering or in the mail. This can occur for a number of reasons. Some elderly church members may forget to complete the check. Others may assume that the church will insert (or stamp) its name as payee, so why bother. Can church members claim a charitable contribution deduction for a blank check? Possibly not, according to a Tax Court case summarized in the following example.

EXAMPLE. A husband and wife claimed a charitable contribution of $34,000 to their church. The couple attempted to substantiate their deductions with canceled checks and carbon copies of checks from their two personal checking accounts on which they left the payee lines blank. The Tax Court ruled that "because these canceled blank checks fail to list [the church] as the donee, these checks do not establish" that the couple made tax-deductible charitable contributions to the church. *Dorris v. Commissioner, T.C. Memo. 1998-324.*

Contributing rebates to charity

A company offers rebates on the sale of certain products and gives consumers the choice of receiving the rebates themselves or donating them to a designated charity. The IRS ruled that consumers who elect to have their rebates donated to charity are entitled to a charitable contribution deduction in the amount of the rebate. *IRS Letter Ruling 199939021.* In reaching this conclusion, the IRS referred to two previous rulings:

- A utility company's customers were entitled to deductions for charitable contributions for payments to the company in excess of their monthly bills for a program designed to help elderly and handicapped persons meet their emergency energy-related needs. Since the utility company was acting as the agent for the charity, the deduction was allowed in the taxable year the payment was made to the utility company. *Revenue Ruling 85-184.*
- A rebate received directly from a seller was a reduction in the purchase price of the item that was not includible in the buyer's taxable income. *Revenue Ruling 76-96.* The IRS cautioned that the special substantiation rules that apply to contributions of $250 or more will apply to rebates (of $250 or more) that a buyer donates to charity.

Tax-free distributions from IRAs for charitable purposes

The Pension Protection Act of 2006 amended the tax code to allow tax-free qualified charitable distributions of up to $100,000 from an IRA to a church or other charity. Note the following rules and conditions:

- A qualified charitable distribution is any distribution from an IRA directly by the IRA trustee to a charitable organization, including a church, that are made on or after the date the IRA owner attains age 70½.
- A distribution will be treated as a qualified charitable distribution only to the extent that it would be includible in taxable income without regard to this provision.
- This provision applies only if a charitable contribution deduction for the entire distribution would be allowable under present law, determined without regard to the generally applicable percentage limitations. For example, if the deductible amount is reduced because the donor receives a benefit in exchange for the contribution of some or all of his or her IRA account, or if a deduction is not allowable because the donor did not have sufficient substantiation, the exclusion is not available with respect to any part of the IRA distribution.

❖ **KEY POINT.** This provision, which was scheduled to expire at the end of 2009, was extended through 2011 by the Tax Relief and Job Creation Act of 2010. It is not available in 2012 or thereafter unless further extended by Congress.

Contributions by credit card and electronic funds transfers

Section 170(a)(1) of the tax code specifies that "there shall be allowed as a deduction any charitable contribution . . . payment of which is made within the taxable year." The term "charitable contribution" is defined in the tax code and regulations as a contribution of cash or property to a qualified charity.

The income tax regulations clarify that a charitable contribution of cash or money includes "a transfer of a gift card redeemable for cash, and a payment made by credit card, electronic fund transfer (as described in section 5061(e)(2)), an online payment service, or payroll deduction."

Section 5061(e)(2) of the tax code defines the term "electronic fund transfer" (EFT) to mean "any transfer of funds, other than a transaction originated by check, draft, or similar paper instrument, which is initiated through an electronic terminal, telephonic instrument, or computer or magnetic tape so as to order, instruct, or authorize a financial institution to debit or credit an account."

The current edition of IRS Publication 526 (Charitable Contributions) confirms this conclusion by noting that "contributions charged on a donor's bank credit card are deductible in the year the donor makes the charge."

EFT is a safe and efficient process for making tax payments that is being used with increasing frequency to pay bills and make various kinds of payments. All transactions are governed by strict, nationally established rules, regulations, and security procedures and occur between financial institutions only at your request. Benefits of making contributions by EFT include the following:

- No paper checks are required.
- Contributions are paid automatically from your bank account.
- Contributions can be scheduled in advance.
- Contributions are made on the day you specify.
- It eliminates the risk of payments getting lost.
- Transactions are secure and confidential.

In order to substantiate a charitable contribution, a donor must maintain adequate records to show that the contribution was made. For contributions by credit cards, which are considered similar to a cash contribution, you must keep the credit card statement that shows the name of the charitable organization, the amount of the contribution, and the date of the contribution. Additional requirements apply to any individual charitable contribution (including by credit card) of $250 or more. Generally, these contributions can be substantiated only with a written acknowledgment from the donee charity that meets certain requirements.

Gift tax returns

The federal gift tax applies to the transfer by gift of any property. The general rule is that any gift is a taxable gift. However, this rule has many exceptions, including gifts of one's entire interest in property to charity, gifts to a spouse, and gifts that are not more than the annual exclusion for the calendar year. A separate annual exclusion applies to each person to whom a taxpayer makes a gift.

For 2012 the annual exclusion was $13,000. This means taxpayers could give up to $13,000 each to any number of people in 2012, and none of the gifts were taxable. The annual exclusion amount is adjusted for inflation in $1,000 increments. It increases to $14,000 for 2013.

The exemption of gifts to charity applies only to gifts of a donor's *entire* interest in property to a church or charity. It does not apply to a gift of a *partial* interest in property.

✳ New in 2013. The annual gift tax exclusion increases to $14,000 for 2013.

> **EXAMPLE.** John contributed $15,000 in cash to his church in 2012. He is not required to file a gift tax return with the IRS, because he has made a gift of his entire interest in the funds to his church.

> **EXAMPLE.** Joan donated her home to her church in 2012. She is not required to file a gift tax return with the IRS, even though the home is worth more than $13,000, because she gave her entire interest in the property to the church.

> **EXAMPLE.** Same facts as the previous example, except that Joan reserved a "life estate" in the home, which permits her to remain in the home for the rest of her life. Joan must file a gift tax return with the IRS, since she made only a partial gift of her property to the church.

> **EXAMPLE.** Jack donated ten acres of land to a church in 2012. The deed provides that if the property ever ceases to be used for church purposes, the title will revert back to Jack or his heirs. Jack has retained a partial interest in the property (since the title may revert to him or his heirs in the future). Jack's interest is known as a "possibility of reverter." He must file a gift tax return with the IRS, since he made only a partial gift of his property to the church.

2. TIME OF CONTRIBUTION

❖ **KEY POINT.** Charitable contributions must be claimed in the year they are delivered. One exception is a check mailed to a charity: it is deductible in the year the check is mailed (and postmarked), even if it is received early in the next year. See Table 8-1 for an overview of when to report end-of-year contributions.

Ordinarily a contribution is made at the time of delivery. For example, a check that is mailed to a church (or other charity) is considered delivered on the date it is mailed. A contribution of real estate generally is deductible in the year that a deed to the property is delivered to the charity. A contribution of stock is deductible in the year that a properly endorsed stock certificate is mailed or otherwise delivered to the charity. A promissory note issued in favor of a charity (and delivered to the charity) does not constitute a contribution until note payments are made. Contributions charged to a bank

═══ **TABLE 8-1** ═══

REPORTING END-OF-YEAR CONTRIBUTIONS

TYPE OF CONTRIBUTION	CHURCH REPORTS AS A 2012 CONTRIBUTION	CHURCH REPORTS AS A 2013 CONTRIBUTION
Checks written in December 2012 and deposited in church offering in January 2013		X
Checks written and deposited in church offering in January 2013 but backdated to December 2012		X
Checks written and deposited in church offering in December 2012 but postdated to January 2013		X
Checks written in and dated December 2012 and deposited in the mail and postmarked in December 2012 but not received by the church until January 2013	X	
Checks written in and dated December 2012 and deposited in the mail in December 2012 but not postmarked until January 2013 and not received by the church until January 2013		X

credit card are deductible in the year the charge was made. Pledges are not deductible until actually paid.

Predated checks

The first worship service in January often presents problems regarding the correct receipting of charitable contributions. For example, the first Sunday in January 2013 falls on January 6. Can a member who contributes a personal check to her church on Sunday, January 6, deduct the check on her 2012 federal tax return if the check is backdated to read "December 31, 2012"?

Many churches advise their congregations during the first worship service in January that checks contributed on that day can be credited to the previous year if they are dated December 31 of the previous year. *This advice is incorrect and should not be given.* Section 1.170A-1(b) of the income tax regulations states: "Ordinarily, a contribution is made at the time delivery is affected. The unconditional delivery or mailing

THE RELEVANCE OF A POSTMARK

Question: I dropped a number of charitable contributions in the mail on December 31, 2012. Some of them were reported as 2012 contributions, but one (for $1,000) was reported as a 2013 contribution. I called the church and was told that this envelope was postmarked January 2, 2013. The rest of the envelopes were postmarked in 2012. The church treasurer informed me that because the postmark date (2013) was controlling, he had to include this as a 2013 contribution. Is this true? Is the check that is mailed in 2012 but postmarked in 2013 deductible in 2013?

Answer: Section 170 of the tax code states that "there shall be allowed as a deduction any charitable contribution payment of which is made within the taxable year." Section 1.170A-1 of the regulations states that "the unconditional delivery or mailing of a check which subsequently clears in due course will constitute an effective contribution on the date of delivery or mailing." Similarly, Publication 526 states that "a check that you mail to a charity is considered delivered on the date you mail it."

In none of these cases is there a requirement that the check be postmarked as well as mailed in a particular year in order for a deduction to be available in that year. However, this is the position that is taken by the vast majority of charities, including major universities, government agencies, the American Bar Association, and the Association of Fundraising Professionals. The reasons are obvious. Charities must determine how to allocate contribution checks that are received in the mail during the first week of each new year. Are they current- or prior-year contributions? The charity could ignore the postmarks and proceed to question all of those donors to ascertain the date they placed their checks in the mail. But few, if any, charities go to this trouble.

It is far more prudent and reasonable to use the postmark as conclusive evidence of when a check was mailed. Yes, this will work to the detriment of a small number of donors who slip their check in the mailbox in the closing moments of the prior year, after the last mail pickup. Technically, those donors could claim a charitable contribution deduction in the prior year, based on the tax code and regulations quoted above. However, keep in mind one additional point. It is the taxpayer who has the burden of proving his or her entitlement to any tax deduction, including a charitable contribution. Donors are certainly free to claim a charitable contribution on their 2012 tax return for checks dropped in the mail on December 31 of that year (but that were not postmarked until January 2013). However, bear in mind that the donor has the burden of proving that this, in fact, was the case. In most cases, this will be a difficult, if not impossible, task.

In other words, what evidence could a donor present to prove that the postmark is wrong? In rare exceptions, this would be possible. For example, a donor asks a disinterested person (a neighbor) to accompany him to a mailbox just before midnight on December 31; has the neighbor examine the contribution check before it is placed in an envelope (making a written record of the name of the donee and the amount of the check); makes a record of the addressee identified on the envelope and ensures that proper postage is affixed; observes the donor place the envelope in the mailbox; and notes and records the precise time that the envelope is placed in the mailbox. How many donors would be able to satisfy their burden of proof in this manner?

For all of these reasons, the vast majority of charities receipt contributions they receive by mail according to the postmark date.

Finally, note that neither the IRS nor any court has ever addressed this question, so there is no definitive precedent either way. However, if this issue is ever raised, the most likely outcome would be that the IRS or a court would rule that the postmark date is the best evidence of when a check is mailed and that a taxpayer has a heavy burden to prove that a check was mailed in a year prior to its postmark date.

---

of a check which subsequently clears in due course will constitute an effective contribution on the date of delivery or mailing."

According to this language, a check dated December 31, 2012, but physically delivered to a church in January 2013, is deductible only on the donor's 2013 federal tax return. This is so whether a donor predated a check to read "December 31, 2012" during the first church service in January 2013 or in fact completed and dated the check on December 31, 2012, but deposited it in a church offering in January of 2013.

The only exception to this rule is a check that is dated, mailed, *and postmarked* in December 2012. The fact that the church does not receive the check until January 2013 does not prevent the donor from deducting it on his or her 2012 federal tax return.

Postdated checks

Churches occasionally receive a postdated check (a check that bears a future date). For example, Frank writes a check for $100 on March 1, 2013, that he dates April 15, 2013. Such checks often are received at the end of the year, when some donors decide they will be better off for tax purposes if they delay their contribution until the following year. Other donors make gifts of postdated checks before leaving on an extended vacation or business trip.

One court defined a postdated check as follows: "A postdated check is not a check immediately payable but is a promise to pay on the date shown. It is not a promise to pay presently and it does not mature until the day of its date, after which it is payable on demand the same as if it had not been issued until that date." In other words, a postdated check is treated like a promissory note. It is nothing more than a promise to pay a stated sum on or after a future date. It is not an enforceable obligation prior to the date specified.

Since a postdated check is no different than a promissory note, it should be treated the same way for tax purposes. If someone issues a note to a church, promising to pay $1,000 in one year, no charitable contribution is made when the note is signed (assuming the donor is a "cash basis" taxpayer). Rather, a contribution is made when the note is paid. Until then, there is only a promise to pay. Like a promissory note, a church ordinarily should simply retain a postdated check until the date on the check occurs. There is no need to return it. A bank may be willing to accept such a check for deposit before the date on the check has occurred, with the understanding that the funds will not be available for withdrawal.

EXAMPLE. Jane writes a check in the amount of $1,000 to her church during the last service of 2012 and drops it in the offering. She dates the check January 1, 2013, however, in order to claim a deduction in 2013 rather than in 2012. She does so because she believes her taxable income will be higher in 2013 and so the deduction will be "worth more" in that year. The check is a postdated check, which on the day it is given to the church is nothing more than a promise to pay, and so no charitable contribution has occurred. The charitable contribution occurs on January 1, 2013. On that date the check becomes more than a mere promise to pay. It is a legally enforceable commitment. The church should record the check as a 2013 contribution.

EXAMPLE. Jack makes weekly contributions of $100 to his church. In anticipation of a month-long business trip, he writes four checks in the amount of $100 each that he postdates for the next four Sundays. He places the checks in the offering during a church service prior to leaving on his trip. The church should record each check as a contribution on the date specified on the check.

EXAMPLE. Lynn mails a check to her church on December 29, 2012, that is dated January 1, 2013, and that is received by the church on January 2, 2013. A contribution in the form of a check is effective on the date of delivery with one exception—a check that is mailed (and postmarked) in one year is deductible in that year, even though it is not received by the church until the next year. This assumes that the check is accepted for deposit by

the bank. In this case, however, the "mailbox rule" does not apply, since the check was postdated. The church treasurer should record Lynn's check as a 2013 contribution.

Promissory notes

Churches occasionally receive gifts of promissory notes. For example, during a church building campaign in 2013, Bob gives his church a promissory note in which he promises to pay the church $10,000 over a three-year term. How much does the church treasurer report as a charitable contribution for year 2013? The full amount of the note? Some other amount?

The Tax Court has addressed this question. An attorney gave his church a promissory note for a substantial amount and then claimed a charitable contribution deduction for the entire face amount of the note, even though very little had been paid that year. The court ruled that the attorney could claim a charitable contribution deduction only for amounts he actually paid on the note in the year in question, not for the entire amount of the note. *Investment Research Associates v. Commissioner, T.C. Memo. 1999-407 (1999).*

Credit card charges

Some church members make charitable contributions using a credit card. When are these donations receiptable? On the date the charge is made? The date that the donor pays the credit card statement? Some other date?

The IRS addressed this question for the first time in a 1971 revenue ruling in which it concluded that a taxpayer who used a bank credit card to contribute to a qualified charity could not deduct any part of the contribution until the year the cardholder made payment of the amount of the contribution to the bank. *Revenue Ruling 71-216.* The IRS concluded that a charitable contribution made by a taxpayer using a credit card was tantamount to a charitable contribution made by the issuance and delivery of a promissory note by the donor to a charitable organization and, therefore, represented a mere promise to pay at some future date that was not currently deductible.

The IRS reconsidered this question in a 1978 ruling in which it revoked its earlier ruling. It concluded:

> *Upon further study, it has been concluded that there are major distinctions between contributions made by the use of credit cards and contributions made by promissory notes. . . . A credit card holder . . . by using the credit card to make the contribution, becomes immediately indebted to a third party (the bank) in such a way that the cardholder cannot thereafter prevent the charitable organization from receiving payment. . . . Since the cardholder's use of the credit card creates the cardholder's own debt to a third party, the use of a bank credit card to make a charitable contribution is equivalent to the use of borrowed funds to make a contribution.*

The general rule is that when a deductible payment is made with borrowed money, the deduction is not postponed until the year in which the borrowed money is repaid. Such expenses must be deducted in the year they are paid and not when the loans are repaid. Accordingly, a taxpayer discussed who makes a contribution to a qualified charity by a charge to the taxpayer's bank credit card is entitled to a charitable contribution deduction in the year the charge was made and the deduction may not be postponed until the taxpayer pays the indebtedness resulting from such charge.

The current edition of IRS Publication 526 (Charitable Contributions) confirms this conclusion by noting that "contributions charged on your bank credit card are deductible in the year you make the charge."

Of course, in order to substantiate a charitable contribution, a donor must maintain adequate records to show that the contribution was made. For contributions by credit cards, which are considered similar to a cash contribution, you must keep the credit card statement that shows the name of the charitable organization, the amount of the contribution and the date of the contribution. Additional requirements apply to any individual charitable contribution (including by credit card) of $250 or more. Generally, these contributions can be substantiated only with a written acknowledgment from the donee charity that meets certain requirements.

3. UNCONDITIONAL AND WITHOUT PERSONAL BENEFIT

The word "contribution" is synonymous with the word "gift," and so a contribution is not deductible unless it is a valid gift. Since no gift occurs unless a donor absolutely and irrevocably transfers title, dominion, and control over the gift, it follows that no charitable contribution deduction is available unless the contribution is unconditional. Similarly, no charitable contribution deduction is permitted if the donor receives a direct and material benefit for the contribution, since a gift by definition is a gratuitous transfer of property without consideration or benefit to the donor other than the feeling of satisfaction it evokes.

If a donor does receive a return benefit in exchange for a contribution, then a charitable contribution exists only to the extent that the cash or property transferred by the donor exceeds the fair market value of the benefit received in return. These two requirements of a charitable contribution—unconditional transfer without personal benefit to the donor—are illustrated by the examples below:

EXAMPLE. A church member purchases a church bond. No charitable contribution will be permitted for this purchase, since the purchaser receives a return benefit. However, a charitable contribution will be available if the member gives the bond back to the church. *Revenue Ruling 58-262.*

EXAMPLE. A religious broadcaster offers a "gift" (a free book) to anyone who contributes $10 or more. Contributors who give $10 and who receive the book can claim a charitable contribution of only the amount by which their check exceeds the fair market value of the book.

EXAMPLE. A taxpayer was interested in purchasing a tract of land owned by a church. Accordingly, he offered to "donate" $5,000 to the church if the church would give him preferential consideration in the purchase of the land. It also was understood that if he purchased the land, the purchase price would be reduced by the amount of the $5,000 "contribution." A federal appeals court denied the taxpayer a charitable contribution deduction under these facts, since the $5,000 payment obviously was not unconditional and without personal benefit to the donor. *Wineberg v. Commissioner, 326 F.2d 157 (9th Cir. 1964).*

EXAMPLE. A church charges a fee of $250 for each marriage occurring on its premises. The fee is designed to reimburse the church for utilities, wear and tear, custodial services, and other costs it incurs as a result of the ceremony. A taxpayer's daughter was married at the church, and he paid the $250 fee. On his federal income tax return for that year, the taxpayer claimed a charitable contribution deduction for this fee. The Tax Court denied the deductibility of the fee, since it was not a charitable contribution. The court noted that the taxpayer received a material benefit in exchange for his fee that was of commensurate value. *Summers v. Commissioner, 33 T.C.M. 696 (1974).*

EXAMPLE. A church operates a religious school. A church member has a child who attends the school. Annual tuition at the school is $2,000. In 2013 the parent makes a check payable to the church for $2,000 in excess of her normal offerings, and in exchange the church permits the member's child to attend the school without charge. The member cannot claim the $2,000 as a charitable contribution, since she received a material return benefit. If tuition were $1,000 per year, then the member would have made a contribution of $1,000. The subjects of tuition and scholarship gifts and "quid pro quo" contributions are addressed later in this chapter.

EXAMPLE. A church trustee lived in the pastor's home. He did not pay rent or any of the expenses of the home. He claimed a charitable contribution deduction to the church that was disallowed by the IRS because the claimed deduction did not exceed the value of the free "room and board" received by the trustee. The Tax Court agreed. It observed: "It is further reasonable to infer that any contributions made by [the trustee] to the [church] benefited him and were in anticipation of such housing or other benefits and, thus, did not proceed from detached and disinterested generosity. Based on the record before us, we hold that [the trustee] has failed to prove that he made a contribution or gift to the church." *Williamson v. Commissioner, 62 T.C. 610 (1991).*

EXAMPLE. A church honors donors of large amounts to a building program by inscribing their names on a memorial plaque. Does the public disclosure, for many years to come, of the major donors' identity on a memorial plaque constitute a benefit received in exchange for the contributions that nullifies any charitable contribution deductions for these donors? The IRS has observed: "Payments an exempt organization receives from donors are nontaxable contributions where there is no expectation that the organization will provide a substantial return benefit. Mere recognition of a . . . contributor as a benefactor normally is incidental to the contribution and not of sufficient value to the contributor to [preclude a charitable contribution deduction]. Examples of mere recognition [that do not nullify a charitable contribution deduction] are naming a . . . building after a benefactor." *IRS News Release IR-92-4.*

EXAMPLE. The Tax Court ruled that a woman who made contributions to a religious organization was not entitled to a charitable contribution deduction because the organization provided her with the necessities of life. *Ohnmeiss v. Commissioner, T.C. Memo. 1991-594.*

❖ **KEY POINT.** Charitable contributions generally are deductible only to the extent they exceed the value of any premium or benefit received by a donor in return for the contribution.

For further discussion of the requirement that a contribution is deductible by a donor only to the extent that it exceeds the fair market value of any premium or merchandise received in exchange, see section D of this chapter.

The income tax regulations specify that if a contribution to a charity is dependent on the performance of some act or the happening of some event in order for it to be effective, then no deduction is allowable unless the possibility that the gift will not become effective is so remote as to be negligible. Further, if the contribution specifies that it will be voided if a specified future event occurs, then no deduction is allowable unless the possibility of the future event occurring is so remote as to be negligible. *Treas. Reg. 1.170A-1(e).*

To illustrate, if a donor transfers land to a church on the condition that the land will be used for church purposes and will revert to the donor if the land ever ceases to be so used, the donor is entitled to a charitable contribution deduction if on the date of the transfer the church plans to use the property for church purposes and the possibility that it will cease to do so is so remote as to be negligible. *IRS Letter Ruling 9443004.*

The United States Supreme Court has summarized these rules as follows:

> The [essence] of a charitable contribution is a transfer of money or property without adequate consideration. The taxpayer,

> therefore, must at a minimum demonstrate that he purposely contributed money or property in excess of any benefit he received in return. [A contribution is deductible] only if and to the extent it exceeds the market value of the benefit received . . . [and] only if the excess payment [was] made with the intention of making a gift. United States v. American Bar Endowment, 106 S. Ct. 2426 (1986).

Returning contributions to a donor

Should churches ever return a contribution to a donor? This is a question that nearly every church leader faces eventually. Such requests can arise in a variety of ways. Consider the following:

EXAMPLE. A church member donates $1,000 to the church building fund in 2011. In 2013 the church abandons its plans to construct a new building. The member asks the church treasurer to return her $1,000 contribution.

EXAMPLE. A church member donates $2,500 to his church during the first six months of 2013. In July 2013, due to a financial crisis, he asks for a refund of his contributions.

EXAMPLE. A church member donates $2,000 to her church during the first six months of 2013. In July 2013 she becomes upset with the pastor and begins attending another church. She later asks the treasurer of her former church for a refund of her contributions.

A charitable contribution is a gift of money or property to a charitable organization. Like any gift, a charitable contribution is an irrevocable transfer of a donor's entire interest in the donated cash or property. Since the donor's entire interest in the donated property is transferred, it generally is impossible for the donor to recover the donated property.

Undesignated contributions

Most charitable contributions are undesignated, meaning that the donor does not specify how the contribution is to be spent. An example would be a church member's weekly contributions to a church's general fund.

Undesignated contributions are unconditional gifts. A church has absolutely no legal obligation to return undesignated contributions to a donor under any circumstances. In fact, a number of problems are associated with the return of undesignated contributions to donors. These are explored below.

Inconsistency. A return of a donor's contributions would be completely inconsistent with the church's previous characterization of the transactions as charitable contributions. As already noted, a charitable contribution is tax-deductible because it is an irrevocable gift to a charity. If a church complies with enough donors' requests to refund their contributions, this raises a serious question as to the deductibility of any contribution made to the church. Contributions under these circumstances might be viewed as no-interest "demand loans"—that is, temporary transfers of funds that are recallable by donors at will. As such, they would not be tax-deductible as charitable contributions.

Amended tax returns. Donors who receive a "refund" of their contributions would need to be advised to file amended federal tax returns if they claimed a charitable contribution deduction for their "contributions" for any of the previous three tax years. This would mean that donors would have to file a Form 1040X with the IRS. In most states donors also would have to file amended state income tax returns.

Church liability. A church that returns a charitable contribution to a donor who does not file an amended tax return to remove a prior charitable contribution deduction faces potential liability for "aiding and abetting" in the substantial understatement of tax. *IRC 6701(b)*.

Inurement. One of the conditions for tax-exempt status under section 501(c)(3) of the tax code is that none of a church's assets inures to the benefit of a private individual. Since undesignated contributions are church assets, a church that voluntarily returns such contributions to donors is distributing its resources to private individuals. It is possible that the return of such contributions would amount to prohibited inurement, thereby jeopardizing the church's tax-exempt status. Inurement is discussed more fully in Chapter 4, section A.

"Refund department." Compliance with a donor's demand for the return of a contribution would morally compel a church to honor the demands of anyone wanting a return of a contribution. This would establish an undesirable precedent.

✿ **KEY POINT.** Churches should resist appeals from donors to return their undesignated contributions. No legal basis exists for doing so, even in emergencies. Honoring such requests can create serious problems, as noted above. Churches should not honor such requests without the recommendation of an attorney.

First Amendment issues. A few courts have concluded that the First Amendment's guarantees of the nonestablishment and free exercise of religion bar the civil courts from refunding charitable contributions to donors if doing so would implicate religious doctrine. The leading cases, *Hawthorne v. Couch* and *McDonald v. Macedonia Missionary Baptist Church*, are summarized below.

In *Hawthorne v. Couch*, 911 So.2d 907 (La. App. 2005), a church member (the "donor") sued a church, seeking repayment of tithes he paid the church and also damages and attorney fees. The lawsuit alleged that the pastor of the church obtained the donor's tithes by exerting a "powerful influence over members of his church, demanding total submission to his authority, and gaining complete control of the members' minds and money." The lawsuit further

alleged that the pastor involved himself in the day-to-day business of a company the donor owned; ordered the donor to pay tithes on the gross income from the business and to increase the tithes paid by the business; and threatened him with "judgment and hell" if he did not pay up. The lawsuit claimed that the pastor knew his teaching was not biblical but that he was "overwhelmed with greed and power" and at some point had the idea that he would take over the donor's business. The donor claimed that his efforts to comply with the pastor's false teaching was bankrupting the company and that the pastor offered to purchase the business for a nominal sum.

The donor insisted that he always intended to tithe on his personal income, as opposed to the gross receipts from his business, and that he donated money to the church under duress. He claimed that the pastor's "misrepresentation of the Bible" constituted fraud, that the pastor knew his teaching was false, and that he knew the donor was relying on that teaching in making excessive contributions to the church's enrichment.

A trial court dismissed the donor's lawsuit, and the case was appealed. A Louisiana state appellate court began its opinion by noting that the First Amendment guaranty of religious freedom forbids the civil courts from interfering in the ecclesiastical matters of religious organizations and that this prohibition "extends to matters of religious discipline, faith, and custom." The court acknowledged that "not all church disputes necessarily involve purely ecclesiastical matters," but it concluded that where a "dispute is rooted in an ecclesial tenet of a church, the court will not have jurisdiction of the matter."

The court noted that the donor's claims "focused almost exclusively on the pastor's teachings regarding tithing. Without question, any legal analysis that would require a court to analyze and pass judgment upon such teachings would violate the [First Amendment]. The issue of tithing is at its core a purely ecclesiastical matter. . . . Accordingly, the trial court correctly concluded that it lacked jurisdiction."

The donor insisted that no religious doctrine had to be considered in the revocation of his donations to the church, and so his claims could be considered. He relied on the general rule that a donation "shall be declared null upon proof that it is the product of influence by the donee or another person that so impaired the volition of the donor as to substitute the volition of the donee or other person for the volition of the donor." However, the court pointed out that the donor's allegations regarding the validity of his consent "are rooted in the religious teachings or beliefs of the pastor and the church":

> *He alleged that the pastor threatened him with judgment and hell if he failed to make proper tithes. Although he claimed not to have free will and his gifts were made under duress due to the fraud allegedly perpetrated by the pastor, he further characterized the pastor's position as false teaching based on his misinterpretation of the Bible. . . . Whereas the donor masks his claims with legal terms such as consent, fraud, and duress, this controversy*

is indeed purely religious. Any consideration of his claims would require a court to examine the interpretation of the Bible on the subject of tithing which was applied by the pastor and then make a determination of whether that interpretation was or was not fraudulent. A civil court is in no position to make a judicial determination of what is and what is not a correct biblical interpretation. Furthermore, to consider whether the pastor was attempting to substitute his volition for the donor's would likewise require a court to consider the biblical basis of the pastor's threats aimed at the donor. A court would have to consider the pastor's intent in directing such statements at the donor, which again would require an interpretation of the basis for the comments, i.e., the Bible. For instance, in considering the allegation that the donor was threatened with judgment and hell for failing to give sufficiently, a court would need to delve into the issue of whether such statement was an actual threat to coerce the donor to donate money or rather a literal interpretation of the Bible as believed by the pastor. Clearly, as discussed herein, such an analysis is outside the jurisdiction of a civil trial court.

Moreover, at all times herein, the donor possessed the free will to simply walk away from this controversy by disassociating himself from the pastor and church. That would have ended the controversy concerning the amount of tithe he did or did not give to the church, and all parties would then have been free to live by any biblical interpretation they chose concerning this subject. By even requesting this or any other civil court to issue a ruling on such a clearly ecclesiastical matter runs the honored issue of separation of church and state to the very edge of the fabric. The Founders showed incredible foresight in setting up our system of government where the lines should never cross on such issues, and the courts should and do maintain a neutral posture.

IRS response to a question submitted by a member of Congress. In 2010 the IRS responded to questions submitted by Congresswoman Kay Granger on behalf of one of her constituents regarding the tax consequences associated with a charity's return of a charitable contribution. The IRS observed:

We are pleased to provide you with the following general information about the federal income consequences to a donor who receives a repayment of a charitable gift plus interest on the repayment. . . .

If a taxpayer receives the full tax benefit of a charitable contribution deduction when making a contribution to a qualified charity, and the charity repays the contribution to the taxpayer in a subsequent year, the "tax benefit rule" requires the taxpayer to include in gross income in that subsequence year the amount of the previously deducted contribution.

A taxpayer who receives interest on a repaid contribution must also include that amount in income. An individual taxpayer

generally includes interest in income when it is available to the taxpayer free of substantial limitations and restrictions. . . .

If the taxpayer uses a repaid contribution to make a new charitable contribution to a different charitable organization, he or she may claim a charitable contribution deduction for the new contribution, subject to the usual restrictions and limitations on charitable contribution deductions.

The tax benefit rule referenced in the above-quoted IRS response is codified in section 111 of the tax code, which states: "Gross income does not include income attributable to the recovery during the taxable year of any amount deducted in any prior taxable year to the extent such amount did not reduce the amount of tax imposed by this chapter."

In several cases the IRS and the courts have ruled that section 111 requires donors who have received a refund of a charitable contribution made in a prior year should report the refund as taxable income in the year of the refund rather than file an amended return for the year of the contribution deleting that contribution. See, e.g., Revenue Ruling 75-150.

✸ **KEY POINT.** Note that Congresswoman Kay Granger's constituent made his designated contribution to charity "more than two decades ago." According to the IRS, this did not affect his obligation to report the refunded contribution as taxable income.

Designated contributions—project not abandoned

Often a donor will make a designated contribution to a church. That is, the donor designates how the contribution is to be spent. For example, a donor contributes a check in the amount of $1,000 and specifies that it be used for missions or the building fund or some other specific project. Some courts have ruled that such designated contributions are held by the church "in trust" for the designated purpose. So long as the church honors the designation or plans to do so in the foreseeable future, it has no legal obligation to return a donor's designated contribution. Quite to the contrary, returning a donor's designated contribution under these circumstances would create the same problems associated with the return of undesignated contributions (summarized above). Those problems should be reviewed again.

In *McDonald v. Macedonia Missionary Baptist Church*, 2003 WL 1689618 (Mich. App. 2003), a married couple donated $4,000 to their church's "new building fund." The congregation planned to construct a new church the following year, but these plans were put on hold when the church received an unused school building. The couple sued their church, seeking a return of their building fund donation on the basis of the church's "breach of contract." Church leaders noted that the church had $500,000 in its new building fund and insisted that it still planned to build a new sanctuary as

Chapter 8   CHARITABLE CONTRIBUTIONS

soon as the fund grew to $6 million. A trial court agreed with the couple and ordered the church to refund their contributions. The church appealed.

A Michigan appeals court reversed the trial court's ruling and dismissed the case. It concluded that the civil courts are barred by the First Amendment guaranty of religious freedom from intervening in such internal church disputes:

> It is well settled that courts, both federal and state, are severely circumscribed by the First Amendment [and the Michigan constitution] in resolution of disputes between a church and its members. Jurisdiction is limited to property rights which can be resolved by application of civil law. Whenever the trial court must stray into questions of ecclesiastical polity or religious doctrine the court loses jurisdiction. . . . We hold that this dispute involves a policy of the church for which our civil courts should not interfere. Because the decision of when and where to build a new church building is exclusively within the province of the church members and its officials, the trial court erred in not dismissing the couple's lawsuit.

Designated contributions—project abandoned

What if a donor contributes money to a church's building fund and the church later abandons its plans to construct a new facility? Should the church refund contributions to donors who stipulated that their contributions were for the building fund? A number of possibilities exist, including the following:

Donors can be identified. If donors can be identified, they should be asked if they want their contributions to be returned or retained by the church and used for some other purpose. Ideally, donors should communicate their decision in writing to avoid any misunderstandings. Churches must provide donors with this option in order to avoid violating their legal duty to use "trust funds" only for the purposes specified.

A church should send a letter to donors who request a refund of a prior designated contribution informing them that (1) there may be tax consequences; (2) they may want to consider filing an amended tax return to remove any deduction claimed during any of the three previous years as a result of their designated contribution; and (3) they should discuss the options with their tax advisor.

Some churches have issued donors a Form 1099-MISC under these circumstances to reduce the church's risk of liability for aiding and abetting in the substantial understatement of tax. *IRC 6701(b).* But this approach presents two problems:

(1) It assumes that the donor claimed a charitable contribution deduction for the designated gift and will not file an amended tax return. In fact, some donors did not get a tax deduction for their gifts because they could not itemize

their deductions on Schedule A. Others received a "discounted" deduction because of the amount of their income (high-income taxpayers only get a partial deduction for their charitable contributions). A church treasurer would have to inspect the actual tax return of each donor who requests a return of his or her contribution. Most church leaders consider such precautions excessive and unnecessary, especially for smaller contributions.

(2) Form 1099-MISC is not designed to report this kind of income. It is designed for nonemployee compensation. In what sense have these donors performed services for the church for which they are being compensated?

In summary, the best approach is for the church to inform donors who request a refund of a designated contribution to address the tax consequences with their tax advisor. They can either do nothing, report the amount of the returned contribution as "other income" on line 21 of their Form 1040, or file an amended return for the year the designated contribution was made, which removes the contribution from Schedule A. Keep in mind that amended returns can be made for only one of the previous three years.

EXAMPLE. Bob gives $1,000 to his church building fund in 2008. In 2013 the church decides to abandon the building project. Bob asks the church to refund his contribution. While it is too late for Bob to file an amended return for 2008, he feels morally compelled to report the $1,000 as income on his 2013 tax return. Doing so, however, is problematic, since Bob may not have been able to claim a deduction in the year of the contribution, or the deduction was reduced. Even if a full deduction was claimed, this only reduced taxable income. A $1,000 contribution to the building fund was not, in other words, worth $1,000. It was worth considerably less, depending on Bob's income and tax bracket. If Bob was in the 15 percent tax bracket in 2008, then the value of the contribution to him was $150. His $1,000 donation reduced taxable income by $1,000, thereby saving him $150 in taxes. Further, if Bob had substantial income in the year of the gift, the value of his donation may have been even less (charitable contribution deductions were partially "phased out" for high-income taxpayers in 2008). So when Bob receives his $1,000 back several years later, it is not a simple matter of reporting $1,000 as taxable income. At best, this should be something for Bob to decide, not the church.

✪ **KEY POINT.** Often donors prefer to let the church retain their designated contributions rather than go through the inconvenience of filing an amended tax return.

Donors cannot be identified. A church may not be able to identify all donors who contributed to the building fund. This is often true of donors who contributed small amounts, or donors who made anonymous cash offerings to the fund. In some cases designated contributions were made many years before the church abandoned its building plans, and there are no records that identify donors. Under these circumstances, the church has a variety of options.

One option is to address the matter in a membership meeting. Inform the membership of the amount of designated contributions in the church building fund that cannot be traced to specific donors, and ask the membership to adopt a resolution with regard to the disposition of the fund. Often the members will authorize the transfer of the funds to the general fund. Note that this procedure is appropriate only for that portion of the building fund that cannot be traced to specific donors. If donors can be identified, use the procedure described above.

Another option is to ask a court for authorization to transfer the building fund to another church fund. Most states have adopted the Uniform Prudent Management of Institutional Funds Act of 2006 (UPMIFA), and this Act permits churches to ask a civil court for authorization to remove a restriction on charitable contributions to permanent endowment funds in some situations. UPMIFA is addressed below.

Other options are available. Churches should consult with an attorney when deciding how to dispose of designated funds if the specified purpose has been abandoned or is no longer feasible.

�֎ **KEY POINT.** Some courts have ruled that a donor has no legal standing to enforce a designated gift to charity. The reason for this rule is simple—a charitable contribution is a gift, and a gift is a transfer of all of a donor's control over the donated property. Allowing a donor to enforce a designated gift is not legally possible because the donor has no remaining interest in the gift. This is true even if the gift was designated. The fact remains that a designated gift is held by a church or charity in trust for the specified purpose. The trust may be expressed in a written trust instrument, but usually no instrument exists and the trust is implied. While the donor may not be able to enforce such a trust, this does not mean that a church or charity can ignore it. Some courts have ruled that the state attorney general can enforce a trust created by a designated gift, and so can any other person with a "special interest" in the trust. While this does not ordinarily include donors, their families or heirs, or even beneficiaries of the gift or trust, it may include fiduciaries (such as a trustee of a written trust).

Some donors can be identified, and some cannot. In most cases, some of the building fund can be traced to specific donors, but some of it cannot. Both of the procedures summarized above may apply.

�֎ **KEY POINT.** This section has focused on building funds. The same analysis is relevant to contributions that designate any other specific purpose or activity. Other examples include contributions designating a new organ, a missions activity, or a new vehicle.

➠ **TIP.** Churches that solicit funds for designated projects face difficult choices when they abandon the project and are left with the task of disposing of funds donated for that project. These problems can be avoided if the church simply includes a statement similar to the following when soliciting funds for a specific project: "By contributing to this project, donors acknowledge that the church has full authority to apply contributions designated for this project to other purposes in the event the project is canceled or oversubscribed." Such a statement should be printed on special offering envelopes used for the project, or on any other materials so long as they provide adequate notice to donors of the policy and reflect donors' consent to it.

The Uniform Prudent Management of Institutional Funds Act of 2006 (UPMIFA)

The Uniform Prudent Management of Institutional Funds Act (UPMIFA) has been adopted, with minor variations, in 47 states. It replaces the Uniform Management of Institutional Funds Act (UMIFA), which was adopted by most states since its inception in 1972. An introductory note to UPMIFA states that one of the reasons for the revision of UMIFA was an update to the provisions "governing the release and modification of restrictions on charitable funds to permit more efficient management of these funds." In this regard, Section 6 of UPMIFA states:

(a) If the donor consents in a record, an institution may release or modify, in whole or in part, a restriction contained in a gift instrument on the management, investment, or purpose of an institutional fund. A release or modification may not allow a fund to be used for a purpose other than a charitable purpose of the institution.

(b) The court, upon application of an institution, may modify a restriction contained in a gift instrument regarding the management or investment of an institutional fund if the restriction has become impracticable or wasteful, if it impairs the management or investment of the fund, or if, because of circumstances not anticipated by the donor, a modification of a restriction will further the purposes of the fund. The institution shall notify the [Attorney General] of the application, and the [Attorney General] must be given an opportunity to be heard. To the extent practicable, any modification must be made in accordance with the donor's probable intention.

(c) If a particular charitable purpose or a restriction contained in a gift instrument on the use of an institutional fund becomes unlawful, impracticable, impossible to achieve, or wasteful, the court, upon application of an institution, may modify the purpose of the fund or the restriction on the use of the fund in a manner consistent with the charitable purposes expressed in the gift instrument. The institution shall notify the [Attorney General] of the application, and the [Attorney General] must be given an opportunity to be heard.

(d) If an institution determines that a restriction contained in a gift instrument on the management, investment, or purpose of an institutional fund is unlawful, impracticable, impossible to achieve, or wasteful, the institution, [60 days] after notification to the [Attorney General], may release or modify the restriction, in whole or part, if:

> *(1) the institutional fund subject to the restriction has a total value of less than [$25,000];*
>
> *(2) more than [20] years have elapsed since the fund was established; and*
>
> *(3) the institution uses the property in a manner consistent with the charitable purposes expressed in the gift instrument.*

UPMIFA defines an institutional fund as "a fund held by an institution exclusively for charitable purposes. The term does not include: (A) program-related assets; (B) a fund held for an institution by a trustee that is not an institution; or (C) a fund in which a beneficiary that is not an institution has an interest, other than an interest that could arise upon violation or failure of the purposes of the fund." Charitable purposes are defined as "the relief of poverty, the advancement of education or religion, the promotion of health, the promotion of a governmental purpose, or any other purpose the achievement of which is beneficial to the community." The Act defines a program-related asset as "an asset held by an institution primarily to accomplish a charitable purpose of the institution and not primarily for investment." An "institution" means any entity organized and operated exclusively for charitable purposes. This would include a church.

An official comment to section 6 (quoted above) states:

> *Subsection (a) permits the release of a restriction if the donor consents. A release with donor consent cannot change the charitable beneficiary of the fund. Although the donor has the power to consent to a release of a restriction, this section does not create a power in the donor that will cause a federal tax problem for the donor. The gift to the institution is a completed gift for tax purposes, the property cannot be diverted from the charitable beneficiary, and the donor cannot redirect the property to another use by the charity. The donor has no retained interest in the fund.*
>
> *Subsection (b) applies the rule of equitable deviation. . . . Under the deviation doctrine, a court may modify restrictions on the way an institution manages or administers a fund in a manner that furthers the purposes of the fund. Deviation implements the donor's intent. A donor commonly has a predominating purpose for a gift and, secondarily, an intent that the purpose be carried out in a particular manner. Deviation does not alter the purpose but rather modifies the means in order to carry out the purpose.*

Sometimes deviation is needed on account of circumstances unanticipated when the donor created the restriction. In other situations the restriction may impair the management or investment of the fund. Modification of the restriction may permit the institution to carry out the donor's purposes in a more effective manner. A court applying deviation should attempt to follow the donor's probable intention in deciding how to modify the restriction. Consistent with the doctrine of equitable deviation in trust law, subsection (b) does not require an institution to notify donors of the proposed modification. Good practice dictates notifying any donors who are alive and can be located with a reasonable expenditure of time and money. Consistent with the doctrine of deviation under trust law, the institution must notify the attorney general who may choose to participate in the court proceeding. The attorney general protects donor intent as well as the public's interest in charitable assets. Attorney general is in brackets in the Act because in some states another official enforces the law of charities.

The cy pres rule

The cy pres doctrine (which has been adopted by most states) generally specifies that if property is given in trust to be applied to a particular charitable purpose, and it is or becomes impossible or impracticable or illegal to carry out the particular purpose, and if the donor manifested a more general intention to devote the property to charitable purposes, the trust will not fail but the court will direct the application of the property to some charitable purpose which falls within the general charitable intention of the donor.

An official comment to section 8 of UPMIFA confirms that

> *subsection (c) applies the rule of cy pres from trust law, authorizing the court to modify the purpose of an institutional fund. The term modify encompasses the release of a restriction as well as an alteration of a restriction and also permits a court to order that the fund be paid to another institution. A court can apply the doctrine of cy pres only if the restriction in question has become unlawful, impracticable, impossible to achieve, or wasteful. . . . Any change must be made in a manner consistent with the charitable purposes expressed in the gift instrument. Consistent with the doctrine of cy pres, subsection (c) does not require an institution seeking cy pres to notify donors. Good practice will be to notify donors whenever possible. As with deviation, the institution must notify the attorney general who must have the opportunity to be heard in the proceeding.*

EXAMPLE. An elderly man drafted a will in 1971 that left most of his estate in trust to his sisters, and upon the death of the surviving sister to a local Congregational church with the stipulation that the funds be used "solely for the building of a new church." The man died in 1981, and his surviving sister died in 1988. Since the Congregational church had no plans to build a new sanctuary, it asked a local court to interpret the will to permit the church to use the trust fund not only for construction of a new facility but also "for the remodeling, improvement, or expansion of the existing church facilities" and for the purchase of real estate that may be needed for future church construction. The church also asked the court for permission to use income from the trust fund for any purposes that the church board wanted. The state attorney general, pursuant to state law, reviewed the church's petition and asked the court to grant the church's requests.

However, a number of heirs opposed the church's position, insisting that the decedent's will was clear and that the church was attempting to use the trust funds "for purposes other than building a new church." They asked the court to distribute the trust fund to the decedent's lawful heirs. The local court agreed with the church on the ground that "gifts to charitable uses and purposes are highly favored in law and will be most liberally construed to make effectual the intended purpose of the donor." The trial court's ruling was appealed by the heirs, and the state supreme court agreed with the trial court and ruled in favor of the church. The supreme court began its opinion by observing that "it is contrary to the public policy of this state to indulge in strained construction of the provisions of a will in order to seek out and discover a basis for avoiding the primary purpose of the [decedent] to bestow a charitable trust."

The court emphasized that the cy pres doctrine clearly required it to rule in favor of the church. Applying the cy pres rule, the court concluded: "The will gave the property in trust for a particular charitable purpose, the building of a new church. The evidence clearly indicated that it was impractical to carry out this particular purpose. Furthermore, the [decedent] did not provide that the trust should terminate if the purpose failed. A trust is not forfeited when it becomes impossible to carry out its specific purpose, and there is no forfeiture or reversion clause." The court concluded that the trial court's decision to permit the church to use the trust fund for the remodeling, improvement, or expansion of the existing church facilities "falls within the [decedent's] general charitable intention." Accordingly, the trial court's decision represented a proper application of the cy pres rule. *Matter of Trust of Rothrock, 452 N.W.2d 403 (Iowa 1990).*

EXAMPLE. A court ruled that church funds earmarked by a donor for a specific purpose could be used by the church for other, related purposes. In 1911 a Quaker church established a fund for the care and maintenance of its graveyard and began soliciting contributions for the fund. By 1988 the fund had increased to nearly $200,000 and had annual income far in excess of expenses. In 1985 the church discussed the possibility of using the excess income for purposes other than graveyard maintenance and ultimately expressed a desire to use excess income from the fund for general church purposes (including upkeep and maintenance of church properties). A church trustee who administered the fund took an unbending position that the fund could not be used for any purpose other than

graveyard maintenance. The church and trustee thereupon sought an opinion ("declaratory judgment") from a local court as to the use of the fund for other purposes.

The trial court ruled that the excess income could be used for general church purposes other than graveyard maintenance, and the trustee appealed the case to a state appeals court on the ground that the trial court's decision "conflicts with the express intent of the donors." The appeals court agreed with the trial court on the basis of the "cy pres" doctrine. The court observed that the cy pres doctrine was created "for the preservation of a charitable trust when accomplishment of the particular purpose of the trust becomes impossible, impractical, or illegal." The court concluded that "if income from a charitable trust exceeds that which is necessary to achieve the donor's charitable objective, cy pres may be applied to the surplus income since there is an impossibility of using the income to advance any of the charitable purposes of the [donor]." Therefore, to the extent that the graveyard fund in question "exceeds maintenance and preservation costs, application of cy pres is appropriate since there is an impossibility of using the excess income to advance the particular purpose expressed by the donors."

The only remaining question was whether the donors manifested an intention to devote excess income to a charitable purpose more general than graveyard maintenance. The court concluded that the donors to the graveyard fund did, in fact, manifest such an intent: "Since the donations were made for the perpetual maintenance of a graveyard, it is logical to assume that the donors expected excess income would be used . . . 'to strengthen the very institution to which [they] entrusted their money' to permit it to survive in perpetuity in order to carry out the donors' intent. A contrary result, that the income be held in the trust and accumulate in perpetuity for maintenance of the graveyard, is both illogical and contrary to the probable intent of the donors. The only sensible conclusion to be reached is that the donors did not intend that the trusts would grow while the [church] itself may cease to exist because of lack of funds. We are also convinced that use of the funds for general meeting purposes is sufficiently similar to the particular purpose of the [donors] to apply the cy pres doctrine." The court emphasized that only trust income in excess of graveyard expenses could be applied for general church purposes and that the church's bylaws required an annual audit of the fund by certified public accountants. *Sharpless v. Medford Monthly Meeting of the Religious Society of Friends, 548 A.2d 1157 (N.J. Super. 1988).*

Conclusions

So long as a church honors donors' designations, or plans to do so in the foreseeable future, it ordinarily has no legal obligation to return such contributions to donors. To the contrary, returning a donor's designated contribution under these circumstances could create one or more of the problems noted above.

If a church abandons a project for which it solicited designated funds from donors, one option would be for the church to ask donors if they want their contributions to be returned or retained by the church and used for some other purpose. Ideally, donors should communicate their decision in writing to avoid any misunderstandings.

What if a church cannot identify all of the donors who contributed to the abandoned project? One option is to address the matter in a membership meeting. Another is to ask a court for authorization to transfer the building fund to another church fund, pursuant to UPMIFA. As noted above, UPMIFA applies only to "institutional funds" (such as endowment funds) that are regarded as permanent. Other options are available. Churches should consult with an attorney when deciding how to dispose of designated funds if the specified purpose has been abandoned or is no longer feasible.

When deciding how to respond to donors' requests for a return of their contributions, it is advisable to seek legal counsel.

The Scientology case

In 1989 the Supreme Court ruled that "contributions" made to the Church of Scientology for "auditing" were not deductible as charitable contributions. *Hernandez v. Commissioner, 109 S. Ct. 2136 (1989).* Auditing involves a counseling session between a church official and a counselee during which the counselor utilizes an electronic device (an "E-meter") to identify areas of spiritual difficulty by measuring skin responses during a question and answer session. Counselees are encouraged to attain spiritual awareness through a series of auditing sessions. The church also offers members doctrinal courses known as "training."

The church charges fixed "donations" for auditing and training sessions (the charges are set forth in published schedules). For example, the published charges for a particular year were $625 for a 12-hour basic auditing session, $750 for a 12-hour specialized auditing session, and $4,250 for a 100-hour package. A 5 percent "discount" was available to persons who paid their charges in advance, and the church offered refunds of the unused portions of prepaid charges in the event that a person discontinued the services before their completion. The system of fixed charges was based on a tenet of Scientology (the doctrine of exchange) that requires persons to pay for any benefit received in order to avoid "spiritual decline."

The Supreme Court ruled that payments made to the Church of Scientology for auditing and training services are not deductible as charitable contributions. The court emphasized that a charitable contribution is a payment made to a qualified charitable organization with no expectation of a return benefit. If a return benefit is received, then the payment is a contribution only to the extent that it exceeds the value of the benefit received in exchange. The court concluded that payments made to the Church of Scientology for auditing and training sessions were a nondeductible reciprocal exchange, since

the Church established fixed price schedules for auditing and training sessions in each branch church; it calibrated particular prices to auditing or training sessions of particular lengths and levels of sophistication; it returned a refund if auditing and training services went unperformed; it distributed account cards on which persons who had paid money to the Church could monitor what prepaid services they had not yet claimed; and it categorically barred provision of auditing or training services for free. Each of these practices reveals the inherently reciprocal nature of the exchange.

In other words, "contributions" to the church (1) were mandatory, in the sense that no benefits or services were available without the prescribed payment, and (2) represented a specified fee for a specified service.

The court rejected the church's claim that it would be unfair to permit members of more conventional churches to deduct contributions for which they undeniably receive benefits (i.e., sacraments, preaching, teaching, counseling) but deny Scientologists a deduction for payments they make for auditing and training. The court emphasized that "the relevant inquiry in determining whether a payment is a [deductible] contribution is, as we have noted, *not whether the payment secures religious benefits or access to religious services, but whether the transaction in which the payment is involved is structured as a quid pro quo exchange*" (emphasis added).

Scientologists clearly receive a specified benefit in exchange for a mandatory and specified fee, and this fact distinguishes payments by Scientologists for auditing and training from most voluntary contributions made by donors to more conventional churches. The typical contribution to a conventional church is voluntary (in the sense that religious benefits ordinarily are not withheld if the individual does not make a contribution), and specified religious benefits are not available only upon the payment of a specified fee. The typical church member receives a number of general benefits, none of which is associated with a prescribed fee, regardless of whether he or she contributes to the church. These facts demonstrate that the typical contribution to a conventional church does not constitute a "quid pro quo exchange" of a specified service for a specified and mandatory fee.

✿ **KEY POINT.** If a donor makes a quid pro quo contribution of more than $75 (that is, a payment that is partly a contribution and partly a payment for goods or services received in exchange), the church must provide a written statement to the donor that satisfies certain conditions. These are addressed in section D of this chapter.

4. CONTRIBUTIONS MADE TO OR FOR THE USE OF A QUALIFIED ORGANIZATION

✿ **KEY POINT.** Charitable contributions must be made to or for the use of a qualified charitable organization.

Only those contributions made to qualified organizations are deductible. Section 170(c) of the tax code defines "qualified organizations" to include, among others, any organization that satisfies all of the following requirements:

(1) created or organized in the United States (or a United States possession);

(2) organized and operated exclusively for religious, educational, or other charitable purposes;

(3) no part of the net earnings of which inures to the benefit of any private individual; and

(4) not disqualified for tax exempt status under section 501(c)(3) by reason of attempting to influence legislation, and which does not participate or intervene in any political campaign on behalf of any candidate for public office.

IRS Publication 78 lists those organizations that have been recognized by the IRS to be qualified organizations. This listing is not ... ing churches, ... ithout filing ... rdinarily do ... are covered ... n A.4).

... published as a ... y on the IRS

... the use of ... irectly to ... ave ruled that ... dy individu- ... uals will, in ... *for the use of* a ... aries under the ... are considered to be deductible on this basis. The contribution is not made to the organization, but it is made for the use of the organization. Similarly, contributions often are made payable to a church, but with a stipulation that the funds be distributed to a specified individual. Common examples include Christmas gifts to a minister, scholarship gifts to a church school, and contributions to a church benevolence fund.

The deductibility of these designated contributions, along with contributions made to foreign missionaries, is considered in detail in section B of this chapter.

Contributions to foreign charities

Church members sometimes make contributions directly to religious organizations or ministries overseas. Or they make contributions to a United States religious organization for distribution to a foreign organization. Are these contributions tax-deductible? Federal law specifies that a charitable contribution, to be tax-deductible, must go to an organization "created or organized in the United States or in any possession thereof." In addition, the organization must be organized and operated exclusively for religious or other charitable purposes. This means that contributions made directly by church members to a foreign church or ministry are not tax-deductible in this country.

A related question addressed by the IRS in a 1963 ruling is whether a donor can make a tax-deductible contribution to an American charity with the stipulation that it be transferred directly to a foreign charity. The IRS ruled that such a contribution is not deductible, since in effect it is made directly to the foreign charity. *Revenue Ruling 63-252.*

✿**KEY POINT.** In its 1963 ruling the IRS did concede that contributions to a U.S. charity are deductible even though they are earmarked for distribution to a foreign charity, so long as the foreign charity "was formed for purposes of administrative convenience and the [U.S. charity] controls every facet of its operations." The IRS concluded: "Since the foreign organization is merely an administrative arm of the [U.S.] organization, the fact that contributions are ultimately paid over to the foreign organization does not require a conclusion that the [U.S.] organization is not the real recipient of those contributions."

EXAMPLE. The Tax Court ruled that a taxpayer who sent contributions to a mosque in his family's hometown in Iran was not entitled to a charitable contribution deduction. The court noted that to be deductible, a charitable contribution must go to a charity organized in the United States. *Alisobhani v. Commissioner, T.C. Memo. 1994-629 (1994).*

The fact that church members cannot claim a charitable contribution deduction for transfers to foreign charities in no way implies that a church cannot make such distributions. Churches can distribute their resources in furtherance of their tax-exempt purposes, even if this means transferring funds to a foreign charity. Individual donors, on the other hand, are confronted with the requirement of the tax code that their charitable contributions must go to a qualified charity (a term that excludes foreign charities).

Gifts to Canadian, Mexican, and Israeli charities

You may be able to deduct contributions to certain Canadian charitable organizations covered under an income tax treaty with Canada. To deduct your contribution to a Canadian charity, you generally must have income from sources in Canada. See IRS Publication 597 (Information on the United States–Canada Income Tax Treaty) for information on how to figure your deduction.

You may be able to deduct contributions to certain Mexican charitable organizations under an income tax treaty with Mexico.

The organization must meet tests that are essentially the same as the tests that qualify U.S. organizations to receive deductible contributions. The organization may be able to tell you if it meets these tests. If not, you can get general information about the tests the organization must meet by writing to the Internal Revenue Service, International Section, P.O. Box 920, Philadelphia, PA 19255-0725.

To deduct your contribution to a Mexican charity, you must have income from sources in Mexico.

You may be able to deduct contributions to certain Israeli charitable organizations under an income tax treaty with Israel. To qualify for the deduction, your contribution must be made to an organization created and recognized as a charitable organization under the laws of Israel. The deduction will be allowed in the amount that would be allowed if the organization was created under the laws of the United States but is limited to 25 percent of your adjusted gross income from Israeli sources.

> **EXAMPLE.** A member (the "donor") of a Catholic church in Texas was an ardent supporter of churches in her native country that were experiencing persecution from the government. Fearing that direct contributions to these churches would be confiscated by the government, the donor wired money to the personal bank account of her cousin. The cousin then transferred the money to selected Catholic churches in that country. Other than her membership in a Catholic church, the cousin did not have any formal role with any other Catholic institutions in that country.
>
> During 2006, the donor wired $25,000 to her cousin's account pursuant to her plan. She claimed these transfers as charitable contributions on her tax return for that year, since the ultimate beneficiary of the transfers was the Roman Catholic Church, a qualified charitable organization. The court disagreed, noting that section 170(c)(2) of the tax code defines a charitable contribution as a contribution or gift "to or for the use of" an organization "created or organized in the United States . . . or under the law of the United States." It added: "[The donor] did not make the wire transfers to or for the use of an organization created or organized in the United States or under the laws of the United States. Her contributions were made to her cousin, who distributed them for the benefit of foreign Catholic churches. Therefore, her wire transfers of $25,000 are not deductible as charitable contributions."
>
> The donor also claimed that the Catholic Church is a universal organization, and therefore Catholic churches in foreign countries are qualified charitable contribution recipients. The court disagreed: "[We have] no basis to find that the Catholic churches in that foreign country to which the donor's wire transfers were sent were created or organized in the United States or under the laws of the United States." The court added that "the language of section 170(c)(2) is explicit, and this court must follow such plain language." *Anonymous v. Commissioner. TC Memo. 2010-87 (2010).*

5. AMOUNT DEDUCTIBLE

❖ **KEY POINT.** The amount of a contribution that is tax-deductible is limited. In some cases the amount of a contribution that exceeds these limits can be carried over and claimed in future years.

In general, donors can deduct contributions they make to most charitable organizations up to 50 percent of their adjusted gross income (AGI). The 50 percent limit applies to contributions to all public charities, including churches and most religious organizations. Donors who contribute noncash property generally can claim a deduction in the amount of the fair market value of the donated property. Donors and churches should keep in mind a number of special rules, explained below.

Property subject to a debt

What if a donor gives property to a church that is subject to a debt (such as a mortgage)? What is the value of the charitable contribution? That depends on whether the donor transfers the debt to the church. If the debt is transferred to the church, then the value of the charitable contribution is the fair market value of the donated property less the amount of the outstanding debt.

Giving property that has decreased in value

A donor who donates property with a current fair market value that is less than the donor's "basis" (cost) can only claim the current value as a charitable contribution deduction. The donor cannot claim a deduction for the amount between the property's basis and its current value.

> **EXAMPLE.** A church member owns a computer that she purchased two years ago for $4,000. The current value of the computer is $1,000. The member donates the computer to her church. The amount of her charitable contribution deduction is the donated property's fair market value ($1,000), not its cost basis ($4,000).

Giving property that has increased in value

A donor who donates property with a fair market value that is more than the donor's basis (cost) in the property may have to reduce the amount of a charitable contribution deduction by the amount of appreciation (increase in value). Consider the following two rules:

Ordinary income property

If a donor contributes appreciated "ordinary income property" that would have resulted in ordinary income had the property been sold at its fair market value on the date of the gift, the amount of the contribution ordinarily is the fair market value of the property less the amount that would have been ordinary income or short-term capital gain if the property had been sold at its fair market value. Generally, this rule limits the deduction to the donor's basis in the property. Ordinary income property includes capital assets (including stocks and bonds, jewelry, coins, cars, and furniture) held for one year or less.

EXAMPLE. Jill donates to her church stock that she held for five months. The fair market value of the stock on the day of the donation was $1,000, but she paid only $800 (her basis). Because the $200 of appreciation would be short-term capital gain if she sold the stock, her deduction is limited to $800 (fair market value less the appreciation).

✿ **KEY POINT.** Do not reduce your charitable contribution if you include the ordinary or capital gain income in your gross income in the same year as the contribution.

Capital gain property

Property is capital gain property if its sale at fair market value on the date of the contribution would have resulted in long-term capital gain. Capital gain property includes capital assets held more than one year. Capital assets include most items of property that are used for personal purposes or investment. Examples are stocks and bonds, jewelry, coin and stamp collections, cars, furniture, or real estate used in the donor's business.

In general, donors who contribute capital gain property can claim a charitable contribution deduction in the amount of the property's fair market value. There are exceptions. In some situations the donor must reduce the fair market value by an amount that would have been long-term capital gain if the property had been sold for its fair market value. In most cases this means reducing the fair market value to the property's basis. A donor must make this reduction in the value of the contribution in either of the following two situations:

- The donor chooses the 50 percent limit instead of the 30 percent limit (discussed below).
- The contributed property is "tangible personal property" (defined below) that (1) is put to an "unrelated use" (defined below) by the charity or (2) has a claimed value of more than $5,000 and is sold, traded, or otherwise disposed of by the qualified organization during the year in which the contribution was made, and the charity has not made the required "certification" of exempt use (see below).

    Tangible personal property is any property, other than land or buildings, that can be seen or touched. It includes furniture, books, jewelry, paintings, and cars.

    An unrelated use is a use that is unrelated to the exempt purpose of the charitable organization.

EXAMPLE. Jane donated an item of jewelry to her church this year. The jewelry was purchased in 1995 for $2,000 but has a

current market value of $8,000. The church sold the jewelry shortly after the contribution but never used it for a "related purpose." Since the church did not use the donated tangible personal property in furtherance of its exempt purposes, Jane's charitable contribution deduction is limited to the property's cost basis ($2,000) rather than its market value ($8,000).

✿ **KEY POINT.** Given the nature of most items of appreciated tangible personal property, it is rare for a church to be able to use a donation of such property for exempt purposes. This means that donors ordinarily will be able to claim a charitable contribution deduction in the amount of their cost basis in the donated property, not the property's fair market value.

No adjustment in the amount of the charitable contribution is made if the charity makes a certification to the IRS by written statement signed under penalties of perjury by an officer of the charity. The statement must either (1) certify that the use of the property by the charity was related to the purpose or function constituting the basis for its exemption and describe how the property was used and how such use furthered such purpose or function; or (2) state the intended use of the property by the charity at the time of the contribution and certify that such use became impossible or infeasible to implement. The charity must furnish a copy of the certification to the donor (for example, as an attachment to Form 8282, a copy of which is supplied to the donor). A valid certification can be made on Part IV of Form 8282 (a copy of this form is reproduced at the end of this chapter).

If a donee charity disposes of donated appreciated tangible personal property within three years of the contribution, the donor is subject to an adjustment of the tax benefit. If the disposition occurs in the tax year of the donor in which the contribution is made, the donor's deduction generally is his or her cost basis rather than the donated property's fair market value. If the disposition occurs in a subsequent year, the donor must include, as ordinary income for the taxable year in which the disposition occurs, an amount equal to the excess (if any) of (1) the amount of the deduction previously claimed by the donor as a charitable contribution with respect to such property, over (2) the donor's basis in such property at the time of the contribution.

A penalty of $10,000 applies to a person who identifies applicable property as having a use that is related to a purpose or function constituting the basis for the donee's exemption, knowing that it is not intended for such a use. *IRC 6720B.*

EXAMPLE. A church member purchased a coin collection in 1992 for $3,000 that is worth $10,000 today. He donated the collection to his church in December 2012. The church sold the collection shortly after the contribution and never used it for a "related purpose." Since the church did not use the donated appreciated tangible personal property in furtherance of its exempt purposes, the member's charitable contribution deduction is limited to the property's cost basis ($3,000) rather than its market value ($10,000). Since the contribution deduction does not exceed $5,000, the donor is not required to obtain a qualified appraisal or complete a qualified appraisal summary (Form 8283, Section B), and the church is not required to file Form 8282 with the IRS upon its sale of the collection.

EXAMPLE. Esther purchased a religious painting in 1996 for $4,000 that is worth $8,000 today. She donates the painting to her church in December 2012. The church displays the painting in a prominent location as a means of facilitating prayer and worship. Since she assumed the painting would be used indefinitely for exempt purposes, Esther claimed a charitable contribution deduction on her 2012 tax return in the amount of the painting's market value ($8,000). In 2014 the church sells the painting for $10,000.

If a donee charity disposes of donated appreciated tangible personal property within three years of the date of the contribution, the donor is subject to an adjustment in the charitable contribution deduction. If the disposition occurs in the year the contribution is made, the donor's deduction generally is his or her cost basis rather than the donated property's fair market value. If the disposition occurs after the year of the contribution, the donor "must include as ordinary income for the taxable year in which the disposition occurs an amount equal to the excess (if any) of (i) the amount of the deduction previously claimed by the donor as a charitable contribution with respect to such property, over (ii) the donor's basis in such property at the time of the contribution." This means that Esther must report $4,000 as additional income on her 2014 tax return (the excess of the deduction claimed in 2012 over the property's cost basis).

EXAMPLE. Same facts as the previous example, except that the church attaches to the Form 8282 that it files with the IRS upon disposing of the painting a written statement signed by a church officer under penalties of perjury, certifying that the use of the property by the church was related to the purpose or function constituting the basis for its exemption, and describes how the property was used and how such use furthered the church's exempt purpose or function. The church also provides Esther a copy of the Form 8282 and the attachment. Under these circumstances Esther is not required to report the difference between her charitable contribution deduction and the property's cost basis on her 2014 tax return.

EXAMPLE. Jon purchased a religious sculpture in 1991 for $3,000 that is worth $7,000 today. He donates the sculpture to his church in December 2012. Assuming that the church will use the sculpture for religious purposes, Jon claims a charitable contribution deduction in the amount of the sculpture's fair market value. The church puts the sculpture in a storeroom until it sells it in 2013. Not wanting to report additional income, Jon persuades the church treasurer to attach a signed statement to the Form 8282 the church submits to the IRS following the sale, certifying that the property was used for exempt purposes. Two consequences should be noted. First, Jon must report additional income of $4,000 on his 2013 tax return, corresponding to the difference between the deduction he claimed in 2012 and the property's cost basis. Second, the church treasurer may be assessed a penalty of $10,000 for certifying that the donated property was used by the church for exempt purposes when he knew that it was not so used.

EXAMPLE. Sarah purchased a musical instrument in 2002 for $4,000 that is worth $6,000 when she donates it to her church in December 2012. The church uses the instrument in worship services on several occasions over the next three years. In 2015 it sells the instrument. Since the church's disposition of the instrument occurred more than three years after the date of Sarah's contribution, she is not required to report any additional income on her tax return. Further, the church is not required to file a Form 8282 with the IRS, since it disposed of the property more than three years after the date of the contribution.

Bargain sales

A bargain sale is a sale of property to a charity at less than its fair market value. Many churches have received substantial contributions through such an arrangement. It is especially attractive to taxpayers who have property that has greatly appreciated in value. The church obtains property at a greatly reduced price, and the donor receives a significant charitable contribution deduction and reduces the amount of taxable gain he or she would have realized had the property been sold for its fair market value.

A bargain sale results in a transaction that is partly a sale and partly a charitable contribution. A special computation must be made to compute (1) the amount of any deductible charitable contribution, and (2) the taxable gain from the part of the transaction that is a sale. In general, the adjusted basis of the property must be allocated between the part sold and the part given to charity.

Charitable contribution

Figure the amount of the charitable contribution in three steps:

(1) Subtract the amount the donor receives for the property from the property's fair market value at the time of sale. The result is the fair market value of the contributed part.

(2) Find the adjusted basis of the contributed part. This is computed by multiplying the adjusted basis of the property by the fair market value of the contributed part, divided by the fair market value of the entire property.

(3) Determine whether the amount of the charitable contribution is the fair market value of the contributed part (step 1) or the adjusted basis of the contributed part (step 2). Generally, if the property sold was capital gain property, the charitable contribution is the fair market value of the

contributed part. If it was ordinary income property, the charitable contribution is the adjusted basis of the contributed part. The terms "capital gain property" and "ordinary income property" are defined above.

Taxable gain on sale

Part of a bargain sale may be a contribution, but part may be a sale that can result in a taxable gain to the donor. If a bargain sale results in a charitable contribution deduction, the adjusted basis of the property must be allocated between the part of the property sold and the part of the property given to charity. The *adjusted basis of the contributed part* is computed by multiplying the adjusted basis of the entire property by the fair market value of the contributed part, divided by the fair market value of the entire property. To determine the *fair market value of the contributed part*, the donor subtracts the amount received from the sale (the selling price) from the fair market value of the entire property. The *adjusted basis of the part sold* is computed by multiplying the selling price by the adjusted basis for the entire property, divided by the fair market value of the entire property.

Bargain sales are illustrated in the following examples:

EXAMPLE. G sells ordinary income property with a fair market value of $10,000 to a church for $2,000. G's basis is $4,000, and his AGI is $20,000. G makes no other contributions during the year. The fair market value of the contributed part of the property is $8,000 ($10,000 - $2,000). The adjusted basis of the contributed part is $3,200 ($4,000 x [$8,000/$10,000]). Because the property is ordinary income property, G's charitable contribution deduction is limited to the adjusted basis of the contributed part. He can deduct $3,200.

EXAMPLE. A church member sells ordinary income property with a fair market value of $10,000 to his church for $4,000. If his basis (cost) in the property is $4,000 and his AGI is $30,000, the contribution from the sale is $6,000 ($10,000 fair market value less $4,000 selling price). But since the amount of ordinary income the donor would have received had he sold the property for its fair market value is $6,000 ($10,000 fair market value less $4,000 basis), and since the contribution must be reduced by this amount, the taxpayer is left with no charitable contribution deduction.

EXAMPLE. Same facts as the preceding example, except that the donated property was capital gain property held for more than one year. Unlike gifts of ordinary income property, which must be reduced by the amount of ordinary income that would have been realized had the property been sold at its fair market value on the date of the contribution, gifts of long-term capital gain property made to a church ordinarily do not have to be reduced. Therefore, a deduction of $6,000 is permitted, assuming the percentage limitations discussed above are not exceeded.

▲ **CAUTION.** *Bargain sale contributions are limited to sales. No charitable contribution deduction is available to persons who lease a building to a church for less than its fair rental value.*

Inventory

If a donor contributes inventory (property sold in the course of the donor's business), the amount that can be claimed as a contribution deduction is the smaller of its fair market value on the day it was contributed or its basis. The basis of donated inventory is any cost incurred for the inventory in an earlier year that would otherwise be included in opening inventory for the year of the contribution.

The amount of any contribution deduction must be removed from opening inventory. It is not part of the cost of goods sold. If the cost of donated inventory is not included in opening inventory, the inventory's basis is zero, and no charitable contribution deduction is available.

EXAMPLE. In 2013, T, an individual using the calendar year as the taxable year and the accrual method of accounting, contributes property to a church from inventory having a fair market value of $600. The closing inventory at the end of 2012 included $400 of costs attributable to the acquisition of such property, and in 2012 T properly deducted under section 162 $50 of administrative and other expenses attributable to such property. The amount of the charitable contribution allowed for 2013 is $400 ($600 - [$600 - $400]). The cost of goods sold to be used in determining gross income for 2013 may not include the $400 which was included in opening inventory for that year. *Treas. Reg. 1.170A-1(c)(4).*

EXAMPLE. Same facts as the previous example, except that the contributed property was acquired in 2013 at a cost of $400. The $400 cost of the property is included in determining the cost of goods sold for 2013, and $50 is allowed as a deduction for that year under section 162. T is not allowed any deduction for the contributed property, since the amount of the charitable contribution is reduced to zero ($600 - [$600 - $0]). *Treas. Reg. 1.170A-1(c)(4).*

Limits on charitable contribution deductions

The amount of a charitable contribution deduction may be limited to either 20 percent, 30 percent, or 50 percent of a donor's adjusted gross income, depending on the type of property given and the nature of the charity.

50 percent limit

A donor's charitable contribution deduction cannot exceed 50 percent of his or her AGI (Form 1040, line 37). The 50 percent limit applies to contributions made to churches, educational organizations, and most other charities supported primarily through public contributions.

30 percent limit

Some charitable contributions are limited to 30 percent of a donor's AGI. This limit applies to the following:

Gifts of capital gain property to "50 percent limit" organizations. However, the 30 percent limit does not apply when a donor elects to reduce the fair market value of the property by the amount that would have been long-term capital gain if the donor had sold the property (explained above). Instead, only the 50 percent limit applies.

Gifts (other than gifts of capital gain property) "for the use of" any organization). This term is explained in section B.3 of this chapter (in connection with the Mormon missionary case).

Gifts (other than gifts of capital gain property) to all qualified charities other than "50 percent limit" organizations. This includes gifts to veterans' organizations, fraternal societies, nonprofit cemeteries, and certain private nonoperating foundations.

20 percent limit

A limit of 20 percent of AGI applies to all gifts of capital gain property to or for the use of qualified organizations (other than gifts of capital gain property to 50 percent limit organizations).

Carryovers of excess contributions

Contributions in excess of the 50 percent or 30 percent ceilings can be carried over and deducted in each of the five succeeding years until they are used up.

EXAMPLE. A church member has AGI of $20,000 in 2012 and contributed $11,000 to her church in that year (she made no other contributions). If she itemizes her deductions, she may deduct $10,000 in 2012 ($20,000 x 50 percent) and may carry over the remaining $1,000 to 2013.

EXAMPLE. A married couple were generous contributors to their church. In 2002 they donated $122,214. In 2003 they donated $33,155. In 2004 they donated $16,995. In 2005 they donated $35,920. In 2004 the IRS selected their 2002 return for an audit examination. The couple's 2002 charitable contributions were substantiated, and it was determined that petitioners had a charitable contribution carryover of $61,150. They did not amend their already-filed 2003 return to claim any part of the carryover amount they were eligible for in that year. When they filed their 2004 federal income tax return, they reported charitable contributions of $16,995 and claimed a carryover of $17,033 from 2002. In 2005 they reported charitable contributions of $35,920. They also claimed a charitable contribution carryover of $10,000 from 2002. The IRS disallowed the $10,000 deduction and determined that the couple was entitled to a carryover of $1,944 from 2002 to 2005.

On appeal the Tax Court noted that the tax code provides that if the amount of a charitable contribution made to a church exceeds 50 percent of a taxpayer's "contribution base" for that year (adjusted gross income calculated without regard to any net

operating loss carryback), any excess contribution is treated as a charitable contribution paid in each of the five succeeding taxable years in order of time, according to a formula contained in section 170(d)(1)(A) of the Code. The court noted that "the carryover is good for the 5 years immediately following the charitable deduction, and some portion of the deduction expires each year whether it is actually used or not." The court rejected the couple's claim that they should have been allowed to use the carryover credit as they saw fit so long as they did so within the allowable time period following the original charitable contribution. *Maddux v. Commissioner, T.C. Summary Opinion 2009-30 (2009).*

Itemized deductions

Charitable contributions are available only as an itemized deduction on Schedule A (Form 1040). This means that taxpayers who do not itemize deductions cannot claim a deduction for charitable contributions. No charitable contribution deduction is available to taxpayers who use Form 1040A or 1040-EZ. As a result, most taxpayers are prevented from deducting any portion of their charitable contributions, since it is estimated that about 70 percent of all taxpayers have insufficient deductions to use Schedule A.

Efforts occasionally are initiated in Congress to resurrect the charitable contribution deduction for nonitemizers. Any developments will be addressed in future editions of this tax guide.

Limitation on charitable contribution deductions for high-income taxpayers

✱ **New in 2012.** In 2001 Congress enacted legislation repealing the limitation on itemized deductions of high-income taxpayers over a five-year period beginning in 2006. The limit on itemized deductions was reduced by one-third in 2006 and 2007 and by two-thirds in 2008 and 2009. The overall limitation was repealed for 2010. The Tax Relief and Job Creation Act of 2010 extends the repeal through 2012. Unless Congress acts, the elimination of the limitation on charitable contribution deductions will not be available after 2012.

Taxpayers may choose to claim either the standard deduction or itemized deductions (subject to certain limitations) for certain expenses incurred during the year. Prior to the enactment of the Economic Growth and Tax Relief Reconciliation Act of 2001 (EGTRRA), the total amount of allowable itemized deductions (with a few exceptions) was reduced by 3 percent of the amount of the taxpayer's adjusted gross income in excess of a specified amount. However, itemized deductions could not be reduced by more than 80 percent. The starting point for the phaseout was adjusted annually for inflation.

EGTRRA repealed this limitation on itemized deductions over a five-year period beginning in 2006. The limit on itemized deductions was reduced by one-third in taxable years beginning in 2006 and 2007, and by two-thirds in taxable years beginning in 2008 and 2009. The overall limitation was repealed in 2010, and this repeal was extended through 2012 by the Tax Relief and Job Creation Act of 2010.

> **EXAMPLE.** Joan has AGI of $175,000 for 2012 and total itemized deductions of $20,000. Her charitable contribution deduction is not reduced by the limitation that applied prior to the enactment of EGTRRA. The same result will apply in 2012 due to an extension of the limitation's repeal by the Tax Relief and Job Creation Act of 2010.

➡ **TIP.** The extension of the repeal of the limits on the deductibility of charitable contributions (and most other itemized deductions) through 2012 will significantly enhance the value and appeal of charitable contributions for higher income donors.

Corporations

Corporations may deduct charitable contributions of up to 10 percent of taxable income computed without regard to certain items. *IRC 170(b)(2)*. They can carry over contributions in excess of this limit over the next five years, with some limitations. *IRC 170(d)(2)*.

6. SUBSTANTIATION

Section 170 of the tax code, which authorizes deductions for charitable contributions, states that a charitable contribution shall be allowable as a deduction only if verified. Because of the importance of this issue, it is addressed in a separate section of this chapter (see section D).

A. THE AUTHORITY OF BANKRUPTCY COURTS TO RECOVER CHARITABLE CONTRIBUTIONS

In the past churches were adversely impacted by federal bankruptcy law in two ways. First, many courts ruled that bankruptcy trustees could recover contributions made to a church by a bankrupt donor within a year of filing a bankruptcy petition. Second, church members who declared bankruptcy were not allowed by some bankruptcy courts to continue making contributions to their church.

These restrictions were eliminated in 1998, when Congress enacted the Religious Liberty and Charitable Donation Protection Act. The Act, which was an amendment to the bankruptcy code, provides significant protection to churches and church members. This section will review the background of the Act, explain its key provisions, and demonstrate its application with practical examples.

1. AUTHORITY OF BANKRUPTCY TRUSTEES TO RECOVER CHARITABLE CONTRIBUTIONS

Section 548(a) of the bankruptcy code authorizes a bankruptcy trustee to "avoid" or recover two kinds of "fraudulent transfers" made by bankrupt debtors within a year of filing for bankruptcy:

- **Intent to defraud.** Section 548(a)(1) gives a bankruptcy trustee the legal authority to recover "any transfer of an interest of the debtor in property . . . that was made or incurred on or within one year before the date of the filing of the petition, if the debtor voluntarily or involuntarily made such transfer or incurred such obligation with actual intent to hinder, delay, or defraud any entity to which the debtor was or became, on or after the date that such transfer was made or such obligation was incurred, indebted."

- **Transfers of cash or property for less than reasonably equivalent value.** Section 548(a)(2) gives a bankruptcy trustee the legal authority to recover "any transfer of an interest of the debtor in property . . . that was made or incurred on or within one year before the date of the filing of the petition, if the debtor voluntarily or involuntarily . . . received less than a reasonably equivalent value in exchange for such transfer or obligation and was insolvent on the date that such transfer was made or such obligation was incurred, or became insolvent as a result of such transfer or obligation . . . or intended to incur, or believed that the debtor would incur, debts that would be beyond the debtor's ability to pay as such debts matured."

In the past many bankruptcy trustees contacted churches, demanding that they return donations made by bankrupt debtors within a year of filing for bankruptcy. They argued that charitable contributions made by bankrupt debtors to a church are for less than "reasonably equivalent value"; therefore they can be recovered by bankruptcy trustees under the second type of "fraudulent transfer" mentioned above.

Donors and churches protested such efforts. They insisted that donors do receive valuable benefits in exchange for their contributions, such as preaching, teaching, sacraments, and counseling. Not so, countered bankruptcy trustees. These benefits would be available regardless of whether a donor gives anything, so it cannot be said that a donor is receiving "reasonably equivalent value" in exchange for a contribution. Many courts agreed with this logic and ordered churches to turn over contributions made by bankrupt debtors. This created a hardship for many churches. After all, most churches had already spent the debtor's contributions before being contacted by the bankruptcy trustee, so returning them (especially if they were substantial) was often difficult.

The Religious Freedom and Charitable Donation Protection Act

In 1998 Congress enacted the Religious Freedom and Charitable Donation Protection Act in order to protect churches and other charities from having to turn over charitable contributions to a bankruptcy trustee. The key to the Act is the following provision, which is an amendment to section 548(a)(2) of the bankruptcy code:

> A transfer of a charitable contribution to a qualified religious or charitable entity or organization shall not be considered to be a transfer [subject to recovery by a bankruptcy trustee] in any case in which—(A) the amount of that contribution does not exceed 15 percent of the gross annual income of the debtor for the year in which the transfer of the contribution is made; or (B) the contribution made by a debtor exceeded the percentage amount of gross annual income specified in subparagraph (A), if the transfer was consistent with the practices of the debtor in making charitable contributions.

⚙ **KEY POINT.** Bankruptcy trustees cannot recover contributions made by a bankrupt debtor within a year of filing for bankruptcy protection if the contributions amount to 15 percent or less of the debtor's gross annual income, or a greater amount if consistent with the "practices of the debtor in making charitable contributions."

⚙ **KEY POINT.** It is critical to note that this provision only amends the second type of "fraudulent transfer" described above—transfers of cash or property made for less than reasonably equivalent value within a year of filing a bankruptcy petition. The Act does not amend the first kind of fraudulent transfer—those made with an actual intent to defraud.

Examples

Let's illustrate the impact of this provision with some practical examples.

THE RELIGIOUS FREEDOM AND CHARITABLE DONATION PROTECTION ACT
A Checklist

This checklist will be a helpful resource in applying the law:

Step 1. Did the bankruptcy debtor make one or more contributions of cash or property to a church within a year preceding the filing of a bankruptcy petition?

- If **NO**, stop here. A bankruptcy trustee cannot recover the debtor's contributions from the church.
- If **YES**, go to step 2.

Step 2. In making contributions to the church, did the debtor have an actual intent to hinder, delay, or defraud his or her creditors? In deciding if an intent to defraud exists, consider the timing, amount, and circumstances surrounding the contributions, as well as any change in the debtor's normal pattern or practice.

- If **YES**, a bankruptcy trustee can recover from the church contributions made by the debtor within a year prior to the filing of the bankruptcy petition.
- If **NO**, go to step 3.

Step 3. Did the debtor receive "reasonably equivalent value" for the contributions made to the church? Note that reasonably equivalent value will not include such "intangible" religious services as preaching, teaching, sacraments, or counseling.

- If **YES**, stop here. A bankruptcy trustee cannot recover the debtor's contributions from the church.
- If **NO**, go to step 4.

Step 4. Is the value of the debtor's contributions 15 percent or less of his or her gross annual income?

- If **YES**, stop here. A bankruptcy trustee cannot recover the debtor's contributions from the church.
- If **NO**, go to step 5.

Step 5. Is the value of the debtor's contributions consistent with the practices of the debtor in making charitable contributions?

- If **YES**, stop here. A bankruptcy trustee cannot recover the debtor's contributions from the church.
- If **NO**, a bankruptcy trustee can recover from the church contributions made by the debtor within a year prior to the filing of the bankruptcy petition.

EXAMPLE. Bob has attended his church for many years. For the past few years, his contributions to his church have averaged roughly $50 per week, or about $2,500 per year. Bob's gross annual income for 2012 and 2013 is about $40,000. On May 15, 2013, Bob files for bankruptcy. A bankruptcy trustee contacts the church treasurer and demands that the church turn over all contributions made by Bob from May 15, 2012, through May 15, 2013. The Religious Freedom and Charitable Donation Protection Act applies directly to this scenario and protects the church from the reach of the trustee, since (1) the amount of Bob's annual contributions in both 2012 and 2013 (the years in which the contributions were made) did not exceed 15 percent of his gross annual income (15 percent of $40,000 = $6,000); and (2) the timing, amount, and circumstances surrounding the contributions, as well as the lack of any change in the debtor's normal pattern or practice, suggest that Bob did not commit intentional fraud, so the trustee cannot recover contributions on this basis. See step 4 in the sidebar.

EXAMPLE. Same facts as the previous example, except that in addition to his weekly giving, Bob made a one-time gift to the church building fund on December 1, 2012, in the amount of $5,000. Bob's total giving for the year preceding the filing of his bankruptcy petition now totals $7,500, or nearly 19 percent of his gross annual income. As a result, he is not eligible for the 15 percent "safe harbor" rule described in step 4 of the sidebar. The trustee will be able to recover the $7,500 in contributions made by Bob to the church within a year of filing the bankruptcy petition unless Bob can demonstrate that giving 19 percent of his gross annual income is consistent with his normal practices in making charitable contributions. It is unlikely that Bob or the church will be able to satisfy this condition, since the gift to the building fund was a one-time, extraordinary gift for Bob that was unlike his giving pattern in any prior year.

EXAMPLE. Barb believes strongly in giving to her church, and for each of the past several years, she has given 20 percent of her income. On June 1, 2013, she files for bankruptcy. A bankruptcy trustee contacts the church treasurer and demands that the church turn over all contributions made by Barb from June 1, 2012, through June 1, 2013. The Religious Freedom and Charitable Donation Protection Act applies directly to this scenario and protects the church from the reach of the trustee, since (1) the amount of Barb's annual contributions in both 2012 and 2013 (the years in which the contributions were made) exceeded 15 percent of her gross annual income, but she had a consistent practice in prior years of giving this amount; and (2) the timing, amount, and circumstances surrounding the contributions, as well as the lack of any change in the debtor's normal pattern or practice, suggest that Barb did not commit intentional fraud, so the trustee cannot recover contributions on this basis. See step 5 in the sidebar.

EXAMPLE. Bill has attended his church sporadically for the past several years. For the past few years, his contributions to his church have averaged less than $1,000 per year. Bill's gross annual income for 2012 and 2013 is about $80,000. Bill is facing a staggering debt load due to mismanagement and unrestrained credit card charges. He wants to declare bankruptcy, but he has a $15,000 bank account that he wants to protect. He decides to give the entire amount to his church in order to keep it from the bankruptcy court and his creditors. He gives the entire balance to his church on June 1, 2013. On July 1, 2013, Bill files for bankruptcy. A bankruptcy trustee contacts the church treasurer, demanding that the church turn over the $15,000 contribution. The Religious Freedom and Charitable Donation Protection Act does not protect Bill or the church. The timing, amount, and circumstances surrounding the contribution of $15,000 strongly indicate that Bill had an actual intent to hinder, delay, or defraud his creditors. This conclusion is reinforced by the fact that the gift was contrary to Bill's normal pattern or practice of giving. As a result, the trustee probably will be able to force the church to return the $15,000. See step 2 in the checklist on page 392.

EXAMPLE. A federal court in California ruled that a bankruptcy trustee could not recover charitable contributions made by a church member to his church in the year preceding his filing of a bankruptcy petition since the amount of his contributions was less than 15 percent of his gross annual income. The court rejected the trustee's claim that gross annual income meant annual income less expenses, or "disposable income." It concluded: "When Congress [enacted] the Religious Freedom and Charitable Donation Protection Act, it was aware of the term 'disposable income' and chose not to use this term. Instead 'gross annual income' was used. . . . If Congress wanted to have business gross income reflect deductions for operation of a business, it would have used the term 'disposable income.'" *In re Lewis, 401 B.R. 431 (C.D. Cal. 2009).*

EXAMPLE. A bankruptcy court in Colorado addressed the authority of bankruptcy trustees to recover charitable contributions made by bankrupt debtors within a year of filing a bankruptcy petition. A married couple (the "debtors") filed for Chapter 7 bankruptcy relief on December 31, 2009. Throughout 2008, the debtors made 25 donations to their church totaling $3,478. In 2009 the debtors' gross earned income was $7,487, and they received $23,164 in Social Security benefits. Throughout 2009, the debtors made seven donations totaling $1,280 to their church. The bankruptcy trustee attempted to avoid these charitable contributions and have the church return them to the court. The court concluded that Social Security benefits are not included in computing gross annual income, and as a result, only 15 percent of the debtors' other income was shielded from the bankruptcy trustee. The court also concluded that if a bankruptcy debtor contributes more than 15 percent of gross annual income to his or her church, the bankruptcy trustee can recover only the contributions in excess of 15 percent of gross annual income. It observed: "It is doubtful that Congress would protect a debtor's right to donate 15 percent of their gross annual income to a charitable organization, but allow a trustee to avoid all donations if one cent over the 15 percent threshold is donated." *In re McGough, 2011 WL 2671253 (D. Colo. 2011).*

✿ **KEY POINT.** When a donor makes a large gift of cash or property to a church, church leaders should be alert to the fact that a bankruptcy trustee may be able to recover the contribution at a later date if the donor files for bankruptcy within a year after making the gift and none of the exceptions described in this chapter applies.

2. MAKING CHARITABLE CONTRIBUTIONS AFTER FILING FOR BANKRUPTCY

Until now, this section has addressed the authority of bankruptcy trustees to recover contributions made by bankrupt debtors within a year prior to filing a bankruptcy petition. However, a second bankruptcy issue is of direct relevance to churches: can church members who file for bankruptcy continue to make regular contributions to their church? This issue was also addressed by the Religious Freedom and Charitable Donation Protection Act. The bankruptcy code says that a court may not approve a bankruptcy plan unless it provides that all of a debtor's "projected disposable income to be received in the three-year period beginning on the date that the first payment is due under the plan will be applied to make payments under the plan." In addition, a court can dismiss a bankruptcy case to avoid "substantial abuse" of the bankruptcy law. Many courts have dismissed bankruptcy cases on the ground that a debtor's plan called for a continuation of charitable contributions.

The Act clarifies that bankruptcy courts no longer can dismiss bankruptcy cases on the ground that a debtor proposes to continue making charitable contributions. This assumes that the debtor's contributions will not exceed 15 percent of his or her gross annual income for the year in which the contributions are made (or a higher percentage if consistent with the debtor's regular practice in making charitable contributions).

The committee report accompanying the Act states:

> In addition [the bill] protects the rights of certain debtors to tithe or make charitable contributions after filing for bankruptcy relief. Some courts have dismissed a debtor's chapter 7 case . . . for substantial abuse under section 707(b) of the bankruptcy code based on the debtor's charitable contributions. The bill also protects the rights of debtors who file for chapter 13 to tithe or make charitable contributions. Some courts have held that tithing is not a reasonably necessary expense or have attempted to fix a specific percentage as the maximum that the debtor may include in his or her budget.

EXAMPLE. Brad files a chapter 7 bankruptcy petition. Brad's plan states that he will use all available disposable income to pay his creditors during the three-year period following the approval of his plan. But the plan permits Brad to continue making contributions to his church, which in the past have averaged 10 percent of his income. Some creditors object to the plan and demand that the court reject it, since Brad will be making contributions to his church rather than using these funds to pay off his lawful debts. The Religious Liberty and Charitable Donation Protection Act specifies that the court cannot reject Brad's bankruptcy plan because of the charitable contributions, since the contributions are less than 15 percent of his gross annual income.

EXAMPLE. Same facts as the previous example, except that Brad's plan proposes to pay contributions to his church in the amount of 25 percent of his gross annual income. Brad would rather that his church receive all available income than his creditors. Several creditors object to this plan. The court probably will deny Brad's request for bankruptcy protection, since the substantial contributions proposed in his plan exceed 15 percent of his gross annual income and are not consistent with his prior practice of making charitable contributions.

EXAMPLE. A young married couple had a premature baby which resulted in substantial medical bills that were not fully covered by insurance. The couple filed for bankruptcy protection under chapter 13 of the bankruptcy law. Under chapter 13 (also known as a "wage earner's plan"), the debtor continues to work and applies all disposable income to the payment of debts. The bankruptcy trustee objected to the couple's plan on the ground that they were not applying all of their disposable income to their debts. In particular, the trustee noted that the couple planned to make monthly contributions of $234 to their church, which amounted to nearly 10 percent of their gross income. The couple conceded that tithing is not required as a condition of membership in their church but is "strongly recommended."

A federal court noted that the bankruptcy law provides that a bankruptcy plan will not be approved unless the debtor's projected disposable income to be received in the next three years will be applied to payments under the plan. However, it noted that the bankruptcy law defines "disposable income" to exclude charitable contributions to a qualified religious or charitable organization in an amount not to exceed 15 percent a debtor's income. Since the couple's monthly tithe was less than 15 percent of their income, it did not meet the definition of "disposable income," and their plan could not be rejected on account of these contributions. *In re Cavanagh, 242 B.R. 707 (D. Mont. 2000).*

EXAMPLE. A couple with $100,000 of debt filed for bankruptcy, but their petition was opposed by a bankruptcy trustee on the ground that the plan allowed them to donate 10 percent of their income to their church. The trustee insisted that the proposed charitable contributions were not "reasonably necessary for the debtors' maintenance and support" and therefore constituted disposable income that should be paid to their creditors. A federal bankruptcy court ruled that the plan could not be denied on the basis of the debtors' proposed contributions to their church. The court noted that the contributions the couple wanted to continue making to their church were less than 15 percent of their annual income, so their bankruptcy plan could not be rejected on the basis of these contributions. This was so despite the size of their debt. However, the court agreed that the couple should be required to prove to the bankruptcy court that they were, in fact, making the contributions to their church. *In re Kirschner, 259 B.R. 416 (M.D. Fla. 2001).*

EXAMPLE. A married couple with over $65,000 of consumer debts filed a chapter 7 bankruptcy petition, seeking to have their debts discharged. The plan called for all of the couple's income to be assigned to the court over and above specified living expenses, which included $615 in monthly contributions to their church. The court noted that bankruptcy plans can be rejected if they would promote a "substantial abuse" of bankruptcy law. The court concluded that allowing the couple to withhold $615 each month for payment to their church was abusive, and it would accept their bankruptcy plan only after reducing monthly charitable contributions to $400.

The court conceded that the law bars rejection of bankruptcy plans on the basis of charitable contributions that do not exceed 15 percent of a debtor's annual income (or a higher percentage if consistent with the debtor's regular practice in making charitable contributions). While the couple's proposed contributions were less then 15 percent of their income, the court noted that "this does not mean that the court must accept the amount of charitable contributions that a debtor lists where the evidence does not reflect that the debtor, in fact, has given or is giving the listed amount to charity." The court noted that the couple had only contributed $450 per month to their church over the previous two years, so it reduced their proposed monthly contributions of $615 to $450 as a condition of accepting the plan. *In re Hallstrom, 2002 WL 1784500 (M.D.N.C. 2003).*

EXAMPLE. A federal court ruled that tuition payments made to a church-operated school were not charitable contributions, and so a married couple's bankruptcy plan could be rejected because of their insistence on continuing to make such payments.

A married couple (the debtors) filed for bankruptcy protection. They had net monthly income of $5,770, expenses of $4,194, and $1,576 in disposable income. The bankruptcy plan provided for 36 monthly payments of $1,576 (totaling $56,736), which would pay $123,714 of unsecured creditors 25 percent of their claims. The debtors were devout Catholics and asked the court

to allow them to continue making monthly tuition expenses of $750 to send their children to a parochial school. They pointed out that the tuition was less than 15 percent of their gross annual income and that the bankruptcy code permits debtors to make charitable contributions of up to 15 percent of their annual income. A federal bankruptcy court rejected the debtors' argument that parochial school tuition payments should be allowed because they constituted a charitable contribution.

The court acknowledged that the bankruptcy code prohibits trustees from rejecting a bankruptcy plan on the basis of charitable contributions (so long as the contributions do not exceed 15 percent of the debtor's annual income), but it concluded that this provision did not apply to tuition payments even if motivated by religious beliefs: "Charitable or religious donations are just that, and in making such contributions the donor is not bargaining for a tangible quid pro quo, but is making a gift to support the religion of his/her choice. Here the debtors propose to purchase, under the guise of a so-called religious donation, a substantial asset—the private education of their children. Based upon the record and the applicable law, I conclude as a matter of law that parochial school tuition payments are not charitable donations within the meaning of the Act, and that the money proposed to be used by the debtors to make said payments is disposable income required to be distributed under the chapter 13 plan." *In re Watson, 299 B.R. 56 (D.R.I. 2003).*

B. DESIGNATED CONTRIBUTIONS

Designated contributions are contributions made to a church for a specified purpose. In most cases a donor either designates a specific project (such as the church building fund) or a specific individual (such as a missionary, student, minister, or needy person). In this section both kinds of designated contribution are addressed. More emphasis is given to contributions designating individuals, since this is the type of designated contribution that has caused the most confusion.

1. CONTRIBUTIONS DESIGNATING A PROJECT OR PROGRAM

If the purpose is an approved project or program of the church, the designation ordinarily will not affect contribution deductibility. An example is a contribution to a church building fund.

IRS Letter Ruling 200530016 (2005) addressed charitable contributions that designate specific projects. A charity began construction of a cultural center and solicited contributions for this project. It asked the IRS for a ruling affirming that contributions toward the project would be deductible even if donors requested that their donations be applied to the project and the charity "provides no more than assurances to such donors that it will attempt in good faith to honor such preferences."

The IRS provided an exhaustive analysis of the deductibility of designated contributions and made the following helpful clarifications and observations:

- In Revenue Ruling 60-367 the issue was gifts to a university for the purpose of constructing housing for a designated fraternity. The college accepted gifts designated for improving or building a house for a designated fraternity and honored such designation so long as it was consistent with the policy, needs, and activities of the college. The college retained and exercised discretion and control, with respect to the amount spent on the fraternity house, consistent with the standards and pattern of the college for other student housing and consistent with the expressed housing policy of the college. The ruling thus held that the contributions made to the college under such circumstances were allowable deductions.
- Where funds are earmarked, it is important that the charity has full control of the donated funds and discretion as to their use, to ensure that the funds will be used to carry out the organization's functions and purposes. If the charity has such control and discretion and the gift is applied in accordance with the organization's exempt purposes, the donation ordinarily will be deductible, despite the donor's expressed hope that the gift will be applied for a designated purpose.
- The charity must maintain discretion and control over all contributions. Accordingly, the charity may endeavor to honor donors' wishes that designate use of donated funds. However, the charity must maintain control over the ultimate determination of how all donated funds are allocated. Donors should be made aware that although the charity will make every effort to honor their contribution designation, contributions become the property of the charity, and the charity has the discretion to determine how best to use all contributions to carry out its functions and purposes.

The IRS concluded, based on this precedent, that charitable contributions to the charity would be deductible even if the donors requested that their donations be used to cover costs and expenses relating to the cultural center and the charity provided no more than assurances to such donors that it would attempt in good faith to honor such preferences.

> **EXAMPLE.** A church establishes a "new building" fund. Bob donates $500 to his church with the stipulation that the money be placed in the "new building" fund. This is a valid charitable contribution and may be treated as such by the church treasurer.

> **EXAMPLE.** Barb would like to help her church's music director buy a new home. She contributes $10,000 to her church with the stipulation that it be used "for a new home for our music director." Neither the church board nor the congregation has ever agreed to assist the music director in obtaining a home. Barb's gift is not a charitable contribution. As a result, the church treasurer should not accept it. Barb should be advised to make her gift directly to the music director. Of course, such a gift will not be tax-deductible by Barb. On the other hand, the music director may be able to treat it as a tax-free gift.

> **EXAMPLE.** A university owned several fraternity houses. The condition of the houses declined to such an extent that student safety was jeopardized. As a result, university officials launched a fundraising drive to raise funds to renovate the houses. Donors were encouraged to contribute for the renovation of a specific fraternity house, and the university assured donors that it would "attempt" to honor their designations. However, the university made it clear to donors that it accepted their designated gifts with the understanding that the designations would not restrict or limit the university's full control over the contributions and that the university could use the designated contributions for any purpose.

The IRS cautioned that for a designated gift to be a tax-deductible charitable contribution, it "must be in reality a gift to the college and not a gift to the fraternity by using the college as a conduit. The college must have the attributes of ownership in respect of the donated property, and its rights as an owner must not, as a condition of the gift, be limited by conditions or restrictions which in effect make a private group the beneficiary of the donated property. . . . [The] university will accept gifts designated for the benefit of a particular fraternity only with the understanding that such designation will not restrict or limit university's full ownership rights in either the donated property or property acquired by use of the donated property. Accordingly, we conclude that contributions made to university for the purpose of reconstructing and remodeling fraternity housing will qualify for a charitable contribution deduction." *Private Letter Ruling 9733015.*

2. CONTRIBUTIONS DESIGNATING A SPECIFIC INDIVIDUAL

If a donor stipulates that a contribution be spent on a designated individual, no deduction ordinarily is allowed unless the church exercises full administrative control over the donated funds to ensure that they are being spent in furtherance of the church's exempt purposes. To illustrate, contributions to a church or missions agency for the benefit of a particular missionary may be tax deductible if the church or missions agency exercises full administrative and accounting control over the contributions and ensures that they are spent in furtherance of the church's mission.

✿ **KEY POINT.** Direct contributions to missionaries, or any other individual, are not tax-deductible, even if they are used for religious or charitable purposes.

As noted above, a charitable contribution must be made to or for the use of a qualified organization. Contributions and gifts made directly to individuals are not deductible. However, contributions to individuals will, in some cases, be deductible on the ground that they were for the use of a qualified organization. Contributions to foreign missionaries under the control and supervision of a religious organization often are deductible on this basis. The contribution is not made *to* the organization, but it is made *for the use of* the organization. Similarly, contributions often are made payable to a church, but with a stipulation that the funds be distributed to a specified individual. Common examples include Christmas gifts to a minister, scholarship gifts to a church school, and contributions to a church benevolence fund. The deductibility of these designated contributions, along with contributions made to foreign missionaries, is considered below.

Of course, donors can designate the specific charitable activity to which they would like their contribution applied. For example, a donor can contribute $500 to a church and specify that the entire proceeds be applied to foreign missions or to a benevolence or scholarship fund. Designating a charitable activity, as opposed to an individual, presents no legal difficulties.

EXAMPLE. A taxpayer made payments to a boys' school on behalf of a ward of the Illinois Children's Home and Aid Society. The court held that the payments were not contributions to or for the use of the charitable organization but were gifts for the benefit of a particular individual. *S.E. Thomason v. Commissioner, 2 T.C. 441 (1943).*

EXAMPLE. An individual gave money to a university, requiring that it use the money to fund the research project of a particular professor. The university had no discretion over the use of the funds. The IRS ruled that the university was a "conduit" only and that the real donee was the professor. As a payment to an individual, the gift was not deductible. *IRS Revenue Ruling 61-66 (1961).*

IRS Letter Ruling 200530016 (2005) addresses charitable contributions that designate specific projects and individuals. The IRS provided an exhaustive analysis of the deductibility of designated contributions and made these clarifications and observations:

- An important element for a taxpayer donor of a qualified charitable contribution is the charity's control over the donated funds. The donor must show that the charity retained control over the funds. To have control over donated funds is to have discretion as to their use. In instances where a donor designates a gift to benefit a particular individual and the individual does benefit from the gift, the determination of whether the gift is deductible depends upon whether the charity has full control of the donated funds and discretion as to their use. Such control and discretion ensures that the funds will be used to carry out the organization's functions and purposes.

- If contributions to a fund are earmarked by the donor for a particular individual and the charity exercises no control or discretion over their use, they are treated as gifts to the designated individual and are not deductible as charitable contributions.

- In *Tripp v. Commissioner,* 337 F.2d 432 (7th Cir. 1964) (see below), a taxpayer's illusory gifts to a scholarship fund subject to the college's discretionary use were, in fact, designated by the donor and used for the sole benefit of a named individual and did not qualify as deductions for charitable contributions.

- When contributions are restricted by the donor to a class of beneficiaries, the class of potential beneficiaries may still be too narrow to qualify as a deductible charitable contribution. Thus, in *Charleston Chair Co. v. United States,* 203 F. Supp. 126 (E.D.S.C. 1962), a corporation was denied a deduction for amounts given to a foundation established to provide educational opportunities for employees and their children. The court noted that the narrow class of persons who might benefit, the more restricted group that did benefit, and the preference given to the son of the director, stockholder, and trustee disclose that the Foundation was not operated exclusively for charitable purposes.

- However, a deduction is allowable where it is established that a gift is intended by the donor for the use of the organization rather than a gift to an individual. *Revenue Ruling 62-113 (see below).* This revenue ruling concerned contributions to a church fund by the parent of one of the church's missionaries. The ruling noted that if contributions to the fund are earmarked by the donor for a particular individual, they are treated, in effect, as being gifts to the designated individual and are not deductible. However, a deduction will be allowable where it is established that a gift is intended by a donor for the use of the organization and not as a gift to an individual. The test in each case is whether the organization has full control of the donated funds and discretion as to their use, so as to insure that they will be used to carry out its functions and purposes. The ruling held that unless the taxpayer's contributions to the fund are distinctly marked by him so that they may be used only for his son or are received by the fund pursuant to a commitment or understanding that they will be so used, they may be deducted by the taxpayer.

- A charitable contribution may be permitted where preferences expressed at the time of contribution are precatory rather than mandatory, or where preference is given to relatives who otherwise qualify as charitable beneficiaries. . . . In addition, retention by the donor, or his family members, of the right to determine which individuals actually receive benefits does not preclude a charitable deduction.

- Where funds are earmarked, it is important that the charity has full control of the donated funds and discretion as to their use, so as to ensure that the funds will be used to carry out the organization's functions and purposes. If the charity has such control and discretion and the gift is applied in accordance with the organization's exempt purposes, the charitable gift ordinarily will be deductible, despite the donor's expressed hope that the gift will be applied for a designated purpose. Thus, in *Peace v. Commissioner*, 43 T.C. 1 (1964) (see below), the court permitted a deduction for funds donated to a church mission society with the stipulation that specific amounts should go to each of four designated missionaries because an examination of the totality of the facts and evidence demonstrated that the contribution went into a common pool and the church retained control of the actual distribution of the funds.

- In *Winn v. Commissioner*, 595 F.2d 1060 (5th Cir. 1979) (see below), at issue was a contribution in response to an appeal by a church to assist a certain person in her church missionary work. Central to the court's finding was that even though the contribution was made payable to a fund named for the individual, an officer of the church took the funds donated and dealt with them as the church wished. That is, possession of the contribution by a church official was held to be one of the elements establishing control by the church. The court concluded, "We also note that a donor can earmark a contribution given to a qualified organization for specific purposes without losing the right to claim a charitable deduction. Such a contribution still would be to or for the use of a charitable entity despite the fact that the donor controlled which of the qualified entity's charitable purposes would receive the exclusive benefit of the gift. . . . Proof that the church sponsored the appeal for the express purposes of collecting funds for this part of its work, that an officer of that church took the funds donated and dealt with them as the church wished, and that the funds went to the support of the work the church intended is sufficient to establish that the funds were donated for the use of the church."

- In summary, funds donated to a charitable organization restricted for the benefit of a private individual are not deductible. This is in contrast to funds contributed for a particular purpose, but the charity maintains control and discretion over actual use of the funds.

- The charity must maintain discretion and control over all contributions. Accordingly, the charity may endeavor to honor donors' wishes that designate the use of donated funds. However, the charity must maintain control over the ultimate determination of how all donated funds are allocated. Donors should be made aware that although the charity will make every effort to honor their contribution designation, contributions become the property of the charity, and the charity

has the discretion to determine how best to use contributions to carry out its functions and purposes.

3. MISSIONARIES

✿ **KEY POINT.** The IRS issued a private letter ruling that addresses charitable contributions that designate specific individuals. The ruling provides an exhaustive analysis of the deductibility of designated contributions and makes several helpful clarifications and observations. The ruling is addressed earlier in this section. *IRS Letter Ruling 200530016 (2005).*

✿ **KEY POINT.** In Revenue Ruling 62-113 the IRS noted that contributions earmarked by a donor for a particular student were gifts to the designated student and were not deductible. However, the IRS acknowledged that a deduction will be allowed if it is established that the gift is intended by the donor for the use of the charitable organization. The test in each case is whether the organization has full control of the donated funds, and discretion as to their use, to ensure that they will be used to carry out the charitable organization's functions and purposes. The IRS has noted that this test is to be used in evaluating the tax-deductibility of contributions that designate a student as well as contributions that designate other individuals "such as a fund to help pay for an organ transplant or to help a particular family rebuild a home destroyed by a tornado . . . [and] religiously motivated programs to support designated missionaries." *IRS Exempt Organizations Continuing Professional Education Technical Instruction Program for 1996.*

Contributions made directly to a missionary may be deductible if it can be established that the contribution was for the use of a charitable organization (i.e., a church or religious denomination exercises control or supervision over the missionary). In 1962 the IRS clarified the application of this principle in a ruling upholding a donor's contribution to a church fund out of which missionaries, including his son, were compensated:

If contributions to the fund are earmarked by the donor for a particular individual, they are treated, in effect, as being gifts to the designated individual and are not deductible. However, a deduction will be allowable where it is established that a gift is intended by a donor for the use of the organization and not as a gift to an individual. The test in each case is whether the organization has full control of the donated funds, and discretion as to their use, so as to insure that they will be used to carry out its functions and purposes. In the instant case, the son's receipt of reimbursements from the fund is alone insufficient to require holding that this test is not met. Accordingly, unless the taxpayer's contributions to the fund are distinctly marked by him so that they may be used only for his son or are received by the fund pursuant to a commitment or understanding that they will be so used, they may be deducted by the taxpayer in computing his taxable income. Revenue Ruling 62-113. *[Emphasis added.]*

This principle has been consistently applied by the courts in determining the deductibility of designated contributions to charitable organizations. Consider the following examples.

Peace v. Commissioner, 43 T.C.1 (1964)

The Tax Court ruled that checks payable to the Sudan Interior Mission were deductible by a donor despite the listing of four missionaries' names on the lower left-hand corner of each check and a letter from the donor requesting that the checks be used for the missionaries. After analyzing all the facts, the court concluded that the donor knew and intended that his contributions would go into a common pool and be administered by the mission and distributed in accordance with stated policies regarding missionary support. As a result, the donor's designation of four individual missionaries "was no more than a manifestation of [his] desire" to have his donations credited to the support allowance of those individuals. The mission maintained "exclusive control, under its own policy, of both the administration and distribution of the funds." The IRS, in a private letter ruling summarized earlier in this section, explained this case as follows: "The court permitted a deduction for funds donated to a church mission society with the stipulation that specific amounts should go to each of four designated missionaries because an examination of the totality of the facts and evidence demonstrated that the contribution went into a common pool and the church retained control of the actual distribution of the funds." *IRS Letter Ruling 200530016 (2005).*

Lesslie v. Commissioner, 36 T.C.M. 495 (1977)

A taxpayer who sent a bank check to a missionary serving in Brazil with the express instruction that the funds be used for Presbyterian mission work was allowed a deduction by the Tax Court. The court noted that while the check was payable directly to the missionary, it was not a gift to him personally, since it was given for the express purpose of Presbyterian mission work. In substance, the court concluded, the funds were contributed "to or for the use of the church in its mission work, with the missionary receiving the funds as its agent."

Winn v. Commissioner, 595 F.2d 1060 (5th Cir. 1979)

A federal appeals court upheld the deductibility of a contribution to a fund established by three Presbyterian churches for the support of a particular missionary, even though the contribution mentioned the missionary's name, since the contribution was for the use of an exempt missions organization. The court noted that a church officer received donated funds and distributed them for the mission work the church intended. The IRS, in a private letter ruling summarized earlier in this section, explained this case as follows:

At issue was a contribution in response to an appeal by a church to assist a certain person in her church missionary work. Central to the court's finding was that even though the contribution was made payable to a fund named for the individual, an officer of the church took the funds donated and dealt with them as the church wished. That is, possession of the contribution by a church official was held to be one of the elements establishing control by the church. The court concluded:

> We also note that a donor can earmark a contribution given to a qualified organization for specific purposes without losing the right to claim a charitable deduction. Such a contribution still would be to or for the use of a charitable entity despite the fact that the donor controlled which of the qualified entity's charitable purposes would receive the exclusive benefit of the gift. . . . Proof that the church sponsored the appeal for the express purposes of collecting funds for this part of its work, that an officer of that church took the funds donated and dealt with them as the church wished, and that the funds went to the support of the work the church intended is sufficient to establish that the funds were donated for the use of the church. IRS Letter Ruling 200530016 (2005).

Ratterman v. Commissioner, 11 T.C. 1140 (1948)

A contribution given to a Jesuit priest was held to be deductible on the theory that members of the Jesuit Order are under a vow of poverty obligating them to give to the Order all property received by them, and accordingly a gift to a priest in reality is a gift to or for the use of the Order.

Davis v. United States, 110 S. Ct. 2014 (1991)

In this ruling the Supreme Court gave its most detailed interpretation of the requirement that a charitable contribution be to or for the use of a qualified charitable organization. The case involved the question of whether the parents of Mormon missionaries can deduct (as charitable contributions) payments they make directly to their sons for travel expenses incurred in performing missionary activities. The parents conceded that their payments were not made to a qualified charity, since the monies went directly to the sons and not to the Mormon Church. However, they insisted that their payments were for the use of the church, since the church "had a reasonable ability to ensure that the contributions primarily served the organization's charitable purposes." They pointed to the church's role in requesting the funds, setting the amount to be donated, and requiring weekly expense sheets from the missionaries.

On the other hand, the IRS interpreted "for the use of" much more narrowly, to mean "in trust for." In other words, for a contribution to be "for the use of" a charity, it must be made to an individual or organization pursuant to a trust or similar legal arrangement for the benefit of the charity. Without such a legal and enforceable arrangement, a contribution to an individual cannot be considered for the use of the charity, since no legal means are in place to ensure that the contribution will be used for the exclusive benefit of the charity. An example of a donation for the use of a qualified charity would be a contribution to a trustee who is required, under the terms of a trust agreement, to spend the trust income solely for the benefit of specified charities. Such a contribution is not *to* a charitable organization, but it should be deductible if made to a trustee who is required to distribute the funds to qualified charities. Obviously, the parents' transfer of funds to their sons' personal checking accounts failed this definition.

The court conceded that the words "for the use of," taken in isolation, could support the interpretation of either the parents or the IRS . However, it reviewed the events leading to the enactment of the phrase "for the use of" in 1921 and concluded that "it appears likely that in choosing the phrase 'for the use of' Congress was referring to donations made in trust or in a similar legal arrangement." The court noted that the parents had presented no evidence supporting their claim that Congress intended the phrase "for the use of" to mean contributions directly to individual missionaries so long as the church "has a reasonable ability to supervise the use of the contributed funds." The court further emphasized that the parents' interpretation

> *would tend to undermine the purposes of [federal tax law] by allowing taxpayers to claim deductions for funds transferred to children or other relatives for their own personal use. Because a recipient of donated funds need not have any legal relationship with a [church], the [IRS] would face virtually insurmountable administrative difficulties in verifying that any particular expenditure benefited a [church]. Although there is no suggestion whatsoever in this case that the transferred funds were used for an improper purpose, it is clear that [the parents'] interpretation would create an opportunity for tax evasion that others might be eager to exploit.*

The court concluded that the parents could not deduct the payments they made directly to their missionary sons because the payments were not made either to or for the use of a church or other qualified charity as required by federal law. The payments could not be considered for the use of a church, since the parents

> *took no steps normally associated with creating a trust or similar legal arrangement. Although the sons may have promised to use the money in accordance with Church guidelines, they did not have any legal obligation to do so; there is no evidence that the [church's] guidelines have any legally binding effect. . . . We conclude that because the [parents] did not donate the funds in trust for the Church, or in a similarly enforceable legal arrangement for the benefit of the Church, the funds were not donated 'for the use of' the Church.*

❖ **KEY POINT.** A Tax Practitioner Newsletter published by the IRS Salt Lake City District specifies: "The LDS Church initiated a new missionary funding program, on January 1, 1991. Under this new funding program, called the Equalized Funding Program, all missionary contributions are made directly to the Church. Contributions under the program then become the property of the Church and are under its control. The Church has the discretion to use those funds as the need appears in the various missions of the Church. By contrast, under the former missionary funding program of the Church, contributions sometimes were made directly to the individual missionaries. The Supreme Court held in *Davis v. United States* that such contributions were not deductible because they were not to or for the use of the Church. The IRS stated that contributions made directly to the Church under the new Equalized Funding Program qualify as deductible contributions under Internal Revenue Code section 170."

Contributions to churches or missions agencies that designate a particular missionary as the recipient of the contributed funds

Assume that a church member makes a contribution of $500 to a denominational missions board and designates on the check (or with a cover letter) that it is for a designated missionary. Is this common practice affected by the Supreme Court's decision in the *Davis* case (summarized above)? In many cases it will not be. In 1962 the IRS ruled that designated contributions are tax-deductible (assuming that all of the other legal requirements applicable to charitable contributions are satisfied) so long as the church or missions board "has full control of the donated funds, and discretion as to their use, so as to insure that they will be used to carry out its functions and purposes."

In other words, if a donor contributes funds to a missions board, designating a particular missionary, the contribution will be deductible so long as the missions board retains *full administrative and accounting control* over the funds. What does this mean? Neither the IRS nor any federal court has addressed this issue directly. Presumably, this test could be satisfied if a missions agency adopts the following procedures:

- Require each missionary to complete a periodic (e.g., quarterly) activity report summarizing all missionary activities conducted for the previous period. This would include services conducted, teaching activities, and any other missionary activities. The summary should list the date and location of each activity.
- Require the missionary to complete a periodic accounting of the donated funds received from the missions agency. The agency should prepare an appropriate form. The form should account for all dollars distributed by the agency. Written receipts should be required for any expense of more than $75. This report should indicate the date, amount, location, and missionary purpose of each expense. It can be patterned after the expense report used for business travel. Keep in mind that "religious purposes" includes not only those expenses related directly to missionary activities but also ordinary and necessary travel and living expenses while serving as a missionary.

- The missions agency must approve each missionary's ministry as a legitimate activity in furtherance of the church's religious mission.
- Prepare a letter of understanding that communicates these terms and conditions. The agency should specifically reserve the right to audit or otherwise verify the accuracy of any information provided to you. For example, you may on occasion wish to verify that the activity reports are accurate.
- Reconcile the expense summaries with the activity summaries. That is, confirm that the expenses claimed on the expense reports correspond with the missionary activities described in the activity reports.

Such procedures can be burdensome for a missions agency. This is the type of accounting and administrative control the Mormon Church was attempting to avoid in the *Davis* case (see above) by its practice of direct person-to-person donations. However, such procedures (or similar ones) will be essential in order to demonstrate that the agency maintains administrative and accounting control over contributions designating specific missionaries.

EXAMPLE. A married couple (the "taxpayers") gave contributions of $6,000, $6,500, and $6,000 directly to three "missionaries" and claimed the total amount ($18,500) as a charitable contribution on their tax return. The three recipients were characterized as missionaries and evangelists for the taxpayers' church. In 2005 the three missionaries worked to establish and develop new local churches. One developed a church in Flint, Michigan. Another developed a church in Raleigh, North Carolina. A third developed a church in South Africa.

The missionaries determined how best to use those funds toward the development of their respective churches. They used these funds to support the recruitment of new members, to purchase and provide religious education materials, and to provide for their basic financial support. Each of the missionaries provided reports to both his local church and the taxpayers. These reports detailed the use of the contributions for their missionary work.

The IRS denied a charitable contribution deduction for any of the donations the taxpayers made to the three missionaries, but the Tax Court ruled that they were entitled to deduct these donations. It began its opinion by restating two basic requirements for charitable contributions:

(1) The charitable donee (a) is created or organized in the United States, (b) is organized and operated exclusively for religious purposes, (c) no part of the net earnings of which inures to the benefit of any individual, and (d) which is not disqualified for tax exemption under section 501(c)(3).
(2) The contribution was given either (a) for the use of or (b) to the charitable donee.

The court conceded that the churches in Michigan and North Carolina met the first requirement. However, the church in South Africa did not. Therefore, contributions made to or for the use of the local church in South Africa are not deductible.

Having determined that the local churches in Michigan and North Carolina were qualified charitable donees, the court addressed the second requirement—were the taxpayers' donations given to the missionaries associated with these two churches made for the use of or to either of those qualified charitable donees? The court concluded that the taxpayers' donations were not made for the use of the Michigan and North Carolina churches, noting that the United States Supreme Court has defined the phrase "for the use of" to mean that the contribution must be "held in a legally enforceable trust for the qualified organization or in a similar legal arrangement." *Davis v. United States, 495 U.S. 472, 485 (1990).* Such legal arrangements "must provide the charitable donee a legally enforceable right against the recipient that ensures the donated funds are used on behalf of the donee."

This requirement was not met in this case, since the taxpayers' donations "were given directly to the two missionaries for the purpose of supporting the missionary and evangelical work performed at the local churches." The taxpayers "made no effort to establish a legally enforceable trust, nor did they succeed in creating a similar legal arrangement." The court rejected the taxpayers' argument that their donations created contractual obligations on the part of the missionaries to use the funds as directed. The court noted that the taxpayers had failed to demonstrate that oral contracts between themselves and the two missionaries "could create a legally enforceable right in the local churches to secure access to the funds." Therefore, their contributions were not given "for the use of" a qualified donee.

Although the contributions were not given for the use of a qualified charitable donee, the contributions could be deductible if the taxpayers gave the contributions "to" a qualified donee. The court noted that contributions to an organization "include contributions given to an agent of the organization." It explained:

Agency is a fiduciary relationship that arises when an agent acts on behalf of and under the control of a principal. Additionally, both the principal and the agent must manifest consent to the relationship. The analysis of agency has two substantive components: (1) The relationship between the principal and the agent and (2) the interaction of the agent with third parties on the principal's behalf.

First [the two missionaries] had appropriately established an agency relationship with their respective local churches in Flint, Michigan, and Raleigh, North Carolina. Religious doctrine forbids the local churches from accepting funds directly from nonmembers. Thus the local churches designated [the missionaries] as their agents to solicit, collect, and disburse funds on their behalf. Additionally, the local churches gave [them] authority to represent the local churches in interactions with the general public in order to facilitate recruitment of additional members. Through the granting of this authority the local churches manifested their assents to [the missionaries'] service as agents. Additionally, the local churches required [the missionaries] to provide regular financial reports to their respective local churches. To ensure [they] complied with the teaching of the [church] the elders of the local churches monitored the distributions of funds and [the missionaries'] interactions with the public. If at any time [they] acted contrary to the wishes of the local churches, the local churches held the authority to terminate the relationship and dismiss either of them as an agent. Therefore [the missionaries] established a proper agency relationship with their respective local churches.

Second [the missionaries] interacted with the taxpayers and other third parties on behalf of their local churches. They provided religious instruction to both members and nonmembers of the local churches. They used this instruction of nonmembers as an opportunity to recruit new members to the local churches. They also purchased radio and newspaper advertisements on behalf of their local churches. [They] solicited and received funds from nonmembers (including the taxpayers) for their local churches. They used these funds to purchase religious instructional materials and advertisements and to provide for their own modest living expenses. All of these interactions with third parties were performed under the authority of the agency relationship between the men and their local churches.

Because [the missionaries] were agents of their respective local churches (qualified donees) and the taxpayers' contributions were given to them in this capacity, their contributions were given "to" a qualified donee within the requirements of [the tax code]. Therefore, they are entitled to deduct the [$12,500 given to these two missionaries]. Wilkes v. Commissioner, T.C. Summary Opinion 2010-53 (2010).

Contributions to a local church designating a particular missionary not associated with any missions board or agency

Are these contributions tax-deductible? According to the IRS 1962 ruling, such contributions are deductible only if the church "has full control of the donated funds, and discretion as to their use, so as to insure that they will be used to carry out its functions and purposes." This means that the local church must assume the role of a missions board and implement the kinds of procedures described above with regard to each such missionary. This is a significant responsibility that many churches will not be willing to assume. The Supreme Court's decision in the *Davis* case (summarized above)

ensures that contributions to local churches for independent missionaries and short-term "lay missionaries" from one's own church are not tax-deductible without such controls.

❖ **KEY POINT.** Persons may still make direct contributions to individual missionaries or religious workers. Such contributions are not illegal—they merely are not tax-deductible as charitable contributions. The fact that 70 percent of all taxpayers are not able to itemize their deductions means that most persons receive no tax benefit from making charitable contributions. It makes no difference whether such persons make their contributions to a missions board or directly to a missionary—the contributions are not deductible in either case.

❖ **KEY POINT.** Some independent missionaries have set up nonprofit, tax-exempt corporations. Individuals are free to make tax-deductible contributions directly to such ministries. Churches also can make distributions to them.

Hubert v. Commissioner, T.C. Memo. 1993-482 (1993)

The Tax Court ruled that contributions to a church were deductible even though they were designated for the support of two missionaries. A member attended an inner-city Baptist church for many years. Due to a lack of funds, the church asked the member to sponsor two missionaries from the church. The member did so for a number of years. One of the missionaries worked in Peru and was responsible for beginning 15 Baptist churches there. The other missionary worked in a variety of assignments overseas in missionary radio. The member was not related to either missionary or personally associated with them in any way other than the fact that he had taught one of them in his Sunday-school class many years before.

In 1982 the member executed a last will and testament that created two trusts funded with $100,000 each. The income of each trust was to be paid to two missions organizations for the missionary work of the two missionaries during their lives, including support during retirement. The member died in 1986, and his estate claimed a charitable contribution deduction for the two $100,000 trusts. The IRS denied a deduction, arguing that the member intended to benefit the missionaries personally and that the missions organizations lacked full control over the use of the funds. The IRS relied in part on the Supreme Court's decision in the *Davis* case (the Mormon missionary case discussed above) denying a charitable contribution deduction to Mormon parents for contributions made directly to their missionary sons.

The Tax Court ruled that the estate *could* claim a charitable contribution deduction for the money placed in the two trusts, despite the fact that the church member specified that the trusts were for the benefit of the two missionaries. The court noted that a charitable contribution, to be deductible, must be to or for the use of a charity.

A contribution is for the use of a charity if it is transferred to a legally enforceable trust for the charity:

> Under [the Supreme Court's decision in the Mormon missionary case] the test is not whether the charitable organization has full control of the funds, but rather is whether the charitable organization has a legally enforceable right to the funds. In [the Mormon missionary case] the charitable organization [did not] actually receive the funds, either directly or in trust. In the case before us, the income and later the principal are held in a legally enforceable trust for [the two missions] organizations which have control over the funds.

The court rejected the IRS argument that the charitable purpose failed because the intent and the actual effect of the gifts was to benefit the two missionaries rather than the church. The court acknowledged that the trusts focused on two specific missionaries. However, it concluded that "we are satisfied, on the facts before us, that decedent intended the bequests to be used to implement the missionary work of the [missions organizations] through the named missionaries, as well as through the building of foreign mission field medical clinics." The court explained:

> The charities have complete discretion to use the funds in any manner which fits the stated purpose, including choosing the amounts of the funds to be used and the methods of using those funds. . . . On these facts, we conclude that decedent intended to benefit the general public, not the two named missionaries. Moreover, we find that the charitable organizations have substantial control over the use of the funds and were not meant to be mere conduits to funnel money to the missionaries. The fact that decedent directed the [missions organizations] to use the funds for specific purposes does not defeat the charitable nature of the bequests. Under general trust principles, the [missions organizations] have a fiduciary duty to use the funds as directed; however, they have complete discretion to determine the most appropriate ways to implement the directed purposes. We conclude that the charitable organizations had sufficient control and enforceable rights over the bequests to ensure that the funds were used for charitable purposes, as is required by [law]. The charitable nature of the bequests is further protected by the Attorneys General of Georgia and the State or States in which the charitable organizations are located. The Attorneys General are charged with ensuring that the charitable purposes of the trust are carried out.

The fact that the trusts were to continue distributing funds to the two missionaries following their retirements did not matter to the court. It observed:

> The retirement provisions further decedent's charitable purpose by ensuring that the missionaries will be able to continue their work without concern for what will happen to them when the time comes to retire. During the retirement period, the [missions organizations] will continue to control the funds and may provide for the retirement of the missionaries as they see fit. Under the provisions of the will, upon retirement of the missionaries, the income and principal of the trusts are to be given to the charities "to provide for" the retirement of the missionaries and their wives.

> The court did caution that "on different facts we might conclude that the charitable organization was a mere conduit to funnel money to an individual and, therefore, lacked sufficient control over the funds. In such a circumstance, because the bequest was intended to benefit one individual rather than the general public, the bequest would not qualify for a charitable deduction."

Conclusions

The *Hubert* case, along with the other precedent summarized above, suggest that contributions to a church or missions organization may be tax-deductible even though they designate a specific missionary in either of two situations:

Situation 1

In 1962 the IRS ruled that contributions to a church or missions organization are tax-deductible even though they designate a particular missionary, so long as the church or missions organization "has full control of the donated funds, and discretion as to their use, so as to insure that they will be used to carry out its functions and purposes." *Revenue Ruling 62-113.* In other words, if a donor contributes funds to a church missions board and designates a particular missionary, the contribution will be deductible so long as the church or missions board retains full administrative and accounting control over the funds.

Situation 2

Contributions *for the use of* a church or missions organization are tax-deductible even though they designate a particular missionary. The phrase "for the use of" means that a contribution is given to a trustee pursuant to a trust or similar legal arrangement for the benefit of a charitable organization. If this test is met, it does not matter that the trustee is directed to distribute funds to a church or missions organization for a specified individual. A contribution is deductible under these circumstances because the trustee has a legal duty to ensure that trust funds are used by the named beneficiary for religious or charitable purposes. This conclusion is reinforced by two additional considerations:

First, churches and missions organizations have a fiduciary duty to distribute funds only for religious or charitable purposes. As a result, if a trust distributes funds to a church or missions organization for the missionary work of a specified individual, the church or missions organization has a fiduciary duty to ensure that trust distributions are used by the missionary for such purposes. As a result, such contributions are for the use of the church or missions organization even though they designate a specific recipient.

Second, state attorneys general are empowered to ensure that the charitable purposes of charitable trusts are carried out.

4. BENEVOLENCE FUNDS

❂ **KEY POINT.** The IRS issued a private letter ruling that addresses charitable contributions that designate specific individuals. The ruling provides an exhaustive analysis of the deductibility of designated contributions and makes several helpful clarifications and observations. The ruling is addressed earlier in this section. *IRS Letter Ruling 200530016 (2005).*

❂ **KEY POINT.** In Revenue Ruling 62-113 the IRS noted that contributions earmarked by a donor for a particular student were gifts to the designated student and were not deductible. However, the IRS acknowledged that a deduction will be allowed if it is established that the gift is intended by the donor for the use of the charitable organization. The test in each case is whether the organization has full control of the donated funds, and discretion as to their use, to ensure that they will be used to carry out the charitable organization's functions and purposes. The IRS has noted that this test is to be used in evaluating the tax-deductibility of contributions that designate a student as well as contributions that designate other individuals "such as a fund to help pay for an organ transplant or to help a particular family rebuild a home destroyed by a tornado . . . [and] religiously motivated programs to support designated missionaries." *IRS Exempt Organizations Continuing Professional Education Technical Instruction Program for 1996.*

Many churches have established benevolence funds to assist needy persons. Typical beneficiaries of such funds include the unemployed, persons with a catastrophic illness, accident victims, and the aged. There is no question that churches may establish benevolence funds. This is both a religious and a charitable function. Undesignated contributions to a church benevolence fund are deductible by the donor if he or she itemizes deductions on Schedule A (Form 1040).

Problems arise when a donor makes a contribution to a church benevolence fund and designates the intended recipient of the contribution. For example, assume that John is a member of a church, that his church has a benevolence fund, that Joan (another church member) is suffering from a catastrophic illness for which she has inadequate medical insurance, and that John contributes $1,000 to the church benevolence fund with the instruction that his contribution be applied to Joan's medical bills. Is John's contribution deductible? The answer to this question depends upon the following two considerations:

- **Contributions to or for a qualified charity.** As noted above, section 170 of the tax code allows a charitable contribution deduction only with respect to donations to or for the use of charitable organizations. Contributions to an individual, however needy, are never deductible, since they can never (unlike certain contributions made to missionaries) be said to be to or for the use of a charitable organization.
- **The donor's intent.** The intent of the donor ordinarily determines whether the transfer should be characterized as a tax-deductible contribution to a church or a nondeductible transfer to an individual. The question to be asked whenever a donor makes a designated contribution to a church benevolence fund is this: did the donor intend to make a contribution to the church, or did the donor only intend to benefit the designated individual (using the church as an intermediary in order to obtain a tax deduction for an otherwise nondeductible gift)? The fact that the payment was made to a church is not controlling, since taxpayers cannot obtain a deduction merely by funneling a payment through a church. As the IRS often asserts, it is the substance and not the form of a transaction that is controlling.

Let's apply these rules to some specific situations below.

Contributions made directly to individuals

Obviously, contributions made directly to individuals are not deductible, no matter how needy the recipient may be. For example, the courts have repeatedly denied deductions for contributions made directly to relatives, ministers, students, military personnel, and needy persons.

EXAMPLE. A church invited members to submit requests for financial assistance. Church leaders (elders) reviewed the requests and selected persons to assist consistently with the church's teachings. A married couple made direct contributions totaling $3,500 to various persons identified by the elders. Recipients used the donations to cover living expenses. The Tax Court, in denying any charitable contribution deduction for these donations, observed:

> *[The taxpayers'] contributions to [the needy church members] are not charitable contributions. . . . [The tax code] allows taxpayers to deduct "a contribution or gift to or for the use of . . . a corporation, trust, or community chest, fund, or foundation . . . created or organized in the United States . . . organized and operated exclusively for religious [or] charitable purposes . . . no part of the net earning of which inures to the benefit of any private individual." Moneys given directly to individuals for their personal benefit are deemed private gifts and are not deductible charitable contributions because they are not given to or for the use of a charitable organization. The taxpayers' contributions were given directly to the needy individuals for their personal use.*

Although the recipients were morally obligated to use the funds in accordance with religious teachings, no organization or entity besides the individuals was the beneficiary of the gift. Therefore, the taxpayers are not entitled to a $3,500 charitable contribution deduction for contributions given to the needy individuals. Wilkes v. Commissioner, T.C. Summary Opinion 2010-53 (2010).

Undesignated contributions made directly to a tax-exempt charitable organization

Contributions made directly to a tax-exempt charitable organization ordinarily are deductible. Accordingly, contributions to a church benevolence fund are deductible by donors who itemize deductions on Schedule A and who do not designate a recipient or beneficiary of their contribution. To illustrate, assume that a church establishes a benevolence fund and that a church member contributed $250 to the fund but made no reference (either orally or in writing) as to a desired recipient of the contribution. Such a contribution ordinarily will be deductible by the donor (assuming he or she is able to itemize deductions on Schedule A) since it is clear that the contribution was made to or for the use of the church.

Anonymous recommendations

Some churches have established a benevolence fund and allow only undesignated contributions to the fund. However, church members are free to make anonymous recommendations (in writing) to the church board regarding desired recipients. Similarly, several churches have appointed a benevolence committee to receive written or oral recommendations from the congregation regarding candidates for benevolence fund distributions and to make recommendations to the church board.

In either case, if the identity of donors to the benevolence fund is undisclosed, and if all church members are free to make recommendations regarding recipients of the fund, then donor contributions may be deductible. However, these procedures will not support the deductibility of contributions if the identity of benevolence fund donors is obvious to the board, and the board distributes such donations consistently with the expressed desires of the donors.

Contributions designating a specific beneficiary

The most difficult kind of benevolence fund contribution to evaluate (but by far the most common) is a contribution that designates a specific recipient. The designation may be written on the face of the check, on an envelope accompanying the contribution, or in a letter; or it may be oral.

To illustrate, a member contributes a check in the amount of $500 to a church's benevolence fund and inserts a note requesting that a designated individual receive the proceeds. Is such a contribution deductible? Ordinarily such designated contributions to a benevolence fund are *not* deductible, since the intent of the donor is to make a transfer of funds *directly to a particular individual* rather than to a charitable organization. This does not make them

illegal—it simply makes them nondeductible by the donor. On the other hand, the recipient ordinarily does not have to report the transfer as taxable income, since it is a nontaxable gift.

The IRS has stated:

If contributions to the fund are earmarked by the donor for a particular individual, they are treated, in effect, as being gifts to the designated individual and are not deductible. However, a deduction will be allowable where it is established that a gift is intended by a donor for the use of the organization and not as a gift to an individual. The test in each case is whether the organization has full control of the donated funds, and discretion as to their use, so as to insure that they will be used to carry out its functions and purposes. Revenue Ruling 62-113.

This test suggests that in some cases it may be possible for a donor to deduct a designated contribution to a church benevolence fund if the circumstances clearly demonstrate that the designation was a mere suggestion or recommendation and that the donor intended the donation to be to or for the use of the church and subject to its control rather than to the control of the designated individual.

The IRS has reached such a conclusion in three rulings:

- **Letter Ruling 200250029 (2002)**—addressed later in this section.
- **Letter Ruling 200530016 (2005)**—addressed earlier in this section.
- **Letter Ruling 8752031 (1987).** A taxpayer contributed money to a philanthropic fund within a charitable organization. Once the taxpayer made the contribution, the charity had complete legal and equitable control over the fund. However, the donor could, from time to time, submit recommendations to the charity regarding recipients of the fund. Such recommendations, however, were advisory only, and the charity could accept or reject them.

Under these facts the IRS reached the following conclusion:

Although the term "contribution" is not defined either in the Internal Revenue Code or in the income tax regulations, it is well-established that in order to be deductible under section 170 of the tax code, a contribution must qualify as a gift in the common sense of being a voluntary transfer of property without consideration.

Revenue Ruling 62-113 [quoted above] holds that contributions to a [tax-exempt] organization that are not earmarked by the donor for a particular individual, will be deductible if it is established that a gift is intended by the donor for the use of the organization and not as a gift to an individual. The test is whether the organization has full control of the donated funds and discretion as to their use, so as to insure that they will be used to carry out its functions and purposes.

From the information submitted and representations made, [the charity] is to have complete legal and equitable control over the funds contributed by [the donor]. [The donor's] right to suggest distributees will be advisory in nature and will not be binding on [the charity]. Moreover, the fund will be used in the furtherance of [the charity's] stated purposes. IRS Letter Ruling 8752031.

While private letter rulings apply only to the parties covered by the ruling and may not be used as precedent in support of a particular position, they reflect the thinking of the IRS on a particular issue and, as a result, can be of considerable relevance. The private letter ruling discussed above suggests that contributions to a church benevolence fund can be deductible, even if the donor mentions a beneficiary, if the facts demonstrate that

- the donor's recommendation is advisory only;
- the church retains "full control of the donated funds, and discretion as to their use"; and
- the donor understands that his or her recommendation is advisory only and that the church retains full control over the donated funds, including the authority to accept or reject the donor's recommendations.

How can these facts be established? One possible way would be for a church to adopt a "benevolence fund policy," making all distributions from a benevolence fund subject to the unrestricted control and discretion of the church board, and to communicate such a policy to all prospective donors. It can be argued that donors willing to make a designated contribution to a church benevolence fund under these conditions are manifesting an intent to make a contribution to the church rather than to the designated individual. A sample policy is printed in Illustration 8-1.

Churches adopting such a policy should make copies available to any person wanting to make a designated contribution to the church benevolence fund. Such a policy does not guarantee that a designated contribution will be rendered deductible. Churches wishing to assure donors that their contributions to church benevolence funds will be deductible should use one of the more certain methods discussed above (e.g., undesignated contributions or undesignated contributions and anonymous designations to the board or benevolence committee).

Obviously, a church can administer a program in such a way as to jeopardize the deductibility of contributions. For example, a church can adopt the benevolence fund policy reproduced in Illustration 8-1, yet honor every recommendation made by a donor. Clearly, no contribution would be deductible under such an arrangement, since the church's alleged control over the donated funds would be illusory. Similarly, if a church receives only a few contributions to

---

ILLUSTRATION 8-1

BENEVOLENCE FUND POLICY OF FIRST CHURCH

First Church, in the exercise of its religious and charitable purposes, has established a benevolence fund to assist persons in financial need. The church welcomes contributions to the fund. Donors are free to suggest beneficiaries of the fund or of their contributions to the fund. However, such suggestions shall be deemed advisory rather than mandatory in nature. The administration of the fund, including all disbursements, is subject to the exclusive control and discretion of the church board. The church board may consider suggested designations, but in no event is it bound in any way to honor them, since they are accepted only on the condition that they are merely nonbinding suggestions or recommendations. As a result, donors will not be entitled to a return of their designated contributions on the ground that the church failed to honor their designations.

Donors wishing to make contributions to the benevolence fund subject to these conditions may be able to deduct their contributions if they itemize their deductions on their federal income tax return. The church cannot guarantee this result and recommends that donors who want assurance that their contributions are deductible seek the advice of a tax professional. Checks should be made payable to the church, with a notation that the funds are to be placed in the church benevolence fund.

The Official Board
First Church

---

its benevolence fund each year and, at the time of each contribution, receives a single anonymous recommendation regarding a recipient, it is reasonably clear that the contributions are associated with the recommendations, and the church's control over the funds will be compromised to the extent that it routinely honors such recommendations.

▲ **CAUTION.** *In 1994 the IRS ruled that donors could not deduct their contributions to a scholarship fund if they designated specific recipients. This ruling is discussed fully in section B.5 of this chapter. It is relevant to a consideration of benevolence fund policies, since the IRS disregarded a religious organization's "scholarship policy" that purported to give the organization full control over contributions that designated specific scholarship recipients. The IRS concluded that the degree of control exercised by the organization over the contributions was insufficient to support a charitable contribution deduction. This ruling must be studied carefully by any church that has implemented a benevolence fund policy allowing donors to designate individual recipients. While it is still possible in some* *cases for a church to exercise sufficient control over designated benevolence fund contributions to support a charitable contribution deduction, the 1994 IRS ruling demonstrates that the degree of control exercised by the church over designated contributions must be real and substantial. Churches that merely rubber-stamp every designated contribution to a benevolence fund will not demonstrate sufficient control.* IRS Letter Ruling 9405003.

Special appeals

Many churches have made special appeals to raise funds for a particular benevolence need. For example, an offering is collected to assist a family with a child who has incurred substantial medical expenses. Are contributions made to such an offering tax-deductible? Unfortunately, neither the IRS nor any federal court has addressed this issue directly. However, it is possible that such contributions would be tax-deductible if the following conditions are met: (1) the offering was preauthorized by the church board; (2) the recipient (or his or her family) is financially needy, and the uninsured medical expenses are substantial; (3) the offering is used exclusively to pay a portion of the medical expenses; (4) immediate family members are not the primary contributors; and (5) no more than one or two such offerings are collected for the same individual. This interpretation of the law is aggressive and should not be adopted without the advice of a competent tax professional.

In 1956 the IRS issued a ruling acknowledging that charities can distribute funds for benevolent purposes so long as certain conditions are satisfied:

> *Organizations privately established and funded as charitable foundations which are organized and actively operated to carry on one or more of the purposes specified in section 501(c)(3) of the Internal Revenue Code of 1954, and which otherwise meet the requirements for exemption from federal income tax are not precluded from making distributions of their funds to individuals, provided such distributions are made on a true charitable basis in furtherance of the purposes for which they are organized. However, organizations of this character which make such distributions should maintain adequate records and case histories to show the name and address of each recipient of aid; the amount distributed to each; the purpose for which the aid was given; the manner in which the recipient was selected and the relationship, if any, between the recipient and (1) members, officers, or trustees of the organization, (2) a grantor or substantial contributor to the organization or a member of the family of either, and (3) a corporation controlled by a grantor or substantial contributor, in order that any or all distributions made to individuals can be substantiated upon request by the Internal Revenue Service.* Revenue Ruling 56-304. [Emphasis added.]

Handling excess contributions

How should the balance of a fund created to assist a cancer victim be distributed in the event of her death? That was the issue faced by a New Jersey appeals court. A woman was diagnosed as suffering from acute leukemia. After chemotherapy proved unsuccessful in treating the disease, her physicians recommended a bone marrow transplant. The woman's health insurance company refused to pay for the transplant on the ground that it was an experimental procedure. The woman's family launched a fund-raising campaign in their community, seeking private donations to defray the anticipated costs of the transplant. Their efforts included advertisements in newspapers, urging readers to mail contributions to a fund established in the woman's name at a local bank. Nearly $21,000 was raised through these efforts. Unfortunately, the woman died before the transplant could be performed. The fund had a balance of nearly $8,000 at the time of the woman's death.

A dispute arose as to the proper distribution of this fund balance. Family members insisted that the fund balance should be distributed to them, and they based their position on affidavits signed by several donors to the fund stating that had they known the leukemia victim would die before the bone marrow transplant, they would have wanted the fund balance distributed to the woman's family. A court refused to distribute the balance to the family. Rather, it ordered the bank (in which the contributed funds were deposited) to distribute the remaining funds on a pro rata basis among the donors. This ruling will be relevant to any church that has created a fund for the benefit of a specified individual or family (ordinarily for benevolent or charitable purposes). The important point is this: when the purpose of the fund no longer exists, any fund balance should not necessarily be distributed to family members. *Matter of Gonzalez, 621 A.2d 94 (N.J. Super. 1992).*

Employer-provided relief to employees

Can a church make benevolence distributions to employees or to family members of employees? Are such distributions consistent with a church's exempt purposes? Note the following five points:

First, section 102(c) of the tax code specifies that the exclusion of gifts from income taxation does not apply to "any amount transferred by or for an employer to, or for the benefit of, an employee." This is a broad prohibition that would appear to preclude employers, under any circumstances, from making nontaxable benevolence distributions to employees.

Second, IRS Publication 3833 (discussed below) contains the following guidance:

> *Frequently, employers fund relief programs through charitable organizations aimed at helping their employees cope with the consequences of a disaster or personal hardship. . . . Public charities can establish employer-sponsored assistance programs to respond to any type of disaster or employee emergency hardship situations, as long as the related employer does not exercise excessive control over the organization.*

To ensure the program is not impermissibly serving the related employer, the following requirements must be met:

- *the class of beneficiaries must be large or indefinite (a "charitable class"),*
- *the recipients must be selected based on an objective determination of need or distress, and*
- *the recipients must be selected by an independent selection committee or adequate substitute procedures must be in place to ensure that any benefit to the employer is incidental and tenuous. The charity's selection committee is independent if a majority of the members of the committee consists of persons who are not in a position to exercise substantial influence over the affairs of the employer.*

If these requirements are met, the public charity's payments to the employer-sponsor's employees and their family members in response to a disaster or emergency hardship are presumed: (1) to be made for charitable purposes and (2) not to result in taxable compensation to the employees.

Third, note that this excerpt from Publication 3833 does not treat all natural disaster or emergency hardship distributions to employees as nontaxable benevolence gifts. Rather, this result is possible only if the three conditions mentioned in the excerpt are satisfied. The first condition is that the class of beneficiaries is large and indefinite (a "charitable class"). This means that Publication 3833 is not addressing church benevolence distribution to one or two employees who are facing an emergency hardship. One or two employees do not constitute a large and indefinite charitable class, so such distributions would be fully taxable. An example of employer distributions to employees that would be nontaxable would be a disaster fund established by a large charitable employer to all employees adversely affected by a natural disaster. However, the same result would not apply to churches with only a small number of employees, since the requirement of a charitable class would not be met.

Fourth, the above-quoted excerpt from Publication 3833 demonstrates that the IRS did not consider section 102(c) of the tax code to be a bar to the nontaxability of disaster and emergency hardship distributions by employers to their employees. However, as noted above, some important conditions must be met.

Fifth, note that Publication 3833 is addressing disaster relief and "emergency hardship" situations. Its preamble states that it "is for people interested in using a charitable organization to provide help to victims of disasters or other emergency hardship situations. These disasters may be caused by floods, fires, riots, storms, or similar large-scale events. Emergency hardship may be caused by illness, death, accident, violent crime, or other personal events." This language is broad enough to encompass many kinds of emergency hardships beyond those directly caused by a natural disaster.

Disaster relief

IRS Publication 3833 (Disaster Relief) provides charities with helpful information on how to handle contributions from individuals who designate a specific benevolence recipient in the context of natural disasters. Here is the key excerpt: "Individuals can also help victims of disaster or hardship by making gifts directly to victims. This type of assistance does not qualify as a tax-deductible contribution since a qualified charitable organization is not the recipient. However, individual recipients of gifts are generally not subject to federal income tax on the value of the gift."

The publication then provides the following example, which will be useful to many church treasurers in evaluating the tax-deductibility of contributions to the church that designate a particular needy person.

Jim, a college student and a counselor at a summer camp, accidentally rolls his old truck into a lake. The other counselors collect several hundred dollars and give the monies directly to Jim to help with the down payment for another truck. Since the counselors are making gifts to a particular individual, the use of a qualified charitable organization would not be appropriate. The counselors cannot claim tax deductions for their gifts to Jim. However, Jim is not subject to federal income tax on the gift amount. [Emphasis added.]

IRS Publication 3833 contains information concerning the distribution of funds by a "disaster relief or emergency hardship organization." The same principles would apply to churches and other religious organizations. Here are the key excerpts directly relevant to many kinds of benevolence gifts made to churches:

Organizations may provide assistance in the form of funds, services, or goods to ensure that victims have the basic necessities, such as food, clothing, housing (including repairs), transportation, and medical assistance (including psychological counseling). The type of aid that is appropriate depends on the individual's needs and resources. Disaster relief organizations are generally in the best position to determine the type of assistance that is appropriate.

For example, immediately following a devastating flood, a family may be in need of food, clothing, and shelter, regardless of their financial resources. However, they may not require long-term assistance if they have adequate financial resources. Individuals who are financially needy or otherwise distressed are appropriate recipients of charity. Financial need and/or distress may arise through a variety of circumstances. Examples include individuals who are:

- *temporarily in need of food or shelter when stranded, injured, or lost because of a disaster;*
- *temporarily unable to be self-sufficient as a result of a sudden and severe personal or family crisis, such as victims of violent crimes or physical abuse;*

- in need of long-term assistance with housing, childcare, or educational expenses because of a disaster;
- in need of counseling because of trauma experienced as a result of a disaster or a violent crime. . . .

The group of individuals that may properly receive assistance from a tax-exempt charitable organization is called a "charitable class." A charitable class must be large enough or sufficiently indefinite that the community as a whole, rather than a pre-selected group of people, benefits when a charity provides assistance. For example, a charitable class could consist of all the individuals in a city, county or state. This charitable class is large enough that the potential beneficiaries cannot be individually identified and providing benefits to this group would benefit the entire community.

If the group of eligible beneficiaries is limited to a smaller group, such as the employees of a particular employer, the group of persons eligible for assistance must be indefinite. To be considered to benefit an indefinite class, the proposed relief program must be open-ended and include employees affected by the current disaster and those who may be affected by a future disaster. Accordingly, if a charity follows a policy of assisting employees who are victims of all disasters, present or future, it would be providing assistance to an indefinite charitable class. If the facts and circumstances indicate that a newly established disaster relief program is intended to benefit only victims of a current disaster without any intention to provide for victims of future disasters, the organization would not be considered to be benefiting a charitable class.

Because of the requirement that exempt organizations must serve a charitable class, a tax-exempt disaster relief or emergency hardship organization cannot target and limit its assistance to specific individuals, such as a few persons injured in a particular fire. Similarly, donors cannot earmark contributions to a charitable organization for a particular individual or family.

The publication provides the following example:

Linda's baby, Todd, suffers a severe burn from a fire requiring costly treatment that Linda cannot afford. Linda's friends and co-workers form the Todd Foundation to raise funds from fellow workers, family members, and the general public to meet Todd's expenses. Since the organization is formed to assist a particular individual, it would not qualify as a charitable organization.

Consider this alternative case: Linda's friends and co-workers form an organization to raise funds to meet the expenses of an open-ended group consisting of all children in the community injured by disasters where financial help is needed. Neither Linda nor members of Linda's family control the charitable organization. The organization controls the selection of aid

recipients and determines whether any assistance for Todd is appropriate. Potential donors are advised that, while funds may be used to assist Todd, their contributions might well be used for other children who have similar needs. The organization does not accept contributions specifically earmarked for Todd or any other individual. The organization, formed and operated to assist an indefinite number of persons, qualifies as a charitable organization.

The publication cautions charities that "an organization must maintain adequate records that demonstrate the victims' needs for the assistance provided. These records must also show that the organization's payments further charitable purposes." It clarifies that documentation should include

- a complete description of the assistance provided
- costs associated with providing the assistance
- the purpose for which the aid was given
- the charity's objective criteria for disbursing assistance under each program
- how the recipients were selected
- the name, address, and amount distributed to each recipient
- any relationship between a recipient and officers, directors or key employees of or substantial contributors to the charitable organization
- the composition of the selection committee approving the assistance

However, the publication concedes that

a charitable organization that is distributing short-term emergency assistance would only be expected to maintain records showing the type of assistance provided, criteria for disbursing assistance, date, place, estimated number of victims assisted (individual names and addresses are not required), charitable purpose intended to be accomplished, and the cost of the aid. Examples of such short-term emergency aid would include the distribution of blankets, hot meals, electric fans, or coats, hats, and gloves. An organization that is distributing longer-term aid should keep the more-detailed type of records described above.

EXAMPLE. Amy is a young mother who recently was diagnosed with a rare kidney disease that will require expensive and continuing treatment in excess of her insurance coverage. Her father hands the treasurer of Amy's church a check in the amount of $10,000, payable to the church, with the stipulation that it be used for Amy's medical expenses. According to IRS Publication 3833, this check should not be accepted by the church, since it is not a tax-deductible contribution.

EXAMPLE. The Smith family loses its home in a fire. The home was not insured adequately for this loss. The family's church has a benevolence fund, and several members make contributions to this fund assuming that their contributions will be distributed to the Smith family. Members' contributions may be tax-deductible if they are advised that while their contributions may be used to assist the Smith family, their contributions might be used for other individuals or families who are in need. Contributions earmarked for the Smith family, specifically, should not be accepted by the church.

IRS Publication 3833 contains the following additional information concerning distributions of aid by charitable organizations for the "needy and distressed."

Needy and distressed test

A charity should have in place a "needy or distressed test," that is, a set of criteria by which it can objectively make distributions to individuals who are financially or otherwise distressed. Adequate records are required to support the basis upon which assistance is provided.

Definition of "needy"

Persons "do not have to be totally destitute to be needy." Rather, "merely lacking the resources to meet basic necessities" qualifies. On the other hand, "charitable funds cannot be distributed to persons merely because they are victims of a disaster. Therefore, an organization's decision about how its funds will be distributed must be based on an objective evaluation of the victim's needs at the time of the grant."

Documentation required

A charity that is distributing short-term emergency assistance may require less documentation, in the way of victims establishing that they need relief assistance, than an organization that is distributing longer-term aid. For example, IRS Publication 3833 states:

A charitable organization that is distributing short-term emergency assistance would only be expected to maintain records showing the type of assistance provided, criteria for disbursing assistance, date, place, estimated number of victims assisted (individual names and addresses are not required), charitable purpose intended to be accomplished, and the cost of the aid. Examples of such short-term emergency aid would include the distribution of blankets, hot meals, electric fans, or coats, hats, and gloves. An organization that is distributing longer-term aid should keep the more detailed type of records described above.

Amount of assistance needed

An individual who is eligible for assistance because the individual is a victim of a disaster or emergency hardship has no automatic right to a charity's funds. For example, a charitable organization that provides disaster or emergency hardship relief does not have to make an individual whole, such as by rebuilding the individual's uninsured home destroyed by a flood or replacing an individual's income after the person becomes unemployed as the result of a civil disturbance.

Excess contributions

A person who is eligible for assistance because he or she is a victim of a disaster or emergency hardship has no automatic right to a charity's funds. This issue "is especially relevant when the volume of contributions received in response to appeals exceeds the immediate needs. A charitable organization is responsible for taking into account the charitable purposes for which it was formed, the public benefit of its activities, and the specific needs and resources of each victim when using its discretion to distribute its funds."

To illustrate, a tornado destroys several homes in a small town. Local churches collect undesignated offerings for disaster relief. The churches receive more donations than are necessary to cover short term and long-term needs of the victims. Any excess donations should be returned to the donors if possible. If this is not possible, the churches could retain the excess donations for use in future emergencies. In some cases a court may be willing to remove any restriction on the use of excess donations.

IRS Private Letter Ruling 200250029

The IRS issued a ruling in a case involving the deductibility of a designated contribution made to a charity that was organized to promote music. The charity accomplished its charitable purpose by hosting composer events, placing composers in residencies with professional arts institutions, funding recordings of new American music, and entering agreements with professional arts institutions to commission works.

A married couple (the donors) informed the charity of their desire to support the work of a particular composer, and a few months later they donated a substantial amount to the charity. At the time of the contribution, the charity did not make any commitment to use the funds to commission the work of the composer, and there was no representation that the funds would be used for that purpose. The charity informed the donors that the funds would be used at its discretion in furtherance of its charitable purpose, and the donors understood this. In a letter to the donors, the charity thanked them for the contribution. The letter stated that there "can be no assurance that the funds contributed will be used to support the work of the composer" and that the funds would be used by the charity "in carrying out its charitable purpose and will not be returned to the donors."

A short time later the charity paid the composer a commissioning fee to compose a new musical work, and it also agreed to reimburse the expenses incurred by the composer in appearing at the premier of his work. The composer agreed to complete a musical work of specified type and duration in a timely manner.

The charity asked the IRS to issue a ruling that the donors' contribution to the charity was tax-deductible and was not affected by the donors' earmarking of their contribution for the support of the composer. The IRS began its ruling by noting that the tax code allows a tax deduction for charitable contributions and that a charitable contribution "is a contribution or gift *to or for the use of* an organization operated exclusively for charitable purposes" (emphasis added). The IRS concluded that the donors' contribution to the charity was tax-deductible, despite their expressed interest in benefiting a specific composer (and the charity's use of the donated funds for that same composer). The IRS observed:

A charitable contribution deduction is not allowed if a charity is used as a conduit, and a payment to a qualifying charity is "earmarked" or designated for the benefit of a particular individual, even if the individual is a member of the class the charity is intended to benefit. The organization must have control and discretion over the contribution, unfettered by a commitment or understanding that the contribution would benefit a designated individual. The donor's intent must be to benefit the organization and not the individual recipient.

In this case donors made a payment to a recognized charity, and expressed an interest in supporting the work of a particular composer. This expression of interest raises the issue of whether the contribution was impermissibly earmarked for this composer. No commitment or understanding existed between the donors and charity that the contribution would benefit the composer. The donors understood that any funds contributed to the charity would be distributed according to the discretion of the charity, and that the charity's officers select the composers. We believe that the instant case is similar to Revenue Ruling 62-113 and Peace [addressed above]. Although the donors expressed an interest in the selection of a particular individual to compose a work for the charity, the common understanding was that the contribution would become part of the general funds of the charity, and would be distributed in the manner chosen by the charity's officers. Therefore, the contribution by the donors to the charity was not impermissibly earmarked for the composer, and therefore is a charitable contribution. [Emphases added.]

The ruling provides useful information on the correct handling of contributions that suggest or recommend a particular recipient. This issue frequently arises in churches when members want to donate funds for a particular needy person or family or for a student or missionary. In the past the IRS has been adamant that such contributions do not qualify as charitable contributions. This ruling suggests that the IRS may be taking a more flexible approach in such cases if the following conditions exist: (1) The church has control and discretion over the contribution, "unfettered by a commitment or understanding that the contribution would benefit a designated individual." (2) No commitment or understanding exists between a donor and the church that a contribution will benefit a person or persons specified by the donor. (3) The donor understands that any funds contributed to the church would be distributed according to its discretion.

Note that a "commitment or understanding" is not the same as a mere expression of interest in a particular individual. A commitment or

understanding connotes some compulsion on the part of the church to distribute donated funds to a person designated by the donor and, in that sense, removes any control by the church over the funds. As a result, such a donation was not to or for the use of the church. On the other and, mere expressions of interest by the donor do not bind a church to distribute donated funds to the person designated by the donor. Instead, the church is left with the discretion to determine how the donated funds are spent and may completely disregard the donor's expression of interest in a specified individual.

The IRS ruling was a private letter ruling. As such, it cannot be used as precedent in other cases. However, such rulings are commonly viewed by tax attorneys as indications of the thinking of the IRS on specific issues, and in this sense they are relevant.

Conclusions

Consider these few final remarks regarding benevolence funds.

Form 1099-MISC

Does the church need to give the recipient of the benevolence distributions a Form 1099-MISC (if the distributions are $600 or more in any one year)? Ordinarily the answer would be no, since the Form 1099-MISC is issued only to nonemployees who receive *compensation* of $600 or more from the church during the year. *IRS Letter Rulings 9314014, 200113031.* To the extent that benevolence distributions to a particular individual represent a legitimate charitable distribution by the church (consistently with its exempt purposes), no Form 1099-MISC would be required. It would be unrealistic to characterize such distributions as compensation for services rendered when the individual performed no services whatever for the church.

How church treasurers should respond

What should church treasurers do when a member attempts to contribute a check for a specified benevolence recipient and it is clear (on the basis of the above information) that the contribution is not tax-deductible? The best option would be to refuse to accept the check. This is the conclusion reached by the IRS in Publication 3833, which states that "contributors may not earmark funds for the benefit of a particular individual or family." Church treasurers should keep this example in mind when church members want to make contributions to the church for the benefit of a specific needy person or family. Since such contributions are not tax-deductible by the donor, the church should not receive them.

Honoring every donor "recommendation"

If a church routinely honors every "recommendation" made by donors regarding the individual recipient of their contributions, this strongly suggests that the church does not exercise sufficient control over those contributions for them to be treated as charitable contributions. The IRS *Exempt Organizations Continuing Professional Education Technical Instruction Program for 1996* contains the following statement: "In circumstances where the organization is directing all, or close to all, donor contributions to the use of individuals specifically preferred by those donors, a review of the facts should . . . determine whether the organization is in control of the funds. If control is not in the hands of the organization, it may be appropriate to refer the [matter to the IRS national office]."

Reviewing the church charter

If your church has established a benevolence fund, you may wish to review your corporate charter or other organizational documents to be sure that your statement of purposes includes "charitable" as well as "religious" purposes. Some legal precedent suggests that benevolence activities are more properly characterized, for tax purposes, as charity rather than religion.

No impact on nonitemizers

With the significant increase in the standard deduction in recent years, it is estimated that as few as 30 percent of all taxpayers are able to claim itemized deductions (including charitable contributions). As a result, as many as 70 percent of all donors receive no tax benefit from a charitable contribution. These individuals are able to designate contributions (or make direct gifts to needy individuals) without concern for the rules summarized in this section.

Definition of "charity"

Benevolence funds typically are established to assist persons in need. The income tax regulations define "charitable" to include "relief of the poor and distressed or of the underprivileged." The regulations define "needy" as

> *being a person who lacks the necessities of life, involving physical, mental, or emotional well-being, as a result of poverty or temporary distress. Examples of needy persons include a person who is financially impoverished as a result of low income and lack of financial resources, a person who temporarily lacks food or shelter (and the means to provide for it), a person who is the victim of a natural disaster (such as fire or flood), a person who is the victim of a civil disaster (such as civil disturbance), a person who is temporarily not self sufficient as a result of a sudden and severe personal or family crisis (such as a person who is the victim of a crime of violence or who has been physically abused).* Treas. Reg. 1.170A-4A(b)(2)(ii)(D).

The church board should carefully scrutinize every distribution to ensure that the recipient meets this test.

➥ **TIP.** One way to determine whether a person or family is sufficiently needy to qualify for benevolence assistance is to see if they fall below the poverty guidelines published each year by the U.S. Department of Health and Human Services (HHS). For example, the 2012 guidelines define poverty for a family of four as income of less than $23,050 (this amount is higher in Alaska and Hawaii). These guidelines are published on the HHS website. Obviously, a church can make a persuasive case that persons or families below

the federal poverty guidelines are needy and can receive distributions from a church's benevolence fund. However, this conclusion has never been adopted by the IRS or any court.

EXAMPLE. The IRS ruled that employee contributions to a nonprofit hospital's benevolence fund were tax-deductible. The IRS noted that the fund was established to assist financially needy persons who suffer economic hardship due to accident, loss, or disaster. Persons eligible for assistance include current employees of the hospital, retirees, former employees, volunteers, and the spouses and children of such persons. It emphasized that employee contributions did not earmark specific recipients. Rather, all distributions from the fund were made by a committee consisting of employees of the hospital. The committee reviews a potential beneficiary's application to determine the need for emergency financial assistance and the availability of resources in the fund to meet that need.

The IRS concluded that employee contributions to the fund were tax-deductible, since the purpose of the fund was consistent with the hospital's charitable purposes and the class of potential beneficiaries was sufficiently large: "All awards of the fund are payable only after a determination of need in the discretion of the committee. Contributions may not be earmarked and there is no guarantee that funds will even be available for past contributors should they have a need arise and apply to the fund for assistance. Thus, contributions cannot be made to the fund with an expectation of procuring a financial benefit. The fund derives its income from voluntary contributions and no part of its income inures to the benefit of any individual. The class of potential beneficiaries consists of several thousand employees. . . . Such a class of beneficiaries is not so limited in size that the donee organization is considered to benefit specified individuals. Accordingly, we rule that contributions to the fund are deductible as charitable contributions."

The IRS cautioned that the hospital needed to comply with various recordkeeping requirements: "Adequate records and case histories should be maintained to show the name and address of each recipient, the amount distributed to each, the purpose for which the aid was given, the manner in which the recipient was selected and the relationship, if any, between the recipient and members, officers, or trustees of the organization, in order that any or all distributions made to individuals can be substantiated upon request by the IRS." *Revenue Ruling 56-304; see also IRS Letter Ruling 9741047.*

EXAMPLE. The IRS ruled that a donor can deduct contributions to a charitable organization on behalf of needy persons in a foreign country. The organization obtained a list of 5,000 needy families in the foreign country from a social welfare agency in that country. From this list 25 families were randomly selected who were given $50 per month in support payments.

The IRS stated the general rule that "contributions by an individual to a charitable organization that are for the benefit of a designated individual are not deductible under [federal tax law] even though the designated individual may be an appropriate beneficiary for a charitable organization. A gift for the benefit of a specific individual is a private gift, not a charitable gift."

However, the IRS concluded that individual donors could deduct their contributions to the relief fund, since the organization's "selection of beneficiaries is done in a way to assure objectivity and to preclude any influence by individual donors in the selection. Therefore, [the charity] is not acting as a conduit for private gifts from its contributors to other individuals. Accordingly, contributions to [the charity] for the relief of needy families in a foreign country will be deductible by donors under the provisions of section 170 of the tax code." *IRS Letter Ruling 8916041.*

5. SCHOLARSHIP GIFTS

❖**KEY POINT.** The IRS issued a private letter ruling that addresses charitable contributions that designate specific individuals. The ruling provides an exhaustive analysis of the deductibility of designated contributions and makes several helpful clarifications and observations. The ruling is addressed earlier in this section. *IRS Letter Ruling 200530016 (2005).*

Many taxpayers have attempted to claim charitable contribution deductions for payments made to a church-operated private school (or to the church that operates the school) in which the taxpayer's child is enrolled. The IRS has emphasized that a charitable contribution is "a voluntary transfer of money or property that is made with no expectation of procuring a financial benefit commensurate with the amount of the transfer." *Revenue Ruling 83-104.* Therefore, payments made by a taxpayer on behalf of a child attending a church-operated school are not deductible as contributions either to the school or to the church if the payments are earmarked in any way for the child.

The fact that payments are not earmarked for a particular child does not necessarily mean they are deductible. The IRS has held that the deductibility of undesignated payments by a taxpayer to a private school in which his child is enrolled depends upon

> *whether a reasonable person, taking all the facts and circumstances of the case in due account, would conclude that enrollment in the school was in no manner contingent upon making the payment, that the payment was not made pursuant to a plan (whether express or implied) to convert nondeductible tuition into charitable contributions, and that receipt of the benefit was not otherwise dependent upon the making of the payment.* Revenue Ruling 83-104.

In resolving this question, the IRS has stated that the presence of one or more of the following four factors creates a presumption that the payment is not a charitable contribution:

- the existence of a contract under which a taxpayer agrees to make a "contribution" and which contains provisions ensuring the admission of the taxpayer's child,
- a plan allowing taxpayers either to pay tuition or to make "contributions" in exchange for schooling,
- the earmarking of a contribution for the direct benefit of a particular individual, or
- the otherwise unexplained denial of admission or readmission to a school of children of taxpayers who are financially able but who do not contribute. *Revenue Ruling 83-104.*

The IRS has observed that if none of these factors is determinative, a combination of several additional factors may indicate that a payment is not a charitable contribution. Such additional factors include but are not limited to the following: (1) the absence of a significant tuition charge, (2) substantial or unusual pressure to contribute applied to parents of children attending a school, (3) contribution appeals made as part of the admissions or enrollment process, (4) the absence of significant potential sources of revenue for operating the school other than contributions by parents of children attending the school, and (5) other factors suggesting that a contribution policy has been created as a means of avoiding the characterization of payments as tuition. If a combination of such factors is not present, payments by a parent will normally constitute deductible contributions, even if the actual cost of educating the child exceeds the amount of any tuition charged for the child's education.

An income tax regulation further specifies that the term "scholarship" does not include "any amount provided by an individual to aid a relative, friend, or other individual in pursuing his studies where the grantor is motivated by family or philanthropic considerations." *Treas. Reg. 1.117-(3)(a).*

Examples from IRS Ruling 83–104

The IRS has illustrated the application of these principles in the following examples (set forth in Revenue Ruling 83-104):

Situation 1

A school requests parents to contribute a designated amount (e.g., $400) for each child enrolled in the school. Parents who do not make the $400 contribution are required to pay tuition of $400 for each child. Parents who neither make the contribution nor pay the tuition cannot enroll their children in the school. A parent who pays $400 to the school is not entitled to a charitable contribution deduction because the parent must either make the contribution or pay the tuition in order for his child to attend the school. Therefore, admission to the school is contingent upon making a payment of $400. Such a payment is not voluntary.

Situation 2

A school solicits contributions from parents of applicants for admission during the school's solicitation for enrollment of students or while applications are pending. The solicitation materials are part of the application materials or are presented in a form indicating that parents of applicants have been singled out as a class for solicitation. Most parents who are financially able make a contribution or pledge to the school. No tuition is charged. The school suggests that parents make a payment of $400. A parent making a payment of $400 to the school is not entitled to a charitable contribution deduction. Because of the time and manner of the solicitation of contributions by the school, and the fact that no tuition is charged, it is not reasonable to expect that a parent can obtain the admission of his child to the school without making the suggested payments. Such payments are in the nature of tuition, not voluntary contributions.

Situation 3

A school admits a significantly larger percentage of applicants whose parents have made contributions to the school than applicants whose parents have not made contributions. Parents who make payments to the school are not entitled to a charitable contribution deduction. The IRS ordinarily will conclude that the parents of applicants are aware of the preference given to applicants whose parents have made contributions. The IRS therefore ordinarily will conclude that a parent could not reasonably expect to obtain the admission of his child to the school without making the payment.

Situation 4

A society for religious instruction has as its sole function the operation of a private school providing secular and religious education to the children of its members. No tuition is charged. The school is funded through the society's general account. Contributions to the account are solicited from all society members, as well as from local churches and nonmembers. Persons other than parents of children attending the school do not contribute a significant portion of the school's support. Funds normally come to the school from parents on a regular, established schedule. At times, parents are solicited by the school to contribute funds. No student is refused admittance because of the failure of his or her parents to contribute to the school. Under these circumstances, the IRS generally will conclude that payments to the society are nondeductible. Unless contributions from sources other than parents are of such magnitude that the school is not economically dependent upon parents' contributions, parents would ordinarily not be certain that the school could provide educational benefits without their payments. This conclusion is further evidenced by the fact that parents contribute on a regular, established schedule.

Situation 5

A private school charges a tuition of $300 per student. In addition, it solicits contributions from parents of students during periods other than the period of the school's solicitation for student enrollments. Solicitation materials indicate that parents of students have been singled out as a class for solicitation and the solicitation materials include a report of the school's cost per student. Suggested amounts of contributions based on an individual's ability to pay are provided. No unusual pressure to contribute is placed upon individuals who have children in the school, and many parents do not contribute. In addition, the school receives contributions from many former students, parents of former students, and other individuals. A parent pays $100 to the school in addition to the $300 tuition payment. Under these circumstances, the IRS generally will conclude that the parent is entitled to claim a charitable contribution deduction of $100. Because a charitable organization normally solicits contributions from those known to have the greatest interest in the organization, the fact that parents are singled out for a solicitation will not in itself create an inference that future admissions or any other benefits depend upon a contribution from the parent.

Situation 6

A church operates a school providing secular and religious education that is attended both by children of parents who are members of the church and by children of nonmembers. The church receives contributions from all of its members. These contributions are placed in the church's general operating fund and are expended when needed to support church activities. A substantial portion of the other activities is unrelated to the school. Most church members do not have children in the school, and a major portion of the church's expenses are attributable to its nonschool functions. The methods of soliciting contributions from church members with children in the school are the same as the methods of soliciting contributions from members without children in the school. The church has full control over the use of the contributions that it receives. Members who have children enrolled in the school are not required to pay tuition for their children, but tuition is charged for the children of nonmembers. A church member whose child attends the school contributes $200 to the church for its general purposes. The IRS ordinarily will conclude that the parent is allowed a charitable contribution deduction of $200 to the church. Because the facts indicate that the church school is supported by the church, that most contributors to the church are not parents of children enrolled in the school, and that contributions from parent members are solicited in the same manner as contributions from other members, a parent's contributions will be considered charitable contributions, and not payments of tuition, unless there is a showing that the contributions by members with children in the school are significantly larger than those of other members. The absence of a tuition charge is not determinative in view of these facts.

Effect of a recommendation

Can donors recommend or suggest that their contributions be distributed by the church to a named individual? Possibly. The question in each case is whether the church has "full control of the donated funds, and discretion as to their use, so as to ensure that they will be used to carry out its functions and purposes." *Revenue Ruling 62-113.* A number of courts and IRS rulings suggest that this test is compatible with mere recommendations or expressions of interest that accompany donors' contributions. To illustrate, the IRS has ruled that the church must have "control and discretion over the contribution, unfettered by a *commitment or understanding* that the contribution benefit a designated individual" (emphasis added). *IRS Letter Ruling 200250029 (summarized above).* Of course, if every recommendation made by donors is honored by the church, this will call into question the reality of the church's control over the designated contributions. The following cases illustrate that not all contributions accompanied by recommendations will be charitable contributions.

- Students at a religious educational institution had their tuition paid by sponsors. In many cases the sponsor was the student's parent. Each sponsor signed a commitment form that set the contribution amount and payment schedule and indicated the names of the sponsor and the student. Space was also provided on the payment envelopes for the student's name. The commitment form provided that contributions were nonrefundable and that the use of money was "solely at the discretion" of the organization. The IRS denied a charitable contribution deduction because deductibility requires both full control by the organization and the intent by the donor to benefit the charity itself and not a particular recipient. The commitment form and the envelopes indicated that the payments were designated for the benefit of particular students. *IRS Revenue Ruling 79-81 (1979).*
- The IRS rejected a charity's claim that parents' donations were deductible because it exercised sufficient control over the use of the funds. The IRS observed: "The organization's statement in their literature that the disposition of all contributions rests with the board of directors is not sufficient to demonstrate control. In fact, the organization in this case refutes its own statement of control by going on to say that it considers designations by donors as a matter of accountability." *IRS Letter Ruling 9405003.*

The Scientology case

In a 1989 ruling the Supreme Court affirmed that tuition payments made to church or school are not tax-deductible as charitable contributions. The court rejected the Church of Scientology's claim that all contributions for which the donor receives religious benefits and services are automatically deductible. *Hernandez v. Commissioner, 109 S. Ct. 2136 (1989).* It noted that if the church's claim were accepted, the effect would be to

expand the charitable contribution deduction far beyond what Congress has provided. Numerous forms of payments to eligible donees plausibly could be categorized as providing a religious benefit or as securing access to a religious service. For example, some taxpayers might regard their tuition payments to parochial

schools as generating a religious benefit or as securing access to a religious service; such payments, however, have long been held not to be charitable contributions under [federal law]. Taxpayers might make similar claims about payments for church-sponsored counseling sessions or for medical care at church-affiliated hospitals that otherwise might not be deductible.

IRS Letter Ruling 9405003

A religious organization solicits contributions from family members and other interested persons to apply toward the tuition expenses of seminary students. Interested parents and family members send in contributions to the organization on behalf of a designated seminary student, and the organization transfers the funds to the student for his or her seminary expenses (less a nominal administrative fee). Most donors give a certain amount every month for the support of a particular student. Literature published by the organization states:

As with all Christian corporations for which donations qualify for tax-exempt status with the Internal Revenue Service, contributions must be directed to [the organization]. A check should not contain the name of the [student] for whose ministry it is given; instead the student's name should be designated on the envelope or a separate paper. Although the disposition of all contributions rests with the board of directors, [the organization] honors the donor's designation whenever possible. If it is not possible, [the organization] notifies the donor about the situation.

The organization's policy manual states that "because of the nonprofit status of [the organization] the distribution of all contributions rests with the board of directors. However, [the organization] takes donors' designations into account as a matter of accountability and integrity." [Emphases added.]

The organization claimed that donors' contributions for specified students were fully deductible, since the organizations' board of directors reserved final authority to distribute all contributed funds. The IRS disagreed, noting that "an individual taxpayer is entitled to a deduction for charitable contributions or gifts to or for the use of qualified charitable organizations, payment of which is made during the taxable year." It added, "[A] gift is not considered a contribution 'to' a charity if the facts show that the charity is merely a conduit to a particular person." The IRS then quoted from Revenue Ruling 62-113 (quoted above) in which it observed:

If contributions to the fund are earmarked by the donor for a particular individual, they are treated, in effect, as being gifts to the designated individual and are not deductible. However, a deduction will be allowable where it is established that a gift is intended by a donor for the use of the organization and not as a gift to an individual. The test in each case is whether the organization has full control of the donated funds, and discretion as to their use, so as to insure that they will be used to carry out its functions and purposes. In the instant case, the son's receipt of reimbursements from the fund is alone insufficient to require holding that this test is not met. Accordingly, unless the taxpayer's contributions to the fund are distinctly marked by him so that they may be used only for his son or are received by the fund pursuant to a commitment or understanding that they will be so used, they may be deducted by the taxpayer in computing his taxable income.

The IRS concluded that contributions designating seminary students did not satisfy this test:

In the present case, the taxpayers' contributions to [the organization] were earmarked for the student not only through the use of account numbers which link donors to seminarians, but also by indicating the student's name on the contribution envelopes. Further, the organization's literature indicates that it will make every effort to use the contributions as the donor requests "as a matter of accountability and integrity." These facts indicate that the program is set up so that donors would expect that their contributions will go to the designated seminarian. Thus, the donor reasonably intends to benefit the individual recipient. In addition, taxpayers in this case have stated that they would not have made donations to this particular organization if their son had not been associated with it. Taxpayers intended their donations to support their son and expected that their son would receive the contributions they made to the organization. It follows from these facts that the organization does not have full control of the donated funds. Thus, under the standard enunciated by Revenue Ruling 62-113 . . . the contributions made by taxpayers to the organization are not deductible . . . because they not only are earmarked but also are received subject to an understanding that the organization will use the funds as the donors designate and because the taxpayers intended to benefit the designated individual rather than the organization.

The IRS rejected the organization's claim that the parents' donations were deductible because the organization exercised control over their distribution. The IRS observed: "[T]he organization's statement in their literature that the disposition of all contributions rests with the board of directors is not sufficient to demonstrate control. In fact, the organization in this case refutes its own statement of control by going on to say that it considers designations by donors as a matter of accountability."

❈ **KEY POINT.** The IRS concluded that contributions on behalf of specific seminary students were not deductible because (1) the contributions designated a specific student; (2) donors understood that their contributions would benefit the students they designated; and (3) the parents intended to benefit designated children rather than the school. This is a useful test for evaluating the deductibility of contributions to churches and schools that earmark a specific student.

In conclusion, contributions by parents and others that designate a particular student are not deductible, even if the school (or other organization) purports to retain full control over the distribution of those contributions. A mere statement that the school exercises control is not enough.

❈ **KEY POINT.** To be tax-deductible, a charitable contribution must be to or for the use of a charitable organization. Gifts that designate a specific project or fund (building fund, new organ) are tax-deductible, since they clearly are made to a church.

EXAMPLE. A church operates a school and charges annual tuition of $2,000. A parent contributes $2,000 to the school's scholarship fund and specifies that the contribution be used for his child's tuition (who attends the school). This "contribution" is not deductible. The church or school should so inform the parent at the time of the contribution and should decline the check.

EXAMPLE. Same facts as the previous example, except that the donor is a neighbor rather than the student's parent. The result is the same.

EXAMPLE. A church establishes a scholarship fund to assist members who are attending seminary. A parent of a seminary student contributes $5,000 to the fund with the stipulation that the contribution be applied toward her son's seminary tuition. Based on IRS Letter Ruling 9405003, this contribution would not be deductible if the parent understood that her contribution would benefit her son and the parent intended to benefit her son rather than the school. (This can be established by asking the donor whether she would have contributed to the scholarship fund if her son were not a seminary student.)

EXAMPLE. A member contributes $2,000 to a scholarship fund. The donor does not designate any student but leaves the distribution of her contribution to the discretion of the school's scholarship committee. This contribution is tax-deductible.

EXAMPLE. A member contributes $1,000 to a church building fund. This contribution is tax-deductible, since it is to a church rather than to a specific individual.

EXAMPLE. A donor disbursed funds to various college scholarship funds to pay tuition and related educational expenses of certain individual students selected by the colleges. The IRS contended that the payments were, in effect, gifts to individual students rather than deductible charitable contributions. A federal appeals court disagreed and held: "Although [the government] contends that the scholarship awards by [the donor] were, in effect, mere gifts to individual students, the record clearly shows that the payments were made to the state teachers colleges themselves and that [the donor] had no part in the selection of any individual recipient of a scholarship." *Sico Foundation v. United States, 295 F.2d 924 (Ct. Cl. 1961).*

EXAMPLE. A donor made contributions to a college scholarship fund. The first contribution was accompanied by a letter stating, in part: "I am interested in the work that your college is doing and I am enclosing my check for [a stated amount], which as I understand it, represents tuition for one term, plus book requirements. Of late, I have been interested in the career of Mr. Robert Roble, who is a very promising young man in my opinion, and whose family lives close to my summer home. I believe he deserves all the help he can get toward his education. I am aware that a donation to a scholarship fund is only deductible if it is unspecified; however, if in your opinion and that of the authorities, it could be applied to the advantage of Mr. Robert Roble, I think it would be constructive." Subsequent contributions from the donor were marked "scholarship grants for Robert Roble."

A federal appeals court concluded: "It is clear from the record that the [donor] intended to aid Roble in securing an education and that the payments to the college were earmarked for that purpose. . . . If a scholarship was involved, it was one the [donor], not the college, awarded Roble. . . . [The donor's payments] were for the sole benefit of one specified person, Robert Roble, rather than gifts to the college for the benefit of an indefinite number of persons. . . . The payments made were not to a general scholarship fund to be used as the college saw fit, but were to be applied to the educational expenses of Roble. . . . A contribution to an individual, no matter how worthy, does not qualify as a charitable deduction." *Tripp v. Commissioner, 337 F.2d 432 (7th Cir. 1964).*

EXAMPLE. In 1968 the IRS approved a charitable contribution deduction for a corporation under the following facts:

The corporation is a large employer that obtains its trained employees principally from graduates of accredited colleges and other educational institutions. To assure an adequate supply of trained young people who may seek employment with the corporation and to respond in a charitable manner to the financial needs of such educational institutions, the corporation established a program for advancement of higher education.

Under the program, amounts were made available to private and public educational institutions for their use in providing individuals with scholarships. The selection of these institutions was made on the following basis: (1) at least one scholarship was made available to each private institution that currently had 20 or more graduates employed by the corporation, and (2) further scholarships were made available to those public institutions from which the corporation drew a substantial number of graduates.

No one institution was awarded more than five scholarships. Each educational institution involved selected the recipients of the scholarships. Upon a determination of the amount of each scholarship, based on the need of the recipient, payment was made to the educational institution, which in turn made disbursements therefrom to or for the account of each student.

Also, under this program, the corporation made grants-in-aid to private institutions in the form of unrestricted funds, the amounts of which were equivalent to the regular tuition charges made by the institutions for students. The recipients of the scholarships were not connected with the corporation in any manner, and the educational benefits they derived from the corporation's expenditures could be utilized by them as they chose, free of any present or future obligations to the corporation. And, in turn, the corporation was free of any responsibility to offer employment to the students who derived these benefits. *Revenue Ruling 68-484.*

EXAMPLE. A donor contributed funds to the college scholarship funds at the colleges in which his son and daughter-in-law were enrolled. The contributions designated the donor's son and daughter-in-law as the intended recipients. The Tax Court, in denying the deductibility of these payments, observed: "The amounts paid to [the two colleges] were distributed by these institutions as scholarships to individuals specifically designated by [the donor] including [his] son and daughter-in-law. The payments were, in effect, tuition payments for specifically designated beneficiaries, and as such are nondeductible personal expenses." *Lloyd v. Commissioner, T.C. Memo. 1970-95.*

EXAMPLE. A prominent donor (who served in the state legislature) established a scholarship fund for the benefit of students in his district. Each year one senior student from each high school was selected by the high-school principal on the basis of need and scholastic merit to receive proceeds from the scholarship fund. The donor did not participate in the selection of students to receive scholarships. Each check drawn on the scholarship fund was signed by the donor and made payable to a student and a college or university as joint payees. The donor claimed these payments as a deduction for charitable contributions.

The IRS denied a charitable contribution deduction for these payments. It claimed that deductions should be disallowed because the identity of the recipient of the scholarship was made known to the donor prior to the time the funds were disbursed.

A federal district court rejected the IRS position and ruled that the donor was entitled to claim a charitable contribution deduction for his payments. The court observed: "I am unwilling to place the ultra-technical interpretation on Section 170 of the Internal Revenue Code which is urged upon us by the Government. Under the facts presented here, the [donor] had no voice in the selection of the individuals who would benefit from the scholarship donations; [the donor] instructed the principals of

CHARITABLE CONTRIBUTIONS EARMARKED FOR AN INDIVIDUAL

In 2012 a member of Congress asked the IRS for an opinion regarding a question submitted by a constituent. The question was whether contributions to a church's scholarship fund are tax-deductible if the donor suggests that the church use the contributions to pay for the college tuition costs of the pastor's daughter. The IRS responded as follows:

> *An individual can take a deduction for a charitable contribution or gift to or for the use of a charitable organization, including a church. . . . However, if a donor earmarks the contribution to a particular individual, the donor must treat it as being a gift to the designated individual and not as a tax-deductible contribution. Various courts have ruled that contributions to a church fund for missionaries are not deductible if there is a commitment or understanding that the church will use the contributions only for a particular individual. The law allows a deduction only if the church has full control of the donated funds and discretion as to their use.*

the various high schools to select a student based upon need and merit. Any contributions which flow into a scholarship program result in benefit to both the educational institution and the individual recipients of those scholarships. No reason or authority is presented which would lead me to the conclusion that benefit by an individual scholarship recipient should defeat the deductibility of the gift; notwithstanding benefit by the individual student, the gift is nevertheless 'for the use of' an exempt entity. . . . The fact that the checks were made to the joint order of the student and the college or university is not inconsistent with plaintiffs' intention to further the educational purposes of the high schools and colleges in question." *Bauer v. United States, 449 F. Supp. 755 (W.D. La. 1978).*

EXAMPLE. Students at a religious educational institution had their tuition paid by sponsors. In many cases the sponsor was the student's parent. Each sponsor signed a commitment form that set the contribution amount and payment schedule and indicated the names of the sponsor and the student. Space was also provided on the payment envelopes for the student's name. The commitment form provided that contributions were non-refundable and that the use of money was "solely at the discretion" of the organization. The IRS denied a charitable contribution deduction because deductibility requires both full control by the organization and the intent by the donor to benefit the

charity itself and not a particular recipient. The commitment form and the envelopes indicated that the payments were designated for the benefit of particular students. *IRS Revenue Ruling 79-81 (1979).*

EXAMPLE. A donor established a scholarship fund with a large gift from his estate, with the stipulation that scholarships would be distributed to persons who bore the donor's family name and attended either of two specified colleges who bore the donor's family name. The IRS concluded that the scholarship gift was not tax-deductible as a charitable contribution, since it did not benefit a large and indefinite class (as is required of a charitable distribution). Rather, "the class of beneficiaries . . . is necessarily limited to a private class of persons." This ruling will be relevant to those churches that have created scholarship funds for designated students (such as church members attending seminary). The smaller the pool of eligible recipients, the more likely that any contributions to the scholarship fund will be deemed nondeductible by the IRS, since they will be seen as benefiting a private class of persons rather than serving a public and charitable purpose by designating a large and indefinite class of potential recipients. *IRS Letter Ruling 9631004.*

EXAMPLE. In 1999 the IRS released an internal memorandum (a "field service advisory") addressing the question of whether parents can claim a charitable contribution deduction for tuition payments they make for their children who attend an Orthodox Jewish school. The parents cited the following facts in supporting their claim that tuition payments they made on behalf of their children were deductible as charitable contributions:

(1) The act of religious study for Orthodox Jews is an observance of their religion that begins at an early age and continues for life. As a result, tuition payments they make to Jewish religious schools are in furtherance of this religious function and are deductible as charitable contributions.

(2) For the Orthodox Jew the obligation to study the Torah and the Talmud is a matter of duty and adherence to Jewish law, a lifelong commitment ranking aside the obligation to pray. The observance of such duties primarily benefits the community, not the individual.

(3) The primary purpose of Jewish schools is religious study. A significant portion of a student's time at a Jewish school is devoted to religious study.

(4) The payment of tuition to Jewish religious schools yields only an incidental benefit to the parent and a direct benefit to the Jewish people, who have had their religion preserved for thousands of years through careful adherence to the study of Judaism by members of the faith.

The IRS rejected all of the parents' arguments and concluded that the tuition payments were not deductible as charitable contributions. It observed that the parents in this case "are required to make specific payments in return for which they receive a benefit—religious and secular education for their children. Under the rationale postulated in Hernandez [discussed above], the parents are not entitled to a charitable contribution deduction for tuition payments made to Jewish religious schools." *FSA 9999-9999-201.*

EXAMPLE. A federal appeals court rejected a married couple's claim that they could deduct 55 percent of the cost of their son's tuition at a religious school because religious instruction comprised 55 percent of the curriculum and constituted an "intangible religious benefit" that did not reduce the value of their charitable contribution.

The court concluded, "Not only has the Supreme Court held that, generally, a payment for which one receives consideration does not constitute a contribution or gift . . . but it has explicitly rejected the contention . . . that there is an exception for payments for which one receives only religious benefits in return."

The parents also argued that they could claim a charitable contribution deduction for the amount by which their tuition payments exceeded the market value of their son's education. They claimed that the value of the education their son received was zero, since the cost of an education at a public school was "free," and therefore they could fully deduct the cost of their son's tuition, since the entire amount exceeded the "value" of the education received.

The court disagreed, noting that the value of their son's education was the cost of a comparable secular education offered by private schools. Further, the court noted that the parents presented no evidence of the tuition that private schools charge for a comparable secular education, so there was no evidence showing that they made an excess payment that might qualify for a tax deduction. *Sklar v. Commissioner, 2002-1 USTC 50,210 (9th Cir. 2002). See also Sklar v. Commissioner, 2008 WL 5192051 (9th Cir. 2008).*

EXAMPLE. Church members made contributions to their church as part of a scheme to deduct tuition payments made to private schools their children were attending. Members contributed to the church an amount equal to or exceeding the amount of their child's tuition at a private school unrelated to the church. The school billed the church for the tuition, and the church paid it. At the end of the year, the church provided a receipt to the members, reflecting their total contributions for the year without any reduction for tuition the church paid. The receipt also stated that the member had received nothing in exchange for the contributions except intangible religious benefits.

The IRS classified this arrangement as a "disguised tuition payment program" that triggered tax penalties for aiding and abetting

the understatement of tax ($1,000 for each person receiving a contribution statement per year) and an additional penalty of $10 for each quid pro quo contribution for which the church failed to provide a written receipt complying with the quid pro quo substantiation requirements (addressed in Chapter 8). *IRS Private Letter Ruling 200623063.*

EXAMPLE. A married couple paid for their son's tuition at a church-affiliated university and claimed the full amount as a charitable contribution deduction on their tax return. The IRS denied the deduction, and the couple appealed to the United States Tax Court. The court agreed with the IRS that the couple could not deduct the tuition payments as a charitable contribution. It concluded: "In order for petitioners to be entitled to a charitable contribution deduction . . . for the payment made to the university, they must show the extent to which the tuition payment exceeds the market value of their son's education and that the excess payment was made with the intention of making a gift. They have failed to establish that the amount paid to the university exceeded the market value of the education received by their son so as to take on the dual character of both a tuition payment and a charitable contribution. . . . Therefore, petitioners are not entitled to a charitable contribution deduction for their son's tuition." *Reece v. Commissioner, T.C. Summary Opinion 2009-59.*

Tax benefits for parents with children in college
Congress has enacted several tax benefits to assist individuals and families with the cost of higher education. See Chapter 7, section I.4.

Church-established scholarship funds
Many churches have established scholarship funds to provide financial assistance to members or their children who are attending college or seminary. Can parents deduct contributions they make to these funds if their child is a potential beneficiary? To illustrate, assume that a church establishes a scholarship fund to provide scholarships to church members who are attending seminary. In 2013 only one member is attending a seminary, and his parents contribute $10,000 to the scholarship fund. While their contribution is undesignated, it is clear that their son will be the sole beneficiary of their contribution, so it is not tax-deductible. Would it make a difference if ten members were attending the seminary?

In order to be tax-deductible as a charitable contribution, a gift to a church or charity must benefit an indefinite class of beneficiaries. Whether undesignated gifts to a scholarship fund are deductible will depend on the number of potential beneficiaries. The more the better, since you have to prove that the class of potential beneficiaries is indefinite. Frankly, this test is not met when only a few potential candidates exist. The problem is that parents of these students, in effect, get to deduct a substantial portion of their contributions to the fund. At some point, however, the number of potential beneficiaries is sufficiently large to allow a deduction.

Church leaders should consider this test in evaluating the deductibility of undesignated contributions by parents to a church-established scholarship fund: the probability of the deductibility of such a gift equals the number of potential recipients. So, if a church adopts a scholarship fund to benefit seminary students and it has 2 students attending seminary, the probability of an undesignated gift to the scholarship fund being tax-deductible would be 2 percent. If 15 students are potential recipients, the probability rises to 15 percent. This test has never been endorsed by the IRS or a court, but it does illustrate an important point: churches should not treat contributions to scholarship funds as tax-deductible unless a significant number of potential recipients exists that comprise a charitable class.

Conclusions

Be sure to review the conclusions at the end of the subsection on designated benevolence contributions (section B.4, above).

6. GIFTS THAT DESIGNATE MINISTERS

Designated gifts to ministers can occur in various ways. For example, churches often collect an offering to honor a minister on a birthday or anniversary, at Christmas, or on another special occasion. Sometimes members make gifts directly to a minister on such occasions. The deductibility of such contributions is discussed in Chapter 4, sections B.2 and B.3, and Chapter 10, section D.

It is also fairly common for individuals to attempt to supplement a minister's compensation by making contributions to a church that are designated for the benefit of a particular minister. To illustrate, assume that Pastor R is a church's youth pastor, that his annual compensation from the church is $20,000, and that his parents (who live in another state) want to supplement his income. As a result, they send $5,000 to the church earmarked for their son, which is paid by the church to Pastor R in addition to his stated salary of $20,000. This contribution is not tax-deductible by the parents, since it clearly was their intent to benefit their son. The church acted simply as an intermediary through which the gift was funneled (in many cases, in an attempt to obtain a charitable contribution deduction).

But what if the church informed the parents that their $5,000 gift would be applied to reducing the church's obligation to pay a $20,000 salary? In other words, if the parents understand that their $5,000 gift will be applied toward the church's commitment to pay a $20,000 salary (leaving the church with an obligation of $15,000), does this make a difference? Does relieving the church of $5,000 of its $20,000 obligation warrant a charitable contribution deduction?

This question was addressed directly by the Tax Court in a 1975 decision. *Davenport v. Commissioner, 34 T.C.M. 1585 (1975).* A couple paid $100 per month toward the housing expenses of their minister son and claimed a charitable contribution deduction for all of their payments. They argued that their payments were tax-deductible, since they were relieving the church of an obligation to provide housing (or a housing allowance) for their son. In denying any charitable contribution deduction to the parents for their monthly payments, the court observed: "The cases are clear that the criteria for determining whether an amount is a charitable contribution is not whether the payment which is not made directly to the charity might incidentally relieve the charity of some cost but rather whether the payment is such that the contribution is 'for the use of' the charity in a meaning similar to 'in trust for.'"

The court referred to an earlier decision in which it denied a charitable contribution deduction for a payment made by a taxpayer directly to an educational institution for the education and maintenance of a child who was a ward of the Illinois Children's Home. *Thomason v. Commissioner, 2 T.C. 441 (1943).* In the prior case the taxpayer had contended that since the Illinois Children's Home would have had to pay for the education and maintenance of this boy had he not done so, his payments were payments "for the use of" that charity and should be tax-deductible. In holding that the amount paid by the taxpayer in the *Thomason* case to the educational institution was not a charitable contribution, the court observed that these payments were earmarked "from the beginning not for a group or class of individuals, not to be used in any manner seen fit by the home, but for the use of a single individual" in whom the taxpayer "felt a keen fatherly and personal interest." The court further observed that "charity begins where certainty in beneficiaries ends," quoting from a Supreme Court case which held that the uncertainty of the objects of the donation is an essential element of charity. After reviewing this precedent, the court concluded:

> *Here, whether the [church] would have chosen to maintain a house . . . for the use of [the taxpayer's] son and his family as living quarters . . . is not shown by this record. It may have been that had the taxpayer paid the [$100 per month] directly to the church, that organization would have chosen to use the funds otherwise. . . . However, even were there something in this record to indicate that the church would have rented a house for the use of the taxpayer's son . . . it would not follow that the deduction would be allowable since by making the payments directly to the landlord the taxpayer took away the option of the church with respect to its use of the funds. As we have pointed out in several cases, the charity must have full control of the funds donated in order for a taxpayer to be entitled to a charitable deduction, and such is not the situation where the funds are designated by the donor for the use of a particular individual. In the instant case, in our view the evidence as a whole shows that it was the taxpayer's intent to benefit his son by insuring that his son had a place to live with his family. . . . Under these circumstances the payments were for the use or benefit of a particular individual, the taxpayer's son, and therefore are not charitable deductible contributions even though incidentally the payments . . . may have relieved the church of the necessity of paying for a place for the taxpayer's son to live.*

Be sure to review the conclusions at the end of the subsection on designated benevolence contributions (section B.4, above).

7. ENFORCING DESIGNATED CONTRIBUTIONS

It is common for donors to make gifts to a church that designate a specific purpose. For example, donors frequently donate funds or property to a church's building fund, missions fund, benevolence fund, or a similar project. In some cases a church does not honor a donor's designation. Does a donor have a legal right to enforce a designated gift if the church ignores the designation? Few courts have addressed this important question, so authoritative legal guidance is sparse. The leading cases and key conclusions are summarized below.

✸ **KEY POINT.** This section does not address transfers of money or property to a church that are not valid charitable contributions. For example, a "donation" of funds to a church with the stipulation that it must be used for a specified needy person or student is not a charitable contribution and should not be accepted by a church. As a result, the questions addressed in this section do not apply.

The definition of "gift" and the requirement of "standing"

Understanding the legal authority of a donor to enforce the terms of a completed gift to charity requires an understanding of two important concepts: (1) the distinction between "gifts" and charitable trusts and (2) the legal requirement of standing.

Gifts and charitable trusts

The first issue to resolve in deciding if a donor has the legal authority to enforce a designated contribution to a church is whether the contribution constitutes a gift or charitable trust. Understanding this distinction is crucial, since donors generally can enforce charitable trusts but not outright gifts. What, then, is the difference between a gift and a charitable trust?

A gift is a transfer of the donor's entire interest in the donated property. As one court explained, "A gift is a voluntary, gratuitous transfer of property by one to another where the donor manifests an intent to make such a gift and absolutely and irrevocably delivers the property to the donee. Moreover to prove a gift it must be shown that the donor has relinquished all present and future dominion and power over the subject matter of the gift." *In re Marriage of Simmons, 409 N.E.2d 321 (Ill. App. 1980).*

According to this definition, a donor whose designated contribution to a church constitutes a gift lacks the legal authority to enforce it, since he or she has "relinquished all present and future dominion and power" over the contribution.

On the other hand, a contribution that is made *in trust* to a church or charity for a specified purpose is a charitable trust. The church or charity holds the contribution as a trustee and must ensure that the donor's specified purpose is honored. The church or charity has no authority to apply the contributed funds or property for a purpose other than what was specified by the donor in creating the trust. One court explained the distinction between gifts and charitable trusts as follows: "We note the difference between an absolute devise or gift and one in trust to a charitable institution. In the former, the property becomes an asset of the corporation to be used in such manner as the corporation deemed best, while in the latter, the property is held by the corporation, not as its own, but in the capacity as a trustee, or as an instrumentality of the [donor] in carrying out the directions."

Are designated contributions to churches gifts that the donors no longer can enforce, or are they charitable trusts that are enforceable? A leading authority on trust law answered this question as follows: "The court will examine carefully all the clauses of the instrument and the situation of the parties in order to decide whether the phrases used were intended to be binding upon the donee and to make him trustee for charity, or whether he was to be an absolute owner with only moral obligations by reason of the suggestions or requests from the donor as to the use of the property given." *Bogert, The Law of Trusts and Trustees § 324.*

One court has noted that "the mere statement in a will of the purpose for which the property is to be used does not create a trust." On the other hand, "as a general proposition charitable trusts are favored by the law." *St. Mary's Medical Center v. McCarthy, 829 N.E.2d 1068 (Ind. App. 2005).*

To summarize, if a designated contribution to a church is a gift, then the church is free to use the contributed funds or property in any manner it chooses, and neither the donor nor anyone else has the legal authority to enforce the original designation. On the other hand, if a designated contribution is deemed to be a charitable trust, then the designation is enforceable. Clearly, this distinction is critical when addressing the enforceability of a designated contribution. Unfortunately, in many cases it is not an easy task to decide whether a contribution is a gift or a charitable trust. Some of the leading cases to address this distinction are summarized below.

EXAMPLE. A woman executed a will in which she left a portion of her estate "to the Chattowah Open Land Trust, Inc., for qualified conservation purposes." The Georgia Supreme Court ruled that this language created a charitable trust that was legally enforceable: "This devise of property reflects all of the composite elements of an express trust: (1) an intention by a [donor] to create a trust; (2) a trust property; (3) a beneficiary; (4) a trustee; and (5) active duties imposed upon a trustee. Decedent devised her property to Chattowah to use for conservation purposes for the benefit of the public. Decedent placed active duties on the trustee to maintain the property in perpetuity. . . . Therefore, the probate court did not err in its finding that decedent's will unambiguously created a charitable trust. Chattowah's argument that the will failed to use the terms 'trust' and 'trustee' does not alter this outcome, as the strict use of these terms is not required to establish a trust." *Chattowah Open Land Trust, Inc. v. Jones, 636 S.E.2d 523 Ga. 2006).*

EXAMPLE. A gift to the Bible Institute Colportage Association of Chicago "to be used in the publication and dissemination of evangelical Christian literature in harmony with its Articles of Incorporation" created a charitable trust that was for the benefit of those who might receive the literature and was binding on the Association's successor as trustee of the bequeathed assets. One of the court's judges filed a concurring opinion in which he noted that the court's decision seemed to conflict with the established rule that a mere statement in a will of an intended purpose for a gift to charity does not convert the gift into a charitable trust. *Bible Institute Colportage Association v. St. Joseph Bank & Trust Co., 75 N.E.2d 666 (Ind. App. 1947).*

EXAMPLE. A donor's will bequeathed assets to the Methodist Church "to the Northwestern Branch of the Women's Foreign Missionary Society to be used for China, India and Africa." A court concluded that this was "a gift absolute without restrictions as to use" and did not create a charitable trust. *Stockton v. Northwestern Branch of Women's Foreign Missionary Society of the Methodist Episcopal Church, 133 N.E.2d 877 (Ind. App. 1956).*

EXAMPLE. An Indiana court addressed the important question of whether a designated gift to charity is legally enforceable, and under the facts presented concluded that a designated gift was not enforceable by an heir of the original donor. In 1950 a woman executed a last will and testament that bequeathed $250,000 to a hospital for the construction of a chapel. Following the donor's death, a chapel was constructed. It contained a plaque noting that it was a memorial to the donor. In 2003 the hospital decided that it would be necessary to expand its facilities and that such expansion would require demolition of the chapel. In 2004 the hospital took steps to dismantle the chapel, including removing the stained-glass windows. A descendant of the donor asked a court to block the demolition of the chapel. A trial court issued an order permanently enjoining the hospital from destroying the chapel and ordering it to restore the chapel to its original condition. The hospital appealed.

The appeals court began its opinion by making a distinction between "an absolute gift and one in trust to a charitable institution. In the former, the property becomes an asset of the corporation to be used in such manner as the corporation deemed best, while in the latter, the property is held by the corporation, not as its own, but in the capacity as a trustee." The court noted that the question of whether the language of a will or other document "was intended to create a charitable trust, binding on the recipient, has been litigated in a number of cases." In answering this question, a court must "examine carefully all the clauses of the instrument and the situation of the parties in order to decide whether the phrases used were intended to be binding upon the charity . . . or whether it was to be an absolute owner with only moral obligations by reason of the suggestions or requests from the donor as to the use of the property given."

The court stressed that "the mere statement in a will of the purpose for which the property is to be used does not create a trust." On the other hand, "as a general proposition charitable trusts are favored by the law."

Did the donor in this case intend to make an outright gift to the hospital, subject to its full discretion and control? Or did she intend to create a perpetual charitable trust that was beyond the power of the hospital to change? The court concluded that there was no question that the donor intended to make a charitable gift of some kind to the hospital. The donor's purpose (funding a chapel) "was met when the chapel was constructed and a plaque memorializing the donor was placed there." Further, "the general rule is that the mere statement of the purpose for a charitable gift does not transform it into a charitable trust." Beyond that, the donor's will "says nothing as to how long the memorial had to exist in order for it to be valid, or what would happen should [the hospital] no longer want the chapel before the end of its useful life." In further support of its conclusion that the donor had not created a perpetual charitable trust, the court noted that the donor's will had been drafted by an experienced attorney who knew how to create a perpetual trust if this had been the donor's desire.

The donor's heir claimed that whenever a designated gift is made to a charity, the charity holds the property subject to a "condition subsequent," meaning that the gift is revoked if the charity uses the property for some other purpose. Once again, the court disagreed: "Although no definite or particular form of expression is absolutely essential to the creation of a condition subsequent, it must be manifest from the terms of the will that the gift was made on condition and the absence of the words usually used for such purpose is significant. Conditions subsequent are not favored in law and always receive a strict construction. A condition subsequent will not be implied from a mere declaration in the deed that the gift is made for a special purpose." The court quoted from a leading treatise on the law of trusts: "The clear majority rule is that nothing short of express provisions for forfeiture and either a reverter, a gift over or a right to retake the property in the donor or his heirs would enable a donor to effectively impose a condition subsequent." The court noted that the donor's will in this case "contained nothing to indicate the required duration of the [chapel]. . . . The will also contains no reverter language to indicate what should happen to the chapel, or the funds used to build it, if the hospital no longer wanted the chapel on its premises. . . . When the language of an instrument does not clearly indicate the grantor's intention that the property is to revert to him in the event it is diverted from the declared use, the instrument does not operate as a restraint upon alienation of the property, but merely expresses the grantor's confidence that the grantee will use the property so far as may be reasonable and practicable to effect the purpose of the grant."

The court concluded by noting that the donor's gift in fact had been used to construct a chapel that had been used continuously for nearly 50 years and that "although charitable gifts should be encouraged so far as possible, charities themselves should not be bound to one particular use of bequeathed property for multiple generations unless they are on clear notice that such is a requirement of the bequest." *St. Mary's Medical Center v. McCarthy, 829 N.E.2d 1068 (Ind. App. 2005).*

EXAMPLE. A woman executed a will that left most of her estate to "be held in trust by the Board of Managers of the Foreign Missionary Society of the Methodist Episcopal Church of the United States of America for the following purposes: After all my debts, bequests, and provision for my burial, etc., be paid, that sufficient funds be used to educate as Bible readers in India six girls . . . the money remaining after that set aside for the education of the aforesaid Bible readers to be applied to the purchase of a building to be used for the education of girls in India." A Maryland court concluded: "We say that this will creates no trust, because none was intended to be created; and the evidence that none was intended to be created is furnished by the fact that the gift, whatever the language used in making it, was to a corporation capable of taking [donations] for its purposes, some of which purposes are precisely those indicated in the will as the ones to which the funds were to be devoted. The gift is, therefore, not to the society in trust, but to it for its legitimate corporate uses, and is free from restrictions other than the conditions that have been indicated." *Women's Foreign Missionary Society of the Methodist Episcopal Church v. Mitchell, 44 A. 737 (Md. 1901).*

EXAMPLE. A church member's will left the balance of his estate as follows: "I give to my executor, Oren D. Becker, the remainder and residue of my estate to hold in trust, to be invested by him and used to perpetuate my name and interest in Hawes Methodist Episcopal Church and to assist needy and worthy causes and persons as he understands my wishes and practice to be when living, and at his death if there be still a residue or remainder of my estate, it shall go to the Elizabeth Gamble Deaconess Home Association." The Ohio Supreme Court ruled that the will created a valid charitable trust that was legally enforceable. The court concluded: "To my mind there was first created by this will a valid charitable trust for the benefit of the Hawes Methodist Episcopal Church, and this direct bequest to the Hawes Methodist Episcopal Church was clear, unambiguous, and enforceable in a court of equity. This state is committed to the universal doctrine that charitable trusts should be liberally construed to carry out the intentions of the testator in the creation and execution of a charitable trust, and that where there is no uncertainty in trustee, beneficiary or object, or manner of execution, a court of equity will not permit the same to fail." *Becker v. Fisher, 147 N.E. 744 (Ohio 1925).*

EXAMPLE. A donor's will bequeathed his house to his church "to be used as a parsonage." An Ohio court concluded that this language did not transfer the home in trust to the church for charitable purposes, and the church received unrestricted title to the property and could sell it rather than using it as a parsonage. *First Presbyterian Church v. Tarr, 26 N.E.2d 597 (Ohio 1939).*

Requirement of standing

A fundamental requirement in any lawsuit is that the plaintiff have "standing." Standing means that the plaintiff has suffered an injury to a legally protected interest that can be redressed by a civil court. Since no gift occurs unless a donor absolutely and irrevocably transfers title, dominion, and control over the gift to the donee, it follows that donors have no legal interest to protect when their designated gifts to charity are not honored. To illustrate, in a frequently cited case, the Supreme Court of Connecticut observed: "At common law, a donor who has made a completed charitable contribution, whether as an absolute gift or in trust, had no standing to bring an action to enforce the terms of his or her gift or trust unless he or she had expressly reserved the right to do so." *Carl J. Herzog Foundation, Inc. v. University of Bridgeport, 699 A.2d 995 (Conn. 1997).*

How can a donor who has made a designated contribution to a church sue to enforce the designation when a charitable contribution, by definition, is a transfer of *all* of the donor's interest in the donated funds or property to the church? Standing poses a significant legal barrier to any donor who is considering litigation as a means of enforcing the terms of a designated gift.

One judge aptly observed: "In considering the subject of standing, I begin with the observation that, when a charitable gift is made, without any provision for a reversion of the gift to the donor or his heirs, the interest of the donor and his heirs is permanently excluded." *Smithers v. St. Luke's-Roosevelt Hospital Center, 723 N.Y.S.2d 426 (2001) (Judge Friedman, dissenting).* This judge quoted from a leading treatise on trust law:

> *There is no property interest left in the [donor] or his heirs, devises, next of kin, or legatees. The donor or his successors may have a sentimental interest in seeing that his wishes are respected, but no financial [interest] which the law recognizes . . . and hence neither he nor they are as a general rule permitted to sue the trustees to compel them to carry out the trust. . . . The better reasoned cases refuse to permit the donor during his lifetime, or his successors after his death, to sue*

merely as donor or successors to compel the execution of the charitable trust. Bogert, Trusts and Trustees, § 415.

The traditional view: no donor enforcement

Section 391 of the *Restatement (Second) of Trusts*, a respected legal treatise that has been adopted in many states, specifies that donors or their heirs may not enforce the terms of a charitable gift: "A suit can be maintained for the enforcement of a charitable trust by the attorney general or other public officer, *or by a co-trustee, or by a person who has a special interest in the enforcement of the charitable trust,* but not by persons who have no special interest or by the [donor] or his heirs, personal representatives or next of kin."

Several courts have concluded that donors lack the legal authority to enforce a designated gift to charity, usually on the basis of one or both of the two principles described above (the definition of a "gift," or a lack of standing). The leading cases are summarized below.

Carl J. Herzog Foundation, Inc. v. University of Bridgeport, 699 A.2d 995 (Conn. 1997)

A charitable foundation (the "donor") made a gift of $250,000 to a university "to provide need-based merit scholarship aid to disadvantaged students for medical related education." A few years later, the university informed the donor that it no longer was using the funds for the specified purpose. The donor sued the university to enforce the terms of the gift. The Connecticut Supreme Court conducted a thorough analysis of the laws and judicial precedent of all 50 states, concluding that donors do not have standing to enforce their completed gifts. The donor insisted that it had standing because the university's decision to discontinue using the donated funds pursuant to the terms of the gift constituted an injury that a court could redress. The donor also claimed that the Uniform Management of Institutional Funds Act (UMIFA) conferred standing on donors to enforce the terms of completed gifts even if no such right was reserved in a gift instrument. UMIFA, which was adopted by most states, provided the boards and trustees of charitable organizations with guidance in handling perpetual endowment funds. It has been replaced in most states by the Uniform Prudent Management of Institutional Funds Act (UPMIFA).

UMIFA provided that "with the written consent of the donor, the governing board may release, in whole or in part, a restriction imposed by the applicable gift instrument on the use or investment of an institutional fund." The donor insisted that it would be illogical for UMIFA to provide for written consent by a donor to change a restriction and then deny that donor access to the courts to complain of a change without such consent. In other words, UMIFA implicitly conferred standing on donors. The Connecticut Supreme Court disagreed, noting that the drafters of UMIFA, in an official comment, stated that "the donor has no right to enforce the restriction, no interest in the fund and no power to change the beneficiary

of the fund. He may only acquiesce in a lessening of a restriction already in effect." *UMIFA, § 7, comment.* The court noted that this comment regarding the power of a donor to enforce restrictions on a charitable gift

arose in the context of debate concerning the creation of potential adverse tax consequences for donors, if UMIFA was interpreted to provide donors with control over their gift property after the completion of the gift. Pursuant to section 170 of the [federal tax code, quoted above] an income tax deduction for a charitable contribution is disallowed unless the taxpayer has permanently surrendered dominion and control over the property or funds in question. Where there is a possibility not so remote as to be negligible that the charitable gift subject to a condition might fail, the tax deduction is disallowed. The drafters of UMIFA worked closely with an impressive group of professionals, including tax advisers, who were concerned with the federal tax implications of the proposed Act. The drafters' principal concern in this regard was that the matter of donor restrictions not affect the donor's charitable contribution deduction for the purposes of federal income taxation. In other words, the concern was that the donor not be so tethered to the charitable gift through the control of restrictions in the gift that the donor would not be entitled to claim a federal charitable contribution exemption for the gift. IRC § 170(a), Treas. Reg. § 1.170A-1(c).

In resolving these concerns, the drafters of UMIFA clearly stated their position in the commentary. "No federal tax problems for the donor are anticipated by permitting release of a restriction. The donor has no right to enforce the restriction, no interest in the fund and no power to change the eleemosynary beneficiary of the fund. He may only acquiesce in a lessening of a restriction already in effect." . . . Indeed, it would have been anomalous for the drafters of UMIFA to strive to assist charitable institutions by creating smoother procedural avenues for the release of restrictions while simultaneously establishing standing for a new class of litigants, donors, who would defeat this very purpose by virtue of the potential of lengthy and complicated litigation.

This ruling directly acknowledges that the deductibility of a charitable contribution would be jeopardized if donors were legally capable of suing to enforce the terms of their completed gifts.

Russell v. Yale University, 737 A.2d 941 (Conn. App. 1999)

A graduate of Yale University died in 1918, leaving a substantial sum of money in trust for the erection of a building that would constitute a fitting memorial reflecting his gratitude and affection for his alma mater. The trustees were given broad discretion in the disposition of these funds. In 1930 the trustees voted to contribute money for the erection of the divinity school quadrangle. The divinity school is one of Yale's graduate professional schools, which educates men and women for the ministry and provides theological education for persons engaged in other professions. In 1996, as a result of a comprehensive study, the university decided to demolish large portions of the divinity school quadrangle. The trustees took exception to this proposal and asked a court to block it on the grounds that it violated the terms of the trust. Relying on the *Herzog* case (summarized above) a Connecticut appellate court concluded that the trustees lacked standing to enforce the terms of the trust: "Although the plaintiffs are sincere in their efforts to maintain the divinity school as a leader in theological education and preparation for the Christian ministry and they acted in good faith based on motives that are beyond question, the plaintiffs, as a matter of law, lack standing to adjudicate the equitable remedies they seek."

Amundson v. Kletzing-McLaughlin Memorial Foundation College, 73N.W.2d 114 (Iowa 1955)

The Iowa Supreme Court ruled that "where the donor has effectually passed out of himself all interest in the fund devoted to a charity, neither he, nor those claiming under him, have any standing in a court of equity as to its disposition and control."

Enforcement by state attorneys general

❂ **KEY POINT.** The Uniform Prudent Management of Institutional Funds Act (summarized above) states that "in all types of modification [to donor-designated charitable contributions] the attorney general continues to be the protector both of the donor's intent and of the public's interest in charitable funds."

While a donor may not have standing to enforce a designated gift to a church, this does not mean the church can ignore it. Most states have enacted laws empowering the attorney general to enforce the terms of such gifts. An official comment to section 348 of the *Restatement (Second) of Trusts*, a respected legal treatise that has been adopted in many states, specifies:

> Where property is given to a charitable corporation, particularly where restrictions are imposed by the donor, it is sometimes said by the courts that a charitable trust is created and that the corporation is a trustee. It is sometimes said, however, that a charitable trust is not created. This is a mere matter of terminology. The important question is whether and to what extent the principles and rules applicable to charitable trusts are applicable to charitable corporations. Ordinarily the principles and rules applicable to charitable trusts are applicable to charitable corporations. Where property is given to a charitable corporation without restrictions as to the disposition of the property, the corporation is under a duty, enforceable at the suit of the attorney general, not to divert the property to other purposes but to apply it to one or more of the charitable purposes for which it is organized. Where property is given to a charitable corporation and it is directed by the terms of the gift to devote the property to a particular one of its purposes, it is under a duty, enforceable at the suit of the [state] attorney general, to devote the property to that purpose *[emphasis added]*. Section 348, comment f.

Another leading legal treatise states: "The public benefits arising from the charitable trust justify the selection of some public official for its enforcement. Since the attorney general is the governmental officer whose duties include the protection of the rights of the people of the state in general, it is natural that he has been chosen as the prosecutor, supervisor, and enforcer of charitable trusts, both in England and in the several states." *Bogert, Trusts and Trustees § 411.* Several courts have recognized the exclusive authority of the state attorney general to enforce the terms of completed gifts.

Carl J. Herzog Foundation, Inc. v. University of Bridgeport, 699 A.2d 995 (Conn. 1997)

The Connecticut Supreme Court, after ruling that donors have no legal right to enforce their gifts to charity, concluded that the attorney general could do so:

> The general rule is that charitable trusts or gifts to charitable corporations for stated purposes are [enforceable] at the instance of the attorney general. . . . Although gifts to a charitable organization do not create a trust in the technical sense, where a purpose is stated a trust will be implied, and the disposition enforced by the attorney general, pursuant to his duty to effectuate the donor's wishes. . . . Connecticut is among the majority of jurisdictions which have . . . entrusted the attorney general with the responsibility and duty to represent the public interest in the protection of any gifts, legacies or devises intended for public or charitable purposes. . . . The theory underlying the power of the attorney general to enforce gifts for a stated purpose is that a donor who attaches conditions to his gift has a right to have is intention enforced. The donor's right, however, is enforceable only at the instance of the attorney general.

Wier v. Howard Hughes Medical Institute, 407 A.2d 1051 (Del. Ch. 1979)

A Delaware court ruled that the state attorney general "has the exclusive power to bring actions to enforce charitable trusts."

Lopez v. Medford Community Center, Inc., 424 N.E.2d 229 (Mass. 1981)

A Massachusetts court ruled that "it is the exclusive function of the attorney general to correct abuses in the administration of a public charity by the institution of proper proceedings" and that donors have no standing to enforce the terms of their gifts when they have not retained a specific right to do so, such as a right of reverter, after relinquishing physical possession of it.

Marin Hospital District v. State Dept. of Health, 154 Cal. Rptr. 838 (Cal. 1979)

A California court concluded that the fact that a charity is bound to use contributions for purposes for which they were given does not confer upon the donor standing to enforce the terms of the gift.

Smith v. Thompson, 266 Ill. App. 165, 169 (Ill. 1932) (quoting Perry, Trusts and Trustees § 732a)

An Illinois court observed:

> As a matter of common law, when a . . . donor of property to a charity fails specifically to provide for a reservation of rights in the trust or gift instrument, neither the donor nor his heirs have any standing in court in a proceeding to compel the proper execution of the trust." The court also noted that "where the donor has effectually passed out of himself all interest in the fund devoted to a charity, neither he nor those claiming under him have any standing in a court of equity as to its disposition and control.

Lefkowitz v. Lebensfeld, 417 N.Y.S.2d 715 (1979)

A New York court observed: "The general rule is that gifts to charitable corporations for stated purposes are [enforceable] at the instance of the attorney general. . . . It matters not whether the gift is absolute or in trust or whether a technical condition is attached to the gift."

Brown v. Concerned Citizens for Sickle Cell, 382 N.E.2d 1155 (Ohio. App. 1978)

An Ohio court concluded:

> One of the recognized powers held by the attorney general at common law was to inquire into any abuses of charitable donations. Clearly, the attorney general's traditional power to protect public donations to charity goes beyond the mere enforcement of express trusts where the formal elements of such a trust manifestation of intent to create a trust, the existence of trust property, and a fiduciary relationship are essential to its creation. The attorney general, in seeking to protect the public interest, may also bring suit to impose a constructive trust on funds collected for charitable purposes but subsequently diverted to other purposes. A constructive trust, although not a formal trust at all, serves as a means to prevent the unjust enrichment of those who would abuse their voluntary roles as public solicitors for charity. For this court to hold that the attorney general can only enforce express charitable trusts would greatly hamper his ability to carry out his statutory and common law duties.

Several other courts have concluded that the attorney general alone may enforce designated gifts to charity. *See, e.g., Denver Foundation v. Wells Fargo Bank, 163 P.3d 1116 (Cal. App. 2007); American Center for Education, Inc. v. Cavnar, 145 Cal. Rptr. 736 (Cal. App. 1978); Greenway v. Irvine's Trustee, 131 S.W.2d 705 (Ky. 1930); Weaver v. Wood, 680 N.E.2d 918 (Mass. 1997); In re James' Estate, 123 N.Y.S.2d 520 (N.Y. Sur. 1953).*

The authority of a state attorney general to enforce donors' designated gifts to charity is largely meaningless, since state attorneys general rarely exercise this power. When they do, it is in cases involving large gifts to prominent charities. Attorneys general rarely, if ever, have enforced designated gifts to a church. *Attorney General v. First United Baptist Church, 601 A.2d 96 (Maine 1992).*

Enforcement by persons having a "special interest"

Section 391 of the *Restatement (Second) of Trusts* specifies that others, in addition to the attorney general, may enforce the terms of a charitable trust: "A suit can be maintained for the enforcement of a charitable trust by the attorney general or other public officer, *or by a co-trustee, or by a person who has a special interest in the enforcement of the charitable trust*, but not by persons who have no special interest or by the [donor] or his heirs, personal representatives or next of kin."

One court concluded that "fiduciaries, such as trustees, have historically been deemed to have a special interest so as to possess standing." *Hartford v. Larrabee Fund Association, 288 A.2d 71 (1971).* However, the court cautioned that the attorney general must be joined as a party to protect the public interest.

Those with no special interest have no standing to bring an action to enforce the conditions of a gift. These include beneficiaries of the charitable gift. *Steeneck v. University of Bridgeport, 668 A.2d 688 (Conn. 1995).*

The California Supreme Court ruled that "the prevailing view of other jurisdictions is that the attorney general does not have exclusive power to enforce a charitable trust and that a trustee or other person having a sufficient special interest may also bring an action for this purpose. This position is adopted by [section 391 of] the Restatement (Second) of Trusts and is supported by many legal scholars." *Holt v. College of Osteopathic Physicians and Surgeons, 40 Cal. Rptr. 244 (1964).*

> **EXAMPLE.** The Alabama Supreme Court ruled that a church lacked standing to enforce a charitable trust that was created to distribute income to religious and charitable institutions. The court noted that "the prevailing view of other jurisdictions is that the attorney general does not have exclusive power to enforce a charitable trust and that a . . . person having a sufficient special interest may also bring an action for this purpose. Beneficiaries of a charitable trust have a right to maintain a suit to enforce the trust or prevent diversion of the funds." The court ruled, however, that not all beneficiaries have a legal right to enforce the terms of a charitable trust. It drew a distinction between "a person or entity that has a vested or fixed right to receive a benefit from a charitable trust and a person or entity that might merely potentially receive a benefit in the discretion of the trustees" and concluded that only beneficiaries with a vested or fixed right to receive distributions from a charitable trust have standing to enforce it. The church and school in this case were mere "potential beneficiaries" who would benefit from the trust only if the trustee selected them out of the large class of religious and charitable

institutions, and such an interest was not sufficient to confer standing. *Rhone v. Adams, 2007 WL 2966822 (Ala. 2007).*

Enforcement by donors who reserved a property interest

By expressly reserving a property interest, such as a right of reverter in a gift instrument, donors may bring themselves and their heirs within the special-interest exception to the general rule that donors and beneficiaries of a charitable trust may not bring an action to enforce the trust but rather are represented exclusively by the attorney general. A right of reverter is created when a property owner transfers title to another with the express stipulation that title will revert back to the prior owner upon the occurrence of a specified condition.

To illustrate, a landowner could convey a home or other property to a church "so long as the property is used for church purposes." If the property ceases to be used for church purposes, then the title reverts back to the former owner by operation of law. Such deeds vest only a "determinable" or "conditional" title in the church, since the title will immediately revert back to the previous owner (or such person's heirs or successors) by operation of law upon a violation of the condition.

Reversionary clauses represent one way for donors to ensure that they will be able to enforce a donation of land or a building to a church for specified purposes. However, note that if a reversionary clause is inserted in a deed as part of a donation of property to a church, the donor may be denied a charitable contribution deduction unless the IRS determines that the possibility of a reversion of title from the church back to the former owner is so remote as to be negligible. As the drafters of UMIFA stated:

> *Pursuant to section 170 of the [federal tax code] an income tax deduction for a charitable contribution is disallowed unless the taxpayer has permanently surrendered dominion and control over the property or funds in question. Where there is a possibility not so remote as to be negligible that the charitable gift subject to a condition might fail, the tax deduction is disallowed. The drafters of UMIFA worked closely with an impressive group of professionals, including tax advisers, who were concerned with the federal tax implications of the proposed Act. The drafters' principal concern in this regard was that the matter of donor restrictions not affect the donor's charitable contribution deduction for the purposes of federal income taxation. In other words, the concern was that the donor not be so tethered to the charitable gift through the control of restrictions in the gift that the donor would not be entitled to claim a federal charitable contribution exemption for the gift.* IRC § 170(a), Treas. Reg. § 1.170A-1 (c).

The income tax regulations specify that a charitable contribution deduction "shall not be disallowed . . . merely because the interest which passes to, or is vested in, the charity may be defeated by the performance of some act or the happening of some event, if on the date of the gift it appears that the possibility that such act or event will occur is so remote as to be negligible."

The language "so remote as to be negligible" has been defined as "a chance which persons generally would disregard as so highly improbable that it might be ignored with reasonable safety in undertaking a serious business transaction. It is likewise a chance which every dictate of reason would justify an intelligent person in disregarding as so highly improbable and remote as to be lacking in reason and substance."

The IRS applies the following factors in deciding if a charitable contribution deduction should be allowed or denied: (1) whether the donor and donee intend at the time of the donation to cause the event's occurrence; (2) the incidence of the event's occurring in the past; (3) the extent to which the occurrence of the event would defeat the donation; and (4) whether the taxpayer has control over the event's occurrence. *IRS Letter Ruling 200610017(2005).*

Court-allowed donor enforcement

In recent years a few courts have rejected the traditional rule that donors cannot enforce their completed gifts and have allowed donors (or their heirs) to sue a charity in order to enforce the terms of a completed gift. The leading cases are summarized below.

L.B. Research and Education Foundation v. UCLA Foundation, 29 Cal.Rptr.3d 710 (Cal. App. 2005)

A donor contributed $1 million to establish an endowed chair at a university medical school, which the school accepted along with the conditions imposed by the donor. Several years later, the donor sued the school for specific performance of the agreement and breach of contract, alleging that the school had failed to honor the conditions specified in the original gift. The court concluded that the gift was a "conditional gift" rather than a charitable trust. It defined a conditional gift as a gift in which "it is expressly provided in the instrument that the donee shall forfeit it or that the donor or his heirs may [sue] for breach of the condition." The court noted that standing is presumed in cases of a conditional gift. It acknowledged that donors have no legal authority to enforce a charitable trust unless they have standing, but it concluded that even if the gift in this case were construed to be a charitable trust rather than a conditional gift, the donor would have standing. The court noted:

> *The attorney general's power to enforce charitable trusts does not . . . deprive the donor of standing to enforce the terms of the trust it created. . . . The prevailing view of other jurisdictions is that the attorney general does not have exclusive power to enforce a charitable trust and that a trustee or other person having a sufficient special interest may also bring an action for this purpose. In addition to the general public interest, however, there is the interest of donors who have directed that their contributions be used for certain charitable purposes.*

Glenn v. University of Southern California, 2002 WL 31022068 (Cal. App. 2003)

A school asked a wealthy individual to donate $1.5 million to endow a professorial chair to support young, untenured researchers in the field of gerontology. The donor agreed to do so and agreed to give $1.5 million within 10 years. The school added that if the donor promised to increase his pledge to keep pace with inflation until he fully funded the endowment, it would immediately establish the professorship and select and fund the chair's holder without waiting for the donation. The donor agreed to these terms, and over the next 10 years transferred $1.6 million to the school. The donor later learned that the school had not used the donated funds for the specified purpose, and he sued the school for promissory fraud and breach of contract.

The court concluded that a breach of contract claim requires proof of (1) a contract, (2) the donor's performance of his contractual obligations, (3) the school's breach of its commitments, and (4) damages. The donor alleged that he had a partly oral, partly written contract with the school to endow a professorial chair, which the school promised to fund while it waited for him to honor his pledge. He claimed that he performed his commitment under the contract when he transferred $1.6 million to the school and that the school breached the contract by not funding the professorship as promised. Finally, he alleged that the school's breach damaged him because he could have put his money to other uses.

The court agreed that the donor had established a claim for breach of contract. The court also agreed that the donor had established a claim for promissory fraud, which it defined as (1) a knowing misrepresentation, (2) made with the intent to induce another's reliance, (3) the other's justifiable reliance, and (4) damages. The donor claimed that the school promised to fund the professorship immediately without intending to do so. He alleged that the school made the promise to encourage him to endow the position, and in giving $1.6 million he justifiably relied on that promise.

Surprisingly, the court did not address the question of whether the donor has standing to enforce the terms of his gift.

Maffei v. Roman Catholic Archbishop, 867 N.E.2d 300 (Mass. 2007)

A church launched a capital fund-raising campaign. A retiree in her eighties (Eileen) contributed $35,000 to the campaign. She later testified, "If I had known that the archdiocese . . . was giving any consideration to closing the church, I would not have made the gift of $35,000." A few years later, the archbishop ordered the closure of the church as part of a reorganization. During one of the last worship services before the church closed, Eileen asked the pastor, "Why didn't you tell us the church was closing?" He replied, "I didn't know." Eileen sued the archbishop, claiming negligent misrepresentation and breach of a fiduciary duty. The

Massachusetts Supreme Judicial Court ruled that Eileen had standing to pursue her claim:

> It is clear that Eileen has alleged an individual stake in this dispute that makes her, and not the state attorney general, the party to bring suit . . . . A gift to a church generally creates a public charity. It is the exclusive function of the attorney general to correct abuses in the administration of a public charity by the institution of proper proceedings. It is his duty to see that the public interests are protected . . . or to decline so to proceed as those interests may require. However, a plaintiff who asserts an individual interest in the charitable organization distinct from that of the general public has standing to pursue her individual claims. In this case, Eileen's claims are readily distinguishable from those of the general class of parishioner beneficiaries. . . . She claims that she lost substantial personal funds as the result of the archbishop's negligent misrepresentation to her. This claim is personal, specific, and exists apart from any broader community interest in keeping the church open. She has alleged a personal right that would, in the ordinary course, entitle her to standing.

As noted below, while the court concluded that Eileen had standing to sue, it rejected her theory of liability.

Smithers v. St. Luke's-Roosevelt Hospital Center, 723 N.Y.S.2d 426 (2001)

A recovered alcoholic devoted the last 40 years of his life to the treatment of alcoholism. In 1971 he announced his intention to make a gift to a hospital of $10 million for the establishment of an alcoholism treatment center. With $1 million from the first installment of the gift the hospital purchased a building for the rehabilitation program. According to the donor's widow, the hospital sought to avoid its obligations under the terms of the gift, and its relationship with the donor was an uneasy one. A year after the donor's death in 1994, the hospital informed his widow that it planned to move the treatment center into a hospital ward and sell the building.

The hospital's plans aroused the suspicions of the donor's widow, and she demanded an accounting of the treatment center's finances. The hospital at first resisted disclosing its financial records, but the widow persisted, and in 1995 the hospital disclosed that it had been misappropriating monies from the endowment fund (funded by the donor's original gift) and transferring them to its general fund, where they were used for purposes unrelated to the treatment center. The widow notified the state attorney general, who investigated the hospital's finances and confirmed that it had transferred restricted assets from the endowment fund to its general fund in what it called "loans." The attorney general demanded the return of these assets, and the hospital returned nearly $5 million to the endowment fund, although it did not restore the income lost on those funds during the intervening years.

The widow was still convinced that the hospital was not fully honoring her husband's gift, so she filed a lawsuit in which she asked a court to compel the hospital to honor the terms of the gift. The state attorney general asked the court to dismiss the widow's lawsuit on the ground that donors lack standing (judicial authority) to enforce the terms of their gifts. The attorney general insisted that standing to enforce the terms of a charitable gift is limited to the attorney general. The court concluded that a donor (or, in this case, a donor's widow acting on his behalf) has the legal authority to enforce the terms of a charitable contribution.

The Episcopal seminary case. The court referred to an earlier decision of the New York Court of Appeals (the highest state court in New York) in a case addressing the question of whether alumni of a seminary, who had donated funds for the endowment of a professorship with specified conditions, could sue to enforce those conditions when they were violated. *Associate Alumni of the General Theological Seminary of the Protestant Episcopal Church v. The General Theological Seminary of the Protestant Episcopal Church, 163 N.Y. 417 (1900).* The court concluded that the donors (alumni) could enforce the conditions of their contributions but could not obtain a return of their contributions. The court described the general rule as follows: "If the trustees of a charity abuse the trust, misemploy the charity fund, or commit a breach of the trust, the property does not revert to the heir or legal representative of the donor unless there is an express condition of the gift that it shall revert to the donor or his heirs, in case the trust is abused, but the redress is by . . . the attorney-general *or other person having the right to sue.*"

The court in the Episcopal seminary case concluded that while the donors were not entitled to a return of their contributions, they "had sufficient standing to maintain an action to enforce the trust."

Conclusion. The court concluded that the Episcopal seminary case "forecloses the conclusion that the attorney general's standing in these actions is exclusive." In other words, the attorney general is not the only person who is legally authorized to enforce the terms of a charitable gift. In some cases, donors can as well. Further, the court concluded that donors may have the right to enforce the terms of charitable gifts even though they do not specifically reserve the right to do so. The court then defended its conclusion that donors can enforce the terms of their gifts to charity:

> The donor of a charitable gift is in a better position than the attorney general to be vigilant and, if he or she is so inclined, to enforce his or her own intent. . . . To hold that, in her capacity as her late husband's representative [the donor's widow] has no standing to institute an action to enforce the terms of the gift is to contravene the well-settled principle that a donor's expressed intent is entitled to protection and the longstanding recognition under New York law of standing for a donor. We have seen no

> New York case in which a donor attempting to enforce the terms of his charitable gift was denied standing to do so. . . .

> Moreover, the circumstances of this case demonstrate the need for co-existent standing for the attorney general and the donor. The attorney general's office was notified of the hospital's misappropriation of funds by [the donor's widow]. Indeed, there is no substitute for a donor, who has a "special, personal interest in the enforcement of the gift restriction" . . . We conclude that the distinct but related interests of the donor and the attorney general are best served by continuing to accord standing to donors to enforce the terms of their own gifts concurrent with the attorney general's standing to enforce such gifts on behalf of the beneficiaries thereof.

Church leaders should be familiar with this case and understand its implications. It is common for churches to receive contributions from donors that are designated for a specific purpose. For example, donors contribute money to the church's building fund or a scholarship fund or missions fund. Can these donors legally enforce their designations if the church decides to divert these contributions to other purposes? This court concluded that they can, even if they retained no right to do so in a written agreement. The attorney general also is authorized to enforce the conditions of a designated gift, but the attorney general's authority is not exclusive. It is "concurrent" with the authority of the donors themselves. As noted above, many courts have rejected this reasoning and have ruled that the authority of the attorney general to enforce charitable gifts is exclusive.

Constitutional considerations

A few courts have concluded that the First Amendment guaranties of nonestablishment and free exercise of religion bar the civil courts from resolving donors' disputes with churches regarding the handling of designated contributions if doing so would implicate religious doctrine.

McDonald v. Macedonia Missionary Baptist Church, 2003 WL 1689618 (Mich. App. 2003)

A Michigan appeals court concluded that the civil courts are barred by the First Amendment guaranty of religious freedom from intervening in such internal church disputes:

> It is well settled that courts, both federal and state, are severely circumscribed by the First Amendment [and the Michigan constitution] in resolution of disputes between a church and its members. Jurisdiction is limited to property rights which can be resolved by application of civil law. Whenever the trial court must stray into questions of ecclesiastical polity or religious doctrine the court loses jurisdiction. . . . We hold that this dispute involves a policy of the church for which our civil courts should not interfere. Because the decision of when and where to build a new church building is exclusively within the province of the church members and its officials, the trial court erred in not dismissing the couple's lawsuit.

Hawthorne v. Couch, 911 So.2d 907 (La. App. 2005)

A Louisiana court concluded:

> *Not all church disputes necessarily involve purely ecclesiastical matters. . . . However, where the dispute is rooted in an ecclesial tenet of the church, the court will not have jurisdiction of the matter. In this case, the testimony focused almost exclusively on the pastor's teachings regarding tithing. Without question, any legal analysis that would require the court to analyze and pass judgment upon such teachings would violate the [First Amendment]. The issue of tithing is at its core a purely ecclesiastical matter.*

To help clarify the true intention of the donor of a designated contribution (at the time of the contribution), the IRS has suggested that the following language be used in a receipt for the contribution: "This contribution is made with the understanding that the donee organization has complete control and administration over the use of the donated funds." *(IRS Exempt Organizations Continuing Professional Education Technical Instruction Program for 1999.)*

Maffei v. Roman Catholic Archbishop, 867 N.E.2d 300 (Mass. 2007)

An Italian immigrant (James) established a successful gravel business and owned several tracts of land. Upon the death of James and his wife, most of their property passed to their six children. The pastor of a Catholic church was interested in acquiring an eight-acre tract from the family as the site of a new sanctuary. Two of the siblings agreed to donate their interest in the land to the church, but the other four siblings were reluctant to transfer their interests until the pastor assured them that the new church would be named "St. James," in honor of their father, and that the church would remain a tribute to James "forever." During the negotiations for the property, the pastor did not inform any members of the family that canon law permitted the closure of the church in the future.

A church was constructed on the land in 1958. By the 1990s, however, question arose concerning the continuing viability of the church. A local newspaper story listed the church among those the archdiocese planned to close. The current pastor of the church assured the congregation that the story was false. The church launched a capital fund-raising campaign. A retiree in her eighties (Eileen) contributed $35,000 to the campaign. She later testified, "If I had known that the archdiocese . . . was giving any consideration to closing St. James, I would not have made the gift of $35,000." In 2004 the archdiocese ordered the closure of St. James. During one of the last worship services before the church closed, Eileen asked the pastor, "Why didn't you tell us the church was closing?" He replied, "I didn't know it."

Eileen, as well as the sole surviving sibling to have transferred the land to the church, sued the archbishop. The lawsuit claimed that the oral assurance by church officials that the church would be named "St. James" forever was a binding and enforceable commitment that was breached by the church's closure. The lawsuit also alleged negligent misrepresentation and breach of a fiduciary duty and asked the court to order a reversion of the property to the surviving sibling.

The Supreme Judicial Court noted that the First Amendment guaranty of religious freedom "places beyond our jurisdiction disputes involving church doctrine, canon law, polity, discipline, and ministerial relationships" and that "among the religious controversies off limits to our courts are promises by members of the clergy to keep a church open." The court concluded that it had jurisdiction over church property disputes "if and to the extent, and only to the extent, that they are capable of resolution under neutral principles of law" involving no inquiry into church doctrine or polity.

The court concluded that the sole surviving sibling who conveyed property to the church had standing, since she gave up her rights in the property in reliance on the pastor's assurance that the property would always be used as a church in memory of James. In other words, her rights were different from members of the congregation generally. Similarly, the court concluded that Eileen had standing to sue:

> *It is clear that Eileen has alleged an individual stake in this dispute that makes her, and not the state attorney general, the party to bring suit . . . . A gift to a church generally creates a public charity. It is the exclusive function of the attorney general to correct abuses in the administration of a public charity by the institution of proper proceedings. It is his duty to see that the public interests are protected . . . or to decline so to proceed as those interests may require. However, a plaintiff who asserts an individual interest in the charitable organization distinct from that of the general public has standing to pursue her individual claims. In this case, Eileen's claims are readily distinguishable from those of the general class of parishioner-beneficiaries. . . . She claims that she lost substantial personal funds as the result of the archbishop's negligent misrepresentation to her. This claim is personal, specific, and exists apart from any broader community interest in keeping the church open. She has alleged a personal right that would, in the ordinary course, entitle her to standing.*

However, the court ruled that the First Amendment prevented it from resolving the sibling's claims. For example, the sibling claimed that the pastor breached a fiduciary duty to her by not informing her at the time she conveyed her interests in the property to the archbishop that the church could be closed according to canon law. In rejecting this argument, the court observed:

> *A ruling that a Roman Catholic priest, or a member of the clergy of any (or indeed every) religion, owes a fiduciary-confidential*

relationship to a parishioner that inheres in their shared faith and nothing more is impossible as a matter of law. Such a conclusion would require a civil court to affirm questions of purely spiritual and doctrinal obligation. The ecclesiastical authority of the archbishop and [the pastor] over the parishioners, the ecclesiastical authority of the archbishop over the pastor, the state of canon law at the date of the property transfer . . . the canonical obligation of the pastor, if any, to inform parishioners of canonical law—all of these inquiries bearing on resolution of the fiduciary claims would take us far afield of neutral principles of law. We decline to hold that, as a matter of civil law, the relationship of a member of the clergy to his or her congregants, without more, creates a fiduciary or confidential relationship grounded in their shared religious affiliation for which redress is available in our courts.

The court also rejected Eileen's claim that the archbishop acted negligently in failing to inform the local pastor of the plans to close the church when he knew he would be soliciting funds to sustain the church "now and for the future." The court noted that Eileen's gift was made in 2002, nearly two years before the archbishop decided to close the church. As a result, the pastor's efforts to raise funds for the maintenance of the church, both now and in the future, was not negligent or a misrepresentation.

Documentation

To help clarify the true intention of the donor of a designated contribution (at the time of the contribution), the IRS has suggested that the following language be used in a receipt for the contribution: "This contribution is made with the understanding that the donee organization has complete control and administration over the use of the donated funds." *IRS Exempt Organizations Continuing Professional Education Technical Instruction Program for 1999.*

This language clearly indicates that donors are transferring all rights in the donated funds or property, and as a result they will be less likely to attempt to enforce their gift designations. It also will weaken any legal basis for doing so.

Tax deduction

Two tax issues are associated with designated contributions. First, can a donor deduct a contribution to a church or other charity that designates a specific project or individual? This question is addressed fully in Chapter 8, section B. Second, is the deductibility of charitable contributions jeopardized if donors are legally capable of suing to enforce the terms of their completed gifts? This question is addressed above in the summary of the *Herzog Foundation* case, which quotes the drafters of the Uniform Management of Institutionalized Funds Act.

Practical considerations

Donors may not have the legal right to enforce a designated gift, but this does not mean that church leaders should ignore

requests by donors to honor their designations. After all, both practical and ethical considerations should be taken into account. As two dissenting judges noted in the *Herzog* case (summarized above): "This decision is simply an approval of a [charity] double crossing the donor, and doing it with impunity unless an elected attorney general does something about it." Do church leaders want to be perceived as "double-crossing" members who make designated gifts?

Further, the dissenting judges noted that the court's decision "will not encourage donations to [charities]." What did they mean? Simply this: Many donors are prompted to make a charitable contribution because of a desire to further a specific purpose or project. If donors realize that they have no legal right to enforce a designated gift, many of them may decide not to give.

The fact is that most donors who make designated gifts to their church do so assuming that the church is ethically, if not legally, bound to honor their designations. Church leaders who violate this perception will be viewed by many donors as guilty of unethical conduct that may lead to internal dissension. Church leaders should consider these potential consequences before making a decision to ignore a donor's designation, and they should consult with legal counsel before doing so to determine whether the designation is legally enforceable under state law, and if so, by whom.

Returning donated funds to donors

Donors whose designated gifts to their church are not honored may seek to enforce their designations in two ways. First, they may ask a civil court to order the church to honor the designation; or, second, they may ask a court to order a return of their contribution. Either option involves a judicial recognition of the legally enforceable nature of the donor's designation. This section is only addressing the legal authority of donors to enforce their designated contributions to charity. The related question of refunding contributions to donors is addressed in the introduction to this chapter (under section 3, Unconditional and Without Personal Benefit).

The Uniform Prudent Management of Institutional Funds Act (UPMIFA)

This Act specifies that "if the donor consents . . . an institution may release or modify, in whole or in part, a restriction contained in a gift instrument on the management, investment, or purpose of an institutional fund. A release or modification may not allow a fund to be used for a purpose other than a charitable purpose of the institution." Further, if written consent of the donor cannot be obtained, a court, "upon application of an institution, may modify a restriction contained in a gift instrument regarding the management or investment of an institutional fund if the restriction has become impracticable or wasteful, if it impairs the management or investment of the fund, or if, because of circumstances not anticipated by the donor, a modification of a restriction will further the purposes of the fund."

UPMIFA is addressed more fully in the introduction to this chapter (under section 3, Unconditional and Without Personal Benefit).

Conclusions

In deciding whether to disregard donors' designations, church leaders should consider several factors, including the following:

(1) In some states donors have the legal authority to enforce their designated gifts in the civil courts.
(2) In many states donors have the legal authority to enforce their designated gifts if they have a "special interest."
(3) In most states the attorney general is empowered to enforce the terms of charitable gifts.
(4) Ethical and practical considerations (mentioned above) are associated with any decision to disregard donors' designations.
(5) The Uniform Prudent Management of Institutional Funds Act (UPMIFA) only applies to perpetual "institutional funds." But if it applies, it will provide a church with a possible way to avoid a restriction on a designated gift.
(6) Church leaders should never disregard donors' designations without first consulting with legal counsel.

C. SHORT-TERM MISSION TRIPS

Many churches send teams on short-term mission trips both inside and outside of the United States. In some cases the participants on such trips are adults, while in others most of the participants are minors. The travel expenses incurred by participants may be paid in whole or in part by the church or by the participants (or in the case of minors, their parents) either directly or through contributions to the church.

Under what circumstances are participants, or nonparticipants who donate funds to defray the travel expenses of one or more participants, entitled to a charitable contribution deduction? Before addressing this question, three important principles must be addressed.

1. THREE IMPORTANT PRINCIPLES

Principle 1: charitable travel expenses

Travel expenses incurred during a short-term mission trip which may qualify a charitable contribution include air, rail, and bus transportation; out-of-pocket car expenses; taxi fares or other costs of transportation between the airport or station and your hotel; lodging costs; and the cost of meals. Since these expenses are not

business related, they are not subject to the limits that apply to the deductibility of business expenses.

Principle 2: substantiation

If a participant in a short-term mission trip is entitled to a charitable contribution deduction for unreimbursed travel expenses of $250 or more, the church must issue an "abbreviated written acknowledgment" in order for the participant to substantiate a deduction. The requirements for such an acknowledgment are set forth in section D.1 of this chapter (under the discussion of Rule 2).

Principle 3: no significant element of personal pleasure

Section 170(j) of the tax code states that no charitable contribution deduction is allowed "for traveling expenses (including amounts expended for meals and lodging) while away from home, whether paid directly or by reimbursement, unless there is no significant element of personal pleasure, recreation, or vacation in such travel." The key phrase is "no significant element of personal pleasure, recreation, or vacation in such travel." Unfortunately, neither the tax code nor regulations define a "significant element of personal pleasure, recreation, or vacation." A conference committee report to section 170(j) provides the following clarification:

The disallowance rule applies whether the travel expenses are paid directly by the taxpayer, or indirectly through reimbursement by the charitable organization. For this purpose, any arrangement whereby a taxpayer makes a payment to a charitable organization and the organization pays for his or her travel expenses is treated as a reimbursement.

In determining whether travel away from home involves a significant element of personal pleasure, recreation, or vacation, the fact that a taxpayer enjoys providing services to the charitable organization will not lead to denial of the deduction. For example, a troop leader for a tax-exempt youth group who takes children belonging to the group on a camping trip may qualify for a charitable deduction with respect to his or her own travel expenses if he or she is on duty in a genuine and substantial sense throughout the trip, even if he or she enjoys the trip or enjoys supervising children. By contrast, a taxpayer who only has nominal duties relating to the performance of services for the charity, or who for significant portions of the trip is not required to render services, is not allowed any charitable deduction for travel costs.

The IRS has provided the following additional clarification in Notice 87-23:

[Section 170(j)] provides that no deduction is allowed for transportation and other travel expenses relating to the performance of services away from home for a charitable organization unless there is no significant element of personal pleasure, recreation, or vacation in the travel. For example, a taxpayer who sails from one Caribbean

TABLE 8-2

SHORT-TERM MISSION TRIPS

A Review of the Tax Consequences

PARTICIPANTS	WHO PAYS TRAVEL EXPENSES (TRANSPORTATION, LODGING, MEALS)?	DOES THE CHURCH RECEIVE DESIGNATED CONTRIBUTIONS FROM PARTICIPANTS OR OTHERS?	TAX CONSEQUENCES (ASSUME THAT THE TRIP WAS PREAUTHORIZED BY THE CHURCH BOARD OR MEMBERSHIP AND FURTHERS THE CHURCH'S EXEMPT PURPOSE)
Adults	Church	No	None
Adults	Church	Yes, from participants, in the amount of their travel expenses paid by the church	• Payments by participants to their church are deductible as charitable contributions if the trip involves "no significant element of personal pleasure, recreation, or vacation." • Participants' payments can be reported by the church treasurer on giving statements (if expenses are $250 or more, the church's receipt must comply with substantiation requirements described in this chapter).
Adults	Church	Yes, from nonparticipants, to cover the travel expenses of participants who cannot afford to pay the expenses themselves	• Payments by nonparticipants to their church are deductible as charitable contributions if the trip involves "no significant element of personal pleasure, recreation, or vacation." • Nonparticipants' payments can be reported by the church treasurer on giving statements (if a contribution is for $250 or more, the church's receipt must comply with substantiation requirements described in this chapter).
Adults	Participants	No	• Unreimbursed travel expenses paid by participants are deductible as charitable contributions if the trip involves "no significant element of personal pleasure, recreation, or vacation." • If a participant is entitled to a charitable contribution deduction for unreimbursed travel expenses of $250 or more, the church must issue an "abbreviated written acknowledgment" in order for the participant to substantiate a deduction.
Minors	Church	No	None
Minors	Church	Yes, from parents, in the amount of their travel expenses paid by the church	• Payments by parents to their church are deductible as charitable contributions if the trip involves "no significant element of personal pleasure, recreation, or vacation." • Parents' payments can be reported by the church treasurer on giving statements (if expenses are $250 or more, the church's receipt must comply with substantiation requirements described in this chapter).
Minors	Parents	No	• Payments made directly by parents to their children who participate on a mission trip are probably not deductible as a charitable contribution.
Minors	Minors	No	None, since minors generally file no tax returns and cannot deduct contributions.

Island to another and spends eight hours a day counting whales and other forms of marine life as part of a project sponsored by a charitable organization generally will not be permitted a charitable deduction. By way of further example, a taxpayer who works on an archaeological excavation sponsored by a charitable organization for several hours each morning, with the rest of the day free for recreation and sightseeing, will not be allowed a deduction even if the taxpayer works very hard during those few hours. In contrast, a *member of a local chapter of a charitable organization who travels to New York City and spends an entire day attending the organization's regional meeting will not be subject to this provision even if he or she attends the theatre in the evening. This provision applies whether the travel expenses are paid directly by the taxpayer or by some indirect means such as by contribution to the charitable organization that pays for the taxpayer's travel expenses.*

The current edition of IRS Publication 526 addresses this issue:

Generally, you can claim a charitable contribution deduction for travel expenses necessarily incurred while you are away from home performing services for a charitable organization only if there is no significant element of personal pleasure, recreation, or vacation in the travel. This applies whether you pay the expenses directly or indirectly. You are paying the expenses indirectly if you make a payment to the charitable organization and the organization pays for your travel expenses.

The deduction for travel expenses will not be denied simply because you enjoy providing services to the charitable organization. Even if you enjoy the trip, you can take a charitable contribution deduction for your travel expenses if you are on duty in a genuine and substantial sense throughout the trip. However, if you have only nominal duties, or if for significant parts of the trip you do not have any duties, you cannot deduct your travel expenses.

IRS Publication 526 (Charitable Contributions) states: "If you are a chosen representative attending a convention of a qualified organization, you can deduct unreimbursed expenses for travel and transportation, including a reasonable amount for meals and lodging, while away from home overnight in connection with the convention. . . . You cannot deduct your expenses in attending a church convention if you go only as a member of your church rather than as a chosen representative. You can deduct unreimbursed expenses that are directly connected with giving services for your church during the convention."

EXAMPLE. Pastor J goes on a short-term mission to Europe. He is in Europe for 10 days and conducts one-hour worship services on two of those days. Pastor J will not be able to claim a charitable contribution deduction for the travel expenses he incurs in making this trip. The same rule would apply to the travel expenses of his wife and children if they accompany him on the trip.

EXAMPLE. Unreimbursed expenses of a delegate to a church conference qualify as deductible charitable contributions. *Revenue Ruling 58-240.*

EXAMPLE. K is a music director at her church. She attends a church convention as a visitor (not as a delegate). After arriving at the location of the meeting, K visits a religious music publisher to consider music for the church. Her unreimbursed expenses in making this side trip can be claimed as a charitable contribution.

However, this does not convert her expenses incurred in traveling to the meeting site to a deductible business expense. This conclusion is supported by the following language in IRS Publication 526: "You can deduct unreimbursed expenses that are directly connected with giving services for your church during the convention."

EXAMPLE. Persons attending church conventions, assemblies, or other meetings in accordance with their rights, privileges, or obligations as members of the church (as opposed to attending such meetings as the duly chosen representative of a congregation or other official church body) are not, by their attendance, rendering gratuitous services to their church. Expenses incurred in attending such meetings do not constitute charitable contributions. Such expenses constitute nondeductible personal expenses under section 262 of the tax code, even if attendance is required or expected of the persons by the tenets of their particular religious group. However, this does not preclude the deduction as charitable contributions of unreimbursed expenditures directly connected with and solely attributable to the rendition of gratuitous services performed for the church during the meeting. *Revenue Ruling 61-46.*

EXAMPLE. A Presbyterian church planned a trip to the Holy Land for 27 of its high-school students in order to "visit the places where Jesus lived and walked; visit and know young people of other backgrounds, cultures and religions; and share in an experience of Christian group living, understanding and friendship through work travel, and worship." For various reasons the destination was changed to Italy, Greece, and Turkey. While in Greece the students assisted in a "farm school" that taught local farmers more advanced techniques. Their primary responsibility involved the construction of a new chicken coop for the school's chickens. The cost of the trip was $1,400 per student, and this cost was paid by several of the parents for their respective children. One of the parents claimed this payment as a charitable contribution, and this position was rejected by the IRS in an audit.

The Tax Court agreed with the IRS. It observed: "We think it apparent that a deduction for expenses incident to the performance of services for the school is not allowable as a charitable contribution to [the church]. Although the church had a history of assisting the school, these are two distinctly separate organizations, and the services were not performed for the benefit of the church. That the trip increased the teenagers' interest in the church program, developed their leadership capabilities, and increased their religious understanding does not aid [the parent's] cause. If the trip, indeed, produced these results, the true beneficiaries were the teenagers themselves. . . . The evidence shows plainly that the 46 day expedition to Europe was primarily a vacation, sightseeing, and cultural trip for the teenagers. . . . Instead of the expenditures in question being incident to the rendition of services, we think the visit to the school and the work which was performed were only incidental to, or part of, a vacation trip. There is nothing to suggest that the expenses would have been less if the group had spent the entire trip solely for sightseeing. . . . While efforts to assist the teenagers in developing deeper religious involvement and concern for the needs of others are laudable, the tax laws do not permit parents to deduct sums which they expend for such purposes specifically on behalf of their own children." *Tate v. Commissioner, 59 T.C. 543 (1973).*

Consider another example. Assume that a layperson goes on a one week mission trip to Germany and, on the way home, stops off in London for a two-week vacation. If he had only gone to Germany, his travel expenses would have been $2,000. But with the addition of the vacation, his unreimbursed expenses are $3,000. How much can he deduct as a charitable contribution: $3,000, $2,000, or $0? The best answer is $0. This conclusion is based on the text of section 170(j), which states that "no deduction shall be allowed under this section for traveling expenses (including amounts expended for meals and lodging) while away from home, whether paid directly or by reimbursement, unless there is no significant element of personal pleasure, recreation, or vacation in such travel." Can it be said that there is "no significant element of personal pleasure, recreation, or vacation" when a layperson spends two weeks in London on vacation following a one-week mission trip to Germany? Probably not.

In summary, it is unlikely that a short-term missionary who spends two weeks in London (on vacation) following a one-week mission trip to Germany could claim a charitable contribution deduction for any of his or her travel expenses. With two out of three weeks being devoted to vacation, it is difficult to conclude that there was "no significant element of personal pleasure, recreation, or vacation in such travel." While existing precedent does not clarify the meaning of a significant element," it almost certainly would include two-thirds of the total trip time.

2. SEVEN COMMON SCENARIOS

The seven most common forms of funding of short-term mission trips, and the tax consequences of each, are summarized below.

❀ **KEY POINT.** In each of the scenarios described below, the deductibility of charitable contributions assumes that the donor is able to itemize deductions on Schedule A (Form 1040) and that the trip does not involve a significant element of personal pleasure, recreation, or vacation.

Scenario 1: adult participants; church pays none of participants' travel expenses

Adult participants on a short-term mission trip can claim their unreimbursed travel expenses as a charitable contribution. The income tax regulations specify:

> Unreimbursed expenditures made incident to the rendition of services to an organization contributions to which are deductible may constitute a deductible contribution. For example, the cost

of a uniform without general utility which is required to be worn in performing donated services is deductible. Similarly, out of pocket transportation expenses necessarily incurred in performing donated services are deductible. Reasonable expenditures for meals and lodging necessarily incurred while away from home in the course of performing donated services are also deductible. Treas. Reg. 1.170A 1(g).

Scenario 2: adult participants; church pays all travel expenses from the general fund or a missions fund, with no contributions from participants (or nonparticipants) to cover travel expenses

Such an arrangement has no tax consequences. The church's payment of the participants' travel expenses is a legitimate expenditure of church funds in furtherance of the church's religious purposes. No questions are raised concerning the deductibility of charitable contributions.

Scenario 3: adult participants; church pays all travel expenses; participants make contributions to the church in the amount of their travel expenses

Are payments made by the participants themselves to their church to cover the cost of their travel expenses deductible as charitable contributions? Yes, according to IRS Publication 526 (Charitable Contributions), so long as no significant element of personal pleasure is involved in the trip:

> You can claim a charitable contribution deduction for travel expenses necessarily incurred while you are away from home performing services for a charitable organization only if there is no significant element of personal pleasure, recreation, or vacation in such travel. This applies whether you pay the expenses directly or indirectly. You are paying the expenses indirectly if you make a payment to the charitable organization and the organization pays for your travel expenses. The deduction will not be denied simply because you enjoy providing services to the charitable organization.

The term "no significant element of personal pleasure" is defined above.

Scenario 4: adult participants; church pays all travel expenses; nonparticipants make contributions to the church to cover the travel expenses of participants who cannot afford to pay all of their own expenses

The question raised by this scenario is whether payments made by donors are deductible as charitable contributions. If donors are contributing to a fund that will defray the travel expenses of unnamed participants who cannot afford to pay all of their own travel expenses, their contributions would be tax-deductible. The same would be true for donations specifying that they be applied to the travel expenses of a named participant. See Chapter 8, section B.3. In both cases it is assumed that the church has preauthorized the mission trip, that the trip will further the exempt purposes of the church, and that the church exercises sufficient control over the funds to ensure that they are used to carry out its purposes.

Scenario 5: minor participants; church pays all travel expenses from the general fund or a missions fund, with no contributions from participants (or nonparticipants) to cover travel expenses

Such an arrangement has no tax consequences. The church's payment of the minor participants' travel expenses is a legitimate expenditure of church funds in furtherance of the church's religious purposes. No questions are raised concerning the deductibility of charitable contributions.

Scenario 6: minor participants; church pays all travel expenses; parents make contributions to the church in the amount of their children's travel expenses

It is common for minors to go on church-sponsored short-term mission trips. If parents pay for their child's travel expenses, can they claim a charitable contribution deduction? That depends. If the parents pay the church an amount sufficient to cover the travel expenses of their child on a church-approved mission trip, it is likely that this payment will be tax-deductible. The United States Supreme Court addressed a related question in a 1990 decision. *Davis v. United States, 110 S. Ct. 2014 (1990)*. The Court reached two conclusions. First, contributions by a parent to a church or missions agency are tax-deductible, even if they designate the donor's missionary child, so long as the church or missions agency exercises full accounting and administrative control over the contribution to be sure it is used for travel and other missions-related expenses of the missionary. Second, payments made directly by a parent to a missionary child are not tax-deductible, since they are not made to a charitable organization exercising administrative control over the payments.

The first ruling in the *Davis* case supports the tax-deductibility of contributions made by parents to their church to cover travel expenses incurred on a church-sponsored mission trip. The church ordinarily will exercise administrative control over the donated funds in such cases and will ensure that funds are expended for missions-related travel expenses; it also will ensure that the children are, in fact, traveling for missions rather than personal purposes. However, if parents pay their child's travel expenses directly or send funds to their children to cover travel expenses, the deduction is in doubt. The Supreme Court observed in the *Davis* case that

> the plain language [of the income tax regulation] indicates that taxpayers may claim deductions only for expenditures made in connection with their own contributions of service to charities . . . [A] taxpayer ordinarily reports his own income and takes his own expenses. . . . It would strain the language of the regulation

> to read it, as [the parents] suggest, as allowing a deduction for expenses made incident to a third party's rendition of services rather than to the taxpayer's own contribution of services.

Scenario 7: minor participants; church pays none of the minor participants' travel expenses

If the minors pay their own expenses through their own fund-raising efforts, there usually will not be a tax question, since the minors will not be filing a tax return and do not need a charitable contribution deduction. On the other hand, if a minor's parents (or other adult nonparticipants) pay for a child's travel expenses, the analysis in the previous sections would apply.

D. SUBSTANTIATION OF CHARITABLE CONTRIBUTIONS

❉ **KEY POINT.** In order to be tax-deductible, a charitable contribution must be substantiated according to the nine rules summarized in this section.

❉ **KEY POINT.** Church leaders need to be familiar with the many legal requirements that apply to charitable contributions so they can determine the deductibility of contributions and advise donors.

❉ **KEY POINT.** Churches are not appraisers and are not responsible for assigning a value to donated property.

Charitable contributions to churches and other tax-exempt organizations are deductible only if they satisfy certain conditions. One important condition is that the donor must be able to substantiate the contribution. The substantiation requirements vary depending on the kind of contribution. They are summarized below.

The many substantiation rules are presented in this section in the form of ten rules. Simply find the rules that apply to a particular contribution and follow the substantiation requirements. The rules apply to the categories of contributions mentioned in Table 8-3.

❉ **KEY POINT.** The rules for substantiating charitable contributions are summarized in Table 8-6 at the end of this chapter.

1. CONTRIBUTIONS OF CASH

Rule 1—requirements for all cash contributions

Donors cannot deduct a cash contribution to a church or charity, regardless of the amount, unless they keep one of the following:

- a bank record (a statement from a financial institution, an electronic fund transfer receipt, a canceled check, a scanned image of both sides of a canceled check obtained from a bank website, or a credit card statement) showing the charity's name, date of the contribution, and the amount of the contribution or
- a written communication (including "electronic mail correspondence") from the charity showing the charity's name, date of the contribution, and the amount of the contribution.

The substantiation requirements *may not be satisfied by maintaining other reliable written records*. In the past donors could substantiate cash contributions of less than $250 with "other reliable written records showing the name of the donee, the date of the contribution, and the amount of the contribution" if no cancelled check or receipt was available. This is no longer allowed.

▲ **CAUTION.** *As noted below, additional substantiation requirements apply to individual contributions of $250 or more, and these must be satisfied as well.*

EXAMPLE. A church member makes cash contributions to his church of between $20 and $50 each week. He uses offering envelopes provided by the church, but the church provides no other receipt or statement substantiating the contributions. The member will not be able to claim a charitable contribution deduction for any of these payments. All cash contributions, regardless of amount, must be substantiated by either a bank record (such as a cancelled check) or a written communication from the donee showing the name of the donee organization, the date of the contribution, and the amount of the contribution. The record-keeping requirements cannot be satisfied by other written records, including offering envelopes.

EXAMPLE. The IRS audits a taxpayer's 2012 federal income tax return and questions an alleged contribution of $100 to a church that was made on February 1, 2012, and for which the taxpayer has no canceled check or church receipt. The taxpayer does maintain a daily diary. A diary entry on the alleged date of the contribution shows that a contribution of $100 was made to the church. This is inadequate substantiation. Cash contributions can only be substantiated with bank records (including cancelled checks) or a written communication from the donee charity showing the name of the donee, the date of the contribution, and the amount of the contribution. They cannot be substantiated with other written records, including diary entries.

➤ **TIP.** To assist members in substantiating cash contributions, churches should keep records showing the amount and date of every contribution (whether in the form of cash or check). Periodically (i.e., quarterly) the church should send contribution summaries to each member, showing the amounts and dates of

each contribution and identifying the member and church by name. Such summaries will satisfy the definition of a church receipt and will support a charitable contribution deduction for cash donors (and donors who misplace canceled checks). Additional requirements apply to individual contributions of cash or property of $250 or more. These are explained fully later in this chapter.

Offering envelopes

Many churches use offering envelopes. They have a number of advantages, including the following:

- they help the church connect cash contributions to individual donors;
- they promote privacy in the collecting of contributions;
- they give members the opportunity to designate specific programs or projects;
- they provide members with a weekly reminder of the need to make contributions and honor pledges; and
- they reduce the risk of offering counters pocketing loose bills.

In the past, another reason for using offering envelopes was to assist donors in substantiating cash contributions of less than $250. Offering envelopes no longer can be used for this purpose. The tax code now states that all cash contributions, regardless of amount, must be

===== **TABLE 8-3** =====

THE 10 RULES FOR SUBSTANTIATING CHARITABLE CONTRIBUTIONS

RULE	COVERS THE FOLLOWING CONTRIBUTIONS
1	All cash contributions
2	Individual cash contributions of $250 or more
3	Individual quid pro quo cash contributions of $75 or less
4	Individual quid pro quo cash contributions of more than $75
5	Individual contributions of noncash property valued by the donor at less than $250
6	Individual contributions of noncash property valued by the donor at $250 to $500
7	Individual contributions of noncash property valued by the donor at more than $500 but not more than $5,000
8	Quid pro quo contributions of noncash property
9	Individual contributions of noncash property valued by the donor at more than $5,000
10	Donations of (a) cars, boats, and planes; (b) stock; and (c) clothing and household items

substantiated with (1) a bank record (such as a cancelled check) or a written communication from the charity (2) showing the charity's name, date of the contribution, and the amount of the contribution. Offering envelopes will not satisfy these requirements and cannot be used to substantiate a donor's cash contributions.

Church leaders often ask how long they must keep offering envelopes. If your church uses offering envelopes, one option is to issue donors a periodic (quarterly, semiannual, or annual) summary of contributions and include in this summary a statement similar to the following: "Any documentation, including offering envelopes, that the church relied upon in preparing this summary will be disposed of within six months. Therefore, please review this summary carefully and inform the church treasurer of any apparent discrepancies within six months of the date of this summary."

Such a statement provides the church with a reasonable basis for destroying envelopes and other written records after the specified period of time. The burden is on members to promptly call attention to discrepancies. Of course, you can change the six-month period to any other length of time you desire. This statement will relieve the church of the responsibility of warehousing offering envelopes and other supporting documentation for long periods of time.

EXAMPLE. A church member ordinarily contributes cash (in church envelopes and in individual amounts of less than $250) rather than checks. Since the member will have no canceled checks to substantiate her contributions, she must rely upon the periodic receipts provided by her church. If the church does not issue the member a receipt, the member will not be able to deduct any of her cash contributions. The offering envelopes will not suffice.

EXAMPLE. A taxpayer attended church regularly. Sometimes he would attend his father's church, and other times his grandfather's, but he contributed to both churches. He made weekly payments using offering envelopes provided by the churches. He put both cash and checks into these envelopes. He also made a contribution by cash or check to the Salvation Army. The taxpayer claimed a deduction of $6,000 for these contributions. The IRS audited his tax return and disallowed any deduction for these contributions on the ground that the taxpayer lacked adequate substantiation. The Tax Court conceded that the taxpayer had no canceled checks or credit card receipts proving his charitable contributions. However, "he did produce letters from the two churches he attended acknowledging contributions of $3,750 and $4,500. These contributions total $8,250, and exceed the $6,000 claimed on the taxpayer's return. The court is satisfied with the credibility of the taxpayer's testimony as verified by his documentation under the cited legal standards and, therefore, allows a charitable contribution deduction of $8,201 for the year at issue." *Jones v. United States, T.C. Summary Opinion 2004-76.*

Payroll deductions

If you make a contribution by payroll deduction, you must keep

(1) a pay stub, Form W-2, or other document furnished by your employer that shows the date and amount of the contribution, and

(2) a pledge card or other document prepared by or for the qualified organization that shows the name of the organization.

If you make a contribution by payroll deduction and your employer withheld $250 or more from a single paycheck, see Rule 2, below.

Rule 2—individual cash contributions of $250 or more

✤ **KEY POINT.** Donors cannot substantiate individual cash contributions of $250 or more with canceled checks.

Written acknowledgment

Donors must substantiate individual cash contributions of $250 or more "by a contemporaneous written acknowledgment of the contribution by the donee organization." *Donors cannot substantiate individual cash contributions of $250 or more with canceled checks.* They must receive a written acknowledgment from the church or other charity.

The IRS has clarified that "as long as it is in writing and contains the information required by law, a contemporaneous written acknowledgment may be in any format." The law specifies that a written acknowledgment must include the following information:

- name of organization;
- amount of cash contribution;
- description (but not the value) of noncash contribution;
- statement that no goods or services were provided by the organization in return for the contribution, if that was the case;
- description and good faith estimate of the value of goods or services, if any, that an organization provided in return for the contribution; and
- statement that goods or services, if any, that an organization provided in return for the contribution consisted entirely of intangible religious benefits (described later) if that was the case.

It is not necessary to include the donor's Social Security number on the acknowledgment.

✤ **KEY POINT.** Although it is a donor's responsibility to obtain a written acknowledgment, a church can assist a donor by providing a timely, written acknowledgment that meets the requirements summarized above.

The IRS has provided the following clarification regarding acceptable written acknowledgments:

A separate acknowledgment may be provided for each single contribution of $250 or more, or one acknowledgment, such as an annual summary, may be used to substantiate several single contributions of $250 or more. There are no IRS forms for the acknowledgment. Letters, postcards, or computer-generated forms with the above information are acceptable. An organization can provide either a paper copy of the acknowledgment to the donor, or an organization can provide the acknowledgment electronically, such as via an e-mail addressed to the donor. A donor should not attach the acknowledgment to his or her individual income tax return, but must retain it to substantiate the contribution. Separate contributions of less than $250 will not be aggregated. An example of this could be weekly offerings to a donor's church of less than $250, even though the donor's annual total contributions are $250 or more. IRS Publication 1771.

Contemporaneous

The tax code requires that written acknowledgments must be contemporaneous. The IRS explains this requirement as follows: "For the written acknowledgment to be considered contemporaneous with the contribution, a donor must receive the acknowledgment by the earlier of the date on which the donor actually files his or her individual federal income tax return for the year of the contribution, or the due date (including extensions) of the return."

EXAMPLE. A taxpayer made several contributions to a church (Church A) during 2007. The contributions to Church A were reported in a letter from the church dated January 19, 2010, indicating that the taxpayer contributed a total of $7,500, and several copies of checks, all for amounts of $250 or more. In addition, the taxpayer made several contributions to a second church (Church B). These contributions were reflected in a "tithing statement" from the church dated January 19, 2010, stating that she contributed a total of $2,255, and several copies of checks, some of which are for amounts less than $250.

The IRS disallowed any charitable contribution deduction for these contributions, and the taxpayer appealed to the Tax Court. The court concluded that the taxpayer was not entitled to deduct the $7,500 she contributed to Church A: "The taxpayer introduced a letter from the church dated January 19, 2010, and copies of several checks, each for more than $250 and made out to the church's pastor and his wife. The letter does not state whether she received goods or services in exchange for contribution and was not received by the earlier of her return's filing date or its due date of April 15, 2008. Thus, there is no contemporaneous written acknowledgment from the donee that would permit petitioner to deduct the contributions."

The court also concluded that the taxpayer could not deduct most of the contributions she made to Church B: "To substantiate the contributions, the taxpayer introduced checks made out to Church B and a 2007 tithing statement from Church B

dated January 19, 2010. Because the taxpayer did not receive the tithing statement by the earlier of her return's filing date or its due date of April 15, 2008, it is not a contemporaneous written acknowledgment. Thus, she does not have proper substantiation for the contributions of $250 or more." *Linzy v. Commissioner, T.C. Memo. 2011-264.*

↝ **TIP.** To avoid jeopardizing the tax deductibility of charitable contributions, churches should advise donors at the end of 2013 not to file their 2013 income tax returns until they have received a written acknowledgment of their contributions from the church. This communication should be in writing. To illustrate, the following statement could be placed in the church bulletin or newsletter for the last few weeks of 2013 or included in a letter to members: "IMPORTANT NOTICE: To ensure the deductibility of your church contributions, please do not file your 2013 income tax return until you have received a written acknowledgment of your contributions from the church. You may lose a deduction for some contributions if you file your tax return before receiving a written acknowledgment of your contributions from the church."

Goods or services

The acknowledgment must describe goods or services a charity provides in exchange for a contribution of $250 or more. It must also provide a good faith estimate of the value of such goods or services, because a donor must generally reduce the amount of the contribution deduction by the fair market value of the goods and services provided by the charity. Goods or services include cash, property, services, benefits, or privileges. However, two important exceptions are described below:

1. Token exception. Insubstantial goods or services a charitable organization provides in exchange for contributions do not have to be described in the acknowledgment. Goods and services are considered to be insubstantial if the payment occurs in the context of a fund-raising campaign in which a charitable organization informs the donor of the amount of the contribution that is a deductible contribution, and (1) the fair market value of the benefits received does not exceed the lesser of 2 percent of the payment or $102; or (2) the payment is at least $51, the only items provided bear the organization's name or logo (e.g., calendars, mugs, or posters), and the cost of these items is within the limits for "low-cost articles," which is $10.20. Free, unordered low-cost articles are also considered to be insubstantial. The amounts mentioned in this paragraph are the 2013 amounts. They are adjusted annually for inflation.

2. Intangible religious benefits exception. If a religious organization provides only intangible religious benefits to a contributor, the acknowledgment does not need to describe or value those benefits. It should simply state that the organization provided intangible religious benefits to the contributor. What are intangible religious benefits? The IRS defines them as follows:

Generally, they are benefits provided by a tax-exempt organization operated exclusively for religious purposes, and are not usually sold in commercial transactions outside a donative (gift) context. Examples include admission to a religious ceremony and a de minimis tangible benefit, such as wine used in a religious ceremony. Benefits that are not intangible religious benefits include education leading to a recognized degree, travel services, and consumer goods. IRS Publication 1771.

To substantiate an individual charitable contribution of $250 or more, a donor must obtain a receipt from the charity that states whether the charity provided any goods or services in exchange for a contribution of $250 or more (other than intangible religious benefits), and if so, a description and good faith estimate of the value of those goods and services.

IRS regulations define a "good faith estimate" as an estimate of the fair market value of the goods or services provided by a charity in return for a donor's contribution. The fair market value of goods or services may differ from their cost to the charity. The charity may use any reasonable method it applies in good faith in making the good faith estimate.

However, a taxpayer is not required to determine how the charity made the estimate. IRS regulations specify that a taxpayer generally may treat an estimate of the value of goods or services as the fair market value for purposes of computing a charitable contribution deduction if the estimate is in a receipt issued by the charity. For example, if a charity provides a book in exchange for a $100 payment and the book is sold at retail prices ranging from $18 to $25, the taxpayer may rely on any estimate of the charity that is within the $18 to $25 range (the charitable contribution deduction is limited to the amount by which the $100 donation exceeds the fair market value of the book that is provided to the donor). However, a taxpayer may not treat an estimate as the fair market value of the goods or services if the taxpayer knows, or has reason to know, that such treatment is unreasonable. For example, if the taxpayer is a dealer in the type of goods or services it receives from a charity, or if the goods or services are readily valued, it is unreasonable for the taxpayer to treat the charity's estimate as the fair market value of the goods or services if that estimate is in error and the taxpayer knows, or has reason to know, the fair market value of the goods or services.

Unreimbursed expenses

If a donor makes a single contribution of $250 or more in the form of unreimbursed expenses (such as out-of-pocket transportation expenses) incurred in order to perform donated services for a church, the donor must obtain a written acknowledgment from the church containing the following information: (1) a description of the services provided by the donor; (2) a statement of whether the organization provided goods or services in return for the contribution; (3) a description and good faith estimate of the value of goods

or services, if any, that an organization provided in return for the contribution; and (4) a statement that goods or services, if any, that an organization provided in return for the contribution consisted entirely of intangible religious benefits (described above) if that was the case. In addition, a donor must maintain adequate records of the unreimbursed expenses. The church's acknowledgment must meet the contemporaneous requirement (see above).

✪ **KEY POINT.** The IRS has observed: "There is precedent for exempting from the substantiation requirements certain types of payments for which a charitable beneficiary cannot provide a receipt, either because the charitable beneficiary has not yet been identified or because the charitable beneficiary has no firsthand knowledge of the amount of the payment. For example . . . the proposed regulations provide an exception from the substantiation requirements for unreimbursed expenses of less than $250 incurred incident to the rendition of services to a charitable organization. Taxpayers claiming deductions for monetary contributions . . . for out of pocket expenses incurred incident to the rendition of services are advised to maintain records of the gifts or expenses."

EXAMPLE. A chosen representative to an annual church convention purchases an airline ticket to travel to the convention. The church does not reimburse the delegate for the $500 ticket. The representative should keep a record of the expenditure, such as a copy of the ticket. The representative should obtain from the church a description of the services the representative provided and a statement that the representative received no goods or services from the organization.

EXAMPLE. Greg participates in a short-term mission project sponsored by his church and incurs $700 of unreimbursed out-of-pocket travel expenses. Here is an example of an abbreviated written acknowledgment that complies with the regulations: "Greg Jones participated in a mission trip sponsored by [name of church] in the nation of Panama in 2013. His services included [working in a medical clinic]. The church provided no goods or services in return for these services." The church should be sure that Greg receives this receipt before the earlier of (1) the date he files a tax return claiming the contribution deduction, or (2) the due date (including extensions) for the tax return for that year.

Examples of written acknowledgments

Here are examples of acceptable written acknowledgments:

- "Thank you for your cash contribution of $300 that First Church received on December 12, 2012. No goods or services were provided in exchange for your contribution, other than intangible religious benefits."
- "Thank you for your cash contribution of $350 that First Church received on May 6, 2012. In exchange for your

contribution, we gave you a cookbook with an estimated fair market value of $30."

- "Thank you for your contribution of a used oak baby crib and matching dresser that First Church received on March 15, 2012. No goods or services were provided in exchange for your contribution other than intangible religious benefits."

Below are a few additional points to note concerning the substantiation rules.

Donor's, not the church's, responsibility

A congressional committee report states that the substantiation requirement for contributions of $250 or more does "not impose an information reporting requirement upon charities; rather, it places the responsibility upon taxpayers who claim an itemized deduction for a contribution of $250 or more to request (and maintain in their records) substantiation from the charity of their contribution (and any good or service received in exchange)."

While the sole risk of failing to comply with substantiation rules for contributions of $250 or more is upon the donor (who will not be able to substantiate a charitable contribution deduction), churches should take an active role in informing donors of the substantiation requirements to ensure the deductibility of contributions.

No reporting to the IRS

A church's written acknowledgments are issued to donors. They are not sent to the IRS. Exceptions exist for some contributions of noncash property and vehicles, as noted later in this chapter.

Why church contribution receipts often are inadequate

Most churches provide some form of periodic written statement to donors, acknowledging their contributions. However, any statements currently being used must be carefully reviewed to ensure compliance with the requirements summarized above. In some cases, they will need to be changed. Here are a few common examples of receipts that do not comply with the law:

- A church's receipts do not specify whether the church provided any goods or services in exchange for each individual contribution of $250 or more.
- A church occasionally provides goods or services to donors in exchange for their contributions of $250 or more, but the receipts it issues to these donors do not include a good-faith estimate of the value of the goods or services the church provided. Note that if such goods or services consist solely of intangible religious benefits, the church's receipt must include a statement to that effect.
- Some churches issue receipts in February or March of the following year. Such a practice will jeopardize the deductibility of every individual contribution of $250 or more to the extent a receipt is received by a donor after a tax return is filed.

The $250 threshold

If a donor makes a $50 cash contribution each week to a church, the substantiation requirements addressed in Rule 2 do not apply, even though the donor will have made $2,600 in contributions for the year, because no individual contribution was $250 or more. The donor can rely on canceled checks to substantiate the contributions or on an acknowledgment provided by the church that satisfies the requirements of Rule 1.

Combining separate contributions of $250

If a donor makes 10 separate contributions of $250 or more to her church during 2013, must the church issue a receipt listing each contribution separately, or can the 10 contributions be combined as one amount? The IRS has provided the following clarification: "A separate acknowledgment may be provided for each single contribution of $250 or more, or one acknowledgment, such as an annual summary, may be used to substantiate several single contributions of $250 or more." *IRS Publication 1771*.

✥ **KEY POINT.** Most churches currently itemize individual contributions on receipts provided to donors, and many will want to continue this practice even though it is not legally required. A receipt that merely provides donors with a lump sum of all their contributions will be of no value to a donor who wants to correct a discrepancy.

✥ **KEY POINT.** This chapter (text, examples, and illustrations) shows receipts that separately list each contribution of $250 or more, since this is the most common church practice, and it provides donors with information that will assist in detecting errors and reconciling discrepancies.

Effect of noncompliance

No penalty is imposed on a church that does not issue written acknowledgments to donors who comply with Rule 2. However, a donor will not be able to substantiate individual charitable contributions of $250 or more if audited, and a deduction for such contributions may be denied. Thus it is essential for church leaders to be familiar with these rules and issue acceptable written acknowledgments to donors who have made one or more individual contributions to the church of $250 or more during the year.

Making contributions through payroll deductions

If you make a contribution by payroll deduction and your employer withheld $250 or more from a single paycheck, you must keep

(1) a pay stub, Form W-2, or other document furnished by your employer that shows the amount withheld as a contribution, and

(2) a pledge card or other document prepared by or for the qualified organization that shows the name of the organization and states the organization does not provide goods or services in return for any contribution made to it by payroll deduction.

CHARITABLE CONTRIBUTIONS

A single pledge card may be kept for all contributions made by payroll deduction regardless of amount as long as it contains all the required information.

If the pay stub, Form W-2, pledge card, or other document does not show the date of the contribution, you must also have another document that does show the date of the contribution. If the pay stub, Form W-2, pledge card, or other document does show the date of the contribution, you do not need any other records except those described in (1) and (2).

EXAMPLE. B is a member of a church. She makes 52 weekly contributions of $10 (for a total of $520) during 2013 and receives only intangible religious benefits in exchange. The substantiation rules that apply to contributions of $250 or more do not affect either B or the church. She will be permitted to deduct her contributions (if she can itemize her deductions on Schedule A), and she can substantiate her contributions using canceled checks or a written statement from the church that meets the requirements summarized under Rule 1 (above).

EXAMPLE. Same facts as the previous example, except that B made a one-time cash contribution of $1,000 to the church's mission fund on June 28, 2013. In order to ensure the deductibility of the $1,000 contribution, B must receive a written acknowledgment from the church not later than the date she files her tax return or the due date of her tax return, whichever is earlier, that (1) reports the date and amount of the $1,000 contribution, and (2) states that the only goods or services received by the donor in return for her $1,000 contribution were intangible religious benefits (assuming this is the case). The $1,000 contribution may be aggregated with the weekly contributions for a total of $1,520, or all of the contributions can be separately itemized.

EXAMPLE. A member made weekly contributions to his church in 2013 that averaged $50 (none is for $250 or more). However, the member made a cash contribution of $500 to the missions fund and an additional cash contribution of $1,000 to the building fund. The church treasurer is aware of the substantiation requirements that apply to donations of $250 or more and plans to issue the member a written acknowledgment by February 15, 2013. The member files his 2013 tax return on February 1, 2013. A contribution of $250 or more must be substantiated with a contemporaneous written acknowledgment, which is defined as an acknowledgment that is received by the donor by the earlier of (1) the date the donor files a tax return claiming a deduction for the contribution, or (2) the due date (including extensions) for filing the return. Since the member filed a tax return on February 1, 2013, a receipt issued by the church on February 15 is not contemporaneous and may result in a loss of a deduction for the $500 and $1,000 contributions. This example illustrates the importance of issuing proper receipts as soon as possible.

➡ **TIP.** Churches should take the following two steps to ensure compliance with the requirement that their written acknowledgments to donors be contemporaneous: (1) issue contribution receipts as soon as possible after the close of the year; and (2) prior to the close of each year, advise donors in writing (through a church newsletter, bulletin, or personal letter) not to file their tax return before receiving all of their contribution receipts for the year.

EXAMPLE. A church treasurer has heard that special substantiation requirements apply to cash contributions of $250 or more, but she assumes that these requirements do not affect her church since it issues annual contribution receipts to each donor. The church's receipts are issued by the end of January of the following year and report the date and amount of each contribution of cash as well as the date and a description of each contribution of property. The treasurer is in error. The church's current reporting is deficient in the following respects:

(1) Since written acknowledgments are issued at the end of January, it is possible that they will be issued to some donors after they have filed their tax returns, meaning that the acknowledgments are not contemporaneous and may result in the nondeductibility of individual contributions of $250 or more (of either cash or property).

(2) The church's written acknowledgment must specify whether the church provided any goods or services in exchange for contribution of $250 or more. If goods or services were provided by the church to the donor in exchange for a particular contribution, the church must include on its written acknowledgment a good faith estimate of the value of the goods or services it provided to the donor. If such goods or services consist solely of intangible religious benefits, the written acknowledgment must include a statement to that effect. The church does not include this information on its current receipts, and accordingly they are insufficient with regard to individual contributions of $250 or more.

(3) The church is not complying with the quid pro quo reporting requirements (described below).

EXAMPLE. M attends a fund-raising breakfast at her church in 2013. M makes a contribution of $300 and receives a free breakfast with a value of $4. The church has two options. First, it can issue a receipt separately identifying both the $300 contribution and the $4 value of the breakfast and informing M that her tax deduction is limited to the amount by which her contribution exceeds the value of the breakfast ($296). Second, since the value of the breakfast meets the definition of "goods or services of insubstantial value" (since it is less than the lesser of $102 or 2 percent of the amount of the contribution), the church's receipt can simply state that no goods or services were provided in connection with the contribution.

EXAMPLE. Same facts as the previous example, except that the value of the breakfast is $10. This does not satisfy the definition of "goods or services of insubstantial value," so the church's receipt may not state that no goods or services were provided in connection with the contribution. It must state a good faith value for the breakfast and indicate on a receipt or separate statement that the contribution is deductible to the extent it exceeds the value of the goods or services provided by the church.

EXAMPLE. A church conducts a fund-raising auction. T buys a bicycle with a value of $200 for an offer of $100. The value of the bicycle does not satisfy the definition of "goods or services of insubstantial value." The church's receipt should not state that no goods or services were provided in connection with the contribution. It must state a good faith value for the bicycle and indicate on its receipt (or in a separate statement) that the contribution is deductible to the extent it exceeds the value of the goods or services provided by the church.

EXAMPLE. The Tax Court ruled that a married couple could not use cancelled checks to substantiate charitable contributions of $250 or more. The couple made donations of $21,000 to various charities and claimed that they could use their personal testimony and cancelled checks to substantiate all of these contributions, including those of $250 or more. The court disagreed, noting that the tax code requires contributions of $250 or more to be substantiated with a written acknowledgment from the charity that meets various requirements. It concluded, "Given that the taxpayers in this case do not have such a written acknowledgment from any of the recipients of the disputed amounts . . . we conclude that they are precluded by the statute from deducting the disputed amounts as charitable contributions." *Hill v. Commissioner, T.C. Memo. 2004-156 (2004).*

EXAMPLE. A woman (the donor) claimed a charitable contribution deduction of $22,000 for cash and property donated to her church. The cash contributions amounted to $12,000 and consisted of 12 monthly contributions ranging from $250 to $450 and several other contributions ranging from $125 for the annual choir concert to $1,200 for the building fund. The donor also made several donations of miscellaneous noncash property, including furniture, kitchen equipment, a television, and several items of clothing. She valued each of these items at more than $250 but less than $5,000.

The IRS audited the donor's tax return and asked her to substantiate her charitable contributions of cash and property. She submitted a receipt from her church that listed each contribution of cash and property. The IRS concluded that the receipt failed to substantiate any contribution of $250 or more because it failed to state whether the church had provided any goods or services in exchange for the contributions, as required by the tax code. Further, the receipt failed to adequately describe the items of donated property. The Tax Court

agreed with the IRS that the contributions of cash and property of $250 or more were not deductible because the church's receipt failed to state "whether the church provided any goods or services in consideration, in whole or in part, for those contributions." The court upheld the imposition of a negligence penalty against the donor. *Kendrix v. Commissioner, T.C. Memo. 2006-9 (2006).*

EXAMPLE. A couple claimed a charitable contribution deduction of $6,500 on their tax return for contributions they made to their church consisting of 10 checks totaling $6,100 (each check was in excess of $250) and an additional eight checks totaling $400 (each check was for less than $250). The IRS audited the couple's tax return and asked them to substantiate their charitable contributions consisting of checks of $250 or more. The couple produced a letter from their church stating that they had made contributions of $6,500 to the church for the year in question. The IRS concluded that this letter failed to substantiate any contribution of $250 or more for two reasons: first, it was not contemporaneous, and second, it failed to state whether the church had provided any goods or services in exchange for the contributions, as required by the tax code. The couple appealed to the Tax Court.

The Tax Court agreed with the IRS that the couple's contributions of $250 or more were not deductible. The court concluded that letter the church sent to the couple (acknowledging contributions of $6,500) was not contemporaneous because the couple did not receive it by the latter of the date they filed their tax return or the due date of their return. Rather, the church did not issue the letter to the couple until two years later, on the day they had their hearing before the court.

The court also noted that "the letter from [the church] does not meet the substantiation requirements set forth in the Internal Revenue Code and regulations. According to the Internal Revenue Code and regulations, the required acknowledgment of the charitable contribution not only must include the amount contributed, but also must state whether the charity provided any goods or services in consideration for the contributions and describe and set forth a good faith estimate of the value of those goods or services. *Gomez v. Commissioner, T.C. Memo. 2008-93.*

EXAMPLE. The Tax Court denied a taxpayer's charitable contribution deduction due to a lack of adequate substantiation. A registered nurse worked for several employers in different cities. She claimed a $17,000 deduction on her federal tax return for charitable contributions, which she reported on line 16 of Schedule A ("Gifts by cash or check"). Next to the $17,000 amount, she wrote, "Church tithes different churches—cash each Sunday." She testified that she attended "any kind of [her denomination's] churches that I could find [and contributed] 10 percent of what I earned that week." She also testified that she donated $1,000 to a charity that failed to provide her with a written acknowledgment of the contribution. The court denied a deduction for this $1,000 contribution since the taxpayer did not receive a written acknowledgment. It concluded that "even if we were persuaded that the taxpayer did make the $1,000 contribution and all the other requirements for a deduction had been met, the statute would prohibit allowance of a deduction for this asserted $1,000 contribution" since the charity failed to comply with the written acknowledgment requirement.

When the IRS pressed the taxpayer on the remaining $16,000 that she allegedly donated to various churches and noted that this was more than 20 percent of her gross income and would have required her to donate more than $300 a week, she testified that "I go to various churches. I don't walk around with $300 in my pocket, but I know when I am leaving work on Saturday night I will stop at whatever church before I go home to sleep, and if it is $100, yes, I will take that along with me." She added, "This isn't a guess or an estimate. If I go back home and think about things, or whatever, I will probably be able to come up with why it is $17,000." The court concluded that the taxpayer was not entitled to any charitable contribution deduction. It also imposed a penalty in the amount of 20 percent of the taxpayer's total tax liability as a result of her understatement of income tax. Section 6662 of the tax code empowers the IRS to assess the 20 percent penalty if an understatement of tax is more than the greater of $5,000 or 10 percent of the amount required to be shown on the tax return. The court affirmed the imposition of this tax, since the taxpayer had understated her tax liability by more than $5,000. *Woodard v. Commissioner, T.C. Summary Opinion 2008-45.*

EXAMPLE. The Tax Court ruled that a married couple could not deduct $26,000 in contributions made to their church due to a lack of adequate substantiation. The husband claimed he lacked substantiating documents for the $26,000 of charitable contributions because he and his wife made anonymous cash donations to their church. He alleged that he was unaware that he needed to substantiate the contributions. However, when asked whether he followed the instructions on the tax return that relate to charitable contributions over $250, he stated: "I don't have to follow [them], I just put whatever is necessary to put the deduction. This is my deduction, the cash plate that I donated." The court agreed with the IRS that the couple was not entitled to any tax deduction for charitable contributions. *Guerrero v. Commissioner, T.C. Memo. 2009-164 (2009).*

EXAMPLE. The Tax Court ruled that a pastor could not deduct cash contributions of $37,000 to her church due to a failure to comply with the substantiation requirements. A woman (the "pastor") was employed as a full-time law enforcement technician and also served as pastor of a church. On her 2004 and 2005 federal income tax returns, she claimed charitable contribution deductions totaling $37,000 for gifts of cash or check to her church.

The IRS audited her tax return and disallowed all of her cash contributions because she "did not verify that the amounts shown were contributions, and paid." The pastor attempted to substantiate her charitable contributions with letters received from church officials and a log she kept that recorded cash contributions she made to her church. The Tax Court ruled that these documents did not provide adequate substantiation of her contributions of $250 or more since they "failed to satisfy the requirement that the organization provide a statement as to whether or not the organization provided any goods or services in consideration for the donation. Therefore, the pastor's charitable contribution deduction is not allowable." *Coleman v. Commissioner, T.C. Summary Opinion 2009-16 (2009). See also Fuentes v. Commissioner, T.C. Summary Opinion 2009-39 (2009).*

EXAMPLE. The Tax Court ruled that a married couple was not entitled to a charitable contribution deduction for contributions of noncash property they had valued at $217,000, since the written acknowledgement they had received from the charity did not contain a statement that no goods or services were provided by the donee in exchange for the contributions. The court concluded that such a statement "is necessary for a charitable contribution deduction under section 170(f)(8)(B)(ii) of the tax code. The donors argue that section 170(f)(8)(B)(ii) can be read to require the statement only when the donee actually furnishes goods or services to the donor. We disagree. Courts must presume that a legislature says in a statute what it means and means in a statute what it says there. In the absence of a clearly expressed legislative intent to the contrary, unambiguous statutory language ordinarily must be regarded as conclusive. Section 170(f)(8)(B)(ii) plainly states that the written acknowledgment is sufficient if it includes information as to whether the donee organization provided any goods or services in consideration, in whole or in part, for any property donated by the taxpayer. The language used is clear and unconditional. There is no reason to read into section 170(f)(8)(B)(ii) the limitation suggested by petitioners." *Friedman v. Commissioner, 99 T.C.M. 1175 (2010). See also Hendrix v. Commissioner, 2010 WL 2900391 (S.D. Ohio 2010).*

EXAMPLE. The Tax Court denied any charitable contribution deduction to a donor who donated property valued at $700,000 to charity because the receipt he received from the charity failed to disclose whether he had received any goods or services in return for his donation. The court concluded that "even if the charity actually provided no consideration for the contribution, the written acknowledgment must say so in order to satisfy the requirement of [the tax code]." It referred to a congressional conference committee report commenting on the substantiation requirements for charitable contributions: "If the donee organization provided no goods or services to the taxpayer in consideration of the taxpayer's contribution, the written substantiation is required to include a statement to that effect." *Schrimsher v. Commissioner, T.C. Memo. 2011-71 (2011).*

EXAMPLE. A married couple (the "taxpayers") timely filed their 2007 income tax return. On their attached Schedule A, the taxpayers claimed a deduction of $25,171 for charitable contributions made by cash or check. Most of the contributions were made by check to their church. Except for five checks totaling $317, the checks the taxpayers wrote to their church were for amounts larger than $250. In 2009 the IRS sent a notice to the taxpayers disallowing their charitable contribution deduction for 2007. In response, the taxpayers produced records of their contributions, including copies of canceled checks and a letter from the church that acknowledged contributions from them during 2007 totaling $22,517 (the "first acknowledgment"). The IRS did not accept the first acknowledgment and informed the taxpayers that it lacked a statement regarding whether any goods or services were provided in consideration for the contributions.

The taxpayers obtained a second letter from the church (the "second acknowledgment") that contained the same information found in the first acknowledgment as well as a statement that no goods or services were provided to them in exchange for their contributions.

The IRS concluded that the taxpayers were not entitled to a deduction for any of their contributions of $250 or more because of their failure to comply with the substantiation requirements. It noted that the church's first letter to the taxpayers failed to comply with the written acknowledgment requirement because it did not include a statement regarding whether any goods or services were provided in consideration for their contribution. And the second letter, which included the statement, was not contemporaneous. The couple conceded that they had not strictly complied with the tax code's substantiation requirements. But they insisted that they had substantially complied with the requirements and therefore were entitled to deduct their contributions.

The Tax Court agreed with the IRS and denied any deduction for contributions of $250 or more. The taxpayers claimed that the omission of a statement regarding goods or services in the church's first letter was sufficient to indicate that no goods or services were provided in consideration for their contributions. The court disagreed, noting that "the express terms of the statute require an affirmative statement." The court also agreed with the IRS that the church's second letter, which included the required statement that no goods or services were provided to the donors in consideration of their contribution, did not meet the tax code's "contemporaneous" requirement because it was issued after the earlier of the date on which the taxpayer files a return for the taxable year in which the contribution was made or the due date (including extensions) for filing such return.

The court rejected the taxpayers' argument that they should be allowed to deduct their donations to their church because they had "substantially complied" with the tax code's substantiation

requirements. It acknowledged that it had found substantial compliance in prior cases that involved compliance with the "essential purpose" of the substantiation requirements despite a lack of strict compliance. But in the present case, the taxpayers had not complied with the "essential purpose" of the law, which includes both the contemporaneous requirement and the requirement that the charity's written acknowledgement indicate whether any goods or services were provided in consideration of the contribution. *Durden v. Commissioner, TC Memo. 2012-140 (2012).*

Rule 3—individual quid pro quo cash contributions of $75 or less

While the special quid pro quo substantiation rules (discussed below) do not apply to contributions of $75 or less, these contributions are still only deductible to the extent they exceed the value of the goods or services provided in exchange. To illustrate, a donor who contributes $50 to a charity and receives a "free" book with a market value of $10 is entitled to a deduction of only $40, since donors may only deduct the amount by which a contribution exceeds the value of any goods or services received in return.

Raffle tickets

Some churches use raffles to raise funds for a project or activity. Numbered tickets are sold to church members, and a ticket is randomly selected as the winner of a prize. Does the possibility of winning a prize make all of the raffle tickets nondeductible? The IRS addressed raffle tickets offered by charities in a 1967 ruling and made the following observation:

> A taxpayer paid $5 for a ticket which entitled him to a chance to win a new automobile. The raffle was conducted to raise funds for the X Charity. Although the payment for the ticket was solicited as a "contribution" to the X Charity and designated as such on the face of the ticket, no part of the payment is deductible as a charitable contribution. Amounts paid for chances to participate in raffles, lotteries, or similar drawings or to participate in puzzle or other contests *for valuable prizes are not gifts in such circumstances, and therefore, do not qualify as deductible charitable contributions.* Revenue Ruling 67-246. [Emphasis added.]

The key language here is "for valuable prizes." To the extent that a raffle ticket entitles a purchaser to valuable prizes, it is nondeductible according to this ruling. The vast majority of religious congregations that use raffles as a means of raising funds do not offer "valuable prizes." Rather, they offer prizes of token value. Everyone is aware that the purpose of the raffle is to raise funds, and the value of the prize is incidental. However, if a congregation offers valuable prizes to raffle ticket purchasers, then the treatment of raffle tickets as charitable contributions is in doubt.

The IRS issued a similar ruling in 1983. *Revenue Ruling 83-130.* It quoted its previous 1967 ruling and noted that "amounts paid for chances to participate in raffles, lotteries, or similar drawings or to participate in puzzle or other contests *for valuable prizes* conducted by a charity are not gifts and therefore do not qualify as charitable contributions" (emphasis added). Again, note that the emphasis is on "valuable prizes."

The Tax Court addressed raffle tickets in a 1966 ruling. *Goldman v. Commissioner, 46 T.C. 136 (1966), aff'd 388 F.2d 476 (6th Cir. 1967).* A taxpayer purchased raffle tickets in the following amounts from the following organizations: Good Samaritan Hospital ($50), Jewish Community Center ($10), Chofetz Chaim (Hebrew School) Bazaar ($10), and Cancer Aid ($10). The taxpayer received tickets for these payments and these tickets were placed in a "blind draw" from which he conceivably might have won something. The taxpayer acknowledged that he would have won something if his ticket number had been drawn in the lottery but contended that in purchasing the tickets he did not intend to gamble on a risk but intended to make a gift, characterizing his payments as "a regular donation that is made year after year, to these institutions." The taxpayer insisted that "the odds of winning were infinitesimal" and that "the amount of the payment far exceeded the actuarial value of the 'chance'."

The taxpayer treated all of these purchases as charitable contributions on his tax return. The IRS challenged these deductions, and the case was appealed to the Tax Court. The court acknowledged that "it is possible to hypothesize a raffle ticket situation where the charitable nature of the gift would scarcely be debated, as where the purchase for $10 is one of one thousand chances and the prize a nosegay of violets." In other words, the purchase of a raffle ticket may be treated as a charitable contribution if either or both of the following conditions is met: (1) the chance of winning a prize is low because of the number of tickets sold; or (2) the value of the prize is low. On the other hand, the court noted that there are other situations in which the purchase of a raffle ticket cannot be treated as a charitable contribution because neither of these two conditions is satisfied.

The court concluded that the raffle tickets could not be treated as charitable contributions, since the prizes offered by the various charities were of "substantial" value, and the taxpayer had failed to establish that his chances of winning were sufficiently low to entitle him to a charitable contribution deduction.

Conclusion

In conclusion, note the following two considerations:

First, the precedent summarized above allows raffle tickets to be treated as a charitable contribution so long as the chance of winning is remote because of the number of tickets sold or the value of the prize is insubstantial. Many congregational raffles satisfy either or both of these conditions, so there is a reasonable basis for treating the tickets as charitable contributions.

Second, these rulings never raised any concerns about the legality of conducting raffles. The IRS addressed various "games of chance"

conducted by charities in Announcement 89-138, I.R.B. 1988-45. The IRS did not express any concerns about the legality of such activities but did note that they may generate unrelated business taxable income if they are "regularly carried on" as opposed to an intermittent activity.

Rule 4—individual quid pro quo cash contributions of more than $75

In addition to providing a written acknowledgment for contributions of $250 or more (as discussed under Rule 2 above), a church must issue a written disclosure statement to persons who make *quid pro quo contributions* of more than $75. A quid pro quo contribution is a payment "made partly as a contribution and partly in consideration for goods or services provided to the donor by the donee organization." For example, a donor contributes $100 to her church, but in return she receives a dinner worth $30.

The written disclosure statement a church or charity provides to a donor of a quid pro quo contribution of more than $75 must

- inform the donor that the amount of the contribution that is tax-deductible is limited to the excess of the amount of any money (or the value of any property other than money) contributed by the donor over the value of any goods or services provided by the church or other charity in return; and
- provide the donor with a good faith estimate of the value of the goods or services furnished to the donor. *IRC 6115.*

EXAMPLE. A donor gives a charitable organization $100 in exchange for a concert ticket with a fair market value of $30. In this example the donor's tax deduction may not exceed $70. Because the donor's payment (quid pro quo contribution) exceeds $75, the charitable organization must furnish a disclosure statement to the donor even though the deductible amount does not exceed $75.

Exceptions to the quid pro quo reporting rule

A written statement need not be issued to a donor of a quid pro contribution in any of the following situations:

Token goods or services are given to the donor by the charity. Token goods or services are defined in either of the following two ways:

- items such as bookmarks, calendars, key chains, mugs, posters, or T-shirts bearing the charity's name or logo and having a cost (as opposed to fair market value) of less than $10.20; or
- in other cases, when the value of goods or services provided to the donor does not exceed the lesser of $102 or 2 percent of the amount of the contribution.

The $102 and $10.20 amounts are adjusted annually for inflation (and represent the 2013 amounts).

The donor receives an intangible religious benefit. The term "intangible religious benefit" is defined by the tax code as "any intangible religious benefit which is provided by an organization organized exclusively for religious purposes and which generally is not sold in a commercial transaction outside the donative context." A congressional committee report states that the term "intangible religious benefit" includes "admission to a religious ceremony" or other insignificant "tangible benefits furnished to contributors that are incidental to a religious ceremony (such as wine)." However, the committee report clarifies that "this exception does apply, for example, to tuition for education leading to a recognized degree, travel services, or consumer goods."

Penalties

The tax code imposes a penalty of $10 per contribution (up to a maximum of $5,000 per fund-raising event or mailing) on charities that fail to make the required quid pro quo disclosures, unless a failure was due to reasonable cause. The penalties will apply if a charity either fails to make the required disclosure in connection with a quid pro quo contribution (as explained above) or makes a disclosure that is incomplete or inaccurate.

Intent to make a charitable contribution

For many years the IRS has ruled that persons who receive goods or services in exchange for a payment to a charity are eligible for a charitable contribution deduction only with respect to the amount by which their payment exceeds the fair rental value of the goods or services they received. The tax regulations add an additional condition: donors may not claim a charitable contribution in such a case unless they intended to make a payment in excess of the fair market value of the goods or services. *Treas. Reg. 1.170A-1(h).*

> **EXAMPLE.** A church sells tickets to a missions banquet. The cost of each ticket is $100, though the fair market value of the meal is only $20. Persons who purchase tickets are eligible to claim a charitable contribution deduction in the amount of $80 if they intended to make a payment in excess of the amount of the dinner.

How will church treasurers know when donors intend to make a payment in excess of goods or services received in exchange? The tax regulations state that "the facts and circumstances" of each case must be considered.

✿ **KEY POINT.** One rule of thumb may help: the greater the amount by which a payment exceeds the market value of goods or services received in exchange, the more likely the donor intended to make a charitable contribution. In the previous example it is clear that donors intend to make a contribution, since the ticket price ($100) obviously exceeds the value of the dinner. This is a good reason to set ticket prices at a level obviously higher than the value of a meal received at an appreciation banquet.

Refusal of benefits

What if a member purchases a $100 ticket to a church's missions banquet (as in the above example) but has no intention of attending the banquet? Is the member entitled to a charitable contribution deduction of $100 or $80? In other words, must a charitable contribution be reduced by the amount of goods or services that a donor refuses to accept? The IRS has ruled that "a taxpayer who has properly rejected a benefit offered by a charitable organization may claim a deduction in the full amount of the payment to the charitable organization." *Revenue Ruling 67-246.* How does a donor reject a benefit? The IRS suggested that charities create a form containing a "check-off box" that donors can check at the time they make a contribution if they want to refuse a benefit.

✿ **KEY POINT.** The IRS distinguishes goods or services that were made available to a donor but not used from those that were properly rejected. To illustrate, donors who purchase a ticket to a missions banquet for $100 must reduce their contribution by the value of the meal ($20 in the above example) even if they decide not to attend the banquet. However, if at the time a donor purchases a ticket, she indicates unequivocally and in writing that she will not be attending the banquet, then the church treasurer can receipt the donor for the full value of the ticket ($100). The IRS has noted that in such a case the receipt issued by the church "need not reflect the value of the rejected benefit." *Revenue Ruling 67-246.*

> **EXAMPLE.** A church conducts an auction to raise funds for missions. Members are asked to donate baked items, which are then auctioned to other members at the highest price. A member donates a pie, which is sold to another member for $150 (assume that it has a value of $5). Do the quid pro quo rules apply to the donor who bought the pie for $150? The answer is yes, since this member made a contribution of more than $75, in return for which she received goods or services other than token items or intangible religious benefits. The pie is not a token item, since its value ($5) exceeds the lesser of $102 or 2 percent of the contribution ($3).

> **EXAMPLE.** A church conducts an auction of donated items. A member purchases a used bicycle (with a value of $50) for $250. This is a quid pro quo contribution, since it is part contribution and part purchase of goods or services. Accordingly, in addition to the substantiation requirements mentioned above, the church must issue the donor a written statement that (1) informs the donor that the amount of the contribution that is tax-deductible is limited to the excess of the amount of any money contributed by the donor over the value of any goods or services provided by the church in return, and (2) provides the donor with a good faith estimate of the value of the goods or services furnished to the donor. Accordingly, the church's written acknowledgment should report the contribution of $250, inform the donor that the contribution is deductible only to the extent it exceeds the value of goods or services received

in exchange, provide the donor with a description and good faith estimate of the value of the bicycle provided in return ($50), and then list the deductible portion of the contribution ($200).

EXAMPLE. A church-affiliated college conducts an annual banquet for persons who have contributed more than $1,000 during the year. The value of the meal provided is $30 per person. Do the quid pro quo reporting requirements apply? At first glance the answer would appear to be yes, since donors are receiving a $30 benefit in exchange for their contributions. However, the tax code defines a quid pro contribution as "a payment made partly as a contribution and partly in consideration for goods or services provided to the payor by the donee organization." When a donor makes a contribution of $1,000 to the college, does he or she do so in order to receive a free dinner? Is the dinner in any sense relevant to the donor in deciding whether to make the contribution?

Obviously, the answer in most cases is no. Most donors do not make their contributions "in consideration for goods or services." Most donors would have made their contributions even if no dinner were provided. As a result, an argument can be made that contributions to the college are not quid quo pro contributions. However, this rationale has never been recognized by the IRS or the courts and should not be adopted without the advice of a tax professional.

EXAMPLE. A religious radio ministry offers a "free" book in exchange for contributions of $50 or more. The book has a value of $10. The quid pro quo rules apply to contributions in excess of $75 but not to contributions of $75 or less. Note, however, that while the quid pro quo rules do not apply to contributions of $75 or less, these contributions are still only deductible to the extent they exceed the value of the goods or services provided in exchange.

EXAMPLE. Many churches conduct sales of merchandise to raise funds for various programs and activities. Examples include bake sales, auctions, and bazaars. Should a church issue a Form 1099-MISC to persons who purchase items at such events? No, ruled the IRS. Charities that sell items in the course of fund-raising events need not issue Forms 1099-MISC to purchasers, since no compensation is being paid to them. Form 1099-MISC is issued to nonemployees who are paid compensation of $600 or more during the year. *IRS Letter Ruling 9517010.*

2. CONTRIBUTIONS OF NONCASH PROPERTY

The substantiation requirements for contributions of noncash property (e.g., land, equipment, stock, books, art, vehicles) are more stringent than for contributions of cash or checks. It is important to note that more than one rule may apply to a particular contribution. For example, any contribution of property valued by the donor at

less than $250 will trigger only Rule 5. But contributions of property valued at $250 or more will trigger Rule 6 and possibly Rule 7 or Rule 10 (depending on the value of the donated property).

Rule 5—individual contributions of noncash property valued by the donor at less than $250

The church's written acknowledgment
The income tax regulations specify that

> *any taxpayer who makes a charitable contribution of property other than money . . . shall maintain for each contribution a receipt from the donee showing the following information:*
>
> *(1) The name of the donee.*
>
> *(2) The date and location of the contribution.*
>
> *(3) A description of the property in detail reasonably sufficient under the circumstances. Although the fair market value of the property is one of the circumstances to be taken into account in determining the amount of detail to be included on the receipt, such value need not be stated on the receipt.* Treas. Reg. 1.170A-13.

A letter or other written communication from the church acknowledging receipt of the contribution and containing the information in (1), (2), and (3) above will serve as a receipt. You are not required to have a receipt where it is impractical to get one (for example, if you leave property at a charity's unattended drop site).

Records maintained by donors
In addition to the receipt provided by the church, donors themselves must keep reliable written records for each item of donated property. Records must include the following information:

- the name and address of the organization to which you contributed.
- the date and location of the contribution.
- a description of the property in detail reasonable under the circumstances. For a security, keep the name of the issuer, the type of security, and whether it is regularly traded on a stock exchange or in an over-the-counter market. The fair market value of the property at the time of the contribution and how you figured the fair market value. If it was determined by appraisal, you should also keep a signed copy of the appraisal.
- the fair market value of the property at the time of the contribution and how the fair market value was determined.
- the cost or other basis of the property if you must reduce its fair market value by appreciation. Your records should also include the amount of the reduction and how you figured it. If you choose the 50 percent limit instead of the special 30 percent limit on certain capital gain property (discussed

earlier), you must keep a record showing the years for which you made the choice, contributions for the current year to which the choice applies, and carryovers from preceding years to which the choice applies.

- the amount you claim as a deduction for the tax year as a result of the contribution, if you contribute less than your entire interest in the property during the tax year. Your records must include the amount you claimed as a deduction in any earlier years for contributions of other interests in this property. They must also include the name and address of each organization to which you contributed the other interests, the place where any such tangible property is located or kept, and the name of any person in possession of the property, other than the organization to which you contributed.
- the terms of any agreement or understanding entered into by the donor which relates to the use, sale, or other disposition of the donated property, including, for example, the terms of any agreement or understanding which (1) restricts the church's right to use or dispose of the donated property, (2) confers upon anyone other than the church any right to the income from the donated property or to the possession of the property, or (3) earmarks donated property for a particular use. *Treas. Reg. 1.170A-13(b)(2)(ii).*

Rule 6—individual contributions of noncash property valued by the donor at $250 to $500

The church's written acknowledgment

Donors who claim a deduction of at least $250 but not more than $500 for a noncash charitable contribution must get and keep an acknowledgment of their contribution from the church. Donors who make more than one contribution of $250 or more must have either a separate acknowledgment for each contribution or one acknowledgment that shows the total contributions. The church's written acknowledgment must contain the same information as under Rule 5 (above). It also must also meet these tests:

- It must be written.
- It must include (1) a description (but not necessarily the value) of the donated property, (2) a statement of whether the church provided any goods or services as a result of the contribution (other than certain token items and membership benefits), and (3) a description and good faith estimate of the value of any goods or services described in (2). If the only benefit provided by the church was an intangible religious benefit (such as admission to a religious ceremony) that generally is not sold in a commercial transaction outside the donative context, the acknowledgment must say so and does not need to describe or estimate the value of the benefit.
- The donor must receive the church's written acknowledgment on or before the earlier of (1) the date the donor files his or her tax return claiming the contribution; or (2) the due date, including extensions, for filing the return.

Records maintained by donors

IRS regulations specify that donors who make contributions of $250 or more, but not more than $500, are required to obtain a contemporaneous written acknowledgment from the donee charity and, in addition, maintain all of the donor records described under Rule 5 above.

Rule 7—individual contributions of noncash property valued by the donor at more than $500 but not more than $5,000

Donors who claim a deduction over $500 but not over $5,000 for a noncash charitable contribution must have the acknowledgment and written records described under Rule 6, and their records must also include

- a description of how the donor acquired the donated property, for example, by purchase, gift, bequest, inheritance, or exchange.
- the approximate date the donor acquired the property.
- the cost or other basis, and any adjustments to the basis, of property held less than 12 months and, if available, the cost or other basis of property held 12 months or more. This requirement, however, does not apply to publicly traded securities.

✲ **KEY POINT.** Donors whose total deduction for all noncash contributions for the year is over $500 must complete Section A of Form 8283 and attach it to Form 1040. However, donors should not complete Section A for items reported on Section B (see Rule 9). The IRS can disallow a deduction for a noncash charitable contribution of more than $500 if a donor does not submit Form 8283 with his or her tax return.

➡ **TIP.** Donors who are not able to provide information on either the date they acquired the property or the cost basis of the property, and who have a reasonable cause for not being able to provide this information, should attach a statement of explanation to their tax return.

Tip. See section 5 of the introduction to this chapter for rules that apply to the deductibility of a contribution of noncash property that has appreciated in value.

Rule 8—quid pro quo contributions of noncash property

The quid pro quo rules are explained fully in the previous section dealing with cash contributions (see Rules 3 and 4). Those rules apply to contributions of property as well and should be reviewed at this time.

Rule 9—individual contributions of noncash property valued by the donor at more than $5,000

In this section the rules for substantiating a contribution of property valued by the donor at more than $5,000 will be reviewed. Unfortunately, many donors and church leaders are not familiar with these rules. This can lead to unfortunate consequences, since

IRS regulations warn that no deduction for any contribution of property valued by the donor at more than $5,000 will be allowed unless these requirements are satisfied.

The requirements discussed below ordinarily are triggered by a contribution of a single item of property valued by the donor at more than $5,000, but they also can be triggered by contributions of *similar items* within a calendar or fiscal year if the combined value claimed by the donor exceeds $5,000.

Publicly traded stock listed on a stock exchange is not subject to these requirements, since its value is readily ascertainable. Note, however, that gifts of publicly traded stock must be substantiated by completing Part A of Form 8283, even if the stock is valued at more than $5,000. Part A does not require a qualified appraisal.

Contributions of nonpublicly traded stock (i.e., stock held by most small, family-owned corporations) are subject to the qualified appraisal requirement, but only if the value claimed by the donor exceeds $10,000.

Contributions of cars, boats, and planes are subject to special rules, as explained in Rule 10.

> **EXAMPLE.** S contributes equipment to a church in September 2013. The equipment has a retail value of $4,000, but S believes $6,000 is a more accurate value and plans to deduct this amount as a charitable contribution on her 2013 federal income tax return. The substantiation rules discussed in this section apply.

> **EXAMPLE.** Same facts as the preceding example, except that S plans to claim a contribution deduction of only $4,000. The substantiation rules discussed in this section do not apply.

> **EXAMPLE.** B contributes a vacant lot and a computer to a church in 2013. B plans to claim a charitable contribution deduction of $4,000 for each item. The substantiation rules discussed in this section (with respect to contributions of noncash property valued at more than $5,000) do not apply. If B had given two lots and planned to claim a contribution deduction of $4,000 for each, the rules discussed in this section would apply, since the lots are similar items whose values must be combined.

The substantiation requirements that apply to contributions of $250 or more were enacted to make it more difficult for donors to improperly reduce taxable income by intentionally overvaluing contributed property and then claiming inflated charitable contribution deductions on their income tax returns.

The donor's obligations

Donors who contribute property valued at more than $5,000 to a church or other charity must satisfy each of the following three requirements in order to claim a charitable contribution deduction:

(1) Obtain a qualified appraisal. A donor's first obligation is to obtain a qualified appraisal. The income tax regulations define a qualified appraisal as an appraisal that (a) is "made, signed, and dated" by a "qualified appraiser"; (b) is made no earlier than 60 days prior to the date the appraised property was donated; (c) does not involve a prohibited appraisal fee (i.e., based on a percentage of the appraised value or on the amount allowed as a deduction); and (d) includes the following information:

- an adequate description of the donated property;
- the physical condition of the property;
- the date (or expected date) of the contribution;
- the terms of any agreement or understanding entered into by or on behalf of the donor pertaining to the use or disposition of the donated property;
- the name, address, and identifying number of the qualified appraiser;
- the qualifications of the qualified appraiser who prepared and signed the qualified appraisal;
- a statement that the appraisal was prepared for income tax purposes;
- the date on which the property was valued;
- the appraised fair market value of the property on the date (or expected date) of the contribution;
- the method of valuation used to determine the fair market value;
- the specific basis for the valuation; and
- a description of the fee arrangement between the donor and appraiser.

In addition, a qualified appraisal must be prepared in accordance with generally accepted appraisal standards and any regulations or other guidance prescribed by the IRS. The income tax regulations define a qualified appraisal as an appraisal prepared by a qualified appraiser in accordance with generally accepted appraisal standards. Generally accepted appraisal standards are defined in the proposed regulations as "the substance and principles of the Uniform Standards of Professional Appraisal Practice (USPAP), as developed by the Appraisal Standards Board of the Appraisal Foundation."

Qualified appraiser. A qualified appraisal, as noted above, is one prepared by a *qualified appraiser*. The regulations define the term "qualified appraiser" as an individual who

- has earned an appraisal designation from a recognized professional appraiser organization or has otherwise met minimum education and experience requirements to be determined by the IRS in regulations.
- has met certain minimum education and experience requirements. For real property, the appraiser must be licensed or certified for the type of property being appraised in the state in which the property is located. For property other

than real property, the appraiser must have successfully completed college or professional-level coursework relevant to the property being valued; must have at least two years of experience in the trade or business of buying, selling, or valuing the type of property being valued; and must fully describe in the appraisal his or her qualifying education and experience.
- regularly prepares appraisals for which he or she is paid.
- demonstrates verifiable education and experience in valuing the type of property being appraised. To do this, the appraiser can make a declaration in the appraisal that, because of his or her background, experience, education, and membership in professional associations, he or she is qualified to make appraisals of the type of property being valued.
- has not been prohibited from practicing before the IRS at any time during the three-year period ending on the date of the appraisal.
- is not an "excluded individual." This term includes the donor or donee of the property, or a party to the transaction in which the donor acquired the property being appraised, unless the property is donated within two months of the date of acquisition and its appraised value is not more than its acquisition price. See IRS Publication 561 for additional information.

The qualified appraisal must be received by the donor before the due date (including extensions) of the federal income tax return on which the deduction is claimed. Finally, note that a qualified appraisal must be obtained for each item of contributed property valued by the donor in excess of $5,000.

Exceptions. You do not need an appraisal if the property is

- nonpublicly traded stock of $10,000 or less;
- a vehicle (including a car, boat, or airplane) for which your deduction is limited to the gross proceeds from its sale (see Rule 10, below);
- publicly traded securities listed on a stock exchange for which quotations are published on a daily basis, or regularly traded in a national or regional over-the-counter market for which published quotations are available; or
- inventory.

❖ **KEY POINT.** The requirement that a donor obtain a qualified appraisal of property donated to charity if the amount of the deduction exceeds $5,000 applies to both individuals and C corporations.

Donors and appraisers may be subject to penalties, as follows:

Penalties against the appraiser. An appraiser who prepares an incorrect appraisal may be subject to a penalty if: (1) the appraiser knows or should have known the appraisal would be used in connection with a return or claim for refund and (2) the appraisal results in the 20 percent or 40 percent penalty for a valuation misstatement described below. The penalty imposed on the appraiser is the smaller of

- the greater of (i) 10 percent of the underpayment due to the misstatement or (ii) $1,000, or
- 125 percent of the gross income received for the appraisal.

In addition, any appraiser who falsely or fraudulently overstates the value of property described in a qualified appraisal of a Form 8283 that the appraiser has signed may be subject to a civil penalty for aiding and abetting as understatement of tax liability and may have his or her appraisal disregarded.

Penalties against the donor. You may be liable for a penalty if you overstate the value or adjusted basis of donated property. The penalty is 20 percent of the underpayment of tax related to the overstatement if

- the value or adjusted basis claimed on the return is 150 percent or more of the correct amount and
- you underpaid your tax by more than $5,000 because of the overstatement.

The penalty is 40 percent, rather than 20 percent, if

- the value or adjusted basis claimed on the return is 200 percent or more of the correct amount and
- you underpaid your tax by more than $5,000 because of the overstatement.

(2) Prepare a qualified appraisal summary. A donor must also complete an appraisal summary and enclose it with the tax return on which the charitable contribution deduction is claimed. The appraisal summary is a summary of the qualified appraisal and is made on Section B (side 2) of IRS Form 8283. Because of the importance of this form, one is reproduced at the end of this chapter. You can obtain copies of Form 8283 by contacting your nearest IRS office, by calling the toll-free IRS forms hotline at 1-800-829-3676, or by downloading them from the IRS website (irs.gov).

Section A (side 1) of Form 8283 is completed by donors who contribute property valued between $500 and $5,000, as noted under Rule 7.

Section B of Form 8283 contains four parts. Part I is completed by the donor or appraiser and sets forth information from the qualified appraisal regarding the donated property, including its appraised value. Part II is completed by the donor and identifies individual items in groups of similar items having an appraised value of not more than $500. Part II contains the appraiser's certification that he or she satisfies the definition of a qualified appraiser. Part IV is a donee acknowledgment, which must be *completed by the church*. The church simply indicates the date on which it received the contribution and agrees to file an information return (Form 8282) with the IRS if it disposes of the donated property within three years. The regulations specify that the church's acknowledgment "does not represent concurrence in the appraised value of the contributed property. Rather, it represents acknowledgment of receipt of the property described in the appraisal summary on the date specified in the appraisal summary."

The instructions for Form 8283 permit a church to complete Part IV before the qualified appraisal is completed. They instruct the donor to "complete at least your name, identification number, and description of the donated property," along with Part II if applicable, before submitting the Form 8283 to the church (or other donee). In other words, the donor should fill in his or her name and Social Security number on the lines provided at the top of page 1 of the form, and also complete line 5(a) of Section B, Part I (on the back page of the form) before submitting the form to the church. After completing Section B, Part IV, the church returns the form to the donor, who then completes the remaining information required in Part I. The donor should also arrange to have the qualified appraiser complete Part II at this time.

If the amount of a contribution of property other than cash, inventory, or publicly traded securities exceeds $500,000 (if art, $20,000), the qualified appraisal must be attached to the donor's tax return. For purposes of the dollar thresholds, property and all similar items of property donated to one or more charities are treated as one property.

(3) Maintain records. The donor's third obligation is to have the acknowledgment and written records described under Rule 7. Many of these items will be contained in the qualified appraisal, which should be retained by the donor.

EXAMPLE. A member contributes equipment valued at $15,000 to his church. The member asks an appraiser who attends the church to appraise the property. Such an appraiser may not satisfy the definition of a qualified appraiser, since his relationship to the church might cause a reasonable person to question his independence.

EXAMPLE. A member contributes property to a church in 2013 that is worth well in excess of $5,000. To assist the member in complying with the substantiation requirements, the church should (1) acknowledge receipt of the contribution in a signed document; (2) inform the member of the necessity of obtaining a qualified appraisal; and (3) inform the member of the obligation to complete an appraisal summary (Form 8283) prior to the due date for the 2013 income tax return (and, as a convenience, give the member a copy of the current form). The church is required to sign Section B, Part IV, of the donor's Form 8283 and to complete and file with the IRS an information return (Form 8282)

within 125 days of the date it disposes of the property (if it does so within 3 years of the date of the contribution).

EXAMPLE. The Tax Court ruled that a taxpayer who donated property to charity had substantially complied with the law even though a separate appraisal had not been obtained and the qualifications of the appraiser were omitted from the appraisal summary attached to the donor's tax return. The court noted that the donor had obtained an appraisal of the property prior to the time he decided to donate it to charity and that this appraisal contained substantially all the information required by law. When the donor later decided to donate the property to charity, he simply enclosed a copy of this appraisal with the tax return on which a charitable contribution was claimed. The court concluded that the qualified appraisal rules are "directory, not mandatory," and therefore they could be met by substantial, rather than strict, compliance. The fact that the donor did not obtain a new appraisal did not preclude a charitable contribution deduction. *Bond v. Commissioner, 100 T.C. 32 (1993).*

EXAMPLE. A donor contributed nonpublicly traded stock worth more than $10,000 to a church but obtained no qualified appraisal and attached no qualified appraisal summary to the tax return on which the charitable contribution deduction was claimed. The Tax Court ruled that the donor was not entitled to a charitable contribution deduction, even though there was no dispute as to the value of the donated stock. *Hewitt v. Commissioner, 109 T.C. 12 (1997).*

EXAMPLE. A donor claimed two charitable contributions of clothing that she valued at $4,000 and $2,000. The IRS denied a charitable contribution deduction for these gifts because the donor failed to comply with the substantiation requirements. The donor appealed to the Tax Court, which agreed with the IRS. The court noted that persons who contribute property valued at more than $5,000 must obtain a qualified appraisal of the property and attach a qualified appraisal summary (IRS Form 8283) to the tax return on which the deduction is claimed. Items of similar property are combined when applying the $5,000 test. Since the donor in this case gave similar property (clothing), the value of the two separate donations had to be combined. And, since the combined value exceeded $5,000, the donor was required by law to obtain a qualified appraisal and attach a qualified appraisal summary to her tax return. Since she failed to comply with these requirements, she was not eligible for any charitable contribution deduction for the gifts of clothing. *Fast v. Commissioner, T.C. Memo. 1998-272 (1998).*

EXAMPLE. A corporation made a sizeable contribution of property to a charity for the care of the needy. The charity issued the corporation a receipt acknowledging the contribution but failing to indicate whether the charity provided any goods or services in return for the contribution. The IRS ruled that the corporation was not entitled to a charitable contribution deduction for three reasons:

First, the income tax regulations require that a charity's written acknowledgment of a contribution be furnished on or before the earlier of the date on which the taxpayer files a return for the taxable year in which the contribution was made or the due date for filing such return. The IRS concluded that this requirement was not met.

Second, the charity's written acknowledgment did not comply with the substantiation requirements for contributions valued at $250 or more, since it did not indicate whether the charity provided any goods or services in return for the contributed property.

Third, since the corporation donated property that it valued at more than $5,000, it was required by the income tax regulations to obtain a qualified appraisal of the property and enclose a summary of the appraisal (on IRS Form 8283) with the tax return on which the contribution deduction was claimed. A Form 8283 was not enclosed with the corporation's tax return. When asked by an IRS agent about the missing Form 8283, the corporation furnished the missing form; but the IRS concluded that this was too late, since the form did not accompany the corporation's tax return. *IRS Letter Ruling 200003005.*

EXAMPLE. A taxpayer claimed a deduction of $950,000 for contributions of several items of property he made to a church. The donated items included historical books and paintings. The taxpayer completed a Form 8283, on which he listed the donated items and his estimate of their market value, but he did not obtain an appraisal for any of the items. The IRS audited the taxpayer and allowed a charitable contribution deduction of only $12,900. On appeal, the Tax Court agreed with the IRS. It noted that the taxpayer failed to obtain a qualified appraisal of the donated items within the time limits specified by law. In general, persons who donate property valued at more than $5,000 must obtain a qualified appraisal no later than the date they file the tax return on which the contribution deduction is claimed. The taxpayer retained an appraiser only after his tax return was audited.

Further, the court noted that the appraiser's valuations were not credible, since "he gave no persuasive explanation of his methodology, made no reference to comparable sales or a valuation rationale, and made no reference to any experience he had that would support the values at which he arrived. Without any reasoned analysis, his report is useless. His opinions are so exaggerated that his testimony is not credible." *Jacobson v. Commissioner, T.C. Memo. 1999-401 (1999).*

EXAMPLE. A married couple (the "taxpayers") donated property having a fair market value of $10,000 to their local Boys and Girls Club. The next year they donated a truck having a fair market value of $14,850 to their church. The taxpayers failed to obtain qualified appraisals for both charitable contributions prior to the due date of their tax returns. They were audited

by the IRS, and only then did they produce letters from two appraisers (dated after the taxpayers filed their tax returns). The IRS disallowed any deduction for either of these contributions, and the taxpayers appealed. The Tax Court noted that the tax code specifies that a taxpayer must obtain a qualified appraisal for donated property (except money and certain publicly traded securities) in excess of $5,000. In addition, the income tax regulations require that the taxpayer attach an appraisal summary to the tax return, and the IRS has prescribed Form 8283 to be used as the appraisal summary.

The Tax Court concluded: "Although we have not demanded that the taxpayer strictly comply with the reporting requirements of [the regulations] we have required that the taxpayer substantially comply with the regulations in order to take the deduction for a charitable contribution. Based on the record, we find that [the taxpayers] did not timely obtain qualified appraisals and failed to include complete appraisal summaries with their tax returns. Because [they] failed to comply substantially with [the regulations] we hold that [they] are not entitled to deduct the noncash charitable contributions." *Jorgenson v. Commissioner, 79 T.C.M. 1444 (2000).*

EXAMPLE. A couple made a gift of privately held corporate stock to a charity and claimed a charitable contribution deduction in the amount of $500,000. The couple based this amount on the opinion of a stockbroker who occasionally traded the stock. The Tax Court ruled that the couple could not deduct any amount for the gift of stock because they failed to comply with the substantiation requirements that apply to gifts of privately held stock.

Gifts of privately held stock (valued at more than $10,000) are not deductible unless (1) the donor obtains a qualified appraisal of the donated shares no earlier than 60 days prior to the date of the contribution, and (2) the donor completes a qualified appraisal summary (IRS Form 8283) and encloses it with the Form 1040 on which the contribution deduction is claimed. Note that the donee (church or other charity) must sign this appraisal summary.

In this case the couple did not obtain a qualified appraisal and did not attach a Form 8283 appraisal summary to their tax return. The court concluded, "We find that the couple failed to meet the substantiation requirements. Accordingly . . . no charitable deductions are allowed to them on account of the transfer of the shares." *Todd v. Commissioner, 118 T.C. No. 19 (2002).*

EXAMPLE. The Tax Court ruled that a church member could not deduct a contribution of a BMW automobile to his pastor, for two reasons. First, the contribution was to an individual rather than to a charity, and "such gifts are not deductible as charitable contributions." Second, the donor failed to obtain a qualified appraisal of the donated car and attach a qualified appraisal summary (Form 8283) to his tax return, as is required for any contribution of noncash property (other than publicly traded stock) with a claimed value of more than $5,000. *Brown v. Commissioner, T.C. Summary Opinion 2002-91 (2002).*

EXAMPLE. A taxpayer donated a "garage full" of obsolete computer equipment to a church and claimed a charitable contribution deduction of $15,320. The Tax Court ruled that the contribution was not deductible for a number of reasons, including the fact that the donor failed to comply with the qualified appraisal requirement. The court noted that the contribution deduction for the computer equipment exceeded $5,000, and therefore the donor was required to obtain a qualified appraisal and attach an appraisal summary (Form 8283, Section B) to his tax return. Since he failed to file an appraisal summary with his tax return, no deduction was permissible. *Castleton v. Commissioner, T.C. Memo. 2005-58 (2005).*

EXAMPLE. The Tax Court denied a charitable contribution deduction of $210,000 for donations of two pieces of property made by a married couple to a charity. The court noted that the couple failed to obtain a timely qualified appraisal of the donated properties. It rejected the donors' claim that they had "substantially complied" with the law: "None of the appraisals the donors obtained is a qualified appraisal. . . . The qualified appraisal requirement is mandatory, not merely directory. Our case law is clear that we cannot apply the doctrine of substantial compliance to excuse a taxpayer's failure to meet this requirement. . . . We also note that the requirements that the appraiser and the donee sign the Form 8283 also appear to be mandatory. By signing the appraiser's declaration, the appraiser potentially subjects himself to a penalty. . . . This requirement . . . discourages the overvaluation of charitable contributions. . . . By signing the donee's acknowledgment, the donee asserts that it is a charitable organization. This requirement thus relates to the substance or essence of whether or not a charitable contribution was actually made." *Ney v. Commissioner, T.C. Summary Opinion 2006-154.*

EXAMPLE. The Tax Court disallowed a donor's charitable contribution deduction of $23,200 due to lack of proper substantiation. The donor claimed that he made several contributions of clothing to various religious organizations and that the total value of the donated items amounted to $5,600. He also claimed a deduction of $5,560 for several items of furniture that he claimed he donated to the same organizations. The rest of his contributions were in the form of cash. The IRS disallowed all of the contributions as a result of inadequate substantiation. On appeal, the Tax Court agreed. It noted that for noncash contributions in excess of $5,000, taxpayers must "(1) obtain a qualified appraisal, (2) attach a fully completed appraisal summary (Form 8283) to the tax return on which the deduction is claimed, and (3) maintain records pertaining to the claimed deduction." The court correctly pointed out that "similar items of property, such as generic items like clothing and furniture, are aggregated when

determining whether the $5,000 threshold is met. In this case the claimed deductions for jackets, clothes, shoes, and bags are aggregated and satisfy the $5,000 threshold. The claimed deduction for furniture also exceeds $5,000."

The donor conceded that he neither obtained a qualified appraisal of the donated clothing and furniture nor attached a Form 8283 to his tax return. The only forms that he attached to his return were a receipt that he filled out and an itemized list of the donated items, which he also compiled. The court concluded that "neither the receipt nor the itemized form meet the requirements prescribed under [the tax code] as they do not meet the requirements for a qualified appraisal made by a qualified appraiser."

The court also denied the donor's cash contributions, since he failed to provide any receipts, canceled checks, or other written records for their claimed contributions. *Obiakor v. Commissioner, T.C. Summary Opinion 2007-185 (2007). See also Tilman v. United States, 2009-2 U.S.T.C. ¶50,549 (S.D.N.Y. 2009).*

EXAMPLE. The Tax Court ruled that a married couple was not entitled to a charitable contribution deduction for contributions of noncash property they had valued at $217,000.

The donors conceded that they had not strictly complied with the appraisal and appraisal summary requirements. But they insisted that they were nonetheless entitled to deduct their contributions since they had "substantially complied" with the substantiation requirements. The Tax Court concluded that even if the contributions were allowable based on substantial compliance with the law, the donors had not satisfied this test since their compliance with the law was far from substantial: "The donors' documents fail to provide an adequate description of or the condition of the donated items. The Forms 8283 and the appraisal reports provide very generic descriptions, stating the items were in 'good working condition' or 'operational, clean and in good saleable condition.' An adequate description is necessary because 'Without a more detailed description the appraiser's approach and methodology cannot be evaluated.' In fact, their documents fail to even indicate the valuation method used or the basis for the appraised values. We have previously held such information to be essential because 'Without any reasoned analysis . . . [the appraiser's] report is useless.' *Friedman v. Commissioner, 99 T.C.M. 1175 (2010).*

EXAMPLE. The Tax Court ruled that a married couple (the "donors") was not eligible for a charitable contribution deduction for a donation of property because their appraisal failed to comply with the qualified appraisal requirements. The donors argued that their appraisal should be accepted because it was in substantial compliance with the law. The court rejected this argument for two reasons. First, the tax code contains no provision suggesting that substantial compliance is sufficient to meet the substantiation requirements enumerated in the code and regulations. Second, even if such an exception existed, it would not benefit the donors, since their compliance was far from substantial:

> *Assuming* arguendo *that the [substantial compliance] doctrine indeed could apply in such taxpayer actions, the court finds that the appraisal at issue wholly lacks even a modicum of content in critical areas to say that it substantially complies with numerous statutory and regulation mandates. The substantial compliance doctrine is not a substitute for missing entire categories of content; rather, it is at most a means of accepting a nearly complete effort that has simply fallen short in regard to minor procedural errors or relatively unimportant clerical oversights. The required content the donors neglected does not constitute such instances of technicalities. Much of the content provides necessary context permitting the Internal Revenue Service to evaluate a claimed deduction. Without, for example, the appraiser's education and background information, it would be difficult if not impossible to gauge the reliability of an appraisal that forms the foundation of a deduction. The simple inclusion of an appraiser's license number does not suffice given that there are distinctions between appraisers that the required information targets. . . .*

> *Nowhere is it more apparent that donors' actions negate the equitable safe haven they pursue than in recognizing that the purpose of the qualified appraisal is to present an understandable rationale for the claimed deduction, and the deduction of $287,400.00 claimed here hardly matches the $520,000.00 appraisal offered.* Hendrix v. Commissioner, 2010 WL 2900391 (S.D. Ohio 2010).

EXAMPLE. A successful real estate broker and appraiser donated several properties to his charitable remainder unitrust and claimed a charitable contribution deduction in the amount of $23 million. The IRS audited the tax return on which the deduction was claimed and denied any deduction on the ground that the donor failed to comply with the substantiation requirements that apply to donations of noncash property valued by the donor in excess of $5,000. Specifically, the donor did not obtain an appraisal of any of the donated properties prior to their donation, and he filled out his federal income tax return himself, including the Form 8283 (Noncash Charitable Contributions), which is used to substantiate donations of property valued at more than $5,000. The donor used his own appraisals of the donated properties. He didn't report his basis in any of the donated properties but stated that he had bought all the properties "in the 1970s and 1980s." The IRS disallowed any charitable contribution deduction on the ground that the substantiation requirements for donations of noncash property were not met.

The Tax Court agreed, noting that the donor's Form 8283 did not constitute a valid qualified appraisal summary because it failed to

comply with several of these requirements: "[The donor] failed to include information about several of these categories on his Form 8283 and the attached statements. For instance, he didn't include his bases in the properties, there is no bargain-sale statement, and there are no statements from a qualified appraiser." In addition, the donor did not seek independent appraisals until after the IRS audit started (well after his returns were due)."

The court rejected the donor's argument that he should be allowed a deduction since he had "substantially complied" with the legal requirements: "The cases make clear that substantial compliance requires a qualified appraisal. . . . Since it is an essential requirement of [the tax code] that the taxpayer obtain a qualified appraisal, we can't excuse failure to do so as substantial compliance." *Mohamed v. Commissioner, 103 T.C.M. 1814 (2012).*

The church's obligations

Churches receiving contributions of property valued by the donor at more than $5,000 have the following two obligations (assuming that the donor plans to claim a deduction for the contribution):

Written acknowledgment. The church should provide the donor with a written acknowledgment described under Rule 7, above.

Form 8283. The church must complete and sign Part IV of Section B of the donor's Form 8283 appraisal summary.

Form 8282. Churches are required to file a Form 8282 (Donee Information Return) with the IRS if three conditions are met: (1) a donor makes a contribution of noncash property to the church that is valued at more than $5,000 (other than publicly traded securities); (2) the donor presented the church with a qualified appraisal summary (Form 8283, Section B, Part IV) for signature; and (3) the church sells, exchanges, consumes, or otherwise disposes of the donated property within three years of the date of contribution. This form is reproduced at the end of this chapter. The purpose of this reporting requirement is to ensure that donors do not claim inflated values for donated property.

Note the following specific rules that apply to the Form 8282 reporting requirement:

(1) When to file. If your church is required to file a Form 8282 (no exception applies), it should file Form 8282 within 125 days of the date it disposed of the property. An exception applies if the church did not file a Form 8282 because there was no reason to believe that the qualified appraisal requirement applied to a donor, but you later learned that it did apply. Then you must file Form 8282 within 60 days of learning of your obligation to file.

(2) Missing information. The instructions for Form 8282 specify that you must complete at least "column a" of Part II. If you do not have enough information to complete the other columns, you may

leave them blank. This may occur if you did not keep a copy of the donor's appraisal summary (Form 8283, Section B).

✦ **KEY POINT.** The IRS has addressed the question of the penalty that should be assessed against a church or other charity that does not list the donor's Social Security number on Form 8282. It concluded that section 6721 of the tax code imposes a penalty in such a case of $50 for each return that does not contain a donor's Social Security number. The IRS pointed out, however, that this penalty can be reduced to $30 per return if a return is filed with the correct information within 30 days following the due date of the return. Further, the instructions for Form 8282 state that the form does not have to be filled out completely if, for example, the information is not available to the church because it does not have the donor's appraisal summary (Form 8283). *IRS Letter Ruling 200101031.*

(3) Where to file. Send the completed Form 8282 to the Department of the Treasury, Internal Revenue Service Center, Ogden, UT 84201-0027.

(4) Informing the donor. You must provide the donor with a copy of the Form 8282 you filed with the IRS.

(5) Exceptions. A Form 8282 does not need to be filed if either or both of the following exceptions apply: (a) The church consumes the donated property or distributes it without charge to another organization or individual. The consumption or distribution must be in furtherance of the church's tax-exempt purposes. (b) At the time the church signed the donor's appraisal summary, the donor had signed a statement on the appraisal summary (Form 8283, Section B, Part II) that the appraised value of the donated property was not more than $500. This exception will apply if a donor contributes several similar items of property (having a combined value in excess of $5,000) to a church during a calendar year, and the church disposes of or consumes one item that is separately valued by the donor at $500 or less.

(6) Certification. The charitable contribution deduction available to donors who contribute tangible personal property to a charity is not reduced (from market value to cost basis) if the donee charity makes a certification to the IRS by written statement, signed under penalties of perjury by an officer of the charity, that either (a) certifies that the use of the property by the charity was related to the purpose or function constituting the basis for its exemption and describes how the property was used and how such use furthered such purpose or function, or (b) states the intended use of the property by the charity at the time of the contribution and certifies that such use became impossible or infeasible to implement. This certification is made in Part IV of Form 8282.

Examples. The following examples illustrate the application of the Form 8282 reporting requirement to churches:

EXAMPLE. A member contributes a house to her church on July 1, 2013. The church sells the property on November 1, 2013. The church must complete and file Form 8282 with the IRS within 125 days of the date of sale and also mail a copy to the donor.

EXAMPLE. A member contributed property to his church on October 1, 2012. The property had an apparent value in excess of $5,000, but the church was never asked to sign a qualified appraisal summary (Form 8283, Section B, Part IV). The church sells the property on July 1, 2013. It is not required to file Form 8282.

EXAMPLE. A member contributed property to her church on May 1, 2013. The property had an apparent value in excess of $5,000. The church sells the property on June 1, 2013, for $8,000. The church was never asked to sign a qualified appraisal summary (Form 8283, Section B, Part IV), so it does not file a Form 8282. However, on November 1, 2013, the donor provides the church treasurer with a qualified appraisal summary for signature. Since November 1 is more than 125 days after the church's disposition of the property, the filing deadline for Form 8282 was missed. However, an exception permits the church to file a Form 8282 within 60 days of learning that it is required to file the form. Since the church treasurer had no reason to believe that a Form 8282 was required until the donor presented the qualified appraisal summary on November 1, the church has 60 days from that date to file the form.

EXAMPLE. A member contributes several shares of publicly traded stock to his church in July 2013. The stock has a market value of $15,000. The church sells the stock within a few weeks. It is not required to file a Form 8282 because it will not be asked to sign a qualified appraisal summary (Form 8283, Section B, Part IV). The qualified appraisal summary requirement does not apply to gifts of publicly traded stock. Note that the qualified appraisal and Form 8282 requirements are designed to ensure that donors claim fair valuations for contributions of noncash property. In the case of publicly traded stock, the valuation is determined each business day by the stock market. There is no question as to proper valuation. As a result, the qualified appraisal summary and Form 8282 requirements do not apply.

EXAMPLE. A member contributed property to her church in June 2012. In November the member has a church board member sign a qualified appraisal summary on behalf of the church. The board member is not familiar with this requirement and so does not inform the pastor, church treasurer, or any other member of the board. In January 2013 the church sold the property. The church treasurer is familiar with the Form 8282 requirement but does not file this form after the property is sold because he was never informed that the church had signed a qualified appraisal summary.

This is a real problem that can occur in any church. It can be prevented in a number of ways. For example, the church could establish a written policy requiring a designated person (such as the senior pastor or church treasurer) to sign any qualified appraisal summary (Form 8283) on behalf of the church and requiring a log or journal to be made of each qualified appraisal summary that is signed. If such a policy is clearly communicated to all staff and board members, it is unlikely that the church will fail to comply with the Form 8282 reporting requirement.

EXAMPLE. A member donates property to his church in June 2013. The church issues the member a receipt acknowledging the contribution. The church uses the property for four years before selling it. It is not required to file Form 8282 because it did not dispose of the property within three years of the date of the gift.

EXAMPLE. A local business contributes food to a church for distribution to the needy. The church is not required to file a Form 8282, even if it is asked to sign a qualified appraisal summary by the donor. The Form 8282 requirement does not apply if a church distributes donated property without charge to another organization or individual in furtherance of the church's tax-exempt purposes.

EXAMPLE. Same facts as the previous example, except that the church distributes the donated food to its members. The Form 8282 reporting requirement may apply. While the donated food is distributed without charge to church members, this may not further the church's tax-exempt purposes unless the congregation is predominantly poor.

EXAMPLE. John donated property to First Church on July 1, 2011. He obtained a qualified appraisal (that valued the property at $9,500), and he had the church sign his qualified appraisal summary (Form 8283, Part B). First Church donates the property to Second Church on May 1, 2013, in furtherance of its religious purposes. First Church is required to file Form 8282. Second Church will also have to file a Form 8282 if it disposes of the property within three years of the date John gave it to First Church—unless it does so at no charge and in direct furtherance of its exempt purposes.

How will Second Church know the date of the original gift? First Church is required to provide Second Church with the following information that will assist Second Church in complying with the Form 8282 reporting requirement: (1) its name, address, and employer identification number, and a copy of John's qualified appraisal summary, within 15 days after the later of the date it transferred the property to Second Church, or the date it signed the qualified appraisal summary (Form 8283, Part B); and (2) an unofficial copy of Form 8282. If First Church does not provide this information, Second Church should request it.

EXAMPLE. Same facts as the previous example, except that Second Church does not dispose of the property until December 2014. Since this is more than three years after John donated the property to First Church, Second Church is not required to file Form 8282.

➡ **TIP.** Be alert to any donation of property that may be valued by the donor at more than $5,000. Be sure the donor is aware of the need to obtain a qualified appraisal and complete a qualified appraisal summary (Form 8283, Section B). It is a good practice to have some of these forms on hand to give to such donors. Designate one person to sign all qualified appraisal summaries on behalf of the church, inform the church board and staff of this policy, and make a record of each of these forms that is signed. This will help to ensure that the church is in full compliance with the Form 8282 reporting requirement.

Rule 10—special rules for donations of (a) cars, boats, and planes; (b) stock; and (c) clothing and household items

Donations of cars, boats, and planes

❂ **KEY POINT.** Persons who contribute to a charity a car that is then sold without significant use cannot claim the fair market value of the car as a charitable contribution deduction. Instead, their deduction is limited to the gross proceeds received by the charity from the sale.

❂ **KEY POINT.** The purpose of the vehicle donation rules is to address the chronic problem of donors greatly inflating the value of vehicles they donate to charity. Limiting a deduction to the sales proceeds received by a charity upon selling a donated car (assuming no significant use by the charity) will reduce or eliminate the incentive of donors to inflate the value of donated cars.

Special rules apply to donations of cars, boats, and planes. It is important for church leaders to be familiar with these rules for two reasons. First, churches have reporting requirements that must be followed; and second, church leaders need to be ready to explain the rules to members who indicate an interest in donating a car (or a boat or plane) to the church.

❂ **KEY POINT.** This section addresses the substantiation requirements that apply to donations of cars valued by the donor at more than $500. The same rules apply to donations of boats and planes.

The substantiation and reporting requirements that apply to donations of cars, boats, and planes are summarized in Table 8-4. Note the following:

- Mere application of the proceeds from the sale of a qualified vehicle to a needy individual to any charitable purpose does not directly further a donee organization's charitable purpose within the meaning of this rule.

VEHICLE DONATION REPORTING RULES WIDELY IGNORED BY DONORS AND CHARITIES

The Treasury Inspector General for Tax Administration (TIGTA) released an audit of taxpayer compliance with reporting requirements for vehicle donations. The report concluded that some taxpayers did not provide the IRS with sufficient documentation to substantiate their deductions for the charitable donation of motor vehicles. TIGTA also found that charities did not properly report these contributions as required by the rules summarized above. Specifically, TIGTA found that an estimated 92,037 taxpayers claimed unsubstantiated motor vehicle donations totaling $204 million in 2007. An estimated 63,972 of those taxpayers may have avoided paying approximately $17 million in taxes. "The IRS's procedures to ensure that taxpayers meet all of the requirements for deducting charitable contributions of motor vehicles continue to be inadequate," commented the Treasury Inspector General for Tax Administration.

TIGTA recommended that the IRS match the information reported by charities on Forms 1098-C with the information reported on taxpayers' returns. TIGTA also recommended that the IRS continue to educate charities on the need to file Form 1098-C for each donated motor vehicle with a value in excess of $500.

- To constitute a significant intervening use, a charity must actually use the donated car to substantially further its regularly conducted activities, and the use must be significant. Incidental use is not a significant intervening use. Whether a use is a significant intervening use depends on its nature, extent, frequency, and duration.
- Material improvement includes a major repair or improvement that improves the condition of a car in a manner that significantly increases the value. To be a material improvement, the improvement may not be funded by an additional payment to the donee organization from the donor of the qualified vehicle. Services that are not considered material improvements include application of paint or other types of finishes (such as rust proofing or wax), removal of dents and scratches, cleaning or repair of upholstery, and installation of theft deterrent devices.
- A donor claiming a deduction for the fair market value of a car must be able to substantiate the fair market value. A reasonable method of determining fair market value is by reference to an established used-vehicle pricing guide. A used-vehicle pricing guide establishes the fair market value of a particular vehicle only if the guide lists a sales price for a vehicle

that is the same make, model, and year, sold in the same area, in the same condition, with the same or substantially similar options or accessories and with the same or substantially similar warranties or guarantees as the vehicle in question.

EXAMPLE. On October 1, 2012, Don donated a vehicle with a fair market value of $2,500 to his church. On December 1, 2012, the vehicle was sold without any significant intervening use or material improvement. Gross proceeds from the sale are $1,000. The church must provide Don with a contemporaneous written acknowledgment of the donation by December 31, 2012. It may use IRS Form 1098-C to ensure that it has met all of the requirements for a contemporaneous written acknowledgment issued to the donor. It must use Form 1098-C to provide the same information to the IRS by February 28, 2013. You may obtain this form from the IRS website (irs.gov).

EXAMPLE. Same facts as the previous example, except that the church plans to use the donated car several times a week in the course of church activities. If the church "significantly uses" the car, it must certify this intended use (and duration) and provide a written acknowledgment to Don within 30 days of the contribution. The church may use IRS Form 1098-C to comply with these requirements. It must use Form 1098-C to provide the same information to the IRS by February 28, 2013.

EXAMPLE. On July 1, 2013, Carrie contributes a used car to a charity whose exempt purposes include helping needy individuals who are unemployed develop new job skills, finding job placements for these individuals, and providing transportation for these individuals who need a means of transportation to jobs in areas not served by public transportation. The charity determines that, in direct furtherance of its charitable purpose, it will sell the qualified vehicle at a price significantly below fair market value to a trainee who needs a means of transportation to a new workplace. On or before July 31, 2013, the charity provides an acknowledgment to Carrie containing her name and taxpayer identification number; the vehicle identification number; a statement that the date of the contribution was July 1, 2013; a certification that it will sell the qualified vehicle to a needy individual at a price significantly below fair market value; and a certification that the sale is in direct furtherance of its charitable purpose. It may use IRS Form 1098-C to ensure that it has met all of the requirements for a contemporaneous written acknowledgment issued to the donor. It must use Form 1098-C to provide the same information to the IRS by February 28, 2014.

Deductions of $500 or less. A donation of a car with a claimed value of at least $250 must be substantiated by a contemporaneous written acknowledgment of the contribution by the charity. For a donation of a car with a claimed value of at least $250 but not more than $500, the acknowledgment must contain the following information (as noted above): the amount of cash and a description (but not value) of any property other than cash contributed; whether the donee organization provided any goods or services in consideration, in whole or in part, for the cash or property contributed; and a description and good faith estimate of the value of any goods or services provided by the donee organization in consideration for the contribution, or, if such

goods or services consist solely of intangible religious benefits, a statement to that effect.

If a donor contributes a car that is sold by the charity without any significant intervening use or material improvement, and if the sale yields gross proceeds of $500 or less, the donor may be allowed a

---

TABLE 8-4

DONATIONS OF VEHICLES TO CHARITY
(for vehicles valued at more than $500)

RULE	FORM OF DONATION	AMOUNT OF CHARITABLE CONTRIBUTION DEDUCTION	CHARITY'S OBLIGATIONS
1	A taxpayer donates a vehicle to a charity, and the charity sells it without any significant use or material improvement.	• Gross proceeds received by the charity from the sale of the vehicle • No deduction allowed unless a donor itemizes expenses on Schedule A and attaches either of the following to the tax return claiming the deduction: (1) IRS Form 8283, Section A and (2) either a "written acknowledgment" (described in next column) or a completed Form 1098-C • Appraisal not required if donor's deduction is limited to the gross proceeds of the sale	• Provide the donor with a written acknowledgment, within 30 days of the sale, containing donor's name and Social Security number; vehicle identification number; date of contribution; date of sale; amount of gross proceeds from the sale; certification that the vehicle was sold in an "arm's length transaction" to an unrelated party; statement that the deductible amount may not exceed the amount of the gross proceeds from the sale; and whether the charity provided any goods or services in consideration of the donation (and a description and good faith estimate of the value of any such goods or services, or, if the goods or services consist solely of intangible religious benefits, a statement to that effect). • IRS Form 1098-C may be used as a written acknowledgment (if provided to the donor within 30 days of the sale). • Submit Form 1098-C to the IRS by February 28 of the following year (April 1 if filed electronically).
2	A taxpayer donates a vehicle to a charity, and the charity "significantly uses" the vehicle (e.g., regular use over an extended period of time in performing the charity's exempt purposes).	• Fair market value of the donated vehicle • No deduction allowed unless a donor itemizes expenses on Schedule A and attaches the following to the tax return claiming the deduction: (1) IRS Form 8283, Section A and (2) either a "written acknowledgment" (described in next column) or a completed Form 1098-C • Qualified appraisal and appraisal summary (Form 8283) required for a deduction in excess of $5,000 if the deduction is not limited to gross proceeds from the sale of the vehicle (a written acknowledgment or Form 1098-C is still required, but not Form 8283, Section A)	• Provide the donor with a written acknowledgment, within 30 days of the contribution, containing donor's name and Social Security number; vehicle identification number; date of contribution; whether the charity provided any goods or services in consideration of the donation (and a description and good faith estimate of the value of any such goods or services, or, if the goods or services consist solely of intangible religious benefits, a statement to that effect); a certification and description of the intended significant intervening use by the charity and the intended duration of the use; and a certification that the vehicle will not be sold before completion of the use. • IRS Form 1098-C may be used as a written acknowledgment (if provided to the donor within 30 days of the contribution). • Submit Form 1098-C to the IRS by February 28 of the following year (April 1 if filed electronically).

(Continued on page 460)

═══ TABLE 8-4 ═══

DONATIONS OF VEHICLES TO CHARITY

(continued)

RULE	FORM OF DONATION	AMOUNT OF CHARITABLE CONTRIBUTION DEDUCTION	CHARITY'S OBLIGATIONS
3	A taxpayer donates a vehicle to a charity, and the charity "materially improves" the vehicle (e.g., major repairs that significantly increase the vehicle's value).	Same as Rule 2	• Provide the donor with a written acknowledgment, within 30 days of the contribution, containing donor's name and Social Security number; vehicle identification number; date of contribution; whether the charity provided any goods or services in consideration of the donation (and a description and good faith estimate of the value of any such goods or services, or, if the goods or services consist solely of intangible religious benefits, a statement to that effect); a certification and description of the intended material improvement by the charity; and a certification that the vehicle will not be sold before completion of the improvement. • IRS Form 1098-C may be used as a written acknowledgment (if provided to the donor within 30 days of the contribution). • Submit Form 1098-C to the IRS by February 28 of the following year (April 1 if filed electronically).
4	A taxpayer donates a vehicle to a charity, and the charity transfers it to a needy person for significantly below market value in furtherance of its charitable purposes.	Same as Rule 2	• Provide the donor with a written acknowledgment, within 30 days of the contribution, containing donor's name and Social Security number; vehicle identification number; date of contribution; whether the charity provided any goods or services in consideration of the donation (and a description and good faith estimate of the value of any such goods or services, or, if the goods or services consist solely of intangible religious benefits, a statement to that effect); and a certification that the charity will sell the vehicle to a needy individual at a price significantly below fair market value (or, if applicable, that it will gratuitously transfer the vehicle to a needy individual) and that the sale (or transfer) will be in direct furtherance of the charity's exempt purpose of relieving the poor and distressed or the underprivileged who are in need of a means of transportation. • IRS Form 1098-C may be used as a written acknowledgment (if provided to the donor within 30 days of the contribution). • Submit Form 1098-C to the IRS by February 28 of the following year (April 1 if filed electronically).

deduction equal to the lesser of the fair market value of the qualified vehicle on the date of the contribution or $500. Under these circumstances the donor must substantiate the fair market value and, if the fair market value is $250 or more, must substantiate the contribution with an appropriate acknowledgment.

Penalties. The tax code imposes penalties on any charity required to furnish an acknowledgment to a donor that knowingly furnishes a false or fraudulent acknowledgment or knowingly fails to furnish an acknowledgment in the manner, at the time, and showing the information required under the rules summarized above. For example, the penalty applicable to an acknowledgment relating to the sale of a donated car is the greater of (1) the product of the highest individual income tax rate (currently 35 percent) and the sales price stated on the acknowledgment, or (2) the gross proceeds from the sale of the qualified vehicle.

The penalty applicable to an acknowledgment relating to a vehicle that was materially improved or used significantly by the church for its religious purposes is the greater of (1) the claimed value of the vehicle multiplied times the highest individual income tax rate or (2) $5,000.

EXAMPLE. A church receives a contribution of a used car. It sells the car without any significant intervening use or material improvement. Gross proceeds from the sale are $300. The church provides an acknowledgment to the donor in which it knowingly includes a false or fraudulent statement that the gross proceeds from the sale of the vehicle were $1,000. The church is subject to a penalty for knowingly furnishing a false or fraudulent acknowledgment to the donor. The amount of the penalty is $350, the product of the sales price stated in the acknowledgment ($1,000) and 35 percent, because that amount is greater than the gross proceeds from the sale of the vehicle ($300).

Donations of stock

With more than half of all Americans now owning stock, it is not surprising that many of them are donating shares of stock to their church. As a result, it is important for church leaders and donors to be familiar with the tax rules that apply to stock donations. Unfamiliarity with these rules can result in additional taxes. This section will review what donors and church leaders need to know.

Why should donors consider donating stock to their church?
Gifts of stock can provide donors with a double tax benefit. First, they may be able to claim a charitable contribution deduction in the amount of the current market value of the donated stock. That is, they can deduct not only the original cost they paid for the donated shares but also the value of any increase in the value of those shares. Second, donors avoid paying taxes on the appreciated value of the donated stock.

EXAMPLE. Bob purchased 100 shares of ABC stock at a cost of $1,000 in 2004, and he donates these shares to his church in 2013, when their value is $3,000. Subject to the limitations discussed later in this section, Bob would be able to deduct the full $3,000 market value, and he would not have to pay capital gains tax on the $2,000 gain in the value of the stock.

Many church members own stock that has appreciated in value. The greater the amount of appreciation, the more capital gains tax the shareholder will face if the stock is sold. But this tax can be avoided if the member donates the stock to his or her church. And remember, the church pays no capital gains tax when it sells the donated stock, so the entire amount of the gift furthers the church's mission.

What about gifts of privately held stock? Most stock is either publicly traded or privately held by the owners of a business that has not offered its shares for sale to the public. When donors make gifts of privately held stock, three special rules must be understood by both donors and church leaders:

Qualified appraisals. If privately held stock valued at more than $10,000 is donated, a donor must obtain a qualified appraisal of the donated shares no earlier than 60 days prior to the date of the contribution. The cost of obtaining a qualified appraisal of privately held shares can be high and has caused some donors to reconsider making such a gift.

Qualified appraisal summaries (Form 8283). The donor must complete a qualified appraisal summary (IRS Form 8283) and enclose it with the Form 1040 on which the contribution deduction is claimed. Note that the church must sign this appraisal summary. Unfortunately, some donors have sent this form to their church for signature only to have it discarded or misplaced. The failure of a donor to submit a properly executed appraisal summary will jeopardize the deductibility of the contribution.

If the donor buys back the donated shares. It is common for donors who donate privately held stock to a church to buy back those shares after the gift. After all, there usually is little if any market for shares in privately held companies, so the church cannot easily sell the shares to anyone else. However, an agreement exists at the time the shares are donated for the donor to buy back the shares or for the church to sell them to the donor, the charitable contribution may be disallowed by the IRS, and any gain in the value of the shares may be taxed to the donor. Such transactions should never be consummated without legal advice.

What limitations apply to gifts of stock? Three limitations apply to a gift of stock that has appreciated in value:

(1) The one-year rule. When contributing capital gain property, such as stock, to a church or other public charity, a donor generally is entitled to claim a deduction in the amount of the fair market value of the donated property on the date of the gift. Property is capital gain property if its sale at fair market value on the date of the contribution would have resulted in long-term capital gain. Capital gain property includes capital assets held more than one year.

Donated stock that was held by the donor for less than one year is not capital gain property. The IRS classifies it as "ordinary income property," since a sale of the stock would result in ordinary taxable income rather than capital gain on any appreciation in value. The amount a donor can deduct for a contribution of ordinary income property is its fair market value less the amount that would have been ordinary income or short-term capital gain if the donor had sold the property for its fair market value on the date of the gift. Generally, this rule limits the deduction to the donor's basis (cost) in the property.

EXAMPLE. Barb donates stock that she held for five months to her church. The fair market value of the stock on the date of the donation was $1,000, but Barb paid only $800 (her "basis") for the stock. Because the $200 of appreciation would be short-term capital gain if she had sold the stock on the date of the contribution, her deduction is limited to $800 (fair market value less the appreciation).

(2) The 30 percent limit. Donors generally can deduct contributions to their church only up to 50 percent of their adjusted gross income (AGI), with any excess being carried over to the next year (up to five years in all, with the 50 percent limit applying to each year).

However, gifts of capital gain property (including stock) to a church are deductible only up to 30 percent of a donor's AGI. The 30 percent limit does not apply to donors who elect to reduce the fair market value of donated property by the amount that would have been long-term capital gain had the property been sold on the date of the gift. In such cases the 50 percent limit applies.

✦ **KEY POINT.** Donors may elect a 50 percent limit for gifts of capital gain property instead of the 30 percent limit. Donors who make this election must reduce the fair market value of the donated property by the appreciation in value that would have been long-term capital gain if the property had been sold on the date of the gift. This choice applies to all capital gain property contributed to churches and other public charities during a tax year. Donors make the election on their tax return or on an amended return filed by the due date for filing the original return.

EXAMPLE. In 2013 Bill has AGI of $50,000 and makes cash contributions of $5,000 to his church. In addition, he donates stock to his church that he purchased in 2009 for $20,000 that has a current market value of $25,000. Ordinarily, gifts of capital gain property are limited to 30 percent of the donor's AGI, or $15,000 in this case (30 percent x $50,000), with any excess being carried over to the next five years. In addition, Bill can deduct his cash contributions of $5,000, for a total contribution deduction of $20,000. However, Bill can elect to claim a deduction of up to 50 percent of his AGI (i.e., $25,000) if he reduces the market value of the donated stock by the appreciation in value that would have been long-term capital gain had the stock been sold. In such a case, the amount of his charitable contribution would be his basis of $20,000 (what he paid for the stock) plus the $5,000 in cash that he donated to his church, for a total deduction of $25,000 or 50 percent of his AGI.

Bill would be better off electing the 50 percent limit, since his charitable contribution deduction would be $5,000 greater. Donors are not always better off electing the 50 percent limit. In general, the more a donor's shares of stock have appreciated in value, the less advantageous the 50 percent election will be. On the other hand, if stock has not appreciated greatly in value, then the 50 percent election may result in a larger charitable contribution deduction.

Donors can carry over contributions that they could not deduct in the current year because they exceed the 30 percent of AGI limit. Donors can deduct the excess in each of the next five years until it is used up, but not beyond that time. Contributions that are carried over are subject to the same percentage limits in the year to which they are carried. For example, contributions subject to the 30 percent limit in the year in which they are made are subject to the same limit in the year to which they are carried. Donors deduct carryover contributions only after deducting all allowable contributions in that category for the current year.

(3) Itemized deductions. Donors claim charitable contribution deductions as itemized expenses on Schedule A of Form 1040. Donors who do not itemize their expenses cannot claim a charitable contribution deduction for a gift of stock.

What about stock that has declined in value? Some donors give their church stock that has declined in value. In general, donors who contribute stock with a fair market value that is less than their basis (cost) are entitled to a deduction in the amount of the stock's fair market value. They cannot claim a deduction for the difference between the stock's basis and its fair market value (the decrease in value). Persons who have stock that has declined in value generally will pay less taxes if they sell the stock, give the proceeds to charity, and then claim a loss on their income tax return.

What about selling the stock and donating the proceeds? Some donors consider selling their stock and then donating the cash proceeds to their church. Is this a good idea? Not if the stock has increased in value. Let's illustrate this with an example. Assume that Bill buys shares of stock for $6,000 in 2009 that is worth $10,000 in 2013. Bill sells the stock for $10,000 and donates the proceeds to his church. By selling the stock, Bill realized capital gains on the appreciation, and he will have to pay taxes on this amount. However, if Bill had donated the stock to his church without selling it, he would have avoided capital gains tax on the appreciation and still could have claimed a charitable contribution. This example is summarized in Table 8-5.

By giving the stock directly to the church, Bill avoids paying tax on the $4,000 gain on his stock investment, and he gets a charitable contribution deduction for the full value of his shares (unless one of the limitations previously mentioned applies).

▲ **CAUTION.** *Stock that has been held more than a year and that has declined in value ordinarily should not be given directly to a church or charity. It often is more desirable, from a tax perspective, for the owner to sell the stock and give the proceeds to charity, because this will create a "realized loss" that the donor may be able to deduct in computing his or her taxes.*

How does a donor value donated stock? As we have seen, donors who contribute publicly traded stock to a church or charity can claim a charitable contribution deduction in the amount of the fair market value of the donated shares, subject to the limitations previously discussed. The fair market value of donated stock is determined by (1) determining the "mean price" of the donated shares by adding the high and low quoted prices of the stock on the day of the gift, and dividing by two; then (2) multiplying the mean price by the number of donated shares.

✦ **KEY POINT.** The date of a gift of stock is addressed in the income tax regulations as follows: "Ordinarily, a contribution is made at the time delivery is effected. The unconditional delivery or mailing of a check which subsequently clears in due course will constitute an effective contribution on the date of delivery or mailing. If a taxpayer unconditionally delivers or mails a properly endorsed stock certificate to a charitable donee or the donee's agent, the gift is completed on the date of delivery or, if such certificate is received in the ordinary course of the mails, on the date of mailing. If the donor delivers the stock certificate to his bank or broker as the donor's agent, or to the issuing corporation or its agent, for transfer into the name of the donee, the gift is completed on the date the stock is transferred on the books of the corporation." *Treas. Reg. 1.170A-1(b).*

▲ **CAUTION.** *Donors often make gifts of stock at the end of the year by calling their stockbroker and asking that the shares be transferred. Donors who expect a year-end charitable contribution deduction should make their desire clear when communicating with their broker. In some cases brokers do not transfer donated shares until the beginning of the new year, resulting in the loss of any deduction for the previous year.*

What are the mechanics of donating stock? Donors can donate stock in a number of ways, including

- by electronic transfer (if available).
- by physical transfer (personally or through the mail). For security purposes, donors usually transfer unsigned stock certificates and separately execute a "stock power" form with a signature guaranteed by the donor's bank or broker. The stock power form should be sent on the same day as the stock certificate but in a separate envelope. If donated stock is held in the names of more than one person, all owners must sign the stock power form. If using the mail, donors should send all documents by registered mail.
- through a stockbroker.

▲ **CAUTION.** *Donors who contribute stock to their church through a broker should be sure that the broker understands that they are donating the stock, not selling it. If the broker sells stock held by the donor for more than one year and transfers the proceeds to the donor's church rather than giving the shares directly to the church, the donor will have to pay capital gains tax on any gain in the value of the stock.*

What about gifts of mutual fund shares? Donors generally determine the fair market value of donated mutual fund shares by multiplying the net asset value on the date of the gift by the number of donated shares.

How do donors substantiate gifts of stock? Gifts of stock are subject to special substantiation rules. Note the following:

- A church is not an appraiser and should never provide donors with a value for donated stock. Instead, provide a receipt that acknowledges the date of gift, the donor's name, the number of shares given, and the name of the company.
- A donor who gives publicly traded stock valued at more than $5,000 is not required to obtain a qualified appraisal or complete a qualified appraisal summary (Section B of Form 8283).
- A donor who gives publicly traded stock valued at more than $500 must complete Section A, Part I, of Form 8283. This requirement applies even if the stock is valued at more than $5,000 (in which case the stock is exempt from the qualified appraisal requirement).
- A donor who gives nonpublicly traded stock valued at $10,000 or less is not required to obtain a qualified appraisal and complete a qualified appraisal summary (Form 8283). However, donors who give nonpublicly traded stock valued at more than $10,000 must obtain a qualified appraisal of the stock no earlier than 60 days prior to the date of the gift, and they must also complete a qualified appraisal summary (IRS Form 8283) that summarizes the qualified appraisal and is enclosed with the tax return on which the deduction is claimed. Failure to comply with these requirements can lead to a loss of any charitable contribution deduction.

EXAMPLE. A donor contributed nonpublicly traded stock worth more than $10,000 to a church but obtained no qualified appraisal and attached no qualified appraisal summary to the tax return on which the charitable contribution deduction was claimed. The Tax Court ruled that the donor was not entitled to a charitable contribution deduction, even though there was no dispute as to the value of the donated stock. *Hewitt v. Commissioner, 109 T.C.12 (1997).*

➥ **TIP.** Do not assume that donors are familiar with the substantiation rules that apply to gifts of stock. Church treasurers should obtain several copies of Form 8283 each January to give to persons who donate stock to the church during the year. You can order multiple copies of Form 8283 by calling the IRS forms hotline at 1-800-TAX-FORM or by downloading them from the IRS website (irs.gov).

TABLE 8-5

STOCK VERSUS SALES PROCEEDS

	GIFT OF STOCK	GIFT OF SALES PROCEEDS
Charitable contribution	$10,000	$10,000
Bill's marginal tax rate	25%	25%
Tax benefit of gift	$2,500	$2,500
Tax on gain	0	$600 ($4,000 gain x 15%)
Net benefit of gift (tax savings)	$2,500	$1,900

Donations of clothing and household items

Americans love to donate used clothing and household items to charity. The IRS reports that the amount claimed as deductions in a recent year for clothing and household items was more than $9 billion. These items are notoriously difficult to value, and the attempt to do so wastes valuable time and resources.

The tax code responds to this dilemma by denying a charitable contribution deduction for a contribution of clothing or household items unless the clothing or household items are in "good used condition or better." The Treasury Department is authorized to deny (by regulation) a deduction for any contribution of clothing or a household item that has minimal monetary value, such as used socks and used undergarments.

A deduction may be allowed for a charitable contribution of an item of clothing or a household item not in good used condition or better only if the amount claimed for the item is more than $500 and the taxpayer obtains a qualified appraisal of the property and attaches a qualified appraisal summary (Form 8283) to the tax return claiming the deduction.

Household items include furniture, furnishings, electronics, appliances, linens, and other similar items. Food, paintings, antiques, and other objects of art, jewelry and gems, and collections are excluded from the definition.

If the donated item is in good used condition or better and a deduction in excess of $500 is claimed, the taxpayer must file a completed Form 8283 (Section A or B, depending on the type of contribution and claimed amount), but a qualified appraisal is required only if the claimed contribution amount exceeds $5,000.

If the donor claims a deduction of less than $250, the donor must obtain a receipt from the church or charity or maintain reliable written records of the contribution. A reliable written record for a contribution of clothing or a household item must include a description of the condition of the item. If the donor claims a deduction of $250 or more, the donor must obtain from the church or charity a receipt that meets the requirements of a contemporaneous written acknowledgment (see Rule 6, above).

3. HOW CHURCH TREASURERS CAN COMPLY WITH THE SUBSTANTIATION RULES

Church treasurers can comply with the substantiation and quid pro quo reporting requirements in a number of ways. Some of the options are summarized below:

Option 1—cash contributions only

In most churches the only contributions donors make are cash contributions. Illustration 8-2 is a receipt that acknowledges only cash contributions and that takes into account the substantiation rules. If a church only receives cash contributions, this form is all that will be required. Illustration 8-2 satisfies all of the substantiation rules with minimal complexity. However, it makes three important assumptions:

- the church provided no goods or services in connection with any individual contribution of $250 or more other than intangible religious benefits,
- no donor made any quid pro quo contribution, and
- only cash contributions were made (not property).

Obviously, these assumptions will hold true for many, if not most, donors. However, if any one or more of these assumptions is not met, appropriate adjustments will be required. For example, if a donor made a quid pro quo contribution, an appropriate statement would need to be incorporated into the form (or issued on a separate form). And if the church provides goods or services of more than insubstantial value in exchange for a contribution of $250 or more, it would need to adapt this form based on Rule 2 above. Illustration 8-3 can be used in conjunction with Illustration 8-2 to substantiate most contributions not covered by the simpler form.

➤ **TIP.** The illustrations in this chapter separately list each contribution because this is the most common church practice, and it provides donors with information that will assist in detecting errors and reconciling discrepancies. However, church treasurers are free to combine all contributions in a single amount. But if donors made any individual contributions of $250 or more, or quid pro quo contributions of more than $75, the contribution statement issued by the church must contain the appropriate language required for the substantiation of these contributions.

Option 2—contributions of property, or quid pro quo contributions

Some churches receive occasional contributions of property, or quid pro quo contributions, in addition to cash contributions. Illustration 8-2 does not address these kinds of contributions. As a result, churches must either

- use Illustration 8-2 plus a second form that acknowledges contributions of property and quid pro quo contributions, or
- use a form that acknowledges cash contributions as well as contributions of property and quid pro quo contributions.

Illustration 8-3 is a form churches can use to acknowledge contributions of property or quid pro quo contributions. It is designed to be used with Illustration 8-2 (the cash contributions receipt). Illustration 8-4 is a form churches can use that acknowledges cash contributions as well as contributions of property and quid pro quo contributions.

Option 3—a unified acknowledgment

Some treasurers will prefer to consolidate all contributions on one form. This approach is shown in Illustration 8-4. The advantage of this option is that donors will receive only one acknowledgment, rather than two or three different acknowledgments. The disadvantage is that the unified form is more complicated and may raise more questions from donors. For many donors, some sections of the unified form will not apply. *Note that in the case of contributions of noncash property, a donor will have some additional recordkeeping requirements (see, for example, Rules 7–10, above).*

Comprehensive example illustrating compliance with the requirements

Assume the following facts:

- First Church issues quarterly contribution receipts to donors.
- John A. Doe made 13 weekly cash contributions of $30 to the church's general fund for the fourth quarter of 2012.
- Mr. Doe made a cash contribution of $500 on October 21 to the church's missions fund.
- Mr. Doe purchased a pie at a fund-raising raffle for $100 on October 5.
- Mr. Doe donated 10 shares of ABC stock (worth $50 per share) to the church on November 15.

- On November 18 Mr. Doe made a cash contribution of $100 to the general fund, and on December 9 he made an additional contribution of $250 to the missions fund.
- Mr. Doe contributed a 2009 Toyota Camry to his church on November 28. The church uses the vehicle significantly for church purposes and so does not immediately sell it. The church issues Mr. Doe a Form 1098-C in lieu of a written acknowledgment.
- Mr. Doe paid $100 for a dinner at a church event on December 8 but received a dinner having an estimated value of $30.

Option 1

The easiest way for church treasurers to comply with the substantiation requirements would be to issue a receipt for cash contributions and an additional receipt to cover those occasional contributions of property or quid pro quo contributions. Illustrations 8-3 and 8-4 illustrate this approach. Note the following points:

- All cash contributions, regardless of amount, must be substantiated with (1) either a bank record (such as a cancelled check) or a written communication from the charity (2) showing the charity's name, date of the contribution, and

---

ILLUSTRATION 8-2

SAMPLE RECEIPT

Cash Contributions Only

First Church, Anytown, Illinois, December 31, 2012
Contributions Statement for October through December 2012 for John A. Doe

For the calendar quarter October through December 2012, our records indicate that you made the following cash contributions. Should you have any questions about any amount reported or not reported on this statement, please notify the church treasurer within 90 days of the date of this statement. Statements not questioned within 90 days will be assumed to be accurate, and any supporting documentation (such as offering envelopes) retained by the church may be discarded. *No goods or services were provided to you by the church in connection with any contribution, or their value was insignificant or consisted entirely of intangible religious benefits.*

CODES: 10=General Fund 20=Building Fund 30=Missions 40=Other

CODE	DATE	AMOUNT	CODE	DATE	AMOUNT	CODE	DATE	AMOUNT
10	Oct. 7	$30	10	Nov. 4	$30	10	Dec. 2	$30
10	Oct. 14	$30	10	Nov. 11	$30	10	Dec. 9	$30
10	Oct. 21	$30	10	Nov. 18	$30	30	Dec. 9	$250
30	Oct. 21	$500	30	Nov. 18	$100	10	Dec. 16	$30
10	Oct. 28	$30	10	Nov. 25	$30	10	Dec. 23	$30
						10	Dec. 30	$30
TOTALS	October	$620		November	$220		December	$400
							QUARTERLY TOTAL	$1,240

the amount of the contribution. These requirements may not be satisfied with any other written records. Illustrations 8-3 and 8-4 comply with these requirements.

- Mr. Doe purchased a pie at a fund-raising raffle on October 5 for $100. Assume that a good faith estimate of the value of the pie would be $5. Since Mr. Doe contributed more than $75 in a quid pro quo exchange, the church will need to (1) inform Mr. Doe that the amount of the contribution that is tax-deductible is limited to the excess of the cash donation over the value of the pie provided by the church in return, and (2) provide Mr. Doe with a good faith estimate of the value of the pie. The quid pro quo reporting rules do not apply if the church only provides goods or services whose value is insignificant (generally, with a value of the lesser of $102 or 2 percent of the amount of the contribution, whichever is less). But this exception does not apply, since a good faith estimate of the value of a homemade pie is $5, which is more than the lesser of $102 or 2 percent of the amount of the contribution ($2).

- The church "significantly uses" the donated car for church purposes rather than selling it. This means that Mr. Doe's charitable contribution deduction will be based on the car's fair market value. The church must (1) provide the donor with a written acknowledgment, within 30 days of the date of the contribution, containing the donor's name and Social Security number, date of contribution, vehicle identification number, certification and detailed description of the intended significant intervening use by the charity and the intended duration of the use or the intended material improvement by the charity and a certification that the qualified vehicle will not be sold before completion of the use or improvement and whether the church provided any goods or services in consideration of the donation (and a description and good-faith estimate of the value of any such goods or services, or, if the goods or services consist solely of intangible religious benefits, a statement to that effect) and (2) submit the same information to the IRS by February 28 of the following year. IRS Form 1098-C must be used to submit the information to the IRS and may be used in lieu of a written acknowledgment for the donor. The church elects to provide Mr. Doe with a completed Form 1098-C in lieu of a written acknowledgment. Since the car is significantly used by the church for church purposes and is valued at more than $5,000, Mr. Doe will need to obtain a qualified appraisal from a qualified appraiser and complete a qualified appraisal summary (IRS Form 8283) and attach it to the tax return on which the charitable contribution deduction is claimed. He does not complete Form 8283, Section A.

- Illustration 8-2 allows the church to separately list multiple contributions made by a donor on the same day. To illustrate, on October 14 the donor made a contribution of $500 to the

mission fund and, in addition, made a separate contribution of $30 to the general fund. Separately identifying contributions on the same day can be important. For example, if a donor attends two scheduled services at the same church on the same day and makes a $150 contribution in each service, the church's receipt will either show two separate contributions of $150, or it will aggregate the contributions and show a single contribution of $300. This can be an important distinction if the church's receipt does not comply with the substantiation requirements, since those requirements are triggered by an individual contribution of at least $250. For this reason it is desirable to have the capacity to show separate contributions made on the same day.

- Illustrations 8-3 and 8-4 easily can be modified to correspond to semiannual or annual reporting periods.

Option 2

Illustration 8-4 combines all of the substantiation and quid pro quo reporting requirements into one form. This form can be used to cover most kinds of contributions that will be made to a church. While it has the advantage of providing donors with a single form, it is far more complex and will confuse many donors. It contains information that is not necessary for the vast majority of donors who only make cash contributions to their church.

✦ **KEY POINT.** Many church leaders are unsure how long to retain records supporting charitable contributions. Such records may include offering envelopes, copies of canceled checks, and periodic contribution statements issued by the church to donors. Must a church keep these records indefinitely? Not at all. In general, such records should be kept for a total of seven years from the date of the records. But this rule can be reduced substantially by placing a notice on contribution statements informing donors that the church will dispose of supporting documentation within a specified number of days (e.g., 90 days) and instructing them to address any apparent discrepancies within that period of time. Such a notice is included in Illustrations 8-2, 8-3, and 8-4.

E. HOW TO CLAIM THE DEDUCTION

Charitable contribution deductions are available only as itemized expenses on Schedule A. This means that taxpayers who do not itemize their deductions get no tax benefit from making charitable contributions. See point 5 in the introduction of this chapter for more details.

ILLUSTRATION 8-3

SAMPLE RECEIPT

Property and Quid Pro Quo Contributions

First Church, Anytown, Illinois, December 31, 2012
Contributions Statement for October through December 2012 for John A. Doe

For the calendar quarter October through December 2012, our records indicate that you made the following individual property contributions and quid pro quo contributions. A quid pro quo contribution is a contribution that is in part a contribution and in part a purchase of goods or services. Should you have any questions about any amount reported or not reported on this statement, please notify the church treasurer within 90 days of the date of this statement. Statements not questioned within 90 days will be assumed to be accurate, and any supporting documentation (such as offering envelopes) retained by the church may be discarded.

This statement includes a good faith estimate of the value of any goods or services you received in exchange for any individual contribution of more than $75. *If no value is listed, this means that no goods or services were provided, or their value was insignificant or consisted entirely of intangible religious benefits.* If you received goods or services in return for your contribution, the deductible portion of your contribution is the amount by which it exceeds the value of the goods or services received in return (as noted below). This assumes that you otherwise qualify for a charitable contribution deduction.

CODES: C=Cash or Check   P=Property   10=General Fund   20=Building Fund   30=Missions   40=Other

CODE	FORM	DATE	GROSS AMOUNT	VALUE AND DESCRIPTION OF GOODS OR SERVICES PROVIDED TO YOU BY THE CHURCH (FOR CONTRIBUTIONS OF MORE THAN $75)	NET AMOUNT OF CASH CONTRIBUTION (TAX-DEDUCTIBLE AMOUNT)	DESCRIPTION (FOR DONATED PROPERTY VALUED BY DONOR AT $250 OR MORE)
10	C	Oct. 5	$100	$5 (pie)	$95	
30	P	Nov. 15				10 shares of ABC stock
30	C	Dec. 8	$100	$30 (dinner)	$70	
TOTAL					$165	

ILLUSTRATION 8-4

SAMPLE RECEIPT

Cash, Property, and Quid Pro Quo Contributions

First Church, Anytown, Illinois, December 31, 2012
Contributions Statement for October through December 2012 for John A. Doe

For the calendar quarter October through December 2012, our records indicate that you made the following contributions. Should you have any questions about any amount reported or not reported on this statement, please notify the church treasurer within 90 days of the date of this statement. Statements not questioned within 90 days will be assumed to be accurate, and any supporting documentation (such as offering envelopes) retained by the church may be discarded.

This statement includes a good faith estimate of the value of any goods or services you received in exchange for any individual contribution of more than $75. *If no value is listed, this means that no goods or services were provided, or their value was insignificant or consisted entirely of intangible religious benefits.* If you received goods or services in return for your contribution, the deductible portion of your contribution is the amount by which it exceeds the value of the goods or services received in return (as noted below). This assumes that you otherwise qualify for a charitable contribution deduction.

CODES: C=Cash or Check   P=Property   10=General Fund   20=Building Fund   30=Missions   40=Other

CODE	FORM	DATE	GROSS AMOUNT	VALUE AND DESCRIPTION OF GOODS OR SERVICES PROVIDED TO YOU BY THE CHURCH (FOR CONTRIBUTIONS OF MORE THAN $75)	NET AMOUNT OF CASH CONTRIBUTION (TAX-DEDUCTIBLE AMOUNT)	DESCRIPTION (FOR DONATED PROPERTY VALUED BY DONOR AT $250 OR MORE)
10	C	Oct. 5	$100	$5 (pie)	$95	
10	C	Oct. 7	$30		$30	
10	C	Oct. 14	$30		$30	
10	C	Oct. 21	$30		$30	
30	C	Oct. 21	$500		$500	
10	C	Oct. 28	$30		$30	
10	C	Nov. 4	$30		$30	
30	P	Nov. 11	$30		$30	
10	C	Nov. 15				10 shares of ABC stock
10	C	Nov. 18	$30		$30	
10	C	Nov. 18	$100		$100	
10	C	Nov. 25	$30		$30	
10	C	Dec. 2	$30		$30	
30	C	Dec. 8	$100	$30 (dinner)	$70	
10	C	Dec. 9	$30		$30	
30	C	Dec. 9	$250		$250	
10	C	Dec. 16	$30		$30	
10	C	Dec. 23	$30		$30	
10	C	Dec. 30	$30		$30	
TOTAL					$1,405	

================ TABLE 8-6 ================

SUBSTANTIATION REQUIREMENTS FOR CHARITABLE CONTRIBUTIONS

(Note: More than one rule may apply to a particular contribution. Follow each rule that applies.)

RULE	FORM OF CONTRIBUTION	SUBSTANTIATION REQUIREMENTS
1	Cash contributions	All cash contributions, regardless of amount, must be substantiated with (1) either a bank record (such as a cancelled check) or a written communication from the charity (2) showing the charity's name, date of the contribution, and the amount of the contribution. *These requirements may not be satisfied with any other written records.*
2	Individual cash contributions of $250 or more	Donors will not be allowed a tax deduction unless they receive a written acknowledgment from the church or charity that satisfies the following requirements: (1) the receipt must be in writing; (2) the receipt must identify the donor by name (a Social Security number is not required); (3) the receipt may combine all contributions, even those that are for $250 or more, in a single amount, or it can list each contribution separately to aid donors in resolving discrepancies; (4) the receipt must state whether the church provided any goods or services to the donor in exchange for the contribution, and if so, the receipt must include a good faith estimate of the value of those goods or services; (5) if the church provides no goods or services to a donor in exchange for a contribution, or if the only goods or services the church provides are intangible religious benefits, the receipt must contain a statement to that effect; (6) the written acknowledgment must be received by the donor on or before the earlier of the following two dates: the date the donor files a tax return claiming a deduction for the contribution, or the due date (including extensions) for filing the return.
3	Quid pro quo cash contributions of $75 or less	Quid pro quo contributions (part contribution and part payment for goods or services received in exchange) of less than $75 are deductible to the extent they exceed the value of the goods or services provided in exchange.
4	Quid pro quo cash contributions of more than $75	In addition to the requirements of Rule 2 (if applicable), the church must provide a written statement to the donor that (1) informs the donor that the amount of the contribution that is tax-deductible is limited to the excess of the amount of cash contributed by the donor over the value of any goods or services provided by the church in return; and (2) provides the donor with a good faith estimate of the value of the goods or services furnished to the donor. **Note:** For 2013, a written statement need not be issued if only token goods or services are provided to the donor having a value of $102 or 2 percent of the amount of the contribution, whichever is less, or if the donor receives solely an intangible religious benefit that generally is not sold in a commercial context outside the donative context.
5	Individual contributions of noncash property valued at less than $250	**Church receipt.** Substantiate with a receipt that lists the donor's name, the church's name, the date and location of the contribution, and a reasonably detailed description (but not value) of the property. **Donor's records.** The income tax regulations require that all donors of noncash property maintain reliable written records with respect to each item of donated property that include the following information: (1) name and address of the church; (2) date and location of contribution; (3) detailed description of property; (4) fair market value of property at time of contribution, including description of how value was determined; (5) cost or other basis of property; (6) if less than the donor's entire interest in property is donated during the year, an explanation of the total amount claimed as a deduction in the current year; and (7) the terms of any agreement between the donor and church relating to the use, sale, or other disposition of the property.
6	Individual contributions of noncash property valued at $250 to $500	**Church receipt.** The church's receipt must contain the same information as under Rule 5 ("church receipt"). It also must also meet these tests: (1) It must be written. (2) It must include (a) a description (but not necessarily the value) of the donated property, (b) a statement of whether the church provided any goods or services as a result of the contribution (other than certain token items and membership benefits), and (c) a description and good faith estimate of the value of any goods or services described in (b). If the only benefit provided by the church was an intangible religious benefit (such as admission to a religious ceremony) that generally is not sold

(Continued on page 470)

== **TABLE 8-6** ==

SUBSTANTIATION REQUIREMENTS FOR CHARITABLE CONTRIBUTIONS
(continued)

RULE	FORM OF CONTRIBUTION	SUBSTANTIATION REQUIREMENTS
(Continued from page 469)		in a commercial transaction outside the donative context, the acknowledgment must say so and does not need to describe or estimate the value of the benefit. (3) The donor must receive the church's written acknowledgment on or before the earlier of (a) the date the donor files his or her tax return claiming the contribution or (b) the due date, including extensions, for filing the return.
		Donor's records. IRS regulations specify that donors who make contributions of $250 or more, but not more than $500, are required to obtain a contemporaneous written acknowledgment from the donee charity and, in addition, maintain all of the donor records described under Rule 5 above.
7	Individual contributions of noncash property valued by the donor at $500 to $5,000	**Church receipt.** See Rule 6. **Donor's records.** Donors who claim a deduction over $500 but not over $5,000 for a noncash charitable contribution must have the acknowledgment and written records described under Rule 6, and their records must also include (1) a description of how the donor acquired the donated property, for example, by purchase, gift, bequest, inheritance, or exchange; (2) the approximate date the donor acquired the property; and (3) the cost or other basis, and any adjustments to the basis, of property held less than 12 months, and, if available, the cost or other basis of property held 12 months or more. This requirement, however, does not apply to publicly traded securities. In addition, a donor must complete the front side (Section A, Part I, and Part II if applicable) of IRS Form 8283 and enclose the completed form with the Form 1040 on which the charitable contribution is claimed.
8	Quid pro quo contributions of noncash property	The quid pro quo rules explained under Rules 3 and 4 apply to contributions of property as well.
9	Individual contributions of noncash property valued at more than $5,000 (single items, or total of similar items)	**Church receipt.** See Rule 6. **Donor's records.** In addition to complying with Rule 7, a donor must obtain a qualified appraisal of the donated property from a qualified appraiser and complete a qualified appraisal summary (Section B of Form 8283) and have the summary signed by the appraiser and a church representative; the completed Form 8283 is then enclosed with the Form 1040 on which the charitable contribution deduction is claimed.
10	Donations of (a) cars, boats, or planes; (b) stock; or (c) clothing and household items	**a) Cars, boats, and planes (valued at more than $500)** **Church sells vehicle with no significant use or alteration.** The church must (1) issue a written acknowledgment to the donor, within 30 days of the sale, containing the donor's name and Social Security number, date of contribution, vehicle identification number, date of sale, certification that the vehicle was sold in an arm's-length transaction, a statement of the gross proceeds from the sale, a statement that the deductible amount may not exceed the amount of the gross proceeds, and whether the church provided any goods or services in consideration of the donation (and a description and good faith estimate of the value of any such goods or services, or, if the goods or services consist solely of intangible religious benefits, a statement to that effect); and (2) submit the same information to the IRS by February 28 of the following year. IRS Form 1098-C must be used to submit the information to the IRS and may be used to provide the required information to the donor. The donor must complete IRS Form 8283, Section A.

(Continued on page 471)

TABLE 8-6

SUBSTANTIATION REQUIREMENTS FOR CHARITABLE CONTRIBUTIONS
(continued)

RULE	FORM OF CONTRIBUTION	SUBSTANTIATION REQUIREMENTS
(Continued from page 470)		**Church sells vehicle at a price significantly below fair market value (or gratuitously transferred) to needy individual in direct furtherance of its exempt purpose.** The church must (1) issue a written acknowledgment to the donor, within 30 days of the date of contribution, containing the donor's name and Social Security number, date of contribution, vehicle identification number, certification that the charity will sell the qualified vehicle to a needy individual at a price significantly below fair market value (or, if applicable, that it will gratuitously transfer the vehicle to a needy individual) and that the sale (or transfer) will be in direct furtherance of the charity's exempt purpose of relieving the poor and distressed or the underprivileged who are in need of a means of transportation, and whether the church provided any goods or services in consideration of the donation (and a description and good faith estimate of the value of any such goods or services, or, if the goods or services consist solely of intangible religious benefits, a statement to that effect); and (2) submit the same information to the IRS by February 28 of the following year. IRS Form 1098-C must be used to submit the information to the IRS and may be used to provide the required information to the donor. The donor must complete IRS Form 8283, Section A.

The church "significantly uses or materially improves" the car. The church must (1) provide the donor with a written acknowledgment, within 30 days of the date of the contribution, containing the donor's name and Social Security number, date of contribution, vehicle identification number, certification and detailed description of the intended significant intervening use by the charity and the intended duration of the use or the intended material improvement by the charity, and a certification that the qualified vehicle will not be sold before completion of the use or improvement, and whether the church provided any goods or services in consideration of the donation (and a description and good faith estimate of the value of any such goods or services, or, if the goods or services consist solely of intangible religious benefits, a statement to that effect); and (2) submit the same information to the IRS by February 28 of the following year. IRS Form 1098-C must be used to submit the information to the IRS and may be used to provide the required information to the donor.

Note: In addition to the above requirements, a qualified appraisal and qualified appraisal summary (Form 8283, Section B—see Rule 9) are required for a deduction in excess of $5,000 for a qualified vehicle if the deduction is not limited to gross proceeds from the sale of the vehicle. But Form 8283, Section A, need not be completed in such a case.

(b) Stock
Gifts of stock are subject to special substantiation rules. Note the following:

- A church is not an appraiser and should never provide donors with a value for donated stock. Instead, provide a receipt that acknowledges the date of gift, the donor's name, the number of shares given, and the name of the company.
- A donor who gives publicly traded stock valued at more than $5,000 is not required to obtain a qualified appraisal or complete a qualified appraisal summary (Section B of Form 8283). A donor who gives publicly traded stock valued at more than $500 must complete Section A, Part 1, of Form 8283. This requirement applies even if the stock is valued at more than $5,000 (in which case the stock is exempt from the qualified appraisal requirement).
- A donor who gives nonpublicly traded stock valued at $10,000 or less is not required to obtain a qualified appraisal and complete a qualified appraisal summary (Form 8283). However, donors who give nonpublicly traded stock valued at more than $10,000 must obtain a qualified appraisal of the stock no earlier than 60 days prior to the date of the gift, and they must also complete a qualified appraisal summary (IRS Form 8283) that

(Continued on page 472)

==== **TABLE 8-6** ====

SUBSTANTIATION REQUIREMENTS FOR CHARITABLE CONTRIBUTIONS
(continued)

RULE	FORM OF CONTRIBUTION	SUBSTANTIATION REQUIREMENTS
(Continued from page 471)		summarizes the qualified appraisal and is enclosed with the tax return on which the deduction is claimed. Failure to comply with these requirements can lead to a loss of any charitable contribution deduction. **(c) Clothing and household items** No deduction is allowed for a contribution of clothing or household items unless the clothing or household items are in "good used condition or better." The Treasury Department is authorized to deny (by regulation) a deduction for any contribution of clothing or a household item that has minimal monetary value, such as used socks and used undergarments. A deduction may be allowed for a charitable contribution of an item of clothing or a household item not in good used condition or better only if the amount claimed for the item is more than $500 and the taxpayer includes with his or her tax return a qualified appraisal with respect to the property. Household items include furniture, furnishings, electronics, appliances, linens, and other similar items. Food, paintings, antiques, and other objects of art, jewelry and gems, and collections are excluded from the provision. If the donated item is in good used condition or better and a deduction in excess of $500 is claimed, the taxpayer must file a completed Form 8283 (Section A or B, depending on the type of contribution and claimed amount), but a qualified appraisal is required only if the claimed contribution amount exceeds $5,000. If the donor claims a deduction of less than $250, the donor must obtain a receipt from the church or charity or maintain reliable written records of the contribution. A reliable written record for a contribution of clothing or a household item must include a description of the condition of the item. If the donor claims a deduction of $250 or more, the donor must obtain from the church or charity a receipt that meets the requirements of a contemporaneous written acknowledgment (see Rule 6, above).

☐ VOID   ☐ CORRECTED

DONEE'S name, street address, city or town, province or state, country, ZIP or foreign postal code, and telephone no.		OMB No. 1545-1959	**Contributions of Motor Vehicles, Boats, and Airplanes**
	1 Date of contribution	20**13**	
		Form **1098-C**	

	2a Year	**2b** Make	**2c** Model	
DONEE'S federal identification number	DONOR'S identification number	**3** Vehicle or other identification number		

DONOR'S name	**4a** ☐ Donee certifies that vehicle was sold in arm's length transaction to unrelated party	
Street address (including apt. no.)	**4b** Date of sale	**Copy D**
City or town, province or state, country, and ZIP or foreign postal code	**4c** Gross proceeds from sale (see instructions) $	**For Donee**

5a ☐ Donee certifies that vehicle will not be transferred for money, other property, or services before completion of material improvements or significant intervening use

5b ☐ Donee certifies that vehicle is to be transferred to a needy individual for significantly below fair market value in furtherance of donee's charitable purpose

5c Donee certifies the following detailed description of material improvements or significant intervening use and duration of use

For Privacy Act and Paperwork Reduction Act Notice, see the **2013 General Instructions for Certain Information Returns.**

6a Did you provide goods or services in exchange for the vehicle? . . . . ▶ Yes ☐   No ☐

6b Value of goods and services provided in exchange for the vehicle
$

6c Describe the goods and services, if any, that were provided. If this box is checked, donee certifies that the goods and services consisted solely of intangible religious benefits . . . . ▶ ☐

7 Under the law, the donor may not claim a deduction of more than $500 for this vehicle if this box is checked . . . . . ▶ ☐

Form **1098-C**   www.irs.gov/form1098c   Department of the Treasury - Internal Revenue Service

Form **8283**
(Rev. December 2012)
Department of the Treasury
Internal Revenue Service

Noncash Charitable Contributions

▶ Attach to your tax return if you claimed a total deduction
of over $500 for all contributed property.

▶ Information about Form 8283 and its separate instructions is at *www.irs.gov/form8283*.

OMB No. 1545-0908

Attachment
Sequence No. **155**

Name(s) shown on your income tax return

Identifying number

Note. Figure the amount of your contribution deduction before completing this form. See your tax return instructions.

Section A. Donated Property of $5,000 or Less and Certain Publicly Traded Securities—List in this section **only** items (or groups of similar items) for which you claimed a deduction of $5,000 or less. Also, list certain publicly traded securities even if the deduction is more than $5,000 (see instructions).

| Part I | Information on Donated Property—If you need more space, attach a statement. |

1	**(a)** Name and address of the donee organization	**(b)** If donated property is a vehicle (see instructions), check the box. Also enter the vehicle identification number (unless Form 1098-C is attached)	**(c)** Description of donated property (For a donated vehicle, enter the year, make, model, condition, and mileage, unless Form 1098-C is attached.)
A		☐	
B		☐	
C		☐	
D		☐	
E		☐	

Note. If the amount you claimed as a deduction for an item is $500 or less, you do not have to complete columns (e), (f), and (g).

	(d) Date of the contribution	**(e)** Date acquired by donor (mo., yr.)	**(f)** How acquired by donor	**(g)** Donor's cost or adjusted basis	**(h)** Fair market value (see instructions)	**(i)** Method used to determine the fair market value
A						
B						
C						
D						
E						

| Part II | Partial Interests and Restricted Use Property—Complete lines 2a through 2e if you gave less than an entire interest in a property listed in Part I. Complete lines 3a through 3c if conditions were placed on a contribution listed in Part I; also attach the required statement (see instructions). |

2a Enter the letter from Part I that identifies the property for which you gave less than an entire interest ▶ _____
If Part II applies to more than one property, attach a separate statement.

b Total amount claimed as a deduction for the property listed in Part I: **(1)** For this tax year ▶ _____
(2) For any prior tax years ▶ _____

c Name and address of each organization to which any such contribution was made in a prior year (complete only if different from the donee organization above):
Name of charitable organization (donee)

_____

Address (number, street, and room or suite no.)

_____

City or town, state, and ZIP code

_____

d For tangible property, enter the place where the property is located or kept ▶ _____
e Name of any person, other than the donee organization, having actual possession of the property ▶ _____

		Yes	No
3a	Is there a restriction, either temporary or permanent, on the donee's right to use or dispose of the donated property?		
b	Did you give to anyone (other than the donee organization or another organization participating with the donee organization in cooperative fundraising) the right to the income from the donated property or to the possession of the property, including the right to vote donated securities, to acquire the property by purchase or otherwise, or to designate the person having such income, possession, or right to acquire?		
c	Is there a restriction limiting the donated property for a particular use?		

For Paperwork Reduction Act Notice, see separate instructions.   Cat. No. 62299J   Form **8283** (Rev. 12-2012)

Form 8283 (Rev. 12-2012)   Page **2**

Name(s) shown on your income tax return	Identifying number

Section B. Donated Property Over $5,000 (Except Certain Publicly Traded Securities)—List in this section only items (or groups of similar items) for which you claimed a deduction of more than $5,000 per item or group (except contributions of certain publicly traded securities reported in Section A). An appraisal is generally required for property listed in Section B (see instructions).

Part I | **Information on Donated Property**—To be completed by the taxpayer and/or the appraiser.

4   Check the box that describes the type of property donated:

a ☐ Art* (contribution of $20,000 or more)   b ☐ Qualified Conservation Contribution   c ☐ Equipment
d ☐ Art* (contribution of less than $20,000)   e ☐ Other Real Estate   f ☐ Securities
g ☐ Collectibles**   h ☐ Intellectual Property   i ☐ Vehicles
j ☐ Other

*Art includes paintings, sculptures, watercolors, prints, drawings, ceramics, antiques, decorative arts, textiles, carpets, silver, rare manuscripts, historical memorabilia, and other similar objects.

**Collectibles include coins, stamps, books, gems, jewelry, sports memorabilia, dolls, etc., but not art as defined above.

Note. In certain cases, you must attach a qualified appraisal of the property. See instructions.

5	(a) Description of donated property (if you need more space, attach a separate statement)	(b) If tangible property was donated, give a brief summary of the overall physical condition of the property at the time of the gift	(c) Appraised fair market value
A			
B			
C			
D			

	(d) Date acquired by donor (mo., yr.)	(e) How acquired by donor	(f) Donor's cost or adjusted basis	(g) For bargain sales, enter amount received	See instructions (h) Amount claimed as a deduction	(i) Average trading price of securities
A						
B						
C						
D						

Part II | **Taxpayer (Donor) Statement**—List each item included in Part I above that the appraisal identifies as having a value of $500 or less. See instructions.

I declare that the following item(s) included in Part I above has to the best of my knowledge and belief an appraised value of not more than $500 (per item). Enter identifying letter from Part I and describe the specific item. See instructions. ▶ _____

Signature of taxpayer (donor) ▶   Date ▶

Part III | **Declaration of Appraiser**

I declare that I am not the donor, the donee, a party to the transaction in which the donor acquired the property, employed by, or related to any of the foregoing persons, or married to any person who is related to any of the foregoing persons. And, if regularly used by the donor, donee, or party to the transaction, I performed the majority of my appraisals during my tax year for other persons.

Also, I declare that I perform appraisals on a regular basis; and that because of my qualifications as described in the appraisal, I am qualified to make appraisals of the type of property being valued. I certify that the appraisal fees were not based on a percentage of the appraised property value. Furthermore, I understand that a false or fraudulent overstatement of the property value as described in the qualified appraisal or this Form 8283 may subject me to the penalty under section 6701(a) (aiding and abetting the understatement of tax liability). In addition, I understand that I may be subject to a penalty under section 6695A if I know, or reasonably should know, that my appraisal is to be used in connection with a return or claim for refund and a substantial or gross valuation misstatement results from my appraisal. I affirm that I have not been barred from presenting evidence or testimony by the Office of Professional Responsibility.

Sign Here

Signature ▶	Title ▶	Date ▶

Business address (including room or suite no.)	Identifying number
City or town, state, and ZIP code	

Part IV | **Donee Acknowledgment**—To be completed by the charitable organization.

This charitable organization acknowledges that it is a qualified organization under section 170(c) and that it received the donated property as described in Section B, Part I, above on the following date ▶ _____

Furthermore, this organization affirms that in the event it sells, exchanges, or otherwise disposes of the property described in Section B, Part I (or any portion thereof) within 3 years after the date of receipt, it will file **Form 8282,** Donee Information Return, with the IRS and give the donor a copy of that form. This acknowledgment does not represent agreement with the claimed fair market value.

Does the organization intend to use the property for an unrelated use?   . . . . ▶ ☐ Yes   ☐ No

Name of charitable organization (donee)	Employer identification number
Address (number, street, and room or suite no.)	City or town, state, and ZIP code
Authorized signature	Title	Date

Form **8283** (Rev. 12-2012)

Form **8282**
(Rev. April 2009)
Department of the Treasury
Internal Revenue Service

Donee Information Return

(Sale, Exchange, or Other Disposition of Donated Property)

▶ See instructions.

OMB No. 1545-0908

Give a Copy to Donor

Parts To Complete

- If the organization is an **original donee,** complete *Identifying Information,* Part I (lines 1a–1d and, if applicable, lines 2a–2d), and Part III.
- If the organization is a **successor donee,** complete *Identifying Information,* Part I, Part II, and Part III.

Identifying Information

Print or Type	Name of charitable organization (donee)	Employer identification number
	Address (number, street, and room or suite no.) (or P.O. box no. if mail is not delivered to the street address)	
	City or town, state, and ZIP code	

Part I Information on ORIGINAL DONOR and SUCCESSOR DONEE Receiving the Property

1a Name of original donor of the property	1b Identifying number(s)

1c Address (number, street, and room or suite no.) (P.O. box no. if mail is not delivered to the street address)

1d City or town, state, and ZIP code

Note. Complete lines 2a–2d only if the organization gave this property to another charitable organization (successor donee).

2a Name of charitable organization	2b Employer identification number

2c Address (number, street, and room or suite no.) (or P.O. box no. if mail is not delivered to the street address)

2d City or town, state, and ZIP code

Part II Information on PREVIOUS DONEES. Complete this part only if the organization was not the first donee to receive the property. See the instructions before completing lines 3a through 4d.

3a Name of original donee	3b Employer identification number

3c Address (number, street, and room or suite no.) (or P.O. box no. if mail is not delivered to the street address)

3d City or town, state, and ZIP code

4a Name of preceding donee	4b Employer identification number

4c Address (number, street, and room or suite no.) (or P.O. box no. if mail is not delivered to the street address)

4d City or town, state, and ZIP code

For Paperwork Reduction Act Notice, see page 4.   Cat. No. 62307Y   Form **8282** (Rev. 4-2009)

Form 8282 (Rev. 4-2009)   Page **2**

Part III	**Information on DONATED PROPERTY**

1. Description of the donated property sold, exchanged, or otherwise disposed of and how the organization used the property. (If you need more space, attach a separate statement.)	**2.** Did the disposition involve the organization's entire interest in the property?		**3.** Was the use related to the organization's exempt purpose or function?		**4.** Information on use of property. • If you answered "Yes" to question 3 and the property was tangible personal property, describe how the organization's use of the property furthered its exempt purpose or function. Also complete Part IV below. • If you answered "No" to question 3 and the property was tangible personal property, describe the organization's intended use (if any) at the time of the contribution. Also complete Part IV below, if the intended use at the time of the contribution was related to the organization's exempt purpose or function and it became impossible or infeasible to implement.
	Yes	**No**	**Yes**	**No**	
A					
B					
C					
D					

		Donated Property			
		A	**B**	**C**	**D**
5	Date the organization received the donated property (MM/DD/YY)	/ /	/ /	/ /	/ /
6	Date the original donee received the property (MM/DD/YY)	/ /	/ /	/ /	/ /
7	Date the property was sold, exchanged, or otherwise disposed of (MM/DD/YY)	/ /	/ /	/ /	/ /
8	Amount received upon disposition	$	$	$	$

Part IV	**Certification**

You must sign the certification below if any property described in Part III above is tangible personal property and:
- You answered "Yes" to question 3 above, or
- You answered "No" to question 3 above and the intended use of the property became impossible or infeasible to implement.

Under penalties of perjury and the penalty under section 6720B, I certify that either: (1) the use of the property that meets the above requirements, and is described above in Part III, was substantial and related to the donee organization's exempt purpose or function; or (2) the donee organization intended to use the property for its exempt purpose or function, but the intended use has become impossible or infeasible to implement.

▶ _____ | _____ | ▶ _____
Signature of officer   Title   Date

Sign Here	Under penalties of perjury, I declare that I have examined this return, including accompanying schedules and statements, and to the best of my knowledge and belief, it is true, correct, and complete. ▶ _____ | _____ ▶ _____ Signature of officer Title Date _____ Type or print name

Form **8282** (Rev. 4-2009)

Chapter 9 SOCIAL SECURITY FOR MINISTERS

If anyone does not provide for his relatives, and especially for his immediate family, he has denied the faith and is worse than an unbeliever.

1 Timothy 5:8

CHAPTER HIGHLIGHTS

■ ***Two tax systems.*** Social Security taxes are paid under two tax systems. Employers and employees pay Social Security and Medicare taxes—which for 2012 and 2013 are 15.3 percent of each employee's wages (the employer and employee split tax, with each paying 7.65 percent). Self-employed persons pay the self-employment tax, which for 2012 and 2013 is 15.3 percent of net self-employment earnings.

■ ***Maximum wages subject to Social Security and Medicare taxes.*** The Social Security and Medicare tax rate (7.65 percent for both employers and employees, or a combined tax of 15.3 percent) did not change in 2013. The 7.65 percent tax rate is comprised of two components: (1) a Medicare hospital insurance tax of 1.45 percent, and (2) an "old-age, survivor and disability" (Social Security) tax of 6.2 percent. There is no maximum amount of wages subject to the Medicare tax (the 1.45 percent tax rate). The tax is imposed on all wages, regardless of amount. For 2013 the maximum wages subject to the 6.2 percent Social Security tax is $113,700. Stated differently, employees who received wages in excess of $113,700 in 2013 pay the full 7.65 percent tax rate for wages up to $113,700 and the Medicare tax (1.45 percent) on all earnings above $113,700, regardless of amount. Employers paid an identical amount.

■ ***Maximum compensation subject to self-employment tax.*** The self-employment tax rate of 15.3 percent consists of two components: (1) a Medicare hospital insurance tax of 2.9 percent, and (2) an "old-age, survivor and disability" (Social Security) tax of 12.4 percent. All net income from self-employment, regardless of amount, is subject to the Medicare tax of 2.9 percent. However, for 2013 the 12.4 percent Social Security tax rate only applies to the first $113,700 of net self-employment earnings. Stated differently, self-employed persons who received compensation in excess of $113,700 in 2013 pay the full 15.3 percent tax rate on net self employment earnings up to $113,700 and the Medicare tax (2.9 percent) on all earnings above $113,700, regardless of amount.

■ ***Payroll tax holiday.*** Congress provided a payroll tax and self-employment tax holiday for 2011 and 2012 of two percentage points off the employee share of Social Security tax and the Social Security component of self-employment taxes. This meant that the employee share of Social Security taxes dropped from 6.2 to 4.2 percent of wages, and the Social Security component of self-employment taxes dropped from 12.4 to 10.4 percent of self-employment earnings. This reduction in taxes was enacted to stimulate the economy by increasing the take-home pay for millions of workers. It is unlikely that this tax holiday will be extended beyond 2012. Check the Social Security Administration website for current information.

■ ***Ministers as self-employed.*** Ministers always are self-employed for Social Security with respect to their ministerial services. This means they pay the self-employment tax, not the employee's share of Social Security and Medicare taxes with respect to such income. Churches must *not* treat clergy as employees for Social Security, even if they treat them as employees for federal income tax reporting.

■ ***Exemption.*** Clergy may exempt themselves from self-employment taxes with respect to their ministerial earnings if several requirements are met. Among other things, the exemption must be filed within a limited time period, and it is available only to clergy who are opposed on the basis of *religious considerations* to the *acceptance* of Social Security benefits based on their ministerial services. The exemption is only effective upon its approval by the IRS.

■ ***Exemption applicable only to ministerial services.*** An exemption from self-employment taxes only applies to ministerial services. Clergy who have exempted themselves from self-employment taxes must pay Social Security taxes on any nonministerial employment. They are eligible for Social Security benefits based on their nonministerial services (assuming that they have worked enough quarters in nonministerial employment).

■ ***Revoking an exemption.*** Many ministers who opted out of Social Security by filing a Form 4361 with the IRS have wanted to rejoin the program—often to qualify for Medicare benefits. In the past ministers have not been permitted to revoke an exemption. The tax code specifies that such exemptions are irrevocable. Congress has enacted legislation in the past giving ministers a limited opportunity to revoke an exemption from self-employment taxes. However, this option is not currently available.

- **Computing the self-employment tax.** The self-employment tax is computed by multiplying net self-employment earnings by the current self-employment tax rate. Net self-employment earnings consist of a minister's total church compensation, including the annual fair rental value of a parsonage or a housing allowance, reduced by most income tax exclusions and business expenses (whether unreimbursed or reimbursed under a nonaccountable plan).

- **Two deductions.** Self-employed persons pay the entire combined Social Security and Medicare tax rate (15.3 percent) that is shared by employers and employees. To partly offset the tax burden that falls on self-employed persons, the law allows them two deductions: (1) an amount equal to 7.65 percent multiplied by their net self-employment earnings (without regard to this deduction) may be deducted in computing earnings subject to the self-employment tax; and (2) half of their self-employment tax is deductible as an adjustment in computing federal income taxes, regardless of whether they can itemize deductions on Schedule A.

- **Religious sects opposed to Social Security coverage.** Members of certain religious sects that are opposed to Social Security coverage and that provide for the welfare and security of their members may become exempt from Social Security coverage if several conditions are met.

INTRODUCTION

The Social Security Act provides a variety of benefits that are designed to assist aged and disabled persons and their dependents. The four major benefits provided under the Social Security system are

- retirement benefits payable to a fully insured person;
- survivors benefits payable to the surviving spouse or dependent children of a deceased worker;
- disability benefits payable to a permanently disabled worker who is not able to engage in substantial gainful activity; and
- medical and hospital benefits payable at age 65 (the Medicare program).

These important benefits are financed primarily through two separate tax systems. Under the Federal Insurance Contributions Act (FICA), a tax is levied against employers and employees, representing a percentage of an employee's wages. Under the Self-employment Contributions Act (SECA), a tax is levied against the net earnings of self-employed persons. FICA taxes are withheld by an employer from an employee's wages and paid to the government, along with the employer's share of the FICA tax, according to the payroll tax procedures summarized later in this chapter and in Chapter 11. Self-employment taxes are paid entirely by the self-employed worker

and ordinarily are paid to the government through the estimated tax procedure (Form 1040-ES).

❖ **KEY POINT.** Throughout this chapter, FICA taxes will be referred to as Social Security and Medicare taxes. This is the terminology the IRS now uses on Form 941 and Form W-2.

A. MINISTERS DEEMED SELF-EMPLOYED

❖ **KEY POINT.** Ministers always are self-employed for Social Security with respect to their ministerial services. This means they pay the self-employment tax, not Social Security and Medicare taxes. Churches must not treat ministers as employees for Social Security, even if they report their income taxes as employees.

For Social Security, a duly ordained, commissioned, or licensed minister is treated as *self-employed* with respect to services performed in the exercise of ministry (with the exception of some chaplains). This is true even if a minister is an employee for income tax purposes. As a result, a minister reports and pays Social Security taxes as a self-employed person (and not as an employee) with respect to services performed in the exercise of ministry. *IRC 3121(b)(8)(A).*

▲ **CAUTION.** *Many churches withhold the employee's share of Social Security and Medicare taxes from ministers' compensation and then pay the employer's share. Such reporting is incorrect.*

It is important to note that ministers are self-employed for Social Security purposes only with respect to "services performed in the exercise of ministry." This significant term is explained fully in Chapter 3 (as is the term "minister").

The treatment of ministers as self-employed for Social Security purposes but as employees for income tax purposes has generated much confusion. In explaining the reason for treating ministers as self-employed for Social Security purposes, the Tax Court has observed: "Congress chose not to place the onus of participation in the old-age and survivors insurance program upon the churches, but to permit ministers to be covered on an individual election basis, as self-employed, whether, in fact, they were employees or actually self-employed." *Silvey v. Commissioner, 35 T.C.M. 1812 (1976).*

In other words, if ministers were treated as employees for Social Security, their employing churches would be required to pay the employer's share of the Social Security and Medicare tax, and this apparently was viewed as inappropriate. This justification ceased to be valid in 1984 when church employees became covered under Social Security.

B. EXEMPTION OF MINISTERS FROM SOCIAL SECURITY COVERAGE

❉ **KEY POINT.** Ministers may exempt themselves from self-employment taxes with respect to services performed in the exercise of ministry if several requirements are met. Among other things, the exemption must be filed within a limited time period, and it is available only to ministers who are opposed on the basis of religious considerations to the acceptance of Social Security benefits based on their ministerial services. The exemption is only effective upon its approval by the IRS. IRS Form 4361 is the exemption application form. A copy of this form is included at the end of this chapter.

1. SIX REQUIREMENTS FOR EXEMPTION

Until 1968, services performed by a duly ordained, commissioned, or licensed minister of a church in the exercise of ministry were exempt from Social Security taxes. A minister could voluntarily elect to be covered under the Social Security program by filing a timely Form 2031 with the IRS.

Since January 1, 1968, ministers have been automatically *covered* under Social Security but may exempt themselves with respect to compensation earned in the performance of ministerial services if they meet the following conditions.

Condition 1—minister status

The minister must be an ordained, commissioned, or licensed minister of a church. Licensed ministers of a church or denomination that both licenses and ordains ministers are eligible for the exemption only if they perform substantially all the religious functions of an ordained minister under the tenets and practices of their church or denomination. *Revenue Ruling 78-301.* See Chapter 3 for a complete explanation of what persons qualify as an ordained, commissioned, or licensed minister.

Condition 2—tax-exempt religious organization

The minister must have been ordained, commissioned, or licensed by a tax-exempt church or convention or association of churches. *Revenue Ruling 80-59.* Form 4361 (the exemption application for ministers) specifies: "You must establish that the body that ordained, commissioned, or licensed you . . . is exempt from federal income tax . . . as a religious organization described in section 501(c)(3) of

the Internal Revenue Code. *You must also establish that the body is a church (or convention or association of churches)*" (emphasis added).

Condition 3—filing a timely Form 4361

The minister must file a timely exemption application (Form 4361) in triplicate with the IRS. A minister certifies on Form 4361, "I am conscientiously opposed to, or because of my religious principles I am opposed to, the acceptance (for services I performed as a minister . . .) of any public insurance that makes payments in the event of death, disability, old age, or retirement, or that makes payments toward the cost of, or provides services for, medical care." The form states that "public insurance includes insurance systems established by the Social Security Act." Three factors are important to note:

1. Conscientious opposition based on religious belief

Section 1402(e) of the tax code and Form 4361 both specify that the exemption is available to a minister who is "conscientiously opposed to, or because of his religious principles is opposed to, the acceptance (with respect to services performed by him as such minister) of any public insurance that makes payments in the event of death, disability, old age, or retirement, or that makes payments toward the cost of, or provides services for, medical care." The regulations interpreting this language specify that

> ministers . . . requesting exemption from Social Security coverage must meet either of two alternative tests:
>
> (1) a religious principles test which refers to the institutional principles and discipline of the particular religious denomination to which he belongs, or
>
> (2) a conscientious opposition test which refers to the opposition because of religious considerations of individual ministers . . . (rather than opposition based upon the general conscience of any such individual or individuals). Treas. Reg. 1.1402(e)-2A(a)(2).

Under both the "religious principles" and "conscientious opposition" tests, a minister must have religion-based opposition to accepting Social Security benefits. The income tax regulations clearly reject the view that ministers can be eligible for exemption from Social Security coverage on the basis of conscientious opposition alone. The conscientious opposite on must be rooted in religious belief. Section 1402(e) of the tax code specifically delegates to the Treasury Department the authority to adopt regulations prescribing the "form and manner" of filing exemption applications. Therefore, though the regulations' rejection of nonreligious conscientious opposition to Social Security benefits as a grounds for exemption seems to contradict the plain meaning of the tax code, it is unlikely that a court would find the regulations to be invalid.

Clearly, economic or any other nonreligious considerations are not a valid basis for the exemption. Regrettably, many ministers have been induced to exempt themselves from Social Security participation because of the recommendation of a financial counselor that they would be "better off financially." In many cases counselors have recommended an alternative investment returning a commission or premium to themselves. Fortunately, such tactics will be significantly reduced because of the verification requirement for exemption, discussed later in this section.

The applicant qualifies for the exemption as long as he or she is *personally* opposed to accepting Social Security benefits on the basis of religious principles, even though his or her ordaining, commissioning, or licensing body is not officially opposed to Social Security participation (i.e., such an applicant would satisfy the conscientious opposition test described above).

2. Opposition to the acceptance of public insurance benefits

The exemption is available only if a minister is opposed on the basis of religious considerations to the *acceptance of public insurance benefits (including Social Security)*—not opposition to payment of an associated tax. A minister may have religious opposition to payment of the tax, but this alone will not suffice. The individual must have religious opposition to accepting Social Security benefits upon his or her retirement or disability. This is an extraordinary claim that few ministers will be able to make in good faith.

3. Participation in private insurance programs permitted

The applicant's opposition must be to accepting benefits under the Social Security program (or any other public insurance system that provides retirement and other specified benefits). As a result, a minister who files the exemption application may still purchase life insurance or participate in retirement programs administered by nongovernmental institutions (such as a life insurance company). *T.A.M. 8741002.*

The income tax regulations specify that the term "public insurance" refers to "governmental, as distinguished from private, insurance and does not include insurance carried with a commercial insurance carrier." *Treas. Reg. 1.1402(e)-2A(a)(2); Revenue Ruling 77-78.* The regulation goes on to clarify that to qualify for the exemption, a minister "need not be opposed to the acceptance of all public insurance," but he "must be opposed *on religious grounds* to the acceptance of any such payment which, in whole or in part, is based on, or measured by earnings from, services performed by him in his capacity as a minister" (emphasis added).

The deadline for filing Form 4361 is the due date, including extensions, of the federal tax return for the second year in which a minister has net earnings from self-employment of $400 or more, any part of which derives from the performance of services in the exercise of ministry. In most cases, this means the form is due by April 15 of the third year of ministry.

EXAMPLE. A federal appeals court ruled that ministers who opt out of Social Security by filing a timely Form 4361 will not be able to claim years later that they qualify for Social Security retirement benefits on the ground that their exemption application was filed after the deadline expired and should never have been approved by the IRS. The court noted that the minister "made a knowing waiver of his Social Security benefits in return for a tax exemption. . . . For over twenty years [he] did not pay self-employment tax and did not notify the IRS nor the Social Security Administration about the 'mistake' in granting his application. The government kept its part of the agreement, and the minister must keep his." *Yoder v. Barnhardt, 56 Fed. Appx. 728 (7th Cir. 2003).*

✿ **KEY POINT.** The IRS is rejecting some ministers' applications for exemption from self-employment taxes (Form 4361) because the applications were filed before the minister has worked at least two years in the ministry. Ministers may exempt themselves from self-employment (Social Security) taxes with regard to services they perform in the exercise of ministry if they file an exemption application (Form 4361) with the IRS by the due date, including extensions, of the federal tax return (Form 1040) for the second year in which they have at least $400 of self-employment earnings, any portion of which comes from ministerial services. The IRS apparently is interpreting this requirement, at least in some cases, to mean that ministers are not eligible to submit Form 4361 until they have worked at least two years. This is an incorrect interpretation of the tax code. The tax code defines the deadline for filing Form 4361 and does not forbid ministers from filing the form until they have been engaged in ministry for at least two years. In fact, such an interpretation is absurd, since it means that some ministers will have to file the form after the deadline has expired.

Condition 4—notifying the religious organization

Applicants for exemption must inform their "ordaining, commissioning, or licensing body" that they are opposed to Social Security coverage for services they perform in the exercise of ministry. *IRC 1402(e)(1).* By signing Form 4361, applicants verify that they have satisfied this requirement. Ministers who plan to apply for exemption from Social Security coverage must be sure to notify the church or denomination that ordained, commissioned, or licensed them regarding their opposition to Social Security coverage and presumably of their intention to file an exemption application. This notification must occur prior to the time the exemption application is filed.

Churches or religious denominations that ordain, commission, or license ministers should be aware that they must be informed by applicants for exemption from Social Security coverage that they are applying for exemption. This requirement apparently was designed to provide churches and denominations with an opportunity to counsel applicants regarding the desirability of seeking exemption. Further, knowledge that a particular minister has applied for exemption will assist the church or denomination in providing appropriate pension counseling to such a person. Churches and denominations should prepare standardized responses, setting forth in detail their response to a minister's claim of exemption.

Ministers are free to obtain an exemption (assuming that they otherwise qualify) even if their church or denomination is officially opposed to the exemption of ministers from Social Security coverage or has never taken a position one way or the other. Such churches and denominations should be sure to state, in detail, their reasons for urging an applicant to reconsider his or her decision to pursue exemption. At a minimum, a response should specify the various Social Security benefits that will be forfeited (i.e., retirement benefits, survivor benefits, disability benefits, and Medicare).

Some denominations have been sued for failing to adequately counsel younger ministers regarding the financial disadvantages that may be associated with an exemption from Social Security. Churches and denominations may wish to have applicants for exemption sign a form acknowledging that the church or denomination counseled against filing an exemption application, and releasing the church or denomination from any liability that may arise out of financial hardships associated with exemption. Of course, these procedures would not be as critical if a church or denomination has no position regarding Social Security exemptions. Even in such cases, however, it may be prudent to point out the benefits that are being forfeited and the financial hardship that an exemption may create.

Condition 5—IRS verification

No application for exemption will be approved unless the IRS "has verified that the individual applying for the exemption is aware of the grounds on which the individual may receive an exemption . . . and that the individual seeks an exemption on such grounds." *IRC 1402(e)(2).* This verification requirement was adopted to prevent the widespread practice of ministers exempting themselves from Social Security coverage solely on the basis of financial considerations. The income tax regulations explain the verification procedure as follows:

> *Upon receipt of an application for exemption from self-employment taxes . . . the IRS will mail to the applicant a statement that describes the grounds on which an individual may receive an exemption under [the law]. The individual filing the application shall certify that he or she has read the statement and that he or she seeks exemption from self-employment taxes on the grounds listed in the statement. The certification shall be made by signing a copy of the statement under penalties of perjury and mailing the signed copy to the IRS Service Center from which the statement was issued not later than 90 days after the date on which the statement was mailed to the individual. If the signed copy of the statement is not mailed to the IRS Service Center within 90 days of the date on which the statement was mailed to the individual, that individual's exemption will not be effective until the date that the signed copy of the statement is received at the Service Center.* Treas. Reg. 1.1402(e)-5A.

In other words, the IRS satisfies the verification requirement by sending each applicant a statement reciting the grounds on which

an exemption is available and having the applicant sign the statement, certifying under penalty of perjury that he or she is seeking exemption on the basis of an available ground. The statement must then be returned to the IRS within 90 days from the date it was originally sent by the IRS. Ministers who fail to return the signed statement within 90 days will delay recognition of their exemption until the date that the signed statement is received by the IRS.

✿ **KEY POINT.** If the IRS returns your application marked "approved" and your only self-employment income was from ministerial services, write "Exempt—Form 4361" on the self-employment tax line (line 56) in the "Other Taxes" section of Form 1040. If you had other self-employment income, see Schedule SE (Form 1040).

Condition 6—no disqualifying election

You cannot be exempt from self-employment tax if you made one of the following elections to be covered under Social Security. These elections are irrevocable.

- You elected to be covered under Social Security by filing Form 2031 (Revocation of Exemption from Self-employment Tax for Use by Ministers, Members of Religious Orders, and Christian Science Practitioners) for your 1986, 1987, 2000, or 2001 tax year.
- You elected before 1968 to be covered under Social Security for your ministerial services.

2. COMMON QUESTIONS

Some common questions pertaining to the exemption from self-employment taxes are addressed below.

When is an exemption effective?

Filing a timely exemption application does not necessarily qualify a minister for exemption. The income tax regulations specify that "the filing of an application for exemption on Form 4361 by a minister . . . does not constitute an exemption from the tax on self-employment income. . . . The exemption is granted only if the application is approved by an appropriate internal revenue officer." In practice, an exemption is effective only when an applicant receives back one of the three 4361 forms (it is filed in triplicate) from the IRS marked "approved." Ministers should be careful not to lose an approved Form 4361. *Treadway v. Commissioner, 47 T.C.M. 1375 (1984).*

What if I cannot prove that I submitted a Form 4361?

➡ **TIP.** If you cannot remember if you filed a timely Form 4361, contact the tax preparer you used to prepare and file your tax returns at the time the form would have been submitted. The preparer may have records that will indicate if a Form 4361 was filed.

Some ministers claim to be exempt from self-employment taxes, but the IRS has no record of a Form 4361 ever having been filed or approved. Are such ministers exempt? Do they owe back taxes? As noted in the answer to the previous question, exemption from self-employment taxes generally is not effective until the IRS *approves* a minister's Form 4361. This poses a potential problem when ministers are audited and cannot produce a copy of their approved Form 4361 (and the IRS has no record of receiving or approving such a form). The courts have addressed this issue in four cases. Each case is summarized below.

Eade v. United States, 792 F.Supp. 476 (W.D. Va. 1991)

A federal court in Virginia ruled that a minister was entitled to exemption from self-employment taxes even though the IRS had no record of ever having received his exemption application (Form 4361). The minister was able to persuade a jury that he qualified for exemption and that he filed a timely exemption application. The court acknowledged that the income tax regulations specify that a minister's exemption is not effective until the IRS marks a copy of the exemption application "approved" and returns it to the minister. However, the court concluded that IRS approval of such applications is a perfunctory act involving no discretion. Accordingly, since the minister had done everything he was required to do in order to claim the exemption and was in fact qualified for it, he was entitled to the exemption despite the apparent mistake of the Post Office or the Internal Revenue Service.

The *Eade* case may resolve a dilemma for many ministers who have submitted a timely application for exemption from self-employment taxes (Form 4361) but who have never received a reply from the IRS. Many of these ministers have assumed that they are exempt. They become alarmed when they discover that the income tax regulations state that the exemption is effective only when the IRS stamps their application "approved" and returns it to them.

The *Eade* case gives hope to these ministers. They will not necessarily be liable for self-employment taxes (plus penalties and interest) for previous years. However, to achieve this result, they must (1) demonstrate that they were eligible for the exemption; (2) convince a jury that they mailed a timely Form 4361; and (3) persuade the court to apply the same reasoning as the Virginia federal district court (i.e., that IRS "approval" of an exemption is a perfunctory, administrative act that is not a requirement for exemption). As the court itself noted, not every minister will be able to persuade a jury that he or she mailed a timely Form 4361.

A few other points should be observed about the *Eade* case. First, the decision does not provide any relief to those ministers who would like to exempt themselves from self-employment taxes after the deadline has expired. Second, the decision does not liberalize the requirements

for qualifying for exemption. To be eligible for the exemption from self-employment taxes, a minister must be opposed on the basis of religious considerations to the acceptance of Social Security benefits. This is an extraordinary claim that few ministers can satisfy. Nothing in the court's decision changes this. Third, the case will be of no help to ministers who cannot recall whether they filed a Form 4361. Fourth, the court in no way was encouraging ministers to opt out of Social Security. Again, few ministers will be able to satisfy the extraordinary requirements for exempt status. This has not changed.

Abdallah v. Commissioner, T.C. Summary Opinion 2002-132

Pastor B graduated from seminary in 1976 and was ordained in 1977. Since his ordination, Pastor B served as the senior pastor of a church. In March 1977 Pastor B completed and signed Form 4361 in the presence of witnesses and mailed it to the IRS. The IRS has no record that the Form 4361 was filed, and Pastor B did not keep a copy of the form he submitted. The IRS audited Pastor B and determined that he was not exempt from self-employment taxes. It relied on a provision in the income tax regulations specifying that an exemption is not effective until approved by the IRS. Pastor B appealed to the Tax Court. Both he and the IRS agreed that a Form 4361 filed in March of 1977 would have been timely. The only issue was whether the form was actually filed.

The court concluded that Pastor B was exempt from self-employment taxes: "We found [Pastor B's] evidence that he had filed for an exemption to be particularly credible. His testimony concerning the filing of the Form 4361 was straightforward and plausible. Further, his testimony was buttressed by the written statement of a witness who observed petitioner complete and sign the Form 4361 in 1977. With regards to whether the application was approved by [IRS], as required by the regulations . . . we believe that such approval must have been given. [Pastor B] consistently has not paid self-employment taxes on his ministerial earnings since 1977. . . . It seems highly peculiar that, if the approval had not been given, he would have filed for 21 years as being exempt without some dispute. Rather, it seems more likely that his file was misplaced at some point in time. Thus, we find that he prepared and filed the Form 4361 in 1977."

The court acknowledged that Pastor B could not produce a copy of the Form 4361 that he allegedly filed, but it concluded that neither the tax code nor regulations require ministers "to retain such a copy."

William and Cathy A. Bennett v. Commissioner, T.C. Memo. 2007-355 (2007)

In one case a minister was commissioned and licensed by a church in 1996 and served as its senior pastor. He received net ministerial income of $400 or more for 1997 through 2002 (except for 2000). In 1998 he paid self-employment taxes on his ministerial income but did not do so for any of these other years based on his belief that he was exempt.

The IRS audited the minister's 2002 tax return and determined that he incorrectly claimed to be exempt from self-employment taxes. Self-employment taxes, plus interest, were assessed. The minister claimed that he was exempt from self-employment taxes since (1) he filed a Form 4361 with the IRS in 1980 that the IRS approved, although he didn't have a copy of the form or the IRS approval; and (2) he filed a new Form 4361 with his tax returns for 1997, 1999, 2000, and 2002.

The IRS claimed that it never received the minister's 1980 exemption application and that the subsequent forms he submitted were all too late. The minister appealed his case to the United States Tax Court. The Tax Court agreed with the IRS that the minister failed to submit his Form 4361 on time.

The 1980 Form 4361. The court concluded that the following facts undermined the minister's claim that he owed no self-employment taxes in 2002 because he filed a timely Form 4361 in 1980 that was approved by the IRS:

- The minister produced no documentation to corroborate that in 1980 he filed a Form 4361.
- The IRS searched relevant files in its Ministerial Unit at the Philadelphia Service Center, which processes all Forms 4361 and which maintains individual folders containing Forms 4361 relating to all ministers, and the folder relating to the minister in this case did not contain any Form 4361 filed by him in 1980.
- The IRS also conducted a search of the minister's other files and archives for the allegedly filed Form 4361, but this search yielded no Form 4361 filed in 1980.
- The fact that, for 1998, the minister actually reported and paid self-employment taxes of $4,191 on his ministerial income undermined his claim that he believed that in 1980 he had filed a Form 4361 that was approved by the IRS.
- After approving or disapproving a Form 4361, the IRS is to submit to the Social Security Administration (SSA) a copy of the approved or disapproved Form 4361, and there is in evidence a Certificate of Lack of Record from the SSA, indicating that the SSA has no record of any Form 4361 filed by the minister in 1980.

The minister claimed that because he failed to pay employment taxes in some years proved that in 1980 he must have received an approved ministerial exemption. The court noted that "his failure to pay employment taxes in some years could be attributed to a number of reasons (e.g., unemployment)."

The other Forms 4361. The court noted that the minister had income of at least $400 for both 1997 and 1998 from the exercise of ministry, and therefore the due date for his Form 4361 was April 15, 1999 (the due date for his federal tax return for the second year that he had net self-employment income of at least $400, any part of

which derived from ministerial services). The minister insisted that he filed timely Forms 4361 (or letters containing the same information) in 1997, 1999, 2000, and 2002, and therefore his ministerial income was exempt from self-employment taxes for 2002. The court disagreed. It addressed each of the minister's submissions as follows:

- His 1997 tax return included a Form 4361, but this return was not submitted until 2000, a year after the filing deadline of April 15, 1999.
- His 1998 tax return was filed on April 15, 1999, and it included a letter requesting exemption from self-employment taxes, but the letter failed to include the "certifications" required for an exemption application. The court acknowledged that the IRS "may accept from a minister, in lieu of a Form 4361, a letter if the letter is timely filed and if the letter includes the required certification statements." Two such statements are required by the tax code: (1) a statement certifying that the minister is conscientiously, or on the basis of religious principles, opposed to the acceptance of public insurance such as Social Security and (2) an additional statement certifying that the minister "has informed the ordaining, commissioning, or licensing body of the church or order that he is opposed to such insurance." *Audit, Internal Revenue Manual, sec. 4.19.6.3.1(3), at 10,779-749-11.* Since the letter the minister enclosed with his 1998 tax return did not contain either of these certifications, it was not a valid application for exemption.
- His 1999 tax return included a Form 4361, but it was filed in 2000 (after the April 15, 1999, deadline for his Form 4361).
- He did not file a tax return for 2000.
- His tax returns for 2000 and 2001 included a Form 4361, but these were filed after the April 15, 1999, deadline for filing his Form 4361.

The minister produced several additional copies of different Forms 4361 prepared and signed by him and dated prior to April 15, 1999, but he "produced no evidence that these Forms 4361 were ever properly addressed, stamped, mailed, and filed with the IRS prior to April 15, 1999."

The court stressed that (1) the Form 4361 filing deadline "is mandatory and is to be complied with strictly" and that (2) ministers "bear the burden of proof to establish that a Form 4361 or letter was timely filed."

Vigil v. Commissioner, T.C. Summary Opinion 2008-6 (2008)

In 1996, during an audit of his 1994 joint tax return, the taxpayer wrote a letter to the IRS stating that in 1987 he had filed a Form 4361 exemption application and that a copy of the approved Form 4361 had been returned to him. He requested that another copy of the approved application be sent to him and enclosed a copy of the signed (but unapproved) Form 4361 that he claimed he filed in 1987. The IRS received his request along with the copy of the unapproved Form 4361. It searched its document and computer files but did not find any record that the taxpayer had been approved for a ministerial exemption or any record that he had filed a request for a ministerial exemption before 1996. The IRS requested that the Social Security Administration search its records and learned that the SSA did not have any record of either the approval or the receipt of a Form 4361 from the taxpayer.

In 1997 the IRS informed the taxpayer of an adjustment to his 1994 federal income tax, together with a negligence penalty, resulting from nonpayment of self-employment taxes. However, a few months later the IRS sent the taxpayer a letter stating that the 1994 examination resulted in no change to the taxes reported.

Several years later the IRS audited the taxpayer's 2001 tax return and determined that he had underpaid his taxes by $12,118, mostly due to a failure to pay self-employment taxes. Again the IRS asserted that it could find no evidence that the taxpayer was exempt. The taxpayer appealed to the Tax Court.

The court noted that the tax code provides specific requirements for a minister to obtain an exemption from self-employment tax: "A minister seeking the exemption must file an application stating that he is opposed, because of religious principles or conscientious beliefs, to the acceptance of certain types of public insurance, such as that provided by the Social Security Act, attributable to his services as a minister. This application must be filed within the specific time limits. . . . Once properly obtained, the exemption from self-employment tax is irrevocable and remains effective for all succeeding taxable years."

The court noted that an application for exemption (Form 4361) must be filed "on or before the later of the following dates: (1) [t]he due date of the return (including any extensions) for the second taxable year for which the taxpayer has net earnings from self-employment of $400 or more, any part of which was derived from the performance of services as a minister, or (2) the due date of the return (including any extensions) for his second taxable year ending after 1967." The court stressed that it had "consistently held that the time limitations are mandatory and taxpayers must strictly comply with them." In addition, ministers bear the burden of proving that they are eligible for the exemption and that they filed a timely Form 4361. The court observed:

> The IRS's "Ministerial Exemption Unit" had conducted a search to determine whether the taxpayer had previously filed a Form 4361 and whether it had been approved. A supervisor of this unit found the taxpayer's 1996 letter asserting that he filed Form 4361 in 1987, requesting another copy of the approved Form 4361, and enclosing a copy of the signed but unapproved Form 4361. The supervisor also found the case history sheet that was completed in 1996 when the IRS received the taxpayer's letter. The case history sheet documented the search at both the IRS and the SSA for any Form 4361 filed by the taxpayer and reflects that the IRS notified him in 1996 that neither the IRS nor the SSA found any record of a Form 4361 for him, either approved or denied. The supervisor queried the SSA again and received a certification, dated May 3, 2007, that the SSA had no record of the taxpayer submitting a Form 4361. Finally, she testified that the SSA retains such records for 75 years.

> The taxpayer's testimony regarding when he filed Form 4361 was vague and inconsistent; he was certain it was filed in the 1980s, but he thought it might have been a couple of years after he was licensed. He signed the Form 4361 on April 7, 1987. The form states that he was licensed in January 1979. His testimony was confusing on this issue; he stated that he was licensed around 1980, but could not say exactly when. He also testified that he worked part time as a minister in 1979 and full time starting in 1980. The Form 4361 states that the first 2 years in which he had net self-employment earnings in excess of $400, at least some of which came from services as a minister, were 1979 and 1980. We find that the taxpayer was licensed in 1979 and that his first 2 earning years as a minister were 1979 and 1980. We conclude that his Form 4361 was due on the due date of his tax return for 1980; i.e., April 15, 1981, with extensions. He signed the Form 4361 and gave it to their certified public accountant (CPA). However, he has not demonstrated that he submitted a Form 4361 to the IRS before his letter in May of 1996 or that an application for exemption was ever approved. Because a search of IRS and SSA records by the IRS for the taxpayer's Form 4361 failed to discover the original form, and since he failed to carry his burden of proving that the form was filed, we find that he did not timely file a request for exemption as required by law.

The taxpayer claimed that his CPA showed the signed Form 4361 to the IRS agent examining his 1994 return and that this documentation ultimately resulted in the no-change letter from the IRS for 1994. He insisted that the decision by the IRS not to change his taxes for 1994 proved that it accepted his exemption for 1994 and established that the application form was on file at that time and, by implication, was approved. As a result, the IRS was barred from denying his exemption. The court disagreed: "It is well established that each tax year stands on its own. Furthermore, errors of law in prior years do not estop the IRS from correcting those errors in later years. In view of the apparent failure of the taxpayer to file Form 4361 timely, acquiescence by IRS agents in accepting his claim of exemption in 1994 was an error of law. Such a mistake does not prevent correction of the error as to 2001. [The tax code] imposes time limitations, and IRS agents have neither the authority nor the power to grant an exemption not complying with the statute."

Will I receive a refund of self-employment taxes I paid before filing Form 4361?

Ministers who file an exemption application close to the deadline will have paid self-employment taxes on their ministerial income for two years. IRS Publication 517 contains the following instructions for claiming a refund of these taxes:

If, after receiving an approved Form 4361, you find that you over-paid SE tax, you can file a claim for refund on Form 1040X before the period of time for filing ends. This is generally within three years from the date you filed the return or within two years from the date you paid the tax, whichever is later. A return you filed, or tax you paid, before the due date is considered to have been filed or paid on the due date. If you file a claim after the three-year period but within 2 years from the time you paid the tax, the credit or refund will not be more than the tax you paid within the 2 years immediately before you file the claim.

Can the period for filing an exemption application be extended or renewed?

As noted above, an exemption application must be submitted by the due date, including extensions, of the federal tax return for the second year in which a minister receives net earnings from self-employment of $400 or more, any portion of which comes from the exercise of ministry. Many ministers have asked, "Is there any way I can submit an exemption application after this deadline has expired?" Consider the following.

Exemption application rules

The general rule—no extension or renewal allowed. A number of ministers have attempted to file exemption applications after the filing deadline expired. However, the courts have never permitted any exceptions to the filing deadline rules—except in one case discussed below.

To illustrate, a number of ministers who failed to file a timely exemption application have argued that their constitutional right to freely exercise their religion is violated if they are forced to pay Social Security taxes against their will. This contention has been consistently rejected by the courts. The United States Supreme Court has observed that "if we hold that ministers have a constitutional right to opt out of the Social Security system when participation conflicts with their religious beliefs, that same right should extend as well to persons with secular employment and to other taxes, since their right to freely exercise their religion is no less than that of ministers." *United States v. Lee, 455 U.S. 252 (1982).*

Other ministers have argued that (1) they were unaware of the deadline; (2) they were certain (but could not prove) that they had filed a timely election; (3) they were given incorrect advice by IRS employees regarding the requirements for exemption; or (4) their opposition to participation in the Social Security program did not arise until after the deadline for filing an exemption application had passed. The courts have rejected all of these arguments. *See, e.g., Ballinger v. Commissioner, 728 F.2d 1287 (10th Cir. 1984); Olsen v. Commissioner, 709 F.2d 278 (4th Cir. 1983); Keaton v. Commissioner, T.C. Memo. 1993-365; Paschall v. Commissioner, 46 T.C.M. 1197 (1983); Hess v. Commissioner, 40 T.C.M. 415 (1980).*

Change of faith accompanied by an untimely exemption application. The general rule applies, and the period for filing an exemption application will not be renewed. In 1984 a federal appeals court ruled that the deadline for filing an application for exemption from self-employment taxes is not renewed or extended simply because a minister undergoes a change of faith. *Ballinger v. Commissioner, 728 F.2d 1287 (10th Cir. 1984).* In the *Ballinger* case a minister was ordained by a Baptist church in 1969 and served as a minister of that church from 1969 through 1972. He did not apply for an exemption from self- employment tax. He became a minister in another faith in 1973 and performed services as a minister of a church affiliated with his new faith in 1973, 1974 and 1975. He paid the appropriate self-employment tax on such earnings during each of these years. In 1978 the minister was formally ordained by his new church, and in the same year he submitted an exemption application (Form 4361) to the IRS, claiming that he followed his new church's teachings in opposition to accepting public or private insurance benefits, such as Social Security benefits in the event of death, disability, or old age.

The IRS denied this application for exemption, and the Tax Court agreed. The Tax Court refused to interpret the time requirements for filing an exemption application as allowing an exemption after a second ordination. The minister appealed this decision to a federal appeals court, which agreed with the IRS and Tax Court. However, it insisted that it did not agree with the Tax Court's sweeping conclusion that an exemption is never permissible in cases of second ordinations. The court observed:

> *The statute makes no distinction between a first ordination and subsequent ordinations. Not all churches or religions have a formally ordained ministry, whether because of the nature of their beliefs, the lack of a denominational structure or a variety of other reasons. Courts are not in a position to determine the merits of various churches nor an individual's conversion from one church to another. Thus, we cannot hold that an individual who functions as a minister in a church which does not ordain, license or commission that individual in a traditional or legally formal manner is not entitled to the exemption. Nor can we hold that an individual who has a change of belief accompanied by a change to another faith is not entitled to the exemption. We interpret Congress' language providing an exemption for any individual who is "a duly ordained, commissioner or licensed minister of a church" to mean that the triggering event is the assumption of the duties and functions of a minister.*

Since the minister in this case began his duties with his new church in 1973, his deadline for filing an exemption application was April 15, 1975. It did not matter that he was not ordained until 1978, since the critical event according to this court is the date a person begins performing the duties of a minister.

Minister who remains in the same church but does not develop religious-based opposition to the acceptance of Social Security benefits until after the deadline has expired. The general rule applies here as well, and an exemption application will be denied. The federal appeals court in the *Ballinger* case (see above) observed:

> The more difficult question is whether an individual, who has already assumed the duties of a minister, belatedly acquires a belief in opposition to the acceptance of public insurance and that change in belief is not accompanied by a change in faiths, is entitled to the exemption if he files within the statutory time frame after acquiring his new belief. We find that the statute does not provide for an exemption in that situation. The triggering event for measuring the statutory time period is the assumption of ministerial duties, combined with earning a particular amount of income. Thus, the statute does not provide for an exemption where a minister belatedly acquires a belief in opposition to public insurance apart from conversion to another faith. The [minister] did not file for the exemption within the applicable time frame.

Possible exception to the general rule—a second ordination in another faith accompanied by a timely exemption application.
In 1994 a federal appeals court for the tenth circuit (Colorado, Kansas, New Mexico, Oklahoma, Utah, and Wyoming) ruled that the deadline for filing an exemption application had to be recomputed after a minister left the ministry for five years and was then reordained by another church. *Hall v. Commissioner, 30 F.3d 1304 (10th Cir. 1994)*. Pastor Hall served as a Methodist minister in 1980 and 1981, and he received net earnings from self-employment in both years of at least $400 from the exercise of his ministry. As a result, the deadline for filing an application for exemption from self-employment taxes was April 15, 1982. During this time, however, Pastor Hall was not opposed to the acceptance of Social Security or other public insurance benefits and did not file for exemption. He left the ministry and worked as an engineer. Five years later he was ordained as a minister by another denomination and immediately filed an application for exemption from self-employment taxes. He insisted that he developed an opposition to accepting Social Security benefits as a result of the influence of his new denomination.

The IRS denied Pastor Hall's exemption application, concluding that the deadline was April 15, 1982. On appeal, the Tax Court agreed with the IRS and denied Pastor Hall's exemption application. The court noted that the tax code does not make any provision for a second application period following a second ordination. Pastor Hall appealed, and a federal appeals court concluded that the deadline for filing an exemption application is renewed when a minister is reordained by another church. The court observed:

> The question before us is whether the taxpayer's return to the ministry after a five-year absence, combined with his ordination in a new church and his acceptance of a new belief in opposition to public insurance, provides an opportunity to opt out of the Social Security system. . . . Without performing a detailed analysis, we express concern that the Tax Court's interpretation

> of [the deadline requirement] could arbitrarily and unconstitutionally interfere with the adherence to sincere religious beliefs by individuals, such as the taxpayer in this case, who undergo a genuine religious conversion, are ordained in a second church, and act within the defined statutory period to exempt themselves from tax on their self-employment income. . . . The plain language of the statute extends the exemption to "any individual who is a duly ordained, commissioned, or licensed minister of a church . . . upon filing an application . . . together with a statement that either he is conscientiously opposed to, or because of religious principles he is opposed to, the acceptance . . . of any public insurance." [Pastor Hall] fits that profile exactly. The code also requires an applicant for exemption to file on or before "the due date of the return . . . for the second taxable year for which he has net earnings from self-employment [from his ministerial services] of $400 or more." As recited above, [Pastor Hall] filed during the first taxable year in which his self-employment income from his new ministry exceeded $400. When an individual enters the ministry anew in a new church, having adopted a new set of beliefs about the propriety of accepting public insurance, it is logical and consistent with the [language of the tax code] to characterize that individual as a "new" minister for the purposes of seeking an exemption. The plain language does not preclude this sensible reading.

> We are not concerned that our decision will open the floodgates for conniving Elmer Gantrys to dupe the Internal Revenue Service and opt out of the Social Security system without documenting a legitimate religious or conscientious reason to justify their exemption from the self-employment tax. It seems unlikely that individuals will forgo the retirement security represented by the Social Security system without a sincere religious objection. Ministers who do not switch churches may not belatedly opt out of the system. Ministers who do switch will still have a limited time frame in which to file for exemption following their assumption of the duties and functions of the new ministry. And once ministers elect exemption, that exemption is irrevocable.

The court's decision in the *Hall* case has not opened the floodgates to other ministers. For the vast majority of ministers who fail to file an exemption application by the deadline summarized above, there is no second chance. They will never be able to exempt themselves from Social Security coverage.

The court's decision in the *Hall* case is a narrow one and applies only to those few ministers who

- change their church affiliation;
- are reordained;
- develop an opposition, based on their new religious convictions, to the acceptance of Social Security benefits; and
- submit an exemption application (Form 4361) by the due date, including extensions, of the federal tax return for the

second year in which they have net self-employment earnings of $400 or more, any part of which comes from the performance of ministerial services in their new faith.

Few ministers will satisfy these requirements. The ruling will *not* apply to ministers who do not change their church affiliation or doctrine. Ministers who did not file an exemption application within the prescribed period and who have served a local church for several years are not given a second chance to opt out of Social Security by this ruling. The court agreed with its decision in an earlier case denying an exemption from Social Security to a minister who changed his religious beliefs, was reordained, and then waited five years before submitting an exemption application. *Ballinger v. Commissioner, 728 F.2d 1287 (10th Cir. 1984).*

❖ **KEY POINT.** The *Hall* case was a decision by a federal appeals court in the 10th federal circuit, which includes the states of Colorado, Kansas, New Mexico, Oklahoma, Utah, and Wyoming. In other states it is at best persuasive, but not binding, precedent. While its authority may have been enhanced by its recognition in IRS Chief Council Advice 200404048 (see below), it is still possible that other federal appeals courts and the Tax Court would reach different conclusions. Despite its limitations, the *Hall* case represents the most authoritative judicial precedent on the question addressed in this section.

Chief Counsel Advice 200404048

The IRS chief counsel issued an opinion in 2003 addressing two questions pertaining to the exemption from self-employment taxes. The questions and the IRS chief counsel's responses are noted below.

Question 1. Pastor G is a duly ordained minister of a church who is not opposed to the acceptance of public insurance. Pastor G subsequently has a change of faith and is ordained as a minister in another church, which results in a change in belief by Pastor G to being opposed to the acceptance of public insurance. Pastor G seeks exemption from self-employment tax.

The chief counsel correctly noted that the *Hall* case (see above) addressed this issue and concluded that a minister under these circumstances would requalify for exemption from Social Security. The chief counsel explained that the *Hall* case "provides that when an individual enters the ministry anew in a new church, having adopted a new set of beliefs about the propriety of accepting public insurance, it is logical and consistent with the [language of the tax code] to characterize that individual as a 'new' minister for the purposes of seeking an exemption." As a result, the chief counsel concluded that "a minister seeking exemption from self employment tax who has a change of faith that results in a change in belief to opposing the acceptance of public insurance . . . merely needs to sign the Form 4361."

Question 2. Pastor T is a duly ordained minister of a church who, because of religious principles, is opposed to the acceptance of

public insurance. Pastor T filed a Form 4361 that the IRS did not approve for reasons of late filing. Pastor T subsequently has a change of faith and is ordained as a minister in another church and has no resulting change in belief regarding public insurance (taxpayer continues to be opposed to the acceptance of public insurance). May the taxpayer file another Form 4361?

The chief counsel answered no to this question. The chief counsel's opinion applied the *Ballinger* and *Hall* cases (see above) to this question and concluded:

> *As in Ballinger and Hall, the taxpayer had a change of faith. But unlike these cases, he did not have a change of belief in opposing the acceptance of public insurance. He has consistently opposed such insurance beginning with his first ministry. When an individual enters the ministry anew in a new church, having adopted a new set of beliefs about the propriety of accepting public insurance, it is logical and consistent with the [language of the tax code] to characterize that individual as a 'new' minister for the purposes of seeking an exemption. Under the facts and circumstances presented, however, the taxpayer had his opportunity based on his beliefs to apply for an exemption after the first ordination, but the exemption was denied because he did not file the application timely as is required under the statute. The tax code does not give him a second opportunity to file a Form 4361 in the stated circumstances due only to a change in faith and entering the ministry in a new church*

❖ **KEY POINT.** In a 1979 General Counsel Memorandum, the IRS concluded that "the clear purpose of [the exemption] is to allow ministers who are opposed to the acceptance of public insurance because of religious principles . . . to be exempt from self-employment tax, provided that the minister claims exemption within the prescribed period." *GCM 38,210 (1979).* It stated that the purposes of the statute are served by allowing a minister who is ordained by a second church and who previously "was not conscientiously opposed to the acceptance of public insurance to qualify for the self-employment tax exemption, by claiming exemption within the prescribed period after the second ordination. Denying exemption in such a situation on the basis that the minister should have requested exemption when ordained by the first church would be unreasonable because the minister was not opposed then to public insurance and thus did not qualify at that time."

Four years later the IRS reversed its opinion on the grounds that the plain language and legislative history of the tax code provided no grounds for such a position. *GCM 39,042 (1983).* This memorandum expressed no concern for burdens on changed religious beliefs, concluding that even if the minister's first church did not oppose public insurance, the minister could have filed for exemption based on personal views.

How far back can the IRS assess Social Security taxes?

This question is relevant whenever a minister has unreported or underreported self-employment taxes. This condition can occur in several ways, including the following:

- A minister submits a timely exemption application (Form 4361) but never receives back an approved copy. The minister assumes that he or she is exempt from self-employment taxes from the date the application is submitted and does not pay self-employment taxes. The IRS rejects the *Eade* case (discussed above).
- Some ministers assume they are automatically exempt from self-employment taxes and so do not submit a Form 4361.
- Some ministers who have submitted a timely exemption application that has been approved by the IRS are later audited, and the validity of their exemption is challenged.
- Some ministers underreport their self-employment taxes because they fail to include their housing allowance (or the fair rental value of a church-provided parsonage) in their taxable income when computing self-employment taxes.

Under any of these circumstances, can the IRS assess back taxes and penalties all the way back to the first year of the person's ministry? This question was answered in a 1982 ruling of the IRS. The ruling involved a farmer who filed a timely Form 1040 for several years, on which he correctly reported his income tax liability but failed to attach a Schedule SE or report or pay any self-employment tax (i.e., Social Security tax for self-employed persons) for any of those years. The question presented to the IRS was whether self-employment taxes could be assessed for *all* the years in question. The IRS noted that section 6501(a) of the tax code specifies that taxes must be assessed within three years after a return is filed, though taxes may be assessed at any time in the case of failure to file a return. In other words, the IRS generally can assess back taxes only for the three years preceding a return, but there is no limit on how far back the IRS can assess taxes if no return is filed.

The IRS concluded that "self-employment taxes are not separate and distinct from individual income taxes" but rather are "in all particulars an integral part of the income tax." Accordingly, "the filing of a Form 1040 that fully reports all income but contains no entry with respect to self-employment tax will be treated as the filing of a valid self-employment tax return," and therefore the "self-employment tax may not be assessed later than three years after the taxpayer files a Form 1040 and fully reports all income but makes no entry with respect to self-employment tax." *Revenue Ruling 82-185. See also Hoffa v. Commissioner, 50 T.C.M. 869 (1985).*

EXAMPLE. Pastor W was ordained in 1990 but never has paid Social Security taxes because of his belief that he submitted a timely exemption application (Form 4361) to the IRS. However, he does not have in his possession a copy of the exemption application, and he does not recall ever receiving back an approved copy from the IRS. In May 2013 he learns that an exemption from Social Security is not effective unless the applicant receives back from the IRS an approved copy of the exemption application. Pastor W is afraid to contact the IRS or Social Security Administration to confirm his exemption out of fear that he will be told that he is not exempt and that he will have to pay Social Security taxes all the way back to 1990 (with penalties and interest).

According to Revenue Ruling 82-185, Pastor W will not be assessed Social Security taxes later than three years after he files a Form 1040 and fully reports all income (but makes no entry with respect to self-employment tax). This means that if Pastor W filed a Form 1040 for each year since 1990, and fully reported all income in each year, he cannot be assessed Social Security taxes for any year prior to 2008 (i.e., three years from the filing deadline for Pastor W's 2008 income tax return would have been April 15, 2013, so it is too late in May 2013 for the IRS to assess taxes for 2006 or any preceding year).

EXAMPLE. In 1993 the Tax Court ruled that a minister, who had not paid self-employment taxes for the years 1983 through 1987 on the ground that the IRS had "improperly denied" his 1980 and 1983 applications for exemption from self-employment taxes, was liable for self-employment taxes for all of the years in question. It is unclear how the IRS could assess back taxes for five years, and for years that clearly were more than three years prior to the IRS audit. In fact, 1983 (one of the years for which the IRS was demanding back taxes) was a decade prior to the court's decision, and nearly a decade prior to the IRS audit. *Reeder v. Commissioner, T.C. Memo. 1993-287.*

Is an exemption from Social Security coverage irrevocable?

The tax code clearly states that ministers who exempt themselves from self-employment taxes cannot revoke their exemption. The decision to become exempt from self-employment taxes is "irrevocable." *IRC 1402(e)(4).* Form 4361 itself warns that "once the application is approved, you cannot revoke it." However, both Congress and the IRS have created limited exceptions as noted below.

Congressional relief

Congress has created three limited windows of time since 1977 to allow exempt ministers to revoke their exemption.

1977 legislation. Congress allowed ministers who were exempt as of December 20, 1977, to revoke their exemption by the due date of their federal income tax return for 1977 (April 15, 1978) by filing a Form 4361-A.

1987 legislation. The Tax Reform Act of 1986 gave exempt ministers another limited opportunity to revoke an exemption from self-employment taxes, by filing a Form 2031 with the IRS by the due date for their federal income tax return for 1987 (April 15, 1988). The decision to revoke an exemption from self-employment tax was irrevocable. Ministers who revoked an exemption did not become liable for self-employment taxes all the way back to the date of their original exemption. Rather, they were required to pay self-employment taxes effective January 1, 1986, or January 1, 1987. Few exempt ministers revoked their exemption under this legislation, because most waited until the deadline and discovered that a revocation of their exemption would obligate them to pay several quarters of back taxes. On modest income, this was a crushing liability that few could afford.

1999 legislation. At the end of 1999, Congress enacted legislation giving ministers the option to revoke an exemption from Social Security by filing Form 2031 with the IRS by April 15, 2002 (August 15, 2002, for ministers who obtained a four-month extension to file their federal tax return by filing a timely Form 4868 with the IRS). Ministers could revoke their exemption beginning on either January 1, 2000, or January 1, 2001. Ministers who revoked an exemption are not permitted to apply for exemption at a later time. The decision to revoke an exemption is irrevocable.

> **EXAMPLE.** Pastor D revoked his exemption from self-employment taxes in April 2003. In 2013 he decides that revoking the exemption was a bad idea, and he wants to revert back to exempt status. He will not be permitted to do so. A decision to revoke an exemption is irrevocable.

> ✿ **KEY POINT.** Will Congress give ministers another opportunity to revoke an exemption from Social Security? It does not look likely, at least for now. No bill has been introduced in Congress since 2005 that would allow ministers a limited time to revoke an exemption from Social Security, and the 2005 bill attracted no cosponsors.

IRS relief

In a 1970 ruling the IRS allowed an exempt minister to revoke his exemption on the ground of mistake. *Revenue Ruling 70-197.* The minister filed a timely Form 4361 with the IRS certifying that he was opposed on the basis of his religious convictions to the acceptance of Social Security or any other public insurance benefits. However, he later explained that he filed the Form 4361 based on erroneous advice and that his filing was based solely on a personal decision that private insurance programs were financially preferable to participation in the Social Security program. The IRS ruled that such a minister was *not legally exempt from self-employment tax*:

> *In this case the taxpayer filed the Form 4361 solely for economic considerations and not because he was conscientiously opposed to, or because of religious principles opposed to, the acceptance of any public insurance of the type described on the form. Accordingly, it is held that the taxpayer did not qualify for the*

> *exemption since the Form 4361 filed solely for economic reasons is a nullity. Therefore, his net earnings from the exercise of his ministry . . . are subject to the [self-employment] tax.*

According to this ruling, which has never been withdrawn or modified by the IRS, a Form 4361 that is filed "solely for economic reasons" is a "nullity."

Many ministers have exempted themselves from self-employment taxes based on economic reasons. Can they revoke their exemption based on the 1970 IRS ruling? Possibly. But before embracing such a conclusion, ministers should carefully consider the following points:

Point 1. While Revenue Ruling 70-197 has never been withdrawn or modified by the IRS, it has never been applied or even mentioned by the IRS in any other published ruling.

Point 2. Revenue Ruling 70-197 has been recognized or applied by only one court since 1970. In 1983 a federal appeals court addressed the legal validity of a Form 2031 filed by a pastor many years before. *Blakely v. Commissioner, 720 F.2d 411 (5th Cir. 1983).* Prior to 1968, ministers were automatically exempt from self-employment taxes unless they filed a Form 2031 waiving their exemption. A pastor signed and filed a Form 2031 in 1957. He paid self-employment taxes for a few years, then ceased doing so. The IRS audited his tax return and claimed that he owed back taxes and penalties for unpaid self-employment taxes. The pastor asserted that he was not liable for these taxes because the Form 2031 that he filed was of no legal effect, since (1) he signed it under the "mistaken impression" that he was "opting out" of Social Security and not into it; and (2) it did not accurately reflect his intent at the time of signing it. The Tax Court agreed with the IRS, and the pastor appealed.

On appeal, the pastor cited Revenue Ruling 70-197 (see above) in support of his position. A federal appeals court rejected the pastor's arguments and ordered him to pay the back taxes and penalties. It concluded:

> *The pastor signed the waiver [that was] exceedingly clear and unambiguous, and irrevocable by its own plain terms. . . . [The pastor] is an intelligent and learned individual, and for the two years immediately following his signing of the waiver reported income from self-employment earnings in conformity with his expressed intent when he signed the waiver. . . . In Revenue Ruling 70-197 the IRS allowed a minister to rescind an opting-out waiver executed after Congress passed the 1967 Social Security amendments. When he decided to revoke his waiver, the minister told the IRS that he opted out of the system for economic reasons, and not because he was conscientiously or religiously opposed to national insurance programs. The pastor in this case similarly asserts that he did not intend to participate in the system when he signed the waiver. Therefore, the waiver is based on a material misstatement of fact. The pastor's reliance on Revenue*

Ruling 70-197 is inappropriate . . . When he executed the waiver, he did not misstate anything. He knew what he was signing and intended to be included in the Social Security system.

The court concluded that the IRS

allows rescission of validly executed waivers only under the narrowest of circumstances. For example, it has allowed a taxpayer to withdraw a waiver within the statutorily prescribed time limits for initial filing of the waiver (Revenue Ruling 61-187), or when the evidence unequivocally leads to the conclusion that the waiver itself is based on a material misstatement of fact (Revenue Ruling 70-197). The IRS's strict policy regarding rescission of waivers is sound. It facilitates certainty. The IRS must be able to rely on the validity and plain meaning of documents executed and submitted by taxpayers.

This case interprets Revenue Ruling 70-197 narrowly but does suggest that it provides a basis for revoking an exemption from self-employment taxes "when the evidence unequivocally leads to the conclusion that the waiver itself is based on a material misstatement of fact."

Point 3. Form 4361 is signed under penalty of perjury. In some cases an attempt to revoke a Form 4361 based on Revenue Ruling 70-197 may expose a pastor to criminal liability for perjury. Clearly, any decision to revoke an exemption (Form 4361) based on Revenue Ruling 70-197 should not be made without the advice of a tax attorney.

What is the legal effect of an exemption based on economic considerations?
See the discussion of Revenue Ruling 70-197 in the previous subsection.

Can ministers who have opted out of Social Security receive retirement and Medicare benefits based on the fully insured status of their spouse?
The Social Security Administration has informed the author of this tax guide that ministers who have opted out of Social Security can become eligible to receive retirement or Medicare benefits based on their spouse's Social Security coverage. This makes sense. A minister's decision to opt out of Social Security is based on religious opposition to the acceptance of Social Security benefits *payable as a result of the minister's services performed in the exercise of ministry*. To the extent that a minister's spouse is fully insured under Social Security as a result of nonministerial services, Social Security benefits the minister receives as a result of the spouse's Social Security coverage are not based on services performed by the minister in the exercise of ministry and so are not covered by the minister's exemption.

❖ **KEY POINT.** Ministers who exempted themselves from self-employment taxes and who receive benefits based on their spouse's Social Security coverage may have their benefits reduced substantially under the so-called windfall elimination provision. Under this provision, the Social Security Administration can reduce the benefits of persons who did not pay Social Security taxes, such as exempt ministers seeking benefits on the basis of their spouse's coverage. For more information, see section J of this chapter.

Can ministers who have opted out of Social Security purchase Medicare insurance after they reach age 65?
Yes, they can. Ministers who have opted out of Social Security and who have less than 40 quarters of secular earnings (and whose spouse has less than 40 quarters of nonministerial earnings subject to Social Security and Medicare taxes) may be able to obtain Part A coverage by paying a Part A premium. The Part A monthly premium for 2013 is $441. A reduced monthly premium of $243 applies to persons with 30–39 quarters of Social Security and Medicare coverage. These amounts are adjusted annually for inflation.

❖ **KEY POINT.** In 2013 a quarter of coverage is received for each $1,160 of wages or self-employment income earned during the year.

Part A coverage is for hospital benefits. Most people get Part A benefits once they turn age 65 because they paid Social Security and Medicare taxes for at least 40 quarters while gainfully employed. No additional premium must be paid. However, they must apply for this coverage after reaching age 65.

Medicare Part B helps pay for doctors' services, outpatient hospital care, and some other medical services that Part A does not cover, such as the services of physical and occupational therapists and some home health care. Part B coverage is optional. It can be purchased for a monthly premium. The amount of the premium depends on a number of variables, including personal income. The standard Medicare Part B monthly premium will be $104.90 in 2013.

The Part B premium a beneficiary pays each month is based on his or her annual income. Specifically, if a beneficiary's modified adjusted gross income is greater than the legislated threshold amounts ($85,000 in 2013 for a beneficiary filing an individual income tax return or married and filing a separate return, and $170,000 for a beneficiary filing a joint tax return), the beneficiary is responsible for a larger portion of the estimated total cost of Part B benefit coverage.

In addition to the standard Part B premium, affected beneficiaries must pay an income-related monthly adjustment amount. About 4 percent of current Part B enrollees are expected to be subject to these higher premium amounts.

3. CONSTITUTIONAL CHALLENGES

Several constitutional challenges have been brought against the exemption of ministers from Social Security coverage. So far, none has been successful. The courts have consistently held that the exemption of ministers who are opposed to participation on the basis of religious principles is mandated by the First Amendment guaranty of religious freedom. To illustrate, a federal appeals court has explained the basis for the exemption as follows: "Congress provided the exemption for ministers to accommodate the free exercise and establishment clauses of the First Amendment to the extent compatible with a comprehensive national insurance program." *Blakely v. Commissioner, 720 F.2d 411 (5th Cir. 1983).*

4. EXAMPLES

The coverage and exemption rules summarized in section B are illustrated by the following examples.

Basis for exemption

EXAMPLE. Pastor D, an ordained minister, is opposed to Social Security on the basis of economic considerations. He is not eligible for the exemption.

EXAMPLE. Pastor L is opposed on the basis of nonreligious conscientious objection to the acceptance of Social Security benefits. He is not eligible for an exemption from Social Security coverage. *Revenue Ruling 75-189.*

EXAMPLE. Pastor N is opposed on the basis of religious principles to paying Social Security taxes. He does not qualify for the exemption, since the opposition must be to the acceptance of benefits.

EXAMPLE. In 1995 the Tax Court upheld the revocation of a minister's exemption from Social Security on the ground that he did not qualify. This case is important, since it illustrates that while ministers cannot revoke an exemption from self-employment taxes, the IRS may do so if it can establish that a minister did not qualify for exemption.

The Tax Court noted that a minister's exemption application had been filed on time, but it concluded that the minister was not eligible for exemption because of comments he made during his trial. Among other things, the minister gave the following response when asked whether he was opposed to accepting Social Security benefits on the basis of religious principles (as required by law to qualify for the exemption): "No. I am not opposed to the—to that, as a religious issue, no. We were advised to—by our accountant, to file for an exemption with the state, providing the state would allow it. And we asked the state to allow it, which they did."

This is an extraordinary ruling that is significant for younger ministers who are trying to decide whether to file an application for exemption from self-employment taxes (Form 4361). The ruling

indicates that filing a timely Form 4361—which contains a certification by the applicant that he or she meets all of the eligibility requirements—may not be enough. The IRS or the courts may later question whether the minister was eligible for the exemption when the Form 4361 was filed.

The court struggled with this conclusion. It acknowledged that the minister "signed an exemption application stating that he was opposed to public insurance because of his religious principles." However, it found the minister's "trial testimony to be more compelling." This conclusion was reinforced by the mistakes that appeared on the Form 4361, which suggested to the court that the minister had not read the form and was not aware that he was ineligible for exemption.

Many ministers have filed a Form 4361 without being eligible for the exemption from self-employment taxes. These ministers must recognize that the validity of their exemption may be questioned in an audit. *Hairston v. Commissioner, T.C. Memo. Dec. 51,025(M) (1995).*

Filing deadline

EXAMPLE. Pastor G graduated from seminary in May 2011 and accepts an associate pastoral position in July of the same year. Assuming that he earns at least $400 in self-employment earnings in 2011 and subsequent years, he must file an exemption application (Form 4361) no later than April 15, 2013 (the due date for the federal income tax return for the second year in which he had net earnings from self-employment of $400 or more, any part of which derived from ministry). If Pastor G obtains an automatic six-month extension for filing his 2013 income tax return by filing a timely Form 4868, his Form 4361 is not due until October 15, 2013.

EXAMPLE. The Tax Court ruled that a minister was not exempt from Social Security, since his exemption application was filed too late. While enrolled in college, a student (John) was licensed as a "student local pastor" for the United Methodist Church ("the Church") and served in a local church in 1983 and 1984. His earnings exceeded $400 each year. John thereafter attended seminary, and during this time he was licensed and served as the local pastor of a church from 1985 to 1987. In 1987 he was ordained a deacon in the Church. In 1990 he was ordained an elder. The ordained ministry of the Church consists of deacons and elders. In 1989 John filed an application for exemption from Social Security (self-employment) taxes by filing a Form 4361 with the IRS . He noted on the form that he had been ordained in 1987, when he was ordained a deacon. Therefore, the form was filed prior to the deadline.

The Tax Court ruled that John's application for exemption had been filed too late, since the duties he performed as a licensed pastor in 1983 and 1984 (when a student) were the performance of services as a minister. The court noted that as a licensed local pastor in 1983 and 1984, John was authorized to preside over the ministration of sacerdotal functions, such as baptism, communion, and marriage, and he conducted religious worship. Therefore, "for those years acted in a manner consistent with the performance of service by a duly ordained, commissioned, or licensed minister within the meaning of [the tax code]."

The court conceded that as a licensed pastor John had no voice or vote on official matters of his denomination. But it noted that "to perform services in the control, conduct, and maintenance of the church or organizations within the church, the minister need only have some participation in the conduct, control, and maintenance of the local church or denomination." It concluded that during 1983 and 1984, as a licensed local pastor, John served "in the control, conduct, and maintenance" of his local church even though as a licensed local pastor he might not have done so with respect to his national denomination. Since John had net earnings of at least $400 derived for the performance of services as a minister in 1983 and 1984, his application for exemption from self-employment tax should have been filed prior to the due date of his 1984 federal income tax return (April 15, 1985). Because it was not, it was filed too late and was not deemed to be effective. *Brannon v. Commissioner, T.C. Memo. 1999-370 (1999).*

The IRS provides the following three examples in Publication 517 that illustrate the filing deadline:

EXAMPLE 1. Rev. Lawrence Jaeger, a clergyman ordained in 2011, has net self-employment earnings of $450 in 2011 and $500 in 2012. He must file his application for exemption by the due date, including extensions, for his 2012 income tax return. However, if Rev. Jaeger does not receive IRS approval for an exemption by April 15, 2013, his SE tax for 2013 is due by that date.

EXAMPLE 2. Rev. Louise Wolfe has $300 in net self-employment earnings as a minister in 2011 but earned more than $400 in 2010 and expects to earn more than $400 in 2012. She must file her application for exemption by the due date, including extensions, for her 2012 income tax return. However, if she does not receive IRS approval for an exemption by April 15, 2013, her SE tax for 2012 is due by that date.

EXAMPLE 3. In 2009 Rev. David Moss was ordained a minister and had $700 in net self-employment earnings as a minister. In 2010 he received $1,000 as a minister, but his related expenses were over $1,000. Therefore, he had no net self-employment earnings as a minister in 2010. Also in 2010, he opened a book store and had $8,000 in net self-employment earnings from the store. In 2011 he had net self-employment earnings of $1,500 as a minister and $10,000 net self-employment earnings from the store. Rev. Moss had net earnings from self-employment in 2009 and 2011 that were $400 or more each year, and part of

the self-employment earnings in each of those years was for his services as a minister, so he must file his application for exemption by the due date, including extensions, for his 2011 income tax return.

Eligibility requirements

EXAMPLE. Pastor M accepts his first pastoral assignment in January 2013. He has decided to exempt himself from self-employment taxes but wants to be sure all of the eligibility requirements are satisfied. He must obtain an exemption application (Form 4361) containing a statement that he has notified his ordaining, commissioning, or licensing body of his opposition to Social Security coverage. Also, his application will not be approved unless the IRS verifies that Pastor M is aware of the basis for the exemption and is claiming the exemption on that basis. This is done by sending Pastor M a statement reciting the grounds on which an exemption is available and having him sign the statement, certifying under penalty of perjury that he is seeking exemption on the basis of an available ground. The statement must then be returned to the IRS within 90 days from the date it was originally sent by the IRS. If Pastor M fails to return the signed statement within 90 days, he will delay recognition of his exemption until the date the signed statement is received by the IRS.

EXAMPLE. Pastor B is a licensed minister in a denomination that also ordains ministers. Pastor B is eligible for the exemption from Social Security coverage only if he is able to perform substantially the same religious duties as an ordained minister under the tenets and practices of his denomination. *IRS Letter Ruling 9221025.*

EXAMPLE. Pastor H testified that he filed a timely exemption application, despite IRS assertions that the form was never received. Pastor H's wife testified that she distinctly remembered signing the application along with her husband. The Tax Court, in rejecting Pastor H's testimony, concluded that he had not been a "credible or convincing witness" and noted in particular that "his wife's signature was neither required nor provided for on the application form." *Holland v. Commissioner, 47 T.C.M. 494 (1983).*

Filing an exemption application after the deadline

EXAMPLE. Pastor F is ordained in 1994. In 2013 he becomes convinced, on the basis of religious principles, that he should not accept Social Security benefits, and he submits an exemption application to the IRS. His exemption will not be accepted, and this will not violate his constitutional rights.

EXAMPLE. Pastor P became convinced that accepting Social Security benefits violated his understanding of the Bible. However, this conviction developed only after the deadline for filing an exemption application (Form 4361) had expired. He is not eligible for the exemption. *Paschall v. Commissioner, 46 T.C.M. 1197 (1983).*

When an exemption takes effect

EXAMPLE. Pastor O filed an exemption application (Form 4361) with the IRS within a year of his ordination in 1995, and he quit paying Social Security taxes that year. Pastor O never received back a copy of his application marked "approved" by the IRS. Even though Pastor O is sure he submitted the form, the income tax regulations specify that "the filing of an application for exemption on Form 4361 by a minister . . . does not constitute an exemption from the tax on self-employment income. . . . The exemption is granted only if the application is approved by an appropriate internal revenue officer." As a result, Pastor O has never been exempt from Social Security coverage, since he did not receive back a copy of his application marked "approved" by the IRS.

Note, however, that a federal court in Virginia has concluded that ministers may qualify for exemption if they (1) demonstrate that they were eligible for the exemption when they submitted an exemption application; (2) convince a jury that they mailed a timely Form 4361; and (3) persuade the IRS or a court to apply the same reasoning as the Virginia federal district court (i.e., that IRS "approval" of an exemption is a perfunctory, administrative act that is not a requirement for exemption). *Eade v. United States*, 792 F.Supp. 476 (W.D. Va. 1991) (discussed above).

Change of faith

EXAMPLE. Pastor B has served as senior pastor of a church for many years. He did not apply for exemption from Social Security before the deadline for doing so expired several years ago, because he was not opposed to receiving Social Security benefits based on his ministerial employment at that time. This year, however, Pastor B learns of IRS Counsel Advice 200404048 (see above) and begins to rethink his position on Social Security. He concludes that he is opposed on the basis of religious convictions to receiving Social Security benefits, and he would like to submit a Form 4361 to claim exemption. He cannot do so. In the *Hall* case (which served as the basis for the chief counsel advice memorandum), a federal appeals court concluded that "ministers who do not switch churches may not belatedly opt out of the system."

EXAMPLE. Pastor G has served as associate pastor of a church for many years. He did not apply for exemption from Social Security before the deadline for doing so expired, because no one told him about this option. However, he was never opposed on the basis of religious convictions to receiving Social Security benefits based on his ministerial employment. This year Pastor G learns of IRS Chief Counsel Advice 200404048 (see above) and views this as an opportunity to "save taxes." He is not eligible to file a Form 4361, for two reasons. First, he does not qualify for exemption, since a desire to "save taxes" is not a valid basis for exemption. Second, in the *Hall* case (which served as the basis for the chief counsel advice memorandum), a federal appeals court

concluded that "ministers who do not switch churches may not belatedly opt out of the system."

EXAMPLE. Pastor D has served as senior pastor of a church for many years. He did not apply for exemption from Social Security before the deadline for doing so expired, because he was not opposed to receiving Social Security benefits based on his ministerial employment. However, over the years Pastor D did develop a sincere opposition, based on religious convictions, to accepting any form of public insurance, including Social Security. He learns of IRS Chief Counsel Advice 200404048 (see above) and plans to file a Form 4361 exemption application. He is not eligible to do so. In the *Hall* case (which served as the basis for the chief counsel advice memorandum), a federal appeals court concluded that "ministers who do not switch churches may not belatedly opt out of the system."

EXAMPLE. Pastor J has served as senior pastor of a church for many years. He did not apply for exemption from Social Security before the deadline for doing so expired, because he was not opposed to receiving Social Security benefits based on his ministerial employment. However, last year Pastor J resigned his pastoral position, joined a new faith, and was ordained as a minister of the new faith. The new faith teaches opposition to receiving any form of public assistance, including Social Security. Pastor J adopts this teaching. He learns of IRS Chief Counsel Advice 200404048 (see above) and plans to file a Form 4361 exemption application this year.

Pastor J is eligible to do so, since he meets all the requirements for renewal of exemption listed by the court in the Hall case and in the chief counsel advice memorandum: (1) change of church affiliation; (2) reordination by the new church; (3) development of opposition, based on one's new faith, to the acceptance of Social Security benefits; and (4) submission of an exemption application (Form 4361) by the due date of the federal tax return for the second year in which one has net self-employment earnings of $400 or more, any part of which comes from the performance of ministerial services in one's new faith.

EXAMPLE. Pastor T was an associate pastor of a church for many years. She did not apply for exemption from Social Security before the deadline for doing so expired, because she was not opposed to receiving Social Security benefits based on her ministerial employment. Five years ago Pastor T resigned her pastoral position, joined a new faith, and was ordained as a minister of the new faith. The new faith teaches opposition to receiving any form of public assistance, including Social Security. Pastor T adopted this teaching but did not file an exemption application (Form 4361). This year she learns of IRS Chief Counsel Advice 200404048 (see above) and plans to file a Form 4361 exemption application. She is not eligible to do so, since the deadline for filing a new application for exemption has expired.

EXAMPLE. Pastor K is the senior pastor of a church. He did not apply for exemption from Social Security before the deadline for doing so expired, because he was not opposed to receiving Social Security benefits based on his ministerial employment. However, last year Pastor K resigned his pastoral position and ordination and became associated with a new faith that teaches opposition to receiving any form of public assistance, including Social Security. The new faith does not ordain ministers, but Pastor K serves as a minister in one of its churches. Pastor K adopts the teaching of his new faith regarding Social Security. He learns of IRS Chief Counsel Advice 200404048 (see above) and plans to file a Form 4361 exemption application this year. It is likely, but not certain, that Pastor K is eligible to do so.

In the *Hall* case, a federal appeals court ruled that the following requirements must be met in order to requalify for exemption from Social Security: (1) change of church affiliation; (2) reordination by the new church; (3) development of an opposition, based on one's new faith, to the acceptance of Social Security benefits; and (4) submission of an exemption application (Form 4361) by the due date of the federal tax return for the second year in which one has net self-employment earnings of $400 or more, any part of which comes from the performance of ministerial services in one's new faith.

Pastor K meets all of these requirements except for the second one (reordination by the new church). The *Hall* case explicitly requires that a minister not only change faiths to requalify for exemption after the original deadline has expired but also that the minister be reordained by the new faith. IRS Chief Counsel Advice 200404048 (see above) contains the same language. It states that the *Hall* case "provides that when an individual enters the ministry anew in a new church, having adopted a new set of beliefs about the propriety of accepting public insurance, it is logical and consistent with the [language of the tax code] to characterize that individual as a 'new' minister for the purposes of seeking an exemption." This language strongly supports the conclusion that reordination is required.

On the other hand, in the *Ballinger* case (discussed above), a federal appeals court made the following observation: "Not all churches or religions have a formally ordained ministry, whether because of the nature of their beliefs, the lack of a denominational structure or a variety of other reasons. Courts are not in a position to determine the merits of various churches nor an individual's conversion from one church to another. Thus, we cannot hold that an individual who functions as a minister in a church which does not ordain, license or commission that individual in a traditional or legally formal manner is not entitled to the exemption. Nor can we hold that an individual who has a change of belief accompanied by a change to another faith is not entitled to the exemption. We interpret Congress' language providing an exemption for any individual who is 'a duly ordained, commissioned or licensed

minister of a church' to mean that the triggering event is the assumption of the duties and functions of a minister."

EXAMPLE. Pastor M is the senior pastor of a church. He did not apply for exemption from Social Security before the deadline for doing so expired, because he was not opposed to receiving Social Security benefits based on his ministerial employment. This year he learns about IRS Chief Counsel Advice 200404048 (see above) and is told by another pastor that if he "switches churches," the deadline for filing an exemption application (Form 4361) will be reset. This advice is incorrect. A change of faiths is only one requirement to requalify for exemption after the original deadline has expired. The other requirements, as noted above, are reordination by the new church; acquiring an opposition, based on one's new faith, to the acceptance of Social Security benefits; and submitting an exemption application (Form 4361) by the due date, including extensions, of the federal tax return for the second year in which one has net self-employment earnings of $400 or more, any part of which comes from the performance of ministerial services in one's new faith. If these additional requirements are not met, Pastor M will not requalify for exemption even if he does change faiths.

EXAMPLE. Pastor L was an associate pastor of a church for many years. This year she accepts a position as senior pastor in a different church associated with the same faith. Pastor L did not apply for exemption from Social Security before the deadline for doing so expired, because she was not opposed to receiving Social Security benefits based on ministerial employment. She learns about IRS Chief Counsel Advice 200404048 (see above) and is told by another pastor that by accepting the new pastoral position, she requalifies for opting out of Social Security if she so chooses. This advice is incorrect. Pastor L does not requalify for exemption, since she has not had a change of faith or been reordained in a new faith.

EXAMPLE. Pastor G has served as senior pastor of a church for many years. He did not apply for exemption from Social Security before the deadline for doing so expired, because he was not opposed to receiving Social Security benefits based on his ministerial employment. However, last year Pastor G resigned his pastoral position, joined a new faith, and was ordained as a minister of the new faith. The new faith has no position on participation in Social Security. This year Pastor G learns of IRS Chief Counsel Advice 200404048 (see above) and sees it as an opportunity to be relieved of the burden of paying self-employment taxes. He does not requalify for exemption, for two reasons:

First, he has not been reordained by a faith that is opposed to the acceptance of public insurance benefits (including Social Security). The chief counsel advice memorandum states, "When an individual enters the ministry anew in a new church, having adopted a new set of beliefs about the propriety of accepting public insurance, it is logical and consistent with the [language of the tax code] to characterize that individual as a 'new' minister for the purposes of seeking an exemption." This language indicates that a change of belief about the propriety of accepting public insurance benefits must reflect the views of one's new faith.

Second, Pastor G's desire to be relieved of the burden of paying self-employment taxes does not qualify as a basis for exemption.

5. IRS AUDIT GUIDELINES FOR MINISTERS

The IRS has issued audit guidelines for its agents to follow when auditing ministers. The guidelines inform agents that in order for ministers to claim exemption from self-employment tax, they must satisfy the following requirements:

- Be an ordained, commissioned, or licensed minister of a church or denomination.
- File Form 4361. This is an application for exemption from self-employment tax for use by ministers.
- Be conscientiously opposed to public insurance (Medicare/Medicaid and Social Security benefits) because of religious beliefs.
- File for exemption for reasons other than economic.
- Notify the church or order that they are opposed to public insurance.
- Establish that the organization that ordained, licensed, or commissioned the minister is a tax-exempt religious organization.
- Establish that the organization is a church or a convention or association of churches.

○ OBSERVATION. The guidelines fail to clarify that a minister must be opposed to the acceptance of benefits under a public insurance program. Opposition to the program is not sufficient.

The guidelines further clarify that

> *Form 4361 must be filed by the due date of the Form 1040 (including extensions) for the second tax year in which at least $400 in self-employment ministerial earnings was received. The 2 years do not have to be consecutive. An approved Form 4361 is effective for all tax years after 1967 for which a minister received $400 or more of self-employed income for ministerial services.*

> *The exemption from self-employment tax applies only to services performed as a minister. The exemption does not apply to other self-employment income. To determine if a minister is exempt from self-employment tax, request that he or she furnish a copy of the approved Form 4361 if it is not attached to the return. If the taxpayer cannot provide a copy, order a transcript for the year under examination. The ADP and IDRS Information handbook*

> *shows where the ministers' self-employment exemption codes are located on the transcripts and what the codes mean. Transcripts will not show exemption status prior to 1988. If the transcript does not show a MIN SE indicator and the taxpayer still claims that he or she is exempt from self-employment tax, the Taxpayer Relations Branch at the Service Center where the Form 4361 was filed can research this information and provide the taxpayer with a copy. The Social Security Administration in Baltimore also can provide the information on exemption for an individual.*

○ OBSERVATION. Many ministers who claim they are exempt from self-employment tax cannot prove that they are exempt. Ministers who file a timely application for exemption that is approved by the IRS will be sent a copy of their exemption application marked "approved." Many ministers who have filed a timely exemption application cannot produce the approved copy of their application. In some cases they have mislaid the application, but in others they mistakenly believe they filed the application many years ago, when in fact they did not. In either case, they may not pay self-employment taxes for several years. If they are audited and asked to verify their exemption from self-employment tax, they may be unable to do so. The guidelines contain some helpful information for ministers in this situation, for they reveal the procedure IRS agents are instructed to follow if a minister who claims to be exempt from self-employment taxes cannot produce an approved application. A number of recommendations are in place that agents can pursue in verifying the exempt status of a minister who cannot produce a copy of an approved exemption application.

The guidelines contain the following four examples (dates have been revised):

EXAMPLE. H had ministerial earnings of $400 in 2011 and $1,800 in 2012. He has until April 15, 2013 (if no extension has been filed) to file Form 4361. If the approved Form 4361 is not received by the due date for the 2011 return, the self-employment tax for 2011 is still due by that date. If he later receives the approved 4361, he may amend his 2011 return.

EXAMPLE. J earned $500 in 2009, $300 in 2010, and $6,000 in 2011 from her ministry. She has until April 15, 2013 (if no extension has been filed) to file Form 4361. If the approval of the exemption is not received by April 15, 2010, J must pay the self-employment tax with her 2009 return, but may amend it after the exemption is approved. J may file a claim for refund (an amended tax return) within three years from the time the return was filed or within two years from the time the tax was paid, whichever is later.

EXAMPLE. K, ordained in 2011, has $7,500 in net earnings as a minister in both 2011 and 2012. He files Form 4361 on March 5, 2013. If the exemption is granted, it is effective for 2011 and all following years.

EXAMPLE. L, an ordained minister, has applied for and received exemption from self-employment tax for his services as a minister. In 2013 he has ministerial income of $12,000 and income from his shoe repair business, a sole proprietorship, of $9,000. He must compute self-employment tax on the $9,000.

❊ **KEY POINT.** The audit guidelines assist IRS agents in the examination of ministers' tax returns. They alert agents to the key questions to ask, and they provide background information along with the IRS position on a number of issues. It is therefore important for ministers be familiar with these guidelines.

C. SERVICES TO WHICH EXEMPTION APPLIES

❊ **KEY POINT.** An exemption from self-employment taxes only applies to ministerial services. Ministers who have exempted themselves from self-employment taxes must pay Social Security taxes on any nonministerial employment. They are eligible for Social Security benefits based on their nonministerial services (assuming that they have worked enough quarters in nonministerial employment).

A minister whose exemption application is duly approved by the IRS is exempt from paying Social Security taxes on compensation earned from the performance of services in the exercise of ministry. The term "services performed in the exercise of ministry" is a technical one that is defined fully in Chapter 3 of this text.

Some ministers who have exempted themselves from Social Security coverage have worked previously in secular employment. Does their exemption prevent them from ever receiving any Social Security benefits? The answer is no. An approved exemption only exempts a minister from Social Security taxes and benefits with respect to services performed in the exercise of ministry. The exemption has no effect on benefits based on employment that is not in the exercise of ministry.

The income tax regulations specify that "a minister performing service in the exercise of his ministry may be eligible to file an application for exemption on Form 4361 even though he is not opposed to the acceptance of benefits under the Social Security Act with respect to service performed by him which is not in the exercise of his ministry." *Treas. Reg. 1.1402(e)-2A(a)(2).* As a result, a minister whose exemption application (Form 4361) has been approved by the IRS will be eligible to receive Social Security benefits based on earnings not covered by the exemption, assuming that such earnings are sufficient to entitle the minister to the benefits. Note also that the longer a minister is exempt from Social Security coverage, the lower his or her Social Security retirement benefits will tend to be.

EXAMPLE. A pastor of a local church also operated a private business as a handyman. The pastor, who had filed for exemption from self-employment taxes, assumed that the exemption applied to his handyman income. As a result, he did not pay self-employment tax on these earnings. The IRS audited his tax return and determined that the secular earnings were subject to the self-employment tax. The Tax Court agreed, noting that "although the income [the pastor] derived from his handyman business may have enabled him to sustain his ministry at [his church] and to fulfill the obligation of supporting his family, those reasons or motives do not cause the handyman business to be integral to the conduct of his ministry." The court acknowledged that ministers can exempt themselves from self-employment taxes if they meet several conditions, but the exemption applies only to "services performed in the exercise of ministry." Such services did not include the pastor's work as a handyman. *Williams v. Commissioner, T.C. Memo. 1999-105.*

D. COMPUTING SELF-EMPLOYMENT TAX

❊ **KEY POINT.** The self-employment tax is reported on Schedule SE and is computed by multiplying net self-employment earnings by the current self-employment tax rate. Net self-employment earnings consist of a minister's total church compensation, including the annual fair rental value of a parsonage or a housing allowance, reduced by most income tax exclusions and business expenses (whether unreimbursed or reimbursed under a nonaccountable plan). Two deductions are allowed in computing net earnings from self-employment (see the next paragraph).

❊ **KEY POINT.** Self-employed persons pay the combined Social Security and Medicare tax rate (15.3 percent) that is shared by employers and employees. To partly offset the tax burden that falls on self-employed persons, the law allows them two deductions: (1) an amount equal to 7.65 percent multiplied by their net self-employment earnings (without regard to this deduction) may be deducted in computing earnings subject to the self-employment tax; and (2) half their self-employment tax is deductible as an adjustment in computing income taxes, regardless of whether they can itemize deductions on Schedule A (Form 1040).

❊ **KEY POINT.** For 2013 the maximum earnings subject to self-employment taxes is $113,700. In addition, all self-employment earnings, regardless of amount, are subject to the 2.9 percent Medicare component of the self-employment tax.

In most cases, ministers must pay self-employment tax on salaries and other income for services performed as a minister. But if you filed Form 4361 and received IRS approval, you will be exempt from paying SE tax on those net earnings. If you had no other income subject to SE tax, enter "Exempt—Form 4361" on Form 1040, line 56. However, if you had other net earnings of $400 or more subject to SE tax, see line A at the top of "long" Schedule SE.

The Social Security tax for ministers who have not filed a timely exemption application is computed by multiplying the applicable self-employment tax rate by the minister's net earnings from self-employment. The computation of self-employment earnings for ministers is summarized in the sidebar "Clergy Self-Employment Earnings" in this chapter.

1. UNREIMBURSED BUSINESS EXPENSES AND NONACCOUNTABLE REIMBURSEMENTS OF BUSINESS EXPENSES

In computing their self-employment tax liability, can ministers deduct their unreimbursed business expenses and business expenses reimbursed by their employing church under a nonaccountable plan? This question has been addressed by the IRS in Revenue Ruling 80-110, Publication 517, and the instructions to Schedule SE (Form 1040), as noted below.

Revenue Ruling 80-110

In Revenue Ruling 80-110 the IRS addressed the following question: could a pastor who is unable to deduct unreimbursed business expenses of $500 in computing income taxes, since he was unable to itemize deductions on Schedule A (Form 1040), deduct the expenses in computing self-employment taxes on Schedule SE (Form 1040)? The IRS concluded that he could. It noted that section 1402 of the tax code says that ministers are treated as self-employed and that they can reduce self-employment earnings in computing their self-employment tax liability by "the deductions attributable to the trade or business" in computing their net earnings from self-employment." There is no requirement here that the minister be allowed to itemize deductions—that limitation only pertains to the deductibility of business expenses in computing income taxes. *IRC 62*. It follows that ministers can deduct any expenses associated with their trade or business of the ministry, including unreimbursed and nonaccountable reimbursed expenses, even if these same expenses are not deductible in computing income taxes. The limitation on deducting these expenses in computing income taxes (the taxpayer must itemize) does not pertain to self-employment tax deductions. There is no requirement in section 1402 that only expenses qualifying for an income tax deduction reduce self-employment earnings.

The IRS observed:

> Section 1402(c)(2)(D) of the tax code provides that the term "trade or business," when used with reference to self-employment income, does not include the services of an employee other than the performance of service by a duly ordained minister of a church in the exercise of the ministry. Section 1402(a) provides that the term "net earnings from self-employment" means the gross income derived by an individual from any trade or business carried on by the individual, less the deductions attributable to the trade or business.... The trade and business deductions of a minister are allowable as deductions for purposes of computing the tax on self-employment income. [Therefore] the $500 is deductible on the Schedule SE (Form 1040) in computing the minister's self-employment tax [emphasis added].

Revenue Ruling 80-110 has never been modified or repealed by the IRS.

IRS Publication 517

The current edition of Publication 517 states:

> When figuring your net earnings from self-employment, deduct all your nonemployee ministerial expenses. These are ministerial expenses you incurred while not working as a common-law employee of the church. They include expenses incurred in performing marriages and baptisms, and in delivering speeches. Deduct these expenses on Schedule C or C-EZ (Form 1040), and carry the net amount to line 2 of Schedule SE (Form 1040), Section A or B.

> Wages earned as a common-law employee (explained earlier) of a church are generally subject to self-employment tax unless an exemption is requested.... Subtract any allowable expenses, including unreimbursed employee business expenses, from those wages, include the net amount on line 2 of Schedule SE (Form 1040), Section A or B, and attach an explanation. Do not complete Schedule C or C-EZ (Form 1040). However, for income tax purposes, the expenses are allowed only as an itemized deduction on Schedule A (Form 1040) if they exceed 2 percent of adjusted gross income....

> Since reimbursements under a nonaccountable plan are included in your gross income, you can deduct your related expenses (for SE tax and income tax purposes) regardless of whether they are more than, less than, or equal to your reimbursement.

Schedule SE instructions

Self-employment taxes are computed on Schedule SE (Form 1040). The instructions to Schedule SE provide: "If you were a duly ordained minister who was an employee of a church and you must pay SE tax, when figuring SE tax, subtract on line 2 allowable expenses from your self-employment earnings and attach an explanation. *Please note that the unreimbursed employee business expenses that you*

CLERGY SELF-EMPLOYMENT EARNINGS

Clergy are deemed to be self-employed for Social Security with respect to services they perform in the exercise of their ministry. This means they pay the self-employment tax rather than the employee's share of Social Security and Medicare taxes. The self-employment tax for 2012 is computed by multiplying net self-employment earnings (up to $110,100) by the self-employment tax rate of 15.3 percent. Only the Medicare component (2.9 percent) of self-employment taxes applies to self-employment earnings in excess of $110,100. Net self-employment earnings are computed as follows:

(1) Church salary

(2) Plus

- other items of church income (including taxable fringe benefits) described in Chapter 4
- fees you receive for marriages, baptisms, funerals, masses, etc.
- self-employment earnings from outside businesses
- annual rental value of a parsonage, including utilities paid by church (unless you are retired)
- a housing allowance (unless you are retired)
- business expense reimbursements (under a nonaccountable plan)
- the value of meals served on the church's premises for the convenience of the employer

- any amount a church pays toward your income tax or self-employment tax

(3) Reduced by

- most income tax exclusions (see Chapter 5) other than meals or lodging furnished for the employer's convenience, and the foreign earned income exclusion
- annual fair rental value of a parsonage provided to you after you retire
- housing allowance provided to you after you retire
- contributions by your church to a tax-sheltered annuity plan set up for you, including any salary reduction contributions (elective deferrals) that are not included in your gross income
- pension payments or retirement allowances you receive for your past ministerial services
- net self-employment earnings (without regard to this deduction) multiplied by 7.65 percent

Note: It may be possible to reduce self-employment earnings by unreimbursed business expenses and business expenses reimbursed by an employing church under a nonaccountable plan even if these expenses cannot be claimed as an income tax deduction due to an inability to itemize deductions. See Section D of this chapter for more information.

---

incurred as an employee of the church are not allowable expenses for SE tax purposes, and are allowed only as an itemized deduction for income tax purposes" (emphasis added).

Conclusion

In summary, the clear implication of the tax code and Revenue Ruling 80-110 is that unreimbursed business expenses and reimbursed business expenses under a nonaccountable plan are deductible by pastors in computing their self-employment tax liability even if they are not able to deduct these expenses in computing their income tax liability because they do not have enough itemized expenses to use Schedule A. The key point is that there is no requirement under section 1402, as there is under section 62, that only those business expenses that can be claimed as an itemized deduction on Schedule A are deductible in computing net earnings from self-employment. This understanding is clearly reflected in Publication 517.

However, this understanding is contradicted by the following statement in the instructions to Schedule SE: "Unreimbursed employee business expenses that you incurred as an employee of the church

are not allowable expenses for SE tax purposes." Note that this statement implies that unreimbursed employee business expenses are never deductible in computing net earnings from SE, regardless of whether they can be claimed as itemized deductions on Schedule A. This statement is clearly wrong, since section 1402 says that self-employed persons can reduce self-employment earnings in computing their self-employment tax liability by "the deductions attributable to the trade or business." This clearly includes unreimbursed business expenses.

Because of the confusion caused by the instructions to Schedule SE, ministers should consult with a tax professional before claiming unreimbursed expenses and nonaccountable reimbursed expenses as deductions in computing self-employment tax liability on Schedule SE.

2. THE DEASON RULE

The IRS has acknowledged that the *Deason* rule does not apply to the deductibility of business expenses on Schedule SE. This means that ministers do not need to reduce their business expense deduction on Schedule SE by the percentage of their total church compensation that consists of a housing allowance. The reason is that the housing allowance is not an exclusion in computing self-employment taxes on Schedule SE. This position is reflected in the current edition of IRS Publication 517 as well as in the IRS audit guidelines for ministers. The *Deason* rule is explained fully in Chapter 7, section F.

3. EXCLUSIONS

The income tax regulations specify that "income which is excludable from gross income under any provision of subtitle A of the Internal Revenue Code is not taken into account in determining net earnings from self-employment," with certain exceptions. *Treas. Reg. 1.1402(a)-2(a).* This means that most income tax exclusions (see Chapter 5) are also excludable in computing self-employment tax. The exceptions, which are included in income for self-employment tax purposes, include (1) the housing allowance (unless provided to a retired minister); (2) the fair rental value of a church-provided home (unless provided to a retired minister); (3) the foreign earned income exclusion; and (4) meals and lodging provided for the convenience of an employer. Apart from these exceptions, the general rule is that the exclusions discussed in Chapter 5 are excludable in computing both income taxes and self-employment taxes.

> **EXAMPLE.** A church provided free meals to ministers who were required to reside in housing on the church's premises in order to fulfill their duties. The IRS concluded that the value of the meals was taxable income to the ministers for self-employment (Social Security) tax purposes. It noted that section 1402(a)(8) of the tax code prevents the exclusion of meals "for the convenience of the employer" (under section 119) from reducing a minister's net earnings. Thus, the value of meals and cash reimbursements for groceries furnished by the church to its ministers "must be included in the ministers' net earnings from self-employment" for self-employment tax purposes. *IRS Letter Ruling 9129037.*

4. PARSONAGES AND HOUSING ALLOWANCES

The definition of net earnings from self-employment includes the fair rental value of a church-owned parsonage provided without charge to a minister, as well as a housing allowance paid to a minister who owns or rents a home. The fair rental value of a parsonage is the fair rental value of a furnished parsonage. This is often a difficult amount to compute. See Chapter 6 for a discussion of this important term.

> ❂ **KEY POINT.** If a church pays the utilities of a minister who lives in a church-owned parsonage, the amount paid must be included in the minister's income for Social Security tax purposes.

❂ **KEY POINT.** As noted in Chapter 10, section E, the annual rental value of a parsonage is not included in net earnings when computing the self-employment tax of retired ministers.

5. FRINGE BENEFITS

Generally, the taxable fringe benefits discussed in Chapter 4 are included in a minister's income for Social Security tax purposes.

6. EARNINGS SUBJECT TO THE SELF-EMPLOYMENT TAX

The 15.3 percent self-employment tax rate consists of two components: (1) a Medicare hospital insurance tax of 2.9 percent; and (2) an "old-age, survivor and disability" (Social Security) tax of 12.4 percent. For 2012 the Medicare component of the self-employment tax (the 2.9 percent tax rate) applied to all net earnings from self-employment, regardless of amount, while the Social Security component (the 12.4 percent tax rate) applied to net earnings from self-employment up to $110,100. As a result, persons who received compensation in excess of $110,100 in 2012 paid the full 15.3 percent tax rate for net self-employment earnings up to $110,100, and the Medicare rate of 2.9 percent on all net earnings, regardless of amount. This provision directly impacts ministers, who always are considered self-employed for Social Security with respect to their ministerial services. But see "Payroll tax holiday" below.

❂ **KEY POINT.** The $110,100 amount increases to $113,700 for 2013.

7. TWO SPECIAL DEDUCTIONS FOR THE SELF-EMPLOYED

Self-employed persons pay the entire Social Security and Medicare tax rate of 15.3 percent. Unlike employees, they do not split the cost with an employer. Because of the unfair burden this places on self-employed persons, the tax code gives them two deductions:

- Persons who are self-employed for Social Security purposes (including ministers, with respect to their ministerial income) can reduce their taxable earnings by 7.65 percent (half of the self-employment tax rate). This is done by multiplying net earnings from self-employment by 0.9235 on line 4 of Schedule SE (Form 1040).
- Persons who are self-employed for Social Security purposes (including ministers, with respect to their ministerial income) can deduct half of their actual self-employment taxes as an adjustment on line 27 of Form 1040, regardless of whether they are able to itemize deductions on Schedule A.

In explaining these changes, Congress stated that its purpose was "to achieve parity between employees and the self-employed" for Social Security purposes. Unfortunately, many ministers fail to claim both of these deductions.

A minister's calculation of estimated taxes should incorporate (1) the application of the Medicare component of the self-employment tax (the 2.9 percent tax rate) to all net earnings from self-employment, regardless of amount; and (2) the two special deductions described above. Many ministers fail to take these rules into account in calculating their estimated taxes.

8. PAYROLL TAX HOLIDAY

Congress provided a temporary payroll tax holiday for 2011 and 2012 of two percentage points off the employee share of Social Security tax and the Social Security component of self-employment taxes. This meant that the employee share of Social Security taxes dropped from 6.2 to 4.2 percent of wages, and the Social Security component of self-employment taxes dropped from 12.4 to 10.4 percent of self-employment earnings for 2012.

This reduction in taxes was enacted to stimulate the economy by increasing the take-home pay for millions of workers. It is unlikely that Congress will extend this tax holiday beyond 2012. Check the Social Security Administration website for current information.

9. CHURCHES THAT PAY HALF OF A PASTOR'S SELF-EMPLOYMENT TAXES

Many churches agree to pay half of their ministers' self-employment taxes in order to "duplicate" the payment of half of a nonminister employee's Social Security and Medicare taxes. This practice is not recommended for two reasons. First, the two special deductions summarized above make it difficult, if not impossible, to determine in advance what half of a minister's self-employment tax will be.

Second, "half" of a minister's self-employment tax liability for a particular year will not be known until the minister files a tax return paying his or her self-employment taxes and the statute of limitations for auditing the minister's tax return has expired. Because of these problems, church leaders should consider the following alternatives:

- Pay half of the self-employment taxes paid by a minister each quarter who uses the estimated tax procedure, with the understanding that this is only an estimate. Only when the minister computes his or her actual self-employment tax liability on Schedule SE (Form 1040) after the end of the year will the church know what half the self-employment taxes actually were. If actual self-employment taxes are more than the quarterly estimates, then the church would need to

THE NONFARM OPTIONAL METHOD OF COMPUTING SELF-EMPLOYMENT INCOME

You may be able to use the nonfarm optional method for figuring your net earnings from self-employment. In general, the nonfarm optional method is intended to permit continued coverage for Social Security and Medicare purposes when your income for the tax year is low. You may use the nonfarm optional method if you meet all the following tests.

(1) You are self-employed on a regular basis. This means that your actual net earnings from self-employment were $400 or more in at least two of the three tax years before the one for which you use this method. The net earnings can be from either farm or nonfarm earnings or both.

(2) You have used this method less than five years (there is a five-year lifetime limit). The years do not have to be one after another.

(3) Your net nonfarm profits were (a) less than $4,894 and (b) less than 72.189 percent of your gross nonfarm income.

If you meet the three tests, use the table below to figure your net earnings from self-employment under the nonfarm optional method.

IF YOUR GROSS NONFARM INCOME IS	THEN YOUR NET EARNINGS ARE EQUAL TO
$6,780 or less	Two-thirds of your gross nonfarm income
More than $6,780	$4,520

pay half of the difference in order to pay half of the minister's self-employment tax liability for the year. If actual self-employment taxes are less than the quarterly estimates, then the church has paid more than half of the minister's self-employment taxes. It could either request a refund of the difference or consider the difference additional taxable income. A church could pay half of a minister's estimated self-employment taxes for the year. This amount is readily ascertainable.

- A church could pay a specified additional amount of compensation to a pastor for the express purpose of assisting with the payment of self-employment taxes. The amount specified could be based on a reasonable estimate of what the pastor's self-employment tax liability for the year will be, keeping in mind that self-employment taxes are assessed against both salary and housing allowances (or the fair rental value of a parsonage).

Churches that pay half of a minister's self-employment tax are putting the minister in a better position than nonminister staff, since the minister can claim the two special deductions summarized above.

10. SCHEDULE SE

Ministers report their self-employment taxes on Schedule SE (Form 1040). Most ministers use the "short" Schedule SE rather than the "long" form. This means that they complete Section A on page 1 of the schedule rather than Section B on page 2. Ministers report their net self-employment earnings on line 2 of Section A. See the sidebar "Clergy Self-employment Earnings" for a summary of how to compute your net self-employment earnings.

11. IRS AUDIT GUIDELINES FOR MINISTERS

The IRS has issued audit guidelines for its agents to follow when auditing ministers. The guidelines inform agents that "to compute self-employment tax, allowable trade or business expenses are subtracted from gross ministerial earnings, then the appropriate rate is applied." The guidelines instruct agents to include the following items in a minister's gross income for self-employment tax:

- salaries and fees for services, including offerings and honoraria received for marriages, funerals, baptisms, etc. (Include gifts which are considered income as discussed under the section on income.);
- any housing allowance or utility allowances;
- fair rental value (FRV) of a parsonage, if provided, including the cost of utilities and furnishings provided;
- any amounts received for business expenses treated as paid under a nonaccountable plan, such as an automobile allowance; and
- income tax or self-employment tax obligation of the minister which is paid by the church.

The guidelines provide the following additional examples:

EXAMPLE. M receives a salary from the church of $20,000. His parsonage/housing allowance is $12,000. The church withholds federal income tax (by mutual agreement) and issues him a Form W-2. He has unreimbursed employee business expenses (before excluding nondeductible amounts attributable to his exempt income) of $5,200. His net earnings for self-employment tax are $26,800 ($20,000 + $12,000 - $5,200). Note that all of M's unreimbursed business expenses are deductible for self-employment

tax purposes, although the portion attributable to the exempt housing allowance is not deductible for federal income tax purposes. IRC § 265 regarding the allocation of business expenses related to exempt income pertains to income tax computations but not self-employment tax computations.

EXAMPLE. G, as shown in Example 8, computes her self-employment taxable income as follows: $12,000 salary plus $9,000 housing allowance plus $3,000 Schedule C income less $4,500 total business expenses equals $19,500 self-employment income.

◉ OBSERVATION. The first example illustrates an important point. Ministers' business expenses should not be reduced in computing their self-employment taxes, since the housing allowance does not represent tax-exempt income when computing self-employment taxes. The so-called *Deason* reduction rule applies only to the computation of income taxes.

⊷ TIP. For more information on the nonfarm optional method, see Publication 334 and the Schedule SE (Form 1040) instructions.

12. ADDITIONAL HOSPITAL INSURANCE TAX ON HIGH-INCOME TAXPAYERS

The FICA tax rate (7.65 percent for both employers and employees, or a combined tax of 15.3 percent) is comprised of a Medicare hospital insurance (HI) tax of 1.45 percent and a Social Security (old-age, survivor, and disability) tax of 6.2 percent. The self-employment tax rate (SECA) is comprised of a Medicare hospital insurance tax of 2.9 percent and an old-age, survivor, and disability (Social Security) tax of 12.4 percent.

Beginning in 2013, the health care reform legislation (Affordable Care Act of 2010) increases the employee portion of the Medicare (HI) tax by an additional tax of 0.9 percent on wages received in excess of the threshold amount. However, unlike the general 1.45 percent HI tax on wages, this additional tax is on the combined wages of the employee and the employee's spouse, in the case of a joint return. The threshold amount is $250,000 in the case of a joint return or surviving spouse, $125,000 in the case of a married individual filing a separate return, and $200,000 in any other case.

In determining the employer's requirement to withhold and liability for the tax, only wages the employee receives from the employer in excess of $200,000 for a year are taken into account, and the employer must disregard the amount of wages received by the employee's spouse. Thus, the employer is only required to withhold on wages in excess of $200,000 for the year, even though the tax may apply to a portion of the employee's wages at or below $200,000, if the employee's spouse also has wages for the year, they are filing a joint return, and their total combined wages for the year exceed $250,000.

EXAMPLE. In 2013 a pastor earns $100,000 in church compensation. His wife, a physician, earns $200,000. The combined income of the husband and wife exceeds the threshold amount of $250,000, and so they are liable for an additional Medicare tax of 0.9 percent times compensation in excess of $250,000. However, neither spouse's employer is required to withhold any portion of this additional tax from their wages, even though the combined wages of the taxpayer and the taxpayer's spouse are over the $250,000 threshold, since neither earned compensation of more than $200,000.

The employee is also liable for this additional 0.9-percent HI tax to the extent the tax is not withheld by the employer. The amount of this tax not withheld by an employer must also be taken into account in determining a taxpayer's liability for estimated tax. This same additional HI tax (0.9 percent) applies to the HI portion of SECA tax on self-employment income in excess of the threshold amount. As in the case of the additional HI tax on employee wages, the threshold amount for the additional SECA HI tax is $250,000 in the case of a joint return or surviving spouse, $125,000 in the case of a married individual filing a separate return, and $200,000 in any other case. The threshold amount is reduced (but not below zero) by the amount of wages taken into account in determining the FICA tax with respect to the taxpayer. No deduction is allowed for the additional SECA tax, and the deduction under 1402(a)(12) is determined without regard to the additional SECA tax rate.

This new tax applies to compensation received and taxable years beginning after December 31, 2012.

E. WORKING AFTER YOU RETIRE

Many churches employ persons who are receiving Social Security retirement benefits. But persons younger than full retirement age may have their Social Security retirement benefits cut if they earn more than a specified amount. Full retirement age (the age at which you are entitled to full retirement benefits) for persons born in 1943 through 1954 is 66 years.

In the year you reach full retirement age, your monthly Social Security retirement benefits are reduced by $1 for every $3 you earn above a specified amount ($3,340 per month for 2013). No reduction in Social Security benefits occurs for income earned in the month full retirement age is attained (and all future months). Persons who begin receiving Social Security retirement benefits prior to the year in which they reach full retirement age will have their benefits reduced by $1 for every $2 of earned income in excess of a specified amount. For 2013 this annual amount increases to $15,120. Table 9-1 shows the full retirement ages based on year of birth.

1. EXAMPLES

EXAMPLE. In 2013 Pastor D attained full retirement age (66 years) on August 15 and began receiving Social Security benefits. He continues to work as a senior pastor of his church throughout the entire year, earning $2,500 each month. None of his Social Security benefits will be reduced, because his monthly income is less than $3,240.

EXAMPLE. Same facts as the previous example, except that Pastor D's monthly salary is $4,000. His Social Security benefits will be reduced by $1 for every $3 of earned income in excess of $3,240 for each month from January through July (the month before he attained full retirement age). This amounts to a reduction in benefits of $253 for each of these months ($4,000 - $3,240 = $760/3 = $253).

EXAMPLE. Pastor T is a retired minister who is hired by a church as its minister of visitation. Pastor T is 63 years old and is receiving Social Security benefits. The church pays him $26,000 of taxable compensation in 2013. Pastor T's Social Security retirement benefits will be reduced by $1 for every $2 of earned income over $14,640. Since Pastor T has earned income of $11,360 in excess of $14,640, his Social Security benefits would be reduced by a whopping $5,680!

2. HOUSING ALLOWANCES AND THE ANNUAL EARNINGS TEST

If a minister elects to receive Social Security retirement benefits prior to full retirement age, does the amount of the minister's compensation designated as a housing allowance count toward the earnings test? To illustrate, assume that Pastor J begins drawing Social Security retirement benefits during 2013, when he is 63 years of age, and continues to work for the church. The church pays Pastor J total compensation of $25,000 for 2013, of which $15,000 is designated as a housing allowance. If the housing allowance is included in applying the earnings test, then Pastor J has earned $9,880 over the earnings test exempt amount ($15,120 for 2013), meaning that his Social Security retirement benefits will be reduced by $4,940 ($1 for every $2 of earned income in excess of $15,120). On the other hand, if the housing allowance is not counted in applying the earnings test, then Pastor J's earnings are $10,000. Since this amount is less than the exempt amount ($15,120), there will be no reduction in Pastor J's Social Security benefits. Obviously, the answer to this question can have a significant financial impact.

Unfortunately, there is no definitive answer to this question. It is likely, however, that a minister's housing allowance *should* be included in applying the earnings test. This conclusion is based on section 1811 of the current *Social Security Handbook*, which states that "the following types of earnings count for earnings test purposes: (A) All wages for employment covered by Social Security . . . (B) All net earnings from self-employment." Since the duties of ministers in the exercise of ministry are not "employment covered by Social Security" (see section B of this chapter), a minister's earnings for purposes of the annual earnings test are limited to "net earnings from self-employment." This important term is defined by section 1402 of the code as follows: "[A]n individual who is a duly ordained, commissioned, or licensed minister of a church . . . shall compute his net earnings from self-employment derived from the performance of service [as a minister] without regard to section 107 (relating to rental value of parsonages)."

In summary, the best evidence supports the conclusion that ministers *should* include housing allowances (and the annual rental value of parsonages) in applying the annual earnings test, since such items are *not* excluded from the definition of net earnings from self-employment under section 1402 of the tax code. Neither the IRS, the Social Security Administration, nor any court has ever addressed this issue directly, but the conclusion summarized above seems to be the most likely result.

The elimination of the annual earnings test for persons who are full retirement age and older has diminished the importance of this question, since few ministers who are under their full

TABLE 9-1

FULL RETIREMENT AGE

YEAR OF BIRTH	FULL RETIREMENT AGE
1937 or before	65
1938	65 and 2 months
1939	65 and 4 months
1940	65 and 6 months
1941	65 and 8 months
1942	65 and 10 months
1943–1954	66
1955	66 and 2 months
1956	66 and 4 months
1957	66 and 6 months
1958	66 and 8 months
1959	66 and 10 months
1960 and later	67

retirement age have any desire to begin receiving Social Security retirement benefits and continue working at the same time (since their benefits are reduced by $1 for every $2 they earn above $15,120 in 2013).

F. EXEMPTION OF MEMBERS OF CERTAIN RELIGIOUS FAITHS

✸ **KEY POINT.** Members of certain religious sects that are opposed to Social Security coverage and that provide for the welfare and security of their members may become exempt from Social Security coverage if several conditions are met.

Section 1402(g) of the tax code permits self-employed members (whether ministers or laypersons) of certain religious faiths to exempt themselves from Social Security coverage if the following conditions are satisfied:

- the member belongs to a recognized religious sect;
- the sect is opposed to the acceptance of "the benefits of any private or public insurance which makes payments in the event of death, disability, old-age, or retirement or makes payments toward the cost of, or provides services for, medical care (including the benefits of any insurance system established by the Social Security Act)" on the basis of its established tenets or teachings;
- the member adheres to the sect's tenets or teachings relating to Social Security coverage;
- the member files an exemption application (Form 4029);
- the member's exemption application is accompanied by evidence of his membership in and adherence to the tenets or teachings of the sect;
- the member waives his right to all Social Security benefits; and
- the Secretary of the Department of Health and Human Services finds that the sect (1) does, in fact, have established tenets or teachings in opposition to Social Security coverage; (2) makes provision for the financial support of its dependent members; and (3) has been in existence continually since December 31, 1950.

Such an application for exemption, if granted, is irrevocable unless the member ceases to be a member of the sect or no longer adheres to the sect's tenets or teachings pertaining to participation in the Social Security system.

The regulations interpreting this statute specify that a member is eligible for the exemption even if he or she is not opposed to obtaining personal liability or property insurance.

The United States Supreme Court emphasized in a 1982 ruling that the exemption applied only to self-employed persons. Accordingly, an Amish employer who employed several persons to work on his farm and in his carpentry shop was not eligible for the exemption despite the fact that both he and his Amish employees were opposed to Social Security coverage on the basis of well-established Amish religious beliefs. *United States v. Lee, 455 U.S. 252 (1982).* The court accepted the contention that compulsory participation in the Social Security program would interfere with the right of the Amish employer and employees to freely exercise their religion. This, however, was only the beginning and not the end of the court's inquiry, since "the state may justify a limitation on religious liberty by showing that it is essential to accomplish an overriding governmental interest." It concluded that the government's interest in "assuring mandatory and continuous participation in and contribution to the Social Security system" was an interest of sufficient magnitude to override the interest of Amish employers and employees in freely exercising their religion.

Congress amended the law in 1988 to extend this exemption to *employees* for tax years beginning in 1989 (in effect, overruling the Supreme Court's decision in *United States v. Lee*). However, the exemption applies only if the employee and employer are both members of a qualifying religious sect (as described above). The exemption is available to both the employer and employee portion of Social Security and Medicare taxes. No time restriction is imposed on the filing of employee exemption applications, and the law prospectively amended section 1402(g)(2) by eliminating the time restrictions on filing exemption applications by self-employed persons. *IRC 3127.*

The courts have strictly enforced the requirement that the member belong to a religious sect having established tenets or teachings in opposition to Social Security coverage and that provides for its dependent members. To illustrate, a Seventh-Day Adventist was denied an exemption despite his claim that he was personally opposed to Social Security coverage on the basis of religious beliefs, since the Seventh-Day Adventist Church had no established tenets or teachings against Social Security coverage and made no provision for the support of its dependent members. *Varga v. United States, 467 F. Supp. 1113 (D. Md. 1979).*

The exemption has been challenged on the ground that it unconstitutionally discriminates against persons who personally are opposed on the basis of religious beliefs to Social Security coverage but who are not members of a religious sect that has established tenets or teachings in opposition to Social Security coverage and that provides for its dependent members. Such challenges thus far have failed. One court has stated:

The limitation by Congress of the exemption of members of certain religious sects with established tenets opposed to insurance and which made reasonable provisions for their dependent members was in keeping with the overall welfare purpose of the Social Security Act. This provision provided assurance that those qualifying for the exemption would be otherwise provided for in the event of their dependency. Palmer v. Commissioner, 52 T.C. 310 (1969). See also Bethel Baptist Church v. United States, 822 F.2d 1334 (3rd Cir. 1987); May v. Commissioner, T.C. Memo. Dec. 51,242(M) (1996).

G. CHECKING YOUR SOCIAL SECURITY EARNINGS

In 1999 the Social Security Administration (SSA) began providing an annual Social Security Statement to most workers age 25 and older who were not receiving Social Security benefits, at a cost of about $70 million a year. Due to budgetary constraints, the SSA suspended statement mailings in April 2011. This action midway through the fiscal year (FY) saved approximately $30 million in printing and postage in FY 2011. In February 2012 the SSA resumed mailing paper statements to workers age 60 and older who are not already receiving Social Security benefits.

As printing and postage rates continue to increase, it could cost taxpayers more than a billion dollars over the next 10 years to mail annual statements to all eligible workers. Therefore, the SSA developed an easy-to-use online version of the statement that provides eligible workers with secure and convenient access to their earnings and benefit information. The online statement was released on May 1, 2012. Later in 2012, the SSA began mailing an initial paper statement to workers at age 25 and decided to continue the practice of mailing statements to workers age 60 and older who are not already receiving benefits.

The statement provides a year-by-year display of a worker's earnings as either a self-employed person or an employee, provided the worker with an estimate of future benefits, and asked the worker to carefully inspect the statement for errors.

H. SOCIAL SECURITY AS AN INVESTMENT

Is Social Security a good investment? Many ministers ask this question when considering an exemption from self-employment taxes. Of course, in one sense, such a question is irrelevant, since ministers are subject to self-employment taxes unless they are opposed to the acceptance of Social Security benefits on the basis of religious principles and they file a timely exemption application.

~

2013 SOCIAL SECURITY AMOUNTS

	2013
Tax rate—employees	7.65%*
Tax rate—self-employed	15.3%
Maximum taxable earnings (Social Security tax only)	$113,700
Maximum taxable earnings (Medicare tax)	No limit
Retirement earnings tax-exempt amount (for workers under full retirement age)†	$15,120

*Churches and their nonminister employees are subject to Social Security and Medicare taxes (except for churches that exempted themselves from these taxes by filing a timely Form 8274 with the IRS, in which case their nonminister employees are treated as self-employed for Social Security purposes). The combined Social Security and Medicare tax rate is 15.3 percent of each employee's wages. This rate is paid equally by the employer and employee, with each paying a tax of 7.65 percent of the employee's wages. This 7.65 percent rate is comprised of two components: (1) a Medicare hospital insurance (HI) tax of 1.45 percent and (2) an old-age, survivor, and disability (Social Security) tax of 6.2 percent. For 2011 and 2012, Congress provided a temporary payroll tax holiday of two percentage points off the employee share of Social Security tax. This meant that the employee's share of Social Security taxes dropped from 6.2 to 4.2 percent of wages for 2011 and 2012. It is unlikely that Congress will extend the lower rates for 2013 or future years. Check the Social Security Administration website for current information.

† Your Social Security retirement benefits are reduced if your earnings exceed a certain level, called a "retirement earnings test exempt amount," and if you are under your "normal retirement age" (NRA). NRA, also referred to as "full retirement age," varies from age 65 to age 67 by year of birth. For persons born in 1943–1954, the NRA is 66 years. For people attaining NRA after 2012, the annual exempt amount in 2013 is $15,120, meaning that you can earn up to this amount with no reduction in Social Security retirement benefits. For every $2 earned above this amount, Social Security retirement benefits are reduced by $1. A modified annual earnings test applies in the year a worker attains full retirement age. Social Security benefits are reduced by $1 for every $3 of earnings above a specified amount for each month prior to full retirement age. (This amount is $3,340 for 2013.) Beginning with the month an individual attains full retirement age, no reduction in Social Security retirement benefits occurs, no matter how much the person earns.

Whether Social Security is a "good investment" has nothing to do with this decision.

Historically, Social Security has been a good investment for most workers, including ministers. But benefits received in the past were based on a larger percentage of workers and a smaller percentage of beneficiaries. In the future, increasingly fewer workers will be supporting larger numbers of beneficiaries. Undoubtedly, changes will have to be made. Taxes may increase. Benefits may be cut or their rate of increase reduced, or they may be denied altogether to those with higher incomes or net worth. The minimum retirement age likely will be increased. These potential changes suggest that Social Security should be viewed as a supplemental benefit plan, as it was originally intended, rather than as an exclusive source of retirement income.

Social Security coverage provides several benefits, including retirement, survivors, disability, and Medicare. While some ministers who have filed an exemption application conceivably could have duplicated the coverage Social Security provides, this is unlikely. Most exempt ministers only think of duplicating the retirement benefits through some form of retirement arrangement, forgetting that Social Security coverage provides far more than these benefits. Social Security benefits have the additional advantages of being inflation-indexed and nontaxable (for most persons).

I. APPLYING FOR BENEFITS

Generally, you should apply for retirement benefits three months before you want your benefits to begin. Even if you don't plan to receive benefits right away, you still should sign up for Medicare three months before you reach age 65.

J. THE WINDFALL ELIMINATION PROVISION

In 1983 Congress amended the Social Security Act to include a "windfall elimination provision" (WEP). The WEP was added to eliminate "windfall" Social Security benefits for retired and disabled workers receiving pensions from employment not covered by Social Security.

The purpose of the provision was to remove an unintended advantage that the weighting in the regular Social Security benefit formula would otherwise provide for persons who have substantial pensions from noncovered employment. This weighting is intended to help workers who spent their whole lives in low-paying jobs by providing them with a benefit that is relatively higher in relation to their prior earnings than the benefit that is provided for higher-paid workers.

However, because benefits are based on average earnings in employment covered by Social Security over a working lifetime (35 years), a worker who has spent part of his or her career in employment not covered by Social Security appears to have lower average lifetime earnings than he or she actually had. Years with no covered earnings are counted as years of zero earnings for purposes of determining average earnings for Social Security benefit purposes. Without the WEP, such a worker would be treated as a low lifetime earner for Social Security benefit purposes and inappropriately receive the advantage of the weighted benefit formula. The WEP provision eliminates the potential windfall by providing for a different, less heavily weighted benefit formula to compute benefits for such persons.

In some cases the WEP may apply to ministers who elected to exempt themselves from self-employment taxes and who are receiving Social Security benefits based on their spouse's coverage. For more information on this important limitation, contact your nearest Social Security Administration office.

Legislation has been introduced in Congress in recent years to eliminate the windfall elimination provision, so far without success.

| Form **4361**
(Rev. January 2011)
Department of the Treasury
Internal Revenue Service | **Application for Exemption From Self-Employment Tax**
for Use by Ministers, Members of Religious Orders
and Christian Science Practitioners | OMB No. 1545-0074

File Original
and Two Copies |

File original and two copies and attach supporting documents. This exemption is granted only if the IRS returns a copy to you marked "approved."

Please type or print

1 Name of taxpayer applying for exemption (as shown on Form 1040)	Social security number
Number and street (including apt. no.)	Telephone number (optional)
City or town, state, and ZIP code	

2 Check **one** box: ☐ Christian Science practitioner ☐ Ordained minister, priest, rabbi
☐ Member of religious order not under a vow of poverty ☐ Commissioned or licensed minister (see line 6)

3 Date ordained, licensed, etc. (Attach supporting document. See instructions.)

4 Legal name of ordaining, licensing, or commissioning body or religious order

Number, street, and room or suite no.

Employer identification number

City or town, state, and ZIP code

5 Enter the first 2 years after the date shown on line 3 that you had net self-employment earnings of $400 or more, any of which came from services as a minister, priest, rabbi, etc.; member of a religious order; or Christian Science practitioner . . . . ▶

6 If you apply for the exemption as a licensed or commissioned minister and your denomination also ordains ministers, please indicate how your ecclesiastical powers differ from those of an ordained minister of your denomination. Attach a copy of your denomination's bylaws relating to the powers of ordained, commissioned, and licensed ministers.

----

7 I certify that I am conscientiously opposed to, or because of my religious principles I am opposed to, the acceptance (for services I perform as a minister, member of a religious order not under a vow of poverty, or Christian Science practitioner) of any public insurance that makes payments in the event of death, disability, old age, or retirement; or that makes payments toward the cost of, or provides services for, medical care. (Public insurance includes insurance systems established by the Social Security Act.)

I certify that as a duly ordained, commissioned, or licensed minister of a church or a member of a religious order not under a vow of poverty, I have informed the ordaining, commissioning, or licensing body of my church or order that I am conscientiously opposed to, or because of religious principles I am opposed to, the acceptance (for services I perform as a minister or as a member of a religious order) of any public insurance that makes payments in the event of death, disability, old age, or retirement; or that makes payments toward the cost of, or provides services for, medical care, including the benefits of any insurance system established by the Social Security Act.

I certify that I have never filed Form 2031 to revoke a previous exemption from social security coverage on earnings as a minister, member of a religious order not under a vow of poverty, or Christian Science practitioner.

I request to be exempted from paying self-employment tax on my earnings from services as a minister, member of a religious order not under a vow of poverty, or Christian Science practitioner, under section 1402(e) of the Internal Revenue Code. I understand that the exemption, if granted, will apply only to these earnings. Under penalties of perjury, I declare that I have examined this application and to the best of my knowledge and belief, it is true and correct.

Signature ▶   **Date** ▶

Caution: *Form 4361 is* **not proof** *of the right to an exemption from federal income tax withholding or social security tax, the right to a parsonage allowance exclusion (section 107 of the Internal Revenue Code), assignment by your religious superiors to a particular job, or the exemption or church status of the ordaining, licensing, or commissioning body, or religious order.*

For Internal Revenue Service Use

☐ Approved for exemption from self-employment tax on ministerial earnings
☐ Disapproved for exemption from self-employment tax on ministerial earnings

By _____   _____
                          (Director's signature)   (Date)

General Instructions

Section references are to the Internal Revenue Code unless otherwise noted.

Purpose of form. File Form 4361 to apply for an exemption from self-employment tax if you have ministerial earnings (defined later) and are:

• An ordained, commissioned, or licensed minister of a church;

• A member of a religious order who has not taken a vow of poverty; or

• A Christian Science practitioner.

Note. If you are a commissioned or licensed minister of a religious denomination or church that ordains its ministers, you may be treated in the same manner as an ordained minister if you perform substantially all the religious functions within the scope of the tenets and practices of your religious denomination or church.

This application must be based on your religious or conscientious opposition to the acceptance (for services performed as a minister, member of a religious order not under a vow of poverty, or Christian Science practitioner) of any public insurance that makes payments for death, disability, old age, or retirement; or that makes payments for the cost of, or provides services for, medical care, including any insurance benefits established by the Social Security Act.

If you are a duly ordained, commissioned, or licensed minister of a church or a member of a religious order not under a vow of poverty, prior to filing this form you must inform the ordaining, commissioning, or licensing body of your church or order that, on religious or conscientious grounds, you are opposed to the acceptance of public insurance benefits based on ministerial service.

For Privacy Act and Paperwork Reduction Act Notice, see page 2   Cat. No. 41586H   Form **4361** (Rev. 1-2011)

Chapter 10 RETIREMENT PLANS

At the age of fifty, they must retire from their regular service and work no longer.

Numbers 8:25

CHAPTER HIGHLIGHTS

■ **Tax advantages.** Several kinds of tax-favored retirement plans are available to ministers and lay church employees. Contributions to such plans ordinarily are partially or fully deductible (or excludable) by the minister for income tax purposes, and taxation of interest earnings generally is deferred until a later date.

■ **The value of early participation.** Ministers can accumulate substantial retirement funds by using tax-deferred retirement plans. How much is accumulated depends on three variables—the amount of the annual contributions to the plan, the interest earned, and the number of years of participation. Younger ministers should discipline themselves to participate in such plans at as early an age as possible, since the value of their contributions will be magnified over time.

■ **Types of retirement plans.** Common retirement plans for ministers include

- IRAs,
- SEPs,
- Keogh plans (for self-employed ministers),
- nonqualified deferred compensation plans,
- tax-sheltered annuities (403(b) plans),
- church retirement income accounts,
- qualified pension plans,
- 401(k) plans (established prior to July 2, 1986, or after 1996), and
- "rabbi trusts."

■ **Legal requirements.** All tax-sheltered retirement plans require compliance with complex rules (summarized in this chapter).

■ **Denominational retirement plans.** Most denominations offer retirement plans to their ministers (and sometimes to lay church employees). These plans often offer unique advantages that make them attractive.

■ **Housing allowances.** Church retirement plans can designate housing allowances for retired ministers if certain conditions are satisfied. This is a significant tax benefit for retired ministers.

■ **Retirement gifts.** Church congregations often distribute a lump-sum retirement gift to a retiring minister. Sometimes the gift is paid out in monthly installments. Ordinarily, these gifts constitute taxable compensation rather than a tax-free gift to the minister.

INTRODUCTION

✹**KEY POINT.** Many tax-favored retirement plan options are available to ministers and lay church employees. Contributions to such plans may be partly or fully tax-deductible (or excludable), and taxation of interest or earnings may be deferred until distribution.

✹**KEY POINT.** Ministers and lay staff members can accumulate substantial retirement funds by using tax-deferred retirement plans. How much is accumulated depends on three variables: the amount of the annual contributions to the plan, the rate of return, and the number of years of participation.

Most ministers and lay church employees are eligible to participate in a tax-favored retirement plan, either through their employing church or through a denominationally sponsored plan. A tax-favored plan is characterized by the following two traits:

(1) contributions made by a church to an employee's account are partially or fully deductible for income tax purposes in the year of contribution, and
(2) the income (or appreciation) earned on the account is tax-deferred, meaning that it is not taxable until distributed. These plans may be funded with employee contributions (typically through salary reductions), by employer contributions, or by a combination of the two.

This chapter will address the following church- or denomination-sponsored retirement plans:

- deferred compensation plans (including rabbi trusts),
- tax-sheltered annuities,
- qualified pension plans, and
- informal plans.

Also covered in this chapter are housing allowances for retired ministers.

Church employees also may establish IRAs. These are fully explained in IRS Publication 590, which can be downloaded from the IRS website (irs.gov).

✤ **KEY POINT.** The deferral of tax on income generated by a retirement plan can result in sizable accumulations of wealth, especially if contributions begin early and are made systematically. See Table 10-1.

Before reviewing the various retirement options available to ministers and lay church workers, two important points must be addressed.

1. CHURCH PLANS

The tax code uses the term *church plan* in several contexts, including the following:

- Section 79(d)(7) exempts church plans from the nondiscrimination rules that apply to the exclusion of up to $50,000 of employer-provided group term life insurance. This section defines a church plan with reference to the definition contained in section 414(e)(1), which states: "The term 'church plan' means a plan established and maintained . . . for its employees (or their beneficiaries) by a church or by a convention or association of churches which is exempt from tax under section 501."
- To qualify under section 401(a), a retirement plan must meet certain requirements, including the minimum participation requirements under §410(a), the minimum coverage

requirements under §410(b), and the minimum vesting requirements under §411. A church plan for which no special election described below has been made (non-electing church plan) is ordinarily not subject to various requirements that apply to tax-qualified plans under section 401(a) of the tax code. As a result, tax code provisions that do not apply to a non-electing church plan include participation standards, vesting standards, funding standards, and prohibited transactions. Section 414(e) of the Internal Revenue Code defines the term *church plan* as follows:

The term "church plan" means a plan established and maintained . . . for its employees (or their beneficiaries) by a church or by a convention or association of churches which is exempt from tax under section 501. . . . A plan established and maintained for its employees (or their beneficiaries) by a church or by a convention or association of churches includes a plan maintained by an organization, whether a civil law corporation or otherwise, the principal purpose or function of which is the administration or funding of a plan or program for the provision of retirement benefits or welfare benefits, or both, for the employees of a church or a convention or association of churches, if such organization is controlled by or associated with a church or a convention or association of churches. . . .

The term "employee of a church" or "a convention or association of churches" shall include—(i) a duly ordained, commissioned, or licensed minister of a church in the exercise of his ministry, regardless of the source of his compensation; (ii) an employee of an

═══════ **TABLE 10-1** ═══════

THE EFFECT OF TAX DEFERRAL

ANNUAL CONTRIBUTION	YEARS TO RETIREMENT	ANNUAL RATE OF INTEREST	VALUE AT RETIREMENT IF . . .		
			CONTRIBUTIONS TAX DEDUCTIBLE AND EARNINGS TAX DEFERRED	CONTRIBUTIONS NOT TAX DEDUCTIBLE AND EARNINGS TAXABLE (15% BRACKET)	CONTRIBUTIONS NOT TAX DEDUCTIBLE AND EARNINGS TAXABLE (25% BRACKET)
$3,000	20	3%	$83,029	$78,985	$76,416
$3,000	20	6%	$116,978	$105,366	$98,349
$3,000	20	9%	$167,294	$142,182	$127,759
$3,000	30	3%	$147,008	$136,148	$129,434
$3,000	30	6%	$251,405	$213,115	$191,257
$3,000	30	9%	$445,726	$343,169	$289,239
$3,000	40	3%	$232,990	$209,679	$195,664
$3,000	40	6%	$492,143	$390,306	$335,540
$3,000	40	9%	$1,104,876	$763,298	$599,550

organization, whether a civil law corporation or otherwise, which is exempt from tax under section 501 and which is controlled by or associated with a church or a convention or association of churches . . . .

An organization, whether a civil law corporation or otherwise, is associated with a church or a convention or association of churches if it shares common religious bonds and convictions with that church or convention or association of churches.

- Section 410(d) of the tax code permits an election to be made under which a church plan would be subject to the same requirements as apply to other qualified plans (electing church plan). Section 1.410(d)-1 of the income tax regulations provides that the election is irrevocable and may be made only by the plan administrator and only in the manner provided in the regulations. If the election is made, the plan must comply with the applicable provisions of the code. In addition, an electing church plan would be covered by and subject to Title I and, if a defined benefit pension plan, Title IV of ERISA.
- Section 4980D exempts church plans from the penalty that applies to group health plans that discriminate in favor of highly compensated employees.
- Section 1402(a)(8) specifies that net earnings from self-employment (in computing the self-employment tax) does not include "the rental value of any parsonage or any parsonage allowance . . . provided after the individual retires, or any other retirement benefit received by such individual from a church plan (as defined in section 414(e)) after the individual retires."
- Section 415(c)(7) provides that church employees who participate in a church plan can elect an increased amount for the limit on annual additions. Under this election, employees can increase their limit on annual additions to $10,000 a year. Total contributions over one's lifetime under this election cannot be more than $40,000.
- The nondiscrimination rules that apply to 403(b) plans do not apply to church plans.
- The instructions for the current IRS Form 5500 state that church plans not electing ERISA coverage under section 410(b) of the tax code are not required to file Form 5500.

Under section 4(b)(2) of ERISA, a non-electing church plan is excluded from coverage under Title I of ERISA. Thus, for example, it is not subject to ERISA's rules governing reporting, disclosure, and fiduciary conduct. In the case of a defined benefit pension plan, the plan is also not covered by the insurance provisions of Title IV of ERISA, which provides for certain benefit guarantees by the Pension Benefit Guaranty Corporation (PBGC) in the event of termination of an underfunded pension plan. These results are not limited to a church plan whose only participants are employees of a church, but may also in some cases include substantial numbers of employees of certain affiliated entities who are participants in a church plan as defined in §414(e).

A non-electing church plan is instead primarily subject to certain qualification requirements that predate the enactment of ERISA. The plan is treated as a tax-qualified plan only if the plan satisfies the participation, vesting, and funding requirements of the tax code as in effect prior to ERISA. Section 514(a) of ERISA generally provides that ERISA supersedes state laws that relate to an employee benefit plan described in section 4(a) of ERISA and not exempt under section 4(b) of ERISA. A non-electing church plan is exempt under section 4(b) of ERISA. Thus, state laws that relate to an employee benefit plan generally would apply to the non-electing church plan.

✤**KEY POINT.** The major advantage derived by a plan that qualifies as a church plan is that it allows the plan sponsor a choice to comply with the participation, vesting, and funding requirements imposed by Title II of ERISA. As well as being exempt from certain provisions of the tax code, church plans are exempt from Titles I and IV of ERISA.

EXAMPLE. A federal court in Minnesota dismissed a lawsuit brought by several participants in a denominational pension plan citing ERISA violations and state law claims for breach of trust, breach of contract, breach of fiduciary duty, and consumer fraud. The court concluded that the retirement plan was a church plan that was exempt from ERISA and dismissed the plaintiffs' ERISA claims. The court concluded: "The court has thoroughly reviewed the applicable law and the arguments of counsel, and finds no support for plaintiffs' position that a single employer benefit plan, established and maintained by an organization controlled by or associated with a church, is not a church plan as defined by ERISA. Rather, the court finds that the statutory language defining 'church plan,' as well as the applicable agency determinations and court decisions support a finding that the plan is a church plan." *Thorkelson v. Publishing House, 764 F.Supp.2d 1119 (D. Minn. 2011).*

2. SELF-EMPLOYED MINISTERS AND CHAPLAINS

Church employees, members of religious orders, and duly ordained, commissioned, or licensed ministers working as ministers or chaplains can participate in tax-sheltered annuity (403(b)) plans. An exception to the above applies if you are a minister or chaplain and, in the exercise of your ministry, you are either self-employed or employed by an organization that is not exempt from tax under section 501(c)(3) of the Internal Revenue Code. If the exception applies to you, you can deduct your contributions to a 403(b) plan as follows:

- If you are self-employed, deduct your contributions on Form 1040, line 28.
- If you are not self-employed and your employer does not exclude your contributions from your earned income, deduct your contributions on Form 1040, line 36. Enter the

amount of your deduction and "403(b)" on the dotted line next to line 36.

Note that these provisions apply only to ministers. Self-employed lay church workers are not covered.

❖**KEY POINT.** Ministers who report their income taxes as self-employed are permitted to participate as fully as employees in tax-favored retirement plans, including tax-sheltered 403(b) annuities.

A. DEFERRED COMPENSATION PLANS

A "nonqualified" deferred compensation plan consists of a promise by an employer to pay an employee (or self-employed person) compensation in the future in exchange for services performed currently. The term "nonqualified" means that the plan is *not* subject to the many conditions that apply to qualified benefit plans under section 401 of the tax code.

Nonqualified deferred compensation arrangements can be funded through salary reduction agreements or employer contributions, or they can be unfunded (a mere unsecured promise by the employer to pay future benefits). I either case, such arrangements ordinarily are attractive only if contributions made by or on behalf of an employee are not currently taxable and earnings can accumulate tax-free.

It often is difficult to determine whether these tax benefits are available because of the "constructive receipt" and "economic benefit" doctrines.

1. DETERMINING AVAILABILITY

Constructive receipt doctrine
The constructive receipt doctrine is set forth in income tax regulation 1.451-2(a):

> *Income although not actually reduced to a taxpayer's possession is constructively received by him in the taxable year during which it is credited to his account, set apart for him, or otherwise made available so that he may draw upon it at any time, or so that he could have drawn upon it during the taxable year if notice of intention to withdraw had been given. However, income is not constructively received if the taxpayer's control of its receipt is subject to substantial limitations or restrictions.*

Economic benefit doctrine
The economic benefit doctrine (codified in section 83 of the tax code) provides that property transferred to a person as compensation for services (including deferred compensation) generally will be taxed at the first time the property can be reasonably valued. For example, this rule applies when assets are unconditionally and irrevocably paid into a fund or trust to be used for an employee's sole benefit. However, the IRS generally rules that no income is includible in an employee's income under the economic benefit doctrine if the source of the deferred compensation remains subject to the general creditors of the employer or was otherwise subject to a "substantial risk of forfeiture."

To illustrate, in Revenue Ruling 72-25 the IRS ruled that an employee did not receive taxable income as a result of his employer's purchase of an insurance contract to provide a source of funds for deferred compensation because the insurance contract was the employer's asset and was subject to the claims of the employer's general creditors.

Section 457 deferred compensation plans
Section 457 of the tax code imposes special rules on the unfunded deferred compensation plans of state and local governments. This section once imposed these same rules on the unfunded deferred compensation plans of churches and other religious organizations. However, section 457 was amended to exempt the following organizations: (1) a church; (2) a convention or association of churches; (3) an elementary or secondary school that is controlled, operated, or principally supported by a church or convention or association of churches; and (4) a "qualified church-controlled organization." *IRC 457(e)(13).*

A qualified church-controlled organization is defined in section 3121(w)(3)(B) of the tax code as

> *any church-controlled tax-exempt organization described in section 501(c)(3), other than an organization which (i) offers goods, services, or facilities for sale, other than on an incidental basis, to the general public, other than goods, services or facilities which are sold at a nominal charge which is substantially less than the cost of providing such goods, services, or facilities; and (ii) normally receives more than 25 percent of its support from either (I) governmental sources, or (II) receipts from admissions, sales of merchandise, performance of services, or furnishing of facilities, in activities which are not unrelated trades or businesses, or both.*

Clearly, local churches, church denominations, and church-controlled elementary and secondary schools qualify as church-controlled organizations. While it is less clear, it is reasonably certain that seminaries and Bible colleges would also qualify. The committee report on the Tax Reform Act of 1986, in construing the term "qualified church-controlled organization" in another context, noted that it includes "the typical seminary, religious retreat center, or burial society, regardless of its funding sources, because it does not offer goods, services, or facilities for sale to the general public." The committee report also noted that the term "qualified church-controlled organization" included

> *a church-run orphanage or old-age home, even if it is open to the general public, if not more than 25 percent of its support is derived from the receipts of admissions, sales of merchandise, performance of services, or furnishing of facilities (in other than unrelated trades or businesses) or from governmental sources. The committee specifically intends that the [term "qualified church-controlled organization" will not include] church-run universities (other than religious seminaries) and hospitals if both conditions (i) and (ii) exist.*

Religious organizations not covered by one of the exemptions noted above are governed by section 457, meaning that their deferred compensation plans must meet the definition of an "eligible deferred compensation plan" in order to entitle employees to the limited tax benefits discussed above. Eligible 457 plans are exempt from the requirements imposed on rabbi trusts and certain other nonqualified deferred compensation plans by section 409A of the tax code (described below).

2. SECTION 409A

Congress added section 409A to the tax code in 2004 in response to public outrage over the Enron scandal. With reports of over $100 million in deferred compensation benefits being paid out to key executives in the months prior to the company's collapse, the public demanded action.

Section 409A imposes strict requirements on most nonqualified deferred compensation arrangements, including rabbi trusts. In order to succeed in deferring immediate taxation of compensation under a nonqualified deferred compensation plan (NQDP), section 409A imposes several requirements that are explained below.

Taxable income

If at any time during a taxable year a nonqualified deferred compensation plan fails to meet the following three requirements, all compensation deferred under the plan for the taxable year and all preceding taxable years are included in taxable income for the taxable year to the extent not subject to a substantial risk of forfeiture and not previously included in taxable income. Other penalties may apply (increased interest rate on underpayment of tax, and a 20 percent additional tax on the amount to be included in income). These three requirements are as follows:

1. Distributions

Compensation deferred under the plan may not be distributed earlier than (1) separation from service (as determined by the IRS);

(2) the date the participant becomes disabled; (3) death; (4) a time specified under the plan at the date of the deferral of such compensation; or (5) the occurrence of an unforeseeable emergency.

The time and form of distributions must be specified at the time of initial deferral. A plan can specify the time and form of payments to be made as a result of a distribution event (e.g., a plan could specify that payments upon separation of service will be paid in lump sum within 30 days of separation from service) or allow participants to elect the time and form of payment at the time of the initial deferral election. Multiple payout events are permissible. For example, a participant could elect to receive 25 percent of his or her account balance at age 50 and the remaining 75 percent at age 60. A plan also can allow participants to elect different forms of payment for different permissible distribution events. For example, a participant could elect to receive a lump sum distribution upon disability but an annuity at age 65.

2. Acceleration of benefits

The plan does not permit the acceleration of the time or schedule of any payment under the plan except as provided in IRS regulations.

3. Elections

The plan provides that compensation for services performed during a taxable year may be deferred at the participant's election only if the election to defer is made not later than the close of the preceding taxable year or at such other time as provided in the regulations. In the case of the first year in which a participant becomes eligible to participate in the plan, such election may be made with respect to services to be performed subsequent to the election within 30 days after the date the participant becomes eligible to participate in the plan.

A nonqualified deferred compensation plan may allow a subsequent election to delay the timing or form of distributions only under certain conditions: (1) the plan requires that such election cannot be effective for at least 12 months after the date on which the election is made; (2) except in the case of elections relating to distributions on account of death, disability, or unforeseeable emergency, the plan requires that the additional deferral with respect to which such election is made is for a period of not less than five years from the date such payment would otherwise have been made; and (3) the plan requires that an election related to a distribution to be made upon a specified time may not be made less than 12 months prior to the date of the first scheduled payment.

If the requirements of section 409A are not met, in addition to current income inclusion, interest at the underpayment rate plus one percentage point is imposed on the underpayments that would have occurred had the compensation been includible in income when first deferred or, if later, when not subject to a substantial risk of forfeiture. The amount required to be included in income is also subject to a 20 percent additional tax. Current income inclusion, interest, and the additional tax apply only if the requirements of section 409A are not met.

Nonqualified deferred compensation plan

Section 409A applies to amounts deferred under a nonqualified deferred compensation plan. A nonqualified deferred compensation plan is any plan that provides for the deferral of compensation, with specified exceptions, such as qualified retirement plans, tax-deferred annuities, simplified employee pensions, and SIMPLEs.

Substantial risk of forfeiture

The regulations specify that compensation is subject to a substantial risk of forfeiture "if entitlement to the amount is conditioned on the performance of substantial future services by any person or the occurrence of a condition related to a purpose of the compensation, and the possibility of forfeiture is substantial."

Reporting requirements

The Act imposed two reporting requirements:

(1) Amounts required to be included in taxable income because the requirements of section 409A are not met are required to be reported on an individual's Form W-2 (or Form 1099) for the year includible in income. This is done in box 12 of Form W-2 using the code Z (this amount is also included in box 1). It is done on Form 1099-MISC in the box 15b (this amount also is included in box 7). Amounts required to be included in income under section 409A are subject to federal income tax withholding requirements.

(2) Employers originally were required to report amounts deferred under a nonqualified deferred compensation plan on an individual's Form W-2 (or Form 1099) for the year deferred even if the amount was not currently includible in income for that taxable year. This was done in box 12 of Form W-2 using code Y (or box 15a on Form 1099-MISC for self-employed workers). However, in 2008 the IRS announced that "until the Treasury Department and the IRS issue further guidance, an employer is not required to report amounts deferred during the year under a nonqualified deferred compensation plan subject to section 409A in box 12 of Form W-2 using code Y. In addition, until the Treasury Department and the IRS issue further guidance, a payer is not required to report amounts deferred during the year under a nonqualified deferred compensation plan subject to section 409A in box 15a of Form 1099-MISC." *IRS Notice 2008-115.*

Final IRS regulations

In 2007 the IRS published final regulations interpreting section 409A. The final regulations define an NQDP broadly to include any plan that provides for the deferral of compensation. This definition is broad enough to include rabbi trusts, some severance agreements, and many other kinds of compensation arrangements.

The final regulations specify that a plan generally provides for the deferral of compensation if an employee has a legally binding right during the current year to compensation that, pursuant to the terms of an NQDP, is payable to the employee in a later year. The final regulations list some exceptions, including section 403(b) annuities, simplified employee pensions (SEPs), qualified retirement plans meeting the requirements of section 401(a) of the tax code, bona fide sick leave or vacation plans, disability plans, death benefit plans, or certain medical expense reimbursement arrangements.

Churches that enter into any type of deferred compensation arrangement with a staff member should pay careful attention to section 409A and the final regulations, since a failure to do so can result in the following significant penalties:

- inclusion of the "deferred" amount in taxable income currently,
- interest on the deferred amount at an enhanced rate, and
- an excise tax of 20 percent of the deferred amount.

The final regulations contain the following provisions of most relevance to church leaders:

Written documentation

Perhaps most importantly, the final regulations require the existence of a written plan demonstrating compliance with the requirements of section 409A. Failure to have such a plan triggers the current taxation of "deferred" compensation, an enhanced rate of interest, and a 20 percent excise tax. If your church has a rabbi trust or any other arrangement that may meet the broad definition of an NQDP, it is imperative that you consult with an attorney to ensure that you have a written plan that satisfies the requirements of the final regulations.

Several persons asked the IRS to publish language meeting the written plan requirement. The IRS responded by stating, "Due to the complex and varied universe of deferred compensation plans, the IRS does not believe that it is feasible to publish model amendments at this time." Also note that the final regulations warn that "savings clauses" in a plan document will not suffice. Such clauses state that the document will be interpreted to comply with section 409A even if they otherwise fail to meet the section 409A requirements. The IRS has stated that "if a plan contains terms that do not meet the requirements of section 409A and these regulations . . . the plan will violate the requirements of section 409A and these regulations regardless of whether the plan contains such a savings clause."

Short-term deferrals

The final regulations adopt a short-term deferral rule. Under this rule, a deferral of compensation does not occur for purposes of section 409A if the arrangement under which a payment is made does not provide for a deferred payment and the payment is made no later than the 15th day of the 3rd month following the end of the employee's taxable year.

Exemptions

The final regulations include various exceptions from the definition of deferred compensation for certain types of separation pay, providing exceptions for the following:

(1) Certain arrangements providing separation pay due solely to an involuntary separation from employment and that do not exceed a specified amount. The regulations provide that if a separation from service is voluntary, it is presumed that the payment results from an acceleration of vesting followed by a payment of the deferred compensation that is subject to section 409A. As a result, any change in the payment schedule to accelerate or defer the payments would be subject to section 409A. This presumption may be rebutted in some cases.

(2) Certain reimbursement arrangements providing for expense reimbursements for a limited period of time following a separation from service.

(3) Certain rights to limited amounts of separation pay (generally less than the current limit on elective deferrals, defined in section B.5 of this chapter).

(4) The regulations include the following exemption for legal settlements:

An agreement to which [an employee] is a party does not provide for a deferral of compensation for purposes of this paragraph (b) to the extent that the agreement provides for amounts paid as settlements or awards resolving bona fide legal claims based on wrongful termination, employment discrimination, the Fair Labor Standards Act, or worker's compensation statutes, including claims under applicable federal, state, local, or foreign laws, or for reimbursements or payments of reasonable attorneys fees or other reasonable expenses incurred by the service provider related to such bona fide legal claims, regardless of whether such settlements, awards, or reimbursement or payment of expenses pursuant to such claims are treated as compensation or wages for federal tax purposes. Whether the execution of a waiver of any or all of such types of claims indicates that the amounts are paid as an award or settlement of an actual bona fide claim for damages under applicable law is determined based on the facts and circumstances. This paragraph does not apply to any deferred amounts that did not arise as a result of an actual bona fide claim for damages under applicable law, such as amounts that would have been deferred or paid regardless of the existence of such claim, even if such amounts are paid or modified as part of a settlement or award resolving an actual bona fide claim.

Separation pay due to voluntary separation

The final regulations provide that where the right to a payment is contingent on a voluntary separation from service following an event that constitutes good reason for the employee to terminate his or her employment, the right may be treated as payable only upon an involuntary separation from service where the good-reason condition is such that the employee's separation from service effectively is an involuntary separation for purposes of section 409A. To be treated as an involuntary separation for purposes of section 409A, avoidance of the requirements of section 409A must not be a purpose of the inclusion of any good-reason condition in the plan or of the actions by the employer in connection with the satisfaction of a condition.

Safe harbor

The final regulations provide a "safe harbor" under which a provision for a payment upon a voluntary separation from service for good reason will be treated, for purposes of section 409A, as providing for a payment upon an actual involuntary separation from service. Those conditions include that the amount be payable only if the employee separates from service within a limited period of time not to exceed two years following the initial existence of the good-reason condition and that the amount, time, and form of payment upon a voluntary separation from service for good reason be identical to the amount, time, and form of payment upon an involuntary separation from service. In addition, the employee must be required to provide notice of the existence of the good-reason condition within a period not to exceed 90 days of its initial existence, and the employer must be provided a period of at least 30 days during which he or she may remedy the good-reason condition.

For these purposes, a good-reason condition may consist of one or more of the following conditions arising without the consent of the employee: (1) a material reduction in the employee's compensation; (2) a material reduction in the employee's authority, duties, or responsibilities; (3) a material reduction in the authority, duties, or responsibilities of the supervisor to whom the employee is required to report; (4) a material reduction in the budget over which the employee retains authority; (5) a material change in geographic location at which the employee must perform the services; or (6) any other action or inaction that constitutes a material breach of the terms of an employment agreement.

Medical expense reimbursements

The final regulations extend the period during which taxable reimbursements of medical expenses may be provided, to cover the period during which the employee would be entitled to continuation coverage under a group health plan of the employer under COBRA if the employee elected such coverage and paid the applicable premiums.

✤ **KEY POINT.** Any church or other organization that has entered into a rabbi trust or any other arrangement that defers compensation to a future year should contact an attorney to have the trust or other arrangement reviewed to ensure compliance with both section 409A and the final regulations. Such a review will protect against the substantial penalties the IRS can assess for noncompliance. It also will help clarify whether a rabbi trust or other deferred compensation arrangement remains a viable option in light of the recent limitations imposed by section 409A and the final regulations.

3. RABBI TRUSTS

▲ **CAUTION.** *The American Jobs Creation Act of 2004 imposed several restrictions on rabbi trusts. These restrictions are explained below. All existing rabbi trusts should be reviewed to ensure compliance with these restrictions, and any new rabbi trusts should comply with them.*

A synagogue asked the IRS whether its rabbi would realize taxable income if it funded a trust for his benefit. The synagogue proposed to create and fund the trust with a specified amount and to pay the net income from the trust to the rabbi at least quarter-annually. Upon his death, disability, retirement, or discharge, the trust would distribute the remaining principal and any accrued interest directly to the rabbi (or his estate).

The trust was irrevocable, and the trust assets were subject to the claims of the synagogue's general creditors (as if they were any other general asset). Further, the trust specified that the rabbi's interest could not be assigned or used by him as collateral, and it was not subject to the claims of his creditors. In a landmark private letter ruling, the IRS concluded that the rabbi was *not* taxable on the funds transferred by the synagogue to the trust. *IRS Letter Ruling 8113107.*

The IRS concluded that the creation of the rabbi trust fund was not taxable to the rabbi under either the economic benefit or constructive receipt rules. These rules were devised by the IRS and the courts to tax income currently rather than in the future.

Economic benefit
The IRS acknowledged that under the economic benefit doctrine, the creation by an employer of a fund in which an employee has vested rights "will result in immediate inclusion" of the fund in the employee's taxable income. Such a taxable fund "is created when an amount is irrevocably placed with a third party, and a taxpayer's interest in the fund is vested if it is nonforfeitable." This rule did not require inclusion of the fund in the rabbi's income, since "the assets of the trust estate are subject to the claims of [the synagogue's] creditors." In other words, the creation of the trust did not result in any present economic benefit to the rabbi.

Constructive receipt
The IRS noted that under the constructive receipt doctrine, "income although not actually reduced to a taxpayer's possession is constructively received by him in the taxable year during which it is credited to his account, set apart for him, or otherwise made available so that he may draw upon it at any time, or so that he could have drawn upon it during the taxable year if notice of intention to withdraw had been given. However, income is not constructively received if

the taxpayer's control of its receipt is subject to substantial limitations or restrictions." *Treas. Reg. 1.451-2(a).* The IRS concluded that the trust fund was not presently taxable to the rabbi, since "the assets of the trust estate are subject to the claims of [the synagogue's] creditors and are not paid or made available within the meaning of section 451 of the tax code." The IRS further noted that "payments of income or principal under the terms of the trust agreement will be includable in [the rabbi's] gross income in the taxable year in which they are actually received or otherwise made available, whichever is earlier."

This ruling unleashed a whirlwind of requests by taxpayers for similar rulings (the rabbi's private letter ruling could not be relied upon by any other taxpayer). The IRS has issued hundreds of rabbi trust rulings since 1980, most to business executives who recognized the value of such a trust. All of these rulings are private letter rulings, meaning that they can be relied upon only by the individual taxpayers who requested them. Again, while a synagogue and its rabbi were responsible for the first such ruling, nearly all of the subsequent rulings were issued to business executives.

In 1992 the IRS acknowledged that it receives a flood of private ruling requests by employers seeking IRS approval of their rabbi trust arrangements. In response, it published a model rabbi trust agreement. *Revenue Procedure 92-64.* The IRS observed:

> The model trust provided in this revenue procedure is intended to serve as a safe harbor for taxpayers that adopt and maintain grantor trusts in connection with unfunded deferred compensation arrangements. If the model trust is used in accordance with this revenue procedure, an employee will not be in constructive receipt of income or incur an economic benefit solely on account of the adoption or maintenance of the trust. However, the desired tax effect will be achieved only if the nonqualified deferred compensation arrangement effectively defers compensation.

The IRS warned that it will not issue any rulings on unfunded deferred compensation arrangements that "use a trust other than the model trust." In other words, churches and other religious employers that have adopted rabbi trust arrangements *should ensure that the language used in their trusts is identical to that in the model IRS form.* The IRS cautioned: "The model language must be adopted verbatim, except where substitute language is expressly permitted. . . . Of course, provisions may be renumbered if appropriate, language in brackets may be omitted, and blanks may be completed. In addition, the taxpayer may add sections to the model language provided that such additions are not inconsistent with the model language."

Summary
In summary, while the first rabbi trust involved a trust adopted by a synagogue for its rabbi, few synagogues or churches have used these trusts. For the most part they have been used by secular businesses as a component of executive compensation. However,

a rabbi trust can be an effective tool for churches and religious organizations, especially for highly compensated ministers who are nearing retirement age. Through proper drafting, it is possible for a church to set aside amounts in trust that would exceed the limits associated with other retirement plans. But keep the following points in mind:

- **Assets.** The trust must provide that the trust assets are subject to the general creditors of the employer under both federal and state law. This is the most significant disadvantage of a rabbi trust and distinguishes it from many other tax-favored retirement plans.

EXAMPLE. A church establishes a rabbi trust for its senior pastor. Over several years the trust accumulates to $250,000. The church is sued as a result of the sexual misconduct of a volunteer worker, and a court awards the victim $1 million in damages. The church's insurance only covers $100,000 of this amount. The victim has the legal right to compel the church to turn over the rabbi trust to her, thereby eliminating the pastor's retirement funds.

- **Beneficiary.** The beneficiary (i.e., the minister) cannot have any legal interest in the trust fund until the trust assets are distributed. The trust should specify that the beneficiary's interest cannot be assigned, transferred, or used as collateral, and it is not subject to his or her creditors prior to distribution. The idea is this—the beneficiary cannot be taxed on the employer's transfer of funds to the rabbi trust, since the beneficiary has no interest in the funds and may never receive them should the employer become insolvent.
- **Funding.** The trust must be funded with the employer's assets. It is unclear whether a rabbi trust can be funded, in whole or in part, with an employee's own compensation (such as through a salary reduction agreement). In a 1997 ruling the IRS did conclude that a rabbi trust could be funded through "salary deferrals" that were executed by employees prior to the beginning of the year in which the salary was earned. *IRS Letter Ruling 9703022.*
- **Section 409A.** Section 409A of the tax code imposes strict requirements on most nonqualified deferred compensation plans (NQDPs). In 2007 the IRS published final regulations interpreting section 409A. The final regulations define an NQDP broadly, to include any plan that provides for the deferral of compensation, with some exceptions as noted above. This definition is broad enough to include rabbi trusts and many other kinds of church compensation arrangements. Any church or other organization that is considering a rabbi trust (or any other arrangement that defers compensation to a future year) should contact an attorney to have the arrangement reviewed to ensure compliance with both section 409A and the final regulations. Such a review will protect against the substantial penalties the IRS can assess for noncompliance. It also will help clarify whether a deferred compensation

arrangement is a viable option in light of the limitations imposed by section 409A and the final regulations.

4. EXAMPLES

EXAMPLE. A federal appeals court ruled that a pastor whose rabbi trust retirement fund was substantially lost by an investment company due to securities law violations could not sue the investment company, since he had no present interest in the trust assets. This case demonstrates that to achieve the benefit of tax deferral, a rabbi trust must deprive employees of all rights in the trust fund. This can have consequences in addition to tax deferral. It also means that employees will not be allowed to sue investment companies in the event that their trust fund is lost or depleted due to securities law violations. *Smith v. Pennington, 352 F.3d 884 (4th Cir. 2003).*

EXAMPLE. The IRS ruled that a rabbi trust that was established by a church for some of its employees and that conformed to the model rabbi trust published by the IRS in 1992 was owned by the church; therefore, the church's periodic contributions to the trust and trust earnings did not result in current taxable income to the trust beneficiaries. The IRS stressed that (1) the trust was revocable; (2) the trust document did not contain any language inconsistent with the language of the model IRS rabbi trust agreement; (3) the trust was a valid trust under state law and that all of the material terms and provisions of the trust, including the creditors' rights clause, were enforceable under state law; (4) an employee's rights to benefits under the trust were not subject in any manner to attachment or garnishment by his or her creditors; and (5) the trust did not provide for any distributions to an employee prior to retirement or voluntary termination. Under the terms of the church's rabbi trust, employees forfeited any rights under the trust if they were terminated for cause or resigned without the church's consent. *IRS Letter Ruling 200434008 (2004).*

B. TAX-SHELTERED ANNUITIES

1. DEFINITION OF A TAX-SHELTERED ANNUITY

One of the most popular retirement plans for church employees is the 403(b) plan (sometimes called a tax-sheltered annuity). Such plans permit employees of churches and other public charities to make nontaxable contributions to their 403(b) account up to the allowable limits prescribed by law. In addition, earnings and gains on 403(b) accounts are tax-deferred, meaning that they are not taxed until distributed.

When section 403(b) accounts were first introduced in 1958, the only investment option available to employees was an annuity (hence the name "tax-sheltered annuity"). In 1974 Congress added section 403(b)(7) to the tax code. This section allows employees of churches and other charities to invest their 403(b) account with a mutual-fund company. These types of 403(b) plans are called 403(b)(7) accounts or custodial accounts. In 1982 Congress added section 403(b)(9) to the tax code, which recognizes retirement income accounts of churches as yet another kind of 403(b) plan. Such accounts may be invested in annuities or mutual funds, and they usually are. But they are not limited to these investments.

To summarize, a 403(b) plan can be any of the following types:

- an annuity contract, which is a contract provided through an insurance company;
- a custodial account, which is an account invested in mutual funds; or
- a retirement income account set up for church employees.

Although 403(b) plans established by churches can be of any of these three types, there are two reasons many churches establish the third kind of 403(b) plan (retirement income account). First, these accounts were designed for church employees. Second, the investment options are more flexible, since church retirement income accounts are not restricted to annuities and regulated mutual funds.

2. TAX ADVANTAGES

A 403(b) plan has several tax advantages:

- You do not pay tax on contributions to your 403(b) plan in the year they are made. You do not pay tax on them until you begin making withdrawals from the 403(b) plan, usually after you retire.
- Earnings and gains on your 403(b) plan are not taxed until you withdraw them, usually after you retire.
- You may be eligible to claim a "qualified retirement savings" tax credit for contributions to your 403(b) plan made by salary reduction.
- Elective contributions (through salary reduction) to a 403(b) plan do not necessarily constitute self-employment earnings in computing the self-employment tax liability of a minister.
- Churches and church pension boards that offer 403(b) plans can designate a portion of a retired minister's distributions as a housing allowance.

3. QUALIFIED EMPLOYER

Only a qualified employer can maintain a 403(b) plan. There are three kinds of qualified employer: (1) public schools; (2) tax-exempt organizations (including churches and most other religious and charitable organizations); and (3) employers that are not tax-exempt but that employ a minister to perform ministerial services (see below).

4. ELIGIBLE EMPLOYEES

Any eligible employee can participate in a 403(b) plan. The following employees are eligible employees.

- Employees of tax-exempt organizations established under section 501(c)(3) of the tax code (includes employees of religious organizations and schools).
- Ministers employed by section 501(c)(3) organizations.
- A self-employed minister treated as employed by a tax-exempt organization that is a qualified employer. The earned income of self-employed ministers becomes their compensation for purposes of calculating permissible contributions to a 403(b) plan, and a self-employed minister "shall be treated as his or her own employer which is an organization described in section 501(c)(3) and exempt from tax." This is an exception to the general rule that only employees of 501(c)(3) organizations are eligible to participate in a 403(b) plan.
- Ministers (chaplains) who meet both of the following requirements: (1) they are employed by organizations that are not section 501(c)(3) organizations, and (2) they function as ministers in their day-to-day professional responsibilities with their employers. A 403(b) plan generally is available only to employees of organizations that are exempt from tax under section 501(c)(3) of the tax code. This includes religious, charitable, and educational organizations (and some others) but does not include government agencies and secular businesses. As a result, ministers employed by the government or a secular business (e.g., as chaplains) were once ineligible to participate in 403(b) tax-sheltered annuities. The tax code was amended to permit ministers employed by an organization not described in section 501(c)(3) of the tax code to participate in a 403(b) plan so long as their duties consist of the exercise of ministry and they do not share "common religious bonds with their employers."

✿ **KEY POINT.** While the tax code permits self-employed ministers to participate in 403(b) plans, the same is not true for nonminister self-employed persons who perform services for churches.

EXAMPLE. Pastor H is employed as the senior pastor of a church, has always reported his income taxes as self-employed, and participates in the church's 403(b) program. Pastor H's participation in such a program is permitted by law.

EXAMPLE. Charles is an ordained minister who is a full-time self-employed itinerant evangelist. He is eligible to establish and contribute to a 403(b) plan. Charles will be treated as his own employer that is presumed to be an exempt organization eligible to participate in a 403(b) tax-sheltered annuity. In addition, he will use his earned income as his compensation for purposes of computing the limits on contributions.

EXAMPLE. L is an ordained minister employed as a chaplain by a state correctional facility. The correctional facility is not an exempt organization described in section 501(c)(3) of the tax code. L is allowed to participate in a 403(b) plan, since she is engaged in the exercise of her ministry while employed as a chaplain by the correctional facility.

EXAMPLE. A minister employed as a chaplain in the United States Army is an eligible employee, since his employer is not a section 501(c)(3) organization and he is employed as a minister.

EXAMPLE. M is an ordained minister who is temporarily working in a secular job as a salesman. In the past he has participated in a denominationally sponsored 403(b) plan. M cannot continue contributing to his annuity, since his present job does not constitute the exercise of ministry.

5. CONTRIBUTIONS

A 403(b) plan can be funded by the following contributions.

- **Elective deferrals.** These are contributions made under a salary reduction agreement. This agreement allows your employer to withhold money from your paycheck to be contributed directly into a 403(b) account for your benefit. Except for Roth contributions (see section E.10, below), you do not pay tax on these contributions until you withdraw them from the account. If your contributions are Roth contributions, you pay taxes on your contributions, but any qualified distributions from your Roth account are tax-free.
- **Nonelective contributions.** These are employer contributions that are not made under a salary reduction agreement. Nonelective contributions include matching contributions, discretionary contributions, and mandatory contributions from your employer. You do not pay tax on these contributions until you withdraw them from the account.
- **After-tax contributions.** These are contributions (that are not Roth contributions) you make with funds that you must include as income on your tax return. A salary payment on which income tax has been withheld is a source of these contributions. If your plan allows you to make after-tax contributions, they are not excluded from income, and you cannot deduct them on your tax return.
- **Combination.** A combination of any of the three contribution types listed above.

Determining maximum amount contributable (MAC)

Generally, for 2013, the MAC is the lesser of (1) the limit on annual additions, or (2) the limit on elective deferrals.

Limit on annual additions

The limit on annual additions is the limit on the total contributions that can be made to your 403(b) plan each year. For 2013 it is the lesser of $51,000 or 100 percent of includible compensation for your most recent year of service. *IRC 415(c).* The $51,000 amount is indexed for inflation in $1,000 increments. This limit is found in section 415(c) of the tax code and is sometimes called the "415(c) limit."

Includible compensation. Includible compensation is defined by the tax code as "the amount of compensation which is received from the employer . . . and which is includible in gross income . . . for the most recent period (ending not later than the close of the taxable year). . . . Such term does not include any amount contributed by the employer for an annuity contract to which this subsection applies." *IRC 403(b)(3).* Includible compensation also includes (1) elective deferrals (employer's contributions made on your behalf under a salary reduction agreement); (2) amounts contributed or deferred by your employer under a section 125 cafeteria plan; (3) wages for personal services earned with the employer that maintains the 403(b) plan; and (4) income otherwise excluded under the foreign earned income exclusion.

Housing allowances. Does the term "includible compensation" include a minister's housing allowance? This is an important question for ministers, since the answer will determine how much can be contributed to a 403(b) plan. If the housing allowance is treated as compensation, then ministers will be able to contribute larger amounts to a 403(b) plan. The tax code's definition of includible compensation (quoted in the preceding paragraph) includes any amount received from an employer "which is includible in gross income." Section 107 of the tax code specifies that a minister's housing allowance (or the annual rental value of a parsonage) is *not* included in the minister's gross income for income tax reporting purposes. Therefore, it would appear that the definition of includible compensation for purposes of computing the limit on annual additions to a 403(b) plan would *not* include the portion of a minister's housing allowance that is excludable from gross income, or the annual rental value of a parsonage. For many years the IRS website contained the following question and answer, which affirm this conclusion:

> **Question.** *I am an employee minister in a local church. Each year, my church permits $25,000 as a yearly tax-free housing allowance. I would like to use my yearly housing allowance as compensation to determine my annual contribution limits (to a 403(b) plan) under section 415(c) of the Internal Revenue Code. May I do so?*
>
> **Answer.** *No. For purposes of determining the limits on contributions under section 415(c) of the Internal Revenue Code, amounts paid to*

an employee minister, as a tax-free housing allowance, may not be treated as compensation pursuant to the definitions of compensation under section 1.415-2(d) of the income tax regulations.

EXAMPLE. Applying pre-2002 law, the IRS ruled that ministers' housing allowances are not "compensation" for purposes of computing the contribution limits to a 403(b) plan. The IRS noted that the general definition of "compensation" for purposes of section 415(c) includes "employee wages . . . and other amounts received for personal services actually rendered in the course of employment with the employer maintaining the plan to the extent that the amounts are includible in gross income." Section 107 of the tax code provides that the gross income of a minister does not include "the rental value of a home furnished to the minister as part of his compensation, or the rental allowance paid to the minister as part of his compensation, to the extent used by the minister to rent or provide a home." Therefore, under the general definition, a housing allowance is not included in compensation under section 415(c).

The IRS also concluded that housing allowances could not be included in compensation under two alternative definitions that applied prior to 2002. This ruling supports the conclusion that in computing the section 415 limit for 403(b) plans after 2001, the term "compensation" should not include a minister's housing allowance or the annual rental value of a parsonage. While the definition of "compensation" is slightly different after 2002, it continues to include employee income that is "includible in gross income," and this is the phrase that was construed by the IRS in this ruling. Therefore, pre-2002 interpretations of this phrase will be relevant in interpreting the identical language in 2002 and thereafter. *IRS Letter Ruling 200135045 (2001). See also IRS Letter Ruling 8416003.*

Limit on elective deferrals

The limit on elective deferrals is a limit on the amount of contributions that can be made to a 403(b) plan through a salary reduction agreement. The general limit on elective deferrals for 2013 is $17,500. It is indexed annually for inflation in $500 increments.

This limit applies to the total of all elective deferrals contributed (even if contributed by different employers) for the year on your behalf to section 401(k) plans, SIMPLE plans, SEP plans, and 403(b)

RETIREMENT SAVINGS CREDIT
(or "saver's credit")

If you make eligible contributions to certain eligible retirement plans or to an individual retirement arrangement (IRA), you may be eligible for a tax credit of up to $1,000 ($2,000 if filing jointly). The amount of the "saver's credit" you can get is generally based on the contributions you make and your credit rate. Refer to Publication 590 or the instructions for Form 8880 for more information. If you are eligible for the credit, your credit rate can be as low as 10 percent or as high as 50 percent, depending on your adjusted gross income. The lower your income, the higher the credit rate; your credit rate also depends on your filing status. These two factors will determine the maximum credit you may be allowed to take. You are not eligible for the credit if your adjusted gross income exceeds a certain amount.

The credit is available with respect to elective deferrals to a 401(k) plan, a 403(b) annuity, a SIMPLE or a simplified employee pension (SEP), contributions to a traditional or Roth IRA, and voluntary after-tax employee contributions to a 403(b) annuity or qualified retirement plan. The amount of the credit for 2013 is described in the following table.

ADJUSTED GROSS INCOME			
Joint Return	Heads of Household	Single Filers	Amount of Credit
$1 to $35,500	$1–28,625	$1–17,750	50 percent of eligible contributions up to $2,000 ($1,000 maximum credit)
$35,501 to $38,500	$28,626 to $28,875	$17,751 to 19,250	20 percent of eligible contributions up to $2,000 ($400 maximum credit)
$38,501 to $59,000	$28,876 to $44,250	$19,251 to $29,500	10 percent of eligible contributions up to $2,000 ($200 maximum credit)
Over $59,000	Over $44,250	Over $29,500	0 percent

*For married couples filing jointly, each spouse is eligible for the credit plans. If you defer more than the allowable amount for a tax year, you must include the excess in your gross income for that year.

Determining which limit applies in computing your MAC

Depending on the type of contributions made to your 403(b) plan in 2013, only one of the two limits described above may apply. If only elective deferrals (through salary reduction) were made to your 403(b) plan, then your MAC is the lesser of the limit on elective deferrals or the limit on annual additions. If only nonelective contributions (employer contributions not made under a salary reduction agreement) were made to your 403(b) plan, then your MAC will be the limit on annual additions. If both elective deferrals and nonelective deferrals were made to your 403(b) plan, you will need to figure both the limit on elective deferrals and the limit on annual additions. Your MAC is your limit on annual additions, but you need to compute the limit on elective deferrals to determine whether the amount contributed to your 403(b) plan is more than your allowable limit.

✦ **KEY POINT.** Computing your MAC can be a complex task. Worksheets in Chapter 9 of IRS Publication 571 can help. You can obtain a copy of this publication by calling the IRS at 1-800-TAX-FORM or by visiting the IRS website (irs.gov).

Special rules for ministers and church employees

Special rules apply to church employees in computing their MAC. A church employee is anyone who is an employee of a church or a convention or association of churches, including an employee of a tax-exempt organization controlled by or associated with a convention or association of churches. Consider the following special rules:

Employees of at least 15 years. If you have at least 15 years of service with a public school system, hospital, home health service agency, health and welfare service agency, church, or convention or association of churches (or associated organization), the limit on elective deferrals to your 403(b) plan is increased by the least of

- $3,000;
- $15,000, reduced by the sum of (1) the additional pre-tax elective deferrals made in prior years because of this rule plus (2) the aggregate amount of designated Roth contributions permitted for prior tax years because of this rule; or
- $5,000 times the number of your years of service for the organization, minus the total elective deferrals made by your employer on your behalf for earlier years.

All years of service by (1) a duly ordained, commissioned, or licensed minister of a church, or (2) a lay employee of a church, a convention or association of churches, and some church-controlled organizations, are considered as years of service for one employer. This means ministers and lay church employees can count their years of service with different churches or denominational agencies as years of service with the same employer.

✦ **KEY POINT.** If you qualify for the 15-year rule, your elective deferrals under this limit can be as high as $20,500 for 2013 ($26,000 with the age 50 catch-up).

Increased limit for church employees. Church employees can elect an increased amount for the limit on annual additions. Under this election, you can increase your limit on annual additions to $10,000 a year. Total contributions over your lifetime under this election cannot be more than $40,000. *IRC 415(c)(7)(A).*

Self-employed ministers. If you are a self-employed minister, you are treated as an employee of a tax-exempt organization that is a qualified employer. Your includible compensation is your net earnings from your ministry minus the contributions made to the retirement plan on your behalf and the deduction for one-half of the self-employment tax.

Foreign missionaries. Includible compensation is figured differently for foreign missionaries. If you are a foreign missionary, your includible compensation does not include contributions made by the church during the year to your 403(b) account. If you are a foreign missionary and your adjusted gross income is $17,000 or less, contributions to your 403(b) account will not be treated as exceeding the limit on annual additions if the contributions are not in excess of $3,000. You are a foreign missionary if you are either a layperson or a duly ordained, commissioned, or licensed minister of a church and you meet both of the following requirements: (1) you are an employee of a church or convention or association of churches; and (2) you are performing services for the church outside the United States.

Changes to years of service. Generally, only service with the employer who maintains your 403(b) account can be counted when figuring your limit on annual additions. Special rules apply to church employees and self-employed ministers. If you are a church employee, treat all of your years of service as an employee of a church or a convention or association of churches as years of service with one employer. If you are a self-employed minister, your years of service include full and partial years during which you were self-employed.

Catch-up contributions

The limit on elective deferrals under a 403(b) plan is increased for individuals who have attained age 50 by the end of the year. Additional contributions may be made by an individual who has attained age 50 before the end of the plan year and with respect to whom no other elective deferrals may otherwise be made to the plan for the year because of the application of any limitation of the tax code (e.g., the annual limit on elective deferrals) or of the plan.

The additional amount of elective contributions that may be made by an eligible individual participating in such a plan is the lesser of (1) the applicable dollar amount, or (2) the participant's compensation for the year reduced by any other elective deferrals of the participant for the year.

The applicable dollar amount for a 403(b) plan is $5,500 for 2013. Catch-up contributions are not subject to any other contribution limits and are not taken into account in applying other contribution limits.

> **EXAMPLE.** In 2013 Gwen is a church employee who is over 50 years of age and who is a participant in a 403(b) plan. Gwen's compensation for the year is $30,000. The maximum annual deferral limit (without regard to the catch-up provision) is $17,500. Under the terms of the plan, the maximum permitted deferral is 10 percent of compensation or, in Gwen's case, $3,000. Under the catch-up rule, Gwen can contribute up to $8,500 for the year ($3,000 under the normal operation of the plan, and an additional $5,500 catch-up contribution).

> ❖ **KEY POINT.** The generous catch-up contribution limits were scheduled to expire at the end of 2010. However, they were made permanent by the Pension Protection Act of 2006.

Excess contributions

If your actual contributions are greater than your MAC, you have an excess contribution. Excess contributions can result in additional taxes and penalties.

Reemployed veterans

Employees who temporarily are absent from work due to military service can make increased contributions to their employer's qualified retirement plan (including 403(b) tax-sheltered annuities) to make up for the contributions they missed while away from their job. Such "make-up contributions" will not affect the tax-favored status of the plan or the employee's account, even though they exceed the limits that otherwise would apply. Of course, make-up contributions cannot exceed the amount the employee would have been permitted to contribute had he or she not been absent from work.

Employers who do not allow employees who are away from work on military leave to make additional contributions to their retirement plan when they return may be in violation of the Uniformed Services Employment and Reemployment Rights Act (USERA).

Voluntary employee contributions

You cannot deduct voluntary employee contributions you make to your 403(b) plan.

Contributions and Social Security

Note the following rules.

Nonminister employees

Contributions to a 403(b) plan under a salary reduction agreement are considered wages for Social Security and Medicare taxes.

The employer must take into account the entire amount of these contributions for Social Security and Medicare tax purposes, whether they are wholly or partially excludable for income tax purposes. These wages are credited to the employee's Social Security account for benefit purposes. However, if the employer makes a contribution to a 403(b) plan that is not under a salary reduction agreement, that amount is not considered wages for Social Security tax purposes.

Religious exemption

A church or church-related organization may have chosen, for religious reasons, to exempt itself from the employer's share of Social Security and Medicare taxes by filing a timely Form 8274 with the IRS. If such an election is in effect, the wages of lay church employees are generally subject to self-employment tax.

Ministers

IRS Publication 517 instructs ministers, when computing self-employment taxes: "Do not include . . . contributions by your church to a tax-sheltered annuity plan set up for you, including any salary reduction contributions (elective deferrals), that are not included in your gross income." *See also Revenue Ruling 68-395 and Revenue Ruling 78-6.*

Further, section 1402(a)(8) of the tax code specifies that "an individual who is a duly ordained, commissioned, or licensed minister of a church . . . shall not include in net earnings from self-employment the rental value of any parsonage or any parsonage allowance (whether or not excludable under section 107) provided after the individual retires, *or any other retirement benefit received by such individual from a church plan after the individual retires*" (emphasis added).

Income tax withholding by employer

Your employer's contributions to your 403(b) plan, to the extent excludable from your gross income, are not subject to income tax withholding. However, any amount contributed to the plan in excess of the applicable limits, or used to purchase current life insurance protection, is subject to withholding (for nonminister church employees and ministers who have elected voluntary withholding).

6. REPORTING CONTRIBUTIONS ON YOUR TAX RETURN

Generally, you do not report contributions to your 403(b) account (except Roth contributions) on your tax return. Your employer will report contributions on your Form W-2. Elective deferrals will be shown in box 12 (code E), and the "retirement plan" box will be checked in box 13. Exceptions to this rule apply to self-employed ministers and chaplains:

- **Self-employed ministers.** If you are a self-employed minister (for income tax reporting purposes), you must report the total contributions as a deduction on your tax return. Deduct your contributions on line 28 of Form 1040.

- **Chaplains.** If you are a chaplain and your employer does not exclude contributions made to your 403(b) account from your earned income, you may be able to take a deduction for those contributions on your tax return. However, if your employer has agreed to exclude the contributions from your earned income, you will not be allowed a deduction on your tax return. If you can take a deduction, enter your contributions on line 36 of Form 1040. Write "403(b)" on the dotted line next to line 36.

If you participate in a 403(b) plan, your employer must report this participation by checking the "retirement plan" box in box 13 on the Form W-2 given to you and the IRS after the end of the year. Also, your employer must report in box 12 (using code E) of your Form W-2 your total elective deferrals, including any excess contributions to a 403(b) plan. Employers and plan administrators must report contributions in excess of the limits that apply. Form 1099-R includes boxes for reporting gross and taxable amounts of total distributions.

7. DISTRIBUTIONS

Generally, a distribution cannot be made from a 403(b) plan until the employee

- reaches age 59½;
- has a severance from employment;
- dies;
- becomes disabled; or
- in the case of salary reduction contributions, encounters financial hardship.

✿ **KEY POINT.** Distributions prior to age 59½ that do not satisfy one of the above exceptions are subject to an additional "tax on early distributions" of 10 percent multiplied by the amount of the distribution.

The term "hardship" is not defined in section 403(b) of the tax code. The same term is used in connection with premature distributions under a 401(k) plan (discussed later in this chapter), and in that context it is defined as a distribution that "is made on account of an immediate and heavy financial need of the employee and is necessary to satisfy the financial need. The determination of the existence of an immediate and heavy financial need and of the amount necessary to meet the need must be made in accordance with non-discriminatory and objective standards set forth in the plan." *Treas. Reg. 1.401(k)-1(d)(2)(i).* This definition probably will be relevant in construing the same term under section 403(b).

In most cases the payments you receive or that are made available to you under your 403(b) plan are taxable in full as ordinary income. In general, the same tax rules apply to distributions from 403(b) plans that apply to distributions from other retirement plans.

Tax on excess accumulation

To make sure most of your retirement benefits are paid to you during your lifetime rather than to your beneficiaries after your death, the payments you receive from a 403(b) plan must begin no later than the required beginning date, which is the later of

- the calendar year in which you reach age 70½ or
- the calendar year in which you retire from employment with the employer maintaining the plan.

The payments each year cannot be less than the "minimum required distribution" (defined below). If the actual distributions to you in any year are less than the minimum required distribution (RMD) for that year, you are subject to an additional tax. The tax equals 50 percent of the part of the required minimum distribution that was not distributed. This tax may be waived if you establish that the shortfall in distributions was due to reasonable error and that reasonable steps are being taken to remedy the shortfall. If you believe you qualify for this relief, you must file Form 5329 with the IRS and attach a letter of explanation.

However, your plan may require you to begin to receive distributions by April 1 of the year that follows the year in which you reach age 70½ even if you have not retired. If you reach age 70½ in 2013, you may be required to receive your first distribution by April 1, 2014. Your required distribution then must be made for 2014 by December 31, 2014.

You reach age 70½ on the date that is six calendar months after the date of your 70th birthday. For example, if your 70th birthday was on June 30, 2013, you reached age 70½ on December 30, 2013. If your 70th birthday was on July 1, 2013, you reached age 70½ on January 1, 2014.

Required minimum distributions

Required Minimum Distributions (RMDs) generally are minimum amounts that a 403(b) account owner must withdraw annually starting with the year that he or she reaches 70½ years of age or, if later, the year in which he or she retires.

An account owner must take the first RMD for the year in which he or she turns 70½. However, the first RMD payment can be delayed until April 1 of the year following the year in which he or she turns 70½. For all subsequent years, including the year in which the first RMD was paid by April 1, the account owner must take the RMD by December 31 of the year.

Generally, an RMD is calculated for each account by dividing the prior December 31 balance of that account by a life expectancy factor the IRS publishes in "Tables" in Publication 590. There are three tables:

(1) The Joint and Last Survivor Table is used by an account owner whose sole beneficiary of the account is his or her spouse and is more than 10 years younger than the account owner.

(2) The Uniform Lifetime Table is used by account owners whose spouse is not the sole beneficiary or whose spouse is not more than 10 years younger.

(3) The Single Life Expectancy Table is used by a beneficiary of an account.

If an account owner fails to withdraw an RMD, fails to withdraw the full amount of the RMD, or fails to withdraw the RMD by the applicable deadline, the amount not withdrawn is taxed at 50 percent. The account owner should file Form 5329, Additional Taxes on Qualified Plans (Including IRAs) and Other Tax-Favored Accounts, with his or her federal tax return for the year in which the full amount of the RMD was not taken.

8. ROLLOVERS

You can generally roll over, tax-free, all or any part of a distribution from a 403(b) plan to a traditional IRA or an eligible retirement plan (defined below) except for any nonqualifying distributions. The most you can roll over is the amount that, except for the rollover, would be taxable. The rollover must be completed by the 60th day following the day on which you receive the distribution. The IRS may waive the 60-day rollover period if the failure to waive such requirement would be against equity or good conscience, including cases of casualty, disaster, or other events beyond the reasonable control of the individual. To obtain a hardship exception, you must apply to the IRS for a waiver of the 60-day rollover requirement.

Contributions from a designated Roth account can only be rolled over to another Roth account or a Roth IRA.

You can roll over, tax-free, all or any part of a distribution from an eligible retirement plan to a 403(b) plan. Additionally, you can roll over, tax-free, all or any part of a distribution from a 403(b) plan to an eligible retirement plan, except for any nonqualifying distributions, described below. If a distribution includes both pre-tax contributions and after-tax contributions, the portion of the distribution that is rolled over is treated as consisting first of pre-tax amounts (contributions and earnings that would be includible in income if no rollover occurred). This means that if you roll over an amount that is at least as much as the pre-tax portion of the distribution, you do not have to include any of the distribution in income.

The following are considered eligible retirement plans: IRAs, Roth IRAs, qualified retirement plans, 403(b) plans, and eligible 457 plans. You cannot roll over, tax-free, any of the following nonqualifying distributions: minimum distributions (generally required to begin at age 70½), substantially equal payments over your life or life expectancy, substantially equal payments over the joint lives or life expectancies of your beneficiary and you, substantially equal payments for a period of 10 years or more, or hardship distributions.

9. FORM 5500

The instructions to the current IRS Form 5500 state that church plans not electing ERISA coverage under section 410(b) of the tax code are not required to file Form 5500. See the introduction to this chapter for a definition of *church plans*.

10. NONDISCRIMINATION RULES

Section 403(b) plans that include employee elective salary deferrals must satisfy a "universal availability" rule demonstrating that salary deferrals, including after-tax Roth deferrals, do not discriminate in favor of highly compensated employees (defined in Chapter 5, section I, in this text). This rule provides that if any employee is permitted to make elective salary deferrals to a 403(b) plan, then all employees, with limited optional exclusions, must be provided the same opportunity. *IRC 403(b)(1)(D) and 403(b)(12).*

The universal availability requirement does not apply to 403(b) plans of (1) a church; (2) a convention or association of churches; (3) an elementary or secondary school that is controlled, operated, or principally supported by a church or convention or association of churches; or (4) a qualified church-controlled organization. *IRC 403(b)(1)(D) and 403(b)(12)(B).* A qualified church-controlled organization is defined in section 3121(w)(3)(B) of the tax code as

> *any church-controlled tax-exempt organization described in section 501(c)(3), other than an organization which (i) offers goods, services, or facilities for sale, other than on an incidental basis, to the general public, other than goods, services or facilities which are sold at a nominal charge which is substantially less than the cost of providing such goods, services, or facilities; and (ii) normally receives more than 25 percent of its support from either (I) governmental sources, or (II) receipts from admissions, sales of merchandise, performance of services, or furnishing of facilities, in activities which are not unrelated trades or businesses, or both.*

Clearly, local churches, church denominations, and church-controlled elementary and secondary schools qualify as church-controlled organizations. The committee report on the Tax Reform Act of 1986, in construing the term "qualified church-controlled organization" in another context, noted that it included "the typical seminary, religious retreat center, or burial society, regardless of its funding sources, because it does not offer goods, services, or facilities for sale to the general public." The committee report also noted that the term "qualified church-controlled organization" includes *a church-run orphanage or old-age home, even if it is open to the general public, if not more than 25 percent of its support is derived from the receipts of admissions, sales of merchandise, performance of services, or furnishing of facilities (in other than unrelated trades or businesses) or from governmental sources. The committee specifically intends that the [term 'qualified church-controlled organization' will not include] church-run universities (other than religious seminaries) and hospitals if both conditions (i) and (ii) exist.*

Application of pre-ERISA nondiscrimination rules to church plans

❀**KEY POINT.** See the introduction to this chapter for a definition of *church plan*.

Church retirement plans are exempt from various requirements imposed by the Employee Retirement Income Security Act of 1974 (ERISA) on pension plans. For example, church plans are not subject to ERISA's vesting, coverage, and funding requirements. However, according to a comment in the conference committee's official report to the Small Business Job Protection Act of 1996, in some cases church plans will be "subject to provisions in effect before the enactment of ERISA," and under these rules, a church plan "cannot discriminate in favor of officers . . . or persons whose principal duties consist in supervising the work of other employees, or highly compensated employees."

What church plans are subject to the pre-ERISA nondiscrimination rules? The general rule is that *qualified church pension plans* under section 401(a) of the tax code must satisfy the pre-ERISA nondiscrimination rules. See section C in this chapter for a discussion of qualified pension plans.

The Act clarifies that church plans subject to these pre-ERISA nondiscrimination rules may not discriminate in favor of "highly compensated employees" as defined under the Act, and this single nondiscrimination rule replaces the pre-ERISA rule banning discrimination in favor of officers or persons whose principal duties consist in supervising the work of other employees (unless they also satisfy the definition of a highly compensated employee). The Act's definition of a highly compensated employee (for 2013) includes an employee who had compensation for the previous year in excess of $115,000 and, if an employer elects, was in the top 20 percent of employees by compensation.

11. ROTH ACCOUNTS AND 403(B) PLANS

Your 403(b) plan may allow you to contribute to a Roth contribution program. Under this program, you can designate all or a portion of your elective deferrals as Roth contributions. Elective deferrals designated as Roth contributions must be maintained in a separate Roth account. Contributions to a designated Roth account are not excluded from your gross income; however, qualified distributions from a Roth account are excluded from your gross income.

The maximum amount of contributions allowed under a Roth contribution program is your limit on elective deferrals, less elective deferrals not designated as Roth contributions.

A distribution from your designated Roth account can only be rolled over to another designated Roth account of yours or a Roth IRA of yours.

A qualified distribution is a distribution that is made after the non-exclusion period and

- when you are age 59½ or over,
- because you are disabled, or
- on or after the death of the plan participant.

A qualified distribution does not include a distribution of excess elective deferrals. Excess elective deferrals in a designated Roth account are treated in the same manner as excess deferrals in a non-Roth account. The nonexclusion period is the five-tax-year period beginning with the earlier of (1) the first tax year in which you made a designated Roth contribution to any Roth account under the same plan; or (2) if a rollover contribution was made to a designated Roth account from a designated Roth account previously established for you under another plan, the first tax year you made a designated Roth contribution to your previously established account.

➡ **TIP.** Ministers and lay church employees who currently are participating in a 403(b) plan should carefully consider whether they want to make designated Roth contributions. For many taxpayers the dual advantages of no taxes on gains or on distributions are compelling and outweigh the loss of any deduction for annual contributions to their account.

12. IRS REGULATIONS

In 2004 the IRS published proposed regulations that provided the first comprehensive guidance on the administration of 403(b) plans in 40 years. The IRS was prompted to act as a result of the massive noncompliance it uncovered in field audits of 403(b) plans. Following publication of the 2004 proposed regulations, comments were received and a public hearing was held. The regulations were adopted as final regulations in 2007. The final regulations took effect on January 1, 2009, for most tax-exempt organizations.

What is the relevance of the 403(b) regulations to churches? Section 403(b) retirement plans are perhaps the most common form of retirement plan for church employees, so it is essential for church leaders to be familiar with the application of the regulations to their 403(b) plan. Failure to comply with the regulations may result in adverse tax consequences.

The provisions in the final regulations of most relevance to churches are summarized below.

Written plan requirement

The final regulations require all 403(b) providers, including churches, to have a plan that, in both form and operation, satisfies the requirements of section 403(b) and the regulations. This means that a plan document must address several issues, including the following:

- employee eligibility,
- contribution limits,
- distributions,
- benefits,
- salary reductions,
- investments (fund providers available under the plan),
- loans,
- hardship withdrawals, and
- allocation of compliance responsibilities to employers and fund providers (vendors).

The final regulations note that a 403(b) plan is permitted to allocate to the employer or to one or more third parties (e.g., investment companies) the responsibility for compliance with section 403(b) and the regulations. Any such allocation must identify who is responsible for compliance with the requirements of section 403(b), including loans and hardship withdrawals. However, the final regulations assert that it is generally inappropriate to allocate these responsibilities to employees.

The final regulations permit the plan to incorporate by reference other documents (including salary-reduction agreements, contracts, and policies) which, as a result of such reference, would become part of the plan. As a result, a plan may include a wide variety of documents, but it is important for the employer adopting the plan to ensure that it does not conflict with other documents that are incorporated by reference. If a plan does incorporate other documents by reference, then, in the event of a conflict with another document, except in rare and unusual cases, the plan would govern.

Active and inactive vendors

Since one of the purposes of a written plan document is the allocation of compliance responsibilities between the employer and fund providers, it is important for the document to identify these parties. However, "frozen" vendors that have not received elective deferrals since January 1, 2005, do not have to be identified in the plan document. Frozen vendors that have received elective deferrals after January 1, 2005, generally must be accounted for in the plan document, pursuant to the following two options: First, the employer can direct the vendor to "freeze" employee accounts,

thereby cutting off access to loans and hardship distributions. Second, the employer can allow the vendor to continue making loans and hardship distributions to employees, but this will require an information-sharing agreement that requires the vendor to share data with the employer that will enable it to approve such transactions and monitor compliance with section 403(b).

Churches that offer a 403(b) plan to their employees should consult with an attorney to ensure full compliance with the final regulations. Churches that use a denominational plan should contact their denomination for assistance with compliance.

Nontaxable exchanges and transfers

The final regulations provide employees with two options for transferring funds out of an existing 403(b) account while the employee is still working for the same employer, without any of the funds being currently taxable: (1) contract exchanges (a change of investment within the same plan) and (2) fund transfers (a plan-to-plan transfer so that another employer plan receives the exchange).

1. Contract exchanges

The final regulations allow an exchange of one contract for another to constitute a nontaxable change of investment within the same plan, but only if certain conditions are satisfied in order to facilitate compliance with tax requirements. The IRS summary that accompanies the final regulations explains:

> *Specifically, the other contract must include distribution restrictions that are not less stringent than those imposed on the contract being exchanged and the employer must enter into an agreement with the issuer of the other contract under which the employer and the issuer will from time to time in the future provide each other with certain information. This includes information concerning the participant's employment and information that takes into account other section 403(b) contracts or qualified employer plans, such as whether a severance from employment has occurred for purposes of the distribution restrictions and whether the hardship withdrawal rules in the regulations are satisfied. Additional information that is required is information necessary for the resulting contract or any other contract to which contributions have been made by the employer to satisfy other tax requirements, such as whether a plan loan constitutes a deemed distribution under section 72(p).*

Clearly, churches that allow employees to invest their 403(b) contract with more than one authorized vendor will be incurring significant additional paperwork and administrative responsibilities. The same is true for any tax-exempt entity that offers multiple investment providers to its employees. An "information sharing agreement" (ISA) will need to be executed with each investment provider to ensure that it is sharing enough information with the employer to enable it to ensure compliance with section 403(b). To illustrate, some of the issues that each ISA must address include loans and hardship distributions to employees. In the past, employees could "self-certify" their eligibility for loans and hardship distributions. The final regulations prohibit this practice. The employer or plan administrator must approve each employee's loan or hardship distribution and ensure compliance with the law.

2. Plan-to-plan transfers.

Under the final regulations, plan-to-plan transfers are permitted if the participant whose assets are being transferred is an employee or former employee of the employer that maintains the receiving plan and certain additional requirements are met. However, the regulations prohibit a plan-to-plan transfer to a qualified plan, a plan under section 457(b), or any other type of plan that is not a section 403(b) plan. Similarly, a section 403(b) plan is not permitted to accept a transfer from a qualified plan, an eligible plan under section 457(b), or any other type of plan that is not a section 403(b) plan.

Special rules for church plans

✿ **KEY POINT.** See the introduction to this chapter for a definition of *church plan*.

The final regulations include a number of special rules for church plans. Under section 403(b)(9), a retirement income account for employees of a church-related organization is treated as an annuity contract for purposes of section 403(b). The regulations define a retirement income account as a defined contribution program established or maintained by a church-related organization under which (a) there is separate accounting for the retirement income account's interest in the underlying assets (namely, it must be possible at all times to determine the retirement income account's interest in the underlying assets and to distinguish that interest from any interest that is not part of the retirement income account); (b) investment performance is based on gains and losses on those assets; and (c) the assets held in the account cannot be used for or diverted to purposes other than for the exclusive benefit of plan participants or their beneficiaries. For this purpose, assets are treated as diverted to the employer if the employer borrows assets from the account.

A retirement income account must be maintained pursuant to a program which is a plan, and the plan document must state (or otherwise evidence in a similarly clear manner) the intent to constitute a retirement income account.

Effect of a failure to satisfy section 403(b)

Section 403(b)(5) of the tax code provides for all of the contracts purchased for an employee by an employer to be treated as a single contract for purposes of section 403(b). As a result, if a contract fails to satisfy any of the section 403(b) requirements, not only that contract but also any other contract purchased for that individual by that employer would fail to be a contract that qualifies for tax deferral under section 403(b).

If a contract includes any amount that fails to satisfy the requirements of the regulations, then, except for special rules relating to vesting conditions and excess contributions (under section 415 or section 402(g)), that contract and any other contract purchased for that individual by that employer does not constitute a section 403(b) contract.

In addition, if a contract is not established pursuant to a written plan, then the contract does not satisfy section 403(b). To illustrate, if an employer fails to have a written plan, any contract purchased by that employer would not be a section 403(b) contract. Similarly, if an employer is not an eligible employer for purposes of section 403(b), none of the contracts purchased by that employer is a section 403(b) contract.

Any operational failure, other than those described in this section, that is solely within a specific contract generally will not adversely affect the contracts issued to other employees that comply with section 403(b). For example, if an employee's elective deferrals under a contract, when aggregated with any other contract, plan, or arrangement of the employer for that employee during a calendar year, exceed the maximum deferral amount permitted under section 403(b), the failure would adversely affect the contracts issued to the employee by that employer but would not adversely affect any other employee's contracts.

Former employees

The final regulations permit employers to make nonelective employer contributions on behalf of a former employee through the fifth year following his or her termination of employment. Nonelective employer contributions for a former employee cannot exceed certain limitations spelled out in the regulations. However, note that nondiscrimination rules that apply to some church-affiliated entities prohibit nonelective employer contributions to discriminate in favor of highly compensated former employees (for 2013, those with annual income of $115,000 or more).

For further assistance

Churches that are affiliated with a denomination that offers a 403(b) plan should check with their denominational plan for compliance-related questions. Churches that offer 403(b) plans through one or more commercial mutual fund or investment firms should check with those vendors for assistance. In addition, the IRS website contains a section devoted to compliance with the regulations.

↪ **TIP.** The author of the regulations is IRS employee Bob Architect. Questions regarding the application of the regulations to your church can be directed to him at (202) 283-9634.

13. CONCLUSION

Tax-sheltered annuities involve complex rules. However, they provide attractive tax benefits, making them worthy of serious consideration. Persons wishing to pursue this subject further should consult with a CPA or tax attorney with experience in handling such arrangements, or with the staff of a denominational pension board.

c. QUALIFIED PENSION PLANS

Some churches and religious denominations have established qualified pension plans to finance retirement benefits for their employees. Such plans enjoy several tax benefits, including the following: (1) the employer gets an immediate tax deduction for contributions to the plan (this benefit is not relevant to tax-exempt churches and religious organizations); (2) fund earnings are tax-exempt; (3) employees are not taxed on their share of the fund until they receive distributions; (4) qualifying distributions can be rolled over tax-free to another plan or IRA; and (5) an employee can elect to have benefits payable to a designated beneficiary after his or her death without incurring gift tax liability.

These various tax benefits are available only if the plan is qualified. Qualification means that the plan satisfies the several conditions enumerated in section 401 of the tax code. Some of the more important requirements for qualification include the following: (1) the plan must be a written program that is communicated to all employees; (2) the plan must be for the exclusive benefit of employees and their beneficiaries; (3) the plan must be properly funded; (4) the plan must begin making payments no later than a specified date; (5) contributions and benefits may not exceed specified limitations; (6) certain employees must be permitted to participate in the plan; and (7) an employee's interest in the plan must vest within a specified time. Additional requirements apply to plans benefiting owner-employees and certain "top-heavy" plans (i.e., plans that disproportionately benefit highly compensated employees).

✸ **KEY POINT.** ERISA is a comprehensive pension law enacted by Congress in 1974 containing numerous provisions regulating pension plans (such as vesting, participation, and nondiscrimination).

✸ **KEY POINT.** See the introduction to this chapter for a definition of *church plan*.

Church plans are exempted from the minimum participation, vesting, funding, and nondiscrimination requirements of ERISA unless they elect to be covered. *IRC 410.* Such an election is irrevocable. Tax code section 414(e) defines the term "church plan" as a plan "maintained for its employees by a church." The income tax regulations clarify that, for the purpose of this definition, the term "church" includes "a religious organization if such organization (1) is an integral part of a church, and (2) is engaged in carrying out the functions of a church, whether as a civil law corporation or otherwise." *Treas. Reg. § 1.414(e)-1(e).*

Qualified pension plans can be either defined benefit or defined contribution plans. In a defined benefit plan, each employee is promised specified benefits upon retirement either for a term of years or for life, based upon such factors as years of service and amount of compensation earned. Employer contributions are actuarially calculated to provide the promised benefits and are not allocated to individual accounts for each employee. In a defined contribution plan, the employer does not promise specified benefits to the employees. Rather, the employer promises specified contributions on behalf of each employee. Such contributions must be allocated to individual accounts for each employee. Retirement benefits are whatever can be provided by the accumulated employer contributions plus any earnings.

The establishment of a qualified pension plan obviously is a complex task that should be handled by an attorney having experience with employee benefits. While IRS approval is not necessary, it ordinarily is advisable. Often employee pension plans are drafted using a master or prototype plan previously approved by the IRS.

The instructions for the current IRS Form 5500 state that church plans not electing ERISA coverage under tax code section 410(b) are not required to file Form 5500.

A plan cannot be a qualified plan if it provides for contributions or benefits in excess of specified amounts. A defined benefit plan cannot provide annual benefits that exceed the lesser of $200,000 (for 2012) or 100 percent of an employee's average compensation for his or her highest three years. Contributions (and any other additions) to a defined contribution plan must not exceed the lesser of $205,000 or 100 percent of an employee's compensation for 2013.

✸ **KEY POINT.** Congress enacted legislation in 1996 replacing any pre-ERISA nondiscrimination rules that still apply to churches with a simplified nondiscrimination rule. This legislation is addressed in section B of this chapter.

D. RETIREMENT DISTRIBUTIONS NOT PURSUANT TO A FORMAL PLAN

Occasionally a church that has made no provision for a minister's retirement will begin making payments to the minister after his or her retirement. For example, assume that Pastor T was employed by a church for 30 years preceding his retirement in 2013 and that the church never established a retirement program for him. The church board, embarrassed that no provision had ever been made for Pastor T's retirement, enacts a resolution in 2013 agreeing to pay Pastor T a monthly sum of $500 until the time of his death. What is the tax effect of such distributions? Are they tax-free gifts to Pastor T or taxable compensation for services rendered?

Prior to 1987 a number of courts ruled that payments to a retired minister constituted a tax-free gift to the minister rather than taxable compensation if all of the following conditions were satisfied: (1) the payments were made by a local church congregation with which the minister was associated; (2) the payments were not made in accordance with any enforceable agreement or established plan; (3) the payments were authorized at or about the time of the minister's retirement; (4) the minister did not perform any further services for the church and was not expected to do so; and (5) the minister was adequately compensated during his or her previous working relationship with the church. *See, e.g., Abernathy v. Commissioner, 211 F.2d 651 (D.C. Cir. 1954); Hershman v. Kavanagh, 210 F.2d 654 (6th Cir. 1954); Mutch v. Commissioner, 209 F.2d 390 (3rd Cir. 1954).*

The IRS concurred with these decisions in a 1955 ruling. *Revenue Ruling 55-422.*

Similarly, a federal appeals court ruled that an annual sum paid to a minister by a former church from which he had to resign because of illness was a gift and not taxable compensation. The minister had served the church for several years when he was stricken with a severe heart attack. After a prolonged recovery, including eight months in a hospital, the minister was advised by his physician to move from Pennsylvania to Florida. The church congregation, aware of the physician's advice and of the minister's lack of funds to make the move, adopted the following resolution:

> *Whereas the pastor of this church . . . has become incapacitated for further service as pastor and has requested the congregation to join in a petition . . . to dissolve the pastoral relation; and whereas the congregation, moved by affectionate regard for him and gratitude for his long and valued ministry among them, desire that he should continue to be associated with them in an honorary relation; now, therefore, be it resolved that . . . [the minister] be constituted pastor emeritus of this church with salary or honorarium amounting to two thousand dollars ($2,000) annually, payable in monthly installments, with no pastoral authority or duty, and that the session of this church be requested to report this action to the presbytery.*

The minister made no request to the congregation for such payments, had no knowledge that the resolution would be adopted, did not agree to render any services in exchange for the payments, and performed no pastoral services for the church following his resignation. Under these facts, the court concluded that the

payments to the minister were nontaxable gifts rather than taxable compensation. Noting that "a gift is none the less a gift because inspired by gratitude for past faithful service," the court observed that the payments were gifts because they were "bestowed only because of personal affection or regard or pity and not with the intent to pay the minister what was due him." *Schall v. Commissioner, 174 F.2d 893 (5th Cir. 1949).*

Another federal appeals court ruled that a $20,000 retirement payment by a church to its retiring minister was a tax-free gift rather than taxable compensation. *Stanton v. Commissioner, 287 F.2d 876 (2d Cir. 1961).*

For a full explanation of the continuing relevance of these cases, see Chapter 4, section B.3 (above).

E. HOUSING ALLOWANCES

✸ **KEY POINT.** Denominational pension plans can designate housing allowances for retired ministers if certain conditions are satisfied. This is a significant tax benefit and is one of the main advantages of denominational pension plans.

Are retired ministers eligible for a housing allowance? In 1989 the IRS announced that this is a question "under extensive study" and that it will "not issue rulings or determination letters on the question . . . until it resolves the issue through publication of a revenue ruling, revenue procedure, regulation, or otherwise." *Revenue Procedure 89-54.*

In 2012 the IRS repeated that the issue of "whether amounts distributed to a retired minister from a pension or annuity plan should be excludable from the minister's gross income as a parsonage allowance" is "an area under extensive study in which rulings or determination letters will not be issued until the Service resolves the issue through publication of a revenue ruling, revenue procedure, regulations, or otherwise." *Revenue Procedure 2012-3.*

Several years of "extensive study" have failed to produce the promised clarification. In the meantime, consider the following.

1. INCOME TAX REGULATIONS

Section 1.107-1(b)

Section 1.107-1(b) of the income tax regulations specifies that ministers may exclude from their taxable income (for federal income tax reporting purposes) that portion of their compensation that is designated as a housing allowance "pursuant to official action taken *by the employing church or other qualified organization* before the payment is made" (emphasis added).

Revenue Ruling 62-117

In 1962 the IRS ruled that a resolution of the executive committee of a national religious denomination could not effectively designate a portion of the salaries of ministers of local congregations as a housing allowance where each local congregation employed and compensated its own minister. The IRS concluded that the national church was not an "employing church or other qualified organization" eligible to designate a housing allowance for local ministers, since local congregations were independent of the national church as to policy and conduct of their local affairs, and ministers were hired and paid by the local congregations. Accordingly, "each congregation was the 'employing church' and only action taken by the individual church could effectively designate a portion of its minister's salary as a [housing allowance]." The IRS conceded that the national church could designate housing allowances for ministers who were employees of the national church.

Revenue Ruling 63-156

The IRS addressed the question of whether a retired minister of the gospel could exclude a housing allowance furnished to him "pursuant to official action taken by the employing qualified organization in recognition of his past services which were the duties of a minister of the gospel in churches of his denomination." The IRS concluded that "the rental allowance paid to him as part of his compensation for past services is excludable . . . to the extent used by him for expenses directly related to providing a home."

Revenue Ruling 72-249

The IRS addressed the question of whether the widow of a retired minister could exclude as a rental allowance amounts she receives from her deceased husband's church. Prior to his retirement and death, the husband was a minister of the gospel and pastor of a church. Shortly before he retired, in recognition of his years of past service, the church, through official action of its governing body, authorized the payment of a specific amount to be paid each month upon retirement, for so long as he lived, with survivor benefits for his wife. The authorization designated a portion of the payment as a rental allowance. The wife was not a minister of the gospel, and she did not perform any services for the church.

The IRS concluded that "until his death, and to the extent used to provide a home, the rental allowance paid to the retired minister was excludable from his gross income since it was paid as part of his compensation for past services and it was paid pursuant to official action of his church. However, the rental allowance exclusion does not apply to amounts paid to his widow since it does not represent compensation for services performed by her as a minister of the gospel."

✿ **KEY POINT.** This ruling suggests that local churches can designate housing allowances out of retirement distributions paid to a retired minister under a church-sponsored plan.

Revenue Ruling 75-22

In 1975 the IRS addressed the question of whether the board of a denominational pension fund can designate a portion of a retired minister's pension distributions as a housing allowance. Could the pension board be deemed to be an "employing church or other qualified organization" eligible to designate housing allowances for retired ministers? The IRS concluded that it was. In reaching its decision, the IRS noted the following factors:

- The general convention of a national denomination (consisting of representatives from affiliated churches) established a pension fund for retired ministers.
- Pursuant to its bylaws and regulations, the general convention enacted a resolution creating a clergy pension plan for all its retired clergy, compensating them for past services to its local churches or to the denomination.
- The resolution specified that the fund was to be governed by a board of trustees elected by the general convention.
- The trustees were empowered to establish such rules and regulations as were necessary to implement the purpose of the fund.
- The trustees were the sole authority of the denomination's retirement program for its ministers.
- The trustees prescribed the eligibility requirements necessary to receive a pension.
- The trustees set the amount of the pension and the amount of the monthly assessment each local church was required to contribute to maintain the fund.
- Neither the individual minister nor the local church could intervene in this process.
- The trustees designated a percentage of the pension paid to retired ministers as a rental allowance.
- Retired ministers have severed their relationship with the local church and are reliant upon the fund for their pension.

Based on these factors, the IRS concluded that the pension board met the requirement of being an "employing church":

> *The fund was created by the general convention and specifically authorized by the formal actions of representatives of the local churches to make all determinations regarding the pensions paid to retired ministers compensating them for past services to the local churches of the denomination or to the denomination.* The trustees of the fund are, therefore, deemed to be acting on behalf of the local churches in matters affecting the unified pension system in compensating retired ministers for such past services. *[Emphasis added.]*

The IRS noted that the facts in this case were distinguishable from those in Revenue Ruling 62-117 (summarized above) "in that the minister, effective with his retirement, has severed his relationship with the local church and is reliant upon the fund for his pension."

IRS Letter Ruling 7734028

The IRS addressed the question of whether the financial board of a denomination's pension fund could designate 40 percent of pensions paid to retired ministers as a housing allowance. The IRS concluded:

We feel that the facts in your case are similar to those presented in Revenue Ruling 75-22. In your situation, the Conference (or the Synod) is the sole authority in the area of retired ministers' pensions. It appears from the information furnished that the local church organizations have no direct control over the amount a retired minister will receive as a pension. Although the exact amount contributed by the local church organization is not specifically prescribed, each participating organization must contribute no less than the specific percentage. It may be stated that, pursuant to the authorization creating the Synod and the Conference, its Constitution and Bylaws, the participating church organizations have appointed the Synod and the Conference to act on their behalf, as their agent, in matters pertaining to the pensions of retired ministers. Accordingly, we conclude that when the Synod or the Conference designates a portion of a retired minister's pension as a rental allowance, it will be considered that the local church or church organization that employed the minister made such designation.

❖ **KEY POINT.** The IRS has issued audit guidelines for its agents to follow when auditing ministers. The guidelines state that the "trustees of a minister's retirement plan may designate a portion of each pension distribution as a parsonage allowance excludable under Code section 107."

Conclusion

The availability of a housing allowance exclusion for denominationally sponsored pension plans has been an attractive benefit for many retired ministers. In many instances retired ministers are able to exclude some or all of their pension income by having the pension plan designate a portion of their income as a housing allowance.

Until further guidance is issued, retired ministers and denominational pension plans may continue to rely on the 1975 IRS ruling (its most recent official guidance) in evaluating whether the designation of housing allowances by denominational pension boards is appropriate.

EXAMPLE. Pastor B was minister of First Church at the time of her retirement in 2013. She had been employed by First Church for 20 years and, prior to coming to First Church, had been employed as a minister in three other churches, all of which were affiliated with Pastor B's denomination. The denomination operates a qualified pension plan for its ministers, and Pastor B was a participant in the plan for the last several years of her active ministry. The plan was designed to compensate retired ministers for their service to local churches, and it is characterized by the same factors as described in Revenue Ruling 75-22. The denomination may declare a portion

of Pastor B's retirement income as a housing allowance, and Pastor B can exclude her actual expenses in owning or providing a home to the extent that they do not exceed the designated allowance or, if Pastor B owns her home, the fair rental value of the home plus the cost of utilities. See Chapter 6 for further details.

2. THE CLERGY HOUSING ALLOWANCE CLARIFICATION ACT OF 2002

The Clergy Housing Allowance Clarification Act of 2002 directly impacts the designation of housing allowances for retired ministers. The Act amended section 107 of the tax code to limit the amount of a housing allowance that is nontaxable. As amended, section 107 specifies that a housing allowance provided to ministers who own their homes is nontaxable (in computing federal income taxes) only to the extent that it does not exceed the lesser of actual housing expenses or the fair rental value of the home (furnished, plus utilities).

Some ministers have accumulated significant amounts in their pension or retirement account, and they may elect a lump-sum distribution to pay for a large down payment or the entire purchase price of a new home, or to pay off a mortgage loan on an existing home. Consider the following example.

EXAMPLE. Pastor T is a recently retired pastor who has accumulated $200,000 in his pension account. He builds a new home costing $200,000, and in 2013 he asks the pension board to distribute the entire balance in his pension account as a lump-sum distribution. He further requests that the entire distribution be designated as a housing allowance. His objective is to pay for the entire cost of his new home with tax-free dollars. Assume that the annual fair rental value of the home (furnished, plus utilities) is $25,000. The $200,000 housing allowance is nontaxable only to the extent that it does not exceed either actual housing expenses or the fair rental value of the home (furnished, plus utilities). Since the lower of these two amounts is $25,000, Pastor T's nontaxable housing allowance is limited to this amount. This means that the excess housing allowance of $175,000 must be reported as taxable income by Pastor T in 2013. This will push him into a higher tax bracket and will result in a significant tax liability.

One additional concern is associated with large lump-sum distributions from church pension plans. If a housing allowance (combined with any other church income that a pastor may receive from a church) is excessive or unreasonable in amount, the IRS may assess intermediate sanctions against the pastor. Intermediate sanctions are excise taxes that the IRS can assess against any "disqualified person" who is involved in an excess benefit transaction. Disqualified persons include officers and directors and their relatives. These excise taxes are substantial. They begin at 25 percent of the amount of compensation the IRS deems to be excessive. If the excess is not returned to the church before the 25 percent tax is assessed, the pastor faces an additional tax of 200 percent of the amount of the excess. Intermediate sanctions and the related issue of inurement and its impact on a church's tax-exempt status are addressed fully in Chapter 4, sections A.1 and A.3.

❖ **KEY POINT.** Church pension board members who approve an excess benefit transaction also face liability (collectively, up to $20,000).

3. LOCAL CHURCH DESIGNATION OF HOUSING ALLOWANCES FOR RETIRED MINISTERS

Some local churches establish their own retirement programs for retired ministers, apart from a denominational plan. In some cases these churches are not affiliated with a denomination, and in others they simply choose not to participate in a denomination-sponsored plan. Can such churches designate a portion of the retirement distributions paid to retired ministers as a housing allowance? The answer would appear to be yes, based on the following precedent:

Revenue Ruling 72-249
In Revenue Ruling 72-249 (summarized above), the IRS concluded that a local church could designate a portion of the retirement distributions it paid to a retired minister as a housing allowance.

Revenue Ruling 75-22
In Revenue Ruling 75-22 the IRS concluded that a denominational pension fund could designate housing allowances out of the distributions paid to retired ministers, since

> [t]he fund was created by the general convention and specifically authorized by the formal actions of representatives of the local churches to make all determinations regarding the pensions paid to retired ministers compensating them for past services to the local churches of the denomination or to the denomination. The trustees of the fund are, therefore, deemed to be acting on behalf of the local churches in matters affecting the unified pension system in compensating retired ministers for such past services. [Emphasis added.]

The denominational pension plan could designate housing allowances because it was acting on behalf of local churches. The implication here is that local churches have the authority to designate housing allowances if they maintain a retirement plan.

IRS Letter Ruling 7734028
In IRS Letter Ruling 7734028, the IRS reached the same result as in Revenue Ruling 75-22:

> It may be stated that, pursuant to the authorization creating the Synod and the Conference, its Constitution and Bylaws, the participating church organizations have appointed the Synod and the Conference to act on their behalf, as their agent, in matters pertaining to the pensions of retired ministers. Accordingly, we conclude that when the Synod or the Conference designates a portion of a retired minister's pension as a rental allowance, it will be considered that the local church or church organization that employed the minister made such designation.

Again, the implication is that local churches can designate housing allowances with regard to distributions made from their own retirement programs.

EXAMPLE. A local church congregation decided that cash should be set aside annually, as the church council deemed appropriate, to provide funding for housing for its senior pastor upon his retirement. The amounts allocated to the fund were deposited in a separate account in the church's name. The funds in that account were assets of the church, and the pastor had no access to them prior to distribution. The church council determined that the total amount in the fund at the date of the pastor's retirement would be used to provide him with retirement housing. The council planned to designate amounts set aside in the fund for the pastor's retirement housing as a housing allowance after his retirement. The IRS ruled that "amounts paid by the church to the pastor as a rental allowance after his retirement, which are designated as rental allowances pursuant to official action taken by the church council in advance of such payment, are excludable from the gross income of the pastor" to the extent they are used for housing expenses and do exceed the fair rental value of the home. *IRS Private Letter Ruling 8344062.*

❖ **KEY POINT.** Housing allowances paid to retired ministers by church or denominational pension plans are not subject to self-employment tax.

4. SECTION 403(b)(7) CUSTODIAL ACCOUNTS

One of the most popular retirement plans for church employees is the 403(b) plan (sometimes called a tax-sheltered annuity). Such plans permit employees of churches and other public charities to make nontaxable contributions to their 403(b) account up to the allowable limits. In addition, earnings and gains on 403(b) accounts are tax-deferred, meaning that they are not taxed until distributed.

When section 403(b) accounts were first introduced in 1958, the only investment option available to employees was an annuity (hence the name "tax-sheltered annuity"). In 1974 Congress added section 403(b)(7) to the tax code. This section allows employees of churches and other charities to invest their 403(b) account with a mutual-fund company. These types of 403(b) plans are called 403(b)(7) accounts or custodial accounts. Then, in 1982, Congress added section 403(b)(9) to the tax code, which recognizes retirement income accounts of churches as yet another kind of 403(b) plan. Such accounts may be invested in annuities or mutual funds, and they usually are. But they are not limited to these investments.

Church employees whose employing church did not maintain a 403(b) plan could establish such a plan directly with an insurance company (tax-sheltered annuity) or mutual fund company (403(b)(7) custodial account). In addition, up until 2009, church employees whose employing church had established a 403(b) retirement income account could transfer their 403(b) account to an outside vendor (such as a mutual-fund company) if they were not satisfied with whatever investment option was provided by their employing church, in what was called a "90-24 exchange." IRS regulations that took effect on January 1, 2009, no longer permit such exchanges. Now church employees must choose an investment option authorized by their employing church. Further, the regulations impose burdensome reporting and compliance requirements on churches that allow multiple investment providers, so most churches and other charities that maintain 403(b) plans for their employees are consolidating the investment options. Many are only recognizing a single provider. In the case of churches that are affiliated with a denomination, the single provider typically is a denominational pension plan. This will make 403(b)(7) custodial accounts less common. However, they are still available to church employees whose employing church has not established a retirement plan. Such employees can go directly to a mutual fund company and establish their own 403(b)(7) custodial account.

Churches and denominational pension plans that have established retirement income accounts for their employees can designate some or all of a retired minister's account distributions as a housing allowance so long as the requirements for a valid housing allowance are met (see chapter 6). But what about church employees who have established a 403(b)(7) custodial account directly with a mutual fund company? Are they eligible for a housing allowance, and if so, who designates it? The mutual fund company? Their former employing church? Their denomination?

The income tax regulations specify that a housing allowance must be designated by a minister's "employing church or other qualified organization before the payment is made." Obviously, retired ministers no longer have an employing church, so who can designate a housing allowance for them? The IRS has ruled that a denominational pension plan can designate some or all of a retired minister's retirement distributions under a plan as a housing allowance if several conditions are satisfied (see Revenue Ruling 75-22, and IRS Letter Ruling 7734028, addressed earlier in this chapter).

But what about ministers who have invested in a 403(b)(7) custodial account with a mutual-fund company without any participation by their church other than reducing their compensation by a specified amount and remitting it to the mutual-fund company? There is no question that these ministers are *eligible* for a housing

allowance, assuming they are credentialed ministers and the 403(b)(7) account was funded with compensation they performed in the exercise of ministry. The question is whether a housing allowance can be *designated* by their "employing church or other qualified organization," as required by the regulations. Neither the IRS nor any court has addressed this issue directly, so no definitive guidance exists as it does for retired ministers who have invested in a denominational retirement plan. Consider these three possibilities:

(1) There is no "employing church or other qualified organization" that can designate a housing allowance. So, while these ministers are eligible for a housing allowance, there is no employing church or other qualified organization that can designate one for them.
(2) The last employing church of these retired ministers can designate some or all of the distributions from their 403(b)(7) account as a housing allowance. But there is no definitive basis for this option.
(3) The mutual fund company that is the investment provider for a retired minister's 403(b)(7) account is an "other qualified organization" that can designate the housing allowance. Note that the term "other qualified organization" has rarely been defined by either the IRS or the courts.

The best attempt to define the term "other qualified organization" was by the Tax Court in a 1981 decision. *Boyd v. Commissioner, 42 T.C.M. 1136 (1981).* An ordained minister was employed as a chaplain by a municipal police department. The police department's chaplain program was established through its joint efforts with a local federation of churches. The minister claimed that amounts designated by the federation as a housing allowance were excludable from his gross income. The IRS maintained that because the minister was employed by the city, and not by the federation, the city was the only "other qualified organization" eligible to designate a housing allowance; and since it failed to do so, the minister could not claim a housing allowance exclusion.

The Tax Court reversed the IRS determination and ruled that the minister was entitled to a housing allowance. It noted that as a police chaplain, the minister was under the direct supervision of the chief of police. However, the federation retained supervision over his ecclesiastical performance and maintained day-to-day contact with him and other chaplains. The federation also was involved in the operation of the police chaplaincy program. If a problem arose concerning a police chaplain, a police-department official would usually contact the federation to resolve the problem. When a vacancy occurred for a chaplain, the federation assumed primary responsibility for finding a qualified person to fill the vacancy.

The federation annually designated a specific amount of the minister's salary, in advance, as a housing allowance even though his salary was paid by the city. The city neither provided him with a home nor designated any portion of his salary as a housing allowance.

The Tax Court concluded that the federation was an "other qualified organization" within the meaning of section 1.107-1(b) of the regulations and that its designation of a portion of the minister's salary as a housing allowance was valid. The court based its decision on the "constant and detailed involvement of the federation" in the city's police chaplaincy program. The IRS later acquiesced in the Tax Court's ruling on the ground that the federation's responsibilities toward the chaplaincy program were similar to those of an employer and that the federation was closely involved with the police department in its employer-employee relationship with the ministers.

Could a mutual-fund company that served merely as an investment provider for a minister pursuant to a 403(b)(7) custodial account be considered an "other qualified organization" capable of designating a housing allowance? It would appear doubtful, based on this Tax Court ruling.

Retired ministers who have participated in a 403(b)(7) custodial account with a mutual fund company should consult with a competent tax professional in assessing their eligibility for a housing allowance and identifying the entity that can designate the allowance. Unfortunately, the IRS has announced that it will not issue letter rulings on this question, so no definitive guidance is possible.

5. SPOUSES OF DECEASED MINISTERS

The IRS ruled that a church pension plan can designate housing allowances for retired ministers, but it cannot designate housing allowances for the surviving spouses of deceased ministers unless (1) they are active or retired ministers, and (2) the housing allowance is designated out of income from a retirement account that was funded from compensation earned by the spouse for the performance of ministerial services. *Revenue Ruling 72-249, IRS Private Letter Ruling 8404101.*

For a more complete analysis of this issue, see Chapter 3, section D, of this text.

6. SELF-EMPLOYMENT TAX

The tax code specifies that self-employment tax does *not* apply to "the rental value of any parsonage or any parsonage allowance (whether or not excludable under section 107) provided after the individual retires, or any other retirement benefit received by such individual from a church plan . . . after the individual retires." *IRC 1402(a)(8).* Five things should be noted about this section of the tax code:

- The portion of a retired minister's retirement distributions designated as a housing allowance are not subject to self-employment taxes.
- The fair rental value of a parsonage provided a retired minister is not subject to self-employment taxes.

- "Any other retirement benefits" paid by a church plan to a retired minister are not subject to self-employment taxes.
- Section 1402(a)(8) of the tax code (quoted above) suggests that the exclusion from self-employment taxes of a housing allowance paid to a retired minister, or the fair rental value of a parsonage provided to a retired minister, only applies if these benefits are provided by a church retirement plan.
- Section 1402(a)(8) specifies that the exclusion from self-employment tax of a housing allowance paid to a retired minister (and the fair rental value of a parsonage provided to a retired minister) applies "whether or not excludable under section 107." This is an interesting statement. Section 107 is the provision in the tax code that excludes housing allowances and the fair rental value of parsonages from federal income tax. Presumably, retired ministers can exclude housing allowances and the fair rental value of a parsonage in computing self-employment tax even though they could not exclude these items in computing federal income taxes. The meaning of this provision is not clear. In most cases a housing allowance is not available under section 107 in computing income taxes because (1) a church failed to designate the allowance in advance, or (2) the minister has little, if any, actual housing expenses. Are church retirement plans able to retroactively designate housing allowances for retired ministers? Can they designate housing allowances in excess of a retired minister's actual housing expenses (or the fair rental value of a minister's home)? Section 1402(a)(8) suggests that the answer to these questions is yes. However, this result is so extraordinary that church retirement plans and ministers should not rely upon it without the advice of legal counsel or until clarification is provided by the IRS or the courts.

EXAMPLE. In 2013 Pastor G retires from many years of ministry. He has participated in a church retirement plan that begins making monthly distributions to him in 2013, some of which are designated as a housing allowance by action of the church plan. Retirement distributions total $9,000 for 2013, of which $5,000 was designated as a housing allowance. Pastor G will not pay self-employment tax on the housing allowance ($5,000) or on the balance of his retirement distributions ($4,000).

EXAMPLE. Pastor T retires from many years of ministry. She is allowed to reside in a church parsonage without any rental charge. Pastor T does not pay self-employment taxes on the fair rental value of the parsonage.

❖**KEY POINT.** Church and denominational retirement plans should inform retired ministers that (1) any portion of their retirement distributions designated in advance by the plan as a housing allowance is not subject to self-employment taxes; and (2) if they are permitted to reside in a parsonage (without charge) following their retirement, the annual rental value of the parsonage is not subject to self-employment taxes.

11 CHURCH REPORTING REQUIREMENTS

Everyone must submit himself to the governing authorities, for there is no authority except that which God has established. The authorities that exist have been established by God. . . . Therefore, it is necessary to submit to the authorities, not only because of possible punishment but also because of conscience.

Romans 13:1, 5

CHAPTER HIGHLIGHTS

- ■ ***Application to churches.*** Federal law (and many states) requires churches to comply with several payroll tax reporting obligations. Almost every church will be subject to at least some of these rules.

- ■ ***Penalties.*** Church leaders must take these rules seriously, since penalties are assessed for noncompliance. For example, church officers may be personally liable for a penalty equal to the amount of payroll taxes that were not withheld or deposited. It is essential for church leaders to understand these rules.

- ■ ***Churches not exempt.*** The courts have rejected the argument that the application of the payroll tax reporting rules to churches violates the constitutional guaranty of religious freedom.

- ■ ***Ministers considered self-employed for Social Security.*** Ministers are always self-employed for Social Security with respect to their ministerial services, and accordingly they pay the self-employment tax rather than the employee's share of FICA taxes—even if they report their federal income taxes as employees. It is incorrect for churches to treat ministers as employees for Social Security and to withhold the employee's share of FICA taxes from their wages.

- ■ ***Clergy compensation not subject to withholding rules.*** Clergy compensation is exempt from federal income tax withholding, whether clergy report their income taxes as employees or as self-employed.

- ■ ***Voluntary withholding.*** Ministers who report their federal income taxes as employees may elect voluntary withholding. Under such an arrangement, the church withholds income taxes from a minister's wages as if he or she were subject to income tax withholding. Such an arrangement also may take into account the minister's self-employment taxes.

- ■ ***Exemption of some churches from FICA.*** Federal law allowed churches that had nonminister employees as of July of 1984 to exempt themselves from the employer's share of FICA taxes by filing a Form 8274 with the IRS by October 30, 1984. Many churches did so. The effect of such an exemption is to treat all nonminister church employees as self-employed for Social Security. Such employees must pay the self-employment tax (just like ministers).

- ■ ***Ten payroll reporting requirements for churches.*** The more common payroll tax reporting requirements that apply to churches include the following:

  (1) Obtain an employer identification number.
  (2) Determine whether each worker is an employee or self-employed, and obtain each worker's Social Security number.
  (3) Obtain a completed Form W-4 (withholding allowance certificate) from each employee.
  (4) Compute employee wages (including many fringe benefits and other taxable items).
  (5) Determine the amount of federal income taxes to withhold from each employee's wages from tables published in IRS Circular E (Publication 15).
  (6) Withhold FICA taxes from employee wages (unless the church filed a timely exemption from the employer's share of FICA taxes, in which case nonminister employees are treated as self-employed for Social Security).
  (7) Deposit withheld taxes (both income taxes and employees' share of FICA taxes) plus the employer's share of FICA taxes by electronic funds transfer using the Electronic Federal Tax Payment System (EFTPS). If you do not want to use EFTPS, you can arrange for your tax professional, financial institution, payroll service, or other trusted third party to make deposits on your behalf.
  (8) File Form 941 (employer's tax return) with the IRS quarterly if the church has any employees who are paid wages or whose wages are subject to tax withholding.
  (9) Issue a Form W-2 to every employee before February 1 of the following year (and send copies of all W-2s to the Social Security Administration before March 1 of the following year with a Form W-3 transmittal form).
  (10) Issue a Form 1099-MISC to any nonemployee worker (who was paid $600 or more) before February 1 of the following year (and send copies to the IRS before March 1 of the following year with a 1096 transmittal form).

- ■ ***Comprehensive examples.*** The payroll tax requirements are illustrated with comprehensive examples (including completed forms) in this chapter.

INTRODUCTION

While churches are exempt from federal income taxes if they satisfy the requirements for exemption in section 501(c)(3) of the tax code, they may be subject to one or more of the following taxes: (1) the employer's share of Social Security (FICA) taxes payable on the wages of nonminister employees; (2) the tax on unrelated business taxable income; (3) state sales tax; (4) property tax on property that is not used exclusively for exempt purposes; and (5) state unemployment taxes.

In addition, many churches are subject to one or more federal reporting requirements, including the following:

- The withholding of federal income taxes and Social Security (FICA) taxes from the wages of nonminister employees, and the reporting of withheld taxes to the IRS by filing a quarterly Form 941.
- Providing each employee with a wage and tax statement (Form W-2) each year.
- Providing each self-employed person (receiving compensation of $600 or more) with an annual statement of nonemployee compensation (Form 1099-MISC).
- Providing each person to whom the church paid interest of $600 or more during the year a Form 1099-INT (a $10 rule applies in some cases).
- Submitting a Form W-3 to the Social Security Administration each year (transmitting copies of all Forms W-2 distributed to employees).
- Submitting a Form 1096 (summary of Forms 1099-MISC) to the IRS each year.
- Completing Part V, Section C, of Form 4562 if the church provides ministers or other employees with a car.
- Filing an annual unrelated business income tax return (Form 990-T) if the church earns unrelated business taxable income.
- Submitting a donee information return (Form 8282) to the IRS if donated property valued by the donor in excess of $5,000 is disposed of within three years of the date of contribution.
- Signing Section B, Part IV, of the qualified appraisal summary (Form 8283) that must be attached to the tax return of a donor who claims a charitable contribution deduction of more than $5,000 for a gift of noncash property to a church.
- Submitting to the IRS each year a certificate of racial nondiscrimination if the church operates a preschool, elementary or secondary school, or college (Form 5578).
- Issuing a completed Form 1098-C to donors who contribute a vehicle to the church that is valued by the donor at more than $500 (a copy of this form must also be filed with the IRS).

Other federal tax returns and reports of relevance to churches and religious organizations include the application for recognition of tax-exempt status (Form 1023), the annual information return (Form 990), and the election to waive Social Security participation (Form 8274). All of these forms and reporting requirements are discussed below.

These are not the only reporting requirements that apply to churches and religious organizations. But the reporting requirements addressed in this chapter represent the most common federal reporting requirements for churches.

A. PAYROLL TAX PROCEDURES FOR 2013

1. WHY CHURCH LEADERS SHOULD TAKE SERIOUSLY THE PAYROLL TAX REPORTING RULES

✿ **KEY POINT.** Federal law requires churches to comply with several payroll tax reporting obligations. Almost every church will be subject to at least some of these rules. Many states have similar provisions.

✿ **KEY POINT.** Church leaders must take these rules seriously, since penalties are assessed for noncompliance. For example, church officers may be personally liable for a penalty equal to the amount of payroll taxes that are not withheld or deposited. It is essential for church leaders to understand these rules.

Without question, the most significant federal reporting obligation of most churches is the withholding and reporting of employee income taxes and Social Security taxes. These requirements apply, in whole or in part, to almost every church. Yet many churches do not comply with them because of unfamiliarity. This can trigger one or more of the penalties summarized in Table 11-1.

Section 6672

One of the most serious penalties is found in section 6672 of the tax code. This section specifies that "any person required to collect, truthfully account for, and pay over any [income tax or FICA tax] who willfully fails to collect such tax, or truthfully account for and pay over such tax, or willfully attempts in any manner to evade or defeat any such tax or the payment thereof, shall, in addition to other penalties provided by law, be liable for a penalty equal to the total amount of the tax evaded, or not collected, or not accounted for and paid over."

TABLE 11-1

SUMMARY OF PAYROLL TAX REPORTING PENALTIES

CODE SECTION	ACTION	PENALTY
3403	Failure to withhold payroll taxes	Employer liable for full amount of taxes (which can be deducted from future wages paid to the same employees)
3509	Failure to withhold payroll taxes from a self-employed worker the IRS later reclassifies as an employee	1. Employer liable for penalty of 1.5 percent x wages paid to the worker (3 percent if no Form 1099-MISC was filed) for income tax purposes, and 20 percent x employee's share of FICA taxes (40 percent if no Form 1099-MISC was filed) 2. Employer liable for full employer's share of FICA taxes 3. Employer generally liable for full amount of taxes if intentionally disregards withholding rules
6721	1. Failure to file a correct information return (Forms 1099-MISC, W-2) with IRS by due date (February 28 of following year, or February 29 if a leap year) 2. Failure to report all required information on a return 3. Including incorrect information on a return	1. A 3-tier penalty: $30 per return (if correct return filed within 30 days after due date); $60 per return (if correct return filed by August 1); $100 per return (if correct return filed after August 1) 2. No penalty if failure due to reasonable cause (not willful neglect) 3. No penalty if no more than 10 returns filed without full information or with incorrect information, and errors corrected by August 1 (and error not due to willful neglect) 4. In case of intentional disregard of filing requirement, penalty of $250 per return or 10 percent of the total amount of items required to be reported correctly, whichever is larger
6722	1. Failure to furnish a correct payee statement (Forms 1099-MISC, W-2) to workers by due date (January 31 of following year) 2. Failure to report all required information on a payee statement 3. Including incorrect information on a payee statement	Same as section 6721 penalties (see above).
6723	Failure to insert taxpayer identification number (employer identification number) on any return or statement (e.g., Forms W-2, 1099-MISC, W-3, 1096, 941)	$50 per failure
6656	Failure to make timely deposits of payroll taxes	A 4-tier penalty: penalty equal to 2 percent of amount of underpayment if failure corrected not more than 5 days after due date; penalty equal to 5 percent of amount of underpayment if failure corrected after 5 days but not more than 15 days after due date; penalty equal to 10 percent of amount of underpayment if failure corrected after 15 days but not more than 10 days after date of first delinquency notice to taxpayer; penalty equal to 15 percent of amount of underpayment if failure not corrected within 10 days after date of first delinquency notice to taxpayer
6672	Willful failure to withhold or deposit payroll taxes	Civil penalty equal to 100 percent of taxes not withheld or deposited assessed against either the employer or its officers (may apply to volunteer officers or directors of nonprofit organizations)
7201	Willful attempt to evade or defeat tax	A felony, with a criminal penalty of up to $100,000 (up to $500,000 for a corporation) and imprisonment of up to 5 years (or both)

(Continued on page 538)

TABLE 11-1

SUMMARY OF PAYROLL TAX REPORTING PENALTIES
(continued)

CODE SECTION	ACTION	PENALTY
7202	Willful failure to withhold or deposit payroll taxes	A felony, with a criminal penalty (in addition to the section 6672 civil penalty) of up to 5 years imprisonment or $10,000 fine (or both), generally applies to officers
7203	Willful failure to file a return, pay a tax, or supply required information	A misdemeanor, with a criminal penalty of up to $25,000 ($100,000 for a corporation) and imprisonment of up to 1 year (or both)
7204	Willful failure to provide a Form W-2 to employees, or willfully including false information on a Form W-2	A misdemeanor, with a criminal penalty of up to $1,000 and imprisonment of up to 1 year (or both)
7207	Willfully providing the IRS with a false return or statement	A misdemeanor, with a criminal penalty of up to $10,000 ($50,000 for a corporation) and imprisonment of up to 1 year (or both)

Stated simply, this section says that if an employer has failed to collect or pay over income and employment taxes, the trust fund recovery penalty may be asserted against those determined to have been *responsible and willful* in failing to pay over the tax. Responsibility and willfulness must both be established.

The withheld income and employment taxes will be collected only once, whether from the business or from one or more of its responsible persons.

Responsibility

The *IRS Internal Revenue Manual* (IRM) states that responsibility is a matter of "status, duty, and authority," that "a determination of responsibility is dependent on the facts and circumstances of each case," and that "potential responsible persons" include an officer or employee of a corporation, or a corporate director. *IRM 5.7.3.3.1.* The IRM further clarifies that a responsible person has: (1) power to direct the act of collecting withheld taxes; (2) accountability for and authority to pay employment taxes; and (3) authority to determine which creditors will or will not be paid. The IRM lists the following "indicators of responsibility":

1. *The full scope of authority and responsibility is contingent upon whether the person had the ability to exercise independent judgment with respect to the financial affairs of the business....*
3. *If a person has the authority to sign checks, the exercise of that authority does not, in and of itself, establish responsibility. Signatory authority may be merely a convenience.*

4. *Persons with ultimate authority over financial affairs may generally not avoid responsibility by delegating that authority to someone else....*
5. *Persons serving as volunteers solely in an honorary capacity as directors and trustees of tax exempt organizations will generally not be considered responsible persons unless they participated in the day-to-day or financial operations of the organization and they had actual knowledge of the failure to withhold or pay over the trust fund taxes. This does not apply if it would result in there being no person responsible [for the section 6672 penalty].*

To determine whether a person has the status, duty, and authority to ensure that employment taxes are paid, the IRM directs IRS agents to consider "the duties of the officers as set forth in the corporate bylaws as well as the ability of the individual to sign checks." In addition, agents are instructed to determine the identity of individuals who

- are officers, directors, or shareholders of the corporation;
- hire and fire employees;
- exercise authority to determine which creditors to pay;
- sign and file the excise tax or employment tax returns, such as Form 941 (Employer's Quarterly Federal Tax Return);
- control payroll and disbursements; and
- make federal tax deposits.

IRS Policy Statement 5-14 specifies:

An employee is generally not a "responsible person" if the employee's function was solely to pay the bills as directed by a superior, rather than to determine which creditors would or would not be paid. However, if an employee . . . has significant control over making the company's other financial decisions about who to pay or has the ability to obtain financing for the company, then such an employee cannot avoid being responsible for the [section 6672 penalty] by merely showing that [the employer] limited his discretion on the specific matter of paying taxes that the company owed.

Here are a few examples that appear in the *IRS Internal Revenue Manual* (they are adapted for church use):

EXAMPLE. A church bookkeeper has check-signing authority, and she pays all of the bills the treasurer gives her. She is not permitted to pay any other bills, and when there are not sufficient funds in the bank account to pay all of the bills, she must ask the treasurer which bills to pay. The bookkeeper should generally not be held responsible for the section 6672 penalty.

EXAMPLE. An employee works as a clerical secretary in the office. She signs checks and tax returns at the direction of and for the convenience of a supervisor. She is directed to pay other vendors, even though payroll taxes are unpaid. The secretary is not a responsible person, because she works under the dominion and control of the owner or a supervisor and is not permitted to exercise independent judgment.

Willfulness

Willful means intentional, deliberate, voluntary, reckless, or knowing, as opposed to accidental. No evil intent or bad motive is required. To show willfulness, the IRS generally must demonstrate that a responsible person was aware or should have been aware of the outstanding taxes and either intentionally disregarded the law or was plainly indifferent to its requirements. A responsible person's failure to investigate or correct mismanagement after being notified that withholding taxes have not been paid satisfies the willfulness requirement.

Application to churches and other nonprofit organizations

Does the penalty imposed by section 6672 apply to churches and other nonprofit organizations? The answer is yes. Consider the following three points.

1. IRS Policy Statement 5-14 (IRM 1.2.14.1.3). In Policy Statement 5-14 (part of the *Internal Revenue Manual*), the IRS states:

In general, non-owner employees of the business entity, who act solely under the dominion and control of others, and who are not in a position to make independent decisions on behalf of the business entity, will not be asserted the trust fund recovery penalty. The penalty shall not be imposed on unpaid, volunteer members of any board of trustees or directors of an organization referred to in section 501 of the Internal Revenue Code to the extent such members are solely serving in an honorary capacity, do not participate in the day-to-day or financial operations of

the organization, and/or do not have knowledge of the failure on which such penalty is imposed.

In order to make accurate determinations, all relevant issues should be thoroughly investigated. An individual will not be recommended for assertion if sufficient information is not available to demonstrate he or she was actively involved in the corporation at the time the liability was not being paid. However, this shall not apply if the potentially responsible individual intentionally makes information unavailable to impede the investigation. [Emphasis added.]

This language indicates that the IRS will not assert the 100 percent penalty against uncompensated, volunteer board members of a church who

- are solely serving in an honorary capacity,
- do not participate in the day-to-day or financial operations of the organization, and
- do not have knowledge of the failure to withhold or pay over withheld payroll taxes.

2. Court cases involving churches. The courts have recognized that church officers can be liable for the section 6672 penalty. Consider the following three cases:

Carter v. United States, 717 F. Supp. 188 (S.D.N.Y. 1989). A federal district court ruling in New York illustrates the importance of complying with the payroll tax procedures discussed in this chapter. A church-operated charitable organization failed to pay over to the IRS withheld income taxes and the employer's and employees' share of Social Security and Medicare taxes for a number of quarters in both 1984 and 1985. Accordingly, the IRS assessed a penalty in the amount of 100 percent of the unpaid taxes ($230,245) against *each* of the four officers of the organization pursuant to section 6672 of the tax code. The officers challenged the validity of the IRS actions. The court observed that federal law requires employers to withhold Social Security and Medicare and income taxes from the wages of their employees and to hold the withheld taxes as a "special trust fund" for the benefit of the United States government until paid or deposited. If an employer fails to make the required payments, "the government may actually suffer a loss because the employees are given credit for the amount of the taxes withheld regardless of whether the employer ever pays the money to the government." Accordingly, "section 6672 of the [tax code] supplies an alternative method for collecting the withheld taxes. Pursuant to this section, the government may assess a penalty, equal to the full amount of the unpaid tax, against a person responsible for paying over the money who willfully fails to do so."

The court observed that a person is liable for the full amount of taxes under section 6672 if "(1) he or she was under a duty to collect, account for, and pay over the taxes (i.e., a 'responsible person'), and (2) the failure to pay the taxes was 'willful.'" The court concluded that the four officers of the church-related charitable organization satisfied both requirements, and accordingly that they were personally liable for the unpaid taxes under section 6672. The officers were "responsible persons," since (1) they were directors as well as officers; (2) they had the authority to sign checks (including payroll checks); and (3) they were involved in "routine business concerns such as corporate funding, bookkeeping, salaries, and hiring and firing." The fact that a nonprofit organization was involved and that the officers donated their services without compensation did not relieve them of liability. The court also ruled that the officers acted willfully and thus met the second requirement of section 6672. It defined "willful action" as "voluntary, conscious and intentional—as opposed to accidental—decisions not to remit funds properly withheld to the government." There need not be "an evil motive or an intent to defraud."

The court specifically held that "the failure to investigate or to correct mismanagement after having notice that withheld taxes have not been remitted to the government is deemed to be willful conduct." Further, the court concluded that payment of employee wages and other debts with the knowledge that the payment of payroll taxes is late constitutes willful conduct.

In re Triplett, 115 B.R. 955 (N.D. Ill. 1990). A federal bankruptcy court in Illinois ruled that a church treasurer was not personally liable for his church's failure to withhold and pay over to the IRS some $100,000 in payroll taxes but that the pastor and chairman of the board of deacons might be. The court concluded that the church treasurer did not have sufficient control over the finances of the church to be liable for the 100 percent penalty. It noted that the chairman of the board of deacons made all decisions regarding which bills would be paid, and he (and the pastor) alone were responsible for day-to-day church operations. While the treasurer did not satisfy the definition of a responsible person, the court suggested that the pastor and chairman of the deacon board would. It observed that "ample evidence exists to indicate that other church employees, like [the pastor and chairman of the deacon board] may be liable. It is fortuitous that the treasurer's assessment has been litigated before assessments against these other persons." This case illustrates that the IRS is committed to assessing the 100 percent penalty under section 6674 of the tax code against church leaders in appropriate cases. While the treasurer in this case did not have sufficient control over church finances to be a "responsible person," there is little doubt that many church treasurers would satisfy the court's definition of a responsible person.

Holmes v. United States, 2004-2 USTC 50,301 (S.D. Tex. 2004). A church operated a private school for primary and secondary students. The school is incorporated, and its board of directors includes parents of students and members of the affiliated church. The board has six directors. The school suffered a substantial drop in enrollment. The loss of tuition made the school insolvent. The

directors chose to pay some creditors while negotiating with others. The board's goal was to keep the school open as long as possible. The school's checks required two signatures. The board's chairman, treasurer, and the school administrator, were signatories. The chairman claimed that he rarely signed checks and only did so when the others were not available.

Because of its financial problems, the school did not deposit its employees' withheld taxes for three quarters. The treasurer informed the chairman about the tax liability from the beginning. The chairman discussed it with the board and suggested cutbacks to free up cash to pay the taxes. He claimed that the board rejected his ideas. Nearly $120,000 in withheld payroll taxes were not deposited for the quarters in question.

A few years later the IRS assessed the full amount of payroll taxes against the treasurer and chairman of the board pursuant to section 6672 of the tax code. Both of these individuals insisted that they were not liable and that the IRS had abused its discretion by not assessing other board members for the taxes. A federal district initially found the treasurer personally liable for the full amount of the payroll tax liability. In a subsequent proceeding, the personal liability of the board chairman was addressed by the court.

The court noted that "under federal law, a company's agent who is responsible for the collection and payment of employment taxes is liable to the government for the amount of the taxes unpaid" and that a responsible person "has some authority over the payment of the taxes, like paying them himself, ordering their payment, or having some control over the company's treasury." The chairman of the board "had enough responsibility to be personally liable for the unpaid taxes. He knew about the tax burden—he signed a return showing that no tax deposits were made for three months. Also, he signed several checks to some of the school's creditors instead of paying the withheld taxes. He could have seen that the taxes were paid but chose not to."

The court rejected the board chairman's argument that his concern over the use of the withheld taxes was ignored or rejected by the board. It observed, "As chairman, he could have protested the use of the funds or refused to follow the directive. Further, that the school required two signatures on its checks is not a defense; it simply shows that at least two people were jointly in control."

The court also ruled that the board chairman was not immune from liability because he was a volunteer for the school, since "he had a real position, he was involved in the financial operations of the school, and he knew about the obligation to the government. His titles, positions, and jobs were not honorary."

The court concluded that along with the treasurer the government would "recover jointly from the board chairman the balance of the unpaid employment taxes because he actively participated in the diversion of the funds. Others may share in the responsibility."

✿**KEY POINT.** The Taxpayer Bill of Rights 2 established important limitations on the authority of the IRS to assess the 100 percent civil penalty against church leaders who fail to withhold or deposit payroll taxes. These limitations are discussed below.

✿**KEY POINT.** The tax code permits personal delivery, as an alternative to delivery by mail, of a preliminary notice that the IRS intends to assess a 100 percent penalty upon a financially responsible person under section 6672 of the tax code.

In re Vaughn, 2011-2 U.S.T.C. ¶50,681 (E.D.N.C. 2011). A federal court in North Carolina ruled that a minister met the definition of a "responsible person" under section 6672 of the tax code, and therefore the IRS could assess a penalty against her in the amount of 100 percent of the payroll taxes that were not withheld or paid over to the government. Although the employer remains liable for unpaid payroll taxes, its officers and agents may incur personal liability for the unpaid payroll taxes. In order for an individual to be held personally liable under section 6672: (1) the party assessed must be a person required to collect, truthfully account for, and pay over the tax, referred to as a "responsible person"; and (2) the responsible person must have "willfully failed" to insure that the withholding taxes were paid.

In deciding whether an officer or employee is a "responsible person," the most important question is whether the person "had the effective power to pay the taxes—that is, whether he had the actual authority or ability, in view of his status within the corporation, to pay the taxes owed." When making the determination of who is a "responsible person," courts have considered several factors which are indicative of this authority, including "whether the employee: (1) served as an officer of the company or as a member of its board of directors; (2) controlled the company's payroll; (3) determined which creditors to pay and when to pay them; (4) participated in the day-to-day management of the corporation; (5) possessed the power to write checks; and (6) had the ability to hire and fire employees."

The court concluded that the minister in this case was a responsible person based on the following considerations:

- The ministry's bylaws stated that the minister was "CEO over all spiritual and business matters" and a member of all boards and committees.
- The bylaws also specified that the minister had "the general powers and duties of supervision and management usually vested in the office of president of a corporation."
- The minister was authorized to cosign loans.
- The minister had the authority, and exercised that authority, to sign checks on behalf of the ministry without any other

signature. Although the minister claimed that she rarely wrote checks, the court concluded that "the issue is not how many checks [she] signed, but whether [she] had authority to do so."
- The minister had the authority to hire and fire employees.

The court concluded that the minister had the "power to compel or prohibit the allocation of corporate funds."

The court acknowledged that responsible person status does not in itself create personal liability under section 6672. Liability arises only if the responsible person acts willfully in failing to collect, account for, or pay over the taxes. The court noted that willfulness can be established if a "responsible person" "(1) has actual or constructive knowledge of the unpaid taxes and the employer continues to pay other creditors in lieu of the United States; (2) lacks actual knowledge of the unpaid taxes, but recklessly disregards the existence of an unpaid deficiency; or (3) becomes aware of the unpaid taxes and fails to use all unencumbered funds to pay the tax liability." The court noted that "reckless disregard" exists when the person "(1) clearly ought to have known that (2) there was a grave risk that withholding taxes were not being paid and if (3) he was in a position to find out for certain very easily." In this case, the minister testified that she had actual knowledge that the ministry had failed to remit is employment taxes in the past and that she was aware that it had entered into an installment payment with the IRS.

The court concluded that the minister

was on notice that the taxes were not being paid, but she failed to engage in any investigation to verify that the subsequent trust fund taxes were being paid. Failing to do so meets the reckless disregard test. This notice placed a duty on her to investigate and confirm that the ministry was paying trust fund taxes. The Form 941s filed by [the ministry] showed significant unpaid taxes and little to no payments for any of the quarters. As CEO and president of the ministry she could have easily confirmed the outstanding liability.

3. Court cases involving other charities. The courts have addressed the liability of officers of nonreligious charities for the section 6672 penalty in a number of cases. Consider the following case.

A charity began experiencing severe financial problems. A consultant informed the board of directors that the charity had not been paying withheld payroll taxes to the IRS. The president resigned following this disclosure, but the board refused to accept his resignation, so he agreed to continue to function under the title of "acting president."

The charity was forced to file for bankruptcy. The IRS sought to recover $50,000 against the president under section 6672 of the tax code, which amounted to the full amount of payroll taxes (plus interest) that the charity had withheld but not paid over to the government. The president insisted that he was not a financially responsible person and so could not be liable for the 100 percent penalty. The Tax Court agreed with the president and refused to impose the penalty.

The court considered the following seven factors in deciding whether the penalty should be assessed: (1) the corporate bylaws; (2) the person's ability to sign checks on the company's bank account; (3) signature on the employer's federal quarterly and other tax returns; (4) payment of other creditors in lieu of the government; (5) identity of officers and directors; (6) identity of individuals in charge of hiring and discharging employees; and (7) identity of individuals in charge of the firm's financial affairs. It concluded that a consideration of these factors did not support the assessment of the 100 percent penalty against the president:

> The charity's bylaws do not allow the president to determine which bills should be paid. They only specify that the board of directors is responsible for the proper conduct of all business of the charity. The bylaws expressly permit the president to cosign checks with the treasurer but do not grant the president sole authority. Additionally, the charity's payroll checks were issued by ADP Incorporated, an independent contractor, who used a facsimile signature of the president on the checks. [Further], the president was only one of several officers, employees and members of the club who sometimes authorized the payment of creditors and the hiring and firing of employees. The evidence does not reveal that he decided to pay the charity's other creditors in lieu of the government. Also, there is no evidence that he signed the charity's tax forms. Although he did sign the charity's bankruptcy petition, he did so after learning of its failure to pay [withheld payroll taxes].

The court also noted that the 100 percent penalty requires proof that a financially responsible person acted willfully and that "a responsible person acts willfully when he pays other creditors in preference to the IRS knowing that the taxes are due, or with reckless disregard for whether taxes have been paid." The court concluded that the IRS failed to prove that the president acted willfully. *In re Lartz, 2003-2 USTC ¶50,674 (2003). See also Verret v. United States, 2008-1 USTC ¶ 50,248 (E.D. Tex. 2008).*

Taxpayer Bill of Rights 2 (TBOR2)

Congress enacted the Taxpayer Bill of Rights 2 in 1996. This law contains four important limitations on the application of the penalty under section 6672:

1. Notice requirement

The IRS must issue a notice to an individual it has determined to be a responsible person with respect to unpaid payroll taxes at least 60 days prior to issuing a notice and demand for the penalty.

2. Disclosure of information if more than one person subject to penalty

TBOR2 requires the IRS, if requested in writing by a person considered by the IRS to be a responsible person, to disclose in writing to that person the name of any other person the IRS has determined to be a responsible person with respect to the tax liability. The IRS is required to disclose in writing whether it has attempted to collect this penalty from other responsible persons, the general nature of those collection activities, and the amount (if any) collected. Failure by the IRS to follow this provision does not absolve any individual from any liability for this penalty.

3. Contribution from other responsible parties

If more than one person is liable for this penalty, each person who paid the penalty is entitled to recover from other persons who are liable for the penalty an amount equal to the excess of the amount paid by such person over such person's proportionate share of the penalty. This proceeding is a federal cause of action and is separate from any proceeding involving IRS collection of the penalty from any responsible party.

4. Volunteer board members of churches and other charities

TBOR2 clarifies that the responsible person penalty is not to be imposed on volunteer, unpaid members of any board of trustees or directors of a tax-exempt organization to the extent such members are solely serving in an honorary capacity, do not participate in the day-to-day or financial activities of the organization, and do not have actual knowledge of the failure. However, this provision cannot operate in such a way as to eliminate all responsible persons from responsibility.

TBOR2 requires the IRS to develop materials to better inform board members of tax-exempt organizations (including voluntary or honorary members) that they may be treated as responsible persons. The IRS is required to make such materials routinely available to tax-exempt organizations. TBOR2 also requires the IRS to clarify its instructions to IRS employees on application of the responsible person penalty with regard to honorary or volunteer members of boards of trustees or directors of tax-exempt organizations.

EXAMPLE. Bill serves as the treasurer of his church. Due to financial difficulties, the pastor decides to use withheld payroll taxes to pay other debts. The IRS later asserts that the church owes $25,000 in unpaid payroll taxes. The church has no means of paying this debt. The IRS insists that Bill and other church board members are personally liable for the debt. It is likely that Bill is a responsible person who may be liable for the 100 percent penalty, since he has authority over the day-to-day financial activities of the church. TBOR2 will not protect him. However, it will protect members of the church board who (1) are volunteer, unpaid members; (2) serve solely in an honorary capacity; (3) do not participate in the day-to-day or financial activities of the organization; and (4) do not have actual knowledge of the failure to pay over withheld taxes to the government.

EXAMPLE. A church board votes to use withheld taxes to pay other debts of the church. Over a three-year period the church fails to deposit $100,000 in withheld taxes. The IRS claims that the board members are personally liable for the 100 percent penalty for failing to deposit withheld taxes. All of the members of the board claim they are protected by the provisions of TBOR2. They are not correct, since TBOR2 specifies that its provisions cannot operate in such a way as to eliminate all responsible persons from responsibility.

Conclusions

The precedents summarized above demonstrate that church officers and directors (and in some cases employees, such as administrators or bookkeepers) can be *personally liable* for the payment of income taxes and Social Security and Medicare taxes that they fail to withhold, account for, or pay over to the government. It does not matter that they serve without compensation, so long as they satisfy the definition of a "responsible person" and act willfully.

Many church officers and directors (and in some cases employees, such as administrators or bookkeepers) will satisfy the definition of a "responsible person," and such persons can be personally liable for unpaid payroll taxes if they act under the liberal definition of "willfully" described above. Clearly, church leaders must be knowledgeable regarding a church's payroll tax obligations and ensure that these obligations are satisfied.

2. APPLICATION OF PAYROLL REPORTING RULES TO MINISTERS

✪ **KEY POINT.** Two special rules apply to ministers under the payroll reporting rules. Unfamiliarity with these two rules has created untold confusion. The first rule is that ministers are always self-employed for Social Security with respect to their ministerial services, so they pay the self-employment tax rather than the employee's share of Social Security and Medicare taxes (even if they report their federal income taxes as employees). The second rule is that ministers' compensation is exempt from federal income tax withholding whether ministers report their income taxes as employees or as self-employed.

Clarification of rules

The application of the payroll reporting rules to ministers has created considerable confusion because of two rather simple rules that are often misunderstood. These two rules are explained below.

Self-employed status for Social Security

The first special rule is that ministers always are self-employed for Social Security with respect to services performed in the exercise of their ministry (with the exception of some government-employed chaplains—see Chapter 3, section B). As a result, ministers pay the self-employment tax rather than the employee's share of Social Security and Medicare taxes—even if they report their federal income taxes as employees. It is incorrect for churches to treat ministers as employees for Social Security and to withhold the employee's share of Social Security and Medicare taxes from their wages. See Chapter 9 for more details. *IRC 3121(b)(8)(A).*

Exemption from income tax withholding

The second special rule is that ministers' compensation is exempt from income tax withholding whether a minister reports his or her income taxes as an employee or as self-employed. While it is true that the tax code requires every employer, including churches and religious organizations, to withhold federal income taxes from employee wages, some exceptions to this rule are made. One exception is wages paid for "services performed by a duly ordained, commissioned, or licensed minister of a church in the exercise of his ministry." *IRC 3401(a)(9).* Therefore, a church need not withhold income taxes from the salary of a minister who is an employee for income tax reporting purposes. See Chapter 3 for a complete explanation of the term "services performed by a duly ordained, commissioned, or licensed minister of a church in the exercise of his ministry." Further, since the income tax withholding requirements only apply to the wages of *employees*, a church should not withhold taxes from the compensation of a minister (or any other worker) who is *self-employed.*

Voluntary withholding for minister-employees

The IRS maintains that a church and a minister-employee may agree voluntarily that federal income taxes be withheld from the minister's wages, but this is not required. Some ministers find voluntary withholding attractive because it eliminates the guesswork, quarterly reports, and penalties associated with the estimated tax procedure (which applies automatically if voluntary withholding is not elected).

Use of voluntary withholding may help to avoid underpayment penalties that may apply to ministers and other taxpayers whose estimated tax payments are less than their actual tax liability. See Chapter 1 for more information on the underpayment penalty.

A minister-employee who elects to enter into a voluntary withholding arrangement with his or her church need only file a completed Form W-4 (employee's withholding allowance certificate) with the church. The filing of this form is deemed to be a request for voluntary withholding.

Voluntary withholding arrangements can be terminated unilaterally by either a minister or the church, or by mutual consent. Alternatively, a minister can stipulate that the voluntary withholding arrangement will terminate on a specified date. In such a case the minister must give the church a signed statement setting forth the date on which the voluntary withholding is to terminate; the minister's name and address; and a statement that he or she wishes to enter into a voluntary withholding arrangement with his or her employer. This statement must be attached to a completed Form W-4. The voluntary withholding arrangement will terminate automatically on the date specified. Either the church or the minister may terminate a voluntary withholding arrangement before a specified or mutually agreed upon termination date by providing a signed notice to the other.

If a church and its minister voluntarily agree that income taxes will be withheld, a minister ordinarily will no longer be subject to the estimated tax requirements with respect to federal income taxes. But what about a minister's self-employment taxes? Ministers who have not exempted themselves from Social Security coverage are required to pay the self-employment tax (Social Security tax for self-employed persons). Can a church withhold the self-employment tax from a minister-employee's wages? The answer is yes. IRS Publication 517 (Social Security and Other Information for Members of the Clergy) states that "if you perform your services as a common-law employee of the church and your salary is not subject to income tax withholding, you can enter into a voluntary withholding agreement with the church to cover any *income and [self-employment] tax* that may be due" (emphasis added).

A church whose minister has elected voluntary withholding (and who is not exempt from Social Security taxes) withholds an additional amount from each paycheck to cover the minister's estimated self-employment tax for the year, and then reports this additional amount as additional *income tax* (not FICA tax) withheld on its quarterly 941 forms. The minister should submit an amended Form W-4 to the church, inserting on line 6 an additional amount of income tax to be withheld that will be enough to cover projected self-employment taxes for the year. The excess income tax withheld is a credit against tax that the minister claims on his or her federal income tax return and is applied against the minister's self-employment tax liability. Further, it is considered to be a timely payment of the minister's self-employment tax obligation, so no penalties for late payment of the quarterly estimates will apply.

Voluntary withholding for self-employed ministers

A self-employed minister is free to enter into an unofficial withholding arrangement whereby the church withholds a portion of his or her compensation each week and deposits it in a church account, then distributes the balance to the minister in advance of each quarterly estimated tax payment due date. However, note that no Form W-4 should be used to initiate such unofficial withholding arrangements, and none of the withheld taxes should be reported to the IRS on the church's Forms 941.

Ministers who report their income taxes as self-employed persons should recognize that the use of a Form W-4 will almost guarantee that they will be deemed to be an employee by the IRS. Only

ministers who report their income taxes as employees should use a Form W-4 to initiate (or amend) voluntary withholding.

3. MANDATORY CHURCH COMPLIANCE WITH THE PAYROLL TAX REPORTING RULES AND VIOLATION OF "SEPARATION OF CHURCH AND STATE"

❖ **KEY POINT.** The courts have rejected the argument that the application of the payroll tax reporting rules to churches violates the constitutional guaranty of religious freedom.

No withholding exemption exists for nonminister church employees. As a result, churches must be careful to follow the withholding requirements discussed below with respect to any nonminister employees (or to minister-employees who have elected voluntary withholding).

Does the imposition of these requirements upon churches violate the constitutional principle of separation of church and state? Every court that has addressed this question has said no. Consider the following three examples.

The Eighth Street Baptist Church case

A church withheld federal payroll taxes from the wages of its organist, pianist, choir director, janitor, and church clerk. It paid the withheld taxes to the government and then filed a refund claim with the IRS. It cited the following five reasons why it was not legally obligated to withhold payroll taxes from its employees: (1) a church cannot be made a trustee or collection agent of the government against its will; (2) the First Amendment prevents the IRS from requiring churches to withhold taxes from the wages of employees; (3) it was not the intent of Congress to require churches to withhold taxes from the wages of employees; (4) if withholding laws apply to churches, then churches would become "servants" of the federal government in violation of their constitutional right of religious freedom; and (5) church employees are exempt because they qualify for the exemption available to members of religious orders. The IRS rejected the church's request for a refund, and the church appealed the case to a federal court.

A federal district court in Kansas rejected all of the church's arguments. It noted that the tax code specifies that *all* wages are subject to withholding, with certain exceptions, and therefore the wages of church employees are subject to withholding unless a specific exception applies. The court concluded that the wages of nonminister church employees are not specifically exempted from the withholding requirements, and therefore a church is legally required to comply with the tax withholding requirements with respect to these employees. Note that the wages of ministers are exempted by law from tax withholding, as noted previously in this chapter, so churches are not required to withhold taxes from the wages of ministers who are being compensated for the performance of ministerial duties. The court also rejected the church's attempt to bring its employees under the exemption available to members of religious orders.

In rejecting the church's constitutional arguments, the court observed: "A taxing statute is not contrary to the provisions of the First Amendment unless it directly restricts the free exercise by an individual of his religion. We think it clear that, within the intendment of the First Amendment, the Internal Revenue Code, in imposing the income tax and requiring the filing of returns and the payment of the tax, is not to be considered as restricting an individual's free exercise of his religion." A federal court rejected a church's challenge to the constitutionality of the tax withholding requirements. *Eighth Street Baptist Church v. United States, 291 F. Supp. 603 (D. Kan. 1968), aff'd, 431 F.2d 1193(10th Cir. 1970); see also, Bethel Baptist Church v. United States, 822 F.2d 1334 (3rd Cir. 1987) Schultz v. Stark, 554 F. Supp. 1219 (D. Wis. 1983); Goldsboro Christian Schools, Inc. v. United States, 436 F. Supp. 1314 (D.S.C. 1976).*

The Indianapolis Baptist Temple case

A church stopped filing federal employment tax returns and withholding or paying federal employment taxes for its employees. Church leaders insisted that the government could not regulate an unincorporated "New Testament church." When IRS attempts to discuss the matter with church leaders failed, the IRS assessed $5.3 million in unpaid taxes and interest. The IRS asked a federal court to enter a judgment for the full $5.3 million and to foreclose on a tax lien the IRS had placed on the church's property.

The church claimed that the First Amendment guaranty of religious freedom prevented the IRS from applying payroll tax reporting requirements to churches opposed on religious grounds to complying with those requirements, and also prohibited the IRS from penalizing noncompliant churches for failing to comply.

The court rejected the church's position, noting that "neutral laws of general application that burden religious practices do not run afoul" of the First Amendment. Since federal employment tax laws are "neutral laws of general application" (they apply to a large class of employers and do not single out religious employers for less favorable treatment), they do not violate the First Amendment.

This case demonstrates that any attempt by a church to avoid compliance with federal payroll tax obligations (including the withholding and payment of income taxes and Social Security taxes) on the basis of the First Amendment will be summarily rejected by the civil courts. *Indianapolis Baptist Temple v. United States, 224 F.3d 627 (7th Cir. 2000).*

305 Fed.Appx. 615 (11th Cir. 2008)

The founder of a parachurch ministry was charged in a 58-count indictment for willfully failing to withhold and deposit federal income

taxes and FICA taxes for employees of his ministry, structuring cash withdrawals to avoid financial reporting requirements, and obstructing the administration of tax laws. He was convicted on all charges and received a prison sentence of 10 years. The court also ordered a forfeiture of all property attributable to the reporting crimes.

On appeal the founder insisted that he had not willfully failed to withhold or pay federal payroll taxes since he did not know of the specific statutes that required him to collect and pay withholding taxes.

A federal appeals court rejected this argument and affirmed his conviction. The court observed that a conviction for willfully failing to collect or withhold payroll taxes only requires that the defendant knew of the "duty purportedly imposed by the tax laws, not that he knew which specific provision created that duty. When a defendant knows of facts constituting an offense, he has acted with the requisite willfulness to violate the law."

The court concluded:

> The government proved that [the founder] knew the tax laws required the collection and payment of withholding taxes, but he refused to comply. Employees of [his parachurch ministry] testified that he disputed the authority of the Internal Revenue Service based on the separation of the church and state, debated the interpretation and application of the withholding requirements, and intentionally characterized [his ministry] as a "church" and his employees as "missionaries" to avoid tax obligations. He had opined to [an attorney] that he was "smarter" than other church officials who had forfeited property after they refused to collect or pay withholding taxes. Although he argued at trial that he was ignorant of the law and the Internal Revenue Service failed to identify a law that required him to collect and pay withholding taxes, the jury was entitled to find that he knew about and deliberately violated the tax laws.

Conclusions

In summary, the wages of nonminister church employees are subject to withholding. This obligation cannot be avoided by labeling a church employee an independent contractor or self-employed, unless the person clearly fails the IRS common-law employee test (explained in Chapter 2).

Church secretaries, teachers, choir directors, preschool workers, and business managers almost always will satisfy the common-law employee test and therefore will be employees of the church (unless they represent temporary help secured from a local temporary help service). Church custodians who work full-time similarly will almost always be employees subject to withholding. However, a custodian who is paid by the job rather than by the hour, who decides when to work and how to perform his or her services, who works substantially less than full-time, and who is not subject to the control of the church with respect to the performance of his or her services, often may properly be characterized as self-employed. The effect of this is that no income taxes or Social Security taxes are withheld from the worker's compensation. Rather, he or she uses the quarterly estimated tax procedure to prepay and report taxes.

If a church worker satisfies the common-law employee definition, he or she will be an employee despite the church's characterization of the person as self-employed (although in a close case, such as the custodian described above, the written characterization of the worker as self-employed will be a relevant factor).

Obviously, if a church concludes that a particular worker is self-employed, it should issue the person a Form 1099-MISC rather than a Form W-2 at year end (assuming the person has received church compensation of at least $600 for the year). Churches should be careful in characterizing any worker as self-employed, since section 3509 of the tax code imposes a penalty on any employer that fails to withhold income taxes or Social Security taxes from the wages of a worker deemed to be self-employed but whom the IRS reclassifies as an employee.

4. THE 10-STEP APPROACH TO COMPLIANCE WITH FEDERAL PAYROLL TAX REPORTING RULES

Church compliance with the payroll tax reporting rules can be understood with the following 10 simple steps. Keep in mind that all 10 steps will not apply to every church. All (or most) of the 10 steps apply only if a church has nonminister employees to whom it pays wages or if its minister is an employee for income tax purposes and has requested voluntary withholding. Smaller churches with no nonminister employees will only be subject to a few of these steps. But regardless of a church's size, its payroll tax reporting obligations will be described by some or all of the following 10 steps.

These 10 steps are illustrated in comprehensive examples at the end of this chapter.

Step 1: Obtain an employer identification number (EIN) from the IRS

This number must be listed on some of the returns listed below and is used to reconcile a church's deposits of withheld taxes with the Forms W-2 it issues to employees. The EIN is a nine-digit number that looks like this: 00-0246810.

❖ **KEY POINT.** The employer identification number is not a tax exemption number and has no relation to your nonprofit corporation status. It merely identifies you as an employer subject to tax withholding and reporting, and ensures that your church receives proper credit for payments of withheld taxes. You can obtain an EIN by submitting a Form SS-4 to the IRS.

❖ **KEY POINT.** Taxpayers can request an Employer Identification Number (EIN) through a web-based system that instantly processes requests and generates identification numbers in real time. Here's how it works. A taxpayer accesses the Internet EIN system through the IRS website (IRS.gov) and enters the required information. If the information passes the automatic validity checks, the IRS issues a permanent EIN to the taxpayer. An EIN assigned through Internet submission is immediately recognized by IRS systems.

The IRS *Tax Guide for Churches and Religious Organizations* contains the following statement about employer identification numbers:

> *Every tax-exempt organization, including a church, should have an Employer Identification Number (EIN), whether or not the organization has any employees. There are many instances in which an EIN is necessary. For example, a church needs an EIN when it opens a bank account, in order to be listed as a subordinate in a group ruling, or if it files returns with the IRS (e.g., Forms W-2, 1099, 990-T). An organization may obtain an EIN by filing Form SS-4, Application for Employer Identification Number, in accordance with the instructions.*

Many pastors and church treasurers think their church has a special "tax exemption number" confirming that it is exempt from federal income tax. This is not the case. While in some states churches have "tax exemption numbers" for sales tax purposes, no corresponding number is issued by the IRS. The IRS *Tax Guide for Churches and Religious Organizations* notes that "the IRS does not assign a special number or other identification as evidence of an organization's exempt status."

Step 2: Determine whether each church worker is an employee or self-employed, and obtain each worker's Social Security number

In some cases it is difficult to determine whether a worker is an employee or self-employed. If in doubt, churches always should treat a worker as an employee, since substantial penalties can be assessed against a church for treating a worker as self-employed whom the IRS later reclassifies as an employee.

In general, a self-employed worker is one who is not subject to the control of an employer with respect to how a job is to be done. Further, a self-employed person typically is engaged in a specific trade or business and offers his or her services to the general public. The IRS and the courts have developed various tests to assist in classifying a worker as an employee or self-employed. These are reviewed in Chapter 2 of this tax guide.

Factors indicating employee status

Factors that tend to indicate employee status include the following:

- The worker is required to follow an employer's instructions regarding when, where, and how to work.

- The worker receives on-the-job training from an experienced employee.
- The worker is expected to perform the services personally and not use a substitute.
- The employer, rather than the worker, hires and pays any assistants.
- The worker has a continuing working relationship with the employer.
- The employer establishes set hours of work.
- The worker is expected to work full time.
- The work is done on the employer's premises.
- The worker must submit regular oral or written reports to the employer.
- The worker's business expenses are reimbursed by the employer.
- The employer furnishes the worker's tools, supplies, and equipment.
- The worker does not work for other employers.
- The worker does not advertise his or her services to the general public.

Not all of these factors must exist for a worker to be an employee. But if most of them do, the worker is considered an employee. Again—if in doubt, treat the worker as an employee.

The IRS and the courts have applied various tests in determining whether *ministers* are employees or self-employed for income tax reporting. Those tests are reviewed in Chapter 2.

✵ **KEY POINT.** Congress has established important limitations on the authority of the IRS to assess penalties against employers for misclassifying workers as self-employed. These are discussed in section A.6 of this chapter ("Section 530 employees").

Backup withholding

After determining whether a worker is an employee or self-employed, you must obtain the worker's Social Security number. A worker who does not have a Social Security number can obtain one by filing Form SS-5. If a self-employed worker performs services for your church (and earns at least $600 for the year) but fails to provide you with his or her Social Security number, the church is required by law to withhold a portion of the worker's compensation as backup withholding. Prior to 2013, the backup withholding rate was 28 percent of the worker's compensation. This rate (which is tied to the income tax rates) increases to 31 percent beginning in 2013 unless Congress acts to extend the lower rate.

A self-employed person can stop backup withholding by providing the church with a correct Social Security number. The church will need the correct number to complete the worker's Form 1099-MISC (discussed later).

Churches can be penalized if the Social Security number they report on a Form 1099-MISC is incorrect, *unless* they have exercised "due diligence." A church will be deemed to have exercised due diligence if it has self-employed persons provide their Social Security numbers using Form W-9. It is a good idea for churches to present self-employed workers (e.g., guest speakers, contract laborers) with a Form W-9 and to "backup withhold" unless the worker returns the form. The church should retain each Form W-9 to demonstrate its due diligence.

The backup withholding requirements were designed to ensure that self-employed persons fully report their income. Without backup reporting, self-employed persons can often underreport their true income (without detection) by simply refusing to provide their Social Security numbers to employers. Of course, to avoid backup withholding, some self-employed persons may consider providing a false Social Security number. The IRS will discover such a scheme when it receives the Form 1099-MISC containing the false number. At such time the IRS will notify the church to commence backup withholding on any future payments to the individual (until a correct Social Security number is provided).

Two additional rules pertain to backup withholding and must be understood.

Form 945. All taxes withheld through backup withholding must be reported to the IRS on Form 945. The Form 945 for 2013 must be filed with the IRS by January 31, 2014. However, if you made deposits on time in full payment of the taxes for the year, you may file the return by February 10, 2014.

Depositing backup withholdings. Deposit all nonpayroll withheld federal income tax, including backup withholding, by electronic funds transfer. Combine all Form 945 taxes for deposit purposes. Do not combine deposits for Form 941 with deposits for Form 945. Generally, the deposit rules that apply to Form 941 also apply to Form 945. However, because Form 945 is an annual return, the rules for determining your deposit schedule (discussed below) are different from those for Form 941.

Two deposit schedules—monthly or semiweekly—are used to determine when you must deposit withheld income tax. These schedules tell you when a deposit is due after a tax liability arises (e.g., you make a payment subject to income tax withholding, including backup withholding). Before the beginning of each calendar year, you must determine which of the two deposit schedules you must use.

For 2013 you are a monthly schedule depositor for Form 945 if the total tax reported on your 2011 Form 945 was $50,000 or less. If the total tax reported for 2011 exceeded $50,000, you are a semiweekly schedule depositor.

✵ **KEY POINT.** If your backup withholdings for the year are less than $2,500, you may enclose a check for the balance with your annual Form 945.

PAYROLL TAX WITHHOLDING CHECKLIST
(a church's withholding obligations)

- Employers are legally required to withhold payroll taxes (income taxes and Social Security and Medicare taxes) from the wages of employees.
- Churches are not required to withhold payroll taxes from wages paid to ministers for ministerial services.
- Ministers who are treated as employees by the church can elect voluntary withholding of income taxes by submitting a Form W-4 to the church. Note, however, that ministers are always treated as self-employed for compensation paid for ministerial services, so churches should not withhold Social Security and Medicare taxes from their wages even if they elect voluntary withholding. However, ministers who elect voluntary withholding can request that their employing church withhold additional income taxes in an amount that will be sufficient to cover their self-employment taxes. These additional income tax withholdings become a credit that can be applied to self-employment taxes on the minister's tax return. The additional income tax withholdings are requested on line 6 of Form W-4.
- Some churches have elected to exempt themselves from the employer's share of Social Security and Medicare taxes by filing a timely Form 8274 with the IRS. The filing of this form has the effect of recharacterizing lay employees as self-employed persons for purposes of Social Security, meaning that the church does not withhold Social Security or Medicare taxes from their wages. However, the church is not relieved of the obligation to withhold income taxes.
- See IRS Publication 15 for information on computing the correct amount of income taxes, as well as Social Security and Medicare taxes, to withhold.
- Employees whose wages are subject to withholding should provide the church with a completed Form W-4. If this is not done, then the church must withhold federal income taxes from an employee's wages as if he or she were single and claiming no withholding allowances.
- Some lay employees are exempt from income tax withholding. To qualify for exempt status, the employee must have had no tax liability for the previous year and must expect to have no tax liability for the current year. However, if the employee can be claimed as a dependent on a parent's or another person's tax return, additional limitations may apply.
- Exemption from withholding is claimed by submitting a properly completed Form W-4 to one's employer. The exemption is claimed by completing lines 1–4 and 7 of the form and signing it. A Form W-4 claiming exemption from withholding is valid for only one calendar year. To continue to be exempt from withholding in the next year, an employee must complete a new Form W-4 claiming exempt status by February 15 of that year. If the employee does not provide the employer with a new Form W-4, the employer must withhold tax as if he or she is single, with no withholding allowances. However, if the employing church has an earlier Form W-4 (not claiming exempt status) for this employee that is valid, it should withhold as it did before.
- Employees should be encouraged to review their Form W-4 annually to see if they need to file a new one with the church. Forms W-4 often become obsolete because of changes in an employee's circumstances. This can result in withholding that is significantly above or below the actual tax liability. There are many reasons an employee's W-4 may be inaccurate, including the birth of a child, a pay raise, or significant medical expenses. These same considerations apply to ministers who have elected voluntary withholding of their taxes. The tax cuts passed by Congress in recent years have reduced taxes for most Americans, and this is another reason some church employees will want to submit a new Form W-4.
- Any unauthorized change or addition to Form W-4 makes it invalid. This includes taking out any language by which the employee certifies that the form is correct. A Form W-4 is also invalid if, by the date an employee gives it to you, he or she indicates in any way that it is false. An invalid Form W-4 should not be used to determine federal income tax withholding. The employee should be informed that it is invalid and asked for another one. If the employee does not provide a valid Form W-4, taxes should be withheld as if the employee were single and claiming no withholding allowances. However, if the employing church has an earlier Form W-4 for this employee that is valid, it should withhold as it did before.
- When requested by the IRS, a church must make original Forms W-4 available for inspection by an IRS employee. A church may also be directed to send certain Forms W-4 to the IRS. Requested copies of Form W-4 should be sent to the IRS at the address provided and in the manner directed by the notice. After submitting a copy of a requested Form W-4 to the IRS, continue to withhold federal income tax based on that Form W-4 if it is valid. However, if the church is later notified in writing by the IRS that the employee is not entitled to claim exemption from withholding or a claimed number of withholding allowances, it should withhold federal income tax based on the effective date, marital status, and maximum number of withholding allowances specified in the notice (commonly referred to as a "lock-in letter").
- Frivolous tax protester arguments, like those summarized above, should never persuade a church to ignore its payroll tax withholding obligations. The only way for an employee to claim exemption from withholding is by submitting a properly completed and signed Form W-4 (lines 1–4 and 7) to the church.

WHY CHURCHES OFTEN FAIL TO COMPLY FULLY WITH THE PAYROLL REPORTING RULES

The risks associated with tax code section 6672 are aggravated by the widespread noncompliance of churches with federal payroll tax reporting obligations. Churches too often fail to comply with the payroll tax reporting obligations—either by failing to withhold taxes or by failing to pay withheld taxes over to the government. As one court observed, "Because these [withheld taxes] accrue on the withholding date but generally are paid on a quarterly basis, they can be a tempting source of available cash to [an employer]."

Why do so many churches fail to comply with these rules? Some of the reasons are listed below.

- Payroll tax reporting rules are complex.
- Unique rules apply to churches, including the exemption of ministers from income tax withholding, the treatment of ministers as self-employed for Social Security, and the availability of an exemption from the employer's share of FICA taxes for some churches that file a timely application. Church treasurers cannot assume that a church can be treated like a secular business.
- Most church treasurers are volunteers who serve for limited terms. Often it is difficult for such individuals to adequately familiarize themselves with the application of federal payroll tax reporting obligations to churches.

EXAMPLE. A church invites a visiting pastor to conduct services for one week in April 2013 and agrees to pay him $1,000. The visiting pastor declines to disclose his Social Security number. As a result, the church must withhold $280 from his compensation as backup withholding (28 percent of total compensation). If the church accumulates less than $2,500 of backup withholding during the year, it simply encloses a check for the full amount when it files its 2013 Form 945 with the IRS by January 31, 2014. This example assumes that the 28 percent backup withholding rate, which increases to 31 percent in 2013, will be extended by Congress. If Congress does not act, then the church would withhold $310.

Step 3: Have each employee complete Form W-4

Form W-4 is used by employees to claim withholding allowances. A church will need to know how many withholding allowances each nonminister employee claims in order to withhold the correct amount of federal income tax. A withholding allowance lowers the amount of tax that will be withheld from an employee's wages. Allowances generally are available for the employee, the employee's spouse, each of the employee's dependents, and in some cases for itemized deductions.

Ask all new employees to give you a signed Form W-4 when they start work. If an employee does not complete such a form, the church must treat the employee as a single person without any withholding allowances or exemptions. Employers must put into effect any Form W-4 that replaces an existing certificate no later than the start of the first payroll period ending on or after the 30th day after the day you received the replacement Form W-4. Of course, you can put a Form W-4 into effect sooner, if you wish.

Employers are not responsible for verifying the withholding allowances employees claim.

✿ **KEY POINT.** Final regulations issued by the IRS eliminate the requirement that employers send copies of potentially questionable Forms W-4 to the IRS. In the past, employers had to send to the IRS any Form W-4 claiming more than 10 allowances or claiming complete exemption from withholding if $200 or more in weekly wages was expected. Forms W-4 are still subject to review by the IRS. However, employers will no longer have to submit them to the IRS unless directed to do so in a written notice.

➦ **TIP.** The withholding calculator found on the IRS website (irs.gov) can help employees determine the proper amount of federal income tax withholding. Another useful resource, Publication 919 (How Do I Adjust My Tax Withholding?), is available on the IRS website.

Step 4: Compute each employee's taxable wages

The amount of taxes a church should withhold from an employee's wages depends on the amount of the employee's wages and the information contained on his or her Form W-4. A church must determine the wages of each employee that are subject to withholding and Social Security and Medicare taxes. Wages subject to federal withholding include pay given to an employee for service performed. The pay may be in cash or in other forms. Measure pay that is not in money (such as property) by its fair market value. Wages include a number of items in addition to salary (see Chapter 4 for more details). Some of these items are listed below.

- Bonuses
- Christmas and special occasion offerings
- Retirement gifts
- The portion of an employee's Social Security tax paid by a church
- Personal use of a church-provided car
- Purchases of church property for less than fair market value
- Business expense reimbursements under a nonaccountable business expense reimbursement arrangement

- Imputed interest on no-interest and low-interest church loans
- Most reimbursements of a spouse's travel expenses
- Forgiven debts
- Noncash compensation

Step 5: Determine the amount of income tax to withhold from each employee's wages

The amount of federal income tax the employer should withhold from an employee's wages may be computed in a number of ways. The most common methods are the *wage bracket method* and the *percentage method*.

Wage bracket method

Under the wage bracket method, the employer locates an employee's taxable wages for the applicable payroll period (i.e., weekly, bi-weekly, monthly) on the wage bracket withholding tables in IRS Publication 15 (Circular E) and determines the tax to be withheld by using the column headed by the number of withholding allowances claimed by the employee on Form W-4. You can view a copy of IRS Publication 15 on the IRS website (irs.gov).

Percentage method

Under the percentage method, the employer multiplies the value of one withholding allowance (derived from a table contained in Publication 15) by the number of allowances an employee claims on Form W-4, subtracts the total from the employee's wages, and determines the amount to be withheld from another table.

➥ **TIP.** Be sure you are using the current version of Publication 15 at the beginning of each calendar year, since it will have updated tables for computing the amount of income taxes to withhold from employees' wages, as well as other helpful information.

Both of these withholding options are explained fully in Publication 15.

Step 6: Withhold Social Security and Medicare taxes from nonminister employees' wages

Churches and their nonminister employees are subject to Social Security and Medicare taxes. The combined tax rate is 15.3 percent of each employee's wages. This rate is paid equally by the employer and employee, with each paying a tax of 7.65 percent of the employee's wages. Churches must withhold the employee's share of Social Security and Medicare taxes from the wages of nonminister employees and, in addition, must pay the employer's share of these taxes. This 7.65 percent rate is comprised of two components: (1) a Medicare hospital insurance (HI) tax of 1.45 percent, and (2) an "old-age, survivor and disability" (Social Security) tax of 6.2 percent.

For 2013 the Medicare tax (the 1.45 percent tax rate) applies to all wages, regardless of amount. The Social Security tax (the 6.2 percent tax rate) applies to wages up to $113,700.

PAYROLL TAX HOLIDAY

Congress enacted legislation providing a temporary payroll tax and self-employment tax "holiday" for 2011 and 2012 of two percentage points off the employee share of Social Security tax and the Social Security component of self-employment taxes. This meant that the employee's share of Social Security taxes dropped from 6.2 to 4.2 percent of wages, and the Social Security component of self-employment taxes dropped from 12.4 to 10.4 percent of self-employment earnings for 2011 and 2012. This reduction in taxes was enacted to stimulate the economy by increasing the take-home pay for millions of workers. The holiday ends at the close of 2012 unless extended further by Congress.

The church must withhold the employee's share of Social Security and Medicare taxes from each wage payment. Simply multiply each wage payment by the applicable percentage above. Special tables in IRS Publication 15 help in making this computation. Wages of less than $108.28 per year paid to a church employee are exempt from Social Security and Medicare taxes.

Beginning in 2013, the health care reform legislation enacted by Congress in 2010 increases the employee portion of the Medicare (HI) tax by an additional tax of 0.9 percent on wages received in excess of the threshold amount. However, unlike the general 1.45 percent HI tax on wages, this additional tax is on the combined wages of the employee and the employee's spouse in the case of a joint return. The threshold amount is $250,000 in the case of a joint return or surviving spouse, $125,000 in the case of a married individual filing a separate return, and $200,000 in any other case.

However, in determining the employer's requirement to withhold and liability for the tax, only wages the employee receives from the employer in excess of $200,000 for a year are taken into account, and the employer must disregard the amount of wages received by the employee's spouse. Thus, the employer is only required to withhold on wages in excess of $200,000 for the year, even though the tax may apply to a portion of the employee's wages at or below $200,000, if the employee's spouse also has wages for the year, they are filing a joint return, and their total combined wages for the year exceed $250,000.

> **EXAMPLE.** In 2013 a pastor earns $100,000 in church compensation. His wife, a physician, earns $200,000. The combined income of the husband and wife exceeds the threshold amount of $250,000, so they are liable for an additional Medicare tax of 0.9 percent times compensation in excess of $250,000. However,

neither spouse's employer is required to withhold any portion of this additional tax from their wages even though the combined wages of the taxpayer and the taxpayer's spouse are over the $250,000 threshold, since neither earned compensation of more than $200,000.

The employee is also liable for this additional 0.9 percent HI tax to the extent the tax is not withheld by the employer. The amount of this tax not withheld by an employer must also be taken into account in determining a taxpayer's liability for estimated tax. This same additional HI tax (0.9 percent) applies to the HI portion of SECA tax on self-employment income in excess of the threshold amount. As in the case of the additional HI tax on employee wages, the threshold amount for the additional SECA HI tax is $250,000 in the case of a joint return or surviving spouse, $125,000 in the case of a married individual filing a separate return, and $200,000 in any other case. The threshold amount is reduced (but not below zero) by the amount of wages taken into account in determining the FICA tax with respect to the taxpayer. No deduction is allowed for the additional SECA tax, and the deduction under 1402(a)(12) is determined without regard to the additional SECA tax rate.

This new tax applies to compensation received and taxable years beginning after December 31, 2012.

Step 7: Deposit withheld taxes

Deposit withheld income taxes and employee's share of Social Security and Medicare taxes, along with the employer's share of Social Security and Medicare taxes, by electronic funds transfer using the Electronic Federal Tax Payment System (EFTPS.) If you do not want to use EFTPS, you can arrange for your tax professional, financial institution, payroll service, or other trusted third party to make deposits on your behalf.

Payment with return

You may make a payment of payroll taxes with Form 941 instead of depositing them if you accumulate less than a $2,500 tax liability during the quarter (line 10 of Form 941) and you pay in full with a timely filed Form 941. However, if you are unsure that you will accumulate less than $2,500, deposit under the appropriate rules so you will not be subject to penalties for failure to deposit.

➥ **TIP.** As noted above, under Step 2, separate deposits are required for backup withholdings. Do not combine deposits for Forms 941 and 945 tax liabilities.

When to deposit

Two deposit schedules (monthly or semiweekly) are used by most churches to determine when to deposit Social Security, Medicare, and withheld income taxes. These schedules tell you when a deposit is due after a tax liability arises (e.g., when you have a payday). Prior to the beginning of each calendar year, you must determine which

of the two deposit schedules you are required to use. The deposit schedule you must use is based on the total tax liability you reported on Form 941 during a four-quarter "lookback period," discussed below. Your deposit schedule is not determined by how often you pay your employees or make deposits.

Lookback period. Your deposit schedule for a calendar year is determined from the total taxes reported on your Forms 941 (line 10) in a four-quarter lookback period. The lookback period begins July 1 and ends June 30 of the previous year. If you reported $50,000 or less of taxes for the lookback period, you are a *monthly* schedule depositor; if you reported more than $50,000, you are a *semiweekly* schedule depositor.

Monthly deposit schedule. You are a monthly schedule depositor for a calendar year if the total taxes on Form 941 (line 10) for the four quarters in your lookback period were $50,000 or less. Under the monthly deposit schedule, deposit Form 941 taxes on payments made during a month by the 15th day of the following month. Monthly schedule depositors should not file Form 941 on a monthly basis.

Semiweekly deposit schedule. You are a semiweekly schedule depositor for a calendar year if the total taxes on Form 941 (line 10) during your lookback period were more than $50,000. Under the semiweekly deposit schedule, deposit Form 941 taxes on payments made on Wednesday, Thursday, and Friday by the following Wednesday. Deposit amounts accumulated on payments made on Saturday, Sunday, Monday, and Tuesday by the following Friday.

➥ **TIP.** If a deposit is required to be made on a day that is not a banking day, the deposit is considered timely if it is made by the close of the next banking day. In addition to federal and state bank holidays, Saturdays and Sundays are treated as nonbanking days. For example, if a deposit is required to be made on a Friday and Friday is not a banking day, the deposit will be considered timely if it is made by the following Monday (if that Monday is a banking day).

➥ **TIP.** The terms "monthly schedule depositor" and "semiweekly schedule depositor" do not refer to how often your business pays its employees or even how often you are required to make deposits. The terms identify which set of deposit rules you must follow when an employment tax liability arises. The deposit rules are based on the dates wages are paid, not on when tax liabilities are accrued.

How to deposit

You must make electronic deposits of all depository taxes (such as employment taxes) using the Electronic Federal Tax Payment System (EFTPS). If you do not want to use EFTPS, you can arrange for your tax professional, financial institution, payroll service, or other trusted third party to make deposits on your behalf.

Deposit penalties

Penalties may apply if you do not make required deposits on time, if you make deposits for less than the required amount, or if you do not use EFTPS when required. The penalties do not apply if any failure to make a proper and timely deposit was due to reasonable cause and not to willful neglect. For amounts not properly or timely deposited, the penalty rates are (1) 2 percent for deposits made 1 to 4 days late; (2) 5 percent for deposits made 6 to 15 days late; (3) 10 percent for deposits made 16 or more days late; (4) 10 percent for deposits made at an unauthorized financial institution, paid directly to the IRS, or paid with your tax return; (5) 10 percent for amounts subject to electronic deposit requirements but not deposited using EFTPS; and (6) 15 percent for amounts still unpaid more than 10 days after the date of the first notice the IRS sent asking for the tax due or the day on which you receive notice and demand for immediate payment, whichever is earlier.

Step 8: File Form 941

Form 941 reports the number of employees and amount of Social Security and Medicare taxes and withheld income taxes that are payable. Form 941 contains a box on line 4 that is checked if wages and other compensation are not subject to Social Security or Medicare tax. This box should be checked if your church filed a timely Form 8274 with the IRS, exempting itself from the employer's share of Social Security and Medicare taxes. See section B of this chapter for more information.

Form 941 is due on the last day of the month following the end of each calendar quarter, as shown below:

QUARTER	ENDING	DUE DATE OF FORM 941
January–March	March 31	April 30
April–June	June 30	July 31
July–September	September 30	October 31
October–December	December 31	January 31

➥ **TIP.** The Form 941 e-file program allows a taxpayer to electronically file Form 941 using a personal computer, modem, and commercial tax preparation software. Contact the IRS at 1-866-255-0654 or visit the IRS website (irs.gov) for more information.

➥ **TIP.** You can call the IRS toll free at 1-800-829-4933 for answers to your questions about completing Form 941, tax deposit rules, or obtaining an EIN.

Clergy wages

The wages of ministers who report their income taxes as employees are reported on line 2 along with the wages of nonminister employees. Do not include a minister's housing allowance on this line, since it will not be reported on the Form W-2 issued to the minister. However, ministers' wages are exempt from tax withholding, so no amount will be entered on line 3 with respect to minister employees unless they have elected voluntary tax withholding.

Ministers are always deemed to be self-employed for Social Security with respect to services performed in the exercise of ministry, so they do not pay the employee's share of Social Security or Medicare taxes, and their employing church does not pay the employer's share of these taxes. Instead, ministers pay the self-employment tax. As a result, no amount is entered on lines 5a through 5d.

Churches with only one employee

Some smaller churches have only one employee (the minister). They also may have another worker, such as a part-time custodian, who is self-employed for tax reporting purposes. Are these churches required to file a Form 941? Consider the following three points:

(1) IRS regulation 31.6011(a)-4T. This regulation states:

> *Every person required to make a return of income tax withheld from wages pursuant to section 3402 shall make a return for the first calendar quarter in which the person is required to deduct and withhold such tax and for each subsequent calendar quarter, whether or not wages are paid therein, until the person has filed a final return.*

According to this regulation, only those employers that are required to withhold income taxes from the wages of employees pursuant to section 3402 of the tax code are required to file a Form 941. Section 3401(a)(9) states that employee wages subject to income tax withholding does not include compensation paid for "services performed by a duly ordained, commissioned, or licensed minister of a church in the exercise of his ministry or by a member of a religious order in the exercise of duties required by such order." As a result, the wages of a minister are not subject to income tax withholding; therefore, according to the above-quoted regulation, the minister's employing church is not required to file a Form 941 if the minister is the only employee.

If the church employs nonminister employees, it would have to file Forms 941, since the wages of these employees would be subject to income tax withholding. The same would be true if a church has only one employee, its minister, who has elected voluntary income tax withholding.

(2) Form 941 instructions. The instructions to IRS Form 941 state: "File your initial Form 941 for the quarter in which you first paid wages that are subject to Social Security and Medicare taxes or subject to federal income tax withholding." Since a church with only one employee (its minister) does not pay wages subject to Social Security or Medicare taxes or to income tax withholding, it is not required to file Form 941.

(3) IRS Publication 15. IRS Publication 15 (Employer's Tax Guide) states: "Each quarter, all employers who pay wages subject to income tax withholding . . . or Social Security and Medicare taxes must file Form 941." Since a church with only one employee (its minister) does not pay wages subject to Social Security or Medicare taxes or to income tax withholding, it is not required to file Form 941.

Each of these three grounds assumes that the minister has not elected voluntary withholding. The same rule would apply to a church with more than one minister-employee, so long as there are no nonminister employees.

Of course, issuing the minister a Form W-2 without filing quarterly Forms 941 will present an apparent discrepancy that may trigger an IRS inquiry. On the other hand, submitting Forms 941 that report a minister's wages but no Social Security and Medicare withholdings will also raise questions. In either case, the apparent discrepancy can be easily explained.

Form 944

Form 944 (Employer's Annual Federal Tax Return) is designed so the smallest employers (those whose annual liability for Social Security, Medicare, and withheld federal income taxes is $1,000 or less) will file and pay these taxes only once a year instead of every quarter using Form 941.

In general, if the IRS has notified you to file Form 944, you must file Form 944 to report all of the following amounts: (1) wages you have paid; (2) federal income tax you withheld; (3) both the employer's and the employee's share of Social Security and Medicare taxes; and (4) advance earned income tax credit (EIC) payments. You must file a Form 944 for each year, even if you have no taxes to report (or you have taxes in excess of $1,000 to report) unless the IRS notifies you that your filing requirement has been changed to Form 941.

If you believe you are eligible to file Form 944, but the IRS did not notify you, call the IRS at 1-800-829-0115 to determine if you can file Form 944. If you contact the IRS and the IRS determines you are eligible to file Form 944, it will send you a written notice that your filing requirement has been changed.

File Form 944 for 2013 by January 31, 2014. If you made deposits in full payment of your taxes for the year by January 31, 2014, you have 10 more calendar days after that date to file your Form 944.

After you file your first Form 944, you must file Form 944 for every year after that, even if you have no taxes to report, or until the IRS notifies you to file Form 941.

File Form 944 only once for each calendar year. If you filed Form 944 electronically, do not also file a paper Form 944.

The IRS matches amounts reported on Form 944 with Form W-2 amounts totaled on Form W-3 (Transmittal of Wage and Tax Statements). If the amounts do not agree, the IRS may contact you.

If your liability for Social Security, Medicare, and withheld federal income taxes is less than $2,500 for the year, you can pay the taxes with your return if you file on time. You do not have to deposit the taxes. However, you may choose to make deposits of these taxes even if your liability is less than $2,500.

Form 944 filers whose payroll grows during the year may be required to make federal tax deposits, but they will still file Form 944 for the year. If your total tax liability for calendar year 2013 is more than $1,000, the IRS will notify you when to begin filing quarterly Forms 941.

If your liability for Social Security, Medicare, and withheld federal income taxes is $2,500 or more for the year, but less than $2,500 for the quarter, you can deposit the taxes by the last day of the month after the end of a quarter. However, if your fourth-quarter tax liability is less than $2,500, you may pay the fourth quarter's tax liability with your timely filed Form 944.

If your liability for Social Security, Medicare, and withheld federal income taxes is $2,500 or more for the quarter, you must deposit monthly or semiweekly, depending on your deposit schedule. See the instructions for Form 944 for details.

Form 941-X

Use Form 941-X to correct errors on a Form 941 that you previously filed. Use Form 941-X to correct

- wages, tips, and other compensation;
- income tax withheld from wages and other compensation;
- taxable Social Security wages;
- taxable Medicare wages; and
- credits for COBRA premium assistance payments.

When you discover an error on a previously filed Form 941, you must

- correct that error using Form 941-X;
- file a separate Form 941-X for each Form 941 that you are correcting; and
- file Form 941-X separately. Do not file Form 941-X with Form 941.

If you did not file a Form 941 for one or more quarters, do not use Form 941-X. Instead, file Form 941 for each of those quarters. However, if you did not file Forms 941 because you improperly treated workers as independent contractors or nonemployees and are now reclassifying them as employees, see the instructions for line 23 of Form 941-X.

Report the correction of underreported and overreported amounts for the same tax period on a single Form 941-X unless you are requesting a refund or abatement. If you are requesting a refund or abatement and are correcting both underreported and overreported amounts, file one Form 941-X correcting the underreported amounts only and a second Form 941-X correcting the overreported amounts. You will use the adjustment process if you underreported employment taxes and are making a payment or if you overreported employment taxes and will be applying the credit to Form 941 for the period during which you file Form 941-X.

❖ **KEY POINT.** Form 941-X corresponds line-by-line with the Form 941 it is correcting. Since the Form 941-X is a stand-alone form, the employer will be able to file Form 941-X when an error is discovered rather than having to wait to file it at the end of the quarter with the next employment tax return.

➥ **TIP.** Form 941-X is used to make adjustments and claim refunds. If an employer is correcting an overpayment for a Form 941, the employer will be able to either make an adjustment or claim a refund. If an adjustment is made, the amount of the overpayment will be applied as a credit to the quarter in which the Form 941-X is filed. Employers correcting underpayments of employment taxes that result in a balance due can pay using EFTPS, by credit card, or by sending a check along with Form 941-X. The IRS will make both the tax and wage corrections to the actual tax period being corrected, resulting in a more accurate record.

Step 9: Complete Forms W-2 and W-3

❖ **KEY POINT.** Health care reform legislation passed by Congress in 2010 contained a provision requiring the 2011 Form W-2 to be modified to include a box for employers to report the value of the health care insurance they provide for their employees. The IRS announced late in 2010 that it will defer this requirement in order to provide employers with the time they need to make changes to their payroll systems or procedures in preparation for compliance with the new reporting requirement. In a public announcement, the IRS stated: "Although reporting the cost of coverage will be optional with respect to 2011, the IRS continues to stress that the amounts reportable are not taxable. Included in the Affordable Care Act passed by Congress in March, the new reporting requirement is intended to be informational only, and to provide employees with greater transparency into overall health care costs." *IRS News Release IR-2010-103.*

A 2012 Form W-2 must be issued to any employee to whom you paid wages in 2012. You may obtain copies of the Form W-2 from your local IRS office or by calling the IRS toll-free forms number (1-800-TAX-FORM). The form must be completed and issued to each employee by January 31, 2013 (if a worker's employment ends before December 31, you may issue a Form W-2 to the person at any time after the termination of employment).

By February 28, 2013 (March 31, 2013, if you file electronically), submit to the Social Security Administration copies of all Forms W-2 (Copy A) that you issued for 2012 compensation, along with the Form W-3 (transmittal form).

❖ **KEY POINT.** This section discusses the issuance of Forms W-2 for compensation paid in 2012. The 2013 Forms W-2 were not available at the time of publication.

➥ **TIP.** Be sure to add cents to all amounts. Make all dollar entries without a dollar sign and comma, but with a decimal point and cents. For example, $1,000 should read "1000.00." Government scanning equipment assumes that the last two figures of any amount are cents. If you report $40,000 of income as "40000," the scanning equipment would interpret this as 400.00 ($400)! If a box does not apply, leave it blank—do not insert "0."

➥ **TIP.** If a worker's employment ends before December 31, you may issue a Form W-2 to the person at any time after the termination of employment.

➥ **TIP.** You can request an automatic 30-day extension to file Copy A of Form W-2 with the SSA by filing Form 8809. You still must issue a Form W-2 to each employee by January 31 unless you obtain an extension from the IRS.

Changes in 2012 Form W-2 and Form W-3

The 2012 Form W-2 and Form W-3 are similar to the 2011 forms, but note the following:

- **Employee Social Security tax withholding.** Congress temporarily reduced the rate of Social Security tax withholding (for employees only) from 6.2 percent to 4.2 percent for wage payments made in 2011 and 2012.
- **Advance earned income credit (EIC) payments.** The advance earned income credit payment is eliminated for tax years beginning after 2011. Box 9, Advance EIC payments, has been deleted from the 2012 Form W-2 and Form W-3.
- **Interim relief for Form W-2 reporting of the cost of coverage of group health insurance.** Code DD is added to box 12 of the 2012 Form W-2 to report the cost of employer-sponsored health coverage. However, this reporting will not be mandatory for 2012.
- **Form W-3, Kind of Employer.** To improve document matching compliance, box b of the 2012 Form W-3 has been expanded to include a new section, Kind of Employer, which contains five new checkboxes. Filers are required to check one of these new checkboxes. Be sure to check the "None apply" checkbox if none of the other checkboxes apply.
- **Future developments.** The IRS has created a Web page for information about Forms W-2 and W-3 and their instructions at irs.gov/w2. Information about any future developments affecting Forms W-2 and W-3 and their instructions (such as future legislation) will be posted on that page.
- **Form W-3c, box b.** Box b of Form W-3c has been expanded to include an additional line for name, address, and ZIP code.

Completing Form W-2

Here are some tips that will assist church treasurers in completing Forms W-2.

Box a. Report the employee's Social Security number. Insert "applied for" if an employee does not have a Social Security number but has applied for one.

Box b. Insert your church's federal employer identification number (EIN). This is a nine-digit number assigned by the IRS. If you do not have one, you can obtain one by submitting a completed Form SS-4 to the IRS.

✸ **KEY POINT.** Some churches have more than one EIN (for example, some churches that operate a preschool have a number for the church and a number for the preschool). Be sure that the EIN listed on an employee's Form W-2 is the one associated with the employee's actual employer. Also, be sure that this box reports the same EIN that appears on the Forms 941 on which the Form W-2 wages and withholdings are reported.

Box c. List your church's name and address.

Box d. You may use this box to identify individual W-2 forms. You are not required to use this box.

Box e. Identify the employee by name as it appears on his or her Social Security card. Do *not* insert titles or academic degrees, such as Dr., Rev., or D.Min., at the beginning or end of an employee's name. Generally, do not enter "Jr.," "Sr.," etc., in the "Suff." box on Copy A *unless* the suffix appears on the employee's Social Security card. However, the Social Security Administration still prefers that you do not enter the suffix on Copy A. If the name does not fit, you may show first name initial, middle initial, and last name (and ignore the vertical line).

> **EXAMPLE.** Identify pastor John Doe, Jr. as "John Doe," not "Rev. John Doe, Jr."

Box f. List the employee's address and zip code.

Box 1. Report all wages *paid* to the employee during the year. If an employee works for only the last week of December in 2012 and is paid in the first week of January 2013, do not issue a 2012 Form W-2, even though the wages were earned in 2012. The wages are reported when paid—on a 2013 Form W-2.

Here are some common items of income that are reported in box 1:

- Salary.
- Taxable fringe benefits (including cost of employer-provided group term life insurance coverage that exceeds $50,000). However, if you provided your employee a vehicle and included 100 percent of its annual lease value in the employee's income, you must separately report this value to the employee in box 14 (or on a separate statement). The employee can then figure the value of any business use of the vehicle and report it on Form 2106. If you used the commuting rule or the vehicle cents-per-mile rule to value the personal use of the vehicle, you cannot include 100 percent of the value of the use of the vehicle in the employee's income.
- The value of the personal use of an employer provided car.
- Bonuses.
- Most Christmas gifts paid by the church.
- Business expense reimbursements paid under a nonaccountable plan (one that does not require substantiation of business expenses, or does not require excess reimbursements to be returned to the church, or reimburses expenses out of salary reductions). Also note that such reimbursements are subject to income tax and Social Security withholding if paid to nonminister employees.
- If you reimburse employee travel expenses under an accountable plan using a per diem rate, include in box 1 the amount by which your per diem rate reimbursements for the year exceed the IRS-approved per diem rates. Also note that such excess reimbursements are subject to income tax and Social Security withholding if paid to nonminister employees or ministers who have elected voluntary tax withholding. Use code L in box 12 to report the amount equal to the IRS-approved rates.
- If you reimburse employee travel expenses under an accountable plan using a standard mileage rate in excess of the IRS-approved rate (55.5 cents per mile for 2012), include in box 1 the amount by which your mileage rate reimbursements for the year exceed the IRS-approved rates. Also note that such excess reimbursements are subject to income tax and Social Security withholding if paid to nonminister employees or ministers who have elected voluntary tax withholding. Use code L in box 12 to report the amount equal to the IRS-approved rates.
- Employer reimbursements of an employee's nonqualified (nondeductible) moving expenses.
- Any portion of a minister's self-employment taxes paid by the church.
- Amounts includible in income under a nonqualified deferred compensation plan because of section 409A.
- Designated Roth contributions made under a section 403(b) salary reduction agreement.

▲ **CAUTION.** *Taxable fringe benefits not reported as income in box 1 may constitute an automatic excess benefit transaction exposing the recipient and members of the church board to intermediate sanctions in the form of substantial excise taxes. See Chapter 4, section A.3, for details.*

✸ **KEY POINT.** Churches should not include in box 1 the annual rental value of a parsonage or a housing allowance provided to a minister as compensation for ministerial services.

NEED HELP COMPLETING A
FORM W-2, W-3, 1099-MISC, OR 1096?

The IRS operates a centralized call site to answer questions about reporting information on these forms. If you have any questions about completing these forms, call the IRS at 1-866-455-7438, Monday through Friday, 8:30 A.M. to 4:30 P.M. Eastern time.

Box 2. List all federal income taxes you withheld from the employee's wages in 2012. The amounts reported in this box (for all employees) should correspond to the amount of withheld income taxes reported on your four Forms 941 for 2012.

You must notify employees who have no income tax withheld that they may be able to claim an income tax refund because of the Earned Income Tax Credit. You can do this by using a Form W-2 containing the EIC notice on the back of Copy B (all forms provided by the IRS contain this notice).

Box 3. Report a nonminister employee's wages subject to Social Security taxes. The amount in this box usually will be the same as the amount in box 1, but not always. For example, certain retirement contributions are included in box 3 that are not included in box 1. To illustrate, contributions to a tax-sheltered annuity may be excludable from income and not reportable in box 1, but they are subject to Social Security taxes, so they represent Social Security wages for nonminister employees and are reported in box 3.

Also include in box 3 (1) the taxable cost of group term life insurance over $50,000 included in box 1; (2) employee and non-excludable employer contributions to an Archer Medical Savings Account or health savings account (HSA); (3) employee contributions to a SIMPLE retirement account; and (4) adoption benefits.

Box 3 does not report compensation paid to ministers for services performed in the exercise of ministry, since ministers (including those who report their income taxes as employees, but excluding some chaplains) are considered self-employed for Social Security purposes with respect to such services. They pay the self-employment tax, not the employee's share of Social Security and Medicare taxes.

✿ **KEY POINT.** Box 3 should not list more than the maximum wage base ($110,100 for 2012 or $113,700 for 2013).

➥ **TIP.** Churches that filed a timely Form 8274, exempting themselves from the employer's share of FICA taxes, do not report the wages of nonminister employees in this box, since these employees

are considered self-employed for Social Security purposes. See Chapter 11, section B.

Box 4. Report the Social Security tax withheld from a nonminister employee's wages. This tax is imposed on all wages up to a maximum of $106,800 in 2012. Ministers who report their income taxes as employees remain self-employed for Social Security purposes with respect to their ministerial services. Box 4 is left blank for ministers with respect to compensation received in the exercise of their ministry.

✿ **KEY POINT.** The employee's share of Social Security and Medicare taxes has been temporarily reduced for 2012 from 6.2 percent to 4.2 percent for wage payments made in 2012.

Box 5. Report a nonminister employee's wages subject to the Medicare tax (1.45 percent of an employee's wages). Note that there is no limit on the amount of wages subject to this tax. For most workers (earning less than $106,800 in 2012), boxes 3 and 5 should show the same amount. Box 5 is left blank for ministers with respect to compensation received in the exercise of ministry.

Box 6. Report Medicare taxes (1.45 percent of an employee's wages) that you withheld from the nonminister employee's wages in 2012. Box 6 is left blank for ministers with respect to compensation received in the exercise of ministry.

Box 11. Report the total amount you distributed to an employee under a nonqualified deferred compensation plan (including a section 457 plan and some rabbi trusts). This amount should also be reported as wages in box 1. Few churches have section 457 plans, but many have established rabbi trusts for their minister. The purpose of box 11 is for the Social Security Administration to determine if any part of the amount reported in box 1 was earned in a prior year. This information is used to verify that the Social Security Administration has correctly applied the annual earnings test and paid the correct amount of benefits.

If you did not make distributions in 2012, show deferrals (plus earnings) under a nonqualified plan that became taxable for Social Security and Medicare taxes during the year (but were for prior-year services), because the deferred amounts were no longer subject to a substantial risk of forfeiture. See Chapter 10, section A, for additional information. Also report these amounts in boxes 3 and 5. Do not report in box 11 deferrals that are included in boxes 3 or 5 and that are for current-year services (such as those having no substantial risk of forfeiture). If your church made distributions and is reporting any deferrals in boxes 3 and 5, do not complete box 11.

Box 12. Complete and code this box for all items described below. Do not report in box 12 any items that are not listed as codes A through BB. On Copy A (Form W-2), do not enter more than four items in box 12. If more than four items need to be reported in box 12, use a separate Form W-2 to report the additional items, but enter no more than four items on each Copy A (Form W-2). On all other copies of Form W-2 (Copies B, C, etc.), you may enter more than four items in box 12.

Use the IRS code designated below for the item you are entering, followed by the dollar amount for that item. Even if only one item is entered, you must use the IRS code designated for that item. Enter the code using a capital letter. Leave at least one space blank after the code, and enter the dollar amount on the same line. Use decimal points but not dollar signs or commas. For example, if you are reporting $5,300.00 in elective deferrals to a section 403(b) plan, the entry would be "E 5300.00" (not "A 5300.00," even though it is the first or only entry in this box). Report the IRS code to the left of the vertical line in boxes 12a–d and money amount to the right of the vertical line.

The codes most relevant to churches are the following:

C You (the church) provided your employee with more than $50,000 of group term life insurance. Report the cost of coverage in excess of $50,000. It should also be included in box 1 (and in boxes 3 and 5 for nonminister employees).

E Report elective deferrals made by the church to an employee's 403(b) tax-sheltered annuity. An elective deferral is one made by an employee through a voluntary salary reduction agreement. While this amount ordinarily is not reported in box 1, it is included in boxes 3 and 5 for nonminister employees, since it is subject to Social Security and Medicare taxes with respect to such workers.

L You (the church) reimbursed the employee for employee business expenses using a mileage rate or per diem rates, and the amount you reimbursed *exceeds* the IRS-approved amounts. Enter code L in box 12, followed by the amount of the reimbursements that *equal* the IRS-approved standard mileage or per diem rates. Any excess reimbursements (above the per diem or standard mileage rates) should be included in box 1. For nonminister employees, report the excess in boxes 3 and 5 as well. Do not include any per diem or mileage allowance reimbursements for employee business expenses in box 12 if the total reimbursements are *less than or equal to* the amount deemed substantiated under the IRS-approved standard mileage rate or per diem rates.

P You (the church) paid qualified moving expenses reimbursements directly to an employee. Report the amount of these reimbursements. Do not report reimbursements of qualified moving expenses that you paid directly to a third party on behalf of the employee (e.g., to a moving company).

R Report employer contributions to an Archer Medical Savings Account on behalf of the employee. Any portion that is not excluded from the employee's income also should be included in box 1.

S Report employee salary reduction contributions to a SIMPLE retirement account. However, if the SIMPLE account is part of a 401(k) plan, use code D.

T Report amounts paid (or expenses incurred) by an employer for qualified adoption expenses furnished to an employee under an adoption assistance program.

W Report employer contributions to a health savings account (HSA).

Y It is no longer necessary to report deferrals under a section 409A nonqualified deferred compensation plan in box 12 using code Y.

Z Enter all amounts deferred (including earnings on amounts deferred) that are includible in income under section 409A because the NQDC plan fails to satisfy the requirements of section 409A. Do not include amounts properly reported on a Form 1099-MISC, corrected Form 1099-MISC, Form W-2, or Form W-2c for a prior year. Also, do not include amounts that are considered to be subject to a substantial risk of forfeiture for purposes of section 409A. The amount reported in box 12 using code Z is also reported in box 1 and is subject to an additional tax reported on the employee's Form 1040. See Chapter 10 for more details.

BB Report designated Roth contributions under a section 403(b) salary reduction agreement. Do not use this code to report elective deferrals under code E.

DD Starting in tax year 2011, the Affordable Care Act requires employers to report the cost of coverage under an employer-sponsored group health plan. To give employers more time to update their payroll systems, IRS Notice 2010-69 made this requirement optional for all employers in 2011. IRS Notice 2011-28 provided further relief for small employers filing fewer than 250 Forms W-2 by making the reporting requirement optional for them for 2012 as well and continuing this optional treatment for small employers until further guidance is issued. The reporting under this provision is for information only; the amounts reported are not included in taxable wages and are not subject to new taxes.

Box 13. Check the appropriate box.

- *Statutory employee.* Churches rarely, if ever, have statutory employees. These include certain drivers, insurance agents, and salespersons.

- *Retirement plan.* Mark this checkbox if the employee was an active participant (for any part of the year) in any of the following: (1) a qualified pension, profit-sharing, or stock bonus plan described in section 401(a) (including a 401(k) plan); (2) a 403(b) annuity; (3) a simplified employee pension (SEP) plan; or (4) a SIMPLE retirement account.
- *Third party sick pay.* Churches generally will not check this box.

Box 14. This box is optional. You may use it to provide information to your employee. Some churches report a church-designated housing allowance in this box (for ministers who

report their income taxes as employees). This is not mandatory, however.

➥ **TIP.** You also may report in box 14 nonelective church contributions made to an employee's tax-sheltered annuity. These are contributions made by the church that are not funded by reducing the employee's salary.

Boxes 15 through 20. Use these boxes to report state and local income tax information. Enter the two-letter abbreviation for the name of the state. An employer's state ID number is assigned by the

DESIGNATING A MINISTER'S ENTIRE SALARY AS A HOUSING ALLOWANCE

Question. We have a part-time associate pastor who has asked the church to designate his entire salary as a housing allowance. Do we need to issue him a W-2 form at the end of the year reporting no income?

Answer. This is a surprisingly complex question. Here's why. Until 1974, section 6051 of the federal tax code required a Form W-2 to be issued to (1) each employee from whom income, Social Security, or Medicare tax is withheld or (2) each employee from whom income tax would have been withheld if the employee had claimed no more than one withholding allowance or had not claimed exemption from withholding on Form W-4. Churches were not required to issue a W-2 to pastors under this provision since their wages are exempt from tax withholding.

In 1974 Congress enacted a massive pension law (the Employee Retirement Income Security Act, or ERISA). This law added the following phrase to section 6051: "Every employer engaged in a trade or business who pays remuneration for services performed by an employee, including noncash payments, must file a Form W-2 for each employee." Unfortunately, the legislative history contains no explanation of why this language was added. In any event, it was broad enough to require churches to issue a Form W-2 to ministers even though they are not subject to tax withholding.

The 1974 amendment created some ambiguities, and the stated question highlights one of them. Read literally, the revised section 6051 requires a church to issue a Form W-2 to a minister even though all of the minister's income is designated as a housing allowance, no amount is shown in box 1 (wages), and no withholdings of income taxes or Social Security or Medicare taxes are reported. Why? Because the church is an employer "engaged in a trade or business who pays remuneration for services

performed by an employee, including noncash payments." Of course, submitting to the IRS a Form W-2 that identifies a minister by name and Social Security number but has blank boxes for income and withholdings is not consistent with the purpose of the form, which is to report wages and withholdings to the IRS to ensure that the correct amount of taxes are paid. This purpose is not furthered by submitting blank forms. This, however, does not necessarily mean that a church is relieved of obligation to issue a Form W-2.

In 2000 the IRS addressed the question of whether election workers should be issued W-2 forms. Election workers are individuals who are generally employed to perform services for states and local governments at election booths in connection with national, state, or local elections. Government agencies typically pay election workers a set fee for each day of work. The IRS quoted section 6051 of the tax code and concluded that this section "does not require reporting of compensation that is not subject to withholding of FICA tax or income tax. . . . Section 6051 requires reporting of compensation subject to either FICA tax or income tax withholding. No reporting is required . . . for items of income that are not subject to withholding of FICA tax or income tax. If an election worker's compensation is subject to withholding of FICA tax, reporting is required by section 6051 regardless of the amount of compensation." *IRS Revenue Ruling 2000-6.*

This ruling suggests that a church may not be required to issue a W-2 to a part-time pastor whose entire income is designated as a housing allowance.

The IRS operates a centralized call site to answer questions about reporting information on W-2 forms. If you have any questions about completing a Form W-2, call the IRS at 1-866-455-7438, Monday through Friday, 8:30 A.M. to 4:30 P.M. Eastern time.

state. The state and local information boxes can be used to report wages and taxes for two states and two localities. Keep each state's and locality's information separated by the broken line. If you need to report information for more than two states or localities, prepare a second Form W-2. Contact your state or locality for specific reporting information.

✿ **KEY POINT.** The Social Security Administration (SSA) is urging employers to be sure that amounts reported on Form W-3 correspond to amounts reported on quarterly Forms 941. The SSA also noted that the main reason Forms W-2 are rejected is the use of incorrect Social Security numbers.

➥ **TIP.** The IRS has provided the following suggestions to reduce the discrepancies between amounts reported on Forms W-2, W-3, and 941: First, be sure the amounts on Form W-3 are the total amounts from Forms W-2. Second, reconcile Form W-3 with your four quarterly Forms 941 by comparing amounts reported for (1) income tax withholding (box 2); (2) Social Security and Medicare wages (boxes 3, 5, and 7); and (3) Social Security and Medicare taxes withholdings (boxes 4 and 6). Amounts reported on Forms W-2, W-3, and 941 may not match for valid reasons. If they do not match, you should confirm that the reasons are valid.

➥ **TIP.** The most common errors the IRS finds on Forms W-2 are using ink that is too faint; entries that are too small; adding dollar signs to dollar amounts (they are not required); and checking the "retirement plan" box when not applicable.

Furnishing Form W-2 to employees electronically

You may set up a system to electronically furnish Forms W-2 to employees who choose to receive them in this format. Each employee participating must consent electronically, and you must notify the employees of all hardware and software requirements to receive the forms. You may not send Form W-2 electronically to any employee who does not consent or who has revoked consent previously provided.

To furnish Forms W-2 electronically, you must meet the following disclosure requirements and provide a clear and conspicuous statement of each of them to your employees.

- The employee must be informed that he or she may receive a paper Form W-2 if consent is not given to receive it electronically.
- The employee must be informed of the scope and duration of the consent.
- The employee must be informed of any procedure for obtaining a paper copy of any Form W-2 (and whether the request for a paper statement is treated as a withdrawal of his or her consent) after giving consent.
- The employee must be notified about how to withdraw consent and the effective date and manner by which the employer will confirm the withdrawn consent.

- The employee must also be notified that the withdrawn consent does not apply to previously issued Forms W-2.
- The employee must be informed about any conditions under which electronic Forms W-2 will no longer be furnished (for example, termination of employment).
- The employee must be informed of any procedures for updating his or her contract information that enables the employer to provide electronic Forms W-2.
- The employer must notify the employee of any changes to the employer's contact information. *Treas. Reg. 31.6051-1(j).*

The employer must furnish the electronic statements by the due date of the paper forms.

✿ **KEY POINT.** Employers can submit Forms W-2 to the Social Security Administration electronically. Visit the SSA website for details.

Internet verification of Social Security numbers

The Social Security Administration (SSA) offers employers two methods for verifying employee SSNs online:

- Verify up to 10 names and numbers (per screen) online using the Social Security Number Verification Service (SSNVS) and receive immediate results. This option is ideal to verify new hires.
- Upload overnight files of up to 250,000 names and SSNs and usually receive results the next government business day. This option is ideal if you want to verify an entire payroll database or if you hire a large number of workers at a time.

While this service is available to all employers and third-party submitters, it can only be used to verify current or former employees and only for wage reporting (Form W-2) purposes.

Why verify names and SSNs online? The Social Security Administration lists the following reasons:

- *Correct names and SSNs on W-2 wage reports are the keys to the successful processing of your annual wage report submission.*
- *It's faster and easier to use than submitting your requests paper listings or using Social Security's telephone verification option.*
- *Results in more accurate wage reports.*
- *Saves you processing costs and reduces the number of W-2s.*
- *Allows Social Security to properly credit your employees' earnings record, which will be important information in determining their Social Security benefits in the future.*

In order to access online verification, you must register. See the Social Security Administration website for information.

Employers have other options for verifying employee SSNs, including telephone and paper options. These are fully explained on the SSA website.

Employee retention of Forms W-2

It is a good practice for employees to keep copies of all Forms W-2 issued to them by their employer until they confirm that the earnings reported on their Forms W-2 correspond to the earnings credited to them on their Social Security Statement. The Social Security Statement is available on the Social Security website and is mailed to workers age 60 or older who are not Social Security recipients.

If earnings reflected on an employee's Social Security Statement are underreported, the easiest way to correct the record is for the employee to present copies of his or her Forms W-2 for the year in question to the nearest Social Security office. While proof of earnings is possible without Forms W-2, it is much more difficult and time-consuming.

➡ **TIP.** Encourage church employees to retain each Form W-2 they receive until they confirm that the earnings reported on the form show up as earnings for the same year on their Social Security Statement. You also may want to include a similar notice to your members in a church bulletin or newsletter.

Completing Form W-3

Anyone required to file Form W-2 must file Form W-3 to transmit Copy A of Forms W-2 to the Social Security Administration. Make a copy of Form W-3 and keep it and Copy D of Forms W-2 with your records for four years. Be sure to use Form W-3 for the correct year. Churches need to file Form W-3 even if they only issue one Form W-2. Form W-3 combines all of the data reported on the individual Forms W-2 issued by an employer. The 2012 Form W-3 is due by February 28, 2013.

❋ **KEY POINT.** The due date for filing Form W-3 for calendar year 2012 is extended to March 31, 2013, for employers that issue their W-2 forms electronically.

❋ **KEY POINT.** Because the Social Security Administration (SSA) processes paper forms by machine, you cannot file Copy A of Forms W-2 and W-3 with the SSA that you download and print from the IRS website. Instead, visit the SSA website at ssa.gov/employer to see if you can file "filled in" versions of Forms W-2 and W-3.

Step 10: Complete Forms 1099-MISC and 1096

A Form 1099-MISC must be issued to any nonemployee who is paid compensation of at least $600 during any year. For compensation paid in 2012, furnish Copy B of this form to the recipient by January 31, 2013, and file Copy A with the IRS by February 28, 2013. If you file electronically, the due date for filing Copy A with the IRS is March 31, 2013. Form 1099-MISC is designed to induce self-employed persons to report their full taxable income.

❋ **KEY POINT.** If you file Form 1099-MISC electronically, the due date for filing with the IRS is postponed to March 31,

2013—a month later than if you file paper forms. The extended due date does not apply to magnetic media filing, and it does not relieve an employer of the obligation to provide workers with a Form 1099-MISC (for 2012) by January 31, 2013. For more information on electronic filing of Form 1099-MISC, see IRS Publication 1220 (available at irs.gov).

The income tax regulations specify that "every person engaged in a trade or business" shall issue a Form 1099-MISC "for each calendar year with respect to payments made by him during the calendar year in the course of his trade or business to another person" of compensation of $600 or more. In other words, a church must issue a Form 1099-MISC to a person only if the following five requirements are satisfied: (1) the church is "engaged in a trade or business"; (2) the church pays the person compensation of $600 or more during the calendar year; (3) the person is self-employed (a nonemployee); (4) the payment is in the course of the church's "trade or business"; and (5) no exception exists.

Is a church engaged in a trade or business? The regulations specify that the term "person engaged in a trade or business" includes not only "those so engaged for gain or profit, but also organizations the activities of which are not for the purpose of gain or profit," including organizations exempt from federal income tax under section 501(c)(3) of the tax code. This includes churches and other religious organizations. There is no doubt that churches are required to issue a Form 1099-MISC if the other requirements are satisfied. Note, however, that various exceptions may apply in a particular case. These are addressed below.

A church should issue a Form 1099-MISC to any person to whom it pays $600 or more in a year in the form of self-employment earnings. These forms can be obtained from any IRS office or by calling the IRS forms hotline at 1-800-829-3676. Self-employment earnings include compensation paid to any individual other than an employee. Examples include ministers who report their income as self-employed for income tax reporting purposes, some part-time custodians, and certain self-employed persons who perform miscellaneous services for the church (plumbers, carpenters, lawn maintenance providers, etc.) who are not incorporated. Exceptions apply, and they are discussed later in this section.

Churches also must issue a Form 1099-MISC to a self-employed person who is paid in property other than money. The regulations state that "if any payment required to be reported in Form 1099-MISC is made in property other than money, the fair market value of the property at the time of payment is the amount to be included on such form." In other words, if a church pays a self-employed minister compensation in the form of a car or other property, the fair market value of the property must be reported on a Form 1099-MISC.

Exceptions

The income tax regulations specify that *no Form 1099-MISC is required* with respect to various kinds of payments, including the following:

Payments of income required to be reported on Forms W-2 or 941. This means that a church should not issue a Form 1099-MISC to any worker who is treated as an employee for income tax and payroll tax reporting.

Payments to a corporation. The Affordable Care Act, enacted by Congress in 2010, contained a provision eliminating the long-standing exemption of payments to corporations from the Form 1099-MISC reporting requirement for payments made after 2012. This provision ignited a firestorm of protest. Congress responded by enacting the Comprehensive 1099 Taxpayer Protection and Repayment of Exchange Subsidy Overpayments Act of 2011, which repealed the Form 1099-MISC requirement for payments made to corporations. The exemption for payments to tax-exempt entities was not affected.

> **EXAMPLE.** In 2013 a church hires a local landscaping contractor to provide landscaping services for the church for an annual fee of $5,000. The contractor is unincorporated and self-employed. The church is required to issue the contractor a Form 1099-MISC reporting the compensation paid to him. It sends a copy of the Form 1099-MISC to the IRS.

> **EXAMPLE.** Same facts as the previous example, except that the contractor is incorporated. The church is not required to issue a Form 1099-MISC to a corporation, since it is assumed that the corporation will issue the appropriate form (W-2 or 1099) to the contractor.

> **EXAMPLE.** A self-employed, incorporated evangelist conducts religious services at a church on two occasions during 2013 and is paid $500 on each occasion. The church also reimburses the evangelist's substantiated travel expenses under its accountable reimbursement plan. The church is not required to issue a Form 1099-MISC to the evangelist, since his ministry is incorporated and his corporation is tax-exempt. It is a good practice for churches to confirm an evangelist's representation that he or she is a tax-exempt corporation. This is easily done by (1) checking with the secretary of state's office in the state in which the evangelist is allegedly incorporated to confirm nonprofit corporate status (in most states this can be done via the secretary of state's website) and (2) confirming that the corporation is tax-exempt by searching the online directory of tax-exempt organizations on the IRS website.

Payments of bills for merchandise, telegrams, telephone, freight, storage, and similar charges. According to this exception, a church need not issue a Form 1099-MISC to the telephone company, UPS, or to vendors from which it purchases merchandise.

Travel expense reimbursements paid under an accountable reimbursement arrangement. According to this exception, a church need not report on a Form 1099-MISC the amount of travel and other business expense reimbursements that it pays to a self-employed worker under an accountable reimbursement arrangement (i.e., expenses are reimbursed only if they are substantiated as to amount, date, place, and business nature, and any excess reimbursements must be returned to the employer).

On the other hand, travel expense reimbursements (or advances) paid to a self-employed person without adequate substantiation are considered to be nonaccountable and must be reported as compensation on the Form 1099-MISC. An example of a non-accountable reimbursement would be a monthly car allowance paid to a minister without any requirement that the minister substantiate that the allowances were used to pay for business expenses. Another common example of a nonaccountable reimbursement would be a church's reimbursement of a guest speaker's travel expenses based on the speaker's oral statement or estimate of the amount of the expenses (without any documentary substantiation).

Payments not made in the course of a trade or business. The income tax regulations specify that organizations must issue a Form 1099-MISC only with respect to payments they make in the course of their trade or business. As a result, the Form 1099-MISC filing requirement does "not apply to an amount paid by the proprietor of a business to a physician for medical services rendered by the physician to the proprietor's child." Similarly, a homeowner need not issue a Form 1099-MISC to a roofer or carpenter who is paid $600 or more during the year, because the payment is not made "in the course of a trade or business." The same result applies to payments most persons make to dentists, physicians, lawyers, photographers, and similar professionals, to the extent that such payments are not made in the course of a trade or business.

Canceled debts

The forgiveness or cancellation of a debt represents taxable income to the debtor. However, the instructions to Form 1099-MISC specify that "a canceled debt is not reportable on Form 1099-MISC." The instructions clarify that only financial institutions are required to report a canceled debt as income, and this is done on Form 1099-C. Of course, if the debtor is an employee, the forgiven debt represents taxable income that should be added to the debtor's compensation that is reported on Form W-2.

Repairs

The instructions for Form 1099-MISC clarify that "payment for services, including payment for parts or materials used to perform the services" are reportable as nonemployee compensation "if supplying the parts or materials was incidental to providing the service. For example, report the entire insurance company payments to an auto repair shop under a repair contract showing an amount for labor and another amount for parts, since furnishing parts was incidental to repairing the auto."

The $600 requirement

As noted above, churches need not issue a person a Form 1099-MISC unless the individual is paid $600 or more in compensation. Let's take a closer look at this rule.

Compensation of less than $600. There is no need to issue a Form 1099-MISC to persons paid less than $600 in self-employment earnings during the year.

Accountable reimbursements of business expenses. Since reimbursements under an accountable business expense reimbursement arrangement are not included in the reportable income of self-employed persons, it is reasonable to assume that such reimbursements should not count toward the $600 threshold for filing a Form 1099-MISC. Under an accountable reimbursement arrangement, an employer reimburses a worker's expenses only if the worker substantiates (with documentary evidence, including receipts for individual expenses of $75 or more) the amount, date, location, and business purpose of each reimbursed expense within a reasonable time. The instructions for Form 1099-MISC state that a "travel reimbursement for which the nonemployee did not account to the payer, if the . . . reimbursement totals at least $600" must be reported on the form. This implies that accountable reimbursements do not count toward the $600 filing amount.

> **EXAMPLE.** A church paid a guest speaker (an ordained minister) $1,000 in 2012, of which $300 represents reimbursement of substantiated travel expenses and $200 represents a church-designated housing allowance. No Form 1099-MISC should be issued, since the church has only paid the speaker $500 of reportable income.

> **EXAMPLE.** Same facts as the previous example, except that the guest speaker "substantiated" travel expenses solely by means of a handwritten note not accompanied by any receipts or other supporting documentary evidence. The church's reimbursement of the $300 of travel expenses under these circumstances constitutes a nonaccountable arrangement. As a result, the reimbursements must be reported as income. Since the travel expense reimbursements and compensation amount to $800, the church must issue a Form 1099-MISC. However, the Form 1099-MISC would only report $800 (the housing allowance would not be included).

Benevolence recipients

Should a church give recipients of benevolence distributions a Form 1099-MISC (for distributions of $600 or more for the year)? Ordinarily, the answer would be no, since the Form 1099-MISC is issued only to nonemployees who receive *compensation* of $600 or more from the church during the year. *IRS Revenue Ruling 2003-12; IRS*

Letter Rulings 9314014, 200113031. To the extent that benevolence distributions to a particular individual represent a legitimate charitable distribution by the church (consistent with its exempt purposes), no Form 1099-MISC would be required. It would be unrealistic to characterize such distributions as compensation for services rendered when the individual performed no services for the church.

Completing the Form 1099-MISC

A Form 1099-MISC is easy to complete. A church (the "payer") should list its name, street address (no post office box numbers), and employer identification number on the form as well as the name, address, and Social Security number (or other tax identification number) of the recipient. Form 1099-MISC includes 14 numbered boxes. The key boxes are 1, 3, 4, and 7. Let's look at these individually.

Box 1. Report in this box amounts paid to recipients for all types of "rents," such as real estate rentals paid for office space, machine rentals, and equipment rentals (e.g., hiring a bulldozer to clear land for a parking lot).

Box 3. Report compensation paid to a worker that is not subject to self-employment tax (and is not reported anywhere else on Form 1099-MISC). Churches ordinarily will not use this box.

Box 4. Report backup withholding (explained elsewhere in this section) in this box.

Box 7. Report compensation paid to a nonemployee (self-employed person) in the course of the payer's "trade or business." This would include compensation a church pays to a pastor who is self-employed for income tax reporting, or to any other self-employed person who performs services on behalf of the church.

FORM 1099-MISC CHECKLIST

Form 1099-MISC is one of the most neglected church reporting requirements. Here is a simple test that may help. In general, a church must issue a Form 1099-MISC to an individual if all of the following five conditions are satisfied:

- The church is "engaged in a trade or business" (includes nonprofit activities).
- The church pays the person compensation of $600 or more during the calendar year.
- The person is self-employed, rather than an employee.
- The payment is in the course of the church's "trade or business."
- No exception exists.

Box 14. Report in *box 7* fees you pay to an attorney who represents you in the course of your church activities ("trade or business"), and report in *box 14* an amount you pay to an attorney that is not reportable in box 7 because it was not compensation you paid to an attorney who represented you. The purpose of this reporting requirement is to disclose settlement payments made to litigants and their attorneys. This box would apply to a church only if it pays a settlement to a litigant in a lawsuit for an uninsured claim.

> **EXAMPLE.** B is a former employee who sues a church for back wages and is represented by attorney C. The claim is not covered under any church insurance policy. The church, out of its own funds, settles the suit for $100,000 that represents taxable wages and writes a settlement check payable jointly to B and C in the amount of $100,000. The church sends the check to C. C retains $50,000 of the payment and disburses the remaining $50,000 to B. The church must issue a Form 1099-MISC to C, reporting the entire settlement amount in box 14.

> **EXAMPLE.** A church pays an attorney $2,000 to review a property transaction. The church issues the attorney a Form 1099-MISC reporting the $2,000 in box 7.

Box 15a. May show current year deferrals as a nonemployee under a nonqualified deferred compensation (NQDC) plan that is subject to the requirements of section 409A, plus any earnings on current and prior year deferrals. However, this is not mandatory.

Backup withholding
Federal law requires that organizations (including churches) that are required to furnish a Form 1099-MISC to a self-employed worker must apply "backup withholding" if (1) the worker fails or refuses to furnish his or her Social Security number (or other taxpayer identification number), *or* (2) the IRS notifies you that the worker's Social Security number is incorrect, *or* (3) the IRS notifies you to apply backup withholding.

Backup withholding means that you must withhold a specified amount of total compensation from the paycheck of the self-employed person and report the withholdings on Form 945. These requirements are explained fully under Step 2, above. The backup withholding rate is 31 percent of compensation for 2013 unless Congress extends the lower 28 percent rate that applied in 2012 and prior years.

➡ **TIP.** You must file Form 1099-MISC for each person from whom you have withheld any federal income tax under the backup withholding rules, regardless of the amount of the payment. This is in addition to Form 945.

Corrected forms
If you issue a Form 1099-MISC with incorrect information, you should issue a corrected Form 1099-MISC. See Table 11-2.

Section 530 employees
Payments to section 530 employees should be reported as nonemployee compensation in box 7. Section 530 employees are defined later in this chapter.

❈ **KEY POINT.** What are the ten most common payroll tax reporting errors made by churches? See Table 11-3.

5. TAXPAYER BILL OF RIGHTS 2

❈ **KEY POINT.** The Taxpayer Bill of Rights 2 contains a number of provisions pertaining to payroll reporting requirements.

In 1996 Congress enacted a second Taxpayer Bill of Rights (TBOR2) that contains a number of provisions pertaining to payroll reporting requirements. Two of these provisions are summarized below.

Civil damages for filing fraudulent Forms 1099-MISC
TBOR2 permits employers who issue fraudulent Forms 1099-MISC or W-2 to be sued by the person who receives them. Damages are the greater of $5,000, or actual damages plus attorney's fees. A committee report contains the following observation regarding this provision:

> *The committee does not want to open the door to unwarranted or frivolous actions or abusive litigation practices. The committee is concerned, for example, about the possibility that an unfounded or frivolous action might be brought under this section by a current or former employee of an employer who is not pleased with one or more items that his or her current or former employer has included on the employee's Form W-2. Therefore, actions brought under this section will be subject to Rule 11 of the Federal Rules of Civil Procedure, relating to the imposition of sanctions in the case of unfounded or frivolous claims, to the same extent as other civil actions.*

> **EXAMPLE.** A church loans $15,000 to Pastor B, its youth pastor, to assist him in making a down payment on a home. Pastor B signs a $15,000 promissory note with a five-year term. After two years, Pastor B leaves the church to accept another position. He still owes the church $14,000 (unpaid principal and accrued interest) but does not respond to several requests by the church for repayment. The church informs Pastor B that if he does not respond, it will have no option but to declare the entire balance due in full and include it on his Form W-2 for the year. The church receives no response, so it issues Pastor B a Form W-2 at the end of the year reporting his wages and the $14,000 unpaid note. Pastor B threatens to sue the church for civil damages under TBOR2. Pastor B has no recourse under TBOR2, since the church's Form W-2 was

===== TABLE 11-2 =====

FILING A CORRECTED FORM 1099-MISC

ERROR ON ORIGINAL FORM 1099-MISC	FILING A CORRECTED FORM

Error 1

No Social Security number; incorrect Social Security number; or incorrect name or address of payee (this will require two separate returns to make the correction properly—read and follow all instructions for both Steps 1 and 2)

Step 1—Identify the incorrect Form 1099-MISC, and then . . .

1. Prepare a new Form 1099-MISC.
2. Enter an "X" in the "CORRECTED" box at the top of the form.
3. Enter the payer, recipient, and account number information exactly as it appeared on the original incorrect return; HOWEVER, enter "0" (zero) for all money amounts.

Step 2—Report correct information

Form 1099-MISC

1. Prepare a new Form 1099-MISC.
2. Do not enter an "X" in the "CORRECTED" box at the top of the form. Prepare the new return as though it were an original.
3. Include all the correct information on the form, including the correct Social Security number, name, and address.

Form 1096

1. Prepare a new transmittal Form 1096.
2. Enter the words "Filed to Correct TIN, Name, and/or Address" in the bottom margin of the form.
3. Provide all requested information on the form as it applies to the returns prepared in Steps 1 and 2.
4. File Form 1096 and Copies A of the returns with the appropriate service center.
5. Do not include a copy of the original returns that were filed incorrectly.

Error 2

Incorrect money amount(s); incorrect address; or a return was filed when one should not have been filed (this error requires only one return to make the correction—follow the instructions for Error 1, instead of these instructions, if you must correct an address and a name or SSN)

Form 1099-MISC

1. Prepare a new information return.
2. Enter an "X" in the "CORRECTED" box at the top of the form.
3. Enter the payer, recipient, and SSN information exactly as it appeared on the original incorrect return; HOWEVER, enter all correct money amounts in the correct boxes as they should have appeared on the original return, and enter the recipient's correct address.

Form 1096

1. Prepare a new transmittal Form 1096.
2. Provide all requested information on the form as it applies to Part A, 1 and 2.
3. File Form 1096 and Copy A of the return with the appropriate service center.
4. Do not include a copy of the original return that was filed incorrectly.

---

not fraudulent. If Pastor B sues, he risks being assessed sanctions for filing a frivolous lawsuit.

IRS investigation of disputed Forms W-2 and 1099-MISC

TBOR2 provides that, in any court proceeding, if a taxpayer asserts a reasonable dispute with respect to any item of income reported on an information return (Form 1099-MISC or W-2) filed by an employer and the taxpayer has fully cooperated with the IRS, then the government has the burden of proving the deficiency (in addition to the information return itself). Fully cooperating with

the IRS includes (but is not limited to) the following: bringing the reasonable dispute over the item of income to the attention of the IRS within a reasonable period of time and providing (within a reasonable period of time) access to and inspection of all witnesses, information, and documents within the control of the taxpayer (as reasonably requested by the IRS).

EXAMPLE. A church employee is issued a Form W-2 that incorrectly reports certain items as income. The employee refuses to pay tax on her full income, and this results in an IRS audit. The case is eventually appealed to a federal court, where she insists that her employer erroneously included various items as wages on her Form W-2. Under TBOR2 the government has the burden of proving the deficiency and cannot rely on the Form W-2 itself—if the employee has fully cooperated with the IRS.

6. SECTION 530

In the 1960s the IRS began vigorously challenging employer attempts to classify workers as self-employed rather than as employees. Predictably, employers complained about what was seen as overreaching by the IRS. Employers also were concerned about being assessed large penalties if the IRS successfully reclassified workers as employees. Congress responded with section 530 of the Revenue Act of 1978. Section 530 was designed to provide employers with relief from hostile IRS attempts to reclassify workers from self-employed to employees. It specifies that an employer can treat a worker as self-employed for employment tax purposes so long as three conditions are met:

(1) **Reasonable basis.** First, you had a reasonable basis for not treating the workers as employees. To establish that you had a reasonable basis for not treating the workers as employees, you can show that

- you reasonably relied on a court case about federal taxes or a ruling issued to you by the IRS;
- your organization was audited by the IRS at a time when you treated similar workers as independent contractors and the IRS did not reclassify those workers as employees. You may not rely on an audit commenced after December 31, 1996, unless such audit included an examination for employment tax purposes of whether the individual involved (or any other individual holding a substantially similar position) should be treated as your employee;
- you treated the workers as independent contractors because you knew that was how a significant segment of your industry treated similar workers; or
- you relied on some other reasonable basis. For example, you relied on the advice of a lawyer or accountant who knew the facts about your organization.

If you did not have a reasonable basis for treating the workers as independent contractors, you do not meet the relief requirements.
(2) **Substantive consistency.** In addition, you must have treated the workers, and any similar workers, as independent contractors. If you treated similar workers as employees, this relief provision is not available.
(3) **Reporting consistency.** Finally, you must have filed all required federal tax returns (including information

returns) consistent with your treatment of each worker as not being employees. This means, for example, that if you treated a worker as an independent contractor and paid him or her $600 or more, you must have filed Form 1099-MISC for the worker. Relief is not available for any year or for any workers for whom you did not file the required information returns.

If you do not meet these relief requirements, the IRS will need to determine whether the workers are independent contractors or employees and whether you owe employment taxes for those workers.

❀ **KEY POINT.** Section 530 relieves employers of penalties that otherwise may apply because of their treatment of certain workers as self-employed rather than as employees. It does not directly apply to a worker's personal tax reporting. To illustrate, section 530 can be used by a church to avoid employment tax penalties that otherwise might apply as a result of treating certain workers as self-employed. But section 530 cannot be used by those workers in defending their self-employed status in reporting their own federal taxes.

A congressional report explaining section 530, and which is an authoritative guide to its meaning, states that section 530 is to be "construed liberally in favor of taxpayers." Remember that the purpose of section 530 was to protect employers from zealous attempts by the IRS to reclassify millions of workers as employees, thereby subjecting employers to substantial penalties for incorrectly treating workers as self-employed.

❀ **KEY POINT.** The IRS audit guidelines for ministers (updated in 2009) specify that section 530 does not apply to ministers "since they are statutorily exempt from FICA and are subject to SECA."

7. VOLUNTARY CLASSIFICATION SETTLEMENT PROGRAM

The Voluntary Classification Settlement Program (VCSP) is a voluntary program that provides an opportunity for employers to reclassify their workers as employees for employment tax purposes for future tax periods with partial relief from federal employment taxes. To participate in this new program, the employer must meet certain eligibility requirements, apply to participate in the VCSP by filing Form 8952, Application for Voluntary Classification Settlement Program, and enter into a closing agreement with the IRS.

The VCSP is available for employers who want to voluntarily change the prospective classification of their workers. The program applies to taxpayers who are currently treating their workers (or a class or group of workers) as independent contractors or other nonemployees and want to prospectively treat the workers as employees.

The employer must have consistently treated the workers as nonemployees and must have filed all required Forms 1099 for the workers to be reclassified under the VCSP for the previous three years to participate in the VCSP. Additionally, the employer cannot currently be under audit by the IRS and cannot be currently under audit concerning the classification of the workers by the Department of Labor or by a state government agency.

If the IRS or the Department of Labor has previously audited a taxpayer concerning the classification of the workers, the taxpayer will be eligible only if the taxpayer has complied with the results of that audit.

Exempt organizations may participate in the VCSP if they meet all of the eligibility requirements.

An employer participating in the VCSP will agree to prospectively treat the class or classes of workers as employees for future tax periods. In exchange, the employer

- will pay 10 percent of the employment tax liability that may have been due on compensation paid to the workers for the most recent tax year;
- will not be liable for any interest and penalties on the amount; and
- will not be subject to an employment tax audit with respect to the worker classification of the workers being reclassified under the VCSP for prior years.

In addition, as part of the VCSP, the employer will agree to extend the period of limitations on assessment of employment taxes for three years for the first, second, and third calendar years beginning after the date on which it has agreed under the VCSP closing agreement to begin treating the workers as employees.

To participate in the VCSP, an employer must apply using Form 8952, Application for Voluntary Classification Settlement Program. The application should be filed at least 60 days from the date the employer wants to begin treating its workers as employees.

B. SOCIAL SECURITY TAXES

❖ **KEY POINT.** Federal law allowed churches that had nonminister employees as of July of 1984 to exempt themselves from the employer's share of Social Security and Medicare taxes by filing a Form 8274 with the IRS by October 30, 1984. Many

churches did so. The effect of such an exemption is to treat all nonminister church employees as self-employed for Social Security. Such employees must pay the self-employment tax (just like ministers).

❖ **KEY POINT.** Many churches pay some or all of a minister's self-employment taxes. When this is the case, the amount paid by a church represents taxable income to the minister and should be so reported.

Since the beginning of the Social Security program in 1937, the employees of churches and most other nonprofit organizations were exempted from mandatory coverage. The exemption was designed to encourage nonprofit organizations by freeing them from an additional tax burden that they ordinarily could not pass along to customers through price increases. Churches and other nonprofit organizations were permitted to waive their exemption by filing Forms SS-15 and SS-15a with the IRS.

In 1983 Congress repealed the exemption for calendar years beginning with 1984. The repeal of the exemption was criticized by some church leaders who viewed it as a "tax" on churches, in violation of the constitutional principle of separation of church and state.

1. A LIMITED EXEMPTION

In the Tax Reform Act of 1984, Congress responded to such criticism by again amending the Social Security Act, this time to give churches a one-time irrevocable election to exempt themselves from Social Security coverage if they were opposed, for religious reasons, to the payment of the employer's share of Social Security and Medicare taxes and if they filed an election (Form 8274, reproduced at the end of this chapter) with the IRS *prior* to the deadline for filing the first quarterly employer's tax return (Form 941) after July 17, 1984, on which the *employer's* share of Social Security and Medicare taxes is reported. Since a Form 941 is due on the last day of the month following the end of each calendar quarter (i.e., April 30, July 31, October 31, and January 31), the election deadline for churches in existence as of July 1984 and having at least one nonminister employee was October 30, 1984 (the day before the deadline for filing Form 941 for the quarter ending September 30). Churches either not in existence as of July 1984, or not having nonminister employees at that time, have until the day prior to the deadline for their first Form 941 to file an election (Form 8274).

To illustrate, a church organized in 1960 that hires its first nonminister employee (a secretary) on September 1, 2013, has until October 30, 2013, to file Form 8274. No deadline exists until a church has at least one nonminister employee, since the deadline corresponds to the next filing date of a church's quarterly tax return

======== **TABLE 11-3** ========

10 COMMON PAYROLL TAX REPORTING ERRORS

COMMON ERROR	CORRECT REPORTING PROCEDURE
1. Treating ministers as self-employed for income taxes	Most ministers are employees for federal income tax reporting purposes.
2. Treating ministers as employees for Social Security	Ministers always are self-employed for Social Security with respect to ministerial services (except some chaplains).
3. Withholding taxes from ministers' pay without authorization	Ministers are exempt from income tax withholding, whether they report their income taxes as employees or self-employed; ministers who report their income taxes as employees can request voluntary withholding by submitting a Form W-4 to the church.
4. Withholding payroll taxes from ministers who report their income taxes and Social Security taxes as self-employed	Do not withhold payroll taxes from self-employed persons.
5. Giving Forms W-2 to self-employed ministers	Provide self-employed workers who are paid $600 or more during the year with a Form 1099-MISC, not a Form W-2.
6. Failure to provide Forms 1099-MISC to nonemployee recipients of $600 or more of annual compensation	A Form 1099-MISC must be issued to such persons.
7. Church employees failing to pay self-employment taxes if their employing church exempted itself from the employer's share of FICA taxes (by filing a Form 8274)	Such employees are treated as self-employed for Social Security with respect to their church compensation and must pay the self-employment tax.
8. Not filing Forms 941	These forms must be filed quarterly by a church with one or more nonminister employees (or a minister who elects voluntary withholding).
9. Not issuing Forms W-2 or 1099-MISC	A Form W-2 must be issued to each employee, and a Form 1099-MISC must be issued to each nonemployee (who received compensation of at least $600 during the year).
10. Not complying with payroll tax deposit requirements	Submit directly to the IRS payroll taxes of less than $2,500 at end of any calendar quarter with Form 941; if accumulated payroll taxes are $2,500 or more at end of any month, deposit them by electronic fund transfer using the Electronic Federal Tax Payment System (EFTPS). If you do not want to use EFTPS, you can arrange for your tax professional, financial institution, payroll service, or other trusted third party to make deposits on your behalf.

reporting the employer's share of Social Security taxes, and no tax or return is due until a church has nonminister employees.

2. NONMINISTER EMPLOYEES

What about a church with only one employee—its minister? As noted in the preceding section, the preferred practice would be for the church to file quarterly 941 forms reporting the minister's compensation, even though no taxes are withheld. But would the church thereby be prevented from filing a Form 8274 at a later date in the event that it hires nonminister employees (on the ground that it already has submitted Forms 941, and accordingly

the deadline for filing Form 8274 has expired)? The answer is no, since section 3121(w) of the tax code defines the deadline for filing Form 8274 as any time prior to the date of a church's first Form 941 "for the tax imposed under section 3111." Section 3111 pertains to the employer's share of Social Security and Medicare taxes, and therefore a church with no nonminister employees does not trigger the deadline for filing a Form 8274 by filing Forms 941 for its minister.

A timely election relieves a church of the obligation to pay the employer's share of Social Security and Medicare taxes (7.65 percent of an employee's wages in 2012 and 2013) and relieves each nonminister employee of the obligation to pay the employee's share of

Social Security and Medicare taxes (an additional 7.65 percent of wages in 2012 and 2013). However, the employee is not relieved of all Social Security tax liability. On the contrary, the nonminister employees of an electing church are required to report and pay their Social Security taxes as self-employed individuals (the self-employment tax) if their annual compensation exceeds $108.28. This tax is significantly greater than the employee's share of Social Security and Medicare taxes.

EXAMPLE. In 2013 the self-employment tax is 15.3 percent of net self-employment earnings. Therefore, a nonminister church employee receiving a salary of $18,000 in 2013 would pay $1,377 in Social Security and Medicare taxes if his or her church did not file an election on Form 8274 (the church would pay an additional $1,377). However, if the church filed the election to exempt itself from the employer's share of Social Security and Medicare taxes, the following consequences occur: (1) the church pays no Social Security and Medicare taxes; (2) the employee pays no Social Security and Medicare taxes; and (3) the employee must report and pay a self-employment tax liability of $2,754 (an additional $1,377 in taxes). The self-employment tax is reduced by an income tax deduction of half the self-employment tax, and also by a similar deduction in computing self-employment taxes (explained fully in Chapter 9). This example assumes that the payroll tax holiday that for 2011 reduced the employee's share of Social Security taxes from 6.2 to 4.2 percent, and the Social Security component of self-employment taxes from 12.4 to 10.4 percent, does not apply in 2013.

The employees of an electing church ordinarily will be required to use the estimated tax procedure (Form 1040-ES) to report and pay their estimated self-employment tax in quarterly installments. Alternatively, an employee of an electing church can request that an additional amount be withheld from his or her wages each pay period to cover the estimated self-employment tax liability. The church simply withholds an additional amount from each paycheck to cover an employee's estimated self-employment tax liability for the year, and then reports this additional amount as additional income tax (not FICA tax) withheld on its quarterly Forms 941. The excess income tax withheld is a credit against tax that each employee may claim on his or her federal income tax return and is applied against an employee's self-employment tax liability. A similar withholding arrangement has been approved by the IRS with respect to a minister-employee's self-employment tax (see IRS Publication 517). Unless an employee makes such a request, a church that has elected to exempt itself from the employer's share of Social Security and Medicare taxes has no obligation to withhold Social Security taxes from the wages of its employees.

Many churches and church employees consider this situation unfair. Churches are free to exempt themselves from Social Security taxes, but only at the cost of increasing the tax liability of their employees. In response, many electing churches have increased the salary of their employees to compensate for the increase in taxes. Of course, this leaves the church in essentially the same position as if it had not elected to be exempt—it is, in effect, paying Social Security taxes indirectly. This dilemma, argued a church in Pennsylvania, unconstitutionally restricts the religious freedom of churches by forcing them (contrary to their religious convictions) to divert church resources away from religious and charitable functions in order to increase employee compensation (and thereby indirectly pay the Social Security tax).

A federal appeals court rejected this contention. The court based its ruling on a 1982 Supreme Court decision that upheld the imposition of the Social Security tax to employees of Amish farmers even though this directly violated the farmers' religious beliefs. The Supreme Court had observed that "tax systems could not function if denominations were allowed to challenge the tax systems because tax payments were spent in a manner that violates their religious belief." It concluded that the broad public interest in the maintenance of the federal tax systems was of such a high order that religious belief in conflict with the payment of the taxes provides no constitutional basis for resisting them.

The appeals court found this precedent controlling in resolving the challenge to Social Security coverage of church employees. The appeals court also rejected the church's argument that the taxation of church employees violates the First Amendment's nonestablishment of religion clause by creating an "excessive entanglement" between church and state. It also rejected the claim that the tax code was impermissibly discriminatory in granting ministers an exemption from Social Security coverage, but not churches or church employees. *Bethel Baptist Church v. United States, 822 F.2d 1334 (3rd Cir. 1987).*

Churches that elected to exempt themselves from the employer's share of Social Security and Medicare taxes have less need to increase the compensation of nonminister employees, since such persons are entitled to deduct half their self-employment taxes for income tax and self-employment tax purposes (this is supposed to partially offset the disadvantages of self-employed persons paying a self-employment tax at the combined Social Security and Medicare tax rate of 15.3 percent). See Chapter 9 for details. Churches that file a timely election application remain subject to income tax withholding and reporting requirements with respect to all nonminister employees and to ministers who have requested voluntary withholding. They must continue to issue Forms W-2 to all nonminister employees and to ministers who are treated as employees for income tax purposes. In addition, they must file the employer's quarterly tax return (Form 941) with the IRS. The law specifies that the IRS can revoke a church's exemption from Social Security coverage if the church fails to issue Forms W-2 for a period of two years or more to nonminister employees or ministers who report their federal income taxes as employees and if the church disregards an IRS request to furnish employees with such forms for the period during which its election has been in effect.

Only churches that are opposed *for religious reasons* to the payment of Social Security taxes are eligible for the exemption. Apparently, a local church will qualify for the exemption if it is opposed, for religious reasons, to the payment of Social Security taxes, even if it is affiliated with a religious denomination that has no official position on the subject. Churches, conventions or association of churches, and elementary and secondary schools that are controlled, operated, or principally supported by a church are all eligible for the exemption. Qualified church-controlled organizations also are eligible for the exemption. Such organizations include most church-controlled tax-exempt organizations described in section 501(c)(3) of the tax code. See Chapter 10, section A, for a full explanation of this term.

A number of churches having nonminister employees (e.g., an office secretary) apparently do not know whether they have elected to exempt themselves from the employer's share of Social Security (FICA) taxes by filing a timely Form 8274. Churches that filed a timely election but that nevertheless paid all employment taxes due from the effective date of their election through December 31, 1986 (a fairly common practice by churches that could not remember if they ever filed the election), are treated as if they never filed the election. *Internal Revenue News Release IR-87-94.*

> **EXAMPLE.** The IRS rejected a church's application for exemption from the employer's share of FICA taxes, since the application (Form 8274) was filed after the deadline. The church asked the IRS to waive the deadline, but the IRS refused. The IRS concluded: "The law setting forth the filing of elections for tax exemption was enacted by Congress, and there are no statutory provisions to permit an exception, for any reason, if the due date is missed. While we can sympathize with your situation, we have no authority to extend the period for filing the Form 8274, or to grant an exception to the timely filing requirement imposed by the law. Accordingly, you should continue to file Form 941." *IRS Letter Ruling 199911025.*

3. REVOKING THE EXEMPTION

Churches that have elected to exempt themselves from the employer's share of Social Security and Medicare taxes (by filing a timely Form 8274) can revoke their exemption. Temporary regulations issued by the Treasury Department specify that churches can revoke their exemption by filing a Form 941 (employer's quarterly tax return) accompanied by full payment of Social Security taxes for that quarter.

To illustrate, if a church with three employees elects in May 2013 to revoke its election to be exempt from Social Security taxes, it should submit Form 941 by July 31, 2013 (the deadline for filing a Form 941 for the second calendar quarter), along with applicable Social Security and Medicare taxes for that quarter. Of course, if a church revokes its exemption, nonminister employees are no longer treated as self-employed for Social Security and should no longer file quarterly estimated tax payments (their Social Security and Medicare taxes will be withheld from their wages).

C. UNEMPLOYMENT TAXES

The application of unemployment taxes to churches is addressed in Chapter 12, section D.

D. FORM 990 (ANNUAL INFORMATION RETURNS)

"Information returns" are financial reports that provide information to the IRS other than an amount of tax due. Some common types of information returns have already been discussed in this chapter (Forms W-2, 1099-MISC, and 941). This section will describe another type of information return that must be filed annually by certain kinds of tax-exempt organizations.

Section 6033 of the tax code requires every organization that is exempt from federal income taxes to file an annual return (Form 990) with the IRS. Form 990 consists of more than 100 questions, requesting detailed information about the finances, services, and administration of the exempt organization. However, section 6033 exempts several organizations from the reporting requirements, including the following:

- A church, an interchurch organization of local units of a church, a convention or association of churches, an integrated auxiliary of a church (such as a men's or women's organization, religious school, mission society, or youth group), and certain church-controlled organizations (see Revenue Procedure 86-23). The term "integrated auxiliary" is defined fully in Chapter 12, section A.4, in this guide.
- A school below college level affiliated with a church (or operated by a religious order).
- A mission society sponsored by or affiliated with one or more churches or church denominations, if more than half of the

society's activities are conducted in, or directed at persons in, foreign countries.

- An exclusively religious activity of any religious order.
- A religious or apostolic organization described in section 501(d) of the tax code (these organizations file Form 1065).
- An exempt organization whose annual gross receipts are normally $50,000 or less (some of these organizations are required to file the simpler Form 990-N, as noted below).

Some members of Congress have suggested that churches (and most other exempt organizations mentioned above) be required to file Form 990 each year as a means of avoiding financial impropriety and fraud. At this time such efforts are merely suggestions.

•➡ **TIP.** Charities with annual gross income of less than $50,000 are exempt from filing an annual information return (Form 990) with the IRS. But they are required by law to furnish to the IRS annually, in electronic format (e-postcard), Form 990-N showing the legal name of the organization, any name under which the organization operates or does business, the organization's mailing address and website address (if any), the organization's taxpayer identification number, the name and address of a principal officer, and evidence of the organization's continuing basis for its exemption from the information return filing requirement. If an organization fails to provide the required notice for three consecutive years, its tax-exempt status is revoked. Churches are exempt from this reporting requirement.

EXAMPLE. The IRS ruled that a separately incorporated, church-controlled private elementary and secondary school was exempt from federal income taxation as a result of its relationship with the church and was not required to file an annual information return (Form 990) with the IRS. The IRS pointed out that (1) the school was created to further the religious purposes of the church by providing education consistent with the church's religious teachings; (2) the spiritual teachings and values of the church were incorporated into all aspects of school life; (3) the school conducted mandatory weekly worship service for all students; (4) the church controlled the school's board of directors; (5) a majority of the school's board were required to be members of the church; and (6) admissions literature clearly identified the school's relationship with the church. *IRS Private Letter Ruling 200615027.*

E. PROOF OF RACIAL NONDISCRIMINATION

✿ **KEY POINT.** Independent religious schools that are not affiliated with a church or denomination, and that file Form 990 (see above), do not file Form 5578. Instead, they make their annual certification of racial nondiscrimination directly on Form 990.

Churches and other religious organizations that operate, supervise, or control a private school must file a certificate of racial nondiscrimination (Form 5578) each year with the IRS. The certificate is due by the 15th day of the fifth month following the end of the organization's fiscal year. This is May 15 of the following year for organizations that operate on a calendar year basis. For example, the Form 5578 for 2012 is due May 15, 2013.

A private school is defined as an educational organization that normally maintains a regular faculty and curriculum and normally has a regularly enrolled body of pupils or students in attendance at the place where its educational activities are regularly conducted. The term includes primary, secondary, preparatory, or high schools; and colleges and universities, whether operated as a separate legal entity or an activity of a church.

✿ **KEY POINT.** The term "school" also includes preschools, and this is what makes the reporting requirement relevant for many churches. As many as 25 percent of all churches operate a preschool program.

Form 5578 is easy to complete. A church official simply identifies the church and the school and certifies that the school has "satisfied the applicable requirements of sections 4.01 through 4.05 of Revenue Procedure 75-50." This reference is to the following requirements:

- The school has a statement in its charter, bylaws, or other governing instrument, or in a resolution of its governing body, that it has a racially nondiscriminatory policy toward students.
- The school has a statement of its racially nondiscriminatory policy toward students in all its brochures and catalogs dealing with student admissions, programs, and scholarships.
- The school makes its racially nondiscriminatory policy known to all segments of the general community served by the school through the publication of a notice of its racially nondiscriminatory policy at least annually in a newspaper of general circulation or through utilization of the broadcast media. However, such notice is not required if one or more exceptions apply. These include the following: (1) During the preceding three years, the enrollment consists of students at least 75 percent of whom are members of the sponsoring church or religious denomination, and the school publicizes its nondiscriminatory policy in religious periodicals distributed in the community. (2) The school draws its students from local communities and follows a racially nondiscriminatory policy toward students and demonstrates that it follows a racially nondiscriminatory policy by

showing that it currently enrolls students of racial minority groups in meaningful numbers.

- The school can demonstrate that all scholarships or other comparable benefits are offered on a racially nondiscriminatory basis.

Filing the certificate of racial nondiscrimination is one of the most commonly ignored federal reporting requirements. Churches that operate a private school (including a preschool), as well as independent schools, may obtain copies of Form 5578 through the IRS website (irs.gov).

A sample Form 5578 is reproduced at the end of this chapter.

F. APPLICATION FOR RECOGNITION OF TAX-EXEMPT STATUS (FORM 1023)

Churches may apply for recognition of exemption from federal income taxes by submitting a Form 1023 to the IRS. This procedure is discussed in Chapter 12, section A.4.

G. UNRELATED BUSINESS INCOME TAX RETURN

Churches that generate unrelated business taxable income may be required to file Form 990-T with the IRS. The unrelated business income tax and Form 990-T are addressed in Chapter 12, section B.

H. CHARITABLE CONTRIBUTIONS

A number of reporting requirements under federal law are associated with charitable contributions. These are discussed fully in Chapter 8 of this tax guide.

I. ILLUSTRATION 1: TAX WITHHOLDING AND REPORTING REQUIREMENTS

2 MINISTER-EMPLOYEES;
4 NONMINISTER EMPLOYEES;
1 SELF-EMPLOYED CUSTODIAN;
CHURCH-OPERATED PRESCHOOL

Note: Since the 2013 payroll tax forms were not available when this book was published, this illustration uses the 2012 forms and reflects the reporting requirements for the fourth quarter of 2012. When appropriate, comments are made regarding changes that take effect in 2013. By studying this illustration, you should have no difficulty completing the corresponding 2013 forms (which will be substantially similar to the 2012 forms).

Assume the following facts:

First Church was organized in 1940 in Anytown, Illinois. Pastor Jacob Ellis has served as senior minister of the church since 2000, and Pastor James Milton has served as associate minister since 2005. Both ministers are ordained, and both report their federal income taxes as employees. However, Pastor Ellis has requested voluntary withholding of his federal income taxes and self-employment taxes, while Pastor Milton has not. Neither minister is exempt from self-employment taxes.

Pastor Ellis's total church compensation was $50,000 in 2012, consisting of a salary of $40,000 and a housing allowance of $10,000. In 2012 the church had an accountable business expense reimbursement arrangement for Pastor Ellis. It reimbursed only those business expenses for which he provided a timely and adequate accounting (substantiating the amount, date, place, and business nature of each expense). The church reimbursed $4,000 of business expenses in 2012.

Pastor Ellis requested voluntary withholding of income taxes in 2012 by submitting a Form W-4 to the church treasurer. He requested that an additional amount ($128) of income taxes be withheld to cover his self-employment tax liability. Note that the church correctly reported this additional withholding as income taxes withheld and not as Social Security or Medicare taxes.

Pastor Milton received $40,000 in compensation from the church in 2012 and, in addition, was permitted to live in the church's parsonage (the parsonage had an annual rental value of $10,000 for 2012).

Pastor Milton did not elect voluntary tax withholding in 2012. He was expected to pay utilities and other miscellaneous expenses associated with living in the parsonage, so the church board declared (in December 2011) $4,000 of his 2012 compensation as a "parsonage allowance." Pastor Milton also was paid a monthly car allowance of $300 in 2012 and was not required to account for any of these reimbursements. As a result, this allowance arrangement was nonaccountable, and all of the reimbursements ($3,600) were reported by the church as taxable income for 2012.

Pastor Milton's total church compensation was $43,600 and consisted of a salary of $36,000, a parsonage allowance of $4,000, and a car allowance of $3,600.

The church employs a full-time secretary, Joan Reed, who was paid an annual salary of $18,000 in 2012. The church employs a full-time bookkeeper, Janice Guerra, who was paid an annual salary of $20,000 in 2012. The church also pays John Rhodes $200 per month to perform all necessary custodial duties. Mr. Rhodes sets his own hours and performs his duties in the manner he chooses (using his own equipment), without any supervision on the part of the church. The church treats Mr. Rhodes as a self-employed person.

Pastor Lane conducted two weeks of special services at the church in November 2012, for which the church paid him $1,000. In addition, the church paid Pastor Lane's travel expenses, which were adequately accounted for under an accountable reimbursement plan.

The church began operating a childcare facility in 1998. In 2012 the facility is attended by 12 preschool-age children. The church has employed two workers to operate the preschool—Susan Peck and Sharon Adams. Both are treated as employees by the church, and each receives a yearly salary of $14,000.

Aside from Mr. Rhodes (the custodian), all workers are paid on a weekly basis. Gross weekly compensation for each worker is as follows: Pastor Ellis—$961.54, including salary and housing allowance ($769.23 net of the housing allowance); Pastor Milton—$838.46, including salary, parsonage allowance, and car allowance (or $761.54 net of the parsonage allowance); Joan Reed—$346.15; Janice Guerra—$384.62; Susan Peck—$269.23; Sharon Adams—$269.23.

1. FILING REQUIREMENTS: THE 10-STEP METHOD

For 2012 the church would have the following filing and reporting requirements. The 10-step method for complying with a church's federal payroll tax reporting obligations (discussed in this chapter) is applied.

Step 1: Obtain an EIN from the IRS
The church obtained an employer identification number (00-0238457) in 1970.

Step 2: Determine workers' status and Social Security numbers
The church determines that each worker is an employee for income tax reporting purposes, except for custodian John Rhodes and guest speaker Pastor Lane (both of whom are self-employed). The church obtains the Social Security numbers for all workers (employees and self-employed).

Step 3: Have employees complete Forms W-4
To enable the church to withhold the proper amount of federal income taxes and Social Security and Medicare taxes from employee wages, the church should be sure that each employee has completed and signed a Form W-4. Each employee did, in fact, prepare a Form W-4 that was effective for 2012, and their forms are set forth below.

Note that Pastor Ellis submitted a revised Form W-4 for 2012 that requested an additional amount of $128 to be withheld from his salary each week to cover his self-employment tax liability. Pastor Ellis estimated that his net self-employment earnings for 2012 would be $50,000 (his total salary of $40,000 plus his housing allowance of $10,000). Note that he properly included his housing allowance in computing his estimated self-employment tax liability. He multiplied his net self-employment earnings of $50,000 by the self-employment tax rate for 2012 (13.3 percent, which reflects the reduction in the Social Security component of self-employment taxes from 12.4 to 10.4 percent for 2012 as a result of the payroll tax holiday authorized by Congress) to obtain his estimated tax liability of $6,650. He divided this amount by 52 to determine the additional amount to be withheld from his salary in 2012 to cover this liability ($128 per week).

Step 4: Compute taxable wages
The church computes the wages of all employees.

Step 5: Determine income tax to be withheld
The church uses the wage bracket method of computing the amount of income taxes to withhold from each employee's wages. Based on the withholding allowances claimed on the employees' Forms W-4 and the wage bracket withholding tables in IRS Publication 15, the church withheld the amounts listed in Table 11-4 each week throughout the year. Note that Ellis, Milton, Reed, and Guerra are married, and Peck and Adams are single. Based on this data, the church withholds income taxes of $194 each week.

The church does not withhold any taxes from the wages of Pastor Milton, but it should advise him of his obligation to report and prepay his federal income taxes and Social Security taxes through use of the estimated tax procedure (Form 1040-ES). Remember that ministers' compensation is exempt from federal payroll tax withholding—even if they report their income taxes as employees. However, ministers who report their income taxes as employees are permitted to elect voluntary withholding (as Pastor Ellis has done). This is not mandatory, so Pastor Milton is free to avoid the withholding rules completely.

TABLE 11-4

WEEKLY PAY AND TAXES WITHHELD

EMPLOYEE	MARITAL STATUS	WITHHOLDING ALLOWANCES	WEEKLY PAY	INCOME TAX WITHHELD	FICA WITHHELD[1]	FICA PAID BY EMPLOYER[2]
Ellis	Married	3	$769.23[3]	$170[4]	$0[5]	$0
Milton	Married	4	$761.54[6]	$0[7]	$0	$0
Reed	Married	3	$346.15	$0	$19.56	$26.48
Peck	Single	2	$269.23	$8	$15.21	$20.60
Adams	Single	1	$269.23	$15	$15.21	$20.60
Guerra	Married	3	$384.62	$1	$21.73	$29.42
TOTAL			$2,800.00	$194	$71.71	$97.10

1. Includes both the Social Security and Medicare tax (combined rate of 5.65% for 2012 due to the payroll tax holiday authorized by Congress).
2. Includes both the Social Security and Medicare tax (combined rate of 7.65%).
3. Wages subject to income tax withholding (Pastor Ellis requested voluntary withholding), net of the housing allowance.
4. The sum of $42 per week (from tax bracket tables) plus an additional $128 per week pursuant to Pastor Ellis's revised Form W-4 (line 6).
5. Ministers, unless exempt, pay self-employment taxes (SECA) rather than FICA taxes.
6. Wages subject to income tax withholding (net of housing allowance), including an average of $69.23 per week ($300 per month) for business expenses under a nonaccountable arrangement.
7. Pastor Milton is exempt from income tax withholding and did not elect voluntary withholding.

Step 6: Withhold Social Security and Medicare taxes from nonminister employees' wages

First Church must withhold from each nonminister employee's wages his or her share of Social Security and Medicare taxes (5.65 percent) and, in addition, must pay the employer's share of Social Security and Medicare taxes (an additional 7.65 percent). The amount of Social Security tax to be withheld from a particular employee's wages is determined by multiplying the current Social Security and Medicare tax rate (5.65 percent) by the employee's taxable wage base. This results in weekly withholding of Social Security and Medicare taxes of $71.71. See Table 11-4.

Step 7: The church must deposit the taxes it withholds

According to the rules discussed in the text, the church deposits these taxes by the 15th day of the following month by electronic funds transfer using the Electronic Federal Tax Payment System (EFTPS). The forms set forth below illustrate the final deposit of 2012 taxes on January 15, 2013. If an employer reported withheld taxes of $50,000 or less during the most recent lookback period (for 2012 the lookback period is July 1, 2010, through June 30, 2011), the taxes are deposited monthly by the 15th day of the following month. Assuming that the total payroll taxes paid by First Church during the lookback period were less than $50,000, the church deposits its payroll taxes for each calendar month in 2012 by the 15th day of the following month.

Step 8: File quarterly Form 941

The church files Forms 941 each quarter (by April 30, July 31, October 31, and January 31). The January 31, 2013, Form 941 (for the final calendar quarter of 2012) is set forth below. Note the following:

- Line 1 is completed only on Form 941 for the first calendar quarter of the year (due April 30).
- Pastor Milton's wages are included on line 2, even though the church withheld no taxes from his wages.
- Pastor Ellis's wages are included on line 2.
- The amount on line 2 equals the combined weekly payroll of all employees for the 13 payroll periods in the fourth quarter.
- The amount on line 3 equals the total amount of all federal income taxes withheld during the 13 payroll periods in the fourth quarter.
- Lines 5a through 5d report wages paid during the quarter that are subject to Social Security and Medicare taxes. Since ministers (Pastor Ellis and Pastor Milton) always are self-employed for Social Security with respect to services performed in the exercise of their ministry, these lines only report wages paid to nonminister employees during the quarter.

Step 9: Issue Forms W-2

Before February 1, 2013, the church issues a Form W-2 to each employee. It also submits an additional copy along with a transmittal Form W-3 to the Social Security Administration before March 1, 2013. *Publication 517 states that ministers who report their income taxes as employees should receive a Form W-2 from their church even though they did not elect voluntary withholding.*

The church included the car allowances ($3,600) on Pastor Milton's Form W-2. The amounts were included with salary in box 1 of Form W-2. The income tax regulations require withholding on all business expense reimbursements paid under a nonaccountable plan (i.e., expenses are reimbursed without any substantiation or accounting by the employee). However, since Pastor Milton's wages are not subject to income tax withholding and he did not elect voluntary withholding, the church is not required to withhold any tax from these reimbursements.

Since Pastor Ellis's business expenses were reimbursed under an accountable arrangement, the church does not include these reimbursements on his Form W-2.

Note that the amount of Pastor Ellis's housing allowance was reported in box 14 of his Form W-2. The annual fair rental value of Pastor Milton's parsonage, plus the parsonage allowance designated by the church, are reported in box 14 of his Form W-2. While such reporting is not required, this is the approach taken by the IRS in Publication 517.

Note that the W-2 forms issued to Pastor Ellis and Pastor Milton do *not* use the title "Rev." The instructions for Form W-2 direct employers not to use professional titles when completing Forms W-2.

Form W-3 (the transmittal form) reports all wages paid during 2012 and all income taxes, Social Security, and Medicare taxes withheld. Box 1 reports wages paid ($145,600); box 2 reports income taxes withheld ($10,088); box 3 reports Social Security wages ($66,000); box 4 reports Social Security taxes withheld ($66,000 x 4.2 percent, or $2,772); box 4 reports Medicare wages ($66,000); and box 5 reports Medicare taxes withheld (66,000 x 1.45 percent, or $ $957).

Step 10: Issue Forms 1099-MISC

The church issues a Form 1099-MISC to Mr. Rhodes before February 1, 2013. It also sends an additional copy to the IRS before March 1, 2013, along with a Form 1096 transmittal form. The church also must issue Pastor Lane (the guest speaker) a Form 1099-MISC before February 1, 2013, reporting the $1,000 in nonemployee compensation. It is incorrect to assume that the church has no obligation to issue Pastor Lane a Form 1099-MISC because it characterized the payment as an "honorarium" or "gift." The church obtained Pastor Lane's Social Security number by having him complete a Form W-9.

2. MISCELLANEOUS REPORTING REQUIREMENTS

In addition to the payroll tax reporting obligations, First Church must comply with other federal reporting rules:

- The church must file a Form 5578 (proof of racial nondiscrimination) by May 15, 2013.
- The church must file a Form 1098-C by February 28, 2013, reporting the sale of the donated car. The same form can be used to provide the donor with a contemporaneous written acknowledgment, as required by law. See Chapter 8 for details.

The church also may wish to remind Pastor Ellis that his housing allowance must be included in income for purposes of computing his self-employment tax liability. The church also may wish to remind Pastor Milton that the fair rental value of the church-owned parsonage, and the parsonage allowance designated by the church, must be included in income for purposes of computing his self-employment tax liability.

Form W-4

Department of the Treasury
Internal Revenue Service

Employee's Withholding Allowance Certificate

▶ Whether you are entitled to claim a certain number of allowances or exemption from withholding is subject to review by the IRS. Your employer may be required to send a copy of this form to the IRS.

OMB No. 1545-0074

2012

1 Your first name and middle initial	Last name		2 Your social security number
Jacob C.	Ellis		011-22-0001

Home address (number and street or rural route)	3 ☐ Single ☑ Married ☐ Married, but withhold at higher Single rate.
112 Main Street	Note. If married, but legally separated, or spouse is a nonresident alien, check the "Single" box.

City or town, state, and ZIP code	4 If your last name differs from that shown on your social security card,
Anytown, IL 61000	check here. You must call 1-800-772-1213 for a replacement card. ▶ ☐

5	Total number of allowances you are claiming (from line **H** above **or** from the applicable worksheet on page 2)	5	3
6	Additional amount, if any, you want withheld from each paycheck	6	$
7	I claim exemption from withholding for 2012, and I certify that I meet **both** of the following conditions for exemption.		

• Last year I had a right to a refund of **all** federal income tax withheld because I had **no** tax liability, **and**
• This year I expect a refund of **all** federal income tax withheld because I expect to have **no** tax liability.
If you meet both conditions, write "Exempt" here . . . . ▶ | 7 |

Under penalties of perjury, I declare that I have examined this certificate and, to the best of my knowledge and belief, it is true, correct, and complete.

Employee's signature
(This form is not valid unless you sign it.) ▶ *Jacob Ellis*   Date ▶ *Jan. 5, 2012*

8 Employer's name and address (Employer: Complete lines 8 and 10 only if sending to the IRS.)	9 Office code (optional)	10 Employer identification number (EIN)

For Privacy Act and Paperwork Reduction Act Notice, see page 2.   Cat. No. 10220Q   Form **W-4** (2012)

Form W-4

Department of the Treasury
Internal Revenue Service

Employee's Withholding Allowance Certificate

▶ Whether you are entitled to claim a certain number of allowances or exemption from withholding is subject to review by the IRS. Your employer may be required to send a copy of this form to the IRS.

OMB No. 1545-0074

2012

1 Your first name and middle initial	Last name		2 Your social security number
Sharon M.	Adams		222-00-1111

Home address (number and street or rural route)	3 ☑ Single ☐ Married ☐ Married, but withhold at higher Single rate.
1400 Lynn Street	Note. If married, but legally separated, or spouse is a nonresident alien, check the "Single" box.

City or town, state, and ZIP code	4 If your last name differs from that shown on your social security card,
Anytown, IL 61000	check here. You must call 1-800-772-1213 for a replacement card. ▶ ☐

5	Total number of allowances you are claiming (from line **H** above **or** from the applicable worksheet on page 2)	5	1
6	Additional amount, if any, you want withheld from each paycheck	6	$
7	I claim exemption from withholding for 2012, and I certify that I meet **both** of the following conditions for exemption.		

• Last year I had a right to a refund of **all** federal income tax withheld because I had **no** tax liability, **and**
• This year I expect a refund of **all** federal income tax withheld because I expect to have **no** tax liability.
If you meet both conditions, write "Exempt" here . . . . ▶ | 7 |

Under penalties of perjury, I declare that I have examined this certificate and, to the best of my knowledge and belief, it is true, correct, and complete.

Employee's signature
(This form is not valid unless you sign it.) ▶ *Sharon Adams*   Date ▶ *Jan. 3, 2012*

8 Employer's name and address (Employer: Complete lines 8 and 10 only if sending to the IRS.)	9 Office code (optional)	10 Employer identification number (EIN)

For Privacy Act and Paperwork Reduction Act Notice, see page 2.   Cat. No. 10220Q   Form **W-4** (2012)

Form **W-4**

Department of the Treasury
Internal Revenue Service

Employee's Withholding Allowance Certificate

▶ Whether you are entitled to claim a certain number of allowances or exemption from withholding is subject to review by the IRS. Your employer may be required to send a copy of this form to the IRS.

OMB No. 1545-0074

20**12**

1 Your first name and middle initial	Last name		2 Your social security number
Susan A.	Peck		010-11-2222

Home address (number and street or rural route)	3 ☑ Single ☐ Married ☐ Married, but withhold at higher Single rate.
501 Elm Street	**Note.** If married, but legally separated, or spouse is a nonresident alien, check the "Single" box.

City or town, state, and ZIP code	4 **If your last name differs from that shown on your social security card,** check here. You must call 1-800-772-1213 for a replacement card. ▶ ☐
Anytown, IL 61000	

5	Total number of allowances you are claiming (from line **H** above **or** from the applicable worksheet on page 2)	**5**	2
6	Additional amount, if any, you want withheld from each paycheck	**6** $	
7	I claim exemption from withholding for 2012, and I certify that I meet **both** of the following conditions for exemption.		
	• Last year I had a right to a refund of **all** federal income tax withheld because I had **no** tax liability, **and**		
	• This year I expect a refund of **all** federal income tax withheld because I expect to have **no** tax liability.		
	If you meet both conditions, write "Exempt" here . . . . ▶	**7**	

Under penalties of perjury, I declare that I have examined this certificate and, to the best of my knowledge and belief, it is true, correct, and complete.

Employee's signature
(This form is not valid unless you sign it.) ▶ *Susan Peck* Date ▶ Jan. 2, 2012

8 Employer's name and address (Employer: Complete lines 8 and 10 only if sending to the IRS.)	9 Office code (optional)	10 Employer identification number (EIN)

For Privacy Act and Paperwork Reduction Act Notice, see page 2. Cat. No. 10220Q Form **W-4** (2012)

Form **W-4**

Department of the Treasury
Internal Revenue Service

Employee's Withholding Allowance Certificate

▶ Whether you are entitled to claim a certain number of allowances or exemption from withholding is subject to review by the IRS. Your employer may be required to send a copy of this form to the IRS.

OMB No. 1545-0074

20**12**

1 Your first name and middle initial	Last name		2 Your social security number
Janice L.	Guerra		203-11-0100

Home address (number and street or rural route)	3 ☐ Single ☑ Married ☐ Married, but withhold at higher Single rate.
17 Birch Drive	**Note.** If married, but legally separated, or spouse is a nonresident alien, check the "Single" box.

City or town, state, and ZIP code	4 **If your last name differs from that shown on your social security card,** check here. You must call 1-800-772-1213 for a replacement card. ▶ ☐
Anytown, IL 61000	

5	Total number of allowances you are claiming (from line **H** above **or** from the applicable worksheet on page 2)	**5**	3
6	Additional amount, if any, you want withheld from each paycheck	**6** $	
7	I claim exemption from withholding for 2012, and I certify that I meet **both** of the following conditions for exemption.		
	• Last year I had a right to a refund of **all** federal income tax withheld because I had **no** tax liability, **and**		
	• This year I expect a refund of **all** federal income tax withheld because I expect to have **no** tax liability.		
	If you meet both conditions, write "Exempt" here . . . . ▶	**7**	

Under penalties of perjury, I declare that I have examined this certificate and, to the best of my knowledge and belief, it is true, correct, and complete.

Employee's signature
(This form is not valid unless you sign it.) ▶ *Janice Guerra* Date ▶ Jan. 2, 2012

8 Employer's name and address (Employer: Complete lines 8 and 10 only if sending to the IRS.)	9 Office code (optional)	10 Employer identification number (EIN)

For Privacy Act and Paperwork Reduction Act Notice, see page 2. Cat. No. 10220Q Form **W-4** (2012)

Form **W-4**	**Employee's Withholding Allowance Certificate**	OMB No. 1545-0074
Department of the Treasury Internal Revenue Service	▶ Whether you are entitled to claim a certain number of allowances or exemption from withholding is subject to review by the IRS. Your employer may be required to send a copy of this form to the IRS.	20**12**

1 Your first name and middle initial	Last name		2 Your social security number
Joan A.	Reed		101-22-1000

Home address (number and street or rural route)	3 ☐ Single ☑ Married ☐ Married, but withhold at higher Single rate.
15 Maple Avenue	**Note.** If married, but legally separated, or spouse is a nonresident alien, check the "Single" box.
City or town, state, and ZIP code	4 If your last name differs from that shown on your social security card,
Anytown, IL 61000	check here. You must call 1-800-772-1213 for a replacement card. ▶ ☐

5	Total number of allowances you are claiming (from line **H** above **or** from the applicable worksheet on page 2)	5	3
6	Additional amount, if any, you want withheld from each paycheck	6	$
7	I claim exemption from withholding for 2012, and I certify that I meet **both** of the following conditions for exemption.		

• Last year I had a right to a refund of **all** federal income tax withheld because I had **no** tax liability, **and**
• This year I expect a refund of **all** federal income tax withheld because I expect to have **no** tax liability.

If you meet both conditions, write "Exempt" here . . . . ▶ | 7 |

Under penalties of perjury, I declare that I have examined this certificate and, to the best of my knowledge and belief, it is true, correct, and complete.

Employee's signature
(This form is not valid unless you sign it.) ▶ *Joan Reed*   Date ▶ *Jan. 3, 2012*

8 Employer's name and address (Employer: Complete lines 8 and 10 only if sending to the IRS.)	9 Office code (optional)	10 Employer identification number (EIN)

For Privacy Act and Paperwork Reduction Act Notice, see page 2.   Cat. No. 10220Q   Form **W-4** (2012)

Void ☐	a Employee's social security number 222-00-1111	OMB No. 1545-0008		

b Employer identification number (EIN) 00-0238457	1 Wages, tips, other compensation 14000.00	2 Federal income tax withheld 780.00
c Employer's name, address, and ZIP code First Church 423 Abel Avenue Anytown, IL 61000	3 Social security wages 14000.00	4 Social security tax withheld 588.00
	5 Medicare wages and tips 14000.00	6 Medicare tax withheld 203.00
	7 Social security tips	8 Allocated tips
d Control number	9	10 Dependent care benefits
e Employee's first name and initial Last name Suff. Sharon M. Adams 1400 Lynn St., Apt. 7 Anytown, IL 61000	11 Nonqualified plans	12a See instructions for box 12
	13 Statutory employee ☐ Retirement plan ☐ Third-party sick pay ☐	12b
	14 Other	12c
		12d
f Employee's address and ZIP code		

15 State Employer's state ID number	16 State wages, tips, etc.	17 State income tax	18 Local wages, tips, etc.	19 Local income tax	20 Locality name

Form **W-2** Wage and Tax Statement   2012   Department of the Treasury—Internal Revenue Service
For Privacy Act and Paperwork Reduction Act Notice, see separate instructions.

Copy D — For Employer.

Void ☐	a Employee's social security number 011-22-0001	OMB No. 1545-0008		
b Employer identification number (EIN) 00-0238457		1 Wages, tips, other compensation 40000.00	2 Federal income tax withheld 8840.00	
c Employer's name, address, and ZIP code First Church 423 Abel Avenue Anytown, IL 61000		3 Social security wages	4 Social security tax withheld	
		5 Medicare wages and tips	6 Medicare tax withheld	
		7 Social security tips	8 Allocated tips	
d Control number		9	10 Dependent care benefits	
e Employee's first name and initial Last name Suff. Jacob C. Ellis 112 Main St. Anytown, IL 61000		11 Nonqualified plans	12a See instructions for box 12	
		13 Statutory employee ☐ Retirement plan ☐ Third-party sick pay ☐	12b	
		14 Other 10000.00 housing allowance	12c	
			12d	
f Employee's address and ZIP code				

15 State Employer's state ID number	16 State wages, tips, etc.	17 State income tax	18 Local wages, tips, etc.	19 Local income tax	20 Locality name

Form **W-2** Wage and Tax Statement **2012** Department of the Treasury—Internal Revenue Service
For Privacy Act and Paperwork Reduction Act Notice, see separate instructions.

Copy D — For Employer.

Void ☐	a Employee's social security number 203-11-0010	OMB No. 1545-0008		
b Employer identification number (EIN) 00-0238457		1 Wages, tips, other compensation 20000.00	2 Federal income tax withheld 52.00	
c Employer's name, address, and ZIP code First Church 423 Abel Avenue Anytown, IL 61000		3 Social security wages 20000.00	4 Social security tax withheld 840.00	
		5 Medicare wages and tips 20000.00	6 Medicare tax withheld 290.00	
		7 Social security tips	8 Allocated tips	
d Control number		9	10 Dependent care benefits	
e Employee's first name and initial Last name Suff. Janice L. Guerra 17 Birch Drive Anytown, IL 61000		11 Nonqualified plans	12a See instructions for box 12	
		13 Statutory employee ☐ Retirement plan ☐ Third-party sick pay ☐	12b	
		14 Other	12c	
			12d	
f Employee's address and ZIP code				

15 State Employer's state ID number	16 State wages, tips, etc.	17 State income tax	18 Local wages, tips, etc.	19 Local income tax	20 Locality name

Form **W-2** Wage and Tax Statement **2012** Department of the Treasury—Internal Revenue Service
For Privacy Act and Paperwork Reduction Act Notice, see separate instructions.

Copy D — For Employer.

Form W-2 — James D. Milton

Void ☐	**a** Employee's social security number 100-22-0030 OMB No. 1545-0008

b Employer identification number (EIN) 00-0238457	**1** Wages, tips, other compensation 39600.00	**2** Federal income tax withheld
c Employer's name, address, and ZIP code First Church 423 Abel Avenue Anytown, IL 61000	**3** Social security wages	**4** Social security tax withheld
	5 Medicare wages and tips	**6** Medicare tax withheld
	7 Social security tips	**8** Allocated tips
d Control number	**9**	**10** Dependent care benefits
e Employee's first name and initial Last name Suff. James D. Milton 1400 Cedar Lane Anytown, IL 61000	**11** Nonqualified plans	**12a** See instructions for box 12
	13 Statutory employee ☐ Retirement plan ☐ Third-party sick pay ☐	**12b**
	14 Other 4000.00 parsonage allowance	**12c**
		12d
f Employee's address and ZIP code		

15 State Employer's state ID number	**16** State wages, tips, etc.	**17** State income tax	**18** Local wages, tips, etc.	**19** Local income tax	**20** Locality name

Form **W-2** Wage and Tax Statement **2012** Department of the Treasury—Internal Revenue Service For Privacy Act and Paperwork Reduction Act Notice, see separate instructions.

Copy D — For Employer.

Form W-2 — Susan A. Peck

Void ☐	**a** Employee's social security number 010-11-2222 OMB No. 1545-0008

b Employer identification number (EIN) 00-0238457	**1** Wages, tips, other compensation 14000.00	**2** Federal income tax withheld 416.00
c Employer's name, address, and ZIP code First Church 423 Abel Avenue Anytown, IL 61000	**3** Social security wages 14000.00	**4** Social security tax withheld 588.00
	5 Medicare wages and tips 14000.00	**6** Medicare tax withheld 203.00
	7 Social security tips	**8** Allocated tips
d Control number	**9**	**10** Dependent care benefits
e Employee's first name and initial Last name Suff. Susan A. Peck 501 Elm St. Anytown, IL 61000	**11** Nonqualified plans	**12a** See instructions for box 12
	13 Statutory employee ☐ Retirement plan ☐ Third-party sick pay ☐	**12b**
	14 Other	**12c**
		12d
f Employee's address and ZIP code		

15 State Employer's state ID number	**16** State wages, tips, etc.	**17** State income tax	**18** Local wages, tips, etc.	**19** Local income tax	**20** Locality name

Form **W-2** Wage and Tax Statement **2012** Department of the Treasury—Internal Revenue Service For Privacy Act and Paperwork Reduction Act Notice, see separate instructions.

Copy D — For Employer.

		a Employee's social security number		
Void ☐		101-22-1080	OMB No. 1545-0008	

b Employer identification number (EIN) 00-0238457		**1** Wages, tips, other compensation 18050.00	**2** Federal income tax withheld
c Employer's name, address, and ZIP code		**3** Social security wages 18000.00	**4** Social security tax withheld 756.00
First Church 423 Abel Avenue Anytown, IL 61000		**5** Medicare wages and tips 18050.00	**6** Medicare tax withheld 261.00
		7 Social security tips	**8** Allocated tips
d Control number		**9**	**10** Dependent care benefits
e Employee's first name and initial Last name Suff.		**11** Nonqualified plans	**12a** See instructions for box 12
Joan A. Reed 15 Maple Avenue Anytown, IL 61000		**13** Statutory employee ☐ Retirement plan ☐ Third-party sick pay ☐	**12b**
		14 Other	**12c**
			12d
f Employee's address and ZIP code			

15 State Employer's state ID number	**16** State wages, tips, etc.	**17** State income tax	**18** Local wages, tips, etc.	**19** Local income tax	**20** Locality name

Form **W-2** Wage and Tax Statement   2012   Department of the Treasury—Internal Revenue Service
For Privacy Act and Paperwork Reduction Act Notice, see separate instructions.

Copy D — For Employer.

Form **941 for 2012:** Employer's QUARTERLY Federal Tax Return
(Rev. January 2012)   Department of the Treasury — Internal Revenue Service

950112

OMB No. 1545-0029

Employer identification number (EIN)   0 0 – 0 2 3 8 4 5 7

Name *(not your trade name)* First Church

Trade name *(if any)*

Address 423 Able Avenue
         Number   Street   Suite or room number
         Anytown   IL   61000
         City   State   ZIP code

Report for this Quarter of 2012
(Check one.)

☐ 1: January, February, March

☐ 2: April, May, June

☐ 3: July, August, September

☒ 4: October, November, December

Prior-year forms are available at *www.irs.gov/form941.*

Read the separate instructions before you complete Form 941. Type or print within the boxes.

Part 1: Answer these questions for this quarter.

1	Number of employees who received wages, tips, or other compensation for the pay period including: *Mar. 12* (Quarter 1), *June 12* (Quarter 2), *Sept. 12* (Quarter 3), or *Dec. 12* (Quarter 4)	1	
2	Wages, tips, and other compensation	2	36400 . 00
3	Income tax withheld from wages, tips, and other compensation	3	2522 . 00
4	If no wages, tips, and other compensation are subject to social security or Medicare tax	☐ Check and go to line 6.	

		Column 1		Column 2
5a	Taxable social security wages .	16500 . 00	× .104 =	1716 . 00
5b	Taxable social security tips . .	.	× .104 =	.
5c	Taxable Medicare wages & tips.	16500 . 00	× .029 =	478 . 00

5d	Add *Column 2* line 5a, *Column 2* line 5b, and *Column 2* line 5c	5d	2194 . 00
5e	Section 3121(q) Notice and Demand—Tax due on unreported tips (see instructions)	5e	.
6	Total taxes before adjustments (add lines 3, 5d, and 5e)	6	4716 . 00
7	Current quarter's adjustment for fractions of cents	7	.
8	Current quarter's adjustment for sick pay	8	.
9	Current quarter's adjustments for tips and group-term life insurance	9	.
10	Total taxes after adjustments. Combine lines 6 through 9	10	4716 . 00
11	Total deposits for this quarter, including overpayment applied from a prior quarter and overpayment applied from Form 941-X or Form 944-X	11	.
12a	COBRA premium assistance payments (see instructions)	12a	.
12b	Number of individuals provided COBRA premium assistance . .		
13	Add lines 11 and 12a	13	.
14	**Balance due.** If line 10 is more than line 13, enter the difference and see instructions	14	4716 . 00
15	**Overpayment.** If line 13 is more than line 10, enter the difference [.] Check one: ☐ Apply to next return. ☐ Send a refund.		

▶ **You MUST complete both pages of Form 941 and SIGN it.**

Next ▶

For Privacy Act and Paperwork Reduction Act Notice, see the back of the Payment Voucher.

Cat. No. 17001Z

Form **941** (Rev. 1-2012)

950212

Name *(not your trade name)*	**Employer identification number (EIN)**
First Church	00-0238457

Part 2: Tell us about your deposit schedule and tax liability for this quarter.

If you are unsure about whether you are a monthly schedule depositor or a semiweekly schedule depositor, see *Pub. 15 (Circular E), section 11.*

16 Check one: ☐ Line 10 on this return is less than $2,500 or line 10 on the return for the prior quarter was less than $2,500, and you did not incur a $100,000 next-day deposit obligation during the current quarter. If line 10 for the prior quarter was less than $2,500 but line 10 on this return is $100,000 or more, you must provide a record of your federal tax liability. If you are a monthly schedule depositor, complete the deposit schedule below; if you are a semiweekly schedule depositor, attach Schedule B (Form 941). Go to Part 3.

☒ **You were a monthly schedule depositor for the entire quarter.** Enter your tax liability for each month and total liability for the quarter, then go to Part 3.

Tax liability: Month 1   1451. 00

Month 2   1451. 00

Month 3   1451. 00

Total liability for quarter   1451. 00   **Total must equal line 10.**

☐ **You were a semiweekly schedule depositor for any part of this quarter.** Complete *Schedule B (Form 941): Report of Tax Liability for Semiweekly Schedule Depositors,* and attach it to Form 941.

Part 3: Tell us about your business. If a question does NOT apply to your business, leave it blank.

17 If your business has closed or you stopped paying wages . . . . ☐ Check here, and

enter the final date you paid wages   /   /   .

18 If you are a seasonal employer and you do not have to file a return for every quarter of the year . . ☐ Check here.

Part 4: May we speak with your third-party designee?

Do you want to allow an employee, a paid tax preparer, or another person to discuss this return with the IRS? See the instructions for details.

☒ Yes. Designee's name and phone number   Jacob Ellis   309-7x2-2345

Select a 5-digit Personal Identification Number (PIN) to use when talking to the IRS.   4 5 6 7 8

☐ No.

Part 5: Sign here. You MUST complete both pages of Form 941 and SIGN it.

Under penalties of perjury, I declare that I have examined this return, including accompanying schedules and statements, and to the best of my knowledge and belief, it is true, correct, and complete. Declaration of preparer (other than taxpayer) is based on all information of which preparer has any knowledge.

X   Sign your name here   *Jacob Ellis*

Print your name here   Jacob C. Ellis

Print your title here   president

Date   1 / 24/ 2013

Best daytime phone   309-7x2-2345

Paid Preparer Use Only	Check if you are self-employed . . . ☐
Preparer's name	PTIN
Preparer's signature	Date / /
Firm's name (or yours if self-employed)	EIN
Address	Phone
City State	ZIP code

☐ VOID ☐ CORRECTED

PAYER'S name, street address, city, state, ZIP code, and telephone no.	1 Rents	OMB No. 1545-0115	
First Church 423 Able Avenue Anytown, IL 61000	$ 2 Royalties $	2012 Form **1099-MISC**	**Miscellaneous Income**
	3 Other income $	4 Federal income tax withheld $	**Copy C**

PAYER'S federal identification number	RECIPIENT'S identification number	5 Fishing boat proceeds	6 Medical and health care payments	**For Payer**
00-0238457	202-22-3030	$	$	

RECIPIENT'S name James E. Lane	7 Nonemployee compensation $ 1000.00	8 Substitute payments in lieu of dividends or interest $	For Privacy Act and Paperwork Reduction Act Notice, see the **2012 General Instructions for Certain Information Returns.**
Street address (including apt. no.) 1225 Willow	9 Payer made direct sales of $5,000 or more of consumer products to a buyer (recipient) for resale ▶ ☐	10 Crop insurance proceeds $	
City, state, and ZIP code Anytown, IL 61000	11	12	

Account number (see instructions)	2nd TIN not. ☐	13 Excess golden parachute payments $	14 Gross proceeds paid to an attorney $	

15a Section 409A deferrals $	15b Section 409A income $	16 State tax withheld $ $	17 State/Payer's state no.	18 State income $ $

Form **1099-MISC**   Department of the Treasury - Internal Revenue Service

---

☐ VOID ☐ CORRECTED

PAYER'S name, street address, city, state, ZIP code, and telephone no.	1 Rents	OMB No. 1545-0115	
First Church 423 Able Avenue Anytown, IL 61000	$ 2 Royalties $	2012 Form **1099-MISC**	**Miscellaneous Income**
	3 Other income $	4 Federal income tax withheld $	**Copy C**

PAYER'S federal identification number	RECIPIENT'S identification number	5 Fishing boat proceeds	6 Medical and health care payments	**For Payer**
00-0234457	303-44-1234	$	$	

RECIPIENT'S name John Rhodes	7 Nonemployee compensation $ 2400.00	8 Substitute payments in lieu of dividends or interest $	For Privacy Act and Paperwork Reduction Act Notice, see the **2012 General Instructions for Certain Information Returns.**
Street address (including apt. no.) 222 Adams St.	9 Payer made direct sales of $5,000 or more of consumer products to a buyer (recipient) for resale ▶ ☐	10 Crop insurance proceeds $	
City, state, and ZIP code Anytown, IL 61000	11	12	

Account number (see instructions)	2nd TIN not. ☐	13 Excess golden parachute payments $	14 Gross proceeds paid to an attorney $	

15a Section 409A deferrals $	15b Section 409A income $	16 State tax withheld $ $	17 State/Payer's state no.	18 State income $ $

Form **1099-MISC**   Department of the Treasury - Internal Revenue Service

DO NOT STAPLE

a Control number **33333**	For Official Use Only ▶ OMB No. 1545-0008

b Kind of Payer (Check one) ▶ 941 ☒ Military ☐ 943 ☐ 944 ☐ CT-1 ☐ Hshld. emp. ☐ Medicare govt. emp. ☐

Kind of Employer (Check one) ▶ None apply ☐ 501c non-govt. ☒ State/local non-501c ☐ State/local 501c ☐ Federal govt. ☐ Third-party sick pay (Check if applicable) ☐

c Total number of Forms W-2 **6**
d Establishment number

1 Wages, tips, other compensation **145600.00**
2 Federal income tax withheld **10088.00**

e Employer identification number (EIN) **00-0238457**

3 Social security wages **66000.00**
4 Social security tax withheld **2772.00**

f Employer's name
First Church
423 Able Avenue
Anytown, IL 61000

5 Medicare wages and tips **66000.00**
6 Medicare tax withheld **951.00**

7 Social security tips
8 Allocated tips

9
10 Dependent care benefits

11 Nonqualified plans
12a Deferred compensation

g Employer's address and ZIP code

h Other EIN used this year
13 For third-party sick pay use only
12b

15 State   Employer's state ID number
14 Income tax withheld by payer of third-party sick pay

16 State wages, tips, etc.
17 State income tax
18 Local wages, tips, etc.
19 Local income tax

Contact person **Janet Jensen**
Telephone number **309-746-1122**
For Official Use Only

Email address **JJensen@connect.com**
Fax number **309-746-1123**

Under penalties of perjury, I declare that I have examined this return and accompanying documents and, to the best of my knowledge and belief, they are true, correct, and complete.

Signature ▶ **Jacob Ellis**   Title ▶ **president**   Date ▶ **2/15/13**

Form **W-3** Transmittal of Wage and Tax Statements   **2012**   Department of the Treasury Internal Revenue Service

Do Not Staple   6969

| Form **1096**
Department of the Treasury
Internal Revenue Service | **Annual Summary and Transmittal of**
U.S. Information Returns | OMB No. 1545-0108
20**12** |

FILER'S name

First Church

Street address (including room or suite number)

423 Able Avenue

City, state, and ZIP code

Anytown, IL 61000

| Name of person to contact
Janet Jensen | Telephone number
309-746-1122 | **For Official Use Only** |
| Email address
JJensen@Connect.com | Fax number
309-746-1123 | |

| 1 Employer identification number
00-0238457 | 2 Social security number | 3 Total number of forms
2 | 4 Federal income tax withheld
$ | 5 Total amount reported with this Form 1096
$ 3400.00 |

6 Enter an "X" in only one box below to indicate the type of form being filed.

7 If this is your **final return,** enter an "X" here ▶ ☐

W-2G 32	1097-BTC 50	1098 81	1098-C 78	1098-E 84	1098-T 83	1099-A 80	1099-B 79	1099-C 85	1099-CAP 73	1099-DIV 91	1099-G 86	1099-H 71	1099-INT 92
☐	☐	☐	☐	☐	☐	☐	☐	☐	☐	☐	☐	☐	☐

1099-K 10	1099-LTC 93	1099-MISC 95	1099-OID 96	1098-PATR 97	1099-Q 31	1099-R 98	1099-S 75	1099-SA 94	3921 25	3922 26	5498 28	5498-ESA 72	5498-SA 27
☐	☐	☒	☐	☐	☐	☐	☐	☐	☐	☐	☐	☐	☐

Return this entire page to the Internal Revenue Service. Photocopies are not acceptable.

Under penalties of perjury, I declare that I have examined this return and accompanying documents, and, to the best of my knowledge and belief, they are true, correct, and complete.

Signature ▶ Jacob Ellis   Title ▶ President   Date ▶ 2/7/13

| Form **5578** (Rev. April 2009) Department of the Treasury Internal Revenue Service | **Annual Certification of Racial Nondiscrimination for a Private School Exempt From Federal Income Tax** (For use by organizations that do not file Form 990 or Form 990-EZ) | OMB No. 1545-0213 **Open to Public Inspection** For IRS Use Only ▶ |

For the period beginning **January 1** , **2012** and ending **December 31** , **2012**

1a Name of organization that operates, supervises, and/or controls school(s).	1b Employer identification number
First Church	
Address (number and street or P.O. box no., if mail is not delivered to street address) — **423 Able Avenue** · Room/suite	**00** ┊ **0238457**
City or town, state, and ZIP + 4 (If foreign address, list city or town, state or province, and country. Include postal code.) — **Anytown, IL 61000**	

2a Name of central organization holding group exemption letter covering the school(s). (If same as 1a above, write "Same" and complete 2c.) If the organization in 1a above holds an individual exemption letter, write "Not Applicable."	2b Employer identification number
not applicable	
Address (number and street or P.O. box no., if mail is not delivered to street address) · Room/suite	2c Group exemption number (see instructions under **Definitions**)
City or town, state, and ZIP + 4 (If foreign address, list city or town, state or province, and country. Include postal code.)	

3a Name of school. (If more than one school, write "See Attached," and attach a list of the names, complete addresses, including postal codes, and employer identification numbers of the schools.) If same as 1a above, write "Same."	3b Employer identification number, if any
Evergreen Preschool	
Address (number and street or P.O. box no., if mail is not delivered to street address) — **423 Able Avenue**	Room/suite
City or town, state, and ZIP + 4 (If foreign address, list city or town, state or province, and country. Include postal code.) — **Anytown, IL 61000**	

Under penalties of perjury, I hereby certify that I am authorized to take official action on behalf of the above school(s) and that to the best of my knowledge and belief the school(s) has (have) satisfied the applicable requirements of sections 4.01 through 4.05 of Rev. Proc. 75-50, 1975-2 C.B. 587, for the period covered by this certification.

Jacob Ellis	President	May 10, 2013
(Signature)	(Type or print name and title.)	(Date)

J. ILLUSTRATION 2: TAX WITHHOLDING AND REPORTING REQUIREMENTS

1 SELF-EMPLOYED MINISTER; 1 SECRETARY; 1 SELF-EMPLOYED CUSTODIAN; CHURCH HAS EXEMPTED ITSELF FROM SOCIAL SECURITY AND MEDICARE COVERAGE

Note: Since the 2013 payroll tax forms were not available when this book was published, this illustration uses the 2012 forms and reflects the reporting requirements for the fourth quarter of 2012. When appropriate, comments are made regarding changes that take effect in 2013. By studying this illustration, you should have no difficulty completing the corresponding 2013 forms (which will be substantially similar to the 2012 forms).

Assume that Second Church (of Anytown, Illinois) has one minister, Pastor Adam M. Hoyle, who has served since 1998, and one office secretary, Anna H. Todd, who was hired in 2002. Pastor Hoyle reports his federal income taxes as a self-employed person, and Anna Todd reports as an employee.

The church filed a Form 8274 in October 1984, waiving its obligation to pay the employer's portion of Social Security (FICA) taxes. The effect of this election is that the church is not liable for the employer's share of any Social Security and Medicare taxes, and nonminister employees are treated as self-employed for Social Security (just like ministers). This means that Ms. Todd must pay the self-employment tax (15.3 percent) rather than just the employee's share of Social Security and Medicare taxes (7.65 percent).

Pastor Hoyle's annual church compensation for 2012 was $45,000 (which included a housing allowance of $8,000), and Ms. Todd's compensation was $17,000 ($326.92 per week).

The church has a self-employed custodian, John Bridges, who receives a lump sum of $200 each month.

The church has an accountable business expense reimbursement policy. It reimburses Pastor Hoyle for any business expense he incurs on behalf of the church and substantiates with adequate records within one month of incurring each expense, up to a maximum of $4,000 per year. For 2012 Pastor Hoyle incurred and substantiated $3,600 in actual business expenses on behalf of the church, and he was reimbursed by the church for all of these expenses.

1. FILING REQUIREMENTS: THE 10-STEP METHOD

For 2012 the church would have the following filing and reporting requirements. The 10-step method for complying with a church's federal payroll tax reporting obligations (discussed in this chapter) is applied.

Step 1: Obtain an employer identification number from the IRS

The church obtained an employer identification number (00-0019283) in 1983.

Step 2: Determine workers' status and Social Security numbers

The church determines that Pastor Hoyle and custodian John Bridges are self-employed, and Ms. Todd is an employee. The church obtains the Social Security numbers for all workers.

Step 3: Have employees complete Forms W-4

To enable the church to withhold the proper amount of federal income taxes from the wages of its sole employee (Anna Todd), the church had Ms. Todd complete and sign an updated Form W-4 early in 2012 (she is married, with two withholding allowances). Ms. Todd's new Form W-4 requested the church to withhold an additional amount of taxes ($43) from her wages to cover her self-employment tax liability (see Step 6, below). The church honored this request beginning with the first payroll period of 2012. Since the other church workers (Pastor Hoyle and Mr. Bridges) are self-employed, they do not complete Form W-4.

Step 4: Compute taxable wages

The church computes the wages of its employee (Ms. Todd).

Step 5: Determine income tax to be withheld

The church uses the wage bracket method of computing the amount of income taxes to withhold from Ms. Todd's wages. Based on the two withholding allowances claimed on her Form W-4 and a weekly salary of $326.92, and using the withholding tables in IRS Publication 15, the church determines that it must withhold $2 in income taxes each week.

Step 6: Withhold Social Security and Medicare taxes from nonminister employees' wages

Since the church filed a Form 8274 waiving participation in the FICA program, it does not withhold any Social Security (FICA) taxes from Ms. Todd's wages, and the church is not responsible for the employer's share of Social Security and Medicare taxes. However, the law requires that Ms. Todd be treated as self-employed for Social Security purposes (because the church filed the Form 8274).

Rather than pay her self-employment taxes using the quarterly estimated tax procedure, Ms. Todd elects to have the church withhold an additional amount of *income taxes* from her wages in 2012 to cover her expected self-employment tax liability. On the Form W-4 that she submitted to the church at the beginning of the year, she requested that an additional $43 be withheld (total wages of $17,000 multiplied by the self-employment tax rate for 2012 of 13.3 percent and divided by 52 weeks) to cover her estimated self-employment tax liability for the year. Ms. Todd will still have to complete a Schedule SE (Form 1040) to report her self-employment tax liability for 2012. However, the excess withheld income taxes reported on line 62 (Form 1040) will offset the self-employment tax liability.

Step 7: The church must deposit the taxes it withholds

Since the church exempted itself in the past from the employer's share of Social Security and Medicare taxes, thereby making its nonminister employee (Ms. Todd) subject to self-employment tax, the only payroll taxes the church accumulates are Ms. Todd's income taxes, which consist of $2 per pay period from the tax withholding tables and an additional $43 per pay period based on her Form W-4. Since the church does not accumulate payroll taxes of more than $2,500 during the quarter, it is not required to deposit the taxes with the government. Instead, it encloses payment with its quarterly Form 941.

The instructions to Form 941 state:

> *If your total taxes (line 10) are less than $2,500 for the current quarter or the preceding quarter, and you did not incur a $100,000 next-day deposit obligation during the current quarter, you do not have to make a deposit. To avoid a penalty, you must pay the amount in full with a timely filed return or you must deposit the amount timely. If you are not sure your total tax liability for the current quarter will be less than $2,500 (and your liability for the preceding quarter was not less than $2,500), make deposits using the semi-weekly or monthly rules so you won't be subject to failure to deposit penalties.*

Step 8: File quarterly Form 941

The church files Forms 941 each quarter (by April 30, July 31, October 31, and January 31). The January 31, 2012, Form 941 (for the final calendar quarter of 2012) is set forth below. Note that the Form 941 only reports wages paid to Anna Todd. Pastor Hoyle reports his income taxes as self-employed, so none of his

compensation is reported on Form 941. Also note that the box on line 4 is checked, indicating that the church filed a timely Form 8274, in which it elected to be exempt from the employer's share of FICA taxes. As a result of this filing, Anna Todd is treated as self-employed for Social Security. This explains why lines 5a through 5d are left blank.

Step 9: Issue Forms W-2

Before February 1, 2013, the church issues a Form W-2 to its sole employee, Ms. Todd. It also submits an additional copy along with a Form W-3 (transmittal form) to the Social Security Administration before March 1, 2013.

Step 10: Issue Forms 1099-MISC

Similarly, the church issues a Form 1099-MISC to Pastor Hoyle and Mr. Bridges before February 1, 2013. It also sends an additional copy to the IRS before March 1, 2013, along with a Form 1096 (transmittal form). Note that Pastor Hoyle's Form 1099-MISC does not include the amount of the church-designated housing allowance. If the church-designated housing allowance exceeds the actual expenses incurred by Pastor Hoyle in owning or maintaining a home in 2012 (or any other applicable limitation), the excess should be reported as "other income" (i.e., excess housing allowance) on Pastor Hoyle's Schedule C (Form 1040). Note that the church does not include on Pastor Hoyle's Form 1099-MISC any of the business expense reimbursements that it paid to him in 2012, since the reimbursements were all paid pursuant to an accountable reimbursement arrangement. See Chapter 7 for details.

All Forms 1099-MISC must contain the telephone number of a contact person who can answer questions the recipient may have about the form. The telephone number of the church's treasurer (G. White) is listed on the Forms 1099-MISC issued by the church. Ms. White is identified by name on the Form 1096 that the church uses to send Forms 1099-MISC to the IRS.

2. MISCELLANEOUS REPORTING REQUIREMENTS

In addition to the payroll tax reporting obligations, First Church may wish to remind Pastor Hoyle that his housing allowance must be included in his income for purposes of computing his self-employment tax liability.

		a Employee's social security number 003-20-3111	OMB No. 1545-0008		
Void ☐					

b Employer identification number (EIN) 00—0019283	1 Wages, tips, other compensation 17000.00	2 Federal income tax withheld 2340.00
c Employer's name, address, and ZIP code Second Church 867 Alton Road Anytown, IL 61000	3 Social security wages	4 Social security tax withheld
	5 Medicare wages and tips	6 Medicare tax withheld
	7 Social security tips	8 Allocated tips
d Control number	9	10 Dependent care benefits
e Employee's first name and initial Last name Suff. Anna H. Todd 301 Estes Avenue Anytown, IL 61000	11 Nonqualified plans	12a See instructions for box 12
	13 Statutory employee ☐ Retirement plan ☐ Third-party sick pay ☐	12b
	14 Other	12c
		12d
f Employee's address and ZIP code		

15 State Employer's state ID number	16 State wages, tips, etc.	17 State income tax	18 Local wages, tips, etc.	19 Local income tax	20 Locality name

Form **W-2** Wage and Tax Statement   2012   Department of the Treasury—Internal Revenue Service
For Privacy Act and Paperwork Reduction Act Notice, see separate instructions.

Copy D — For Employer.

DO NOT STAPLE

33333	a Control number		For Official Use Only ▶ OMB No. 1545-0008

| b Kind of Payer (Check one) ▶ | 941 ☒ CT-1 ☐ | Military ☐ Hshld. emp. ☐ | 943 ☐ Medicare govt. emp. ☐ | 944 ☐ | Kind of Employer (Check one) ▶ | None apply ☐ State/local non-501c ☐ | 501c non-govt. ☒ State/local 501c ☐ Federal govt. ☐ | | Third-party sick pay (Check if applicable) ☐ |

c Total number of Forms W-2 _1_	d Establishment number	1 Wages, tips, other compensation **17000.00**	2 Federal income tax withheld **2340.00**
e Employer identification number (EIN) **00-0019283**		3 Social security wages	4 Social security tax withheld
f Employer's name **Second Church**		5 Medicare wages and tips	6 Medicare tax withheld
867 Alton Road		7 Social security tips	8 Allocated tips
Anytown, IL 61000		9	10 Dependent care benefits
		11 Nonqualified plans	12a Deferred compensation
g Employer's address and ZIP code			
h Other EIN used this year		13 For third-party sick pay use only	12b
15 State Employer's state ID number		14 Income tax withheld by payer of third-party sick pay	
16 State wages, tips, etc.	17 State income tax	18 Local wages, tips, etc.	19 Local income tax

Contact person **G. White**	Telephone number **319-4×4-2222**	For Official Use Only
Email address **Gwhite@conect.com**	Fax number **319-4×4-2223**	

Under penalties of perjury, I declare that I have examined this return and accompanying documents and, to the best of my knowledge and belief, they are true, correct, and complete.

Signature ▶ **A. Hoyle**   Title ▶ **President**   Date ▶ **2/15/13**

Form **W-3** Transmittal of Wage and Tax Statements   **2012**   Department of the Treasury Internal Revenue Service

---

Form **W-4** Department of the Treasury Internal Revenue Service	**Employee's Withholding Allowance Certificate** ▶ Whether you are entitled to claim a certain number of allowances or exemption from withholding is subject to review by the IRS. Your employer may be required to send a copy of this form to the IRS.	OMB No. 1545-0074 **2012**

1 Your first name and middle initial Anna H.	Last name Todd	2 Your social security number 002-22-3111
Home address (number and street or rural route) 301 Estes Avenue	3 ☐ Single ☑ Married ☐ Married, but withhold at higher Single rate. Note. If married, but legally separated, or spouse is a nonresident alien, check the "Single" box.	
City or town, state, and ZIP code Anytown, IL 61000	4 If your last name differs from that shown on your social security card, check here. You must call 1-800-772-1213 for a replacement card. ▶ ☐	

5	Total number of allowances you are claiming (from line **H** above **or** from the applicable worksheet on page 2)	5	2
6	Additional amount, if any, you want withheld from each paycheck	6	$ 43.00
7	I claim exemption from withholding for 2012, and I certify that I meet **both** of the following conditions for exemption.		

• Last year I had a right to a refund of **all** federal income tax withheld because I had **no** tax liability, **and**
• This year I expect a refund of **all** federal income tax withheld because I expect to have **no** tax liability.
If you meet both conditions, write "Exempt" here . . . . ▶ | 7 |

Under penalties of perjury, I declare that I have examined this certificate and, to the best of my knowledge and belief, it is true, correct, and complete.

Employee's signature (This form is not valid unless you sign it.) ▶ **Anna Todd**   Date ▶ **Jan. 2, 2012**

8 Employer's name and address (Employer: Complete lines 8 and 10 only if sending to the IRS.)	9 Office code (optional)	10 Employer identification number (EIN)

For Privacy Act and Paperwork Reduction Act Notice, see page 2.   Cat. No. 10220Q   Form **W-4** (2012)

Form **941 for 2012:** Employer's QUARTERLY Federal Tax Return
(Rev. January 2012)   Department of the Treasury — Internal Revenue Service

950112

OMB No. 1545-0029

Employer identification number (EIN) 0 0 — 0 0 1 9 2 8 3

Name *(not your trade name)* Second Church

Trade name *(if any)*

Address 867 Alton Road
Number   Street   Suite or room number

Anytown   IL   61000
City   State   ZIP code

Report for this Quarter of 2012
(Check one.)

☐ 1: January, February, March

☐ 2: April, May, June

☐ 3: July, August, September

☒ 4: October, November, December

Prior-year forms are available at *www.irs.gov/form941.*

Read the separate instructions before you complete Form 941. Type or print within the boxes.

Part 1: Answer these questions for this quarter.

1 Number of employees who received wages, tips, or other compensation for the pay period including: *Mar. 12* (Quarter 1), *June 12* (Quarter 2), *Sept. 12* (Quarter 3), or *Dec. 12* (Quarter 4) **1**

2 Wages, tips, and other compensation . . . . **2** 4250 . 00

3 Income tax withheld from wages, tips, and other compensation . . . . **3** 585 . 00

4 If no wages, tips, and other compensation are subject to social security or Medicare tax ☒ Check and go to line 6.

	Column 1		Column 2
5a Taxable social security wages .	.	× .104 =	.
5b Taxable social security tips . .	.	× .104 =	.
5c Taxable Medicare wages & tips.	.	× .029 =	.

5d Add *Column 2* line 5a, *Column 2* line 5b, and *Column 2* line 5c . . . . . **5d** .

5e Section 3121(q) Notice and Demand—Tax due on unreported tips (see instructions) . . **5e** .

6 Total taxes before adjustments (add lines 3, 5d, and 5e) . . . . **6** 585 . 00

7 Current quarter's adjustment for fractions of cents . . . . . . **7** .

8 Current quarter's adjustment for sick pay . . . . **8** .

9 Current quarter's adjustments for tips and group-term life insurance . . . . . **9** .

10 Total taxes after adjustments. Combine lines 6 through 9 . . . . **10** 585 . 00

11 Total deposits for this quarter, including overpayment applied from a prior quarter and overpayment applied from Form 941-X or Form 944-X . . . . . . **11** .

12a COBRA premium assistance payments (see instructions) . . . . . . **12a** .

12b Number of individuals provided COBRA premium assistance . .

13 Add lines 11 and 12a . . . . **13** .

14 Balance due. If line 10 is more than line 13, enter the difference and see instructions . . . **14** 585 . 00

15 Overpayment. If line 13 is more than line 10, enter the difference . Check one: ☐ Apply to next return. ☐ Send a refund.

▶ You MUST complete both pages of Form 941 and SIGN it.

Next ▶

For Privacy Act and Paperwork Reduction Act Notice, see the back of the Payment Voucher.   Cat. No. 17001Z   Form **941** (Rev. 1-2012)

591

950212

Name *(not your trade name)*	Employer identification number (EIN)
Second Church	00-0019283

Part 2: Tell us about your deposit schedule and tax liability for this quarter.

If you are unsure about whether you are a monthly schedule depositor or a semiweekly schedule depositor, see *Pub. 15 (Circular E), section 11.*

16 Check one: [X]   Line 10 on this return is less than $2,500 or line 10 on the return for the prior quarter was less than $2,500, and you did not incur a $100,000 next-day deposit obligation during the current quarter. If line 10 for the prior quarter was less than $2,500 but line 10 on this return is $100,000 or more, you must provide a record of your federal tax liability. If you are a monthly schedule depositor, complete the deposit schedule below; if you are a semiweekly schedule depositor, attach Schedule B (Form 941). Go to Part 3.

[ ]   **You were a monthly schedule depositor for the entire quarter.** Enter your tax liability for each month and total liability for the quarter, then go to Part 3.

Tax liability: Month 1   [.   ]

Month 2   [.   ]

Month 3   [.   ]

Total liability for quarter   [.   ]   Total must equal line 10.

[ ]   **You were a semiweekly schedule depositor for any part of this quarter.** Complete *Schedule B (Form 941): Report of Tax Liability for Semiweekly Schedule Depositors,* and attach it to Form 941.

Part 3: Tell us about your business. If a question does NOT apply to your business, leave it blank.

17 If your business has closed or you stopped paying wages . . . .   [ ] Check here, and

enter the final date you paid wages   [/   /   ] .

18 If you are a seasonal employer and you do not have to file a return for every quarter of the year . .   [ ] Check here.

Part 4: May we speak with your third-party designee?

Do you want to allow an employee, a paid tax preparer, or another person to discuss this return with the IRS? See the instructions for details.

[X] Yes. Designee's name and phone number   [Adam M. Hoyle]   [319-4x4-2222]

Select a 5-digit Personal Identification Number (PIN) to use when talking to the IRS.   [2] [2] [3] [3] [4]

[ ] No.

Part 5: Sign here. You MUST complete both pages of Form 941 and SIGN it.

Under penalties of perjury, I declare that I have examined this return, including accompanying schedules and statements, and to the best of my knowledge and belief, it is true, correct, and complete. Declaration of preparer (other than taxpayer) is based on all information of which preparer has any knowledge.

X   **Sign your name here**   *Adam Hoyle*

Print your name here   [Adam M. Hoyle]

Print your title here   [President]

Date   [1 / 10 / 13]

Best daytime phone   [319-4x4-2222]

Paid Preparer Use Only   Check if you are self-employed . . . [ ]

Preparer's name		PTIN	
Preparer's signature		Date	/ /
Firm's name (or yours if self-employed)		EIN	
Address		Phone	
City		State	ZIP code

☐ VOID   ☐ CORRECTED

PAYER'S name, street address, city, state, ZIP code, and telephone no.	1 Rents	OMB No. 1545-0115	
Second Church 867 Alton Road Anytown, IL 61000 319-4x4-2222	$	**2012**	**Miscellaneous Income**
	2 Royalties		
	$	Form **1099-MISC**	
	3 Other income	4 Federal income tax withheld	
	$	$	**Copy C**

PAYER'S federal identification number	RECIPIENT'S identification number	5 Fishing boat proceeds	6 Medical and health care payments	**For Payer**
00-0019283	303-30-0003	$	$	

RECIPIENT'S name	7 Nonemployee compensation	8 Substitute payments in lieu of dividends or interest	For Privacy Act and Paperwork Reduction Act Notice, see the **2012 General Instructions for Certain Information Returns.**
Adam M. Hoyle	$ 37000.00	$	

Street address (including apt. no.)	9 Payer made direct sales of $5,000 or more of consumer products to a buyer (recipient) for resale ▶ ☐	10 Crop insurance proceeds	
641 Eastgate Blvd.		$	

City, state, and ZIP code	11	12	
Anytown, IL 61000			

Account number (see instructions)	2nd TIN not.	13 Excess golden parachute payments	14 Gross proceeds paid to an attorney	
	☐	$	$	

15a Section 409A deferrals	15b Section 409A income	16 State tax withheld	17 State/Payer's state no.	18 State income
$	$	$ $		$ $

Form **1099-MISC**   Department of the Treasury - Internal Revenue Service

---

☐ VOID   ☐ CORRECTED

PAYER'S name, street address, city, state, ZIP code, and telephone no.	1 Rents	OMB No. 1545-0115	
Second Church 867 Alton Road Anytown, IL 61000 319-4x4-2222	$	**2012**	**Miscellaneous Income**
	2 Royalties		
	$	Form **1099-MISC**	
	3 Other income	4 Federal income tax withheld	
	$	$	**Copy C**

PAYER'S federal identification number	RECIPIENT'S identification number	5 Fishing boat proceeds	6 Medical and health care payments	**For Payer**
00-0019283	200-03-0100	$	$	

RECIPIENT'S name	7 Nonemployee compensation	8 Substitute payments in lieu of dividends or interest	For Privacy Act and Paperwork Reduction Act Notice, see the **2012 General Instructions for Certain Information Returns.**
John L. Bridges	$ 2400.00	$	

Street address (including apt. no.)	9 Payer made direct sales of $5,000 or more of consumer products to a buyer (recipient) for resale ▶ ☐	10 Crop insurance proceeds	
1700 National Avenue		$	

City, state, and ZIP code	11	12	
Anytown, IL 61000			

Account number (see instructions)	2nd TIN not.	13 Excess golden parachute payments	14 Gross proceeds paid to an attorney	
	☐	$	$	

15a Section 409A deferrals	15b Section 409A income	16 State tax withheld	17 State/Payer's state no.	18 State income
$	$	$ $		$ $

Form **1099-MISC**   Department of the Treasury - Internal Revenue Service

Do Not Staple **6969**

Form **1096**	Annual Summary and Transmittal of U.S. Information Returns	OMB No. 1545-0108
Department of the Treasury Internal Revenue Service		20**12**

FILER'S name
Second Church

Street address (including room or suite number)
867 Alton Road

City, state, and ZIP code
Anytown, IL 61000

For Official Use Only

Name of person to contact	Telephone number
G. White	*319-444-2222*
Email address	Fax number
GWhite@connect.com	*319-444-2223*

1 Employer identification number	2 Social security number	3 Total number of forms	4 Federal income tax withheld	5 Total amount reported with this Form 1096
00-0019283		*2*	$	$ *39400.00*

6 Enter an "X" in only one box below to indicate the type of form being filed.

7 If this is your final return, enter an "X" here ▶ ☐

W-2G 32	1097-BTC 50	1098 81	1098-C 78	1098-E 84	1098-T 83	1099-A 80	1099-B 79	1099-C 85	1099-CAP 73	1099-DIV 91	1099-G 86	1099-H 71	1099-INT 92
☐	☐	☐	☐	☐	☐	☐	☐	☐	☐	☐	☐	☐	☐

1099-K 10	1099-LTC 93	1099-MISC 95	1099-OID 96	1099-PATR 97	1099-Q 31	1099-R 98	1099-S 75	1099-SA 94	3921 25	3922 26	5498 28	5498-ESA 72	5498-SA 27
☐	☐	☒	☐	☐	☐	☐	☐	☐	☐	☐	☐	☐	☐

Return this entire page to the Internal Revenue Service. Photocopies are not acceptable.

Under penalties of perjury, I declare that I have examined this return and accompanying documents, and, to the best of my knowledge and belief, they are true, correct, and complete.

Signature ▶ *A. Hoyle*   Title ▶ *President*   Date ▶ *1/26/13*

K. ILLUSTRATION 3: TAX WITHHOLDING AND REPORTING REQUIREMENTS

1 SELF-EMPLOYED MINISTER; NO OTHER COMPENSATED CHURCH WORKERS

Assume that Third Church (of Anytown, Illinois) has one minister, Pastor Jane Frank, who reports her income taxes as a self-employed person. The church has no other compensated workers. Pastor Frank lives in a church-owned parsonage. Under these facts, the church has only one reporting obligation—it must issue a Form 1099-MISC to Pastor Frank before February 1, 2013 (assuming she receives at least $600 in compensation from the church). The Form 1099-MISC reports compensation paid to Pastor Frank (do not include the fair rental value of the parsonage). The church also sends an additional copy to the IRS before March 1, 2013, with a Form 1096 (transmittal form).

The church has no other reporting obligations. Pastor Frank uses the estimated tax procedure (Form 1040-ES) to report both her federal income taxes and her self-employment taxes. Note that the fair rental value of the parsonage is included in Pastor Frank's earnings for purposes of determining her self-employment tax liability. The same would be true of any parsonage allowance designated by the church. The church may wish to so advise Pastor Frank.

Form **8274**
(Rev. September 2006)

Department of the Treasury
Internal Revenue Service

Certification by Churches and Qualified Church-Controlled Organizations Electing Exemption From Employer Social Security and Medicare Taxes

File Two Copies

Please type or print	Full name of organization

Employer identification number (EIN)

Address (number and street or P.O. box number if mail is not delivered to street address)

City, state, and ZIP code

Date wages first paid

If exemption is based on a group ruling, give full name of central organization

Group exemption number

Sign Here ▶

I certify that the above named organization is a church or qualified church-controlled organization which, as defined in section 3121(w) of the Internal Revenue Code, is opposed for religious reasons to the payment of employer social security and Medicare taxes, and elects not to be subject to such taxes.

(Signature of authorized official)   (Title)   (Date)

Section references are to the Internal Revenue Code unless otherwise noted.

Purpose of form. Churches and qualified church-controlled organizations (defined below) that are opposed, for religious reasons, to the payment of social security and Medicare taxes may elect exemption from the payment of the employer's share of these taxes by filing Form 8274.

Effect of election. This election applies to services performed by all current and future employees of the electing organization. However, this election **does not** apply to services as ministers of a church, members of a religious order, or to services performed in an unrelated trade or business of the church or qualified church-controlled organization.

The electing organization must continue to withhold federal income tax on wages, tips, and other compensation, and to report this income and the tax withheld on Form W-2, Wage and Tax Statement. The organization must also file Form 941, Employer's QUARTERLY Federal Tax Return, or Form 944, Employer's ANNUAL Federal Tax Return, to report both the wages covered by this election and the wages of any employees engaged in unrelated business activities whose wages are not covered by this election and are subject to employer taxes.

Employees (except ministers of a church or members of religious orders) who receive wages of $108.28 or more in a year from an electing church or qualified church-controlled organization are subject to self-employment tax on the earnings. They will be considered employees for all other purposes of the Internal Revenue Code, including federal income tax withholding.

Churches and qualified church-controlled organizations. The term "church" means a church described in sections 501(c)(3) and 170(b)(1)(A)(i). The term "church" includes conventions or associations of churches. It also includes any elementary or secondary school that is controlled, operated, or principally supported by a church (or conventions or associations of churches).

A "qualified church-controlled organization" includes any church-controlled tax-exempt organization described in section 501(c)(3) unless the organization both:

● Offers goods, services, or facilities for sale to the general public, other than on an incidental basis or for a nominal charge, and

● Normally receives more than 25% of its support from governmental sources and/or receipts from admissions, sales of merchandise, services, or facilities in related trade or business activities.

Eligibility for election. Any organization that meets both of the above conditions is **not** eligible to file this form. For example, a church-controlled hospital generally will meet both conditions and will not qualify to make the election. However, seminaries, religious retreat centers, or burial societies generally will be eligible, regardless of funding sources, because they don't offer goods, services, or facilities for sale to the general public.

A church-run orphanage or home for the elderly that is open to the general public may qualify if not more than 25% of its support is from admissions, sales of merchandise, services or facilities in related trades or businesses, or from governmental sources. Church pension boards, fund-raising organizations, and auxiliary organizations such as youth groups and ladies auxiliaries generally may make the election.

Revocation of election. Either the electing church or organization or the IRS may revoke this election. The electing church or organization can permanently revoke the election by paying social security and Medicare taxes for wages covered by this election. The IRS will permanently revoke the election if the organization does not file Form W-2 for 2 years or more and does not provide the information within 60 days after a written request by the IRS.

Employer identification number (EIN). If you do not have an EIN, you may apply for one online. Go to the IRS website at *www.irs.gov/businesses* and click on the "Employer ID Numbers (EINs)" link. You may also apply for an EIN by calling 1-800-829-4933 (hours of operation are Monday - Friday, 7:00 a.m. to 10:00 p.m. local time), or you can fax or mail Form SS-4, Application for Employer Identification Number, to the IRS.

Signature. An official authorized to sign tax returns for the church or qualified church-controlled organization must sign Form 8274.

When to file. File Form 8274 after you hire employees, but before the first date on which a quarterly or annual employment tax return is due (or would be due except for this election). Keep a copy for your records.

Where to file. Send two copies of Form 8274 to: Internal Revenue Service, Ogden, Utah 84201–0027.

Cat. No. 61933Q   Form **8274** (Rev. 9-2006)

| Form **5578**
(Rev. April 2009)
Department of the Treasury
Internal Revenue Service | **Annual Certification of Racial Nondiscrimination for a Private School Exempt From Federal Income Tax**
(For use by organizations that do not file Form 990 or Form 990-EZ) | OMB No. 1545-0213
Open to Public Inspection
For IRS Use Only ▶ |

For the period beginning , and ending ,

| 1a | Name of organization that operates, supervises, and/or controls school(s). | 1b | Employer identification number |

Address (number and street or P.O. box no., if mail is not delivered to street address) Room/suite

City or town, state, and ZIP + 4 (If foreign address, list city or town, state or province, and country. Include postal code.)

| 2a | Name of central organization holding group exemption letter covering the school(s). (If same as 1a above, write "Same" and complete 2c.) If the organization in 1a above holds an individual exemption letter, write "Not Applicable." | 2b | Employer identification number |

Address (number and street or P.O. box no., if mail is not delivered to street address) Room/suite

2c Group exemption number (see instructions under **Definitions**)

City or town, state, and ZIP + 4 (If foreign address, list city or town, state or province, and country. Include postal code.)

| 3a | Name of school. (If more than one school, write "See Attached," and attach a list of the names, complete addresses, including postal codes, and employer identification numbers of the schools.) If same as 1a above, write "Same." | 3b | Employer identification number, if any |

Address (number and street or P.O. box no., if mail is not delivered to street address) Room/suite

City or town, state, and ZIP + 4 (If foreign address, list city or town, state or province, and country. Include postal code.)

Under penalties of perjury, I hereby certify that I am authorized to take official action on behalf of the above school(s) and that to the best of my knowledge and belief the school(s) has (have) satisfied the applicable requirements of sections 4.01 through 4.05 of Rev. Proc. 75-50, 1975-2 C.B. 587, for the period covered by this certification.

(Signature) (Type or print name and title.) (Date)

General Instructions

Section references are to the Internal Revenue Code unless otherwise noted.

Note. This form is open to public inspection.

Purpose of Form

Form 5578 may be used by organizations that operate tax-exempt private schools to provide the Internal Revenue Service with the annual certification of racial nondiscrimination required by Rev. Proc. 75-50 (the relevant part of which is reproduced in these instructions).

Who Must File

Every organization that claims exemption from federal income tax under section 501(c)(3) of the Internal Revenue Code and that operate(s), supervises, or controls a private school(s) must file a certification of racial nondiscrimination. If an organization is required to file Form 990, Return of Organization Exempt From Income Tax, or Form 990-EZ, Short Form Return of Organization Exempt From Income Tax, either as a separate return or as part of a group return, the certification must be made on Schedule E (Form 990 or 990-EZ), Schools, rather than on this form.

An authorized official of a central organization may file one form to certify for the school activities of subordinate organizations that would otherwise be required to file on an individual basis, but only if the central organization has enough control over the schools listed on the form to ensure that the schools maintain a racially nondiscriminatory policy as to students.

Definitions

A *racially nondiscriminatory policy as to students* means that the school admits the students of any race to all the rights, privileges, programs, and activities generally accorded or made available to students at that school and that the school does not discriminate on the basis of race in the administration of its educational policies, admissions policies, scholarship and loan programs, and other school-administered programs.

The IRS considers discrimination on the basis of race to include discrimination on the basis of color or national or ethnic origin.

A *school* is an educational organization that normally maintains a regular faculty and curriculum and normally has a regularly enrolled body of pupils or students in attendance at the place where its educational activities are regularly carried on. The term includes primary,

secondary, preparatory, or high schools and colleges and universities, whether operated as a separate legal entity or as an activity of a church or other organization described in section 501(c)(3). The term also includes preschools and any other organization that is a school as defined in section 170(b)(1)(A)(ii).

A *central organization* is an organization that has one or more subordinates under its general supervision or control. A subordinate is a chapter, local, post, or other unit of a central organization. A central organization may also be a subordinate, as in the case of a state organization that has subordinate units and is itself affiliated with a national organization.

The *group exemption number (GEN)* is a four-digit number issued to a central organization by the IRS. It identifies a central organization that has received a ruling from the IRS recognizing on a group basis the exemption from federal income tax of the central organization and its covered subordinates.

When To File

Under Rev. Proc. 75-50, a certification of racial nondiscrimination must be filed annually by the 15th day of the 5th month following the end of the organization's calendar year or fiscal period.

For Paperwork Reduction Act Notice, see page 3. Cat. No. 42658A Form **5578** (Rev. 4-2009)

"Bring me a denarius and let me look at it." They brought the coin, and he asked them,
"Whose portrait is this? And whose inscription?" "Caesar's," they replied.
Then Jesus said to them, "Give to Caesar what is Caesar's and to God what is God's."

Mark 12:15–17

CHAPTER HIGHLIGHTS

■ ***Churches subject to some taxes.*** Churches are subject to a variety of taxes, including property taxes, sales taxes, federal and state payroll taxes, the unrelated business income tax, and various excise taxes.

■ ***Federal income taxes.*** Churches are exempt from federal income taxes if they meet six requirements: (1) the church is a corporation; (2) the church is organized exclusively for exempt purposes; (3) the church is operated exclusively for exempt purposes; (4) none of the church's net earnings inures to the benefit of any private individuals, (5) the church does not engage in substantial efforts to influence legislation; and (6) the church does not intervene or participate in political campaigns.

■ ***Inurement.*** One of the six requirements for exemption from federal income tax is that none of a church's funds or assets inures to the benefit of a private individual, other than as reasonable compensation for services rendered. Inurement may occur in many ways, including excessive compensation, payment of excessive rent, receipt of less than fair market value in sales or exchanges of property, inadequately secured loans, and the payment of personal expenses of an officer that the church did not characterize as compensation at the time of payment.

■ ***Lobbying activities.*** In order to remain exempt from federal income tax, a church must not engage in "substantial efforts" to influence legislation. Insubstantial attempts to influence legislation do not jeopardize a church's tax-exempt status.

■ ***Campaign activities.*** To remain exempt from federal income tax, a church may neither intervene nor participate in a political campaign on behalf of or in opposition to any candidate for public office. There is no exception for "insubstantial" campaign activities.

■ ***Basis of tax-exempt status.*** Many courts have ruled that the exemption of churches from federal income tax is a matter of "legislative grace" that is not required by the First Amendment's "free exercise of religion" and "nonestablishment of religion" clauses.

■ ***Securing exempt status.*** Churches are automatically exempt from federal income tax, assuming they meet the conditions summarized above. They may seek IRS recognition of exempt status in order to facilitate the deductibility of donors' contributions.

■ ***Group exemptions.*** Conventions and associations of churches are allowed to obtain a "group exemption ruling" from the IRS. Such a ruling provides recognition of exempt status to all subordinate organizations described in the group exemption ruling request.

■ ***Unrelated business income tax (UBIT).*** The tax code imposes an unrelated business income tax on the unrelated business taxable income of churches and other charities. Unrelated business income generally is income from the operation of a trade or business that is regularly carried on. Certain exceptions apply.

■ ***Unemployment taxes.*** The following activities are exempt from unemployment taxes in most states: (1) service performed in the employ of a church or a convention or association of churches; (2) service performed in the employ of an unincorporated, church-controlled elementary or secondary school; (3) service performed in the employ of an incorporated religious elementary or secondary school if it is operated primarily for religious purposes and is operated, supervised, controlled, or principally supported by a church or a convention or association of churches; (4) service performed by a duly ordained, commissioned, or licensed minister of a church in the exercise of ministry or by a member of a religious order in the exercise of duties required by such order.

■ ***State sales taxes.*** Most states impose a tax on the sale of tangible personal property or the rendering of various services for compensation. Religious organizations are exempt from sales taxes in most states, although the nature of the exemption varies from state to state. Sales made to religious organizations are exempted from sales taxes in many states. Some states exempt sales made by religious organizations, and others exempt sales to or by religious organizations. Many states that exempt sales of property made to religious organizations stipulate that the exemption is available only if the organization uses the purchased property for exempt purposes. Some states are even more restrictive, and some have no specific exemption for sales by or to religious organizations. Table 12-3 at the end of this chapter contains the text of the sales tax exemption statutes of all 50 states.

- **State property taxes.** All 50 states exempt some church-owned property from property tax. However, the extent of the exemption varies from state to state. Some states exempt property used exclusively for religious worship, while others exempt property used for religious purposes. Parsonages are exempt in many states. Table 12-4 at the end of this chapter contains the text of the property tax exemption statutes of all 50 states.

INTRODUCTION

Federal, state, and local governments have enacted a variety of tax laws to finance the enormous costs of government. The primary sources of federal revenue are individual and corporate income taxes and Social Security taxes. Other federal taxes include unemployment, estate, and excise taxes. State and local governments often impose income, sales, and property taxes and, in addition, provide employment security through unemployment taxes.

The applicability of any of these various taxes to churches depends upon the following factors: (1) whether the statute that imposes the tax specifically exempts churches; (2) if churches are exempt, whether all conditions to exempt status have been satisfied; and (3) whether a tax that purports to apply to churches is permissible under state and federal constitutions.

A. FEDERAL INCOME TAXATION

1. DEFINITION OF "CHURCH"

The tax code uses the term "church" in many contexts, including the following:

- charitable giving limitations,
- various retirement plan rules,
- unrelated business income,
- exemption from applying for recognition of tax-exempt status,
- unemployment tax exemption,
- exemption from filing annual information returns, and
- restrictions on IRS examinations.

Despite numerous references to the term "church," the tax code provides no definition. This is understandable, since a definition that is too narrow may interfere with the constitutional guaranty of religious freedom, while a definition that is too broad may encourage abuses in the name of religion. The United States Supreme Court has noted that "the great diversity in church structure and organization among religious groups in this country . . . makes it impossible, as Congress perceived, to lay down a single rule to govern all church-related organizations." *St. Martin Evangelical Lutheran Church v. South Dakota, 451 U.S. 772 (1981).*

Several other courts have noted the difficulty of defining the term "church," including the following:

- "There is very little guidance for courts to use in making decisions [as to church status]." *Spiritual Outreach Society v. Commissioner, 927 F.2d 335 (8th Cir. 1991).*
- "Deciding what constitutes a church for federal tax purposes is not an easy task. There is very little guidance for courts to use in making decisions." *Spiritual Outreach Society v. Commissioner, 927 F.2d 335 (8th Cir. 1991).*
- "While federal tax authorities must apply the word church in a variety of contexts, there is no ready definition. . . . It is generally accepted that Congress intended a more restricted definition for a 'church' than for a 'religious organization,' but probably because of First Amendment considerations it has provided virtually no guidance on this distinction." *Spiritual Outreach Society v. Commissioner, 927 F.2d 335 (8th Cir. 1991).*
- "The Internal Revenue Code is silent as to the definition of the term 'church,' as are the regulations." *VIA v. Commissioner, 68 T.C.M. 212 (1994).*
- "Although it is settled that Congress intended a more limited concept for 'church' than for the previously identified 'religious organization,' Congress has offered virtually no guidance as to precisely what is meant. Nor does a coherent definition emerge from reviewing the Internal Revenue Service's rulings or regulations, or the limited instances of judicial treatment. One court concluded after thorough review of the relevant statutes and regulations that what is a 'church' must be determined in light of general or traditional understandings of the term. Such understandings are not easily achieved for at least two reasons. There is no bright line beyond which certain organized activities undertaken for religious purposes coalesce into a 'church' structure. And the range of 'church' structures extant in the United States is enormously diverse and confusing." *American Guidance Foundation, Inc. v. United States, 490 F.Supp. 304 (D.C.D.C. 1980).*

In the absence of any meaningful guidance in the tax code and regulations, the courts have developed three different approaches to determine whether an organization qualifies as a church: the *De La Salle* approach, the associational test, and the IRS's 14 criteria. These approaches are explained below.

The De La Salle approach

In *De La Salle Institute v. United States*, 195 F.Supp. 891, 898 (N.D. Cal. 1961), a federal court in California issued a ruling in a case brought by an organization contending that it was exempt from taxation imposed upon its unrelated business income due to its qualification as a church under section 511 of the tax code.

The court in *De La Salle* concluded that in the absence of a congressional definition of the term "church," the term is properly defined by "the common meaning and usage of the word." In decisions subsequent to *De La Salle*, courts have declined to adopt the approach taken by the *De La Salle* court. To illustrate, in *American Guidance Foundation, Inc. v. United States*, 490 F.Supp. 304 (D.C.D.C. 1980), the court stated that a general or traditional understanding of the term is elusive because "there is no bright line beyond which certain organized activities undertaken for religious purposes coalesce into a 'church' structure and the range of 'church' structures extant in the United States is enormously diverse and confusing."

The associational test

Courts also have followed *American Guidance* in finding that a church may be distinguished from other religious organizations by fulfillment of an "associational role": "The means by which an avowedly religious purpose is accomplished separates a 'church' from other forms of religious enterprise. At a minimum, a church includes a body of believers or communicants that assembles regularly in order to worship. Unless the organization is reasonably available to the public in its conduct of worship, its educational instruction, and its promulgation of doctrine, it cannot fulfill this associational role."

The IRS's 14 criteria

Several courts have applied a 14-criteria standard introduced in 1977 by Jerome Kurtz, then Commissioner of Internal Revenue, and thereafter applied by the IRS to evaluate whether an organization qualifies for church status. The Tax Court has applied the 14 criteria in several cases. The criteria are:

(1) a distinct legal existence;
(2) a recognized creed and form of worship;
(3) a definite and distinct ecclesiastical government;
(4) a formal code of doctrine and discipline;
(5) a distinct religious history;
(6) a membership not associated with any church or denomination;
(7) an organization of ordained ministers;
(8) ordained ministers selected after completing prescribed studies;
(9) a literature of its own;
(10) established places of worship;
(11) regular congregations;
(12) regular religious services;
(13) Sunday schools for religious instruction of the young; and
(14) schools for the preparation of its ministers.

One court noted:

> *Due partly to concerns over a mechanical application of rigid criteria to a diverse set of religious organizations, some courts have deemed a few of the criteria within the fourteen-factor IRS test to be of special, or "central" importance. The leading case is* American Guidance, *in which the United States District Court for the District of Columbia articulated the following standard: "While some of the [fourteen criteria applied by the IRS] are relatively minor, others, e.g., the existence of an established congregation served by an organized ministry, the provision of regular religious services and religious education for the young, and the dissemination of a doctrinal code, are of central importance."*

A federal appeals court made the following observation regarding the 14 criteria: "We are mindful of [the plaintiff's] claim that the criteria discriminate unfairly against rural, newly formed churches which lack the monetary resources held by other churches. [The plaintiff] is not alone in this position. In large part it is for this reason we have emphasized what we view as the core requirements of the fourteen criteria." *Spiritual Outreach Society v. Commissioner, 927 F.2d 335 8th Cir. 1991).*

The IRS has acknowledged that "no single factor is controlling, although all 14 may not be relevant to a given determination." These criteria have been recognized by a number of courts, as illustrated in the following examples.

EXAMPLE. The first federal court to recognize the IRS "14 criteria" test involved a claim by a husband and wife that they and their minor child constituted a church. The family insisted that it was a church, since the father often preached and disseminated religious instruction to his son; the family conducted "religious services" in their home; and the family often prayed together at home. The court agreed with the IRS that the family was not a church, basing its decision on the 14 criteria. In commenting upon the 14 criteria, the court noted that "while some of these are relatively minor, others, e.g., the existence of an established congregation served by an organized ministry, the provision of regular religious services and religious education for the young, and the dissemination of a doctrinal code, are of central importance. The means by which an avowedly religious purpose is accomplished separates a 'church' from other forms of religious enterprise." In concluding that the family was not a church, the court observed: "At a minimum, a church includes a body of believers or communicants that assembles regularly in order to worship. Unless the organization is reasonably available to the public in its conduct of worship, its educational instruction, and its promulgation of doctrine, it cannot fulfill this associational role."

American Guidance Foundation v. United States, 490 F. Supp. 304 (D.D.C. 1980). See also Lutheran Social Service of Minnesota v. United States, 758 F.2d 1283 (8th Cir. 1985).

EXAMPLE. The United States Tax Court ruled that a religious organization formed to "spread the message of God's love and hope throughout the world" and to "provide a place in which those who believe in the existence of God may present religious music to any persons interested in hearing such" was not a church. The organization maintained an outdoor amphitheater on its property, at which musical programs and an occasional "retreat" or "festival" were conducted about 12 times each year. No other regularly scheduled religious or musical services were conducted. Most of the musical events were held on Saturdays so that persons could attend their own churches on Sundays.

Musical services consisted of congregational singing of religious music. A minister always opened and closed these events with prayer. While it did not charge admission to its events, its published schedule of "donations" was similar to admission charges. The organization also maintained a chapel on its property that was open to the public for individual prayer.

The Tax Court concluded that the organization was not a church. It refused to accept the 14 criteria as the only test for determining whether a particular organization is a church. It did concede, however, that the 14 criteria are helpful in deciding such cases. The court noted that the organization met at least a few of the 14 criteria and that some would not be relevant to "a newly created rural organization." On the other hand, the court noted that the organization had no ecclesiastical government, formal creed,

ARE MISSIONS AGENCIES CHURCHES?
(A Summary of Three IRS Rulings)

Note: In a series of three private letter rulings in 2007, the IRS ruled that three missions agencies were not churches. The IRS applied the 14-criteria test in reaching its conclusions. In each ruling it concluded that the italicized factors (below) "are not distinctive characteristics of a church, but are common to both churches and non-church religious organizations" and that "meeting these criteria is not sufficient to establish [that an entity is] a church." The factors of "central importance" include "the existence of an established congregation, the provision of regular worship services and religious education for the young, and the dissemination of a doctrinal code."

14 FACTORS	RULING 200727021	RULING 200712047	RULING 200712046
1. *Distinct legal existence*	Yes	Yes	Yes
2. *Recognized creed and form of worship*	Yes	Yes	Yes
3. Definite and distinct ecclesiastical government	No	No	No
4. *Formal code of doctrine and discipline*	Yes	Yes	Yes
5. *A distinct religious history*	Yes	Yes	Yes
6. A membership not associated with any other church or denomination	No	No	No
7. An organization of ordained ministers	No	No	No
8. Ordained ministers selected after completing prescribed studies	No	No	No
9. *A literature of its own*	Yes	Yes	Yes
10. Established places of worship	No	No	No
11. Regular congregations	No	No	No
12. Regular religious services	No	No	No
13. Sunday schools for the religious instruction of the young	No	No	No
14. *Schools for the preparation of ministers*	Yes	Yes	Yes
Conclusion: was the agency a church?	No	No	No

organization of ordained clergy, seminary, or Sunday school for the training of youth. Further, it did not produce its own religious literature (it sold literature produced by other religious organizations).

The court concluded, "While a definitive form of ecclesiastical government or organizational structure may not be required, we are not persuaded that musical festivals and revivals (even if involving principally gospel singing . . .) and gatherings for individual meditation and prayer by persons who do not regularly come together as a congregation for such purposes should be held to satisfy the cohesiveness factor which we think is an essential ingredient of a 'church.'" *Spiritual Outreach Society v. Commissioner of Internal Revenue, 58 T.C.M. 1284 (1990), affirmed, 927 F.2d 335 (8th Cir. 1991).*

EXAMPLE. A church conducted three or four weekly worship services on its premises for a number of years. These services were attended by up to 350 persons. Over time the church stopped conducting regular worship services and embarked upon radio and publishing activities and occasional regional seminars, where the church's founder disseminated his religious views, counseled the audience, and raised funds. The IRS concluded that the church had ceased to qualify as a church for federal tax purposes. In reaching its decision, the IRS noted that the organization failed most of the 14 criteria used by the IRS in identifying churches.

The IRS concluded that "while some of these are relatively minor, others, e.g., the existence of an established congregation served by an ordained ministry, the provision of regular religious services and religious education for the young, and the dissemination of a doctrinal code, are of central importance." Conceding that "there is no bright-line test as to whether an organization is a church," the IRS concluded, based on an analysis of the 14 criteria, that the organization no longer qualified as a church. It observed, "Most important, it no longer possesses the regular church services which have been held to be a prerequisite for church status. It no longer has the minimum for church status—a body of believers or communicants that assembles regularly in order to worship. It no longer has a defined congregation of worshipers, nor an established place of worship, nor regular religious services. Nor does it have other substantial church characteristics. Its ministers officiated at no more than [a few] weddings or other ministerial events or sacerdotal functions during the years." *IRS Letter Ruling 200437040. See also IRS Letter Rulings 200912039, 200926049.*

Difficulties with the criteria

The examples above demonstrate the continuing viability of the 14 criteria. Nevertheless, these criteria are troubling because they are so restrictive that many, if not most, bona fide churches fail to satisfy several of them. In part the problem stems from the use of

criteria that apply to both local churches and religious denominations. To illustrate, few local churches would meet criteria 7, 9, and 14, since these ordinarily would pertain only to religious denominations. In addition, many newer, independent churches often will fail criteria 1 and 5 and may also fail 2, 3, 4, 6, and 8. It is therefore possible for a legitimate church to fail as many as 10 of the 14 criteria.

⊙ OBSERVATION. The original Christian churches described in the New Testament book of Acts would have failed most of the 14 criteria.

The criteria clearly are vague and inadequate. Some apply exclusively to local churches; others do not. And the IRS does not indicate how many criteria an organization must meet in order to be classified as a church, or if some criteria are more important than others. The vagueness of the criteria means that their application in any particular case will depend on the discretion of a government agent. This is the very kind of conduct that the courts repeatedly have condemned in other contexts as unconstitutional.

To illustrate, the courts have invalidated municipal ordinances that condition the rights of speech and assembly on compliance with criteria that are so vague that decisions are a matter of administrative discretion. The United States Supreme Court has held that "it is a basic principle of due process that an enactment is void for vagueness if its prohibitions are not clearly defined. . . . A vague law impermissibly delegates basic policy matters to [government officials] for resolution on an ad hoc and subjective basis with the attendant dangers of arbitrary and discriminatory application." *Grayned v. City of Rockford, 408 U.S.104 (1972).*

This same reasoning should apply in the context of other fundamental constitutional rights, such as the First Amendment right to freely exercise one's religion. The IRS should not be permitted to effectively limit the right of churches and church members to freely exercise their religion on the basis of a test, such as the 14 criteria, that not only is inherently vague but whose application is a matter of administrative discretion.

The criteria also are constitutionally suspect on the related ground of "overbreadth." The Supreme Court

> *has repeatedly held that a governmental purpose to control or prevent activities constitutionally subject to state regulation may not be achieved by means which sweep unnecessarily broadly and thereby invade the area of protected freedoms. The power to regulate must be so exercised as not, in attaining a permissible end, unduly to infringe the protected freedom. Even though the governmental purpose be legitimate and substantial, that purpose cannot be pursued by means that broadly stifle fundamental personal liberties when the end can be more narrowly achieved.* N.A.A.C.P. v. Alabama, 377 U.S. 288, 307-08 (1964).

Congress and the IRS undoubtedly have the authority to identify those churches that are not qualified for the tax benefits afforded by federal law, but they may not do so on the basis of criteria that sweep so broadly as to jeopardize the standing of legitimate churches. The courts understandably find the task of defining the term "church" perplexing. But when a definition is needed, they should reject the 14 criteria as a guide.

✿ **KEY POINT.** Unfortunately, the IRS refers to the 14 criteria in its *Tax Guide for Churches and Religious Organizations* (Publication 1828).

Conflict of interest policy

In a 2008 private letter ruling, the IRS ruled that an organization did not qualify as a church for tax purposes in part because it did not have a conflict of interest policy. The organization applied to the IRS for recognition of tax-exempt status as a church. Its application for exemption disclosed the following: (1) Its stated purposes were to "operate for the advancement of Christianity and for other charitable purposes." (2) It did not have a regular group of people that come together to worship, nor did it conduct regular services. Instead, it claimed that it was engaged in "street ministry." (3) It did not have an organization of ordained ministers. (4) It did not own or rent a building in which it held religious services. (5) It did not maintain a religious school for the education of the young. (6) The organization's board of directors consisted of four individuals—the founder (who was the chairman of the board) and his wife and two sons.

The IRS ruled that the organization was not eligible for exemption as a church. It relied on the 14-factor test it has applied in recent years in deciding if an organization is a church. The IRS has observed that "while some of these are relatively minor, others, e.g. the existence of an established congregation served by an ordained ministry, the provision of regular religious services and religious education for the young, and the dissemination of a doctrinal code, are of central importance." Further, the IRS has acknowledged that an organization need not satisfy all 14 criteria to be classified as a church.

In concluding that the organization was not a church, the IRS stated:

> You lack all of the significant elements used to determine whether an organization is a church for tax purposes. You do not have a group of people who come together on a regular basis and you do not hold regular religious services. Your organization consists only of four members of a single family and you do not even hold regular services for those individuals. Furthermore, you have provided no evidence that you are actively seeking new members. You have not provided specific details regarding any religious activities sufficient to demonstrate that you are a church. Thus, all of the significant factors used in determining church status weigh against you.

> You also lack many of the other elements associated with churches: you do not have an established place of worship, you do not have a membership distinct from another church or denomination, and you do not maintain schools or education activities either for the young or to prepare ministers. You have stated an intention to create a Sunday School in the future once you are fully established, but have not provided sufficient details about this planned activity nor given a timeframe. Even if you had, this element would not outweigh the many facts that indicate you are not a church. You lack all of the significant factors and most of the other factors used to determine whether an organization is a church. Therefore, we have concluded that you are not operating as a church.

The IRS noted that the organization was ineligible for exempt status for a second reason: it was operated for private rather than public purposes. To qualify for exemption, an organization must be operated for public rather than private purposes, and "the organization has the burden of demonstrating this by showing that it is not operated for the benefit of private individuals, such as its creator and his family." *Treas. Reg. 1.501(c)(3)-1(d)(1)(ii).* The IRS observed:

> Your board of directors consists entirely of [the founder's] family and there are no other members of the organization. In addition, you have not stated that none of your family members will be compensated in the future, only that you do not currently intend to do so. Even if no direct compensation is paid to [your family members] the family exercises complete control over your organization and its assets could be used to benefit the family.

> You have not adopted bylaws or provided specific information about the governance of your organization, nor have you adopted a conflict of interest policy. In addition, you do not have any members outside of your family and no other organization exercises significant influence over you.

> The structure of your organization indicates that it can be used to benefit private individuals, such as [the founder] and his family, and you lack safeguards that would help to prevent such use. In addition, you have provided no evidence that the organization will not be used for the benefit of private individuals. Therefore, you have not met your burden to prove that you will be operated for public rather than private purposes. Consequently, you are not eligible for exemption under section 501(c)(3) of the code even if you did conduct activities in furtherance of an exempt purpose. [Emphasis added.]

This ruling is significant because of the importance the IRS assigned to a conflict of interest policy despite the fact that neither the tax code nor regulations specifically require that a church have such a policy. The IRS concluded that the lack of a conflict of interest policy tends to show that a family-governed entity is operated for private rather than public interests and is therefore ineligible for exemption. *IRS Letter Ruling 200830028.*

Convention or association of churches

The tax code and regulations refer in several places to "conventions or associations of churches." For example, an organization that qualifies as a convention or association of churches is not required to file an annual return (Form 990), is subject to the church tax inquiry and church tax examination provisions applicable to churches, and is treated like a church for the following tax code sections:

- section 402(g)(8)(B) (limitation on elective deferrals);
- section 403(b)(9)(B) (definition of retirement income account);
- section 410(d) (election to have participation, vesting, funding, and certain other provisions apply to church plans);
- section 414(e) (definition of church plan);
- section 415(c)(7) (certain contributions by church plans);
- section 501(h)(5) (disqualification of certain organizations from making the section 501(h) election regarding lobbying expenditure limits);
- section 501(m)(3) (definition of commercial-type insurance);
- section 508(c)(1)(A) (exception from requirement to file application seeking recognition of exempt status); section 512(b)(12) (allowance of up to $1,000 deduction for purposes of determining unrelated business taxable income);
- section 514(b)(3)(E) (definition of debt-financed property);
- section 3121(w)(3)(A) (election regarding exemption from Social Security taxes);
- section 3309(b)(1) (application of federal unemployment tax provisions to services performed in the employ of certain organizations);
- section 6043(b)(1) (requirement to file a return upon liquidation or dissolution of the organization); and section 7702(j)(3)(A) (treatment of certain death benefit plans as life insurance).

Despite these numerous references to conventions or associations of churches, neither the tax code nor regulations define the term. A committee report to the Pension Protection Act of 2006 observed:

> *The term "convention or association of churches" was added to the code to ensure that hierarchical churches and congregational churches would not be treated dissimilarly for federal income tax purposes merely because of their organizational and governance structures. The committee understands that some congregational church organizations have only churches as members, and that others have both churches and individuals as members. The committee is concerned that an organization with the characteristics of a convention or association of churches, including having a substantial number of churches as members, might fail to be regarded as a convention or association of churches merely because it includes individuals in its membership. The committee intends that a congregational church organization that otherwise constitutes a convention or association of churches not*

> *be denied recognition as such merely because its membership includes individuals as well as churches.*

As a result, the Pension Protection Act of 2006 included a provision clarifying that an organization that otherwise is a convention or association of churches does not fail to so qualify merely because the membership of the organization includes individuals as well as churches or because individuals have voting rights in the organization. *IRC 7701.*

Mail-order churches

The term *mail-order church* refers to an organization set up pursuant to a "church charter" purchased through the mail from an organization claiming that the charter and other "ministerial credentials" can be used to reduce or eliminate an individual's federal income tax liability. Although a mail-order church is not precluded from exemption, since it is possible for one to be organized and operated exclusively for religious purposes, the IRS and the courts have ruled that many fail to qualify for tax-exempt status because they are operated for the private benefit of those who control the organization.

To illustrate, in one case a professional nurse founded an organization under the name ABC Church after purchasing a "certificate of ordination" from an organization selling such certificates and church charters. The nurse was the organization's minister, director, and principal officer. The nurse executed a vow of poverty and transferred all of her assets, including a home and an automobile, and income to the organization. The organization also assumed all of her liabilities, including a home mortgage and credit card balances. The organization paid all her living expenses, and she continued to use the house and automobile for personal purposes. The IRS concluded that the organization did not qualify for exemption under section 501(c)(3) because it operated to serve the private interests of a designated individual rather than a public interest. *Revenue Ruling 81-94 (1981).*

Several court cases have held that, in situations similar to that described in Revenue Ruling 81-94, an organization that serves the private interests of a designated individual rather than a public interest does not qualify for exemption. *See, e.g., Basic Bible Church v. Commissioner, 74 T.C. 846 (1980); Church of the Transfiguring Spirit, Inc. v. Commissioner, 76 T.C. 1 (1981); People of God Community v. Commissioner, 75 T.C. 127 (1980); The Southern Church of Universal Brotherhood Assembled, Inc. v. Commissioner, 74 T.C. 1223 (1980); Bubbling Well Church of Universal Love v. Commissioner, 74 T.C. 531 (1980); and Unitary Mission Church of Long Island v. Commissioner, 74 T.C. 507 (1980); aff'd, 647 F. 2d 163 (2d Cir. 1981).*

The IRS has observed:

> *In many situations where the organization selling the church charters and ministerial credentials has been recognized as exempt under 501(c)(3) (but has not received a group exemption), the organization purchasing the charter claims that it is covered by the selling organization's exempt status. This argument was made in* Basic

Bible Church *where the petitioner contended that as an auxiliary of the Basic Bible Church, it shared that organization's tax exempt status (the organization had not received a group ruling). The court concluded, however, that the petitioner was legally separate and distinct from the parent church and, therefore, had to qualify for exemption under 501(c)(3) on its own merits. See also* United States v. Toy National Bank, *79–1 USTC ¶ 9344 (N.D.Iowa 1979), and* Brown v. Commissioner, *T.C.M. 1980–553, which held that organizations that had obtained a charter from the Universal Life Church, Inc. (ULC) were not covered by that organization's individual exemption. The courts in these cases concluded that because ULC had an individual rather than a group exemption, the chartered organizations had to qualify for exemption on their own merits.* Internal Revenue Manual 7.25.3.6.12 (1999).

2. REQUIREMENTS FOR EXEMPTION

Section 501(a) of the tax code exempts organizations described in section 501(c) from federal income taxation. Section 501(c)(3) lists several exempt organizations, including

> corporations . . . organized and operated exclusively for religious, charitable . . . or educational purposes . . . no part of the net earnings of which inures to the benefit of any private shareholder or individual, no substantial part of the activities of which is carrying on propaganda, or otherwise attempting, to influence legislation . . . and which does not participate in, or intervene in (including the publishing or distributing of statements), any political campaign on behalf of any candidate for public office.

This section exempts churches from federal income taxation. Note that the exemption is conditioned upon the following six factors: (1) the church is a corporation; (2) the church is organized exclusively for exempt purposes; (3) the church is operated exclusively for exempt purposes; (4) none of the church's net earnings inures to the benefit of any private individuals; (5) the church does not engage in substantial efforts to influence legislation; and (6) the church does not intervene or participate in political campaigns. These factors will be considered separately.

Church as corporation
While section 501(c)(3) would appear to exempt only those churches that are incorporated, the IRS maintains that unincorporated churches are eligible for exemption. The IRS *Internal Revenue Manual* states that "the typical nonprofit association formed under a constitution or bylaws, with elective officers empowered to act for it, would be treated as a corporation." *IRM § 7.25.3.2.3 (1999).*

Organized exclusively for exempt purposes
To be exempt from federal income tax, a church must be organized exclusively for exempt purposes. This requirement is referred to by the IRS as the "organizational test" of tax-exempt status.

The income tax regulations state that an organization will be deemed to be organized exclusively for exempt purposes only if its articles of incorporation limit the purposes of the organization to one or more of the exempt purposes listed in section 501(c)(3) of the tax code and do not empower the organization to engage, other than as an insubstantial part of its activities, in activities that are not in furtherance of one or more exempt purposes. *Treas. Reg. 1.501(c)(3)-1(b)(1)(i).* Note that the regulations require these limitations to appear in an exempt organization's articles of incorporation, and not in its bylaws.

A church's purposes may be as broad as, or more specific than, the purposes stated in section 501(c)(3) (cited above). But in no event will a church be considered organized exclusively for one or more exempt purposes if its articles of incorporation recite purposes broader than the purposes stated in section 501(c)(3). *Treas. Reg. 1.501(c)(3)-1(b)(1)(iv).* The fact that the actual operation of a church whose purposes are broader than those stated in section 501(c)(3) is exclusively in furtherance of one or more exempt purposes will not be sufficient to permit the church to satisfy the organizational test. Similarly, a church whose purposes are broader than those stated in section 501(c)(3) will not meet the organizational test as a result of statements or other evidence that its members intend to operate it solely in furtherance of one or more exempt purposes. In summary, a church can be organized for purposes other than religious if such purposes are among those listed in section 501(c)(3).

Feeder organizations
Section 502 of the tax code states that "an organization operated for the primary purpose of carrying on a trade or business for profit shall not be exempt from taxation under section 501 on the ground that all of its profits are payable to one or more organizations exempt from taxation under section 501." Such organizations are referred to as "feeder organizations."

To illustrate, in Revenue Ruling 73-164 the IRS ruled that a church-controlled commercial printing corporation whose business earnings were paid to the church but that had no other significant charitable activity was a feeder organization that did not qualify for exemption under section 501(c)(3). Section 502(b) specifies that an organization will not be considered to be a feeder organization if (1) its earnings consist of rents that would be excluded from the definition of unrelated business income under section 512 of the tax code; (2) substantially all of its work is performed without compensation; or (3) its earnings derive from the selling of merchandise, substantially all of which was received as gifts or contributions.

Dissolution clauses
The income tax regulations specify that an organization is not organized exclusively for exempt purposes unless its assets are dedicated to an exempt purpose, and that an organization's assets will be presumed to be dedicated to an exempt purpose if, upon dissolution, the assets would, by reason of a provision in the organization's articles of incorporation, be distributed to another exempt organization.

The IRS has drafted the following paragraphs, which if inserted in a church's articles of incorporation, will indicate compliance with the organizational test:

> *Said corporation is organized exclusively for charitable, religious, and educational . . . purposes, including, for such purposes, the making of distributions to organizations that qualify as exempt organizations under section 501(c)(3) of the Internal Revenue Code, or the corresponding section of any future federal tax code.*
>
> *No part of the net earnings of the corporation shall inure to the benefit of, or be distributable to its members, trustees, officers, or other private persons, except that the corporation shall be authorized and empowered to pay reasonable compensation for services rendered and to make payments and distributions in furtherance of the purposes set forth [herein]. No substantial part of the activities of the corporation shall be the carrying on of propaganda, or otherwise attempting to influence legislation, and the corporation shall not participate in, or intervene in (including the publishing or distribution of statements) any political campaign on behalf of any candidate for public office. Notwithstanding any other provision of these articles, the corporation shall not carry on any other activities not permitted to be carried on (a) by a corporation exempt from federal income tax under section 501(c)(3) of the Internal Revenue Code, or corresponding section of any future federal tax code, or (b) by corporation, contributions to which are deductible under section 170(c)(2) of the Internal Revenue Code, or corresponding section of any future federal tax code.*
>
> *Upon the dissolution of the corporation, assets shall be distributed for one or more exempt purposes within the meaning of section 501(c)(3) of the Internal Revenue Code, or corresponding section of any future federal tax code, or shall be distributed to the federal government, or to a state or local government, for a public purpose. Any such assets not so disposed of shall be disposed of by the Court of Common Pleas of the county in which the principal office of the corporation is then located, exclusively for such purposes or to such organization or organizations, as said Court shall determine, which are organized and operated exclusively for such purposes.* IRS Publication 557. See also Revenue Procedure 82-2.

EXAMPLE. One court ruled that a church satisfied the organizational test even though its articles of incorporation did not call for the distribution of church assets to other tax-exempt organizations upon dissolution, since (1) the church's minister interpreted his denomination's constitution to call for the distribution of church assets to other churches in the denomination upon dissolution; and (2) state law prohibited church property from being distributed for private use so long as there was someone who would carry on its use for church purposes. *Bethel Conservative Mennonite Church v. Commissioner, 746 F.2d 388 (7th Cir. 1984).*

EXAMPLE. A Pennsylvania court addressed the issue of whether a church acted properly when it dissolved due to declining attendance, sold its assets, and transferred most of the $750,000 sales price to the pastor as compensation for wages it was previously unable to pay. The state had claimed that by voting to approve the compensation package, the pastor and other members of the church board violated a fiduciary duty imposed by the nonprofit corporation law and engaged in "self-dealing to inure benefits to private individuals." A state appeals court dismissed the church's appeal on a technical ground. But as the trial court in this case noted, such dispositions of the proceeds from the sale or church assets have a number of potential legal and tax consequences, including potential inurement of the church's assets for the private benefit of an individual in violation of the tax code.

The court also noted that to be exempt from federal income tax, a church must be organized exclusively for exempt purposes. This requirement is referred to as the "organizational test" of tax-exempt status. The income tax regulations specify that an organization is not organized exclusively for exempt purposes unless its assets are dedicated to an exempt purpose and that an organization's assets will be presumed to be dedicated to an exempt purpose if, upon dissolution, the assets would, by reason of a provision in the organization's articles of incorporation, be distributed to another exempt organization. This did not happen in this case.

In summary, the distribution of church assets to a minister or other private individual raises an array of legal and tax issues of considerable importance. Such transactions should never be contemplated without the assistance of legal counsel. *In re First Church, 2011 WL 2302540 (Pa. Common. 2011).*

Religious purpose

It is difficult to define what is meant by a "religious purpose." The IRS, in its *Internal Revenue Manual*, acknowledges that the term "religion" cannot be defined with precision. The IRS does agree with federal court rulings defining religion to include beliefs not encompassing a Supreme Being in the conventional sense, such as Taoism, Buddhism, and secular humanism. *IRM § 7.25.3.6 (1999).* The IRS also maintains that religion is not confined to a sect or a ritual. Activities carried on in furtherance of the belief must be exclusively religious. Religious organizations that engage in substantial legislative activity are disqualified from tax exemption regardless of the motivation or purpose of that activity.

✿ **KEY POINT.** Religious organizations that engage in substantial legislative activity are disqualified from tax exemption regardless of the motivation or purpose of that activity. *Christian Echoes National Ministry, Inc. v. U.S., 470 F.2d 849 (10th Cir. 1972).*

Religious publishing

Several courts have ruled that religious publishing is a commercial, nonexempt activity, regardless of religious motivation, if literature is sold to the general public at a profit. *See, e.g., Parker v. Commissioner, 365 F.2d 792 (8th Cir. 1966); Incorporated Trustees of the Gospel Worker Society v. United States, 510 F. Supp. 374 (D.D.C. 1981), aff'd, 672 F.2d 894 (D.C. Cir. 1981); Fides Publishers Assoc. v. United States, 263 F. Supp. 924 (N.D. Ind. 1967); Scripture Press Foundation v. United States, 285 F.2d 800 (Ct. Cl. 1961); Christian Manner International v. Commissioner, 71 T.C. 661 (1979); Revenue Ruling 73-164; Revenue Ruling 68-26.*

The IRS *Internal Revenue Manual* states:

> *Publishing literature is an important method of disseminating religious views. Publishing may also be a business operating in competition with commercial enterprises. The following are some of the items to consider in determining whether or not the activity is an unrelated business:*
>
> *1. Does the organization charge fees for its services and/or publications? If so, secure a schedule of fees charged.*
>
> *2. Does the organization operate a bookstore or engage in publishing activities of any nature (printing, publications, or distribution of its own material, or that printed or published by others and distributed by the organization)?*
>
> *3. What is the nature of the operations? Does the organization make sales to the general public, what kind of literature is involved, and how do such activities further the organization's exempt purposes?*
>
> *4. Does the organization have literature of its own? If so, secure a list of several of the chief works, giving the author and title.*
>
> *5. Who selects any publishing projects and how are they selected? What are the criteria used for making selections?*
>
> *6. How are the publishing activities distinguishable from those of a for-profit enterprise?*
>
> *7. Is the literature distributed free of charge? If not, what basis is used in determining the sales price?*
>
> *8. How does the organization distribute the literature?*
>
> *9. Is the literature copyrighted? If so, in whose name will the copyright be held?* IRM § 4.76.6.6 (2003).

The IRS Internal Revenue Manual contains the following summary of applicable precedent:

> *Publishing literature is an important method of disseminating religious views. However, publishing may also be a business operating in competition with commercial enterprises. The Service has held that publishing and distributing a monthly newspaper carrying church news of interdenominational interest accomplishes a charitable purpose by contributing to the advancement of religion. In that case subscriptions were obtained through individual churches and church associated groups and revenues did not cover the costs of operation.* Revenue Ruling 68-306.
>
> *In a Tax Court case, an organization sold a large volume of literature to the general public by mail. Some of the literature had little or no connection to the beliefs held by the organization. The surrounding circumstances tended to show that the individual who dominated the organization regarded the enterprise "simply as a money making operation." The court held that this was not a religious organization, but rather a trade or business.* Foundation for Divine Meditation, Inc., 24 T.C.M. 411 (1965), affirmed M.E. Parker v. Commissioner, 365 F.2d 792 (8th Cir. 1966), cert. denied, 385 U.S. 1026 (1967).
>
> *In cases where religious literature is published by an organization to promote its beliefs, the activity may further exclusively religious purposes even though it produces an operating profit.* Saint Germain Foundation, 26 T.C. 648 (1956); Unity School of Christianity, 4 B.T.A. 61 (1926). *See also Pulpit Resource v. Commissioner, 70 T.C. 594 (1978), in which the court reversed the Service's denial of exemption to an organization that sold a publication containing prepared sermons for use by ministers.*
>
> *However, in* Scripture Press Foundation v. United States, 285 F.2d 800 (1961), *cert. den., 363 U.S. 985 (1962), a separately organized publishing corporation that sold a large volume of religious literature, periodicals, and Sunday school supplies at a substantial profit was held not exempt. The court found that operating profits and accumulated earnings were disproportionately large and there was no clear purpose to further any particular religious beliefs. The general character of the operation was that of a commercial publishing house catering to religious customers. Thus, the court concluded it was a trade or business and not exempt. The existence of a modest program of expenditures for religious and educational purposes unconnected with the publishing did not have a decisive effect.* See also Christian Manner International v. Commissioner, 71 T.C. 661 (1979).
>
> *One case places a great weight on the existence of an operating profit and a commercial pricing pattern. In* Fides Publishers Association v. United States, 263 F. Supp. 924 (1967*), a corporate publisher of religious books priced at commercial levels that showed moderate but consistent operating profits was held not to be exempt. The court said that although the "publishing activities further the exempt purpose of educating the lay apostolate," nevertheless, there was a substantial nonexempt purpose—"the publication and sale of religious literature at a profit."*
>
> *In another case, an organization that published religious literature was held to no longer qualify as tax exempt in view of an abrupt*

increase in salaries of top personnel of the organization's press, a large amount of accumulated profits, and the fact that the press was in direct competition with a number of commercial publishers. The facts showed that the organization's primary purpose was to operate as a commercial business producing net profits. Incorporated Trustees of the Gospel Workers Society v. U.S., 520 F. Supp. 374 (D.D.C. 1981).

On the other hand, the Third Circuit Court of Appeals upheld the exempt status of another religious publishing organization, concluding that its accumulation of capital for physical expansion and its increased profit due to unexpected increases in popularity of one of the publisher's authors did not show a substantial nonexempt purpose. Presbyterian and Reformed Publishing Co. v. Commissioner, 743 F.2d 148 (3rd Cir. 1984). IRM § 7.25.3.6.8 (1999).

If a religious organization publishes literature to promote its own beliefs, and revenues are used to defray expenses and to further the religious purposes of the organization, the activity is considered to be religious. *Elisian Guild, Inc. v. United States, 412 F.2d 121 (1st Cir. 1969); Pulpit Resource v. Commissioner, 70 T.C. 594 (1978); Saint Germain Foundation v. Commissioner, 26 T.C. 648 (1956); Unity School of Christianity v. Commissioner, 4 B.T.A. 61 (1962); Revenue Ruling 68-26.* The IRS *Internal Revenue Manual* acknowledges that "in cases where religious literature is published by an organization to promote its beliefs, the activity may further exclusively religious purposes even though it produces an operating profit." *IRM § 7.25.3.6.8 (1999).*

EXAMPLE. A federal appeals court upheld the exempt status of a religious publishing organization that was closely associated (though not legally affiliated) with the Orthodox Presbyterian Church, and whose primary purpose was the publication of books furthering the reformed faith, concluding that its accumulation of capital for physical expansion and its increased profit due to unexpected increases in popularity of one of the publisher's authors did not show a substantial nonexempt purpose. *Presbyterian and Reformed Publishing Co. v. Commissioner, 743 F.2d 148 (3rd Cir. 1984).*

EXAMPLE. The Tax Court ruled that a church did not qualify for tax-exempt status because its publishing activities constituted a substantial nonexempt activity. The pastor of the church wrote a number of books and pamphlets that were published and sold by the church. He claimed that the church's book publishing activities were a significant aspect of the church's activities.

The court concluded, "Although the books had a religious theme, writing and publishing books is not a religious activity unless petitioner can prove the primary purpose for publishing the books was not for profit but for the furtherance of a nonexempt purpose. [The pastor] testified that the church distributed the books at cost; however, he introduced no evidence in support of this statement. Absent introduction of any financial statements from

the church whatsoever, the court cannot evaluate whether the church did not in fact profit from the publishing and distribution of books. Therefore, the court finds that the publishing and distributing of books by the church was a substantial nonexempt activity. The existence of this substantial nonexempt purpose precludes the church from qualifying as an exempt organization."

The court further concluded, "The nature of this nonexempt activity, publishing books, was conducted for the exclusive benefit of the pastor, not the public. [He] authored each of the books the church published. He then paid all publishing costs from his personal bank account and deducted the costs as a charitable deduction on his federal income tax returns. The IRS argues that the pastor essentially incorporated the church to enable the publishing of books he authored. This argument is well founded. A substantial percentage of the pastor's earnings went to the church; yet, his was the sole authorized signature of this account. No evidence was offered to establish that the church had members or received contributions from others. It did not maintain any books and records. In effect, the pastor was using a claimed church as his pocket book. Therefore . . . the church fails the 'private inurement' test of section 501(c)(3)." *Triplett v. Commissioner, T.C. Summary Opinion 2005-148.*

Religious broadcasting

The IRS *Internal Revenue Manual* states:

Broadcasting is an activity analogous to publishing. In Revenue Ruling 68-513, a religious broadcasting station was held exempt under IRC 501(c)(3), where broadcast time was devoted to worship services and other programs having religious content. Although the station was operated on a commercial license, it did not sell commercial or advertising time. Revenue Ruling 68-563 was amplified in Revenue Ruling 78-385, which held a religious and educational television station exempt under IRC 501(c)(3) even though it devoted an insubstantial amount of broadcast time to commercially sponsored programs. However, the commercially sponsored programs are unrelated trade or business under IRC 513. IRM § 7.25.3.6.9. (1999).

Other activities deemed to be religious

The following activities also have been found to be sufficiently religious in nature to entitle the organization to exempt status:

- A nonprofit organization formed by local churches to operate a supervised facility, known as a coffeehouse, in which persons of college age were brought together with church leaders, educators, and businessmen for discussion of religion and current events. *Revenue Ruling 68-72.*
- A nonprofit organization formed to complete genealogical research data on its family members in order to perform religious ordinances in accordance with the precepts of the

religious denomination to which family members belonged. *Revenue Ruling 71-580.*

- A nonprofit organization that supervised the preparation and inspection of food products prepared commercially in order to ensure that they satisfied the dietary rules of a particular religion, thereby assisting members of the religion to comply with its tenets. *Revenue Ruling 74-575.*

- An organization formed and controlled by an exempt conference of churches that borrowed funds from individuals and made mortgage loans at less than commercial rates of interest to affiliated churches to finance the construction of church buildings. *Revenue Ruling 75-282.*

- An organization established to provide temporary low-cost housing and related services for missionary families on furlough in the United States from their assignments abroad. *Revenue Ruling 75-434.*

- An organization formed to arrange for the construction of housing for sale to individuals associated with a religious denomination. The housing was to be constructed on the grounds of a retreat center owned by a denominational agency. The IRS concluded that the housing would substantially further the nonexempt purpose of providing recreational and vacation opportunities to the purchasers. The Tax Court concluded that because only active participants in the religious activities conducted at the center would be permitted to purchase the housing, the organization was organized and operated exclusively to further religious purposes. *Janaluska Assembly Housing Inc. v. Commissioner, 86 T.C. 1114 (1986).*

Activities deemed not to be religious

Not every organization claiming to be religious is entitled to exemption from federal income taxes. The IRS has denied tax-exempt status to several organizations on the ground that they were not organized exclusively for religious purposes. To illustrate, the following activities were denied exempt status:

- A religious organization whose primary activity was the operation of a commercial restaurant. *Riker v. Commissioner, 244 F.2d 220 (9th Cir. 1957).*

- A church that engaged in substantial social and political activities. *First Libertarian Church v. Commissioner, 74 T.C. 396 (1980).*

- An organization incorporated for religious purposes but which conducted no religious services and whose primary activity was making investments to accumulate monies for its "building fund." *Western Catholic Church v. Commissioner, 73 T.C. 196 (1979), aff'd, 631 F.2d 736 (7th Cir. 1980).*

- An alleged religious organization that conducted few if any religious activities, and one of its directors engaged in extensive counseling on the use of private churches to reduce taxes. *Church of Ethereal Joy v. Commissioner, 83 T.C. 20 (1984).*

- A central religious organization providing assistance to local "family missions" in incorporating under state law and in

obtaining tax-exempt status. *National Association of American Churches v. Commissioner, 82 T.C. 18 (1984).*

- An organization offering financial and estate planning advice to wealthy individuals referred to it by prospective charitable donees. *Christian Stewardship Assistance, Inc. v. Commissioner, 70 T.C. 1037 (1978).*

- A direct-mail religious organization that promised spiritual blessings in exchange for monetary contributions. *Church by Mail, Inc. v. Commissioner, 48 T.C.M. 471 (1984).*

- A "church" consisting of three family members that held Christmas and Easter services but otherwise engaged in no regular or substantial religious activities. *Bubbling Well Church of Universal Love, Inc. v. Commissioner, 74 T.C. 531 (1980), aff'd, 670 F.2d 104 (9th Cir. 1981).*

- An organization that was incorporated for religious purposes but whose major activities were the operation of a debt collection agency, a magazine subscription clearinghouse, and a health insurance plan. *Universal Church of Jesus Christ, Inc., 55 T.C.M. 144 (1988).*

Charitable purposes

Charitable purposes, like religious purposes, constitute a basis for exemption under the tax code. Many churches define their purposes as including both religious and charitable purposes. The income tax regulations define the term "charitable" as follows:

> *Relief of the poor and distressed or of the underprivileged; advancement of religion; advancement of education or science; erection or maintenance of public buildings, monuments, or works; lessening of the burdens of Government; and promotion of social welfare by organizations designed to accomplish any of the above purposes, or (i) to lessen neighborhood tensions; (ii) to eliminate prejudice and discrimination; (iii) to defend human and civil rights secured by law; or (iv) to combat community deterioration and juvenile delinquency. Treas. Reg. § 1.501(c)(3)-1(d)(2).*

The IRS has provided additional guidance on the meaning of "charitable":

> *A charitable organization or trust must be set up for the benefit of an indefinite class of individuals, not for specific persons. A trust or corporation organized and operated for the benefit of specific individuals is not charitable. Thus, a trust to benefit John Jones is not a charitable trust even though the facts may show that John Jones is impoverished. However, an organization set up with the general charitable purpose of benefiting needy individuals in a particular community is a charitable organization and it may select John Jones as a beneficiary.*

> *A trust set up for the benefit of an aged clergyman and his wife was held not to be an exempt organization in Carrie A. Maxwell Trust, Pasadena Methodist Foundation v. Commissioner, 2 TCM 905 (1943). The court found the trust to be a private, rather than*

charitable trust, despite the fact that the elderly gentleman was in financial need. However, an organization may properly have a purpose to benefit a comparatively small class of beneficiaries, provided the class is open and the identities of the individuals to be benefited remain indefinite. It has been held that a foundation set up to award scholarships solely to undergraduate members of a designated fraternity could be exempt as a charitable foundation. Revenue Ruling 56–403.

Churches occasionally engage in activities of a charitable nature. Examples include day-care centers, homes for the aged, orphanages, and halfway houses. Although a church may contend that these activities are religious, it is clear that the IRS views them as charitable. *IRM § 7.25.3.5 (1999).* Therefore, it is important for a church contemplating any such activities to be sure that its articles of incorporation or other organizing document lists "charitable" purposes among its purposes.

Educational purposes

Educational purposes, like religious and charitable purposes, constitute a basis for exemption. The income tax regulations define "educational" as "the instruction or training of the individual for the purpose of improving or developing his capabilities; or the instruction of the public on subjects useful to the individual and beneficial to the community." *Treas. Reg. § 1.501(c)(3)-1(d)(3).*

The IRS maintains that even if a school is operated by a church, it is an educational organization if it has a regularly scheduled curriculum, a regular faculty, and a regularly enrolled body of students in attendance at a place where the educational activities are regularly carried on. *Treas. Reg. § 1.501(c)(3)-1(d)(3)(ii).* As a result, the IRS would view many church-operated primary and secondary schools as educational rather than religious institutions.

On the other hand, some courts have ruled that church-operated schools can be considered a religious function. *Concord v. New Testament Baptist Church, 382 A.2d 377 (N.H. 1978); Employment Division v. Archdiocese of Portland, 600 P.2d 926 (Ore. 1979).* Churches that operate schools or preschools should review their articles of incorporation to see if their statement of purposes includes "educational" activities as well as religious activities.

Insubstantial nonexempt activities

The income tax regulations specify that an organization can be exempt from taxation even if it engages in activities that are not in furtherance of one or more exempt purposes if such activities compose no more than an "insubstantial" part of the organization's total activities. *Treas. Reg. § 1.501(c)(3)-1(b)(1)(i).* Neither the tax code nor the regulations define the term "insubstantial." Therefore, this is an issue that must be determined under the facts and circumstances of each case.

To illustrate, a charitable organization was determined to be exempt despite its participation in a profit-seeking limited partnership.

Plumstead Theater Society, Inc. v. Commissioner, 675 F.2d 244 (9th Cir. 1981). Another organization whose primary purpose was to raise funds for missionaries was found to be exempt despite its unrelated activity of distributing 10 percent of its net income in the form of grants and loans to applicants conducting scientific research in the area of energy resources. *World Family Corp. v. Commissioner, 81 T.C. 958 (1983).* The court emphasized that it was not establishing a general rule that 10 percent was insubstantial. In an earlier decision, the Tax Court ruled that a religious organization which made cash grants of approximately 20 percent of its net income to private individuals, including its officers, was not exempt, since such grants were more than an insubstantial nonexempt activity. *Church in Boston v. Commissioner, 71 T.C. 102 (1978).* The court stated that "while the facts in the instant case merit a denial of exempt status . . . we do not set forth a percentage test which can be relied upon for future reference with respect to nonexempt activities of an organization. Each case must be decided upon its own unique facts and circumstances." The Tax Court also denied exempt status to a religious retreat facility on the ground that it was operated primarily for recreational and social purposes and therefore was engaged to more than an insubstantial degree in nonexempt activities. *Schoger Foundation v. Commissioner, 76 T.C. 380 (1981).*

Operated exclusively for exempt purposes

To be exempt from federal income taxes, section 501(c)(3) of the tax code requires that a church be "operated exclusively" for exempt purposes. This requirement is referred to as the operational test. The regulations specify that an organization will be regarded as operated exclusively for one or more exempt purposes only if it engages primarily in activities that accomplish one or more of the exempt purposes specified in section 501(c)(3) and if no more than an insubstantial part of its activities are not in furtherance of an exempt purpose.

To illustrate, the tax-exempt status of the following religious organizations was revoked on the ground that they were not operated exclusively for exempt purposes:

- A church-sponsored insurance company that provided members and their families with financial and casualty insurance. *Mutual Aid Association of the Church of the Brethren v. United States, 578 F. Supp. 1451 (D. Kan. 1983).*
- A religious retreat that offered recreational and social activities for a fee similar to those of most other commercial vacation resorts. *Schoger Foundation v. Commissioner, 76 T.C. 380 (1981). But see Revenue Ruling 77-340 (exempt status of religious retreat upheld since no fees were charged). See also Alive Fellowship of Harmonious Living v. Commissioner, 47 T.C.M. 1134 (1984).*
- A religious organization that operated a commercial restaurant. *Christ's Church of Golden Rule v. Commissioner, 244 F.2d 220 (9th Cir. 1957).*
- A church that conducted no religious services and whose primary activity was the accumulation of contributions for its

building fund. *Western Catholic Church v. Commissioner, 73 T.C. 196 (1979), aff'd, 631 F.2d 736 (7th Cir. 1980).*

- A church that conducted purely social and political meetings. *First Libertarian Church v. Commissioner, 74 T.C. 396 (1980).*
- An independent publisher that sold religious literature to the general public at a profit. *Parker v. Commissioner, 365 F.2d 792 (8th Cir. 1966); Scripture Press Foundation v. United States, 285 F.2d 800 (Ct. Cl. 1961). But see Presbyterian and Reformed Publishing Co. v. Commissioner, 743 F.2d 148 (3rd Cir. 1984).*

A federal appeals court ruled that profitability in and of itself does not necessarily mean that an exempt organization is no longer operated exclusively for exempt purposes. *Presbyterian and Reformed Publishing Co. v. Commissioner, 743 F.2d 148 (3rd Cir. 1984).* To determine whether such an organization should retain its exemption, the court proposed a two-pronged test: first, what is the purpose of the organization; and second, to whose benefit do its activities and earnings inure? The court upheld the tax-exempt status of a profitable religious publisher that continued to adhere to its exempt religious purposes and that diverted none of its net earnings to the personal benefit of any individual. The court concluded that "success in terms of audience reached and influence exerted, in and of itself should not jeopardize the tax-exempt status of organizations which remain true to their stated goals."

No inurement of net earnings to private individuals

In order to be tax exempt under section 501(c)(3) of the tax code, no part of a church's net earnings may inure to the personal benefit of an insider, and the church must not provide a substantial "private benefit" to anyone. The related concepts of inurement and private benefit are summarized below.

Inurement defined

A church is not entitled to exemption from federal income taxes if any part of its net earnings inures or accrues to the benefit of a private individual other than as reasonable compensation for services rendered or as distributions in direct furtherance of the church's exempt purposes. The IRS construes this requirement as follows:

Churches and religious organizations, like all exempt organizations under IRC section 501(c)(3), are prohibited from engaging in activities that result in inurement of the church's or organization's income or assets to insiders (i.e., persons having a personal and private interest in the activities of the organization). Insiders could include the minister, church board members, officers, and in certain circumstances, employees. Examples of prohibited inurement include the payment of dividends, the payment of unreasonable compensation to insiders, and transferring property to insiders for less than fair market value. The prohibition against inurement to insiders is absolute; therefore, any amount of inurement is, potentially, grounds for loss of tax-exempt status. In addition, the insider involved may be subject to excise tax. See

the following section on Excess benefit transactions. Note that prohibited inurement does not include reasonable payments for services rendered, payments that further tax-exempt purposes, or payments made for the fair market value of real or personal property. IRS Publication 1828.

The IRS *Internal Revenue Manual* lists several examples of unreasonable compensation, including the withdrawal of an exempt organization's earnings by an officer under the guise of salary payments; receipt of less than fair market value in sales of property; and inadequately secured loans to an officer.

❈ **KEY POINT.** The related concepts of unreasonable compensation, excess benefit transactions, and intermediate sanctions are addressed in Chapter 4, section A, of this text.

Examples of inurement

The IRS found private inurement in each of the following situations:

- A church, consisting mostly of family members and conducting few, if any, religious services, that paid rent on a residence for the church's "ministers," paid for a church car that was used by church members, and purchased a "church camp" for church members. *Riemers v. Commissioner, 42 T.C.M. 838 (1981).*
- A religious denomination whose assets could be distributed to members upon dissolution. *General Conference of the Free Church of America v. Commissioner, 71 T.C. 920 (1979).*
- A church that made cash grants of 20 percent of its income to officers and other individuals based on no fixed criteria and with no provision for repayment. *Church in Boston v. Commissioner, 71 T.C. 102 (1978).*
- A church that received almost all of its income from its minister and, in turn, paid back 90 percent of such income to the minister in the form of living expenses. *People of God Community v. Commissioner, 75 T.C. 127 (1980).*
- A church comprised of three minister-members that paid each minister a salary based on a fixed percentage of the church's gross receipts. *New Life Tabernacle v. Commissioner, 44 T.C.M. 309 (1982).*
- A church that paid an unreasonable and excessive salary to its pastor. *United States v. Dykema, 666 F.2d 1096 (7th Cir. 1981); Unitary Mission Church v. Commissioner, 74 T.C. 507 (1980).*
- The founder of a church who was paid 10 percent of the church's gross income, received a residence and car at the church's expense, and received loans and unexplained reimbursements from the church. The court held that an organization's net earnings may inure to the benefit of a private individual in ways other than excessive salaries, such as loans. The court also emphasized that the tax code specifies that "no part" of the net earnings of a religious organization may inure to the benefit of a private individual, and therefore the amount or extent of benefit is immaterial. *The Founding Church of Scientology v. United States, 412 F.2d 1197 (Ct. Cl. 1969), cert.*

denied, 397 U.S. 1009 (1970). See also Church of the Chosen People v. United States, 548 F. Supp. 1247 (D. Minn. 1982); Truth Tabernacle v. Commissioner, 41 T.C.M. 1405 (1981).

✣ **KEY POINT.** Another result of inurement is the potential disqualification of a church to receive tax-deductible charitable contributions. In one case a religious ministry paid for a minister-employee's personal expenses, including scholarship pledges made in the minister's name and a season ticket for a local college football team. The tax code allows a charitable contribution deduction for contributions made to a charity, "no part of the net earnings of which inures to the benefit of any private shareholder or individual." *IRC 170.* The court noted that the minister received payments from his employer (football tickets and scholarship pledges) and that these payments inured to his benefit. In addition, the minister failed to establish that the payments were compensation. Accordingly, the minister was not allowed to deduct the contributions he made to his employer. *Whittington v. Commissioner, T.C. Memo. 2000-296 (2000).*

EXAMPLE. The Tax Court ruled that a church did not qualify for tax-exempt status because its publishing activities constituted a substantial nonexempt activity. The pastor of the church wrote a number of books and pamphlets that were published and sold by the church. He claimed that the church's book publishing activities were a significant aspect of its activities.

The court concluded, "Although the books had a religious theme, writing and publishing books is not a religious activity unless petitioner can prove the primary purpose for publishing the books was not for profit but for the furtherance of a nonexempt purpose. [The pastor] testified that the church distributed the books at cost; however, he introduced no evidence in support of this statement. Absent introduction of any financial statements from the church whatsoever, the court cannot evaluate whether the church did not in fact profit from the publishing and distribution of books. Therefore, the court finds that the publishing and distributing of books by the church was a substantial nonexempt activity. The existence of this substantial nonexempt purpose precludes the church from qualifying as an exempt organization."

The court further concluded, "The nature of this nonexempt activity, publishing books, was conducted for the exclusive benefit of the pastor, not the public. [He] authored each of the books the church published. He then paid all publishing costs from his personal bank account and deducted the costs as a charitable deduction on his federal income tax returns. The IRS argues that the pastor essentially incorporated the church to enable the publishing of books he authored. This argument is well founded. A substantial percentage of the pastor's earnings went to the church; yet, his was the sole authorized signature of this account. No evidence was offered to establish that the church had members or received contributions from others. It did not maintain any books

and records. In effect, the pastor was using a claimed church as his pocket book. Therefore . . . the church fails the 'private inurement' test of section 501(c)(3)." *Triplett v. Commissioner, T.C. Summary Opinion 2005-148.*

EXAMPLE. The IRS denied tax-exempt status to a religious organization (the "applicant") as a result of no-interest loans it made to various individuals that served a private rather than a charitable or religious purpose. The applicant's corporate charter described its purposes to include the maintenance of a house of worship and seminary. The governing board of the applicant was comprised of three individuals, all of whom have both family and business relationships. The applicant's religious tenets prohibited it from charging interest on loans.

The IRS, in denying tax-exempt status to the applicant, noted that the applicant had made loans to a business operated by its three board members, and additional loans to its treasurer, and to three outsiders to assist with their for-profit businesses. The IRS observed: "Each of these five loans is questionable as the intent of each loan does not appear charitable. While the loan documentation stipulates a return of a contribution in lieu of interest, thereby potentially lessening the private gain of a loan, this does not appear to have occurred. Each appears to be furthering the private interest of an individual or business causing both private benefit and inurement."

The IRS concluded: "Overall, while the applicant does conduct religious services, the loan activities they have directed disqualify them from exemption as the structure and intention has only served related parties and private interests. The organization itself seems to be an outlet for distributions from a related for-profit entity for the purpose of distributions and loans. While by definition some of the recipients of these loans could be deemed needy the purposes listed for which the loans were made further no 501(c)(3) purposes in eliminating direct charitable need. The facts in the application and supplemental correspondence show that the board had been controlling all aspects of the applicant for their private interests and not for the benefit of the public." *IRS Private Letter Ruling 200926037 (2009).*

EXAMPLE. A Pennsylvania court addressed the issue of whether a church acted properly when it dissolved due to declining attendance, sold its assets, and transferred most of the $750,000 sales price to the pastor as compensation for wages it was previously unable to pay. The state had claimed that by voting to approve the compensation package, the pastor and other members of the church board violated a fiduciary duty imposed by the nonprofit corporation law and engaged in "self-dealing to inure benefits to private individuals." A state appeals court dismissed the church's appeal on a technical ground. But as the trial court in this case noted, such dispositions of the proceeds from the sale or church assets have a number of potential legal and tax consequences, including potential inurement of the church's assets for the private benefit of an individual in violation of the tax code. *In re First Church, 2011 WL 2302540 (Pa. Common. 2011).*

Private benefit distinguished from inurement

Closely related to but distinguishable from inurement is the concept of private benefit. The IRS defines private benefit as follows:

> *An IRC section 501(c)(3) organization's activities must be directed exclusively toward charitable, educational, religious, or other exempt purposes. Such an organization's activities may not serve the private interests of any individual or organization. Rather, beneficiaries of an organization's activities must be recognized objects of charity (such as the poor or the distressed) or the community at large (for example, through the conduct of religious services or the promotion of religion). Private benefit is different from inurement to insiders. Private benefit may occur even if the persons benefited are not insiders. Also, private benefit must be substantial in order to jeopardize tax-exempt status. IRS Publication 1828.*

Note the following two important distinctions between inurement and private benefit:

(1) Inurement applies to insiders; private benefit applies to anyone receiving benefits from a public charity.

(2) Inurement involves any use of a charity's resources for the private benefit of an insider, regardless of amount; private benefit must be substantial in order to jeopardize tax-exempt status.

No substantial efforts to influence legislation

✵ **KEY POINT.** The tax code prohibits religious organizations from engaging in "substantial" efforts to influence legislation. A few courts have attempted to clarify the key word "substantial." One court concluded that the "substantial" requirement is not met if less than 5 percent of an organization's time and effort is devoted to lobbying activities. *Seasongood v. Commissioner, 227 F.2d 907 (6th Cir. 1955).* Another court ruled that an organization that devoted 16–20 percent of its budget to lobbying activities was engaged in substantial efforts to influence legislation. *Haswell v. U.S., 500 F.2d 1133 (Ct. Cl. 1974).* The IRS has never endorsed a percentage definition of the word "substantial."

Section 501(c)(3) of the tax code exempts from federal income taxation a church or religious organization organized and operated exclusively for exempt purposes and "no substantial part of the activities of which is carrying on propaganda, or otherwise attempting to influence legislation, and which does not participate in, or intervene in (including the publishing or distributing of statements), any political campaign on behalf of any candidate for public office."

Note that there are two distinct limitations. First, churches may not engage in substantial efforts to influence legislation. Second, churches may not participate or intervene in any political campaign, even to an insubstantial degree. The first of these limitations is addressed in this subsection. The second limitation is addressed in the following subsection.

To be exempt from federal income taxation, no "substantial part" of a church's activities can be the "carrying on of propaganda, or otherwise attempting to influence legislation." This limitation was enacted by Congress in 1934. Unfortunately, however, it is not entirely clear why the limitation was adopted. The following reasons have been suggested:

- The exemption from federal income taxation was designed to promote charitable activities, not lobbying.
- The limitation is required to preserve the constitutional principle of separation of church and state.
- Congress was unwilling to permit business organizations, which in 1934 could not deduct lobbying expenses as a business expense, to achieve the same result by deducting contributions to exempt organizations engaged in lobbying activities.
- Allowing exempt organizations to lobby with tax-free dollars gave them an unfair advantage, in 1934, over nonexempt organizations that were both taxable and unable to deduct lobbying expenditures.

One commentator has observed that "it is fair to assume that Congress gave virtually no thought to what it was doing when it enacted the [limitation on legislative activities], and it is highly unlikely that it ever imagined that the [limitation] might be applied to threaten a church." *Note, Church Lobbying: The Legitimacy of the Controls, 16 Houston L. Rev. 480 (1979).*

Before analyzing this limitation in more detail, it must be emphasized that it is seldom enforced against churches, despite many potential violations. For example, many churches and religious denominations have lobbied actively for or against specific legislation concerning civil rights, workers' rights, peace, nuclear disarmament, aid to the poor, women's rights, abortion, various treaties, education, sale and advertising of alcoholic beverages, Sunday closing restrictions, sales and property tax exemptions, lotteries, and gambling. Despite the long history of legislative activity, only one religious organization has lost its tax-exempt status as a result of political activities. That case is discussed in detail later in this subsection. Nevertheless, in recent years the political activities of churches and religious organizations have been scrutinized more aggressively by the IRS, Congress, the public, and various special interest groups.

Why has the limitation on substantial legislative activity been enforced so infrequently? One reason is the limitation's ambiguity. Specifically, what is meant by the terms "legislation," "attempts to influence legislation," and "substantial"? These definitional problems, coupled with the limitation's uncertain purpose and the reluctance of the courts (and to a lesser extent the IRS) to attack the exempt status of churches, have all contributed to the sporadic enforcement of the "legislative activity" limitation.

The income tax regulations, interpreting the legislative activity limitation, provide that neither a church nor any other organization can be exempt from federal income taxation if its charter empowers it "to devote more than an insubstantial part of its activities to attempting to influence legislation by propaganda or otherwise," or if "a substantial part of its activities is attempting to influence legislation by propaganda or otherwise." *Treas. Reg. §1.501(c)(3)-1(c)(3)(ii).*

The regulations further provide that

> *an organization will be regarded as attempting to influence legislation if the organization (a) contacts, or urges the public to contact, members of a legislative body for the purpose of proposing, supporting, or opposing legislation; or (b) advocates the adoption or rejection of legislation. The term "legislation" . . . includes action by the Congress, by any State legislature, by any local council or similar governing body, or by the public in a referendum, initiative, constitutional amendment, or similar procedure. An organization will not fail to meet the operational test merely because it advocates, as an insubstantial part of its activities, the adoption or rejection of legislation.*

This language helps clarify the meaning of "legislation" and "attempts to influence legislation" but does not define the critical term "substantial." The regulations also provide that an organization cannot be exempt if is has the following two characteristics:

> *(a) Its main or primary objective or objectives (as distinguished from its incidental or secondary objectives) may be attained only by legislation or a defeat of proposed legislation; and (b) it advocates, or campaigns for, the attainment of such main or primary objective or objectives as distinguished from engaging in nonpartisan analysis, study, or research, and making the results thereof available to the public. In determining whether an organization has such characteristics, all the surrounding facts and circumstances, including the articles and all activities of the organization, are to be considered.* Treas. Reg. § 1.501(c)(3)-1(c)(iii).

The regulations also provide that "the fact that an organization, in carrying out its primary purpose, advocates social or civic changes or presents opinion on controversial issues with the intention of molding public opinion or creating public sentiment to an acceptance of its views does not preclude such organization from qualifying under section 501(c)(3) so long as it [does not violate any of the regulations quoted above]." *Treas. Reg. § 1.501(c)(3)-1(d)(2).*

The IRS *Internal Revenue Manual* provides the following additional information regarding the limitation on legislative activities:

> *Attempts to influence legislation are not limited to direct appeals to members of the legislature (direct lobbying). Indirect appeals to legislators through the electorate or general public (indirect or "grass roots" lobbying) also constitute attempts to influence legislation. Both direct and indirect lobbying are nonexempt activities subject to the IRC 501(c)(3) limitation on substantial legislative action. . . . Whether a communication or an appeal constitutes an attempt to influence legislation is determined on the basis of the facts and circumstances surrounding the communication in question. . . . Attempting to influence legislation includes requesting that an executive body support or oppose legislation. Attempting to influence legislation does not include appearing before a legislative committee in response to an official request for testimony. . . . Study, research, and discussion of matters pertaining to government and even to specific legislation, may, under certain circumstances, be educational activities rather than attempts to influence legislation. This is so where the study, research, and discussion do not serve merely as a preparatory stage for the advocacy of legislation. (Of course, the primary inquiry is the purpose of the study, research, or discussion.)* IRM § 7.25.3.17.1 (1999).

> *Attempts to influence legislation that are less than a substantial part of the organization's activities will not deprive it of exemption. Whether a specific activity of an exempt organization constitutes a "substantial" portion of its total activities is a factual issue, and there is no simple rule as to what amount of activities is substantial. The earliest case on this subject,* Seasongood v. Commissioner, *held that attempts to influence legislation that constituted 5 percent of total activities were not substantial.* Seasongood *provides only limited guidance because the court's view of activities to measure is no longer supported by the weight of precedent. Further, it is not clear how the court arrived at the 5 percent figure. Most courts have not attempted to measure activities by percentage or have stated that a percentage test is not conclusive.* IRM § 7.25.3.17.2 (1999).

The courts, with one notable exception, have held that exempt religious organizations have not violated the ban on legislative activities.

EXAMPLE. A federal appeals court ruled that the Methodist Episcopal Church was exempt despite lobbying activities carried on by its "Board of Temperance, Prohibition and Public Morals," since such activities were motivated by religious beliefs. The court observed: "Religion includes a way of life as well as beliefs upon the nature of the world; and the admonitions to be 'doers of the word and not hearers only' (James 1:22) and 'go ye therefore, and teach all nations' (Matthew 28:19) are as old as the Christian Church. The step from acceptance by the believer to his seeking to influence others in the same direction is a perfectly natural one, and is found in countless religious groups. The next step, equally natural, is to secure the sanction of organized society for or against certain outward practices thought to be essential." *Girard Trust Co. v. Commissioner, 122 F.2d 108 (3rd Cir. 1941).*

EXAMPLE. A federal court concluded that a religious organization that had been established to promote observance of the Sabbath was exempt despite its opposition to legislation that would permit commercial activity on Sundays, since such legislative efforts were "incidental" to its religious purposes. *Lord's Day Alliance v. United States, 65 F. Supp. 62 (E.D. Pa. 1946).*

EXAMPLE. A federal appeals court concluded that a church-related organization was tax-exempt despite the fact that it proposed 36 legislative bills (18 of which were enacted). Again, the legislative activity was considered to be consistent with the organization's exempt status, since it all related directly to the organization's religious purposes. *International Reform Federation v. District Unemployment Compensation Board, 131 F.2d 337 (D.C. Cir. 1942).*

The Christian Echoes case

The one case in which a religious organization's tax-exempt status was revoked because of political activities was *Christian Echoes National Ministry, Inc. v. United States, 470 F.2d 849 (10th Cir. 1972).* Christian Echoes was a religious organization founded to disseminate conservative Christian principles through radio and television broadcasts and literature. Publications and broadcasts appealed to the public to react to a wide variety of issues in specific ways, including: (1) write their representatives in Congress in order to influence political decisions; (2) work in politics at the precinct level; (3) support a constitutional amendment restoring prayer in the public schools; (4) demand a congressional investigation of the biased reporting of major television networks; (5) demand that Congress limit foreign aid spending; (6) discourage support of the World Court; (7) cut off diplomatic relations with communist countries; (8) reduce the federal payroll and balance the federal budget; (9) stop federal aid to education, socialized medicine, and public housing; (10) abolish the federal income tax; (11) withdraw from the United Nations; and (12) restore stringent immigration laws. The organization also attempted to influence legislation by molding public opinion on the issues of firearms control, the Panama Canal treaty, and civil rights legislation.

In 1966 the IRS notified the organization that its exemption was being revoked for three reasons: (1) it was not operated exclusively for charitable, educational, or religious purposes; (2) it had engaged in substantial activity aimed at influencing legislation; and (3) it had directly and indirectly intervened in political campaigns on behalf of candidates for public office. Christian Echoes filed suit in federal court, challenging the IRS action, and a federal district court ruled in its favor. This ruling was reversed by a federal appeals court.

The federal appeals court began its opinion by observing that "tax exemption is a privilege, a matter of grace rather than right," and that the limitations on exempt status set forth in section 501(c)(3)

of the tax code are valid restrictions on the privilege. The limitations on political activity "stem from the congressional policy that the United States Treasury should be neutral in political affairs and that substantial activities directed to attempts to influence legislation or affect a political campaign should not be subsidized." The court emphasized that prohibited legislative activity was not limited to attempts to influence specific legislation before Congress. Quoting the income tax regulations (excerpted above), the court concluded that efforts to influence legislation must be interpreted much more broadly and include all indirect attempts to influence legislation through a "campaign to mold public opinion." The fact that specific legislation is not mentioned is irrelevant.

The court rejected the "5 percent test" applied by a federal appeals court in a previous case as a measure of substantial legislative activities, noting that "a percentage test to determine whether the activities were substantial obscures the complexity of balancing the organization's activities in relation to its objectives and circumstances." *Seasongood v. Commissioner, 227 F.2d 907 (6th Cir. 1955) (5 percent of an organization's time devoted to lobbying was not substantial).*

Christian Echoes' contention that revocation of its tax-exempt status violated the constitutional guaranty of religious freedom was rejected by the court. Rejecting the notion that the guaranty of religious freedom "assures no restraints, no limitations and, in effect, protects those exercising the right to do so unfettered," the court concluded that the limitations on political activities set forth in section 501(c)(3) of the tax code were constitutionally valid: "The free exercise clause of the First Amendment is restrained only to the extent of denying tax exempt status and then only in keeping with an overwhelming and compelling governmental interest: that of guarantying that the wall separating church and state remains high and firm."

From the perspective of many churches, the *Christian Echoes* decision is unsatisfactory for at least three reasons. First, the court gave an excessively broad definition of the term "attempts to influence legislation," including within that term indirect attempts to mold public opinion despite the income tax regulations' statement (quoted above) that an organization's exempt status is not jeopardized if it, in carrying out its primary purpose, "advocates social or civic changes or presents opinion on controversial issues with the intention of molding public opinion or creating public sentiment to an acceptance of its views." Second, the court rejected the 5 percent test for determining whether legislative activity is substantial but replaced it with an ambiguous "balancing test." Churches can never know in advance whether their legislative activities are substantial under the *Christian Echoes* standard. Third, the court gave insufficient weight to the constitutional guaranty of religious freedom.

The United States Supreme Court refused to review the *Christian Echoes* case, and it has not directly addressed the issue of the validity of the limitations on church political activity. However, the Supreme Court has rendered two decisions that are relevant to this issue.

First, in a 1970 opinion upholding the constitutionality of state property tax exemptions for church sanctuaries, the court observed: "Adherents of particular faiths and individual churches frequently take strong positions on public issues including . . . vigorous advocacy of legal or constitutional positions. Of course, churches as much as secular bodies and private citizens have that right." *Walz v. Tax Commission, 397 U.S. 664 (1970).* This is a recognition that churches have a right to engage in "vigorous advocacy" of legal or constitutional positions.

Second, in 1983 the court was presented with a direct challenge to the constitutionality of the limitation on substantial legislative activity. *Regan v. Taxation With Representation, 461 U.S. 540 (1983).* Taxation With Representation (TWR), a nonprofit taxpayers' rights organization, was denied tax-exempt status by the IRS on account of its legislative activities. TWR appealed to the courts, arguing that the limitation on legislative activities was unconstitutional. The Supreme Court disagreed. Noting that tax exemptions are "a matter of grace that Congress can disallow as it chooses," the court concluded that "Congress is not required by the First Amendment to subsidize lobbying." Significantly, the court observed that a section 501(c)(3) organization is free to establish an exempt organization under section 501(c)(4) of the tax code to conduct lobbying activities. Section 501(c)(4) exempts from federal income taxation those "civic leagues" organized and operated for the "promotion of social welfare." Such organizations are exempt from tax and can engage in lobbying but cannot receive tax-deductible contributions. As a result, the court suggested that TWR establish a separate 501(c)(4) organization to conduct its lobbying activities and then apply for exemption under section 501(c)(3). The court noted that "the IRS apparently requires only that the two groups be separately incorporated and keep records adequate to show that tax-deductible contributions are not used to pay for lobbying."

Conclusions

The legal precedent summarized above suggests several conclusions. They are listed below, along with a few additional observations.

Tax-exempt status at risk. Churches will jeopardize their tax-exempt status by engaging in substantial efforts to influence legislation. Whether particular efforts are "substantial" will depend upon a balancing of the facts and circumstances of each case. Accordingly, churches have no clear standard to guide them. Nevertheless, it is clear that certain activities would be insubstantial, such as the circulation of a few petitions each year addressing legislative issues. Also, it ordinarily is the exempt organization itself that must engage in the legislative activities, not individual members. To illustrate, the IRS has ruled that a university's exempt status was not jeopardized by the legislative activities of a student newspaper. *Revenue Ruling 72-513.*

Limiting exercise of religion. The limitation on legislative activity may violate the constitutional right of churches to exercise their religion. The *Christian Echoes* decision rejected such a claim, but no

other federal court has addressed this issue since the *Christian Echoes* decision. As noted above, in 1970 the Supreme Court observed that the "adherents of particular faiths and individual churches frequently take strong positions on public issues including . . . vigorous advocacy of legal or constitutional positions. Of course, churches as much as secular bodies and private citizens have that right." *Walz v. Tax Commission, 397 U.S. 664 (1970).*

Broad definition. The *Christian Echoes* decision construed the term "attempting to influence legislation" broadly, so as to include all indirect attempts to influence legislation through a "campaign to mold public opinion," even though no specific legislation is ever mentioned. This interpretation seems to contradict the income tax regulations themselves, which provide that an organization's exempt status is not jeopardized if it, in carrying out its primary purpose, "advocates social or civic changes or presents opinion on controversial issues with the intention of molding public opinion or creating public sentiment to an acceptance of its views." The court's liberal interpretation of the term "attempting to influence to legislation" has not been endorsed by any other federal court (including the Supreme Court) with respect to a church or religious organization.

Limited geographic application. The *Christian Echoes* ruling is binding only in the tenth federal circuit (which includes the states of Colorado, Kansas, New Mexico, Oklahoma, Utah, and Wyoming). In addition, in 1976 Congress took the extraordinary step of refusing to approve or disapprove of the *Christian Echoes* decision.

Limited precedent. To date, only one religious organization has lost its tax-exempt status for substantial attempts to influence legislation.

Establishing a 501(c)(4) exempt organization. The United States Supreme Court has suggested that 501(c)(3) organizations desiring to engage in substantial legislative activities should establish a 501(c)(4) exempt organization. Section 501(c)(4) organizations are exempt and can engage in legislative activities, but they cannot receive tax-deductible contributions.

Ineligible organizations. The income tax regulations specify that an organization cannot be exempt from federal income taxation if its charter empowers it to devote more than an insubstantial part of its activities to attempting to influence legislation. The IRS has drafted the following clause that exempt organizations may wish to consider including in their charter or bylaws, which will satisfy this requirement:

> *No substantial part of the activities of the corporation shall be the carrying on of propaganda, or otherwise attempting to influence legislation, and the corporation shall not participate in, or intervene in (including the publishing or distribution of statements) any political campaign on behalf of or in opposition to any candidate for public office. Notwithstanding any other provision of these articles, the corporation shall not carry on*

any other activities not permitted to be carried on (a) by a corporation exempt from federal income tax under section 501(c)(3) of the Internal Revenue Code, or the corresponding provision of any future federal tax code, or (b) by a corporation contributions to which are deductible under section 170(c)(2) of the Internal Revenue Code, or corresponding section of any future federal tax code. IRS Publication 557.

The expenditure test. To establish more precise standards for determining whether an exempt organization's legislative activities are substantial, Congress enacted section 501(h) of the federal tax code. Section 501(h) gives some public charities the option to elect an "expenditure" test in lieu of the "substantial part" test of section 501(c)(3). This option is available to some religious organizations but not to churches. The IRS *Tax Guide for Churches and Religious Organizations* explains this expenditure test as follows:

Although churches are not eligible, religious organizations may elect the expenditure test under IRC section 501(h) as an alternative method for measuring lobbying activity. Under the expenditure test, the extent of an organization's lobbying activity will not jeopardize its tax-exempt status, provided its expenditures, related to such activity, do not normally exceed an amount specified in IRC section 4911. This limit is generally based upon the size of the organization and may not exceed $1,000,000.

Religious organizations electing to use the expenditure test must file IRS Form 5768, Election/Revocation of Election by an Eligible IRC Section 501(c)(3) Organization To Make Expenditures To Influence Legislation, at any time during the tax year for which it is to be effective. The election remains in effect for succeeding years unless it is revoked by the organization. Revocation of the election is effective beginning with the year following the year in which the revocation is filed. Religious organizations may wish to consult their tax advisors to determine their eligibility for, and the advisability of, electing the expenditure test.

The IRS *Tax Guide for Churches and Religious Organizations.* The IRS has published a *Tax Guide for Churches and Religious Organizations* (the "Guide"). *IRS Publication 1828.* The Guide notes that "a church or religious organization will be regarded as *attempting to influence legislation* if it contacts, or urges the public to contact, members or employees of a legislative body for the purpose of proposing, supporting, or opposing legislation, or if the organization advocates the adoption or rejection of legislation."

On the other hand, some lobbying activities will not jeopardize a church's exempt status: "Churches and religious organizations may, however, involve themselves in issues of public policy without the activity being considered lobbying. For example, churches may conduct educational meetings, prepare and distribute educational materials, or otherwise consider public policy issues in an educational manner without jeopardizing their tax-exempt status."

Only substantial lobbying activity will jeopardize a church's exempt status. The tax code does not define the term "substantial." The Guide clarifies that

whether a church or religious organization's attempts to influence legislation constitute a substantial part of its overall activities is determined on the basis of all the pertinent facts and circumstances in each case. The IRS considers a variety of factors, including the time devoted (by both compensated and volunteer workers) and the expenditures devoted by the organization to the activity, when determining whether the lobbying activity is substantial. Churches must use the substantial part test since they are not eligible to use the expenditure test described in the next section.

It is truly lamentable that the IRS continues to refuse to provide churches with any meaningful guidance as to the definition of "substantial" lobbying activities. Churches may engage in insubstantial efforts to influence legislation, but once such efforts become substantial, the church's tax-exempt status is in jeopardy. For now, church leaders must remain in the dark concerning the definition of these terms. The only clarification the Guide provides is that the IRS will consider both time and expenses devoted to lobbying activities in assessing whether those activities are substantial. But what amount of time or expenses constitutes substantial activity?

The prohibition of more than insubstantial efforts to influence legislation is illustrated by the following examples.

EXAMPLE. A few times each year, members of First Church circulate petitions among church members following worship services. The petitions enable members to express their support of or opposition to bills pending before Congress or the state legislature. The petitions do not identify the church, and the church itself takes no official position on any of the issues addressed. Such activities clearly do not jeopardize the church's tax-exempt status, for two reasons. First, they are not substantial. While this term has not been defined with clarity, it could not reasonably be construed in such a way as to cover the activities that occur at First Church. No precedent suggests that such activities are substantial. They involve an expenditure of neither funds nor time by the church. Second, the church itself is not directly involved in the activity. Rather, concerned members of the congregation are simply using the occasion of church services as an opportunity to canvass their fellow members. A church is a public forum, and as such it is an appropriate location for citizens to exercise their constitutional right to petition their government, as long as the church itself is not involved in supporting or opposing specific legislation.

EXAMPLE. Church members are permitted to post materials addressing legislative issues on a bulletin board at Grace Church. The church does not screen materials placed on the board. This practice will not jeopardize the church's tax-exempt status, since it does not constitute an attempt to influence legislation.

EXAMPLE. Calvary Church adopts a resolution at a church business meeting, expressing support for a constitutional amendment banning abortions. This resolution, by itself, should not jeopardize the church's exempt status, since it does not constitute a substantial attempt to influence legislation.

EXAMPLE. Peace Church permits a group dedicated to nuclear disarmament and world peace to use a room in the church for a two-hour meeting once each month. No rent is charged, and the room would otherwise be vacant if not used by the group. This activity, by itself, will not jeopardize the church's tax-exempt status, since it does not constitute a substantial attempt to influence legislation. The church is expending no funds and allows only a minimal or incidental use of its facilities.

No intervention or participation in political campaigns

❖ **KEY POINT.** "Although charities are precluded from intervening in political campaigns, the IRS has seen a growth in the number and variety of allegations of such behavior by section 501(c)(3) organizations during election cycles. The increase in allegations, coupled with the dramatic increases in money spent during political campaigns, has raised concerns about whether prohibited funding and activity are emerging in section 501(c)(3) organizations. If left unaddressed, the potential for charities, including churches, being used as arms of political campaigns and parties will erode the public's confidence in these institutions." (Excerpt from a 2006 IRS executive summary of its final report on the Political Activities Compliance Initiative.)

Background

The participation by churches and church leaders in political campaigns is an American tradition. Common examples include

- inviting candidates to speak during worship services,
- distributing "voter education" literature reflecting candidates' views on selected topics,
- voter registration activities,
- enlisting volunteers for a particular candidate's campaign,
- collecting contributions for a particular candidate, and
- statements by ministers during worship services either supporting or opposing various candidates.

Unfortunately, it is not well understood that these kinds of activities, as well-meaning as they may be, jeopardize a church's exemption from federal income taxation. This is because section 501(c)(3) of the tax code prohibits tax-exempt organizations (including churches) from any intervention or participation in political campaigns on behalf of or in opposition to any candidate

for public office. To be sure, there have been massive violations of this prohibition during every presidential election year with not a word of protest from the IRS. But things are changing. In 1999 the IRS, for the first time, revoked the exempt status of a church for its involvement in a political campaign, and over the past few years the IRS has made a number of pronouncements indicating that church political activities no longer will be ignored.

❖ **KEY POINT.** A good example of church intervention in political campaigns was the 1988 presidential election. Not only were two ordained ministers seeking the office of president (Jesse Jackson and Pat Robertson), but each was actively and enthusiastically supported by large numbers of churches.

❖ **KEY POINT.** It is absolutely essential for church leaders to understand the ban on church involvement in political campaigns and to evaluate church practices to ensure compliance.

The legal basis—section 501(c)(3)

The legal basis for the limitation on church political activities is section 501(c)(3) of the tax code, which exempts from federal income taxation any church organized and operated exclusively for religious, charitable, educational, or other exempt purposes and "no substantial part of the activities of which is carrying on propaganda, or otherwise attempting to influence legislation, and which does not participate in, or intervene in (including the publishing or distributing of statements), any political campaign on behalf of any candidate for public office."

Note two distinct limitations here. First, churches may not engage in *substantial efforts to influence legislation*. Second, churches may not *participate or intervene in any political campaign*, even to an insubstantial degree. The first limitation is referred to as the "lobbying" limitation, and it was addressed in the previous subsection. The second limitation is referred to as the "campaign" limitation, and it is addressed in this subsection.

It should be emphasized that none of the political activities described above is illegal. The primary legal consequence of church political activity is that the church's exemption from federal income taxation may be jeopardized.

History of the prohibition against political activities

To be exempt from federal income taxation, a church may not "participate in, or intervene in (including the publishing or distributing of statements), any political campaign on behalf of any candidate for public office." This limitation has an unusual and unfortunate history. It was proposed in 1954 by then Senator Lyndon B. Johnson of Texas as a floor amendment to the tax code, and it was passed without explanation. Apparently, Senator Johnson was attempting to limit the political activities of a private foundation that had supported one of his opponents in a Texas election. It is clear that few, if any, Senators contemplated in 1954 that the newly enacted limitation could be used to threaten the tax-exempt status of churches. However, the limitation is worded in absolute terms—prohibiting any attempts by churches or any other tax-exempt organizations to participate or intervene in a political campaign—and therefore does pose a significant threat to churches. Unlike the limitation on attempts to influence legislation, there is no requirement that the participation or intervention in a political campaign be *substantial*. Presumably, one isolated event could be construed as intervention in a political campaign.

Despite the absolute and unconditional prohibition against church intervention in political campaigns, and repeated flagrant violations of it by churches, only one church has lost its exempt status for transgressing this limitation. A few other religious organizations that were not churches lost their exempt status, in part because of their intervention in political campaigns. Also, the IRS threatened to revoke the exempt status of a prominent televangelist's ministry because of his intervention in a political campaign. These cases are discussed later in this chapter. But in general the IRS has chosen not to enforce the ban on political activities by churches. Why has the IRS been reluctant to enforce this limitation? A number of explanations are possible:

- The IRS wants to avoid constitutional battles that would unleash a firestorm of opposition.
- By failing to enforce the limitation for nearly half a century, the IRS has induced churches to justifiably assume that the limitation is either nonexistent or is not absolute and unconditional. Continued nonenforcement of a statute raises questions as to its validity and effect.
- The meaning of the limitation is unclear. For example, what is the meaning of "participation" or "intervention"? Even more fundamentally, how can one distinguish between action by a church and action by its members or ministers? To illustrate, a campaign representative of the Jesse Jackson presidential campaign justified an offering taken up in many churches in 1988 on the ground that the appeal was directed to individuals, not churches.

These definitional problems, coupled with the limitation's uncertain purpose and the reluctance of the courts (and to a lesser extent the IRS) to attack the exempt status of churches, have all contributed to the sporadic enforcement of the campaign limitation. Let's turn to the relevant provisions of the income tax regulations and the *Internal Revenue Manual*, as well as court decisions and IRS rulings, for these shed additional light on the meaning of this significant limitation.

Income tax regulations

The income tax regulations interpreting the limitation on political campaign intervention provide that neither a church nor any other organization can be exempt from federal income taxation if its charter empowers it "directly or indirectly to participate in, or intervene in (including the publishing or distributing of statements), any

political campaign on behalf of or in opposition to any candidate for public office." The regulations further provide:

> The term "candidate for public office" means an individual who offers himself, or is proposed by others, as a contestant for an elective public office, whether such office be national, state, or local. Activities which constitute participation or intervention in a political campaign on behalf of or in opposition to a candidate include, but are not limited to, the publication or distribution of written or printed statements or the making of oral statements on behalf of or in opposition to such a candidate. Treas. Reg. 1.501(c)(3)-1(c)(3)(iii).

This regulation provides some clarification. In particular:

- A candidate for public office includes local, state, and national candidates.
- The prohibited intervention or participation in a political campaign can be satisfied either by the making of oral statements or by the publishing or distribution of written statements.
- Statements made in opposition to as well as on behalf of a particular candidate are prohibited.

The IRS Tax Guide for Churches and Religious Organizations

The IRS has published a *Tax Guide for Churches and Religious Organizations* (the "Guide") that provides churches with basic information on compliance with federal tax law. *IRS Publication 1828*. The Guide addresses political campaign activities more fully than any other issue. Below are some of the key clarifications. (Also see Table 12-1 for a summary analysis of political activities.)

Political campaign activity—individual political activity by religious leaders. The Guide acknowledges that the campaign activity prohibition "is not intended to restrict free expression on political matters by leaders of churches or religious organizations speaking for themselves, as *individuals*" (emphasis added). Nor are leaders "prohibited from speaking about important issues of public policy." However, "religious leaders cannot make partisan comments in official organization publications or at official church functions." To avoid potential "attribution" of their comments outside of church functions and publications, "religious leaders who speak or write in their individual capacity are encouraged to clearly indicate that their comments are personal and not intended to represent the views of the organization." The Guide illustrates political activity by religious leaders with the following examples.

EXAMPLE. Minister A is the minister of Church J, a section 501(c)(3) organization, and is well known in the community. With their permission, Candidate T publishes a full-page ad in the local newspaper listing five prominent ministers who have personally endorsed Candidate T, including Minister A. Minister A is identified in the ad as the minister of Church J. The ad states, "Titles and affiliations of each individual are provided for identification purposes only." The ad is paid for by Candidate T's

═══ **TABLE 12-1** ═══

POLITICAL CAMPAIGN ACTIVITIES BY CHURCHES
An Analysis of Selected Activities

CAMPAIGN ACTIVITY	IMPACT ON TAX-EXEMPT STATUS	BASIS
Contributions to political campaign funds.	Prohibited	IRS *Tax Guide for Churches and Religious Organizations*
Public statements of position (verbal and written) in favor of or in opposition to candidates for office—in official church publications and at official church functions.	Prohibited	IRS *Tax Guide for Churches and Religious Organizations*
Providing a nonpartisan forum for all candidates to address the church.	Permitted	IRS *Tax Guide for Churches and Religious Organizations*
Public comments made by ministers and other church employees in connection with political campaigns, not made at church facilities or in church publications and accompanied by statement that the comments are strictly personal and are not intended to represent the church.	Permitted	IRS *Tax Guide for Churches and Religious Organizations*; Jimmy Swaggart Ministries settlement with IRS; Revenue Ruling 2007-41
A church invites all candidates for a political office to address the congregation and informs the congregation before each candidate's speech that the views expressed are those of the candidate and not the church and that the church does not endorse any candidate.	Permitted	Revenue Ruling 74-574; IRS *Tax Guide for Churches and Religious Organizations*
A church invites only one candidate in a political campaign to address the congregation.	Prohibited	Revenue Ruling 2007-41
The church provides an opportunity for a candidate to speak in a noncandidate capacity (for example, as a member of the church, public figure, or expert in a nonpolitical field) without providing equal access to all political candidates for the same office. The church ensures that the candidate speaks in a noncandidate capacity; no reference is made to the person's candidacy; the church mentions the capacity in which the candidate is appearing (without mentioning the person's political candidacy); and no campaign activity occurs.	Permitted	IRS *Tax Guide for Churches and Religious Organizations*
A church distributes a compilation of voting records of all members of Congress on major legislative issues involving a wide range of subjects; the publication contains no editorial opinion, and its contents and structure do not imply approval or disapproval of any members or their voting records.	Permitted	Revenue Ruling 78-248
A church distributes a voter guide containing questions demonstrating a bias on certain issues.	Prohibited	Revenue Ruling 78-248
The endorsement of candidates.	Prohibited	Int. Rev. News Release IR-96-23
Campaign activities by employees within the context of their employment.	Prohibited	FSA 1993-0921-1
A church fails to "disavow" the campaign activities of persons under "apparent authorization" from the church by repudiating those acts "in a timely manner equal to the original actions" and taking steps "to ensure that such unauthorized actions do not recur."	Prohibited	FSA 1993-0921-1
Engaging in fund-raising on behalf of a candidate.	Prohibited	Int. Rev. News Release IR-96-23
Neutral voter registration drives.	Permitted	11 C.F.R. § 111.4(c)(4)

(Continued on page 621)

=== **TABLE 12-1** ===

POLITICAL CAMPAIGN ACTIVITIES BY CHURCHES
An Analysis of Selected Activities (continued)

CAMPAIGN ACTIVITY	IMPACT ON TAX-EXEMPT STATUS	BASIS
Newspaper ads urging voters to vote for or against a candidate.	Prohibited	*Branch Ministries, Inc. v. Commissioner*, 99-1 USTC ¶50,410 (D.D.C. 1999), aff'd, *Branch Ministries v. Rossotti*, 2000 USTC ¶50,459 (D.C. Cir. 2000)
Church websites that contain information either supporting or opposing candidates for public office.	Prohibited	Revenue Ruling 2007-41
Church websites containing a link to candidate-related material, if the facts and circumstances indicate that one or more candidates are being supported or opposed.	Prohibited	Revenue Ruling 2007-41
A minister who is well-known in the community attends a press conference at a political candidate's campaign headquarters and states that the candidate should be reelected. The minister does not say he is speaking on behalf of his church. His endorsement is reported on the front page of the local newspaper, and he is identified in the article as the minister of his church.	Permitted	Revenue Ruling 2007-41
The Sunday before the November election, a minister invites a political candidate to preach to her congregation during worship services. During his remarks the candidate states, "I am asking not only for your votes, but for your enthusiasm and dedication, for your willingness to go the extra mile to get a very large turnout on election day." The minister invites no other candidate to address her congregation during the campaign.	Prohibited	Revenue Ruling 2007-41
A church maintains a website that includes biographies of its ministers, times of services, details of community outreach programs, and activities of members of its congregation. A member of the congregation is running for a seat on the town council. Shortly before the election, the church posts the following message on its website: "Lend your support to your fellow parishioner in Tuesday's election for town council."	Prohibited	Revenue Ruling 2007-41

campaign committee. Since the ad was not paid for by Church J, the ad is not otherwise in an official publication of Church J, and the endorsement is made by Minister A in a personal capacity, the ad does not constitute campaign intervention by Church J.

EXAMPLE. Minister B is the minister of Church K, a section 501(c)(3) organization, and is well known in the community. Three weeks before the election, he attends a press conference at Candidate V's campaign headquarters and states that Candidate V should be reelected. Minister B does not say he is speaking on behalf of Church K. His endorsement is reported on the front page of the local newspaper, and he is identified in the article as the minister of Church K. Because Minister B did not make the endorsement at an official church function, in an official church publication or otherwise use the church's assets, and did not state

that he was speaking as a representative of Church K, his actions do not constitute campaign intervention by Church K.

EXAMPLE. Minister C is the minister of Church I, a section 501(c)(3) organization. Church I publishes a monthly church newsletter that is distributed to all church members. In each issue, Minister C has a column titled "My Views." The month before the election, Minister C states in the "My Views" column, "It is my personal opinion that Candidate U should be reelected." For that one issue, Minister C pays from his personal funds the portion of the cost of the newsletter attributable to the "My Views" column. Even though he paid part of the cost of the newsletter, the newsletter is an official publication of the church. Because the endorsement appeared in an official publication of Church I, it constitutes campaign intervention attributed to Church I.

EXAMPLE. Minister D is the minister of Church M, a section 501(c)(3) organization. During regular services of Church M shortly before the election, Minister D preached on a number of issues, including the importance of voting in the upcoming election, and concluded by stating, "It is important that you all do your duty in the election and vote for Candidate W." Because Minister D's remarks indicating support for Candidate W were made during an official church service, they constitute political campaign intervention by Church M.

Political campaign activity—inviting a candidate to speak. Many churches have invited political candidates to address the congregation during a worship service. Sometimes the candidate is a member of the church. In other cases the candidate contacts the senior pastor and asks for permission to address the congregation. Do such activities jeopardize a church's tax-exempt status? The Guide addresses these questions directly in two separate contexts: (1) political candidates who address a church congregation as a candidate, and (2) political candidates who do not address a church congregation as a candidate.

Speaking as a candidate. The Guide notes that when a candidate is invited to speak at a church as a political candidate, the factors to consider in deciding whether the church participated or intervened in a political campaign include the following:

- whether the church provides an equal opportunity to the political candidates seeking the same office;
- whether the church indicates any support of or opposition to the candidate (this should be stated explicitly when the candidate is introduced and in communications concerning the candidate's attendance);
- whether political fund-raising occurs;
- whether the individual is chosen to speak solely for reasons other than candidacy for public office;
- whether the church maintains a nonpartisan atmosphere on the premises or at the event where the candidate is present; and
- whether the church clearly indicates the capacity in which the candidate is appearing and does not mention the individual's political candidacy or the upcoming election in the communications announcing the candidate's attendance at the event.

The Guide notes that in determining whether candidates are given an equal opportunity to participate, a church should consider the nature of the event to which each candidate is invited, in addition to the manner of presentation. For example, "a church that invites one candidate to speak at its well attended annual banquet, but invites the opposing candidate to speak at a sparsely attended general meeting, will likely be found to have violated the political campaign prohibition, even if the manner of presentation for both speakers is otherwise neutral."

Sometimes a church invites several candidates to speak at a public forum. The Guide warns that if such a forum is operated to show a bias for or against any candidate, it would be prohibited campaign activity, since it would be considered intervention or participation in a political campaign. The Guide suggests that when a church invites several candidates to speak at a forum, it should consider the following factors: (1) whether questions for the candidate are prepared and presented by an independent, nonpartisan panel; (2) whether the topics discussed by the candidates cover a broad range of issues that the candidates would address if elected to the office sought and are of interest to the public; (3) whether each candidate is given an equal opportunity to present his or her views on the issues discussed; (4) whether the candidates are asked to agree or disagree with positions, agendas, platforms or statements of the organization; and (5) whether a moderator comments on the questions or otherwise implies approval or disapproval of the candidates.

The Guide illustrates these rules with the following examples.

EXAMPLE. Minister E is the minister of Church N, a section 501(c)(3) organization. In the month prior to the election, Minister E invited the three Congressional candidates for the district in which Church N is located to address the congregation, one each on three successive Sundays, as part of regular worship services. Each candidate was given an equal opportunity to address and field questions on a wide variety of topics from the congregation. Minister E's introduction of each candidate included no comments on their qualifications or any indication of a preference for any candidate. The actions do not constitute political campaign intervention by Church N.

EXAMPLE. The facts are the same as in the preceding example except that four candidates are in the race rather than three, and one of the candidates declines the invitation to speak. In the publicity announcing the dates for each of the candidate's speeches, Church N includes a statement that the order of the speakers was determined at random and that the fourth candidate declined the church's invitation to speak. Minister E makes the same statement in his opening remarks at each of the meetings in which one of the candidates is speaking. Church N's actions do not constitute political campaign intervention.

EXAMPLE. Minister F is the minister of Church O, a section 501(c)(3) organization. The Sunday before the November election, Minister F invited Senate Candidate X to preach to her congregation during worship services. During his remarks, Candidate X stated, "I am asking not only for your votes, but for your enthusiasm and dedication, for your willingness to go the extra mile to get a very large turnout on Tuesday." Minister F invited no other candidate to address her congregation during the Senatorial campaign. Because these activities took place during official church services, they are attributed to Church O. By selectively providing church facilities to allow Candidate X to speak in support of his campaign, Church O's actions constitute political campaign intervention.

Speaking as a noncandidate. The Guide acknowledges that a church may invite political candidates (including church members) to speak in a *noncandidate* capacity. For example, some candidates are invited to speak at church services because they are public figures (such as an expert in a nonpolitical field, a celebrity, or one who has led a distinguished military, legal, or public service career). When a candidate is invited to speak at an event in a noncandidate capacity, *it is not necessary for the church or religious organization to provide equal access to all political candidates.* However, if the candidate is publicly recognized by the church or if the candidate is invited to speak, the Guide lists the following factors to be considered in deciding if the candidate's appearance results in political campaign intervention:

- whether the individual speaks only in a noncandidate capacity;
- whether either the individual nor any representative of the church makes any mention of his or her candidacy or the election;
- whether any campaign activity occurs in connection with the candidate's attendance;
- whether the individual is chosen to speak solely for reasons other than candidacy for public office;
- whether the church maintains a nonpartisan atmosphere on the premises or at the event where the candidate is present; and
- whether the church clearly indicates the capacity in which the candidate is appearing and does not mention the individual's political candidacy or the upcoming election in the communications announcing the candidate's attendance at the event.

In addition, "the church should clearly indicate the capacity in which the candidate is appearing and should not mention the individual's political candidacy or the upcoming election in the communications announcing the candidate's attendance at the event."

✿ **KEY POINT.** Note that the significance of a candidate speaking in a noncandidate capacity is that the church is not required to give other candidates an equal opportunity to address the congregation.

The Guide lists the following examples of a public official appearing at a church in an official capacity and not as a candidate.

EXAMPLE. Church P, a section 501(c)(3) organization, is located in the state capital. Minister G customarily acknowledges the presence of any public officials present during services. During the state gubernatorial race, Lieutenant Governor Y, a candidate, attended a Wednesday evening prayer service in the church. Minister G acknowledged the Lieutenant Governor's presence in his customary manner, saying, "We are happy to have worshiping with us this evening Lieutenant Governor Y." Minister G made no reference in his welcome to the Lieutenant Governor's candidacy or the election. Minister G's actions do not constitute political campaign intervention by Church P.

EXAMPLE. Minister H is the minister of Church Q, a section 501(c)(3) organization. Church Q is building a community center. Minister H invites Congressman Z, the representative for the district containing Church Q, to attend the groundbreaking ceremony for the community center. Congressman Z is running for reelection at the time. Minister H makes no reference in her introduction to Congressman Z's candidacy or the election. Congressman Z also makes no reference to his candidacy or the election and does not do any fund-raising while at Church Q. Church Q has not intervened in a political campaign.

EXAMPLE. Mayor G attends a concert performed by a choir of Church S, a section 501(c)(3) organization, in City Park. The concert is free and open to the public. Mayor G is a candidate for reelection, and the concert takes place after the primary and before the general election. During the concert, Church S's minister addresses the crowd and says, "I am pleased to see Mayor G here tonight. Without his support, these free concerts in City Park would not be possible. We will need his help if we want these concerts to continue next year, so please support Mayor G in November as he has supported us." As a result of these remarks, Church S has engaged in political campaign intervention.

Political campaign activity—voter education. Some churches engage in voter education activities by distributing voter guides. Voter guides, generally, are distributed during an election campaign and provide information on how candidates stand on various issues. A church will jeopardize its tax-exempt status if it distributes a voter guide that favors or opposes candidates for public elected office, since this will amount to prohibited political campaign activity.

The Guide lists the following factors to consider in deciding whether a voter guide constitutes prohibited political campaign activity:

- whether the candidates' positions are compared to the organization's position;
- whether the guide includes a broad range of issues that the candidates would address if elected to the office sought;
- whether the description of issues is neutral;
- whether all candidates for an office are included; and
- whether the descriptions of candidates' positions are either (1) the candidates' own words in response to questions, or (2) a neutral, unbiased, and complete compilation of all candidates' positions.

The Guide addresses voter guides with the following examples.

EXAMPLE. Church R, a section 501(c)(3) organization, distributes a voter guide prior to elections. The voter guide consists of a brief statement from the candidates on each issue made in response to a questionnaire sent to all candidates for governor of State I. The issues on the questionnaire cover a wide variety of topics and were selected by Church R based solely on their importance and interest to the electorate as a whole. Neither the questionnaire nor the voter guide, through their content or structure, indicate a bias or preference for any candidate or group of candidates. Church R is not participating or intervening in a political campaign.

EXAMPLE. Church S, a section 501(c)(3) organization, distributes a voter guide during an election campaign. The voter guide is prepared using the responses of candidates to a questionnaire sent to candidates for major public offices. Although the questionnaire covers a wide range of topics, the wording of the questions evidences a bias on certain issues. By using a questionnaire structured in this way, Church S is participating or intervening in a political campaign.

EXAMPLE. Church T, a section 501(c)(3) organization, sets up a booth at the state fair where citizens can register to vote. The signs and banners in and around the booth give only the name of the church, the date of the next upcoming statewide election, and notice of the opportunity to register. No reference to any candidate or political party is made by volunteers staffing the booth or in the materials available in the booth, other than the official voter registration forms, which allow registrants to select a party affiliation. Church T is not engaged in political campaign intervention when it operates this voter registration booth.

EXAMPLE. Church C is a section 501(c)(3) organization. C's activities include educating its members on family issues involving moral values. Candidate G is running for state legislature, and an important element of her platform is challenging the incumbent's position on family issues. Shortly before the election, C sets up a telephone bank to call registered voters in the district in which Candidate G is seeking election. In the phone conversations, C's representative tells the voter about the moral importance of family issues and asks questions about the voter's views on these issues. If the voter appears to agree with the incumbent's position, C's representative thanks the voter and ends the call. If the voter appears to agree with Candidate G's position, C's representative reminds the voter about the upcoming election, stresses the importance of voting in the election and offers to provide transportation to the polls. C is engaged in political campaign intervention when it conducts this get-out-the-vote drive.

✿ **KEY POINT.** Voter education activities are permissible and will not constitute intervention in political campaigns so long as the activities are neutral and nonpartisan. If the questions or presentation of the voter education activity demonstrate a particular bias in favor of or in opposition to a particular candidate or candidates, then the church's exempt status is threatened.

In a fact sheet issued in 2006, the IRS made the following two clarifications regarding voter guides:

- "In assessing whether a voter guide is unbiased and nonpartisan, every aspect of the voter guide's format, content and distribution must be taken into consideration. If the organization's position on one or more issues is set out in the guide so that it can be compared to the candidates' positions, the guide will constitute political campaign intervention."
- "An organization may be asked to distribute voter guides prepared by a third party. Each organization that distributes one or more voter guides is responsible for its own actions. If the voter guide is biased, distribution of the voter guide is an act of political campaign intervention. Therefore, an organization should reach its own independent conclusion about whether a voter guide prepared by itself or prepared by a third party covers a broad scope of issues and uses neutral form and content." *IRS Fact Sheet FS-2006-17 (2006).*

IRS rulings

IRS rulings addressing campaign activities by religious and charitable organizations are summarized below.

IRS General Counsel Memorandum 39811—biased surveys of political candidates. The IRS revoked the tax-exempt status of a religious organization (not a church) for intervening in a political campaign. The organization was established for religious and charitable purposes, including the protection of (1) religious liberty, (2) the rights of unborn children, and (3) the rights of parents to raise their children without government interference.

The organization encouraged members to run for local political office, and it published a voter survey presenting the views of presidential and vice-presidential candidates on abortion, homosexuality, school prayer, secular humanism, and the "equal rights amendment." The survey also reported the positions of state political candidates on a variety of issues including the state income tax, parents' rights, abortion, the equal rights amendment, homosexual rights, church school freedom, evolution, state lotteries, and prostitution. The survey disclaimed any attempt to judge a candidate's private morality or to "rate" or endorse any candidate. The stated purpose of the surveys was to present the candidates' positions on family and moral issues.

The organization did represent that the survey was designed to "enable Christians to vote intelligently." The organization also claimed great success in defeating state legislation abridging Christian rights, and it announced its legislative agenda for the following year. It contacted legislators concerning proposed legislation and urged members to do the same. Nearly 76 percent of its total budget was spent on legislative activities.

The IRS General Counsel's Office ruled that the organization's tax-exempt status would have to be revoked on the basis of its political activities. It began its opinion by noting that section 501(c)(3) of the tax code (under which churches and many religious organizations are exempt) requires that an exempt organization not participate or intervene in any political campaign on behalf of (or in opposition to) any candidate for public office. The IRS concluded that the organization violated this requirement. It observed:

> The [organization's] officers, directors, employees and members are united in their belief that "God wants Christians to assume civil authority." The organization pursued two complementary strategies to achieve this objective—voters surveys and election of [local politicians]. In the short term, the [organization] encouraged its members to "vote intelligently" for righteous or Christian candidates in the primary and general elections. The voters surveys clearly identified Christian candidates by their positions on the issues. The [organization] also strove to identify righteous candidates in order to publicize such candidates, presumably through future voters surveys or other means. The organization also advocated that Christians dominate the political parties so that more Christian candidates would be nominated and elected to public office. The first step in the [organization's] long-term strategy was to encourage members to be elected as precinct committeemen. These individuals could then exert influence within the party apparatus.

The IRS went on to provide important clarification as to the meaning of "participation" or "intervention" in political campaigns. The IRS observed:

> Organizations intervene in political campaigns in diverse ways. The traditional, direct approach is to criticize or praise candidates running in the general election. At earlier stages in the elective process, an organization may intervene in a primary election or dispatch members to influence the selection of candidates at party caucuses or conventions. The [organization] sought, through its advocacy in its publications, to build a cadre of precinct committeemen in order to further its ultimate objective: the nomination and election of candidates who shared the [organization's] beliefs. Intervention at this early stage in the elective process is, we believe, sufficient to constitute intervention in a political campaign.

The IRS noted that some doubt existed as to whether precinct committeemen were candidates for public office, but it concluded that they were. It also conceded that the organization could allege that it merely educated its members on civics and government and therefore was furthering its exempt purposes. However, it rejected such a view on the basis of all the facts. This ruling represents the view of the IRS national office, and it should be carefully considered by any church or religious organization contemplating similar activities.

Revenue Ruling 74-574—equal time given to all candidates. The IRS announced in 1974 that an exempt organization that operated a broadcasting station presenting religious, educational, and public interest programs was not participating in political campaigns on

behalf of candidates for public office by providing reasonable air time equally available to all legally qualified candidates for election to public office and by endorsing no candidate or viewpoint. The IRS observed that

> the provision of broadcasting facilities to bona fide legally qualified candidates for elective public office . . . furthered the education of the electorate by providing a public forum for the exchange of ideas and the debate of public issues which instructs them on subjects useful to the individual and beneficial to the community. . . . The fact that the organization makes its facilities equally available to the candidates for public office does not make the expression of political views by the candidates the acts of the broadcasting station within the intendment of section 501(c)(3) of the tax code.

The IRS also emphasized that before and after each broadcast, the organization stated that the views expressed were those of the candidate and not the station, that the station endorsed no candidate or viewpoint, that the presentation was made as a public service to educate the electorate, and that equal opportunity would be presented to all bona fide, legally qualified candidates for the same public office to present their views.

❈ **KEY POINT.** Several rulings of the IRS have applied the ban on intervention in political campaigns to "voter education" activities. Such rulings demonstrate that certain nonpartisan voter education activities do not constitute prohibited political activity. However, certain other so-called voter education activities may violate the ban on political activities.

Revenue Ruling 78-248—voter education scenarios. In 1978 the IRS evaluated four voter education activities. The relevant portion of the ruling is set forth below:

Situation 1

Organization A has been recognized as exempt under section 501(c)(3) of the tax code by the Internal Revenue Service. As one of its activities, the organization annually prepares and makes generally available to the public a compilation of voting records of all members of Congress on major legislative issues involving a wide range of subjects. The publication contains no editorial opinion, and its contents and structure do not imply approval or disapproval of any members or their voting records.

The "voter education" activity of Organization A is not prohibited political activity within the meaning of section 501(c)(3) of the tax code.

Situation 2

Organization B has been recognized as exempt under section 501(c)(3) of the tax code by the Internal Revenue Service. As one of its activities in election years, it sends a questionnaire to all candidates for governor in State M. The questionnaire solicits a brief statement of each candidate's position on a wide variety of issues. All responses are published in a voters guide that it makes generally available to the public. The issues covered are selected by the organization solely on the basis of their importance and interest to the electorate as a whole. Neither the questionnaire nor the voters guide, in content or structure, evidences a bias or preference with respect to the views of any candidate or group of candidates.

The "voter education" activity of Organization B is not prohibited political activity within the meaning of section 501(c)(3) of the tax code.

Situation 3

Organization C has been recognized as exempt under section 501(c)(3) of the tax code by the Internal Revenue Service. Organization C undertakes a "voter education" activity patterned after that of Organization B in Situation 2. It sends a questionnaire to candidates for major public offices and uses the responses to prepare a voters guide which is distributed during an election campaign. Some questions evidence a bias on certain issues. By using a questionnaire structured in this way, Organization C is participating in a political campaign in contravention of the provisions of section 501(c)(3) and is disqualified as exempt under that section.

Situation 4

Organization D has been recognized as exempt under section 501(c)(3) of the tax code. It is primarily concerned with land conservation matters.

The organization publishes a voters guide for its members and others concerned with land conservation issues. The guide is intended as a compilation of incumbents' voting records on selected land conservation issues of importance to the organization and is factual in nature. It contains no express statements in support of or in opposition to any candidate. The guide is widely distributed among the electorate during an election campaign.

While the guide may provide the voting public with useful information, its emphasis on one area of concern indicates that its purpose is not nonpartisan voter education.

By concentrating on a narrow range of issues in the voter's guide and widely distributing it among the electorate during an election campaign, Organization D is participating in a political campaign in contravention of the provisions of section 501(c)(3) and is disqualified as exempt under that section.

Revenue Ruling 80-282—an example of permissible voter education. This ruling amplified Revenue Ruling 78-248 (quoted above). An exempt organization engaged in various charitable and educational activities, maintained an office that monitored and reported on judicial and legislative activities and developments, and distributed a monthly newsletter to some 2,000 interested persons nationwide. The monthly newsletter contained expressions of the organization's views on a broad range of legislative and judicial issues and occasionally encouraged readers to contact governmental officials to support or oppose specific action.

Following each session of Congress, the organization published a summary of the voting records of all incumbent members of Congress on selected legislative issues important to it, together with an expression of the organization's position on those issues. Each incumbent's votes were reported in a way that illustrated whether he or she voted in accordance with the organization's position of each issue. However, the newsletter was politically nonpartisan and contained no reference to any political campaigns, candidates, or statements endorsing or rejecting any incumbent as a candidate for public office. Further, no mention was made of an individual's overall qualification for public office, nor was there any comparison with candidates that might be competing with the incumbents in future political campaigns. Publication of voting records usually occurred after the adjournment of a particular session of Congress and was not geared to the conduct of any particular election.

Under these circumstances, the IRS ruled that the organization had not engaged in prohibited political activity:

> *The format and content of the publication are not neutral, since the organization reports each incumbent's votes and its own views on selected legislative issues and indicates whether the incumbent supported or opposed the organization's view. On the other hand, the voting records of all incumbents will be presented, candidates for reelection will not be identified, no comment will be made on an individual's overall qualifications for public office, no statements expressly or impliedly endorsing or rejecting any candidate for public office will be offered, no comparison of incumbents with other candidates will be made, and the organization will point out the inherent limitations of judging the qualifications of an incumbent on the basis of certain selected votes by stating the need to consider such unrecorded matters as performance on subcommittees and constituent advice.*

> *In view of the foregoing, other factors must be examined to determine whether in the final analysis the organization is participating or intervening in a political campaign.*

> *In the instant case, the organization will not widely distribute its compilation of incumbents' voting records. The publication will be distributed to the organization's normal readership who number only a few thousand nationwide. This will result in a very small distribution in any particular state or congressional district. No attempt will be made to target the publication toward particular*

areas in which elections are occurring nor to time the date of publication to coincide with an election campaign.

In view of these facts, Situations 3 and 4 of Revenue Ruling 78-248 [quoted above] are distinguishable from the present case, and the organization will not be considered to be engaged in prohibited political campaign activity.

Internal Revenue News Release IR-96-23—examples of prohibited campaign activities. In this news release the IRS issued guidance to tax-exempt organizations, including churches, on the prohibition of involvement in political campaigns. Here is the full text of the IRS guidance:

Charities should be careful that their efforts to educate voters stay within the Internal Revenue Service guidelines for political campaign activities.

Organizations exempt from federal income tax as organizations described in section 501(c)(3) of the Internal Revenue Code are prohibited by the terms of their exemption from participating or intervening, directly or indirectly, in any political campaign on behalf of, or in opposition to, any candidate for public office. Charities, educational institutions, and religious organizations, including churches, are among those tax exempt under this code section.

These organizations cannot endorse any candidates, make donations to their campaigns, engage in fund raising, distribute statements, or become involved in any other activities that may be beneficial or detrimental to any candidate.

Whether an organization is engaging in prohibited political campaign activity depends upon all the facts and circumstances in each case. For example, organizations may sponsor debates or forums to educate voters. But if the forum or debate shows a preference for or against a certain candidate, it becomes a prohibited activity.

The motivation of an organization is not relevant in determining whether the political campaign prohibition has been violated. The U.S. Court of Appeals for the Second Circuit held that "voter education activities" of the Association of the Bar of the City of New York constituted prohibited campaign activities, even though these activities were nonpartisan and in the public interest. The association rates and publishes the ratings of candidates for elective judicial office. The association had been tax-exempt as an organization described in section 501(c)(6) (a provision that permits some political campaign activity) and had requested reclassification as an organization described in section 501(c)(3). The Service denied the reclassification on the grounds that the association's rating of candidates violates the political campaign prohibition of that section. The Second Circuit upheld the action. Thus, activities that encourage people to vote for or against a particular candidate on

the basis of nonpartisan criteria nevertheless violate the political campaign prohibition of section 501(c)(3).

If the Service finds a section 501(c)(3) organization engaged in prohibited political campaign activity, the organization could lose its exempt status and, further, could be subject to an excise tax on the amount of money spent on that activity. In cases of flagrant violation of the law, the Service has specific statutory authority to make an immediate determination and assessment of tax. Also, the Service can ask a federal district court to enjoin the organization from making further political expenditures. In addition, contributions to organizations that lose their status as section 501(c)(3) organizations because of political activities are not deductible by the donors for federal income tax purposes.

What is the significance of this IRS announcement? Consider three points.

First, it indicates that the IRS intends to focus more directly on the political activities of exempt organizations, including churches. Future presidential campaigns may not be "business as usual" in terms of IRS nonenforcement of the ban on political activities by exempt organizations.

Second, the announcement clearly specifies five activities of exempt organizations that the IRS deems inappropriate. These are

- the endorsement of candidates,
- making donations to a candidate's campaign,
- engaging in fund-raising on behalf of a candidate,
- distributing statements supporting or opposing a political candidate, and
- becoming involved in any other activities that may be beneficial or detrimental to any candidate.

Third, the news release indicates that the IRS is relying on the federal appeals court's decision in *The Association of the Bar of the City of New York v. Commissioner*, 858 F.2d 876 (2nd Cir. 1988). In the "New York Bar" case, a federal appeals court ruled that the New York City bar association did not qualify for exemption from federal income taxation under section 501(c)(3) of the tax code, since its practice of rating candidates for judgeships constituted a prohibited participation in political campaigns. The bar association claimed that its rating system did not constitute prohibited participation in political campaigns, since the ratings (1) were nonpartisan, (2) involved merely the collection and dissemination of objective data, and (3) were not a substantial part of its activities. The court rejected these claims and revoked the exempt status of the bar association.

In rejecting the association's first claim (that its ratings were nonpartisan), the court observed that "a candidate who receives a 'not qualified' rating will derive little comfort from the fact that the rating may have been made in a nonpartisan manner." As to the association's second claim (that the ratings were mere presentations of objective facts), the court observed that "a representation that a candidate is able and has proper character and temperament is a subjective expression of opinion" rather than a mere recital of facts. Finally, the court rejected the association's argument that its exempt status was not affected because the ratings were not a substantial part of its activities. "The short answer to this argument," noted the court "is that Congress did not write the statute that way." While section 501(c)(3) provides that an exempt organization's attempts to *influence legislation* will not jeopardize its exempt status unless such activities are substantial in nature, the requirement of substantiality does not apply to participation in political campaigns.

The court did refer with approval to Revenue Ruling 80-282 (summarized above) upholding the exempt status of an organization that published a voter education newsletter. The IRS emphasized the following factors: (1) the voting records of all incumbents were presented; (2) candidates for reelection were not identified; (3) no comments were made about a candidate's overall qualifications for public office; (4) no statements were made endorsing or rejecting any incumbent as a candidate for public office; (5) the organization did not widely distribute its compilation of incumbents' voting records; and (6) no attempt was made to target the publication toward particular areas in which elections were occurring, nor was the publication timed to coincide with election campaigns.

The appeals court's decision, and the IRS reliance on it, is of relevance to churches for a number of reasons. It demonstrates that

- intervention or participation in political campaigns will jeopardize a church's exemption from federal income taxation;
- the participation or intervention in political campaigns need not be a substantial part of a church's activities;
- participation or intervention in political campaigns cannot be justified on the basis of nonpartisanship without compliance with strict guidelines; and
- statements to the effect that a particular candidate is "fit," "qualified," or "capable" are not mere "statements of fact" that will have no effect upon a church's exempt status.

IRS Letter Ruling 200437040 (2004). During one of its radio broadcasts, a church's founder told the audience that they should not vote for a particular candidate for president in the general election. On a second occasion the founder again told listeners that the named candidate should not be elected president of the United States. The founder offered no disclaimer indicating that the views were his own and not those of his church. He insisted that his statements did not constitute intervention by the church in a political campaign on behalf of, or in opposition to, a candidate for public office, since (1) his statements were taken out of context; (2) the statements reflected his personal views and not those of the church; and (3) the political activity, even if a technical violation, was insubstantial given the overall volume of

statements made by the founder and disseminated through books, pamphlets, audio and videotapes.

The IRS rejected each of these claims and concluded that the church had violated section 501(c)(3)'s ban on campaign intervention. First, it noted that the founder had stated during his radio broadcasts that it would be "dangerous to be an American" and that he would likely "go into exile" if a particular candidate were elected. These were "clear statements in opposition to a candidate" made on behalf of the church that were "clearly and unequivocally intended to influence listeners on how to vote in the presidential election." Second, the IRS rejected the founder's claim that his statements were his own and should not be imputed to his church. It observed:

> *Where an official publication or [broadcast] of an organization contains the organization's opposition to a candidate, the statement of opposition should be imputed to the organization, particularly when the statement is represented to reflect the views of its minister. A religious organization's publications and the acts of the minister at official functions of the organization are the principal means by which an organization communicates its official views to its members. It is, therefore, evident that the statements made by the minister on the organization's official broadcast should be imputed to the organization. The only exception would be where the organization has clearly informed the members prior to the act that the publication or broadcast does not speak for the organization and the organization does not utilize either the minister or the publication to generally represent the views of the organization. Thus, the founder's opposition to [a presidential candidate] should be imputed to the church since he was a minister of the church, and the statement of opposition (and implied endorsement of his principal opponent) was contained in an official program of the church.*

Finally, the IRS rejected the church's argument that the political statements should be disregarded because they were insubstantial. The IRS noted that section 501(c)(3) contains no exception for insubstantial campaign intervention (although an exception does exist for insubstantial attempts to influence legislation).

IRS Fact Sheet FS-2006-17 (2006). In 2006 the IRS issued a nine page fact sheet to help churches and other public charities comply with the tax code's prohibition of campaign activities. The fact sheet explains that "with the 2006 campaign season approaching, the IRS is launching enhanced education and enforcement efforts, based on the findings and analysis of the 2004 election cycle. The IRS is providing this fact sheet to help ensure that charities have enough advance notice of the types of problems that have occurred, the legal strictures against engaging in political activities and how to avoid these problems."

The IRS fact sheet includes much of the same information that is included in the IRS *Tax Guide for Churches and Religious Organizations* (summarized above). It contains the following additional information that will be helpful to church leaders in understanding the prohibition of campaign activities.

Voter registration and "get-out-the-vote" drives. The fact sheet clarifies that charities "may encourage people to participate in the electoral process through voter registration and get-out-the-vote drives, conducted in a non-partisan manner." On the other hand, "voter education or registration activities conducted in a biased manner that favors (or opposes) one or more candidates is prohibited."

Issue advocacy versus political campaign intervention. The fact sheet acknowledges that churches and other charities may "take positions on public policy issues, including issues that divide candidates in an election for public office." However, they

> must avoid any issue advocacy that functions as political campaign intervention. Even if a statement does not expressly tell an audience to vote for or against a specific candidate, an organization delivering the statement is at risk of violating the political campaign intervention prohibition if there is any message favoring or opposing a candidate. A statement can identify a candidate not only by stating the candidate's name but also by other means such as showing a picture of the candidate, referring to political party affiliations, or other distinctive features of a candidate's platform or biography. All the facts and circumstances need to be considered to determine if the advocacy is political campaign intervention.

The fact sheet lists the following factors that will be considered in deciding if a communication results in political campaign intervention:

- whether the statement identifies one or more candidates for a given public office;
- whether the statement expresses approval or disapproval for one or more candidates' positions and/or actions;
- whether the statement is delivered close in time to the election;
- whether the statement makes reference to voting or an election;
- whether the issue addressed in the communication has been raised as an issue distinguishing candidates for a given office;
- whether the communication is part of an ongoing series of communications by the organization on the same issue that are made independent of the timing of any election; and
- whether the timing of the communication and identification of the candidate are related to a nonelectoral event, such as a scheduled vote on specific legislation by an officeholder who also happens to be a candidate for public office.

The fact sheet cautions that "a communication is particularly at risk of political campaign intervention when it makes reference to candidates or voting in a specific upcoming election. Nevertheless, the communication must still be considered in context before arriving at any conclusions."

Websites. The fact sheet cautions that "if an organization posts something on its website that favors or opposes a candidate for public office, the organization will be treated the same as if it distributed printed material, oral statements or broadcasts that favored or opposed a candidate." With regard to links to candidate-related material on a church's website, the fact sheet notes:

> Links to candidate-related material, by themselves, do not necessarily constitute political campaign intervention. The IRS will take all the facts and circumstances into account when assessing whether a link produces that result. The facts and circumstances to be considered include, but are not limited to, the context for the link on the organization's web site, whether all candidates are represented, any exempt purpose served by offering the link, and the directness of the links between the organization's web site and the web page that contains material favoring or opposing a candidate for public office.

The fact sheet contains the following examples:

EXAMPLE. M, a section 501(c)(3) organization, maintains a web site and posts an unbiased, nonpartisan voter guide that is prepared consistent with the principles discussed in the voter guide section above. For each candidate covered in the voter guide, M includes a link to that candidate's official campaign web site. The links to the candidate web sites are presented on a consistent neutral basis for each candidate, with text saying "For more information on Candidate X, you may consult [URL]." M has not intervened in a political campaign because the links are provided for the exempt purpose of educating voters and are presented in a neutral, unbiased manner that includes all candidates for a particular office.

EXAMPLE. Church P, a section 501(c)(3) organization, maintains a web site that includes such information as biographies of its ministers, times of services, details of community outreach programs, and activities of members of its congregation. B, a member of the congregation of Church P, is running for a seat on the town council. Shortly before the election, Church P posts the following message on its web site, "Lend your support to B, your fellow parishioner, in Tuesday's election for town council." Church P has intervened in a political campaign on behalf of B.

Voter guides. The fact sheet made the following two clarifications regarding voter guides:

> [1] In assessing whether a voter guide is unbiased and nonpartisan, every aspect of the voter guide's format, content and distribution must be taken into consideration. If the organization's position on one or more issues is set out in the guide so that it can be compared to the candidates' positions, the guide will constitute political campaign intervention.

[2] An organization may be asked to distribute voter guides prepared by a third party. Each organization that distributes one or more voter guides is responsible for its own actions. If the voter guide is biased, distribution of the voter guide is an act of political campaign intervention. Therefore, an organization should reach its own independent conclusion about whether a voter guide prepared by itself or prepared by a third party covers a broad scope of issues and uses neutral form and content.

IRS Revenue Ruling 2007-41. This ruling presents 21 examples involving campaign activities, along with the IRS analysis. The IRS notes that each of these examples involves only one type of activity and that "in the case of an organization that combines one or more types of activity, the interaction among the activities may affect the determination of whether or not the organization is engaged in political campaign intervention." The 21 examples are segregated under various topics. Most involve secular charities. Three examples addressing church practices are summarized below:

EXAMPLE. Minister C is the minister of Church L, a section 501(c)(3) organization, and Minister C is well known in the community. Three weeks before the election, he attends a press conference at Candidate V's campaign headquarters and states that Candidate V should be reelected. Minister C does not say he is speaking on behalf of Church L. His endorsement is reported on the front page of the local newspaper, and he is identified in the article as the minister of Church L. The IRS concluded that "because Minister C did not make the endorsement at an official church function, in an official church publication or otherwise use the church's assets, and did not state that he was speaking as a representative of Church L, his actions do not constitute campaign intervention by Church L."

EXAMPLE. Minister F is the minister of Church O, a section 501(c)(3) organization. The Sunday before the November election, Minister F invites Senate Candidate X to preach to her congregation during worship services. During his remarks, Candidate X states, "I am asking not only for your votes, but for your enthusiasm and dedication, for your willingness to go the extra mile to get a very large turnout on Tuesday." Minister F invites no other candidate to address her congregation during the senatorial campaign. Because these activities take place during official church services, they are attributed to Church O. The IRS concluded that "by selectively providing church facilities to allow Candidate X to speak in support of his campaign, Church O's actions constitute political campaign intervention."

EXAMPLE. Church P, a section 501(c)(3) organization, maintains a website that includes such information as biographies of its ministers, times of services, details of community outreach programs, and activities of members of its congregation. B, a member of the congregation of Church P, is running for a seat on the town council. Shortly before the election, Church P posts the following message on its website: "Lend your support to B, your fellow parishioner, in Tuesday's election for town council." The IRS concluded that "Church P has intervened in a political campaign on behalf of B."

Court decisions

Court decisions addressing campaign activities by religious organizations are summarized below.

Branch Ministries, Inc. v. Commissioner, **99-1 USTC ¶50,410 (D.D.C. 1999), aff'd, 211 F.3d 137 (D.C. Cir. 2000.** On October 30, 1992, four days before a presidential election, Branch Ministries, Inc., doing business as the Church at Pierce Creek (the "church"), expressed its concern about the moral character of candidate Bill Clinton in a full-page advertisement in the *Washington Times* and in *USA Today*. The advertisement proclaimed, "Christian Beware. Do not put the economy ahead of the Ten Commandments." It asserted that Bill Clinton supported abortion on demand, homosexuality, and the distribution of condoms to teenagers in public schools. The advertisement cited various biblical passages and stated that "Bill Clinton is promoting policies that are in rebellion to God's laws." It concluded with the question, "How then can we vote for Bill Clinton?" At the bottom of the advertisement, in fine print, was the following notice: "This advertisement was co-sponsored by The Church at Pierce Creek . . . and by churches and concerned Christians nationwide. Tax-deductible donations for this advertisement gladly accepted. Make donations to: The Church at Pierce Creek," and a mailing address was provided. The IRS later issued a letter stating that the church's status as a section 501(c)(3) tax-exempt organization was revoked.

The church filed a lawsuit challenging the revocation of its exempt status. The church claimed that the decision of the IRS to revoke its tax-exempt status was unconstitutionally motivated due to the conservative political and religious beliefs of the church. The court noted that to win a selective prosecution claim, the church must clearly establish "(1) that the prosecutorial decision had a discriminatory effect, and (2) that it was motivated by a discriminatory purpose or intent." The court continued:

A showing of discriminatory effect requires [the church] to demonstrate that similarly situated persons of other religions or political beliefs have not been prosecuted. Discriminatory purpose may be established either with direct evidence of intent or with "evidence concerning the unequal application of the law, statistical disparities and other indirect evidence of intent." For obvious reasons, the selective prosecution standard is a "demanding one," and [the church] must present "clear evidence" of both discriminatory effect and intent in order to establish their claim.

The court concluded that the church had failed to present "clear evidence" of either requirement, and the IRS therefore was entitled to summary judgment on this claim:

[The church has] presented little or no evidence of discriminatory effect. As the government has pointed out [the church has] not identified any "similarly situated" organization that retained its section 501(c)(3) status. [The church's] evidence of similarly situated entities relates only to churches that have allowed political leaders to appear at religious services or churches that have used the pulpit to advocate a certain message. For purposes of deciding whether to begin an investigation, however, those entities are not similarly situated to the church. The IRS decided to revoke the tax-exempt . . . because the church had run a print advertisement in two national newspapers that was fully attributable to the church and that solicited donations. [The church has] pointed to no other instance in which a church so brazenly claimed responsibility for a political advertisement in a national newspaper and solicited tax-deductible donations for that political advertisement. In fact, [the church has] provided no evidence of an instance in which a political act could so easily be attributed to a tax-exempt church.

Virtually all of the 65 examples cited by [the church] are of candidates or other political figures speaking from the pulpits of churches or at synagogues—Reverend Jesse Jackson, Senators Al Gore, Charles Robb, Frank Lautenberg and Tom Harkin, Senate candidates Oliver North and Harvey Gantt, Governors Bill Clinton, Mario Cuomo and Douglas Wilder, gubernatorial candidates James Gilmore, III and Don Beyers, Jr., Mayors Marion Barry, Kurt Schmoke and Rudolph Giuliani, and numerous others. [The church maintains] that this conduct is similar to that of the church because, like the advertisement at issue here, those instances involve "public declarations" urging people to vote for or against particular candidates. As the court previously noted, however, "candidates giving speeches from pulpits or churches or churches sponsoring political debates or forums . . . are substantially dissimilar to the instant case."

The church also asserted that the revocation of its tax-exempt status violated the right to free exercise of religion guaranteed by the Religious Freedom Restoration Act (RFRA) and the First Amendment. The court concluded that the church had failed to establish that the revocation of its tax-exempt status substantially burdened its right to freely exercise its religion: "A substantial burden exists where the government puts substantial pressure on an adherent to modify his behavior and to violate his beliefs, or where the government forces an individual to choose between following the precepts of her religion and forfeiting benefits, on the one hand, and abandoning one of the precepts of her religion."

The church claimed that the decision of the IRS to revoke its section 501(c)(3) status had imposed a number of burdens, including exposure to federal income taxation, and the likelihood that contributions will decrease, since donors will not be eligible to deduct their contributions to the church. The court acknowledged that the church was "probably correct" in claiming that the revocation had

imposed these burdens, but it insisted that the church had "failed to establish that the revocation has imposed a burden *on their free exercise of religion*" (emphasis added). The court emphasized that the church had a choice—it "could engage in partisan political activity and forfeit its section 501(c)(3) status or it could refrain from partisan political activity and retain its section 501(c)(3) status." The court insisted that this choice was unconnected to the church's ability to freely exercise its religion.

This ruling was affirmed by federal appeals court in 2000. *Branch Ministries v. Rossotti, 2000 USTC ¶50,459 (D.C. Cir. 2000).*

Christian Echoes National Ministry, Inc. v. United States, **470 F.2d 849 (10th Cir. 1972).** The first case in which a religious organization's tax-exempt status was revoked because of political activities was the *Christian Echoes* case. Christian Echoes was a religious organization founded to disseminate conservative Christian principles through radio and television broadcasts and literature. While the federal appeals court that upheld the IRS revocation of the organization's exempt status focused primarily on the organization's efforts to influence legislation (discussed in the previous subsection), it also relied in part on the organization's participation in political campaigns:

In addition to influencing legislation, Christian Echoes intervened in political campaigns. Generally it did not formally endorse specific candidates for office but used its publications and broadcasts to attack candidates and incumbents who were considered too liberal. It attacked President Kennedy in 1961 and urged its followers to elect conservatives like Strom Thurmond. . . . It urged followers to defeat Senator Fulbright and attacked President Johnson and Senator Hubert Humphrey. The annual convention endorsed Senator Barry Goldwater. These attempts to elect or defeat certain political leaders reflected Christian Echoes' objective to change the composition of the federal government.

A disturbing and often-overlooked aspect of this decision is the fact that Christian Echoes lost its exempt status in part because it "attacked President Kennedy in 1961," even though the next presidential election was three years away. The ban on intervention in political campaigns refers specifically to statements made in support of or in opposition to "candidates" for public office. The court apparently concluded that any office holder is a candidate. If this is true, then the ruling effectively prohibits churches and other exempt organizations from ever criticizing any office holder. Fortunately, no other court, or the IRS, has agreed with this result. In fact, a subsequent ruling of the United States Supreme Court seems to repudiate this radical conclusion.

In *First National Bank of Boston v. Belloti*, 435 U.S. 765 (1978), the Court ruled that business corporations have a constitutional right to speak out on public issues, and therefore it was impermissible for a state to penalize corporations for doing so. The Court observed that "if a legislature may direct business corporations to 'stick to business,' it also may limit other corporations—religious, charitable, or civic—to their respective 'business' when addressing the public. Such power in government to channel the expression of views is unacceptable under the First Amendment." At the least, this language can be read to repudiate the expansive interpretation given by the *Christian Echoes* court to the limitation on church intervention in political campaigns. It is possible that the Supreme Court's ruling also undermines the entire limitation, though such an interpretation cannot at this time be made with confidence.

Christian Echoes' contention that revocation of its tax-exempt status violated the constitutional guaranty of religious freedom was rejected by the court. Rejecting the notion that the guaranty of religious freedom "assures no restraints, no limitations and, in effect, protects those exercising the right to do so unfettered," the court concluded that the limitations on political activities set forth in section 501(c)(3) of the tax code were constitutionally valid: "The free exercise clause of the First Amendment is restrained only to the extent of denying tax exempt status and then only in keeping with an overwhelming and compelling governmental interest: that of guarantying that the wall separating church and state remains high and firm."

From the perspective of many churches, the *Christian Echoes* decision is unsatisfactory for at least two reasons. First, the court gave an excessively broad definition of the limitation on intervention in political campaigns. Second, the court gave insufficient weight to the constitutional guaranty of religious freedom.

The United States Supreme Court refused to review the *Christian Echoes* case, and it has not directly addressed the issue of the validity of the limitation on church political activity. However, as noted above, its opinion in the Belloti case certainly undermines the validity of the limitation.

***Citizens United v. Federal Election Commission*, 130 S.Ct. 876 (2010).** In ruling that portions of the federal Bipartisan Campaign Reform Act of 2002 (BCRA) were unconstitutional, the United States Supreme Court observed: "The government may not suppress political speech on the basis of the speaker's corporate identity. No sufficient governmental interest justifies limits on the political speech of nonprofit or for-profit corporations." This ruling provides indirect support for challenging the constitutionality of section 501(c)(3)'s ban on campaign intervention by churches and other religious organizations.

✿ **KEY POINT.** The Supreme Court's ruling in *First National Bank of Boston v. Belloti*, 435 U.S. 765 (1978), seems to preclude a broad interpretation of the ban on political activities. The court observed that "if a legislature may direct business corporations to 'stick to business,' it also may limit other

corporations—religious, charitable, or civic—to their respective 'business' when addressing the public. Such power in government to channel the expression of views is unacceptable under the First Amendment."

Penalties

As noted above, a church's exemption from federal income tax may be revoked by the IRS if it violates the ban on intervention or participation in a political campaign. This is a severe penalty that the IRS has imposed against only one church (and a few other religious organizations).

Section 4955 of the tax code permits the IRS to assess a tax against an exempt organization that spends funds for political activities in violation of the 501(c)(3) limits discussed in this chapter. This tax can be assessed in addition to revocation of exempt status, or instead of revocation. The tax is equal to 10 percent of political expenditures made by an exempt organization. An additional tax of 2.5 percent of the amount of political expenditures can be assessed against any "manager" who authorized the expenditure unless the manager did not act willfully or his or her decision was based on reasonable cause. If the exempt organization does not correct its political expenditure, the tax can be increased to 100 percent of the amount of a political expenditure (for the organization) or 50 percent (for the manager). "Correction" is defined as "recovering part or all of the expenditure to the extent recovery is possible, establishment of safeguards to prevent future political expenditures, and where full recovery is not possible, such additional corrective action as is prescribed by the [income tax regulations]." The income tax regulations (adopted by the IRS in December 1995) specify that

> *an organization manager's agreement to an expenditure is ordinarily not considered knowing or willful and is ordinarily considered due to reasonable cause if the manager, after full disclosure of the factual situation to legal counsel (including house counsel), relies on the advice of counsel expressed in a reasoned written legal opinion that an expenditure is not a political expenditure under section 4955 (or that expenditures conforming to certain guidelines are not political expenditures).*

Note that the tax imposed by section 4955 only applies when an exempt organization expends funds on political activities. It will not apply to those political activities described in this chapter that involve little, if any, political expenditures.

EXAMPLE. The IRS concluded that revocation of a church's exempt status because of its pastor's vocal opposition to certain political candidates was not warranted. Instead, it imposed a tax under section 4955 of the tax code. The IRS noted that the church made a political expenditure when it purchased broadcast airtime for the broadcasts in which the statements were made opposing a presidential candidate. As a result, the church was liable for a tax equal to 10 percent of the amount of each political expenditure. In addition, the founder "is an organization manager liable for a tax of 2.5 percent of the value of each political expenditure." Further, there was "no evidence to suggest that his political statements on those shows were not willful or were due to reasonable cause. Accordingly, waiver of the tax is not warranted."

Since the political expenditures were not corrected by the church within the taxable period, the church was liable for a 100 percent tax on the amount of each political expenditure, as provided in section 4955, and the founder was liable for a tax of 50 percent of the amount of each political expenditure. The IRS concluded that the church's other directors did not have "sufficient knowledge to be held jointly and severally liable with the founder for the taxes under section 4955." *IRS Letter Ruling 200437040.*

✿ **KEY POINT.** Responding to public criticism that it audits churches for political activity based on political ideology, the IRS asked the Treasurer Inspector General for Tax Administration (TIGTA) to examine its selection procedures. The TIGTA randomly selected 60 IRS cases of suspected church political activity and found no evidence of ideological bias, since 26 of the cases involved proconservative churches (43 percent), 16 involved proliberal churches (26 percent), and in the remaining cases the churches had no known ideological preference.

3. BASIS FOR EXEMPTION

Is the exemption of churches and other religious organizations from federal income taxation mandated by the First Amendment, or is it merely a matter of legislative grace? Several courts have held that religious organizations have no constitutional right to be exempted from federal income taxes and that tax exemptions are "a matter of grace rather than right." To illustrate, one court has observed:

> *We believe it is constitutionally permissible to tax the income of religious organizations. In fact there are those who contend that the failure to tax such organizations violates the "no establishment clause" of the First Amendment. Since the government may constitutionally tax the income of religious organizations, it follows that the government may decide not to exercise this power and grant reasonable exemptions to qualifying organizations, while continuing to tax those who fail to meet these qualifications. The receiving of an exemption is thus a matter of legislative grace and not a constitutional right.* Parker v. Commissioner, 365 F.2d 792 (8th Cir. 1966).

On the other hand, for as long as federal income taxes have had any potential impact on churches, religious organizations have been exempted from such taxes. *Walz v. Tax Commission, 397 U.S. 664 (1970).* Significantly, the exemption of churches is automatic. Unlike other charities, churches are not required to apply for and

receive IRS recognition of tax-exempt status. *IRC 508(c)(1)(A).* This assumes that the church satisfies the conditions enumerated in section 501(c)(3) of the tax code. Whether this legislative history indicates a congressional determination that tax exemption of churches is constitutionally mandated is unclear. As noted previously in this chapter, churches and other religious organizations that engage in substantial efforts to influence legislation, that intervene in political campaigns, that are not operated exclusively for religious purposes, that are not organized exclusively for religious purposes, or the net earnings of which inures to the benefit of a private individual are not entitled to exemption. Further, in 1969 Congress elected to tax the unrelated business income of all religious organizations, including churches. *IRC 511(a)(2)(A).* Certainly such factors militate against the conclusion that religious organizations are constitutionally immune from taxation.

The United States Supreme Court, in upholding the constitutionality of state property tax exemptions for properties used solely for religious worship, suggested that a constitutional basis may exist for property tax exemptions. *Walz v. Tax Commission, 397 U.S. 664 (1970).* The court emphasized that the First Amendment forbids the government from following a course of action, be it taxation of churches or exemption that results in an excessive governmental entanglement with religion. The court reasoned that eliminating the tax exemption of properties used exclusively for religious worship would be unconstitutional, since it would expand governmental entanglement with religion: "Elimination of exemption would tend to expand the involvement of government by giving rise to tax valuation of church property, tax liens, tax foreclosures, and the direct confrontations and conflicts that follow in the train of those legal processes."

The court observed that "exemption creates only a minimal and remote involvement between church and state and far less than taxation of churches" and that "the hazards of churches supporting government are hardly less in their potential than the hazards of government supporting churches." The court concluded that the grant of a tax exemption is not an impermissible sponsorship of religion, since "the government does not transfer part of its revenue to churches but simply abstains from demanding that the church support the state." Such reasoning suggests that the exemption of religious organizations from federal income taxation may be rooted in part in the United States Constitution, at least to the extent that it can be demonstrated that the taxation of religious organizations would lead to substantial governmental entanglement with religion far greater than the entanglement occasioned by exemption.

On the other hand, the Supreme Court ruled unanimously in 1990 that the State of California could tax the sale of religious literature by Jimmy Swaggart Ministries, a religious organization organized "for the purpose of establishing and maintaining an evangelistic outreach for the worship of Almighty God . . . by all available means, both at home and in foreign lands," including evangelistic crusades, missionary endeavors, radio broadcasting, television broadcasting, and publishing. *Jimmy Swaggart Ministries v. Board of Equalization, 110 S. Ct. 688 (1990).*

In 1982 the court ruled that the First Amendment guaranty of religious freedom was not violated by requiring Amish employers to withhold Social Security taxes from their employees' wages. *United States v. Lee, 455 U.S. 252 (1981).* The court acknowledged that subjecting Amish employers to compulsory withholding of Social Security taxes violated their religious convictions. However, the court concluded that this interference with religious convictions was outweighed by an "overriding governmental interest":

> *Because the social security system is nationwide, the governmental interest is apparent. The social security system in the United States serves the public interest by providing a comprehensive insurance system with a variety of benefits available to all participants, with costs shared by employers and employees. The social security system is by far the largest domestic governmental program in the United States today, distributing approximately $11 billion monthly to 36 million Americans. The design of the system requires support by mandatory contributions from covered employers and employees. This mandatory participation is indispensable to the fiscal vitality of the social security system. . . . Moreover, a comprehensive national social security system providing for voluntary participation would be almost a contradiction in terms and difficult, if not impossible, to administer. Thus, the Government's interest in assuring mandatory and continuous participation in and contribution to the social security system is very high.*

The court concluded that "because the broad public interest in maintaining a sound tax system is of such a high order, religious belief in conflict with the payment of taxes affords no basis for resisting the tax." This language would appear to diminish the availability of a constitutionally mandated exemption of churches from federal income taxation.

The exemption of religious organizations from federal income taxation does not constitute an impermissible "establishment of religion" in violation of the First Amendment. *United States v. Dykema, 666 F.2d 1096 (7th Cir. 1981); Swallow v. United States, 325 F.2d 97 (10th Cir. 1963).* The United States Supreme Court has observed that "there is no genuine nexus between tax exemption and establishment of religion." *Walz v. Tax Commission, 397 U.S. 664 (1970).*

4. RECOGNITION OF EXEMPTION

Before 1969 there was no legal requirement that an organization file with the IRS an application for tax-exempt status. Rather, an organization was automatically exempt if it met the requirements set forth in section 501(c)(3) of the tax code. In general, those requirements are as follows: (1) the organization is organized exclusively

for exempt (e.g., religious, charitable, educational) purposes; (2) the organization is operated exclusively for exempt purposes; (3) none of the organization's net earnings inures to the benefit of any private individuals; (4) the organization does not engage in substantial efforts to influence legislation; and (5) the organization does not intervene or participate in political campaigns. Although many organizations voluntarily applied for IRS recognition of exempt status by filing a Form 1023 (Application for Recognition of Exemption) under Section 501(c)(3) of the tax code, many did not.

The Tax Reform Act of 1969 added section 508 to the tax code. This section stipulated that after October 9, 1969, no organization, with a few exceptions, would be treated as exempt unless it gave notice to the IRS, in the manner prescribed by regulation, that it was applying for recognition of exempt status under section 501(c)(3). This is commonly referred to as the "508(a) notice." The income tax regulations state that the 508(a) notice is given by submitting a properly completed Form 1023 to the appropriate IRS district director.

Section 508(c) and the income tax regulations state that the following organizations are exempted from the 508(a) notice requirement and therefore are not required to file a Form 1023 to be exempt from federal income tax:

- churches, interchurch organizations of local units of a church, conventions and associations of churches, or integrated auxiliaries of a church, such as a men's or women's organization, religious seminary, mission society, or youth group;
- any organization that is not a private foundation and the gross receipts of which in each taxable year are normally not more than $5,000; and
- subordinate organizations covered by a group exemption letter.

The recognition of the exempt status of an organization without the need for complying with the section 508(a) notice requirement of course assumes that all of the prerequisites contained in section 501(c)(3) of the tax code have been satisfied.

The IRS maintains that although such organizations are not required to file a Form 1023 to be exempt from federal income taxes or to receive tax-deductible charitable contributions, they may "find it advantageous to obtain recognition of exemption." *IRS Publication 557.* Presumably, such organizations might voluntarily wish to obtain IRS recognition of tax-exempt status in order to assure contributors who itemize their deductions that donations will be tax-deductible.

The IRS publishes a cumulative listing (Publication 78) of organizations that have been determined to be exempt from federal income tax, contributions to which are tax-deductible. Contributions made to an organization whose name does not appear in Publication 78 may be questioned by the IRS, in which case the contributor would have to substantiate the deductibility of his or her contributions by demonstrating that the donee met the requirements of section

501(c)(3) and was exempt from the notice requirements. Similarly, some potential contributors may be reluctant to contribute to a religious organization not listed in Publication 78.

Group exemptions

Each year, tens of thousands of organizations file individual applications with the IRS for recognition of tax-exempt status. But for more than 70 years, the IRS has also had procedures permitting certain affiliated organizations to obtain recognition of their exemption on a group basis rather than by filing separate applications. Under the group procedure, an organization (called the central organization) submits a request for recognition of exemption for a group of organizations that are affiliated with it and under its general supervision or control (called the subordinate organizations). If the IRS grants this request, the central organization is authorized to add other similar subordinates to the group as well as to delete subordinates that no longer meet the group exemption requirements. As a result of the group exemption procedure, subordinate organizations covered by group exemptions are relieved from filing their own individual applications for recognition of exemption with the IRS.

Currently, there are more than 4,300 group exemptions covering some 500,000 subordinate organizations. These statistics do not include church group exemptions because they are not required to file annual information reports with the IRS regarding additions and deletions of subordinate organizations from their group exemptions. Some church group exemptions cover thousands and even tens of thousands of subordinate organizations. ACT estimates that there are 100,000 to 150,000 churches covered by group exemptions. About 700 of the more than 4,300 nonreligious central organizations holding group exemptions elect to file group Form 990 information returns on behalf of some or all of their subordinate organizations.

The group exemption procedure has simplified the process for obtaining exempt status for hundreds of thousands of organizations over the years. However, there have been some significant changes in the law over the years that are not reflected in the current group exemption procedure that dates back to IRS Revenue Procedure 80-27 in 1980 (see Table 12-2).

✸ **KEY POINT.** Many denominational agencies that have obtained group exemptions have not fully complied with the requirements summarized in Table 12-2. Some do not even meet a majority of them. Obviously, these "requirements" do not mean much. This undermines the significance of the "general supervision or control" language.

In 2006 the IRS issued Publication 4573, which contains a series of questions and answers about group exemptions. That publication, most recently revised in 2007, provides basic information about some of the most important aspects of group exemptions. Publication 4573 made one substantive change in the group exemption

procedure—it states that churches holding group exemptions are not required to file an annual report updating the IRS on changes in their subordinates. The obvious impact of this change has left the IRS without updated and accurate information about the identity of the subordinates covered by church group exemptions, at least for those churches that do not voluntarily submit such annual reports.

In 1994 the Exempt Organizations Committee of the American Bar Association's Section of Taxation submitted comments to the IRS recommending that Revenue Procedure 80-27 be modified to remove the requirement that the central organization have "general supervision or control" of subordinates, at least in the case of churches and religious organizations, and to replace that with a requirement that the central organization have sufficient "affiliation bonds" that it will be able to provide accurate, timely, and regular information to the IRS regarding the subordinates covered by the group exemption.

These comments were prompted by several considerations, including the following:

- any churches and other religious organizations are prohibited by theological doctrine or practices from controlling or supervising other entities within the denomination or religious association; and
- central churches and religious associations should not have to represent that they control or supervise affiliated entities, since such representations are frequently used against the central church or religious association in tort litigation.

The latter consideration is reflected in the case of *Barr v. United Methodist Church*, 153 Cal. Rptr. 322 (1979), in which a court used information from a central organization's group ruling application to hold that the entire denomination could be sued in a dispute involving some retirement homes affiliated with a regional body of the church.

ACT's recommendations

The IRS Advisory Committee on Tax Exempt and Government Entities (ACT) issued a report in 2011 that addressed a number of tax compliance issues, including group exemption rulings. The report caught the attention of many church leaders, since thousands of churches have obtained recognition of tax-exempt status by being included in the group exemption ruling of a parent denomination. Unfortunately, the report has caused needless concern, in part because of the false claims of some seminar leaders that the IRS is going to "revoke the group exemptions of churches by the end of the year." The good news is that the IRS is not going to revoke group exemptions. ACT concluded that the group exemption procedure should be retained. Its final report states:

ACT believes that the group exemption process provides an appropriate mechanism for central organizations to seek

===== TABLE 12-2 =====

GROUP EXEMPTION REQUIREMENTS

REQUIREMENT	ACTION
1	"[C]entral organization . . . must establish that the subordinates to be included in the group exemption letter are affiliated with it."
2	"[C]entral organization . . . must establish that the subordinates to be included in the group exemption letter are . . . subject to its general supervision or control."
3	"[C]entral organization . . . must establish that the subordinates to be included in the group exemption letter are . . . all exempt under the same paragraph of section 501(c) of the tax code."
4	"[C]entral organization . . . must establish that the subordinates to be included in the group exemption letter are . . . not private foundations."
5	"[C]entral organization . . . must establish that the subordinates to be included in the group exemption letter are . . . all on the same accounting period."
6	"[E]ach subordinate must authorize the central organization to include it in the application for the group exemption letter."
7	The application for a group exemption must include "a sample copy of a uniform governing instrument (charter, trust indenture, articles of association, etc.) adopted by the subordinates."
8	The application for a group exemption must include "a detailed description of the purposes and activities of the subordinates."
9	The application for a group exemption must include "an affirmation that . . . the purposes and activities of the subordinates are as set forth" in requirements 8 and 9.
10	The application for a group exemption must include "a list of subordinates to be included in the group exemption letter."
11	The application for a group exemption must include "the information required by Revenue Procedure 75-50" (pertaining to racially nondiscriminatory policies of schools).
12	The application for a group exemption must include "a list of the . . . employer identification numbers of subordinates to be included in the group exemption letter."
13	"[T]he central organization must submit with the exemption application a completed Form SS-4 on behalf of each subordinate not having" an employer identification number.
14	Each year the central organization must provide the IRS with lists of "(a) subordinates that have changed their names or addresses during the year, (b) subordinates no longer to be included in the group exemption letter because they have ceased to exist, disaffiliated, or withdrawn their authorization to the central organization, and (c) subordinates to be added to the group exemption letter."

recognition of exemption on a group basis for organizations under their general supervision or control. The original objective of the group exemption procedures was to lessen the administrative burden on subordinate organizations and on the IRS, and we believe that remains a valid rationale for subordinate organizations and the IRS alike. . . .

If group rulings were eliminated, hundreds of thousands of (former) subordinate organizations would need to file individual exemption applications with the IRS. These applications would be in addition to the already significant normal volume of applications currently being processed with limited IRS resources. . . .

The group exemption process provides another benefit to the IRS with respect to its administration of the tax laws in the case of organizations that are not required to seek recognition of exemption on an individual organization basis, including churches. . . . Under the group exemption procedures, all categories of exempt organizations (including churches) must apply to the IRS to obtain a group exemption for their subordinate organizations. This provides the IRS with a base of information that it might not otherwise have about a significant cadre of exempt organizations. This is particularly the case with respect to churches, which would otherwise be invisible to the IRS. Moreover, even though churches are not required to file an annual report to the

IRS listing organizations added to and deleted from the group exemption, some voluntarily choose to do so, which provides the IRS with updated information about their subordinates that can be incorporated into the Exempt Organizations Business Master File (EOBMF). . . .

In summary, ACT believes that group exemptions should be retained because they significantly lessen the administrative burden on the IRS and group ruling members, they provide an additional level of oversight that would not be present otherwise, and they insure consistent treatment of similarly situated entities. We do recognize that, to some degree, there would be more transparency, accountability, and responsibility if there were no group rulings. But we believe the benefits gained by eliminating group rulings would not justify an incredibly difficult and disruptive transition process for all involved. Instead, as we discuss below, we believe that these benefits can be largely achieved through smaller, more targeted reforms of the current group ruling procedures.

In the process of reviewing existing group exemption procedures, ACT members met with representatives of church group exemption holders. The principal issues raised by church group exemption holders included the following:

- the challenge associated with providing donors with acceptable levels of assurance as to the deductibility of contributions made to subordinate organizations covered by a group exemption;
- applying the general supervision or control standard of Revenue Procedure 80-27 in the context of churches;
- complaints expressed by some church group exemption holders about inadequate training given to IRS personnel who respond to calls from donors and others inquiring about the tax-exempt status of their subordinate organizations; and
- frustration expressed by some church group exemption holders over numerous incidents related to inaccurate information in IRS databases concerning their subordinate organizations.

The ACT report concludes with the following nonbinding recommendations to the IRS:

(1) Eliminate group returns. Prohibit central organizations from filing annual information returns (Form 990) with the IRS. Churches and most other religious organizations are exempt from the Form 990 requirement, so this recommendation will not affect them.

(2) Define "general supervision or control." The ACT report recommends that the concept of "general supervision or control" (that central organizations must exercise over their subordinates) be clarified. The report notes that the purpose of the "supervision and control" requirement in the group exemption procedure is not supervision and control per se, but rather "to insure that the central

organization has sufficient information about the on-going operations and activities of the subordinate organizations so that it may act to bring non-compliant subordinates into compliance, and if necessary, remove them from the group."

The report lists several factors that the IRS could consider in determining if general supervision and control exists, and it recommends that the IRS issue a new revenue procedure listing these and other factors.

The report addressed two key issues in applying a supervision and control requirement in the context of group exemptions for churches: (i) recognition that middle-level or "subunits" of a church, rather than just the central organization, can exercise the requisite level of supervision or control over the subordinate organizations; and (ii) that the level of supervision or control over subordinate organizations should vary depending on the type of subordinate organizations (e.g., churches, integrated auxiliaries of a church, or other church-affiliated organizations). The report addresses these issues as follows:

(i) General Supervision or Control by Subunits of the Church

As a testament to the autonomy granted by the First Amendment, churches are organized in a countless variety of ways, many of which do not fit into a conventional legal or corporate paradigm of supervision or control. At one end of the spectrum are purely hierarchical denominations where one entity has complete control over all the constituent entities of the church. At the other end of the spectrum are purely congregational denominations where the constituent entities share common beliefs, but otherwise operate independently of one another. And there are church polities that lie virtually everywhere between the two ends of this spectrum. . . . Because of theological doctrine or practice, many church denominations are prohibited from having one central entity exercise supervision or control (in the conventional legal or corporate sense) over other entities within the denomination. Therefore, there should be another model for general supervision or control in the church group exemption context.

In many church group exemptions, the central organization is not always the "closest" church entity to the subordinate organizations. Instead, there are middle-level or regional "subunits" of the church that exercise more direct supervision or control over the subordinate organizations. For example, the middle-level church entities may own or have an interest in the property held by lower-level church entities. But more significantly, the middle-level entities (or their officials) may exercise religious or ecclesial supervision or control over lower-level church bodies and their leaders (i.e., clergy). And this type of supervision or control can be extremely powerful. Indeed, in some denominations, the clergy leadership of non-compliant subordinate organizations can be summarily removed from their positions by middle-level entities (or their officials)—even in the absence of any corporate board type of control over the subordinate organizations.

In summary, ACT believes that the centralized, conventional legal or corporate model of general supervision or control simply does not work for church group exemptions. Middle-level entities or subunits of the church should be permitted to provide the requisite level of ongoing supervision or control over the subordinate organizations in church group exemptions. These subunits would then provide the central organization with the basic information necessary for it to determine whether to remove a particular subordinate organization from the church group exemption.

(ii) General Supervision or Control that Varies Depending on the Type of Subordinate Organization

We believe that there should not be any specified level of general supervision or control over subordinate organizations that are churches, integrated auxiliaries of churches, or conventions or associations of churches. For other types of church-affiliated subordinate organizations, the requisite level of general supervision or control should be similar to the standard required for non-church group exemptions (with subunits of the church, rather than just the central organization, being permitted to exercise the requisite general supervision or control, as discussed above).

There are several reasons for applying this liberal standard for subordinate organizations that are churches, integrated auxiliaries of churches, or conventions or associations of churches. First, this standard would permit virtually all churches, even congregational churches, to have a group exemption covering these types of entities. Second, in many denominational group exemptions, individual local churches (for doctrinal reasons) and integrated auxiliaries (for financial reasons) typically already have a close, oversight-type of relationship with the central organization or some other subunit of the church. Finally, the IRS is not losing any transparency, accountability, or responsibility by having a more liberal standard for these types of subordinate organizations.

On this last point, one concern about section 501(c)(3) group exemptions is that the IRS is delegating to the central organization the determination of whether a given subordinate organization is indeed tax-exempt. But by statute, churches, integrated auxiliaries of churches, and conventions or associations of churches are not required to apply to the IRS for recognition of their exempt status. Also, there is the concern about ongoing monitoring of the operations and activities of subordinate organizations in group exemptions. But again, by statute, churches, integrated auxiliaries of churches, and conventions or associations of churches are not required to file annual information returns to the IRS. Thus, with respect to these types of organizations, the group exemption process does not deprive the IRS of any information

it would otherwise have in the absence of group exemptions. Indeed, the application for the church group exemption provides the IRS with more information about these types of subordinate organizations than it would have otherwise. The group exemption application provides the IRS insight into the structure, organization, and activities of the subordinate organizations, and assists the IRS in preventing abuse by organizations improperly claiming church status.

In summary, a liberal general supervision or control standard for subordinate organizations that are churches, integrated auxiliaries of churches, or conventions or associations of churches would permit virtually all types of churches to have group exemptions at little or no "cost" to the IRS in terms of losing transparency, accountability, and responsibility. Moreover, because these types of organizations do not file annual information returns, the ongoing oversight provided within the church group exemption is more than what the IRS would be able to do itself. Indeed, this additional level of oversight is one of the advantages of group exemptions, which can be particularly significant in the church context.

As for subordinate organizations other than churches, integrated auxiliaries of churches, or conventions or associations of churches, the calculus of balancing the interests of churches with the interests of the IRS is different. In the absence of group exemptions, many of these types of subordinate organizations would have to file individual applications for recognition of exemption. Thus, in this case, the IRS is deprived of some information about these organizations it would otherwise have in the absence of group exemptions. (On the other hand, some of these church-affiliated subordinate organizations that are not churches, integrated auxiliaries of churches, or conventions or associations of churches are required to file annual information returns.)

In balancing these interests, we believe that the standard for general supervision or control in church group exemptions with respect to subordinate organizations that are not churches, integrated auxiliaries of churches, or conventions or associations of churches should be similar to that for non-church group exemptions. However, because of the unique circumstances presented by church group exemptions, we recommend that the standard allow for consideration of additional facts and circumstances similar to those listed in Treasury Regulations section 1.6033-2(h)(2).

(3) Donor reliance. The report notes that one of the principal concerns that many section 501(c)(3) group exemption holders have is that their subordinate organizations are not listed in the official directory of tax-exempt organizations (IRS Publication 78). This is a frustration for donors as well, since many donors have become reliant on Publication 78 to confirm that prospective donees are eligible to receive charitable contributions. The ACT report concludes:

ACT believes that the inclusion of section 501(c)(3) subordinate organizations in Publication 78 would further the goals of transparency and make it possible for a variety of stakeholders readily to confirm the exempt status of subordinate organizations. Publication 78 is intended, first and foremost, as a service to donors to facilitate the making of contributions to qualified section 501(c)(3) organizations. The fact that donors lack this service with respect to more than 250,000 section 501(c)(3) organizations (not counting 100,000–150,000 churches) that have recognition of exemption under the group exemption procedures is a source of concern to subordinate organizations and their donors. We understand that this is a source of concern to the IRS as well, which is one reason it issued Publication 4573. But group exemption holders have told the ACT that while Publication 4573 is helpful in some cases, it is not sufficient to address the problem.

If it is not possible to include subordinate organizations on Publication 78, ACT recommends that the IRS work with affected organizations to consider additional ways to enhance the reliance by donors on the section 501(c)(3) status of subordinate organizations covered by group exemptions. Possible options might include the following:

(1) Make sure that all church group exemption holders are aware that the IRS will input and update information about their subordinate organizations on the EOBMF if that information is provided in the required format. Work with churches that are interested in this option to develop a process for obtaining and inputting such information.

(2) Have a separate "group exemption" page on the IRS website that includes a list of central organizations and their subordinates (to the extent the IRS has such information) with an explanation that the subordinates received recognition of exemption under the group exemption procedures and confirmation that donors can rely on such exemption. Also include an explanation of how donors may search the EOBMF for names of subordinate organizations, and explain that in the case of subordinate organizations under church group exemptions, they may not be included on the EOBMF.

(3) Include a list of the names and contact information (including Internet address) of central organizations on a separate "group exemption" page of the IRS website, with an explanation of the group exemption procedures and confirmation that donors may rely on information they receive from the central organizations as to the exempt status of their subordinate organizations.

Conclusions

The ACT report comes as welcome news for churches. If its findings are adopted, this will lead to the following positive results.

(1) Group exemption procedure. The group exemption procedure will be retained, and the exempt status of the thousands of churches covered by a denominational group exemption will be preserved. As the report points out, churches are not required to apply for exemption from federal income taxes. Their exemption is automatic, so long as they comply with the conditions listed in section 501(c)(3) of the tax code. But obtaining official recognition of exemption, either by applying for exempt status directly or by being included in a group exemption ruling, has several advantages. Most notably, donors are assured that their donations are tax-deductible.

(2) General supervision and control requirement. The report recognizes the difficulty of applying the group exemption procedure's general supervision and control requirement to religious organizations, in particular to those that are congregational rather than hierarchical in polity. It affirms: "ACT believes that the centralized, conventional legal or corporate model of general supervision or control simply does not work for church group exemptions." The report makes welcome suggestions to resolve this dilemma, including allowing "middle-level entities or subunits of the church . . . to provide the requisite level of ongoing supervision or control over the subordinate organizations. . . . These subunits would then provide the central organization with the basic information necessary for it to determine whether to remove a particular subordinate organization from the church group exemption."

(3) Specified level of supervision or control over subordinate organizations. The report recommends that "there should not be any specified level of general supervision or control over subordinate organizations that are churches, integrated auxiliaries of churches, or conventions or associations of churches." This recommendation would greatly resolve the difficulty encountered in applying the current group exemption procedure (with its general supervision and control requirement) to denominations that are congregational in polity. This would also reduce if not eliminate the ability of trial attorneys to use the general supervision and control requirement in the group exemption procedure as a basis for imposing tort liability on denominational agencies for the acts or obligations of affiliated churches.

(4) Ecclesiastical versus temporal governance. The report notes that the general supervision and control requirement may be construed in light of ecclesiastical rather than temporal governance, thereby reducing the risk that a group exemption ruling can be used to find denominations liable for the acts and obligations of affiliated churches.

In 1994 the IRS issued its first *Tax Guide for Churches and Religious Organizations* (the "Guide"). The Guide clarified that "a church or other organization with a parent organization may wish to contact the parent to see if the parent has a group exemption letter." The Guide further explained:

An organization has a parent if, for example, another organization manages, financially or ecclesiastically, the first organization. If the parent holds a group exemption letter, then the organization seeking exemption may already be recognized as exempt by the

USING A GROUP EXEMPTION RULING AS EVIDENCE OF DENOMINATIONAL LIABILITY

Any attempt to use a group exemption ruling as evidence of denominational liability for the obligations of affiliated churches faces formidable obstacles, including the following:

- No court has recognized such a basis of liability. No court in the history of this country has found a denominational agency liable on the basis of a group exemption ruling for the acts or obligations of affiliated churches.
- A few courts have rejected this basis of liability. In only one reported case was a group exemption ruling cited as evidence in support of an ascending liability claim. *Kersh v. The General Council of the Assemblies of God, 804 F.2d 546 (9th Cir. 1986).* In this case a federal appeals court upheld a district court's summary judgment in favor of the national Assemblies of God church (the General Council of the Assemblies of God) in a case claiming that the national church was legally responsible for the alleged securities fraud of an affiliated church. In addition, some state trial courts have dismissed denominational agencies as defendants from civil lawsuits and rejected plaintiffs' claims that they were liable on the basis of a group exemption ruling.

IRS. Under the group exemption process, one organization, the parent organization, becomes the holder of a group exemption ruling naming other affiliated churches as included within the ruling. Under these rules, a church is recognized as exempt if it is included in the annual update of the parent organization. If the church is included on such a list, it need take no further action in order to obtain such recognition.

This language was significant because it explicitly recognized that the control needed in order to qualify for a group exemption could be ecclesiastical. Unfortunately, all subsequent editions of the Guide delete this helpful recognition of ecclesiastical control. The current Guide contains the following discussion of group exemption rulings:

A church with a parent organization may wish to contact the parent to see if it has a group ruling. If the parent holds a group ruling, then the IRS may already recognize the church as tax-exempt. Under the group exemption process, the parent organization becomes the holder of a group ruling that identifies other affiliated churches or other affiliated organizations. A church is recognized as tax-exempt if it is included in a list provided by

the parent organization. The parent is then required to submit an annual group exemption update to the IRS in which it provides additions, deletions and changes within the group. If the church or other affiliated organization is included on such a list, it does not need to take further action in order to obtain recognition of tax-exempt status.

This language needlessly exposes denominations that are congregational in polity and that have obtained a group exemption to increased risk of liability for the acts and obligations of their affiliates. This is unfortunate, because many of these denominations do not exercise *any* supervision or control over affiliated congregations. The ACT report provides several options that would avoid this result.

The current group exemption procedure that grants favored status only to connectional church organizations is suspect under the Supreme Court's interpretation of the First Amendment's non-establishment of religion clause. In 1982 the court invalidated a Minnesota law that imposed certain registration and reporting requirements upon religious organizations soliciting more than 50 percent of their funds from nonmembers. *Larson v. Valente, 410 U.S. 437 (1982).* The court observed that "when we are presented with a state law granting a denominational preference, our precedents demand that we treat the law as suspect and that we apply strict scrutiny in adjudging its constitutionality." The court concluded that any law granting a denominational preference must be "invalidated unless it is justified by a compelling governmental interest, and unless it is closely fitted to further that interest."

Similarly, a federal appeals court, in construing section 6033 of the tax code, observed: "If 'church' were construed as meaning only hierarchical churches such as the Catholic Church—[this] would result in an unconstitutional construction of the statute [IRC 6033] because favorable tax treatment would be accorded to hierarchical churches while being denied to congregational churches, in violation of the First Amendment." *Lutheran Social Services v. United States, 758 F.2d 1283 (8th Cir. 1985).*

No conceivable governmental interest would justify the government's stated preference for connectional church organizations in the present group exemption procedure.

(5) Demonstrating tax-exempt status. The ACT report addresses another significant concern: demonstrating the tax-exempt status of churches covered by group rulings. Such churches are not listed in the IRS directory of exempt organizations (Publication 78), and this can act as a disincentive for some donors to contribute. The report provides some creative ways to resolve this dilemma.

Integrated auxiliaries

As noted above and in section D, integrated auxiliaries are exempt from filing an annual information return (Form 990) and are automatically deemed to be exempt from federal income taxes without the need for filing an exemption application with the IRS. Section 1.6033-2(h) of the income tax regulations defines an integrated auxiliary as an organization that is

- described in section 501(c)(3) of the tax code;
- affiliated with a church or a convention or association of churches; and
- internally supported.

The first of these requirements needs no explanation. The second and third requirements are addressed below.

The affiliation requirement

An organization meets the "affiliation" test in any one of the following three ways: (1) it is covered by a group exemption letter (see above); (2) it is operated, supervised, or controlled by or in connection with a church or convention or association of churches; or (3) relevant facts and circumstances show that it is so affiliated. Factors to be considered include the following:

- The organization's enabling instrument (corporate charter, trust instrument, articles of association, constitution, or similar document) or bylaws affirm that the organization shares common religious doctrines, principles, disciplines, or practices with the church or convention or association of churches.
- The church or convention or association of churches has authority to appoint or remove or to control the appointment or removal of at least one of the organization's officers or directors.
- The church or convention or association of churches receives reports, at least annually, on the financial and general operations of the organization.
- The corporate name of the organization indicates an institutional relationship, which relationship is affirmed by the church or convention or association of churches or a designee thereof; or if the corporate name of the organization does not indicate an institutional relationship, this institutional relationship is affirmed by the church or convention or association of churches or designee thereof.
- In the event of dissolution, the assets are required to be distributed to the church or convention or association of churches or to an affiliate thereof within the meeting of this revenue procedure.
- Any other relevant fact or circumstance.

The absence of one or more of the above factors does not necessarily preclude classification of an organization as being affiliated with a church or convention or association of churches.

The internal support requirement

An organization satisfies this requirement *unless it both*

- offers admissions, goods, services, or facilities for sale, other than on an incidental basis, to the general public (except

goods, services, or facilities sold at a nominal charge or substantially less than cost); and
- normally receives more than 50 percent of its support from a combination of governmental sources; public solicitation of contributions (such as through a community fund drive); and receipts from the sale of admissions, goods, performance of services, or furnishing of facilities in activities that are not unrelated trades or businesses.

Three points should be noted:

First, the first disqualifying test is satisfied only if an organization offers admissions, goods, services, or facilities *for sale*. If an organization offers services or facilities without charge, this disqualifying test is not met. This is so even though persons and organizations are free to voluntarily make contributions.

Second, the admissions, goods, services, or facilities must be offered for sale *to the general public*. If an organization offers its services primarily to its own constituency (such as members of an affiliated denomination), this disqualifying test is not met.

Third, the second disqualifying test is satisfied only if an organization receives more than 50 percent of its support from governmental sources, public solicitation of contributions, or receipts from the sale of services to the general public. An organization that receives more than 50 percent of its support from soliciting contributions from a narrow constituency (such as members of an affiliated denomination) will not meet this disqualifying test, since it is not receiving support from a "public" solicitation. This conclusion is reinforced and supported by the following example that is set forth in the IRS regulations that define integrated auxiliaries:

EXAMPLE. Organization A is described in sections 501(c)(3) and 509(a)(2) and is affiliated . . . with a church. Organization A publishes a weekly newspaper as its only activity. On an incidental basis, some copies of Organization A's publication are sold to nonmembers of the church with which it is affiliated. Organization A advertises for subscriptions at places of worship of the church. Organization A is internally supported, regardless of its sources of financial support, because it does not offer admissions, goods, services, or facilities for sale, other than on an incidental basis, to the general public. Organization A is an integrated auxiliary.

This example confirms the understanding expressed above that organizations that do not offer their services for sale to the general public, and that do not engage in public solicitation of contributions, satisfy the "internally supported" test. The example demonstrates that religious organizations that solicit and *receive contributions solely from affiliated churches* are not engaged in public solicitation of contributions and are internally supported.

The income tax regulations contain the following additional examples:

> **EXAMPLE.** Organization B is a retirement home described in sections 501(c)(3) and 509(a)(2). Organization B is affiliated . . . with a church. Admission to Organization B is open to all members of the community for a fee. Organization B advertises in publications of general distribution appealing to the elderly and maintains its name on non-denominational listings of available retirement homes. Therefore, Organization B offers its services for sale to the general public on more than an incidental basis. Organization B receives a cash contribution of $50,000 annually from the church. Fees received by Organization B from its residents total $100,000 annually. Organization B does not receive any government support or contributions from the general public. Total support is $150,000 ($100,000 + $50,000), and $100,000 of that total is from receipts from the performance of services (two-thirds of total support). Therefore, Organization B receives more than 50 percent of its support from receipts from the performance of services. Organization B is not internally supported and is not an integrated auxiliary.

> **EXAMPLE.** Organization C is a hospital that is described in sections 501(c)(3) and 509(a)(1). Organization C is affiliated (within the meaning of this paragraph (h)) with a church. Organization C is open to all persons in need of hospital care in the community, although most of Organization C's patients are members of the same denomination as the church with which Organization C is affiliated. Organization C maintains its name on hospital listings used by the general public, and participating doctors are allowed to admit all patients. Therefore, Organization C offers its services for sale to the general public on more than an incidental basis. Organization C annually receives $250,000 in support from the church, $1,000,000 in payments from patients and third party payors (including Medicare, Medicaid and other insurers) for patient care, $100,000 in contributions from the public, $100,000 in grants from the federal government (other than Medicare and Medicaid payments) and $50,000 in investment income. Total support is $1,500,000 ($250,000 + $1,000,000 + $100,000 + $100,000 + $50,000), and $1,200,000 ($1,000,000 + $100,000 + $100,000) of that total is support from receipts from the performance of services, government sources, and public contributions (80 percent of total support). Therefore, Organization C receives more than 50 percent of its support from receipts from the performance of services, government sources, and public contributions. Organization C is not internally supported and is not an integrated auxiliary.

These examples illustrate that some church-affiliated institutions will not be deemed internally supported and therefore will not be integrated auxiliaries. Here is another example from the regulations:

> **EXAMPLE.** Organization D is a seminary for training ministers of a church and is described in sections 501(c)(3) and 509(a)(1).

Organization D is affiliated (within the meaning of this paragraph (h)) with a church. Organization D is open only to members of the denomination of the church with which it is affiliated. Organization D annually receives $100,000 in support from the church with which it is affiliated and $300,000 in tuition payments from students. Therefore, Organization D is internally supported (even though more than 50 percent of its total support comes from receipts from the performance of services) because it does not offer admissions, goods, services, or facilities for sale, other than on an incidental basis, to the general public. Organization D is an integrated auxiliary.

In general, the philosophy of the tax code and regulations is that if an organization is internally supported by a church or religious denomination, there is no compelling reason why that organization should file annual information returns (Form 990) or an application for exemption from federal income tax (Form 1023). On the other hand, if an organization is not internally supported by a church or denomination but instead is supported through public donations or the sale of products or services, then there is a compelling interest in having the public accountability that annual information returns and applications for exemption can provide.

5. NOTIFYING THE IRS OF CHANGES IN CHARACTER, PURPOSES, OR OPERATION

The income tax regulations specify that an organization that has been determined by the IRS to be exempt may rely upon such determination "so long as there are no substantial changes in the organization's character, purposes, or methods of operation." *Treas. Reg. § 1.501(a)-1(a)(2)*. As a result, all exempt organizations are under a duty to notify the IRS of any substantial changes in character, purposes, or methods of operation.

6. ANNUAL INFORMATION RETURN REQUIREMENTS

Most organizations exempt from federal income tax must file an annual information return with the IRS on Form 990. The Form 990 requirement, and its application to religious organizations, is addressed in Chapter 11, section D.

7. LOSS OF EXEMPTION

An exemption ruling or determination letter may be revoked or modified by a ruling or determination letter addressed to the organization or by a revenue ruling or other statement published in the Internal Revenue Bulletin. The revocation or modification may be retroactive if the organization omitted or misstated a material fact or operated in a manner materially different from that originally represented. *Treas. Reg. § 601.201(n)(6)(i).* In any event, revocation or modification ordinarily will take effect no earlier than the time at which the organization received written notice that its exemption ruling or determination letter might be revoked or modified.

Loss of a church's exempt status would have a variety of negative consequences, including some or all of the following.

- The church's net income would be subject to federal income taxation.
- The church's net income would be subject to state income taxation (except in the few states not having an income tax).
- Donors no longer could deduct charitable contributions they make to the church.
- The church would be ineligible to establish or maintain 403(b) tax-sheltered annuities.
- The church could lose its property tax exemption under state law.
- The church could lose its sales tax exemption under state law.
- The church could lose its exemption from unemployment tax under state and federal law.
- The church's status under local zoning law may be affected.
- The church could lose its preferential mailing rates.
- The church could lose its exemption from registration of securities under state law.
- Nondiscrimination rules pertaining to various fringe benefits (including an employer's payment of medical insurance premiums) would apply.
- In some cases a minister's housing allowance may be affected.
- In some cases the exempt status of ministers who opted out of Social Security may be affected.
- The significant protections available to a church under the Church Audit Procedures Act would not apply.
- The exemption of the church under the state charitable solicitation law may be affected.
- The exemption of the church from the ban on religious discrimination under various federal and state employment discrimination laws may be affected.
- The exemption of the church from the public accommodation provisions of the Americans with Disabilities Act may be affected.

Clearly, any activity that jeopardizes a church's exemption from federal income taxation is something that must be taken seriously.

8. THE CHURCH AUDIT PROCEDURES ACT

✿**KEY POINT.** The Church Audit Procedures Act provides churches with a number of important protections in the event of an IRS inquiry or examination. However, there are some exceptions.

Section 7602 of the tax code gives the IRS broad authority to examine or subpoena the books and records of any person or organization for the purposes of (1) ascertaining the correctness of any federal tax return, (2) making a return where none has been filed, (3) determining the liability of any person or organization for any federal tax, or (4) collecting any federal tax. This authority has been held to apply to churches. *See, e.g., United States v. Coates, 692 F.2d 629 (9th Cir. 1982); United States v. Dykema, 666 F.2d 1096 (7th Cir. 1981); United States v. Freedom Church, 613 F.2d 316 (1st Cir. 1979).*

In 1984 Congress enacted the Church Audit Procedures Act to provide churches with important protections when faced with an IRS audit. The Act's protections are contained in section 7611 of the tax code. Section 7611 imposes detailed limitations on IRS examinations of churches. The limitations can be summarized as follows.

Church tax inquiries
Section 7611 refers to church tax inquiries and church tax examinations. A church tax inquiry is defined as any IRS inquiry to a church (with exceptions noted below) for the purpose of determining whether the organization qualifies for tax exemption as a church or whether it is carrying on an unrelated trade or business or is otherwise engaged in activities subject to tax. An inquiry is considered to commence when the IRS requests information or materials from a church of a type contained in church records.

The IRS may begin a church tax inquiry only if

- an appropriate high-level Treasury official (a regional IRS commissioner, or higher Treasury official) reasonably believes on the basis of written evidence that the church is not exempt (by reason of its status as a church), may be carrying on an unrelated trade or business, or is otherwise engaged in activities subject to taxation; and
- the IRS sends the church written inquiry notice containing an explanation of the following: (1) the specific concerns which gave rise to the inquiry, (2) the general subject matter of the inquiry, and (3) the provisions of the tax code that authorize the inquiry and the applicable administrative and constitutional provisions, including the right to an informal conference with the IRS before any examination of church records, and the First Amendment principle of separation of church and state.

✿**KEY POINT.** In 2009 a federal court in Minnesota ruled that the IRS Director of Exempt Organizations, Examinations, was not a "high-level Treasury official" and therefore was not authorized to make a reasonable belief determination that sufficient written evidence existed to warrant a church tax inquiry. The court concluded that only a regional IRS commissioner, or higher Treasury official, qualified as a high-level Treasury official. It rejected the IRS's argument that certain lower-level officials were better qualified to make this determination. *U.S. v. Living Word Christian Center, 2009 WL 250049 (D. Minn. 2009).*

Church tax examinations

The IRS may begin a church tax examination of the church records or religious activities of a church only under the following conditions: (1) the requirements of a church tax inquiry have been met; and (2) an examination notice is sent by the IRS to the church at least 15 days after the day on which the inquiry notice was sent, and at least 15 days before the beginning of such an examination, containing the following information: (a) a copy of the inquiry notice, (b) a specific description of the church records and religious activities which the IRS seeks to examine, (c) an offer to conduct an informal conference with the church to discuss and possibly resolve the concerns giving rise to the examination, and (d) a copy of all documents collected or prepared by the IRS for use in the examination, and the disclosure of which is required by the Freedom of Information Act.

Church records

Church records (defined as all corporate and financial records regularly kept by a church, including corporate minute books and lists of members and contributors) may be examined only to the extent necessary to determine the liability for and amount of any income, employment, or excise tax.

Religious activities

Religious activities may be examined only to the extent necessary to determine whether an organization claiming to be a church is, in fact, a church.

Deadline for completing church tax inquiries

Church tax inquiries not followed by an examination notice must be completed not later than 90 days after the inquiry notice date. Church tax inquiries and church tax examinations must be completed not later than two years after the examination notice date. The two-year limitation can be suspended (1) if the church brings a judicial proceeding against the IRS; (2) if the IRS brings a judicial proceeding to compel compliance by the church with any reasonable request for examination of church records or religious activities; (3) for any period in excess of 20 days (but not more than six months) in which the church fails to comply with any reasonable request by the IRS for church records; or (4) if the IRS and church mutually agree.

⚙ **KEY POINT.** A federal appeals court ruled that the revocation of a church's tax-exempt status by the IRS could not be challenged on the ground that the IRS's examination of the church exceeded the two-year limit imposed by the Church Audit Procedures Act. The court noted that the Act specifies that "no suit may be maintained, and no defense may be raised in any proceeding . . . by reason of any noncompliance by the [IRS] with the requirements of this section." *Music Square Church v. United States, 2000-2 USTC ¶50,578 (Fed. Cir. 2000).*

Written opinion of IRS legal counsel

The IRS can make a determination, based on a church tax inquiry or church tax examination, that an organization is not a church that is exempt from federal income taxation, or that is qualified to receive tax-deductible contributions, or that otherwise owes any income, employment, or excise tax (including the unrelated business income tax), only if the appropriate regional legal counsel of the IRS determines in writing that there has been substantial compliance with the limitations imposed under section 7611 and approves in writing of such revocation of exemption or assessment of tax.

Statute of limitations

Church tax examinations involving tax-exempt status or the liability for any tax other than the unrelated business income tax may be begun only for any one or more of the three most recent taxable years ending before the examination notice date. For examinations involving unrelated business taxable income, or if a church is proven not to be exempt for any of the preceding three years, the IRS may examine relevant records and assess tax as part of the same audit for a total of six years preceding the examination notice date. For examinations involving issues other than revocation of exempt status or unrelated business taxable income (such as examinations pertaining to employment taxes), no limitation period applies if no return has been filed.

Limitation on repeat inquiries and examinations

If any church tax inquiry or church tax examination is completed and does not result in a revocation of exemption or assessment of taxes, then no other church tax inquiry or church tax examination may begin with respect to such church during the five-year period beginning on the examination notice date (or the inquiry notice date if no examination notice was sent) unless such inquiry or examination is (1) approved in writing by the Assistant Commissioner of Employee Plans and Exempt Organizations of the IRS, or (2) does not involve the same or similar issues involved in the prior inquiry or examination. The five-year period is suspended if the two-year limitation on the completion of an examination is suspended.

Exceptions

The limitations on church tax inquiries and church tax examinations do not apply to

- inquiries or examinations pertaining to organizations other than churches (the term "church" is defined by section 7611 as any organization claiming to be a church, and any convention or association of churches; the term does not include separately incorporated church-affiliated schools or other separately incorporated church-affiliated organizations).
- any case involving a knowing failure to file a tax return or a willful attempt to defeat or evade taxes.
- criminal investigations.
- the tax liability of a contributor to a church, or inquiries regarding assignment of income to a church or a vow of poverty by an individual followed by a transfer of property. See, e.g., *St. German of Alaska Eastern Orthodox Catholic Church v. Commissioner, 840 F.2d 1087 (2nd Cir. 1988); United States v. Coates, 692 F.2d 629 (9th Cir. 1982); United States v. Life*

Science Church of America, 636 F.2d 221 (8th Cir. 1980);
United States v. Holmes, 614 F.2d 895 (5th Cir. 1980); United
States v. Freedom Church, 613 F.2d 316 (1st Cir. 1979).

- the tax liability of pastors and other church staff members. *See,*
  e.g., Thomas F. v. Commissioner, 101 T.C.M. 1550 (2011); Pen-
  nington v. U.S. 2010 WL 417410 (W.D. Tex. 2010).
- routine IRS inquiries, including (1) the filing or failure to file
  any tax return or information return by the church; (2) compliance with income tax or FICA tax withholding; (3) supplemental information needed to complete the mechanical
  processing of any incomplete or incorrect return filed by a
  church; (4) information necessary to process applications
  for exempt status, letter ruling requests, or employment tax
  exempt requests; or (5) confirmation that a specific business is
  or is not owned by a church.

Application to excess benefit transactions

For many years, the IRS asked Congress to provide a remedy other
than outright revocation of exemption that it could use to combat
excessive compensation paid by exempt organizations. In 1996
Congress responded by enacting section 4958 of the tax code. Section 4958 empowers the IRS to assess intermediate sanctions in the
form of substantial excise taxes against insiders (called "disqualified
persons") who benefit from an excess benefit transaction.

Section 4958 also allows the IRS to assess excise taxes against a
charity's board members who approved an excess benefit transaction. These excise taxes are called "intermediate sanctions" because
they represent a remedy the IRS can apply short of revocation of a
charity's exempt status. While revocation of exempt status remains
an option whenever a tax-exempt organization enters into an excess
benefit transaction with a disqualified person, it is less likely that
the IRS will pursue this remedy now that intermediate sanctions are
available.

The tax regulations specify that

> the procedures of section 7611 will be used in initiating and
> conducting any inquiry or examination into whether an excess
> benefit transaction has occurred between a church and a dis-
> qualified person. For purposes of this rule, the reasonable belief
> required to initiate a church tax inquiry is satisfied if there is a
> reasonable belief that a section 4958 tax is due from a disqualified
> person with respect to a transaction involving a church. Treas.
> Reg. 53.4958-8(b).

Remedy for IRS violations

If the IRS has not complied substantially with (1) the notice
requirements, (2) the requirement that an appropriate high-level
Treasury official approve the commencement of a church tax inquiry, or (3) the requirement of informing the church of its right to
an informal conference, the church's exclusive remedy is a stay of the
inquiry or examination until such requirements are satisfied.

The fact that the IRS has authority to examine church records and
the religious activities of a church or religious denomination does
not necessarily establish its right to do so. The courts have held
that an IRS summons or subpoena directed at church records must
satisfy the following conditions to be enforceable.

Issued in good faith

Good faith in this context means that (1) the investigation will be
conducted pursuant to a legitimate purpose; (2) the inquiry is necessary to that purpose; (3) the information sought is not already within
the IRS's possession; and (4) the proper administrative steps have been
followed. In *United States v. Powell*, 379 U.S. 48 (1964), the United
States Supreme Court held that in order to obtain judicial enforcement of a summons or subpoena, the IRS must prove "that the investigation will be conducted pursuant to a legitimate purpose, that the
inquiry may be relevant to the purpose, that the information sought
is not already in the Commissioner's possession, and that the administrative steps required by the tax code have been followed." Powell did
not involve an IRS examination of church records. In *United States
v. Holmes*, 614 F.2d 985 (5th Cir. 1980), a federal appeals court held
that section 7605(c) narrowed the scope of the second part of the
Powell test from mere relevancy to necessity in the context of church
records, since it required that an examination of church records be
limited "to the extent necessary." The "necessity test" should apply
to church inquiries or examinations conducted under section 7611,
since the same language is employed. *United States v. Church of Scientology*, 90-2 U.S.T.C. ¶ 50,349 (D. Mass. 1990).

No violation of the church's First Amendment right to freely exercise its religion

An IRS subpoena will not violate a church's First Amendment
rights unless it substantially burdens a legitimate and sincerely
held religious belief and is not supported by a compelling governmental interest that cannot be accomplished by less restrictive means. This is a difficult test to satisfy, not only because few
churches can successfully demonstrate that enforcement of an IRS
summons or subpoena substantially burdens an actual religious
tenet, but also because the courts have ruled that maintenance of
the integrity of the government's fiscal policies constitutes a compelling governmental interest that overrides religious beliefs to the
contrary. *See, e.g., St. German of Alaska Eastern Orthodox Catholic
Church v. Commissioner, 840 F.2d 1087 (2nd Cir. 1988); United
States v. Coates, 692 F.2d 629 (9th Cir. 1982); United States v. Life
Science Church of America, 636 F.2d 221 (8th Cir. 1980); United
States v. Holmes, 614 F.2d 895 (5th Cir. 1980); United States v.
Freedom Church, 613 F.2d 316 (1st Cir. 1979).*

No impermissible entanglement of church and state

*See generally United States v. Coates, 692 F.2d 629 (9th Cir. 1982);
United States v. Grayson County State Bank, 656 F.2d 1070 (5th Cir.
1981); EEOC v. Southwestern Baptist Theological Seminary, 651 F.2d
277 (5th Cir. 1981) (application of 1964 Civil Rights Act's reporting
requirements to seminary did not violate First Amendment).*

Federal law provides that if the IRS wants to retroactively revoke the tax-exempt status of a church, it must show either that the church "omitted or misstated a material fact" in its original exemption application or that the church has been "operated in a manner materially different from that originally represented." *Treas. Reg. 601.201(n)(6)(i).*

Although IRS authority to examine and subpoena church records is broad, it has limits. To illustrate, one subpoena was issued against all documents relating to the organizational structure of a church since its inception; all correspondence files for a three-year period; the minutes of the officers, directors, trustees, and ministers for the same three-year period; and a sample of every piece of literature pertaining to the church. *United States v. Holmes, 614 F.2d 985 (5th Cir. 1980). See also United States v. Trader's State Bank, 695 F.2d 1132 (9th Cir. 1983) (IRS summons seeking production of all of a church's bank statements, correspondence, and records relating to bank accounts, safe deposit boxes, and loans held to be overly broad).* A court concluded that this subpoena was "too far reaching" and declared it invalid. It noted, however, that a "properly narrowed" subpoena would not violate the First Amendment. Another federal court that refused to enforce an IRS subpoena directed at a church emphasized that "the unique status afforded churches by Congress requires that the IRS strictly adhere to its own procedures when delving into church activities." *United States v. Church of Scientology of Boston, 739 F.Supp. 46 (D. Mass. 1990).*

The court also stressed that the safeguards afforded churches under federal law prevent the IRS from "going on a fishing expedition into church books and records."

Examples

The limitations of section 7611 are illustrated by the following examples.

EXAMPLE. First Church receives substantial rental income each year from several residential properties it owns in the vicinity of the church. The IRS has learned of the rental properties and would like to determine whether the church is engaged in an unrelated trade or business. It sends the church an inquiry notice in which the only explanation of the concerns giving rise to the inquiry is a statement that "you may be engaged in an unrelated trade or business." This inquiry notice is defective, since it does not specify the activities which may result in unrelated business taxable income.

EXAMPLE. The IRS receives a telephone tip that First Church may be engaged in an unrelated trade or business. A telephone tip cannot serve as the basis for a church tax inquiry, since such an inquiry may commence only if an appropriate high-level Treasury official reasonably believes, on the basis of written evidence, that a church is not tax-exempt, is carrying on an unrelated trade or business, or otherwise is engaged in activities subject to taxation.

EXAMPLE. The IRS sends First Church written notice of a church tax inquiry on March 1. On March 10 of the same year

it sends written notice that it will examine designated church records on April 15. The examination notice is defective. While it was sent at least 15 days before the beginning of the examination, it was sent less than 15 days after the date the inquiry notice was sent. The church's only remedy is a stay of the examination until the IRS sends a valid examination notice.

EXAMPLE. An IRS inquiry notice does not mention the possible application of the First Amendment principle of separation of church and state to church audits. Such a notice is defective. A church's only remedy is a stay of the inquiry until the IRS sends a valid inquiry notice.

EXAMPLE. An IRS examination notice specifies that the religious activities of First Church will be examined as part of an investigation into a possible unrelated business income tax liability. Such an examination is inappropriate, since the religious activities of a church may be examined by the IRS under section 7611 only to the extent necessary to determine if a church is, in fact, a bona fide church entitled to tax-exempt status.

EXAMPLE. The IRS sends First Church written notice of a church tax inquiry on August 1. As of October 20 of the same year, no examination notice had been sent. The church tax inquiry must be concluded by November 1.

EXAMPLE. In 2008 the IRS conducted an examination of the tax-exempt status of First Church. It concluded that the church was properly exempt from federal income taxation. In 2012 the IRS commences an examination of First Church to determine if it is engaged in an unrelated trade or business and if it has been withholding taxes from nonminister employees. Such an examination is not barred by the prohibition against repeated examinations within a five-year period, since it does not involve the same or similar issues.

EXAMPLE. First Church knowingly fails to withhold federal income taxes from wages paid to its nonminister employees despite its knowledge that it is legally required to do so. The limitations imposed upon the IRS by section 7611 do not apply.

EXAMPLE. The IRS commences an examination of a separately incorporated private school that is controlled by First Church. The limitations of section 7611 do not apply.

9. TITLE-HOLDING CORPORATIONS

Some church leaders have pondered the use of separate corporations for one or more of the following reasons:

(1) To generate revenue for the church. The idea is simple. Create a separate corporation that exists for the sole purpose of

generating income and transferring it to the church. The assumption is that the separate corporation would qualify for tax-exempt status, since all of its net earnings are returned to the church, and so all of its profits could be turned over to the church without being reduced by taxes.

(2) To protect church property from litigation claims. The extent to which this objective can be achieved through a title-holding corporation depends on how the corporation is organized and operated, its relationship to the exempt organization, and the other specific circumstances.

✿ **KEY POINT.** In some cases, use of a title-holding corporation will not succeed in insulating the exempt organization from liability. While it is true that a title-holding corporation, like any corporation, generally is responsible for its own liabilities and obligations, it is also true that if a sufficient "unity of interest" exists between the exempt organization and its title-holding corporation, a plaintiff may be able to "pierce the corporate veil" and make the exempt organization responsible for the obligations and liabilities of the title-holding corporation. Courts generally will pierce the corporate veil only in extreme cases. It is reserved for those cases in which the officers or directors utilized the corporate entity as a sham to perpetuate a fraud, to shun personal liability, or to encompass other truly unique situations. Several factors may persuade a court to pierce the corporate veil, including (1) failure by the title-holding corporation to follow corporate formalities (meetings, etc.); (2) undercapitalization of the title-holding corporation; (3) commingling of assets; and (4) common management.

For many years the tax code has exempted certain title-holding corporations from federal income taxation. This exemption originally was created to overcome state laws prohibiting charities from holding title to property, although in more recent years the objective has increasingly been protection against legal liability.

Currently, title-holding companies are recognized as exempt under sections 501(c)(2) and 501(c)(25) of the federal tax code. Section 501(c)(2) provides for recognition of exemption of single-parent title-holding companies, and section 501(c)(25) describes multiple-parent title-holding companies. Each section is described below.

Section 501(c)(2) title-holding corporations

Section 501(c)(2) of the tax code provides that "corporations organized for the exclusive purpose of holding title to property, collecting income therefrom, and turning over the entire amount thereof, less expenses, to [a tax-exempt organization]" qualify for tax-exempt status. The IRS has observed:

> Section 501(c)(2) exempts corporations that hold title to property on behalf of another exempt organization. The statutory predecessor to section 501(c)(2) goes back to 1916. The statute was enacted largely to overcome state law obstacles against the direct

holding of title by an exempt organization, including property used in the organization's exempt function (e.g., a church's church building). Thereafter, section 501(c)(2) organizations increasingly came to be used for holding investment property. A major reason for having a title-holding company is for the company's owner to limit its liability resulting from ownership (by placing the property in the title-holding company, a separate entity). Other reasons are to improve the owner's ability to borrow; clarify title; simplify accounting; or comply with state law requirements.

The following rules apply to section 501(c)(2) title-holding corporations:

- A title-holding corporation under section 501(c)(2) cannot engage in the active management or operation of real estate. Its role is strictly limited to holding title to property and passively collecting the income from that property.
- The regulations note that since a corporation described in section 501(c)(2) cannot be exempt if it engages in any business other than that of holding title to property and collecting income therefrom, it cannot have unrelated business taxable income (see section B of this chapter), with some exceptions. One exception is for debt-financed income. While such income generally is subject to the unrelated business income tax (UBIT), it will not cause the loss of a title-holding corporation's tax exemption. Another exception, added by an amendment to section 501(c)(2) in 1993, provides that a title-holding corporation may receive up to 10 percent of its gross income from unrelated business income incidentally derived from the holding of property without jeopardizing its exempt status. Examples include income from vending machines, laundry facilities, and parking facilities. This income remains taxable, but will not result in the loss of exemption.
- A section 501(c)(2) title-holding corporation cannot accumulate income and retain its exemption, but instead must turn over the entire amount of income, less expenses, to a tax-exempt organization. *Treas. Reg. 1.501(c)(2)-1(b).* Section 501(c)(2) uses the term "corporation." However, section 7701(a)(3) of the tax code clarifies that this term includes unincorporated associations and some trusts.
- Section 501(c)(2) organizations, though exempt from federal income taxation, are not eligible to receive tax-deductible charitable contributions.
- Section 501(c)(2) organizations generally are required to file an annual information return with the IRS (Form 990).
- Organizations seeking exemption under section 501(c)(2) must be "organized for the exclusive purpose" of holding title to property and collecting income therefrom. An organization's purposes can be established by reviewing its activities, the actual language in its organizational documents, and all events surrounding the incorporation of the organization. Any language in the organizational documents that empowers

the organization to engage in any other business would be evidence that the organization was not formed for the exclusive purpose required by section 501(c)(2).

- A section 501(c)(2) organization does not necessarily have to be a nonprofit corporation under state law. As long as the organizational documents do not impose any broad powers outside of holding title to property, collecting income, and turning over the income to an exempt organization, the requirements of section 501(c)(2) are met.

- The tax code does not specify the relationship required between a title-holding corporation and the exempt organization receiving its income. Traditionally, the relationship is parent and subsidiary (i.e., the exempt organization owns the title-holding corporation).

- Section 501(c)(2) and the regulations make clear that title-holding corporations are strictly limited to holding title to property and collecting the income therefrom. They generally may not, with few exceptions, have income from an unrelated trade or business. Investments in stocks, bonds, and real estate are permissible sources of income for section 501(c)(2) organizations.

- Permitting title-holding corporations to invest in real estate implies that they can earn income by renting this real estate to the general public. An IRS revenue ruling describes a corporation that held title to a building containing offices that were rented to the general public. The corporation collected the rents, paid the expenses incurred in operating and maintaining the building, and turned over the remainder to a parent charitable organization. The title-holding company rendered no substantial services to the tenants other than normal maintenance of the building and grounds. The IRS concluded that income from renting offices to the general public did not preclude exemption under section 501(c)(2). Note that the title-holding corporation itself collected the rent, paid the expenses, and provided normal maintenance services. There is no requirement that a title-holding corporation hire a management company to carry out these activities. *Revenue Ruling 69-381.*

- IRS Publication 598 states: "When an exempt title-holding corporation, described in section 501(c)(2), pays any of its net income to an organization that itself is exempt from tax under section 501(a), such as a church or a convention or association of churches, and files a consolidated return with that organization, the title-holding corporation is treated, for unrelated business income tax purposes, as organized and operated for the same purposes as the exempt organization. As a result, a title-holding corporation whose source of income is related to the exempt purposes of the payee organization is not subject to the unrelated business income tax if the title-holding corporation and the payee organization file a consolidated return. However, if the source of the income is not so related, the title-holding corporation is subject to unrelated business income tax."

- While title-holding corporations are eligible for exemption from federal income taxation, they may be subject to a franchise tax in some states.

Section 501(c)(25) title-holding corporations

Congress added section 501(c)(25) to the tax code in 1986. In enacting this section, Congress allowed certain pension trusts, governmental entities, and 501(c)(3) organizations wider latitude to pool their resources in their real property investments than permitted for section 501(c)(2) title-holding companies. Even though the purpose of section 501(c)(25) was to recognize title-holding companies with multiple parents as exempt from federal tax, the vast majority of section 501(c)(25) applicants have a single parent.

> *Section 501(c)(25) specifies that a corporation or trust may qualify for tax-exempt status if it has no more than 35 shareholders or beneficiaries; has only one class of stock or beneficial interest; and is organized for the exclusive purposes of acquiring, holding title to, and collecting income from real property and remitting the entire amount of income from such property (less expenses) to one or more organizations described in section 501(c)(25)(C) (including religious and other organizations, government entities, and pension funds).*

The following rules apply to section 501(c)(25) title-holding corporations:

- Many 501(c)(25) applicants are formed under general corporation laws and are not nonprofit corporations. However, as long as the organizational requirements are met, it does not matter what type of corporation is used. For nonstick corporations, the term "member" is used and is considered synonymous with "shareholder." Most 501(c)(25) title-holding companies are organized by real-estate investment management firms as Delaware business corporations. An organization seeking exemption under section 501(c)(25) may have as its shareholder an organization described in section 501(c)(3), including a church or other public charity.

- Generally, the receipt of unrelated business income by an IRC 501(c)(25) title-holding company will subject it to loss of exempt status because a title-holding company cannot be exempt from taxation if it engages in any business other than that of holding title to real property and collecting income therefrom. Income derived from a business operation or the business of acquiring, improving, and selling real property is income from an unrelated trade or business and will result in the loss of exempt status.

- Congress amended the tax code in 1993 to allow both 501(c)(2) and 501(c)(25) organizations to receive unrelated business income of up to 10 percent of their gross income provided that the unrelated business income is incidentally derived from the holding of real property. Examples of incidentally derived income are parking revenue and income from vending machines. Income from manufacturing, for example, would not be considered incidental to the holding of real property.

Section 502 "feeder organizations"

Section 502 of the tax code specifies that "an organization operated for the primary purpose of carrying on a trade or business for profit shall not be exempt from taxation under section 501 on the ground that all of its profits are payable to one or more organizations exempt from taxation under section 501." However, section 502(b) excludes various types of activities from the term "trade or business," including "the deriving of rents" that would be excluded from unrelated business taxable income (UBTI) under section 512(b)(3) of the tax code. Section 512(b)(3) excludes from UBTI "all rents from real property," subject to various exceptions. Section 512(b)(4) provides, however, that notwithstanding this exclusion, rents from "debt-financed property" are included in UBTI.

Church leaders may wish to consult with an attorney to explore the feasibility and possible advantages of using a title-holding corporation for one or more of the reasons mentioned above. Given the complexity of such an arrangement, it is essential that church leaders retain an attorney with experience in creating title-holding corporations.

✻ **KEY POINT.** Limited liability corporations (LLCs) are another device used by some charities to insulate themselves from liability for the obligations of affiliated entities. This is another option that should be considered along with title-holding corporations.

B. TAX ON UNRELATED BUSINESS INCOME

1. GENERAL PRINCIPLES

Prior to 1950 a growing number of exempt organizations were engaged in profitable business activities in competition with taxable organizations. In some cases these business activities had little or no relation to the exempt organization's purposes other than the production of revenue to carry out those purposes. This led Congress, in the Revenue Act of 1950, to impose a tax—the unrelated business income tax (UBIT)—on the unrelated business income of certain otherwise exempt organizations. The Report of the Senate Finance Committee stated the purpose of the new tax as follows:

The problem at which the tax on unrelated business income is directed is primarily that of unfair competition. The tax-free status of section [501] organizations enables them to use their profits tax-free to expand operations, while their competitors can expand only with

the profits remaining after taxes. In neither the House bill nor your committee's bill does this provision deny the exemption where the organizations are carrying on unrelated active business enterprises, nor require that they dispose of such businesses. Both provisions merely impose the same tax on income derived from an unrelated trade or business as is borne by their competitors. In fact it is not intended that the tax imposed on unrelated business income will have any effect on the tax-exempt status of any organization.

The Revenue Act of 1950 exempted certain organizations from the unrelated business income tax provisions, including churches and conventions or associations of churches. However, it soon became apparent that many of the exempted organizations were engaging, or were apt to engage, in unrelated business. For example, churches were involved in various types of commercial activities, including publishing houses, hotels, factories, radio and television stations, parking lots, newspapers, bakeries, and restaurants. Congress responded in the Tax Reform Act of 1969 by subjecting almost all exempt organizations, including churches and conventions or associations of churches, to the tax on unrelated business income. *IRC 511(a)(2)(A).* Accordingly, for taxable years beginning after December 31, 1969, churches and conventions or associations of churches became subject to the tax on unrelated business income.

2. UNRELATED BUSINESS INCOME

Tax code definitions

Section 511 of the tax code imposes a tax on unrelated business taxable income. Section 512 defines unrelated business taxable income as "the gross income derived by any organization from any unrelated trade or business regularly carried on by it" less certain deductions. Section 513 defines the term "unrelated trade or business" as "any trade or business the conduct of which is not substantially related (aside from the need of such organization for income or funds or the use it makes of the profits derived) to the exercise or performance by such organization of its charitable, educational, or other purpose or function constituting the basis for its exemption under section 501."

As a result, the following three conditions must be met before an activity of an exempt organization may be classified as an unrelated trade or business and the gross income of such activity subjected to the tax on unrelated business taxable income: (1) the activity must be a trade or business; (2) the trade or business must be regularly carried on; and (3) the trade or business must not be substantially related to exempt purposes. Each of these requirements is addressed below.

Trade or business

The term "trade or business" generally includes any activity carried on for the production of income from the sale of goods or performances of services. The term may include such activities as selling goods at a church bazaar; selling commercial advertising in an exempt organization's magazine; and the operation of factories, bingo games, publishing houses, hotels, radio and television stations, grocery stores, restaurants, newspapers, parking lots, record companies, and cleaners.

The regulations state that an activity does not lose its identity as a trade or business merely because it is carried on within a larger aggregate of similar activities or within a larger complex of other endeavors which may or may not be related to the exempt purposes of the organization. *Treas. Reg. § 1.513-1(b).* To illustrate, if a church's parking lot is used by the church as a commercial lot during the week, the fees received are income from an unrelated trade or business, even though the lot is necessary for the church's exempt purposes. Similarly, commercial advertising does not lose its identity as a trade or business simply because it is contained in a magazine published by an exempt organization.

Regularly carried on

To be subject to the tax on unrelated business income, an activity constituting a trade or business must be regularly carried on. The regulations specify that in determining whether a trade or business is regularly carried on, regard must be given to the "frequency and continuity with which the activities . . . are conducted and the manner in which they are pursued." *Treas. Reg. § 1.513-1(b).* The regulations further stipulate that this requirement must be applied in light of the purpose of the unrelated business income tax to place the business activities of exempt organizations on the same tax basis as the taxable business endeavors with which they compete. If a particular income-producing activity is of a kind normally conducted by taxable commercial organizations on a year-round basis, the conduct of such activities by an exempt organization over a period of only a few weeks does not constitute the regular carrying on of a trade or business. For example, the operation of a sandwich stand by a church for only one or two weeks at a county fair is not "regularly carried on," since such a stand would not compete with a similar facility of a commercial organization that ordinarily would operate on a year-round basis.

On the other hand, if a particular income-producing activity is of a type that is ordinarily conducted on a seasonable basis by commercial organizations, then a similar activity conducted by a church for a substantial part of the season would be "regularly carried on." The IRS maintains that an activity carried on one day a week on a year-round basis, such as the use of a church parking lot for commercial parking every Saturday, is regularly carried on. *Treas. Reg. § 1.513-1(c)(2)(i).* However, the income tax regulations specify that certain intermittent income-producing activities occur so infrequently that they will not be regarded as a trade or business regularly carried on. *Treas. Reg. § 1.513-1(c)(2)(iii).* For example, an income-producing activity lasting for a short period of time and conducted on an annual basis will not be considered regularly carried on. This regulation states that "income derived from the conduct of an annual dance or similar fund raising event for charity would not be income from trade or business regularly carried on."

Not substantially related to an exempt purpose

An activity will not be considered an unrelated trade or business if it is *substantially related to exempt purposes.* The income tax regulations specify that for the conduct of a trade or business to be substantially related, the activity must "contribute importantly to the accomplishment of those purposes." *Treas. Reg. § 1.513-1(d)(2).* If a particular activity does not contribute importantly to the accomplishment of an organization's exempt purposes, the income realized from the activity does not derive from the conduct of a related trade or business. Whether a particular activity contributes importantly to the accomplishment of an organization's exempt purposes depends in each case upon the facts and circumstances involved.

The regulations specify that in determining whether a particular activity contributes importantly to the accomplishment of an exempt purpose, the size and extent of the activity involved must be considered "in relation to the nature and extent of the exempt function which they purport to serve." *Treas. Reg. § 1.513-1(d)(3).* For example, if an exempt organization generates income from activities that are in part related to the performance of its exempt functions but that are conducted on a larger scale than is reasonably necessary for the performance of such functions, the gross income attributable to that portion of the activities in excess of the needs of exempt functions constitutes gross income from the conduct of an unrelated trade or business.

The sale of religious articles and publications with substantial religious content generally is related to the exempt purposes of a church, as is a church's operation of a religious school, since religious training contributes importantly to the exempt purposes of the church. However, it is important to recognize that the accomplishment of a church's exempt purposes does not include a church's need for income or its ultimate use of income. If a church receives income from an unrelated trade or business, the income is taxable, even though it is used exclusively for religious purposes such as maintaining the church building, purchasing hymnals, or supporting missions.

❖ **KEY POINT.** The income tax regulations specify that an exempt organization will not lose its tax-exempt status so long as its nonexempt activities or purposes comprise an "insubstantial part of its activities." *Treas. Reg. 1.501(c)(3)-1.* As a result, if a church's nonexempt activities comprise more than an insubstantial part of its overall activities, then the issue is loss of exempt status and not the unrelated business income tax.

Bookstores

Occasionally a church will operate a bookstore. Is such an enterprise an unrelated trade or business subject to the tax on unrelated business income? This will depend on several considerations, including the following: (1) Is the business operated within the church building, or is it located in another facility? (2) Does the bookstore sell only religious merchandise (books, tapes, records, etc.), or does it also sell nonreligious items such as pen and pencil sets, radios, stationery, and film?

If it sells nonreligious items, what percentage of gross sales comes from such sales? (3) Is the bookstore separately incorporated, or does it come under the church's corporate umbrella? (4) If the bookstore is on church premises, is it open only during those times when the church is in use? (5) Is the bookstore open to the general public? (6) Does the bookstore engage in advertising? (7) What is the relative size of the bookstore's revenue in comparison with church revenues?

As has been noted previously, the fact that a bookstore's net earnings are used exclusively for religious purposes is not controlling. The tax on unrelated business income is designed primarily to eliminate the unfair competitive advantage that nonprofit organizations would enjoy if they could sell products to the public in direct competition with taxable enterprises selling the same or similar merchandise. Even if a bookstore's activities suggest that it is an unrelated trade or business, it will not be liable for the tax on unrelated business income if it fits within any of the three exceptions described in the following subsection.

3. EXCEPTIONS

Section 513(a) of the tax code states that the term "unrelated trade or business" does not include

- activities in which substantially all the work is performed by unpaid volunteers; activities carried on by a church or other charitable organization primarily for the convenience of its members, students, or employees; or
- selling merchandise, substantially all of which has been received by the exempt organization as gifts or contributions.

Several income-producing activities of churches are exempt from the tax on unrelated business income for more than one reason. For example, church bake sales ordinarily are exempt because all of the work is performed by unpaid volunteers, the bakery goods are donated to the church, and the activity is not regularly carried on. Similarly, income from a thrift shop operated by a church or other exempt organization ordinarily is exempt from the tax on unrelated business income because all or most of the work is performed by unpaid volunteers and because most of the merchandise sold by the thrift shop is donated. Car washes, fund-raising dinners, bazaars, and many similar income-producing activities of churches are exempt from the tax on unrelated business income because of one or more of the exceptions discussed above or because the activity is not regularly carried on.

EXAMPLE. A Catholic religious order owned and maintained a 1,600-acre farm that produced crops and livestock for commercial markets. The IRS insisted that the farm was generating unrelated business taxable income, but the Tax Court disagreed. The court, while rejecting the order's contentions that it was not operated for profit and that its farming operation was substantially

related to its tax-exempt purpose, concluded that the farm earnings were not unrelated business taxable income, since 91 percent of the labor was provided, without compensation, by members of the order. The court rejected the government's contention that the members of the order received noncash compensation for their labor in the form of room and board, since the members would have received such amenities even if they performed no work or the farm operations ceased.

EXAMPLE. The Tax Court concluded that a religious organization was engaged in an unrelated trade or business: A religious organization was engaged in evangelizing and rehabilitating drug addicts and street people in a communal setting. Persons in the program were expected to work in one of the organization's businesses, which included forestry, housecleaning, and painting. The Tax Court ruled that such businesses were not substantially related to the organization's religious purposes, and therefore the income derived from the businesses was taxable as unrelated business income. The court distinguished the St. Joseph Farms case (see the previous example) with respect to the applicability of the volunteer labor exception. In the St. Joseph Farms case the members would have been provided food and shelter even if they were not engaged in farming operations, while in this case the members would not have received food, shelter, clothing, medical care, and other benefits if they did not work. *Shiloh Youth Revival Centers v. Commissioner, 88 T.C. 29 (1987).*

Bingo games

The income tax regulations provide that bingo games conducted by a church do not constitute an unrelated trade or business so long as such games are legal under state or local law and bingo games ordinarily are not carried out on a commercial basis by for-profit organizations in the same state. The regulations further specify that

> normally, the entire state will constitute the appropriate jurisdiction for determining whether bingo games are ordinarily carried out on a commercial basis. However, if state law permits local jurisdictions to determine whether bingo games may be conducted by for-profit organizations, or if state law limits or confines the conduct of bingo games by for-profit organizations to specific local jurisdictions, then the local jurisdiction will constitute the appropriate jurisdiction for determining whether bingo games are ordinarily carried out on a commercial basis.

The regulations give the following example, which is preceded by the comment that "it is assumed that the bingo games referred to are operated by individuals who are compensated for their services. Accordingly, none of the bingo games would be excluded from the term 'unrelated trade or business' under section 513(a)(1)."

EXAMPLE. Church Z, a tax-exempt organization, conducts weekly bingo games in State O. State and local laws in State O expressly provide that bingo games may be conducted by tax-exempt organizations. Bingo games are not conducted in State O by any for-profit businesses. Since Z's bingo games are not conducted in violation of state or local law and are not the type of activity ordinarily carried out on a commercial basis in State O, Z's bingo games do not constitute unrelated trade or business.

Rental income, gains from the sale of property, dividends, royalties, and interest income

Section 512(b) exempts dividends, interest, annuities, royalties, capital gains and losses, and rents from real property from the tax on unrelated business income. These exemptions are subject to the following two limitations.

1. Debt-financed property

Section 514 of the tax code states that income from dividends, interest, annuities, royalties, rents, and capital gains and losses must be included in the definition of unrelated business taxable income to the extent it derives from *debt-financed property*. The amount of income included is proportionate to the debt on the property.

Debt-financed property is any property held to produce income and that is subject to an "acquisition indebtedness," such as a mortgage, at any time during the tax year. *IRC 514(b).*

Income derived from debt-financed property generally is included in unrelated business taxable income unless the property falls within one of the following exceptions.

The 85 percent rule. Substantially all (85 percent or more) of the property is used for exempt purposes. *Treas. Reg. § 1.514(b)-1(b)(1).* Property is not used for exempt purposes merely because income derived from the property is expended for exempt purposes. If less than 85 percent of the use of property is devoted to exempt purposes, only that part of the property that is not used to further exempt purposes is treated as unrelated debt-financed property.

> **EXAMPLE.** A church owns a building that is used 90 percent of the time for religious purposes. The building is sold for $300,000. At the time of sale, the building has an existing mortgage debt of $150,000. In general, when a charity sells debt-financed property, it must include, in computing unrelated business taxable income, a percentage of any gain or loss. The percentage is that of the highest acquisition indebtedness with respect to the property during the 12-month period preceding the date of disposition, in relation to the property's average adjusted basis. However, since the church's property was used at least 85 percent of the time for exempt purposes, the gain from the sale of the property is not subject to the unrelated business income tax.

> **EXAMPLE.** A church rents a room to a local government agency. The room comprises 8 percent of the church building.

The remainder of the church's property is used for religious purposes. While rental income from debt-financed property generally is subject to the unrelated business income tax, an exception is made for debt-financed property that is used at least 85 percent of the time for exempt purposes.

Income taken into account. Income from debt-financed property is otherwise taken into account in computing the gross income of any unrelated trade or business.

Volunteer workers. The property is used in a trade or business that is substantially supported by volunteer workers; that is carried on primarily for the convenience of its members, students, or employees; or that involves the selling of merchandise, substantially all of which has been received by the organization as gifts or contributions. *IRC 514(b)(1).*

The neighborhood land rule—general application. The tax code specifies that if an exempt organization acquires real property mainly to use it for exempt purposes within 10 years, it will not be treated as debt-financed property if it is in the neighborhood of other property that the organization uses for exempt purposes and if the intent to use the property for exempt purposes within 10 years is not abandoned. This exception to the definition of debt-financed property is referred to as the "neighborhood land rule." *IRC 514(b)(3).*

The neighborhood land rule does not apply to property 10 years after its acquisition. Further, the rule applies after the first five years only if the organization satisfies the IRS that use of the land for exempt purposes is reasonably certain before the 10-year period expires. The organization need not show binding contracts to satisfy this requirement; but it must have a definite plan detailing a specific improvement and a completion date, and it must show some affirmative action toward the fulfillment of the plan. This information should be forwarded to the following address for a ruling at least 90 days before the end of the fifth year after acquisition of the land:

> Internal Revenue Service
> Commissioner, TE/GE
> Attention: TEORA
> P.O. Box 120, Ben Franklin Station
> Washington, DC 20044

The income tax regulations authorize the IRS to grant a reasonable extension of time for requesting the ruling if the organization can show good cause. *Treas. Reg. § 1.9100-1.* If the neighborhood land rule does not apply because the acquired land is not in the neighborhood of other land used for an organization's exempt purposes or because the organization fails to establish after the first five years of the 10-year period that the property will be used for exempt purposes, but the land is used eventually by the organization for its exempt purposes within the 10-year period, the property is not treated as debt-financed property for any period before the conversion.

The neighborhood land rule—application to churches. The neighborhood land rule applies to churches and associations and conventions of churches, but with two important differences:

- the period during which the organization must demonstrate the intent to use the acquired property for exempt purposes is increased from 10 to 15 years, and
- the land need not be in the "neighborhood" of other property of the organization that is used for exempt purposes.

As a result, if a church or an association or convention of churches acquires real property for the primary purpose of using the land in the exercise or performance of its exempt purposes, beginning within 15 years after the time of acquisition, the property is not treated as debt-financed property as long as the organization does not abandon its intent to use the land in this manner within the 15-year period.

This exception for a church or association or convention of churches does not apply to any property after the 15-year period expires. Further, this rule will apply after the first five years of the 15-year period only if the church or convention or association of churches establishes to the satisfaction of the IRS that use of the acquired land in furtherance of the organization's exempt purposes is reasonably certain before the 15-year period expires. *IRS Letter Ruling 9603019.*

If a church or an association or convention of churches (for the period after the first five years of the 15-year period) cannot establish to the satisfaction of the IRS that use of acquired property for its exempt purpose is reasonably certain within the 15-year period, but the land is, in fact, converted to an exempt use within the 15-year period, the land is not to be treated as debt-financed property for any period before the conversion. The same rule for demolition or removal of structures (discussed below) applies to a church or an association or convention of churches.

> **EXAMPLE.** A church purchased an adjacent apartment building with the intent to demolish it after the mortgage loan was paid off and to build a parking lot for the additional spaces needed for its congregation. Rental income received from the apartment building would be used to help defray the cost of demolition and paving. The church expected that in the next few years after the mortgage was paid off, it would use the parking lot exclusively for its members. The church asked the IRS for a ruling that the neighborhood land rule resulted in none of the rental income being subject to the unrelated business income tax.
>
> The IRS agreed and granted the ruling. It noted that rental income from debt-financed property generally is subject to the unrelated business income tax. But under the neighborhood land rule, if a church acquires property for the purpose of using it in the exercise of its exempt purpose within 15 years of the time of acquisition, the property will not be treated as debt-financed property so long as the church does not abandon its intent to use the land in such

APPLYING THE NEIGHBORHOOD LAND RULE TO CHURCHES

Section 514 provides a special "neighborhood land rule" that exempts rents from debt-financed church property from the unrelated business income tax so long as a church

- has a definite plan to use the land for exempt purposes within 15 years, including a "specific improvement and a completion date, and some affirmative action toward the fulfillment of such a plan";
- informs the IRS of its plan at least 90 days before the end of the fifth year after acquiring the land, and requests a ruling;
- does not abandon its intent during the 15 years following acquisition; and
- demolishes any structures on the property as part of its plans to use the property for exempt purposes.

a manner within the 15-year period. Further, the neighborhood land rule applies after the first five years of the 15-year period only if the church establishes to the satisfaction of the IRS that future use of the acquired land in furtherance of its exempt purpose before the expiration of the 15-year period is reasonably certain. This information must be forwarded to the IRS for a ruling at least 90 days before the end of the fifth year after acquisition of the land.

The IRS concluded: "The property located adjacent to the church was acquired within the five years of the date of the ruling request. The church will be using the property after its conversion to a parking lot in accordance to its exempt purpose. Since the church has a definite plan, and has taken some affirmative action toward the fulfillment of such a plan, it is reasonably certain that future use will be made of the property in furtherance of the church's exempt purpose before the expiration of the 15-year period. Accordingly, we rule that the property located adjacent to the church will not be treated as debt-financed property so long as the church does not abandon its intent to use the land in furtherance of its exempt purpose within the 15-year period." *IRS Letter Ruling 7850071 (1978).*

EXAMPLE. A church purchased two adjacent parcels of land with debt financing. The land had no structures other than a ground-level parking lot. The church used the land in part for church parking. It also leased the property to a company under a 10-year lease for public parking during periods (most of the week) when the church was not in session. The rent payments were a flat fee. The lessee was responsible for paving, lighting, and cleaning.

The church purchased the land for church expansion. Its proposed plans called for constructing a building that would be used for church activities. The church submitted a letter to the IRS asking for a ruling that the property would be exempt from the unrelated business income tax based on the neighborhood land rule.

The IRS issued a ruling in which it concluded: "You purchased land with debt financing and leased it to a third party for operating a parking lot. The amounts derived appear to constitute rents from real property excepted from unrelated business taxable income . . . unless the land is debt-financed property. You have requested a ruling that the neighborhood land rule applies to exempt the land from the definition of debt-financed property for 15 years from acquisition. You submitted your ruling request in a timely manner, and the information submitted satisfies us that it is reasonably certain that you will use the land in an exempt purpose or function within 15 years of acquisition. Accordingly, we rule that it is reasonably certain that the land will be used for an exempt purpose within 15 years of its acquisition, and that the properties are exempt from the debt-financed property provisions of the tax code as a result of the neighborhood land rule for 15 years beginning with the dates that you acquired them." *IRS Letter Ruling 200537037 (2005).*

EXAMPLE. A church purchased a tract of land one mile from it's main location to facilitate future programs and activities. The property included two buildings. The church developed a plan to construct an additional building on the property for church activities. Architectural plans were approved, and a formal fund-raising campaign was launched. The church asked the IRS for a ruling to the effect that rental income it received from the two buildings on the property was exempt from the unrelated business income tax as a result of the neighborhood land rule. The IRS concluded that the neighborhood land rule applied: "You have requested a ruling that the neighborhood land rule applies to exempt the land from the definition of debt-financed property for 15 years from acquisition. You submitted your ruling request in a timely manner, and the information submitted indicates that it is reasonably certain that you will use the land in an exempt purpose or function within 15 years of acquisition. Accordingly, we rule that it is reasonably certain that the land will be used for an exempt purpose within 15 years of its acquisition, and that the properties are exempt from the debt-financed property provisions of sections 512(b)(4) and 514 of the Code as a result of the neighborhood land rule under section 514(b)(3) for 15 years beginning with the dates that you acquired them."

The IRS ruling stressed: "The regulations provide that in order to satisfy the IRS that future use of the acquired land in furtherance of the organization's exempt purpose before the expiration of the relevant period is reasonably certain, the organization does not necessarily have to show binding contracts. However, it must at least have a definite plan detailing a specific improvement

and a completion date, and some affirmative action toward the fulfillment of such a plan. This information shall be forwarded to the Commissioner of Internal Revenue . . . for a ruling at least 90 days before the end of the fifth year after acquisition of the land. . . . [The neighborhood land rule] shall apply after the first 5 years of the 15-year period only if the church or association or convention of churches establishes to the satisfaction of the Commissioner that use of the acquired land in furtherance of the organization's exempt purpose before the expiration of the 15-year period is reasonably certain." *IRS Letter Ruling 200821036.*

EXAMPLE. A church purchased property for future expansion. The property was paid for with a loan secured by a mortgage on the property. For the first five years, the church rented the property to four separate tenants under three-year leases. Four years after the purchase, the church's long-range planning committee awarded a contract to an architectural firm to conduct a space-and-facilities study of the property to determine how it could be used to fulfill long-range needs. One year later, the committee accepted the firm's new plan. The scheduled completion date for the renovation and conversion of the property was 12 years after purchase.

According to the plan, the church would build a retreat center on the property. The first floor would provide spaces for classes, lectures, study groups, and other events. The second floor would provide private apartments for visiting pastors and retreat guests. Although the existing structure on property was not a registered historic landmark, any changes were subject to local review and approval. Since the local review board preferred renovation to demolition of historic structures, the plan recommended refurbishing the front, adding new construction, and only demolishing the rear of the existing building.

Within 90 days prior to the fifth year after acquisition of the property, the church submitted a request to the IRS for a ruling that the rental income from its debt-financed property would be exempt from the unrelated business income tax as a result of the neighborhood land rule. The IRS ruled that the neighborhood land rule did not apply after the fifth year:

To benefit from the neighborhood land rule, you must meet the requirements set forth in . . . the regulations. First, you must establish with reasonable certainty that you will use the property to further your exempt purpose before the 15-year expiration date. To make this showing, you must forward a definite plan detailing a specific improvement, a completion date and some affirmative action toward the fulfillment of the plan to the IRS with a request for a ruling at least 90 days before the end of the fifth year after acquiring the property. You forwarded this ruling request within the time specified and submitted definite plans detailing the specific improvements you will make and actions you have taken, along with an estimated completion date set well before the expiration of the 15-year time period.

However, the special rules for churches . . . reference additional limitations . . . with regard to the structures on property subject to the neighborhood land rule. The limitations apply the rule to the land and the existing structure on the date of acquisition only if the intended future use of the land requires that you demolish or remove the structure in order to use the land to further your exempt purposes. The rule does not apply to structures erected on the land after acquisition.

Therefore, since you did not abandon your intent to demolish the structure on your property for the first five years, the neighborhood land rule will exclude income produced by your property from tax. However, on the sixth year after acquisition, your long range planning committee accepted the architectural firm's plan, which does not require you to demolish or remove the original structures to use the property to further your exempt purposes. . . . When you accepted the plan, you abandoned your intent to demolish or remove all of the original structure to use the land to further your exempt purposes. Therefore, for the sixth and subsequent years after acquisition, the neighborhood land rule will not exclude income produced by your property from tax as unrelated business income. IRS Letter Ruling 201020022.

EXAMPLE. A church purchased land through the use of debt financing in the neighborhood of its existing facility in order to build a larger facility. The land consisted of several acres of land that was undeveloped with the exception of two small buildings. The church borrowed funds to buy the land. It rented a portion of the property for cattle grazing and also received royalty payments from a lease of mineral rights to an oil company. The church asked the IRS for a ruling that the neighborhood land rule applied, and therefore the rental and royalty income the church received from its debt-financed property was not subject to the unrelated business income tax.

The IRS noted that the church had submitted its ruling request in a timely manner, at least 90 days prior to five years after the date of acquisition of the land at issue. It further noted that "within the required period, you have taken steps to convert the land to your exempt use. You have demolished structures that existed on the land at the time of acquisition. You have constructed a new church campus of buildings and put it into use for your congregation. You have put your former location up for sale. While the property allows room for future growth, your church campus is substantially complete and converted to exempt use within 15 years of the land acquisition. Thus, your property will not be treated as debt-financed land . . . because you qualify for the exception under the neighborhood land special rule for churches."

Since the church's property is not treated as debt-financed land for 15 years from the date of acquisition, "any rents or royalties received during that time period will not be treated as unrelated business taxable income," and it is "not subject to imposition of tax on unrelated business income for such rents or royalties for the stated period."

The IRS concluded: "Based on the information you have submitted, it is reasonably certain that the debt-financed land will be used for an exempt church purpose within 15 years of its acquisition. Therefore, the property is exempt from the debt-financed property unrelated business taxable income provisions of [the tax code] as a result of the neighborhood land rule exception . . . for 15 years beginning on the date the land was acquired." *IRS Letter Ruling 201206018.*

EXAMPLE. A church congregation is growing rapidly. The church purchases property as a site for a future facility. The property consists of 10 acres of land and a building. The purchase price was $100,000. The church plans to construct a new sanctuary on the property within three years. The church later changes its plans and purchases a different tract of land. It sells the 10-acre tract for $150,000. At the time of sale, the property had a mortgage debt of $80,000. Is the gain from the sale of this property subject to the unrelated business income tax? No, because of the neighborhood land rule. If a church acquires real property with the intention of using the land for exempt purposes within 15 years, it will not be treated as debt-financed property, regardless of whether it is in the neighborhood of other property that the church uses for exempt purposes. As noted below, this rule applies only if the church intends to demolish any existing structures and use the land for exempt purposes within 15 years and this intent is not abandoned.

EXAMPLE. A church purchases a home at the edge of its parking lot so it can later demolish the home to expand the parking lot if the need arises. The home cost $100,000, and the church paid this amount without incurring any indebtedness. The church begins renting the home to a family. Is rental income received by the church subject to the unrelated business income tax? The answer is no. Rental income is exempted from the definition of unrelated business income, except for rental income received from the rental of debt-financed property. Since the home is not debt-financed, the rental income is not taxable.

EXAMPLE. Same facts as the previous example, except that the church borrowed $75,000 from a bank to purchase the home. While rental income from debt-financed property generally is subject to the unrelated business income tax, an exception is made if a church intends to use the property for exempt purposes within 15 years (and this exempt use will require the demolition of any structure on the property). This is the so-called neighborhood land rule. Note, however, that the neighborhood land rule applies after the first five years following acquisition of the property only if the church satisfies the IRS that use of the land for exempt purposes is reasonably certain before the 15-year period expires. The church need not show binding contracts to satisfy this requirement; but it must have a definite plan detailing a specific improvement and a completion date, and it must show some affirmative action toward the fulfillment of the plan. This information should be forwarded to the IRS (to the address noted above) for a ruling at least 90 days before the end of the fifth year after acquisition of the property.

The demolition rule. The neighborhood land rule applies to any structure on the land when acquired, only so long as the intended future use of the land in furtherance of the organization's exempt purpose requires that the structure be *demolished or removed* in order to use the land in this manner. Thus, during the first five years after acquisition (and for later years if there is a favorable ruling), improved property is not debt-financed so long as the organization does not abandon its intent to demolish the existing structures and use the land in furtherance of its exempt purpose. If an actual demolition of these structures occurs, the use made of the land need not be the one originally intended as long as its use furthers the organization's exempt purpose.

The neighborhood land rule does not apply to structures erected on land after its acquisition.

When the neighborhood land rule does not initially apply, but the land is used eventually for exempt purposes, a refund or credit of any overpaid taxes will be allowed for a prior tax year. A claim must be filed within one year after the close of the tax year in which the property is actually used for exempt purposes.

The tax regulations contain the following examples illustrating the demolition rule. Note that these examples all involve a university, so the 10-year rule applies. In the case of a church, the 10-year rule is increased to 15 years.

> **EXAMPLE.** An exempt university acquires a contiguous tract of land on which there is an apartment building. The university intends to demolish the apartment building and build classrooms and does not abandon this intent during the first four years after acquisition. In the fifth year after acquisition it abandons the intent to demolish and sells the apartment building. Under these circumstances, such property is not debt-financed property for the first four years after acquisition even though there was no eventual demolition or use made of such land in furtherance of the university's exempt purpose However, such property is debt-financed property as of the time in the fifth year that the intent to demolish the building is abandoned and any gain on the sale of the property is subject to section 514.

> **EXAMPLE.** Assume the facts as stated in the previous example except that the university did not abandon its intent to demolish the existing building and construct a classroom building until the eighth year after acquisition when it sells the property. Assume further that the university did not receive a favorable ruling [from

the IRS that future use of the acquired land in furtherance of the organization's exempt purpose before the expiration of the 10-year period is reasonably certain]. Under these circumstances, the building is debt-financed property for the sixth, seventh, and eighth years. It is not, however, treated as debt-financed property for the first five years after acquisition.

> **EXAMPLE.** Assume the facts as stated in the previous example except that the university received a favorable ruling [from the IRS that future use of the acquired land in furtherance of the organization's exempt purpose before the expiration of the 10-year period is reasonably certain]. Under these circumstances, the building is not debt-financed property for the first seven years after acquisition. It only becomes debt-financed property as of the time in the eighth year when the university abandoned its intent to demolish the existing structure.

> **EXAMPLE.** Assume that a university acquired a contiguous tract of land containing an office building for the principal purpose of demolishing the office building and building a modern dormitory. Five years later the dormitory has not been constructed, and the university has failed to satisfy the IRS that the office building will be demolished and the land will be used in furtherance of its exempt purpose and consequently has failed to obtain a favorable ruling [from the IRS that future use of the acquired land in furtherance of the organization's exempt purpose before the expiration of the 10-year period is reasonably certain]. In the ninth taxable year after acquisition the university converts the office building into an administration building. Under these circumstances, during the sixth, seventh, and eighth years after acquisition, the office building is treated as debt-financed property because the office building was not demolished or removed. Therefore, the income derived from such property during these years shall be subject to the tax on unrelated business income.

> **EXAMPLE.** Assume the facts as stated in the previous example except that instead of converting the office building to an administration building, the university demolishes the office building in the ninth taxable year after acquisition and then constructs a new administration building. Under these circumstances, the land would not be considered debt-financed property for any period following the acquisition, and the university would be entitled to a refund of taxes paid on the income derived from such property for the sixth through eighth taxable years after the acquisition.

2. Controlled organizations

The second limitation on the exemption of dividends, interest, annuities, royalties, capital gains and losses, and rents from the tax on unrelated business income relates to the interest, annuities, royalties, and rents of organizations that are controlled by a tax-exempt organization. Under section 512(b)(13) of the tax code, the exclusion of interest, annuities, royalties, and rents from the definition of unrelated business income does not apply if such amounts are derived from organizations that are controlled by a church or other tax-exempt organization. When a tax-exempt organization controls another organization, the interest, annuities, royalties, and rents from the controlled organization are taxable to the controlling organization at a specific ratio, depending on whether the controlled organization is exempt or nonexempt. All deductions directly connected with amounts included in an organization's gross income under this provision are allowed.

The organization from which the interest, annuities, royalties, and rents are received is called the *controlled organization*, and the exempt organization receiving these amounts is called the *controlling organization*. In the case of a nonstock organization, the term "control" means that at least 80 percent of the directors or trustees of such organization are either representatives of or directly or indirectly controlled by the controlling organization. A trustee or director is controlled by an exempt organization if the organization has the power to remove the trustee or director and designate a new trustee or director.

When the controlled organization is an exempt organization, the interest, annuities, royalties, and rents received by the controlling organization are includable in its unrelated business taxable income in the same ratio as the ratio of the controlled organization's unrelated business taxable income to its taxable income determined as if the exempt controlled organization were not tax-exempt.

Rental income from parking lots and storage units

Some churches rent spaces in their parking lot to patrons of neighboring businesses during the week. Other churches have constructed storage units on their property and rent excess units to the public. Is the rental income from such activities subject to the unrelated business income tax? Does it matter that the church owns the property debt-free? The answer to these questions is contained in the following tax regulation:

> Payments for the use or occupancy of rooms and other space where services are also rendered to the occupant, such as for the use or occupancy of rooms or other quarters in hotels, boarding houses, or apartment houses furnishing hotel services, or in tourist camps or tourist homes, motor courts or motels, or for the use or occupancy of space in parking lots, warehouses, or storage garages, do not constitute rent from real property. Generally, services are considered rendered to the occupant if they are primarily for his convenience and are other than those usually or customarily rendered in connection with the rental of rooms or other space for occupancy only. The supplying of maid service, for example, constitutes such service; whereas the furnishing of heat and light, the cleaning of public entrances, exits, stairways, and lobbies, the collection of trash, etc., are not considered as services rendered to the occupant. Payments for the use or occupancy of entire private residences or living quarters in duplex or multiple housing units, of offices in any office building, etc., are generally rent from real property. Treas. Reg. 1.512(b)-1(c)(5).

This regulation clearly removes payments for the use of parking lot spaces from the definition of "rental income," and therefore such payments are not exempt from unrelated business income tax on that basis. In addition, the IRS has applied this regulation to rental income from storage units. Consider the following example.

EXAMPLE. A charity provided storage rental units on its property. It insisted that the rental income it earned was not taxable, since the property was owned debt-free.

The IRS disagreed: "Although rents from real and personal property are generally considered to be excluded from the computations to determine an organization's unrelated business income pursuant to section 1.512(b)-1(c)(2)(i) of the regulations, section 1.512(b)-1(c)(5) provides specifically that payments for the use or occupancy of space in parking lots, warehouses, or storage garages does not constitute rent from real property. Although income from the use or occupancy of rooms (such as in hotels, boarding houses, and apartment houses furnishing hotel services) is considered to be rent within the meaning of section 1.512(b)-1(c)(2)(i) only if services are not rendered to the occupant, the mere use or occupancy of space in parking lots, warehouses, and storage garages is considered to be sufficient rendering of services for section 1.512(b)-1(c)(5) to be applicable. Since [the charity's] storage activity is precisely described in section 1.512(b)-1(c)(5), income from its rental of the storage space would not be excluded from the computation of unrelated business income, and the activity would qualify as an unrelated trade or business." *IRS Letter Rulings 9822006 and 9821067.*

The IRS *Tax Guide for Churches and Religious Organizations* (Publication 1828) clarifies that income from the rental of spaces in a church parking lot is taxable only if spaces are used by the general public. In the unlikely event that a church charges its own members a fee for using its parking lot, these payments would not be taxable. The Guide contains the following paragraph:

> If a church owns a parking lot that is used by church members and visitors while attending church services, any parking fee paid to the church would not be subject to UBIT. However, if a church operates a parking lot that is used by members of the general public, parking fees would be taxable, as this activity would not be substantially related to the church's exempt purpose, and parking fees are not treated as rent from real property. If the church enters into a lease with a third party who operates the church's parking lot and pays rent to the church, such payments would not be subject to tax, as they would constitute rent from real property.

Rental income from communications towers on church property

Many churches allow telecommunications companies to install towers or antennae on their property in exchange for a monthly or annual rental fee. Are such fees subject to the unrelated business

RENTING CHURCH BUILDINGS
TO OUTSIDE GROUPS

Before renting buildings on church-owned property, church leaders should be familiar with

- the debt-financed property exception to the exemption of rental income from the unrelated business income tax;
- the eligibility requirements for application of the neighborhood land rule; and
- the demolition rule.

income tax? In 1998 the IRS said no. It reasoned that "rentals from the lease of real property" were exempt from the unrelated business income tax, and this exemption should apply to any items (including communications towers) permanently affixed to real estate. *IRS Letter Ruling 9816027.*

In 2001 the IRS revoked its 1998 ruling and concluded that rents received by charities for the use of communications towers or antennae constructed on their property *are* subject to the unrelated business income tax. It conceded that the tax code exempts rents from real property from the unrelated business income tax. But it concluded that "for purposes of the unrelated business income tax, broadcasting towers are considered personal property," and so rental income from the use of such towers is not exempt from the unrelated business income tax on the basis of the rental of real estate exception. The IRS limited its ruling to "receipts attributable solely to the rental of the broadcasting tower." This suggests that the rental of a specified area of *church property* on which a communications tower is erected *may* be partially or wholly exempt from the unrelated business income tax. The IRS did not specifically address this issue in its 2001 ruling. *IRS Letter Ruling 200104031.*

Qualified sponsorship activities
Soliciting and receiving qualified sponsorship payments is not an unrelated trade or business, and the payments are not subject to unrelated business income tax. A qualified sponsorship payment is any payment made by a person engaged in a trade or business for which the person will receive no substantial benefit other than the use or acknowledgment of the business name, logo, or product lines in connection with the organization's activities. "Use or acknowledgment" does not include advertising the sponsor's products or services.

The organization's activities include all its activities, regardless of whether related to its exempt purposes. For example: if, in return for

receiving a sponsorship payment, an organization promises to use the sponsor's name or logo in acknowledging the sponsor's support for an educational or fund-raising event, the payment is a qualified sponsorship payment and is not subject to the unrelated business income tax. Providing facilities, services, or other privileges (e.g., pro-am playing spots in golf tournaments, or receptions for major donors) to a sponsor or the sponsor's designees in connection with a sponsorship payment does not affect whether the payment is a qualified sponsorship payment. Instead, providing these goods or services is treated as a separate transaction in determining whether the organization has unrelated business income from the event. Generally, if the services or facilities are not a substantial benefit or if providing them is a related business activity, the payments will not be subject to the unrelated business income tax.

If part of a payment would be a qualified sponsorship payment if paid separately, that part is treated as a separate payment. For example, if a sponsorship payment entitles the sponsor to both product advertising and the use or acknowledgment of the sponsor's name or logo by the organization, then the unrelated business income tax does not apply to the part of the payment that is more than the fair market value of the product advertising. A payment is not a qualified sponsorship payment if, in return, the organization advertises the sponsor's products or services.

Advertising includes:

- messages containing qualitative or comparative language, price information, or other indications of savings or value;
- endorsements; and
- inducements to purchase, sell, or use the products or services.

The use of promotional logos or slogans that are an established part of the sponsor's identity is not, by itself, advertising. In addition, mere distribution or display of a sponsor's product by the organization to the public at a sponsored event, whether for free or for remuneration, is considered use or acknowledgment of the product rather than advertising.

A payment is not a qualified sponsorship payment if its amount is contingent, by contract or otherwise, upon the level of attendance at one or more events, broadcast ratings, or other factors indicating the degree of public exposure to one or more events. However, the fact that a sponsorship payment is contingent upon an event actually taking place or being broadcast does not, by itself, affect whether a payment qualifies.

A payment is not a qualified sponsorship payment if it entitles the payer to the use or acknowledgment of the business name, logo, or product lines in the organization's periodical. For this purpose, a periodical is any regularly scheduled and printed material (for example, a monthly journal) published by or on behalf of the organization. It does not include material that is related to and primarily distributed in connection with a specific event conducted by the organization (such as a program or brochure distributed at a sponsored event).

The treatment of payments that entitle the payer to the depiction of the payer's name, logo, or products in an organization's periodical is determined under the rules that apply to advertising activities.

A trade or business that consists of selling merchandise, substantially all of which the organization received as gifts or contributions, is not an unrelated trade or business. For example, a thrift shop operated by a tax-exempt organization that sells donated clothes and books to the general public, with the proceeds going to the exempt organization, is not an unrelated trade or business.

Works made for hire

Many churches have creative employees on staff who create literary or musical works in their church office, using church equipment, in the course of their employment. Under the so-called "work for hire" doctrine, the employer owns the copyright on such works unless the parties have agreed otherwise in a signed writing. What if a church refuses to renounce its copyright ownership in a work for hire, and instead sells it to an outside company? Is the sales price taxable to the church as unrelated business income? This is a relevant question for any church that chooses to retain the copyright ownership in works created by employees in the scope of their employment. The IRS addressed this issue in a private letter ruling.

A church employee designed a database-management software program for his church within the scope of his employment. Quite unexpectedly, several other churches learned of the program and wanted to use it, and for-profit entities began making inquiries about purchasing the intellectual property rights to it.

The church treated the program as a work for hire, since it was created by its employee in the scope of his employment. As a result, the church regarded itself to own the copyright in the work. The church decided to sell its intellectual property rights in the program to a for-profit company for a one-time cash payment. The church reserved a perpetual license to use the program at no cost.

Following the sale of the intellectual property rights in the program, the church had no further duties in developing the program, and the sales agreement prohibited the church from engaging in any further development relating to the program except as a user.

The church was concerned that the price it received from the sale of the software might be subject to the unrelated business income tax. As a result, it asked the IRS for a private letter ruling addressing the application of UBIT to the sales proceeds. In its ruling request, the church represented that it did not plan to engage in the future sale of computer software; the sale of the intellectual property

rights in the program was a one-time only transaction; and the sale of intellectual property rights to computer software will not be an ongoing income-producing activity. The church asked the IRS to confirm that income it received from the sale of the intellectual property rights in the software did not constitute unrelated business income and, therefore, was not subject to unrelated business income taxation.

The IRS began its ruling by observing:

> Section 511 [of the tax code] imposes a tax on unrelated business income of . . . tax-exempt organizations. Under section 512, unrelated business taxable income includes gross income derived from an unrelated trade or business activity or transaction that a tax-exempt organization carries on regularly. Further [the regulations specify that] income derived from an activity is unrelated business taxable income, if the activity (1) is a trade or business; (2) is regularly carried on; and (3) is not substantially related to the tax-exempt organization's exercise or performance of its tax-exempt functions or purpose, a three part test. The activity must meet all three tests before income from the activity is taxable under section 512.

The IRS proceeded to apply each of these requirements to the facts of this case.

Trade or business

Did the church's sale of its intellectual property rights in the software program constitute a trade or business? The IRS noted that the income tax regulations specify that "any activity carried on for the production of income from the sale of goods or the performance of services, is a trade or business." The IRS concluded that "because you earned income from the sale of the entire intellectual property rights . . . you performed or carried on a trade or business."

Regularly carried on

Only income from a trade or business that is regularly carried on is subject to the unrelated business income tax. Was the church's trade or business "regularly carried on"? The IRS said no:

> [The income tax regulations] define "regularly carried on" to mean a trade or business activity frequently and continuously pursued by a tax-exempt organization in a manner generally similar to comparable commercial activities of non-exempt organizations. . . . Your sale of the intellectual property rights is not a continuous and consistent income producing activity because you performed or carried on this activity once. You have not developed and sold intellectual property rights to computer software in the past. Further, the sales agreement restricts you from further developing the software. Finally, you represent that you do not plan to engage in the future sale of computer software; that the sale of the intellectual property rights was a one-time only transaction; and that the sale of intellectual property rights

to computer software will not be an ongoing income producing activity by you. Thus, your sale of the intellectual property rights failed to meet the second test of [the definition of unrelated business taxable income].

Not substantially related to an exempt purpose

The third element in the definition of unrelated business taxable income is that the income-generating activity is not substantially related to the tax-exempt organization's exercise or performance of its tax-exempt functions or purpose. The IRS noted that income from an activity is taxable as unrelated business income if the activity meets all three elements of the definition of unrelated business taxable income. It concluded: "Because your sale of the intellectual property rights did not meet the [regularly carried on] test, though it met the trade or business activity test, it is not necessary for us to continue with the consideration on whether your sale of the software is not substantially related to your tax-exempt purpose. Having failed one of the tests . . . the income from your sale of the software is not taxable."

Conclusions

While the one who creates a work generally is its author and the initial owner of the copyright in the work, section 201(b) of the Copyright Act specifies that "in the case of a work made for hire, the employer or other person for whom the work was prepared is considered the author . . . and, unless the parties have expressly agreed otherwise in a written instrument signed by them, owns all of the rights comprised in the copyright."

The Copyright Act defines a "work made for hire" as "a work prepared by an employee within the scope of his or her employment." The Act does not define the scope of employment. However, the United States Supreme Court has found that Congress intended to incorporate common law agency principles, as defined in the Restatement (Second) of Agency, to decide whether an employee has created a work within the scope of his or her employment for purposes of the work made for hire doctrine. Under the Restatement (Second) of Agency § 228(1), a work is prepared within the scope of one's employment if it meets a three-prong test:

(1) it is the kind of work the author is employed to perform;
(2) the creation of the work occurred substantially within authorized work hours and space; and
(3) the creation of the work was actuated, at least in part, by a purpose to serve the employer.

Section 201(b) of the Copyright Act specifies that the employer owns the copyright in a work for hire unless the parties have expressly agreed otherwise in a written instrument signed by them. This provision recognizes a presumption that employers are the authors of works made for hire and own the copyright in such works.

Church leaders should understand that the church has the following two options in handling works for hire created by employees within the scope of their employment and that each option involves legal and tax issues that need to be addressed:

The church retains copyright ownership in works for hire. Many churches do not relinquish copyright ownership in works for hire, either intentionally or inadvertently through the execution of an inadequate signed, written agreement (see below). There are a number of issues to consider in such cases, including the following:

(1) *Inurement.* One of the conditions for exemption from federal income taxation under section 501(c)(3) of the federal tax code is that none of a church's assets inures to the personal benefit of any individual other than as reasonable compensation for services. If the church pays a "bonus" or some other form of taxable compensation to the employee-author of a work for hire, this raises the possibility of prohibited inurement.

(2) *Unrelated business taxable income.* Churches that elect to retain the copyright in a work for hire can sell the work, or they can retain it and receive royalties. In either case, the church may be required to pay the unrelated business income tax and file Form 990-T with the IRS. The church involved in the IRS ruling summarized in this article chose to retain the copyright in the work for hire created by one of its employees, and it sold the rights in the work to a for-profit company. According to the IRS, this did not trigger the unrelated business income tax, since it was a one-time sale that did not satisfy the "regularly carried on" element of the definition of unrelated business income.

If the church instead had elected to receive periodic royalties in lieu of a lump sum amount as a result of its sale of the work to the for-profit company, it is more likely (through not certain) that the unrelated business income tax would apply. In this regard, note that rents from real property, royalties, capital gains, and interest and dividends are not subject to the unrelated business income tax unless financed with borrowed money.

(3) *The "operational test" under section 501(c)(3).* To be exempt from federal income taxes, section 501(c)(3) of the tax code requires that a church be "operated exclusively" for exempt purposes. This requirement is referred to as the operational test. The income tax regulations specify that an organization will be regarded as operated exclusively for one or more exempt purposes only if it engages primarily in activities that accomplish one or more of the exempt purposes specified in section 501(c)(3) and if no more than an insubstantial part of its activities are not in furtherance of an exempt purpose.

If a church receives a substantial amount of royalties through the publication and sale of a work for hire in which it retained the copyright, an argument could be made that this amounts to a substantial nonexempt function that jeopardizes its tax-exempt status.

The church relinquishes copyright ownership in works for hire with a signed agreement. An employer can relinquish its ownership of the copyright in a work for hire if it and the employee who created the work execute a written, signed agreement that recognizes the employee as the owner of "all of the rights comprised in the copyright" in the specified work.

If a policy or agreement purporting to vest copyright ownership in works for hire in the employees who create them fails to comply with the requirements for such an agreement under section 201(b) of the Copyright Act, then the church owns the copyright in such works and has the exclusive right to publish or distribute them. This outcome raises a number of issues, including the following: (1) the application of the federal unrelated business income tax to royalties received by the church from a publisher that publishes a work made for hire in which the church retains the copyright; and (2) the possible violation of the "operational test" for tax-exempt status under section 501(c)(3) of the federal tax code. Both of these issues are addressed below.

(1) *The church's tax-exempt status: inurement.* One of the conditions for exemption from federal income taxation under section 501(c)(3) of the federal tax code is that none of a church's assets inures to the personal benefit of any individual other than as reasonable compensation for services. If a church transfers the copyright in a work made for hire to an employee pursuant to a written agreement, this may be viewed by the IRS as private inurement of the church's resources to an individual. If so, this could jeopardize the church's tax-exempt status.

(2) *Excess benefit transactions.* Section 4958 of the tax code empowers the IRS to assess "intermediate sanctions" in the form of substantial excise taxes against insiders (called "disqualified persons") who benefit from an "excess benefit transaction." Generally, disqualified persons include officers or directors and their relatives. Intermediate sanctions may be assessed against ministers, and possibly members of a church board, in a couple of ways:

(a) Ministers and other church employees who retain ownership of a work made for hire because of a written agreement by which the church divests itself of copyright ownership may be subject to this penalty. The point is this—since the church is the legal owner of the copyright in a work made for hire, it is legally entitled to any income generated from sales of the work. By letting an employee retain the copyright, and all rights to royalties, the church may be viewed as paying additional compensation to the employee in this amount. If the work generates substantial income, then this may trigger

CHURCH COPYRIGHT POLICIES

Can the presumption of employer ownership of the copyright in works for hire be negated by a generic "copyright policy" that purports to apply to all employees? To illustrate, some churches have adopted a generic policy (often as part of a policy manual) that purports to disclaim church ownership of works created by employees even if the works meet the definition of works made for hire. The intent of these policies is to have a written agreement that comports with section 201(b). Do such policies overcome the presumption that the employer owns the copyright in works made for hire?

No court has addressed this question in a case involving a church, but a number of courts have ruled that generic copyright policies adopted by private universities that purport to relinquish the university's copyright ownership of professors' works for hire are not legally effective unless they strictly comply with the requirements of the Copyright Act. To illustrate, some courts have ruled that a generic policy in a policy manual is not effective to the extent that it is not signed by both parties and does not explicitly state that the employer is divesting its copyright ownership in specified works. According to these cases, a generic copyright policy will not divest a church of its copyright ownership in works for hire, since such a policy typically will fail one or more of the three requirements specified in section 201(b) of the Copyright Act (see above) for overcoming the presumption of employer ownership of such works.

intermediate sanctions if the employee's total compensation exceeds what is reasonable.

(b) If the church elects to retain the copyright in works made for hire but pays a minister additional compensation (e.g., a fee, or a percentage of royalties) in recognition of the effort involved in creating a work, this may result in excess compensation triggering intermediate sanctions if the amount of the additional compensation is substantial.

✿ **KEY POINT.** Several important legal and tax issues are associated with works for hire. If your church has one or more employees who write articles or books or compose music within the scope of their employment, legal counsel should be consulted.

4. COMPUTATION OF THE TAX

Section 511 imposes a tax on unrelated business taxable income. Section 512 defines "unrelated business taxable income" as the gross income derived from any unrelated trade or business regularly carried on less the deductions directly connected with such trade or business, both computed with the modifications set forth in section 512(b). To qualify as an allowable deduction, an expense must qualify as an income tax deduction and be directly connected with the carrying on of the unrelated trade or business. Expenses that are incurred to carry out both an unrelated trade or business and an organization's exempt functions must be allocated between the two uses on a reasonable basis. For example, if an exempt organization pays its president an annual salary of $60,000, and the president devotes approximately 10 percent of his time to an unrelated trade or business conducted by the organization, a deduction of $6,000 (10 percent of $60,000) would be allowable as a salary expense in computing unrelated business taxable income.

Expenses attributable to an unrelated trade or business that exploits exempt activities for commercial gain, such as the sale of commercial advertising in the periodical of an exempt organization, are deductible if (1) the unrelated trade or business is the kind carried on for profit by taxable organizations; (2) the activity being exploited is of a type normally carried on by taxable corporations; (3) the expenses exceed the income from or attributable to the exempt activity; and (4) the allocation of the excess expenses to the unrelated business does not result in a loss from the unrelated trade or business. Thus, the expenses are allocated first to the exempt activity to the extent of any income derived from or attributable to that activity. Any excess expense is allocated to the unrelated business, but only to the extent that the allocation does not result in a loss carryover or carryback to the unrelated business.

In addition to allowable deductions, an exempt organization is entitled to various modifications in computing unrelated business taxable income. These include (1) dividends, interest, annuities, and royalties, except with respect to the limitations that apply in connection with debt-financed property and controlled organizations; (2) rents from real property; (3) capital gains and losses; (4) charitable contributions of up to 10 percent of unrelated business taxable income; and (5) a specific deduction of $1,000.

The specific deduction is limited to $1,000 regardless of the number of unrelated businesses in which an organization is engaged. An exception is provided in the case of a diocese, province of a religious order, or a convention or association of churches that may claim for each parish, individual church, district, or other local unit a specific deduction limited to the lower of $1,000 or the gross income derived from an unrelated trade or business regularly carried on by the local unit. *Treas. Reg. § 1.512(b)(1)(h)(2).* This exception applies only to parishes, districts, or other local units that are not separate legal entities but are components of a larger entity (diocese, province, convention or association of churches) filing Form 990-T (the unrelated business income tax return). The parent organization must file a return reporting the unrelated business gross income and related deductions of all units that are not separate legal entities.

The local units cannot file separate returns. However, each local unit that is separately incorporated must file its own return and cannot include, or be included with, any other entity.

All tax-exempt organizations subject to the tax on unrelated business income must include, with this income, unrelated debt-financed income from debt-financed property. Once all available deductions and modifications have been considered and unrelated business taxable income is determined, the tax is computed by multiplying unrelated business taxable income by the corporate income tax rates.

5. RETURNS

An exempt organization subject to the tax on unrelated business income must file its income tax return on Form 990-T (Exempt Organization Business Income Tax Return) and attach any required supporting schedules and forms. The return is filed with the appropriate IRS Service Center.

This return is required only if the gross income from an unrelated trade or business is $1,000 or more—even if the church or charity will pay not tax because of expenses and the $1,000 deduction. The obligation to file the Form 990-T is in addition to the obligation to file any other required forms or returns. Form 990-T must be filed not later than the fifteenth day of the fifth month after the tax year ends (i.e., May 15 of the following year for an organization on a calendar-year basis).

A tax-exempt organization must make quarterly estimated tax payments if it expects an unrelated business income tax liability for the year to be $500 or more. Tax-exempt organizations should use Form 990-W (worksheet) to figure estimated taxes. For a calendar-year organization, quarterly estimated tax payments of one-fourth of the total tax liability are due by April 15, June 15, September 15, and December 15. If any due date falls on a Saturday, Sunday, or legal holiday, the payment is due on the next business day. Deposit quarterly tax payments electronically using the EFTPS procedure.

Failure to make the required estimated tax payments when due can result in an underpayment penalty for the period of underpayment. Generally, to avoid the estimated tax penalty, the organization must make estimated tax payments that total 100 percent of the organization's current tax year liability. However, an organization can base its required estimated tax payments on 100 percent of the tax shown on its return for the preceding year (unless no tax is shown) if its taxable income for each of the three preceding tax years was less than $1 million. Any tax due with Form 990-T must be paid in full when the return is filed, but no later than the date the return is due (determined without extensions).

An annual unrelated business income tax return (Form 990-T) is subject to public inspection. The tax code specifies that such forms shall be made available by such organization for inspection during regular business hours by any individual at the principal office of such organization and, if such organization regularly maintains one or more regional or district offices having three or more employees, at each such regional or district office, and upon request of an individual made at such principal office or such a regional or district office, a copy of such return . . . shall be provided to such individual without charge other than a reasonable fee for any reproduction and mailing costs. The request . . . must be made in person or in writing. If such request is made in person, such copy shall be provided immediately and, if made in writing, shall be provided within 30 days.

Certain information may be withheld by the organization from public disclosure and inspection if public availability would "adversely affect" the organization.

> **EXAMPLE.** A church operates a bookstore on its premises that is open to the general public. Net earnings from the bookstore are $15,000 this year. The church pays the unrelated business income tax on this income, using Form 990-T. This form is subject to public inspection. This means that the church must make the form available for inspection during regular business hours to any person who asks to see it, without charge other than a reasonable fee for any reproduction or mailing costs. The request to inspect may be made in person or in writing. If made in person, the copy must be provided immediately; if made in writing, it must be provided within 30 days.

6. EFFECT ON TAX-EXEMPT STATUS

A tax-exempt organization will not lose its exempt status by engaging in an unrelated trade or business so long as the trade or business does not constitute more than an insubstantial part of its activities.

7. EXAMPLES

The following examples will illustrate the application of the unrelated business income tax (UBIT).

Catering

> **EXAMPLE.** A charity operated a catering service that provided meals to members of the general public. The IRS ruled that income generated from this activity was not taxable as unrelated business income, since the activity was operated by volunteer workers. This same exception applies to many church fund-raising activities, including bake sales and car washes. Income from these activities almost always will be exempt from the tax on unrelated business income because they are conducted by volunteer workers. Other exceptions also may apply in some cases. *IRS Letter Ruling 9605001.*

Concerts

> **EXAMPLE.** The IRS ruled that income received by a church from selling tickets to gospel concerts at its facilities does not result in unrelated business taxable income. The concerts were not advertised in any commercial publications but were mentioned in the church section of a local newspaper, in local church bulletins, and on a religious television program. Tickets were sold for the concerts to limit the size of the audience to the capacity of the church. Gospel singers and musicians who perform the concerts receive either a predetermined fixed fee or voluntary donations that are collected at the concerts. The singers and musicians are allowed to sell items during the concerts, including cassette tapes of gospel music, T-shirts, books, and Bibles.

The IRS concluded: "Your exempt purpose is to spread the Gospel of Jesus Christ through Christian television broadcasting, missionary, and humanitarian efforts. Music is an integral part of most of these activities. Gospel singers regularly perform on your programs and are part of many of your other missionary and humanitarian efforts. The music presented in these activities helps to spread the Gospel message. The concerts, which you will host, will not be an end unto themselves but will simply be another means of accomplishing your exempt purposes. In some cases, you will be reaching people with Gospel music who would not otherwise be able to attend such concerts. Therefore, the activity of hosting the concerts will be substantially related to your exempt purposes. Based on the discussion set forth above, we rule that income received by you from the sale of tickets for Gospel concerts, which you will host at your facilities, will not be unrelated business taxable income." *IRS Letter Ruling 9325062.*

> **EXAMPLE.** The IRS ruled that revenue generated from a fund-raising concert was subject to UBIT. A charity conducted two concerts each year to raise funds. The concerts in no way furthered the charity's exempt purposes, other than the raising of revenue. The IRS acknowledged that intermittent activities are not "regularly carried on" and therefore cannot be a taxable unrelated trade or business. However, it insisted that the "preparatory time for an event must be taken into account in determining whether an activity is regularly carried on." Since the charity in this case spent up to six months preparing for each concert, the concerts were "regularly carried on." *IRS Letter Ruling 9712001.*

Gift shops

> **EXAMPLE.** The IRS issued a private letter ruling addressing the application of the tax on unrelated business income to various items sold in a charity's gift shop. While the ruling involved a museum rather than a church, it will be of interest to any church that conducts similar activities. The museum sells a wide variety of merchandise at retail, wholesale, and by mail order. Items for sale include everything from replicas of artwork to gum and candy.

The IRS noted that exempt organizations must pay an unrelated business income tax on net earnings generated from an unrelated trade or business that is not substantially related to the organization's exempt purposes. The IRS concluded that the museum's various sales activities constituted a trade or business and that some sales were exempt from UBIT, since they were substantially related to the museum's exempt purposes. This category included sales of replicas of artwork; sales of books and tapes relating to the museum and its collections; and sales of miscellaneous products such as film, batteries, and umbrellas which are sold for the convenience of visitors and enable them to devote a greater portion of their time to viewing the museum.

On the other hand, the sale of other items was not sufficiently related to the museum's exempt purposes to be exempt from the tax on unrelated business income. These items included the sales of newspapers, magazines, candy, pain relievers, toothpaste, golf clothing and accessories, neckties, caps, shirts, and books, which do not relate to museum collections; sales of souvenirs and mementos; and sales of items that were mere "interpretations" rather than reproductions of items in the museum's collections (such as the depiction of artwork on furniture, dinnerware, silverware, rugs, lamps, jewelry, place mats, and tote bags). *IRS Letter Ruling 9550003.*

Rental income

EXAMPLE. A charity's rental income was not subject to UBIT, said the IRS. A charity rented a portion of its premises to another charity with similar purposes. The IRS noted that rental income received by a charity from debt-financed property generally is subject to UBIT. However, an exception applies to rental agreements that are substantially related to the charity's exempt purposes. This test was met, the IRS concluded, because the rental agreement "will contribute importantly to the accomplishment of [the charity's] purposes" and will help further its "charitable goals." The IRS noted that a rental agreement will be "substantially related" to a charity's exempt purposes if it meets any one or more of the following conditions: (1) it has a "causal relationship to the achievement of exempt purposes (other than through the production of income)"; (2) it contributes importantly to the accomplishment of those purposes; (3) the entire property is devoted to the charity's exempt purposes at least 85 percent of the time; or (4) at least 85 percent of the property (in terms of physical area) is used for the charity's exempt purposes. *IRS Letter Ruling 9726005.*

EXAMPLE. A charity purchased land to build a facility to carry out its charitable and educational functions. It planned to rent some of the building to the public for wedding receptions and other functions. The IRS acknowledged that the tax code excludes rents from real estate from the unrelated business income tax. But this exception does not apply if the rented property is debt-financed. The IRS noted that the charity purchased the land and planned to construct its building without incurring any debt. As a result, it concluded that "the rental income . . . is excludable from the unrelated business tax." *IRS Letter Ruling 199940034.*

EXAMPLE. The IRS ruled that the rental of meeting space by a public museum did not affect its tax-exempt status or generate unrelated business income. The IRS concluded that rental of the space furthered the museum's exempt purpose, since it attracted visitors and produced income used to fund the museum. The IRS also concluded that the rental income was not subject to UBIT, since rental income generally is "excluded in determining unrelated business taxable income so long as any services [the exempt organization] might render in connection with the rental of the meeting space are those usually and customarily rendered in connection with the rental of rooms or other space for occupancy only." *IRS Letter Ruling 200222030 (2002); IRS Letter Ruling 201131029 (2011).*

Sales of property

EXAMPLE. The IRS ruled that gains realized by a charity from the sale of land were not taxable as unrelated business income. The IRS noted that federal law imposes a tax on the unrelated business income of tax-exempt organizations (including churches). However, "all gains or losses from the sale, exchange, or other disposition of property" are excluded from this tax, other than gains from the sale of property "held primarily for sale to customers in the ordinary course of the trade or business." The IRS referred to a Supreme Court ruling addressing the standard to be applied in determining whether property is held primarily for sale to customers in the ordinary course of business. The court interpreted the word "primarily" to mean "of first importance" or "principally." The IRS concluded that "by this standard, ordinary income would not result unless a sales purpose is dominant." *IRS Letter Ruling 9412039.*

EXAMPLE. The sale of charity-owned property was not subject to UBIT, ruled the IRS. A school was given land by a donor with the understanding that it would use the land for school purposes and not sell it unless absolutely necessary. The school attempted to lease the property for many years, but the school's trustees eventually decided that the land had to be sold.

The IRS ruled that taxable income would not result "unless a sales purpose is dominant." The IRS concluded that this standard had not been met in this case because of the following factors: (1) the land was held for "a significant period of time" before it was sold (contrary to the "short turn around period experienced by a typical buyer and seller of property"); (2) the school did not "regularly sell real estate"; (3) the school's "management activities with respect to the property have been minimal" and have consisted of collecting rents and providing routine maintenance and repairs; and (4) the school had not been "involved in any way with improving the land or providing services to tenants." The IRS concluded that "these facts distinguish [this sale] from the sale of property held primarily for sale to customers in the ordinary course of business." Therefore, "income from the sale of this property is excluded from the computation of unrelated business taxable income." *IRS Letter Ruling 9651014.*

Vocational training

EXAMPLE. The IRS ruled that income generated by a charity from various vocational training programs was not subject to UBIT. The IRS concluded that the charity's proposed activities "are being undertaken to further the goals of the existing programs for residents, and not for the production of income. The proposed activities are a natural extension of existing programs for residents. The scale of the operations is no larger than is necessary for the organization to accomplish its charitable purposes. This is evidenced by the fact that the individuals providing labor for these facilities are residents who are employed as part of your rehabilitation program, and your staff. Supervision will be provided by members of your staff who will not receive additional pay for performing this duty." Therefore, income generated from the sale of products is not subject to UBIT. *IRS Letter Ruling 9718034. See also Revenue Rulings 76-37, 73-128, and 73-127; IRS Letter Ruling 9641011.*

c. SOCIAL SECURITY

The application of Social Security and Medicare taxes to churches is addressed in Chapter 11, section B.

d. UNEMPLOYMENT TAXES

Congress enacted the Federal Unemployment Tax Act (FUTA) in 1935 in response to the widespread unemployment that accompanied the Great Depression. The Act called for a cooperative federal-state program of benefits to unemployed workers. It is financed by a federal excise tax on wages paid by employers in covered employment. An employer, however, is allowed a credit of up to 90 percent of the federal tax for "contributions" paid to a state fund established under a federally approved state unemployment compensation law. All 50 states have employment security laws implementing the federal mandatory minimum standards of coverage. States are free to expand their coverage beyond the federal minimum.

From 1960 to 1970 the Act excluded from the definition of covered employment all "service performed in the employ of a religious, charitable, educational, or other organization described in section 501(c)(3) which is exempt from income tax under section 501(a)." A 1970 amendment, in effect, narrowed this broad exemption of nonprofit organizations by conditioning federal approval of state compensation plans on the coverage of all nonprofit organizations except those specifically exempted. The Act was then amended to exempt service performed

> (1) in the employ of (A) a church or convention or association of churches, or (B) an organization which is operated primarily for religious purposes and which is operated, supervised, controlled, or principally supported by a church or convention or association of churches; (2) a duly ordained, commissioned, or licensed minister of a church in the exercise of his ministry or by a member of a religious order in the exercise of duties required by such order; (3) in the employ of a school which is not an institution of higher education. IRC 3309(b).

The Act continues the exemption of "service performed in the employ of a religious . . . organization" from the federal tax. Thus, while the exemption of religious organizations under federal law remains broad, the requirement imposed on states has been significantly narrowed.

In 1976 Congress eliminated the exemption of services performed "in the employ of a school which is not an institution of higher education" from the categories of employment that could be exempted from coverage under state programs without loss of federal approval.

In 1978 the Secretary of the Department of Labor announced that the elimination of this exemption required mandatory coverage of all the employees of church-related schools. This ruling was followed by many states, prompting a number of lawsuits.

In 1981 the United States Supreme Court ruled that the elimination of service performed "in the employ of a school which is not an institution of higher education" did not require the coverage of the employees of unincorporated church-related schools, since the continuing exemption of church employees was broad enough to cover the employees of unincorporated church-controlled elementary and secondary schools. *St. Martin Evangelical Lutheran Church v. South Dakota, 451 U.S. 772 (1981).* The court concluded that the employees of separately incorporated church schools are exempt from coverage only if the school is operated primarily for religious purposes and is operated, supervised, controlled, or principally supported by a church or convention or association of churches.

A 1997 amendment to FUTA established an additional exemption for service performed for "an elementary or secondary school which is operated for primarily religious purposes, which is described in section 501(c)(3), and which is exempt from tax." *IRC § 3309(b)(1)(C).*

In summary, the following activities ordinarily are exempt from state unemployment taxes:

- service performed in the employ of a church, a convention or association of churches, or an organization that is operated primarily for religious purposes and that is operated, supervised, controlled, or principally supported by a church or convention or association of churches. The exemption is not limited to employees performing strictly religious duties.
- service performed in the employ of an unincorporated church-controlled elementary or secondary school.
- service performed in the employ of an incorporated religious elementary or secondary school if it is operated primarily for religious purposes and is operated, supervised, controlled, or principally supported by a church or a convention or association of churches.
- service performed for an elementary or secondary school that is operated primarily for religious purposes and is not operated, supervised, controlled, or principally supported by a church or a convention or association of churches.
- service performed by a duly ordained, commissioned, or licensed minister of a church in the exercise of his ministry or by a member of a religious order in the exercise of duties required by such order.

❖ **KEY POINT.** Some churches that operate private schools have separately incorporated them in order to reduce the church's risk of liability. Unfortunately, separate incorporation will have little effect on the church's liability for the obligations of the school—unless the church relinquishes control of the school. If a church is willing to relinquish control, then the school becomes largely independent. This has a number of consequences, including the following: (1) liability of the church is reduced; and (2) employees of the school are not covered by federal or state unemployment law in most states.

1. MAINE

The Maine Supreme Court ruled that services performed for the Maine Sea Coast Missionary Society (the Mission) might qualify for exemption from unemployment taxes as "service performed in the employ of . . . an organization which is operated primarily for religious purposes and which is operated, supervised, controlled or principally supported by a church or convention or association of churches." The court reviewed the activities and governing documents of the Mission and concluded that it was operated primarily for religious purposes. It conceded that much of the Mission's work was "charitable" in nature but concluded that "the fact that an organization has a charitable purpose and does charitable work does not require the conclusion that its purposes are not primarily religious."

The court also ruled that the "principally supported" requirement is not limited to financial support but includes "contributed goods and services, and organizational backing and support" and that a group of supporting churches could constitute an "association" of churches. However, the court concluded that there was insufficient evidence that the Mission was principally supported by the contributions of finances, goods, and services by the association of churches, and as a result it remanded the case back to the trial court for further deliberations on this point. *Schwartz v. Unemployment Insurance Commission, 895 A.2d 965 (Me. 2006).*

2. MASSACHUSETTS

The Massachusetts Supreme Court ruled that a religious school whose corporate purposes included maintaining a place of worship according to Orthodox Jewish rites and instructing Jewish students in the teachings of Orthodox Judaism was exempt from the state unemployment tax, since it was an organization that was operated primarily for religious purposes and was "principally supported" by a "church or convention or association of churches." The court concluded that the term "church" included "synagogues or other non-Christian organized religious bodies." It also concluded that the term "support" was not limited to financial support:

> [The school] is supported by synagogues and other Jewish organizations in diverse ways. The school recruits from area synagogues the students who pay the tuition and fees that account for a significant part of the school's operating budget. There was uncontested evidence that it relies on members of surrounding Jewish synagogues to operate the school: the board of directors and school committee both include rabbis and members from local synagogues. The school requires that rabbis, presumably drawn from local Jewish synagogues, head the elementary and high schools, as well as the synagogue on its premises. Teachers providing religious instruction are Orthodox Jews, also presumably drawn from local synagogues. The school raises funds from local synagogues, as well as from Combined Jewish Philanthropies, which is itself an organization that raises and distributes funds to Jewish institutions such as [the school]. . . . The school's existence depends upon these essential relationships with members of other temples, synagogues and Jewish organizations, to provide financial and moral support. For all of these reasons . . . [the school] is exempt from the state unemployment tax as an organization "operated primarily for religious purposes" that is "principally supported" by a "church or convention or association of churches."

The school was not exempt under the 1997 amendment to FUTA, which exempts "an elementary or secondary school which is operated for primarily religious purposes, which is described in section 501(c)(3), and which is exempt from tax," since Massachusetts had not adopted this exemption at the time this case was decided. *Bleich v. Maimonides School, 849 N.E.2d 185 (Mass. 2006).*

3. MINNESOTA

A Minnesota court ruled that a former church employee was not eligible for unemployment benefits. A church employed a woman as its business administrator for two years. The church's employment handbook indicated that the church paid unemployment taxes and implied that its employees would receive unemployment benefits if they lost their jobs. The administrator's employment ended through no fault of her own, and she applied for unemployment benefits and attempted to establish a benefit account but was notified by state Department of Employment and Economic Development (the "Department") that employment with a church could not be used to establish a benefit account. She appealed.

Under state law, the Department pays unemployment benefits to an applicant who meets certain requirements. First, the applicant must file an application for unemployment benefits and establish a benefit account. After the application is filed, the Department calculates the applicant's weekly benefit amount and the maximum unemployment benefits available, if any, based on "all the covered employment in the base period." To establish a benefit account, however, the applicant must have earned a certain minimum dollar amount of "wage credits." Wage credits are defined as "the amount of wages paid within an applicant's base period for covered employment." Employment for a church that is operated primarily for religious purposes is "noncovered employment."

A state appeals court observed: "It is undisputed that [the employing church] met these criteria; thus [the administrator's] employment with the church is noncovered employment." The court acknowledged that a church may elect to have employment performed for it considered covered employment, and the Department has the discretion to approve such an election. However, the court found no evidence showing that the church had elected to do so. The court rejected the following four arguments made by the former administrator:

(1) **The church's employment manual.** The court acknowledged that the church's employment manual stated, incorrectly, that unemployment benefits might be available to church employees separated from employment through no fault of their own. However, it rejected the former administrator's claim that manual constituted an affirmative election of unemployment coverage: "Representations by an employer regarding eligibility for unemployment benefits are not binding on the Department."

(2) **Medicare and Social Security taxes.** The former administrator argued that since the church pays Medicare and Social Security taxes, it is a "taxpaying employer" that

should have to pay unemployment taxes as well. The court disagreed: "The fact that the employer and employee pay other taxes is irrelevant to whether the employer must pay unemployment taxes; instead, the latter issue is decided under the provisions of unemployment-insurance law."

(3) **Posting notices.** The former administrator argued that because the state unemployment law requires employers to post and maintain a printed notice of the right to unemployment benefits, the church should have been required to post notices or inform its employees that they did not have the right to unemployment benefits. In rejecting this argument, the court noted that "the statute contains no such requirement, and [the administrator's] argument would be more appropriately addressed to the legislature, which solely has the power to amend the law."

(4) **Equitable relief.** The former administrator, citing the purpose of the unemployment law and its remedial nature, argued that she should receive benefits because she was unemployed through no fault of her own. She cited the statutory provision that "the public good is promoted by providing workers who are unemployed through no fault of their own a temporary partial wage replacement to assist the unemployed worker to become reemployed." Once again, the court rejected this argument: "The Department will pay unemployment benefits only to an applicant who meets all of the requirements. Without having met the requirement of establishing an unemployment-benefit account, [the former administrator] cannot obtain unemployment benefits, and no liberal construction of the statute in favor of its remedial purpose or narrow construction of ineligibility requirements can allow us to reach the result she seeks. . . . Consequently, she cannot prevail on her argument that she should receive unemployment benefits as a matter of equity." *Irvine v. St. John's Lutheran Church of Mound, 779 N.W.2d 101 (Minn. App. 2010).*

4. NEW YORK

A New York state court ruled that a state law exempting "persons employed at a place of religious worship" from unemployment benefits did not violate the First Amendment's nonestablishment of religion clause. *Claim of Klein, 563 N.Y.S.2d 132 (Sup. Ct. 1990).* A teacher who had been employed by a religious school sought unemployment benefits. Benefits were denied on the ground that she had been employed by a religious school. The teacher claimed that the state law exempting religious employees from unemployment coverage was unconstitutional. A state appeals court disagreed. It applied a three-part test announced in 1971 by the United States Supreme Court. *Lemon v. Kurtzman, 403 U.S. 602 (1971).* Under this so-called Lemon test (named after the 1971 Supreme Court case), a law that appears to favor religion will be invalid unless it satisfies three conditions: (1) a secular purpose, (2) a primary effect that neither advances nor inhibits religion, and (3) no "excessive entanglement" between church and state. The court concluded that the New York law exempting religious employees from unemployment benefits satisfied this test. It further noted that the Supreme Court has ruled that "government policies with secular objectives may incidentally benefit religion." Such was the case here.

EXAMPLE. A New York court ruled that a woman employed by a church-operated childcare facility was entitled to unemployment benefits following her termination. The church claimed that it was exempt from paying unemployment benefits under a state law exempting any "person employed at a place of religious worship . . . for the performance of duties of a religious nature." The church asserted that because the day-care center was established in furtherance of the church's religious mission and its primary purpose was to inculcate biblical teachings at the earliest possible age, the employee's duties, while including the basic care of the children, were primarily religious in nature.

A state court rejected the church's position and ruled that the employee was entitled to unemployment benefits. It concluded, "We find that the record contains abundant evidence that [the employee's] duties were primarily secular and thus not excluded from coverage. It is uncontroverted that most, if not all, of [her] working day was spent tending to the basic needs of these young children, all of whom were still in diapers. For a portion of each day, she alone was responsible for the supervision and care of at least 10 children 24 months old and younger. That [her] services were rendered on behalf of a religious organization does not alter their essential secular character." *Jones v. Center Road Baptist Church, 689 N.Y.S.2d 284 (Sup. Ct. 1999).*

5. OHIO

An Ohio court ruled that a former teacher at a church-affiliated school was not eligible for unemployment benefits. A state law denies benefits to persons "in the employ of a church or convention or association of churches, or in an organization which is operated primarily for religious purposes and which is operated, supervised, controlled, or principally supported by a church or convention or association of churches." The court concluded that both tests were met. As to the first test, it noted that "[the] reason for creating and operating a school affiliated with a religious denomination is to offer a learning experience dominated by a religious environment; a situation distinctly different than that offered in public schools. Consequently . . . the primary purpose of operating a school of this type is religious in nature, regardless of whether the school or the local church [is a teacher's] employer." As to the second test, the court noted that "the only individuals authorized to sign paychecks for the school were the principal and the church's pastor," and "the pastor of the church exercised substantial control over the operations and spending of the school, as his consent was required to hire new

teachers and to purchase supplies." *Miller v. Saints Peter and Paul School, 711 N.E.2d 311 (Ohio 1999).*

6. OREGON

In a highly controversial decision, the Oregon Supreme Court ruled in 1989 that all religious organizations, including churches, are subject to state unemployment taxes. *Employment Division v. Rogue Valley Youth for Christ, 770 P.2d 588 (Ore. 1989).* As noted above, the Federal Unemployment Tax Act contains a set of guidelines that a state's unemployment tax program must meet in order to avoid federal unemployment taxes. Although compliance with the federal guidelines is optional, states normally comply in order to avoid subjecting local employers to double taxation (under both federal and state law). One of the federal guidelines with which states must comply exempts services performed in the employ of a church, a convention or association of churches, or certain church-controlled organizations from unemployment tax. There is no exemption for religious organizations not affiliated with a church or convention or association of churches. Accordingly, under FUTA, states *must* subject non-church-affiliated religious organizations to state unemployment tax or risk losing their exemption from federal unemployment tax.

However, the Oregon Supreme Court previously had ruled that the state could *not* make distinctions between church-affiliated and non-church-affiliated religious organizations, since such a distinction "contravenes the equality among pluralistic faiths and kinds of religious organizations embodied in the Oregon constitution's guarantees of religious freedom." How should these conflicting provisions be reconciled? The Employment Division of the Oregon Department of Human Resources (the agency responsible for enforcing the Oregon unemployment law) took the position that it had to assess unemployment taxes against *all* religious organizations—including churches—in order to keep Oregon in compliance with FUTA guidelines and the Oregon constitution. The Oregon Supreme Court agreed. It emphasized that in order to satisfy the state constitution's requirement of "treating all religious organizations similarly," it had two options: (1) completely exempt all religious organizations (whether church-affiliated or not); or (2) eliminate the exemption of all religious organizations (including churches). The court elected the second alternative, since the other option would have led to a broader exemption than permitted by FUTA and accordingly would have subjected Oregon employers to double unemployment tax under both state and federal law.

The court acknowledged that taxing all religious organizations "creates potential constitutional problems involving the free exercise of religion." However, it concluded that its decision did not violate the constitutional guaranty of religious freedom. The Oregon Supreme Court's decision remains an unfortunate precedent that has not been followed by any other court.

EXAMPLE. An Oregon court ruled that a church's constitutional rights were not violated by an award of unemployment benefits to a dismissed youth pastor. The church insisted that the constitutional guaranty of religious freedom prohibited the state from including ministers in the unemployment compensation system. The court conceded that the state unemployment compensation law excluded services performed for a church and services performed by a minister of a church. But the court ruled that this exemption was invalid, since it improperly singled out ministers who performed services for a church, or who had been credentialed by a church, and excluded ministers employed or credentialed by other kinds of religious organizations. As such, the law violated the "constitutional rule that Oregon must treat all religious organizations similarly whether or not they would qualify as churches."

The church also asserted that the state unemployment law denied benefits to employees who are dismissed because of misconduct and that the church's determination that the youth pastor had been dismissed for misconduct could not be questioned by the government, since this would amount to an unconstitutional interference with a church's selection of its ministers. The court disagreed, noting that "by including ministers in the unemployment compensation system, a church retains substantial discretion to choose and control its ministers. That is so because, despite the outcome of the benefits process, the [state] has no authority in any case to change or modify a church's discharge decision. . . . In the absence of direct coercion, [a] church's claimed right to free exercise is best described as concerning generally its right to remain free of any requirement that it explains to the state its ministerial employment decisions. We agree that such an explanation is offensive to principles of church autonomy. However, because the inquiry does not by itself have the power to change a church's decision as to a minister's work status, it is in that sense reasonably characterized as an incidental burden on church's free exercise rights." As a result, the court concluded that the church's First Amendment rights were not violated by the award of unemployment benefits to the dismissed youth minister. *Newport Church of the Nazarene v. Hensley, 983 P.2d 1072 (Ore. App. 1999).*

EXAMPLE. An Oregon court ruled that a church was required to pay state unemployment taxes on its pastor, since he was an employee. Oregon is the only state that currently requires churches to pay unemployment taxes on their pastors. The church in this case argued that it was not required to pay unemployment taxes on its pastor, since he was an independent contractor rather than an employee.

The court acknowledged that employers are not required to pay unemployment taxes on independent contractors, but it concluded that the pastor was not an independent contractor. In support of this conclusion, the court noted that the pastor was subject to dismissal by the church for failing to carry out his duties consistently with what the church regarded as biblical doctrine. The court also rejected the church's argument that requiring

it to pay unemployment taxes violated its constitutional right of religious freedom. The church had argued that requiring it to acknowledge that it was the pastor's employer conflicted with its religious belief that his employer was God, not the church.

The court concluded, "The state's unemployment taxation law applies to all employers, regardless of the religious beliefs of the employers or their employees, and is intended to protect the economic security of the state's residents, not to inhibit or promote any particular religious beliefs. Any effect on the religious beliefs of the church are purely incidental. Requiring the church to report to the department as an employer, therefore, is not prohibited by [the First Amendment guaranty of religious freedom]." *Church at 295 S. 18th Street v. Employment Department, 28 P.3d 1185 (Or. App. 2001).*

7. RHODE ISLAND

A federal appeals court ruled that the exemption of churches from unemployment tax did not violate the First Amendment's nonestablishment of religion clause. *Rojas v. Fitch, 127 F.3d 184 (1st Cir. 1997).* The Salvation Army dismissed an employee in Rhode Island for budgetary reasons. The employee applied for unemployment benefits and was informed that she was not eligible, since her former employer was a religious organization that was exempt from unemployment tax. The employee filed a lawsuit claiming that the exemption of religious organizations from the unemployment law violated the First Amendment. The court disagreed in an important decision that reaffirms the historic exemption of churches from unemployment taxes. The court applied the three-part *Lemon* test (described above) in deciding that the exemption of churches from the Rhode Island unemployment law did *not* create an impermissible establishment of religion.

8. WASHINGTON

A Washington state appeals court ruled that the exemption of churches from the state unemployment compensation law did not violate state or federal constitutional provisions prohibiting the establishment of religion. *Saucier v. Employment Security Department, 954 P.2d 285 (Wash. App. 1999).*

E. STATE TAXES

1. STATE INCOME TAXES

Most states impose a tax on the gross income of corporations. Although nearly all the income of most religious organizations is in the form of gifts that generally are excludable from the done organization's income, most states specifically exempt religious organizations from the tax on corporate income. Some state corporate income tax laws exempt any corporation that is exempt from federal income tax. Others specifically exempt various charitable organizations, including religious and educational organizations. A number of states impose a tax on the unrelated business income of exempt organizations.

2. STATE SALES TAXES

✤ **KEY POINT.** The application of all state sales tax laws to churches is addressed in Table 12-3 at the end of this chapter.

Most states impose a tax on the sale of tangible personal property or the rendering of various services for compensation. Religious organizations are exempt from sales taxes in most states, although the nature of the exemption varies from state to state. See Table 12-3 for a review of the state sales tax exemptions in all 50 states. Sales made *to* religious organizations are exempted from sales taxes in many states. Some states exempt sales made *by* religious organizations, and others exempt sales *to or by* religious organizations. Many states that exempt sales of property made to religious organizations stipulate that the exemption is available only if the organization uses the purchased property for exempt purposes. Some states are even more restrictive, and some have no specific exemption for sales by or to religious organizations.

The exemption of religious organizations from state sales taxes is available only to nonprofit religious organizations and ordinarily is available only to those organizations that make application. One court ruled a religious organization was properly denied an exemption from a state's sales tax, since it had refused to submit sufficient information with its exemption application to establish that it was, in fact, a religious organization. *First Lutheran Mission v. Department of Revenue, 613 P.2d 351 (Colo. 1980).*

The Texas Monthly case
In 1989 the United States Supreme Court ruled that a Texas law exempting religious periodicals from state sales tax violated the First Amendment's nonestablishment of religion clause. *Texas Monthly, Inc. v. Bullock, 109 S. Ct. 890 (1989).* From 1984 until 1987 Texas law imposed a sales tax upon all periodicals except those "published or distributed by a religious faith and that consist wholly of writings sacred to a religious faith." This law was challenged by a secular publisher, and the United States Supreme Court agreed that the Texas law violated the First Amendment.

The court's ruling is significant, since it probed the meaning of the First Amendment's language prohibiting the establishment of a religion. The court noted that the First Amendment nonestablishment of religion clause "prohibits, at the very least, legislation that constitutes an endorsement of one or another set of religious beliefs or of religion generally." It observed that the "core notion" underlying the First Amendment is that the government "may not place its prestige,

coercive authority, or resources behind a single religious faith or behind religious faith in general, compelling nonadherents to support the practices or proselytizing of favored religious organizations and conveying the message that those who do not contribute gladly are less than full members of the community."

The court was quick to add that government policies that are designed to implement a broad secular purpose are not invalid merely because they incidentally benefit religion. For example, the court noted that it had previously upheld a New York property tax exemption law because it exempted a wide variety of charitable organizations including churches. *Walz v. Tax Commission, 397 U.S. 664 (1970).* The court concluded:

> *Every tax exemption constitutes a subsidy that affects nonqualifying taxpayers, forcing them to become indirect and vicarious donors. Insofar as that subsidy is conferred upon a wide array of nonsectarian groups as well as religious organizations in pursuit of some legitimate secular end, the fact that religious groups benefit incidentally does not [violate the First Amendment]. However, when government directs a subsidy exclusively to religious organizations . . . and that either burdens nonbeneficiaries markedly or cannot reasonably be seen as removing a significant state-imposed deterrent to the free exercise of religion, as Texas has done, it provides unjustifiable awards of assistance to religious organizations and cannot but convey a message of endorsement to slighted members of the community. This is particularly true where, as here, the subsidy is targeted at writings that promulgate the teachings of religious faith. It is difficult to view Texas' narrow exemption as anything but state sponsorship of religious belief.*

The court emphasized that if Texas chose to grant a tax exemption to "all groups that contributed to the community's cultural, intellectual, and moral betterment," then the exemption for religious publications could be retained." The court specifically ruled that a statute exempting organizations created for "religious, educational, or charitable purposes" from the payment of state sales tax would be a "model" exemption statute.

The Jimmy Swaggart case
In 1990 the United States Supreme Court ruled unanimously that the state of California could tax the sale of religious literature by Jimmy Swaggart Ministries (JSM). *Jimmy Swaggart Ministries v. Board of Equalization, 110 S. Ct. 688 (1990).* JSM is a religious organization organized "for the purpose of establishing and maintaining an evangelistic outreach for the worship of Almighty God . . . by all available means, both at home and in foreign lands," including evangelistic crusades, missionary endeavors, radio broadcasting, television broadcasting, and publishing. From 1974 to 1981 (the years in question), JSM conducted 23 crusades in California. At the crusades, JSM conducted religious services and sold religious books, tapes, records, and other religious merchandise. JSM also offered its

products for sale through radio and television broadcasts and in its monthly magazine, *The Evangelist.*

In 1980 the state of California informed JSM that religious materials were not exempt from the state sales tax and requested that it register as a seller to facilitate the payment of the tax. California law imposes a 6 percent tax on the sale of most items of tangible personal property. Churches and other religious organizations are not exempted from this tax. State law also requires certain out-of-state sellers to collect a 6 percent "use tax" on sales of property to California residents. JSM responded that the constitutional guaranty of religious freedom exempted it from collecting or paying sales or use taxes.

In 1981 the state of California audited JSM and again asked it to register as a seller and to collect sales taxes on all sales made at its California crusades and to collect use taxes on mail-order sales to California residents. The state concluded that from 1974 through 1981 JSM sold religious merchandise valued at $240,000 at its California crusades, and religious merchandise valued at $1.7 million through mail-order sales to California residents. Both figures represented sales of merchandise with specific religious content—Bibles, Bible study manuals, printed sermons and collections of sermons, audiocassette tapes of sermons, religious books and pamphlets, and religious music in the form of songbooks, tapes, and records. Based on these sales figures, the state notified JSM that it owed sales and use taxes of $120,000 plus interest of $36,000 and penalties of $11,000. JSM did not contest the state's assessment of sales and use taxes on sales of nonreligious merchandise.

JSM challenged the tax assessments on the basis of the First Amendment's guaranty of religious freedom. The state rejected this defense, and JSM appealed to the state courts. Both a trial court and state appeals court ruled in favor of the state, and the state supreme court denied review. JSM appealed the case directly to the United States Supreme Court. The Supreme Court agreed that JSM's sales of religious literature have as "high a claim to constitutional protection" as more orthodox forms of religious exercise, but it disagreed that the constitutional guaranty of religious freedom was violated by the California sales tax. The court based its ruling on six considerations.

First, it noted that "the free exercise [of religion] inquiry asks whether government has placed a substantial burden on the observation of a central religious belief or practice, and, if so, whether a compelling governmental interest justifies the burden." The court concluded that JSM's "religious beliefs do not forbid payment of the sales tax" and accordingly that the tax "imposes no constitutionally significant burden on [JSM's] religious practices or beliefs."

Second, the court rejected JSM's claim that its position was supported by two previous Supreme Court decisions. The earlier cases (decided in the 1940s) involved city ordinances that prohibited home solicitations or the sale of literature without the payment of

a license tax. *Murdock v. Pennsylvania, 319 U.S. 105 (1943), and Follett v. McCormick, 321 U.S. 573 (1944).* The court concluded that these ordinances violated the constitutional rights of itinerant ministers engaged in evangelistic efforts (including the sale of religious literature) in residential neighborhoods. The ordinances were invalid, since they "restrained in advance those constitutional liberties of press and religion and inevitably tended to suppress their exercise." In contrast, the California sales tax "is not imposed as a precondition of disseminating the message." The court further noted that in one of the two earlier cases, it had emphasized that "we do not mean to say that religious groups and the press are free from all financial burdens of government," and it affirmed that "a tax on the income of one who engages in religious activities or a tax on property used or employed in connection with those activities" would not violate the constitution. It concluded that "the tax at issue in this case is akin to a generally applicable income or property tax, which [the two previous decisions] state may constitutionally be imposed on a religious activity."

Third, the California sales tax was "not a tax on the right to disseminate religious information," since it was applied neutrally to all retail sales of tangible personal property (whether by for-profit or nonprofit organizations). Religious organizations were not "singled out for special and burdensome treatment."

Fourth, the sales tax "represents only a small fraction of any retail sale" and accordingly could not meaningfully affect JSM's religious beliefs or practices.

Fifth, the sales tax only requires religious organizations to collect the tax from customers and remit collected taxes to the state. They are not required to pay it themselves. Such "pass through" taxes pose no significant burden on religious beliefs or practices, the court concluded.

Sixth, the court rejected JSM's claim that the marginally higher price that customers would have to pay for its literature (because of the 6 percent sales tax) violated its religious freedoms by driving away potential customers unwilling to pay the higher prices. The court found this argument "not constitutionally significant." The court did acknowledge that "a more onerous tax rate . . . might effectively choke off an adherent's religious practices." Such an argument, however, could not be made with respect to a 6 percent sales tax.

The court rejected the claim of JSM that applying the sales tax to a religious organization violated the nonestablishment of religion clause of the First Amendment. The court acknowledged that a government practice will violate this clause if it creates an "excessive entanglement" between church and state. JSM alleged that taxing its sales would create such an entanglement, since it would require "on-site inspections of evangelistic crusades, lengthy on-site audits, examination of [its] books and records, threats of criminal prosecution, and layers of administrative and judicial proceedings."

In rejecting this claim, the court noted three considerations. First, any "administrative burden" was reduced by the fact that JSM "had a sophisticated accounting staff and had recently computerized its accounting." Second, requiring JSM to collect and remit sales and use taxes "does not enmesh government in religious affairs [and] contrary to [JSM's] contentions requires neither the involvement of state employees in, nor on-site continuing inspection of, [its] day-to-day operations." Third, applying the sales tax to the sale of religious materials "does not require the state to inquire into the religious content of the items sold or the religious motivation for selling or purchasing the items."

Finally, the court refused to consider JSM's claim that it did not have a sufficient presence in California to subject it to sales or use taxes on mail-order sales of religious literature to California residents. This claim was barred, the court concluded, because it had not been raised by JSM in its initial challenge to the state's assessment of taxes. Ordinarily, new issues cannot be raised before the Supreme Court.

What is the relevance of this ruling to churches and religious organizations? Consider the following.

States can impose sales taxes on the in-state sales of religious literature by religious organizations provided that the tax is not onerous and applies generally to most sales of property by nonprofit as well as for-profit organizations. The impact of the court's ruling will be minimized by the fact that nearly 20 states exempt sales of religious literature *to* churches and other religious organizations. About 16 states exempt sales of religious literature *by* a religious organization. Four states have no sales tax at all. Only a few states (like California) have no sales tax exemption that applies to sales either *by or to* religious organizations. In many cases state sales tax exemptions are mandated by the state's constitution. This makes any change in a state's sales tax law very unlikely.

The Supreme Court did not decide whether a state can impose a use tax on the mail-order sales of out-of-state religious organizations to persons living in that state. Many states provide some form of exemption from the use tax for religious organizations. And the courts have ruled that out-of-state sellers cannot be required to collect use taxes unless they have a sufficient relationship with the state seeking to impose the taxes. For example, in 1967 the Supreme Court ruled that a state cannot assess sales or use taxes against an out-of-state seller whose only "presence" in the state is advertising and mail-order sales. *National Bellas Hess, Inc. v. Department of Revenue, 386 U.S. 753 (1967).*

The ruling probably does not make it more likely that church property or income will be taxed. Note that the sales tax is different from either property or income taxes in the sense that the sales tax is merely *collected* by the seller from the purchasers of its products. The tax is not paid out of the seller's own resources but rather is simply

added to the cost of merchandise. This is significantly different from property or income taxes, both of which are paid directly out of an organization's resources. In other words, the burden or impact of property or income taxes on religious organizations is much greater than a sales tax. In 1970 the Supreme Court ruled (by a vote of 8 to 1) that a state law exempting places of religious worship from state property taxation was constitutionally permissible. *Walz v. Tax Commission, 397 U.S. 664 (1970).* With few exceptions, church income is exempt from taxation in all 50 states and under federal law.

The court acknowledged that (1) any tax that imposes a "prior restraint" or precondition on the exercise of religious beliefs or practices would violate the First Amendment; and (2) a sales tax might violate the First Amendment if it was so large as to discourage potential purchasers of religious literature from making purchases, or if it singled out religious organizations for special or more burdensome treatment.

EXAMPLE. The Ohio Supreme Court rejected a state's contention that a religious organization was not exempt from sales taxes, since it was not a church. Ohio law exempts from sales tax any sale of property to churches. State law further provides that no exemption applies to sales made in the course of any trade or business. The state assessed taxes on most purchases made by a religious organization. It disputed the organization's claim that it was a church, and it concluded that the organization's sales of books and tapes constituted a trade or business that precluded any tax exemption.

The state supreme court ruled in favor of the organization. First, it concluded that the organization was a church: "It has adherents. It adopts the Bible as the main source of its dogma, it propagates a comprehensive set of religious objectives and beliefs which attempt to answer its adherents' religious concerns, and it conducts services. . . . It employs ministers who preside at sacramental ceremonies, operates schools to train ministers, and sends forth missionaries to spread its beliefs."

Second, the court ruled that the organization's sale of tapes and records did not constitute a trade or business. It concluded that the organization "advances religion by selling these materials. Despite receiving more for these items than it paid for them, [the organization] did not distribute any profit to its trustees, officers, or employees, but, instead, paid them modest salaries. [The organization] accumulated these profits and expanded its operations, including building a new church facility. Moreover, [the organization's] prime source of funding came from voluntary contributions. [Its] motive is to advance its religion, and it employs books and tapes in a functionally related way to accomplish this. Selling books and tapes to its followers is not a business but a means to its religious ends." *The Way International v. Limbach, 552 N.E.2d 908 (Ohio 1990).*

EXAMPLE. A religious organization operated a variety of retail businesses, including a restaurant, grocery store, two service stations, a clothing store, and an auto repair shop. Members of the organization performed services for these businesses without compensation other than the receipt of food, shelter, and clothing at no cost. A state agency determined that the organization's provision of food and clothing to members in exchange for services constituted sales subject to state sales tax. A trial court upheld the tax assessment, and the organization appealed.

The Arkansas Supreme Court agreed that the transfers of food and clothing were sales subject to tax, since they were "transfers for valuable consideration." The court rejected the organization's argument that its constitutional right of religious freedom was being abridged, since "religious organizations entering the commercial and secular world necessarily do so with the understanding that they no longer enjoy the constitutional protections afforded religious organizations. There are no shields once they cross the line that separates church and state. They are no longer considered a church or religious organization, because they are not acting like one. . . . The [organization] elected to operate retail businesses for profit and, having made that choice, it must abide by the same rules under which all secular businesses operate, including taxation." *Tony & Susan Alamo Foundation v. Ragland, 746 S.W.2d 45 (Ark. 1988).*

3. PROPERTY TAXES

✿ **KEY POINT.** The statute (or constitutional provision) exempting church property from the property tax is set forth in Table 12-4 at the end of this chapter.

The exemption of religious organizations from property taxes is a practice that dates back to ancient times. The Bible records that "Joseph established it as a law concerning land in Egypt . . . that a fifth of the produce belongs to Pharaoh. It was only the land of the priests that did not become Pharaoh's" (Genesis 47:26).

The emperor Constantine exempted churches from property taxes in the fourth century. Medieval Europe generally exempted church property from property taxes. This tradition of exemption was adopted by the American colonies. All 50 states presently recognize some form of exemption of religious organizations from property taxes. The exemption of church property from taxation has been challenged on a number of occasions on the ground that such exemptions violate the First Amendment's nonestablishment of religion clause. The Supreme Court historically viewed such challenges as frivolous. *Walz v. Tax Commission, 397 U.S. 664, 686 n.6 (1970).* In 1970 the court upheld the constitutionality of New York's property tax exemption statute, which exempted property used exclusively for religious purposes.

Every state exempts from taxation buildings that are used exclusively as places of worship. Much variety exists, however, regarding the exemption of other forms of church-owned property. The exemption of some common forms of church-owned property is evaluated below.

Houses of religious worship

Little doubt exists regarding the exemption of buildings used exclusively for religious worship. Every state exempts such buildings from taxation. To illustrate, many state laws exempt "houses of religious worship." Others exempt "places used for religious worship" or "buildings for religious worship" or "property used exclusively for worship." Many states simply exempt all property used exclusively for religious purposes or religious worship. Such an exemption certainly is broad enough to include buildings used for religious worship.

Questions may arise, however, in several ways, including the following: (1) How much of the church-owned property surrounding the sanctuary is exempt? (2) What if a portion of the church property is rented or otherwise used for commercial or investment purposes? (3) If a portion of church-owned property is rented or otherwise used for nonexempt purposes, does the entire property lose its exempt status, or only the portion rented? (4) What if the sanctuary is under construction? Some or all of these questions may not be addressed in an exemption statute, and this can lead to confusion and even litigation. Each of these issues is discussed below.

Surrounding grounds

How much of the property surrounding a church sanctuary is exempt from taxation? Many statutes do not address this issue directly but rather exempt all property used exclusively for religious purposes. Some statutes simply state that the "grounds" or land adjacent or appurtenant to the sanctuary are exempt, without any attempt to clarify how much land is contemplated by the exemption. Other statutes clarify that the land surrounding the sanctuary is exempt to the extent that it is reasonably necessary to the accomplishment of church's purposes. A few statutes specify how much of a church's property is exempt. For example, one state constitution specifies that up to one-half acre is exempt in cities or towns, and up to two acres "in the country." Other state laws exempt church grounds up to five acres, 15 acres, 30 acres, and 320 acres.

EXAMPLE. An Ohio court ruled that a nonprofit religious radio broadcast facility was exempt from property tax as a "house used exclusively for religious worship." The court conceded that the term "houses used exclusively for public worship" could be interpreted to apply to "structures in which the worshipful rites and ordinances of a religious society are celebrated or observed by members of the society." However, it refused to interpret the term this narrowly. It observed: "The programs broadcast by [the radio station] are primarily religious, and they are received for a worshipful purpose by those who subscribe and listen to them. The broadcast and reception constitute a form of public worship and the persons who participate in those exercises constitute a religious society. The property for which [the station] seeks an exemption is used primarily to facilitate the celebration and observance of that particular religious society." *World Evangelistic Enterprise Corporation v. Tracy, 644 N.E.2d 678 (Ohio App. 2 Dist. 1994).*

Effect of rental income

Churches occasionally rent a portion of their property. Does this affect the exempt status of the property? Some statutes specify that church property is not eligible for exempt status if it is rented or otherwise used for commercial, investment, or other nonexempt purposes. The same result may be presumed under state laws exempting property that is used exclusively for religious purposes. Other states recognize the "partial exemption" rule, under which the rental of a portion of exempt property does not affect the exempt status of the entire property but only of that portion actually rented. This rule is summarized in the following subsection. A few courts have concluded that the existence of rental income does not necessarily affect the exempt status of church-owned property. *University Christian Church v. City of Austin, 724 S.W.2d 94 (Tex. App. 1986) (a church rented two of its parking lots).*

EXAMPLE. The Alabama Supreme Court ruled that the rental of a charitable organization's property resulted in the loss of the property's exemption from taxation, despite the fact that the rent was used for charitable purposes. A charity rented a portion of its facilities to various commercial organizations and used all of the rental income (after expenses) for charitable purposes. The state supreme court ruled that the property in question had lost its tax exemption due to the rental activity.

The court observed: "When a property owner allows another party to use his property for religious, educational, or charitable purposes, and the owner derives no income or benefit from the property, then the property is used exclusively for a religious, educational, or charitable use, and the property owner is entitled to an exemption. However, if the owner receives any income or benefit from the property, the property is not used exclusively for religious, educational, or charitable purposes, and the property owner is not entitled to an exemption." The court further noted that exempt property must be used exclusively for religious, educational, or charitable purposes, and "exclusive" means that "the property must be used solely, only, or wholly for a religious, educational, or charitable purpose." Finally, the court rejected the charity's claim that its property was entitled to exemption because all of the rental income (after expenses) was used for charitable purposes. *Most Worshipful Grand Lodge v. Norred, 603 So.2d 996 (Ala. 1992).*

Partial exemption

Many states recognize the "partial exemption" rule. Under this rule, property that is used in part for exclusively religious purposes is entitled to a partial exemption based on the percentage of use or occupancy that is devoted to an exempt use. The rule is based on statute in some states and upon judicial decisions in others. To illustrate, one state statute specifies:

If any portion of the property which might otherwise be exempted under this section is used for commercial or other purposes not within the conditions necessary for exemption (including any use

the primary purpose of which is to produce income even though such income is to be used for or in furtherance of the exempt purposes) that portion of the premises shall not be exempt but the remaining portion of the premises shall not be deprived of the exemption if the remaining portion is used exclusively for purposes within the conditions necessary for exemption. In the event of an exemption of a portion of a building, the tax shall be assessed upon so much of the value of the building (including the land thereunder and the appurtenant premises) as the proportion of the floor space of the nonexempt portion bears to the total floor space of the building.

Another statute provides: "If any portion of such real property is not so used exclusively to carry out thereupon one or more of such purposes but is leased or otherwise used for other purposes, such portion shall be subject to taxation and the remaining portion only shall be exempt."

Several courts have recognized the principle of partial exemption. On the other hand, a few courts have ruled that if any part of a building is used for commercial purposes, the entire facility is subject to tax.

EXAMPLE. The education wing of a parish center used for Sunday school on Sunday but as a commercial child-care center during the week was not used primarily for public worship and was denied exemption. *Summit United Methodist Church v. Kinney, 455 N.E.2d 669 (Ohio 1983).*

EXAMPLE. Where one substantial part of a building was used by a religious organization and another substantial part was used for commercial purposes, the building was taxable on a pro rata basis. *Sisters of Charity v. County of Bernalillo, 596 P.2d 255 (N.M. 1979).*

Property under construction

Is a church building under construction exempt from property taxes? Unfortunately, few statutes address this question directly. One statute specifies that "all grounds and buildings used or *under construction* by . . . religious institutions and societies" (emphasis added) are exempt from tax. Another statute specifies:

[Church property] from which no revenue is derived shall be exempt though not in actual use therefore by reason of the absence of suitable buildings or improvements thereon if (a) the construction of such buildings or improvements is in progress or is in good faith contemplated by such corporation or association or (b) such real property is held by such corporation or association upon condition that the title thereto shall revert in case any building not intended and suitable for one or more such purposes shall be erected upon such premises or some part thereof.

EXAMPLE. A New York statute specifies that if property for which an exemption is sought is "not in actual use" for exempt purposes, such as where it is unimproved or, in its current state, lacks "suitable buildings or improvements," the owner may qualify for the exemption by demonstrating that "the construction of such buildings or improvements is *in progress* or is *in good faith contemplated* by such corporation." Such a showing that improvements are "in good faith contemplated" requires the owner to set forth "*concrete* and *definite* plans for utilizing and adopting the property for exempt purposes within the reasonably foreseeable future." *World Buddhist Ch'an Jing Center, Inc. v. Schoeberl, 846 N.Y.S.2d 392 (N.Y.A.D. 2007).*

EXAMPLE. A church purchased property that it was renovating for church use. The Nebraska Supreme Court ruled that the property was not entitled to exemption: "This court has consistently held that the intention to use property in the future for an exempt purpose is not a use of the property for [exempt] purposes. . . . [We reject the church's argument] that its purchase of the property showed that it had more than intent to use the property for an exempt purpose. The ownership of property is not evidence of use under the statute." *St. Monica's v. Lancaster County Board of Equalization, 751 N.W.2d 604 (Nebr. 2008).*

Leased property

Some churches lease the property they use for worship services and other activities. Does the fact that a church leases the property it uses qualify the property for exemption from tax? Most property tax exemption statutes only apply to property that is *owned* by a church or other specified charity. The fact that a church leases property does not ordinarily render the property exempt from tax. Some statutes refer to property that is used for religious purposes. Property leased by a church for religious purposes may qualify for exemption under such a statute.

EXAMPLE. An Illinois court ruled that a building owned by a church did not lose its tax-exempt status as a result of being leased to a local charity for a nominal fee. The church "leased" a building that it owned to a local charity for a onetime payment of $1. The charity used the property three days each week to accept, distribute, and sell donated furniture, clothing, and household goods. The court noted that Illinois law exempts from taxation "all property used exclusively for religious purposes . . . and not leased or otherwise used with a view to profit."

The court concluded that the property was used exclusively for religious purposes. It acknowledged that the exemption statute requires that property that is used exclusively for religious purposes not be "leased or otherwise used with a view to profit." The court concluded that the property met this test as well: "Whether property is used with a view toward profit depends on the intent of the owner in using the property. It is clear that [the church] did not use the property for profit. [The charity] paid the sum total of one dollar for its use of the property. [The church] uses the property for religious purposes, fulfilling its missions to

provide charity to the community through distribution of food, clothing, furniture, and Christmas gifts to those in need. While some revenues are generated through the sales of clothing and furniture, this is not the primary purpose in using the property. [The church's] use of the property falls within the [requirements of the statute]. Therefore, the property should be exempt from taxation." *First Presbyterian Church v. Zehnder, 715 N.E.2d 1209 (Ill. App. 1999).*

EXAMPLE. The Indiana Supreme Court ruled that property owned by a for-profit entity and leased to a church for religious purposes did not qualify for exemption from property taxation under a state law exempting property "owned, occupied, and used by a person for . . . religious purposes." The court concluded: "[The lessor] has failed to demonstrate an exempt purpose separate from that of [the church]. At most what it has proven is that it leased and primarily used its property for religious and charitable purposes. This is laudable. But in order to qualify for an exemption the property, among other things, must be owned for religious and charitable purposes. And absent evidence that an owner of leased property possesses an exempt purpose separate and distinct from the exempt purpose of its lessee, the owner holds the property for its own benefit, not that of the public, and thus its property is not entitled to the statutory exemption." *Hamilton County Property Tax Assessment Board of Appeals v. Oaken Bucket Partners, LLC, 938 N.E.2d 654 (Ind. 2010).*

EXAMPLE. An Illinois appeals court concluded that a building leased by a church for use as a sanctuary by its parishioners was exempt from property taxation under Illinois law. The court based this conclusion on a state law exempting "all property used exclusively for religious purposes" from tax. The court noted that under this law "the taxable status of property is determined by its use, not by its ownership." *Faith Christian Fellowship v. Department of Revenue, 589 N.E.2d 796 (Ill. App.. 1992).*

EXAMPLE. The Nebraska Supreme Court ruled that a portion of a church's property that it leased to a public school was entitled to exemption from property taxes. The court concluded: "It is the exclusive use of the property that determines the exempt status. The Constitution and the statutes do not require that the ownership and use must be by the same entity. Ownership and use may be by separate entities. . . . The lease of the property by the church to the school did not create a taxable use. Both of the uses were exempt. The property was used for a combination of exempt uses. . . . The lease by the church to the school did not create a non-exempt use of the property. The property continued to be used exclusively for religious and educational purposes." *Fort Calhoun Baptist church v. Washington County Board of Equalization, 759 N.W.2d 475 (Neb. 2009).*

EXAMPLE. The Texas Supreme Court ruled that a church's parking lots were exempt from property taxation, despite the fact that they were rented for most of the week to a neighboring business. It noted that "for purposes of the tax exemption, a place of religious worship includes not only the sanctuary, but also those grounds and structures surrounding the sanctuary which are necessary for the use and enjoyment of the church. Thus, a parking lot may qualify as a place of religious worship." In concluding that the parking lots in this case satisfied the requirements for exemption, the court stressed that the lots were used regularly by church members attending worship services on Sunday mornings and on Sunday and Wednesday evenings. They also were used by members attending special events and activities at the church. This evidence convinced the court that the lots were "used primarily for religious purposes."

The court insisted that the exemption of church property must be analyzed both quantitatively and qualitatively. That is, the test for exemption is not a "mere mathematical calculation" of the number of hours that a church and its members physically occupy the parking lots or other church property. While such an analysis is important, it is not the sole test for evaluating the exempt status of church property. The courts also must consider the qualitative use of the property. That is, how significant is the use of the property in terms of the church's mission? Clearly, most churches could not exist without parking lots, and therefore such lots are entitled to exemption, even though they may be used only a few hours each week by church members. *First Baptist Church v. Bexar County, 833 S.W.2d 108 (Tex. 1992).*

EXAMPLE. A District of Columbia appeals court ruled that property owned by a religious organization but used by a school was exempt from property tax. A religious organization leased a portion of its facilities to a nonprofit music school. The lease provided that the religious organization would pay any real estate taxes on its property resulting from the lease and that the school would reimburse any such payments. The religious organization filed an application seeking to have its leased property declared exempt from property taxes. This request was denied by a local taxing authority on the ground that the property was owned and operated by two different types of nonprofit entities.

An appeals court concluded that limiting the property tax exemption to property that is both owned and operated by the same kind of nonprofit organization "would be an anomaly and contrary to the legislative intent to permit nonprofit charitable organizations, schools, and religious groups to operate in the District of Columbia without the burden of taxation. . . . There is nothing in the legislative history which would show [an intent] to deny a tax exemption where the property is both owned and used by the types of entities exempt from taxation under the statute simply because the owner and user would qualify ordinarily under different sections of the statute." *Sisters of the Good Shepherd v. District of Columbia, 746 A.2d 310 (D.C. App. 2000).*

EXAMPLE. An Illinois court concluded that a church preschool was exempt from property taxation even though children had to pay a fee to attend. The state property tax law exempted property used exclusively for religious or "school and religious" purposes as long as it was not used "with a view to profit." The court reviewed the church's bylaws and concluded that the operation of a preschool was consistent with its religious purposes. Also, "just because [the preschool] charges tuition and fees to keep the doors open, it does not necessarily follow that it operates the child-care center and preschool with a view to profit." *Faith Builders Church, Inc. v. Department of Revenue, 882 N.E.2d 1256 (Ill. App. 2008).*

Youth activities buildings

Some churches have separate buildings that are used for the church's youth ministries. Such buildings may be exempt from property taxes.

EXAMPLE. The Minnesota tax court ruled that a building owned by a church and used for various youth activities was exempt from property tax. The building was located two miles from the sanctuary and consisted of two stories and 12,000 square feet of space that contained a gymnasium, auditorium, tanning salon, weight room, prayer room, bookstore, offices, and video arcade. The building was used primarily as the location of the church's youth ministry, and it was used for Sunday youth activities, religious services, special events, athletic events, prayer meetings, and concerts.

The church claimed that it used the building to fulfill its mission to "win souls for Christ" through religious activities and events. It noted that the building was constructed to attract youths and that it provided a place both for the youths to gather in a family environment and for the gospel to be preached to the users of the buildings various facilities. Christian music was played over the loudspeakers at all times. The church's youth group and staff were trained to approach others to share their religious message. Proselytizing took place in the weight room and with people waiting to use the tanning room. In addition, the rooms contained Christian messages and pictures on posters lining the walls.

The court concluded that the entire building was exempt from property tax on the ground that it was being used for church purposes. *Country Bible Church v. County of Grant, (Minn. Tax Court 2003).*

Parsonages

A parsonage is a church-owned property used as a residence by a minister. Many states exempt such properties from taxation. Some states impose restrictions on the exemption. For example, a few states exempt parsonages only up to a specified dollar value, exempt only one parsonage for each church, or exempt the grounds surrounding a parsonage only up to a specified area. The exemption does not extend to residences owned by ministers themselves. To illustrate, one court ruled that a parsonage was no longer entitled to exemption after the church sold it to its minister. *Watts v. Board of Assessors, 414 N.E.2d 1003 (Mass. 1981).* The minister had title to the parsonage conveyed to himself and his wife as trustees of the church, with the understanding that if he ever relocated, the church would buy the property back by paying him the purchase price he had paid plus the appreciation value. The court concluded that the "parsonage" was owned by a private individual, not by the church, and therefore was not entitled to exemption.

A few courts have ruled that church-owned parsonages may be exempt from property taxation even though they enjoy no specific statutory exemption. For example, one court concluded that a church-owned parsonage that served various religious purposes, such as a meeting place for church groups and a place for providing religious services, including pastoral counseling, was exempted from taxation by the general exemption of property used exclusively for religious purposes. *Immanuel Baptist Church v. Glass, 497 P.2d 757 (Okla. 1972).* But several other courts have ruled that parsonages are taxable unless they are specifically exempted. *Salt Lake County v. Tax Commission ex rel. Good Shepherd Lutheran Church, 548 P.2d 630 (Utah 1976).*

In general, to be exempt from property taxation, a parsonage must be actually and exclusively used as an integral part of the operations of the church rather than as a mere convenience to a minister. *Clinton Township v. Camp Brett-Endeavor, Inc., 1 N.J. Tax 54 (1980).* To illustrate, one court concluded that a dwelling used for several hours a week by a clergyman for commercial purposes did not qualify for a property tax exemption. *Ballard v. Supervisor of Assessments, 306 A.2d 506 (Md. 1973).* However, one court upheld the exemption of a parsonage even though the clergyman's wife engaged in a part-time interior designing business and occasionally used a bedroom for business purposes. *Congregation Beth Mayer, Inc. v. Board of Assessors, 417 N.Y.S.2d 754 (1979).* In holding that a parsonage can meet the definition of "property used exclusively for religious purposes," one court observed that "a parsonage qualifies for an exemption even if it reasonably and substantially facilitates the aims of religious worship and religious instruction because the pastor's religious duties require him to live in close proximity to the church or because the parsonage has unique facilities for religious worship and instruction or is primarily used for such purposes." *McKenzie v. Johnson, 456 N.E.2d 73 (Ill. 1983).*

Residences that are not parsonages
Summarized below are cases in which the courts have concluded that various housing arrangements did not constitute tax-exempt parsonages.

- A home occupied by a full-time evangelist. *Blackwood Brothers Evangelistic Association v. State Board of Equalization, 614 S.W.2d 364 (Tenn. 1980).*
- A home owned by a denominational agency and occupied by one of its officers, an executive of a religious denomination.

Pentecostal Church of God of America v. Hughlett, 601 S.W.2d 666 (Mo. 1980); Pacific Northwest Annual Conference of the United Methodist Church v. Walla Walla County, 508 P.2d 1361 (Wash. 1973). East Coast Conference of Evangelical Covenant Church of America, Inc. v. Supervisor of Assessments, 388 A.2d 177 (Md. 1978).

- A home owned by a denominational agency and occupied by one of its officers, even though the officer was provided with an office at the agency's offices where he performed most of his religious responsibilities. *Nebraska Annual Conference of the United Methodist Church v. Scotts Bluff County Board of Equalization, 499 N.W.2d 543 (Neb. 1993).*
- A duplex owned by a state conference of Seventh Day Adventists. *Seventh-Day Adventists v. Board of Tax Commissioners, 512 N.E.2d 936 (Ind. Tax 1987).*
- A church-owned residence used by an unordained minister of music. *In re Marlow, 237 S.E.2d 57 (S.C. 1977).*
- A church-owned residence used by a superintendent of a church-operated school. *St. Matthew Lutheran Church v. Delhi Township, 257 N.W.2d 183 (Mich. 1977).*
- A church-owned residence used by an instructor at a church-operated school. *St. Matthew Lutheran Church v. Delhi Township, 257 N.W.2d 183 (Mich. 1977).*
- A church-owned residence used by an unordained youth minister. *Borough of Cresskill v. Northern Valley Evangelical Free Church, 312 A.2d 641 (N.J. 1973).*
- A church-owned residence used by the widow of a deceased minister. *Borough of Cresskill v. Northern Valley Evangelical Free Church, 312 A.2d 641 (N.J. 1973).*
- A church-owned residence occupied by a church custodian. *Episcopal Parish of Christ Church v. Kinney, 389 N.E.2d 847 (Ohio 1979); Wauwatosa Avenue United Methodist Church v. City of Wauwatosa, 776 N.W.2d 280 (Wisc. App. 2009).*
- A residence owned by a rescue mission and used by one of its minister-employees. *Goodwill Home and Mission, Inc. v. Garwood Borough, 658 A.2d 1330 (N.J. App. 1995).*
- A church-owned rectory no longer occupied by the parish priest but used for church activities and occupied by a couple in exchange for providing custodial and security services for the church. *Sacred Heart of Brewster Catholic Church v. County of Nobles, 1999 WL 832408 (Minn. Tax 1999).*

Residences that are tax-exempt parsonages
Other courts have construed the term "parsonage" more broadly and have found the following dwellings to be tax-exempt parsonages under applicable state law.

- Dwellings owned by a religious denomination and used by denominational executives. *McCreless v. City of San Antonio, 454 S.W.2d 393 (Tex. 1970); Cudlipp v. City of Richmond, 180 S.E.2d 525 (Va. 1971).*
- A three-story, 16-unit apartment building owned by a missions organization and rented to missionaries temporarily

home on furlough. *Evangelical Alliance Mission v. Department of Revenue, 517 N.E.2d 1178 (Ill. App. 1987).*

- A church-owned home used by an ordained minister of music. *City of Amarillo v. Paramount Terrace Christian Church, 530 S.W.2d 323 (Tex. 1975).*
- A home owned by a denominational agency and used by one of its officers. *Corporation of Presiding Bishop v. Ada County, 849 P.2d 83 (Idaho 1993).*

✧ **KEY POINT.** A few statutes specifically include housing of denominational officials within the definition of parsonage. See Table 12-4 at the end of this chapter.

Generally, the courts have concluded that a church is not limited to one parsonage. As a result, unless the state property tax law specifies otherwise, a church having two or more full-time ministers may provide a tax-free parsonage to each. *Congregation B'Nai Jacob v. City of Oak Park, 302 N.W.2d 296 (Mich. 1981); In re Marlow, 237 S.E.2d 57 (S.C. 1977); Cudlipp v. City of Richmond, 180 S.E. 525 (Va. 1971).*

EXAMPLE. A New York court ruled that a church-owned residence occupied by a nonordained choir director was exempt from property taxes, not because it qualified as a parsonage, but because of the many religious functions that occurred there. The religious uses included choir rehearsals, weekly Bible studies, youth retreats, and occasional housing for visiting clergy. *Holy Trinity Orthodox Church v. O'Shea, 720 N.Y.S.2d 904 (2001).*

Vacant land

Many churches own tracts of vacant land for purposes of recreation or future expansion. Are such properties exempt from taxation? Courts have come to both conclusions. The key decisions are summarized below.

Exemption recognized

EXAMPLE. A Colorado court ruled that two vacant lots owned by a church were exempt from property tax because they were used one day each year for religious purposes. The church in question owned two vacant lots—one near the church and the second some distance away. The church was the only user of the two lots, and it used each lot one day each year for activities it claimed were in furtherance of its religious mission. The church hoped to construct structures on each lot for church use, but it lacked the funds to do so. A local tax assessor ruled that the lots did not qualify for exemption because the quantity and extent of the church's use was insufficient.

The court disagreed. It concluded: "We note that property tax exemptions are determined on an annual basis . . . based on the use of the property in each tax year. Implicit in this scheme is the requirement that, in order for the property to qualify for tax exemption for that tax year, there be at least some actual use of the

property for tax exempt purposes in that tax year. Apart from this minimal implicit requirement, however, we decline to hold . . . that any particular frequency or quantity of use religious in character is required to satisfy the foregoing . . . standards for exemption based on religious use." The court noted that while the tax assessor considered the church's use of the lots just one day each year to be insufficient for exemption, he "was unable to quantify the frequency or amount of such use that would be considered sufficient." *Pilgrim Rest Baptist Church v. PTA, 971 P.2d 270 (Colo. App. 1998).*

EXAMPLE. A Florida court ruled that vacant land owned by a religious agency and used occasionally for religious purposes was exempt from property taxation. A denominational agency (the "church") purchased 2.5 acres of vacant land. After purchasing the land, the church used it occasionally for religious purposes. This use included prayer services on the property by small groups of church leaders and frequent visits to the property for site development planning and fund-raising. A tax assessor ruled that the "inaccessible, weed-covered lot" was not exempt and that the religious activities that occurred on the property were incidental.

A state appeals court disagreed with the assessor's decision and ruled that the property was exempt from tax. The court concluded: "The record demonstrates that the church's property was used exclusively for religious purposes. There is no evidence that the property was used for any nonexempt purpose. Thus, the church's use of the property cannot be characterized as incidental." *Robbins v. Florida Conference Association of Seventh Day Adventists, 641 So.2d 893 (Fla. App. 3 Dist. 1994).*

EXAMPLE. A Florida state court ruled that a church-owned unimproved lot was exempt from real estate taxes. The court observed that "while the land was substantially vacant and unimproved and was not used by the church continuously, nevertheless, the land was being actually and presently used by the church for religious purposes sporadically and improvements and greater physical use were planned. The church's present religious use of the property, while not evidenced by improvements and not continuous, was exclusive of any other use and was not incidental to any nonexempt use." *Hausman v. First Baptist Church, 513 So.2d 767 (Fla. App. 1987).*

EXAMPLE. An Illinois court ruled that a church's property was exempt from tax. The court concluded: "As the land in question was used exclusively for religious purposes, insofar as it was at least minimally used for religious purposes, was not used for secular purposes, and was in the actual process of development and adaptation for religious use in the tax year in question," it was entitled to exemption. *Grace Community Church Assemblies of God v. Illinois Dept. of Revenue, 950 N.E.2d 1151(Ill. App. 2011).*

EXAMPLE. The Tax Court of Indiana ruled that an undeveloped tract of church-owned property was exempt from property taxation under Indiana law. The land had been purchased by the church under a land sales contract providing for the transfer of title to the church only after payment of the full purchase price over a term of two years. The church claimed that the property was exempt from taxation under a state law exempting "land . . . purchased for the purpose of erecting a building which is to be owned, occupied, and used" for exempt purposes. The state board of tax commissioners rejected the church's claim of exemption, arguing that the church could not be considered to have purchased property that it held under a land sales contract. The tax court upheld the church's claim of exemption, noting that the church planned to erect a new sanctuary on the property and that it satisfied the definition of a purchaser when it entered into the land sales contract. *Community Christian Church, Inc. v. Board of Tax Commissioners, 523 N.E.2d 462 (Ind. T.C. 1988).*

EXAMPLE. The Kentucky Supreme Court ruled that a 10-acre tract of largely vacant property that a church had acquired for future expansion was exempt from property taxation due to its occasional use for church purposes. A church purchased 10 acres of land, including two houses. The acreage was divided into two parcels, each consisting of approximately five acres, with a single family dwelling located on each parcel. It was the stated purpose of the church to build a new, larger facility on this property, as well as to provide for an activity center and other related church facilities as soon as finances allowed. The two houses were rented to individuals for residential purposes, with the rental income being used by the church building fund to service a mortgage on the property. The field on the side of these houses is used by the church for recreational purposes about once a year. On two occasions, the church has held an annual church picnic on the property. And while there have been no improvements or permanent structures erected by the church, a cross and bench were erected on a small portion of the property with permission of the tenants. This area is used for meditation by some of the parishioners.

The tax assessor determined that the property was subject to taxation. The church appealed to the state supreme court, claiming that the property was exempt on the basis of a provision in the state constitution exempting from taxation "property owned and occupied by . . . institutions of religion." The court, in concluding that the property was entitled to exemption, observed: "While the evidence does not indicate a continuous use of these grounds by [the church] it does support the finding of the trial court as to periodic use, such as horseshoe pitching, volleyball, softball, and tugs of war during the occasional outings by the church membership. There is also a portion used as a prayer and meditation area, including a bench and a large wooden cross. In essence, the congregation has used this property like a park, although not on either a daily or weekly basis. However, it would seem that it has been utilized by the church with the same frequency as many, if not most, churches use outdoor land that adjoins their main

sanctuaries. Therefore, we find that substantial evidence supports the findings by the trial court that the land owned by the church, but not occupied by the tenants, is, in fact, occupied by the church for purposes of the Kentucky Constitution."

The court then made the following significant comment: "We recognize that churches are unique. For the most part, they are never 'occupied' in the conventional sense. A vast majority of properties owned by 'institutions of religion' such as churches, mosques, tabernacles, temples, and the like, are used for places of worship at specified times and may remain vacant for substantial periods during the week. We further recognize that adjacent facilities, such as activity buildings, gymnasiums, even shelters, may be owned by religious institutions, but perhaps utilized irregularly on an as needed basis. School buildings owned by religious institutions may, in fact, sit idle for a great deal of time. This would not preclude these buildings from being 'occupied'. . . . It is precisely for these reasons that we find that the trial court's findings were supported substantially by the evidence in this case as to the property not being rented out as residences."

This case is significant for two reasons. First, it demonstrates that occasional use of church-owned vacant land for religious purposes may be sufficient for exemption from taxation. Second, the court made the important observation that many buildings owned by religious, educational, and charitable institutions are vacant for significant periods of time but are nevertheless entitled to exemption because of their occasional exempt use. A university classroom building comes to mind. Such buildings are often vacant for several months during the year. The same is true for many churches, whose property is used for religious purposes for no more than a few hours each week. In many states, the exemption of church property from taxation is limited to property that is "used exclusively for religious worship." And yet, the exempt status of churches that conduct a single, one-hour worship service weekly has never been questioned on the ground of infrequent use. *Freeman v. St. Andrew Orthodox Church, Inc., 294 S.W.3d 425 (Ky. 2009).*

EXAMPLE. The Maryland Court of Appeals ruled that 16 acres of undeveloped land owned by a church was exempt from property taxation. It observed, "The 16 acres are part of the land on which the church sits and that parcel is not subject to another, non-church use. The applicable covenants and zoning restrictions prohibit that property from being put to other than open space use; there simply can be no commercial, residential, or other non-worship related development on that property. The land, then, may be used only for church purposes, either in tangible, such as the construction of a prayer garden, or in nontangible, i.e. reflective or spiritual, ways. . . . A church is more than four walls built of stone, marble or concrete. . . . In the present case, it does not follow that, merely because the church has been required, or decided, to leave a large portion of the church property undeveloped, the property is not being used—it clearly is as the site of the church—or that the congregation will not use the property in its natural state to enrich its worship experience. . . . Nor is there any merit to the argument that the use of the 16-acre tract is not related to the furtherance of public worship. . . . The primary purpose of the non-developed land is to preserve the environmental aesthetics of the neighboring community and present the primary structure in a visually pleasing and understated manner. The development envelope is balanced by the open space, non-use area, much as a garden, lawn, or yard balances many residential parcels. . . . In this case the 16 acres provide a natural setting for the church and, thus, the religious worship use. As such, they are being actively used by the church for religious worship." *Supervisor of Assessments v. Keeler, 764 A.2d 821 (Md. 2001).*

EXAMPLE. A North Carolina state appeals court concluded that a five-acre undeveloped lot located next to (and owned by) a Baptist church was exempt from property taxes. The church purchased the lot for future expansion and also as a buffer to preserve the church from the burgeoning industrial area surrounding it (which included a plastics factory, a textile mill, and a proposed industrial park). Though the lot remained in an unimproved condition, it was used by the church for youth activities (recreation, camping, etc.) and as a religious retreat for men from a local rescue mission.

A local governmental agency ruled that the lot did not qualify for exemption under a state law exempting "buildings, the land they actually occupy, and additional adjacent land reasonably necessary for the convenient use of any building . . . if wholly and exclusively used by its members for religious purposes." The agency concluded that the property had been acquired for future expansion and was not presently used "wholly and exclusively" for religious purposes.

A state appeals court rejected this conclusion and ruled in favor of the church. It acknowledged that the present use of property determines whether it is exempt, not its intended future use, because "no public purpose is served by permitting land to lie unused and untaxed." Nevertheless, the court concluded that the land was presently being used "wholly and exclusively" for exempt purposes. The court pointed to the church's use of the property as a religious retreat by men from the rescue mission and as a recreational center for its youth group. The court concluded that the property also qualified for exemption because of its present use as a buffer zone insulating the church from surrounding factories. Using the property for this purpose was "reasonably necessary for the convenient use of [church] buildings" and accordingly qualified the property for exemption from tax under the statute. Further, use of the property as a buffer zone "to protect the sanctity and serenity of the church from encroaching industrial development was a permissible religious purpose and present use

entitling the property to exemption." *Matter of Worley, 377 S.E.2d 270 (N.C. App. 1989).*

EXAMPLE. A church-owned 15-acre tract of land was granted an exemption by a state court, since the land was used for neighborhood recreational activities and for Boy Scout and Girl Scout activities, and was reasonably necessary for the convenient use of the church's existing structures. *Appeal of Southview Presbyterian Church, 302 S.E.2d 298 (N.C. App. 1983).*

EXAMPLE. The Supreme Court of Ohio ruled that a three-acre tract of undeveloped land owned by a synagogue and located on its premises was properly exempt from real estate taxes. Ohio law exempts "houses used exclusively for religious worship . . . and the grounds attached to such buildings necessary for the proper occupancy, use, and enjoyment thereof, and not leased or otherwise used with a view to profit." The synagogue in question owned 14 acres, 11 of which consisted of the synagogue building, a parking lot, and a landscaped lawn area. The additional three acres were a largely undeveloped grove of trees. The tax commissioner ruled that the three-acre tract was not exempt from real estate taxes, since it was "not necessary for the proper occupancy, use and enjoyment of the synagogue."

This determination was reversed by the state board of tax appeals, and an appeal was taken to the Ohio Supreme Court. The court, in upholding the exemption, observed that "the land added aesthetic qualities to the existing site. It also served as a sound barrier as well as providing a wooded backdrop for outdoor services and congregational activities." The court added that "for outdoor services to be appreciated, it is certainly important to hear them." Accordingly, the use of a grove of trees "as a sound barrier to the noise of traffic traveling by the property" was a necessary means of enabling the congregation to enjoy its property. *Congregation Brith Emeth v. Limbach, 514 N.E.2d 874 (Ohio 1987).*

EXAMPLE. The Supreme Court of Ohio ruled that a 21-acre tract of land owned by a church and used for recreational purposes qualified for exemption from property taxation on the basis of charitable use. The property included two softball fields, a soccer field, and a jogging trail and was used by an estimated 3,000 community members per year at no charge. The court rejected the tax assessor's argument that merely holding the property open to the public and allowing various third parties to use it was not a charitable use and did not qualify the property for exemption. The court concluded: "If the use to which property is put otherwise qualifies as charitable, neither the fact of ownership by a religious organization nor the existence of religious motives in connection with the charitable use will defeat the claim of exemption." *The Chapel v. Testa, 950 N.E.2d 142 (Ohio 2011).*

EXAMPLE. Vacant church-owned property was granted an exemption, since the church had prepared plans and raised funds for the construction of a house of worship within a reasonable time after the filing of the application for exemption. *Holy Trinity Episcopal Church v. Bowers, 173 N.E.2d 682 (Ohio 1961).*

These cases demonstrate that undeveloped land acquired by a church for future expansion may be eligible for tax exemption if it is not used commercially and it either (1) is needed as a buffer zone to insulate the adjacent church facility from industrial development; or (2) is used by church youth groups and other groups associated with the church for religious purposes or recreational purposes, or is otherwise integrated into the church's activities.

Exemption denied

A number of courts have held that vacant land ordinarily is not used exclusively for religious purposes and does not qualify for exemption. This almost always will be the result if the land is used for commercial purposes (such as farming) or if no religious or charitable activities occur on the land or such uses are insignificant.

EXAMPLE. A Connecticut court ruled that an undeveloped tract of land owned by a church was not entitled to exemption from property taxation, since it was not used exclusively for religious purposes. The church property was an unimproved, wooded lot that contained no structures or buildings other than a volleyball court. The court noted that the state property tax law exempts property belonging to a religious organization that is not in actual use for religious purposes because of "the absence of suitable buildings and improvements thereon, if the construction of such buildings or improvements is in progress." Despite the church's assertion that the property was used for religious purposes, in that "prayer walks" were occasionally conducted on the property, the court ruled that the property was not exempt, because it "contains neither any building or other improvement used for charitable purposes, nor such improvements in the process of being constructed." *Grace n' Vessels of Christ Ministries, Inc. v. City of Danbury, 733 A.2d 283 (Conn. App. 1999).*

EXAMPLE. A Florida court ruled that vacant land acquired by a church as a site for a future sanctuary was not exempt from state property taxes. A church, which usually had 800 to 1,000 people attending Sunday services in a rented building, purchased 47 acres of unimproved land for $4 million, on which it planned to build a sanctuary. The property was not adjacent to the building the church was renting. No church services were conducted on the property before January 1, 2000. However, on two occasions in 1999, a few members of the church and staff walked around the property, discussed plans as to where things would be located, and offered some prayers (such as thanking God for the land). A tax assessor determined that the property was not entitled to exemption from tax under a state law exempting property "used predominantly for charitable or religious purposes." A state appeals court agreed: "Property is

not necessarily exempt merely because small groups walked on it twice between the time the church closed on the property, and the assessment date." *Palm Beach Community Church v. Nikolits, 835 So.2d 1274 (Fla. App. 2002).*

EXAMPLE. The Indiana tax court ruled that a church-owned tract of land was not eligible for property tax exemption. A church owned a tract of land on which it planned, one day, to construct a new sanctuary. For several years the land was not used for any purpose. A state tax board denied the church's application to have the property declared exempt from property taxes under a state law exempting property "purchased for the purpose of erecting a building which is to be owned, occupied, and used" exclusively for church purposes. The state tax court agreed that the church-owned property was not eligible for exemption. It conceded that church-owned property could be exempt under state law prior to the actual construction of a church building, and that the law specified no time period in which a proposed church facility had to be constructed. Still, the court denied the exemption in this case, noting that "it would not serve any purpose to grant an exemption for property merely owned by a church, with no reasonable expectation of the property ever being used for its intended purpose."

The court noted that the congregation, which numbered 35 members, planned to construct a "world class tabernacle" on the site costing $5 million. The court concluded: "The intent to use such property for an exempt purpose must be one of substance and not a mere dream that sometime in the future, if funds can be obtained, the [church] would so use such property." *Foursquare Tabernacle Church of God in Christ v. State Board of Tax Commissioners, 550 N.E.2d 850 (Ind. Tax 1990).*

EXAMPLE. A Michigan court ruled that an undeveloped tract of church-owned property on which a sanctuary was about to be constructed was not exempt from state property taxation under a Michigan statute exempting "houses of public worship . . . used predominantly for religious services or for teaching of religious truths." The court concluded that "actual use of a building, not merely preparation for construction or even initiation of actual construction, is a prerequisite to an exemption from taxation" under the Michigan statute, since "by the statute's own terms, a prerequisite to an exemption is that the house of public worship be used predominantly for religious services or for teaching the religious truths and beliefs." The court rejected contrary rulings in other states with the observation that such rulings were "based on the particular language of those states' exemption statutes." *St. Paul Lutheran Church v. City of Riverview, 418 N.W.2d 412 (Mich. App. 1987).*

EXAMPLE. The Minnesota Tax Court ruled that there was insufficient support for the exemption of three church-owned wooded lots from property taxation to grant the church's motion for summary judgment in its favor. The church claimed that the lots were entitled to exemption because they were devoted to and reasonably necessary to the accomplishment of church purposes. It pointed out that the lots were used for prayer, reflection, and Christian education, including a Vacation Bible School. The court, in denying the church's request, noted that the only support for its position were "self-serving statements" about the actual use of the lots without an adequate factual basis. *Advent Evangelical Lutheran Church v. County of Ramsey, 2008 WL 3892374 (Minn. Tax Court 2008).*

EXAMPLE. The Utah Supreme Court ruled that a parcel of vacant land purchased by a church was not exempt from property taxes, despite the church's use of the land for occasional worship services. The land was purchased as a site for a new church building. The church maintained the land but did not begin construction of a new church building. However, the church did use the property for religious purposes. For approximately two hours each year, the church held religious services on the property. The court noted that state law exempts from property taxes "property used exclusively for religious purposes." It concluded that the land in question failed this test. It insisted that in order for land to be used exclusively for religious purposes, it must be "actually used or committed to a use that is exclusively religious." The church argued that the land was used exclusively for religious purposes even though it was used for religious services for only a few hours each year, since "for 8,758 hours out of the year the land is committed to no use at all." The court disagreed, noting that "property held for future development is being used." *Corporation of the Episcopal Church v. Utah State Tax Commission, 919 P.2d 556 (Utah 1996).*

Church-owned retreats and campgrounds

Church-owned retreats and campgrounds have presented considerable difficulty for tax assessors. Several courts have concluded that a campground or retreat center owned and operated by a religious organization is exempt from property taxation if the activities conducted on the property are directly related to the religious purposes for which the organization was established. A few state property tax statutes specifically exempt church-owned campgrounds.

EXAMPLE. A Georgia state appeals court ruled that a campground owned and operated by an association of churches was exempt from property taxes. The association owns a 640-acre campground that contains various improvements, including worship facilities, a dining hall, cabins, meeting rooms, a swimming pool, and ball fields. About one-third of the property is undeveloped but is used for nature walks, outdoor Bible studies, and prayer. While user fees are charged for use of the facilities, they are not enough to cover operating expenses, and the deficit is made up through subsidies provided by the association. The facilities are used exclusively by adult and youth church groups of various denominations. The association requires that each group

conduct a religious program during its stay, and it previews each program to ensure that scheduled events include "worship and knowledge of God, Bible study, and prayer." Recreational activities, such as swimming and softball, are regularly incorporated into such programs.

A county tax assessor attempted to tax the entire 640-acre campground (arguing that the facility was operated primarily as an income-producing recreational facility), and the association appealed. A state appeals court affirmed the exempt status of the campground under a state law exempting properties used as a "place of religious worship." The court concluded that "the evidence establishes without dispute that religious activities are an integral part of every aspect of the use of the property. Although the recreational facilities which are provided to visitors are secular in nature, their use was shown to be intimately connected and intertwined with the religious activities to which the property is primarily dedicated. The fact that visitors are charged fees which are applied towards the operating expenses of the facility does not alter its fundamentally religious character. In light of the foregoing authorities, and on the basis of the uncontroverted evidence in the present case, we hold that the trial court did not err in concluding as a matter of law that the property was exempt from taxation as a place of religious worship." *Pickens County Board of Tax Assessors v. Atlanta Baptist Association, Inc., 381 S.E.2d 419 (Ga. App. 1989).*

EXAMPLE. An Illinois state appeals court ruled that a 1.6-acre "religious park" owned by a denominational agency was exempt from property taxation. *Illinois Conference of the United Church of Christ v. Illinois Department of Revenue, 518 N.E.2d 755 (Ill. App. 1988).* The park was established "to provide a unique setting outdoors for individuals and groups to experience and live out the biblical faith, and to experience a place for recreation and reflection." The park was used regularly for religious activities, including morning spiritual meditations, evening vespers, and religious retreats. Under these circumstances the court concluded that the park qualified for exemption as "property used exclusively for religious purposes." It rejected the contention that the presence of a small caretaker's residence on the tract prevented the property from being "used exclusively for religious purposes" and similarly ignored court rulings from other states under state property tax exemption statutes "far more restrictive than the statutory authority in our state." *Illinois Conference of the United Church of Christ v. Illinois Department of Revenue, 518 N.E.2d 755 (Ill. App. 1988).*

EXAMPLE. A Michigan court ruled that an 1,800-acre retreat owned by a parachurch ministry was exempt from property tax as a "house of public worship." The court concluded that the property could be viewed as a house of public worship, noting that "although [the ministry] may not fall within the traditional definition of a religious society, that does not mean that it is not entitled to an exemption as a religious society under the house of public worship exemption." The court refused to limit the property tax exemption to those portions of the 1,800 acres actually used for religious teaching and worship, since engaging in such an analysis "would unnecessarily intrude into the affairs of religious organizations." The court noted that the ministry conducted religious seminars on the property and "provides its seminar attendees access to the lakes on the property and has paved seven miles of road for bicycling. The large areas of undeveloped land permit the participants to walk through the woods and think about what they have heard. . . . The record contains no evidence that the property was being used for purposes outside those enumerated in [the ministry's] bylaws." *Institute in Basic Life Principles, Inc. v. Watermeet Township, 551 N.W. 2d 199 (Mich. App. 1996).*

EXAMPLE. The New Hampshire Supreme Court ruled that a church-operated campground did not qualify for exemption from property tax, except for a small chapel. The court based this conclusion on the fact that the operation of the campground did not benefit "the general public or a substantial and indefinite segment of the general public" because of the following factors: (1) the church's organizational documents state that the camp was to be used for members of the church; (2) the camp's own rules specify that "our programs and facilities are primarily reserved for the members of our [church]"; (3) no advertisements for the camp are sent to those outside of the church's membership; (4) while the camp is used by secular groups, this use is only "occasional and infrequent"; and (5) people who stay at the camp, even those associated with secular groups, must agree with the basic beliefs of the church.

The court concluded, "Where an organization makes efforts to limit its services, and targets its benefits only to its members, that organization is not obligated to serve an indefinite segment of the population . . . and is not eligible for a charitable tax exemption." The court also ruled that the camp did not qualify for exemption based on its religious nature, except for the chapel and "those portions of the administrative offices, maintenance center, barn and workshop that are reasonably related to the function of the chapel." *East Coast Conference of the Evangelical Covenant Church of America v. Town of Swanzey, 786 A.2d 88 (N.H. 2001).*

EXAMPLE. A New York court denied exemption to a church camp that derived 25 percent of its income from nonexempt uses, since the nonexempt uses were substantial enough to preclude a finding that the property was used exclusively for religious purposes. *Mount Tremper Lutheran Camp, Inc. v. Board of Assessors, 417 N.Y.S.2d 796 (1979).*

EXAMPLE. The New York Court of Appeals (the highest state court in New York) ruled that 64 bungalows, 6 house trailers, and a 10-acre wooded section of a 31-acre religious campground were exempt from property taxes as property "used exclusively for religious purposes." The court concluded that the bungalows, trailers, and 10-acre wooded section all met this test. It observed: "If [the organization] was unable to provide residential housing accommodations to its faculty, staff, students and their families, its primary purposes of providing rigorous religious and educational instruction . . . would be seriously undermined. Thus, these housing facilities are 'necessary and reasonably incidental' to the primary purpose of the facility, and this is so notwithstanding the existence of limited housing facilities nearby." For the same reasons, the court concluded that the trailer provided to the full-time caretaker was exempt. The court also concluded that the 10-acre wooded section was exempt, since it, too, was "incidental to the primary religious purpose of the entire 31-acre parcel." *Hapletah v. Town of Fallsburg, 590 N.E.2d 1182 (N.Y. 1992). See also Eternal Flame of Hope Ministries v. King, 908 N.Y.S.2d 456 (N.Y.A.D. 2010).*

EXAMPLE. A New York court ruled that a campground owned and operated by a religious organization was not exempt from property taxation. The religious organization consists of lay church members. It owns and operates a campground, which is open to the general public and is attended primarily by persons who are not members of the church. The camping program includes whirlpool and sauna treatments, instruction to assist persons who want to quit smoking, video programs on a variety of health issues, outdoor activities, and classes in cooking. Guests are not required to attend or participate in any religious activities. Advertisements for the camping program do not indicate that it is religious in nature or related to the church. In ruling that the campgrounds were not exempt from property taxation, the court observed: "Although health and physical well being are central concerns of the [church], in this case the health-related services are directed . . . to nonadherents of its religious principles. The fact that advertising for those services is aimed at the public as a whole supports the conclusion that the camp is not used primarily for . . . religious purposes. Also significant is the fact that guests are not required to participate in any prayer services, indoctrination, or similar activities." *Living Springs Retreat v. County of Putnam, 626 N.Y.S.2d 268 (A.D. 2 Dept. 1995).*

EXAMPLE. A North Carolina court ruled that a 532-acre church camp was exempt from property taxation because it was used primarily for religious purposes. In response to the county's argument that the camp could not be exempt from property tax, since it charges some campers a fee, sold some timber from a portion of the property, and allows the facilities to be used by nonchurch groups, the court observed: "There is substantial evidence in this record that the primary purpose of the camp was to serve the religious and spiritual needs of the members of the Methodist Church. The fact that others were permitted to use the camp and that some were charged a fee is not determinative. The fee was small and there is no evidence that there was any effort by the camp to make a profit. Furthermore, the sale of the timber on a portion of the larger tract is not a basis for converting the entire tract into a commercial venture." *Appeal of Mount Shepherd Methodist Camp, 462 S.E.2d 229 (N.C. App. 1995).*

EXAMPLE. Exemption was denied to a 155-acre church camp used for recreational, craft, and religious activities, since the property tax law exempted only actual places of religious worship from the tax. However, a chapel and a minister's residence located on the property were deemed exempt. *Davies v. Meyer, 541 S.E.2d 827 (Tex. 1976).*

Denominational administrative offices

Administrative regional or national offices of religious denominations may be exempt from taxation, depending on the wording of the exemption statute and the property's actual use.

EXAMPLE. The Ohio Supreme Court ruled that property owned by a denominational agency (the "regional church") and used as an administrative office was not exempt from property taxation. The property was used for several purposes, including (1) executive offices; (2) support staff; (3) conference rooms and classrooms for church leadership meetings and ministerial teaching and training; (4) offices for youth and Christian education, women's ministries, evangelism, and home missions; and (5) religious publishing for affiliated churches. The regional church summed up the use of the property as "facilitating the proclamation of the Gospel of Jesus Christ and supporting public worship." Its application for property tax exemption was denied on the ground that the property was being used "for purposes that are merely supportive of public worship" and therefore did not qualify for exemption under a state law that exempted from taxation property used exclusively for public worship or charitable purposes. *Church of God v. Levin, 918 N.E.2d 981 (Ohio 2009).*

Retirement homes

A few state property tax statutes specifically exempt church-operated retirement homes. In other states the courts have been asked to determine the exempt status of such facilities. Predictably, different conclusions have been reached. Courts that have found such facilities to be exempt generally do so on the basis of an exemption applicable to property used for *charitable* rather than religious purposes.

EXAMPLE. A Florida appeals court ruled that a nursing home operated by the Archdiocese of Miami was exempt from state property taxes. Since one-third of the residents living at the facility were private paying patients (the remaining two-thirds were Medicare or Medicaid patients), a local tax appraiser argued that only two-thirds of the facility was entitled to exemption.

In concluding that the entire property was entitled to exemption, the court cited the following considerations: (1) most of the residents were over 65 years of age (a majority were in their

80s); (2) charges owed by private paying patients were routinely written off; (3) patients were admitted on a first-come, first-served basis, with no preference given to private paying patients; (4) all patients (whether private paying, Medicare, or Medicaid) received the same quality facilities and services; (5) private paying patients who became unable to pay could become Medicaid patients, in which case they occupied the same bed and received the same services; (6) Medicaid and Medicare reimbursements were below the cost of caring for these patients; and (7) the home did not make a profit on its private paying patients. These factors, concluded the court, demonstrated the exempt status of the entire facility.

The court rejected the tax appraiser's position that "if there is any patient who somehow has enough income to pay for his or her bed at the home," that bed must be removed from the exemption, since such an income test "has reference more to the personal economics of a resident or residents of an apartment or room in a home for the aged than to the overall purpose or use of a home as a religious or charitable institution." In other words, the focus should be on the charitable object of the facility as a whole rather than on the ability of some patients to pay for their services. This certainly is a sensible conclusion and one that will be helpful to church-operated nursing homes in Florida and in other states with similar exemption provisions. *Markham v. Broward County Nursing Home, Inc., 540 So.2d 940 (Fla. App. 1989).*

EXAMPLE. The Oklahoma Supreme Court ruled that a nursing home operated by the Baptist Health Care Corporation was exempt from county real estate taxes. The facility was built and is operated as a statewide ministry to the elderly. Revenues from residents do not cover expenses incurred in operating the facility, and contributions from Baptist churches are used to cover the deficit. The court applied an eight-part test in determining whether a retirement facility qualifies for property tax exemption as a charitable institution: (1) whether rent receipts are applied to upkeep, maintenance, and equipment of the institution or are otherwise applied; (2) whether residents receive the same treatment regardless of their ability to pay; (3) whether the facilities are open to all, regardless of their ability to pay; (4) whether the facilities are open to all, regardless of race, creed, color, religion, or ability to pay; (5) whether charges are made to all patients and, if made, whether lesser charges are made to the poor or any charges made to the indigent; (6) whether a charitable trust fund is created by benevolent and charitably minded persons for the needy or donations made for the use of such persons; (7) whether the institution operated without a profit or private advantage to its founders and officials in charge; and (8) whether the articles or bylaws of the corporation make provision for the disposition of surplus assets upon dissolution. The court concluded that the facility in question met all eight criteria and accordingly was exempt. *Baptist Health Care Corporation v. Okmulgee County Board of Equalization, 750 P.2d 127 (Okla. 1988).*

EXAMPLE. A Pennsylvania state appeals court ruled that a 96-unit apartment building located on a 40-acre retirement community operated by an agency of the Lutheran Church in America was exempt from property taxation. The court concluded that the apartments qualified for exemption under a state law exempting "institutions of benevolence or charity . . . founded, endowed, and maintained by public or private charity," since the facility "charges monthly apartment fees that are by no means exorbitant and that are below actual operating cost; it does not request or receive financial information from apartment applicants before admission, and it routinely grants exonerations from payment of a portion of the monthly fee to residents who later demonstrate financial need." However, the court ruled that 81 cottage units located on the same property were not exempt, since the cottage operation consistently realized a substantial profit, and only a few residents were receiving a subsidy on the payment of fees. *Appeal of Lutheran Social Services, 539 A.2d 895 (Pa. Common. 1988).*

EXAMPLE. A Texas state appeals court ruled that a nursing facility, operated by a Christian Science church as part of its religious and charitable purposes, was exempt from property taxation. The facility admitted persons without regard to their religious faith. However, all patients had to agree to rely entirely upon the Christian Science method of healing (the sole method practiced at the facility), and all were expected and encouraged to study Christian Science literature. The facility charged a fee for its services but did not turn away patients unable to pay. Its total operating revenue generally was well below its operating expenses. Such facts, concluded the court, clearly established the facility's exemption under a state law exempting from property taxation any facility organized exclusively for religious or charitable purposes that was engaged exclusively in providing support or housing to elderly persons without regard to their ability to pay. The court rejected the state's contention that the facility's discrimination against non–Christian Scientists prevented its property from being exempt from taxation: "As long as a nursing home provides care to persons who would otherwise become burdens upon the state, it meets the requirement that its services benefit the general public, regardless of the religious motivations of its operators." *Dallas County Appraisal District v. The Leaves, Inc., 742 S.W.2d 424 (Tex. App. 1987).*

Other courts have concluded that church-operated retirement homes are not exempt from taxation.

EXAMPLE. A Connecticut appeals court ruled that a state law exempting from property taxes any property used exclusively for carrying out charitable purposes did not apply to a housing project for the elderly operated by a church. *United Church of Christ v. Town of West Hartford, 519 A.2d 1217 (Conn. App. 1987).* The court, noting that the housing was not restricted to the poor, sick, or infirm, concluded that the facility "provides an attractive retirement environment for those among the elderly who have the health to enjoy it and who can afford to pay for it." This simply could not be considered a "charitable purpose," said the court.

EXAMPLE. The Nebraska Supreme Court concluded that a 31-unit apartment complex operated in conjunction with a nursing home was not exempt from property taxes. *Evangelical Lutheran Good Samaritan Society v. Board of Equalization, 430 N.W.2d 502 (Nebr. 1988).* The apartments were located at St. Luke's Good Samaritan Village, which was operated by the Evangelical Lutheran Good Samaritan Society. Apartment residents were required to be at least 55 years of age and physically capable of living in an apartment without supervised medical care. They were assessed a monthly rent of $220. The court concluded that the apartments did not qualify for exemption as a charitable use. While acknowledging that a nursing home operated on a nonprofit basis "is exempt from taxation as a charitable institution," the court concluded that apartment units operated in conjunction with a nursing home were not exempt, since they constituted "low-rent housing," which was not a charitable use under Nebraska law.

Religious publishing

The tax-exempt status of property used for the publication of religious literature is another question that has been addressed by a number of courts. Most courts have concluded that property owned by a religious organization and used for religious purposes is exempt under statutes exempting property used exclusively for religious purposes. To illustrate, the following printing operations have been held to be exempt from tax.

- A printing facility owned by a religious denomination and which printed religious periodicals and Sunday-school materials for affiliated churches. *Himes v. Free Methodist Publishing House, 251 N.E.2d 486 (Ind. 1969); Christian Reformed Church in North America v. City of Grand Rapids, 303 N.W.2d 913 (Mich. 1981) (press sold all products at cost and operated at a loss).*
- A printing facility that promoted religion. *State Board of Tax Commissioners v. Warner Press, Inc., 248 N.E.2d 405 (Ind. 1969), modified, 258 N.E.2d 621 (Ind. 1970).*
- A printing facility that published two magazines devoted to religious purposes, with no diversion to commercial or secular uses, even though the magazines contained some political and economic views. *America Press, Inc. v. Lewisohn, 345 N.Y.S.2d 396 (1973), aff'd, 372 N.Y.S.2d 194 (1975).*
- A church-owned printing facility that published a weekly newspaper informing members of the work of the church. *Archdiocese of Portland v. Department of Revenue, 513 P.2d 1137 (Ore. 1973).*

A few courts have denied tax-exempt status to property used for religious publishing. To illustrate, a Pennsylvania court ruled that a nonprofit corporation that published religious materials was not exempt from property taxes. *Scripture Union v. Deitch, 572 A.2d 51 (Pa. Common. 1990).* The publisher (which was not affiliated with a church or denomination) published quarterly Bible study guides that it made available for a suggested annual donation of $20. The court noted that the property of "purely public charities" is exempt from taxation under state law and that an institution qualifies as a purely public charity only if it (1) advances a charitable purpose, (2) donates a substantial portion of its services, (3) benefits a substantial and indefinite class of persons who are legitimate subjects of charity, (4) relieves the government of some of its burdens, and (5) operates entirely free from the private profit motive.

The court concluded that the publisher failed to satisfy a number of these requirements. For example, only 14 percent of its materials were distributed without charge—too low to comprise a substantial portion of its total materials. Further, the court rejected the publisher's claim that its operating deficits for the previous two years demonstrated that it operated on a nonprofit basis. The court observed that the deficits existed only because of large expenses labeled in the publisher's financial statements simply as "other expenses." When questioned about the nature of these expenses, the publisher's president could not identify them. The court found this evidence insufficient to support the publisher's contention that it operated without a profit motive. The court concluded that the publisher failed to demonstrate that it relieved the government of some of its burden. The publisher had emphasized that "our purpose is to introduce people to God through the Jewish Christian scriptures in such a way that they are made aware of the difference between right and wrong, and the importance of choosing the right, and in such a way that they are introduced to the importance of loving their neighbor and of fulfilling a responsible role in their families, their workplace, and in society." While acknowledging that this indeed was a laudable objective, the court could not agree that the publisher was relieving a governmental burden, since the constitution "prohibits the government from endorsing any religion."

Another court denied exemption to a Bible society that printed and distributed Bibles but that was not affiliated with any particular religion or denomination. *American Bible Society v. Lewisohn, 369 N.Y.S.2d 725 (1975), aff'd, 386 N.Y.S.2d 49 (1976).* It is unlikely that a church-owned printing facility would qualify for an exemption in those states that exempt only buildings and property used exclusively for religious worship. Even in these states, however, church-owned printing facilities may be exempt as a charitable organization. *Missouri Conference Association of Seventh Day Adventists v. State Tax Commission, 727 S.W.2d 940 (Mo. App. 1987) (a Seventh Day Adventist bookstore was ruled to be exempt under a Missouri law exempting property used for purely charitable purposes).*

Exclusive use

Many statutes exempt property used exclusively for religious purposes. An exclusive use generally is construed to mean a primary,

inherent, or principal use, in contrast to secondary or incidental uses. The courts have ruled that the term "exclusively" does not necessarily mean "directly" or "immediately"; that a use that is incidental and reasonably necessary to an exempt use is properly exempted from tax; and that the exemption of property used exclusively for exempt purposes does not require constant activity or vigorous or obvious activity, but rather requires that the property be devoted to no other use than that which warrants the exemption. If part of church-owned property is used for commercial purposes, the entire property cannot be considered to be used exclusively for religious purposes. However, as noted previously, some states recognize the partial exemption rule, under which only the portion of church-owned property that is used for nonexempt purposes is denied exempt status.

EXAMPLE. A Pennsylvania court ruled that a church's weekly Bible study classes, held in the fellowship hall, constituted "religious worship," and therefore the fellowship hall was exempt from property taxes. The church treasurer testified that the building was used for the following religious purposes: (1) "lock-ins" and other overnight activities for the youth group; (2) a weekly Bible study and other church meetings and dinners; (3) wedding receptions; and (4) Boy Scout troop meetings. The court concluded that the fellowship hall was used weekly for the weekly Bible study and that the "regularity and constancy" of this worship brought the primary use of this part of the building within the standards for a place of regularly stated worship. The court added that an unfinished second floor above the fellowship hall also was exempt, since it was not being used at all. *Connellsville Street Church of Christ v. Fayette County Board of Assessment, 838 A.2d 848 (Pa. App. 2003).*

Application for exemption

The fact that a religious organization has received a determination letter from the IRS acknowledging that it is exempt from federal income taxation as an organization described in section 501(c)(3) of the tax code does not necessarily entitle the organization to a property tax exemption. It is important to recognize that in many states property used for religious purposes is not automatically exempt from taxation. An application must be filed with local tax authorities in such states. Failure to do so will result in loss of exemption, at least for the current year.

EXAMPLE. The Minnesota Supreme Court ruled that a church's property was not exempt from property taxes, since it had not been acquired by the assessment date of July 1 as required by state law. The court rejected the church's arguments that an oral understanding to acquire the property plus the signing of a letter of intent with the seller satisfied the acquisition requirement. *Crossroads Church v. County of Dakota, 800 N.W.2d 608 (Minn. 2011).*

EXAMPLE. The Nebraska Supreme Court ruled that a church can be denied an exemption from real estate taxes as a result of its failure to file an application for exemption. The court relied on the United States Supreme Court ruling that those "claiming the benefits of the religious-organization exemption should not automatically enjoy those benefits. Rather, in order to receive them, [they] may be required by the state to provide that [they] are a religious organization within the meaning of the act." *Indian Hills Church v. County Board of Equalization, 412 N.W.2d 459 (Neb. 1987).*

EXAMPLE. The Ohio Supreme Court concluded: "We regard as settled the general proposition that the taxable or exempt status of property should be determined as of the tax lien date, which is January 1 of whatever tax year is at issue." *Sylvania Church of God v. Levin, 888 N.E.2d 408 (Ohio 2008).*

EXAMPLE. An Oregon court ruled that a church's property was subject to tax because the church failed to timely appeal an assessor's decision to place it on the tax roll. *Taft Church v. Department of Revenue, 14 Or. Tax 119 (1997).*

EXAMPLE. The Oregon Tax Court ruled that a church's property was subject to taxation because it failed to file a timely exemption application, despite the fact that the tax assessor's office used an incorrect address to inform the church of the need to file a timely exemption application. The court acknowledged that the church did not receive notice of the exemption status change or the tax statements because the assessor sent the notices to the wrong address. The church claimed that the assessor was obligated to determine the church's correct address through a search of its internal records or of other available sources. Additionally, the church claimed that the assessor could have searched other sources, such as the Internet, and learned that no mail was accepted at the address on the deed.

In rejecting the church's request that a property tax exemption be granted for prior years based on the assessor's failure to send notices to the correct address, the court observed: "While it is definitely a good idea for the county to examine its returned mail, arguing about whether the county might have found the [plaintiff] earlier overlooks the point that the county ought not to have had to look for the [plaintiff] at all. . . . It is not the county's obligation to search for the taxpayer. Instead, it is the taxpayer's responsibility to search the county and make sure its records are correct.

"The legislature has placed the burden on taxpayers to notify county assessors of their true and correct address. [The assessor] did not have a duty to locate any other address for the plaintiff either by searching its internal records or by searching some other source."

This case illustrates that in most jurisdictions it is the responsibility of the property owner to ensure that the local tax assessor's records contain a correct mailing address. Church leaders should not assume that church property will be entitled to exemption from tax if no exemption application is filed, even if the failure to

RELEVANCE OF THE SUPREME COURT'S MINISTERIAL EXCEPTION RULING TO CHURCH PROPERTY TAX EXEMPTIONS

In a ringing endorsement of religious liberty, the United States Supreme Court unanimously affirmed the so-called "ministerial exception" barring civil court review of employment disputes between churches and ministers. The case involved a claim by a "called" teacher at a church-related school in Michigan that the school committed unlawful disability discrimination in terminating her employment. The Court concluded that the ministerial exception applied to a called teacher in a parochial school despite the fact that she only devoted a few minutes each school day to religious activities. The Court concluded that a finding of ministerial status cannot be based solely on the amount of time a person spends on religious functions.

In rejecting a federal appeals court's conclusion that the ministerial exception did not apply because of the limited time the teacher devoted to religious tasks, the Court observed: "The issue before us, however, is not one that can be resolved by a stopwatch. The amount of time an employee spends on particular activities is relevant in assessing that employee's status, but that factor cannot be considered in isolation, without regard to the nature of the religious functions performed."

The Court acknowledged that the teacher's religious duties "consumed only 45 minutes of each workday, and that the rest of her day was devoted to teaching secular subjects." However, the Court noted that it was unsure whether any church employees devoted all their time to religious tasks: "The heads of congregations themselves often have a mix of duties, including secular ones such as helping to manage the congregation's finances, supervising purely secular personnel, and overseeing the upkeep of facilities."

The Court's ruling has potential significance to church property tax exemptions, since it suggests that church property may be entitled to exemption based on exclusive use even though only used infrequently for overtly religious purposes. *Hosanna-Tabor Evangelical Lutheran Church and School v. E.E.O.C., 132 S.Ct. 694 (2012).*

apply for an exemption was due to the fact that the local assessor sent tax statements and related information to the wrong address. *Byzantine Catholic Bishop v. County Assessor, 2011 WL 4444186 (Ore. Tax 2012).*

Assessment date

In most states, property acquired by a church *after the tax assessment date* is not entitled to exemption for the current year, even though it is used exclusively for religious purposes. To illustrate, under New Jersey law the taxable or exempt status of any tract of property is determined as of the tax assessment date (October 1 of the preceding calendar year). A church purchased property on December 12 and used it immediately for exclusively religious purposes. The church applied for a tax exemption for that year but was informed that no exemption would be available, since the property was not owned by the church as of October 1. The church claimed that it was doctrinally opposed, on the basis of biblical passages, to paying taxes with funds obtained from tithes and contributions and that requiring the church to pay property taxes would violate the constitutional guaranty of religious freedom.

A state court acknowledged that "the free exercise of religious beliefs can be crushed and closed out by the sheer weight of the tribute which is exacted." *Bethany Baptist Church v. Deptford Township, 542 A.2d 505 (N.J. Super. 1988).* However, it also noted that "it is equally well-settled that religious groups are not free from all financial burdens of government" and that "not all burdens on religion are unconstitutional." A state may "justify a limitation on religious liberty by showing that it is essential to accomplish an overriding governmental interest" and that there exists "no less restrictive means" of achieving the state's interest.

The court emphasized that the issue was not the tax-exempt status of church property—since New Jersey law clearly exempted such properties from tax. Rather, the issue was whether the constitutional guaranty of religious freedom requires church-owned property to be exempt from taxation the moment it is acquired. The court concluded that the church's religious freedom claim was outweighed by a compelling state interest—the "broad public interest in maintaining a sound tax system." Specifically, the court observed that "mid-year cancellation of tax liability by reason of a property so listed becoming exempt during the year would result in major dislocation and an unfair burden to the remaining taxpayers." Further, "a requirement imposed by the [courts] mandating that property acquired by an exempt owner must receive an exemption at the exact time of its acquisition would severely impair the ability of the tax authorities to predict revenues for the tax year."

In conclusion, the court observed that the maintenance of "an organized society that guarantees religious freedom to a great variety of faiths requires that some religious practices yield to the common good."

EXAMPLE. A Pennsylvania court ruled that a church's property was entitled to exemption from the date the property was purchased, even though this was after the tax assessment date for the year, because a state law authorized the recognition of exemption

TIMELY APPLICATIONS FOR PROPERTY TAX EXEMPTIONS

Church leaders should pay special attention to property tax exemption requirements when purchasing a building or land, even from another church or charity. Here are some important tips:

- Do not assume that a property tax exemption automatically "goes with the land" to a new owner.
- When purchasing property, be sure your church's mailing address is correctly listed on the deed, since this is the address typically used by the assessor's office.
- If you do not hear from the assessor's office within a reasonable time after acquiring property, this may indicate a problem with the property's tax exemption that should be addressed promptly.
- Find out what requirements must be met in order for newly acquired church property to become exempt from property taxes. Go to the assessor's office and obtain the necessary forms.
- Confirm that the assessor's office has the correct address for the church. And, just as importantly, be sure the assessor's office has the correct name of the church. It is common for churches to change their name from time to time, and this can result in confusion when important notices are received at the church's correct address but to an addressee whose name is unfamiliar to the person opening mail in the church office.
- Periodically contact the assessor's office to confirm the exempt status of church property as well as the church's name and address.
- The services of an attorney can be helpful in obtaining and maintaining a church's exemption from property taxes.

for properties that were acquired and used for exempt purposes after the tax assessment date. *In re Jubilee Ministries International, 2 A.3d 706 (Pa. Cmwlth. 2010).*

EXAMPLE. A church purchased a parcel of land in March 1997. A local tax assessor later sued the church for unpaid property taxes. A court ruled that under state law the exempt status of property is determined on January 1 of each year, and since on January 1, 1997, the church did not own the property in question, it was not entitled to exemption. Many states have similar laws specifying that the tax status of property is determined on a specified date each year. It is for this reason that churches may have to pay property taxes for at least a portion of a year on newly acquired property, even if the property is immediately used for church purposes. *St. Joseph Orthodox Christian Church v. Spring Branch Independent School District, 2003 WL 1922580 (Tex. App. Houston 2003).*

EXAMPLE. A Wisconsin statutes exempts from taxation any property owned by a church or religious association and used exclusively for the purposes of the church or religious association. A church called a new pastor who chose to purchase a home rather than live in the church-owned parsonage. The church decided to convert the parsonage into a "hospitality house," providing accommodations for low-income persons visiting loved ones in area hospitals. The tax status of property under Wisconsin law is determined by its use on January 1 of each year. On January 1, 2008, the parsonage was vacant, since it had not yet been modified to serve as a hospitality house.

A federal district court concluded that "property that is vacant and unoccupied at the time of assessment is not exempt." It conceded that "property that has yet to begin serving a tax exempt purpose may, however, be exempt if the taxpayer can be considered as readying the property for such a purpose." The court rejected the church's argument that on January 1, 2008, it was in the process of readying the property for its future exempt use and thus was entitled to exemption for that year: "While the church had agreed on October 7, 2007, that the house could be converted from a parsonage to a hospitality house, the ball did not really start to roll on the project until several months after its assessment. It was not until April 2008 that the [church conference] approved the congregation's decision. Further, the church did not apply for the necessary zoning and use permits until April 2008, bids for necessary construction were not requested until March and April 2008, actual construction did not begin until June 2008 and the house did not open its doors for use as a hospitality house until September 2008." As a result, the church "was far from readying the former parsonage for [an exempt] purpose by the assessment date." *Asbury United Methodist Church v. City of La Crosse, 2010 WL 3363378 (W.D. Wis. 2010).*

4. FEES AND SPECIAL ASSESSMENTS

Does a state or local government have the authority to assess a fee or special assessment against church property in lieu of a direct tax? A few courts have addressed this question, with conflicting results.

EXAMPLE. A Florida appeals court ruled that churches can be required to pay special assessments only if their property is directly benefited. A county ordinance imposed special assessments against various property owners, including churches, to pay for fire and rescue services as well as storm-water management services. A group of churches protested payment of these special assessments, claiming that they were exempt from property taxes. A state appeals court ruled that the exemption of church property from property taxes does not exempt such property from special assessments. However, it acknowledged that the distinction between a property tax and a special assessment often is difficult to make. It noted that a property tax does not necessarily provide any direct benefit to the property it taxes, while a special assessment always does.

The court concluded that fees imposed on churches for fire and rescue services met the definition of a special assessment and therefore could be assessed against a church consistently with the church's exemption from property tax. The court cautioned that "if services are allowed to routinely become special assessments then potentially the exemption of churches from taxation will be largely illusory." It noted that a significant number of items "comprising the ad valorem tax base are services by nature," and that "a domino effect could ensue if special assessments are continually expanded to include generic services." *Sarasota County v. Sarasota Church of Christ, 641 So.2d 900 (Fla. App. 2 Dist. 1994).*

EXAMPLE. A New Jersey appeals court ruled that an annual registration fee of $115 assessed against a church-operated school and childcare center was constitutionally permissible. New Jersey law imposes an annual registration fee on several categories of public buildings, including schools and childcare centers. The purpose of the fee is to help pay the cost of an annual inspection to determine compliance with state fire and safety regulations. A church that operated both a school and childcare program opposed the fee on the ground that it amounted to a tax on churches that violated the First Amendment guaranty of religious freedom.

A state appeals court rejected the church's claim. The court observed: "If the primary purpose of a fee is to raise revenue, it is a tax. . . . In contrast to a tax, a fee is imposed under the government's police power to regulate [to promote the public health, safety, and welfare]. A fee is not judged a tax so long as the amount of the fee bears a reasonable relationship to the cost incurred by the government to regulate. If a fee's primary purpose is to reimburse the municipality for services reasonably related to development, it is a permissible regulatory exaction." The court concluded that the registration fee in this case was a fee rather than a tax, since its purpose was to recover the cost of conducting the annual safety inspection of the church's school and childcare center. The court rejected the church's claim that its constitutional right to freely exercise its religion was violated by the fee. *New Life Gospel Church v. Department of Community Affairs, 608 A.2d 397 (N.J. App. 1992).*

EXAMPLE. A Wisconsin court ruled that a city could assess a fee against all utility customers, including churches, to pay for the cost of providing water in the event of a fire. A church refused to pay the additional fee, arguing that it amounted to an unconstitutional "tax" on religion in violation of the First Amendment.

A state appeals court observed that "the primary purpose of a tax is to obtain revenue for the government, while the primary purpose of a fee is to cover the expense of providing a service." It concluded that the additional charge added to utility customers' bills was a fee rather than a tax: "Here, the purpose of the [additional charge] is to cover the public utility's expense of making water available, storing the water and ensuring that water will be delivered in case it is needed to fight fires at the utility customers' properties. . . . Because the purpose of the [additional charge] is to cover the public utility's expense of making water available, storing the water and ensuring that water will be delivered in case it is needed to fight fires at the utility customers' properties, its substance is consistent with a fee, not a tax." The court pointed out that the additional charges lacked some of the common characteristics of a property tax. For example, the statute authorizing the additional charge was not part of a property tax law, and liens could not be imposed on properties of customers who did not pay the additional charge. The court stated that "because we concluded that the [additional charge] is a fee and not a tax, the church's constitutional challenge . . . must fail." *River Falls v. St. Bridget's Catholic Church, 513 N.W.2d 673 (Wis. App. 1994).*

EXAMPLE. A city ordinance exempted property "owned by any religious corporation actually dedicated and used exclusively as a place of public worship" from water and sewer charges. A city denied a church's request for exemption from these charges because the church property contained apartments for three staff members (the pastor, church business administrator, and a full-time teacher at a church-operated school). The city assessed $12,000

in back charges against the church and imposed a tax lien on the church's property. The church appealed. A state appeals court ruled that the exemption of religious corporations from water and sewer charges "should be interpreted as applying to all property used in furtherance of the corporation's purpose," and in this case "that would include the housing provided its pastor, teacher and administrator staff promoting the primary purpose of the institution." The court added that even if the staff members who were provided housing were not promoting the purposes of the church, the city should have granted a "partial exemption" for all of the church's property less the three apartments. The city's denial of any exemption was "legally wrong, arbitrary and capricious." *Bathelite Community Church v. Department of Environmental Protection, 797 N.Y.S.2d 707 (N.Y. Sup. Ct. 2004).*

EXAMPLE. An Illinois court ruled that a storm-drainage service charge based on the amount of a property owner's runoff surface was a fee, not a tax, that could be assessed against churches without violating a state law exempting churches from property taxation. The court noted that a tax "is a charge having no relation to the service rendered and is assessed to provide general revenue rather than compensation." A user fee, on the other hand, "is proportional to a benefit or service rendered." The court concluded that the storm water service charge was clearly a user fee, since there was a "direct and proportional relationship between imperviousness and storm water run-off, thus creating a rational relationship between the amount of the fee and the contribution of a parcel to the use of the storm water system." The court reviewed several similar cases in other states and concluded that "the more recent case law favors the position that storm water service charges are a fee." *Church of Peace v. City of Rock Island, 2005 WL 1140427 (Ill. App. 2005).*

=== **TABLE 12-3** ===

STATE SALES TAX EXEMPTIONS FOR RELIGIOUS ORGANIZATIONS
State-by-State Analysis

Note: Listed below are state sales tax exemption statutes exempting sales by or to religious organizations. Note that some states do not have sales taxes, and some states with a sales tax do not exempt religious organizations. All laws are subject to change. To determine the current text of any statute, you should visit a library, contact your local or county property tax office, check the website maintained by your state department of revenue, or consult with an attorney.

ALABAMA

Code § 40-23-62 (2012)
The storage, use or other consumption in this state of the following tangible personal property is hereby specifically exempted from the [use tax] . . . (20) the storage, use or other consumption in this state of religious magazines and publications. For the purpose of this subdivision the words "magazines and publications" shall be construed to mean printed or illustrated lessons, notes and explanations distributed by churches or other organizations free of charge to pupils or students in Sunday schools, Bible classes or other educational facilities established and maintained by churches or similar organizations in this state.

ALASKA

No sales tax

ARIZONA

Rev. Stat. Ann § 42-5061 (2012) ("transaction privilege tax")
A. The retail classification is comprised of the business of selling tangible personal property at retail. The tax base for the retail classification is the gross proceeds of sales or gross income derived from the business. The tax imposed on the retail classification does not apply to the gross proceeds of sales or gross income from . . . (4) sales of tangible personal property by any nonprofit organization organized and operated exclusively for charitable purposes and recognized by the United States internal revenue service under section 501(c)(3) of the Internal Revenue Code.

Rev. Stat. Ann § 42-5074 (2012) restaurant classification
3. Sales [of food] by churches, fraternal benefit societies and other nonprofit organizations, as these organizations are defined in the federal internal revenue code which do not regularly engage or continue in the restaurant business for the purpose of fund-raising.

ARKANSAS

Stat. § 26-52-401 (2011)
There is specifically exempted from [the sales tax] . . . (1) The gross receipts or gross proceeds derived from the sale of tangible personal property or services by churches, except when the organizations may be engaged in business for profit; (2) The gross receipts or gross proceeds derived from the sale of tangible personal property or service by charitable organizations, except when the organizations may be engaged in business for profit.

CALIFORNIA

Rev. & Tax Code § 6363.5 (1976)
There are exempted from the taxes imposed by this part the gross receipts from the sale of, and the storage, use or other consumption in this state of, meals and food products for human consumption furnished or served by any religious organization at a social or other gathering conducted by it or under its auspices, if the purpose in furnishing or serving the meals and food products is to obtain revenue for the functions and activities of the organization and the revenue obtained from furnishing or serving the meals and food products is actually used in carrying on such functions and activities.

COLORADO

Rev. Stat. § 39-26-718 (2008)
(1) The following shall be exempt from taxation under the provisions of part 1 of this article: (a) All sales made to charitable organizations, in the conduct of their regular charitable functions and activities . . . (b) (I) . . . all occasional sales by a charitable organization. (II) For purposes of this paragraph (b), "occasional sales" means retail sales of tangible personal property, including concessions, for fund-raising purposes if: (A) The sale of tangible personal property or concessions by the charitable organization takes place no more than twelve days, whether consecutive or not, during any one calendar year; (B) The funds raised by the charitable organization through these sales are retained by the organization to be used in the course of the organization's charitable service; and (C) The funds raised by the charitable organization through these sales do not exceed twenty-five thousand dollars during any one calendar year.

CONNECTICUT

Gen. Stat. § 12-412 (2012)
Taxes imposed by this chapter shall not apply to the gross receipts from the sale of and the storage, use or other consumption in this state with respect to the following items . . . (8) Sales of tangible personal property or services to any organization that is exempt from federal income tax under Section 501(a) of the Internal Revenue Code of 1986 . . . and that the United States Treasury Department has expressly determined, by letter, to be an organization that is described in section 501(c)(3) or (13) of said Internal Revenue Code. At the time of the sale that is exempt under this subsection, the organization shall, in order to qualify for said exemption, do one of the following: (A) Present to the retailer (i) a copy of the United States Treasury

=== **TABLE 12-3** ===

STATE SALES TAX EXEMPTIONS FOR RELIGIOUS ORGANIZATIONS
State-by-State Analysis (continued)

Department determination letter that was issued to such organization and (ii) a certificate, in such form as the commissioner may prescribe, certifying that a United States Treasury Department determination letter has been issued to such organization and has not been revoked and that the tangible personal property or services that are being purchased from the retailer by such organization are to be used or consumed exclusively for the purposes for which such organization was established or (B) present to the retailer (i) a copy of the exemption permit that was issued pursuant to this subsection by the commissioner to such organization before July 1, 1995, after a determination of eligibility by the commissioner and (ii) a certificate, in such form as the commissioner may prescribe, certifying that an exemption permit was issued pursuant to this subsection by the commissioner to such organization before July 1, 1995, and was not revoked and that the tangible personal property or services that are being purchased from the retailer by such organization are to be used or consumed exclusively for the purposes for which the organization was established. The organization shall be liable for the tax otherwise imposed if such tangible personal property or services are not used or consumed exclusively for the purposes for which the organization was established.

DELAWARE

No sales tax

FLORIDA

Stat. § 212.06(9)(2009)

(9) The taxes imposed by this chapter do not apply to the use, sale, or distribution of religious publications, bibles, hymn books, prayer books, vestments, altar paraphernalia, sacramental chalices, and like church service and ceremonial raiments and equipment.

Stat. § 212.08(7)(m) (2012)

1. There are exempt from the tax imposed by this chapter transactions involving sales or leases directly to religious institutions when used in carrying on their customary nonprofit religious activities or sales or leases of tangible personal property by religious institutions having an established physical place for worship at which nonprofit religious services and activities are regularly conducted and carried on.

2. As used in this paragraph, the term "religious institutions" means churches, synagogues, and established physical places for worship at which nonprofit religious services and activities are regularly conducted and carried on. The term "religious institutions" includes nonprofit corporations the sole purpose of which is to provide free transportation services to church members, their families, and other church attendees. The term "religious institutions" also includes nonprofit state, nonprofit district, or other nonprofit governing or administrative offices the function of which is to assist or regulate the customary activities of religious institutions. The term "religious institutions" also includes any nonprofit corporation that is qualified as nonprofit under section 501(c)(3) of the Internal Revenue Code of 1986, as amended, and that owns and operates a Florida television station, at least 90 percent of the programming of which station consists of programs of a religious nature and the financial support for which, exclusive of receipts for broadcasting from other nonprofit organizations, is predominantly from contributions from the general public. The term "religious institutions" also includes any nonprofit corporation that is qualified as nonprofit under section 501(c)(3) of the Internal Revenue Code of 1986, as amended, the primary activity of which is making and distributing audio recordings of religious scriptures and teachings to blind or visually impaired persons at no charge. The term "religious institutions" also includes any nonprofit corporation that is qualified as nonprofit under section 501(c)(3) of the Internal Revenue Code of 1986, as amended, the sole or primary function of which is to provide, upon invitation, nonprofit religious services, evangelistic services, religious education, administrative assistance, or missionary assistance for a church, synagogue, or established physical place of worship at which nonprofit religious services and activities are regularly conducted.

GEORGIA

Code § 48-8-3 (2012)

The sales and use taxes levied or imposed by this article shall not apply to . . . (15) Sales: (A) Of any religious paper in this state when the paper is owned and operated by religious institutions or denominations and no part of the net profit from the operation of the institution or denomination inures to the benefit of any private person; (B) By religious institutions or denominations when: (i) The sale results from a specific charitable fund-raising activity; (ii) The number of days upon which the fund-raising activity occurs does not exceed 30 in any calendar year; (iii) No part of the gross sales or net profits from the sales inures to the benefit of any private person; and (iv) The gross sales or net profits from the sales are used for the purely charitable purposes of: (I) Relief to the aged; (II) Church related youth activities; (II) Religious instruction or worship; or (IV) Construction or repair of church buildings or facilities; (15.1) Sales of pipe organs or steeple bells to any church which qualifies as an exempt religious organization under section 501(c)(3) of the Internal Revenue Code. . . . (16) The sale or use of Holy Bibles, testaments, and similar books commonly recognized as being Holy Scripture regardless of by or to whom sold.

[Note: In 2006 a federal district court in Georgia ruled that the exemptions found in sections 15(A) and (16) were unconstitutional. In 2007, the same court ordered the state of Georgia to cease enforcing these exemptions.]

TABLE 12-3

STATE SALES TAX EXEMPTIONS FOR RELIGIOUS ORGANIZATIONS
State-by-State Analysis (continued)

HAWAII

Rev. Stat. § 237-23 (2012)
[Hawaii does not have a state sales tax. Instead, it has a retail excise tax. However, this tax does not apply to "(4) Corporations, associations, trusts, or societies organized and operated exclusively for religious, charitable . . . or educational purposes."]

IDAHO

Code § 63-3622I. Literature (1999)
There is exempted from the taxes imposed by this chapter the sale or purchase, or the storage, use or other consumption of literature, pamphlets, periodicals, tracts and books published and sold by an entity qualified under section 501(c)(3) of the Internal Revenue Code, no part of the net earnings of which inures to the benefit of a private individual or shareholder. As used in this section, "literature" includes information available in alternative forms, including audio-visual and magnetic, optical or other machine-readable media.

Code § 63-3622J. School, church and senior citizen meals (1984)
There is exempted from the taxes imposed by this chapter . . . the sale of meals by a church to its members at a church function.

Code § 63-3622KK. Incidental sales by religious corporations or societies (1996)
Whenever any religious corporation or society . . . purchases tangible personal property upon which it has paid the tax imposed by this chapter, or acquires tangible personal property via gift, the sale of such property . . . by the religious corporation or society shall be exempt from the taxes imposed in this chapter. . . . If at any time, tangible personal property [is] offered for sale to or used by the general public in the open market in regular competition with commercial enterprise, the sale shall be subject to the taxes imposed by this chapter.

ILLINOIS

35 Compiled Statutes 120/2-5 (2012)
Gross receipts from proceeds from the sale of the following tangible personal property are exempt from the tax imposed by this Act . . . (11) Personal property sold to a . . . corporation, society, association, foundation, or institution organized and operated exclusively for charitable, religious, or educational purposes. . . . On and after July 1, 1987, however, no entity otherwise eligible for this exemption shall make tax-free purchases unless it has an active identification number issued by the Department.

INDIANA

Code § 6-2.5-5-26 (2002)
(a) Sales of tangible personal property are exempt from the state gross retail tax, if: (1) the seller is an organization that is described in section 21(b)(1) of this chapter [includes an organization that is organized and operated exclusively for religious, charitable, or educational]; (2) the organization makes the sale to make money to carry on a not-for-profit purpose; and (3) the organization does not make those sales during more than thirty (30) days in a calendar year. (b) Sales of tangible personal property are exempt from the state gross retail tax, if: (1) the seller is an organization described in section 21(b)(1) of this chapter; (2) the seller is not operated predominantly for social purposes; (3) the property sold is designed and intended primarily either for the organization's educational, cultural, or religious purposes, or for improvement of the work skills or professional qualifications of the organization's members; and (4) the property sold is not designed or intended primarily for use in carrying on a private or proprietary business. (c) The exemption provided by this section does not apply to an accredited college or university's sales of books, stationery, haberdashery, supplies, or other property.

IOWA

Code § 423.3 (2011)
78. The sales price from sales or rental of tangible personal property, or services rendered by any entity where the profits from the sales or rental of the tangible personal property, or services rendered are used by or donated to a nonprofit entity which is exempt from federal income taxation pursuant to section 501(c)(3) of the Internal Revenue Code . . . or a nonprofit private educational institution, and where the entire proceeds from the sales, rental, or services are expended for any of the following purposes: (1) Educational. (2) Religious. (3) Charitable. A charitable act is an act done out of goodwill, benevolence, and a desire to add to or to improve the good of humankind in general or any class or portion of humankind, with no pecuniary profit inuring to the person performing the service or giving the gift. . . . This exemption does not apply to the sales price from games of skill, games of chance, raffles, and bingo games as defined in chapter 99B. This exemption is disallowed on the amount of the sales price only to the extent the profits from the sales, rental, or services are not used by or donated to the appropriate entity and expended for educational, religious, or charitable purposes.

KANSAS

Stat. Ann. § 79-3606 (2012)
The following shall be exempt from the tax imposed by this act . . . (aaa) all sales of tangible personal property and services purchased by a religious organization which is exempt from federal income taxation pursuant to section 501(c)(3) of the federal internal revenue code, and used exclusively for religious purposes, and all sales of tangible personal property or services

STATE SALES TAX EXEMPTIONS FOR RELIGIOUS ORGANIZATIONS
State-by-State Analysis (continued)

purchased by a contractor for the purpose of constructing, equipping, reconstructing, maintaining, repairing, enlarging, furnishing or remodeling facilities for any such organization which would be exempt from taxation under the provisions of this section if purchased directly by such organization. Nothing in this subsection shall be deemed to exempt the purchase of any construction machinery, equipment or tools used in the constructing, equipping, reconstructing, maintaining, repairing, enlarging, furnishing or remodeling facilities for any such organization. When any such organization shall contract for the purpose of constructing, equipping, reconstructing, maintaining, repairing, enlarging, furnishing or remodeling facilities, it shall obtain from the state and furnish to the contractor an exemption certificate for the project involved, and the contractor may purchase materials for incorporation in such project. The contractor shall furnish the number of such certificate to all suppliers from whom such purchases are made, and such suppliers shall execute invoices covering the same bearing the number of such certificate. Upon completion of the project the contractor shall furnish to such organization concerned a sworn statement, on a form to be provided by the director of taxation, that all purchases so made were entitled to exemption under this subsection. All invoices shall be held by the contractor for a period of five years and shall be subject to audit by the director of taxation. If any materials purchased under such a certificate are found not to have been incorporated in the building or other project or not to have been returned for credit or the sales or compensating tax otherwise imposed upon such materials which will not be so incorporated in the building or other project reported and paid by such contractor to the director of taxation not later than the 20th day of the month following the close of the month in which it shall be determined that such materials will not be used for the purpose for which such certificate was issued, such organization concerned shall be liable for tax on all materials purchased for the project, and upon payment thereof it may recover the same from the contractor together with reasonable attorney fees. Any contractor or any agent, employee or subcontractor thereof, who shall use or otherwise dispose of any materials purchased under such a certificate for any purpose other than that for which such a certificate is issued without the payment of the sales or compensating tax otherwise imposed upon such materials, shall be guilty of a misdemeanor and, upon conviction therefore, shall be subject to the penalties provided for in subsection (g) of K.S.A. 79-3615, and amendments thereto. Sales tax paid on and after July 1, 1998, but prior to the effective date of this act upon the gross receipts received from any sale exempted by the amendatory provisions of this subsection shall be refunded. Each claim for a sales tax refund shall be verified and submitted to the director of taxation upon forms furnished by the director and shall be accompanied by any additional documentation required by the director. The director shall review each claim and shall refund that amount of sales tax paid as determined under the provisions of this subsection. All refunds shall be paid from the sales tax refund fund upon warrants of the director of accounts and reports pursuant to vouchers approved by the director or the director's designee.

KENTUCKY

Rev. Stat. § 139.495 (2009)
The taxes imposed by this chapter shall apply to resident, nonprofit educational, charitable, and religious institutions which have qualified for exemption from income taxation under Section 501(c)(3) of the Internal Revenue Code as follows: (1) Tax does not apply to sales of tangible personal property, digital property, or services to such institutions provided the tangible personal property, digital property, or service is to be used solely within the educational, charitable, or religious function. (2) Tax does not apply to sales of food to students in school cafeterias or lunchrooms. (3) Tax does not apply to sales by school bookstores of textbooks, workbooks, and other course materials. (4) Tax does not apply to sales by nonprofit, school sponsored clubs and organizations, provided such sales do not include tickets for athletic events. . . . (7) All other sales made by nonprofit educational, charitable, and religious institutions are taxable and the tax may be passed on to the customer as provided in KRS 139,210.

LOUISIANA

Code § 47:305.14(A) (2011)
A(1)(a). The sales and use taxes . . . shall not apply to sales of tangible personal property at, or admission charges for, outside gate admissions to, or parking fees associated with, events sponsored by domestic, civic, educational, historical, charitable, fraternal, or religious organizations, which are nonprofit, when the entire proceeds, except for the necessary expenses such as fees paid for guest speakers, chair and table rentals, and food and beverage utility related items connected therewith, are used for educational, charitable, religious, or historical restoration purposes, including the furtherance of the civic, educational, historical, charitable, fraternal, or religious purpose of the organization. In addition, newspapers published in this state by religious organizations shall also be exempt from such taxes, provided that the price paid for the newspaper or a subscription to the newspaper does not exceed the cost to publish such newspaper.

(b) Notwithstanding any other provision of this Section, the sales and use tax imposed by taxing authorities shall not apply to an event sponsored by a domestic nonprofit organization that is exempt from tax under section 501(c)(3) of the Internal Revenue Code when the event provides Louisiana heritage, culture, crafts, art, food, and music, and the sponsor has contracted for production management and financing services for the event. Such services shall constitute necessary expenses of the sponsor for purposes of the event. The provisions of this Subparagraph shall apply only to the sales of tangible personal property and admission

TABLE 12-3

STATE SALES TAX EXEMPTIONS FOR RELIGIOUS ORGANIZATIONS
State-by-State Analysis (continued)

charges for, outside gate admissions to, or parking fees associated with an event when the sales, charges, and fees are payable to or for the benefit of the sponsor of the event. The provisions of this Subparagraph shall apply only to an event which transpires over a minimum of seven but not more than twelve days and has a five-year annual average attendance of at least three hundred thousand over the duration of the event. For purposes of determining the five-year annual average attendance, the calculation shall include the total annual attendance for each of the five most recent years.

(2) The exemption provided herein shall not apply to any event intended to yield a profit to the promoter or to any individual contracted to provide services or equipment, or both, for the event.

(3) This Section shall not be construed to exempt any organization or activity from the payment of sales or use taxes otherwise required by law to be made on purchases made by these organizations.

(4) This Section shall not be construed to exempt regular commercial ventures of any type such as bookstores, restaurants, gift shops, commercial flea markets, and similar activities that are sponsored by organizations qualifying hereunder which are in competition with retail merchants. However, the exemption provided in this Section shall apply to thrift shops located on military installations, the operation of which is deemed to be an "event" for purposes of this exemption.

MAINE

Rev. Stat. Ann. title 36, § 1760 (2012)
No tax on sales . . . shall be collected upon or in connection with . . . sales to . . . (16) . . . M. Regularly organized churches or houses of religious worship.

MARYLAND

Tax Code § 11-204 (2012)
(a) The sales and use tax does not apply to . . . (3) a sale to a nonprofit organization made to carry on its work, if the organization: (i) 1. is located in the State; 2. is located in an adjacent jurisdiction and provides its services within the State on a routine and regular basis; or 3. is located in an adjacent jurisdiction whose law: A. does not impose a sales or use tax on a sale to a nonprofit organization made to carry on its work; or B. contains a reciprocal exemption from sales and use tax for sales to nonprofit organizations located in adjacent jurisdictions similar to the exemption allowed under this subsection; (ii) is a charitable, educational, or religious organization; (iii) is not the United States; and (iv) except for the American National Red Cross, is not a unit or instrumentality of the United States. . . .

(b) The sales and use tax does not apply to a sale by: (1) a bona fide church or religious organization, if the sale is made for the general purposes of the church or organization.

MASSACHUSETTS

Gen. Laws ch. 64H, § 6 (2011)
The following sales and the gross receipts therefrom shall be exempt from the tax imposed by this chapter . . . (e) Sales to any corporation, foundation, organization or institution, which is exempt from taxation under the provisions of section five hundred and one (c)(3) of the federal Internal Revenue Code, as amended, and in effect for the applicable period; provided, however, that such sales shall not be exempt unless (1) the tangible personal property or services which are the subject of such sales is used in the conduct of such religious, charitable, educational or scientific enterprise, (2) such corporation, foundation, organization or institution shall have first obtained a certification from the commissioner stating that it is entitled to such exemption, and (3) the vendor keeps a record of the sales price of each such separate sale, the name of the purchaser, the date of each such separate sale, and the number of such certificate. The certificate of exemption issued by the commissioner under clause (2) shall be effective for a period of 10 years from the date of its issuance or until January first, nineteen hundred and eighty-four, whichever shall last expire provided that ninety days prior to said date the commissioner shall notify such corporation, foundation, organization or institution of the expiration date of said certificate. Such corporation, foundation, organization or institution must obtain from the commissioner a renewal of such certificate in order to be entitled to a continuance of such exemption beyond the expiration date of any existing certificate. (f) Sales of building materials and supplies to be used in the construction, reconstruction, alteration, remodeling or repair of . . . (2) any building or structure owned by or held in trust for the benefit of any corporation, foundation, organization or institution described in paragraph (e) and used exclusively in the conduct of its religious, scientific, charitable or educational purposes . . . provided, however, that such . . . organization or institution shall have first obtained a certificate from the commissioner stating that it is entitled to such exemption and the vendor keeps a record of the sales price of each such separate sale, the name of the purchaser, the date of each such separate sale and the number of such certificate. . . .(m) Sales of newspapers, magazines, books required for instructional purposes in educational institutions, books used for religious worship, publications of any corporation, foundation, organization or institution described in paragraph (e) of this section, and motion picture films for commercial exhibition. . . .(cc) . . . meals prepared by the members thereof and served on its premises by any

---

TABLE 12-3

STATE SALES TAX EXEMPTIONS FOR RELIGIOUS ORGANIZATIONS
State-by-State Analysis (continued)

---

church or synagogue or by any church or synagogue organization to any organization of such church or synagogue the proceeds of which are to be used for religious or charitable purposes.

MICHIGAN

Comp. Laws § 205.54a (2012)
Sec. 4a. (1) . . . [T]he following are exempt from the tax under this act: (a) A sale of tangible personal property not for resale to a nonprofit school, nonprofit hospital, or nonprofit home for the care and maintenance of children or aged persons operated by . . . a regularly organized church, religious, or fraternal organization . . . or a corporation incorporated under the laws of this state, if the income or benefit from the operation does not inure, in whole or in part, to an individual or private shareholder, directly or indirectly, and if the activities of the entity or agency are carried on exclusively for the benefit of the public at large and are not limited to the advantage, interests, and benefits of its members or any restricted group. . . . (b) A sale of tangible personal property not for resale to a regularly organized church or house of religious worship, except the following: (i) Sales in activities that are mainly commercial enterprises. (ii) Sales of vehicles licensed for use on public highways other than a passenger van or bus with a manufacturer's rated seating capacity of 10 or more that is used primarily for the transportation of persons for religious purposes.

MINNESOTA

Stat. § 297A.70, subdivision 4 (2011)
(a) All sales, except those listed in paragraph (b), to the following "nonprofit organizations" are exempt: (1) a corporation, society, association, foundation, or institution organized and operated exclusively for charitable, religious, or educational purposes if the item purchased is used in the performance of charitable, religious, or educational functions. . . .(b) This exemption does not apply to the following sales: (1) building, construction, or reconstruction materials purchased by a contractor or a subcontractor as a part of a lump-sum contract or similar type of contract with a guaranteed maximum price covering both labor and materials for use in the construction, alteration, or repair of a building or facility; (2) construction materials purchased by tax-exempt entities or their contractors to be used in constructing buildings or facilities that will not be used principally by the tax-exempt entities; and (3) lodging as defined under section 297A.61, subdivision 3, paragraph (g), clause (2), and prepared food, candy, soft drinks, and alcoholic beverages as defined in 297A.61, subdivision 2, except wine purchased by an established religious organization for sacramental purposes.

MISSISSIPPI

Code § 27-65-22 (2007)
(3) The tax imposed by this section shall not be levied or collected upon:

(a) Any admissions charged at any place of amusement operated by a religious, charitable or educational organization, or by a nonprofit civic club or fraternal organization (i) when the net proceeds of such admissions do not inure to any one or more individuals within such organization and are to be used solely for religious, charitable, educational or civic purposes; or (ii) when the entire net proceeds are used to defray the normal operating expenses of such organization, such as loan payments, maintenance costs, repairs and other operating expenses;

(b) Any admissions charged to hear gospel singing when promoted by a duly constituted local, bona fide nonprofit charitable or religious organization, irrespective of the fact that the performers and promoters are paid out of the proceeds of admissions collected, provided the program is composed entirely of gospel singing and not generally mixed with hillbilly or popular singing.

Code § 27-65-111 (2009)
(e) Sales of tangible personal property to an orphanage or old men's or ladies' home supported wholly or in part by a religious denomination fraternal nonprofit organization or other nonprofit organization. . . .(j) Sales of tangible personal property or services to the Salvation Army.

MISSOURI

Rev. Stat. § 144.030 (2012)
2. There are also specifically exempted from the provisions of the local sales tax law . . . (20) All sales made by or to religious and charitable organizations and institutions in their religious, charitable or educational functions and activities and all sales made by or to all elementary and secondary schools operated at public expense in their educational functions and activities.

MONTANA

No sales tax

NEBRASKA

Rev. Stat. § 77-2704.12 (2012)
Sales and use taxes shall not be imposed on the gross receipts from the sale, lease, or rental of and the storage, use, or other consumption in this state of purchases by (a) any nonprofit organization created exclusively for religious purposes. . . . (2) Any organization listed in subsection (1) of this section shall apply for an exemption on forms provided by the Tax Commissioner.

TABLE 12-3

STATE SALES TAX EXEMPTIONS FOR RELIGIOUS ORGANIZATIONS
State-by-State Analysis (continued)

The application shall be approved and a numbered certificate of exemption received by the applicant organization in order to be exempt from the sales and use tax.

NEVADA

Rev. Stat. § 374.3305 (1995)
There are exempted from the taxes imposed by this act the gross receipts from the sale of . . . any tangible personal property sold by or to a nonprofit organization created for religious, charitable or educational purposes.

NEW HAMPSHIRE

No sales tax

NEW JERSEY

Rev. Stat. § 54:32B-9 (2011)
(b) Except as otherwise provided in this section any sale or amusement charge by or to any of the following or any use or occupancy by any of the following, where such sale, charge, use or occupancy is directly related to the purposes for which the following have been organized, shall not be subject to the sales and use taxes imposed under this act: a corporation, association, trust, or community chest, fund or foundation, organized and operated exclusively (1) for religious, charitable, scientific, testing for public safety, literary or educational purposes. . . . Such a sale, charge, use or occupancy by, or a sale or charge to, an organization enumerated in this subsection, shall not be subject to the sales and use taxes only if no part of the net earnings of the organization inures to the benefit of any private shareholder or individual, no substantial part of the activities of the organization is carrying on propaganda, or otherwise attempting to influence legislation, and the organization does not participate in, or intervene in (including the publishing or distributing of statements), any political campaign on behalf of any candidate for public office.

NEW MEXICO

Stat. § 7-9-29 (1990)
A. Exempted from the gross receipts tax are the receipts of organizations that demonstrate to the department that they have been granted exemption from the federal income tax . . . as organizations described in Section 501(c)(3) of the United States Internal Revenue Code. . . . This section does not apply to receipts derived from an unrelated trade or business as defined in Section 513 of the United States Internal Revenue Code.

NEW YORK

Tax Law § 1116 (2008)
Any sale or amusement charge by or to any of the following or any use or occupancy by any of the following shall not be subject to the sales and compensating use taxes imposed under this article . . . (4) Any corporation, association, trust, or community chest, fund, foundation, or limited liability company, organized and operated exclusively for religious, charitable, scientific, testing for public safety, literary or educational purposes, or to foster national or international amateur sports competition (but only if no part of its activities involve the provision of athletic facilities or equipment), or for the prevention of cruelty to children or animals, no part of the net earnings of which inures to the benefit of any private shareholder or individual, no substantial part of the activities of which is carrying on propaganda, or otherwise attempting to influence legislation . . . and which does not participate in, or intervene in (including the publishing or distributing of statements), any political campaign on behalf of any candidate for public office.

NORTH CAROLINA

Gen. Stat. §§ 105-164.13 and 14 (2012)
13. The sale at retail, the use, storage or consumption in this State of the following tangible personal property is specifically exempted from the tax imposed by this Article . . . (31) Sales of meals not for profit to elderly and incapacitated persons by charitable or religious organizations not operated for profit . . . when such meals are delivered to the purchasers at their places of abode. (31a) Food sold by a church or religious organization not operated for profit when the proceeds of the sales are actually used for religious activities. . . .

14. (b) Nonprofit Entities and Hospital Drugs. A nonprofit entity is allowed a semiannual refund of sales and use taxes paid by it under this Article on direct purchases of tangible personal property and services, other than electricity, telecommunications service, and ancillary service, for use in carrying on the work of the nonprofit entity. Sales and use tax liability indirectly incurred by a nonprofit entity on building materials, supplies, fixtures, and equipment that become a part of or annexed to any building or structure that is owned or leased by the nonprofit entity and is being erected, altered, or repaired for use by the nonprofit entity for carrying on its nonprofit activities is considered a sales or use tax liability incurred on direct purchases by the nonprofit entity. A request for a refund must be in writing and must include any information and documentation required by the Secretary. A request for a refund for the first six months of a calendar year is due the following October 15; a request for a refund for the second six months of a calendar year is due the following April 15. . . .

The following nonprofit entities are allowed a refund under this subsection . . . An organization that is exempt from income tax under section 501(c)(3) of the Code.

STATE SALES TAX EXEMPTIONS FOR RELIGIOUS ORGANIZATIONS
State-by-State Analysis (continued)

NORTH DAKOTA

Cent. Code § 57-39.2-04 (2011)
There are specifically exempted from the provisions of this chapter and from computation of the amount of tax imposed by it the following . . .

4b. Gross receipts from educational, religious, or charitable activities, when the entire amount of net receipts is expended for educational, religious, or charitable purposes. The exemption specified in this subsection does not apply to: (1) Gross receipts from taxable sales in excess of ten thousand dollars per event if the activities are held in a publicly owned facility; or (2) Gross receipts from activities if the seller competes with retailers by maintaining inventory, conducting retail sales on a regular basis from a permanent or seasonal location, or soliciting sales from a website prepared for or maintained by the seller. . . .

5. Gross receipts from sales of textbooks to regularly enrolled students of a private or public school and from sales of textbooks, yearbooks, and school supplies purchased by a private nonprofit elementary school, secondary school, or any other nonprofit institution of higher learning conducting courses of study similar to those conducted by public schools in this state.

25. Gross receipts from the sale of Bibles, hymnals, textbooks, and prayer books sold to nonprofit religious organizations.

OHIO

Rev. Code § 5739.02 (2012)
The tax does not apply to the following . . . (9) Sales of services or tangible personal property, other than motor vehicles, mobile homes, and manufactured homes, by churches or by nonprofit organizations operated exclusively for charitable purposes . . . provided that the number of days on which such tangible personal property or services, other than items never subject to the tax, are sold does not exceed six in any calendar year. If the number of days on which such sales are made exceeds six in any calendar year, the church or organization shall be considered to be engaged in business and all subsequent sales by it shall be subject to the tax. In counting the number of days, all sales by groups within a church or within an organization shall be considered to be sales of that church or organization. . . . (12) Sales of tangible personal property or services to churches. . . .

(13) . . . building materials and services sold to a construction contractor for incorporation into a house of public worship or religious education.

OKLAHOMA

Stat. title 68, § 1356 (2012)
There are hereby specifically exempted from the tax levied by this article . . .

7. Sale of tangible personal property or services to or by churches, except sales made in the course of business for profit or savings, competing with other persons engaged in the same or a similar business or sale of tangible personal property or services by an organization exempt from federal income tax pursuant to section 501(c) of the Internal Revenue Code of 1986, as amended, made on behalf of or at the request of a church or churches if the sale of such property is conducted not more than once each calendar year for a period not to exceed three (3) days by the organization and proceeds from the sale of such property are used by the church or churches or by the organization for charitable purposes. . . .

27. Sales of tangible personal property or services occurring on or after June 1, 1995, to children's homes which are supported or sponsored by one or more churches, members of which serve as trustees of the home. . . .

29. Sales of tangible personal property or services to youth camps which are supported or sponsored by one or more churches, members of which serve as trustees of the organization.

65. Sales of boxes of food by a church or by an organization, which is exempt from taxation pursuant to the provisions of the Internal Revenue Code, 26 U.S.C., Section 501 (c)(3). To qualify under the provisions of this paragraph, the organization must be organized for the primary purpose of feeding needy individuals or to encourage volunteer service by requiring such service in order to purchase food. These boxes shall only contain edible staple food items.

66. Sales of tangible personal property or services to any person with whom a church has duly entered into a construction contract, necessary for carrying out such contract or to any subcontractor to such a construction contract.

========= **TABLE 12-3** =========

STATE SALES TAX EXEMPTIONS FOR RELIGIOUS ORGANIZATIONS
State-by-State Analysis (continued)

OREGON   No sales tax

PENNSYLVANIA   **Stat. title 72, § 7204 (2012)**
The [sales tax] shall not be imposed on . . . (10) The sale at retail to or use by . . . a religious organization for religious purposes of tangible personal property or services other than pursuant to a construction contract: Provided, however, That the exclusion of this clause shall not apply with respect to any tangible personal property or services used in any unrelated trade or business carried on by such organization or institution or with respect to any materials, supplies and equipment used and transferred to such organization or institution in the construction, reconstruction, remodeling, renovation, repairs and maintenance of any real estate structure, other than building machinery and equipment, except materials and supplies when purchased by such organizations or institutions for routine maintenance and repairs. . . .

(28) The sale at retail or use of religious publications sold by religious groups and Bibles and religious articles. . . .

(57) The sale at retail to or use by a construction contractor of building machinery and equipment and services thereto that are: (i) transferred pursuant to a construction contract for any . . . religious organization for religious purposes, provided that the building machinery and equipment and services thereto are not used in any unrelated trade or business.

RHODE ISLAND   **Gen. Laws § 44-18-30 (2012)**
There are exempted from the taxes imposed by this chapter the following gross receipts . . . (5) (i) From the sale to as herein defined, and from the storage, use, and other consumption in this state or any other state of the United States of America of tangible personal property by . . . churches . . . and other institutions or organizations operated exclusively for religious or charitable purposes. . . .
(ii) In the case of contracts entered into with . . . churches . . . and other institutions or organizations operated exclusively for religious or charitable purposes, the contractor may purchase such materials and supplies . . . as are to be utilized in the construction of the projects being performed under the contracts without payment of the tax. . . . (16) Camps. From the rental charged for living quarters, or sleeping or housekeeping accommodations at camps or retreat houses operated by religious, charitable, educational, or other organizations and associations mentioned in subdivision (5), or by privately owned and operated summer camps for children.

SOUTH CAROLINA   **Code §§ 12-36-2110(c) (2009) and 2120 (2011)**
2110(C). For the sale of each musical instrument, or each piece of office equipment, purchased by a religious organization exempt under Internal Revenue Code Section 501(c)(3), the maximum tax imposed by this chapter is three hundred dollars. The musical instrument or office equipment must be located on church property and used exclusively for the organization's exempt purpose. The religious organization must furnish to the seller an affidavit on forms prescribed by the commission. The affidavit must be retained by the seller.

2120. Exempted from the taxes imposed by this chapter are the gross proceeds of sales, or sales price of . . . (8) newsprint paper, newspapers, and religious publications, including the Holy Bible.

SOUTH DAKOTA   **Codified Laws § 10-45-10 (2011)**
There are hereby specifically exempted from the provisions of this chapter and from the computation of the amount of tax imposed by it, the gross receipts from sales of tangible personal property . . . to any nonprofit charitable organization maintaining a physical location within this state which devotes its resources exclusively to the relief of the poor, distressed or underprivileged, and has been recognized as an exempt organization under § 501(c)(3) of the Internal Revenue Code.

Codified Laws § 10-45-13 (2012)
There are specifically exempted from the provisions of this chapter and from the computation of the amount of tax imposed by it, the gross receipts from the following . . . (5) Religious, benevolent, fraternal, youth association or charitable activities, including any bingo or lottery conducted pursuant to § 22-25-25, where the entire amount of such receipts after deducting all costs directly related to the conduct of such activities is expended for religious, benevolent, fraternal, youth association or charitable purposes, and, except for any bingo or lottery, the receipts are not the result of engaging in business for more than three consecutive days. For the purposes of determining whether this business has been engaged in for more than three days, days necessary to set up, organize, prepare for, take down, or disassemble the business or activity may not be construed as days engaged in business. However, receipts from tangible personal property or services purchased for use in the activity are included in the measure of sales tax . . .

(9) Religious, benevolent, fraternal, youth association or charitable activities conducted at county fairs, if the entire amount of such receipts after deducting all costs directly related to the conduct of such activities is expended for religious, benevolent,

STATE SALES TAX EXEMPTIONS FOR RELIGIOUS ORGANIZATIONS

State-by-State Analysis (continued)

fraternal, youth association or charitable purposes, and the receipts are not the result of engaging in business for more than five consecutive days. However, receipts from tangible personal property or services purchased for use in the activity are included in the measure of sales tax;

(10) Admissions to circus performances sponsored or operated by religious, benevolent, fraternal or youth associations, if the entire amount of the receipts after deducting all costs directly related to the conduct of the circus performances is expended for religious, benevolent, fraternal, youth associations or charitable purposes;

(11) Admissions to events or receipts from activities sponsored and operated by religious, benevolent, or charitable organizations for a period not to exceed thirty days in any calendar year, if the entire amount of the receipts after deducting all costs directly related to the conduct of the event or activity is expended for the benefit of homeless persons.

TENNESSEE

Code Ann. § 67-6-322 (2011)
(a) There is exempt from the provisions of this chapter any sales or use tax upon tangible personal property, computer software, or taxable services sold, given, or donated to any . . . church, temple, synagogue or mosque.

TEXAS

Tax Code §§ 151.310 (2011) and 312 (1999)
310. (a) A taxable item sold, leased, or rented to, or stored, used, or consumed by, any of the following organizations is exempted from the taxes imposed by this chapter: (1) an organization created for religious, educational, or charitable purposes if no part of the net earnings of the organization benefits a private shareholder or individual and the items purchased, leased, or rented are related to the purpose of the organization. . . .

312. Periodicals and writings that are published or distributed by a religious, philanthropic, charitable, historical, scientific, or other similar organization that is not operated for profit, but excluding an educational organization, are exempted from the taxes imposed by this chapter.

UTAH

Code § 59-12-104 (2012)
The following sales and uses are exempt from the taxes imposed by this chapter . . .
(8) sales made to or by religious or charitable institutions in the conduct of their regular religious or charitable functions and activities, if the requirements of section 59-12-104.1 are fulfilled [see below].

Code § 59-12-104.1 (2008)
(1) . . . sales made by religious or charitable institutions or organizations are exempt from the sales and use tax imposed by this chapter if the sale is made in the conduct of the institution's or organization's regular religious or charitable functions or activities.

(2) (a) . . . sales made to a religious or charitable institution or organization are exempt from the sales and use tax imposed by this chapter if the sale is made in the conduct of the institution's or organization's regular religious or charitable functions and activities.

(b) In order to facilitate the efficient administration of the exemption granted by this section, the exemption shall be administered as follows: (i) the exemption shall be at point of sale if the sale is in the amount of at least $1,000; (ii) except as provided in Subsection (2)(b)(iii), if the sale is less than $1,000, the exemption shall be in the form of a refund of sales or use taxes paid at the point of sale; and (iii) notwithstanding Subsection (2)(b)(ii), the exemption under this section shall be at point of sale if the sale is: (A) made pursuant to a contract between the seller and the charitable or religious institution or organization; or (B) made by a public utility . . . to a religious or charitable institution or organization.

(3) (a) Religious or charitable institutions or organizations entitled to a refund under Subsection (2)(b)(ii) may apply to the commission for the refund of sales or use taxes paid.

VERMONT

Stat. title 32, § 9743 (2011)
Any sale, service or amusement charged by or to any of the following or any use by any of the following are not subject to the sales and use taxes imposed under this chapter. . . . (3) Organizations which qualify for exempt status under the provisions of section 501(c)(3) of the United States Internal Revenue Code. . . . The organization first shall have obtained a certificate from the commissioner stating that it is entitled to the exemption. . . . (4) Sales of building materials and supplies to be used in the construction, reconstruction, alteration, remodeling or repair of . . . any building or structure owned by or held in trust for the benefit of any organization described in subdivision (3) and used exclusively for the purposes upon which its exempt status is based.

TABLE 12-3

STATE SALES TAX EXEMPTIONS FOR RELIGIOUS ORGANIZATIONS
State-by-State Analysis (continued)

VIRGINIA

Code § 58.1-609.11 (2009)

A. Any nonprofit organization that holds a valid certificate of exemption from the Department of Taxation, or any nonprofit church that holds a valid self-executing certificate of exemption, that exempts it from collecting or paying state and local retail sales or use taxes as of June 30, 2003 . . . shall remain exempt from the collection or payment of such taxes under the same terms and conditions as provided under such sections as such sections existed on June 30, 2003, until . . . (iii) July 1, 2004, for the first one-half of such entities that were exempt under [former] section 58.1-609.8, except churches, which will remain exempt under the same criteria and procedures in effect for churches on June 30, 2003; (iv) July 1, 2005, for the second one-half of such entities that were exempt under section 58.1-609.8. . . . At the end of the applicable period of such exemptions, to maintain or renew an exemption for the period of time set forth in subsection E, each entity must follow the procedures set forth in subsection B and meet the criteria set forth in subsection C. Provided, however, that any entity that was exempt from collecting sales and use tax shall continue to be exempt from such collection, provided that it follows the other procedures set forth in subsection B and meets the criteria set forth in subsection C.

B. On and after July 1, 2004, in addition to the organizations described in subsection A, the tax imposed by this chapter . . . shall not apply to purchases of tangible personal property for use or consumption by any nonprofit entity that, pursuant to this section, (i) files an appropriate application with the Department of Taxation, (ii) meets the applicable criteria, and (iii) is issued a certificate of exemption from the Department of Taxation for the period of time covered by the certificate.

C. To qualify for the exemption under subsection B, a nonprofit entity must meet the applicable criteria under this subsection as follows:

1. a. The entity is exempt from federal income taxation (i) under section 501(c)(3) of the Internal Revenue Code . . . or

b. The entity has annual gross receipts less than $5,000, and the entity is organized for at least one of the purposes set forth in section 501(c)(3) of the Internal Revenue Code . . . and

2. The entity is in compliance with all applicable state solicitation laws, and where applicable, provides appropriate verification of such compliance; and

3. The entity's annual general administrative costs, including salaries and fundraising, relative to its annual gross revenue, under generally accepted accounting principles, is not greater than 40 percent; and

4. If the entity's gross annual revenue was at least $750,000 in the previous year, then the entity must provide a financial review performed by an independent certified public accountant. However, for any entity with gross annual revenue of at least $1 million in the previous year, the Department may require that the entity provide a financial audit performed by an independent certified public accountant. If the Department specifically requires an entity with gross annual revenue of at least $1 million in the previous year to provide a financial audit performed by an independent certified public accountant, then the entity shall provide such audit in order to qualify for the exemption under this section, which audit shall be in lieu of the financial review; and

5. If the entity filed a federal 990 or 990 EZ tax form, or the successor forms to such forms, with the Internal Revenue Service, then it must provide a copy of such form to the Department of Taxation; and

6. If the entity did not file a federal 990 or 990 EZ tax form, or the successor forms to such forms, with the Internal Revenue Service, then the entity must provide the following information:

a. A list of the Board of Directors or other responsible agents of the entity, composed of at least two individuals, with names and addresses where the individuals physically can be found; and

b. The location where the financial records of the entity are available for public inspection.

D. On and after July 1, 2004, in addition to the criteria set forth in subsection C, the Department of Taxation shall ask each entity for the total taxable purchases made in the preceding year, unless such records are not available through no fault of the entity. If the records are not available through no fault of the entity, then the entity must provide such information to the Department the following year. No information provided pursuant to this subsection (except the failure to provide available information) shall be a basis for the Department of Taxation to refuse to exempt an entity.

═══════════════ **TABLE 12-3** ═══════════════

STATE SALES TAX EXEMPTIONS FOR RELIGIOUS ORGANIZATIONS
State-by-State Analysis (continued)

E. Any entity that is determined under subsections B, C, and D by the Department of Taxation to be exempt from paying sales and use tax shall also be exempt from collecting sales and use tax, at its election, if (i) the entity is within the same class of organization of any entity that was exempt from collecting sales and use tax on June 30, 2003, or (ii) the entity is organized exclusively to foster, sponsor, and promote physical education, athletic programs, and contests for youths in the Commonwealth.

F. The duration of each exemption granted by the Department of Taxation shall be no less than five years and no greater than seven years. During the period of such exemption, the failure of an exempt entity to maintain compliance with the applicable criteria set forth in subsection C shall constitute grounds for revocation of the exemption by the Department. At the end of the period of such exemption, to maintain or renew the exemption, each entity must provide the Department of Taxation the same information as required upon initial exemption and meet the same criteria.

WASHINGTON

Rev. Code § 82.08.02573 (2010)
The [sales tax] does not apply to a sale made by a nonprofit organization or library, if the gross income from the sale is exempt [from tax].

WEST VIRGINIA

Code § 11-15-9 (2007)
The following sales of tangible personal property and/or services are exempt as provided in this subsection . . .

(5) Sales of property or services to churches which make no charge whatsoever for the services they render: Provided, that the exemption granted in this subdivision applies only to services, equipment, supplies, food for meals and materials directly used or consumed by these organizations, and does not apply to purchases of gasoline or special fuel. . . .

(6) Sales of tangible personal property or services to a corporation or organization which has a current registration certificate . . . which is exempt from federal income taxes under Section 501(c)(3) or (c)(4) of the Internal Revenue Code of 1986, as amended, and which is: (A) A church or a convention or association of churches as defined in Section 170 of the Internal Revenue Code of 1986, as amended. . .

(24) Food for the following are exempt . . . (C) Food purchased or sold by a charitable or private nonprofit organization . . .under a program to provide food to low-income persons at or below cost . . . (F) Food sold by any religious organization at a social or other gathering conducted by it or under its auspices, if the purpose in selling the food is to obtain revenue for the functions and activities of the organization and the revenue obtained from selling the food is actually used in carrying on those functions and activities: Provided, That purchases made by the organizations are not exempt as a purchase for resale.

(25) Sales of food by little leagues, midget football leagues, youth football or soccer leagues, band boosters or other school or athletic booster organizations supporting activities for grades kindergarten through twelve and similar types of organizations, including scouting groups and church youth groups, if the purpose in selling the food is to obtain revenue for the functions and activities of the organization and the revenues obtained from selling the food is actually used in supporting or carrying on functions and activities of the groups: Provided, That the purchases made by the organizations are not exempt as a purchase for resale.

WISCONSIN

Stat. §§ 77.54(7m) and (9a(f)) (2011)
(7m) Occasional sales of tangible personal property, or items, property, or goods under section 77.52(1)(b), (c), and (d), or services, including admissions or tickets to an event; by a neighborhood association, church, civic group, garden club, social club or similar nonprofit organization; not involving entertainment for which payment in the aggregate exceeds $500 for performing or as reimbursement of expenses unless access to the event may be obtained without payment of a direct or indirect admission fee; conducted by the organization if the organization is not engaged in a trade or business and is not required to have a seller's permit. For purposes of this subsection, an organization is engaged in a trade or business and is required to have a seller's permit if its sales of tangible personal property, and items, property, and goods under section 77.52(1)(b), (c), and (d), and services, not including sales of tickets to events, and its events occur on more than 20 days during the year, unless its receipts do not exceed $25,000 during the year. The exemption under this subsection does not apply to the sales price from the sale of bingo supplies to players or to the sale, rental or use of regular bingo cards, extra regular cards and special bingo cards.

9f. Any corporation, community chest fund, foundation or association organized and operated exclusively for religious, charitable, scientific or educational purposes, or for the prevention of cruelty to children or animals . . . no part of the net income of which inures to the benefit of any private stockholder, shareholder, member or corporation.

TABLE 12-3

STATE SALES TAX EXEMPTIONS FOR RELIGIOUS ORGANIZATIONS
State-by-State Analysis (continued)

WYOMING

Stat. § 39-15-105(a) (2012)

(iv) For the purpose of exempting sales of services and tangible personal property sold to . . . charitable and nonprofit organizations. . . the following are exempt . . . (B) Sales made to religious or charitable organizations including nonprofit organizations providing meals or services to senior citizens as certified to the department of revenue by the department of health in or for the conduct of the regular religious, charitable or senior citizen functions and activities and sales of meals made to persons in regular conduct of senior citizen centers functions and activities; (C) Occasional sales made by religious or charitable organizations for fund raising purposes for the conduct of regular religious or charitable functions and activities, and not in the course of any regular business. For the purposes of this subparagraph, "regular business" means the habitual or regular activity of the organization excluding any incidental or occasional operation.

TABLE 12-4

STATE PROPERTY TAX EXEMPTIONS FOR RELIGIOUS ORGANIZATIONS
State-by-State Analysis

Note: Listed below are the property tax exemptions of all 50 states pertaining to property owned by religious organizations. All laws are subject to change. To determine the current text of any statute, you should visit a library, contact your local or county property tax office, check the website maintained by your state department of revenue, or consult with an attorney.

ALABAMA

Code § 40-9-1. Persons and property generally (1990)
The following property and persons shall be exempt from ad valorem taxation and none other:

(1) All . . . cemeteries, all property, real and personal, used exclusively for religious worship, for schools or for purposes purely charitable; provided, that property, real or personal, owned by any educational, religious or charitable institution, society or corporation let for rent or hire or for use for business purposes shall not be exempt from taxation, notwithstanding that the income from such property shall be used exclusively for education, religious or charitable purposes. . . .

(6) The libraries of ministers of the gospel, all libraries other than those of a professional character and all religious books kept for sale by ministers of the gospel and colporteurs.

ALASKA

Stat. § 29.45.030. Required exemptions (subsection (a) effective through 2017)
(a) The following property is exempt from general taxation: . . . (3) property used exclusively for nonprofit religious, charitable, cemetery, hospital, or educational purposes. . . .

(b) In (a) of this section, "property used exclusively for religious purposes" includes the following property owned by a religious organization: (1) the residence of an educator in a private religious or parochial school or a bishop, pastor, priest, rabbi, minister, or religious order of a recognized religious organization; for purposes of this paragraph, "minister" means an individual who is (A) ordained, commissioned, or licensed as a minister according to standards of the religious organization for its ministers; and (B) employed by the religious organization to carry out a ministry of that religious organization; (2) a structure, its furniture, and its fixtures used solely for public worship, charitable purposes, religious administrative offices, religious education, or a nonprofit hospital; (3) lots required by local ordinance for parking near a structure defined in (2) of this subsection.

(c) Property described in (a)(3) or (4) of this section from which income is derived is exempt only if that income is solely from use of the property by nonprofit religious, charitable, hospital, or educational groups. If used by nonprofit educational groups, the property is exempt only if used exclusively for classroom space.

ARIZONA

Rev. Stat. Ann. § 42-11109. Property subject to taxation; exceptions (2001)
Property or buildings that are used or held primarily for religious worship, including land, improvements, furniture and equipment, are exempt from taxation if the property is not used or held for profit. Within ten days after receiving an initial affidavit of eligibility submitted . . . by a nonprofit organization that owns property used primarily for religious worship, the county assessor, on request, shall issue a receipt for the affidavit. If the organization files with the assessor evidence of the organization's tax exempt status under section 501(c)(3) of the Internal Revenue Code . . . the organization is exempt from the requirement of filing subsequent affidavits . . . until all or part of the property is conveyed to a new owner or is no longer used for religious worship. At that time the organization shall notify the assessor of the change in writing. If a nonprofit organization that holds title to property used primarily for religious worship fails to file the affidavit required by § 42-11152 in a timely manner, but otherwise qualifies for exemption, the county board of supervisors, on petition by the organization, shall direct the county treasurer to: 1. Refund any property taxes paid by the organization for a tax year if the organization submits a claim for the refund to the county treasurer within one year after the date the taxes were paid. The county treasurer shall pay the claim within thirty days after it is submitted to the treasurer. The county treasurer is entitled to credit for the refund in the next accounting period with each taxing jurisdiction to which the tax monies may have been transmitted. 2. Forgive and strike off from the tax roll any property taxes and accrued interest and penalties that are due but not paid.

ARKANSAS

Stat. § 26-3-301. Property exempt from taxes generally (2007)
All property described in this section, to the extent limited, shall be exempt from taxation:

(1) Public school buildings and buildings used exclusively for public worship and the grounds attached to these buildings necessary for the proper occupancy, use, and enjoyment of the buildings, not leased or otherwise used with a view to profit. . . .

TABLE 12-4

STATE PROPERTY TAX EXEMPTIONS FOR RELIGIOUS ORGANIZATIONS
State-by-State Analysis (continued)

(3) All lands used exclusively as graveyards or grounds for burying the dead, except those held by any person, company, or corporation with a view to profit or for the purpose of speculation in the sale of the lands. . . .

(12)(A) Under the provisions of this section, all dedicated church property, including the church building used as a place of worship, buildings used for administrative or missional purposes, the land upon which the church buildings are located, all church parsonages, any church educational building operated in connection with the church including a family life or activity center, a recreation center, a youth center, a church association building, a day-care center, a kindergarten, or private church school shall be exempt. (B) However, in the event any property is used partially for church purposes and partially for investments or other commercial or business purposes, the property shall be exempt from the ad valorem tax.

Stat. § 26-3-303. Parsonages (1945)
Parsonages owned by churches and used as homes for pastors shall be exempt from all taxes on real property, except improvement district taxes.

CALIFORNIA

Rev. & Tax Code § 207. Property used exclusively for religious purposes; religious exemption; effective date (1983)
Property used exclusively for religious purposes shall be exempt from taxation. Property owned and operated by a church and used for religious worship, preschool purposes, nursery school purposes, kindergarten purposes, school purposes of less than collegiate grade, or for purposes of both schools of collegiate grade and schools less than collegiate grade but excluding property used solely for purposes of schools of collegiate grade, shall be deemed to be used exclusively for religious purposes under this section. The exemption provided by this section is granted pursuant to the authority in subdivision (b) of Section 4 of Article XI of the California Constitution, and shall be known as the "religious exemption." This section shall be effective for the 1977-78 fiscal year and fiscal years thereafter.

Rev. & Tax Code § 207.1. Personal property leased to church; religious purposes (1998)
Personal property leased to a church and used exclusively for the purposes described in Section 207 shall be deemed to be used exclusively for religious purposes under that section.

COLORADO

Rev. Stat. § 39-3-106. Property—religious purposes—exemption—legislative declaration (2004)
(1) Property, real and personal, which is owned and used solely and exclusively for religious purposes and not for private gain or corporate profit shall be exempt from the levy and collection of property tax.

(2) In order to guide members of the public and public officials alike in the making of their day-to-day decisions, to provide for a consistent application of the laws, and to assist in the avoidance of litigation, the general assembly hereby finds and declares that religious worship has different meanings to different religious organizations; that the constitutional guarantees regarding establishment of religion and the free exercise of religion prevent public officials from inquiring as to whether particular activities of religious organizations constitute religious worship; that many activities of religious organizations are in the furtherance of the religious purposes of such organizations; that such religious activities are an integral part of the religious worship of religious organizations; and that activities of religious organizations which are in furtherance of their religious purposes constitute religious worship for purposes of section 5 of article X of the Colorado constitution. This legislative finding and declaration shall be entitled to great weight in any and every court.

Rev. Stat. § 39-3-106.5. Tax-exempt property—incidental use—exemption—limitations (2011)
(1) If any property, real or personal, which is otherwise exempt from the levy and collection of property tax pursuant to the provisions of section 39-3-106, is used for any purpose other than the purposes specified in sections 39-3-106 to 39-3-113, such property shall be exempt from the levy and collection of property tax if:

(a) The property is used for such purposes for less than two hundred eight hours, adjusted for partial usage if necessary on the basis of the relationship that the amount of time and space used for such other purpose bears to the total available time and space, during the calendar year; or (b) The use of the property for such purposes results in either: (I) Less than ten thousand dollars of gross income to the owner of such property which is derived from any unrelated trade or business, as determined pursuant to the provisions of sections 511 to 513 of the federal "Internal Revenue Code of 1986", as amended; or (II) Less than ten thousand dollars of gross rental income to the owner of such property.

(1.5) Notwithstanding the provisions of subsection (1) of this section, for property tax years commencing on or after January 1, 1994, if any property, real or personal, which is otherwise exempt from the levy and collection of property tax pursuant to the provisions of section 39-3-106, is used for any purpose other than the purposes specified in sections 39-3-106 to 39-3-113, such property shall be exempt from the levy and collection of property tax if:

(a) The property is used for such purposes for less than two hundred eight hours, adjusted for partial usage if necessary on the basis of the relationship that the amount of time and space used for such other purpose bears to the total available time and space, during the calendar year; or

(b) The use of the property for such purposes results in:

(I) Less than ten thousand dollars of gross income to the owner of such property which is derived from any unrelated trade or business, as determined pursuant to the provisions of sections 511 to 513 of the federal "Internal Revenue Code of 1986," as amended; and

(II) Less than ten thousand dollars of gross rental income to the owner of such property.

(2) Except as otherwise provided in section 39-3-108(3) and subsection (3) of this section, if any property, real or personal, that is otherwise exempt from the levy and collection of property tax pursuant to the provisions of sections 39-3-107 to 39-3-113 is used on an occasional, noncontinuous basis for any purpose other than the purposes specified in sections 39-3-106 to 39-3-113, such property shall be exempt from the levy and collection of property tax if:

(a) The property is used for such purposes for less than two hundred eight hours, adjusted for partial usage if necessary on the basis of the relationship that the amount of time and space used for such other purpose bears to the total available time and space, during the calendar year; or

(b) The use of the property for such purposes results in less than twenty-five thousand dollars of gross rental income to the owner of such property.

(3) The requirement that property be used on an occasional basis in order to qualify for the exemption set forth in subsection (2) of this section shall not apply to property, real or personal, that is otherwise exempt from the levy and collection of property tax pursuant to the provisions of section 39-3-111 that is used for any purpose other than the purposes specified in sections 39-3-106 to 39-3-113.

Rev. Stat. § 39-3-109. Residential property—integral part of tax-exempt entities—charitable purposes—exemption—limitation (2002)
(1) Property, real and personal, which is owned and used solely and exclusively for strictly charitable purposes and not for private gain or corporate profit shall be exempt from the levy and collection of property tax if such property is residential and the structure and the land upon which such structure is located are used as an integral part of a church, an eleemosynary hospital, an eleemosynary licensed health care facility, a school, or an institution whose property is otherwise exempt from taxation pursuant to the provisions of this Part 1 and which is not leased or rented at any time to persons other than: (a) Persons who are attending such school as students; or (b) Persons who are actually receiving care or treatment from such hospital, licensed health care facility, or institution for physical or mental disabilities and who, in order to receive such care or treatment, are required to be domiciled within such hospital, licensed health care facility, or institution, or within affiliated residential units.

(2) Persons residing within residential units specified in paragraph (b) of subsection (1) of this section may submit to the administrator, on a form prescribed by the administrator, a certificate signed by a physician licensed to practice in the state of Colorado that the medical condition of such individual requires the individual to reside in such residential unit. If a person residing within such residential unit submits such signed certificate to the administrator pursuant to the provisions of this subsection (2), the portion of such residential property that is utilized by qualified occupants shall be deemed to be property used solely and exclusively for strictly charitable purposes and not for private gain or corporate profit and such portion, but only such portion, shall be exempt under the provisions of subsection (1) of this section. The determination as to what portion of such structure is so utilized shall be made by the administrator on the basis of the facts existing on the annual assessment date for such property, and the administrator shall have the authority to determine a ratio which reflects the value of the non-exempt portion of such structure in relation to the total value of the whole structure and the land upon which such structure is located and which is identical to the ratio of the number of residential units occupied by nonqualified occupants to the total number of occupied residential units in such structure.

TABLE 12-4

STATE PROPERTY TAX EXEMPTIONS FOR RELIGIOUS ORGANIZATIONS
State-by-State Analysis (continued)

(2.5) No requirement shall be imposed that use of property which is otherwise exempt pursuant to the provisions of this section shall benefit the people of Colorado in order to qualify for said exemption.

(3) Any exemption claimed pursuant to the provisions of this section shall comply with the provisions of section 39-2-117.

CONNECTICUT

Gen. Stat. § 12-81. Exemptions (2011)
The following-described property shall be exempt from taxation . . .

(12) Personal property of religious organizations devoted to religious or charitable use. Personal property within the state owned by, or held in trust for, a Connecticut religious organization, whether or not incorporated, if the principal or income is used or appropriated for religious or charitable purposes or both;

(13) Houses of religious worship. Subject to the provisions of section 12-88, houses of religious worship, the land on which they stand, their pews, furniture and equipment owned by, or held in trust for the use of, any religious organization;

(14) Property of religious organizations used for certain purposes. Subject to the provisions of section 12-88, real property and its equipment owned by, or held in trust for, any religious organization and exclusively used as a school, a Connecticut nonprofit camp or recreational facility for religious purposes, a parish house, an orphan asylum, a home for children, a thrift shop, the proceeds of which are used for charitable purposes, a reformatory or an infirmary or for two or more of such purposes;

(15) Houses used by officiating clergymen as dwellings. Subject to the provisions of section 12-88, dwelling houses and the land on which they stand owned by, or held in trust for, any religious organization and actually used by its officiating clergymen . . .

(58) Property leased to a charitable, religious or nonprofit organization. Subject to authorization of the exemption by ordinance in any municipality, any real or personal property leased to a charitable, religious or nonprofit organization, exempt from taxation for federal income tax purposes, provided such property is used exclusively for the purposes of such charitable, religious or nonprofit organization.

Gen. Stat. § 12-88. When property otherwise taxable may be completely or partially exempted (1949)
Real property belonging to, or held in trust for, any organization mentioned in subdivision (7), (10), (11), (13), (14), (15), (16) or (18) of section 12-81, which real property is so held for one or more of the purposes stated in the applicable subdivision, and from which real property no rents, profits or income are derived, shall be exempt from taxation though not in actual use therefore by reason of the absence of suitable buildings and improvements thereon, if the construction of such buildings or improvements is in progress. The real property belonging to, or held in trust for, any such organization, not used exclusively for carrying out one or more of such purposes but leased, rented or otherwise used for other purposes, shall not be exempt. If a portion only of any lot or building belonging to, or held in trust for, any such organization is used exclusively for carrying out one or more of such purposes, such lot or building shall be so exempt only to the extent of the portion so used and the remaining portion shall be subject to taxation.

DELAWARE

Code Ann. title 9, § 8105. Property owned by governmental, religious, educational or charitable agency (1995)
Property belonging to . . . any church or religious society, and not held by way of investment, or any college or school and used for educational or school purposes, except as otherwise provided, shall not be liable to taxation and assessment for public purposes by any county or other political subdivision of this State. Nothing in this section shall be construed to apply to ditch taxes, sewer taxes and/or utility fees. Corporations created for charitable purposes and not held by way of investment that are in existence on July 14, 1988, together with existing and future charitable affiliates of such corporations that are also not held by way of investment, shall not be liable to taxation and assessment for public purposes by any county, municipality or other political subdivision of this State.

FLORIDA

Stat. § 196.012. Definitions (2012)
(1) "Exempt use of property" or "use of property for exempt purposes" means predominant or exclusive use of property owned by an exempt entity for educational, literary, scientific, religious, charitable, or governmental purposes, as defined in this chapter.

Stat. § 196.192. Exemptions from ad valorem taxation (2008)
Subject to the provisions of this chapter:

TABLE 12-4

STATE PROPERTY TAX EXEMPTIONS FOR RELIGIOUS ORGANIZATIONS
State-by-State Analysis (continued)

(1) All property owned by an exempt entity, including educational institutions, and used exclusively for exempt purposes shall be totally exempt from ad valorem taxation.

(2) All property owned by an exempt entity, including educational institutions, and used predominantly for exempt purposes shall be exempted from ad valorem taxation to the extent of the ratio that such predominant use bears to the nonexempt use.

(3) All tangible personal property loaned or leased by a natural person, by a trust holding property for a natural person, or by an exempt entity to an exempt entity for public display or exhibition on a recurrent schedule is exempt from ad valorem taxation if the property is loaned or leased for no consideration or for nominal consideration. For purposes of this section, each use to which the property is being put must be considered in granting an exemption from ad valorem taxation, including any economic use in addition to any physical use. For purposes of this section, property owned by a limited liability company, the sole member of which is an exempt entity, shall be treated as if the property were owned directly by the exempt entity. This section does not apply in determining the exemption for property owned by governmental units pursuant to section 196.199.

Stat. § 196.195. Criteria for determining profit or nonprofit status of applicant (2001)

(1) Applicants requesting exemption shall supply such fiscal and other records showing in reasonable detail the financial condition, record of operation, and exempt and nonexempt uses of the property, where appropriate, for the immediately preceding fiscal year as are requested by the property appraiser or the value adjustment board.

(2) In determining whether an applicant for a religious, literary, scientific, or charitable exemption under this chapter is a nonprofit or profit-making venture or whether the property is used for a profit making purpose, the following criteria shall be applied: (a) The reasonableness of any advances or payment directly or indirectly by way of salary, fee, loan, gift, bonus, gratuity, drawing account, commission, or otherwise (except for reimbursements of advances for reasonable out-of-pocket expenses incurred on behalf of the applicant) to any person, company, or other entity directly or indirectly controlled by the applicant or any officer, director, trustee, member, or stockholder of the applicant; (b) The reasonableness of any guaranty of a loan to, or an obligation of, any officer, director, trustee, member, or stockholder of the applicant or any entity directly or indirectly controlled by such person, or which pays any compensation to its officers, directors, trustees, members, or stockholders for services rendered to or on behalf of the applicant; (c) The reasonableness of any contractual arrangement by the applicant or any officer, director, trustee, member, or stockholder of the applicant regarding rendition of services, the provision of goods or supplies, the management of the applicant, the construction or renovation of the property of the applicant, the procurement of the real, personal, or intangible property of the applicant, or other similar financial interest in the affairs of the applicant; (d) The reasonableness of payments made for salaries for the operation of the applicant or for services, supplies and materials used by the applicant, reserves for repair, replacement, and depreciation of the property of the applicant, payment of mortgages, liens, and encumbrances upon the property of the applicant, or other purposes; and (e) The reasonableness of charges made by the applicant for any services rendered by it in relation to the value of those services, and, if such charges exceed the value of the services rendered, whether the excess is used to pay maintenance and operational expenses in furthering its exempt purpose or to provide services to persons unable to pay for the services.

(3) Each applicant must affirmatively show that no part of the subject property, or the proceeds of the sale, lease, or other disposition thereof, will inure to the benefit of its members, directors, or officers or any person or firm operating for profit or for a nonexempt purpose.

(4) No application for exemption may be granted for religious, literary, scientific, or charitable use of property until the applicant has been found by the property appraiser or, upon appeal, by the value adjustment board to be nonprofit as defined in this section.

Stat. § 196.196 Determining whether property is entitled to charitable, religious, scientific, or literary exemption (2011)

(1) In the determination of whether an applicant is actually using all or a portion of its property predominantly for a charitable, religious, scientific, or literary purpose, the following criteria shall be applied:

(a) The nature and extent of the charitable, religious, scientific, or literary activity of the applicant, a comparison of such activities with all other activities of the organization, and the utilization of the property for charitable, religious, scientific, or literary activities as compared with other uses.

(b) The extent to which the property has been made available to groups who perform exempt purposes at a charge that is equal to or less than the cost of providing the facilities for their use. Such rental or service shall be considered as part of the exempt purposes of the applicant.

====== **TABLE 12-4** ======

STATE PROPERTY TAX EXEMPTIONS FOR RELIGIOUS ORGANIZATIONS
State-by-State Analysis (continued)

(2) Only those portions of property used predominantly for charitable, religious, scientific, or literary purposes shall be exempt. In no event shall an incidental use of property either qualify such property for an exemption or impair the exemption of an otherwise exempt property.

(3) Property owned by an exempt organization is used for a religious purpose if the institution has taken affirmative steps to prepare the property for use as a house of public worship. The term "affirmative steps" means environmental or land use permitting activities, creation of architectural plans or schematic drawings, land clearing or site preparation, construction or renovation activities, or other similar activities that demonstrate a commitment of the property to a religious use as a house of public worship. For purposes of this subsection, the term "public worship" means religious worship services and those other activities that are incidental to religious worship services, such as educational activities, parking, recreation, partaking of meals, and fellowship.

(4) Except as otherwise provided herein, property claimed as exempt for literary, scientific, religious, or charitable purposes which is used for profitmaking purposes shall be subject to ad valorem taxation. Use of property for functions not requiring a business or occupational license conducted by the organization at its primary residence, the revenue of which is used wholly for exempt purposes, shall not be considered profit making. In this connection the playing of bingo on such property shall not be considered as using such property in such a manner as would impair its exempt status.

(5)(a) Property owned by an exempt organization qualified as charitable under section 501(c)(3) of the Internal Revenue Code is used for a charitable purpose if the organization has taken affirmative steps to prepare the property to provide affordable housing to persons or families that meet the extremely-low-income, very-low-income, low-income, or moderate-income limits, as specified in section 420.0004. The term "affirmative steps" means environmental or land use permitting activities, creation of architectural plans or schematic drawings, land clearing or site preparation, construction or renovation activities, or other similar activities that demonstrate a commitment of the property to providing affordable housing.

(b) 1. If property owned by an organization granted an exemption under this subsection is transferred for a purpose other than directly providing affordable homeownership or rental housing to persons or families who meet the extremely-low-income, very-low-income, low-income, or moderate-income limits, as specified in section 420.0004, or is not in actual use to provide such affordable housing within 5 years after the date the organization is granted the exemption, the property appraiser making such determination shall serve upon the organization that illegally or improperly received the exemption a notice of intent to record in the public records of the county a notice of tax lien against any property owned by that organization in the county, and such property shall be identified in the notice of tax lien. The organization owning such property is subject to the taxes otherwise due and owing as a result of the failure to use the property to provide affordable housing plus 15 percent interest per annum and a penalty of 50 percent of the taxes owed.

2. Such lien, when filed, attaches to any property identified in the notice of tax lien owned by the organization that illegally or improperly received the exemption. If such organization no longer owns property in the county but owns property in any other county in the state, the property appraiser shall record in each such other county a notice of tax lien identifying the property owned by such organization in such county which shall become a lien against the identified property. Before any such lien may be filed, the organization so notified must be given 30 days to pay the taxes, penalties, and interest.

3. If an exemption is improperly granted as a result of a clerical mistake or an omission by the property appraiser, the organization improperly receiving the exemption shall not be assessed a penalty or interest.

4. The 5-year limitation specified in this subsection may be extended if the holder of the exemption continues to take affirmative steps to develop the property for the purposes specified in this subsection.

GEORGIA   **Code § 48-5-41. Property exempt from taxation (2011)**
(a) The following property shall be exempt from all ad valorem property taxes in this state . . . (2.1)(A) All places of religious worship; and (B) All property owned by and operated exclusively as a church, an association or convention of churches, a convention mission agency, or as an integrated auxiliary of a church or convention or association of churches, when such entity is qualified as an exempt religious organization under Section 501(c)(3) of the Internal Revenue Code of 1986, as amended, and such property is used in a manner consistent with such exemption under Section 501(c)(3) of the Internal Revenue Code of 1986, as amended; (3) All property owned by religious groups and used only for single-family residences when no income is derived from the property. . . .

(d)(1) Except as otherwise provided in paragraph (2) of this subsection, this Code section, excluding paragraph (1) of subsection (a) of this Code section, shall not apply to real estate or buildings which are rented, leased, or otherwise used for the

TABLE 12-4

STATE PROPERTY TAX EXEMPTIONS FOR RELIGIOUS ORGANIZATIONS
State-by-State Analysis (continued)

primary purpose of securing an income thereon and shall not apply to real estate or buildings which are not used for the operation of religious, educational, and charitable institutions. Donations of property to be exempted shall not be predicated upon an agreement, contract, or other instrument that the donor or donors shall receive or retain any part of the net or gross income of the property.

(2) With respect to paragraph (4) of subsection (a) of this Code section, a building which is owned by a charitable institution that is otherwise qualified as a purely public charity and that is exempt from taxation under section 501(c)(3) of the Internal Revenue Code and which building is used by such charitable institution exclusively for the charitable purposes of such charitable institution, and not more than 15 acres of land on which such building is located, may be used for the purpose of securing income so long as such income is used exclusively for the operation of that charitable institution.

HAWAII

Rev. Stat. § 246-32. Charitable, etc., purposes (1996)
(a) There shall be exempt from real property taxes real property designated in subsection (b) or (c) and meeting the requirements stated therein, actually and (except as otherwise specifically provided) exclusively used for nonprofit purposes. If an exemption is claimed under one of these subsections (b) or (c), an exemption for the same property may not also be claimed under the other of these subsections.

(b) This subsection applies to property owned in fee simple, leased, or rented for a period of one year or more, by the person using the property for the exempt purposes, hereinafter referred to as the person claiming the exemption. If the property for which exemption is claimed is leased or rented, the lease or rental agreement shall be in force and recorded in the bureau of conveyances.

Exemption is allowed by this subsection to the following property . . . (3) Property used for church purposes, including incidental activities, parsonages, and church grounds, the property exempt from taxation being limited to realty exclusive of burying grounds (exemption for which may be claimed under paragraph (4)). . . .

(d) If any portion of the property which might otherwise be exempted under this section is used for commercial or other purposes not within the conditions necessary for exemption (including any use the primary purpose of which is to produce income even though such income is to be used for or in furtherance of the exempt purposes) that portion of the premises shall not be exempt but the remaining portion of the premises shall not be deprived of the exemption if the remaining portion is used exclusively for purposes within the conditions necessary for exemption. In the event of an exemption of a portion of a building, the tax shall be assessed upon so much of the value of the building (including the land thereunder and the appurtenant premises) as the proportion of the floor space of the nonexempt portion bears to the total floor space of the building.

(e) The term "for nonprofit purposes", as used in this section requires that no monetary gain or economic benefit inure to the person claiming the exemption, or any private shareholder, member, or trust beneficiary. "Monetary gain" includes without limitation any gain in the form of money or money's worth. "Economic benefit" includes without limitation any benefit to a person in the course of the person's business, trade, occupation, or employment.

IDAHO

Code § 63-602B. Property exempt from taxation—religious corporations or societies (2008)
(1) The following property is exempt from taxation: property belonging to any religious limited liability company, corporation or society of this state, used exclusively for and in connection with any combination of religious, educational, or recreational purposes or activities of such religious limited liability company, corporation or society, including any and all residences used for or in furtherance of such purposes.

(2) If the entirety of any property belonging to any such religious limited liability company, corporation or society is leased by such owner, or if such religious limited liability company, corporation or society uses the entirety of such property for business or commercial purposes from which a revenue is derived, then the same shall be assessed and taxed as any other property. If any such property is leased in part or used in part by such religious limited liability company, corporation or society for such business or commercial purposes, the assessor shall determine the value of the entire exempt property, and the value of the part used or leased for such business or commercial purposes, and that part used or leased for such business or commercial purposes shall be taxed as any other property. The Idaho state tax commission shall promulgate rules establishing a method of determining the value of the part used or leased for such business or commercial purposes. If the value of the part used or leased for such business or commercial purposes is determined to be three percent (3%) or less of the value of the entirety, the whole of said property shall remain exempt. If the value of the part used or leased for such business or commercial purposes

TABLE 12-4

STATE PROPERTY TAX EXEMPTIONS FOR RELIGIOUS ORGANIZATIONS
State-by-State Analysis (continued)

is determined to be more than three percent (3%) of the value of the entirety, the assessor shall assess such proportionate part of such property, and shall assess the trade fixtures used in connection with the sale of all merchandise for such business or commercial purposes, provided however, that the use or lease of any property by any such religious limited liability company, corporation or society for athletic or recreational facilities, residence halls or dormitories, meeting rooms or halls, auditoriums, or club rooms for and in connection with the purposes for which such religious limited liability company, corporation or society is organized, shall not be deemed a business or commercial purpose, even though fees or charges be imposed and revenue derived therefrom.

ILLINOIS

35 Compiled Statutes 200/15-40. Religious purposes, orphanages, or school and religious purposes (2001)
(a) Property used exclusively for: (1) religious purposes, or (2) school and religious purposes, or (3) orphanages qualifies for exemption as long as it is not used with a view to profit.

(b) Property that is owned by (1) churches or (2) religious institutions or (3) religious denominations and that is used in conjunction therewith as housing facilities provided for ministers (including bishops, district superintendents and similar church officials whose ministerial duties are not limited to a single congregation), their spouses, children and domestic workers, performing the duties of their vocation as ministers at such churches or religious institutions or for such religious denominations, including the convents and monasteries where persons engaged in religious activities reside also qualifies for exemption.

A parsonage, convent or monastery or other housing facility shall be considered under this Section to be exclusively used for religious purposes when the persons who perform religious related activities shall, as a condition of their employment or association, reside in the facility.

INDIANA

Code § 6-1.1-10-16. Buildings and land used for educational, literary, scientific, religious, or charitable purposes (2011)
(a) All or part of a building is exempt from property taxation if it is owned, occupied, and used by a person for educational, literary, scientific, religious, or charitable purposes. . . .

(c) A tract of land . . . is exempt from property taxation if: (1) a building that is exempt under subsection (a) or (b) is situated on it; (2) a parking lot or structure that serves a building referred to in subdivision (1) is situated on it; or (3) the tract: (A) is owned by a nonprofit entity established for the purpose of retaining and preserving land and water for their natural characteristics; (B) does not exceed five hundred (500) acres; and (C) is not used by the nonprofit entity to make a profit.

(d) A tract of land is exempt from property taxation if:

(1) it is purchased for the purpose of erecting a building that is to be owned, occupied, and used in such a manner that the building will be exempt under subsection (a) or (b); and

(2) not more than four (4) years after the property is purchased, and for each year after the four (4) year period, the owner demonstrates substantial progress and active pursuit towards the erection of the intended building and use of the tract for the exempt purpose. To establish substantial progress and active pursuit under this subdivision, the owner must prove the existence of factors such as the following:

(A) Organization of and activity by a building committee or other oversight group.

(B) Completion and filing of building plans with the appropriate local government authority.

(C) Cash reserves dedicated to the project of a sufficient amount to lead a reasonable individual to believe the actual construction can and will begin within four (4) years.

(D) The breaking of ground and the beginning of actual construction.

(E) Any other factor that would lead a reasonable individual to believe that construction of the building is an active plan and that the building is capable of being completed within eight (8) years considering the circumstances of the owner.

(e) Personal property is exempt from property taxation if it is owned and used in such a manner that it would be exempt under subsection (a) or (b) if it were a building.

=== **TABLE 12-4** ===

STATE PROPERTY TAX EXEMPTIONS FOR RELIGIOUS ORGANIZATIONS
State-by-State Analysis (continued)

IOWA

Code § 427.1. Exemptions (2012)
The following classes of property shall not be taxed . . . 8. Property of religious, literary, and charitable societies. All grounds and buildings used or under construction by . . . religious institutions and societies solely for their appropriate objects, not exceeding three hundred twenty acres in extent and not leased or otherwise used or under construction with a view to pecuniary profit.

KANSAS

Stat. Ann. § 79-201. Property exempt from taxation; religious, educational, literary, scientific, benevolent, alumni association, veterans' organization or charitable purposes; parsonages; community service organizations providing humanitarian services (2009)
The following described property, to the extent herein specified, shall be and is hereby exempt from all property or ad valorem taxes levied under the laws of the state of Kansas:

First. All buildings used exclusively as places of public worship . . . with the furniture and books therein contained and used exclusively for the accommodation of religious meetings . . . together with the grounds owned thereby if not leased or otherwise used for the realization of profit, except that . . . (b) any building, or portion thereof, used as a place of worship, together with the grounds upon which the building is located, shall be considered to be used exclusively for the religious purposes of this section when used as a not-for-profit day care center for children which is licensed pursuant to K.S.A. 65-501 et seq., and amendments thereto, or when used to house an area where the congregation of a church society and others may purchase tracts, books and other items relating to the promulgation of the church society's religious doctrines.

Second. All real property, and all tangible personal property, actually and regularly used exclusively for . . . religious, benevolent or charitable purposes, including property used exclusively for such purposes by more than one agency or organization for one or more of such exempt purposes. Except with regard to real property which is owned by a religious organization, is to be used exclusively for religious purposes and is not used for a nonexempt purpose prior to its exclusive use for religious purposes which property shall be deemed to be actually and regularly used exclusively for religious purposes for the purposes of this paragraph, this exemption shall not apply to such property, not actually used or occupied for the purposes set forth herein, nor to such property held or used as an investment even though the income or rentals received therefrom is used wholly for such . . . religious, benevolent or charitable purposes. In the event any such property which has been exempted pursuant to the preceding sentence is not used for religious purposes prior to its conveyance which results in its use for nonreligious purposes, there shall be a recoupment of property taxes in an amount equal to the tax which would have been levied upon such property except for such exemption for all taxable years for which such exemption was in effect. . . . This exemption shall not be deemed inapplicable to property which would otherwise be exempt pursuant to this paragraph because an agency or organization: (a) Is reimbursed for the provision of services accomplishing the purposes enumerated in this paragraph based upon the ability to pay by the recipient of such services; or (b) is reimbursed for the actual expense of using such property for purposes enumerated in this paragraph; or (c) uses such property for a nonexempt purpose which is minimal in scope and insubstantial in nature if such use is incidental to the exempt purposes of this paragraph; (d) charges a reasonable fee for admission to cultural or educational activities or permits the use of its property for such activities by a related agency or organization, if any such activity is in furtherance of the purposes of this paragraph; or (e) is applying for an exemption pursuant to this paragraph for a motor vehicle that is being leased for a period of at least one year. . . .

Seventh. All parsonages owned by a church society and actually and regularly occupied and used predominantly as a residence by a minister or other clergyman of such church society who is actually and regularly engaged in conducting the services and religious ministrations of such society, and the land upon which such parsonage is located to the extent necessary for the accommodation of such parsonage. . . .

Tenth. For all taxable years commencing after December 31, 1986, any building, and the land upon which such building is located to the extent necessary for the accommodation of such building, owned by a church or nonprofit religious society or order which is exempt from federal income taxation pursuant to section 501(c)(3) of the federal internal revenue code of 1986, and actually and regularly occupied and used exclusively for residential and religious purposes by a community of persons who are bound by vows to a religious life and who conduct or assist in the conduct of religious services and actually and regularly engage in religious, benevolent, charitable or educational ministrations or the performance of health care services.

KENTUCKY

Const. § 170. Property exempt from taxation (1998)
There shall be exempt from taxation . . . real property owned and occupied by, and personal property both tangible and intangible owned by, institutions of religion.

TABLE 12-4

STATE PROPERTY TAX EXEMPTIONS FOR RELIGIOUS ORGANIZATIONS
State-by-State Analysis (continued)

LOUISIANA

Const. Art. 7, § 21. Other property exemptions (2011)
In addition to the homestead exemption provided for in Section 20 of this Article, the following property and no other shall be exempt from ad valorem taxation . . . (B)(1)(a)(i) Property owned by a nonprofit corporation or association organized and operated exclusively for religious, dedicated places of burial, charitable, health, welfare, fraternal, or educational purposes, no part of the net earnings of which inure to the benefit of any private shareholder or member thereof and which is declared to be exempt from federal or state income tax. . . . None of the property listed in Paragraph (B) shall be exempt if owned, operated, leased, or used for commercial purposes unrelated to the exempt purposes of the corporation or association.

MAINE

Rev. Stat. Ann. title 36, § 652. Property of institutions and organizations (2009)
1. Property of institutions and organizations. The property of institutions and organizations is exempt from taxation as provided in this subsection.

G. Houses of religious worship, including vestries, and the pews and furniture within them; tombs and rights of burial; and property owned and used by a religious society as a parsonage up to the value of $20,000, and personal property not exceeding $6,000 in value are exempt from taxation, except that any portion of a parsonage that is rented is subject to taxation. For purposes of this paragraph, "parsonage" means the principal residence provided by a religious society for its cleric whether or not the principal residence is located within the same municipality as the house of religious worship where the cleric regularly conducts religious services.

H. Real estate and personal property owned by or held in trust for fraternal organizations, except college fraternities, operating under the lodge system that are used solely by those fraternal organizations for meetings, ceremonials or religious or moral instruction, including all facilities that are appurtenant to that property and used in connection with those purposes are exempt from taxation. If a building is used in part for those purposes and in part for any other purpose, only the part used for those purposes is exempt.

Further conditions to the right of exemption under this paragraph are that:

(1) A director, trustee, officer or employee of any organization claiming exemption may not receive directly or indirectly any pecuniary profit from the operation of that organization, except as reasonable compensation for services in effecting its purposes or as a proper beneficiary of its purposes;

(2) All profits derived from the operation of the organization and the proceeds from the sale of its property must be devoted exclusively to the purposes for which it is organized; and

(3) The institution, organization or corporation claiming exemption under this paragraph must file with the assessors upon their request a report for its preceding fiscal year in such detail as the assessors may reasonably require.

MARYLAND

Tax-Property Code § 7-204. Religious groups or organizations (1985)
Property that is owned by a religious group or organization is not subject to property tax if the property is actually used exclusively for: (1) public religious worship; (2) a parsonage or convent; or (3) educational purposes.

MASSACHUSETTS

Gen. Laws Ann. ch. 59, § 5. Persons and property exempt from taxation (2012)
Tenth, Personal property owned by or held in trust within the commonwealth for religious organizations, whether or not incorporated, if the principal or income is used or appropriated for religious, benevolent or charitable purposes.

Eleventh, Notwithstanding the provisions of any other general or special law to the contrary, houses of religious worship owned by, or held in trust for the use of, any religious organization, and the pews and furniture and each parsonage so owned, or held in irrevocable trust, for the exclusive benefit of the religious organizations, and including the official residences occupied by district superintendents of the United Methodist Church and the Christian and Missionary Alliance and of the Church of the Nazarene, and by district executives of the Southern New England District of the Assemblies of God, Inc., Unitarian-Universalist Churches and the Baptist General Conference of New England, and the official residence occupied by the president of the New England Synod of the Lutheran Church in America, Inc., and the official residence occupied by a person who has been designated by the congregation of a Hebrew Synagogue or Temple as the rabbi thereof, but such exemption shall not, except as herein provided, extend to any portion of any such house of religious worship appropriated for purposes other than religious worship or instruction. The occasional or incidental use of such property by an organization exempt from taxation under the provisions of 26 USC Sec. 501(c)(3) of the federal Internal Revenue Code shall not be deemed to be an appropriation for purposes other than religious worship or instruction.

TABLE 12-4

STATE PROPERTY TAX EXEMPTIONS FOR RELIGIOUS ORGANIZATIONS
State-by-State Analysis (continued)

MICHIGAN

Comp. Laws § 211.7s. Houses of public worship, parsonages (1980)
Houses of public worship, with the land on which they stand the furniture therein and all rights in the pews, and any parsonage owned by a religious society of this state and occupied as a parsonage are exempt from taxation under this act. Houses of public worship includes buildings or other facilities owned by a religious society and used predominantly for religious services or for teaching the religious truths and beliefs of the society.

MINNESOTA

Stat. § 272.02. Exempt property (2011)
All property described in this section to the extent limited in this section shall be exempt from taxation. . . . 6. All churches, church property, and houses of worship are exempt.

Stat. § 317A.909. Nonprofit Corporations—Special Provisions (2009)
(3) Except for property leased or used for profit, personal and real property that a religious corporation necessarily uses for a religious purpose is exempt from taxation.

MISSISSIPPI

Code Ann. § 27-31-1. What property exempt (2009)
The following shall be exempt from taxation . . . (d) All property, real or personal, belonging to any religious society, or ecclesiastical body, or any congregation thereof, or to any charitable society, . . . and used exclusively for such society or association and not for profit; not exceeding, however, the amount of land which such association or society may own as provided in Section 79-11-33 [see below].

Code Ann. § 79-11-33. Religious organizations, property permitted (1978)
Any religious society, ecclesiastical body and/or any congregation thereof may hold and own the following real property, but no other, viz.:

(a) Each house or building used as a place of worship, with a reasonable quantity of ground annexed to such building or house.

(b) Each house or building, together with a reasonable quantity of ground thereto annexed, used: (i) As a parish house; (ii) As a community facility; (iii) As a Sunday school facility; (iv) As an educational facility; (v) For the care of children on a nonprofit basis.

(c) Each house used for a place of residence for its minister, bishop or representative, together with a reasonable quantity of ground thereto annexed. For purposes of this paragraph, the term "minister" shall mean a minister, priest, pastor, rabbi, nun or other clergy who: (i) has been duly ordained, licensed or qualified according to the principles and procedures prescribed by his religious society, (ii) is regularly engaged as a vocation in preaching and teaching the beliefs of his religious society, in administering its rites and sacraments, and in conducting public worship services in the tradition of his religious society, and (iii) who discharges the duties of a minister in the tradition of his religious society. . . .

(e) All buildings used by a school, college or seminary of learning contiguous to and/or a part of the college or seminary plant, for administration, classrooms, laboratories, observatories, dormitories, and for housing the faculty and students thereof, together with a reasonable quantity of land in connection therewith. . . .

(g) All buildings used for a campground or assembly for religious purposes, together with a reasonable quantity of land in connection therewith. . . .

(i) All buildings and grounds used for denominational headquarters and/or administrative purposes, together with a reasonable quantity of ground annexed thereto. The title to any buildings and grounds heretofore acquired under this subsection shall not be hereafter held invalid because of the lack of authority of the owner thereof to obtain or hold such title. Provided, however, that the provisions of this subsection shall not affect any pending litigation.

(j) Any land which is maintained and used as a parking area for the convenience of the members of the congregation, church, cathedral, mission or other unit or administrative unit from which the society receives no revenue, fee, charge or assessment. The land on which the parking area is located may be noncontiguous to the land on which the building used as the place of worship is located.

MISSOURI

Rev. Stat. § 137.100. Certain property exempt from taxes (2007)
The following subjects are exempt from taxation for state, county or local purposes . . . (5) All property, real and personal, actually and regularly used exclusively for religious worship . . . and not held for private or corporate profit, except that the exemption herein

TABLE 12-4

STATE PROPERTY TAX EXEMPTIONS FOR RELIGIOUS ORGANIZATIONS
State-by-State Analysis (continued)

granted does not include real property not actually used or occupied for the purpose of the organization but held or used as investment even though the income or rentals received therefrom is used wholly for religious, educational or charitable purposes.

MONTANA

Code Ann. § 15-6-201. Exempt categories (2011)
(1) The following categories of property are exempt from taxation . . . (b) buildings and furnishings in the buildings that are owned by a church and used for actual religious worship or for residences of the clergy, not to exceed one residence for each member of the clergy, together with the land that the buildings occupy and adjacent land reasonably necessary for convenient use of the buildings, which must be identified in the application, and all land and improvements used for educational or youth recreational activities if the facilities are generally available for use by the general public but may not exceed 15 acres for a church or 1 acre for a clergy residence after subtracting any area required by zoning, building codes, or subdivision requirements;

(2)(b) For the purposes of subsection (1)(b), the term "clergy" means, as recognized under the federal Internal Revenue Code: (i) an ordained minister, priest, or rabbi; (ii) a commissioned or licensed minister of a church or church denomination that ordains ministers if the person has the authority to perform substantially all the religious duties of the church or denomination; (iii) a member of a religious order who has taken a vow of poverty; or (iv) a Christian Science practitioner.

NEBRASKA

Rev. Stat. § 77-202. Property taxable; exemptions enumerated (2013)
(1) The following property shall be exempt from property taxes . . . (d) Property owned by educational, religious, charitable, or cemetery organizations, or any organization for the exclusive benefit of any such educational, religious, charitable, or cemetery organization, and used exclusively for educational, religious, charitable, or cemetery purposes, when such property is not (i) owned or used for financial gain or profit to either the owner or user, (ii) used for the sale of alcoholic liquors for more than twenty hours per week, or (iii) owned or used by an organization which discriminates in membership or employment based on race, color, or national origin.

NEVADA

Rev. Stat. § 361.125. Exemption of churches and chapels (1999)
1. Except as otherwise provided in subsection 2, churches, chapels, other than marriage chapels, and other buildings used for religious worship, with their furniture and equipment, and the lots of ground on which they stand, used therewith and necessary thereto, owned by some recognized religious society or corporation, and parsonages so owned, are exempt from taxation.

2. Except as otherwise provided in NRS 361.157, when any such property is used exclusively or in part for any other than church purposes, and a rent or other valuable consideration is received for its use, the property must be taxed.

3. The exemption provided by this section must be prorated for the portion of a fiscal year during which the religious society or corporation owns the real property. For the purposes of this subsection, ownership of property purchased begins on the date of recording of the deed to the purchaser.

NEW HAMPSHIRE

Rev. Stat. Ann. § 72:23. Real estate and personal property tax exemption (2011)
The following real estate and personal property shall, unless otherwise provided by statute, be exempt from taxation. . . .
III. Houses of public worship, parish houses, church parsonages occupied by their pastors, convents, monasteries, buildings and the lands appertaining to them owned, used and occupied directly for religious training or for other religious purposes by any regularly recognized and constituted denomination, creed or sect, organized, incorporated or legally doing business in this state and the personal property used by them for the purposes for which they are established.

NEW JERSEY

Rev. Stat. § 54:4-3.6. Exemption of property of nonprofit organizations (2011)
The following property shall be exempt from taxation under this chapter: all buildings actually used for colleges, schools, academies or seminaries, provided that if any portion of such buildings are leased to profit-making organizations or otherwise used for purposes which are not themselves exempt from taxation, said portion shall be subject to taxation and the remaining portion only shall be exempt; . . . all buildings actually used in the work of associations and corporations organized exclusively for religious purposes, including religious worship, or charitable purposes, provided that if any portion of a building used for that purpose is leased to a profit-making organization or is otherwise used for purposes which are not themselves exempt from taxation, that portion shall be subject to taxation and the remaining portion shall be exempt from taxation, and provided further that if any portion of a building is used for a different exempt use by an exempt entity, that portion shall also be exempt from taxation; . . . the buildings, not exceeding two, actually occupied as a parsonage by the officiating clergymen of any religious corporation of this State, together with the accessory buildings located on the same premises; the land whereon any of the buildings hereinbefore mentioned are erected, and which may be necessary for the fair enjoyment thereof, and which is devoted to the purposes above

mentioned and to no other purpose and does not exceed five acres in extent; the furniture and personal property in said buildings if used in and devoted to the purposes above mentioned; . . . provided, in case of all the foregoing, the buildings, or the lands on which they stand, or the associations, corporations or institutions using and occupying them as aforesaid, are not conducted for profit, except that the exemption of the buildings and lands used for charitable, benevolent or religious purposes shall extend to cases where the charitable, benevolent or religious work therein carried on is supported partly by fees and charges received from or on behalf of beneficiaries using or occupying the buildings; provided the building is wholly controlled by and the entire income therefrom is used for said charitable, benevolent or religious purposes; and any tract of land purchased pursuant to subsection (n) of section 21 of P.L.1971, c. 199, and located within a city of the first, second, third or fourth class, actually used for the cultivation and sale of fresh fruits and vegetables and owned by a duly incorporated nonprofit organization or association which includes among its principal purposes the cultivation and sale of fresh fruits and vegetables, other than a political, partisan, sectarian, denominational or religious organization or association. The foregoing exemption shall apply only where the association, corporation or institution claiming the exemption owns the property in question and is incorporated or organized under the laws of this State and authorized to carry out the purposes on account of which the exemption is claimed. . . .

NEW MEXICO

N.M. Const. Art. 8, § 3. [Tax-exempt property] (1972)
[A]ll church property not used for commercial purposes, all property used for educational or charitable purposes . . . shall be exempt from taxation. Provided, however, that any property acquired by . . . churches, property acquired and used for educational or charitable purposes . . . where such property was, prior to such transfer, subject to the lien of any tax or assessment or the principal or interest of any bonded indebtedness shall not be exempt from such lien, nor from the payment of such taxes or assessments.

NEW YORK

N.Y. Real Prop. Tax Law § 420-a. Nonprofit organizations; mandatory class (2010)
1. (a) Real property owned by a corporation or association organized or conducted exclusively for religious, charitable, hospital, educational, or moral or mental improvement of men, women or children purposes, or for two or more such purposes, and used exclusively for carrying out thereupon one or more of such purposes either by the owning corporation or association or by another such corporation or association as hereinafter provided shall be exempt from taxation as provided in this section.

(b) Real property such as specified in paragraph (a) of this subdivision shall not be exempt if any officer, member or employee of the owning corporation or association shall receive or may be lawfully entitled to receive any pecuniary profit from the operations thereof, except reasonable compensation for services in effecting one or more of such purposes, or as proper beneficiaries of its strictly charitable purposes; or if the organization thereof for any such avowed purposes be a guise or pretense for directly or indirectly making any other pecuniary profit for such corporation or association or for any of its members or employees; or if it be not in good faith organized or conducted exclusively for one or more of such purposes.

2. If any portion of such real property is not so used exclusively to carry out thereupon one or more of such purposes but is leased or otherwise used for other purposes, such portion shall be subject to taxation and the remaining portion only shall be exempt; provided, however, that such real property shall be fully exempt from taxation although it or a portion thereof is used (a) for purposes which are exempt pursuant to this section or sections 420-b, 422, 424, 426, 428, 430, or 450 of this chapter by another corporation which owns real property exempt from taxation pursuant to such sections or whose real property if it owned any would be exempt from taxation pursuant to such sections, (b) for purposes which are exempt pursuant to section 406 or section 408 of this chapter by a corporation which owns real property exempt from taxation pursuant to such section or if it owned any would be exempt from taxation pursuant to such section, (c) for purposes which are exempt pursuant to section 416 of this chapter by an organization which owns real property exempt from taxation pursuant to such section or whose real property if it owned any would be exempt from taxation pursuant to such section or (d) for purposes relating to civil defense pursuant to the New York state defense emergency act, including but not limited to activities in preparation for anticipated attack, during attack, or following attack or false warning thereof, or in connection with drill or test ordered or directed by civil defense authorities; and provided further that such real property shall be exempt from taxation only so long as it or a portion thereof, as the case may be, is devoted to such exempt purposes and so long as any moneys paid for such use do not exceed the amount of the carrying, maintenance and depreciation charges of the property or portion thereof, as the case may be.

3. Such real property from which no revenue is derived shall be exempt though not in actual use therefor by reason of the absence of suitable buildings or improvements thereon if (a) the construction of such buildings or improvements is in progress or is in good faith contemplated by such corporation or association or (b) such real property is held by such corporation or association upon condition that the title thereto shall revert in case any building not intended and suitable for one or more such purposes shall be erected upon such premises or some part thereof.

TABLE 12-4

STATE PROPERTY TAX EXEMPTIONS FOR RELIGIOUS ORGANIZATIONS
State-by-State Analysis (continued)

N.Y. Real Prop. Tax Law § 460. Clergy (2010)

(1) Real property owned by a minister of the gospel, priest or rabbi of any denomination, an actual resident and inhabitant of this state, who is engaged in the work assigned by the church or denomination of which he or she is a member, or who is unable to perform such work due to impaired health or is over seventy years of age, and real property owned by his or her unremarried surviving spouse while an actual resident and inhabitant of this state, shall be exempt from taxation to the extent of fifteen hundred dollars.

(2) An exemption may be granted pursuant to this section only upon application by the owner of the property on a form prescribed or approved by the commissioner. The application shall be filed with the assessor of the appropriate county, city, town or village on or before the taxable status date of such county, city, town or village.

(3) Notwithstanding the provisions of this section or any other provision of law, in a city having a population of one million or more, applications for the exemption authorized pursuant to this section shall be considered timely filed if they are filed on or before the fifteenth day of March of the appropriate year.

N.Y. Real Prop. Tax Law § 462. Religious corporations; property used for residential purposes (2010)

In addition to the exemption provided in section 420-a of this article, property owned by a religious corporation while actually used by the officiating clergymen thereof for residential purposes shall be exempt from taxation. An exemption may be granted pursuant to this section only upon application by the owner of the property on a form prescribed or approved by the commissioner. The application shall be filed with the assessor of the appropriate county, city, town or village on or before the taxable status date of such county, city, town or village. Notwithstanding the provisions of this section or any other provision of law, in a city having a population of one million or more, applications for the exemption authorized pursuant to this section shall be considered timely filed if they are filed on or before the fifteenth day of March of the appropriate year.

NORTH CAROLINA   **N.C. Gen. Stat. § 105-278.3. Real and personal property used for religious purposes (2005)**

(a) Buildings, the land they actually occupy, and additional adjacent land reasonably necessary for the convenient use of any such building shall be exempted from taxation if wholly owned by an agency listed in subsection (c), below, and if:

(1) Wholly and exclusively used by its owner for religious purposes as defined in subsection (d)(1), below; or (2) Occupied gratuitously by one other than the owner and wholly and exclusively used by the occupant for religious, charitable, or nonprofit educational, literary, scientific, or cultural purposes.

(b) Personal property shall be exempted from taxation if wholly owned by an agency listed in subsection (c), below, and if:

(1) Wholly and exclusively used by its owner for religious purposes; or (2) Gratuitously made available to one other than the owner and wholly and exclusively used by the possessor for religious, charitable, or nonprofit educational, literary, scientific, or cultural purposes.

(c) The following agencies, when the other requirements of this section are met, may obtain exemption for their properties:
(1) A congregation, parish, mission, or similar local unit of a church or religious body; or (2) A conference, association, presbytery, diocese, district, synod, or similar unit comprising local units of a church or religious body.

(d) Within the meaning of this section: (1) A religious purpose is one that pertains to practicing, teaching, and setting forth a religion. Although worship is the most common religious purpose, the term encompasses other activities that demonstrate and further the beliefs and objectives of a given church or religious body. Within the meaning of this section, the ownership and maintenance of a general or promotional office or headquarters by an owner listed in subdivision (2) of subsection (c), above, is a religious purpose and the ownership and maintenance of residences for clergy, rabbis, priests or nuns assigned to or serving a congregation, parish, mission or similar local unit, or a conference, association, presbytery, diocese, district, synod, province or similar unit of a church or religious body or residences for clergy on furlough or unassigned, is also a religious purpose. However, the ownership and maintenance of residences for other employees is not a religious purpose for either a local unit of a church or a religious body or a conference, association, presbytery, diocese, district, synod, or similar unit of a church or religious body. Provided, however, that where part of property which otherwise qualifies for the exemption provided herein is made available as a residence for an individual who provides guardian, janitorial and custodial services for such property, or who oversees and supervises qualifying activities upon and in connection with said property, the entire property shall be considered as wholly and exclusively used for a religious purpose. . . .

STATE PROPERTY TAX EXEMPTIONS FOR RELIGIOUS ORGANIZATIONS
State-by-State Analysis (continued)

(e) Notwithstanding the exclusive-use requirement of subsection (a), above, if part of a property that otherwise meets that subsection's requirements is used for a purpose that would require exemption if the entire property were so used, the valuation of the part so used shall be exempted from taxation. . . .

(g) Notwithstanding the exclusive-use requirement of subsection (a), above, any parking lot wholly owned by an agency listed in subsection (c), above, may be used for parking without removing the tax exemption granted in this section; provided, the total charge for said uses shall not exceed that portion of the actual maintenance expenditures for the parking lot reasonably estimated to have been made on account of said uses. This subsection shall apply beginning with the taxable year that commences on January 1, 1978.

NORTH DAKOTA   **N.D. Cent. Code § 57-02-08. Property exempt from taxation (2011)**
All property described in this section to the extent herein limited shall be exempt from taxation. . . .

6. All property belonging to schools, academies, colleges, or other institutions of learning, not otherwise used with a view to profit, and all dormitories and boarding halls, including the land upon which they are situated, owned and managed by any religious corporation for educational or charitable purposes for the use of students in attendance upon any educational institution, if such dormitories and boarding halls are not managed or used for the purpose of making a profit over and above the cost of maintenance and operation. . . .

8. All buildings belonging to institutions of public charity, including public hospitals and nursing homes licensed pursuant to section 23-16-01 under the control of religious or charitable institutions, used wholly or in part for public charity, together with the land actually occupied by such institutions not leased or otherwise used with a view to profit.

a. The exemption provided by this subsection includes any dormitory, dwelling, or residential-type structure, together with necessary land on which such structure is located, owned by a religious or charitable organization recognized as tax exempt under section 501(c)(3) of the Internal Revenue code which is occupied by members of said organization who are subject to a religious vow of poverty and devote and donate substantially all of their time to the religious or charitable activities of the owner.

b. For purposes of this subsection . . . property is not used wholly or in part for public charity or charitable or other public purposes if that property is residential rental units leased to tenants based on income levels that enable the owner to receive a federal low-income housing income tax credit.

9. All buildings owned by any religious corporation or organization and used for the religious services of the organization, and if on the same parcel, dwellings with usual outbuildings, intended and ordinarily used for the residence of the bishop, priest, rector, or other minister in charge of services, land directly under and within the perimeter of those buildings, improved off-street parking or reasonable landscaping or sidewalk area adjoining the main church building, and up to a maximum of two additional acres [.81 hectare] must be deemed to be property used exclusively for religious services, and exempt from taxation, whether the real property consists of one tract or more. If the residence of the bishop, priest, rector, or other minister in charge of services is located on property not adjacent to the church, that residence with usual outbuildings and land on which it is located, up to two acres [.81 hectare], is exempt from taxation. The exemption for a building used for the religious services of the owner continues to be in effect if the building in whole, or in part, is rented to another otherwise tax-exempt corporation or organization, provided no profit is realized from the rent.

OHIO   **Ohio Rev. Code Ann. § 5709.07. Exemption of schools, churches, and colleges (2011)**
(A) The following property shall be exempt from taxation . . . (2) Houses used exclusively for public worship, the books and furniture in them, and the ground attached to them that is not leased or otherwise used with a view to profit and that is necessary for their proper occupancy, use, and enjoyment; (3) Real property owned and operated by a church that is used primarily for church retreats or church camping, and that is not used as a permanent residence. Real property exempted under division (A)(3) of this section may be made available by the church on a limited basis to charitable and educational institutions if the property is not leased or otherwise made available with a view to profit. . . .(D)(1) As used in this section, "church" means a fellowship of believers, congregation, society, corporation, convention, or association that is formed primarily or exclusively for religious purposes and that is not formed for the private profit of any person.

OKLAHOMA   **Okla. Stat. title 68, § 2887. Property exempt from ad valorem taxation (2010)**
The following property shall be exempt from ad valorem taxation . . .

TABLE 12-4

STATE PROPERTY TAX EXEMPTIONS FOR RELIGIOUS ORGANIZATIONS
State-by-State Analysis (continued)

7. All property used exclusively and directly for fraternal or religious purposes within this state. For purposes of administering the exemption authorized by this section and in order to determine whether a single family residential property is used exclusively and directly for fraternal or religious purposes, the fair cash value of a single family residential property, for which an exemption is claimed as authorized by this subsection, in excess of Two Hundred Fifty Thousand Dollars ($250,000.00) for the applicable assessment year shall not be exempt from taxation. . . .

11. All libraries and office equipment of ministers of the Gospel actively engaged in ministerial work in the State of Oklahoma, where said libraries and office equipment are being used by said ministers in their ministerial work, shall be deemed to be used exclusively for religious purposes and are declared to be within the meaning of the term "religious purposes" as used in Article X, Section 6 of the Constitution of the State of Oklahoma.

OREGON

Or. Rev. Stat. § 307.140. Property of religious organizations (1993)
Upon compliance with ORS 307.162, the following property owned or being purchased by religious organizations shall be exempt from taxation:

(1) All houses of public worship and other additional buildings and property used solely for administration, education, literary, benevolent, charitable, entertainment and recreational purposes by religious organizations, the lots on which they are situated, and the pews, slips and furniture therein. However, any part of any house of public worship or other additional buildings or property which is kept or used as a store or shop or for any purpose other than those stated in this section shall be assessed and taxed the same as other taxable property.

(2) Parking lots used for parking or any other use as long as that parking or other use is permitted without charge for no fewer than 355 days during the tax year.

(3) Land and the buildings thereon held or used solely for cemetery or crematory purposes, including any buildings solely used to store machinery or equipment used exclusively for maintenance of such lands.

Or. Rev. Stat. § 307.145 Certain child care facilities, schools and student housing (2003)
(1) If not otherwise exempt by law, upon compliance with ORS 307.162, the child care facilities, schools, academies and student housing accommodations, owned or being purchased by incorporated eleemosynary institutions or by incorporated religious organizations, used exclusively by such institutions or organizations for or in immediate connection with educational purposes, are exempt from taxation.

(2) Property described in subsection (1) of this section which is exclusively for or in the immediate connection with educational purposes shall continue to be exempt when leased to a political subdivision of the State of Oregon, or to another incorporated eleemosynary institution or incorporated religious organization for an amount not to exceed the cost of repairs, maintenance and upkeep.

(3)(a) As used in this section, "child care facility" means a child care center certified by the Child Care Division of the Employment Department under ORS 657A.280 to provide educational child care.

(b) Before an exemption for a child care facility is allowed under this section, in addition to any other information required under ORS 307.162, the statement shall:

(A) Describe the property and declare or be accompanied by proof that the corporation is an eleemosynary institution or religious organization.

(B) Declare or be accompanied by proof that the division has issued a certificate of approval to the child care facility to provide educational child care.

(C) Be signed by the taxpayer subject to the penalties for false swearing.

PENNSYLVANIA

Pa. Stat. Ann. title 72, § 5020-204. Exemptions from taxation (1992)
(a) The following property shall be exempt from all county, city, borough, town, township, road, poor and school tax, to wit:
(1) All churches, meeting-houses, or other actual places of regularly stated religious worship, with the ground thereto annexed necessary for the occupancy and enjoyment of the same.

========= **TABLE 12-4** =========

STATE PROPERTY TAX EXEMPTIONS FOR RELIGIOUS ORGANIZATIONS
State-by-State Analysis (continued)

RHODE ISLAND

R.I. Gen. Laws § 44-3-3. Property exempt (2011)
The following property shall be exempt from taxation. . . . (5) Buildings for free public schools, buildings for religious worship, and the land upon which they stand and immediately surrounding them, to an extent not exceeding five (5) acres so far as the buildings and land are occupied and used exclusively for religious or educational purposes; (6) Dwellings houses and the land on which they stand, not exceeding one acre in size, or the minimum lot size for zone in which the dwelling house is located, whichever is the greater, owned by or held in trust for any religious organization and actually used by its officiating clergy; provided, further that in the town of Charlestown, where the property previously described in this paragraph is exempt in total, along with dwelling houses and the land on which they stand in Charlestown, not exceeding one acre in size, or the minimum lot size for zone in which the dwelling house is located, whichever is the greater, owned by or held in trust for any religious organization and actually used by its officiating clergy, or used as a convent, nunnery, or retreat center by its religious order. (7) Intangible personal property owned by, or held in trust for, any religious or charitable organization, if the principal or income is used or appropriated for religious or charitable purposes. (8) Buildings and personal estate owned by any corporation used for a school, academy, or seminary of learning, and of any incorporated public charitable institution, and the land upon which the buildings stand and immediately surrounding them to an extent not exceeding one acre, so far as they are used exclusively for educational purposes, but no property or estate whatever is hereafter exempt from taxation in any case where any part of its income or profits or of the business carried on there is divided among its owners or stockholders.

SOUTH CAROLINA

S.C. Code Ann. § 12-37-220. General exemptions from taxes (2010)
(A) Pursuant to the provisions of Section 3 of Article X of the State Constitution and subject to the provisions of Section 12-4-720, there is exempt from ad valorem taxation . . . (3) all property of all public libraries, churches, parsonages, and burying grounds, but this exemption for real property does not extend beyond the buildings and premises actually occupied by the owners of the real property . . .

(B) In addition to the exemptions provided in subsection (A), the following classes of property are exempt from ad valorem taxation subject to the provisions of section 12-4-720 [pertaining to the filing of applications for recognition of exemption] . . .

(16)(a) The property of any religious, charitable, eleemosynary, educational, or literary society, corporation, or other association, when the property is used by it primarily for the holding of its meetings and the conduct of the business of the society, corporation, or association and no profit or benefit therefrom inures to the benefit of any private stockholder or individual.

(16)(b) The property of any religious, charitable, or eleemosynary society, corporation, or other association when the property is acquired for the purpose of building or renovating residential structures on it for not-for-profit sale to economically disadvantaged persons. The total properties for which the religious, charitable, or eleemosynary society, corporation, or other association may claim this exemption in accordance with this paragraph may not exceed fifty acres per county within the State.

(16)(c) The exemption allowed pursuant to subitem (a) of this item extends to real property owned by an organization described in subitem (a) and which qualifies as a tax exempt organization pursuant to Internal Revenue Code section 501(c)(3), when the real property is held for a future use by the organization that would qualify for the exemption allowed pursuant to subitem (a) of this item or held for investment by the organization in sole pursuit of the organization's exempt purposes and while held this real property is not rented or leased for a purpose unrelated to the exempt purposes of the organization and the use of the real property does not inure to the benefit of any private stockholder or individual. Real property donated to the organization which receives the exemption allowed pursuant to this subitem is allowed the exemption for no more than three consecutive property tax years. If real property acquired by the organization by purchase receives the exemption allowed pursuant to this subitem and is subsequently sold without ever having been put to the exempt use, the exemption allowed pursuant to this subitem is deemed terminated as of December thirty-first preceding the year of sale and the property is subject to property tax for the year of sale to which must be added a recapture amount equal to the property tax that would have been due on the real property for not more than the four preceding years in which the real property received the exemption allowed pursuant to this subitem. The recapture amount is deemed property tax for all purposes for payment and collection.

SOUTH DAKOTA

S.D. Codified Laws § 10-4-9. Property owned by religious society and used exclusively for religious purposes exempt—Sale of property by religious society (1995)
Property owned by any religious society and used exclusively for religious purposes, is exempt from taxation. Property of a religious society is exempt from taxation if such property is a building or structure used exclusively for religious purposes, is a lot owned by a religious society for the exclusive purpose of parking vehicles owned by members of such society and is not rented or leased to nonmembers of such society, is an educational plant owned and operated by a religious society or is a building

TABLE 12-4

STATE PROPERTY TAX EXEMPTIONS FOR RELIGIOUS ORGANIZATIONS
State-by-State Analysis (continued)

or structure used to house any cleric of a religious society. However, any property which is sold by a religious society under a contract for deed shall be taxed as other property of the same class, unless such property is sold to an entity which is exempt from taxation pursuant to this chapter and the property is used for an exempt purpose.

TENNESSEE

Tenn. Code Ann. § 67-5-212. Religious, charitable, scientific, educational institutions (2011)

(a)(1) There shall be exempt from property taxation the real and personal property, or any part thereof, owned by any religious . . . institution that is occupied and actually used by such institution or its officers purely and exclusively for carrying out thereupon one (1) or more of the exempt purposes for which the institution was created or exists. There shall further be exempt from property taxation the property, or any part thereof, owned by an exempt institution that is occupied and actually used by another exempt institution for one (1) or more of the exempt purposes for which it was created or exists under an arrangement in which the owning institution receives no more rent than a reasonably allocated share of the cost of use, excluding the cost of capital improvements, debt service, depreciation and interest, as determined by the state board of equalization. . . .

(3)(A) The property of such institution shall not be exempt, if:

(i) The owner, or any stockholder, officer, member or employee of such institution shall receive or may be lawfully entitled to receive any pecuniary profit from the operations of that property in competition with like property owned by others that is not exempt, except reasonable compensation for services in effecting one (1) or more of such purposes, or as proper beneficiaries of its strictly religious, charitable, scientific or educational purposes; or

(ii) The organization thereof for any such avowed purpose be a guise or pretense for directly or indirectly making any other pecuniary profit for such institution, or for any of its members or employees, or if it be not in good faith organized or conducted exclusively for one (1) or more of these purposes.

(B) The real property of any such institution not so used exclusively for carrying out thereupon one (1) or more of such purposes, but leased or otherwise used for other purposes, whether the income received therefrom be used for one (1) or more of such purposes or not, shall not be exempt; but, if a portion only of any lot or building of any such institution is used purely and exclusively for carrying out thereupon one (1) or more of such purposes of such institution, then such lot or building shall be so exempt only to the extent of the value of the portion so used, and the remaining or other portion shall be subject to taxation.

(4) No church shall be granted an exemption on more than one (1) parsonage, and an exempt parsonage may not include within the exemption more than three (3) acres.

(b)(1) Any owner of real or personal property claiming exemption under this section . . . shall file an application for the exemption with the state board of equalization on a form prescribed by the board, and supply such further information as the board may require to determine whether the property qualifies for exemption. No property shall be exempted from property taxes under these sections, unless the application has been approved in writing by the board. A separate application shall be filed for each parcel of property for which exemption is claimed. . . .

(3)(B) If a religious institution acquires property that was duly exempt at the time of transfer from a transferor who had previously been approved for a religious use exemption of the property, or if a religious institution acquires property to replace its own exempt property, then the effective date of exemption shall be three (3) years prior to the date of application, or the date the acquiring institution began to use the property for religious purposes, whichever is later. The purpose of this subdivision is to provide continuity of exempt status for property transferred from one exempt religious institution to another in the specified circumstances. For purposes of this subdivision, property transferred by a lender following foreclosure shall be deemed to have been transferred by the foreclosed debtor, whether or not the property was assessed in the name of the lender during the lender's possession.

(n) There shall be exempt from property taxation the real and personal property, or any part thereof, that is owned by a religious or charitable institution and that is occupied and used by such institution for a thrift shop; provided, that: (1) The institution is exempt from payment of federal income taxes under section 501(c)(3) of the Internal Revenue Code; (2)(A) The thrift shop is operated as a training venue for persons in need of occupational rehabilitation; or (B) The thrift shop is operated primarily by volunteers; (3) The inventory of the thrift shop is obtained by donation to the institution that owns and operates the shop; (4) Goods are priced at levels generally ascribed to used property; (5) Goods are given to persons whose financial situations preclude payment; and (6) The net proceeds of the thrift shop are used solely for the charitable purposes of the institution that owns and operates the shop.

(o) Land not necessary to support exempt structures or site improvements associated with exempt structures, including land used for recreation, retreats or sanctuaries, shall not be eligible for exemption beyond a maximum of one hundred (100) acres per county for each religious, charitable, scientific or nonprofit educational institution qualified for exemption pursuant to this section. For purposes of applying this limit, land owned by an exempt institution shall be aggregated with land owned by related exempt institutions having common ownership or control. Qualifying land in excess of the limit shall be classified as forest land upon application submitted pursuant to section 67-5-1006, or as open space land upon application submitted pursuant to section 67-5-1007, and the effective date of the classification shall be the date the property might otherwise have qualified for exemption.

TEXAS

Tex. Tax Code § 11.20. Religious organizations (2005)

(a) An organization that qualifies as a religious organization as provided by Subsection (c) is entitled to an exemption from taxation of:

(1) the real property that is owned by the religious organization, is used primarily as a place of regular religious worship, and is reasonably necessary for engaging in religious worship;

(2) the tangible personal property that is owned by the religious organization and is reasonably necessary for engaging in worship at the place of worship specified in Subdivision (1);

(3) the real property that is owned by the religious organization and is reasonably necessary for use as a residence (but not more than one acre of land for each residence) if the property: (A) is used exclusively as a residence for those individuals whose principal occupation is to serve in the clergy of the religious organization; and (B) produces no revenue for the religious organization;

(4) the tangible personal property that is owned by the religious organization and is reasonably necessary for use of the residence specified by Subdivision (3);

(5) the real property owned by the religious organization consisting of: (A) an incomplete improvement that is under active construction or other physical preparation and that is designed and intended to be used by the religious organization as a place of regular religious worship when complete; and (B) the land on which the incomplete improvement is located that will be reasonably necessary for the religious organization's use of the improvement as a place of regular religious worship;

(6) the land that the religious organization owns for the purpose of expansion of the religious organization's place of regular religious worship or construction of a new place of regular religious worship if: (A) the religious organization qualifies other property, including a portion of the same tract or parcel of land, owned by the organization for an exemption under Subdivision (1) or (5); and (B) the land produces no revenue for the religious organization; and

(7) the real property owned by the religious organization that is leased to another person and used by that person for the operation of a school that qualifies as a school under section 11.21(d).

(b) An organization that qualifies as a religious organization as provided by Subsection (c) of this section is entitled to an exemption from taxation of those endowment funds the organization owns that are used exclusively for the support of the religious organization and are invested exclusively in bonds, mortgages, or property purchased at a foreclosure sale for the purpose of satisfying or protecting the bonds or mortgages. However, foreclosure-sale property that is held by an endowment fund for longer than the two-year period immediately following purchase at the foreclosure sale is not exempt from taxation.

(c) To qualify as a religious organization for the purposes of this section, an organization (whether operated by an individual, as a corporation, or as an association) must:

(1) be organized and operated primarily for the purpose of engaging in religious worship or promoting the spiritual development or well-being of individuals;

(2) be operated in a way that does not result in accrual of distributable profits, realization of private gain resulting from payment of compensation in excess of a reasonable allowance for salary or other compensation for services rendered, or realization of any other form of private gain;

TABLE 12-4

STATE PROPERTY TAX EXEMPTIONS FOR RELIGIOUS ORGANIZATIONS
State-by-State Analysis (continued)

(3) use its assets in performing the organization's religious functions or the religious functions of another religious organization; and

(4) by charter, bylaw, or other regulation adopted by the organization to govern its affairs direct that on discontinuance of the organization by dissolution or otherwise the assets are to be transferred to this state, the United States, or a charitable, educational, religious, or other similar organization that is qualified as a charitable organization under section 501(c)(3) of the Internal Revenue Code.

(d) Use of property that qualifies for the exemption prescribed by Subsection (a)(1) or (2) or by Subsection (h)(1) for occasional secular purposes other than religious worship does not result in loss of the exemption if the primary use of the property is for religious worship and all income from the other use is devoted exclusively to the maintenance and development of the property as a place of religious worship.

(e) For the purposes of this section, "religious worship" means individual or group ceremony or meditation, education, and fellowship, the purpose of which is to manifest or develop reverence, homage, and commitment in behalf of a religious faith.

(f) A property may not be exempted under Subsection (a)(5) for more than three years.

(g) For purposes of Subsection (a)(5), an incomplete improvement is under physical preparation if the religious organization has engaged in architectural or engineering work, soil testing, land clearing activities, or site improvement work necessary for the construction of the improvement or has conducted an environmental or land use study relating to the construction of the improvement.

(h) Property owned by this state or a political subdivision of this state, including a leasehold or other possessory interest in the property, that is held or occupied by an organization that qualifies as a religious organization as provided by Subsection (c) is entitled to an exemption from taxation if the property: (1) is used by the organization primarily as a place of regular religious worship and is reasonably necessary for engaging in religious worship; or (2) meets the qualifications for an exemption under Subsection (a)(5).

(i) For purposes of the exemption provided by Subsection (h), the religious organization may apply for the exemption and take other action relating to the exemption as if the organization owned the property.

(j) A tract of land that is contiguous to the tract of land on which the religious organization's place of regular religious worship is located may not be exempted under Subsection (a)(6) for more than six years. A tract of land that is not contiguous to the tract of land on which the religious organization's place of regular religious worship is located may not be exempted under Subsection (a)(6) for more than three years. For purposes of this subsection, a tract of land is considered to be contiguous with another tract of land if the tracts are divided only by a road, railroad track, river, or stream.

UTAH

Utah Code Ann. § 59-2-1101. Exemption of certain property—Proportional payments for certain property—County legislative body authority to adopt rules or ordinances (2011)
(3)(a) The following property is exempt from taxation . . . (iv) property owned by a nonprofit entity which is used exclusively for religious, charitable, or educational purposes.

VERMONT

Vt. Stat. Ann. title 32, § 3802. Property tax (2011)
The following property shall be exempt from taxation . . . (4) Real and personal estate granted, sequestered or used for public, pious or charitable uses; real property owned by churches or church societies or conferences and used as parsonages and personal property therein used by ministers engaged in full time work in the care of the churches of their fellowship within the state.

VIRGINIA

Va. Code § 58.1-3606. Property exempt from taxation by classification (2005)
A. Pursuant to the authority granted in Article X, Section 6(a)(6) of the Constitution of Virginia to exempt property from taxation by classification, the following classes of real and personal property shall be exempt from taxation . . . 2. Buildings with land they actually occupy, and the personal property owned by churches or religious bodies, including (i) an incorporated church or religious body and (ii) a corporation mentioned in section 57-16-1 [pertaining to property of an unincorporated church held by a corporation] and exclusively occupied or used for religious worship or for the residence of the minister of any church or religious body, and such additional adjacent land reasonably necessary for the convenient use of any such building.

TABLE 12-4

STATE PROPERTY TAX EXEMPTIONS FOR RELIGIOUS ORGANIZATIONS
State-by-State Analysis (continued)

WASHINGTON

Wash. Rev. Code § 84.36.030. Property used for character building, benevolent, protective or rehabilitative social services—Camp facilities—Veteran or relief organization owned property—property of nonprofit organizations that issue debt for student loans or that are guarantee agencies (2006)
The following real and personal property shall be exempt from taxation . . . (2) Property owned by any nonprofit church, denomination, group of churches, or an organization or association, the membership of which is comprised solely of churches or their qualified representatives, which is utilized as a camp facility if used for organized and supervised recreational activities and church purposes as related to such camp facilities. The exemption provided by this paragraph shall apply to a maximum of two hundred acres of any such camp as selected by the church, including buildings and other improvements thereon.

Wash. Rev. Code § 84.36.020. Cemeteries, churches, parsonages, convents, and grounds (2010; effective until December 31, 2020)
The following real and personal property is exempt from taxation:

(1) All lands, buildings, and personal property required for necessary administration and maintenance, used, or to the extent used, exclusively for public burying grounds or cemeteries without discrimination as to race, color, national origin or ancestry;

(2) All churches, personal property, and the ground, not exceeding five acres in area, upon which a church of any nonprofit recognized religious denomination is or will be built, together with a parsonage, convent, and buildings and improvements required for the maintenance and safeguarding of such property. The area exempted in any case includes all ground covered by the church, parsonage, convent, and buildings and improvements required for the maintenance and safeguarding of such property and the structures and ground necessary for street access, parking, light, and ventilation, but the area of unoccupied ground exempted in such cases, in connection with church, parsonage, convent, and buildings and improvements required for the maintenance and safeguarding of such property, does not exceed the equivalent of one hundred twenty by one hundred twenty feet except where additional unoccupied land may be required to conform with state or local codes, zoning, or licensing requirements. The parsonage and convent need not be on land contiguous to the church property. Except as otherwise provided in this subsection, to be exempt the property must be wholly used for church purposes. The loan or rental of property otherwise exempt under this subsection to a nonprofit organization, association, or corporation, or school for use for an eleemosynary activity or for use for activities related to a farmers market, does not nullify the exemption provided in this subsection if the rental income, if any, is reasonable and is devoted solely to the operation and maintenance of the property. However, activities related to a farmers market may not occur on the property more than fifty-three days each assessment year. For the purposes of this section, "farmers market" has the same meaning as "qualifying farmers market" as defined in RCW 66.24.170.

Wash. Rev. Code § 84.36.032. Administrative offices of nonprofit religious organizations (1975)
The real and personal property of the administrative offices of nonprofit recognized religious organizations shall be exempt to the extent that the property is used for the administration of the religious programs of the organization and such other programs as would be exempt under RCW 84.36.020 and 84.36.030 as now or hereafter amended.

WEST VIRGINIA

W. Va. Code § 11-3-9. Property exempt from taxation (2008)
(a) All property, real and personal, described in this subsection, and to the extent herein limited, is exempt from taxation . . .
(5) Property used exclusively for divine worship; (6) Parsonages and the household goods and furniture pertaining thereto; (7) Mortgages, bonds and other evidence of indebtedness in the hands of bona fide owners and holders hereafter issued and sold by churches and religious societies for the purposes of securing money to be used in the erection of church buildings used exclusively for divine worship, or for the purpose of paying indebtedness thereon; (8) Cemeteries. . . .

(d) Notwithstanding any other provisions of this section, this section does not exempt from taxation any property owned by, or held in trust for, educational . . . religious or other charitable corporations or organizations . . . unless such property, or the dividends, interest, rents or royalties derived therefrom, is used primarily and immediately for the purposes of the corporations or organizations.

WISCONSIN

Wis. Stat. § 70.11. Property exempted from taxation (2011)
The property described in this section is exempted from general property taxes. . . . Leasing a part of the property described in this section does not render it taxable if the lessor uses all of the leasehold income for maintenance of the leased property, construction debt retirement of the leased property or both and if the lessee would be exempt from taxation under this chapter if it owned the property. Any lessor who claims that leased property is exempt from taxation under this chapter shall, upon request

TABLE 12-4

STATE PROPERTY TAX EXEMPTIONS FOR RELIGIOUS ORGANIZATIONS
State-by-State Analysis (continued)

by the tax assessor, provide records relating to the lessor's use of the income from the leased property. Property exempted from general property taxes is . . . (4) Educational, religious and benevolent institutions; women's clubs; historical societies; fraternities; libraries. Property owned and used exclusively by educational institutions offering regular courses 6 months in the year; or by churches or religious, educational or benevolent associations, including benevolent nursing homes and retirement homes for the aged, and also including property owned and used for housing for pastors and their ordained assistants, members of religious orders and communities, and ordained teachers, whether or not contiguous to and a part of other property owned and used by such associations or churches. . . . but not exceeding 10 acres of land necessary for location and convenience of buildings while such property is not used for profit. Property owned by churches or religious associations necessary for location and convenience of buildings, used for educational purposes and not for profit, shall not be subject to the 10-acre limitation but shall be subject to a 30-acre limitation. Property that is exempt from taxation under this subsection and is leased remains exempt from taxation only if, in addition to the requirements specified in the introductory phrase of this section, the lessee does not discriminate on the basis of race. . . . (11) Bible camps. All real property not exceeding 30 acres and the personal property situated therein, of any Bible camp conducted by a religious nonprofit corporation organized under the laws of this state, so long as the property is used for religious purposes and not for pecuniary profit of any individual.

WYOMING

Wyo. Stat. § 39-11-105. Exemptions (2011)
(a) The following property is exempt from property taxation . . . (vii) Real property used exclusively for religious worship, church schools and church parsonages.

13 CLERGY TAX REPORTING: AN ILLUSTRATED EXAMPLE

Note: This example is based on an illustrated example contained at the end of IRS Publication 517.

INTRODUCTORY FACTS

Rev. John Michaels is the minister of the First United Church. He is married and has one child. The child is considered a qualifying child for the child tax credit. Mrs. Michaels is not employed outside the home. Rev. Michaels is a common-law employee of the church, and he has not applied for an exemption from SE tax. The church paid Rev. Michaels a salary of $45,000. In addition, as a self-employed person, he earned $4,000 during the year for weddings, baptisms, and honoraria. He made estimated tax payments during the year totaling $12,000. He taught a course at the local community college, for which he was paid $3,400. Rev. Michaels owns a home next to the church. He makes a $1,125 per month mortgage payment of principal and interest only. His utility bills and other housing-related expenses for the year totaled $1,450, and the real estate taxes on his home amounted to $1,750 for the year. The church paid him $1,400 per month as his parsonage allowance. The home's fair rental value is $1,380 per month (including furnishings and utilities).

The parts of Rev. and Mrs. Michaels's income tax return are explained in the order they are completed. They are illustrated in the order Rev. Michaels will assemble the return to send it to the IRS.

A. FORM W-2 FROM CHURCH

The church completed Form W-2 for Rev. Michaels as follows:

Box 1. The church entered Rev. Michaels's $45,000 salary.

Box 2. The church left this box blank because Rev. Michaels did not request federal income tax withholding.

Boxes 3 through 6. Rev. Michaels is considered a self-employed person for purposes of Social Security and Medicare tax withholding, so the church left these boxes blank.

Box 14. The church entered Rev. Michaels's total parsonage allowance for the year and identified it.

✔ **TURBOTAX TIP.** Listed below are tips for ministers who use TurboTax to complete their returns. We have listed our recommended responses to some of the questions asked by the software when entering your Form W-2 information from your church. These tips should not be construed as an endorsement or recommendation of the TurboTax software.

(1) **"Do any of these apply to this W-2?"** Be sure to check the box that says "I earned this income for religious employment (clergy, nonclergy, religious sect)."
(2) **"About your religious employment."** Please note that ministers fall under the category of clergy employment.
(3) **"Tell us about your clergy housing."** TurboTax then asks for the Parsonage or Housing Allowance as well as the amount of qualifying expenses. The amount you should enter for qualifying expenses is the lesser of your actual housing expenses, the annual fair rental value of your home (including furnishings and utilities), or the amount of your pay that was designated as ministerial housing allowance by your church.
(4) **"How would you like us to calculate clergy self-employment tax?"** Please note that self-employment tax should be paid on wages and housing allowance. See Schedule SE TurboTax Tip for additional information.

B. FORM W-2 FROM COLLEGE

The community college gave Rev. Michaels a Form W-2 that showed the following.

Box 1. The college entered Rev. Michaels's $3,400 salary.

Box 2. The college withheld $272 in federal income tax on Rev. Michaels's behalf.

Boxes 3 and 5. As an employee of the college, Rev. Michaels is subject to Social Security and Medicare withholding on his full salary from the college.

Box 4. The college withheld $142.80 in Social Security taxes.

Box 6. The college withheld $49.30 in Medicare taxes.

c. SCHEDULE C-EZ (FORM 1040)

Some of Rev. Michaels's entries on Schedule C-EZ are explained here.

Line 1b. Rev. Michaels reports the $4,000 from weddings, baptisms, and honoraria.

Line 2. Rev. Michaels reports his expenses related to the line 1b amount. The total consisted of $87 for marriage and family booklets and $253 for 456 miles of business use of his car, mainly in connection with honoraria. Rev. Michaels used the standard mileage rate to figure his car expense. He multiplied the standard mileage rate of 55.5 cents by 456 miles, for a total of $253. These expenses total $340 ($253 + $87). However, he cannot deduct the part of his expenses allocable to his tax-free parsonage allowance. He attaches the required statement, Attachment 1 (shown later) to his return showing that 25 percent (or $85) of his business expenses are not deductible because they are allocable to that tax-free allowance. He subtracts the $85 from the $340 and enters the $255 difference on line 2.

Line 3. He enters his net profit of $3,745 both on line 3 and on Form 1040, line 12.

Lines 4 through 8b. Rev. Michaels fills out these lines to report information about his car.

✔ **TURBOTAX TIP.** TurboTax does not appear to calculate the nondeductible portion of the expenses that should be allocated to the tax-free portion of the housing allowance. The taxpayer will need to adjust the expenses (as shown in Attachment 1) and input the reduced figure into the software form.

d. FORM 2106-EZ

Rev. Michaels fills out Form 2106-EZ to report the unreimbursed business expenses he had as a common-law employee of First United Church.

Line 1. Before completing line 1, Rev. Michaels fills out Part II because he used his car for church business. His records show that he drove 2,577 business miles, which he reports in Part II. On line

1 he multiplies 2,577 miles driven by the mileage rate of 55.5 cents. The combined result of $1,430 is reported on line 1.

Line 4. He enters $219 for his professional publications and booklets.

Line 6. Before entering the total expenses on line 6, Rev. Michaels must reduce them by the amount allocable to his tax-free parsonage allowance. On the required Attachment 1 (shown later), he shows that 25 percent (or $412) of his employee business expenses are not deductible because they are allocable to the tax-free parsonage allowance. He subtracts $412 from $1,649 and enters the result, $1,237, on line 6. He also enters $1,237 on line 21 of Schedule A (Form 1040).

✔ **TURBOTAX TIP.** TurboTax does not appear to calculate the nondeductible portion of the expenses that should be allocated to the tax-free portion of the housing allowance. The taxpayer will need to adjust the expenses (as shown in Attachment 1) and input the reduced figure into the software form.

e. SCHEDULE A (FORM 1040)

Rev. Michaels fills out Schedule A as explained here.

Line 5. In 2011 a taxpayer could elect to take an itemized deduction for state and local general sales taxes instead of the itemized deduction permitted for state and local income tax. This provision is not available for 2012. Since Rev. and Mrs. Michaels do not pay state income tax, no deduction is available to them on line 5.

Line 6. Rev. Michaels deducts $1,750 in real estate taxes.

Line 10. He deducts $6,810 of home mortgage interest.

Line 16. Rev. and Mrs. Michaels contributed $4,800 in cash during the year to various qualifying charities. Each individual contribution was less than $250. For each contribution, Rev. and Mrs. Michaels maintain the required bank record (such as a cancelled check) or written communication from the charity showing the charity's name, the amount of the contribution, and the date of the contribution. (This substantiation is required in order for any contribution of money (cash, check, or other monetary instrument) made in 2007 and thereafter to be deductible.)

Line 21. Rev. Michaels enters his unreimbursed employee business expenses from Form 2106-EZ, line 6.

Lines 25, 26, and 27. He can deduct only the part of his employee business expenses that exceeds 2 percent of his adjusted gross income. He fills out these lines to figure the amount he can deduct.

Line 29. The total of all the Michaelses' itemized deductions is $13,639, which they enter on line 29 and on Form 1040, line 40.

F. SCHEDULE SE (FORM 1040)

After Rev. Michaels prepares Schedule C-EZ and Form 2106-EZ, he fills out Schedule SE (Form 1040). He reads the chart on page 1 of the schedule, which tells him he can use Section A—Short Schedule SE to figure his self-employment tax. Rev. Michaels is a minister, so his salary from the church is not considered church employee income. Thus he does not have to use Section B—Long Schedule SE. He fills out the following lines in Section A.

Line 2. Rev. Michaels attaches a statement (see Attachment 2, later) that explains how he figures the amount ($63,811) he enters here.

Line 4. He multiplies $63,811 by .9235 to get his net earnings from self-employment ($58,929).

Line 5. The amount on line 4 is less than $110,100, so Rev. Michaels multiplies the amount on line 4 ($58,929) by .133 to get his self-employment tax of $7,838. He enters that amount here and on Form 1040, line 56.

Line 6. Rev. Michaels multiplies the amount on line 5 by .5751 to get his deduction for the employer-equivalent portion of self-employment tax of $4,508. He enters that amount here and on Form 1040, line 27.

✔ **TURBOTAX TIP.** The software asks about self-employment tax on clergy wages. The taxpayer should check the box to pay self-employment tax on wages and housing allowance (assuming, as shown in this example, that the minister has not applied for exemption from the SE tax). Please note that the software does not appear to reduce self-employment wages by the business expenses allocated to tax-free income. The taxpayer will need to adjust net self-employment income (as shown in Attachment 2) and input the reduced figure into the software form.

G. FORM 1040

After Rev. Michaels prepares Form 2106-EZ and the other schedules, he fills out Form 1040. He files a joint return with his wife. First he fills out the address area and completes the appropriate lines for his filing status and exemptions. Then he fills out the rest of the form as follows:

Line 7. Rev. Michaels reports $48,640. This amount is the total of his $45,000 church salary, $3,400 college salary, and $240, the excess of the amount designated and paid to him as a parsonage allowance over the lesser of his actual expenses and the fair rental value of his home (including furnishings and utilities). The two salaries were reported to him in box 1 of the Forms W-2 he received.

Line 12. He reports his net profit of $3,745 from Schedule C-EZ, line 3.

Line 27. He enters $4,508, the deductible part of his SE tax from Schedule SE, line 6.

Line 37. Subtract line 36 from line 22. This is his adjusted gross income, and he carries this amount forward to line 38.

Line 40. He enters the total itemized deductions from Schedule A, line 29.

Line 42. He multiplies the number of exemptions claimed (3 from line 6d) by $3,800 and enters an exemption amount of $11,400 on line 42.

Line 51. The Michaelses can take the child tax credit for their daughter, Jennifer. Rev. Michaels figures the credit by completing the Child Tax Credit Worksheet (not shown) contained in the Form 1040 general instructions. He enters the $1,000 credit. (Note: The Michaelses are not required to attach Schedule 8812 to claim the child tax credit, since their daughter does not have an individual taxpayer identification number (ITIN). The IRS issues ITINs to foreign nationals and others who have federal tax reporting or filing requirements and do not qualify for Social Security numbers (SSNs). Since Jennifer has a SSN, she is not required to obtain an ITIN, and therefore Schedule 8812 is not applicable.)

Line 56. He enters the self-employment tax from Schedule SE, line 5.

Line 62. He enters the federal income tax shown in box 2 of his Form W-2 from the college.

Line 63. He enters the $12,000 estimated tax payments he made for the year.

a Employee's social security number 011-00-1111	OMB No. 1545-0008	Safe, accurate, FAST! Use	IRS e-file	Visit the IRS website at www.irs.gov/efile

b Employer identification number (EIN) 00-0246810	**1** Wages, tips, other compensation 45,000.00	**2** Federal income tax withheld

c Employer's name, address, and ZIP code	**3** Social security wages	**4** Social security tax withheld

First United Church
1042 Main Street
Hometown, Texas 77099

	5 Medicare wages and tips	**6** Medicare tax withheld
	7 Social security tips	**8** Allocated tips

d Control number	**9**	**10** Dependent care benefits

e Employee's first name and initial Last name Suff.	**11** Nonqualified plans	**12a** See instructions for box 12

John E. Michaels
1040 Main Street
Hometown, Texas 77099

13 Statutory employee ☐ Retirement plan ☐ Third-party sick pay ☐	**12b**
14 Other	**12c**

Parsonage
Allowance
$16,800

| | | **12d** |

f Employee's address and ZIP code

15 State Employer's state ID number	**16** State wages, tips, etc.	**17** State income tax	**18** Local wages, tips, etc.	**19** Local income tax	**20** Locality name

Form **W-2** Wage and Tax Statement   2012   Department of the Treasury—Internal Revenue Service

Copy B—To Be Filed With Employee's FEDERAL Tax Return.
This information is being furnished to the Internal Revenue Service.

---

a Employee's social security number 011-00-1111	OMB No. 1545-0008	Safe, accurate, FAST! Use	IRS e-file	Visit the IRS website at www.irs.gov/efile

b Employer identification number (EIN) 00-1357913	**1** Wages, tips, other compensation 3,400.00	**2** Federal income tax withheld 272.00

c Employer's name, address, and ZIP code	**3** Social security wages 3,400.00	**4** Social security tax withheld 142.80

Hometown College
40 Honor Road
Hometown, Texas 77099

	5 Medicare wages and tips 3,400.00	**6** Medicare tax withheld 49.30
	7 Social security tips	**8** Allocated tips

d Control number	**9**	**10** Dependent care benefits

e Employee's first name and initial Last name Suff.	**11** Nonqualified plans	**12a** See instructions for box 12

John E. Michaels
1040 Main Street
Hometown, Texas 77099

13 Statutory employee ☐ Retirement plan ☐ Third-party sick pay ☐	**12b**
14 Other	**12c**
	12d

f Employee's address and ZIP code

15 State Employer's state ID number	**16** State wages, tips, etc.	**17** State income tax	**18** Local wages, tips, etc.	**19** Local income tax	**20** Locality name

Form **W-2** Wage and Tax Statement   2012   Department of the Treasury—Internal Revenue Service

Copy B—To Be Filed With Employee's FEDERAL Tax Return.
This information is being furnished to the Internal Revenue Service.

Form **1040** Department of the Treasury—Internal Revenue Service (99)

U.S. Individual Income Tax Return **20**12 OMB No. 1545-0074 | IRS Use Only—Do not write or staple in this space.

For the year Jan. 1–Dec. 31, 2012, or other tax year beginning , 2012, ending , 20 | See separate instructions.

Your first name and initial	Last name	Your social security number
John E.	Michaels	0 1 1 0 0 1 1 1 1
If a joint return, spouse's first name and initial	Last name	Spouse's social security number
Susan R.	Michaels	0 1 1 0 0 2 2 2 2

Home address (number and street). If you have a P.O. box, see instructions. | Apt. no.

▲ Make sure the SSN(s) above and on line 6c are correct.

1040 Main Street

City, town or post office, state, and ZIP code. If you have a foreign address, also complete spaces below (see instructions).

Presidential Election Campaign

Hometown, Texas 77099

Check here if you, or your spouse if filing jointly, want $3 to go to this fund. Checking a box below will not change your tax or refund. ☐ You ☐ Spouse

Foreign country name	Foreign province/state/county	Foreign postal code

Filing Status

Check only one box.

1 ☐ Single
2 ☑ Married filing jointly (even if only one had income)
3 ☐ Married filing separately. Enter spouse's SSN above and full name here. ▶
4 ☐ Head of household (with qualifying person). (See instructions.) If the qualifying person is a child but not your dependent, enter this child's name here. ▶
5 ☐ Qualifying widow(er) with dependent child

Exemptions

6a ☑ **Yourself.** If someone can claim you as a dependent, **do not** check box 6a
b ☑ **Spouse**

c Dependents:

(1) First name Last name	(2) Dependent's social security number	(3) Dependent's relationship to you	(4) ✓ if child under age 17 qualifying for child tax credit (see instructions)
Jennifer Michaels	0 1 1 0 0 3 3 3 3	Daughter	☑
			☐
			☐
			☐

If more than four dependents, see instructions and check here ▶ ☐

Boxes checked on 6a and 6b — **2**
No. of children on 6c who:
• lived with you — **1**
• did not live with you due to divorce or separation (see instructions)
Dependents on 6c not entered above
Add numbers on lines above ▶ **3**

d Total number of exemptions claimed

Income

Attach Form(s) W-2 here. Also attach Forms W-2G and 1099-R if tax was withheld.

If you did not get a W-2, see instructions.

Enclose, but do not attach, any payment. Also, please use Form 1040-V.

7	Wages, salaries, tips, etc. Attach Form(s) W-2 Excess parsonage allowance $240	7	48,640
8a	**Taxable** interest. Attach Schedule B if required	8a	
b	Tax-exempt interest. **Do not** include on line 8a 8b		
9a	Ordinary dividends. Attach Schedule B if required	9a	
b	Qualified dividends 9b		
10	Taxable refunds, credits, or offsets of state and local income taxes	10	
11	Alimony received	11	
12	Business income or (loss). Attach Schedule C or C-EZ	12	3,745
13	Capital gain or (loss). Attach Schedule D if required. If not required, check here ▶ ☐	13	
14	Other gains or (losses). Attach Form 4797	14	
15a	IRA distributions 15a	b Taxable amount	15b	
16a	Pensions and annuities 16a	b Taxable amount	16b	
17	Rental real estate, royalties, partnerships, S corporations, trusts, etc. Attach Schedule E	17	
18	Farm income or (loss). Attach Schedule F	18	
19	Unemployment compensation	19	
20a	Social security benefits 20a	b Taxable amount	20b	
21	Other income. List type and amount	21	
22	Combine the amounts in the far right column for lines 7 through 21. This is your **total income** ▶	22	52,385

Adjusted Gross Income

23	Reserved 23		
24	Certain business expenses of reservists, performing artists, and fee-basis government officials. Attach Form 2106 or 2106-EZ 24		
25	Health savings account deduction. Attach Form 8889 25		
26	Moving expenses. Attach Form 3903 26		
27	Deductible part of self-employment tax. Attach Schedule SE 27 4,508		
28	Self-employed SEP, SIMPLE, and qualified plans 28		
29	Self-employed health insurance deduction 29		
30	Penalty on early withdrawal of savings 30		
31a	Alimony paid b Recipient's SSN ▶ 31a		
32	IRA deduction 32		
33	Student loan interest deduction 33		
34	Reserved 34		
35	Domestic production activities deduction. Attach Form 8903 35		
36	Add lines 23 through 35	36	4,508
37	Subtract line 36 from line 22. This is your **adjusted gross income** ▶	37	47,877

For Disclosure, Privacy Act, and Paperwork Reduction Act Notice, see separate instructions. Cat. No. 11320B Form **1040** (2012)

Form 1040 (2012)   Page **2**

Tax and Credits

Line	Description		Amount
38	Amount from line 37 (adjusted gross income)	38	47,877
39a	Check if: ☐ **You** were born before January 2, 1948, ☐ Blind. ☐ **Spouse** was born before January 2, 1948, ☐ Blind. } Total boxes checked ▶ 39a		
b	If your spouse itemizes on a separate return or you were a dual-status alien, check here ▶ 39b ☐		

Standard Deduction for—
- People who check any box on line 39a or 39b **or** who can be claimed as a dependent, see instructions.
- All others:

Single or Married filing separately, $5,950

Married filing jointly or Qualifying widow(er), $11,900

Head of household, $8,700

Line	Description		Amount
40	**Itemized deductions** (from Schedule A) **or** your **standard deduction** (see left margin)	40	13,639
41	Subtract line 40 from line 38	41	34,238
42	**Exemptions.** Multiply $3,800 by the number on line 6d	42	11,400
43	**Taxable income.** Subtract line 42 from line 41. If line 42 is more than line 41, enter -0-	43	22,838
44	**Tax** (see instructions). Check if any from: **a** ☐ Form(s) 8814 **b** ☐ Form 4972 **c** ☐ 962 election	44	2,554
45	**Alternative minimum tax** (see instructions). Attach Form 6251	45	
46	Add lines 44 and 45 ▶	46	2,554
47	Foreign tax credit. Attach Form 1116 if required	47	
48	Credit for child and dependent care expenses. Attach Form 2441	48	
49	Education credits from Form 8863, line 19	49	
50	Retirement savings contributions credit. Attach Form 8880	50	
51	Child tax credit. Attach Schedule 8812, if required	51	1,000
52	Residential energy credit. Attach Form 5695	52	
53	Other credits from Form: **a** ☐ 3800 **b** ☐ 8801 **c** ☐	53	
54	Add lines 47 through 53. These are your **total credits**	54	1,000
55	Subtract line 54 from line 46. If line 54 is more than line 46, enter -0- ▶	55	1,554

Other Taxes

Line	Description		Amount
56	Self-employment tax. Attach Schedule SE	56	7,838
57	Unreported social security and Medicare tax from Form: **a** ☐ 4137 **b** ☐ 8919	57	
58	Additional tax on IRAs, other qualified retirement plans, etc. Attach Form 5329 if required	58	
59a	Household employment taxes from Schedule H	59a	
b	First-time homebuyer credit repayment. Attach Form 5405 if required	59b	
60	Other taxes. Enter code(s) from instructions	60	
61	Add lines 55 through 60. This is your **total tax** ▶	61	9,392

Payments

If you have a qualifying child, attach Schedule EIC.

Line	Description		Amount
62	Federal income tax withheld from Forms W-2 and 1099	62	272
63	2012 estimated tax payments and amount applied from 2011 return	63	12,000
64a	**Earned income credit (EIC)**	64a	
b	Nontaxable combat pay election	64b	
65	Additional child tax credit. Attach Schedule 8812	65	
66	American opportunity credit from Form 8863, line 8	66	
67	Reserved	67	
68	Amount paid with request for extension to file	68	
69	Excess social security and tier 1 RRTA tax withheld	69	
70	Credit for federal tax on fuels. Attach Form 4136	70	
71	Credits from Form: **a** ☐ 2439 **b** ☐ Reserved **c** ☐ 8801 **d** ☐ 8885	71	
72	Add lines 62, 63, 64a, and 65 through 71. These are your **total payments** ▶	72	12,272

Refund

73	If line 72 is more than line 61, subtract line 61 from line 72. This is the amount you **overpaid**	73	2,880
74a	Amount of line 73 you want **refunded to you.** If Form 8888 is attached, check here ▶ ☐	74a	

Direct deposit? See instructions.
- **b** Routing number
- ▶ **c** Type: ☐ Checking ☐ Savings
- **d** Account number

Line	Description		Amount
75	Amount of line 73 you want **applied to your 2013 estimated tax** ▶ 75	2,880	

Amount You Owe

76	**Amount you owe.** Subtract line 72 from line 61. For details on how to pay, see instructions ▶	76	
77	Estimated tax penalty (see instructions) 77		

Third Party Designee

Do you want to allow another person to discuss this return with the IRS (see instructions)? ☐ **Yes.** Complete below. ☐ **No**

Designee's name ▶   Phone no. ▶   Personal identification number (PIN) ▶

Sign Here

Under penalties of perjury, I declare that I have examined this return and accompanying schedules and statements, and to the best of my knowledge and belief, they are true, correct, and complete. Declaration of preparer (other than taxpayer) is based on all information of which preparer has any knowledge.

Joint return? See instructions. Keep a copy for your records.

Your signature	Date	Your occupation	Daytime phone number
John Michaels	3/15/13	**Minister**	**212-444-5555**
Spouse's signature. If a joint return, **both** must sign.	Date	Spouse's occupation	If the IRS sent you an Identity Protection PIN, enter it here (see inst.)
Susan Michaels	3/15/13	**Homemaker**	

Paid Preparer Use Only

Print/Type preparer's name	Preparer's signature	Date	Check ☐ if self-employed	PTIN

Firm's name ▶   Firm's EIN ▶

Firm's address ▶   Phone no.

Form **1040** (2012)

SCHEDULE A (Form 1040) Department of the Treasury Internal Revenue Service (99)	**Itemized Deductions** ▶ Information about Schedule A and its separate instructions is at *www.irs.gov/form1040*. ▶ **Attach to Form 1040.**			OMB No. 1545-0074 20**12** Attachment Sequence No. **07**

Name(s) shown on Form 1040				Your social security number
John E. & Susan R. Michaels				011-00-1111

Medical and Dental Expenses		**Caution.** Do not include expenses reimbursed or paid by others.			
	1	Medical and dental expenses (see instructions)	**1**		
	2	Enter amount from Form 1040, line 38 **2**			
	3	Multiply line 2 by 7.5% (.075)	**3**		
	4	Subtract line 3 from line 1. If line 3 is more than line 1, enter -0-		**4**	
Taxes You Paid	5	State and local			
		a ☐ Income taxes			
		b ▨ Reserved ⎫	**5**		
	6	Real estate taxes (see instructions) . . .	**6**	1,750	
	7	Personal property taxes	**7**		
	8	Other taxes. List type and amount ▶ _____			
			8		
	9	Add lines 5 through 8		**9**	1,750
Interest You Paid **Note.** Your mortgage interest deduction may be limited (see instructions).	10	Home mortgage interest and points reported to you on Form 1098	**10**	6,810	
	11	Home mortgage interest not reported to you on Form 1098. If paid to the person from whom you bought the home, see instructions and show that person's name, identifying no., and address ▶ _____ _____	**11**		
	12	Points not reported to you on Form 1098. See instructions for special rules	**12**		
	13	Reserved	**13**		
	14	Investment interest. Attach Form 4952 if required. (See instructions.)	**14**		
	15	Add lines 10 through 14		**15**	6,810
Gifts to Charity If you made a gift and got a benefit for it, see instructions.	16	Gifts by cash or check. If you made any gift of $250 or more, see instructions	**16**	4,800	
	17	Other than by cash or check. If any gift of $250 or more, see instructions. You **must** attach Form 8283 if over $500 . . .	**17**		
	18	Carryover from prior year	**18**		
	19	Add lines 16 through 18		**19**	4,800
Casualty and Theft Losses	20	Casualty or theft loss(es). Attach Form 4684. (See instructions.)		**20**	
Job Expenses and Certain Miscellaneous Deductions	21	Unreimbursed employee expenses—job travel, union dues, job education, etc. Attach Form 2106 or 2106-EZ if required. (See instructions.) ▶ _____	**21**	1,237	
	22	Tax preparation fees	**22**		
	23	Other expenses—investment, safe deposit box, etc. List type and amount ▶ _____			
			23		
	24	Add lines 21 through 23	**24**	1,237	
	25	Enter amount from Form 1040, line 38 **25** 47,877			
	26	Multiply line 25 by 2% (.02)	**26**	958	
	27	Subtract line 26 from line 24. If line 26 is more than line 24, enter -0-		**27**	279
Other Miscellaneous Deductions	28	Other—from list in instructions. List type and amount ▶ _____ _____		**28**	
Total Itemized Deductions	29	Add the amounts in the far right column for lines 4 through 28. Also, enter this amount on Form 1040, line 40		**29**	13,639
	30	If you elect to itemize deductions even though they are less than your standard deduction, check here . . . . ▶ ☐			

For Paperwork Reduction Act Notice, see Form 1040 instructions.   Cat. No. 17145C   Schedule A (Form 1040) 2012

SCHEDULE C-EZ (Form 1040) Department of the Treasury Internal Revenue Service (99)	**Net Profit From Business** (Sole Proprietorship) ▶ **Partnerships, joint ventures, etc., generally must file Form 1065 or 1065-B.** ▶ **Attach to Form 1040, 1040NR, or 1041.** ▶ **See instructions on page 2.**	OMB No. 1545-0074 20**12** Attachment Sequence No. **09A**
Name of proprietor John E. Michaels		Social security number (SSN) 011-00-1111

Part I General Information

You May Use Schedule C-EZ Instead of Schedule C Only If You:	• Had business expenses of $5,000 or less. • Use the cash method of accounting. • Did not have an inventory at any time during the year. • Did not have a net loss from your business. • Had only one business as either a sole proprietor, qualified joint venture, or statutory employee.	**And You:**	• Had no employees during the year. • Are not required to file **Form 4562,** Depreciation and Amortization, for this business. See the instructions for Schedule C, line 13, to find out if you must file. • Do not deduct expenses for business use of your home. • Do not have prior year unallowed passive activity losses from this business.

A Principal business or profession, including product or service
Minister

B Enter business code (see page 2)
▶ 5 4 1 9 9 0

C Business name. If no separate business name, leave blank.

D Enter your EIN (see page 2)

E Business address (including suite or room no.). Address not required if same as on page 1 of your tax return.
1042 Main Street
City, town or post office, state, and ZIP code
Hometown, Texas 77099

F Did you make any payments in 2012 that would require you to file Form(s) 1099? (see the Schedule C instructions) . . . .   ☐ Yes ☑ No

G If "Yes," did you or will you file required Forms 1099? . . . .   ☐ Yes ☐ No

Part II Figure Your Net Profit

1	**Gross receipts. Caution.** If this income was reported to you on Form W-2 and the "Statutory employee" box on that form was checked, see *Statutory Employees* in the instructions for Schedule C, line 1, and check here . . . . ▶ ☐	1	4,000	
2	**Total expenses** (see page 2). If more than $5,000, you **must** use Schedule C	2	255	*
3	**Net profit.** Subtract line 2 from line 1. If less than zero, you **must** use Schedule C. Enter on both **Form 1040, line 12,** and **Schedule SE, line 2,** or on **Form 1040NR, line 13** and **Schedule SE, line 2** (see instructions). (Statutory employees, **do not** report this amount on Schedule SE, line 2.) Estates and trusts, enter on **Form 1041, line 3**	3	3,745	

Part III Information on Your Vehicle. Complete this part **only** if you are claiming car or truck expenses on line 2.

4 When did you place your vehicle in service for business purposes? (month, day, year) ▶   07/15/07   .

5 Of the total number of miles you drove your vehicle during 2012, enter the number of miles you used your vehicle for:

a Business   456   **b** Commuting (see page 2)   0   **c** Other   7,466

6 Was your vehicle available for personal use during off-duty hours? . . . .   ☑ Yes ☐ No

7 Do you (or your spouse) have another vehicle available for personal use? . . . .   ☑ Yes ☐ No

8a Do you have evidence to support your deduction? . . . .   ☑ Yes ☐ No

b If "Yes," is the evidence written? . . . .   ☑ Yes ☐ No

For Paperwork Reduction Act Notice, see your tax return instructions.   Cat. No. 14374D   Schedule C-EZ (Form 1040) 2012

SCHEDULE SE
(Form 1040)

Department of the Treasury
Internal Revenue Service (99)

Self-Employment Tax

▶ Information about Schedule SE and its separate instructions is at *www.irs.gov/form1040*.
▶ **Attach to Form 1040 or Form 1040NR.**

OMB No. 1545-0074

20**12**

Attachment
Sequence No. **17**

Name of person with **self-employment** income (as shown on Form 1040)	Social security number of person with **self-employment** income ▶
John E. Michaels	011-00-1111

Before you begin: To determine if you must file Schedule SE, see the instructions.

May I Use Short Schedule SE or Must I Use Long Schedule SE?

Note. Use this flowchart **only if** you must file Schedule SE. If unsure, see *Who Must File Schedule SE* in the instructions.

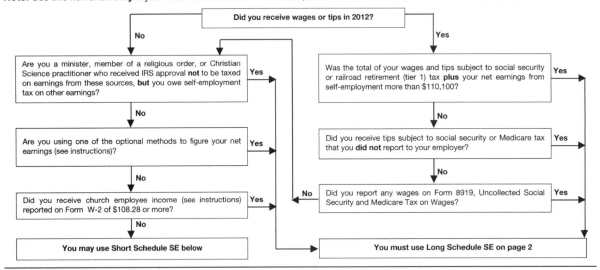

Section A—Short Schedule SE. Caution. Read above to see if you can use Short Schedule SE.

1a	Net farm profit or (loss) from Schedule F, line 34, and farm partnerships, Schedule K-1 (Form 1065), box 14, code A	**1a**		
b	If you received social security retirement or disability benefits, enter the amount of Conservation Reserve Program payments included on Schedule F, line 4b, or listed on Schedule K-1 (Form 1065), box 20, code Y	**1b**	(	)
2	Net profit or (loss) from Schedule C, line 31; Schedule C-EZ, line 3; Schedule K-1 (Form 1065), box 14, code A (other than farming); and Schedule K-1 (Form 1065-B), box 9, code J1. Ministers and members of religious orders, see instructions for types of income to report on this line. See instructions for other income to report	**2**	63,811	*
3	Combine lines 1a, 1b, and 2	**3**	63,811	
4	Multiply line 3 by 92.35% (.9235). If less than $400, you do not owe self-employment tax; **do not** file this schedule unless you have an amount on line 1b . . . . . . ▶	**4**	58,929	
	Note. If line 4 is less than $400 due to Conservation Reserve Program payments on line 1b, see instructions.			
5	**Self-employment tax.** If the amount on line 4 is:			
	• $110,100 or less, multiply line 4 by 13.3% (.133). Enter the result here and on **Form 1040, line 56,** or **Form 1040NR, line 54**			
	• More than $110,100, multiply line 4 by 2.9% (.029). Then, add $11,450.40 to the result. Enter the total here and on **Form 1040, line 56,** or **Form 1040NR, line 54**	**5**	7,838	
6	**Deduction for employer-equivalent portion of self-employment tax.** If the amount on line 5 is:			
	• $14,643.30 or less, multiply line 5 by 57.51% (.5751)			
	• More than $14,643.30, multiply line 5 by 50% (.50) and add $1,100 to the result. Enter the result here and on **Form 1040, line 27,** or **Form 1040NR, line 27**	**6**	4,508	

For Paperwork Reduction Act Notice, see your tax return instructions.

Cat. No. 11358Z

Schedule SE (Form 1040) 2012

* See statement attached.

Schedule SE (Form 1040) 2012 | Attachment Sequence No. **17** | Page **2**

Name of person with **self-employment** income (as shown on Form 1040)

John E. Michaels

Social security number of person with **self-employment** income ▶ 011-00-1111

Section B—Long Schedule SE

Part I Self-Employment Tax

Note. If your only income subject to self-employment tax is **church employee income,** see instructions. Also see instructions for the definition of church employee income.

A If you are a minister, member of a religious order, or Christian Science practitioner **and** you filed Form 4361, but you had $400 or more of **other** net earnings from self-employment, check here and continue with Part I . . . . . . ▶ ☐

1a Net farm profit or (loss) from Schedule F, line 34, and farm partnerships, Schedule K-1 (Form 1065), box 14, code A. **Note.** Skip lines 1a and 1b if you use the farm optional method (see instructions) | **1a**

b If you received social security retirement or disability benefits, enter the amount of Conservation Reserve Program payments included on Schedule F, line 4b, or listed on Schedule K-1 (Form 1065), box 20, code Y | **1b** ( )

2 Net profit or (loss) from Schedule C, line 31; Schedule C-EZ, line 3; Schedule K-1 (Form 1065), box 14, code A (other than farming); and Schedule K-1 (Form 1065-B), box 9, code J1. Ministers and members of religious orders, see instructions for types of income to report on this line. See instructions for other income to report. **Note.** Skip this line if you use the nonfarm optional method (see instructions) . . . . | **2**

3 Combine lines 1a, 1b, and 2 . . . . . . | **3**

4a If line 3 is more than zero, multiply line 3 by 92.35% (.9235). Otherwise, enter amount from line 3 | **4a**
Note. If line 4a is less than $400 due to Conservation Reserve Program payments on line 1b, see instructions.

b If you elect one or both of the optional methods, enter the total of lines 15 and 17 here . . | **4b**

c Combine lines 4a and 4b. If less than $400, **stop**; you do not owe self-employment tax. **Exception.** If less than $400 and you had **church employee income,** enter -0- and continue ▶ | **4c**

5a Enter your **church employee income** from Form W-2. See instructions for definition of church employee income . . . | **5a**

b Multiply line 5a by 92.35% (.9235). If less than $100, enter -0- . . . . . . | **5b**

6 Add lines 4c and 5b . . . . . . | **6**

7 Maximum amount of combined wages and self-employment earnings subject to social security tax or the 4.2% portion of the 5.65% railroad retirement (tier 1) tax for 2012 . . . . . | **7** | 110,100 00

8a Total social security wages and tips (total of boxes 3 and 7 on Form(s) W-2) and railroad retirement (tier 1) compensation. If $110,100 or more, skip lines 8b through 10, and go to line 11 | **8a**

b Unreported tips subject to social security tax (from Form 4137, line 10) | **8b**

c Wages subject to social security tax (from Form 8919, line 10) | **8c**

d Add lines 8a, 8b, and 8c . . . . . . | **8d**

9 Subtract line 8d from line 7. If zero or less, enter -0- here and on line 10 and go to line 11 ▶ | **9**

10 Multiply the **smaller** of line 6 or line 9 by 10.4% (.104) . . . . . . | **10**

11 Multiply line 6 by 2.9% (.029) . . . . . . | **11**

12 **Self-employment tax.** Add lines 10 and 11. Enter here and on **Form 1040, line 56,** or **Form 1040NR, line 54** | **12**

13 **Deduction for employer-equivalent portion of self-employment tax.** Add the two following amounts.
• 59.6% (.596) of line 10.
• One-half of line 11.
Enter the result here and on **Form 1040, line 27,** or **Form 1040NR, line 27** . . . . . . | **13**

Part II Optional Methods To Figure Net Earnings (see instructions)

Farm Optional Method. You may use this method **only** if **(a)** your gross farm income[1] was not more than $6,780, **or (b)** your net farm profits[2] were less than $4,894.

14 Maximum income for optional methods . . . . . . | **14** | 4,520 00

15 Enter the **smaller** of: two-thirds (²⁄₃) of gross farm income[1] (not less than zero) **or** $4,520. Also include this amount on line 4b above . . . . . . | **15**

Nonfarm Optional Method. You may use this method **only** if **(a)** your net nonfarm profits[3] were less than $4,894 and also less than 72.189% of your gross nonfarm income,[4] **and (b)** you had net earnings from self-employment of at least $400 in 2 of the prior 3 years. **Caution.** You may use this method no more than five times.

16 Subtract line 15 from line 14 . . . . . . | **16**

17 Enter the **smaller** of: two-thirds (²⁄₃) of gross nonfarm income[4] (not less than zero) **or** the amount on line 16. Also include this amount on line 4b above . . . . . . | **17**

[1] From Sch. F, line 9, and Sch. K-1 (Form 1065), box 14, code B.
[2] From Sch. F, line 34, and Sch. K-1 (Form 1065), box 14, code A—minus the amount you would have entered on line 1b had you not used the optional method.
[3] From Sch. C, line 31; Sch. C-EZ, line 3; Sch. K-1 (Form 1065), box 14, code A; and Sch. K-1 (Form 1065-B), box 9, code J1.
[4] From Sch. C, line 7; Sch. C-EZ, line 1; Sch. K-1 (Form 1065), box 14, code C; and Sch. K-1 (Form 1065-B), box 9, code J2.

Schedule SE (Form 1040) 2012

Form **2106-EZ**

Department of the Treasury
Internal Revenue Service (99)

Unreimbursed Employee Business Expenses

▶ Attach to Form 1040 or Form 1040NR.

▶ Information about Form 2106 and its separate instructions is available at *www.irs.gov/form2106*.

OMB No. 1545-0074

20**12**

Attachment
Sequence No. **129A**

Your name	Occupation in which you incurred expenses	Social security number
John E. Michaels	Minister	011 ¦ 00 ¦ 1111

You Can Use This Form Only if All of the Following Apply.

• You are an employee deducting ordinary and necessary expenses attributable to your job. An ordinary expense is one that is common and accepted in your field of trade, business, or profession. A necessary expense is one that is helpful and appropriate for your business. An expense does not have to be required to be considered necessary.

• You **do not** get reimbursed by your employer for any expenses (amounts your employer included in box 1 of your Form W-2 are not considered reimbursements for this purpose).

• If you are claiming vehicle expense, you are using the standard mileage rate for 2012.

Caution: *You can use the standard mileage rate for 2012 only if: (a) you owned the vehicle and used the standard mileage rate for the first year you placed the vehicle in service, or (b) you leased the vehicle and used the standard mileage rate for the portion of the lease period after 1997.*

Part I	Figure Your Expenses		
1	Complete Part II. Multiply line 8a by 55.5¢ (.555). Enter the result here	**1**	1,430
2	Parking fees, tolls, and transportation, including train, bus, etc., that **did not** involve overnight travel or commuting to and from work	**2**	
3	Travel expense while away from home overnight, including lodging, airplane, car rental, etc. **Do not** include meals and entertainment	**3**	
4	Business expenses not included on lines 1 through 3. **Do not** include meals and entertainment	**4**	219
5	Meals and entertainment expenses: $ _____ × 50% (.50). (Employees subject to Department of Transportation (DOT) hours of service limits: Multiply meal expenses incurred while away from home on business by 80% (.80) instead of 50%. For details, see instructions.)	**5**	
6	**Total expenses.** Add lines 1 through 5. Enter here and on **Schedule A (Form 1040), line 21** (or on **Schedule A (Form 1040NR), line 7**). (Armed Forces reservists, fee-basis state or local government officials, qualified performing artists, and individuals with disabilities: See the instructions for special rules on where to enter this amount.)	**6**	1,237 *

Part II	Information on Your Vehicle. Complete this part **only** if you are claiming vehicle expense on line 1.

7 When did you place your vehicle in service for business use? (month, day, year) ▶ 07 / 15 / 07

8 Of the total number of miles you drove your vehicle during 2012, enter the number of miles you used your vehicle for:

a Business 2,577 **b** Commuting (see instructions) _____ **c** Other 5,112

9 Was your vehicle available for personal use during off-duty hours? . . . . ☑ Yes ☐ No

10 Do you (or your spouse) have another vehicle available for personal use? . . . . ☑ Yes ☐ No

11a Do you have evidence to support your deduction? . . . . ☑ Yes ☐ No

b If "Yes," is the evidence written? . . . . ☑ Yes ☐ No

For Paperwork Reduction Act Notice, see your tax return instructions. Cat. No. 20604Q Form **2106-EZ** (2012)

* See statement attached.

Attachment 1. Computation of expenses, allocable to tax-free ministerial income, that are nondeductible.

	Taxable	Tax-Free	Total
Salary as a minister	$ 45,000		$ 45,000
Parsonage allowance:			
Amount designated and paid by church ($1,400 x 12) $ 16,800			
Actual expenses			
(Mortgage $1,125 x 12, Utilities/other $1,450, Real estate taxes $1,750) 16,700			
Fair rental value of home (including furnishings and utilities) ($1,380 x 12) 16,560			
Taxable portion of allowance			
(excess of amount designated & paid over lesser of actual expenses or fair rental value) $ 240	240		240
Tax-free portion of allowance (lesser of amount designated, actual expenses or fair rental value)		16,560	16,560
Gross income from weddings, baptisms, and honoraria	4,000		4,000
Ministerial Income	$ 49,240	$ 16,560	$ 65,800
% of nondeductible expenses: $16,560/$65,800 = 25%			

Schedule C-EZ Deduction Computation

Marriage and family booklets	$ 87
Business use of car:	
456 miles x 55.5¢	253
Unadjusted Schedule C-EZ expenses	340
Minus:	
Nondeductible part of Schedule C-EZ expenses (25% x $340)	(85)
Schedule C-EZ deductions (line 2)	$ 255

Form 2106-EZ - Employee Business Expense Deduction Computation

Car expenses for church business:	
2,577 miles x 55.5¢	$ 1,430
Publications and booklets	219
Unadjusted Form 2106-EZ expenses	1,649
Minus:	
Nondeductible part of Form 2106-EZ expenses (25% x $1,649)	(412)
Employee business expense deduction - Form 2106-EZ line 6	$ 1,237

None of the other deductions claimed in the return are allocable to tax-free income.

Attachment 2. Attachment to Schedule SE (Form 1040)

Church wages		$ 45,000
Parsonage allowance		16,800
Net profit from Schedule C-EZ		3,745
		65,545
Less:		
Schedule C-EZ expenses allocable to tax-free income	$ 85	
Ministerial employee business expenses		
(unadjusted Form 2106-EZ expenses)	1,649	(1,734)
Net Self-Employment Income		
Schedule SE, Section A, line 2		$ 63,811

INDEX

**For additional copies of this book,
call 800-222-1840
between 8 AM and 4:30 PM ET.
Visit our website at YourChurchResources.com.**